MW01042060

EDITORIAL BOARD

ROBERT C. CLARK
DIRECTING EDITOR
Distinguished Service Professor and Austin Wakeman Scott
Professor of Law and Former Dean of the Law School
Harvard University

DANIEL A. FARBER
Sho Sato Professor of Law and Director, Environmental Law Program
University of California at Berkeley

HEATHER K. GERKEN
J. Skelly Wright Professor of Law
Yale University

SAMUEL ISSACHAROFF
Bonnie and Richard Reiss Professor of Constitutional Law
New York University

HERMA HILL KAY
Barbara Nachtrieb Armstrong Professor of Law and
Former Dean of the School of Law
University of California at Berkeley

HAROLD HONGJU KOH
Sterling Professor of International Law and
Former Dean of the Law School
Yale University

SAUL LEVMORE
William B. Graham Distinguished Service Professor of Law and
Former Dean of the Law School
University of Chicago

THOMAS W. MERRILL
Charles Evans Hughes Professor of Law
Columbia University

ROBERT L. RABIN
A. Calder Mackay Professor of Law
Stanford University

CAROL M. ROSE
Gordon Bradford Tweedy Professor Emeritus of Law and Organization and
Professorial Lecturer in Law
Yale University
Lohse Chair in Water and Natural Resources
University of Arizona

UNIVERSITY CASEBOOK SERIES®

CIVIL PROCEDURE

REPRESENTING CLIENTS IN CIVIL LITIGATION

R. LAWRENCE DESSEM
Timothy J. Heinsz Professor of Law
University of Missouri

FOUNDATION
PRESS

The publisher is not engaged in rendering legal or other professional advice, and this publication is not a substitute for the advice of an attorney. If you require legal or other expert advice, you should seek the services of a competent attorney or other professional.

University Casebook Series is a trademark registered in the U.S. Patent and Trademark Office.

© 2016 LEG, Inc. d/b/a West Academic
    444 Cedar Street, Suite 700
    St. Paul, MN 55101
    1-877-888-1330

Printed in the United States of America

ISBN: 978-1-60930-355-6

To My Civil Procedure Students in 2014–15 and 2015–16

Your Enthusiasm, Questions, and Hard Work
Made this a Better Text.

PREFACE

After teaching civil procedure for many years, I decided to write my own textbook. The result is this book, which I've enjoyed using for the last two years with my students at the University of Missouri. I have the luxury of five credit-hours for my course (which extends from the fall to the spring semester), and this permits me to devote class periods to assignments such as an in-class review of a final exam, a student visit to observe court proceedings, the completion of a CALI discovery exercise, a guest speaker on class action practice, and classes devoted to exam review at the end of each semester. As suggested in the teacher's manual to this text, the text also lends itself well to a four-hour civil procedure course or sequence. And, if you have a six-hour sequence, the text offers you the ability to spend more time on the material included.

One of my goals in writing this text was to provide professors with great flexibility in teaching year-long civil procedure courses or more condensed one-semester offerings. The text puts students in the position of lawyers and asks them to consider the strategic, tactical, and ethical choices they will confront in practice. The cases selected, many at the district court level, are contemporary in both the law applied and case subject matter—including actions involving same-sex marriage, mortgage-default litigation, electronic discovery, and the recusal of the federal district judge handling the challenge to New York City's "stop and frisk" litigation. The initial case in the text, *Leonard v. PepsiCo*, is one that students are likely to encounter in their contracts course but that presents rich procedural questions as well.

Ethical issues are stressed throughout the text, including the ethical choices presented to the lawyers in the text's cases and citations to the Model Rules of Professional Conduct and applicable state ethical rules. These references should sensitize students to the ethical issues presented in civil procedure and their other first-year courses.

The chapters conclude with both essay and multiple-choice questions that can be assigned by the professor for exam practice or in-class discussion. These also can be used by individual students to review each chapter's material. I share with students my answers to these questions (contained in the teacher's manual), but I suggest that students first attempt to answer the questions before consulting my answers. I've also included more than 40 figures showing aspects of civil procedure in tabular and visual form.

The text incorporates the December 1, 2015, amendments to the Federal Rules of Civil Procedure and the most recent statutes and cases, rather than simply adding new developments onto an older text. I have done a light edit on most cases, showing the deletion of text by * * *. I do not indicate omitted footnotes or the deletion of authorities from within original opinions or text. For the opinion footnotes that I have kept, I have retained the original footnote numbering. As for my own comments, questions and other text, I flipped a coin (quite literally) to determine the gender of lawyers, clients, and judges. As a result of that coin flip, the lawyers are generally women and the judges and clients generally men.

I welcome your questions and comments concerning this text. I especially am interested in portions of the text that are unclear or that don't "teach" for you, as well as your thoughts on particular matter that should be added to the text. With your input, I'm confident that the text will become even better in the years ahead.

R. LAWRENCE DESSEM

Columbia, Missouri
October 27, 2015

ACKNOWLEDGMENTS

Whether or not it "takes a village" for success in every endeavor, it certainly does for writing a book such as this. The acknowledgments that follow cannot fully indicate my true gratitude to all those who helped to make this book possible.

Initially, my thanks and my love go to Beth for indulging me on this project for the last several years and supporting me as a law professor and in so many other ways for the last several decades.

At the University of Missouri, there are many people who made significant contributions to this text. Student Emily Fiore worked on this project in its very early stages, followed by Jared Guemmer, who nicely picked up the work thereafter. The two students who brought this project across the finish line were Alyssa Kenyon-Cordero and Alex Langley, with a last-minute assist from Cailynn Hayter. They may not have fully appreciated the size of the task they had undertaken, but they always were able to juggle their other commitments and find time to do essential work on this book.

I am blessed with wonderful colleagues at my law school, and several of them made specific contributions to this book. Professor Rafael Gely, after researching contracts text books, suggested that *Leonard v. PepsiCo, Inc.* would make a good contracts case with which to start the text. Professor Dennis Crouch shared the wonderful statement by Justice Breyer that I quote in Chapter 15 ("I'm not interested in the real world. I am interested in the record.").

Among the staff, John Dethman deserves special thanks for searching for, and finding, pretty much anything that I sought. He sometimes brought me things for which I didn't even know I was looking, which was appreciated even more. Other staff and wise friends who also helped include Robin Nichols, Cheryl Poelling, Judy Tayloe, and Resa Kerns (who produced surveys through which students critiqued the book's manuscript).

Thanks, also, to Dean Gary Myers, for supporting my work on the book with a faculty research fellowship and to the University of Missouri Law School Foundation for supporting some of my summer work on this book.

At West Academic, John Bloomquist was supportive of this project and initially guided me in the right direction. Soon thereafter Tessa Boury became my "go to" person at West Academic, and her guidance, patience, and support have been much appreciated.

This book is dedicated to my civil procedure students in 2014–15 and 2015–16, who "field-tested" the manuscript of the book. While their feedback most directly made this the book that it became, I offer my sincere thanks to all my students over the last thirty years for making civil procedure and my other courses such fun experiences for me at three different law schools.

Finally, I thank those who have granted me permission to reproduce portions of the following books and articles:

ABA MODEL CODE OF JUDICIAL CONDUCT. Copyright © 2010 by the American Bar Association. All rights reserved. Reprinted with permission.

ABA MODEL RULES OF PROFESSIONAL CONDUCT. Copyright © 2013 by the American Bar Association. All rights reserved. Reprinted with permission.

BLACK'S LAW DICTIONARY (B. Garner ed. 10th ed. 2014). Copyright © 2014 LEG, Inc. d/b/a West Academic. Reprinted with the permission of West Academic Publishing.

CIVIL PROCEDURE STORIES (K. Clermont ed., 2nd ed. 2008). Copyright © 2008 LEG, Inc. d/b/a West Academic. Reprinted with the permission of West Academic Publishing.

Ely, "The Irrepressible Myth of Erie," 87 HARV. L. REV. 693 (1974). Copyright © 1974. Reprinted with permission of the Harvard Law Review via Copyright Clearance Center.

L. Hansberry, TO BE YOUNG, GIFTED AND BLACK: LORRAINE HANSBERRY IN HER OWN WORDS (adapted by R. Nemiroff 1969). Reprinted with the permission of Simon & Schuster, Inc. Copyright © 1969 by Robert Nemiroff and Robert Nemiroff as Executor of the Estate of Lorraine Hansberry. All rights reserved.

Jackson, "Tribute to Country Lawyers: A Review," A.B.A.J., Mar. 1944, at 136. Reprinted by permission, © 1944. The ABA Journal is published by the American Bar Association.

Kahan et al., "Whose Eyes Are You Going to Believe? Scott v. Harris and the Perils of Cognitive Illiberalism," 122 HARV.L.REV. 837 (2009). Copyright © 2009. Reprinted with permission of the Harvard Law Review via Copyright Clearance Center.

McCORMICK ON EVIDENCE (K. Broun ed. 7th ed. 2014). Copyright © 2014 LEG, Inc. d/b/a West Academic. Reprinted with the permission of West Academic Publishing.

McElhaney, "Make 'Em Laugh" A.B.A.J., Oct. 2002, at 52-53. Reprinted by permission, © 2002. The ABA Journal is published by the American Bar Association.

Moore, "Recent Trends in Judicial Interpretation in Railroad Cases Under the Federal Employers' Liability Act," 29 MARQUETTE L.REV. 73 (1946). Copyright © 1946. Reprinted with permission of the Marquette Law Review.

NEWBERG ON CLASS ACTIONS (5th ed. 2013). Copyright © 2013 Thomson Reuters. Reprinted with permission of Thomson Reuters.

O'Connor, "The Essentials and Expendables of the Missouri Plan," 74 MO. L. REV. 479 (2009). Copyright © 2009. Reprinted with permission of the Missouri Law Review.

T. Petzinger, Jr. OIL AND HONOR (1987). Reprinted by permission of the Putnam Publishing Group from OIL AND HONOR by Thomas Petzinger, Jr. Copyright © 1987 by Thomas Petzinger, Jr.

RESTATEMENT (SECOND) OF CONFLICT OF LAWS, copyright © 1971 by the American Law Institute. All rights reserved. Reprinted with permission.

RESTATEMENT (SECOND) OF THE LAW OF JUDGMENTS, copyright © 1982 by the American Law Institute. All rights reserved. Reprinted with permission.

RESTATEMENT OF THE LAW OF JUDGMENTS, copyright © 1942 by the American Law Institute. All rights reserved. Reprinted with permission.

Rizzi, "Erie Memoirs Reveal Drama, Tragedy," HARV. L. REC., Sept. 24, 1976, at 2. Copyright © 1976. Reprinted with permission of the Harvard Law Record.

Roosevelt, "Choice of Law in Federal Courts: from *Erie* and *Klaxon* to CAFA and *Shady Grove*," 106 NW.U.L.REV. 1 (2012). Copyright © 2012 and reprinted by special permission of Northwestern University School of Law, Northwestern University Law Review.

Trubek et al., "The Costs of Ordinary Litigation," 31 UCLA L. Rev. 72 (1983). Copyright © 1983. Reprinted with permission of the Regents of the University of California. All rights reserved.

C. Wright et al., FEDERAL PRACTICE AND PROCEDURE: CIVIL (3rd & 4th eds. 2015). Copyright © 2015 Thomson Reuters. Reprinted with permission of Thomson Reuters.

C. Wright et al., FEDERAL PRACTICE AND PROCEDURE: CRIMINAL (4th ed. 2015). Copyright © 2015 Thomson Reuters. Reprinted with permission of Thomson Reuters.

Zeisel, ". . . And Then There Were None: The Diminution of the Federal Jury," 38 U.CHI.L.REV. 710 (1971). Copyright © 1971. Reprinted with permission of the University of Chicago Law Review via Copyright Clearance Center.

SUMMARY OF CONTENTS

TABLE OF CONTENTS

TABLE OF CASES

The principal cases are in bold type.

TABLE OF STATUTES

TABLE OF RULES AND RESTATEMENT PROVISIONS

UNIVERSITY CASEBOOK SERIES®

CIVIL PROCEDURE

REPRESENTING CLIENTS IN CIVIL LITIGATION

CHAPTER 1

INTRODUCTION: "SECURING A JUST, SPEEDY, AND INEXPENSIVE DETERMINATION."

I. INTRODUCTION

A. "THE MORE PEPSI YOU DRINK, THE MORE GREAT STUFF YOU'RE GOING TO GET!"

In October 1995, a young man watches a television commercial in which PepsiCo, Inc. introduces a new advertising campaign. The commercial highlights several items that can be obtained in exchange for "Pepsi Points" that are attached to specially-marked Pepsi products. The items featured in the commercial include a tee shirt (for 75 Pepsi Points), sunglasses (175 Pepsi Points), and a leather jacket (1450 Pepsi Points). The commercial ends with a shot of a student landing a fighter jet outside his high school, stating for the camera, "Sure beats the bus." The following words then flash on the screen: "HARRIER FIGHTER 7,000,000 PEPSI POINTS."

Although he soon realized how difficult it would be to buy enough Pepsi products to amass 7,000,000 Pepsi Points, John Leonard discovered that the Pepsi Stuff Catalogue stated that, although at least 15 Pepsi Points must be presented to obtain any of the offered prizes, additional Pepsi Points could be purchased for tens cents per point. Leonard then presented to PepsiCo 15 Pepsi Points and a check for $700,008.50. In return, he asked that PepsiCo provide him with a Harrier Jet such as the one featured in the original Pepsi television commercial. Perhaps not surprisingly, PepsiCo officials told Leonard that the television commercial was not really an offer to supply drinkers of Pepsi with a fighter jet. It instead stated that this aspect of the commercial was "clearly a joke," that Leonard could not reasonably have assumed that PepsiCo was offering its customers the opportunity to secure a military aircraft, and that it was returning his check to him.

Although the specific facts underlying this dispute are a bit out of the ordinary, the nature of the dispute is not atypical of those arising on a regular basis across the country and around the world. Two people have engaged in a transaction, and one of them believes he has been injured by the action of the other. The aggrieved person chooses to formalize his dispute by filing a civil action against the other in a

United States District Court. This chapter uses this dispute and the resulting federal civil action (*Leonard v. PepsiCo, Inc.*) to illustrate how lawsuits are filed, litigated, and determined. As you examine this case, you also should become familiar with procedural terminology and the processes commonly used to resolve civil actions in federal and state courts in this country.

B. BUT ISN'T *LEONARD V. PEPSICO, INC.* A CONTRACTS CASE?

Leonard v. PepsiCo, Inc. is a case found in most contracts casebooks. Chances are that you will study this case in your contracts course. The case garnered a significant amount of media attention, there is a Wikipedia discussion of the case,[1] and the Pepsi Stuff television commercial(s) can be found on YouTube.[2] The case is included in contracts textbooks to illustrate the traditional prerequisites for a valid contract offer in a contemporary factual context.

However, the case also nicely illustrates the manner in which lawyers use the civil litigation process to attempt to translate contracts, torts or property claims into relief for their clients. The quality of a claim under the substantive law of contracts is not useful to your client unless it is credited by the opposing party (who offers a settlement prior to trial) or the judge (who renders a judgment in favor of your client).

Thus not only *Leonard*, but virtually all of the cases you will read in your first year of law school, are not just contracts, torts, or property cases—but civil procedure cases as well. You therefore can enhance your learning of civil procedure by the way in which you approach the "non-civil procedure" cases that you read in your other courses.

How can you do this? When reading any case, ask yourself the following questions:

- In what court (state or federal) was the case filed?
- Is the case still in the trial court or is it now in a court of appeals or supreme court?
- If the case is in federal court, what is the basis of subject-matter jurisdiction?
- Is it clear that the court has personal jurisdiction over the defendant?
- What is the procedural posture of the case as reported in your textbook (*e.g.*, is the case being considered because the defendant has filed a motion to dismiss or for summary judgment)?

---

[1] http://en.wikipedia.org/wiki/Leonard_v._Pepsico,_Inc.
[2] http://www.youtube.com/watch?v=ZdackF2H7Qc.

- How does the procedural posture of the case lead to the court's ultimate decision (*i.e.*, does the court of appeals affirm the trial court not because it necessarily agrees with that court but because the trial court has not abused its discretion)?

By approaching the cases in all of your courses in this fashion, you will gain a greater appreciation of how civil procedure works in practice. Perhaps most importantly, you should be alert to the procedural significance of cases in which the defendant has filed a motion to dismiss for failure to state a claim upon which relief can be granted.[3] In ruling on such a motion, the court must presume that all of the allegations of the complaint are true and construe those allegations most favorably to the plaintiff.[4]

This means that motions to dismiss typically test the substance of the legal claim asserted in a complaint, rather than the underlying facts. Assume, for instance, that a student filed a civil action alleging that she suffered emotional distress because a professor wore to class each day "the ugliest neckties in the entire world." The professor's likely response to such a complaint would be to file a motion to dismiss for failure to state a claim upon which relief can be granted. In ruling on that motion, the court would not seek to determine whether the neckties were truly "the ugliest in the entire world." Instead, the judge would presume that this allegation was true and then determine whether, even if the ties were that ugly, the student is entitled to legal relief for being subjected to such an awful sight. Fortunately for the professor, there is no tort or other substantive law that provides a valid claim for such a student. The judge's resulting dismissal of the student complaint therefore would not determine the actual beauty of the neckties. Instead, it would represent a determination that being subjected to even the "ugliest neckties in the entire world" does not constitute a violation of law entitling one to a legal remedy.

The overwhelming majority of the cases that you will read in law school involve civil procedure in some manner. Your sensitivity to this fact will enhance your understanding of both civil procedure and your other courses. It also will make you a more discerning lawyer once you enter practice, where cases are not pre-sorted into categories of torts, contracts, or civil procedure.

---

[3] These motions are recognized by Federal Rule of Civil Procedure 12(b)(6) and are sometimes referred to as "12(b)(6) motions."

[4] *Scheuer v. Rhodes*, 416 U. S. 232, 236 (1974). *But see Ashcroft v. Iqbal*, 556 U.S. 662, 678–79 (2009) (In considering a motion to dismiss, "Threadbare recitals of the elements of a cause of action, supported by mere conclusory statements, do not suffice. . . . [and] only a complaint that states a plausible claim for relief survives a motion to dismiss."); *Bell Atlantic Corp. v. Twombly*, 550 U.S. 544 (2007). The *Iqbal* and *Twombly* cases are discussed in Chapter 2.

II. THE INITIAL CLIENT INTERVIEW

Assume that you are a newly licensed attorney and that John Leonard schedules an appointment with you concerning his desire to obtain a Harrier Jet from PepsiCo for $700,000. What should you tell him? Most likely you will tell him little and use the initial interview to garner from him all potentially relevant facts. After initial pleasantries are exchanged, you would ask Leonard to describe his problem, obtain underlying factual details (ask him to "tell his story"), and determine the relief that he desires.[5]

At the conclusion of your initial interview with Leonard, you probably will tell him that you need to do further research concerning his possible contract claim and ask him to provide you with additional information (such as, for instance, any written communications with PepsiCo and descriptions of the advertising campaign offering Pepsi Stuff). In addition to researching his potential contract claims, you probably also will conduct at least some research concerning the procedural routes to the vindication of those claims in a federal or state court.

If Leonard decides to retain you as counsel, further conversation will be necessary to determine just how to pursue his claims against PepsiCo. Attorneys are governed by rules of ethics adopted by the highest court in each state and the District of Columbia. Most of these rules are based on, or are identical to, the American Bar Association's Model Rules of Professional Conduct. Thus Leonard's New York counsel were bound by the New York Rules of Professional Conduct, Rule 1.2(a) of which in part provides that, with certain limited exceptions, a "lawyer shall abide by a client's decisions concerning the objectives of representation and * * * shall consult with the client as to the means by which they are to be pursued."

The initial question that your client must answer is whether to actually proceed with the filing of a lawsuit against PepsiCo. As Figure 1–1 illustrates, only 5 percent of grievances result in the actual filing of a civil lawsuit.

---

[5]   R. L. Dessem, *Pretrial Litigation: Law, Policy & Practice* 12–18 (5th ed. 2011).

As you will see in Sections III(C) and (D) of Chapter 10, an attorney's interview with her client is generally protected from later disclosure by the attorney-client privilege, while the attorney's investigation and other pretrial preparation should be protected by the work-product doctrine.

FIGURE 1–1
A DISPUTE PYRAMID: THE GENERAL PATTERN
NO. PER 1,0000 GRIEVANCES[6]

Court Filings	50
Lawyers	103
Disputes	449
Claims	718
Grievances	1,000

There are, in fact, many reasons why an individual might not want to file a civil action. Lawsuits are expensive in time, money, and disruption of lives and working relationships. There also may be alternatives to litigation that can provide some redress to an injured person. Indeed, in some states attorneys are expected to discuss with their clients alternatives to civil actions such as mediation, arbitration, and negotiation.[7]

Assume that you have confirmed that your new client wants to file a civil action. You then must research the governing substantive law (for John Leonard, the law of contracts). As you will explore in Chapter 2, Rule 11(b) of the Federal Rules of Civil Procedure requires counsel to conduct "an inquiry reasonable under the circumstances" to confirm that:

- A civil action would not be presented for any improper purpose, such as to harass, cause unnecessary delay, or needlessly increase the cost of litigation (Rule 11(b)(1));

- The claims you will bring on behalf of John Leonard are warranted under existing contract law or you can make a nonfrivolous argument for extending existing law to support such claims (Rule 11(b)(2)); and

- There is evidentiary support for John Leonard's claims or, if specifically identified in the complaint, there will likely be evidentiary support for those claims after a reasonable opportunity for further investigation or discovery (Rule 11(b)(3)).[8]

---

[6] Trubek, et al., "The Costs of Ordinary Litigation," 31 *UCLA L. Rev.* 72, 87 (Figure 2) (1983).

[7] *E.g.*, Colorado Rules of Professional Conduct Rule 2.1; Georgia Aspirational Statements on Professionalism (Specific Aspirational Ideals as to Clients).

[8] As discussed in Chapter 2, the attorney's signature on a civil complaint or other litigation document is a certification that these requirements have been met. Rule 11(b)(1)–(3) of the Federal Rules of Civil Procedure.

Your focus as an attorney now moves from the substantive law of contracts to the various procedural possibilities that you might invoke in a civil action against PepsiCo.

A. STATE OR FEDERAL COURT?

In addition to determining whether her client has suffered legal harm, the attorney must decide where she might file a civil action to seek legal relief for her client. The usual choices will be (1) in a state court of general jurisdiction or (2) in a United States District Court.

Whether a court can hear a specific type of civil action is dependent upon the court's subject-matter jurisdiction—or judicial power over that specific type of action. State trial courts of general jurisdiction have subject-matter jurisdiction to hear all cases, except categories of cases that are specifically excluded from that court's jurisdiction. Many state courts of general jurisdiction are precluded from hearing cases in which the parties claim less than a minimum monetary amount, with such claims instead being heard by a municipal, small claims, or other state court. All states also have an appellate court that reviews judgments of the state trial courts. Some states (particularly larger states) have both an intermediate court of appeals and a state supreme court. In these states, final judgments of the trial courts can be appealed to the intermediate court of appeals, while the state's highest appellate court has jurisdiction to review judgments of the intermediate court of appeals.

The names of state trial and appellate courts vary from state to state. In most states the highest appellate court is called the "supreme court," and the intermediate court of appeals is called the "court of appeals." However, in New York the highest appellate court is the "Court of Appeals," while the trial court of general jurisdiction is called the "Supreme Court."

In addition to the 50 state court systems, there is a separate system of federal courts with jurisdiction to hear many civil actions. United States District Courts initially were established in the Judiciary Act of 1791, 1 Stat. 73 (1789), and today there are 94 such courts: in all 50 states, the District of Columbia, Puerto Rico, the Virgin Islands, Guam, and the Northern Mariana Islands. Each state has at least one federal district court, while some states (such as California, New York and Texas) are divided into four separate federal judicial districts. While there is only a single United States District Court for the District of Idaho, California contains the United States District Courts for the Eastern District of California, the Central District of California, the Northern District of California, and the Southern District of California.

Final judgments in the United States District Courts can be appealed by the losing party to one of the twelve regional United States Courts of Appeals. The geographic boundaries of the 94 federal district courts and the 12 regional courts of appeals are shown in Figure 1–2. In addition to the 11 numbered regional courts of appeals shown in Figure 1–2, there is a separate court of appeals, the United States Court of Appeals for the District of Columbia Circuit, which considers appeals from the United States District Court for the District of Columbia. The final federal court of appeals shown in Figure 1–2 is the United States Court of Appeals for the Federal Circuit, which handles specialized federal appeals from across the country such as some patent actions and appeals from the Court of International Trade and the Court of Federal Claims.

FIGURE 1–2
GEOGRAPHIC BOUNDARIES OF UNITED STATES COURTS OF APPEALS AND UNITED STATES DISTRICT COURTS[9]

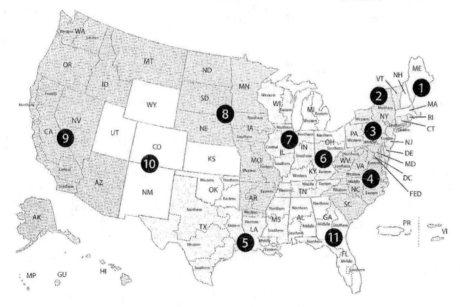

At the head of the federal judiciary is the United States Supreme Court. The Supreme Court can hear cases from the United States Courts of Appeals and some decisions of the highest courts of the 50 states, the District of Columbia, and Puerto Rico. In contrast to appeals from federal district courts to the United States Courts of Appeal, the United States Supreme Court is required to hear very few cases. Instead, through the grant of a writ of certiorari, the Supreme Court has the discretion to determine what cases it will hear. However, in its review of state court decisions, the Supreme Court only has the

---

[9]   http://www.uscourts.gov/uscourts/images/CircuitMap.pdf.

jurisdiction to interpret federal law, with the highest court of each state being the ultimate authority on the interpretation of that state's law.

In a country in which laws are enacted by both the United States Congress and 50 state legislatures, it might make sense to ask state courts to adjudicate only disputes involving state law and federal courts to hear only civil actions involving federal law. This is not, however, the way in which the jurisdiction of state and federal courts is allocated. Instead, many civil actions involving federal law (such as, for instance, federal civil rights claims) can be heard and decided in either state or federal courts; federal and state courts have concurrent jurisdiction over such claims.

There are, though, some claims arising under federal law, such as those involving antitrust, admiralty, and bankruptcy, that only the federal courts can hear. In these cases, Congress has statutorily provided that the federal courts' subject-matter jurisdiction is exclusive (meaning that the state courts cannot exercise jurisdiction over such claims). Whether federal district courts have jurisdiction that is concurrent with state courts or have exclusive power to hear claims arising under federal law, this jurisdictional power, or subject-matter jurisdiction, is provided by the congressional grant of jurisdiction contained in 28 U.S.C. § 1331 or in another specific federal jurisdictional statute.[10] Such federal subject-matter jurisdiction over claims arising under federal law is referred to as "federal-question jurisdiction."

Not only can state courts adjudicate many claims arising under federal law, but federal district courts can hear claims arising under state law in many circumstances. In addition to the federal subject-matter jurisdiction conveyed by 28 U.S.C. § 1331 for civil actions "arising under the Constitution, laws, or treaties of the United States," 28 U.S.C. § 1332 conveys "diversity of citizenship" jurisdiction. This, the second major grant of federal subject-matter jurisdiction, generally provides a federal judicial forum for civil actions involving citizens of different states.

Federal diversity jurisdiction under 28 U.S.C. § 1332 also extends to civil actions between citizens of a state and citizens of a foreign state or a foreign state itself. In contrast to federal-question actions, which require no minimum amount in controversy, 28 U.S.C. § 1332(a) provides that federal diversity actions must involve a "matter in controversy [that] exceeds the sum or value of $75,000, exclusive of interest and costs." In addition, 28 U.S.C. § 1367 provides that, if a federal district court can exercise subject matter jurisdiction over federal diversity or federal-question claims, it also may be able to

---

[10] The United States Code is the official compilation of federal statutes enacted by the United States Congress. Title 28 is the section of the Code that contains the federal statutes concerning the federal courts and federal judicial procedure. Thus 28 U.S.C. § 1331 refers to Section 1331 of Title 28 of the United States Code.

exercise subject-matter jurisdiction over related non-federal (state law) claims. These three major types of federal subject-matter jurisdiction are considered in Chapter 3, but the basic parameters of such jurisdictional bases are set forth in Figure 1–3.

FIGURE 1–3
TYPES OF FEDERAL SUBJECT-MATTER JURISDICTION

Type of Subject-Matter Jurisdiction	Statutory Provision	Basis of Federal Subject-Matter Jurisdiction
Federal Question Jurisdiction	28 U.S.C. § 1331	Action "arise[s] under the Constitution, laws, or treaties of the United States"
Federal Diversity Jurisdiction	28 U.S.C. § 1332(a)	Complete Diversity of Citizenship and more than $75,000 in Controversy
Supplemental Federal Jurisdiction	28 U.S.C. § 1367	If district courts have original jurisdiction, supplemental jurisdiction is generally available "over all other claims that are so related to claims in the action within such original jurisdiction that they form part of the same case or controversy under Article III of the United States Constitution."

So, depending upon the substantive law upon which the claim is based (state or federal) or whether the parties to the civil action are citizens of different states, counsel may have the option of filing the lawsuit in either state or federal court. In making the decision as to the court in which to file the civil action, counsel should consider which judicial forum will be the most advantageous for her client. This may depend upon the judges likely to hear the case in the different courts, the likely jury pool, prior interpretations of the substantive and procedural law in the different trial and appellate courts, the probable time it will take to reach trial in these courts, the relative convenience of the courts for counsel, the parties, and witnesses, and counsel's ultimate sense that her client will "do better" in one jurisdiction than another.

If the decision is made that a United States District Court is the optimal forum to hear the civil action, counsel must determine whether the procedural requirements for filing such a civil action can be met. Those requirements are discussed in the following section of this text.

B. PROCEDURAL PREREQUISITES AND POSSIBILITIES IN THE FEDERAL COURTS.

Your client has told you that he would like to file a civil action to obtain redress for the injury that he has suffered. Before actually filing that lawsuit, you must ensure that all of the prerequisites for a civil action have been satisfied. Although these requirements will be discussed in much greater detail later in this text, a summary of the major requirements is included in Rule 12(b) of the Federal Rules of Civil Procedure. Rule 12(b) provides, in effect, a checklist for the filing of a civil action in a United States District Court and should guide counsel to ask the following questions:

1. DOES THE COMPLAINT STATE A CLAIM UPON WHICH RELIEF CAN BE GRANTED? [RULE 12(b)(6)]

Before considering the procedural means by which the client's claims might be asserted in the state or federal courts, the attorney should determine whether her client has a good claim for relief under the law of torts, contracts, property, or other substantive law. In the event that the facts alleged in the complaint do not set forth a valid claim, Rule 12(b)(6) of the Federal Rules of Civil Procedure authorizes the defendant to move to dismiss the action for "failure to state a claim upon which relief can be granted."

In the *PepsiCo* case, John Leonard's attorney must research the common (non-statutory) law governing contracts, fraud, and specific performance, as well as state and federal statutes (such as consumer protection laws) under which Leonard might bring his claims. Rule 11(b)(2) requires that Leonard's attorney determine "that to the best of [that attorney's] knowledge, information, and belief, formed after an inquiry reasonable under the circumstances * * * the claims [asserted in the complaint] are warranted by existing law or by a nonfrivolous argument for extending, modifying, or reversing existing law or for establishing new law."

2. DOES THE COURT HAVE SUBJECT-MATTER JURISDICTION? [RULE 12(b)(1)]

In order for a court to entertain any civil action, the court must have subject-matter jurisdiction over that action, which is the judicial power to entertain that particular type of case. Because federal district courts are courts of limited jurisdiction, the subject-matter jurisdiction of those courts must be explicitly authorized by Congress. As we will see in Chapter 3, the major types of federal subject-matter jurisdiction are federal-question jurisdiction (under 28 U.S.C. § 1331) and diversity of citizenship jurisdiction (under 28 U.S.C. § 1332). If a federal court does not possess subject-matter jurisdiction, the defendant can move at any time to dismiss the civil action pursuant to Federal Rule of Civil Procedure 12(b)(1).

3. DOES THE COURT HAVE PERSONAL JURISDICTION? [RULE 12(b)(2)]

In addition to subject-matter jurisdiction over the particular type of civil action, the court also must have personal jurisdiction over the parties to the lawsuit. By filing its action in a particular jurisdiction, the plaintiff subjects himself to the personal jurisdiction of that court. As we will see in Chapter 4, determining whether the court has personal jurisdiction over a defendant can be more difficult. The defendant can challenge the court's personal jurisdiction by filing a motion to dismiss under Federal Rule of Civil Procedure 12(b)(2).

4. DOES THE COURT HAVE VENUE? [RULE 12(b)(3)]

Even if a court system can assert both subject-matter and personal jurisdiction over an action, this may not mean that every court in that court system can entertain that claim. State and federal venue rules allocate cases to specific courts within a court system based upon the nexus between the parties or the case to that court. Pursuant to Rule 12(b)(3) of the Federal Rules of Civil Procedure, a defendant can move to dismiss an action because the court does not have venue over that action.

5. IS THE PROCESS SUFFICIENT? [RULE 12(b)(4)]

"Process" generally refers to the summons and complaint with which a defendant must be served to notify him that a civil action has been filed against him. Rule 4 of the Federal Rules of Civil Procedure governs the content, issuance, and service of process, and Rule 12(b)(4) authorizes the defendant to seek dismissal of the action if the process itself is insufficient. Rule 4(a) lists the contents of the summons, and an electronic summons form is available on the website of the Administrative Office of the United States Courts.[11] The civil summons is the document that formally informs a defendant that he has been sued and that an answer or Rule 12 motion must be filed within 21 days (unless the defendant is the United States or a United States agency, officer, or employee, in which case Rule 12(a)(3) allows 60 days for the defendant's response).

6. IS THE SERVICE OF PROCESS SUFFICIENT? [RULE 12(b)(5)]

Rule 12(b)(5) recognizes the defense of insufficient service of process. Thus, not only must the process (summons) be sufficient, but the plaintiff must serve the defendant in the manner specifically

---

[11] http://www.uscourts.gov/uscourts/FormsAndFees/Forms/AO440.pdf. A civil summons form also can be obtained from the clerk's office in the district in which the case will be filed.

provided by Rule 4 of the Federal Rules of Civil Procedure. Traditionally, this meant that the summons and complaint had to be personally handed to the defendant or that the process had to at least be left for the defendant at his dwelling or with an authorized agent. Rule 4, though, now authorizes separate means by which defendants can be served in a foreign country or by which minors, incompetent persons, corporations, the United States, and other governments can be served.

Although Rule 4 authorizes several methods by which the plaintiff can effect service of process upon a defendant, Rule 4(d) allows competent adults, corporations, and associations to waive formal service of process. Rule 4(d)(1) allows the plaintiff to send such defendants by first-class mail "or other reliable means" a copy of the complaint and a written request that they waive formal service of process. Both a carrot and a stick are offered the defendant to induce his agreement to waive formal service.

If a defendant agrees to waive formal service of process, Rule 4(d)(3) extends the defendant's time to answer the complaint to 60 days (or 90 days, if the waiver request was sent to the defendant outside any judicial district of the United States). In addition, Rule 4(d)(2) provides:

> If a defendant located within the United States fails, without good cause, to sign and return a waiver requested by a plaintiff located within the United States, the court must impose on the defendant:
>
> (A) the expenses later incurred in making service; and
>
> (B) the reasonable expenses, including attorney's fees, of any motion required to collect those service expenses.

Thus there are good reasons to expedite the forward movement of a civil action by agreeing to waive formal service of process.

7.   HAVE ALL NECESSARY PARTIES BEEN JOINED PURSUANT TO RULE 19? [RULE 12(b)(7)]

Federal Rule of Civil Procedure 12(b)(7) recognizes the defense of "failure to join a party under Rule 19." As you will learn in Chapter 4, Rule 19(a) of the Federal Rules of Civil Procedure requires that a federal civil action include any person (1) who is subject to service of process; (2) whose joinder will not deprive the court of subject-matter jurisdiction; and (3) who is situated in relation to the civil action so that either (A) "in that person's absence, the court cannot accord complete relief among existing parties" or (B) that person is so situated that disposing of the action in that person's absence may (i) as a practical matter impair or impede the person's ability to protect its interest relating to the subject of the action or (ii) leave an existing party to the lawsuit subject to a substantial risk of incurring double, multiple, or otherwise inconsistent obligations because of the interest. While a person cannot be bound by a lawsuit to which he is not a party, Rule 19(a) requires the joinder of a person to a civil action if, as a practical matter, rights of either that person or existing parties to the lawsuit will be impaired in that person's absence from the action.

8.   HAVE PROCEDURAL PREREQUISITES OTHER THAN THOSE LISTED IN RULE 12(b) BEEN SATISFIED?

In addition to the procedural requirements listed in Rule 12(b), Federal Rule of Civil Procedure 8(a)(3) requires that the complaint contain "a demand for the relief sought." A question that John Leonard and his attorney undoubtedly discussed before Leonard's complaint was filed was whether he really wanted to seek a court order requiring PepsiCo to provide him with the Harrier Jet or instead would be satisfied with money damages to compensate him for PepsiCo's failure to provide him with the jet. Leonard's amended complaint sought both specific performance (a court order requiring that PepsiCo provide him with the jet) and, in the alternative, the damages that he suffered by PepsiCo's refusal to fulfill the terms of the purported contract by providing the jet.

In addition to the suit prerequisites set forth in Rule 12(b), there may be other requirements that must be satisfied to ensure the successful prosecution of a federal civil action. Before actually filing the complaint with the court, it usually makes sense to contact those named as defendants in the complaint in an effort to settle the parties' dispute. Once the civil action is filed, parties' positions harden. The defendant also may be at least somewhat inclined to settle in order to avoid having been named as a defendant in a formal legal proceeding. Thus counsel for plaintiffs often send a demand letter to the opposing parties, offering to discuss settlement before the action is filed. In order to add credibility to the demand letter, a copy of the complaint that will be filed if settlement is not reached may be attached to the demand letter.

In some jurisdictions, and with respect to some claims, there may be a requirement that certain administrative remedies be exhausted before the civil lawsuit can commence. For example, an employment discrimination complaint cannot be filed seeking relief under the federal Civil Rights Act of 1964 unless the plaintiff first files an administrative charge with the Equal Employment Opportunity Commission or counterpart state agency.[12]

Finally, the local rules of the federal district court in which the action will be filed should be checked to be sure that all applicable requirements are met. These rules may specify, for instance, the information that attorneys must include in the signature lines of the complaint, the font typeface size to be used in all court documents, to

---

[12]   42 U.S.C. § 2000e–5. *See also* 28 U.S.C. § 2675 (Federal Tort Claims Act); 42 U.S.C. § 6972(b) (citizen suits under Resource Conservation and Recovery Act of 1976).

whom the check for the required fee must be made payable, and the civil cover sheet that must be filed with a complaint in the federal district courts.[13]

The procedural prerequisites for a federal civil action are summarized in Figure 1–4.

FIGURE 1–4
PREREQUISITES FOR A FEDERAL CIVIL ACTION*

SUIT PREREQUISITE	Subject Matter Jurisdiction Rule 12(b)(1)	Personal Jurisdiction Rule 12(b)(2)	Venue Rule 12(b)(3)	Process Rule 12(b)(4)	Service of Process Rule 12(b)(5)
TEST(S)	1) Fed. Question: action "arise[s] under the Constitution, laws or treaties of the United States," 28 U.S.C. § 1331; or 2) Diversity of Citizenship: Complete diversity of citizenship and more than $75,000 in controversy, 28 U.S.C. § 1332.	Minimum contacts test of International Shoe Co. v. Washington, 326 U.S. 310 (1945): 1) Minimum contacts with forum state; 2) Suit arises from contacts (unless general jurisdiction exists); and 3) Suit does not offend "traditional notions of fair play and substantial justice."	1) Specified in substantive statute; or 2) 28 U.S.C. § 1391: a) where any defendant resides (if all in same state); b) where a substantial part of events/ omissions giving rise to claim occurred or subject property is situated; or, if no other venue, (c) where any defendant is subject to personal jurisdiction.	Federal Rule of Civil Procedure 4(a) and (b).	Federal Rule of Civil Procedure 4(c)–(n).

* In addition to the prerequisites shown, the complaint must state a claim upon which relief can be granted (Rule 12(b)(6)) and any Rule 19 required parties must be joined (Rule 12(b)(7)). There also are special federal statutes governing subject-matter jurisdiction and venue that have not been shown.

C. WHAT QUESTIONS SHOULD I ASK?

Rule 1.1(a) of the New York Rules of Professional Conduct is identical to Rule 1 of the ABA Model Rule of Professional Conduct. It sets forth the lawyer's first duty to her clients:

> A lawyer shall provide competent representation to a client. Competent representation requires the legal knowledge, skill, thoroughness and preparation reasonably necessary for the representation.

---

[13] *E.g.*, Civil Rule 5 of the United States District Court for the District of Rhode Island.

How does an attorney, especially a new attorney, acquire the "legal knowledge, skill, thoroughness and preparation reasonably necessary for the representation"? While legal skill develops over time, newer attorneys can attempt to compensate for their relative inexperience by the thoroughness and preparation that comes from their hard work on behalf of their clients.[14]

The legal knowledge required by Rule 1.1 includes knowledge of the substantive law addressed in courses such as Contracts, Torts, and Property. In a contracts case, for instance, the attorney might ask her client about any offer(s) the defendant made, whether and how the defendant accepted any offers, what consideration was involved, and the damages that allegedly were suffered due to the failure to fulfill any accepted offers.

In a matter likely to result in civil litigation, Rule 1.1 also requires that the attorney have knowledge of the procedural law taught in Civil Procedure. In interviewing her client, just how should an attorney address such procedural law?

Federal Rule of Civil Procedure 12(b)(6) is a bridge between substantive and procedural law, requiring that the client must be able to "state a claim upon which relief can be granted" under the governing substantive law. So, in representing someone such as John Leonard, the lawyer should research contract law to determine what facts must be true for the client to state a valid claim against potential defendants. Thus, if John Leonard wanted to explore a federal civil action against PepsiCo, counsel should determine whether, when and where he watched the Pepsi commercial; whether he believed the commercial; whether he has any other relationship(s) with PepsiCo; what, if any, documents he has concerning this matter; and what relief he ultimately would like to obtain from PepsiCo. As you will learn in your other courses, there are specific elements that must be proven to establish each specific substantive claim, and these elements provide a handy checklist suggesting necessary questions to ask your client or otherwise determine through pretrial investigation.

In addition to confirming that contract or other substantive law will allow her client to "state a claim upon which relief can be granted" as required by Rule 12(b)(6), the lawyer must ensure that the other procedural prerequisites discussed in section II(B), *supra*, can be satisfied. As you will see in Chapter 3, if a proper basis of federal subject-matter jurisdiction is not asserted in the complaint, the defendant can move to dismiss the action pursuant to Rule 12(b)(1).

The two major bases for federal subject-matter jurisdiction are federal-question jurisdiction under Section 1331 of Title 28 of the

---

[14] A strong work ethic also helps to ensure that attorneys satisfy the requirements of Rule 1.3(a) of the New York Rules of Professional Conduct (and corresponding ABA Model Rule). Rule 1.3(a) provides: "A lawyer shall act with reasonable diligence and promptness in representing a client."

United States Code and federal diversity jurisdiction under Section 1332 of Title 28 of the United States Code. Section 1331 of Title 28 states: "The district courts shall have original jurisdiction of all civil actions arising under the Constitution, laws, or treaties of the United States." Section 1332(a) of Title 28 provides, in part:

> The district courts shall have original jurisdiction of all civil actions where the matter in controversy exceeds the sum or value of $75,000, exclusive of interest and costs, and is between—

> (1) citizens of different states * * *.

Thus there would be proper subject-matter jurisdiction for a federal court to hear an action by John Leonard against PepsiCo if either (1) Leonard asserts a claim against PepsiCo "arising under" federal law or (2) Leonard raises a claim for more than $75,000 and he and PepsiCo are "citizens of different states." Questions in the initial client interview should be used to determine whether the facts exist to establish either type of subject-matter jurisdiction. For instance, in order to determine the existence of federal diversity jurisdiction, counsel will want to determine the state of Leonard's citizenship and the approximate size of his monetary losses due to PepsiCo's failure to provide him with the Harrier Jet.

Counsel also must use the initial client interview to determine whether the other prerequisites for a federal action exist. Because PepsiCo is incorporated in North Carolina and has its principal place of business in New York, it is likely that federal courts in those states could exercise personal jurisdiction and venue over PepsiCo. Indeed, because of PepsiCo's size and national operations, it's possible that personal jurisdiction and venue might exist in other districts. However, personal jurisdiction and venue may exist over individuals and more localized companies in only a single district, allowing the defendant to move successfully to dismiss an action pursuant to Rule 12(b)(2) or 12(b)(3) due to lack of personal jurisdiction and venue. A motion to dismiss also can be filed under Rule 12(b)(4) (if there is insufficient process), 12(b)(5) (if the service of that process is insufficient), or 12(b)(7) (if a required party has not been joined to the action pursuant to Rule 19). From her research of the procedural law concerning a particular action, the attorney should learn whether there are additional administrative or other requirements that must be satisfied before suit is filed.

Both substantive and procedural requirements must be satisfied for the filing of a successful civil action. Through her client interviews and other pretrial investigation, counsel must confirm that these requirements are met. Indeed, Rule 11(b) provides that, by the submission of her client's complaint to the federal court, the attorney certifies that "to the best of [that attorney's] knowledge, information, and belief, formed after an inquiry reasonable under the circumstances," the complaint is not being presented for an improper purpose, the claims in the complaint "are warranted by existing law or by a nonfrivolous argument for extending, modifying, or reversing existing law or for establishing new law," and the factual contentions "have evidentiary support or, if specifically so identified, will likely have evidentiary support after a reasonable opportunity for further investigation or discovery." Because these attorney certifications are essential to professional legal practice, they are discussed in more detail in Chapter 2, Section III.

III. THE COURSE OF A FEDERAL CIVIL ACTION

After the attorney interviews her client, she must conduct the factual and legal research required by Rule 11 of the Federal Rules of Civil Procedure, consider settlement or other possible resolution of the dispute outside the courts, and satisfy any administrative requirements (such as filing a complaint with a state or federal administrative agency). Her next task will be to draft the complaint on behalf of her client, file that complaint with a federal district court that has subject-matter jurisdiction, personal jurisdiction, and venue over her client's claims, and serve the complaint upon the defendant.

Only about one percent of federal civil actions actually reach trial.[15] The path to trial is similar in federal and most state courts, proceeding from the filing of the complaint to the trial judge's entry of final judgment. This process is set forth in the following description of a federal civil action from the website of the Administrative Office of the United States Courts.[16]

> A federal civil case involves a legal dispute between two or more parties. A civil action begins when a party to a dispute files a complaint, and pays a filing fee required by statute. A plaintiff who is unable to pay the fee may file a request to proceed in forma pauperis. If the request is granted, the fee is waived.
>
> The Process
>
> To begin a civil lawsuit in federal court, the plaintiff files a complaint with the court and "serves" a copy of the complaint on the defendant. The complaint describes the plaintiff's damages or injury, explains how the defendant caused the harm, shows that the court has jurisdiction, and asks the court to order relief. A plaintiff may seek money to compensate for the damages, or may ask the court to order the defendant to

---

[15] Administrative Office of the United States Courts, Table C–4 (U.S. District Courts—Civil Cases Terminated, by Nature of Suit and Action Taken, During the 12-Month Period Ending Dec. 31, 2014), http://www.uscourts.gov/statistics/table/c–4/statistical-tables-federal-judiciary/2014/06/30.

[16] http://www.uscourts.gov/aboutfederal-courts/types-cases/civil-cases.

stop the conduct that is causing the harm. The court may also order other types of relief, such as a declaration of the legal rights of the plaintiff in a particular situation.

Case Preparation

There may be "discovery," where the litigants must provide information to each other about the case, such as the identity of witnesses and copies of any documents related to the case. The purpose of discovery is to prepare for trial by requiring the litigants to assemble their evidence and prepare to call witnesses. Each side also may file requests, or "motions," with the court seeking rulings on the discovery of evidence, or on the procedures to be followed at trial.

Discovery may include a deposition, requiring a witness to answer questions about the case before the trial. The witness answers questions from the lawyer under oath, in the presence of a court reporter, who produces a word-for-word account called a transcript.

Settling Differences

To avoid the expense and delay of having a trial, judges encourage the litigants to try to reach an agreement resolving their dispute. The courts encourage the use of mediation, arbitration, and other forms of alternative dispute resolution, designed to produce a resolution of a dispute without the need for trial or other court proceedings. As a result, litigants often agree to a "settlement." Absent a settlement, the court will schedule a trial. In a wide variety of civil cases, either side is entitled under the Constitution to request a jury trial. If the parties waive their right to a jury, then a judge without a jury will hear the case.

Trial Process

By applying rules of evidence, the judge determines which information may be presented in the courtroom. So that witnesses speak from their own knowledge and do not change their story based on what they hear another witness say, they are kept out of the courtroom until they testify. A court reporter keeps a record of the trial proceedings, and a deputy clerk of court keeps a record of each person who testifies and any documents, photographs, or other items introduced into evidence.

The opposing attorney may object if a question it invites the witness to say something that is not based on the witness's personal knowledge, is unfairly prejudicial, or is irrelevant to the case. Generally, the judge either overrules or sustains—allows—the objection. If the objection is sustained, the witness does not answer the question, and the attorney must move on to his next question. The court reporter records the objections so that a court of appeals can review the arguments later if necessary.

Closing

After evidence is heard, each side gives a closing argument. In a jury trial, the judge will explain the law that is relevant to the case and the decisions the jury needs to make. The jury generally is asked to determine whether the defendant is responsible for harming the plaintiff in some way, and then to determine the amount of damages that the defendant will be required to pay. If the case is tried before a judge without a jury, known as a "bench" trial, the judge will decide these issues or order some kind of relief to the prevailing party. In a civil case, the plaintiff must convince the jury by a "preponderance of the evidence" (i.e., that it is more likely than not) that the defendant is responsible for the harm the plaintiff has suffered.

———————

If shown as a flow chart, the basic steps in a civil action might look something like Figure 1–5.

FIGURE 1–5
TYPICAL PROGRESSION OF A FEDERAL CIVIL ACTION

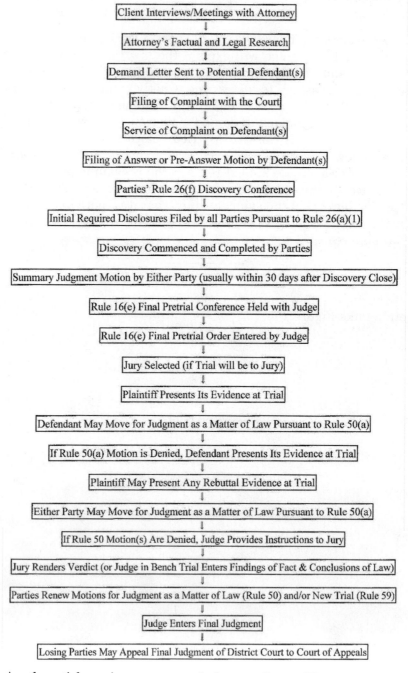

As the stickers in new car windows tell us, "Your Mileage May Vary," and a particular civil action may not proceed in precisely the manner shown in Figure 1–5. The federal district judge or magistrate judge will determine the details by which each individual civil action progresses in the district court. Attorneys always should follow Rule 16(b) pretrial scheduling orders, while in most actions the judge will enter an order governing the trial of an action after the Rule 16(e) final pretrial conference. While some judges and judicial districts approach pretrial and trial matters a bit differently, the basic approach set forth in Figure 1–5 is typical of what attorneys will encounter in most federal district courts.

IV. A CIVIL PROCEDURE GLOSSARY

An important part of becoming an attorney is learning a new language. Legal dictionaries define thousands of words with special meaning for lawyers and the legal system. In reading the case of *Leonard v. PepsiCo, Inc.* and your other law school cases, consider the following glossary of legal terms.[17] During your legal training, you will master this new vocabulary. Remember, though, that you were not conversant with these terms before coming to law school, and be sure to explain these words to your clients and other non-lawyers in the years ahead.

Affidavit*

A written or printed statement made under oath.

Answer*

The formal written statement by a defendant in a civil case that responds to a complaint, articulating the grounds for defense.

Choice of Law

Especially in actions with parties from different states or from a state other than the one in which a claim arises, the court will have to determine from which state to choose the law to apply in the civil action.

Complaint*

A written statement that begins a civil lawsuit, in which the plaintiff details the claims against the defendant.

Common Law*

The legal system that originated in England and is now in use in the United States, which relies on the articulation of legal principles in a historical succession of judicial decisions. Common law principles can be changed by legislation.

---

[17] The definitions of words with asterisks are taken from the glossary contained on the website of the Administrative Office of the United States Courts: http://www.uscourts.gov/glossary. This website also has links to the federal rules of practice and procedure (including the Federal Rules of Civil Procedure), proposed amendments to those rules, the local rules of each of the federal district courts, statistics concerning federal civil and criminal cases, court records, forms and fees, and various other educational resources.

Damages*

Money that a defendant pays a plaintiff in a civil case if the plaintiff has won. Damages may be compensatory (for loss or injury) or punitive (to punish and deter future misconduct).

Declaratory Judgment

A declaratory judgment is recognized by 28 U.S.C. § 2201 and Federal Rule of Civil Procedure 57. So long as there is an actual controversy between the parties and subject-matter jurisdiction and other procedural prerequisites are satisfied, federal courts may declare the respective rights of the parties (rather than or in addition to the award of damages or other remedies).

Defendant*

In a civil case, the person or organization against whom the plaintiff brings suit; in a criminal case, the person accused of the crime.

Discovery*

Procedures used to obtain disclosure of evidence before trial.

Dismissal with Prejudice*

Court action that prevents an identical lawsuit from being filed later.

Dismissal Without Prejudice*

Court action that allows the later filing. [Dismissals without prejudice typically are sought pursuant to Federal Rule of Civil Procedure 41(a) by a claimant who has decided, at least for now, not to proceed with its claims. Such dismissals are generally called voluntary dismissals.]

File*

To place a paper in the official custody of the clerk of court to enter into the files or records of a case.

Final Judgment Rule

The final judgment rule is a restriction on the jurisdiction of the federal courts of appeals created by 28 U.S.C. § 1291. The rule generally limits federal appellate jurisdiction to appeals from a federal district court's final judgment, rather than permitting parties to appeal orders as they are entered by the trial judge throughout the course of the district court proceedings.

Genuine Issue to Be Tried

Rule 56(a) in part provides: "The court shall grant summary judgment if the movant shows that there is no genuine dispute as to any material fact and the movant is entitled to judgment as a matter of law." Thus if there is a genuine dispute as to any material fact, the court must deny summary judgment and that factual dispute will be resolved at trial. Prior to its amendment in 2010, Rule 56 precluded summary judgment if there was "no genuine issue as to any material fact," rather than "no genuine dispute as to any material fact," and this test is also expressed as whether there is a "genuine issue to be tried" in *Leonard v. PepsiCo, Inc.*

Injunction*

A court order preventing one or more named parties from taking some action. A preliminary injunction often is issued to allow fact-finding, so a judge can determine whether a permanent injunction is justified.

Judgment*

The official decision of a court finally resolving the dispute between the parties to the lawsuit.

Jurisdiction

The two main types of jurisdiction are subject-matter jurisdiction (the legal authority or power of a court to hear and decide a certain type of action) and personal jurisdiction (the power of a court to entertain an action against a particular person).

Lawsuit*

A legal action started by a plaintiff against a defendant based on a complaint that the defendant failed to perform a legal duty which resulted in harm to the plaintiff.

Litigation*

A case, controversy, or lawsuit. Participants (plaintiffs and defendants) in lawsuits are called litigants.

Local Rules

In addition to the Federal Rules of Civil Procedure, individual United States District Courts have the authority pursuant to Rule 83 of the Federal Rules of Civil Procedure to adopt additional rules governing practice in that federal district court. Local rules must be consistent with the Federal Rules of Civil Procedure but not duplicate them. Instead, these rules are to fill in details not contained in the Federal Rules (such as, for instance, the form requirements for documents filed with the court).

Motion*

A request by a litigant to a judge for a decision on an issue relating to the case.

Motion to Dismiss

The motion to dismiss is provided by Rule 12(b) of the Federal Rules of Civil Procedure and allows the party opposing a claim (typically the defendant) to obtain a judicial ruling on the seven Rule 12(b) threshold defenses at the outset of a civil action.

Objective vs. Subjective Legal Standard

An objective standard focuses not on the particular individuals who may have been involved in the case, but on what an objective, "reasonable person" might have thought or how such a reasonable person might have acted. In contrast, a subjective standard is determined by the individual, subjective state of mind of an individual person (typically a plaintiff or defendant).

Opinion*

A judge's written explanation of the decision of the court. Because a case may be heard by three or more judges in the court of appeals, the opinion in appellate decisions can take several forms. If all the judges completely agree on the result, one judge will write the opinion for all. If all the judges do not agree, the formal decision will be based upon the view of the majority, and one member of the majority will write the opinion. The judges who did not agree with the majority may write separately in dissenting or concurring opinions to present their views. A dissenting opinion disagrees with the majority opinion because of the reasoning and/or the principles of law the majority used to decide the case. A concurring opinion agrees with the decision of the majority opinion, but offers further comment or clarification or even an entirely different reason for reaching the same result. Only the majority opinion can serve as binding precedent in future cases. See also precedent.

Personal Jurisdiction

The court's ability to render a judgment concerning a particular party to a civil action. While a plaintiff subjects himself to the personal jurisdiction of the court by filing the action, personal jurisdiction can become an issue when the plaintiff seeks to bind defendants who are geographically distant from the court and do not have significant ties or contacts with the state in which the court sits.

Plaintiff*

A person or business that files a formal complaint with the court.

Pleadings*

Written statements filed with the court that describe a party's legal or factual assertions about the case.

Precedent*

A court decision in an earlier case with facts and legal issues similar to a dispute currently before a court. Judges will generally "follow precedent"—meaning that they use the principles established in earlier cases to decide new cases that have similar facts and raise similar legal issues. A judge will disregard precedent if a party can show that the earlier case was wrongly decided, or that it differed in some significant way from the current case.

Procedure*

The rules for conducting a lawsuit; there are rules of civil procedure, criminal procedure, evidence, bankruptcy, and appellate procedure.

Removal

Removal is the procedure provided in 28 U.S.C. § 1441 that permits a defendant to move certain cases from the state court in which the plaintiff filed the action to a federal district court within that same geographic locale.

Restatement of Law

Founded in 1923, the American Law Institute (ALI) is comprised of leading judges, lawyers and law professors who produce treatises restating basic legal principles typically derived from jurisdictions across the country. In *Leonard v. PepsiCo, Inc.*, the court cites and relies upon the *Restatement (Second) of Contracts*.

Specific Performance

The form of judicial relief in which a court orders a party to take or not take specific action. In *Leonard v. PepsiCo, Inc.*, John Leonard sought not only damages from PepsiCo, but also specific performance requiring PepsiCo to provide him with the fighter jet that he alleged was promised in the Pepsi contest.

Statement of Uncontested Facts

Local rules in many federal district courts require the parties to submit a statement of uncontested facts in connection with motions for summary judgment or, later, as part of the parties' final pretrial order. Because the parties themselves reach agreement on relevant facts that are not in dispute, the court does not have to resolve such factual issues.

Subject-Matter Jurisdiction.

A court's power to hear and decide a particular type of case. The primary types of federal subject-matter jurisdiction are federal-question jurisdiction (in which a federal court can hear an action arising under federal substantive law) and diversity jurisdiction (in which a federal court can hear an action involving parties from different states; citizens of a state and citizens of a foreign state; or between a foreign state as plaintiff and citizens of one or more states).

Stipulation

A stipulation is an agreement between the parties concerning a question of fact or law relevant to a civil action. One form of stipulation is a statement of uncontested facts, which may be created in connection with a motion for summary judgment or offered as part of the parties' pretrial order. However, the parties may agree to oral or written stipulations at many other points before or during trial.

Summary Judgment

A decision made pursuant to Rule 56 of the Federal Rules of Civil Procedure on the basis of evidence presented before trial. Summary judgment may be possible when there is no real dispute between the parties concerning the relevant facts and, based on those undisputed facts, one party is entitled to judgment as a matter of law.

Transfer

The movement of a case from one court in a judicial system to another court within that same system. Cases can be transferred from one federal district court to another federal district court pursuant to 28 U.S.C. § 1404. However, there is no comparable procedure for transferring an action from one state court to a court in another state.

Venue*

The geographic area in which a court has jurisdiction. A change of venue is a change or transfer of a case from one judicial district to another.

V. How Do I Read a Case?

You now know the basic course of a civil action and are beginning to master the legal terminology. Governing legal principals of "the law" most typically are expressed in judicial opinions, statutes, and rules. In the book's next chapter you will be introduced to the application and interpretation of legal rules, specifically, the Federal Rules of Civil Procedure. In the next section of the present chapter you will read this text's first judicial opinion—from the case of *Leonard v. PepsiCo, Inc.* This is one of hundreds of cases that you will read in your first year of law school and one of thousands of cases that you will read over your professional career. How should you approach the reading of such cases?

A. Civil Actions, Parties, and Individual Claims.

All judicial decisions involve parties, one or more claims, and one or more civil actions. It's crucial that those reading a judicial opinion understand who is suing whom, for what, and where. It therefore may be helpful to sketch the parties, claims, and civil actions (if there are more than one). The case that follows, *Leonard v. PepsiCo, Inc.*, could be simply represented as follows:

Plaintiff John Leonard vs. Defendant PepsiCo, Inc. (S.D.N.Y.)

This alignment of parties can be taken from the case caption. The notation "S.D.N.Y." indicates that the case is pending in the United States District Court for the Southern District of New York.

When a plaintiff files a civil action, he or she typically asserts more than a single claim in that action. Not all of these claims may be relevant to the major holding of a judicial opinion, but it may be important to understand if there is more than one major claim asserted.

The two principal claims discussed in Judge Wood's opinion in *Leonard v. PepsiCo, Inc.* might be shown as follows:

Plaintiff John Leonard vs. Defendant PepsiCo, Inc. (S.D.N.Y.)

(1) Plaintiff Leonard → Defendant PepsiCo (Breach of Contract Claim)

(2) Plaintiff Leonard → Defendant PepsiCo (Fraud Claim)

In some civil actions, one or more defendants may themselves assert claims against the plaintiff(s) or other parties. It may be easier to understand the procedural posture of a case by diagraming these claims, too.

As you read *Leonard v. PepsiCo, Inc.*, you will learn that there actually were two separate civil actions that were consolidated in the United States District Court for the Southern District of New York. They might be diagramed as follows:

Case #1:

Plaintiff PepsiCo, Inc. vs. Defendant John Leonard (S.D.N.Y.— declaratory judgment)

Case #2:

Plaintiff John Leonard vs. Defendant PepsiCo, Inc. (Fl. State Court S.D.Fla. S.D.N.Y.)

(1) Plaintiff Leonard → Defendant PepsiCo (Breach of Contract Claim)

(2) Plaintiff Leonard → Defendant PepsiCo (Fraud Claim)

Although Case #2 ultimately reached the Southern District of New York, it initially was filed by John Leonard in state court in Florida. PepsiCo then removed this action from state court to federal district court in Florida, after which PepsiCo transferred the case to the United States District Court for the Southern District of New York.[18] The judge assigned to the first case (filed by PepsiCo in the United States District Court for the Southern District of New York), Judge Kimba Wood, dismissed PepsiCo's original action seeking a declaratory judgment. Then, in the opinion that follows, Judge Wood considered the motion for summary judgment filed by PepsiCo seeking dismissal of the claims that Leonard initially filed in Florida state court. These claims had been removed to federal court in Florida, and a federal judge in Florida ultimately transferred them to the United States District Court for the Southern District of New York.

Most of the cases that you will read in the first year of law school will not be as procedurally complex as was the litigation between John

---

[18] Removal from state to federal court is possible in certain circumstances pursuant to 28 U.S.C. § 1441, while transfer ("change of venue") from one federal district to another federal district court is provided in 28 U.S.C. § 1404. Removal is discussed in Chapter 3 of this text, while change of venue is considered in Chapter 4.

Leonard and PepsiCo, Inc. Regardless of the procedural complexity of a case, it is important that students (and lawyers) understand the procedural setting underlying the judicial opinions that they read. By quickly sketching the parties, civil actions, and claims leading to the judicial opinions they study, students will better understand the context, subtleties, and limits of those opinions.

B. CASE BRIEFING

To better understand the judicial opinions assigned in first-year courses, law students are advised to "brief" those cases. This structured analysis is a discipline that requires students to consolidate their understanding of cases and distill from judicial opinions the holdings or legal principles established by those cases. There are various structures for case briefing, and you should follow the recommendation of your professors as to the specific type of analysis that they suggest. It's much more important that you analyze your cases in some systematic fashion, rather than choose any particular analytic format. Regardless of the form of case briefing, it's crucial that you include in your analysis information about the procedural posture of the case and separate out the civil action(s), parties, and individual claims.

After an initial section setting forth the facts and procedural posture of the case, the case brief should continue with further analysis of the judicial opinion in question. One common structure for this further case briefing is "IRAC," which requires the reader to include in her case brief the Issue, Rule, Analysis, and Conclusion. The issue is the student's statement of the question decided by the court, such as: "Did the complaint contain sufficient facts to state a claim upon which relief can be granted under the Federal Rules of Civil Procedure?"[19] The rule section of the brief then sets forth the common law rule, statute, or other legal provision that is at issue in the case, such as "Rule 8(a) of the Federal Rules of Civil Procedure requires that a pleading contain a 'short and plain statement of the claim.'" The next IRAC section, the analysis, is the most important section of the case brief, for it is in this section that the student (or lawyer) traces the logic by which the court reaches its conclusion. The analysis should contain not only the arguments relied upon by the court in reaching its conclusion, but the arguments rejected by the court.[20] Finally, the IRAC case brief should conclude with a simple answer to the issue originally posed; *e.g.*, "Because Rule 8(a) merely requires a 'short and plain statement of the claim,' plaintiffs' complaint was sufficient to withstand a motion to dismiss and the court of appeals is reversed."

Whatever case briefing technique is used, it's important that the initial section of the brief set forth the facts underlying the case. These

---

[19] *E.g. Conley v. Gibson*, 355 U.S. 41 (1957), *infra* p. 69.

[20] These rejected arguments also may appear in the portion of the case brief devoted to any dissent to the majority or plurality opinion.

facts should include the "real world" facts outside the confines of the courthouse (*e.g.*, the parties were in a car accident, the Acme Company failed to fulfill its promise to Consumer, or Charles sold property to Susan). Just as importantly, this section should contain the procedural facts relevant to the civil action (*e.g.*, the court granted Acme's motion to dismiss, summary judgment was denied, or Charles refused to provide Susan with the report of his expert witness).

Whether in your law school courses or as an practicing attorney, it's important to keep a written record of the cases that you read. You will read many cases over the course of a semester, and attorneys read many cases doing legal research for matters that they handle. If a record is not kept of the cases read, and their holdings, you later may need to retrace your steps and reread cases that you read before. Notes also may save you time in preparing for other courses or future cases. Perhaps most importantly, preparing your own case briefs should help you learn the many cases that you will read during your legal training.

VI. THE CASE OF *LEONARD V. PEPSICO, INC.*

Having discussed what lawyers and clients might do in seeking judicial resolution of disputes, let's look at the procedural steps actually taken by the parties in John Leonard's attempt to obtain a Harrier Jet through his federal civil action against PepsiCo.

Leonard v. Pepsico, Inc.

United States District Court, Southern District of New York, 1999
88 F. Supp. 2d 116 *Affirmed Per Curiam*, 210 F.3d 88 (2d Cir. 2000)

OPINION & ORDER

■ KIMBA M. WOOD, DISTRICT JUDGE.

Plaintiff brought this action seeking, among other things, specific performance of an alleged offer of a Harrier Jet, featured in a television advertisement for defendant's "Pepsi Stuff" promotion. Defendant has moved for summary judgment pursuant to Federal Rule of Civil Procedure 56. For the reasons stated below, defendant's motion is granted.

I. Background

This case arises out of a promotional campaign conducted by defendant, the producer and distributor of the soft drinks Pepsi and Diet Pepsi. (See PepsiCo Inc.'s Rule 56.1 Statement ("Def. Stat.") ¶ 2.)[1] The promotion, entitled "Pepsi Stuff," encouraged consumers to collect "Pepsi Points" from specially marked packages of Pepsi or Diet Pepsi and redeem these points for merchandise featuring the Pepsi logo. Before introducing the promotion nationally, defendant conducted a test

---

[1] The Court's recitation of the facts of this case is drawn from the statements of uncontested facts submitted by the parties pursuant to Local Civil Rule 56.1. * * *

of the promotion in the Pacific Northwest from October 1995 to March 1996. A Pepsi Stuff catalog was distributed to consumers in the test market, including Washington State. Plaintiff is a resident of Seattle, Washington. While living in Seattle, plaintiff saw the Pepsi Stuff commercial that he contends constituted an offer of a Harrier Jet.

A. The Alleged Offer

Because whether the television commercial constituted an offer is the central question in this case, the Court will describe the commercial in detail. The commercial opens upon an idyllic, suburban morning, where the chirping of birds in sun-dappled trees welcomes a paperboy on his morning route. As the newspaper hits the stoop of a conventional two-story house, the tattoo of a military drum introduces the subtitle, "MONDAY 7:58 AM." The stirring strains of a martial air mark the appearance of a well-coiffed teenager preparing to leave for school, dressed in a shirt emblazoned with the Pepsi logo, a red-white-and-blue ball. While the teenager confidently preens, the military drumroll again sounds as the subtitle "T-SHIRT 75 PEPSI POINTS" scrolls across the screen. Bursting from his room, the teenager strides down the hallway wearing a leather jacket. The drumroll sounds again, as the subtitle "LEATHER JACKET 1450 PEPSI POINTS" appears. The teenager opens the door of his house and, unfazed by the glare of the early morning sunshine, puts on a pair of sunglasses. The drumroll then accompanies the subtitle "SHADES 175 PEPSI POINTS." A voiceover then intones, "Introducing the new Pepsi Stuff catalog," as the camera focuses on the cover of the catalog.

The scene then shifts to three young boys sitting in front of a high school building. The boy in the middle is intent on his Pepsi Stuff Catalog, while the boys on either side are each drinking Pepsi. The three boys gaze in awe at an object rushing overhead, as the military march builds to a crescendo. The Harrier Jet is not yet visible, but the observer senses the presence of a mighty plane as the extreme winds generated by its flight create a paper maelstrom in a classroom devoted to an otherwise dull physics lesson. Finally, the Harrier Jet swings into view and lands by the side of the school building, next to a bicycle rack. Several students run for cover, and the velocity of the wind strips one hapless faculty member down to his underwear. While the faculty member is being deprived of his dignity, the voiceover announces: "Now the more Pepsi you drink, the more great stuff you're gonna get."

The teenager opens the cockpit of the fighter and can be seen, helmetless, holding a Pepsi. "Looking very pleased with himself," (Pl. Mem. at 3,) the teenager exclaims, "Sure beats the bus," and chortles. The military drumroll sounds a final time, as the following words appear: "HARRIER FIGHTER 7,000,000 PEPSI POINTS." A few seconds later, the following appears in more stylized script: "Drink Pepsi—Get Stuff." With that message, the music and the commercial end with a triumphant flourish.

Inspired by this commercial, plaintiff set out to obtain a Harrier Jet. Plaintiff explains that he is "typical of the 'Pepsi Generation' . . . he is young, has an adventurous spirit, and the notion of obtaining a Harrier Jet appealed to him enormously." (Pl. Mem. at 3.) Plaintiff consulted the Pepsi Stuff Catalog. The Catalog features youths dressed in Pepsi Stuff regalia or enjoying Pepsi Stuff accessories, such as "Blue Shades" ("As if you need another reason to look forward to sunny days."), "Pepsi Tees" ("Live in 'em. Laugh in 'em. Get in 'em."), "Bag of Balls" ("Three balls. One bag. No rules."), and "Pepsi Phone Card" ("Call your mom!"). The Catalog specifies the number of Pepsi Points required to obtain promotional merchandise. The Catalog includes an Order Form which lists, on one side, fifty-three items of Pepsi Stuff merchandise redeemable for Pepsi Points. Conspicuously absent from the Order Form is any entry or description of a Harrier Jet. The amount of Pepsi Points required to obtain the listed merchandise ranges from 15 (for a "Jacket Tattoo" ("Sew 'em on your jacket, not your arm.")) to 3300 (for a "Fila Mountain Bike" ("Rugged. All-terrain. Exclusively for Pepsi.")). It should be noted that plaintiff objects to the implication that because an item was not shown in the Catalog, it was unavailable.

The rear foldout pages of the Catalog contain directions for redeeming Pepsi Points for merchandise. These directions note that merchandise may be ordered "only" with the original Order Form. The Catalog notes that in the event that a consumer lacks enough Pepsi Points to obtain a desired item, additional Pepsi Points may be purchased for ten cents each; however, at least fifteen original Pepsi Points must accompany each order.

Although plaintiff initially set out to collect 7,000,000 Pepsi Points by consuming Pepsi products, it soon became clear to him that he "would not be able to buy (let alone drink) enough Pepsi to collect the necessary Pepsi Points fast enough." (Affidavit of John D. R. Leonard, Mar. 30, 1999 ("Leonard Aff."), ¶ 5.) Reevaluating his strategy, plaintiff "focused for the first time on the packaging materials in the Pepsi Stuff promotion," and realized that buying Pepsi Points would be a more promising option. Through acquaintances, plaintiff ultimately raised about $700,000.

B.   Plaintiff's Efforts to Redeem the Alleged Offer

On or about March 27, 1996, plaintiff submitted an Order Form, fifteen original Pepsi Points, and a check for $700,008.50. Plaintiff appears to have been represented by counsel at the time he mailed his check; the check is drawn on an account of plaintiff's first set of attorneys. At the bottom of the Order Form, plaintiff wrote in "1 Harrier Jet" in the "Item" column and "7,000,000" in the "Total Points" column. In a letter accompanying his submission, plaintiff stated that the check was to purchase additional Pepsi Points "expressly for obtaining a new Harrier jet as advertised in your Pepsi Stuff commercial." (See Declaration of David Wynn, Mar. 18, 1999 ("Wynn Dec."), Exh. A.)

On or about May 7, 1996, defendant's fulfillment house rejected plaintiff's submission and returned the check, explaining that:

> The item that you have requested is not part of the Pepsi Stuff collection. It is not included in the catalogue or on the order form, and only catalogue merchandise can be redeemed under this program.

> The Harrier jet in the Pepsi commercial is fanciful and is simply included to create a humorous and entertaining ad. We apologize for any misunderstanding or confusion that you may have experienced and are enclosing some free product coupons for your use.

Plaintiff's previous counsel responded on or about May 14, 1996, as follows:

> Your letter of May 7, 1996 is totally unacceptable. We have reviewed the video tape of the Pepsi Stuff commercial . . . and it clearly offers the new Harrier jet for 7,000,000 Pepsi Points. Our client followed your rules explicitly. . . .

> This is a formal demand that you honor your commitment and make immediate arrangements to transfer the new Harrier jet to our client. If we do not receive transfer instructions within ten (10) business days of the date of this letter you will leave us no choice but to file an appropriate action against Pepsi. . . .

This letter was apparently sent onward to the advertising company responsible for the actual commercial, BBDO New York ("BBDO"). In a letter dated May 30, 1996, BBDO Vice President Raymond E. McGovern, Jr., explained to plaintiff that:

> I find it hard to believe that you are of the opinion that the Pepsi Stuff commercial ("Commercial") really offers a new Harrier Jet. The use of the Jet was clearly a joke that was meant to make the Commercial more humorous and entertaining. In my opinion, no reasonable person would agree with your analysis of the Commercial.

On or about June 17, 1996, plaintiff mailed a similar demand letter to defendant.

Litigation of this case initially involved two lawsuits, the first a declaratory judgment action brought by PepsiCo in this district (the "declaratory judgment action"), and the second an action brought by Leonard in Florida state court (the "Florida action"). PepsiCo brought suit in this Court on July 18, 1996, seeking a declaratory judgment stating that it had no obligation to furnish plaintiff with a Harrier Jet. That case was filed under docket number 96 Civ. 5320. In response to

PepsiCo's suit in New York, Leonard brought suit in Florida state court on August 6, 1996, although this case had nothing to do with Florida. That suit was removed to the Southern District of Florida in September 1996. In an Order dated November 6, 1996, United States District Judge James Lawrence King found that, "Obviously this case has been filed in a form[um] that has no meaningful relationship to the controversy and warrants a transfer pursuant to 28 U.S.C. § 1404(a)." *Leonard v. PepsiCo*, 96–2555 Civ.–King, at 1 (S.D.Fla. Nov. 6, 1996). The Florida suit was transferred to this Court on December 2, 1996, and assigned the docket number 96 Civ. 9069.

Once the Florida action had been transferred, Leonard moved to dismiss the declaratory judgment action for lack of personal jurisdiction. In an Order dated November 24, 1997, the Court granted the motion to dismiss for lack of personal jurisdiction in case 96 Civ. 5320, from which PepsiCo appealed. Leonard also moved to voluntarily dismiss the Florida action. While the Court indicated that the motion was proper, it noted that PepsiCo was entitled to some compensation for the costs of litigating this case in Florida, a forum that had no meaningful relationship to the case. In an Order dated December 15, 1997, the Court granted Leonard's motion to voluntarily dismiss this case without prejudice, but did so on condition that Leonard pay certain attorneys' fees.

In an Order dated October 1, 1998, the Court ordered Leonard to pay $88,162 in attorneys' fees within thirty days. Leonard failed to do so, yet sought nonetheless to appeal from his voluntary dismissal and the imposition of fees. In an Order dated January 5, 1999, the Court noted that Leonard's strategy was " 'clearly an end-run around the final judgment rule.' " (Order at 2 (quoting *Palmieri v. Defaria*, 88 F.3d 136 (2d Cir.1996)).) Accordingly, the Court ordered Leonard either to pay the amount due or withdraw his voluntary dismissal, as well as his appeals therefrom, and continue litigation before this Court. Rather than pay the attorneys' fees, Leonard elected to proceed with litigation, and shortly thereafter retained present counsel.

On February 22, 1999, the Second Circuit endorsed the parties' stipulations to the dismissal of any appeals taken thus far in this case. Those stipulations noted that Leonard had consented to the jurisdiction of this Court and that PepsiCo agreed not to seek enforcement of the attorneys' fees award. With these issues having been waived, PepsiCo moved for summary judgment pursuant to Federal Rule of Civil Procedure 56. The present motion thus follows three years of jurisdictional and procedural wrangling.

II.   Discussion

A.   The Legal Framework

1.   Standard for Summary Judgment

On a motion for summary judgment, a court "cannot try issues of fact; it can only determine whether there are issues to be tried." *Donahue v. Windsor Locks Bd. of Fire Comm'rs*, 834 F.2d 54, 58 (2d Cir.1987). To prevail on a motion for summary judgment, the moving party therefore must show that there are no such genuine issues of material fact to be tried, and that he or she is entitled to judgment as a matter of law. See Fed.R.Civ.P. 56(c) [now Rule 56(a)]; *Celotex Corp. v. Catrett*, 477 U.S. 317, 322 (1986); *Citizens Bank v. Hunt*, 927 F.2d 707, 710 (2d Cir.1991). The party seeking summary judgment "bears the initial responsibility of informing the district court of the basis for its motion," which includes identifying the materials in the record that "it believes demonstrate the absence of a genuine issue of material fact." *Celotex Corp.*, 477 U.S. at 323.

Once a motion for summary judgment is made and supported, the non-moving party must set forth specific facts that show that there is a genuine issue to be tried. See *Anderson v. Liberty Lobby, Inc.*, 477 U.S. 242, 251–52 (1986). Although a court considering a motion for summary judgment must view all evidence in the light most favorable to the non-moving party, and must draw all reasonable inferences in that party's favor, the nonmoving party "must do more than simply show that there is some metaphysical doubt as to the material facts." *Matsushita Elec. Indus. Co. v. Zenith Radio Corp.*, 475 U.S. 574, 586 (1986). If, based on the submissions to the court, no rational fact-finder could find in the non-movant's favor, there is no genuine issue of material fact, and summary judgment is appropriate. See *Anderson*, 477 U.S. at 250.

The question of whether or not a contract was formed is appropriate for resolution on summary judgment. As the Second Circuit has recently noted, "Summary judgment is proper when the 'words and actions that allegedly formed a contract [are] so clear themselves that reasonable people could not differ over their meaning.'" *Krumme v. Westpoint Stevens, Inc.*, 143 F.3d 71, 83 (2d Cir.1998) (quoting *Bourque v. FDIC*, 42 F.3d 704, 708 (1st Cir.1994)). Summary judgment is appropriate in such cases because there is "sometimes no genuine issue as to whether the parties' conduct implied a 'contractual understanding.' . . . . In such cases, 'the judge must decide the issue himself, just as he decides any factual issue in respect to which reasonable people cannot differ.'" *Bourque*, 42 F.3d at 708 (quoting *Boston Five Cents Sav. Bank v. Secretary of Dep't of Housing & Urban Dev.*, 768 F.2d 5, 8 (1st Cir.1985)).

2.   Choice of Law

The parties disagree concerning whether the Court should apply the law of the state of New York or of some other state in evaluating whether defendant's promotional campaign constituted an offer. Because this action was transferred from Florida, the choice of law rules of Florida, the transferor state, apply. See *Ferens v. John Deere Co.*, 494 U.S. 516, 523–33 (1990). Under Florida law, the choice of law in a contract case is determined by the place "where the last act necessary to complete the contract is done." *Jemco, Inc. v. United Parcel Serv., Inc.*, 400 So.2d 499, 500–01 (Fla.Dist.Ct.App.1981).

The parties disagree as to whether the contract could have been completed by plaintiff's filling out the Order Form to request a Harrier Jet, or by defendant's acceptance of the Order Form. If the commercial constituted an offer, then the last act necessary to complete the contract would be plaintiff's acceptance, in the state of Washington. If the commercial constituted a solicitation to receive offers, then the last act necessary to complete the contract would be defendant's acceptance of plaintiff's Order Form, in the state of New York. The choice of law question cannot, therefore, be resolved until after the Court determines whether the commercial was an offer or not. The Court agrees with both parties that resolution of this issue requires consideration of principles of contract law that are not limited to the law of any one state. Most of the cases cited by the parties are not from New York courts. As plaintiff suggests, the questions presented by this case implicate questions of contract law "deeply ingrained in the common law of England and the States of the Union."

B.   Defendant's Advertisement Was Not An Offer

1.   Advertisements as Offers

The general rule is that an advertisement does not constitute an offer. The *Restatement (Second) of Contracts* explains that:

> Advertisements of goods by display, sign, handbill, newspaper, radio or television are not ordinarily intended or understood as offers to sell. The same is true of catalogues, price lists and circulars, even though the terms of suggested bargains may be stated in some detail. It is of course possible to make an offer by an advertisement directed to the general public (see § 29), but there must ordinarily be some language of commitment or some invitation to take action without further communication.

Restatement (Second) of Contracts § 26 cmt. b (1979). Similarly, a leading treatise notes that:

> It is quite possible to make a definite and operative offer to buy or sell goods by advertisement, in a newspaper, by a handbill, a catalog or circular or on a placard in a store window. It is not customary to do this, however; and the presumption is the other way. . . . Such advertisements are understood to be mere requests to consider and examine and negotiate; and no one can reasonably regard them as otherwise unless the

circumstances are exceptional and the words used are very plain and clear.

Arthur Linton Corbin & Joseph M. Perillo, *Corbin on Contracts* § 2.4, at 116–17 (rev. ed.1993). New York courts adhere to this general principle.

An advertisement is not transformed into an enforceable offer merely by a potential offeree's expression of willingness to accept the offer through, among other means, completion of an order form. * * * Under these principles, plaintiff's letter of March 27, 1996, with the Order Form and the appropriate number of Pepsi Points, constituted the offer. There would be no enforceable contract until defendant accepted the Order Form and cashed the check.

* * *

The Court finds, in sum, that the Harrier Jet commercial was merely an advertisement. The Court now turns to the line of cases upon which plaintiff rests much of his argument.

2.   Rewards as Offers

In opposing the present motion, plaintiff largely relies on a different species of unilateral offer, involving public offers of a reward for performance of a specified act. Because these cases generally involve public declarations regarding the efficacy or trustworthiness of specific products, one court has aptly characterized these authorities as "prove me wrong" cases. See *Rosenthal v. Al Packer Ford*, 36 Md.App. 349 (1977). The most venerable of these precedents is the case of *Carlill v. Carbolic Smoke Ball Co.*, 1 Q.B. 256 (Court of Appeal, 1892), a quote from which heads plaintiff's memorandum of law: "[I]f a person chooses to make extravagant promises . . . he probably does so because it pays him to make them, and, if he has made them, the extravagance of the promises is no reason in law why he should not be bound by them." *Carbolic Smoke Ball*, 1 Q.B. at 268 (Bowen, L.J.).

Long a staple of law school curricula, *Carbolic Smoke Ball* owes its fame not merely to "the comic and slightly mysterious object involved," A.W. Brian Simpson. "Quackery and Contract Law: *Carlill v. Carbolic Smoke Ball Company* (1893), in *Leading Cases in the Common Law*" 259, 281 (1995), but also to its role in developing the law of unilateral offers. The case arose during the London influenza epidemic of the 1890s. Among other advertisements of the time, for Clarke's World Famous Blood Mixture, Towle's Pennyroyal and Steel Pills for Females, Sequah's Prairie Flower, and Epp's Glycerine Jube-Jubes, see Simpson, *supra*, at 267, appeared solicitations for the Carbolic Smoke Ball. The specific advertisement that Mrs. Carlill saw, and relied upon, read as follows:

> 100 £ reward will be paid by the Carbolic Smoke Ball Company
> to any person who contracts the increasing epidemic influenza,
> colds, or any diseases caused by taking cold, after having used

the ball three times daily for two weeks according to the printed directions supplied with each ball. 1000 £ is deposited with the Alliance Bank, Regent Street, shewing our sincerity in the matter.

During the last epidemic of influenza many thousand carbolic smoke balls were sold as preventives against this disease, and in no ascertained case was the disease contracted by those using the carbolic smoke ball.

Carbolic Smoke Ball, 1 Q.B. at 256–57. "On the faith of this advertisement," *id.* at 257, Mrs. Carlill purchased the smoke ball and used it as directed, but contracted influenza nevertheless.[8] The lower court held that she was entitled to recover the promised reward.

Affirming the lower court's decision, Lord Justice Lindley began by noting that the advertisement was an express promise to pay £ 100 in the event that a consumer of the Carbolic Smoke Ball was stricken with influenza. See *id.* at 261. The advertisement was construed as offering a reward because it sought to induce performance, unlike an invitation to negotiate, which seeks a reciprocal promise. As Lord Justice Lindley explained, "advertisements offering rewards . . . are offers to anybody who performs the conditions named in the advertisement, and anybody who does perform the condition accepts the offer." *Id.* at 262; see also *id.* at 268 (Bowen, L.J.). Because Mrs. Carlill had complied with the terms of the offer, yet contracted influenza, she was entitled to £ 100.

* * *

In the present case, the Harrier Jet commercial did not direct that anyone who appeared at Pepsi headquarters with 7,000,000 Pepsi Points on the Fourth of July would receive a Harrier Jet. Instead, the commercial urged consumers to accumulate Pepsi Points and to refer to the Catalog to determine how they could redeem their Pepsi Points. The commercial sought a reciprocal promise, expressed through acceptance of, and compliance with, the terms of the Order Form. As noted previously, the Catalog contains no mention of the Harrier Jet. Plaintiff states that he "noted that the Harrier Jet was not among the items described in the catalog, but this did not affect [his] understanding of the offer." It should have.

Carbolic Smoke Ball itself draws a distinction between the offer of reward in that case, and typical advertisements, which are merely offers to negotiate. As Lord Justice Bowen explains:

---

[8] Although the Court of Appeals's opinion is silent as to exactly what a carbolic smoke ball was, the historical record reveals it to have been a compressible hollow ball, about the size of an apple or orange, with a small opening covered by some porous material such as silk or gauze. The ball was partially filled with carbolic acid in powder form. When the ball was squeezed, the powder would be forced through the opening as a small cloud of smoke. See Simpson, *supra*, at 262–63. At the time, carbolic acid was considered fatal if consumed in more than small amounts. See *id.* at 264.

> It is an offer to become liable to any one who, before it is
> retracted, performs the condition. . . . It is not like cases in
> which you offer to negotiate, or you issue advertisements that
> you have got a stock of books to sell, or houses to let, in which
> case there is no offer to be bound by any contract. Such
> advertisements are offers to negotiate—offers to receive
> offers—offers to chaffer, as, I think, some learned judge in one
> of the cases has said.

Carbolic Smoke Ball, 1 Q.B. at 268. Because the alleged offer in this
case was, at most, an advertisement to receive offers rather than an
offer of reward, plaintiff cannot show that there was an offer made in
the circumstances of this case.

C. An Objective, Reasonable Person Would Not Have Considered the Commercial an Offer

Plaintiff's understanding of the commercial as an offer must also be
rejected because the Court finds that no objective person could
reasonably have concluded that the commercial actually offered
consumers a Harrier Jet.

1. Objective Reasonable Person Standard

In evaluating the commercial, the Court must not consider
defendant's subjective intent in making the commercial, or plaintiff's
subjective view of what the commercial offered, but what an objective,
reasonable person would have understood the commercial to convey. An
obvious joke, of course, would not give rise to a contract. On the other
hand, if there is no indication that the offer is "evidently in jest," and
that an objective, reasonable person would find that the offer was
serious, then there may be a valid offer. See *Barnes*, 549 P.2d at 1155
("[I]f the jest is not apparent and a reasonable hearer would believe that
an offer was being made, then the speaker risks the formation of a
contract which was not intended."); see also *Lucy v. Zehmer*, 196 Va.
493 (1954) (ordering specific performance of a contract to purchase a
farm despite defendant's protestation that the transaction was done in
jest as " 'just a bunch of two doggoned drunks bluffing' ").

2. Necessity of a Jury Determination

Plaintiff also contends that summary judgment is improper
because the question of whether the commercial conveyed a sincere
offer can be answered only by a jury. Relying on dictum from *Gallagher
v. Delaney*, 139 F.3d 338 (2d Cir.1998), plaintiff argues that a federal
judge comes from a "narrow segment of the enormously broad American
socio-economic spectrum," and, thus, that the question whether the
commercial constituted a serious offer must be decided by a jury
composed of, inter alia, members of the "Pepsi Generation," who are, as
plaintiff puts it, "young, open to adventure, willing to do the
unconventional." Plaintiff essentially argues that a federal judge would

view his claim differently than fellow members of the "Pepsi Generation."

Plaintiff's argument that his claim must be put to a jury is without merit. Gallagher involved a claim of sexual harassment in which the defendant allegedly invited plaintiff to sit on his lap, gave her inappropriate Valentine's Day gifts, told her that "she brought out feelings that he had not had since he was sixteen," and "invited her to help him feed the ducks in the pond, since he was 'a bachelor for the evening.'" *Gallagher*, 139 F.3d at 344. The court concluded that a jury determination was particularly appropriate because a federal judge lacked "the current real-life experience required in interpreting subtle sexual dynamics of the workplace based on nuances, subtle perceptions, and implicit communications." *Id.* at 342. This case, in contrast, presents a question of whether there was an offer to enter into a contract, requiring the Court to determine how a reasonable, objective person would have understood defendant's commercial. Such an inquiry is commonly performed by courts on a motion for summary judgment.

3.   Whether the Commercial Was "Evidently Done In Jest"

Plaintiff's insistence that the commercial appears to be a serious offer requires the Court to explain why the commercial is funny. Explaining why a joke is funny is a daunting task; as the essayist E.B. White has remarked, "Humor can be dissected, as a frog can, but the thing dies in the process. . . ." The commercial is the embodiment of what defendant appropriately characterizes as "zany humor."

First, the commercial suggests, as commercials often do, that use of the advertised product will transform what, for most youth, can be a fairly routine and ordinary experience. The military tattoo and stirring martial music, as well as the use of subtitles in a Courier font that scroll terse messages across the screen, such as "MONDAY 7:58 AM," evoke military and espionage thrillers. The implication of the commercial is that Pepsi Stuff merchandise will inject drama and moment into hitherto unexceptional lives. The commercial in this case thus makes the exaggerated claims similar to those of many television advertisements: that by consuming the featured clothing, car, beer, or potato chips, one will become attractive, stylish, desirable, and admired by all. A reasonable viewer would understand such advertisements as mere puffery, not as statements of fact, and refrain from interpreting the promises of the commercial as being literally true.

Second, the callow youth featured in the commercial is a highly improbable pilot, one who could barely be trusted with the keys to his parents' car, much less the prize aircraft of the United States Marine Corps. Rather than checking the fuel gauges on his aircraft, the teenager spends his precious preflight minutes preening. The youth's concern for his coiffure appears to extend to his flying without a helmet. Finally, the teenager's comment that flying a Harrier Jet to school "sure beats the bus" evinces an improbably insouciant attitude toward the relative difficulty and danger of piloting a fighter plane in a residential area, as opposed to taking public transportation.

Third, the notion of traveling to school in a Harrier Jet is an exaggerated adolescent fantasy. In this commercial, the fantasy is underscored by how the teenager's schoolmates gape in admiration, ignoring their physics lesson. The force of the wind generated by the Harrier Jet blows off one teacher's clothes, literally defrocking an authority figure. As if to emphasize the fantastic quality of having a Harrier Jet arrive at school, the Jet lands next to a plebeian bike rack. This fantasy is, of course, extremely unrealistic. No school would provide landing space for a student's fighter jet, or condone the disruption the jet's use would cause.

Fourth, the primary mission of a Harrier Jet, according to the United States Marine Corps, is to "attack and destroy surface targets under day and night visual conditions." *United States Marine Corps, Factfile: AV-8B Harrier II* (last modified Dec. 5, 1995) . Manufactured by McDonnell Douglas, the Harrier Jet played a significant role in the air offensive of Operation Desert Storm in 1991. The jet is designed to carry a considerable armament load, including Sidewinder and Maverick missiles. As one news report has noted, "Fully loaded, the Harrier can float like a butterfly and sting like a bee—albeit a roaring 14-ton butterfly and a bee with 9,200 pounds of bombs and missiles." Jerry Allegood, "Marines Rely on Harrier Jet, Despite Critics," *News & Observer (Raleigh)*, Nov. 4, 1990, at C1. In light of the Harrier Jet's well-documented function in attacking and destroying surface and air targets, armed reconnaissance and air interdiction, and offensive and defensive anti-aircraft warfare, depiction of such a jet as a way to get to school in the morning is clearly not serious even if, as plaintiff contends, the jet is capable of being acquired "in a form that eliminates [its] potential for military use."

Fifth, the number of Pepsi Points the commercial mentions as required to "purchase" the jet is 7,000,000. To amass that number of points, one would have to drink 7,000,000 Pepsis (or roughly 190 Pepsis a day for the next hundred years—an unlikely possibility), or one would have to purchase approximately $700,000 worth of Pepsi Points. The cost of a Harrier Jet is roughly $23 million dollars, a fact of which plaintiff was aware when he set out to gather the amount he believed necessary to accept the alleged offer. Even if an objective, reasonable person were not aware of this fact, he would conclude that purchasing a fighter plane for $700,000 is a deal too good to be true.

Plaintiff argues that a reasonable, objective person would have understood the commercial to make a serious offer of a Harrier Jet because there was "absolutely no distinction in the manner" in which the items in the commercial were presented. Plaintiff also relies upon a press release highlighting the promotional campaign, issued by defendant, in which "[n]o mention is made by [defendant] of humor, or anything of the sort." These arguments suggest merely that the humor of the promotional campaign was tongue in cheek. Humor is not limited to what Justice Cardozo called "[t]he rough and boisterous joke . . . [that] evokes its own guffaws." *Murphy v. Steeplechase Amusement Co.*, 250 N.Y. 479, 483 (1929). In light of the obvious absurdity of the commercial, the Court rejects plaintiff's argument that the commercial was not clearly in jest.

4.   Plaintiff's Demands for Additional Discovery

In his Memorandum of Law, and in letters to the Court, plaintiff argues that additional discovery is necessary on the issues of whether and how defendant reacted to plaintiff's "acceptance" of their "offer"; how defendant and its employees understood the commercial would be viewed, based on test-marketing the commercial or on their own opinions; and how other individuals actually responded to the commercial when it was aired.

Plaintiff argues that additional discovery is necessary as to how defendant reacted to his "acceptance," suggesting that it is significant that defendant twice changed the commercial, the first time to increase the number of Pepsi Points required to purchase a Harrier Jet to 700,000,000, and then again to amend the commercial to state the 700,000,000 amount and add "(Just Kidding)." Plaintiff concludes that, "Obviously, if PepsiCo truly believed that no one could take seriously the offer contained in the original ad that I saw, this change would have been totally unnecessary and superfluous." The record does not suggest that the change in the amount of points is probative of the seriousness of the offer. The increase in the number of points needed to acquire a Harrier Jet may have been prompted less by the fear that reasonable people would demand Harrier Jets and more by the concern that unreasonable people would threaten frivolous litigation. Further discovery is unnecessary on the question of when and how the commercials changed because the question before the Court is whether the commercial that plaintiff saw and relied upon was an offer, not that any other commercial constituted an offer.

Plaintiff's demands for discovery relating to how defendant itself understood the offer are also unavailing. Such discovery would serve only to cast light on defendant's subjective intent in making the alleged offer, which is irrelevant to the question of whether an objective, reasonable person would have understood the commercial to be an offer. Indeed, plaintiff repeatedly argues that defendant's subjective intent is irrelevant.

Finally, plaintiff's assertion that he should be afforded an opportunity to determine whether other individuals also tried to accumulate enough Pepsi Points to "purchase" a Harrier Jet is unavailing. The possibility that there were other people who interpreted the commercial as an "offer" of a Harrier Jet does not render that belief any more or less reasonable. The alleged offer must be evaluated on its own terms. Having made the evaluation, the Court concludes that summary judgment is appropriate on the ground that no reasonable, objective person would have understood the commercial to be an offer.[14]

D. The Alleged Contract Does Not Satisfy the Statute of Frauds [which requires that certain contracts are not enforceable unless made in writing and signed by the party against whom enforcement is sought.]

* * *

E.   Plaintiff's Fraud Claim

In addition to moving for summary judgment on plaintiff's claim for breach of contract, defendant has also moved for summary judgment on plaintiff's fraud claim. The elements of a cause of action for fraud are " 'representation of a material existing fact, falsity, scienter, deception and injury.' " *New York Univ. v. Continental Ins. Co.*, 87 N.Y.2d 308 (1995) (quoting *Channel Master Corp. v. Aluminium Ltd. Sales, Inc.*, 4 N.Y.2d 403, 407 (1958)).

To properly state a claim for fraud, "plaintiff must allege a misrepresentation or material omission by defendant, on which it relied, that induced plaintiff" to perform an act. See *NYU*, 639 N.Y.S.2d at 289. "General allegations that defendant entered into a contract while lacking the intent to perform it are insufficient to support the claim." See *id.* Instead, the plaintiff must show the misrepresentation was collateral, or served as an inducement, to a separate agreement between the parties.

* * *

Plaintiff in this case does not allege that he was induced to enter into a contract by some collateral misrepresentation, but rather that defendant never had any intention of making good on its "offer" of a Harrier Jet. Because this claim "alleges only that the defendant entered into a contract with no intention of performing it," *Grappo*, 56 F.3d at 434, judgment on this claim should enter for defendant.

III. Conclusion

In sum, there are three reasons why plaintiff's demand cannot prevail as a matter of law. First, the commercial was merely an advertisement, not a unilateral offer. Second, the tongue-in-cheek attitude of the commercial would not cause a reasonable person to conclude that a soft drink company would be giving away fighter planes

---

[14]   Even if plaintiff were allowed discovery on all of these issues, such discovery would be relevant only to the second basis for the Court's opinion, that no reasonable person would have understood the commercial to be an offer. That discovery would not change the basic principle that an advertisement is not an offer, as set forth in Section II.B of this Order and Opinion, *supra*; nor would it affect the conclusion that the alleged offer failed to comply with the Statute of Frauds, as set forth in Section II.D, *infra*.

as part of a promotion. Third, there is no writing between the parties sufficient to satisfy the Statute of Frauds.

For the reasons stated above, the Court grants defendant's motion for summary judgment. The Clerk of Court is instructed to close these cases. Any pending motions are moot.

COMMENTS AND QUESTIONS CONCERNING *LEONARD V. PEPSICO, INC.*

1.   It is likely that in your contracts course you will discuss *Leonard v. PepsiCo, Inc.*, with its unique facts and interesting contract issues. The inclusion of this opinion in this text is not to provide a basis for extended discussion of contract law. Instead, the focus here is on the procedural aspects of this litigation. One goal of the inclusion in the text of this opinion is to sensitize you to the procedural aspects of all the cases you will read in law school. By considering the procedural posture of all the cases that you read, your understanding of civil procedure should be enhanced.

2.   By understanding the procedural posture in which questions are presented to the courts, you also should better appreciate the substantive law enunciated by those courts. For instance, if a question is presented to the court in the context of a motion to dismiss, the court must assume that all facts alleged in the complaint are true. However, this is not the case when the court is presented with a Rule 56 motion for summary judgment and must determine whether there is a "genuine dispute as to any material fact."

3.   Sometimes civil actions are filed as a result of unexpected events, such as an accident, with attorneys becoming involved only after the fact. At other times, civil actions are planned so as to present the parties' claims in the most favorable light. In her opinion Judge Wood notes that Leonard "appears to have been represented by counsel at the time he mailed his check [to PepsiCo]." Why does Judge Wood consider this significant enough to mention in her opinion?

4.   In footnote 1 of her opinion, Judge Wood notes: "The Court's recitation of the facts of this case is drawn from the statements of uncontested facts submitted by the parties pursuant to Local Civil Rule 56.1." Rule 83 of the Federal Rules of Civil Procedure permits United States District Courts to adopt local rules governing practice within each district, so long as those rules are consistent with and do not duplicate the Federal Rules of Civil Procedure or other federal law. The first sentence of the local rule in question provides: "Upon any motion for summary judgment pursuant to Rule 56 of the Federal Rules of Civil Procedure, there shall be annexed to the notice of motion a separate, short and concise statement, in numbered paragraphs, of the material facts as to which the moving party contends there is no genuine issue to be tried." Rule 56.1(a) of the United States District Court for the Southern District of New York.

5.   As this case illustrates, not all civil actions are decided by the court that the plaintiff initially selected. Lawyers must anticipate possible litigation moves by other counsel. While plaintiff's counsel chooses the

initial forum, through the doctrines of transfer (typically pursuant to 28 U.S.C. § 1404), forum non conveniens, and removal from state to federal court, the defendant may be able to move the case from that initial forum to a court perceived to be more favorable to the defendant.

6.   As Judge Wood notes in her opinion, PepsiCo filed the initial civil action in the United States District Court for the Southern District of New York seeking a judicial declaration of the rights of the parties in this dispute. How would such a declaratory judgment have been helpful to PepsiCo? Why was PepsiCo's action filed in federal court in New York?

7.   Rather than immediately respond to the New York action, John Leonard filed a separate action in Florida state court. Why file such a separate action? Why in Florida? Why in state court?

8.   Rather than respond to Leonard's action in Florida state court, PepsiCo removed that action to federal court in Florida pursuant to 28 U.S.C. § 1441 and then moved to transfer the action to the United States District Court for the Southern District of New York (where PepsiCo's declaratory judgment action had been filed). Why wouldn't PepsiCo simply litigate Leonard's action in Florida state court?

9.   In her opinion, Judge Wood states: "The present motion * * * follows three years of jurisdictional and procedural wrangling." Do the parties and their lawyers have the right to engage in such "jurisdictional and procedural wrangling"? Do the courts have the ability to constrain such wrangling? Who is paying for all this? Consider New York Rule of Professional Conduct 3.2: "In representing a client, a lawyer shall not use means that have no substantial purpose other than to delay or prolong the proceeding or to cause needless expense." *See also* ABA Model Rule of Professional Conduct 3.2 ("A lawyer shall make reasonable efforts to expedite litigation consistent with the interests of the client.").

10.   Before determining whether a contract was formed and breached, the court first must determine what state's law should be applied. This is referred to as the "choice of law" question, which arises not infrequently in actions in which the parties are from different states and some of the major events leading to the action occurred in still another state. Judge Wood was spared having to decide this choice-of-law question, because she agreed "with both parties that resolution of this issue requires consideration of principles of contract law that are not limited to the law of any one state [and] * * * the questions presented * * * implicate questions of contract law 'deeply ingrained in the common law of England and the States of the Union.'" Judge Wood then interpreted that law to conclude that the television advertisement did not constitute an offer, that an objective, reasonable person would not have considered the advertisement an offer, and that no writing between the parties satisfied the Statute of Frauds.

11.   As you will see in the discussion of judges and juries in Chapter 12, counsel typically seek a judge or jury based on the presumed sympathy of those decision-makers to the attorney and her client. John Leonard argued "that a federal judge comes from a 'narrow segment of the enormously broad American socio-economic spectrum,' * * * and, thus, that

the question whether the commercial constituted a serious offer must be decided by a jury composed of, inter alia, members of the 'Pepsi Generation,' who are, as plaintiff puts it, 'young, open to adventure, willing to do the unconventional.'" Was Leonard successful in this argument?

12. Federal Rule of Civil Procedure 56(d)(2) provides: "If a nonmovant shows by affidavit or declaration that, for specified reasons, it cannot present facts essential to justify its opposition [to a motion for summary judgment], the court may * * * allow time to obtain affidavits or declarations or to take discovery." Why did Judge Wood deny plaintiff Leonard's request to conduct additional discovery seeking information to support his opposition to PepsiCo's motion for summary judgment?

VII. CONCLUSION

Of the thousands of civil actions filed in state and federal court each year, very few result in published opinions—especially published opinions that later are included in law school textbooks. For this and other reasons, *Leonard v. PepsiCo, Inc.* is an atypical case. In at least one respect, though, *Leonard* nicely illustrates the functioning of our state and federal judicial systems. Just as did John Leonard and his attorney, parties and their attorneys initially formalize a dispute by filing a civil action seeking judicial resolution of that dispute. They then make many strategic decisions to obtain the most favorable judicial (or non-judicial) resolution for their clients.

The judges assigned to these civil actions resolve issues as they are presented to them by the parties. Appreciating the innumerable decisions that attorneys and judges make as an action moves to final judgment will enhance your study of civil procedure and other law school courses. It also will make you a better attorney as you represent clients in the years to come.

CHAPTER 2

THE INITIATION OF THE LAWSUIT: "A SHORT AND PLAIN STATEMENT OF THE CLAIM."

I. INTRODUCTION

You now have read your first "civil procedure" opinion, recognizing that procedure is an essential component of all judicial opinions in civil cases. The first chapter also provides a summary overview of the civil litigation process, a sketch of the state and federal court systems, and some basic civil procedure vocabulary. Assume that you have interviewed your client, determined that the most favorable forum for his action is a federal district court, and confirmed that his action should satisfy the prerequisites for a federal action. You now must draft the complaint to initiate that federal civil action. This is the focus of the current chapter.

The Federal Rules of Civil Procedure specify what must be included in a federal complaint and with what specificity that complaint must be pled. Just as importantly, those Rules place duties on counsel as she investigates relevant facts and law prior to filing the complaint. Attorneys owe duties to both their clients and the court, and counsel must be cognizant of those duties before, during, and after the initiation of a federal civil action by the filing of the complaint.

II. THE FEDERAL RULES OF CIVIL PROCEDURE

The Federal Rules of Civil Procedure are the rules by which civil litigation is handled in the 94 United States District Courts. These Rules were authorized by the Rules Enabling Act of 1934, 28 U.S.C. § 2072, and, after having been drafted by a blue ribbon panel of lawyers and law professors, became effective in the federal district courts in 1938.[1] While these Rules only apply in the United States District Courts, many states have used them as a model for their own statutes or rules governing civil procedure.

---

[1] *See generally* Burbank, "The Rules Enabling Act of 1934," 130 *U.Pa.L.Rev.* 1015 (1982); Clark, "Two Decades of the Federal Civil Rules," 58 *Col. L. Rev.* 435 (1958).

THE INITIATION OF THE LAWSUIT: "A SHORT AND PLAIN
STATEMENT OF THE CLAIM."

48

CHAPTER 2

A. THE FEDERAL RULEMAKING PROCESS

The following is a description of the federal rulemaking process
that resulted in the original Federal Rules of Civil Procedure in 1938
and the many amendments to those Rules in the years since.[2]

> The Federal Rules of Practice and Procedure govern the
> conduct of trials, appeals, and cases under Title 11 of the
> United States Code. The system of federal rules began with the
> Rules Enabling Act of 1934 (28 U.S.C. § 2071–2077). The Act
> authorized the Supreme Court to promulgate rules of
> procedure, which have the force and effect of law.
>
> Over time, the work and oversight of the rulemaking process
> was delegated by the Court to committees of the Judicial
> Conference, the principal policy-making body of the U.S.
> Courts. In 1988, amendments to the Rules Enabling Act
> formalized this committee process. Today, the Judicial
> Conference's Committee on Rules of Practice and Procedure,
> ("Standing Committee") and its five advisory rules committees
> "carry on a continuous study of the operation and effect" of the
> federal rules as directed by the Rules Enabling Act.
>
> Advisory Committees on Appellate, Bankruptcy, Civil,
> Criminal, and Evidence Rules evaluate suggestions (i.e.
> proposals) for rules amendments in the first instance. If an
> advisory committee pursues a proposal, it may seek permission
> from the Standing Committee to publish a draft of the
> contemplated amendment. Based on comments from the bench,
> bar, and general public, the advisory committee may then
> choose to discard, revise, or transmit the amendment as
> contemplated to the Standing Committee. The Standing
> Committee independently reviews the findings of the advisory
> committees and, if satisfied, recommends changes to the
> Judicial Conference, which in turn recommends changes to the
> Supreme Court. The Court considers the proposals and, if it
> concurs, officially promulgates the revised rules by order
> before May 1, to take effect no earlier than December 1 of the
> same year unless Congress enacts legislation to reject, modify,
> or defer the pending rules.

It is important to realize that, while the Federal Rules of Civil
Procedure cover most procedural issues in the United States District
Courts, other sources of law may supersede and supplement the Federal
Rules. All statutes and rules governing civil litigation must be
consistent with the United States Constitution. The Fifth Amendment
to the Constitution requires that persons shall not be deprived of life,

---

[2] Administrative Office of the United States Courts, "How the Rulemaking Process
Works," http://www.uscourts.gov/rules-policies/about-rulemaking-process/how-rulemaking-
process-works.

liberty, or property without due process of law, while the Seventh Amendment to the Constitution preserves the right to jury trial in certain federal civil actions. No federal statute, rule, or judicial action can deprive a person of these constitutionally guaranteed rights.

The next most authoritative source of procedural law is provided in federal statutes. Through statutes Congress has, for instance, established the United States District Courts (28 U.S.C. § 132); prescribed the jurisdiction of the federal courts (*e.g.*, 28 U.S.C. § 1331 (federal-question jurisdiction) and 28 U.S.C. § 1332 (diversity jurisdiction)); and specified the number of challenges to prospective jurors in civil actions (28 U.S.C. § 1870). In the event that a federal statute is inconsistent with a provision of the United States Constitution, that statute is superseded by the constitutional provision.

The Federal Rules of Civil Procedure are authorized by the Rules Enabling Act, 28 U.S.C. § 2072. Not only must such Rules generally be consistent with the Constitution and governing federal statutes, but the Rules Enabling Act itself provides: "Such rules shall not abridge, enlarge or modify any substantive right." 28 U.S.C. § 2072(b).

While the Federal Rules of Civil Procedure govern procedure in all United States District Courts, Rule 83 of those Rules recognizes that federal district courts and individual federal district judges may adopt their own rules or orders to cover matters not addressed in the Federal Rules. Rule 83(a) authorizes federal judges within a particular United States District Court to adopt rules governing practice within that district, such as, for instance, the details of electronic filing, discovery, or motion practice in that particular district. Going to an even finer level of detail, some individual judges also adopt standing orders specifying the manner of practice before that particular judge. However, Rule 83(b) specifies that such standing orders, and individual orders entered in a particular case, must be "consistent with federal law, rules adopted under 28 U.S.C. §§ 2072 and 2075 [the Federal Rules of Civil Procedure and Federal Rules of Bankruptcy Procedure], and the district's local rules."

Figure 2–1 shows the various sources of procedural law in the United States District Courts, progressing from the most powerful (provisions of the United States Constitution) to the least powerful (standing and individual orders of individual United States District Judges). Thus an order of an individual district judge can be challenged as inconsistent with any of the sources of law shown above it in Figure 2–1 (constitutional law, statutory law, the Federal Rules of Civil Procedure, or the Local Rules of the United States District Court).

FIGURE 2–1
SOURCES OF FEDERAL PROCEDURAL LAW

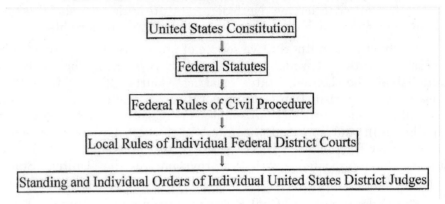

The Federal Rules of Civil Procedure and other governing procedural law are a work in progress, subject to periodic amendment. Just as athletes may gain an edge by their knowledge of the rules of their sport, lawyers with a comprehensive knowledge of the Federal Rules of Civil Procedure and other procedural law gain an advantage in civil litigation. Indeed, because the Federal Rules of Civil Procedure provide at least a starting point for the rules of procedure adopted in most states, knowledge of the Federal Rules can result in a decided litigation advantage in both federal and state courts.

B. READING THE FEDERAL RULES OF CIVIL PROCEDURE

In most of your first-year courses, you will read appellate cases. From these court of appeals and supreme court opinions, you will need to extract the governing rule. However, in the Federal Rules of Civil Procedure, the Civil Rules Advisory Committee has done this work for you—and presented you with the governing rule.

Is this a great deal or what? All you need to do is read the rule and apply it to the situation at hand, and all problems are solved. Unfortunately, things are not quite that simple, and legal judgment is required to apply the Federal Rules to real-world disputes. This is where lawyers and lawyer judgment (*i.e.*, "thinking like a lawyer") come into play.

Even though the Federal Rules were written to provide concrete guidance concerning procedure in the federal district courts, interpretative questions nevertheless sometimes arise. Help in interpreting, and finding, applicable Rules is available in the Table of Rules, which is a basic table of contents for the Federal Rules of Civil Procedure. The Table of Rules groups the Rules as follows:

I.   Scope of Rules; Form of Action (Rules 1–2)

II.   Commencing an Action; Service of Process, Pleadings, Motions and Orders (Rules 3–6)

As you read individual Rules, it can be helpful to check the Table of Rules to see just where a specific Rule fits within the overall spectrum of all 86 Rules.

Each Rule has its own title, which may be helpful for an attorney handling federal civil litigation or a student in a civil procedure examination. Individual subsections of the Rules also have captions, which can be useful as finding and interpretative aids.

In addition to the Rules themselves, the Advisory Committee provided Notes to the original Rules in 1938, and amendments to the Rules since 1938 have been accompanied by Advisory Committee Notes. Thus there are many Notes to some Rules. These Notes contain explanations of what the Advisory Committee was attempting to achieve with a particular Rule or amendment, as well as a history of the evolution of particular Rules over time.

The Federal Rules of Civil Procedure provide the governing procedural law applied in the federal district courts, and the Advisory Committee Notes are an important interpretative aid for those Rules. Rule 11, the focus of the next section of this chapter, provides an example of how one of the Federal Rules has been amended and interpreted over the years.

III. RULE 11 OF THE FEDERAL RULES OF CIVIL PROCEDURE

In 1938 Rule 11 of the Federal Rules of Civil Procedure read, in its entirety:

> Every pleading of a party represented by an attorney shall be signed by at least one attorney of record in his individual name, whose address shall be stated. A party who is not represented by an attorney shall sign his pleading and state his address. Except when otherwise specifically provided by rule or statute, pleadings need not be verified or accompanied by affidavit. The rule in equity that the averments of an

answer under oath must be overcome by the testimony of two witnesses or of one witness sustained by corroborating circumstances is abolished. The signature of an attorney constitutes a certificate by him that he has read the pleading; that to the best of his knowledge, information, and belief there is good ground to support it; and that it is not interposed for delay. If a pleading is not signed or is signed with intent to defeat the purpose of the rule, it may be stricken as sham and false and the action may proceed as though the pleading had not been served. For a wilful violation of this rule an attorney may be subjected to appropriate disciplinary action. Similar action may be taken if scandalous or indecent matter is inserted.[3]

This Rule was largely ignored for over forty years, until its amendment in 1983. It was also amended in 1993 to, in part, again make Rule 11 sanctions discretionary, as they had been prior to the 1983 amendment to the Rule. Significantly amended in 1983 and 1993, and with minor amendments in 1987 and 2007, Rule 11 has grown from the single paragraph above to a rule with several subsections filling two pages of text.

While Rule 11 has expanded greatly since the Federal Rules of Civil Procedure became effective in 1938, the current version of Rule 11 still divides into three major parts:

- A requirement that court papers be signed by at least one attorney representing each party or by the party personally if the party is not represented by an attorney (Rule 11(a));

- A provision that the signature of the attorney or unrepresented party certifies certain specific things to the court (Rule 11(b)); and

- A provision authorizing the court to sanction an attorney, party, or law firm for a violation of the Rule 11(b) certification requirement (Rule 11(c)).[4]

The discussion that follows initially focuses on what Rule 11(a) and (b) require of the attorney. It then considers the possibility of Rule 11(c) sanctions if the attorney violates the Rule 11(b) certification requirements.

---

[3] 5A C. Wright & A. Miller, *Federal Practice and Procedure* § 1331, at 459 (3d ed. 2004).

[4] In addition to major provisions contained in sections (a), (b), and (c) of Rule 11, Rule 11(d) provides: "This rule does not apply to disclosures and discovery requests, responses, objections, and motions under Rules 26 through 37." However, Rule 26(g) contains requirements very similar to those of Rule 11 and applies them to disclosures and discovery requests, responses, and objections, while Rule 37 provides for the award of expenses in connection with disclosure and discovery motions.

A. THE ATTORNEY'S SIGNATURE AND REPRESENTATIONS TO THE COURT

Rule 11(a) and (b) require an attorney to sign litigation documents, thereby making specific certifications to the court. While the Rule 11(a) signature requirement is relatively straightforward, the Rule 11(b) certification requirement has been much litigated in a myriad of factual situations.

1. RULE 11(a): THE ATTORNEY'S SIGNATURE

Rule 11(a) begins: "Every pleading, written motion, and other paper must be signed by at least one attorney of record in the attorney's name—or by a party personally if the party is unrepresented." Federal Rule of Civil Procedure 5(d)(3) authorizes individual federal district courts to provide for electronic filing, in which case the attorney's use of the electronic filing system constitutes a signature for the purposes of Rule 11. Thus Rule 5.5(g) of the United States District Court for the District of Arizona provides: "The log-in and password required to submit documents to the ECF System constitute the Registered User's signature on all electronic documents filed with the Court for purposes of Rule 11 of the Federal Rules of Civil Procedure." In the event that a party is unrepresented in a civil action, Rule 11(a) provides that this party must personally sign every litigation document.

2. RULE 11(b): REPRESENTATIONS TO THE COURT

The second major section of Rule 11, Rule 11(b), sets forth specific representations to the court that an attorney makes by "presenting to the court a pleading, written motion, or other paper." These representations typically stem from the attorney's signature of a litigation document, as required by Rule 11(a). Rule 11(b) further provides that these same representations are considered made by parties who are not represented by counsel but who themselves present litigation papers to the court. Moreover, certifications under Rule 11(b) extend beyond the mere signing of a document to include "signing, filing, submitting, or later advocating" a specific document in a civil action.

Rule 11(b) provides that the presentation of a litigation document to the court by an attorney or unrepresented party constitutes a certification that "to the best of the person's knowledge, information, and belief, formed after an inquiry reasonable under the circumstances":

> (1) [the paper] is not being presented for any improper purpose, such as to harass, cause unnecessary delay, or needlessly increase the cost of litigation;

> (2) the claims, defenses, and other legal contentions are warranted by existing law or by a nonfrivolous argument for

extending, modifying, or reversing existing law or for establishing new law;

(3) the factual contentions have evidentiary support or, if specifically so identified, will likely have evidentiary support after a reasonable opportunity for further investigation or discovery; and

(4) the denials of factual contentions are warranted on the evidence or, if specifically so identified, are reasonably based on belief or a lack of information.

In the next subsection, we will explore the meaning of these certifications, and then consider the sanctions that may be imposed upon an attorney who violates the Rule 11(b) certification requirements.

B. WHAT DO THE RULE 11 CERTIFICATIONS MEAN IN PRACTICE?

What does it mean for an attorney to certify to Rule 11(b) statements to the best of the attorney's "knowledge, information, and belief, formed after an inquiry reasonable under the circumstances"? Assume that John Leonard, the plaintiff in *Leonard v. PepsiCo, Inc.*, seeks your advice in connection with a possible civil action against PepsiCo, Inc. Consider how the following provisions of Rule 11(b) should impact your pre-filing legal and factual inquiries.

1. RULE 11(b)(1)

(a) What types of questions would you ask John Leonard to confirm that the civil action that he would like to file is not being contemplated "for any improper purpose, such as to harass, cause unnecessary delay, or needlessly increase the cost of litigation"?

(b) Suppose Leonard tells you that he "really hates PepsiCo and hopes that his lawsuit will subject them to some really bad publicity"?

(c) What if Leonard says that he's "looking forward to tricking PepsiCo at their own game"?

(d) Even if the filing of a civil action in these circumstances would not constitute a violation of Rule 11(b)(1), should you consider such statements in deciding whether to represent Leonard?

2. RULE 11(b)(2)

(a) What if there are decisions of the New York Court of Appeals (New York's highest court) holding that neither an advertisement nor a reward constitutes a contractual offer?

(b) What if those cases are more than 50 years old?

(c)   What if these are opinions of the New York Supreme Court (a New York trial court)?

(d)   What if the courts of Wyoming and North Dakota recently concluded that an advertisement could constitute an offer in certain circumstances?

(e)   What do you need to confirm concerning the federal subject-matter jurisdiction, personal jurisdiction, and venue for filing a civil action in a particular United States District Court?

3.   RULE 11(b)(3)

(a)   How would you confirm that John Leonard's "factual contentions have evidentiary support"?

(b)   What specific facts would you need to confirm before filing a civil action?

(c)   How would you confirm these specific facts?

(d)   How can you test Leonard's assertion that he actually believed that PepsiCo was offering a Harrier Jet in its advertising campaign?

(e)   Are there documents or other material that you would review before filing a civil action?

(f)   Can you file an action simply hoping to uncover a "smoking gun" from PepsiCo in discovery?

C.   SANCTIONS UNDER RULE 11

What if the court determines that an attorney has violated one or more of the Rule 11(b) certification requirements? Rule 11 originally provided: "For a wilful violation of this rule an attorney may be subjected to appropriate disciplinary action."[5] However, in response to concerns about perceived litigation abuse, Rule 11 was amended in 1983 to create an objective, rather than subjective, standard to determine Rule 11 violations. While Rule 11 initially only authorized sanctions for a "wilful violation" of that Rule, attorneys now are deemed to have violated Rule 11 if their inquiries are not "reasonable under the circumstances"—regardless of their subjective belief that they acted appropriately. Thus attorneys cannot invoke a subjective "empty-head, pure-heart" defense to alleged violations of Rule 11.[6]

Even more significantly, the 1983 amendment to Rule 11 made sanctions mandatory in cases in which the Rule 11(b) certification requirements were violated. Not surprisingly, this resulted in a

---

[5]   5A C. Wright & A. Miller, *Federal Practice and Procedure* § 1331, at 459 (3d ed. 2004).

[6]   Advisory Committee Note to 1993 Amendment to Rule 11, 146 F.R.D. 401, 586–87 (1993).

tremendous increase in Rule 11 litigation.[7] Both opponents and proponents of the 1983 version of the Rule 11 argued that it deterred certain litigation conduct and required attorneys to "stop and think" before filing a paper, advocating a position, or taking a case.[8] Critics differed, though, as to whether this deterrence was a good or a bad development. There also was a concern that "the financial cost of satellite litigation resulting from imposing sanctions perhaps exceeded the benefits resulting from any increased tendency of lawyers to 'stop and think.' "[9]

As a result, Rule 11 was again significantly amended in 1993, and the award of sanctions for Rule 11 violations was made discretionary, rather than mandatory (as had been the case under Rule 11 from 1983 to 1993). The first sentence of Rule 11(c)(1) now provides (with emphasis added): "If, after notice and a reasonable opportunity to respond, the court determines that Rule 11(b) has been violated, the court *may* impose an appropriate sanction on any attorney, law firm, or party that violated the rule or is responsible for the violation."

In addition to giving the judge discretion as to whether to impose sanctions for a violation of the Rule 11(b) certification requirements, the 1993 amendment to Rule 11 also created a 21 day "safe harbor" provision. Pursuant to Rule 11(b)(2), a motion seeking Rule 11 sanctions is not to be filed with the court in the first instance. Instead, the party seeking sanctions must serve on the person from whom sanctions are sought a motion describing the conduct allegedly violating Rule 11. Rule 11(b)(2) states that this motion "must not be filed or be presented to the court if the challenged paper, claim, defense, contention, or denial is withdrawn or appropriately corrected within 21 days after service or within another time the court sets." Thus courts only need consider motions for Rule 11 sanctions if the alleged violator of Rule 11 has declined to withdraw or correct the document in question and the party seeking sanctions has filed the sanctions motion with the court.

---

[7]   Although there were only about two dozen reported decisions involving Rule 11 from its adoption in 1938 until its amendment in 1983, Stempel, "Sanctions, Symmetry, and Safe Harbors: Limiting Misapplication of Rule 11 by Harmonizing it with Pre-Verdict Dismissal Devices," 60 *Fordham L. Rev.* 257, 257 (1991), within five years of its 1983 amendment there were more than 100 federal appellate decisions and 1000 total reported federal decisions involving Rule 11. Committee on Trial Practice, Section of Litigation, American Bar Association, "Standards and Guidelines for Practice Under Rule 11 of the Federal Rules of Civil Procedure," 121 F.R.D. 101, 104 (1988). Popular culture, too, has been impacted by the expansion of Rule 11 sanctions. *Christian v. Mattel, Inc.*, 286 F.3d 1118, 1121 (9th Cir. 2002) ("In her wildest dreams, Barbie could not have imagined herself in the middle of Rule 11 proceedings.").

[8]   A. Miller, *The August 1983 Amendments to the Federal Rules of Civil Procedure: Promoting Effective Case Management and Lawyer Responsibility* 15 (1984).

[9]   Committee on Rules of Practice and Procedure, Judicial Conference of the United States, *Call for Written Comments on Rule 11 of the Federal Rules of Civil Procedure and Related Rules*, 131 F.R.D. 335, 346 (1990).

Whether imposed on the motion of a party or on the court's own initiative pursuant to Rule 11(b)(3), Rule 11(b)(4) provides that any sanctions "must be limited to what suffices to deter repetition of the conduct or comparable conduct by others similarly situated." Rule 11(c)(4) further provides that the sanction ultimately imposed may include:

- nonmonetary directives;

- an order to pay a penalty into court; or

- if imposed on motion and warranted for effective deterrence, an order directing payment to the movant of part or all of the reasonable attorney's fees and other expenses directly resulting from the violation.

As you will see from the *Haisha* decision that follows, Rule 11 provides only one of several bases for sanctioning attorneys and parties.

D. *HAISHA V. COUNTRYWIDE BANK, FSB*

As you read the following case, consider the range of sanctions contemplated by the district judge. Are all of these sanctioning possibilities necessary? Did any of them actually deter the challenged actions by the attorney and his clients?

Haisha v. Countrywide Bank, FSB

United States District Court, Eastern District of Michigan, 2011
2011 WL 3268104

OPINION AND ORDER
GRANTING IN PART AND DENYING IN PART DEFENDANTS'
MOTION FOR SANCTIONS AND DIRECTING DEFENDANTS
TO ACCOUNT FOR ATTORNEY FEES

■ ROBERT H. CLELAND, DISTRICT JUDGE.

Defendants Bank of America, N.A. ("BANA"), as successor in interest to Countrywide Bank, FSB ("Countrywide"), and BAC Home Loans Servicing, LP ("BAC"), removed this matter from state court on March 29, 2011. Defendants moved to dismiss the case against them on April 5, 2011. Plaintiffs did not respond to that motion. The court determined a hearing on the matter was not necessary and granted Defendants' motion to dismiss on June 8, 2011. On May 12, 2011, Defendants filed a motion for sanctions against Plaintiffs and their counsel under Federal Rule of Civil Procedure 11, 28 U.S.C. § 1927, and the court's inherent power to sanction. Pursuant to Federal Rule of Civil Procedure 11(c)(2), Defendants gave Plaintiffs twenty-one days' notice of their intention to seek sanctions to allow Plaintiffs to withdraw the complaint. Plaintiffs did not respond within that twenty-one day period, or to the motion for sanctions. In fact, Plaintiffs have done nothing at all in this litigation other than start it. A hearing on the motion is not necessary. E.D. Mich. LR 7.1(f)(2). The court will grant in part and deny in part Defendants' motion for sanctions under Rule 11 and § 1927. The motion will be granted as to Plaintiffs' counsel and Plaintiff Steven Haisha, but denied as to Plaintiff Nadia Haisha.

I. BACKGROUND

The relevant facts of the underlying case are recorded in the order of dismissal. Therefore, only the facts germane to the pending motion will be recited here.

Plaintiffs' counsel has filed at least four substantially similar complaints in this court in the past year. Each was dismissed based on the pleadings because the claims lacked either factual or legal support. Defendants aver that Plaintiffs' counsel has also filed four substantially similar complaints in various state courts in Michigan, all of which have been dismissed on the pleadings.

The complaint filed in this matter presented multiple factual inaccuracies, including: Plaintiffs' counsel's allegation that Plaintiffs received a negative amortization loan when his own exhibit clearly evidenced a fixed-rate loan; the reference to "Defendant Comerica," presumed to be a typographical error stemming from the use of a form complaint, as Comerica is not a named Defendant in this case; and the fabrication of a nonexistent loan modification agreement. Additionally, most of the complaint lacked a sound legal basis for the reasons stated in the dismissal order.

II. STANDARD

A. Rule 11

Pursuant to Rule 11, an attorney's signature on a pleading certifies that, to the best of the attorney's knowledge, information, and belief, formed after a reasonable inquiry:

(1) [the document] is not being presented for any improper purpose, such as to harass, cause unnecessary delay, or needlessly increase the cost of litigation;

(2) the claims, defenses, and other legal contentions are warranted by existing law or by a nonfrivolous argument for extending, modifying, or reversing existing law or for establishing new law;

(3) the factual contentions have evidentiary support or, if specifically so identified, will likely have evidentiary support after a reasonable opportunity for further investigation or discovery; and

(4) the denials of factual contentions are warranted on the evidence or, if specifically so identified, are reasonably based on belief or a lack of information.

Fed.R.Civ.P. 11. Rule 11 requires an attorney who has signed a pleading to fulfill three obligations. *Jackson v. Law Firm of O'Hara, Ruberg, Osborne and Taylor*, 875 F.2d 1224, 1229 (6th Cir.1989). First, the attorney must conduct a reasonable inquiry to determine that the document is well grounded in fact. Second, the attorney must conduct a reasonable inquiry to determine that the positions taken are warranted by existing law or as good faith arguments for extension or modification of existing law. Third, the document must not be filed for any improper purpose. "The court judges the attorney's conduct by 'an objective standard of reasonableness under the circumstances.'" *Id.* (quoting *INVST Fin. Grp. Inc. v. Chem-Nuclear Sys., Inc.*, 815 F.2d 391, 401 (6th Cir.1987)). There is no good-faith defense to Rule 11 sanctions because these obligations imposed by Rule 11 require more than mere good-faith litigation. *Id.* Rule 11 imposes a "continuing duty of candor" on litigants, authorizing sanctions for the continued pursuit of unsupportable claims. *Ridder v. City of Springfield*, 109 F.3d 288, 293 (6th Cir. 1997).

Sanctions for a Rule 11 violation are discretionary. The primary purpose of a Rule 11 sanction is deterrence rather than compensation. Any Rule 11 sanction "must be limited to what suffices to deter repetition of the conduct or comparable conduct by others similarly situated." Fed.R.Civ.P. 11(c)(4). While the amended Rule 11 de-emphasizes monetary sanctions and direct payouts, it also recognizes that "if imposed on motion and warranted for effective deterrence," sanctions may include "an order directing payment to the movant of part or all of the reasonable attorney's fees and other expenses directly resulting from the violation." Fed.R.Civ.P. 11(c)(4). Parties may be sanctioned under Rule 11, as representation by counsel does not immunize a party from all Rule 11 sanctions. Fed.R.Civ.P. 11(c)(1). However, when sanctions are issued due to a frivolous legal position, only attorneys may be held liable. Fed.R.Civ.P. 11(c)(5)(A).

B. Title 28 U.S.C. § 1927

Courts may issue sanctions under 28 U.S.C. § 1927 when an attorney "multiplies the proceedings in any case unreasonably and vexatiously." Only attorneys or others "admitted to conduct cases" may be sanctioned under 1927. The Sixth Circuit recognizes the court's ability to sanction an attorney under § 1927 "'despite the absence of any conscious impropriety.'" *Rentz*, 556 F.3d at 396 (quoting *Jones v. Cont'l Corp.*, 789 F.2d 1225, 1230 (6th Cir.1986)). If an attorney knows or reasonably should know that either the claim he or she is pursuing is frivolous, or his or her litigation tactic will needlessly obstruct the litigation of nonfrivolous claims, sanctions may be warranted absent any finding of bad faith. "Under this objective standard, '§ 1927 sanctions require a showing of something less than subjective bad faith, but something more than negligence or incompetence.'" *Id.* (quoting *Red Carpet Studios Div. of Source Advantage, Ltd. v. Sater*, 465 F.3d

642, 646 (6th Cir.2006)). As an exception to the general "American
Rule" prohibiting fee shifting, *Alyeska Pipeline Serv. Co. v. Wilderness
Soc'y*, 421 U.S. 240, 247 (1975), § 1927 authorizes requiring an attorney
to reimburse the opposing side for excess costs, expenses, and attorney
fees reasonably incurred because of his or her unreasonable conduct.

C.   The Court's Inherent Power

In *Chambers v. NASCO, Inc.*, 501 U.S. 32, 46 (1991), the Supreme
Court recognized a federal court's inherent power to sanction bad-faith
conduct in litigation. To impose sanctions for bad-faith litigation under
its inherent power, a district court in this circuit must find: (1) the
claims advanced were meritless; (2) counsel for the offending party
knew or had reason to know the claims were meritless; and (3) the
motive for filing the suit was an improper purpose such as harassment.
Conduct "tantamount to bad faith" satisfies the bad-faith requirement
imposed by the Supreme Court in *Chambers*, and the improper-purpose
requirement of the three-prong test. *BDT Prods.*, 602 F.3d at 752.
Courts may rely on their inherent power to sanction parties and
attorneys for litigating in bad faith.

Chambers stressed the importance of exercising caution when
relying on inherent power to ensure compliance " 'with the mandates of
due process, both in determining that the requisite bad faith exists and
in assessing fees.' " *First Bank of Marietta*, 307 F.3d at 511 (quoting
Chambers, 501 U.S. at 50). The Court stated that district courts
"ordinarily should rely on the Rules rather than the inherent power"
when sanctioning. *Chambers*, 501 U.S. at 50. The Court clarified,
however, that a federal court is not forbidden from sanctioning bad-
faith conduct under its inherent power simply because the same
conduct could be sanctioned under other statutes or rules. *Id.*

A district court is not required to exhaust consideration of all other
statutes and rules before relying on its inherent power to issue
sanctions in this circuit. Moreover, the Sixth Circuit has previously
affirmed sanctions imposed under the district court's inherent power,
absent express consideration of other rules of civil procedure
authorizing sanctions. The Sixth Circuit suggests district courts inform
the parties they are considering using inherent power to allow parties
to present those rules or statutes that may be more appropriate. * * *

In *BDT Products*, the Sixth Circuit confronted ambiguity in the
case law concerning whether a meritless lawsuit was, on its own,
sufficient to prove bad faith and an "improper purpose." 602 F.3d at
752–53. The court held that the " 'mere fact that an action is without
merit does not amount to bad faith.' " *Id.* at 753 (quoting *Miracle Mile
Assocs. v. City of Rochester*, 617 F.2d 18, 21 (2d Cir.1980)). However, a
"pattern of asserting meritless claims and advancing baseless and
previously rejected arguments" can establish that an attorney and his
firm acted in bad faith or with an improper purpose. *Issa v. Provident*

Funding Grp., Inc., No. 09–12595, 2010 WL 3245408, at 4 (E.D.Mich. Aug.17, 2010).

III. DISCUSSION

A. Sanctions Against Plaintiffs' Counsel

Sanctions under Rule 11 against Plaintiffs' counsel, Mr. Levant, are appropriate. According to Rule 11, Mr. Levant was obligated to conduct a reasonable inquiry to ensure each of the allegations made in the complaint were factually and legally supported before signing and filing the complaint. Not one of the counts he presented survived the Defendants' motion to dismiss. Each of the ten counts was dismissed for lack of factual or legal merit, or a lack of compliance with the relevant law or procedural rule.

The complaint is fraught with factual inaccuracies. Plaintiffs alleged they received a negative amortization loan. Attached to Plaintiffs' own complaint, filed by Mr. Levant himself, are the note and TILA disclosure statement which clearly show Plaintiffs received a fixed-rate loan. More troubling is the allegation that Plaintiffs received a loan modification from Defendants. Exhibit 3 to the complaint includes a signature page containing Plaintiff Steven Haisha's signature, purported to be the signature page from that loan modification agreement. However, the pagination and text of that signature page suggest, and Defendants assert, it is in fact the signature page from a different document. This second example implies fraud upon the court. See Mich. R. Prof'l Conduct 3.3; see also E.D. Mich. LR 83.22(b) (applying Michigan Rules of Professional Conduct to attorneys practicing in this court).

Additionally, most of the counts lack a legal foundation. To give just one example, Count II alleges violation of the Mortgage Brokers, Lenders, and Servicers Licensing Act, even though the statute does not apply to depository financial institutions. As explained in the June 8 opinion and order, Defendants in this action are well within the statute's definition of a "depository financial institution."

Mr. Levant's conduct is even more deserving of sanctions because he has filed many of these same claims in Michigan courts and they have been repeatedly dismissed on the pleadings. He was therefore on notice that the claims lacked legal support. The advisory notes to Rule 11 state for emphasis that, in certain situations, it may be appropriate to consider factors such as: "whether [the improper conduct] was part of a pattern of activity, or an isolated event; whether it infected the entire pleading, or only one particular count or defense; [and] whether the person has engaged in similar conduct in other litigation." Fed.R.Civ.P. 11 advisory committee notes to the 1993 amendments. To the court's knowledge, Mr. Levant filed four other substantially similar complaints alleging nearly identical counts in this court, all of which were dismissed on the pleadings, before he filed the complaint in this matter.

* * * This pattern of behavior warrants sanctions to deter Mr. Levant from continuing to file baseless form complaints without conducting "an inquiry reasonable under the circumstances," Fed.R.Civ.P. 11(b), to ensure there is an adequate factual and legal basis for each claim made. Considering the language of Rule 11, the case law surrounding Rule 11 violations, and each of the factors emphasized in the advisory notes to Rule 11, sanctions against Mr. Levant under Rule 11 are appropriate.

Mr. Levant is also sanctionable under 28 U.S.C. § 1927 for the same underlying reasons. As an attorney, Mr. Levant either knew or reasonably should have known the claims were frivolous due to the immense lack of factual and legal support and repeated prior dismissals. The litigation was frivolous from the filing of the complaint onward, and therefore all attorney fees were incurred by Defendants in this case as a result of the unreasonable conduct of Mr. Levant. See Mich. R. Prof'l Conduct 3.1 ("A lawyer shall not bring or defend a proceeding, or assert or controvert an issue therein, unless there is a basis for doing so that is not frivolous."). Under Rule 11 and § 1927, payment of at least the total amount of Defendants' reasonable attorney fees is an appropriate sanction for Mr. Levant. After Defendants have accounted for their attorney fees, the court will determine the total amount of sanctions, which the court emphasizes may sum to more than just the attorney fees.

Because Federal Rule of Civil Procedure 11 and 28 U.S.C. § 1927 are sufficient to adequately sanction Mr. Levant, the court declines the invitation to rely on its inherent power.

Finally with respect to Mr. Levant, the court observes that this is not the first time he has been cited for being less than candid with a tribunal. Mr. Levant has been the subject of investigations of the Michigan Attorney Grievance Commission more than once. In one case, the Attorney Discipline Board wrote that Mr. Levant's "contradictory testimony to the hearing panel [ ] is so replete with inconsistencies and inaccuracies that we must assign appropriate weight to the cumulative effect of respondent's untruthfulness."

Considering his record and recent conduct before the court, the court thinks mere monetary sanctions may not go far enough. Accordingly, the court will forward a copy of the relevant court documents from this case to the Michigan Attorney Grievance Commission, and will also refer the matter to Chief Judge Gerald E. Rosen of this court for possible disciplinary action.

B.   Sanctions Against Plaintiffs

Rule 11(c)(5)(A) prohibits issuing a monetary sanction against a represented party when the basis for the sanction is a lack of legal support for contentions presented to the court. Fed.R.Civ.P. 11(c)(5)(A). In general, however, parties with counsel may still be sanctioned pursuant to Rule 11(c)(1). The advisory committee notes to Rule 11 explain that courts are permitted to consider whether "the party itself should be held accountable for [its] part in causing a violation." Fed.R.Civ.P. 11 advisory committee notes to the 1993 amendments. The notes further state that "[w]hen appropriate, the court can make an additional inquiry in order to determine whether the sanction should be imposed on ... parties either in addition to or, in unusual circumstances, instead of the person actually making the presentation to the court." *Id.* Courts in general do not sanction represented parties. *Rentz*, 556 F.3d at 398. However, the Sixth Circuit has upheld Rule 11 sanctions on parties when the parties "misrepresented key facts during depositions and at trial." *Id.* (citing *Union Planters Bank v. L & J Dev. Co.*, 115 F.3d 378, 384–85 (6th Cir.1997)).

Plaintiffs here authorized their attorney to file the complaint alleging the same meritless contentions that were the grounds, in part, for counsel's sanctions. That is all Plaintiff Nadia Haisha did and, given the general trend against sanctioning represented parties, Plaintiffs' counsel's pattern of submitting similar complaints, and the fact that this case was dismissed on the pleadings (and therefore Nadia did not misrepresent facts in discovery or at trial), the court will not sanction her.

However, Plaintiff Steven Haisha did more. He signed and swore to the allegations in the verified complaint before a notary public in Oakland County. The court cannot afford to overlook sworn false statements by parties, even if represented, and however desperate. Consequently, the court will sanction Steven in a moderated amount to be determined following Defendant's accounting of attorney fees.

IV. CONCLUSION

IT IS ORDERED that Defendants Countrywide Bank, FSB, and BAC Home Loans Servicing, LP's "Motion for Sanctions" is GRANTED IN PART and DENIED IN PART. It is GRANTED with respect to Plaintiffs' counsel and Plaintiff Steven Haisha but DENIED with respect to Plaintiff Nadia Haisha.

IT IS FURTHER ORDERED that Defendants are DIRECTED to file an accounting of attorney fees reasonably incurred in defending this action no later than fourteen days from the entry of this order. Plaintiffs' counsel and Plaintiff Steven Haisha shall then have fourteen days from the date of Defendants' submission to file objections, if any, to Defendants' calculations. Thereafter, the court will file an order directing Mr. Levant and Plaintiff Steven Haisha to pay specified sanctions.

COMMENTS AND QUESTIONS CONCERNING *HAISHA v. COUNTRYWIDE BANK, FSB*

1. This action originally was filed in Michigan state court. Why did the plaintiff homeowners choose this state forum? Why did the defendant

banks remove the case to federal court? How did they do so? *See* 28 U.S.C. § 1441(a); (b).

2.   Consider the court's characterization of the plaintiffs: "Plaintiffs have done nothing at all in this litigation other than start it." Assuming that they had filed a complaint without the factual and legal problems identified in this case, would they be subject to sanctions for simply filing the complaint and then doing nothing? Why should this case be treated differently?

3.   The district judge considers sanctioning plaintiffs and their counsel under Rule 11 of the Federal Rules of Civil Procedure, the federal statute 28 U.S.C. § 1927, and his own inherent power as a federal judge. Why are there such overlapping authorities to accomplish the same result? Why should district courts "ordinarily * * * rely on the Rules rather than the inherent power" when sanctioning litigants or their attorneys?

4.   In addition to the inherent power of the court, Rule 11, and 28 U.S.C. § 1927, the court notes that the Michigan Rules of Professional Conduct apply to at least some of attorney Levant's actions in this case. Each state has its own rules of professional conduct governing attorney conduct, most of which are based upon the Model Rules of Professional Conduct promulgated and adopted by the American Bar Association. The district judge refers this matter to not only the Michigan attorney grievance commission, but also to the chief judge of the United States District Court to initiate an independent determination as to whether Mr. Levant should remain admitted to practice in that federal court.

5.   The first two sentences of Rule 3.1 of the Michigan Rules of Professional Conduct provide:

> A lawyer shall not bring or defend a proceeding, or assert or controvert an issue therein, unless there is a basis for doing so that is not frivolous. A lawyer may offer a good-faith argument for an extension, modification, or reversal of existing law.

See also ABA Model Rule of Professional Conduct 3.1. Does this language sound familiar?

6.   Concerning attorney Levant's actions, Judge Cleland states: "After Defendants have accounted for their attorney fees, the court will determine the total amount of sanctions, which the court emphasizes may sum to more than just the attorney fees." Wouldn't payment of the defendants' total attorney fees make defendants whole? Would additional sanctions be needed either to compensate defendants or deter similar conduct by Levant or other attorneys in the future?

7.   Why does Rule 11(c)(5)(A) prohibit the imposition of monetary sanctions against a represented party for violating Rule 11(b)(2)?

8.   On what basis did the judge determine to sanction plaintiff Steven Haisha but not Nadia Haisha? Is their involvement in the case really distinguishable?

9.   If attorney Levant was in a partnership with another attorney, would that attorney be subject to sanctions in this case? *See* Rule 11(c)(1)

("Absent exceptional circumstances, a law firm must be held jointly responsible for a violation committed by its partner, associate, or employee."). What is the rationale for extending potential Rule 11 liability in this fashion?

IV. PLEADING UNDER THE FEDERAL RULES OF CIVIL PROCEDURE

Rule 8 of the Federal Rules of Civil Procedure contains the basic rules for pleading a complaint in the United States District Courts. Rule 8(a) provides:

A pleading that states a claim for relief must contain:

(1) a short and plain statement of the grounds for the court's jurisdiction, unless the court already has jurisdiction and the claim needs no new jurisdictional support;

(2) a short and plain statement of the claim showing that the pleader is entitled to relief; and

(3) a demand for the relief sought, which may include relief in the alternative or different types of relief.

Note that Rule 8(a) requires "short and plain" statements of the court's jurisdiction and of the claim asserted. As Judge Frank Easterbrook stated for the United States Court of Appeals for the Seventh Circuit: "Rule 8(a) requires parties to make their pleadings straightforward, so that judges and adverse parties need not try to fish a gold coin from a bucket of mud." *U.S. ex rel. Garst v. Lockheed-Martin Corp.*, 328 F.3d 374, 378 (7th Cir.), *cert. denied*, 540 U.S. 968 (2003).

Prior to its abrogation in 2015, an Appendix to the Federal Rules contained a set of sample forms that were approved and amended in the same manner as the Rules.[10] Federal Rule of Civil Procedure 84, also abrogated in 2015, established the authority given these forms: "The forms in the Appendix suffice under these rules and illustrate the simplicity and brevity that these rules contemplate."

Forms 1, 2, 7, and 11 illustrated the manner in which the case caption, attorney signature lines, statement of jurisdiction, and the body of a complaint for negligence might be pled. A composite of these four forms illustrates what a simple complaint for negligence might look like:

---

[10] *See* Advisory Committee Note to 2007 Amendments to Forms 1–82, 550 U.S. 1003, 1147 (2007).

United States District Court

for the

_____ District of _____

A B, Plaintiff   )
)
v.   )   Civil Action No. _____
)
C D, Defendant   )

COMPLAINT

1. (*For diversity-of-citizenship jurisdiction.*) The plaintiff is [a citizen of <u>Michigan</u>] [a corporation incorporated under the laws of <u>Michigan</u> with its principal place of business in <u>Michigan</u>]. The defendant is [a citizen of <u>New York</u>] [a corporation incorporated under the laws of <u>New York</u> with its principal place of business in <u>New York</u>]. The amount in controversy, without interest and costs, exceeds the sum or value specified by 28 U.S.C. § 1332.

2. On <u>date</u>, at <u>place</u>, the defendant negligently drove a motor vehicle against the plaintiff.

3. As a result, the plaintiff was physically injured, lost wages or income, suffered physical and mental pain, and incurred medical expenses of $_____.

Therefore, the plaintiff demands judgment against the defendant for $_____, plus costs.

Date _____   _____

(Signature of the attorney or unrepresented party)

_____

(Printed name)

_____

(Address)

_____

(E-mail address)

_____

(Telephone number)[11]

---

[11] Attorneys are creatures of habit. Once a court approves a pleading or other document, attorneys will continue to mimic the approved format for many years. However, why not substitute for the phrase "motor vehicle" in the above form the simple, one-syllable word "car?"

A. PLEADING PRETEST: YOU BE THE JUDGE!

Pleading a federal complaint sounds pretty simple. Indeed, the simplicity of pleading was one of the real breakthroughs brought about by the Federal Rules of Civil Procedure in 1938. To test your understanding, consider which of the following sets of allegations satisfy the Rule 8(a)(2) requirement that federal complaints contain "a short and plain statement of the claim showing that the pleader is entitled to relief." These factual allegations are premised upon federal civil actions in which the sufficiency of the complaint was considered by the United States Supreme Court.

    a.   In an action alleging racial discrimination constituting a violation of plaintiffs' rights under the Railway Labor Act:

1.   On or about May 1, 1954, the Texas and New Orleans Railroad posted a notice at the Freight House abolishing 45 jobs.

2.   All of these jobs were held by Negro members of the craft.

3.   No advance notice of the abolition of the jobs was given to plaintiffs and those similarly situated as required by the collective bargaining agreement.

4.   Such jobs were not in fact abolished, for immediately thereafter many white persons were hired to perform the same work, and, subsequently, some of the same Negro employees who had been previously fired were rehired, but without seniority.

5.   None of the white members of the craft were discharged or displaced.

6.   The defendant Brotherhood of Railway and Steamship Clerks permitted plaintiffs' jobs to be abolished because of plaintiffs' race.

7.   The defendant Brotherhood repeatedly refused to grant plaintiffs a hearing concerning their discharge and declined to come to their aid.

8.   The defendant Brotherhood's actions and inactions constituted a planned course of conduct designed to discriminate against plaintiffs, solely because of their race or color.

9.   By reason of said acts and in refusing to represent them and to give them protection equal to that afforded the white members of the craft, the Brotherhood breached the statutory duty imposed upon it by the Railway Labor Act to represent all members of the craft fairly and impartially.

See Conley v. Gibson, 355 U.S. 41 (1957).

68
THE INITIATION OF THE LAWSUIT: "A SHORT AND PLAIN STATEMENT OF THE CLAIM."

CHAPTER 2

b.   In a complaint alleging municipal liability due to inadequate training of law enforcement officers:

1.   In May 1989 the Leatherman home was entered and searched by law enforcement officers employed by and under the control of TCNICU, Tarrant and Lake Worth.

2.   During the course of the search two dogs belonging to the Leathermans were shot to death.

3.   The officers threatened to shoot two of the Leathermans.

4.   After the officers realized that none of the items described in the warrant pursuant to which they entered the Leatherman home were present, the officers frolicked in the driveway and yard of the residence.

5.   The conduct of the law enforcement officers deprived the Leathermans of rights they have under the Fourth and Fourteenth Amendments of the United States Constitution.

See *Leatherman v. Tarrant County Narcotics Intelligence and Coordination Unit*, 507 U.S. 163 (1993).

c.   In a complaint alleging national origin and age discrimination:

1.   Plaintiff Swierkiewicz, a 53-year old native of Hungary, was fired due to his national origin and age.

2.   Plaintiff was demoted by Mr. Chavel in 1995 in favor of Nicholas Papadopoulo, a substantially younger and less qualified French national.

3.   Plaintiff's firing had nothing to do with his own performance, which had been stellar, but rather, was due to his national origin and his age.

4.   After Plaintiff's demotion he suffered two years of continuous discrimination—which took the form of being isolated and excluded from meetings and being bypassed for assignments in favor of far less qualified non-protected class employees.

5.   Plaintiff protested these unsatisfactory working conditions in a memorandum he sent to Mr. Chavel.

6.   Fifteen days later, without notice or cause, he was fired by Mr. Chavel.

7.   Plaintiff was then denied any severance benefits despite the fact that the defendant company routinely provided these benefits to other executives [five of whom were identified by name] who, unlike him, were terminated for cause.

See *Swierkiewicz v. Sorema, N. A.*, 534 U.S. 506 (2002).

d.   In an action alleging a conspiracy in restraint of trade in violation of the Sherman Antitrust Act:

1. Defendants Local Exchange Carriers (ILECs) have avoided infringing upon each other's markets and have refused to permit nonincumbent competitors to access their networks.

2. Defendants ILECs have agreed not to compete with one another and otherwise allocated customers and markets to one another.

3. Richard Notebaert, the former CEO of one ILEC has stated that competing in a neighboring ILEC's territory "might be a good way to turn a quick dollar but that doesn't make it right."

4. Defendants ILECs have communicated amongst themselves through numerous industry associations.

5. Defendants ILECs entered into a contract, combination or conspiracy to prevent competitive entry in their respective local telephone and/or high speed internet services markets and have agreed not to compete with one another and otherwise allocated customers and markets to one another.

See Bell Atlantic Corp. v. Twombly, 550 U.S. 544 (2007).

B. THE SUPREME COURT'S PLEADING JURISPRUDENCE

Rule 8(a)(2) simply requires that a complaint or other pleading contain "a short and plain statement of the claim showing that the pleader is entitled to relief." To the extent that this requirement is interpreted liberally, civil actions are more likely to survive Rule 12(b)(6) motions to dismiss for failure to state a claim upon which relief can be granted. To the extent that the Rule 8(a)(2) requirement is interpreted more strictly, it is more likely that civil actions will be dismissed before plaintiffs have an opportunity to obtain disclosure or discovery. As the following three cases illustrate, the strictness with which the Supreme Court has interpreted Rule 8(a)(2) has varied over time.

1. NOTICE PLEADING UNDER *CONLEY V. GIBSON*

Conley v. Gibson

Supreme Court of the United States, 1957
355 U.S. 41

■ JUSTICE BLACK delivered the opinion of the Court.

Once again, Negro employees are here under the Railway Labor Act asking that their collective bargaining agent be compelled to represent them fairly. In a series of cases beginning with *Steele v. Louisville & Nashville R. Co.*, 323 U.S. 192, this Court has emphatically and repeatedly ruled that an exclusive bargaining agent under the Railway Labor Act is obligated to represent all employees in the

70   THE INITIATION OF THE LAWSUIT: "A SHORT AND PLAIN STATEMENT OF THE CLAIM."

CHAPTER 2

bargaining unit fairly and without discrimination because of race, and has held that the courts have power to protect employees against such invidious discrimination.

This class suit was brought in a Federal District Court in Texas by certain Negro members of the Brotherhood of Railway and Steamship Clerks, petitioners here, on behalf of themselves and other Negro employees similarly situated against the Brotherhood, its Local Union No. 28 and certain officers of both. In summary, the complaint made the following allegations relevant to our decision: Petitioners were employees of the Texas and New Orleans Railroad at its Houston Freight House. Local 28 of the Brotherhood was the designated bargaining agents under the Railway Labor Act for the bargaining unit to which petitioners belonged. A contract existed between the Union and the Railroad which gave the employees in the bargaining unit certain protection from discharge and loss of seniority. In May, 1954, the Railroad purported to abolish 45 jobs held by petitioners or other Negroes, all of whom were either discharged or demoted. In truth, the 45 jobs were not abolished at all, but instead filled by whites as the Negroes were ousted, except for a few instances where Negroes were rehired to fill their old jobs, but with loss of seniority. Despite repeated pleas by petitioners, the Union, acting according to plan, did nothing to protect them against these discriminatory discharges and refused to give them protection comparable to that given white employees. The complaint then went on to allege that the Union had failed in general to represent Negro employees equally and in good faith. It charged that such discrimination constituted a violation of petitioners' right under the Railway Labor Act to fair representation from their bargaining agent. And it concluded by asking for relief in the nature of declaratory judgment, injunction and damages.

The respondents appeared and moved to dismiss the complaint on several grounds: (1) the National Railroad Adjustment Board had exclusive jurisdiction over the controversy; (2) the Texas and New Orleans Railroad, which had not been joined, was an indispensable party defendant; and (3) the complaint failed to state a claim upon which relief could be given. The District Court granted the motion to dismiss holding that Congress had given the Adjustment Board exclusive jurisdiction over the controversy. The Court of Appeals for the Fifth Circuit, apparently relying on the same ground, affirmed. Since the case raised an important question concerning the protection of employee rights under the Railway Labor Act we granted certiorari.

We hold that it was error for the courts below to dismiss the complaint for lack of jurisdiction. * * *

* * *

Turning to respondents' final ground, we hold that, under the general principles laid down in the *Steele, Graham*, and *Howard* cases the complaint adequately set forth a claim upon which relief could be granted. In appraising the sufficiency of the complaint, we follow, of course, the accepted rule that a complaint should not be dismissed for failure to state a claim unless it appears beyond doubt that the plaintiff can prove no set of facts in support of his claim which would entitle him to relief. Here, the complaint alleged, in part, that petitioners were discharged wrongfully by the Railroad and that the Union, acting according to plan, refused to protect their jobs as it did those of white employees or to help them with their grievances all because they were Negroes. If these allegations are proven, there has been a manifest breach of the Union's statutory duty to represent fairly and without hostile discrimination all of the employees in the bargaining unit. This Court squarely held in *Steele* and subsequent cases that discrimination in representation because of race is prohibited by the Railway Labor Act. * * *

* * *

The respondents also argue that the complaint failed to set forth specific facts to support its general allegations of discrimination, and that its dismissal is therefore proper. The decisive answer to this is that the Federal Rules of Civil Procedure do not require a claimant to set out in detail the facts upon which he bases his claim. To the contrary, all the Rules require is "a short and plain statement of the claim" that will give the defendant fair notice of what the plaintiff's claim is and the grounds upon which it rests. The illustrative forms appended to the Rules plainly demonstrate this. Such simplified "notice pleading" is made possible by the liberal opportunity for discovery and the other pretrial procedures established by the Rules to disclose more precisely the basis of both claim and defense and to define more narrowly the disputed facts and issues.[9] Following the simple guide of Rule 8(f) [now, Rule 8(e)] that "all pleadings shall be so construed as to do substantial justice," we have no doubt that petitioners' complaint adequately set forth a claim and gave the respondents fair notice of its basis. The Federal Rules reject the approach that pleading is a game of skill in which one misstep by counsel may be decisive to the outcome, and accept the principle that the purpose of pleading is to facilitate a proper decision on the merits.

The judgment is reversed, and the cause is remanded to the District Court for further proceedings not inconsistent with this opinion.

It is so ordered.

---

[9] *See, e.g.,* Rule 12(e) (motion for a more definite statement); Rule 12(f) (motion to strike portions of the pleading); Rule 12(c) (motion for judgment on the pleadings); Rule 16 (pretrial procedure and formulation of issue); Rules 26–37 (depositions and discovery); Rule 56 (motion for summary judgment); Rule 15 (right to amend).

COMMENTS AND QUESTIONS CONCERNING *CONLEY V. GIBSON*

1.   Before considering his discussion of pleading sufficiency, what does Justice Black mean in stating that the Supreme Court "granted certiorari" in this case? *See* 28 U.S.C. § 1254.

2.   What is the significance of the Court's holding that "the complaint adequately set[s] forth a claim upon which relief could be granted?" Does this mean that plaintiffs have prevailed in this civil action? That they ultimately will prevail in the action?

3.   In the decades after *Conley v. Gibson*, plaintiffs opposing Rule 12(b)(6) motions to dismiss for failure to state a claim upon which relief can be granted often cited the following language from *Conley*:

> In appraising the sufficiency of the complaint, we follow, of course, the accepted rule that a complaint should not be dismissed for failure to state a claim unless it appears beyond doubt that the plaintiff can prove no set of facts in support of his claim which would entitle him to relief.

Why should plaintiffs not be required to actually prove those facts in response to the motion to dismiss? Why should it be sufficient to simply argue that they may at some future point be able to prove a set of facts that would entitle them to relief? In *Bell Atlantic Corp. v. Twombly*, the Supreme Court stated that "this famous observation has earned its retirement." 550 U.S. 544, 563 (2007).

4.   What is the "notice pleading" endorsed by the Court in *Conley*? Why does the Court believe that such notice pleading is possible?

2.   PLEADING EMPLOYMENT DISCRIMINATION UNDER *SWIERKIEWICZ V. SOREMA N. A.*

Swierkiewicz v. Sorema N. A.

Supreme Court of the United States, 2002
534 U.S. 506

■ JUSTICE THOMAS delivered the opinion of the Court.

This case presents the question whether a complaint in an employment discrimination lawsuit must contain specific facts establishing a prima facie case of discrimination under the framework set forth by this Court in *McDonnell Douglas Corp. v. Green*, 411 U. S. 792 (1973). We hold that an employment discrimination complaint need not include such facts and instead must contain only "a short and plain statement of the claim showing that the pleader is entitled to relief." Fed. Rule Civ. Proc. 8(a)(2).

I

Petitioner Akos Swierkiewicz is a native of Hungary, who at the time of his complaint was 53 years old.[1] In April 1989, petitioner began working for respondent Sorema N. A., a reinsurance company headquartered in New York and principally owned and controlled by a French parent corporation. Petitioner was initially employed in the position of senior vice president and chief underwriting officer (CUO). Nearly six years later, François M. Chavel, respondent's Chief Executive Officer, demoted petitioner to a marketing and services position and transferred the bulk of his underwriting responsibilities to Nicholas Papadopoulo, a 32-year-old who, like Mr. Chavel, is a French national. About a year later, Mr. Chavel stated that he wanted to "energize" the underwriting department and appointed Mr. Papadopoulo as CUO. Petitioner claims that Mr. Papadopoulo had only one year of underwriting experience at the time he was promoted, and therefore was less experienced and less qualified to be CUO than he, since at that point he had 26 years of experience in the insurance industry.

Following his demotion, petitioner contends that he "was isolated by Mr. Chavel . . . excluded from business decisions and meetings and denied the opportunity to reach his true potential at SOREMA." Petitioner unsuccessfully attempted to meet with Mr. Chavel to discuss his discontent. Finally, in April 1997, petitioner sent a memo to Mr. Chavel outlining his grievances and requesting a severance package. Two weeks later, respondent's general counsel presented petitioner with two options: He could either resign without a severance package or be dismissed. Mr. Chavel fired petitioner after he refused to resign.

Petitioner filed a lawsuit alleging that he had been terminated on account of his national origin in violation of Title VII of the Civil Rights Act of 1964, 42 U.S.C. 2000e et seq., and on account of his age in violation of the Age Discrimination in Employment Act of 1967 (ADEA), 29 U.S.C. 621 et seq. The United States District Court for the Southern District of New York dismissed petitioner's complaint because it found that he "ha[d] not adequately alleged a prima facie case, in that he ha[d] not adequately alleged circumstances that support an inference of discrimination." The United States Court of Appeals for the Second Circuit affirmed the dismissal, relying on its settled precedent, which requires a plaintiff in an employment discrimination complaint to allege facts constituting a prima facie case of discrimination under the framework set forth by this Court in *McDonnell Douglas, supra,* at 802. The Court of Appeals held that petitioner had failed to meet his burden because his allegations were "insufficient as a matter of law to raise an inference of discrimination." We granted certiorari to resolve a split

---

[1] Because we review here a decision granting respondent's motion to dismiss, we must accept as true all of the factual allegations contained in the complaint. *See, e.g., Leatherman v. Tarrant County Narcotics Intelligence and Coordination Unit,* 507 U. S. 163, 164 (1993).

among the Courts of Appeals concerning the proper pleading standard for employment discrimination cases, and now reverse.

II

Applying Circuit precedent, the Court of Appeals required petitioner to plead a prima facie case of discrimination in order to survive respondent's motion to dismiss. In the Court of Appeals' view, petitioner was thus required to allege in his complaint: (1) membership in a protected group; (2) qualification for the job in question; (3) an adverse employment action; and (4) circumstances that support an inference of discrimination.

The prima facie case under *McDonnell Douglas*, however, is an evidentiary standard, not a pleading requirement. In *McDonnell Douglas*, this Court made clear that "[t]he critical issue before us concern[ed] the order and allocation of proof in a private, non-class action challenging employment discrimination." 411 U. S., at 800. In subsequent cases, this Court has reiterated that the prima facie case relates to the employee's burden of presenting evidence that raises an inference of discrimination.

This Court has never indicated that the requirements for establishing a prima facie case under *McDonnell Douglas* also apply to the pleading standard that plaintiffs must satisfy in order to survive a motion to dismiss. For instance, we have rejected the argument that a Title VII complaint requires greater "particularity," because this would "too narrowly constric[t] the role of the pleadings." *McDonald v. Santa Fe Trail Transp. Co.*, 427 U. S. 273, 283, n.11 (1976). Consequently, the ordinary rules for assessing the sufficiency of a complaint apply. *See, e.g., Scheuer v. Rhodes*, 416 U. S. 232, 236 (1974) ("When a federal court reviews the sufficiency of a complaint, before the reception of any evidence either by affidavit or admissions, its task is necessarily a limited one. The issue is not whether a plaintiff will ultimately prevail but whether the claimant is entitled to offer evidence to support the claims").

In addition, under a notice pleading system, it is not appropriate to require a plaintiff to plead facts establishing a prima facie case because the *McDonnell Douglas* framework does not apply in every employment discrimination case. For instance, if a plaintiff is able to produce direct evidence of discrimination, he may prevail without proving all the elements of a prima facie case. Under the Second Circuit's heightened pleading standard, a plaintiff without direct evidence of discrimination at the time of his complaint must plead a prima facie case of discrimination, even though discovery might uncover such direct evidence. It thus seems incongruous to require a plaintiff, in order to survive a motion to dismiss, to plead more facts than he may ultimately need to prove to succeed on the merits if direct evidence of discrimination is discovered.

Moreover, the precise requirements of a prima facie case can vary depending on the context and were "never intended to be rigid, mechanized, or ritualistic." *Furnco Constr. Corp. v. Waters*, 438 U. S. 567, 577 (1978). Before discovery has unearthed relevant facts and evidence, it may be difficult to define the precise formulation of the required prima facie case in a particular case. Given that the prima facie case operates as a flexible evidentiary standard, it should not be transposed into a rigid pleading standard for discrimination cases.

Furthermore, imposing the Court of Appeals' heightened pleading standard in employment discrimination cases conflicts with Federal Rule of Civil Procedure 8(a)(2), which provides that a complaint must include only "a short and plain statement of the claim showing that the pleader is entitled to relief." Such a statement must simply "give the defendant fair notice of what the plaintiff's claim is and the grounds upon which it rests." *Conley v. Gibson*, 355 U. S. 41, 47 (1957) . This simplified notice pleading standard relies on liberal discovery rules and summary judgment motions to define disputed facts and issues and to dispose of unmeritorious claims. * * *

Rule 8(a)'s simplified pleading standard applies to all civil actions, with limited exceptions. Rule 9(b), for example, provides for greater particularity in all averments of fraud or mistake.[3] This Court, however, has declined to extend such exceptions to other contexts. In *Leatherman* we stated: "[T]he Federal Rules do address in Rule 9(b) the question of the need for greater particularity in pleading certain actions, but do not include among the enumerated actions any reference to complaints alleging municipal liability under § 1983. Expressio unius est exclusio alterius." 507 U. S., at 168. Just as Rule 9(b) makes no mention of municipal liability under Rev. Stat. § 1979, 42 U.S.C. § 1983, neither does it refer to employment discrimination. Thus, complaints in these cases, as in most others, must satisfy only the simple requirements of Rule 8(a).[4]

Other provisions of the Federal Rules of Civil Procedure are inextricably linked to Rule 8(a)'s simplified notice pleading standard. Rule 8(e)(1) states that "[n]o technical forms of pleading or motions are required," and Rule 8(f) provides that "[a]ll pleadings shall be so construed as to do substantial justice." Given the Federal Rules' simplified standard for pleading, "[a] court may dismiss a complaint only if it is clear that no relief could be granted under any set of facts that could be proved consistent with the allegations." *Hishon v. King &*

---

[3] "In all averments of fraud or mistake, the circumstances constituting fraud or mistake shall be stated with particularity. Malice, intent, knowledge, and other condition of mind of a person may be averred generally."

[4] These requirements are exemplified by the Federal Rules of Civil Procedure Forms, which "are sufficient under the rules and are intended to indicate the simplicity and brevity of statement which the rules contemplate." Fed. Rule Civ. Proc. 84. For example, Form 9 sets forth a complaint for negligence in which plaintiff simply states in relevant part: "On June 1, 1936, in a public highway called Boylston Street in Boston, Massachusetts, defendant negligently drove a motor vehicle against plaintiff who was then crossing said highway."

THE INITIATION OF THE LAWSUIT: "A SHORT AND PLAIN
STATEMENT OF THE CLAIM."

76

CHAPTER 2

Spalding, 467 U. S. 69, 73 (1984). If a pleading fails to specify the allegations in a manner that provides sufficient notice, a defendant can move for a more definite statement under Rule 12(e) before responding. Moreover, claims lacking merit may be dealt with through summary judgment under Rule 56. The liberal notice pleading of Rule 8(a) is the starting point of a simplified pleading system, which was adopted to focus litigation on the merits of a claim. See *Conley*, *supra*, at 48 ("The Federal Rules reject the approach that pleading is a game of skill in which one misstep by counsel may be decisive to the outcome and accept the principle that the purpose of pleading is to facilitate a proper decision on the merits").

Applying the relevant standard, petitioner's complaint easily satisfies the requirements of Rule 8(a) because it gives respondent fair notice of the basis for petitioner's claims. Petitioner alleged that he had been terminated on account of his national origin in violation of Title VII and on account of his age in violation of the ADEA. His complaint detailed the events leading to his termination, provided relevant dates, and included the ages and nationalities of at least some of the relevant persons involved with his termination. These allegations give respondent fair notice of what petitioner's claims are and the grounds upon which they rest. In addition, they state claims upon which relief could be granted under Title VII and the ADEA.

Respondent argues that allowing lawsuits based on conclusory allegations of discrimination to go forward will burden the courts and encourage disgruntled employees to bring unsubstantiated suits. Whatever the practical merits of this argument, the Federal Rules do not contain a heightened pleading standard for employment discrimination suits. A requirement of greater specificity for particular claims is a result that "must be obtained by the process of amending the Federal Rules, and not by judicial interpretation." *Leatherman*, *supra*, at 168. Furthermore, Rule 8(a) establishes a pleading standard without regard to whether a claim will succeed on the merits. "Indeed it may appear on the face of the pleadings that a recovery is very remote and unlikely but that is not the test." *Scheuer*, 416 U. S., at 236.

For the foregoing reasons, we hold that an employment discrimination plaintiff need not plead a prima facie case of discrimination and that petitioner's complaint is sufficient to survive respondent's motion to dismiss. Accordingly, the judgment of the Court of Appeals is reversed, and the case is remanded for further proceedings consistent with this opinion.

It is so ordered.

COMMENTS AND QUESTIONS CONCERNING
SWIERKIEWICZ V. SOREMA N. A.

1.   If plaintiff must prove a prima facie case at trial, why shouldn't he be required to plead such facts in his complaint?

2.   Under the *McDonald Douglas* standard as interpreted by the Court of Appeals, plaintiff had to show at trial: (1) membership in a protected group; (2) qualification for the job in question; (3) an adverse employment action; and (4) circumstances that support an inference of discrimination. Why would it be difficult for plaintiff to include such allegations in his complaint?

3.   Justice Thomas states in his opinion:

> Whatever the practical merits of this argument, the Federal Rules do not contain a heightened pleading standard for employment discrimination suits. A requirement of greater specificity for particular claims is a result that "must be obtained by the process of amending the Federal Rules, and not by judicial interpretation." *Leatherman, supra*, at 168.

What are the benefits, and costs, of "trans-substantive" Federal Rules of Civil Procedure that apply in the same fashion to very different types and complexities of civil actions? *See* Cover, "For James Wm. Moore: Some Reflections on a Reading of the Rules," 84 *Yale L. J.* 718 (1975); Carrington, "Making Rules to Dispose of Manifestly Unfounded Assertions: An Exorcism of the Bogy of Non-Trans-Substantive Rules of Civil Procedure," 137 *U. Pa. L. Rev.* 2067 (1989); Subrin, "The Limitations of Transsubstantive Procedure: An Essay on Adjusting the 'One Size Fits All' Assumption," 87 *Den. U. L. Rev.* (2010).

4.   Justice Thomas notes that "Rule 8(a) establishes a pleading standard without regard to whether a claim will succeed on the merits. 'Indeed it may appear on the face of the pleadings that a recovery is very remote and unlikely but that is not the test.' *Scheuer*, 416 U.S., at 236." As recognized in footnote 1 of the opinion, "Because we review here a decision granting respondent's motion to dismiss, we must accept as true all of the factual allegations contained in the complaint."

In determining whether to grant a motion to dismiss a complaint, why shouldn't the court consider the likelihood that the plaintiff will be able to succeed on the merits of his action at trial?

3.   FACTUAL PLEADING UNDER *ASHCROFT V. IQBAL*

Ashcroft v. Iqbal

Supreme Court of the United States, 2009
556 U.S. 662

■ JUSTICE KENNEDY delivered the opinion of the Court.

Respondent Javaid Iqbal is a citizen of Pakistan and a Muslim. In the wake of the September 11, 2001, terrorist attacks he was arrested in the United States on criminal charges and detained by federal officials. Respondent claims he was deprived of various constitutional protections while in federal custody. To redress the alleged deprivations, respondent filed a complaint against numerous federal officials, including John Ashcroft, the former Attorney General of the United States, and Robert Mueller, the Director of the Federal Bureau of Investigation (FBI). Ashcroft and Mueller are the petitioners in the case now before us. As to these two petitioners, the complaint alleges that they adopted an unconstitutional policy that subjected respondent to harsh conditions of confinement on account of his race, religion, or national origin.

In the District Court petitioners raised the defense of qualified immunity and moved to dismiss the suit, contending the complaint was not sufficient to state a claim against them. The District Court denied the motion to dismiss, concluding the complaint was sufficient to state a claim despite petitioners' official status at the times in question. Petitioners brought an interlocutory appeal in the Court of Appeals for the Second Circuit. The court, without discussion, assumed it had jurisdiction over the order denying the motion to dismiss; and it affirmed the District Court's decision.

Respondent's account of his prison ordeal could, if proved, demonstrate unconstitutional misconduct by some governmental actors. But the allegations and pleadings with respect to these actors are not before us here. This case instead turns on a narrower question: Did respondent, as the plaintiff in the District Court, plead factual matter that, if taken as true, states a claim that petitioners deprived him of his clearly established constitutional rights. We hold respondent's pleadings are insufficient.

I

Following the 2001 attacks, the FBI and other entities within the Department of Justice began an investigation of vast reach to identify the assailants and prevent them from attacking anew. The FBI dedicated more than 4,000 special agents and 3,000 support personnel to the endeavor. By September 18 "the FBI had received more than 96,000 tips or potential leads from the public." Dept. of Justice, Office of Inspector General, The September 11 Detainees: A Review of the Treatment of Aliens Held on Immigration Charges in Connection with the Investigation of the September 11 Attacks 1, 11–12 (Apr. 2003) (hereinafter OIG Report).

In the ensuing months the FBI questioned more than 1,000 people with suspected links to the attacks in particular or to terrorism in general. Of those individuals, some 762 were held on immigration charges; and a 184-member subset of that group was deemed to be "of 'high interest' " to the investigation. The high-interest detainees were held under restrictive conditions designed to prevent them from communicating with the general prison population or the outside world.

Respondent was one of the detainees. According to his complaint, in November 2001 agents of the FBI and Immigration and Naturalization Service arrested him on charges of fraud in relation to identification documents and conspiracy to defraud the United States. Pending trial for those crimes, respondent was housed at the Metropolitan Detention Center (MDC) in Brooklyn, New York. Respondent was designated a person "of high interest" to the September 11 investigation and in January 2002 was placed in a section of the MDC known as the Administrative Maximum Special Housing Unit (ADMAX SHU). As the facility's name indicates, the ADMAX SHU incorporates the maximum security conditions allowable under Federal Bureau of Prison regulations. ADMAX SHU detainees were kept in lockdown 23 hours a day, spending the remaining hour outside their cells in handcuffs and leg irons accompanied by a four-officer escort.

Respondent pleaded guilty to the criminal charges, served a term of imprisonment, and was removed to his native Pakistan. He then filed a *Bivens* action in the United States District Court for the Eastern District of New York against 34 current and former federal officials and 19 "John Doe" federal corrections officers. *See Bivens v. Six Unknown Fed. Narcotics Agents*, 403 U. S. 388 (1971). The defendants range from the correctional officers who had day-to-day contact with respondent during the term of his confinement, to the wardens of the MDC facility, all the way to petitioners—officials who were at the highest level of the federal law enforcement hierarchy. First Amended Complaint in No. 04–CV–1809 (JG)(JA), ¶¶ 10–11 (hereinafter Complaint).

The 21-cause-of-action complaint does not challenge respondent's arrest or his confinement in the MDC's general prison population. Rather, it concentrates on his treatment while confined to the ADMAX SHU. The complaint sets forth various claims against defendants who are not before us. For instance, the complaint alleges that respondent's jailors "kicked him in the stomach, punched him in the face, and dragged him across" his cell without justification, *id.*, ¶ 113; subjected him to serial strip and body-cavity searches when he posed no safety risk to himself or others, *id.*, ¶¶ 143–145; and refused to let him and other Muslims pray because there would be "[n]o prayers for terrorists," *id.*, ¶ 154.

The allegations against petitioners are the only ones relevant here. The complaint contends that petitioners designated respondent a person of high interest on account of his race, religion, or national origin, in contravention of the First and Fifth Amendment s to the Constitution. The complaint alleges that "the [FBI], under the direction of Defendant MUELLER, arrested and detained thousands of Arab Muslim men . . . as part of its investigation of the events of September 11." *Id.*, ¶ 47. It further alleges that "[t]he policy of holding post-September-11th detainees in highly restrictive conditions of confinement until they were 'cleared' by the FBI was approved by

Defendants ASHCROFT and MUELLER in discussions in the weeks
after September 11, 2001." *Id.*, ¶ 69. Lastly, the complaint posits that
petitioners "each knew of, condoned, and willfully and maliciously
agreed to subject" respondent to harsh conditions of confinement "as a
matter of policy, solely on account of [his] religion, race, and/or national
origin and for no legitimate penological interest." *Id.*, ¶ 96. The pleading
names Ashcroft as the "principal architect" of the policy, *id.*, ¶ 10, and
identifies Mueller as "instrumental in [its] adoption, promulgation, and
implementation." *Id.*, ¶ 11.

Petitioners moved to dismiss the complaint for failure to state
sufficient allegations to show their own involvement in clearly
established unconstitutional conduct. The District Court denied their
motion. Accepting all of the allegations in respondent's complaint as
true, the court held that "it cannot be said that there [is] no set of facts
on which [respondent] would be entitled to relief as against" petitioners.
Invoking the collateral-order doctrine petitioners filed an interlocutory
appeal in the United States Court of Appeals for the Second Circuit.
While that appeal was pending, this Court decided *Bell Atlantic Corp. v.
Twombly*, 550 U. S. 544 (2007), which discussed the standard for
evaluating whether a complaint is sufficient to survive a motion to
dismiss.

The Court of Appeals considered *Twombly*'s applicability to this
case. Acknowledging that *Twombly* retired the *Conley* no-set-of-facts
test relied upon by the District Court, the Court of Appeals' opinion
discussed at length how to apply this Court's "standard for assessing
the adequacy of pleadings." It concluded that *Twombly* called for a
"flexible 'plausibility standard,'" which obliges a pleader to amplify a
claim with some factual allegations in those contexts where such
amplification is needed to render the claim plausible." The court found
that petitioners' appeal did not present one of "those contexts" requiring
amplification. As a consequence, it held respondent's pleading adequate
to allege petitioners' personal involvement in discriminatory decisions
which, if true, violated clearly established constitutional law.

Judge Cabranes concurred. He agreed that the majority's
"discussion of the relevant pleading standards reflect[ed] the uneasy
compromise ... between a qualified immunity privilege rooted in the
need to preserve the effectiveness of government as contemplated by
our constitutional structure and the pleading requirements of Rule 8(a)
of the Federal Rules of Civil Procedure." Judge Cabranes nonetheless
expressed concern at the prospect of subjecting high-ranking
Government officials—entitled to assert the defense of qualified
immunity and charged with responding to "a national and international
security emergency unprecedented in the history of the American
Republic"—to the burdens of discovery on the basis of a complaint as
nonspecific as respondent's. Reluctant to vindicate that concern as a
member of the Court of Appeals, Judge Cabranes urged this Court to

address the appropriate pleading standard "at the earliest opportunity." We granted certiorari and now reverse.

II

* * *

[W]e conclude that the Court of Appeals had jurisdiction to hear petitioners' appeal. The District Court's order denying petitioners' motion to dismiss turned on an issue of law and rejected the defense of qualified immunity. It was therefore a final decision "subject to immediate appeal." * * *

* * *

III

In *Twombly*, the Court found it necessary first to discuss the antitrust principles implicated by the complaint. Here too we begin by taking note of the elements a plaintiff must plead to state a claim of unconstitutional discrimination against officials entitled to assert the defense of qualified immunity.

* * *

The factors necessary to establish a *Bivens* violation will vary with the constitutional provision at issue. Where the claim is invidious discrimination in contravention of the First and Fifth Amendments, our decisions make clear that the plaintiff must plead and prove that the defendant acted with discriminatory purpose. *Church of Lukumi Babalu Aye, Inc. v. Hialeah*, 508 U.S. 520, 540–541 (1993) (First Amendment); *Washington v. Davis*, 426 U.S. 229, 240 (1976) (Fifth Amendment). Under extant precedent purposeful discrimination requires more than "intent as volition or intent as awareness of consequences." *Personnel Administrator of Mass. v. Feeney*, 442 U.S. 256, 279 (1979). It instead involves a decisionmaker's undertaking a course of action " 'because of,' not merely 'in spite of,' [the action's] adverse effects upon an identifiable group." *Ibid.* It follows that, to state a claim based on a violation of a clearly established right, respondent must plead sufficient factual matter to show that petitioners adopted and implemented the detention policies at issue not for a neutral, investigative reason but for the purpose of discriminating on account of race, religion, or national origin.

* * * [R]espondent believes a supervisor's mere knowledge of his subordinate's discriminatory purpose amounts to the supervisor's violating the Constitution. We reject this argument. * * * Absent vicarious liability, each Government official, his or her title notwithstanding, is only liable for his or her own misconduct. In the context of determining whether there is a violation of clearly established right to overcome qualified immunity, purpose rather than knowledge is required to impose *Bivens* liability on the subordinate for unconstitutional discrimination; the same holds true for an official charged with violations arising from his or her superintendent responsibilities.

IV

A

We turn to respondent's complaint. Under Federal Rule of Civil Procedure 8(a)(2), a pleading must contain a "short and plain statement of the claim showing that the pleader is entitled to relief." As the Court held in *Twombly*, the pleading standard Rule 8 announces does not require "detailed factual allegations," but it demands more than an unadorned, the-defendant-unlawfully-harmed-me accusation. A pleading that offers "labels and conclusions" or "a formulaic recitation of the elements of a cause of action will not do." 550 U.S., at 555. Nor does a complaint suffice if it tenders "naked assertion[s]" devoid of "further factual enhancement." *Id.*, at 557.

To survive a motion to dismiss, a complaint must contain sufficient factual matter, accepted as true, to "state a claim to relief that is plausible on its face." *Id.*, at 570. A claim has facial plausibility when the plaintiff pleads factual content that allows the court to draw the reasonable inference that the defendant is liable for the misconduct alleged. *Id.*, at 556. The plausibility standard is not akin to a "probability requirement," but it asks for more than a sheer possibility that a defendant has acted unlawfully. *Ibid.* Where a complaint pleads facts that are "merely consistent with" a defendant's liability, it "stops short of the line between possibility and plausibility of 'entitlement to relief.'" *Id.*, at 557.

Two working principles underlie our decision in *Twombly*. First, the tenet that a court must accept as true all of the allegations contained in a complaint is inapplicable to legal conclusions. Threadbare recitals of the elements of a cause of action, supported by mere conclusory statements, do not suffice. Rule 8 marks a notable and generous departure from the hyper-technical, code-pleading regime of a prior era, but it does not unlock the doors of discovery for a plaintiff armed with nothing more than conclusions. Second, only a complaint that states a plausible claim for relief survives a motion to dismiss. Determining whether a complaint states a plausible claim for relief will, as the Court of Appeals observed, be a context-specific task that requires the reviewing court to draw on its judicial experience and common sense. But where the well-pleaded facts do not permit the court to infer more than the mere possibility of misconduct, the complaint has alleged—but it has not "show[n]"—"that the pleader is entitled to relief." Fed. Rule Civ. Proc. 8(a)(2).

In keeping with these principles a court considering a motion to dismiss can choose to begin by identifying pleadings that, because they are no more than conclusions, are not entitled to the assumption of truth. While legal conclusions can provide the framework of a complaint, they must be supported by factual allegations. When there are well-pleaded factual allegations, a court should assume their veracity and then determine whether they plausibly give rise to an entitlement to relief.

* * *

B

Under *Twombly*'s construction of Rule 8, we conclude that respondent's complaint has not "nudged [his] claims" of invidious discrimination "across the line from conceivable to plausible." *Ibid.*

We begin our analysis by identifying the allegations in the complaint that are not entitled to the assumption of truth. Respondent pleads that petitioners "knew of, condoned, and willfully and maliciously agreed to subject [him]" to harsh conditions of confinement "as a matter of policy, solely on account of [his] religion, race, and/or national origin and for no legitimate penological interest." Complaint ¶ 96. The complaint alleges that Ashcroft was the "principal architect" of this invidious policy, *id.*, ¶ 10, and that Mueller was "instrumental" in adopting and executing it, *id.*, ¶ 11. These bare assertions, much like the pleading of conspiracy in *Twombly*, amount to nothing more than a "formulaic recitation of the elements" of a constitutional discrimination claim, 550 U.S., at 555, namely, that petitioners adopted a policy " 'because of,' not merely 'in spite of,' its adverse effects upon an identifiable group." *Feeney*, 442 U.S., at 279. As such, the allegations are conclusory and not entitled to be assumed true. To be clear, we do not reject these bald allegations on the ground that they are unrealistic or nonsensical. We do not so characterize them any more than the Court in *Twombly* rejected the plaintiffs' express allegation of a " 'contract, combination or conspiracy to prevent competitive entry,' " *id.*, at 551, because it thought that claim too chimerical to be maintained. It is the conclusory nature of respondent's allegations, rather than their extravagantly fanciful nature, that disentitles them to the presumption of truth.

We next consider the factual allegations in respondent's complaint to determine if they plausibly suggest an entitlement to relief. The complaint alleges that "the [FBI], under the direction of Defendant MUELLER, arrested and detained thousands of Arab Muslim men . . . as part of its investigation of the events of September 11." Complaint ¶ 47. It further claims that "[t]he policy of holding post-September-11th detainees in highly restrictive conditions of confinement until they were 'cleared' by the FBI was approved by Defendants ASHCROFT and MUELLER in discussions in the weeks after September 11, 2001." *Id.*, ¶ 69. Taken as true, these allegations are consistent with petitioners' purposefully designating detainees "of high interest" because of their race, religion, or national origin. But given more likely explanations, they do not plausibly establish this purpose.

The September 11 attacks were perpetrated by 19 Arab Muslim hijackers who counted themselves members in good standing of al Qaeda, an Islamic fundamentalist group. Al Qaeda was headed by another Arab Muslim—Osama bin Laden—and composed in large part of his Arab Muslim disciples. It should come as no surprise that a legitimate policy directing law enforcement to arrest and detain individuals because of their suspected link to the attacks would produce a disparate, incidental impact on Arab Muslims, even though the purpose of the policy was to target neither Arabs nor Muslims. On the facts respondent alleges the arrests Mueller oversaw were likely lawful and justified by his nondiscriminatory intent to detain aliens who were illegally present in the United States and who had potential connections to those who committed terrorist acts. As between that "obvious alternative explanation" for the arrests, *Twombly, supra,* at 567, and the purposeful, invidious discrimination respondent asks us to infer, discrimination is not a plausible conclusion.

But even if the complaint's well-pleaded facts give rise to a plausible inference that respondent's arrest was the result of unconstitutional discrimination, that inference alone would not entitle respondent to relief. It is important to recall that respondent's complaint challenges neither the constitutionality of his arrest nor his initial detention in the MDC. Respondent's constitutional claims against petitioners rest solely on their ostensible "policy of holding post-September-11th detainees" in the ADMAX SHU once they were categorized as "of high interest." Complaint ¶ 69. To prevail on that theory, the complaint must contain facts plausibly showing that petitioners purposefully adopted a policy of classifying post-September-11 detainees as "of high interest" because of their race, religion, or national origin.

This the complaint fails to do. Though respondent alleges that various other defendants, who are not before us, may have labeled him a person of "of high interest" for impermissible reasons, his only factual allegation against petitioners accuses them of adopting a policy approving "restrictive conditions of confinement" for post-September-11 detainees until they were " 'cleared' by the FBI." Accepting the truth of that allegation, the complaint does not show, or even intimate, that petitioners purposefully housed detainees in the ADMAX SHU due to their race, religion, or national origin. All it plausibly suggests is that the Nation's top law enforcement officers, in the aftermath of a devastating terrorist attack, sought to keep suspected terrorists in the most secure conditions available until the suspects could be cleared of terrorist activity. Respondent does not argue, nor can he, that such a motive would violate petitioners' constitutional obligations. He would need to allege more by way of factual content to "nudg[e]" his claim of purposeful discrimination "across the line from conceivable to plausible." *Twombly*, 550 U.S., at 570.

* * * [R]espondent's pleadings do not suffice to state a claim. Unlike in *Twombly*, where the doctrine of respondeat superior could bind the corporate defendant, here, as we have noted, petitioners cannot be held liable unless they themselves acted on account of a constitutionally protected characteristic. Yet respondent's complaint does not contain any factual allegation sufficient to plausibly suggest petitioners' discriminatory state of mind. His pleadings thus do not meet the standard necessary to comply with Rule 8.

It is important to note, however, that we express no opinion concerning the sufficiency of respondent's complaint against the defendants who are not before us. Respondent's account of his prison ordeal alleges serious official misconduct that we need not address here. Our decision is limited to the determination that respondent's complaint does not entitle him to relief from petitioners.

C

Respondent offers three arguments that bear on our disposition of his case, but none is persuasive.

1

Respondent first says that our decision in *Twombly* should be limited to pleadings made in the context of an antitrust dispute. This argument is not supported by *Twombly* and is incompatible with the Federal Rules of Civil Procedure. Though *Twombly* determined the sufficiency of a complaint sounding in antitrust, the decision was based on our interpretation and application of Rule 8. That Rule in turn governs the pleading standard "in all civil actions and proceedings in the United States district courts." Fed. Rule Civ. Proc. 1. Our decision in *Twombly* expounded the pleading standard for "all civil actions," and it applies to antitrust and discrimination suits alike.

2

Respondent next implies that our construction of Rule 8 should be tempered where, as here, the Court of Appeals has "instructed the district court to cabin discovery in such a way as to preserve" petitioners' defense of qualified immunity "as much as possible in anticipation of a summary judgment motion." We have held, however, that the question presented by a motion to dismiss a complaint for insufficient pleadings does not turn on the controls placed upon the discovery process. *Twombly, supra*, at 559 ("It is no answer to say that a claim just shy of a plausible entitlement to relief can, if groundless, be weeded out early in the discovery process through careful case management given the common lament that the success of judicial supervision in checking discovery abuse has been on the modest side").

Our rejection of the careful-case-management approach is especially important in suits where Government-official defendants are entitled to assert the defense of qualified immunity. The basic thrust of the qualified-immunity doctrine is to free officials from the concerns of litigation, including "avoidance of disruptive discovery." *Siegert v. Gilley*, 500 U.S. 226, 236 (1991) (Kennedy, J., concurring in judgment). There are serious and legitimate reasons for this. If a Government official is to devote time to his or her duties, and to the formulation of sound and responsible policies, it is counterproductive to require the substantial diversion that is attendant to participating in litigation and making informed decisions as to how it should proceed. * * *

It is no answer to these concerns to say that discovery for petitioners can be deferred while pretrial proceedings continue for other defendants. It is quite likely that, when discovery as to the other parties proceeds, it would prove necessary for petitioners and their counsel to participate in the process to ensure the case does not develop in a misleading or slanted way that causes prejudice to their position. Even if petitioners are not yet themselves subject to discovery orders, then, they would not be free from the burdens of discovery.

We decline respondent's invitation to relax the pleading requirements on the ground that the Court of Appeals promises petitioners minimally intrusive discovery. That promise provides especially cold comfort in this pleading context, where we are impelled to give real content to the concept of qualified immunity for high-level officials who must be neither deterred nor detracted from the vigorous performance of their duties. Because respondent's complaint is deficient under Rule 8, he is not entitled to discovery, cabined or otherwise.

3

Respondent finally maintains that the Federal Rules expressly allow him to allege petitioners' discriminatory intent "generally," which he equates with a conclusory allegation. It follows, respondent says, that his complaint is sufficiently well pleaded because it claims that petitioners discriminated against him "on account of [his] religion, race, and/or national origin and for no legitimate penological interest." Were we required to accept this allegation as true, respondent's complaint would survive petitioners' motion to dismiss. But the Federal Rules do not require courts to credit a complaint's conclusory statements without reference to its factual context.

It is true that Rule 9(b) requires particularity when pleading "fraud or mistake," while allowing "[m]alice, intent, knowledge, and other conditions of a person's mind [to] be alleged generally." But "generally" is a relative term. In the context of Rule 9, it is to be compared to the particularity requirement applicable to fraud or mistake. Rule 9 merely excuses a party from pleading discriminatory intent under an elevated pleading standard. It does not give him license to evade the less rigid— though still operative—strictures of Rule 8. And Rule 8 does not empower respondent to plead the bare elements of his cause of action, affix the label "general allegation," and expect his complaint to survive a motion to dismiss.

V

We hold that respondent's complaint fails to plead sufficient facts to state a claim for purposeful and unlawful discrimination against petitioners. The Court of Appeals should decide in the first instance whether to remand to the District Court so that respondent can seek leave to amend his deficient complaint.

The judgment of the Court of Appeals is reversed, and the case is remanded for further proceedings consistent with this opinion.

It is so ordered.

■ JUSTICE SOUTER, with whom JUSTICE STEVENS, JUSTICE GINSBURG, and JUSTICE BREYER join, dissenting.

* * *

II

[T]he complaint satisfies Rule 8(a)(2). Ashcroft and Mueller admit they are liable for their subordinates' conduct if they "had actual knowledge of the assertedly discriminatory nature of the classification of suspects as being 'of high interest' and they were deliberately indifferent to that discrimination." Iqbal alleges that after the September 11 attacks the Federal Bureau of Investigation (FBI) "arrested and detained thousands of Arab Muslim men," Complaint ¶ 47, that many of these men were designated by high-ranking FBI officials as being " 'of high interest,' " *id.*, ¶¶ 48, 50, and that in many cases, including Iqbal's, this designation was made "because of the race, religion, and national origin of the detainees, and not because of any evidence of the detainees' involvement in supporting terrorist activity," *id.*, ¶ 49. The complaint further alleges that Ashcroft was the "principal architect of the policies and practices challenged," *id.*, ¶ 10, and that Mueller "was instrumental in the adoption, promulgation, and implementation of the policies and practices challenged," *id.*, ¶ 11. According to the complaint, Ashcroft and Mueller "knew of, condoned, and willfully and maliciously agreed to subject [Iqbal] to these conditions of confinement as a matter of policy, solely on account of [his] religion, race, and/or national origin and for no legitimate penological interest." *Id.*, ¶ 96. The complaint thus alleges, at a bare minimum, that Ashcroft and Mueller knew of and condoned the discriminatory policy their subordinates carried out. Actually, the complaint goes further in alleging that Ashcroft and Muller affirmatively acted to create the discriminatory detention policy. If these factual allegations are true, Ashcroft and Mueller were, at the very least, aware of the discriminatory policy being implemented and deliberately indifferent to it.

Ashcroft and Mueller argue that these allegations fail to satisfy the "plausibility standard" of *Twombly*. They contend that Iqbal's claims are implausible because such high-ranking officials "tend not to be personally involved in the specific actions of lower-level officers down the bureaucratic chain of command." But this response bespeaks a fundamental misunderstanding of the enquiry that *Twombly* demands. *Twombly* does not require a court at the motion-to-dismiss stage to consider whether the factual allegations are probably true. We made it clear, on the contrary, that a court must take the allegations as true, no matter how skeptical the court may be. The sole exception to this rule lies with allegations that are sufficiently fantastic to defy reality as we know it: claims about little green men, or the plaintiff's recent trip to Pluto, or experiences in time travel. That is not what we have here.

Under *Twombly*, the relevant question is whether, assuming the factual allegations are true, the plaintiff has stated a ground for relief that is plausible. That is, in *Twombly*'s words, a plaintiff must "allege facts" that, taken as true, are "suggestive of illegal conduct." 550 U.S., at 564, n. 8. In *Twombly*, we were faced with allegations of a conspiracy to violate § 1 of the Sherman Act through parallel conduct. The difficulty was that the conduct alleged was "consistent with conspiracy, but just as much in line with a wide swath of rational and competitive business strategy unilaterally prompted by common perceptions of the market." *Id.*, at 554. We held that in that sort of circumstance, "[a]n allegation of parallel conduct is . . . much like a naked assertion of conspiracy in a § 1 complaint: it gets the complaint close to stating a claim, but without some further factual enhancement it stops short of the line between possibility and plausibility of 'entitlement to relief.' " *Id.*, at 557. Here, by contrast, the allegations in the complaint are neither confined to naked legal conclusions nor consistent with legal conduct. The complaint alleges that FBI officials discriminated against Iqbal solely on account of his race, religion, and national origin, and it alleges the knowledge and deliberate indifference that, by Ashcroft and Mueller's own admission, are sufficient to make them liable for the illegal action. Iqbal's complaint therefore contains "enough facts to state a claim to relief that is plausible on its face." *Id.*, at 570.

I do not understand the majority to disagree with this understanding of "plausibility" under *Twombly*. Rather, the majority discards the allegations discussed above with regard to Ashcroft and Mueller as conclusory, and is left considering only two statements in the complaint: that "the [FBI], under the direction of Defendant MUELLER, arrested and detained thousands of Arab Muslim men . . . as part of its investigation of the events of September 11," Complaint ¶ 47, and that "[t]he policy of holding post-September-11th detainees in highly restrictive conditions of confinement until they were 'cleared' by the FBI was approved by Defendants ASHCROFT and MUELLER in discussions in the weeks after September 11, 2001," *id.*,¶ 69. I think the majority is right in saying that these allegations suggest only that Ashcroft and Mueller "sought to keep suspected terrorists in the most secure conditions available until the suspects could be cleared of terrorist activity," and that this produced "a disparate, incidental impact on Arab Muslims." And I agree that the two allegations selected by the majority, standing alone, do not state a plausible entitlement to relief for unconstitutional discrimination.

But these allegations do not stand alone as the only significant, nonconclusory statements in the complaint, for the complaint contains many allegations linking Ashcroft and Mueller to the discriminatory practices of their subordinates. *See* Complaint ¶ 10 (Ashcroft was the "principal architect" of the discriminatory policy); *id.*, ¶ 11 (Mueller was "instrumental" in adopting and executing the discriminatory policy); *id.*, ¶ 96 (Ashcroft and Mueller "knew of, condoned, and willfully and maliciously agreed to subject" Iqbal to harsh conditions "as a matter of policy, solely on account of [his] religion, race, and/or national origin and for no legitimate penological interest").

The majority says that these are "bare assertions" that, "much like the pleading of conspiracy in *Twombly*, amount to nothing more than a 'formulaic recitation of the elements' of a constitutional discrimination claim" and therefore are "not entitled to be assumed true." Ante, at 1951 (quoting *Twombly*, *supra*, at 555). The fallacy of the majority's position, however, lies in looking at the relevant assertions in isolation. The complaint contains specific allegations that, in the aftermath of the September 11 attacks, the Chief of the FBI's International Terrorism Operations Section and the Assistant Special Agent in Charge for the FBI's New York Field Office implemented a policy that discriminated against Arab Muslim men, including Iqbal, solely on account of their race, religion, or national origin. See Complaint ¶¶ 47–53. Viewed in light of these subsidiary allegations, the allegations singled out by the majority as "conclusory" are no such thing. * * *

* * * By my lights, there is no principled basis for the majority's disregard of the allegations linking Ashcroft and Mueller to their subordinates' discrimination.

I respectfully dissent.

COMMENTS AND QUESTIONS CONCERNING *ASHCROFT V. IQBAL*

1.   Before considering the sufficiency with which the complaint was pleaded, Justice Kennedy, in Section II of his opinion, addresses the jurisdiction of the Court of Appeals to review the district court order denying defendants' motion to dismiss. Why was this of concern to the Supreme Court?

2.   As is discussed in Chapter 15 of this text, the usual rule in the federal courts is that the courts of appeals only have jurisdiction to consider appeals from final judgments of United States District Courts. 28 U.S.C.

§ 1291. A final judgment "generally is one which ends the litigation on the merits and leaves nothing for the [trial] court to do but execute the judgment." *Catlin v. United States*, 324 U.S. 229, 233 (1945). Why, then, is the collateral-order doctrine recognized as an exception to the final judgment rule? Why was application of the collateral-order doctrine particularly appropriate in this case?

The Supreme Court has described the collateral order exception to the final judgment rule as follows:

> The collateral order doctrine is a "narrow exception," *Firestone [Tire & Rubber Co. v. Risjord]*, *supra*, 449 U.S., at 374, whose reach is limited to trial court orders affecting rights that will be irretrievably lost in the absence of an immediate appeal. To fall within the exception, an order must at a minimum satisfy three conditions: It must "conclusively determine the disputed question," "resolve an important issue completely separate from the merits of the action," and "be effectively unreviewable on appeal from a final judgment." *Coopers & Lybrand v. Livesay*, 437 U.S. 463, 468 (1978).

Richardson-Merrell, Inc. v. Koller, 472 U.S. 424, 430–31 (1985).

3.　Two years before its decision in *Ashcroft v. Iqbal.* the Supreme Court decided *Bell Atlantic Corp. v. Twombly*, 550 U.S. 544 (2007). In *Twombly* the Court addressed the following language from *Conley v. Gibson* that had been widely quoted and relied upon for fifty years: "In appraising the sufficiency of the complaint we follow, of course, the accepted rule that a complaint should not be dismissed for failure to state a claim unless it appears beyond doubt that the plaintiff can prove no set of facts in support of his claim which would entitle him to relief." 355 U.S. 41, 45–46 (1957). Of this language from *Conley*, the *Twombly* majority said:

> *Conley*'s "no set of facts" language has been questioned, criticized, and explained away long enough. To be fair to the *Conley* Court, the passage should be understood in light of the opinion's preceding summary of the complaint's concrete allegations, which the Court quite reasonably understood as amply stating a claim for relief. But the passage so often quoted fails to mention this understanding on the part of the Court, and after puzzling the profession for 50 years, this famous observation has earned its retirement. The phrase is best forgotten as an incomplete, negative gloss on an accepted pleading standard: once a claim has been stated adequately, it may be supported by showing any set of facts consistent with the allegations in the complaint.

Bell Atlantic Corp. v. Twombly, 550 U.S. 544, 562–63 (2007).

4.　*Bell Atlantic Corp. v. Twombly* had been interpreted by some as raising pleading requirements only in antitrust actions such as *Twombly* itself. However, Justice Kennedy's opinion in *Iqbal* makes clear that *Twombly* should not be so narrowly interpreted:

> This argument is not supported by *Twombly* and is incompatible with the Federal Rules of Civil Procedure. Though *Twombly*

determined the sufficiency of a complaint sounding in antitrust, the decision was based on our interpretation and application of Rule 8. That Rule in turn governs the pleading standard "in all civil actions and proceedings in the United States district courts." Fed. Rule Civ. Proc. 1. Our decision in *Twombly* expounded the pleading standard for "all civil actions," *ibid.*, and it applies to antitrust and discrimination suits alike.

So, just as in *Swierkiewicz v. Sorema N. A.*, the Court concluded that the requirements of Rule 8(a) apply to all types of civil actions. In *Swierkiewicz* this led the Court to refuse to apply a stricter standard for the pleading of employment discrimination actions than for other civil actions. In *Iqbal* this conclusion led the Court to refuse to limit the *Twombly* standard to antitrust actions.

5.   Justice Kennedy explains the impact of *Twombly* as follows:

Two working principles underlie our decision in *Twombly*. First, the tenet that a court must accept as true all of the allegations contained in a complaint is inapplicable to legal conclusions. Threadbare recitals of the elements of a cause of action, supported by mere conclusory statements, do not suffice. * * * Rule 8 marks a notable and generous departure from the hyper-technical, code-pleading regime of a prior era, but it does not unlock the doors of discovery for a plaintiff armed with nothing more than conclusions. Second, only a complaint that states a plausible claim for relief survives a motion to dismiss. Determining whether a complaint states a plausible claim for relief will, as the Court of Appeals observed, be a context-specific task that requires the reviewing court to draw on its judicial experience and common sense. But where the well-pleaded facts do not permit the court to infer more than the mere possibility of misconduct, the complaint has alleged—but it has not "show[n]"— "that the pleader is entitled to relief." Fed. Rule Civ. Proc. 8(a)(2).

Is it always an easy task to separate legal from non-legal conclusions? What standards should guide a district court in its "context-specific task" of determining whether pleading in a complaint states a plausible claim for relief?

6.   Although numerous federal officials were sued in *Iqbal*, and the complaint made specific allegations about these officials, the Supreme Court considered only the claims against former Attorney General John Ashcroft and FBI Director Robert Mueller. The Court stated: "It is important to note * * * that we express no opinion concerning the sufficiency of respondent's complaint against the defendants who are not before us. Respondent's account of his prison ordeal alleges serious official misconduct that we need not address here. Our decision is limited to the determination that respondent's complaint does not entitle him to relief from petitioners."

7.   Justice Kennedy distinguishes *Iqbal* from *Twombly* as follows:

Unlike in *Twombly*, where the doctrine of respondeat superior
could bind the corporate defendant, here, as we have noted,
petitioners cannot be held liable unless they themselves acted on
account of a constitutionally protected characteristic. Yet
respondent's complaint does not contain any factual allegation
sufficient to plausibly suggest petitioners' discriminatory state of
mind. His pleadings thus do not meet the standard necessary to
comply with Rule 8."

What would a "factual allegation sufficient to plausibly suggest
petitioners' discriminatory state of mind" look like? Why can't plaintiff
make such an allegation? Where and how might he obtain information
upon which he could base such an allegation?

8.   Federal Rule of Civil Procedure 9(b) provides:

In alleging fraud or mistake, a party must state with
particularity the circumstances constituting fraud or mistake.
Malice, intent, knowledge, and other conditions of a person's mind
may be alleged generally.

Why do the Rules require more specific allegations in alleging fraud or
mistake? Why does Rule 9(b) state that such particularity is not required in
alleging conditions of mind?

9.   In addition to the heightened pleading standard of Rule 9(b),
Congress has demanded greater specificity in certain federal securities
fraud actions, requiring that complaints "shall, with respect to each act or
omission alleged to violate [these federal provisions], state with
particularity facts giving rise to a strong inference that the defendant acted
with the required state of mind." 15 U.S.C. § 78u–4(b)(2).

10. The *Iqbal* majority declined to adopt a "careful-case-management
approach," under which a district court's restriction of discovery to facts
relevant to the defense of qualified immunity would justify a more liberal
pleading standard. Why shouldn't the trial judge's ability to protect
defendants from broad-ranging discovery justify a less stringent pleading
standard?

11. Justice Souter, who wrote a dissent for four justices in *Iqbal*,
authored the majority opinion in which seven justices joined in *Twombly*.
Does he interpret *Twombly* differently than does the *Ashcroft* majority? Or
does he conclude that the factual allegations in *Ashcroft* are of a different
nature than those in *Twombly*?

12. Might *Iqbal* be considered an example of the maxim that "hard
cases make bad law"?

13. After holding that plaintiff's complaint failed to allege sufficient
facts to state a claim for purposeful and unlawful discrimination, the
Supreme Court majority noted that the Court of Appeals "should decide in
the first instance whether to remand to the District Court so that
respondent can seek leave to amend his deficient complaint." Amendment
of pleadings is discussed in Section IV(E), *infra*.

14. State courts have differed in applying the heightened pleading standard of *Twombly* and *Iqbal* to state rules identical or comparable to Federal Rule of Civil Procedure 8(a). *Compare Walsh v. U.S. Bank, N.A.*, 851 N.W.2d 598, 603 (Minn. 2014) ("[W]e * * * decline to engraft the plausibility standard from *Twombly and Iqbal* onto our traditional interpretation of Minn. R. Civ. P. 8.01. We decline to do so despite the fact that the relevant text of Fed.R.Civ.P. 8(a)(2) is identical to the text of Minn. R. Civ. P. 8.01."), *with Data Key Partners v. Permira Advisers LLC*, 356 Wis. 2d 665, 680 (2014) ("*Twombly* makes clear the sufficiency of a complaint depends on substantive law that underlies the claim made because it is the substantive law that drives what facts must be pled. Plaintiffs must allege facts that plausibly suggest they are entitled to relief.").

C. PLEADING IN PRACTICE

1. HOW MUCH SPECIFICITY IS REQUIRED?

In his majority opinion in *Iqbal*, Justice Kennedy states: "Determining whether a complaint states a plausible claim for relief will * * * be a context-specific task that requires the reviewing court to draw on its judicial experience and common sense." Because the task is "context-specific," it can be quite difficult to determine in practice whether a complaint satisfies Rule 8(a)(2)'s requirement that the complaint set forth "a short and plain statement of the claim showing that the pleader is entitled to relief." Although it is difficult to make this determination without knowledge of the full factual context of a specific civil action, consider how that determination might be made in the following situations.

Reconsider the four sets of factual allegations set forth in Section IV(A) of this chapter, *supra* pp. 67–69 ("Pleading Pretest: You Be the Judge!"). In the first three of these civil actions (*Conley v. Gibson*, *Leatherman v. Tarrant County Narcotics Intelligence and Coordination Unit*, and *Swierkiewicz v. Sorema N. A.*), the Supreme Court found the complaints to be sufficient. However, in the final action (*Bell Atlantic Corp. v. Twombly*), the Court held that the complaint failed to state a claim upon which relief could be granted.

2. PLEADING BEFORE DISCOVERY

One of the challenges for plaintiffs after the Supreme Court's opinions in *Twombly* and *Iqbal* (referred to jointly as *"Twiqbal"* by some) is having sufficient information to satisfy the pleading requirements of those cases before having access to disclosure and discovery from the defendants. However, before filing a civil action the plaintiff's attorney typically conducts informal discovery outside the formal litigation process. Consider, for instance, the informal investigation upon which the following paragraph from the amended complaint in *Leonard v. PepsiCo, Inc.* was based:

7. To promote the sale of its products in the United
States, PepsiCo launched the Pepsi Stuff campaign, which
PepsiCo described in its press releases as a "massive consumer
outreach" and "the single biggest consumer event in the
company's history." The theme of the Pepsi Stuff campaign
was "Drink Pepsi, Get Stuff." The Pepsi Stuff campaign
utilized various forms of media to promote this campaign, the
most significant of which was the use of television
commercials.

¶ 7 of Amended Complaint in *Leonard v. PepsiCo, Inc.*, No. 96 Civ. 9069
(KMW) (March 8, 1999).

What if a plaintiff and his counsel believe that a certain fact may
be true, but are not certain of that fact? Rule 11(b)(3) provides that an
attorney or unrepresented person certifies "that to the best of the
person's knowledge, information, and belief, formed after an inquiry
reasonable under the circumstances * * * the factual contentions have
evidentiary support or, if specifically so identified, will likely have
evidentiary support after a reasonable opportunity for further
investigation or discovery."

This ability to plead matters likely to be confirmed in discovery
won't be helpful in actions in which the plaintiff has no basis for
inferring likely conduct by the defendants or others. However, in other
actions this provision may permit a plaintiff to allege facts likely to be
confirmed after the filing of the complaint. Consider, for instance, the
following paragraph from John Leonard's amended complaint:

12. Upon information and belief, the Harrier jet
commercial was conceived of and developed in New York by
PepsiCo, with the assistance of its advertising agency, BBDO
of New York.

¶ 12 of Amended Complaint in *Leonard v. PepsiCo, Inc.*, No. 96 Civ.
9069 (KMW) (March 8, 1999).

3.   PLEADING FRAUD, MISTAKE, OR STATE OF MIND

Rule 9(b) specifically addresses the specificity with which
allegations of fraud, mistake, and state of mind must be pled. Rule 9(b)
provides:

In alleging fraud or mistake, a party must state with
particularity the circumstances constituting fraud or mistake.
Malice, intent, knowledge, and other conditions of a person's
mind may be alleged generally.

In his action against PepsiCo, Inc., John Leonard included a claim
of fraud. Among his allegations were the following:

34. PepsiCo, by and through its national Pepsi Stuff
campaign, featuring a Harrier jet knowingly made false

statements and representations to Leonard (and the general public), concerning the availability for sale of a Harrier jet as one of the prizes which could be obtained in the Pepsi Stuff promotional campaign.

35. Specifically, PepsiCo misrepresented the material fact that a Harrier jet could be acquired by a member of the general public in exchange for 7 million Pepsi Points, when in fact, PepsiCo had absolutely no intention of fulfilling its promise to deliver the jet under any circumstances.

¶¶ 34–35 of Amended Complaint in *Leonard v. PepsiCo, Inc.*, No. 96 Civ. 9069 (KMW) (March 8, 1999).

What was the basis for Leonard's allegation that "PepsiCo had absolutely no intention of fulfilling its promise to deliver the jet under any circumstances?" Do Leonard's allegations satisfy the requirements of Rules 8(a) and 9(b)? Are there other facts that Leonard could have alleged to satisfy the particularity requirement of Rule 9(b)?

4. PLEADING INCONSISTENT CLAIMS OR DEFENSES

Although pleadings must be filed before discovery, it is difficult to be certain what specific facts ultimately will be proven at trial. Federal Rule of Civil Procedure 8(d)(3) states: "A party may state as many separate claims or defenses as it has, regardless of consistency." Assuming that this is not done for an improper purpose, *see* Rule 11(b)(1), the plaintiff might allege in her complaint both that the defendant was negligent and that she acted intentionally in injuring plaintiff.

While Rule 8(d)(3) permits the assertion of inconsistent claims or defenses in the pleadings, by the time of trial parties generally should proceed with consistent claims or defenses. The downside of offering inconsistent claims or defenses at trial is illustrated in the following description from Professor James McElhaney of attorney Robert Hanley's response to a myriad of inconsistent defenses raised by AT & T in a major antitrust action.

"* * * A farmer has a patch of cabbages. His neighbor has a goat. The goat breaks loose, gets in the cabbage patch and eats all the cabbages. The farmer brings a lawsuit against his neighbor. He says, 'I had a patch of cabbages worth $100. Your goat ate my cabbages. Give me my $100.'"

"And if he was represented by these lawyers for AT & T," said Hanley, pointing at the defense table, "what would the owner of the goat say?"

"1. You had no cabbages.

"2. If you had any cabbages, they were not eaten.

"3. If your cabbages were eaten, it was not by a goat.

"4. If your cabbages were eaten by a goat, it wasn't my goat.

"5. And if it was my goat, he was insane!"

Everyone laughed except the defense, and the jury returned a verdict of $1.8 billion.

McElhaney, "Make 'Em Laugh" *A.B.A.J.*, Oct. 2002, at 52–53.

The fact that the Rules or other governing law permit an attorney to do something does not mean that taking that action necessarily constitutes good advocacy.

D. THE ALLOCATION OF PLEADING BURDENS

Rule 8(a)(2) requires that the plaintiff plead "a short and plain statement of the claim showing that the pleader is entitled to relief." However, in some cases it may not be clear whether a specific matter is included in the claim that plaintiff must plead. Both governing substantive law and practical considerations may influence whether a party is required to plead a specific matter as an element of its claim. In *Gomez v. Toledo*, 446 U.S. 635 (1980), the Supreme Court held that the plaintiff in an action brought under 42 U.S.C. § 1983 need not allege that the defendant had acted in bad faith in taking certain action against him. In reaching this conclusion, the Court considered both the liberal construction to be afforded Section 1983 and the fact that a public official's state of mind is a fact peculiarly within the knowledge of the official. *Id.* at 638–41.

By placing a higher pleading burden upon plaintiffs or by increasing the facts that plaintiffs must plead to set forth a particular legal claim, it becomes more difficult for plaintiffs to "state a claim upon which relief can be granted" sufficient to survive a Rule 12(b)(6) motion to dismiss. In reading the following case, consider the way in which pleading rules can be used to restrict plaintiffs' ability to successfully assert legal claims in the federal courts. To the extent that pleading rules are used in this fashion, should those more restrictive rules be fashioned by Congress or the federal courts?

Jones v. Bock

Supreme Court of the United States, 2007
549 U.S. 199

■ CHIEF JUSTICE ROBERTS delivered the opinion of the Court.

In an effort to address the large number of prisoner complaints filed in federal court, Congress enacted the Prison Litigation Reform Act of 1995 (PLRA), 42 U.S.C. § 1997e et seq. Among other reforms, the PLRA mandates early judicial screening of prisoner complaints and requires prisoners to exhaust prison grievance procedures before filing suit. 28 U.S.C. § 1915A; 42 U.S.C. § 1997e(a). The Sixth Circuit, along with some other lower courts, adopted several procedural rules designed to implement this exhaustion requirement and facilitate early judicial screening. These rules require a prisoner to allege and demonstrate exhaustion in his complaint, permit suit only against defendants who were identified by the prisoner in his grievance, and require courts to dismiss the entire action if the prisoner fails to satisfy the exhaustion requirement as to any single claim in his complaint. Other lower courts declined to adopt such rules. We granted certiorari to resolve the conflict and now conclude that these rules are not required by the PLRA, and that crafting and imposing them exceeds the proper limits on the judicial role.

I

Prisoner litigation continues to "account for an outsized share of filings" in federal district courts. *Woodford v. Ngo*, 548 U.S. 81, 94, n. 4 (2006). In 2005, nearly 10 percent of all civil cases filed in federal courts nationwide were prisoner complaints challenging prison conditions or claiming civil rights violations. Most of these cases have no merit; many are frivolous. Our legal system, however, remains committed to guaranteeing that prisoner claims of illegal conduct by their custodians are fairly handled according to law. The challenge lies in ensuring that the flood of nonmeritorious claims does not submerge and effectively preclude consideration of the allegations with merit.

Congress addressed that challenge in the PLRA. What this country needs, Congress decided, is fewer and better prisoner suits. To that end, Congress enacted a variety of reforms designed to filter out the bad claims and facilitate consideration of the good. Key among these was the requirement that inmates complaining about prison conditions exhaust prison grievance remedies before initiating a lawsuit.

The exhaustion provision of the PLRA states:

"No action shall be brought with respect to prison conditions under [42 U.S.C. § 1983], or any other Federal law, by a prisoner confined in any jail, prison, or other correctional facility until such administrative remedies as are available are exhausted." 42 U.S.C. § 1997e(a).

Requiring exhaustion allows prison officials an opportunity to resolve disputes concerning the exercise of their responsibilities before being haled into court. This has the potential to reduce the number of inmate suits, and also to improve the quality of suits that are filed by producing a useful administrative record. In an attempt to implement the exhaustion requirement, some lower courts have imposed procedural rules that have become the subject of varying levels of disagreement among the federal courts of appeals.

The first question presented centers on a conflict over whether exhaustion under the PLRA is a pleading requirement the prisoner must satisfy in his complaint or an affirmative defense the defendant must plead and prove. The Sixth Circuit, adopting the former view, requires prisoners to attach proof of exhaustion-typically copies of the grievances-to their complaints to avoid dismissal. If no written record of the grievance is available, the inmate must plead with specificity how and when he exhausted the grievance procedures.

* * *

A

Petitioners are inmates in the custody of the Michigan Department of Corrections (MDOC). At the time petitioners filed their grievances, MDOC Policy Directive 03.02.130 (Nov. 1, 2000) set forth the applicable grievance procedures. The policy directive describes what issues are grievable and contains instructions for filing and processing grievances.

Inmates must first attempt to resolve a problem orally within two business days of becoming aware of the grievable issue. If oral resolution is unsuccessful, the inmate may proceed to Step I of the grievance process, and submit a completed grievance form within five business days of the attempted oral resolution. The Step I grievance form provided by MDOC (a one-page form on which the inmate fills out identifying information and is given space to describe the complaint) advises inmates to be "brief and concise in describing your grievance issue." The inmate submits the grievance to a designated grievance coordinator, who assigns it to a respondent-generally the supervisor of the person being grieved.

If the inmate is dissatisfied with the Step I response, he may appeal to Step II by obtaining an appeal form within five business days of the response, and submitting the appeal within five business days of obtaining the form. The respondent at Step II is designated by the policy (e.g., the regional health administrator for medical care grievances). If still dissatisfied after Step II, the inmate may further appeal to Step III using the same appeal form; the MDOC director is designated as respondent for all Step III appeals.

Lorenzo Jones

Petitioner Lorenzo Jones is incarcerated at MDOC's Saginaw Correctional Facility. In November 2000, while in MDOC's custody, Jones was involved in a vehicle accident and suffered significant injuries to his neck and back. Several months later Jones was given a work assignment he allegedly could not perform in light of his injuries. According to Jones, respondent Paul Morrison-in charge of work assignments at the prison-made the inappropriate assignment, even though he knew of Jones's injuries. When Jones reported to the assignment, he informed the staff member in charge—respondent Michael Opanasenko—that he could not perform the work; Opanasenko allegedly told him to do the work or "suffer the consequences." Jones performed the required tasks and allegedly aggravated his injuries. After unsuccessfully seeking redress through MDOC's grievance process, Jones filed a complaint in the Eastern District of Michigan under 42 U.S.C. § 1983 for deliberate indifference to medical needs, retaliation, and harassment. Jones named as defendants, in addition to Morrison and Opanasenko, respondents Barbara Bock (the warden), Valerie Chaplin (a deputy warden), Janet Konkle (a registered nurse), and Ahmad Aldabaugh (a physician).

A Magistrate Judge recommended dismissal for failure to state a claim with respect to Bock, Chaplin, Konkle, and Aldabaugh, and the District Court agreed. With respect to Morrison and Opanasenko, however, the Magistrate Judge recommended that the suit proceed, finding that Jones had exhausted his administrative remedies as to those two. The District Court Judge disagreed. In his complaint, Jones provided the dates on which his claims were filed at various steps of the MDOC grievance procedures. He did not, however, attach copies of the grievance forms or describe the proceedings with specificity. Respondents attached copies of all of Jones's grievances to their own motion to dismiss, but the District Judge ruled that Jones's failure to meet his burden to plead exhaustion in his complaint could not be cured by respondents. The Sixth Circuit agreed, holding both that Jones failed to comply with the specific pleading requirements applied to PLRA suits, and that, even if Jones had shown that he exhausted the claims against Morrison and Opanasenko, dismissal was still required under the total exhaustion rule.

* * *

II

There is no question that exhaustion is mandatory under the PLRA and that unexhausted claims cannot be brought in court. What is less clear is whether it falls to the prisoner to plead and demonstrate exhaustion in the complaint, or to the defendant to raise lack of exhaustion as an affirmative defense. The minority rule, adopted by the Sixth Circuit, places the burden of pleading exhaustion in a case covered by the PLRA on the prisoner; most courts view failure to exhaust as an affirmative defense.

We think petitioners, and the majority of courts to consider the question, have the better of the argument. Federal Rule of Civil Procedure 8(a) requires simply a "short and plain statement of the claim" in a complaint, while Rule 8(c) identifies a nonexhaustive list of affirmative defenses that must be pleaded in response. The PLRA itself is not a source of a prisoner's claim; claims covered by the PLRA are typically brought under 42 U.S.C. § 1983, which does not require exhaustion at all. Petitioners assert that courts typically regard exhaustion as an affirmative defense in other contexts, and respondents do not seriously dispute the general proposition. * * * The PLRA dealt extensively with the subject of exhaustion, but is silent on the issue whether exhaustion must be pleaded by the plaintiff or is an affirmative defense. This is strong evidence that the usual practice should be followed, and the usual practice under the Federal Rules is to regard exhaustion as an affirmative defense.

In a series of recent cases, we have explained that courts should generally not depart from the usual practice under the Federal Rules on the basis of perceived policy concerns. Thus, in *Leatherman v. Tarrant County Narcotics Intelligence and Coordination Unit*, 507 U.S. 163 (1993), we unanimously reversed the Court of Appeals for imposing a heightened pleading standard in § 1983 suits against municipalities. We explained that "[p]erhaps if [the] Rules . . . were rewritten today, claims against municipalities under § 1983 might be subjected to the added specificity requirement. . . . But that is a result which must be obtained by the process of amending the Federal Rules, and not by judicial interpretation." *Id.*, at 168.

In *Swierkiewicz v. Sorema N.A.*, 534 U.S. 506 (2002), we unanimously reversed the Court of Appeals for requiring employment discrimination plaintiffs to specifically allege the elements of a prima facie case of discrimination. We explained that "the Federal Rules do not contain a heightened pleading standard for employment discrimination suits," and a "requirement of greater specificity for particular claims" must be obtained by amending the Federal Rules. *Id.*, at 515 (citing *Leatherman*). And just last Term, in *Hill v. McDonough*, 547 U.S. 573 (2006), we unanimously rejected a proposal that § 1983 suits challenging a method of execution must identify an acceptable alternative: "Specific pleading requirements are mandated by the Federal Rules of Civil Procedure, and not, as a general rule, through case-by-case determinations of the federal courts." *Id.*, at 582 (citing *Swierkiewicz*).

The Sixth Circuit and other courts requiring prisoners to plead and demonstrate exhaustion in their complaints contend that if the "new regime" mandated by the PLRA for prisoner complaints is to function effectively, prisoner complaints must be treated outside of this typical framework. These courts explain that the PLRA not only imposed a new mandatory exhaustion requirement, but also departed in a fundamental way from the usual procedural ground rules by requiring judicial screening to filter out nonmeritorious claims: Courts are to screen inmate complaints "before docketing, if feasible, or, . . . as soon as practicable after docketing," and dismiss the complaint if it is "frivolous, malicious, . . . fails to state a claim upon which relief may be granted[,] or . . . seeks monetary relief from a defendant who is immune from such relief." 28 U.S.C. § 1915A(a), (b). All this may take place before any responsive pleading is filed-unlike in the typical civil case, defendants do not have to respond to a complaint covered by the PLRA until required to do so by the court, and waiving the right to reply does not constitute an admission of the allegations in the complaint. According to respondents, these departures from the normal litigation framework of complaint and response mandate a different pleading requirement for prisoner complaints, if the screening is to serve its intended purpose.

We think that the PLRA's screening requirement does not-explicitly or implicitly-justify deviating from the usual procedural practice beyond the departures specified by the PLRA itself. Before the PLRA, the in forma pauperis provision of § 1915, applicable to most prisoner litigation, permitted sua sponte dismissal only if an action was frivolous or malicious. 28 U.S.C. § 1915(d). In the PLRA, Congress added failure to state a claim and seeking monetary relief from a defendant immune from such relief as grounds for sua sponte dismissal of in forma pauperis cases, § 1915(e)(2)(B), and provided for judicial screening and sua sponte dismissal of prisoner suits on the same four grounds, § 1915A(b); 42 U.S.C. § 1997e(c)(1). Although exhaustion was a "centerpiece" of the PLRA, *Woodford*, 548 U.S., at 84, failure to exhaust was notably not added in terms to this enumeration. There is thus no reason to suppose that the normal pleading rules have to be altered to facilitate judicial screening of complaints specifically for failure to exhaust.

Some courts have found that exhaustion is subsumed under the PLRA's enumerated ground authorizing early dismissal for "fail[ure] to state a claim upon which relief may be granted." 28 U.S.C. § 1915A(b)(1), 1915(e)(2)(B); 42 U.S.C. § 1997e(c)(1). The point is a bit of a red herring. A complaint is subject to dismissal for failure to state a claim if the allegations, taken as true, show the plaintiff is not entitled to relief. If the allegations, for example, show that relief is barred by the applicable statute of limitations, the complaint is subject to dismissal for failure to state a claim; that does not make the statute of limitations any less an affirmative defense, *see* Fed. Rule Civ. Proc. 8(c). Whether a particular ground for opposing a claim may be the basis for dismissal for failure to state a claim depends on whether the allegations in the complaint suffice to establish that ground, not on the nature of the ground in the abstract. * * * Determining that Congress meant to include failure to exhaust under the rubric of "failure to state a claim" in the screening provisions of the PLRA would thus not support treating exhaustion as a pleading requirement rather than an affirmative defense.

The argument that screening would be more effective if exhaustion had to be shown in the complaint proves too much; the same could be said with respect to any affirmative defense. The rejoinder that the PLRA focused on exhaustion rather than other defenses simply highlights the failure of Congress to include exhaustion in terms among the enumerated grounds justifying dismissal upon early screening. As noted, that is not to say that failure to exhaust cannot be a basis for dismissal for failure to state a claim. It is to say that there is no basis for concluding that Congress implicitly meant to transform exhaustion from an affirmative defense to a pleading requirement by the curiously indirect route of specifying that courts should screen PLRA complaints and dismiss those that fail to state a claim.

Respondents point to 42 U.S.C. § 1997e(g) as confirming that the usual pleading rules should not apply to PLRA suits, but we think that provision supports petitioners. It specifies that defendants can waive their right to reply to a prisoner complaint without the usual consequence of being deemed to have admitted the allegations in the complaint. This shows that when Congress meant to depart from the usual procedural requirements, it did so expressly.

We conclude that failure to exhaust is an affirmative defense under the PLRA, and that inmates are not required to specially plead or demonstrate exhaustion in their complaints. We understand the reasons behind the decisions of some lower courts to impose a pleading requirement on plaintiffs in this context, but that effort cannot fairly be viewed as an interpretation of the PLRA. "Whatever temptations the statesmanship of policy-making might wisely suggest," the judge's job is to construe the statute-not to make it better. Frankfurter, "Some Reflections on the Reading of Statutes," 47 *Colum. L.Rev.* 527, 533 (1947). The judge "must not read in by way of creation," but instead abide by the "duty of restraint, th[e] humility of function as merely the translator of another's command." *Id.*, at 533–534. Given that the PLRA does not itself require plaintiffs to plead exhaustion, such a result "must be obtained by the process of amending the Federal Rules, and not by judicial interpretation." *Leatherman*, 507 U.S., at 168.

[Chief Justice Roberts then concluded that the Prison Litigation Reform Act did not support a judicial requirement that each defendant in the civil action must have been named in a prisoner's initial administrative grievance or that no claim can be considered until the prisoner has exhausted administrative remedies on all claims.]

* * *

We are not insensitive to the challenges faced by the lower federal courts in managing their dockets and attempting to separate, when it comes to prisoner suits, not so much wheat from chaff as needles from haystacks. We once again reiterate, however-as we did unanimously in *Leatherman, Swierkiewicz*, and *Hill*—that adopting different and more onerous pleading rules to deal with particular categories of cases should be done through established rulemaking procedures, and not on a case-by-case basis by the courts.

The judgments of the United States Court of Appeals for the Sixth Circuit are reversed, and the cases are remanded for further proceedings consistent with this opinion.

It is so ordered.

COMMENTS AND QUESTIONS CONCERNING *JONES V. BOCK*

1.   *Jones v. Bock* was decided by a unanimous Supreme Court four months before its decision in *Bell Atlantic Corp v. Twombly.* Is there any inconsistency between the two decisions?

2.   Do administrative exhaustion requirements make sense in disputes such as this? Why might they be particularly well-suited to this type of dispute? Can such requirements interfere with a claimant's right to bring his claim before a federal or state court?

3.   Rule 8(c) lists almost twenty separate affirmative defenses that must be specifically set forth in responding to a pleading (typically, in the answer, which responds to the complaint). Exhaustion of administrative remedies is not listed among those affirmative defenses. Is this significant?

4.   What difference does this case make? Is it exalting form over substance to require that administrative exhaustion must be pled as an affirmative defense by defendants rather than as part of the plaintiffs' cause of action? On the other hand, would such a requirement impose any significant burden upon defendants?

5.   Does the burden of pleading have any implications for the trial burdens of production and of persuasion? Reconsider this question after studying those burdens in Chapter 13, *infra.*

6.   The Supreme Court having determined that failure to exhaust administrative remedies must be pled as an affirmative defense by defendants in prison litigation, what is the consequence for a defendant who does not include this defense in his answer? *See* Federal Rule of Civil Procedure 8(c). *See also Haskell v. Washington Township,* 864 F.2d 1266, 1273 (6th Cir. 1988); *Depositors Trust Co. v. Slobusky,* 692 F.2d 205, 208– 209 (1st Cir. 1982). *But see Lafreniere Park Foundation v. Broussard,* 221 F.3d 804, 808 (5th Cir. 2000); *Brinkley v. Harbour Recreation Club,* 180 F.3d 598, 611–13 (4th Cir. 1999) (absent unfair surprise or prejudice to the plaintiff, affirmative defense is not waived because it is first raised in dispositive pretrial motion).

7.   Why did Congress enact legislation concerning prison litigation? Was congressional action a better way to address these issues than the process used to amend the Federal Rules of Civil Procedure?

8.   Does it make sense to have different pleading rules for different types of litigants and claims? One of the traditional advantages of the Federal Rules of Civil Procedure is that they are "trans-substantive" and apply to all civil actions—whether a routine car crash or a complex antitrust action. Is it appropriate for Congress to enact special rules for certain claimants? *E.g.,* Prison Litigation Reform Act of 1995, 110 Stat. 1321–71, as amended, 42 U.S.C. §§ 1997e–et seq.; Private Securities Litigation Reform Act of 1995, Pub. L. No. 104–67, 109 Stat. 737 (codified as amended in scattered sections of Title 15 of the United States Code).

9.   Do you agree with Chief Justice Roberts and Justice Frankfurter that " 'Whatever temptations the statesmanship of policy-making might wisely suggest,' the judge's job is to construe the statute—not to make it

better." Is it realistic to expect Congress to enact new legislation to simply "clean up" issues in a manner consistent with its original intent?

E. AMENDED AND SUPPLEMENTAL PLEADINGS

Rule 15 of the Federal Rules of Civil Procedure, as its title suggests, governs amended and supplemental pleadings. While it's always best to plead one's action properly in the first instance, the Federal Rules liberally permit parties to amend their pleadings before, during, and after trial.

Rule 15(a) deals with the most common situation in which an amended pleading might be in order: before trial. Rule 15(a)(1) gives parties the right to amend their pleadings once "as a matter of course" (*i.e.*, without needing the permission of the judge or opposing parties) in the following circumstances:

> A party may amend its pleading once as a matter of course within:
>
> (A) 21 days after serving it; or
>
> (B) if the pleading is one to which a responsive pleading is required, 21 days after service of a responsive pleading or 21 days after service of a motion under Rule 12(b), (e), or (f), whichever is earlier.

A complaint is a pleading "to which a responsive pleading is required,"[12] and thus falls within Rule 15(a)(1)(B). It therefore can be amended, without permission of the court or opposing party, 21 days after either a "responsive pleading" (*i.e.*, the answer) or a Rule 12(b), (e), or (f) motion is filed. If the pleading is not "one to which a responsive pleading is required" (such as an answer), the party filing the pleading has 21 days after serving that pleading to amend it "as a matter of course."

But what if an answer to the complaint was filed more than 21 days before? Can the plaintiff still file an amended complaint? Yes, this is possible pursuant to Rule 15(a)(2), although "only with the opposing party's written consent or the court's leave." In many situations, the opposing party is unlikely to consent to the filing of an amended pleading. Rule 15(a)(2), though, provides: "The court should freely give leave when justice so requires." Consider whether "justice so require[d]" such an amendment in the case that follows.

---

[12] Rule 7(a) defines the seven pleadings and specifies to which of these pleadings a responsive pleading must be filed.

1. AMENDED PLEADINGS UNDER RULE 15

Beeck v. Aquaslide 'N' Dive Corp.

United States Court of Appeals, Eighth Circuit, 1977
562 F.2d 537

■ PAUL BENSON, DISTRICT JUDGE.

This case is an appeal from the trial court's exercise of discretion on procedural matters in a diversity personal injury action.

Jerry A. Beeck was severely injured on July 15, 1972, while using a water slide. He and his wife, Judy A. Beeck, sued Aquaslide 'N' Dive Corporation (Aquaslide), a Texas corporation, alleging it manufactured the slide involved in the accident, and sought to recover substantial damages on theories of negligence, strict liability and breach of implied warranty.

Aquaslide initially admitted manufacture of the slide, but later moved to amend its answer to deny manufacture; the motion was resisted. The district court granted leave to amend. On motion of the defendant, a separate trial was held on the issue of "whether the defendant designed, manufactured or sold the slide in question." This motion was also resisted by the plaintiffs. The issue was tried to a jury, which returned a verdict for the defendant, after which the trial court entered summary judgment of dismissal of the case. Plaintiffs took this appeal, and stated the issues presented for review to be:

1. Where the manufacturer of the product, a water slide, admitted in its Answer and later in its Answer to Interrogatories both filed prior to the running of the statute of limitations that it designed, manufactured and sold the water slide in question, was it an abuse of the trial court's discretion to grant leave to amend to the manufacturer in order to deny these admissions after the running of the statute of limitations?

2. After granting the manufacturer's Motion for Leave to Amend in order to deny the prior admissions of design, manufacture and sale of the water slide in question, was it an abuse of the trial court's discretion to further grant the manufacturer's Motion for a Separate Trial on the issue of manufacture?

I.   Facts.

A brief review of the facts found by the trial court in its order granting leave to amend, and which do not appear to have been in dispute, is essential to a full understanding of appellants' claims.

In 1971 Kimberly Village Home Association of Davenport, Iowa, ordered an Aquaslide product from one George Boldt, who was a local distributor handling defendant's products. The order was forwarded by

Boldt to Sentry Pool and Chemical Supply Co. in Rock Island, Illinois, and Sentry forwarded the order to Purity Swimming Pool Supply in Hammond, Indiana. A slide was delivered from a Purity warehouse to Kimberly Village, and was installed by Kimberly employees. On July 15, 1972, Jerry A. Beeck was injured while using the slide at a social gathering sponsored at Kimberly Village by his employer, Harker Wholesale Meats, Inc. Soon after the accident investigations were undertaken by representatives of the separate insurers of Harker and Kimberly Village. On October 31, 1972, Aquaslide first learned of the accident through a letter sent by a representative of Kimberly's insurer to Aquaslide, advising that "one of your Queen Model #Q–3D slides" was involved in the accident. Aquaslide forwarded this notification to its insurer. Aquaslide's insurance adjuster made an on-site investigation of the slide in May, 1973, and also interviewed persons connected with the ordering and assembly of the slide. An inter-office letter dated September 23, 1973, indicates that Aquaslide's insurer was of the opinion the "Aquaslide in question was definitely manufactured by our insured." The complaint was filed October 15, 1973.[3] Investigators for three different insurance companies, representing Harker, Kimberly and the defendant, had concluded that the slide had been manufactured by Aquaslide, and the defendant, with no information to the contrary, answered the complaint on December 12, 1973, and admitted that it "designed, manufactured, assembled and sold" the slide in question.[4]

The statute of limitations on plaintiff's personal injury claim expired on July 15, 1974. About six and one-half months later Carl Meyer, president and owner of Aquaslide, visited the site of the accident prior to the taking of his deposition by the plaintiff.[5] From his on-site inspection of the slide, he determined it was not a product of the defendant. Thereafter, Aquaslide moved the court for leave to amend its answer to deny manufacture of the slide.

II.   Leave to Amend.

Amendment of pleadings in civil actions is governed by Rule 15(a), F.R.Civ.P., which provides in part that once issue is joined in a lawsuit, a party may amend his pleading "only by leave of court or by written consent of the adverse party; and leave shall be freely given when justice so requires." [Although Rule 15 has been amended since the *Beeck* litigation, the substance of the quoted language remains the same and now appears in Rule 15(a)(2).]

In *Foman v. Davis*, 371 U.S. 178 (1962), the Supreme Court had occasion to construe that portion of Rule 15(a) set out above:

[3]   Aquaslide 'N' Dive Corporation was the sole defendant named in the complaint.

[4]   In answers to interrogatories filed on June 3, 1974, Aquaslide again admitted manufacture of the slide in question.

[5]   Plaintiffs apparently requested Meyer to inspect the slide prior to the taking of his deposition to determine whether it was defectively installed or assembled.

Rule 15(a) declares that leave to amend "shall be freely given when justice so requires," this mandate is to be heeded. . . . If the underlying facts or circumstances relied upon by a plaintiff may be a proper subject of relief, he ought to be afforded an opportunity to test his claim on the merits. In the absence of any apparent or declared reason such as undue delay, bad faith or dilatory motive on the part of the movant, repeated failure to cure deficiencies by amendments previously allowed, undue prejudice to the opposing party by virtue of allowance of the amendment, futility of amendment, etc. the leave sought should, as the rules require, be "freely given." Of course, the grant or denial of an opportunity to amend is within the discretion of the District Court, ...

371 U.S. at 182.

This Court in *Hanson v. Hunt Oil Co.*, 398 F.2d 578, 582 (8th Cir. 1968), held that "(p)rejudice *must be shown*." (Emphasis added). The burden is on the party opposing the amendment to show such prejudice. In ruling on a motion for leave to amend, the trial court must inquire into the issue of prejudice to the opposing party, in light of the particular facts of the case.

Certain principles apply to appellate review of a trial court's grant or denial of a motion to amend pleadings. First, as noted in *Foman v. Davis*, allowance or denial of leave to amend lies within the sound discretion of the trial court, *Zenith Radio Corp. v. Hazeltine Research*, 401 U.S. 321, 330 (1971), and is reviewable only for an abuse of discretion. *Mercantile T. C. N. A. v. Inland Marine Products*, 542 F.2d 1010, 1012 (8th Cir. 1976). The appellate court must view the case in the posture in which the trial court acted in ruling on the motion to amend.

It is evident from the order of the district court that in the exercise of its discretion in ruling on defendant's motion for leave to amend, it searched the record for evidence of bad faith, prejudice and undue delay which might be sufficient to overbalance the mandate of Rule 15(a), F.R.Civ.P., and *Foman v. Davis*, that leave to amend should be "freely given." Plaintiffs had not at any time conceded that the slide in question had not been manufactured by the defendant, and at the time the motion for leave to amend was at issue, the court had to decide whether the defendant should be permitted to litigate a material factual issue on its merits.

In inquiring into the issue of bad faith, the court noted the fact that the defendant, in initially concluding that it had manufactured the slide, relied upon the conclusions of three different insurance companies, each of which had conducted an investigation into the circumstances surrounding the accident. This reliance upon investigations of three insurance companies, and the fact that "no contention has been made by anyone that the defendant influenced this

THE INITIATION OF THE LAWSUIT: "A SHORT AND PLAIN
STATEMENT OF THE CLAIM."

108   CHAPTER 2

possibly erroneous conclusion," persuaded the court that "defendant has not acted in such bad faith as to be precluded from contesting the issue of manufacture at trial." The court further found "(t)o the extent that 'blame' is to be spread regarding the original identification, the record indicates that it should be shared equally."

In considering the issue of prejudice that might result to the plaintiffs from the granting of the motion for leave to amend, the trial court held that the facts presented to it did not support plaintiffs' assertion that, because of the running of the two year Iowa statute of limitations on personal injury claims, the allowance of the amendment would sound the "death knell" of the litigation. In order to accept plaintiffs' argument, the court would have had to assume that the defendant would prevail at trial on the factual issue of manufacture of the slide, and further that plaintiffs would be foreclosed, should the amendment be allowed, from proceeding against other parties if they were unsuccessful in pressing their claim against Aquaslide. On the state of the record before it, the trial court was unwilling to make such assumptions,[7] and concluded "(u)nder these circumstances, the Court deems that the possible prejudice to the plaintiffs is an insufficient basis on which to deny the proposed amendment." The court reasoned that the amendment would merely allow the defendant to contest a disputed factual issue at trial, and further that it would be prejudicial to the defendant to deny the amendment.

The court also held that defendant and its insurance carrier, in investigating the circumstances surrounding the accident, had not been so lacking in diligence as to dictate a denial of the right to litigate the factual issue of manufacture of the slide.

On this record we hold that the trial court did not abuse its discretion in allowing the defendant to amend its answer.

III. Separate Trials.

After Aquaslide was granted leave to amend its answer, it moved pursuant to Rule 42(b), F.R.Civ.P., for a separate trial on the issue of manufacture of the slide involved in the accident. The grounds upon which the motion was based were:

---

[7] The district court noted in its order granting leave to amend that plaintiffs may be able to sue other parties as a result of the substituting of a "counterfeit" slide for the Aquaslide, if indeed this occurred. The court added:

> (a)gain, the Court is handicapped by an unclear record on this issue. If, in fact, the slide in question is not an Aquaslide, the replacement entered the picture somewhere along the Boldt to Sentry, Sentry to Purity, Purity to Kimberly Village chain of distribution. Depending upon the circumstances of its entry, a cause of action sounding in fraud or contract might lie. If so, the applicable statute of limitations period would not have run. Further, as defendant points out, the doctrine of equitable estoppel might possibly preclude another defendant from asserting the two-year statute as a defense.

67 F.R.D. at 415.

(1) a separate trial solely on the issue of whether the slide was manufactured by Aquaslide would save considerable trial time and unnecessary expense and preparation for all parties and the court, and

(2) a separate trial solely on the issue of manufacture would protect Aquaslide from substantial prejudice.

The court granted the motion for a separate trial on the issue of manufacture, and this grant of a separate trial is challenged by appellants as being an abuse of discretion.

A trial court's severance of trial will not be disturbed on appeal except for an abuse of discretion.

The record indicates that Carl Meyer, president and owner of Aquaslide, designs the slides sold by Aquaslide. The slide which plaintiff Jerry A. Beeck was using at the time of his accident was very similar in appearance to an Aquaslide product, and was without identifying marks. Kimberly Village had in fact ordered an Aquaslide for its swimming pool, and thought it had received one. After Meyer's inspection and Aquaslide's subsequent assertion that it was not an Aquaslide product, plaintiffs elected to stand on their contention that it was in fact an Aquaslide. This raised a substantial issue of material fact which, if resolved in defendant's favor, would exonerate defendant from liability.

Plaintiff Jerry A. Beeck had been severely injured, and he and his wife together were seeking damages arising out of those injuries in the sum of $2,225,000.00. Evidence of plaintiffs' injuries and damages would clearly have taken up several days of trial time, and because of the severity of the injuries, may have been prejudicial to the defendant's claim of non-manufacture. The jury, by special interrogatory, found that the slide had not been manufactured by Aquaslide. That finding has not been questioned on appeal. Judicial economy, beneficial to all the parties, was obviously served by the trial court's grant of a separate trial. We hold the Rule 42(b) separation was not an abuse of discretion.

The judgment of the district court is affirmed.

COMMENTS AND QUESTIONS CONCERNING
BEECK V. AQUASLIDE 'N' DIVE CORP.

1.   Defendant Aquaslide admitted in its answer, as well as in an interrogatory answer, that it manufactured the slide that was involved in Jerry Beeck's accident. The applicable statute of limitations, which normally would preclude the Beecks from filing another civil action, then ran. Six months later, defendant Aquaslide sought to amend its answer to deny that it manufactured the slide. By then the time had passed for Aquaslide to amend its answer "as a matter of course" under Rule 15(a), and the Beecks presumably would not consent to such an amendment to

the answer. Make the argument that the court nevertheless should have permitted Aquaslide to amend the answer because "justice so require[d]."

2.   Even assuming that the statute of limitations would not have barred the assertion of a civil action against the company that actually manufactured the slide, would there be practical difficulties in pursuing a claim against that company some five years after Jerry Beeck's accident? On the other hand, would justice have been served by precluding Aquaslide from contesting the manufacture of a slide that it apparently had not manufactured?

3.   Did the court of appeals determine that, had those judges been sitting as the trial judge, they would have granted leave to amend the answer and the motion for a separate trial on the issue of manufacture? If the district judge had denied either of these motions and Aquaslide appealed after the entry of final judgment in the trial court, is it likely that the court of appeals would have concluded that these motions should have been granted? Or is this a case in which, due to the discretionary nature of these decisions and the abuse of discretion standard of review, the court of appeals is likely to have affirmed whatever decisions the district judge made?

4.   Rule 42(b) of the Federal Rules of Civil Procedure provides:

> For convenience, to avoid prejudice, or to expedite and economize, the court may order a separate trial of one or more separate issues, claims, crossclaims, counterclaims, or third-party claims. When ordering a separate trial, the court must preserve any federal right to a jury trial.

How should a trial judge weigh and balance issues of convenience, prejudice, and economy?

5.   In seeking a separate trial on the question of slide manufacture, Aquaslide asserted that such a trial "would save considerable trial time and unnecessary expense and preparation for all parties and the court." While this argument may be attractive to a district judge, is this the real reason why Aquaslide sought a separate trial?

Once Aquaslide prevailed in the separate trial, didn't this defeat any claims the Beecks had against Aquaslide? Would the evidence relevant to just the question of manufacture be different from the evidence presented in a trial encompassing the questions of manufacture, Aquaslide's liability, and Jerry Beeck's damages? Would a jury be more or less likely to find that Aquaslide had manufactured the slide if it considered that question in a trial that did not include evidence concerning Aquaslide's alleged liability and Beeck's damages?

6.   At the separate trial concerning manufacture of the slide, could the plaintiff have offered as evidence the original answer and the interrogatory answers in which Aquaslide admitted that it manufactured the slide in question? If so, why would the Beecks be prejudiced by permitting Aquaslide to amend its answer?

7.   While Rule 15(a) governs amendments prior to trial, Rule 15(b) specifically addresses amendments during or after trial.

Rule 15(b)(1) provides:

> If, at trial, a party objects that evidence is not within the issues raised in the pleadings, the court may permit the pleadings to be amended. The court should freely permit an amendment when doing so will aid in presenting the merits and the objecting party fails to satisfy the court that the evidence would prejudice that party's action or defense on the merits. The court may grant a continuance to enable the objecting party to meet the evidence.

Thus, to the extent that the evidence is not too separate from the issues raised in the pleadings, the court is more likely to permit that evidence to be offered at trial (perhaps adjourning the trial to enable the objecting party to gather its own evidence or obtain some quick discovery—such as a deposition—from the party offering the evidence).

Rule 15(b)(2) deals with the situation in which evidence relevant to an issue not raised by the pleadings is offered at trial and there is no objection:

> When an issue not raised by the pleadings is tried by the parties' express or implied consent, it must be treated in all respects as if raised in the pleadings. A party may move—at any time, even after judgment—to amend the pleadings to conform them to the evidence and to raise an unpleaded issue. But failure to amend does not affect the result of the trial of that issue.

Note, however, that the surfacing of a "new issue" at trial may require amendment of not only a pleading, but also of the Rule 16 final pretrial order. This may not be as easy as amending the pleading, because Rule 16(e) provides: "The court may modify the order issued after a final pretrial conference only to prevent manifest injustice."

8.   In addition to amended pleadings, Rule 15(d) provides authority for the filing of supplemental pleadings "setting out any transaction, occurrence, or event that happened after the date of the pleading to be supplemented." In what types of actions might a supplemental pleading be necessary?

9.   Why did a United States District Judge write this opinion for the United States Court of Appeals for the Eighth Circuit?

2.   "RELATION BACK" OF AMENDED PLEADINGS

Even if a party can amend her complaint, answer, or other pleading pursuant to Rule 15(a) or (b), the question will remain as to whether that amendment "relates back" to the date on which the original pleading was filed. The practical effect of this is that, if an amendment "relates back" to an earlier pleading, it will be considered to have been filed at the same time as that pleading. Why might this be important? If the statute of limitations has run between the time that the original pleading was filed and the time of the filing of the amended pleading, the party will have filed a time-barred claim or defense—unless that claim or defense relates back to the earlier pleading. As you read the next case, consider the possible operation of Rule 15(c) to permit the relation back of amended pleadings.

Krupski v. Costa Crociere S. p. A.

Supreme Court of the United States, 2010
560 U.S. 538

■ JUSTICE SOTOMAYOR delivered the opinion of the Court.

Rule 15(c) of the Federal Rules of Civil Procedure governs when an amended pleading "relates back" to the date of a timely filed original pleading and is thus itself timely even though it was filed outside an applicable statute of limitations. Where an amended pleading changes a party or a party's name, the Rule requires, among other things, that "the party to be brought in by amendment . . . knew or should have known that the action would have been brought against it, but for a mistake concerning the proper party's identity." Rule 15(c)(1)(C). In this case, the Court of Appeals held that Rule 15(c) was not satisfied because the plaintiff knew or should have known of the proper defendant before filing her original complaint. The court also held that relation back was not appropriate because the plaintiff had unduly delayed in seeking to amend. We hold that relation back under Rule 15(c)(1)(C) depends on what the party to be added knew or should have known, not on the amending party's knowledge or its timeliness in seeking to amend the pleading. Accordingly, we reverse the judgment of the Court of Appeals.

I

On February 21, 2007, petitioner, Wanda Krupski, tripped over a cable and fractured her femur while she was on board the cruise ship Costa Magica. Upon her return home, she acquired counsel and began the process of seeking compensation for her injuries. Krupski's passenger ticket—which explained that it was the sole contract between each passenger and the carrier included a variety of requirements for obtaining damages for an injury suffered on board one of the carrier's ships. The ticket identified the carrier as

> "Costa Crociere S. p. A., an Italian corporation, and all Vessels and other ships owned, chartered, operated, marketed or provided by Costa Crociere, S. p. A., and all officers, staff members, crew members, independent contractors, medical providers, concessionaires, pilots, suppliers, agents and assigns onboard said Vessels, and the manufacturers of said Vessels and all their component parts."

The ticket required an injured party to submit "written notice of the claim with full particulars . . . to the carrier or its duly authorized agent within 185 days after the date of injury." The ticket further required any lawsuit to be "filed within one year after the date of injury" and to be "served upon the carrier within 120 days after filing." For cases arising from voyages departing from or returning to a United States port in which the amount in controversy exceeded $75,000, the ticket designated the United States District Court for the Southern District of Florida in Broward County, Florida, as the exclusive forum for a lawsuit. The ticket extended the "defenses, limitations and exceptions . . . that may be invoked by the CARRIER" to "all persons who may act on behalf of the CARRIER or on whose behalf the CARRIER may act," including "the CARRIER's parents, subsidiaries, affiliates, successors, assigns, representatives, agents, employees, servants, concessionaires and contractors" as well as "Costa Cruise Lines N. V.," identified as the "sales and marketing agent for the CARRIER and the issuer of this Passage Ticket Contract." The front of the ticket listed Costa Cruise Lines' address in Florida and stated that an entity called "Costa Cruises" was "the first cruise company in the world" to obtain a certain certification of quality.

On July 2, 2007, Krupski's counsel notified Costa Cruise Lines of Krupski's claims. On July 9, 2007, the claims administrator for Costa Cruise requested additional information from Krupski "[i]n order to facilitate our future attempts to achieve a pre-litigation settlement." The parties were unable to reach a settlement, however, and on February 1, 2008—three weeks before the 1-year limitations period expired—Krupski filed a negligence action against Costa Cruise, invoking the diversity jurisdiction of the Federal District Court for the Southern District of Florida. The complaint alleged that Costa Cruise "owned, operated, managed, supervised and controlled" the ship on which Krupski had injured herself; that Costa Cruise had extended to its passengers an invitation to enter onto the ship; and that Costa Cruise owed Krupski a duty of care, which it breached by failing to take steps that would have prevented her accident. The complaint further stated that venue was proper under the passenger ticket's forum selection clause and averred that, by the July 2007 notice of her claims, Krupski had complied with the ticket's presuit requirements. Krupski served Costa Cruise on February 4, 2008.

Over the next several months—after the limitations period had expired—Costa Cruise brought Costa Crociere's existence to Krupski's attention three times. First, on February 25, 2008, Costa Cruise filed its answer, asserting that it was not the proper defendant, as it was merely the North American sales and marketing agent for Costa Crociere, which was the actual carrier and vessel operator. Second, on March 20, 2008, Costa Cruise listed Costa Crociere as an interested party in its corporate disclosure statement. Finally, on May 6, 2008, Costa Cruise moved for summary judgment, again stating that Costa Crociere was the proper defendant.

On June 13, 2008, Krupski responded to Costa Cruise's motion for summary judgment, arguing for limited discovery to determine whether

THE INITIATION OF THE LAWSUIT: "A SHORT AND PLAIN
STATEMENT OF THE CLAIM."

114

CHAPTER 2

Costa Cruise should be dismissed. According to Krupski, the following sources of information led her to believe Costa Cruise was the responsible party: The travel documents prominently identified Costa Cruise and gave its Florida address; Costa Cruise's Web site listed Costa Cruise in Florida as the United States office for the Italian company Costa Crociere; and the Web site of the Florida Department of State listed Costa Cruise as the only "Costa" company registered to do business in that State. Krupski also observed that Costa Cruise's claims administrator had responded to her claims notification without indicating that Costa Cruise was not a responsible party. With her response, Krupski simultaneously moved to amend her complaint to add Costa Crociere as a defendant.

On July 2, 2008, after oral argument, the District Court denied Costa Cruise's motion for summary judgment without prejudice and granted Krupski leave to amend, ordering that Krupski effect proper service on Costa Crociere by September 16, 2008. Complying with the court's deadline, Krupski filed an amended complaint on July 11, 2008, and served Costa Crociere on August 21, 2008. On that same date, the District Court issued an order dismissing Costa Cruise from the case pursuant to the parties' joint stipulation, Krupski apparently having concluded that Costa Cruise was correct that it bore no responsibility for her injuries.

Shortly thereafter, Costa Crociere—represented by the same counsel who had represented Costa Cruise—moved to dismiss, contending that the amended complaint did not relate back under Rule 15(c) and was therefore untimely. The District Court agreed. Rule 15(c), the court explained, imposes three requirements before an amended complaint against a newly named defendant can relate back to the original complaint. First, the claim against the newly named defendant must have arisen "out of the conduct, transaction, or occurrence set out—or attempted to be set out—in the original pleading." Fed. Rules Civ. Proc. 15(c)(1)(B), (C). Second, "within the period provided by Rule 4(m) for serving the summons and complaint" * * *, the newly named defendant must have "received such notice of the action that it will not be prejudiced in defending on the merits." Rule 15(c)(1)(C)(i). Finally, the plaintiff must show that, within the Rule 4(m) period, the newly named defendant "knew or should have known that the action would have been brought against it, but for a mistake concerning the proper party's identity." Rule 15(c)(1)(C)(ii).

The first two conditions posed no problem, the court explained: The claim against Costa Crociere clearly involved the same occurrence as the original claim against Costa Cruise, and Costa Crociere had constructive notice of the action and had not shown that any unfair prejudice would result from relation back. But the court found the third condition fatal to Krupski's attempt to relate back, concluding that Krupski had not made a mistake concerning the identity of the proper party. Relying on Eleventh Circuit precedent, the court explained that the word "mistake" should not be construed to encompass a deliberate decision not to sue a party whose identity the plaintiff knew before the statute of limitations had run. Because Costa Cruise informed Krupski that Costa Crociere was the proper defendant in its answer, corporate disclosure statement, and motion for summary judgment, and yet Krupski delayed for months in moving to amend and then in filing an amended complaint, the court concluded that Krupski knew of the proper defendant and made no mistake.

The Eleventh Circuit affirmed in an unpublished per curiam opinion. Rather than relying on the information contained in Costa Cruise's filings, all of which were made after the statute of limitations had expired, as evidence that Krupski did not make a mistake, the Court of Appeals noted that the relevant information was located within Krupski's passenger ticket, which she had furnished to her counsel well before the end of the limitations period. Because the ticket clearly identified Costa Crociere as the carrier, the court stated, Krupski either knew or should have known of Costa Crociere's identity as a potential party. It was therefore appropriate to treat Krupski as having chosen to sue one potential party over another. Alternatively, even assuming that she first learned of Costa Crociere's identity as the correct party from Costa Cruise's answer, the Court of Appeals observed that Krupski waited 133 days from the time she filed her original complaint to seek leave to amend and did not file an amended complaint for another month after that. In light of this delay, the Court of Appeals concluded that the District Court did not abuse its discretion in denying relation back.

We granted certiorari to resolve tension among the Circuits over the breadth of Rule 15(c)(1)(C)(ii), and we now reverse.

II

Under the Federal Rules of Civil Procedure, an amendment to a pleading relates back to the date of the original pleading when:

"(A) the law that provides the applicable statute of limitations allows relation back;

"(B) the amendment asserts a claim or defense that arose out of the conduct, transaction, or occurrence set out—or attempted to be set out—in the original pleading; or

"(C) the amendment changes the party or the naming of the party against whom a claim is asserted, if Rule 15(c)(1)(B) is satisfied and if, within the period provided by Rule 4(m) for serving the summons and complaint, the party to be brought in by amendment:

"(i) received such notice of the action that it will not be prejudiced in defending on the merits; and "(ii) knew or should have known that the action would have been brought against it, but for a mistake concerning the proper party's identity." Rule 15(c)(1).

In our view, neither of the Court of Appeals' reasons for denying relation back under Rule 15(c)(1)(C)(ii) finds support in the text of the Rule. We consider each reason in turn.

A

The Court of Appeals first decided that Krupski either knew or should have known of the proper party's identity and thus determined that she had made a deliberate choice instead of a mistake in not naming Costa Crociere as a party in her original pleading. By focusing on Krupski's knowledge, the Court of Appeals chose the wrong starting point. The question under Rule 15(c)(1)(C)(ii) is not whether Krupski knew or should have known the identity of Costa Crociere as the proper defendant, but whether Costa Crociere knew or should have known that it would have been named as a defendant but for an error. Rule 15(c)(1)(C)(ii) asks what the prospective defendant knew or should have known during the Rule 4(m) period, not what the plaintiff knew or should have known at the time of filing her original complaint.

Information in the plaintiff's possession is relevant only if it bears on the defendant's understanding of whether the plaintiff made a mistake regarding the proper party's identity. For purposes of that inquiry, it would be error to conflate knowledge of a party's existence with the absence of mistake. * * * That a plaintiff knows of a party's existence does not preclude her from making a mistake with respect to that party's identity. A plaintiff may know that a prospective defendant—call him party A—exists, while erroneously believing him to have the status of party B. Similarly, a plaintiff may know generally what party A does while misunderstanding the roles that party A and party B played in the "conduct, transaction, or occurrence" giving rise to her claim. If the plaintiff sues party B instead of party A under these circumstances, she has made a "mistake concerning the proper party's identity" notwithstanding her knowledge of the existence of both parties. The only question under Rule 15(c)(1)(C)(ii), then, is whether party A knew or should have known that, absent some mistake, the action would have been brought against him.

Respondent urges that the key issue under Rule 15(c)(1)(C)(ii) is whether the plaintiff made a deliberate choice to sue one party over another. We agree that making a deliberate choice to sue one party instead of another while fully understanding the factual and legal differences between the two parties is the antithesis of making a mistake concerning the proper party's identity. We disagree, however, with respondent's position that any time a plaintiff is aware of the existence of two parties and chooses to sue the wrong one, the proper defendant could reasonably believe that the plaintiff made no mistake. * * *

This reading is consistent with the purpose of relation back: to balance the interests of the defendant protected by the statute of limitations with the preference expressed in the Federal Rules of Civil Procedure in general, and Rule 15 in particular, for resolving disputes on their merits. A prospective defendant who legitimately believed that the limitations period had passed without any attempt to sue him has a strong interest in repose. But repose would be a windfall for a prospective defendant who understood, or who should have understood, that he escaped suit during the limitations period only because the plaintiff misunderstood a crucial fact about his identity. Because a plaintiff's knowledge of the existence of a party does not foreclose the possibility that she has made a mistake of identity about which that party should have been aware, such knowledge does not support that party's interest in repose.

Our reading is also consistent with the history of Rule 15(c)(1)(C). That provision was added in 1966 to respond to a recurring problem in suits against the Federal Government, particularly in the Social Security context. *Advisory Committee's 1966 Notes* 122. Individuals who had filed timely lawsuits challenging the administrative denial of benefits often failed to name the party identified in the statute as the proper defendant—the current Secretary of what was then the Department of Health, Education, and Welfare—and named instead the United States; the Department of Health, Education, and Welfare itself; the nonexistent "Federal Security Administration"; or a Secretary who had recently retired from office. *Ibid.* By the time the plaintiffs discovered their mistakes, the statute of limitations in many cases had expired, and the district courts denied the plaintiffs leave to amend on the ground that the amended complaints would not relate back. Rule 15(c) was therefore "amplified to provide a general solution" to this problem. It is conceivable that the Social Security litigants knew or reasonably should have known the identity of the proper defendant either because of documents in their administrative cases or by dint of the statute setting forth the filing requirements. Nonetheless, the Advisory Committee clearly meant their filings to qualify as mistakes under the Rule.

* * *

B

The Court of Appeals offered a second reason why Krupski's amended complaint did not relate back: Krupski had unduly delayed in seeking to file, and in eventually filing, an amended complaint. The Court of Appeals offered no support for its view that a plaintiff's dilatory conduct can justify the denial of relation back under Rule 15(c)(1)(c), and we find none. The Rule plainly sets forth an exclusive list of requirements for relation back, and the amending party's diligence is not among them. Moreover, the Rule mandates relation back once the Rule's requirements are satisfied; it does not leave the decision whether to grant relation back to the district court's equitable discretion. See Rule 15(c)(1) ("An amendment . . . relates back . . . when" the three listed requirements are met).

The mandatory nature of the inquiry for relation back under Rule 15(c) is particularly striking in contrast to the inquiry under Rule 15(a), which sets forth the circumstances in which a party may amend its pleading before trial. By its terms, Rule 15(a) gives discretion to the district court in deciding whether to grant a motion to amend a pleading to add a party or a claim. Following an initial period after filing a pleading during which a party may amend once "as a matter of course," "a party may amend its pleading only with the opposing party's written consent or the court's leave," which the court "should freely give . . . when justice so requires." Rules 15(a)(1)–(2). We have previously explained that a court may consider a movant's "undue delay" or "dilatory motive" in deciding whether to grant leave to amend under Rule 15(a). *Foman v. Davis*, 371 U. S. 178, 182 (1962). As the contrast between Rule 15(a) and Rule 15(c) makes clear, however, the speed with which a plaintiff moves to amend her complaint or files an amended complaint after obtaining leave to do so has no bearing on whether the amended complaint relates back.

Rule 15(c)(1)(C) does permit a court to examine a plaintiff's conduct during the Rule 4(m) period, but not in the way or for the purpose respondent or the Court of Appeals suggests. As we have explained, the question under Rule 15(c)(1)(C)(ii) is what the prospective defendant reasonably should have understood about the plaintiff's intent in filing the original complaint against the first defendant. To the extent the plaintiff's postfiling conduct informs the prospective defendant's understanding of whether the plaintiff initially made a "mistake concerning the proper party's identity," a court may consider the conduct. * * * The plaintiff's postfiling conduct is otherwise immaterial to the question whether an amended complaint relates back.[5]

C

Applying these principles to the facts of this case, we think it clear that the courts below erred in denying relation back under Rule 15(c)(1)(C)(ii). The District Court held that Costa Crociere had "constructive notice" of Krupski's complaint within the Rule 4(m) period. Costa Crociere has not challenged this finding. Because the complaint made clear that Krupski meant to sue the company that "owned, operated, managed, supervised and controlled" the ship on which she was injured, and also indicated (mistakenly) that Costa

---

[5] Similarly, we reject respondent's suggestion that Rule 15(c) requires a plaintiff to move to amend her complaint or to file and serve an amended complaint within the Rule 4(m) period. Rule 15(c)(1)(C)(i) simply requires that the prospective defendant has received sufficient "notice of the action" within the Rule 4(m) period that he will not be prejudiced in defending the case on the merits. The Advisory Committee Notes to the 1966 Amendment clarify that "the notice need not be formal." Advisory Committee's 1966 Notes 122.

Cruise performed those roles Costa Crociere should have known, within the Rule 4(m) period, that it was not named as a defendant in that complaint only because of Krupski's misunderstanding about which "Costa" entity was in charge of the ship—clearly a "mistake concerning the proper party's identity."

Respondent contends that because the original complaint referred to the ticket's forum requirement and presuit claims notification procedure, Krupski was clearly aware of the contents of the ticket, and because the ticket identified Costa Crociere as the carrier and proper party for a lawsuit, respondent was entitled to think that she made a deliberate choice to sue Costa Cruise instead of Costa Crociere. As we have explained, however, that Krupski may have known the contents of the ticket does not foreclose the possibility that she nonetheless misunderstood crucial facts regarding the two companies' identities. Especially because the face of the complaint plainly indicated such a misunderstanding, respondent's contention is not persuasive. Moreover, respondent has articulated no strategy that it could reasonably have thought Krupski was pursuing in suing a defendant that was legally unable to provide relief.

Respondent also argues that Krupski's failure to move to amend her complaint during the Rule 4(m) period shows that she made no mistake in that period. But as discussed, any delay on Krupski's part is relevant only to the extent it may have informed Costa Crociere's understanding during the Rule 4(m) period of whether she made a mistake originally. Krupski's failure to add Costa Crociere during the Rule 4(m) period is not sufficient to make reasonable any belief that she had made a deliberate and informed decision not to sue Costa Crociere in the first instance. Nothing in Krupski's conduct during the Rule 4(m) period suggests that she failed to name Costa Crociere because of anything other than a mistake.

It is also worth noting that Costa Cruise and Costa Crociere are related corporate entities with very similar names; "crociera" even means "cruise" in Italian. *Cassell's Italian Dictionary* 137, 670 (1967). This interrelationship and similarity heighten the expectation that Costa Crociere should suspect a mistake has been made when Costa Cruise is named in a complaint that actually describes Costa Crociere's activities. * * * In addition, Costa Crociere's own actions contributed to passenger confusion over "the proper party" for a lawsuit. The front of the ticket advertises that "Costa Cruises" has achieved a certification of quality, without clarifying whether "Costa Cruises" is Costa Cruise Lines, Costa Crociere, or some other related "Costa" company. Indeed, Costa Crociere is evidently aware that the difference between Costa Cruise and Costa Crociere can be confusing for cruise ship passengers.

In light of these facts, Costa Crociere should have known that Krupski's failure to name it as a defendant in her original complaint was due to a mistake concerning the proper party's identity. We therefore reverse the judgment of the Court of Appeals for the Eleventh Circuit and remand the case for further proceedings consistent with this opinion.

It is so ordered.

■ JUSTICE SCALIA, concurring in part and concurring in the judgment.

I join the Court's opinion except for its reliance, at n. 5, on the Notes of the Advisory Committee as establishing the meaning of Federal Rule of Civil Procedure 15(c)(1)(C). The Advisory Committee's insights into the proper interpretation of a Rule's text are useful to the same extent as any scholarly commentary. But the Committee's intentions have no effect on the Rule's meaning. Even assuming that we and the Congress that allowed the Rule to take effect read and agreed with those intentions, it is the text of the Rule that controls.

COMMENTS AND QUESTIONS CONCERNING
KRUPSKI V. COSTA CROCIERE, S. P. A.

1.   It may be easier to understand this case by writing down the dates recited in the first portion of Justice Sotomayor's opinion. Which dates are particularly significant?

2.   The discussion of the limitations period in this case does not refer to a statute of limitations but, instead, to time periods set forth in Wanda Krupski's ticket. Can Costa Crociere (or Costa Cruise) dictate the limitations period that applies to any claims filed against it?

3.   Describe the ways by which Costa Crociere "knew or should have known that the action would have been brought against it, but for a mistake concerning the proper party's identity."

4.   Justice Sotomayor mentions in her opinion that Costa Crociere's motion to dismiss was filed by the same counsel who had represented Costa Cruise. Why might this be significant?

5.   Whether an amended pleading seeks to change the party or the naming of the party against whom a claim is asserted, or seeks to amend the pleading without changing the party or naming of the party, in order to relate back the amended claim or defense must arise "out of the conduct, transaction or occurrence set out—or attempted to be set out—in the original pleading." Why does Rule 15(c)(1)(B) contain this requirement? Variants of this "conduct, transaction, or occurrence" language also occur in Rule 13(a) (compulsory counterclaims) and Rule 13(g) (crossclaims against a coparty). *See also* 28 U.S.C. § 1367 (supplemental jurisdiction).

6.   Justice Scalia concurs in the Court's unanimous opinion, except for footnote 5. Do you agree with Justice Scalia on this point of textual interpretation?

V. CONCLUSION

The pleadings, typically plaintiff's complaint and defendant's answer, set the stage for all that follows—from discovery, to motion practice, to any eventual trial. Rule 11 requires that attorneys conduct reasonable factual and legal inquiries before filing pleadings and provides that their signatures on pleadings and other court documents constitute specific certifications concerning those documents.

Counsel must not only adhere to the requirements of Rule 11, but also draft pleadings that satisfy Rule 8's general rules of pleading, the more specific pleading requirements of Rule 9, and the interpretation of those Rules by the United States Supreme Court. To satisfy all these requirements can be challenging at times. However, successful pleading provides the framework for success in civil litigation, and the time and effort devoted at the outset of a civil action pays dividends as the action proceeds toward trial.

VI. CHAPTER ASSESSMENT

A.   Multiple-Choice Questions. Answer the following questions, reviewing the sections of the chapter noted in connection with each question.

1.   After a car accident involving a pedestrian and a driver, the pedestrian brings a federal diversity action against the driver in United States District Court. The pedestrian does not have an attorney, but files the action on her own behalf. She signs her complaint, in which she alleges that she has suffered "more than $50,000 in medical expenses and has lost her job" as a result of the driver's negligence. The pedestrian's actual medical expenses have been $6500 and she has not been employed since two months before the accident.

The driver's attorney drafts a motion for sanctions under Rule 11 of the Federal Rules of Civil Procedure and files the motion with the court.

Review Sections III(A) and III(C) and choose the best answer from the following choices:

(a) The court should grant the motion, because the factual allegations of the complaint do not have evidentiary support.

(b) The court should grant the motion, because the court is required to impose sanctions if Rule 11 is violated.

(c) The court should deny the motion, because it was not served upon the pedestrian before being filed with the court.

(d) The court should deny the motion, because only attorneys can be sanctioned pursuant to Rule 11.

2.   A patient filed a diversity action in federal district court against his doctor, alleging that the doctor had committed malpractice in operating on the patient. In her answer, the doctor alleged that the

patient had no evidentiary support for the factual contentions in his complaint and that a recently-enacted state statute barred the patient's claim.

The judge ordered the patient and his attorney to show cause why they should not be sanctioned. The patient responded that, as indicated in his complaint, he would be able to point to facts supporting his allegations after an opportunity for discovery and that the validity of the recently-enacted state statute currently was being litigated in other cases. The court rejected these arguments, dismissed the complaint, and ordered the patient to pay the doctor $10,000 because of the need to defend the action.

Did the court properly impose the sanctions on the plaintiff?

Review Sections III(A) and III(C) and choose the best answer from the following choices:

(a) Yes, because the patient's claims were not warranted by existing law.

(b) Yes, because at the time that the complaint was filed, the patient's factual contentions had no evidentiary support.

(c) No, because monetary sanctions cannot be awarded pursuant to Rule 11.

(d) No, because the defendant did not move for these sanctions.

3.   A protester was injured in a political demonstration involving the police. The protester files a federal civil rights action against a police officer in federal district court, seeking $100,000 in damages.

The protester's complaint, in its entirety, alleges:

1.   This action arises under the First Amendment to the United States Constitution.

2.   On July 1, 2014, the defendant officer unconstitutionally violated the first amendment rights of plaintiff.

3.   As a result, plaintiff suffered damages of $100,000.

Therefore, plaintiff demands judgment against the defendant for $100,000 plus costs.

The defendant files a motion to dismiss. Should the court grant that motion?

Review Section IV(B)(3) and choose the best answer from the following choices:

(a) The court should grant the motion, because it is not possible that the defendant violated the constitutional rights of the plaintiff.

(b) The court should grant the motion, because legal conclusions are not enough to satisfy the pleading required for a federal complaint.

(c) The court should deny the motion, because the claim asserts a denial of constitutional rights.

(d) The court should deny the motion, because the complaint contains a short and plain statement of the claim showing that the plaintiff is entitled to relief.

4. A borrower brings an action in federal court, asserting that a bank violated federal law by not fully disclosing the terms of the bank's loan. The bank answered the complaint, the parties engaged in discovery lasting two years, and the trial of the action lasted for seven days.

After the trial testimony had concluded, the bank's lawyer raised for the first time an argument that the action had not been filed within the applicable statute of limitations. The bank's attorney then made a motion to dismiss the action due to the borrower's failure to comply with the statutes of limitations.

Should the court grant the motion and dismiss the action?

Review Section IV(D) and choose the best answer from the following choices:

(a) No, because the bank did not include the defense of statute of limitations in its answer.

(b) No, because the statute of limitations is a disfavored defense and the action should be decided on the merits.

(c) Yes, because the party seeking relief on a federal claim must plead satisfaction of the statute of limitations in its complaint.

(d) Yes, because whether or not the consumer had satisfied the statute of limitations was uniquely within the knowledge of the borrower and his attorney.

5. A Michigan pedestrian was walking across a street in Chicago, Illinois, when she was struck in a crosswalk by a bus. She was badly injured, but read the sign "Jack Rabbit" on the back of the bus as it continued down the road after hitting her. Although neither the pedestrian nor her counsel knew this, the bus that hit her was owned and operated by Jack Rabbit (Illinois).

On the day before the statute of limitations ran on her claim, the pedestrian's counsel filed a federal diversity action on her behalf against Jack Rabbit, Inc. Chicago attorney Lonnie Lawyer received service of the action the same day. Lonnie represents both Jack Rabbit (Illinois) and Jack Rabbit, Inc. Lonnie called counsel for the pedestrian, telling her that Jack Rabbit, Inc. does not operate busses, but that Jack Rabbit (Illinois) does. As a result, the pedestrian's lawyer filed an amended complaint 15 days after the filing of the original complaint. The amended complaint is identical to the complaint against Jack Rabbit, Inc., but names Jack Rabbit (Illinois) as the defendant.

THE INITIATION OF THE LAWSUIT: "A SHORT AND PLAIN
STATEMENT OF THE CLAIM."

124

CHAPTER 2

Jack Rabbit (Illinois) files a motion seeking dismissal of the action because of the statute of limitations. Should the court dismiss the action because of the statute of limitations?

Review Section IV(E) and choose the best answer from the following choices:

(a) No, because the amended complaint asserts the same claim as the original complaint and, within 90 days after the complaint was filed, Jack Rabbit (Illinois) received such notice of the action that it would not be prejudiced in defending on the merits and knew or should have known that the action would have been brought against it except for a mistake concerning the identity of the proper defendant.

(b) No, because the amended complaint was filed within 21 days after the filing of the original complaint.

(c) Yes, because the pedestrian delayed in moving to amend the complaint.

(d) Yes, because the pedestrian intentionally filed the complaint against the wrong defendant.

B. Essay Questions. To test your understanding of this chapter's material, outline or write an answer to the following questions.

1.   Sanctions for All!

Peter Plaintiff had worked for the Ford Motor Company for 15 years when he applied for a promotion as Ford's regional sales manager. The promotion went instead to Sally Success, who had worked for Ford for 8 years. After learning that Success, rather than he, would be promoted, Peter Plaintiff consulted Lori Lawyer and informed her that he believes he, Peter, was denied the promotion because of his gender. When asked why he believed this, Peter responded, "She's a woman and I'm a man. She got the job and I didn't. Need I say more? I really hate the Ford Motor Company!" As a result of this interview, Lori Lawyer files an action against Ford in federal district court. Lawyer signs the federal complaint, but Plaintiff does not. The complaint alleges that Ford illegally discriminated against Peter Plaintiff on the basis of his gender.

Rather than answering the complaint, Ford immediately moves for summary judgment. Accompanying its summary judgment motion is an affidavit from Edsel Edmonds stating that he chose Sally Success for the promotion because she was the best qualified applicant for the supervisory position and denying that either Sally's or Peter's gender had anything to do with the promotion. Edmonds also states in his affidavit that Peter has been repeatedly disciplined for late arrival and early departures from work and for failure to file required paperwork. In response, Peter files an affidavit stating that "I'm a man and I was denied a promotion that went to a woman. If that's not illegal discrimination, I don't know what is!"

The court grants the motion for summary judgment, and Ford then files with the court a Rule 11 motion seeking sanctions due to the filing of the complaint. Ford asks the court to order that Lawyer pay Ford $100,000; that Lawyer's law firm pay Ford an additional $100,000; and that Plaintiff also pay Ford $5500 ($5500 being the amount that Ford expended in attorneys' fees on this lawsuit). Is this Rule 11 motion likely to be successful?

2.   A "Short and Plaint Statement of the Claim."

A group of non-U.S. citizens who either are Arab or Muslim, or are perceived as Arab or Muslim, were arrested and detained in response to the 9/11 terrorism attacks. They brought suit against the Attorney General, the Director of the FBI, and other law enforcement officials. The plaintiffs incorporated by reference into their complaint two reports of the Justice Department's Office of Inspector General concerning the response of law enforcement officials to the 9/11 attacks.

In their complaint plaintiffs alleged that defendants Ashcroft and Mueller developed "a policy whereby any Muslim or Arab man encountered during the investigation of a tip received in the 9/11 terrorism investigation . . . and discovered to be a non-citizen who had violated the terms of his visa, was arrested" and that Attorney General Ashcroft created a "hold until cleared" policy, under which individuals arrested were not to be released from custody until FBI headquarters affirmatively cleared them of terrorist ties. The complaint further alleged that the Director of the FBI "ran the 9/11 investigation out of FBI Headquarters" and that the Attorney General and FBI Director received detailed daily reports of the arrests and detentions.

The complaint challenged the conditions of plaintiffs' detentions, including allegations that, pursuant to a strategy developed by a small working group containing representatives of each defendant's office, the plaintiffs and other detainees were "placed in tiny cells for over 23 hours a day;" "strip searched every time they were removed from or returned to their cell[s], . . . even when they had no conceivable opportunity to obtain contraband;" provided "meager and barely edible" food,; denied sleep by bright lights left on in their cells for 24 hours a day, and, "on some occasions, correctional officers walked by every 20 minutes throughout the night, kicked the doors to wake up the detainees, and yelled" highly degrading and offensive comments; [they were] constructively denied recreation and exposed to the elements; "denied access to basic hygiene items like toilet paper, soap, towels, toothpaste, [and] eating utensils;" and prohibited [detainees] from moving around the unit, using the telephone freely, using the commissar or accessing MDC handbooks, which explained how to file complaints about mistreatment.

The defendants filed a motion to dismiss for failure to state a claim upon which relief can be granted. Should the court grant that motion? *See Turkmen v. Hasty*, 789 F.3d 218 (2nd Cir. 2015).

CHAPTER 3

SUBJECT-MATTER JURISDICTION: "CAN WE MAKE A FEDERAL CASE OUT OF THIS?"

I. INTRODUCTION

As you know, one of the prerequisites for a court to adjudicate a civil action is subject-matter jurisdiction over that action. Subject-matter jurisdiction is the court's power to hear a particular type of civil action, sometimes referred to as the court's competence to hear a particular case.

Congressional grants of subject-matter jurisdiction must not only provide for jurisdiction over the specific civil action before the court, but must be consistent with the power provided to the federal courts by Article III of the United States Constitution. "The district courts of the United States . . . are 'courts of limited jurisdiction. They possess only that power authorized by Constitution and statute.' "[1] Because federal courts are courts of limited jurisdiction, grants of subject-matter jurisdiction must be explicitly conveyed by Congress in federal jurisdictional statutes. This also means that the burden to establish federal subject-matter jurisdiction is on the party seeking to invoke the jurisdiction of the federal courts (typically the plaintiff).[2]

Thus in determining whether a federal court has subject-matter jurisdiction (judicial power) over an action, the plaintiff must show that:

(1) The action falls within a specific grant of federal jurisdictional power; and

(2) The federal statute authorizing that grant of power is consistent with the federal judicial power recognized in the United States Constitution.

---

[1] *Exxon Mobil Corp. v. Allapattah Services, Inc.*, 545 U.S. 546, 552 (2005), quoting *Kokkonen v. Guardian Life Ins. Co. of America*, 511 U.S. 373, 377 (1994).

In contrast to federal district courts, state courts of general jurisdiction have the power to hear all actions except those specifically excluded from that court's subject-matter jurisdiction. For instance, a state legislature might enact a statute providing that a state court of general (subject-matter) jurisdiction cannot hear actions seeking less than a certain monetary amount. A federal court, though, only can hear actions over which Congress has expressly authorized federal subject-matter jurisdiction.

[2] *Kokkonen v. Guardian Life Ins. Co. of America*, 511 U.S. 373, 377 (1994); *Thomson v. Gaskill*, 315 U.S. 442, 446 (1942).

Consider, for instance, a federal action in which Paul Parker, a citizen of Virginia, seeks $150,000 in damages from Lucy London, a citizen of Kentucky. Title 28 of the United States Code is the Judicial Code of the United States, and it contains the federal statutes concerning the organization of the courts, the jurisdiction and venue of those courts, and the statutory procedure to be applied in federal courts. Section 1332(a) of Title 28 of the United States Code provides:

> The district courts shall have original jurisdiction of all civil actions where the matter in controversy exceeds the sum or value of $75,000, exclusive of interest and costs, and is between—(1) citizens of different States; * * *

Parker's action is (1) a civil action; (2) with a matter in controversy ($150,000) that exceeds $75,000; and (3) between citizens of different States (Virginia and Kentucky). Thus there is a federal statute authorizing the exercise of federal subject-matter jurisdiction over this civil action. In addition, Article III, Section 2 of the United States Constitution provides that the "judicial Power shall extend to all Cases, in Law and Equity, * * * between Citizens of different States." So Section 1332(a) is authorized by the Constitution. The exercise of federal subject-matter jurisdiction over this action is appropriate because (1) jurisdiction is authorized by a federal statute (Section 1332(a) of Title 28) and (2) that jurisdictional statute is an appropriate exercise of the federal judicial power authorized by Article III, Section 2 of the U.S. Constitution.

While Congress has authorized the exercise of federal subject-matter jurisdiction in other individual statutes, the major grants of federal subject-matter jurisdiction are:

(1)   Federal-question Jurisdiction under 28 U.S.C. § 1331;

(2)   Diversity Jurisdiction under 28 U.S.C. § 1332;

(3)   Supplemental Jurisdiction under 28 U.S.C. § 1367; and

(4)   Removal Jurisdiction under 28 U.S.C. § 1441.

Each of these grants of federal subject-matter jurisdiction will be considered in turn.

II. FEDERAL-QUESTION JURISDICTION

The first portion of Article III, Section 2 of the United States Constitution provides: "The judicial Power shall extend to all Cases, in Law and Equity, arising under this Constitution, the Laws of the United States, and Treaties made, or which shall be made, under their Authority." Acting pursuant to this authority, Congress enacted 28 U.S.C. Section 1331, which confers federal-question, or "arising under," subject-matter jurisdiction on the United States District Courts.

Section 1331 of Title 28 in its entirety provides:

The district courts shall have original jurisdiction of all civil actions arising under the Constitution, laws, or treaties of the United States.

Consider whether a United States District Court would have subject-matter jurisdiction over the following civil actions:

(1) A civil action seeking $100,000 and asserting that an agent of the Federal Bureau of Investigation had beaten the plaintiff during a march to protest local governmental action.

(2) A civil action seeking $100 and asserting that an agent of the Federal Bureau of Investigation surreptitiously photographed the plaintiff during a march to protest local governmental action.

(3) A civil action seeking an injunction against surveillance and harassment by the Federal Bureau of Investigation at an upcoming protest march.

(4) A civil action seeking an injunction against surveillance and harassment by the Missouri State Highway Patrol at an upcoming protest march.

(5) A civil action seeking $50,000 brought by the mayor of Metropolis, Illinois against the local newspaper for libel due to a newspaper editorial headlined "We Have a First-Amendment Right to Criticize our Mayor."

As it turns out, federal subject-matter jurisdiction would allow a federal district court to hear the first four of these actions. Until 1980, 28 U.S.C. Section 1331 required that there be more than $10,000 in controversy for a federal court to entertain a civil action under that statute. However, there is no longer any "jurisdictional minimum" required to bring an action under Section 1331. The first amendment right to freedom of assembly has been held to protect against actions of state, as well as federal, officials,[3] so a federal court would have the power to entertain the fourth civil action as well as those challenging actions of federal officials.[4]

---

[3] *Edwards v. South Carolina*, 372 U.S. 229, 235 (1963).

[4] For subject-matter jurisdiction to exist under Section 1331, a claim can "arise under" the Constitution, laws (including regulations), or treaties of the United States. In addition to the congressional grant of subject-matter jurisdiction provided by Section 1331, Rule 12(b)(6) of the Federal Rules of Civil Procedure requires that the complaint must state a valid claim upon which relief can be granted. The Supreme Court has held that such a claim can arise directly under the United States Constitution—without statutory authorization for that cause of action. *Bivens v. Six Unknown Named Agents of Federal Bureau of Narcotics*, 403 U.S. 388 (1971).

In addition, the Supreme Court has concluded, as a matter of statutory construction, that a federal cause of action can be implied from more explicit congressional enactments. *Cannon v. University of Chicago*, 441 U.S. 677 (1979). However, for most civil actions, there will be a specific statute explicitly creating a federal cause of action—in addition to the required federal

But what about the fifth action, seeking damages against a newspaper that asserts that it has a federal constitutional right to publish an allegedly libelous editorial? This would seem to be a logical case for the federal courts to adjudicate, because the case will turn on the interpretation of the First Amendment of the United States Constitution. Before answering this question, consider the Supreme Court's decision in *Louisville & Nashville Railroad Co. v. Mottley* and the "well-pleaded complaint" rule established in that case.

A. THE WELL-PLEADED COMPLAINT RULE

Louisville & Nashville Railroad Company v. Mottley

Supreme Court of the United States, 1908
211 U.S. 149

OPINION

■ [The Court's opinion was preceded by the following fact statement by JUSTICE MOODY:

The appellees (husband and wife), being residents and citizens of Kentucky, brought this suit in equity in the circuit court of the United States for the western district of Kentucky against the appellant, a railroad company and a citizen of the same state. The object of the suit was to compel the specific performance of the following contract:

Louisville, Ky., Oct. 2d, 1871.

The Louisville & Nashville Railroad Company, in consideration that E. L. Mottley and wife, Annie E. Mottley, have this day released company from all damages or claims for damages for injuries received by them on the 7th of September, 1871, in consequence of a collision of trains on the railroad of said company at Randolph's Station, Jefferson County, Kentucky, hereby agrees to issue free passes on said railroad and branches now existing or to exist, to said E. L. & Annie E. Mottley for the remainder of the present year, and thereafter to renew said passes annually during the lives of said Mottley and wife or either of them.

The bill alleged that in September, 1871, plaintiffs, while passengers upon the defendant railroad, were injured by the defendant's negligence, and released their respective claims for damages in consideration of the agreement for transportation during their lives, expressed in the contract. It is alleged that the contract was performed by the defendant up to January 1, 1907, when the defendant declined to renew the passes. The bill then alleges that the refusal to comply with the contract was based solely upon that part of the act of

---

statute, such as 28 U.S.C. § 1331, conveying subject-matter jurisdiction on the federal courts to hear such a cause of action.

Congress of June 29, 1906, which forbids the giving of free passes or free transportation. The bill further alleges: First, that the act of Congress referred to does not prohibit the giving of passes under the circumstances of this case; and, second, that, if the law is to be construed as prohibiting such passes, it is in conflict with the 5th Amendment of the Constitution, because it deprives the plaintiffs of their property without due process of law. The defendant demurred to the bill. The judge of the circuit court overruled the demurrer, entered a decree for the relief prayed for, and the defendant appealed directly to this court.]

■ MR. JUSTICE MOODY, after making the foregoing statement, delivered the opinion of the court:

Two questions of law were raised by the demurrer to the bill, were brought here by appeal, and have been argued before us. They are, first, whether that part of the act of Congress of June 29, 1906, which forbids the giving of free passes or the collection of any different compensation for transportation of passengers than that specified in the tariff filed, makes it unlawful to perform a contract for transportation of persons who, in good faith, before the passage of the act, had accepted such contract in satisfaction of a valid cause of action against the railroad; and, second, whether the statute, if it should be construed to render such a contract unlawful, is in violation of the 5th Amendment of the Constitution of the United States. We do not deem it necessary, however, to consider either of these questions, because, in our opinion, the court below was without jurisdiction of the cause. Neither party has questioned that jurisdiction, but it is the duty of this court to see to it that the jurisdiction of the circuit court, which is defined and limited by statute, is not exceeded. This duty we have frequently performed of our own motion.

There was no diversity of citizenship, and it is not and cannot be suggested that there was any ground of jurisdiction, except that the case was a "suit . . . arising under the Constitution or laws of the United States." It is the settled interpretation of these words, as used in this statute [28 U.S.C. § 1331], conferring jurisdiction, that a suit arises under the Constitution and laws of the United States only when the plaintiff's statement of his own cause of action shows that it is based upon those laws or that Constitution. It is not enough that the plaintiff alleges some anticipated defense to his cause of action, and asserts that the defense is invalidated by some provision of the Constitution of the United States. Although such allegations show that very likely, in the course of the litigation, a question under the Constitution would arise, they do not show that the suit, that is, the plaintiff's original cause of action, arises under the Constitution. In *Tennessee v. Union & Planters' Bank*, 152 U. S. 454, the plaintiff, the state of Tennessee, brought suit in the circuit court of the United States to recover from the defendant certain taxes alleged to be due under the laws of the state. The plaintiff alleged that the defendant claimed an immunity from the taxation by virtue of its charter, and that therefore the tax was void, because in violation of the provision of the Constitution of the United States, which forbids any state from passing a law impairing the obligation of contracts. The cause was held to be beyond the jurisdiction of the circuit court, the court saying, by Mr. Justice Gray (p. 464): "A suggestion of one party, that the other will or may set up a claim under the Constitution or laws of the United States, does not make the suit one arising under that Constitution or those laws." Again, in *Boston & M. Consol. Copper & S. Min. Co. v. Montana Ore Purchasing Co.* 188 U.S. 632, the plaintiff brought suit in the circuit court of the United States for the conversion of copper ore and for an injunction against its continuance. The plaintiff then alleged, for the purpose of showing jurisdiction, in substance, that the defendant would set up in defense certain laws of the United States. The cause was held to be beyond the jurisdiction of the circuit court, the court saying, by Mr. Justice Peckham (pp. 638, 639):

> It would be wholly unnecessary and improper, in order to prove complainant's cause of action, to go into any matters of defense which the defendants might possibly set up, and then attempt to reply to such defense, and thus, if possible, to show that a Federal-question might or probably would arise in the course of the trial of the case. To allege such defense and then make an answer to it before the defendant has the opportunity to itself plead or prove its own defense is inconsistent with any known rule of pleading, so far as we are aware, and is improper.

> The rule is a reasonable and just one that the complainant in the first instance shall be confined to a statement of its cause of action, leaving to the defendant to set up in his answer what his defense is, and, if anything more than a denial of complainant's cause of action, imposing upon the defendant the burden of proving such defense.

> Conforming itself to that rule, the complainant would not, in the assertion or proof of its cause of action, bring up a single Federal-question. The presentation of its cause of action would not show that it was one arising under the Constitution or laws of the United States.

> The only way in which it might be claimed that a Federal-question was presented would be in the complainant's statement of what the defense of defendants would be, and complainant's answer to such defense. Under these circumstances the case is brought within the rule laid down in *Tennessee v. Union & Planters' Bank, supra.* That case has been cited and approved many times since.

The interpretation of the act which we have stated was first announced in *Metcalf v. Watertown*, 128 U.S. 586, and has since been repeated and applied in [many cited cases]. The application of this rule to the case at bar is decisive against the jurisdiction of the circuit court.

It is ordered that the judgment be reversed and the case remitted to the circuit court with instructions to dismiss the suit for want of jurisdiction.

COMMENTS AND QUESTIONS CONCERNING
LOUISVILLE & NASHVILLE RAILROAD COMPANY V. MOTTLEY

1. This civil action initially was filed in the "circuit court of the United States for the western district of Kentucky." Today this action would be filed in the United States District Court for the Western District of Kentucky—one of the 94 federal district courts across the United States.

2. What does Justice Moody mean when he states that the "defendant demurred to the bill"? The relief sought by the Mottleys was specific performance, an equitable decree requiring the Railroad to continue to renew their railroad passes. They thus filed a "bill in equity" setting forth their claim, rather than a complaint as would be filed today in a United States District Court.

When faced with a complaint or bill in equity, the defendant traditionally could test the legal sufficiency of that claim by filing a demurrer. The defendant thereby asserted that, even if all facts alleged by the plaintiff are true, there is no legal basis upon which plaintiff can prevail. Federal Rule of Civil Procedure 12(b)(6) represents the modern-day equivalent of a demurrer. In ruling on a Rule 12(b)(6) motion to dismiss, the court must presume that all facts alleged in the complaint are true and must construe the allegations of the complaint favorably to the plaintiff.

3. Consider a civil action seeking $50,000 brought by the mayor of Metropolis, Illinois against the local newspaper. The mayor asserts a claim for libel due to a newspaper editorial headlined "We Have a First-Amendment Right to Criticize our Mayor." Does this action "arise under" federal law so as to provide a basis for federal subject-matter jurisdiction? In determining your answer consider (1) on what law the mayor is basing his cause of action and (2) the law upon which the newspaper bases its defense.

4. Neither the Mottleys nor the Railroad questioned the subject-matter jurisdiction of the trial court over this action. A lack of subject-matter jurisdiction, concerning a court's power or competence to entertain an action, can be raised by any party or the court at any time—even for the first time on appeal. *See also* Federal Rule of Civil Procedure 12(h)(3) ("If the court determines at any time that it lacks subject-matter jurisdiction, the court must dismiss the action.").

However, once the direct appeal of an action is complete, the parties may be unable to collaterally (*i.e.*, in a second action) challenge the judgment entered by a court without subject-matter jurisdiction. *See Chicot*

County Drainage District v. Baxter State Bank, 308 U.S. 371 (1940), and the discussion of claim preclusion in Chapter 14. *See also Jones v. State of South Carolina*, 3:05–CV–0251–MBS–JRM, 2005 WL 2837537, at 2 (D.S.C. 2005) ("To the extent that *Mottley* stands for the proposition that subject matter jurisdiction can be raised at any time, 28 U.S.C. § 2244 supersedes and provides for a one-year statute of limitations for filing a habeas petition by persons in custody pursuant to the judgment of a state court.").

5.   Does it seem a bit strange that, in settlement of claims for injuries due to a train collision, the Mottleys would accept free lifetime passes to continue to ride the Louisville & Nashville Railroad? Why might this be an attractive settlement for the Mottleys? Why might it be an attractive settlement for the Railroad? Is this a remedy that a court could have ordered in the first instance?

6.   After the Supreme Court determined that the federal courts had no jurisdiction to hear their claim, are the Mottleys without a remedy? As we will see in Chapter 14, the doctrine of claim preclusion (or res judicata) normally allows a party to sue only once on a claim in either state or federal court. However, an exception to that doctrine allows a second civil action in a different court if the initial action was dismissed because the first court had no subject-matter jurisdiction (and the statute of limitations does not bar the later action). Acting pursuant to that doctrine, the Mottleys refiled their action against the Railroad in Kentucky state court. The state trial court granted the relief sought by the Mottleys—an order specifically enforcing their settlement agreement with the Railroad. This order was affirmed on appeal, despite the Railroad's argument that a federal statute enacted after the parties entered into their settlement forbid the Railroad from honoring any agreement permitting the Mottleys to ride the railroad for free.

7.   The Supreme Court held that the federal courts had no subject-matter jurisdiction over the Mottley's original civil action, so one might assume that the decision of the Kentucky court to specifically enforce the settlement would be the end of the matter. However, the Railroad was able to obtain review of the decision of the Kentucky appellate court in the United States Supreme Court. Having determined that neither it nor the lower federal courts could exercise subject-matter jurisdiction over the Mottley's initial action, how could the Supreme Court consider the Railroad's defense after the state court had agreed to specifically enforce the settlement agreement?

8.   In entertaining the Railroad's challenge to specific enforcement of the settlement agreement by the Kentucky state court, the Supreme Court recognized that "a refusal to enforce the agreement of 1871 will operate as a great hardship upon the [Mottleys]." *Louisville & Nashville Railroad Co. v. Mottley*, 219 U.S. 467, 474 (1911). The Court, however, continued:

> But that consideration cannot control the determination of this controversy. Our duty is to ascertain the intention of Congress in passing the statute upon which the railroad company relies as prohibitive of the further enforcement of the agreement in suit.

* * * The court cannot mold a statute simply to meet its views of justice in a particular case. Having, in the mode indicated, ascertained the will of the legislative department, the statute as enacted must be executed, unless found to be inconsistent with the supreme law of the land.

Id.

The Court then held:

In our opinion, the relief asked by the plaintiffs must, upon principle and authority, be denied; that the railroad company rightly refused, after the passage of the commerce act, further to comply with the agreement of 1871; and, that the decree requiring performance of its provisions by issuing annual passes was erroneous.

219 U.S. at 486.

9. So was this the end of the line for the Mottleys? The Supreme Court noted at the end of its second opinion:

Whether, without enforcing the contract in suit, the defendants in error may, by some form of proceeding against the railroad company, recover or restore the rights they had when the railroad collision occurred, is a question not before us, and we express no opinion on it.

219 U.S. at 486. Perhaps because it had again ruled against the Mottleys, is the Court hinting that they still may be able to obtain some redress from the Louisville & Nashville Railroad?

10. To say that there is federal subject-matter jurisdiction over a particular civil action does not necessarily mean that only a federal court can hear the action. Unless the federal courts have **exclusive** subject-matter jurisdiction over a particular type of action, that action also can be adjudicated by a state court. State and federal courts have **concurrent** subject-matter jurisdiction over most civil actions, meaning that those actions can be heard in either state or federal court. Thus, unless a federal statute specifically provides to the contrary, even cases "arising under" federal laws can be determined by either a state or federal court.

Consider, though, Section 1338 of Title 28, the first portion of which provides:

The district courts shall have original jurisdiction of any civil action arising under any Act of Congress relating to patents, plant variety protection, copyrights and trademarks. No State court shall have jurisdiction over any claim for relief arising under any Act of Congress relating to patents, plant variety protection, or copyrights.

Do both state and federal courts have subject-matter jurisdiction over a copyright action? What about a trademark action?

B. "ARISING UNDER" JURISDICTION OVER A STATE-LAW CLAIM PRESENTING A SUBSTANTIAL FEDERAL ISSUE

Grable & Sons Metal Products, Inc. v. Darue Engineering & Manufacturing

Supreme Court of the United States, 2005
545 U.S. 308

OPINION

■ JUSTICE SOUTER delivered the opinion of the Court.

The question is whether want of a federal cause of action to try claims of title to land obtained at a federal tax sale precludes removal to federal court of a state action with nondiverse parties raising a disputed issue of federal title law. We answer no, and hold that the national interest in providing a federal forum for federal tax litigation is sufficiently substantial to support the exercise of federal-question jurisdiction over the disputed issue on removal, which would not distort any division of labor between the state and federal courts, provided or assumed by Congress.

I

In 1994, the Internal Revenue Service seized Michigan real property belonging to petitioner Grable & Sons Metal Products, Inc., to satisfy Grable's federal tax delinquency. Title 26 U.S.C. § 6335 required the IRS to give notice of the seizure, and there is no dispute that Grable received actual notice by certified mail before the IRS sold the property to respondent Darue Engineering & Manufacturing. Although Grable also received notice of the sale itself, it did not exercise its statutory right to redeem the property within 180 days of the sale, § 6337(b)(1), and after that period had passed, the Government gave Darue a quitclaim deed, § 6339.

Five years later, Grable brought a quiet title action in state court, claiming that Darue's record title was invalid because the IRS had failed to notify Grable of its seizure of the property in the exact manner required by § 6335(a), which provides that written notice must be "given by the Secretary to the owner of the property [or] left at his usual place of abode or business." Grable said that the statute required personal service, not service by certified mail.

Darue removed the case to Federal District Court as presenting a federal-question, because the claim of title depended on the interpretation of the notice statute in the federal tax law. The District Court declined to remand the case at Grable's behest after finding that the "claim does pose a 'significant question of federal law,'" and ruling that Grable's lack of a federal right of action to enforce its claim against Darue did not bar the exercise of federal jurisdiction. On the merits, the court granted summary judgment to Darue, holding that although

§ 6335 by its terms required personal service, substantial compliance with the statute was enough.

The Court of Appeals for the Sixth Circuit affirmed. On the jurisdictional question, the panel thought it sufficed that the title claim raised an issue of federal law that had to be resolved, and implicated a substantial federal interest (in construing federal tax law). The court went on to affirm the District Court's judgment on the merits. We granted certiorari on the jurisdictional question alone, to resolve a split within the Courts of Appeals on whether *Merrell Dow Pharmaceuticals Inc. v. Thompson*, 478 U.S. 804 (1986), always requires a federal cause of action as a condition for exercising federal-question jurisdiction. We now affirm.

II

Darue was entitled to remove the quiet title action if Grable could have brought it in federal district court originally, 28 U.S.C. § 1441(a), as a civil action "arising under the Constitution, laws, or treaties of the United States," § 1331. This provision for federal-question jurisdiction is invoked by and large by plaintiffs pleading a cause of action created by federal law (*e.g.*, claims under 42 U.S.C. § 1983). There is, however, another longstanding, if less frequently encountered, variety of federal "arising under" jurisdiction, this Court having recognized for nearly 100 years that in certain cases federal-question jurisdiction will lie over state-law claims that implicate significant federal issues. The doctrine captures the commonsense notion that a federal court ought to be able to hear claims recognized under state law that nonetheless turn on substantial questions of federal law, and thus justify resort to the experience, solicitude, and hope of uniformity that a federal forum offers on federal issues, *see* ALI, *Study of the Division of Jurisdiction Between State and Federal Courts* 164–166 (1968).

The classic example is *Smith v. Kansas City Title & Trust Co.*, 255 U.S. 180 (1921), a suit by a shareholder claiming that the defendant corporation could not lawfully buy certain bonds of the National Government because their issuance was unconstitutional. Although Missouri law provided the cause of action, the Court recognized federal-question jurisdiction because the principal issue in the case was the federal constitutionality of the bond issue. Smith thus held, in a somewhat generous statement of the scope of the doctrine, that a state-law claim could give rise to federal-question jurisdiction so long as it "appears from the [complaint] that the right to relief depends upon the construction or application of [federal law]." *Id.*, at 199.

The Smith statement has been subject to some trimming to fit earlier and later cases recognizing the vitality of the basic doctrine, but shying away from the expansive view that mere need to apply federal law in a state-law claim will suffice to open the "arising under" door. As early as 1912, this Court had confined federal-question jurisdiction over state-law claims to those that "really and substantially involv[e] a dispute or controversy respecting the validity, construction or effect of [federal] law." *Shulthis v. McDougal*, 225 U.S. 561. This limitation was the ancestor of Justice Cardozo's later explanation that a request to exercise federal-question jurisdiction over a state action calls for a "common-sense accommodation of judgment to [the] kaleidoscopic situations" that present a federal issue, in "a selective process which picks the substantial causes out of the web and lays the other ones aside." *Gully v. First Nat. Bank in Meridian*, 299 U.S. 109, 117–118 (1936). It has in fact become a constant refrain in such cases that federal jurisdiction demands not only a contested federal issue, but a substantial one, indicating a serious federal interest in claiming the advantages thought to be inherent in a federal forum.

But even when the state action discloses a contested and substantial federal question, the exercise of federal jurisdiction is subject to a possible veto. For the federal issue will ultimately qualify for a federal forum only if federal jurisdiction is consistent with congressional judgment about the sound division of labor between state and federal courts governing the application of § 1331. Thus, *Franchise Tax Bd.[v. Construction Laborers Vacation Trust for Southern Cal.*, 463 U.S. 1 (1983)] explained that the appropriateness of a federal forum to hear an embedded issue could be evaluated only after considering the "welter of issues regarding the interrelation of federal and state authority and the proper management of the federal judicial system." *Id.*, at 8. Because arising-under jurisdiction to hear a state-law claim always raises the possibility of upsetting the state-federal line drawn (or at least assumed) by Congress, the presence of a disputed federal issue and the ostensible importance of a federal forum are never necessarily dispositive; there must always be an assessment of any disruptive portent in exercising federal jurisdiction.

These considerations have kept us from stating a "single, precise, all-embracing" test for jurisdiction over federal issues embedded in state-law claims between nondiverse parties. *Christianson v. Colt Industries Operating Corp.*, 486 U.S. 800, 821 (1988) (STEVENS, J., concurring). We have not kept them out simply because they appeared in state raiment, as Justice Holmes would have done, *see Smith, supra,* at 214 (dissenting opinion), but neither have we treated "federal issue" as a password opening federal courts to any state action embracing a point of federal law. Instead, the question is, does a state-law claim necessarily raise a stated federal issue, actually disputed and substantial, which a federal forum may entertain without disturbing any congressionally approved balance of federal and state judicial responsibilities.

III

A

This case warrants federal jurisdiction. Grable's state complaint must specify "the facts establishing the superiority of [its] claim," Mich.

Ct. Rule 3.411(B)(2)(c) (West 2005), and Grable has premised its superior title claim on a failure by the IRS to give it adequate notice, as defined by federal law. Whether Grable was given notice within the meaning of the federal statute is thus an essential element of its quiet title claim, and the meaning of the federal statute is actually in dispute; it appears to be the only legal or factual issue contested in the case. The meaning of the federal tax provision is an important issue of federal law that sensibly belongs in a federal court. The Government has a strong interest in the "prompt and certain collection of delinquent taxes," *United States v. Rodgers*, 461 U.S. 677, 709, (1983), and the ability of the IRS to satisfy its claims from the property of delinquents requires clear terms of notice to allow buyers like Darue to satisfy themselves that the Service has touched the bases necessary for good title. The Government thus has a direct interest in the availability of a federal forum to vindicate its own administrative action, and buyers (as well as tax delinquents) may find it valuable to come before judges used to federal tax matters. Finally, because it will be the rare state title case that raises a contested matter of federal law, federal jurisdiction to resolve genuine disagreement over federal tax title provisions will portend only a microscopic effect on the federal-state division of labor.

This conclusion puts us in venerable company, quiet title actions having been the subject of some of the earliest exercises of federal-question jurisdiction over state-law claims. In *Hopkins*, 244 U.S., at 490–491, the question was federal jurisdiction over a quiet title action based on the plaintiffs' allegation that federal mining law gave them the superior claim. Just as in this case, "the facts showing the plaintiffs' title and the existence and invalidity of the instrument or record sought to be eliminated as a cloud upon the title are essential parts of the plaintiffs' cause of action."[3] *Id.*, at 490. As in this case again, "it is plain that a controversy respecting the construction and effect of the [federal] laws is involved and is sufficiently real and substantial." *Id.*, at 489. This Court therefore upheld federal jurisdiction in *Hopkins*, as well as in the similar quiet title matters * * *. Consistent with those cases, the recognition of federal jurisdiction is in order here.

B

Merrell Dow Pharmaceuticals Inc. v. Thompson, 478 U.S. 804 (1986), on which Grable rests its position, is not to the contrary. *Merrell Dow* considered a state tort claim resting in part on the allegation that

---

[3]   The quiet title cases also show the limiting effect of the requirement that the federal issue in a state-law claim must actually be in dispute to justify federal-question jurisdiction. In *Shulthis v. McDougal*, 225 U.S. 561 (1912), this Court found that there was no federal-question jurisdiction to hear a plaintiff's quiet title claim in part because the federal statutes on which title depended were not subject to "any controversy respecting their validity, construction, or effect." *Id.*, at 570. As the Court put it, the requirement of an actual dispute about federal law was "especially" important in "suit[s] involving rights to land acquired under a law of the United States," because otherwise "every suit to establish title to land in the central and western states would so arise [under federal law], as all titles in those States are traceable back to those laws." *Id.*, at 569–570.

the defendant drug company had violated a federal misbranding prohibition, and was thus presumptively negligent under Ohio law. The Court assumed that federal law would have to be applied to resolve the claim, but after closely examining the strength of the federal interest at stake and the implications of opening the federal forum, held federal jurisdiction unavailable. Congress had not provided a private federal cause of action for violation of the federal branding requirement, and the Court found "it would . . . flout, or at least undermine, congressional intent to conclude that federal courts might nevertheless exercise federal-question jurisdiction and provide remedies for violations of that federal statute solely because the violation . . . is said to be a . . . 'proximate cause' under state law." *Id.*, at 812.

Because federal law provides for no quiet title action that could be brought against Darue, Grable argues that there can be no federal jurisdiction here, stressing some broad language in *Merrell Dow* (including the passage just quoted) that on its face supports Grable's position. But an opinion is to be read as a whole, and *Merrell Dow* cannot be read whole as overturning decades of precedent, as it would have done by effectively adopting the Holmes dissent in *Smith*, and converting a federal cause of action from a sufficient condition for federal-question jurisdiction into a necessary one.

In the first place, *Merrell Dow* disclaimed the adoption of any bright-line rule, as when the Court reiterated that "in exploring the outer reaches of § 1331, determinations about federal jurisdiction require sensitive judgments about congressional intent, judicial power, and the federal system." 478 U.S., at 810. The opinion included a lengthy footnote explaining that questions of jurisdiction over state-law claims require "careful judgments," *id.*, at 814, about the "nature of the federal interest at stake," *id.*, at 814, n. 12. And as a final indication that it did not mean to make a federal right of action mandatory, it expressly approved the exercise of jurisdiction sustained in *Smith*, despite the want of any federal cause of action available to Smith's shareholder plaintiff. 478 U.S., at 814, n. 12. *Merrell Dow* then, did not toss out, but specifically retained, the contextual enquiry that had been *Smith*'s hallmark for over 60 years. At the end of *Merrell Dow*, Justice Holmes was still dissenting.

Accordingly, *Merrell Dow* should be read in its entirety as treating the absence of a federal private right of action as evidence relevant to, but not dispositive of, the "sensitive judgments about congressional intent" that § 1331 requires. The absence of any federal cause of action affected *Merrell Dow*'s result two ways. The Court saw the fact as worth some consideration in the assessment of substantiality. But its primary importance emerged when the Court treated the combination of no federal cause of action and no preemption of state remedies for misbranding as an important clue to Congress's conception of the scope of jurisdiction to be exercised under § 1331. The Court saw the missing cause of action not as a missing federal door key, always required, but as a missing welcome mat, required in the circumstances, when exercising federal jurisdiction over a state misbranding action would have attracted a horde of original filings and removal cases raising other state claims with embedded federal issues. For if the federal labeling standard without a federal cause of action could get a state claim into federal court, so could any other federal standard without a federal cause of action. And that would have meant a tremendous number of cases.

One only needed to consider the treatment of federal violations generally in garden variety state tort law. "The violation of federal statutes and regulations is commonly given negligence per se effect in state tort proceedings." *Restatement (Third) of Torts* § 14, Reporters' Note, Comment a, p.195 (Tent. Draft No. 1, Mar. 28, 2001). A general rule of exercising federal jurisdiction over state claims resting on federal mislabeling and other statutory violations would thus have heralded a potentially enormous shift of traditionally state cases into federal courts. Expressing concern over the "increased volume of federal litigation," and noting the importance of adhering to "legislative intent," *Merrell Dow* thought it improbable that the Congress, having made no provision for a federal cause of action, would have meant to welcome any state-law tort case implicating federal law "solely because the violation of the federal statute is said to [create] a rebuttable presumption [of negligence] . . . under state law." 478 U.S., at 811–812. In this situation, no welcome mat meant keep out. *Merrell Dow*'s analysis thus fits within the framework of examining the importance of having a federal forum for the issue, and the consistency of such a forum with Congress's intended division of labor between state and federal courts.

As already indicated, however, a comparable analysis yields a different jurisdictional conclusion in this case. Although Congress also indicated ambivalence in this case by providing no private right of action to Grable, it is the rare state quiet title action that involves contested issues of federal law. Consequently, jurisdiction over actions like Grable's would not materially affect, or threaten to affect, the normal currents of litigation. Given the absence of threatening structural consequences and the clear interest the Government, its buyers, and its delinquents have in the availability of a federal forum, there is no good reason to shirk from federal jurisdiction over the dispositive and contested federal issue at the heart of the state-law title claim.[7]

---

[7] At oral argument Grable's counsel espoused the position that after *Merrell Dow*, federal-question jurisdiction over state-law claims absent a federal right of action could be recognized only where a constitutional issue was at stake. There is, however, no reason in text or otherwise to draw such a rough line. As *Merrell Dow* itself suggested, constitutional questions may be the more likely ones to reach the level of substantiality that can justify

IV

The judgment of the Court of Appeals, upholding federal jurisdiction over Grable's quiet title action, is affirmed.

It is so ordered.

■ JUSTICE THOMAS, concurring.

The Court faithfully applies our precedents interpreting 28 U.S.C. § 1331 to authorize federal-court jurisdiction over some cases in which state law creates the cause of action but requires determination of an issue of federal law. In this case, no one has asked us to overrule those precedents and adopt the rule Justice Holmes set forth in *American Well Works Co. v. Layne & Bowler Co.*, 241 U.S. 257 (1916), limiting § 1331 jurisdiction to cases in which federal law creates the cause of action pleaded on the face of the plaintiff's complaint. In an appropriate case, and perhaps with the benefit of better evidence as to the original meaning of § 1331's text, I would be willing to consider that course.*

Jurisdictional rules should be clear. Whatever the virtues of the *Smith* standard, it is anything but clear. *Ante*, at 2367 (the standard "calls for a 'common-sense accommodation of judgment to [the] kaleidoscopic situations' that present a federal issue, in 'a selective process which picks the substantial causes out of the web and lays the other ones aside'" (quoting *Gully v. First Nat. Bank in Meridian*, 299 U.S. 109, 117–118 (1936))); *ante*, at 2368 ("[T]he question is, does a state-law claim necessarily raise a stated federal issue, actually disputed and substantial, which a federal forum may entertain without disturbing any congressionally approved balance of federal and state judicial responsibilities"); *ante*, at 2370 ("'[D]eterminations about federal jurisdiction require sensitive judgments about congressional intent, judicial power, and the federal system'"; "the absence of a federal private right of action [is] evidence relevant to, but not dispositive of, the 'sensitive judgments about congressional intent' that § 1331 requires" (quoting *Merrell Dow*, *supra*, at 810)).

Whatever the vices of the *American Well Works* rule, it is clear. Moreover, it accounts for the "'vast majority'" of cases that come within § 1331 under our current case law—further indication that trying to sort out which cases fall within the smaller *Smith* category may not be worth the effort it entails. Accordingly, I would be willing in appropriate circumstances to reconsider our interpretation of § 1331.

---

federal jurisdiction. But a flat ban on statutory questions would mechanically exclude significant questions of federal law like the one this case presents.

*   This Court has long construed the scope of the statutory grant of federal-question jurisdiction more narrowly than the scope of the constitutional grant of such jurisdiction. I assume for present purposes that this distinction is proper-that is, that the language of 28 U.S.C. § 1331, "[t]he district courts shall have original jurisdiction of all civil actions arising under the Constitution, laws, or treaties of the United States," is narrower than the language of Art. III, 2, cl. 1, of the Constitution, "[t]he judicial Power shall extend to all Cases, in Law and Equity, arising under this Constitution, the Laws of the United States, and Treaties made, or which shall be made, under their Authority. . . ."

COMMENTS AND QUESTIONS CONCERNING *GRABLE & SONS METAL PRODUCTS, INC. V. DARUE ENGINEERING & MANUFACTURING*

1.   Section 1441 of Title 28 permits defendants to remove to federal district court certain civil actions filed in state court. One prerequisite for such removal is that a federal district court "have original jurisdiction" over the removed action. 28 U.S.C. § 1441(a). Thus the federal court must have been able to have exercised subject-matter jurisdiction over the action had it initially been filed in federal court. The Supreme Court's discussion of federal subject-matter jurisdiction would have been the same had Grable initially sued in either state or federal court.

2.   According to Justice Souter, "[T]he question is, does a state-law claim necessarily raise a stated federal issue, actually disputed and substantial, which a federal forum may entertain without disturbing any congressionally approved balance of federal and state judicial responsibilities." Will this test be easy to apply in all cases? In most cases?

3.   Justice Souter concludes his opinion by stating that "there is no good reason to shirk from federal jurisdiction over the dispositive and contested federal issue at the heart of the state-law title claim." Does this mean that federal courts should resolve close cases as to their jurisdictional power in favor of exercising jurisdiction? What if federal courts did not assert their subject-matter jurisdiction in such cases?

4.   In considering whether the federal courts should exercise subject-matter jurisdiction over this particular action, Justice Souter states, "Finally, because it will be the rare state title case that raises a contested matter of federal law, federal jurisdiction to resolve genuine disagreement over federal tax title provisions will portend only a microscopic effect on the federal-state division of labor." Why is it significant that, under the test articulated by the Court, there will be very few actions such as Grable's over which federal courts will exercise jurisdiction? If there is a disputed and substantial federal issue presented, why shouldn't the federal courts be able to resolve that issue?

5.   Do you agree with Justice Thomas that it may be more important to have a rule that clearly resolves the great majority of jurisdictional disputes than to adopt a more flexible test to consider the subtleties presented by more difficult cases? As Justice Thomas states:

> Whatever the vices of the *American Well Works* rule, it is clear. Moreover, it accounts for the " 'vast majority' " of cases that come within § 1331 under our current case law—further indication that trying to sort out which cases fall within the smaller *Smith* category may not be worth the effort it entails.

545 U.S. at 321.

6.   The test advocated by Justice Holmes, and recommended by Justice Thomas, is that a "suit arises under the law that creates the cause of action." *American Well Works Co. v. Layne & Bowler Co.*, 241 U.S. 257, 260 (1916). Would the adoption of this standard make the determination of federal jurisdiction easier? Would such a standard cover all cases? Would

the decision in *Grable* come out the same under the *American Well Works*
standard? Why did other justices not endorse this standard in *Grable*?

7.   An individual plans to sue his former attorney for legal
malpractice in connection with an action for patent infringement. Section
1338(a) of Title 28 gives the federal courts exclusive jurisdiction over "any
claim for relief arising under any Act of Congress relating to patents" and
"arising under" has been interpreted identically under Sections 1331 and
1338(a) of Title 28. Must the legal malpractice action be brought in federal
court? *See Gunn v. Minton*, 133 S. Ct. 1059 (2013).

III. FEDERAL DIVERSITY JURISDICTION

In addition to Section 1331 federal-question jurisdiction, Congress
has authorized a second major grant of federal subject-matter
jurisdiction—federal diversity jurisdiction—in Section 1332 of Title 28.
Indeed, federal diversity jurisdiction initially was enacted as one
portion of the Judiciary Act of 1789. Act of Sept. 24, 1789, § 11, 1 Stat.
73, 78. Because (1) PepsiCo was a citizen of New York and North
Carolina while John Leonard was citizen of Washington and (2) there
was more than $75,000 in controversy in the action, a federal, rather
than state, court ultimately decided those parties' state-law contract
dispute.

Section 1332(a) provides:

> The district courts shall have original jurisdiction of all
> civil actions where the matter in controversy exceeds the sum
> or value of $75,000, exclusive of interest and costs, and is
> between—
>
> (1) citizens of different States;
>
> (2) citizens of a State and citizens or subjects or a foreign
> state, except that the district courts shall not have original
> jurisdiction under this subsection of an action between
> citizens of a State and citizens or subjects of a foreign
> state who are lawfully admitted for permanent residence
> in the United States and are domiciled in the same State;
>
> (3) citizens of different States and in which citizens or
> subjects of a foreign state are additional parties; and
>
> (4) a foreign state, defined in section 1603(a) of this title,
> as plaintiff and citizens of a State or of different States.

All of these congressional grants of subject-matter jurisdiction are
based upon the federal judicial power recognized in Article III, Section 2
of the United States Constitution.

While Section 1331 of Title 28 confers subject-matter jurisdiction
on the federal district courts to entertain a particular type of civil action
(those "arising under" federal law), the subject-matter jurisdiction
conferred by Section 1332(a) is based upon the citizenship of the parties

to an action. There is some debate as to precisely why the framers of the Constitution provided for diversity jurisdiction. Many have argued that this was to insure that an out-of-state defendant could obtain a judicial forum that would be more neutral than a state court in plaintiff's home state, while others have argued that the framers were concerned about providing a federal forum to protect commercial interests from hostile state courts.[5] Whatever the reason for the creation of diversity jurisdiction, it remains a significant basis of federal subject-matter jurisdiction.

There also is some debate as to the continuing wisdom of devoting limited federal judicial resources to the resolution of actions that arise under state, rather than federal, law. Thus a federal study committee recommended the abolition of most diversity jurisdiction in 1990, concluding:

> On the one hand, no other class of cases has a weaker claim on federal judicial resources. On the other hand, no other step will do anywhere nearly as much to reduce federal caseload pressures and contain the growth of the federal judiciary. Given all the demands on the federal courts, there is little reason to use them for contract disputes or automobile accident suits simply because the parties live across state boundaries— especially when litigants who do not live in different states must bring otherwise identical suits in state courts.[6]

Short of total elimination of diversity jurisdiction, recommendations have been made to limit it by not permitting plaintiffs to bring diversity actions in a federal court within their home state.[7] However, although the jurisdictional minimum has been raised over the years, federal diversity jurisdiction remains a significant basis of subject-matter jurisdiction for the federal district courts. Indeed, in recent years Congress has enacted the Multiparty, Multiforum Trial Jurisdiction Act of 2002[8] and the Class Action Fairness Act of 2005[9] that have further expanded the diversity of citizenship jurisdiction of the federal courts.

While Section 1332(a) diversity jurisdiction is authorized by the Constitution's Article III judicial power, Congress has never conferred the full Article III diversity jurisdiction on the federal courts.[10] Thus in order to invoke Section 1332(a) diversity jurisdiction, the plaintiff must

---

[5]   C. Wright, A. Miller & E. Cooper, 13E *Federal Practice and Procedure* § 3601, at 12–22 (3rd ed. 2009).

[6]   101st Cong., *Report of the Federal Courts Study Committee* 39 (1990).

[7]   American Law Institute, *Study of the Division of Jurisdiction Between State and Federal Courts* 109 (1969).

[8]   Pub. L. No. 107–273, § 11020(b)(1), 116 Stat. 1826 (2002) (codified in 28 U.S.C. § 1369).

[9]   Pub. L. No. 109–2, 119 Stat. 4 (2005) (codified in 28 U.S.C. §§ 1332(d), 1453, and 1711–15).

[10]   *Saadeh v. Farouki*, 107 F.3d 52, 54 (D.C. Cir. 1997).

establish that more than $75,000 (exclusive of interest and costs) is in controversy, although Article III contains no similar jurisdictional minimum.

Although Article III, Section 2 of the Constitution states that the "judicial Power shall extend to all Cases, in Law and Equity, * * * between Citizens of different States," Chief Justice Marshall in *Strawbridge v. Curtiss*, 7 U.S. (3 Cranch) 267 (1806), interpreted the federal statutory grant of diversity jurisdiction to require "complete diversity." Thus diversity does not exist under 28 U.S.C. § 1332 unless there is no plaintiff who is a citizen of the same state as any defendant. In contrast to the statutory requirement of complete diversity, Article III, Section 2 merely requires "minimal diversity," with at least one plaintiff being a citizen of a state different than the state of citizenship of at least one defendant. But Congress has not conferred the full Article III judicial power on the federal district courts under Section 1332.[11]

The following examples illustrate complete and minimal diversity and the impact of such diversity upon the ability of a federal district court to hear such cases.

Civil Action A:

Plaintiff #1 (citizen of Texas)	Defendant #1 (citizen of Louisiana)
v.	
Plaintiff #2 (citizen of Texas)	Defendant #2 (citizen of Louisiana)

Because there is no plaintiff who is a citizen of the same state as any defendant, complete diversity exists and there would be subject-matter jurisdiction if plaintiffs satisfy the jurisdictional minimum amount in controversy. "Complete diversity" does not mean or require that co-parties (all plaintiffs or all defendants) be citizens of different states.

Civil Action B:

Plaintiff #1 (citizen of Texas)	Defendant #1 (citizen of Louisiana)
v.	
Plaintiff #2 (citizen of Texas)	Defendant #2 (citizen of Texas)

---

[11] The Supreme Court has noted that "Chief Justice Marshall [in *Strawbridge v. Curtiss*] there purported to construe only 'The words of the act of congress,' not the Constitution itself. And in a variety of contexts this Court and the lower courts have concluded that Article III poses no obstacle to the legislative extension of federal jurisdiction, founded on diversity, so long as any two adverse parties are not co-citizens." *State Farm Fire & Cas. Co. v. Tashire*, 386 U.S. 523, 531 (1967).

Because Defendant #2 is a citizen of the same state as at least one of the plaintiffs (Texas), there is not complete diversity of citizenship. Minimal diversity exists because Defendant #1 is a citizen of a state (Louisiana) of which no plaintiff is a citizen. Although this minimal diversity would be sufficient for Article III, Congress has required complete diversity under Section 1332. Thus a federal district court could not exercise subject-matter jurisdiction over Action B.

Judicial interpretation also has limited the jurisdictional grant conferred by Section 1332(a) in two other significant ways. The Supreme Court has held that diversity jurisdiction does not extend to the issuance of a divorce, alimony, or child custody decree[12] nor to the probate of a will or administration of an estate.[13]

A. DETERMINING CORPORATE CITIZENSHIP

Hertz Corp. v. Friend

Supreme Court of the United States, 2010
559 U.S. 77

OPINION

■ JUSTICE BREYER delivered the opinion of the Court.

The federal diversity jurisdiction statute provides that "a corporation shall be deemed to be a citizen of any State by which it has been incorporated and of the State where it has its principal place of business." 28 U.S.C. § 1332(c)(1). We seek here to resolve different interpretations that the Circuits have given this phrase. In doing so, we place primary weight upon the need for judicial administration of a jurisdictional statute to remain as simple as possible. And we conclude that the phrase "principal place of business" refers to the place where the corporation's high level officers direct, control, and coordinate the corporation's activities. Lower federal courts have often metaphorically called that place the corporation's "nerve center." We believe that the "nerve center" will typically be found at a corporation's headquarters.

I

In September 2007, respondents Melinda Friend and John Nhieu, two California citizens, sued petitioner, the Hertz Corporation, in a California state court. They sought damages for what they claimed were violations of California's wage and hour laws. And they requested relief

---

[12] *Ankenbrandt v. Richards*, 504 U.S. 689, 704 (1992) ("As a matter of judicial economy, state courts are more eminently suited to work of this type than are federal courts, which lack the close association with state and local government organizations dedicated to handling issues that arise out of conflicts over divorce, alimony, and child custody decrees"); *Ohio ex rel. Papovici v. Agler*, 280 U.S. 379, 383 (1930).

[13] *Marshall v. Marshall*, 547 U.S. 293, 311–12 (2006) ("[T]he probate exception reserves to state probate courts the probate or annulment of a will and the administration of a decedent's estate; it also precludes federal courts from endeavoring to dispose of property that is in the custody of a state probate court."); *O'Callaghan v. O'Brien*, 199 U.S. 89 (1905).

on behalf of a potential class composed of California citizens who had allegedly suffered similar harms.

Hertz filed a notice seeking removal to a federal court. 28 U.S.C. §§ 1332(d)(2), 1453. Hertz claimed that the plaintiffs and the defendant were citizens of different States. §§ 1332(a)(1), (c)(1). Hence, the federal court possessed diversity-of-citizenship jurisdiction. Friend and Nhieu, however, claimed that the Hertz Corporation was a California citizen, like themselves, and that, hence, diversity jurisdiction was lacking.

To support its position, Hertz submitted a declaration by an employee relations manager that sought to show that Hertz's "principal place of business" was in New Jersey, not in California. The declaration stated, among other things, that Hertz operated facilities in 44 States; and that California—which had about 12% of the Nation's population—accounted for 273 of Hertz's 1,606 car rental locations; about 2,300 of its 11,230 full-time employees; about $811 million of its $4.371 billion in annual revenue; and about 3.8 million of its approximately 21 million annual transactions, i.e., rentals. The declaration also stated that the "leadership of Hertz and its domestic subsidiaries" is located at Hertz's "corporate headquarters" in Park Ridge, New Jersey; that its "core executive and administrative functions . . . are carried out" there and "to a lesser extent" in Oklahoma City, Oklahoma; and that its "major administrative operations . . . are found" at those two locations.

The District Court of the Northern District of California accepted Hertz's statement of the facts as undisputed. But it concluded that, given those facts, Hertz was a citizen of California. In reaching this conclusion, the court applied Ninth Circuit precedent, which instructs courts to identify a corporation's "principal place of business" by first determining the amount of a corporation's business activity State by State. If the amount of activity is "significantly larger" or "substantially predominates" in one State, then that State is the corporation's "principal place of business." If there is no such State, then the "principal place of business" is the corporation's " 'nerve center,' " i.e., the place where " 'the majority of its executive and administrative functions are performed.' "

Applying this test, the District Court found that the "plurality of each of the relevant business activities" was in California, and that "the differential between the amount of those activities" in California and the amount in "the next closest state" was "significant." Hence, Hertz's "principal place of business" was California, and diversity jurisdiction was thus lacking. The District Court consequently remanded the case to the state courts.

Hertz appealed the District Court's remand order. 28 U.S.C. § 1453(c). The Ninth Circuit affirmed in a brief memorandum opinion. Hertz filed a petition for certiorari. And, in light of differences among the Circuits in the application of the test for corporate citizenship, we granted the writ.

II

[The Court rejected plaintiffs' jurisdictional objection to Supreme Court review of this case.]

III

We begin our "principal place of business" discussion with a brief review of relevant history. The Constitution provides that the "judicial Power shall extend" to "Controversies . . . between Citizens of different States." Art. III, § 2. This language, however, does not automatically confer diversity jurisdiction upon the federal courts. Rather, it authorizes Congress to do so and, in doing so, to determine the scope of the federal courts' jurisdiction within constitutional limits.

Congress first authorized federal courts to exercise diversity jurisdiction in 1789 when, in the First Judiciary Act, Congress granted federal courts authority to hear suits "between a citizen of the State where the suit is brought, and a citizen of another State." The statute said nothing about corporations. In 1809, Chief Justice Marshall, writing for a unanimous Court, described a corporation as an "invisible, intangible, and artificial being" which was "certainly not a citizen." *Bank of United States v. Deveaux*, 5 Cranch 61, 86 (1809). But the Court held that a corporation could invoke the federal courts' diversity jurisdiction based on a pleading that the corporation's shareholders were all citizens of a different State from the defendants, as "the term citizen ought to be understood as it is used in the constitution, and as it is used in other laws. That is, to describe the real persons who come into court, in this case, under their corporate name." *Id.*, at 91–92.

In *Louisville, C. & C.R. Co. v. Letson*, 2 How. 497 (1844), the Court modified this initial approach. It held that a corporation was to be deemed an artificial person of the State by which it had been created, and its citizenship for jurisdictional purposes determined accordingly. *Id.*, at 558–559. Ten years later, the Court in *Marshall v. Baltimore & Ohio R. Co.*, 16 How. 314 (1854), held that the reason a corporation was a citizen of its State of incorporation was that, for the limited purpose of determining corporate citizenship, courts could conclusively (and artificially) presume that a corporation's shareholders were citizens of the State of incorporation. * * *

In 1928 this Court made clear that the "state of incorporation" rule was virtually absolute. It held that a corporation closely identified with State A could proceed in a federal court located in that State as long as the corporation had filed its incorporation papers in State B, perhaps a State where the corporation did no business at all. *See Black and White Taxicab & Transfer Co. v. Brown and Yellow Taxicab & Transfer Co.*, 276 U.S. 518, 522–525 (refusing to question corporation's reincorporation motives and finding diversity jurisdiction). Subsequently, many in Congress and those who testified before it pointed out that this interpretation was at odds with diversity jurisdiction's basic rationale, namely, opening the federal courts' doors to those who might otherwise suffer from local prejudice against out-of-state parties. Through its choice of the State of incorporation, a corporation could manipulate federal-court jurisdiction, for example, opening the federal courts' doors in a State where it conducted nearly all its business by filing incorporation papers elsewhere. Although various legislative proposals to curtail the corporate use of diversity jurisdiction were made, none of these proposals were enacted into law.

At the same time as federal dockets increased in size, many judges began to believe those dockets contained too many diversity cases. A committee of the Judicial Conference of the United States studied the matter. And on March 12, 1951, that committee, the Committee on Jurisdiction and Venue, issued a report (hereinafter *Mar. Committee Rept.*).

Among its observations, the committee found a general need "to prevent frauds and abuses" with respect to jurisdiction. *Id.*, at 14. The committee recommended against eliminating diversity cases altogether. *Id.*, at 28. Instead it recommended, along with other proposals, a statutory amendment that would make a corporation a citizen both of the State of its incorporation and any State from which it received more than half of its gross income. *Id.*, at 14–15 (requiring corporation to show that "less than fifty per cent of its gross income was derived from business transacted within the state where the Federal court is held"). If, for example, a citizen of California sued (under state law in state court) a corporation that received half or more of its gross income from California, that corporation would not be able to remove the case to federal court, even if Delaware was its State of incorporation.

During the spring and summer of 1951 committee members circulated their report and attended circuit conferences at which federal judges discussed the report's recommendations. Reflecting those criticisms, the committee filed a new report in September, in which it revised its corporate citizenship recommendation. It now proposed that "'a corporation shall be deemed a citizen of the state of its original creation . . . [and] shall also be deemed a citizen of a state where it has its principal place of business.'" Judicial Conference of the United States, *Report of the Committee on Jurisdiction and Venue* 4 (Sept. 24, 1951) (hereinafter *Sept. Committee Rept.*)—the source of the present-day statutory language. The committee wrote that this new language would provide a "simpler and more practical formula" than the "gross income" test. *Sept. Committee Rept.* 2. * * *

* * *

The House Committee reprinted the Judicial Conference Committee Reports along with other reports and relevant testimony and circulated it to the general public "for the purpose of inviting further suggestions and comments." *Id.*, at III. Subsequently, in 1958,

Congress both codified the courts' traditional place of incorporation test and also enacted into law a slightly modified version of the Conference Committee's proposed "principal place of business" language. A corporation was to "be deemed a citizen of any State by which it has been incorporated and of the State where it has its principal place of business." § 2, 72 Stat. 415.

IV

The phrase "principal place of business" has proved more difficult to apply than its originators likely expected. * * *

After Congress' amendment, courts were * * * uncertain as to where to look to determine a corporation's "principal place of business" for diversity purposes. If a corporation's headquarters and executive offices were in the same State in which it did most of its business, the test seemed straightforward. The "principal place of business" was located in that State.

But suppose those corporate headquarters, including executive offices, are in one State, while the corporation's plants or other centers of business activity are located in other States? In 1959 a distinguished federal district judge, Edward Weinfeld, relied on the Second Circuit's interpretation of the Bankruptcy Act to answer this question in part:

"Where a corporation is engaged in far-flung and varied activities which are carried on in different states, its principal place of business is the nerve center from which it radiates out to its constituent parts and from which its officers direct, control and coordinate all activities without regard to locale, in the furtherance of the corporate objective. The test applied by our Court of Appeals, is that place where the corporation has an 'office from which its business was directed and controlled'—the place where 'all of its business was under the supreme direction and control of its officers.'" *Scot Typewriter Co.*, 170 F.Supp., at 865.

Numerous Circuits have since followed this rule, applying the "nerve center" test for corporations with "far-flung" business activities.

Scot's analysis, however, did not go far enough. For it did not answer what courts should do when the operations of the corporation are not "far-flung" but rather limited to only a few States. When faced with this question, various courts have focused more heavily on where a corporation's actual business activities are located.

Perhaps because corporations come in many different forms, involve many different kinds of business activities, and locate offices and plants for different reasons in different ways in different regions, a general "business activities" approach has proved unusually difficult to apply. Courts must decide which factors are more important than others: for example, plant location, sales or servicing centers; transactions, payrolls, or revenue generation.

The number of factors grew as courts explicitly combined aspects of the "nerve center" and "business activity" tests to look to a corporation's "total activities," sometimes to try to determine what treatises have described as the corporation's "center of gravity." * * *

This complexity may reflect an unmediated judicial effort to apply the statutory phrase "principal place of business" in light of the general purpose of diversity jurisdiction, *i.e.*, an effort to find the State where a corporation is least likely to suffer out-of-state prejudice when it is sued in a local court. But, if so, that task seems doomed to failure. After all, the relevant purposive concern—prejudice against an out-of-state party—will often depend upon factors that courts cannot easily measure, for example, a corporation's image, its history, and its advertising, while the factors that courts can more easily measure, for example, its office or plant location, its sales, its employment, or the nature of the goods or services it supplies, will sometimes bear no more than a distant relation to the likelihood of prejudice. At the same time, this approach is at war with administrative simplicity. And it has failed to achieve a nationally uniform interpretation of federal law, an unfortunate consequence in a federal legal system.

V

A

In an effort to find a single, more uniform interpretation of the statutory phrase, we have reviewed the Courts of Appeals' divergent and increasingly complex interpretations. Having done so, we now return to, and expand, Judge Weinfeld's approach, as applied in the Seventh Circuit. *See, e.g., Scot Typewriter Co.*, 170 F.Supp., at 865; *Wisconsin Knife Works*, 781 F.2d, at 1282. We conclude that "principal place of business" is best read as referring to the place where a corporation's officers direct, control, and coordinate the corporation's activities. It is the place that Courts of Appeals have called the corporation's "nerve center." And in practice it should normally be the place where the corporation maintains its headquarters—provided that the headquarters is the actual center of direction, control, and coordination, *i.e.*, the "nerve center," and not simply an office where the corporation holds its board meetings (for example, attended by directors and officers who have traveled there for the occasion).

Three sets of considerations, taken together, convince us that this approach, while imperfect, is superior to other possibilities. First, the statute's language supports the approach. The statute's text deems a corporation a citizen of the "State where it has its principal place of business." 28 U.S.C. § 1332(c)(1). The word "place" is in the singular, not the plural. The word "principal" requires us to pick out the "main, prominent" or "leading" place. 12 *Oxford English Dictionary* 495 (2d ed. 1989) (def.(A)(I)(2)). And the fact that the word "place" follows the words "State where" means that the "place" is a place within a State. It is not the State itself.

A corporation's "nerve center," usually its main headquarters, is a single place. The public often (though not always) considers it the corporation's main place of business. And it is a place within a State. By contrast, the application of a more general business activities test has led some courts, as in the present case, to look, not at a particular place within a State, but incorrectly at the State itself, measuring the total amount of business activities that the corporation conducts there and determining whether they are "significantly larger" than in the next-ranking State.

This approach invites greater litigation and can lead to strange results, as the Ninth Circuit has since recognized. Namely, if a "corporation may be deemed a citizen of California on th[e] basis" of "activities [that] roughly reflect California's larger population . . . nearly every national retailer—no matter how far flung its operations—will be deemed a citizen of California for diversity purposes." *Davis v. HSBC Bank Nev., N. A.*, 557 F.3d 1026, 1029–1030 (2009). But why award or decline diversity jurisdiction on the basis of a State's population, whether measured directly, indirectly (say proportionately), or with modifications?

Second, administrative simplicity is a major virtue in a jurisdictional statute. Complex jurisdictional tests complicate a case, eating up time and money as the parties litigate, not the merits of their claims, but which court is the right court to decide those claims. Complex tests produce appeals and reversals, encourage gamesmanship, and, again, diminish the likelihood that results and settlements will reflect a claim's legal and factual merits. Judicial resources too are at stake. Courts have an independent obligation to determine whether subject-matter jurisdiction exists, even when no party challenges it. So courts benefit from straightforward rules under which they can readily assure themselves of their power to hear a case.

Simple jurisdictional rules also promote greater predictability. Predictability is valuable to corporations making business and investment decisions. Predictability also benefits plaintiffs deciding whether to file suit in a state or federal court.

A "nerve center" approach, which ordinarily equates that "center" with a corporation's headquarters, is simple to apply comparatively speaking. The metaphor of a corporate "brain," while not precise, suggests a single location. By contrast, a corporation's general business activities more often lack a single principal place where they take place. That is to say, the corporation may have several plants, many sales locations, and employees located in many different places. If so, it will not be as easy to determine which of these different business locales is the "principal" or most important "place."

Third, the statute's legislative history, for those who accept it, offers a simplicity-related interpretive benchmark. The Judicial Conference provided an initial version of its proposal that suggested a numerical test. A corporation would be deemed a citizen of the State that accounted for more than half of its gross income. The Conference changed its mind in light of criticism that such a test would prove too complex and impractical to apply. That history suggests that the words "principal place of business" should be interpreted to be no more complex than the initial "half of gross income" test. A "nerve center" test offers such a possibility. A general business activities test does not.

B

We recognize that there may be no perfect test that satisfies all administrative and purposive criteria. We recognize as well that, under the "nerve center" test we adopt today, there will be hard cases. For example, in this era of telecommuting, some corporations may divide their command and coordinating functions among officers who work at several different locations, perhaps communicating over the Internet. That said, our test nonetheless points courts in a single direction, towards the center of overall direction, control, and coordination. Courts do not have to try to weigh corporate functions, assets, or revenues different in kind, one from the other. Our approach provides a sensible test that is relatively easier to apply, not a test that will, in all instances, automatically generate a result.

We also recognize that the use of a "nerve center" test may in some cases produce results that seem to cut against the basic rationale for 28 U.S.C. § 1332. For example, if the bulk of a company's business activities visible to the public take place in New Jersey, while its top officers direct those activities just across the river in New York, the "principal place of business" is New York. One could argue that members of the public in New Jersey would be less likely to be prejudiced against the corporation than persons in New York—yet the corporation will still be entitled to remove a New Jersey state case to federal court. And note too that the same corporation would be unable to remove a New York state case to federal court, despite the New York public's presumed prejudice against the corporation.

We understand that such seeming anomalies will arise. However, in view of the necessity of having a clearer rule, we must accept them. Accepting occasionally counterintuitive results is the price the legal system must pay to avoid overly complex jurisdictional administration while producing the benefits that accompany a more uniform legal system.

The burden of persuasion for establishing diversity jurisdiction, of course, remains on the party asserting it. When challenged on allegations of jurisdictional facts, the parties must support their allegations by competent proof. And when faced with such a challenge, we reject suggestions such as, for example, the one made by petitioner that the mere filing of a form like the Securities and Exchange Commission's Form 10–K listing a corporation's "principal executive offices" would, without more, be sufficient proof to establish a corporation's "nerve center." Such possibilities would readily permit jurisdictional manipulation, thereby subverting a major reason for the insertion of the "principal place of business" language in the diversity statute. Indeed, if the record reveals attempts at manipulation—for example, that the alleged "nerve center" is nothing more than a mail drop box, a bare office with a computer, or the location of an annual executive retreat—the courts should instead take as the "nerve center" the place of actual direction, control, and coordination, in the absence of such manipulation.VI

Petitioner's unchallenged declaration suggests that Hertz's center of direction, control, and coordination, its "nerve center," and its corporate headquarters are one and the same, and they are located in New Jersey, not in California. Because respondents should have a fair opportunity to litigate their case in light of our holding, however, we vacate the Ninth Circuit's judgment and remand the case for further proceedings consistent with this opinion.

It is so ordered.

COMMENTS AND QUESTIONS CONCERNING *HERTZ CORP. V. FRIEND*

1.   Justice Breyer cites three reasons for adopting the "nerve center" definition for a corporation's principal place of business: (1) the language of 28 U.S.C. Section 1332(c)(1); (2) the relative administrative simplicity of such a definition; and (3) the legislative history of Section 1332(c)(1). Which of these reasons do you believe provides the strongest argument in support of the Court's interpretation of "principal place of business"?

2.   Straightforward   jurisdictional   rules   promote   greater predictability. The Court notes several other reasons why "simplicity is a major virtue in a jurisdictional statute."

> Complex jurisdictional tests complicate a case, eating up time and money as the parties litigate, not the merits of their claims, but which court is the right court to decide those claims. Complex tests produce appeals and reversals, encourage gamesmanship, and, again, diminish the likelihood that results and settlements will reflect a claim's legal and factual merits. Judicial resources too are at stake. Courts have an independent obligation to determine whether subject-matter jurisdiction exists, even when no party challenges it. So courts benefit from straightforward rules under which they can readily assure themselves of their power to hear a case.

Do you agree that a simple jurisdictional test saves time and money for litigants, conserves judicial resources, and permits non-litigants to better plan their affairs due to the greater predictability engendered by a simple test?

3.   As discussed in the case that follows, *Swiger v. Allegheny Energy, Inc.*, an unincorporated partnership is considered a citizen of each state in which one of its partners is a citizen. Why are corporations treated

differently from unincorporated entities? Is a plaintiff more likely to be able to obtain federal diversity jurisdiction in an action against General Motors or an unincorporated partnership?

4.   Conversely, if sued in state court, is it more likely that General Motors or the unincorporated partnership will be able to remove the action to federal court? *Friend v. Hertz Corp.* was removed by Hertz from state court under a removal provision in the Class Action Fairness Act of 2005 permitting defendants to remove class actions from state court to presumably more defendant-friendly federal courts. 28 U.S.C. § 1453.

5.   In addition to the definition of corporate citizenship provided in 28 U.S.C. Section 1332(c)(1), Section 1332(c)(2) provides that "the legal representative of the estate of a decedent shall be deemed to be a citizen only of the same State as the decedent, and the legal representative of an infant or incompetent shall be deemed to be a citizen only of the same State as the infant or incompetent." What problems (and possibilities) might arise if the citizenship of the legal representative of an estate, infant, or incompetent person were considered to be the personal citizenship of that representative rather than the citizenship of the estate or person represented? Compare this with the jurisdictional manipulation that occurred when corporations were considered to be citizens of only their state of incorporation and not also their principal places of business.

6.   Plaintiffs must not only establish complete diversity of citizenship, but also show that the jurisdictional minimum has been met. Thus a plaintiff must show that more than $75,000 is "in controversy," which should not be difficult if there are measurable damages that can be asserted. But what if the plaintiff seeks equitable relief or a declaratory judgment? The Supreme Court has concluded: "In actions seeking declaratory or injunctive relief, it is well established that the amount in controversy is measured by the value of the object of the litigation." *Hunt v. Washington State Apple Adver. Comm.*, 432 U.S. 333, 347 (1977).

In most cases this amount will be the same, whether valued from the perspective of the plaintiff (and what it will gain from the relief sought) or the defendant (and what it will cost to comply with the injunctive or declaratory relief sought). When these are not the same, there is some disagreement as to whether the amount in controversy should be viewed from the perspective of the plaintiff or defendant. 14AA C. Wright, A. Miller & E. Cooper, *Federal Practice and Procedure* § 3703 (4th ed. 2011). *But see Glenwood Light & Water Co. v. Mutual Light, Heat & Power Co.*, 239 U.S. 121, 126 (1915) ("[T]he jurisdictional amount is to be tested by the value of the object to be gained by complainant. * * * The relief sought is the protection of that right [to conduct plaintiff's business], now and in the future, and the value of that protection is determinative of the jurisdiction.").

7.   What if the plaintiff brings a federal diversity action alleging more than $75,000, but does not actually recover that amount at trial? The Supreme Court has held that this does not retroactively divest the federal district court of subject-matter jurisdiction. *St. Paul Mercury Indemnity*

Corp. v. Red Cab Co., 303 U.S. 283 (1938). The Court concluded: "[T]he sum claimed by the plaintiff controls if the claim is apparently made in good faith. It must appear to a legal certainty that the claim is really for less than the jurisdictional amount to justify dismissal." 303 U.S. at 288–89. While the recovery of less than the jurisdictional minimum may not divest the federal court of jurisdiction, 28 U.S.C. Section 1332(b) provides that in such situations, the district court may deny costs to the plaintiff and may, in fact, impose court costs on plaintiff.

B. THE CITIZENSHIP OF NON-NATURAL, NON-CORPORATIONS

Swiger v. Allegheny Energy, Inc.
United States Court of Appeals, Third Circuit, 2008
540 F.3d 179

OPINION

■ TASHIMA, CIRCUIT JUDGE:

We must decide whether a federal district court has diversity jurisdiction over a lawsuit involving a partnership where one of its partners is a dual American-British citizen domiciled in a foreign state. The district court held that it lacked diversity jurisdiction over such an entity, and we affirm.

I. APPELLATE JURISDICTION & STANDARD OF REVIEW

We have jurisdiction pursuant to 28 U.S.C. § 1291 over a dismissal for lack of subject-matter jurisdiction, and our review for lack of subject matter jurisdiction is plenary.

II. FACTUAL AND PROCEDURAL BACKGROUND

Plaintiff Clifton G. Swiger sued Allegheny Energy, Inc., Allegheny Energy Supply Co., LLC, Allegheny Energy Services Corp., and Morgan, Lewis & Bockius LLP ("Morgan Lewis"), (collectively "Defendants"), on several state law claims, including abuse of process, wrongful use of civil proceedings, invasion of privacy, and wrongful discharge, in the Eastern District of Pennsylvania based upon diversity jurisdiction.

Morgan Lewis, joined by the other Defendants, moved to dismiss the complaint pursuant to Federal Rule of Civil Procedure 12(b)(1), on the ground that complete diversity between the parties was lacking. Morgan Lewis is a partnership that, at the time of the filing of the lawsuit, had among its partners, Charles Lubar, a dual United States and United Kingdom citizen domiciled in the United Kingdom. The district court dismissed the case for lack of jurisdiction, concluding that "[g]iven that for diversity purposes, the court must consult the citizenship of *all* of the members of an artificial entity such as a general or limited partnership and because a United States citizen who is not domiciled in one of the United States cannot invoke diversity jurisdiction in one particular state, we must conclude that we are without jurisdiction to act in this matter." Swiger timely appealed.

III. ANALYSIS

Swiger argues that the district court erred in holding that it lacked diversity jurisdiction because, according to Swiger, a single partner who is not a citizen of a state does not render the entire partnership stateless for diversity purposes. * * * For the reasons set forth below, we * * * hold that if a partner of a partnership is a United States citizen permanently living abroad, there can be no diversity of jurisdiction over the partnership because the partner is neither a citizen of a state nor a citizen of a foreign country.

Swiger also argues that even if the stateless partner destroys diversity, the district court nevertheless had alienage jurisdiction because Lubar, as a dual citizen of the United States and the United Kingdom, is a citizen or subject of a foreign state. This argument, however, is foreclosed by our recent decision in *Frett-Smith*, 511 F.3d at 400, in which we held that, for purposes of diversity jurisdiction, we consider only the American citizenship of a dual American-foreign national. We consider each of Swiger's arguments in turn.

A.   Diversity Jurisdiction and the "Stateless" Partner

Under 28 U.S.C. 1332(a):

> district courts . . . have original jurisdiction of all civil actions where the matter in controversy exceeds the sum or value of $75,000, exclusive of interest and costs, and is between—(1) citizens of different States; (2) citizens of a State and citizens or subjects of a foreign state; (3) citizens of different States and in which citizens or subjects of a foreign state are additional parties; and (4) a foreign state, defined in section 1603(a) of this title, as plaintiff and citizens of a State or of different States.

A natural person is deemed to be a citizen of the state where she is domiciled. A corporation is a citizen both of the state where it is incorporated and of the state where it has its principal place of business. 28 U.S.C. § 1332(c).

Partnerships and other unincorporated associations, however, unlike corporations, are not considered "citizens" as that term is used in the diversity statute. *See Carden v. Arkoma Assocs.*, 494 U.S. 185, 187–92 (1990) (holding that a limited partnership is not a citizen under the jurisdictional statute).

Given that partnerships are not citizens for diversity purposes, the Supreme Court has long applied the rule of *Chapman v. Barney*: that courts are to look to the citizenship of all the partners (or members of other unincorporated associations) to determine whether the federal district court has diversity jurisdiction. *See* 13B Charles Alan Wright et al., *Federal Practice & Procedure* § 3630 (2d ed. 1984) ("[W]henever a partnership, a limited partnership . . . , a joint venture, a joint stock company, a labor union, a religious or charitable organization, a governing board of an unincorporated institution, or a similar association brings suit or is sued in a federal court, the actual citizenship of each of its members must be considered in determining whether diversity jurisdiction exists."). * * *

Further, in the context of partnerships, the complete diversity requirement demands that all partners be diverse from all parties on the opposing side. * * *

Partnerships which have American partners living abroad pose a special problem. "In order to be a citizen of a State within the meaning of the diversity statute, a natural person must be both a citizen of the United States and be domiciled within the State." *Newman-Green, Inc. v. Alfonzo-Larrain*, 490 U.S. 826, 828 (1989). An American citizen domiciled abroad, while being a citizen of the United States is, of course, not domiciled in a particular state, and therefore such a person is "stateless" for purposes of diversity jurisdiction. Thus, American citizens living abroad cannot be sued (or sue) in federal court based on diversity jurisdiction as they are neither "citizens of a State," see 28 U.S.C. § 1332(a)(1), nor "citizens or subjects of a foreign state," *see id.* § 1332(a)(2).

Putting these principles together, that is, that the citizenship of the individual partners must be shown to be wholly diverse from that of the opposing party (or those of the opposing parties) and that American citizens living abroad cannot sue (or be sued) in federal court based on diversity jurisdiction, our sister circuits and other federal courts have concluded that if a partnership has among its partners any American citizen who is domiciled abroad, the partnership cannot sue (or be sued) in federal court based upon diversity jurisdiction.

Swiger, however, asks us to disregard these cases and create an exception to the *Chapman* tradition. He argues that we should ignore Lubar's lack of state citizenship and focus only on the partners who are citizens of a state. Morgan Lewis has American partners domiciled in, among other states, Pennsylvania, New York, and California; therefore, Morgan Lewis, according to Swiger, is a citizen of Pennsylvania, New York, California, and so on. Although Morgan Lewis has a stateless partner, Swiger contends that the partnership can hardly be characterized as "stateless"; indeed, under this view, Morgan Lewis is quite "stateful." That is, according to Swiger, one party, Morgan Lewis, is a citizen of Pennsylvania, New York, and California, and so on, and the other party, Swiger, is a citizen of West Virginia, ipso facto, the parties are "citizens of different States."

We cannot agree. First, the Supreme Court has explicitly held, and consistently stated, as we have already noted, that a partnership is not a "citizen" for purpose of diversity jurisdiction. Instead, for purposes of diversity jurisdiction, a partnership's citizenship as a party is determined by reference to all partners, and all partners must be diverse from all parties on the opposing side. Second, Morgan Lewis, as an entity, is just as "stateless" as it is "stateful": Morgan Lewis is not an American citizen, and it "has no domicile in any state." But rather than treating partnerships as stateless, the *Chapman* rule determines the partnership's citizenship for purposes of diversity by referring to the citizenship of each partner. The rule of *Chapman* is a legal construct that allows a real legal entity, though a non-citizen, to sue and be sued in federal court based upon diversity by looking through the partnership to the citizenship of each partner.

Because Morgan Lewis has a stateless partner, and thus, all partners of Morgan Lewis are not diverse from all parties on the opposing side, the district court correctly held that it lacked diversity jurisdiction over this action.

B. Alienage Jurisdiction

Swiger argues that even if jurisdiction based on diversity of state citizenship is lacking, the district court nevertheless had diversity jurisdiction under 28 U.S.C. § 1332(a)(2), because Lubar, as a dual citizen of the United States and the United Kingdom would still be a "citizen[ ] or subject[ ] of a foreign state," and as such, Lubar would be diverse from Swiger within the meaning of § 1332(a)(2). That is, complete diversity would exist because Swiger is a citizen of West Virginia and Lubar is a citizen of the United Kingdom. After this appeal was briefed, but before oral argument, we decided this question in *Frett-Smith*, in which we held "that for purposes of diversity jurisdiction, only the American nationality of a dual national is recognized." 511 F.3d at 400. Because Lubar is a United States citizen, any reliance on § 1332(a)(2)'s alienage jurisdiction would be in error. Thus, "[o]nly if [Lubar] was domiciled in a particular state of the United States at the time the suit was filed, and that state was diverse from that of [Swiger], would subject-matter jurisdiction be present" as against Morgan Lewis. *Id.*

IV. CONCLUSION

Whenever a partnership (or other unincorporated association) brings suit or is sued in a federal court, the citizenship of each of its partners (or members) must be considered in determining whether diversity jurisdiction exists, and all partners (or members) must be diverse from all parties on the opposing side. Lubar, a Morgan Lewis partner and American citizen domiciled abroad, is "stateless" for purposes of diversity jurisdiction. Because Lubar, as a stateless person, cannot sue or be sued in federal court based upon diversity jurisdiction, neither can Morgan Lewis. The judgment of the district court is AFFIRMED.

■ McKEE, CIRCUIT JUDGE, concurring in the judgment.

I agree that the authority relied upon by my colleagues strongly suggests the analysis the lead opinion has adopted and the result my colleagues have reached. I am therefore reluctant to disagree with that conclusion even though I do not think that the result we reach today is necessarily compelled by precedent of this court or the Supreme Court. I am, in fact, concerned that our decision today unnecessarily extends two conventions of diversity jurisprudence and thereby inappropriately circumscribes that jurisdiction. I think my colleagues would agree that it would be more logical to treat "stateless" partners in situations like this as "jurisdictional zeroes," rather than as citizens of the plaintiff's state; but we are not writing on a blank slate.

I realize, of course, that it is not the province of this or any other lower court to undermine the *Carden* rule or the "stateless person" doctrine discussed in the lead opinion. Nevertheless, applying the *Carden* rule and "stateless person" doctrine here results in a ruling that is inconsistent with both reality and common sense. Accordingly, although I concur in the result, I hope that Congress will one day see fit to clarify that our diversity jurisdiction does extend to this situation.

I.

Article III of the Constitution provides, in pertinent part, that "[t]he judicial Power shall extend to ... Controversies ... between Citizens of different States." In its current form, the diversity statute provides that "[t]he district courts shall have original jurisdiction of all civil actions where the matter in controversy exceeds ... $75,000 ... and is between ... citizens of different States. . . ." 28 U.S.C. § 1332(a). In *Chapman v. Barney*, 129 U.S. 677 (1889), the Supreme Court established that the "citizenship" of an unincorporated association (such as a partnership) is defined by the citizenship of its individual members. Unincorporated associations are thus treated differently than corporations which, under a 1958 amendment to the diversity statute, are considered to be citizens of their state of incorporation and of their primary places of business. See 28 U.S.C. § 1332(c)(1).

The Supreme Court has recognized that the disparate treatment of partnerships and corporations may not conform with modern business realities, but the Court has rejected invitations to reinterpret the rule. Indeed, in *Carden*, the Court stated that this rule "can validly be characterized as technical, precedent-bound, and unresponsive to policy considerations raised by the changing realities of business organization." 494 U.S. at 196. Yet, the Court viewed the 1958 amendment to 28 U.S.C. § 1332(c) as evidence of Congress' tacit approval of the rule regarding citizenship of associations, as "[n]o provision was made for the treatment of artificial entities other than corporations." Id. at 196–97. The Court concluded that the limited scope of the amendment meant that Congress was content with the existing method of determining the citizenship of unincorporated associations such as partnerships. Accordingly, the Court declared that any change to the *Carden* rule must come from Congress, as "[s]uch accommodation is not only performed more legitimately by Congress than by courts, but it is performed more intelligently by legislation than by interpretation of the statutory word 'citizen.'" *Id.*

Nevertheless, despite its apparent relevance to this jurisdictional dispute, *Carden* does not definitively answer the specific question here. In *Carden*, an Arizona limited partnership brought a diversity action against two Louisiana citizens. The partnership asserted that complete diversity was satisfied because none of its general partners shared the same citizenship as any adverse party. The citizenship of its limited partners, it argued, was irrelevant to the presence of diversity jurisdiction. The Court rejected that position and held that complete diversity was lacking because one of the limited partners was, like the defendants, a citizen of Louisiana, thus precluding complete diversity. The Court held that the citizenship of partnerships is determined by the citizenship of all of its partners, not just the general partners.

* * *

In contrast to *Carden* * * *, no member of Morgan Lewis (nor any of the other defendants) shares the citizenship of the plaintiff in this case. Swiger is a citizen of West Virginia. Morgan Lewis is a limited liability partnership registered in Pennsylvania with its principal place of business in Philadelphia, Pennsylvania. In addition to its stateless partner, Lubar, Morgan Lewis has partners who are citizens of Pennsylvania, New York and California. It is undisputed that no Morgan Lewis partner is a citizen of West Virginia. Ideally, that should be the beginning and end of our jurisdictional inquiry.

* * *

III.

It is certainly not our job to create law. We are, however, charged with filling gaps in statutes when unforeseen circumstances create ambiguities. For example, Congress has declared that a corporation is "deemed to be a citizen of any State by which it has been incorporated and of the State where it has its principal place of business." 28 U.S.C. § 1332(c)(1). However, that statute does not determine if a court has jurisdiction when a U.S. corporation has its principal place of business outside of the United States, or has no principal place of business at all. When presented with this situation, courts have not concluded that such a corporation is "stateless" and thereby beyond the reach of diversity jurisdiction. Rather, courts have held that the citizenship of the corporation defaults to the only state citizenship that can be determined-that of the state of incorporation.

Likewise, if partners in a partnership are citizens of several states, but one (or more) partner is not a citizen of any state, there is no reason to necessarily conclude that subject-matter jurisdiction is defeated. Thus, were we free to address the issue of Lubar's citizenship on a clean slate, I hope that we would readily concede that it adds nothing to the diversity equation and that there is no reason to allow it to defeat diversity jurisdiction. Lubar's residence in England makes him a jurisdictional nullity, and his citizenship should be treated that way for purposes of determining subject-matter jurisdiction. *Carden* and *Grupo Dataflux* [*v. Atlas Global Group, L.P.*, 541 U.S. 567 (2004),] are not necessarily to the contrary. They merely hold that it is the citizenship of all the members of a partnership that must be examined, they say nothing about the lack of a partner's citizenship.

IV.

The traditional explanation of the purpose of diversity jurisdiction is "the fear that state courts would be prejudiced against out-of-state litigants." See 13B Charles Alan Wright and Arthur R. Miller, *Federal Practice and Procedure* § 3601 (2008). Morgan Lewis is a nationally prominent law firm whose main office is in Philadelphia, Pennsylvania. It is certainly not unreasonable to believe that local bias might operate in state court in favor of a litigant that is as prominent and influential in the local community as Morgan Lewis. That is the rationale for allowing Swiger to sue in federal court—assuming complete diversity. The rationale is not undermined one iota merely because one of Morgan Lewis' many hundreds of partners has been residing in England and will apparently continue to reside there indefinitely. So long as none of Morgan Lewis' partners is a citizen of Swiger's home state of West Virginia, the purpose of diversity jurisdiction is fully served, and Swiger should be permitted to test the merits of his claim in a federal forum. Lubar's lack of citizenship in any state should not be the jurisdictional equivalent of citizenship in the same state as Swiger. Accordingly, we should be able to conclude that this suit presents "two adverse parties [who] are not co-citizens." *Grupo Dataflux*, 541 U.S. at 579.

V.

According to one 2004 survey, roughly 10,000 of the 110,000 lawyers at the top 250 U.S. firms work overseas. Michael D. Goldhaber & Carlyn Kolker, *Supersonic Lawyers, American Lawyer* (May 2004). As business ventures and legal relationships become more global in depth and breadth, the situation we face today will become increasingly common. When the expanding business universe and shrinking globe are considered along with the growing population of expatriates and the apparently increasing popularity of non-corporate business forms, courts will no doubt be confronted with applying the *Carden* rule and the "stateless" person doctrine in this context with increasing regularity. Unless Congress takes up the problem and clarifies the meaning of 28 U.S.C. 1332(a), persons suing large partnerships will increasingly be barred from bringing their claim in federal court. Hopefully, Congress will address this situation and put the *Carden* genie back in its jurisdictional bottle. However, that day is not yet here, and I therefore concur in this judgment.

COMMENTS AND QUESTIONS CONCERNING
SWIGER V. ALLEGHENY ENERGY, INC.

1.   The court notes "A natural person is deemed to be a citizen of the state where she is domiciled." As the United States Court of Appeals for the Fifth Circuit stated in *Mas v. Perry*, 489 F.2d 1396, 1399 (5th Cir. 1974):

> To be a citizen of a State within the meaning of section 1332, a natural person must be both a citizen of the United States and a domiciliary of that State. For diversity purposes, citizenship means domicile; mere residence in the State is not sufficient.
>
> A person's domicile is the place of "his true, fixed, and permanent home and principal establishment, and to which he has the intention of returning whenever he is absent therefrom. . . ." *Stine v. Moore*, 5 Cir., 1954, 213 F.2d 446, 448. A change of domicile may be effected only by a combination of two elements: (a) taking up residence in a different domicile with (b) the intention to remain there.

2.   Assume that John, a citizen of Ohio, wants to sue Sally, also a citizen of Ohio, for a tort that allegedly resulted in damages of more than $75,000.

(a)   Would the federal courts have subject-matter jurisdiction over an action by John if he moved to Indiana before filing the action?

(b)   What would have to be true about John's move to Indiana?

(c)   The relevant time for determining subject-matter jurisdiction, citizenship, and diversity of citizenship is when the complaint is filed. *Dole Food Co. v. Patrickson*, 538 U.S. 468, 478 (2003); *Wisconsin Dept. of Corrections v. Schacht*, 524 U.S. 381, 390–91 (1998), and jurisdiction is unaffected by subsequent changes in the citizenship of the parties. *Grupo Dataflux v. Atlas Global Group, L.P.*, 541 U.S. 567, 574–77 (2004); *Smith v. Sperling*, 354 U.S. 91, 93 n. 1 (1957). Can you see any advantages to such a rule, in effect taking a "snapshot" of the parties citizenship at the time the complaint is filed?

3.   Assume that Clifton Swiger, a citizen of West Virginia, brings an action in federal district court seeking more than $75,000 for wrongful discharge against a partnership with several hundred partners.

(a)   Would the federal district court have subject-matter jurisdiction to hear this action if all the partners were citizens of a state other than West Virginia?

(b)   What if there were no West Virginia citizens among the firm's partners, but one of the partners was a citizen of the United

Kingdom. Would a federal district court have jurisdiction to hear this action?

(c)   What if there were no West Virginia partners, but one of the partners was a dual citizen of the United States and the United Kingdom, domiciled in Pennsylvania?

(d)   What if there were no West Virginia partners, but one of the partners was a dual citizen of the United States and the United Kingdom, domiciled in the United Kingdom? In terms of the purposes of federal diversity jurisdiction, how does this case differ from the prior hypotheticals?

4.   In his concurrence, Judge McKee quotes from the Supreme Court's opinion in *Carden v. Arkoma Associates* as follows: "Accordingly, the Court declared that any change to the *Carden* rule must come from Congress, as '[s]uch accommodation is not only performed more legitimately by Congress than by courts, but it is performed more intelligently by legislation than by interpretation of the statutory word "citizen." ' " Do you agree? How likely is it that Congress will act to address this situation?

5.   If you were Charles Lubar, would you prefer to be considered a "stateless person," a "jurisdictional zero," or a "jurisdictional nullity"?

IV. SUPPLEMENTAL JURISDICTION

As we have seen, Congress must confer the Article III judicial power upon federal courts for them to exercise subject-matter jurisdiction. Nevertheless, federal courts historically have exercised jurisdiction over claims that, while not falling within their congressionally-delineated jurisdiction, are closely related to claims over which the courts do have jurisdiction under statutes such as 28 U.S.C. §§ 1331 or 1332. The Supreme Court historically considered the power of the federal district courts to exercise power over the following types of claims that fall outside specific statutory grants of subject-matter jurisdiction:

- **ancillary claims** (state-law claims asserted by defendants or others brought involuntarily into a civil action, such as compulsory counterclaims, crossclaims, and third-party claims);

- **pendent claims** (state claims that arise from the same "common nucleus of operative fact" as a federal claim asserted in the complaint); and

- **pendent-party claims** (state claims arising from the same "common nucleus of operative fact" as a federal claim asserted in the complaint, but which require subject-matter jurisdiction over a person who was not a party to the original civil action).

Historically, the Supreme Court upheld the subject-matter jurisdiction of federal district courts over **ancillary** claims such as compulsory counterclaims, crossclaims, and third-party claims. *Owen Equipment & Erection Co. v. Kroger*, 437 U.S. 365, 375 n.18 (1978); *Moore v. New York Cotton Exchange*, 270 U.S. 593 (1926).

In addition to such ancillary jurisdiction, the Court in *United Mine Workers v. Gibbs*, 383 U.S. 715, 725 (1966), recognized **pendent claim** jurisdiction over claims arising from the same "common nucleus of operative fact" as a federal claim over which the district court could exercise federal subject-matter jurisdiction. Thus a federal court exercising Section 1331 subject-matter jurisdiction over a claim arising under federal law also could hear a state-law claim factually related to the federal claim.

However, the Supreme Court did not recognize the subject-matter jurisdiction of federal district courts over claims involving those not parties to the original civil action—even when those **pendent-party claims** arose from the same "common nucleus of operative fact" as a federal claim asserted in the complaint. *Finley v. United States*, 490 U.S. 545 (1989).

In order to understand the operation of non-statutory subject-matter jurisdiction, consider the following examples. These examples are based on cases decided by the United States Supreme Court, and all but the first case are discussed in *Exxon Mobil Corp. v. Allapattah*, which follows.

(A) Plaintiff brings a federal antitrust claim in federal district court, alleging that the defendant commodity exchange and defendant market reporting service entered into an illegal contract under which only those who trade on the commodity exchange are provided reports of selling prices on the exchange. In their answers, defendants admit they have refused to provide market data to plaintiff and plead a counterclaim alleging that plaintiff illegally stole this market data. There is no diversity between the parties and no federal question presented by the counterclaim. Can the federal court entertain subject-matter jurisdiction over the counterclaim? *See Moore v. New York Cotton Exchange*, 270 U.S. 593 (1926).

(B) Plaintiff brings an action in federal court, alleging both a violation of federal labor law and a claim based on state law for unlawful interference with plaintiff's contract rights. Both claims arise from the same series of alleged actions by the defendant labor union. Assuming that it has federal-question jurisdiction over the federal claim, can the court also exercise subject-matter jurisdiction over the state-law claim? *See United Mine Workers v. Gibbs*, 383 U.S. 715 (1966).

(C) Plaintiff brings a federal civil rights claim against her supervisor, claiming that her dismissal as an employee violated her federal civil rights. In addition, she brings a claim challenging her dismissal against the county for which she had worked, even though the county is not subject to suit under federal civil rights laws and there is no diversity of citizenship. Assuming that the federal district court in which the action is filed can exercise federal-question subject-matter jurisdiction over plaintiff's claim against her supervisor, can it also exercise subject-matter jurisdiction over the state-law claim against the county? *See Aldinger v. Howard,* 427 U.S. 1 (1976).

(D) Plaintiff, a citizen of Kansas, brings a class action in federal court, alleging that defendant, a citizen of New York, has violated state consumer protection laws. Plaintiff alleges damages of $100,000, but no other member of the class that she seeks to certify alleges damages of more than $75,000. Assuming that the federal court can exercise diversity jurisdiction over plaintiff's individual claim, can the court also exercise subject-matter jurisdiction over the claims of the other class members? *See Zahn v. International Paper Co.* 414 U.S. 291 (1973); *Exxon Mobil Corp. v. Allapattah Services, Inc.,* 545 U.S. 546 (2005).

As you consider these cases and supplemental jurisdiction more generally, think about whether the Federal Rules of Civil Procedure provide a basis for the assertion of the above claims. Don't Rules 13(a), 13(g), and 14(a) provide for compulsory counterclaims, crossclaims, and third-party claims? Doesn't Rule 18(a) permit a "party asserting a claim * * * [to] join, as independent or alternative claims, as many claims as it has against an opposing party"?

Yes, they do, but the Rules Enabling Act only authorizes the Supreme Court to "prescribe general rules of practice and procedure," 28 U.S.C. § 2072(a), and "federal courts, in adopting rules, [are] not free to extend or restrict the jurisdiction conferred by a statute." *Willy v. Coastal Corp.,* 503 U.S. 131, 135 (1992). As Rule 82 of the Federal Rules of Civil Procedure explicitly provides: "These rules do not extend or limit the jurisdiction of the district courts or the venue of actions in those courts." In order for a federal district court to consider a claim, there must be both (1) a Federal Rule of Civil Procedure permitting the assertion of that claim and (2) an independent jurisdictional basis, usually a statute such as 28 U.S.C. §§ 1331 or 1332, authorizing the court to hear that claim.

In an effort to codify and clarify the doctrines of pendent and ancillary subject-matter jurisdiction, Congress enacted 28 U.S.C. § 1367 in 1990. Section 1367(a) provides:

Except as provided in subsections (b) and (c) or as expressly provided otherwise by Federal statute, in any civil action of which the district courts have original jurisdiction, the district courts shall have supplemental jurisdiction over all other claims that are so related to claims in the action within such original jurisdiction that they form part of the same case or controversy under Article III of the United States Constitution. Such supplemental jurisdiction shall include claims that involve the joinder or intervention of additional parties.

As you read the next case, consider whether Section 1367 did more than codify the doctrines of ancillary and pendent jurisdiction as they had been recognized previously by the Supreme Court. To what extent did Congress extend district court jurisdiction through its enactment of Section 1367?

Exxon Mobil Corporation v. Allapattah Services, Inc.

Supreme Court of the United States, 2005
545 U.S. 546

OPINION

■ JUSTICE KENNEDY delivered the opinion of the Court.

These consolidated cases present the question whether a federal court in a diversity action may exercise supplemental jurisdiction over additional plaintiffs whose claims do not satisfy the minimum amount-in-controversy requirement, provided the claims are part of the same case or controversy as the claims of plaintiffs who do allege a sufficient amount in controversy. Our decision turns on the correct interpretation of 28 U.S.C. § 1367. The question has divided the Courts of Appeals, and we granted certiorari to resolve the conflict.

We hold that, where the other elements of jurisdiction are present and at least one named plaintiff in the action satisfies the amount-in-controversy requirement, § 1367 does authorize supplemental jurisdiction over the claims of other plaintiffs in the same Article III case or controversy, even if those claims are for less than the jurisdictional amount specified in the statute setting forth the requirements for diversity jurisdiction. * * *

I

In 1991, about 10,000 Exxon dealers filed a class-action suit against the Exxon Corporation in the United States District Court for the Northern District of Florida. The dealers alleged an intentional and systematic scheme by Exxon under which they were overcharged for fuel purchased from Exxon. The plaintiffs invoked the District Court's § 1332(a) diversity jurisdiction. After a unanimous jury verdict in favor of the plaintiffs, the District Court certified the case for interlocutory review, asking whether it had properly exercised § 1367 supplemental jurisdiction over the claims of class members who did not meet the jurisdictional minimum amount in controversy.

* * *

In the other case now before us the Court of Appeals for the First Circuit took a different position on the meaning of § 1367(a). In that case, a 9-year-old girl sued Star-Kist in a diversity action in the United States District Court for the District of Puerto Rico, seeking damages for unusually severe injuries she received when she sliced her finger on a tuna can. Her family joined in the suit, seeking damages for emotional distress and certain medical expenses. The District Court granted summary judgment to Star-Kist, finding that none of the plaintiffs met the minimum amount-in-controversy requirement. The Court of Appeals for the First Circuit, however, ruled that the injured girl, but not her family members, had made allegations of damages in the requisite amount.

* * *

II

A

The district courts of the United States, as we have said many times, are "courts of limited jurisdiction. They possess only that power authorized by Constitution and statute," *Kokkonen v. Guardian Life Ins. Co. of America*, 511 U.S. 375, 377 (1994). In order to provide a federal forum for plaintiffs who seek to vindicate federal rights, Congress has conferred on the district courts original jurisdiction in federal-question cases—civil actions that arise under the Constitution, laws, or treaties of the United States. 28 U.S.C. § 1331. In order to provide a neutral forum for what have come to be known as diversity cases, Congress also has granted district courts original jurisdiction in civil actions between citizens of different States, between U.S. citizens and foreign citizens, or by foreign states against U.S. citizens. § 1332. To ensure that diversity jurisdiction does not flood the federal courts with minor disputes, § 1332(a) requires that the matter in controversy in a diversity case exceed a specified amount, currently $75,000.

Although the district courts may not exercise jurisdiction absent a statutory basis, it is well established—in certain classes of cases—that, once a court has original jurisdiction over some claims in the action, it may exercise supplemental jurisdiction over additional claims that are part of the same case or controversy. The leading modern case for this principle is *Mine Workers v. Gibbs*, 383 U.S. 715 (1966). In *Gibbs*, the plaintiff alleged the defendant's conduct violated both federal and state law. The District Court, *Gibbs* held, had original jurisdiction over the action based on the federal claims. *Gibbs* confirmed that the District Court had the additional power (though not the obligation) to exercise supplemental jurisdiction over related state claims that arose from the same Article III case or controversy.

As we later noted, the decision allowing jurisdiction over pendent state claims in *Gibbs* did not mention, let alone come to grips with, the text of the jurisdictional statutes and the bedrock principle that federal courts have no jurisdiction without statutory authorization. *Finley v. United States*, 490 U.S. 545, 548 (1989). In *Finley*, we nonetheless reaffirmed and rationalized *Gibbs* and its progeny by inferring from it the interpretive principle that, in cases involving supplemental jurisdiction over additional claims between parties properly in federal court, the jurisdictional statutes should be read broadly, on the assumption that in this context Congress intended to authorize courts to exercise their full Article III power to dispose of an " 'entire action before the court [which] comprises but one constitutional "case." ' " 490 U.S., at 549 (quoting *Gibbs*, *supra*, at 725).

We have not, however, applied *Gibbs'* expansive interpretive approach to other aspects of the jurisdictional statutes. For instance, we have consistently interpreted § 1332 as requiring complete diversity: In a case with multiple plaintiffs and multiple defendants, the presence in the action of a single plaintiff from the same State as a single defendant deprives the district court of original diversity jurisdiction over the entire action. The complete diversity requirement is not mandated by the Constitution or by the plain text of § 1332(a). The Court, nonetheless, has adhered to the complete diversity rule in light of the purpose of the diversity requirement, which is to provide a federal forum for important disputes where state courts might favor, or be perceived as favoring, home-state litigants. The presence of parties from the same State on both sides of a case dispels this concern, eliminating a principal reason for conferring § 1332 jurisdiction over any of the claims in the action. The specific purpose of the complete diversity rule explains both why we have not adopted *Gibbs'* expansive interpretive approach to this aspect of the jurisdictional statute and why *Gibbs* does not undermine the complete diversity rule. In order for a federal court to invoke supplemental jurisdiction under *Gibbs*, it must first have original jurisdiction over at least one claim in the action. Incomplete diversity destroys original jurisdiction with respect to all claims, so there is nothing to which supplemental jurisdiction can adhere.

In contrast to the diversity requirement, most of the other statutory prerequisites for federal jurisdiction, including the federal-question and amount-in-controversy requirements, can be analyzed claim by claim. True, it does not follow by necessity from this that a district court has authority to exercise supplemental jurisdiction over all claims provided there is original jurisdiction over just one. Before the enactment of § 1367, the Court declined in contexts other than the pendent-claim instance to follow *Gibbs'* expansive approach to interpretation of the jurisdictional statutes. The Court took a more restrictive view of the proper interpretation of these statutes in so-called pendent-party cases involving supplemental jurisdiction over claims involving additional parties—plaintiffs or defendants—where the district courts would lack original jurisdiction over claims by each of the parties standing alone.

Thus, with respect to plaintiff-specific jurisdictional requirements, the Court held in *Clark v. Paul Gray, Inc.*, 306 U.S. 583 (1939), that every plaintiff must separately satisfy the amount-in-controversy requirement. Though *Clark* was a federal-question case, at that time federal-question jurisdiction had an amount-in-controversy requirement analogous to the amount-in-controversy requirement for diversity cases. * * * The Court reaffirmed this rule, in the context of a class action brought invoking § 1332(a) diversity jurisdiction, in *Zahn v. International Paper Co.*, 414 U.S. 291 (1973). It follows "inescapably" from *Clark*, the Court held in *Zahn*, that "any plaintiff without the jurisdictional amount must be dismissed from the case, even though others allege jurisdictionally sufficient claims." 414 U.S., at 300.

The Court took a similar approach with respect to supplemental jurisdiction over claims against additional defendants that fall outside the district courts' original jurisdiction. In *Aldinger v. Howard*, 427 U.S. 1 (1976), the plaintiff brought a 42 U.S.C. § 1983 action against county officials in District Court pursuant to the statutory grant of jurisdiction in 28 U.S.C. § 1343(3). The plaintiff further alleged the court had supplemental jurisdiction over her related state-law claims against the county, even though the county was not suable under § 1983 and so was not subject to § 1343(3)'s original jurisdiction. The Court held that supplemental jurisdiction could not be exercised because Congress, in enacting § 1343(3), had declined (albeit implicitly) to extend federal jurisdiction over any party who could not be sued under the federal civil rights statutes. "Before it can be concluded that [supplemental] jurisdiction [over additional parties] exists," *Aldinger* held, "a federal court must satisfy itself not only that Art[icle] III permits it, but that Congress in the statutes conferring jurisdiction has not expressly or by implication negated its existence." *Id.*, at 18.

In *Finley v. United States*, 490 U.S. 545 (1989), we confronted a similar issue in a different statutory context. The plaintiff in *Finley* brought a Federal Tort Claims Act negligence suit against the Federal Aviation Administration in District Court, which had original jurisdiction under § 1346(b). The plaintiff tried to add related claims against other defendants, invoking the District Court's supplemental jurisdiction over so-called pendent parties. We held that the District Court lacked a sufficient statutory basis for exercising supplemental jurisdiction over these claims. Relying primarily on *Zahn*, *Aldinger*, and [*Owen Equipment & Erection Co. v.*]

Kroger, [437 U.S. 365 (1978),] we held in *Finley* that "a grant of jurisdiction over claims involving particular parties does not itself confer jurisdiction over additional claims by or against different parties." 490 U.S., at 556. While *Finley* did not "limit or impair" *Gibbs'* liberal approach to interpreting the jurisdictional statutes in the context of supplemental jurisdiction over additional claims involving the same parties, 490 U.S., at 556, *Finley* nevertheless declined to extend that interpretive assumption to claims involving additional parties. *Finley* held that in the context of parties, in contrast to claims, "we will not assume that the full constitutional power has been congressionally authorized, and will not read jurisdictional statutes broadly." *Id.*, at 549.

As the jurisdictional statutes existed in 1989, then, here is how matters stood: First, the diversity requirement in § 1332(a) required complete diversity; absent complete diversity, the district court lacked original jurisdiction over all of the claims in the action. Second, if the district court had original jurisdiction over at least one claim, the jurisdictional statutes implicitly authorized supplemental jurisdiction over all other claims between the same parties arising out of the same Article III case or controversy. Third, even when the district court had original jurisdiction over one or more claims between particular parties, the jurisdictional statutes did not authorize supplemental jurisdiction over additional claims involving other parties.

B

In *Finley* we emphasized that "[w]hatever we say regarding the scope of jurisdiction conferred by a particular statute can of course be changed by Congress." 490 U.S., at 556. In 1990, Congress accepted the invitation. It passed the Judicial Improvements Act, 104 Stat. 5089, which enacted § 1367, the provision which controls these cases.

Section 1367 provides, in relevant part:

"(a) Except as provided in subsections (b) and (c) or as expressly provided otherwise by Federal statute, in any civil action of which the district courts have original jurisdiction, the district courts shall have supplemental jurisdiction over all other claims that are so related to claims in the action within such original jurisdiction that they form part of the same case or controversy under Article III of the United States Constitution. Such supplemental jurisdiction shall include claims that involve the joinder or intervention of additional parties.

"(b) In any civil action of which the district courts have original jurisdiction founded solely on section 1332 of this title, the district courts shall not have supplemental jurisdiction under subsection (a) over claims by plaintiffs against persons made parties under Rule 14, 19, 20, or 24 of the Federal Rules of Civil Procedure, or over claims by persons proposed to be joined as plaintiffs under Rule 19 of such rules, or seeking to intervene as plaintiffs under Rule 24 of such rules, when exercising supplemental jurisdiction over such claims would be inconsistent with the jurisdictional requirements of section 1332."

All parties to this litigation and all courts to consider the question agree that § 1367 overturned the result in *Finley*. There is no warrant, however, for assuming that § 1367 did no more than to overrule *Finley* and otherwise to codify the existing state of the law of supplemental jurisdiction. * * * In order to determine the scope of supplemental jurisdiction authorized by § 1367, then, we must examine the statute's text in light of context, structure, and related statutory provisions.

Section 1367(a) is a broad grant of supplemental jurisdiction over other claims within the same case or controversy, as long as the action is one in which the district courts would have original jurisdiction. The last sentence of § 1367(a) makes it clear that the grant of supplemental jurisdiction extends to claims involving joinder or intervention of additional parties. The single question before us, therefore, is whether a diversity case in which the claims of some plaintiffs satisfy the amount-in-controversy requirement, but the claims of other plaintiffs do not, presents a "civil action of which the district courts have original jurisdiction." * * *

We now conclude the answer must be yes. When the well-pleaded complaint contains at least one claim that satisfies the amount-in-controversy requirement, and there are no other relevant jurisdictional defects, the district court, beyond all question, has original jurisdiction over that claim. The presence of other claims in the complaint, over which the district court may lack original jurisdiction, is of no moment. If the court has original jurisdiction over a single claim in the complaint, it has original jurisdiction over a "civil action" within the meaning of § 1367(a), even if the civil action over which it has jurisdiction comprises fewer claims than were included in the complaint. Once the court determines it has original jurisdiction over the civil action, it can turn to the question whether it has a constitutional and statutory basis for exercising supplemental jurisdiction over the other claims in the action.

Section 1367(a) commences with the direction that §§ 1367(b) and (c), or other relevant statutes, may provide specific exceptions, but otherwise § 1367(a) is a broad jurisdictional grant, with no distinction drawn between pendent-claim and pendent-party cases. In fact, the last sentence of § 1367(a) makes clear that the provision grants supplemental jurisdiction over claims involving joinder or intervention of additional parties. The terms of § 1367 do not acknowledge any distinction between pendent jurisdiction and the doctrine of so-called ancillary jurisdiction. Though the doctrines of pendent and ancillary jurisdiction developed separately as a historical matter, the Court has recognized that the doctrines are "two species of the same generic problem," *Kroger*, 437 U.S., at 370. Nothing in § 1367 indicates a congressional intent to recognize, preserve, or create some meaningful, substantive distinction between the jurisdictional categories we have historically labeled pendent and ancillary.

If § 1367(a) were the sum total of the relevant statutory language, our holding would rest on that language alone. The statute, of course, instructs us to examine § 1367(b) to determine if any of its exceptions apply, so we proceed to that section. While § 1367(b) qualifies the broad rule of § 1367(a), it does not withdraw supplemental jurisdiction over the claims of the additional parties at issue here. The specific exceptions to § 1367(a) contained in § 1367(b), moreover, provide additional support for our conclusion that § 1367(a) confers supplemental jurisdiction over these claims. Section 1367(b), which applies only to diversity cases, withholds supplemental jurisdiction over the claims of plaintiffs proposed to be joined as indispensable parties under Federal Rule of Civil Procedure 19, or who seek to intervene pursuant to Rule 24. Nothing in the text of § 1367(b), however, withholds supplemental jurisdiction over the claims of plaintiffs permissively joined under Rule 20 (like the additional plaintiffs in No. 04–79) or certified as class-action members pursuant to Rule 23 (like the additional plaintiffs in No. 04–70). The natural, indeed the necessary, inference is that § 1367 confers supplemental jurisdiction over claims by Rule 20 and Rule 23 plaintiffs. This inference, at least with respect to Rule 20 plaintiffs, is strengthened by the fact that § 1367(b) explicitly excludes supplemental jurisdiction over claims against defendants joined under Rule 20.

We cannot accept the view, urged by some of the parties, commentators, and Courts of Appeals, that a district court lacks original jurisdiction over a civil action unless the court has original jurisdiction over every claim in the complaint. As we understand this position, it requires assuming either that all claims in the complaint must stand or fall as a single, indivisible "civil action" as a matter of definitional necessity—what we will refer to as the "indivisibility theory"—or else that the inclusion of a claim or party falling outside the district court's original jurisdiction somehow contaminates every other claim in the complaint, depriving the court of original jurisdiction over any of these claims—what we will refer to as the "contamination theory."

The indivisibility theory is easily dismissed, as it is inconsistent with the whole notion of supplemental jurisdiction. If a district court must have original jurisdiction over every claim in the complaint in order to have "original jurisdiction" over a "civil action," then in *Gibbs* there was no civil action of which the district court could assume original jurisdiction under § 1331, and so no basis for exercising supplemental jurisdiction over any of the claims. The indivisibility theory is further belied by our practice—in both federal-question and diversity cases—of allowing federal courts to cure jurisdictional defects by dismissing the offending parties rather than dismissing the entire action. *Clark*, for example, makes clear that claims that are jurisdictionally defective as to amount in controversy do not destroy original jurisdiction over other claims. If the presence of jurisdictionally problematic claims in the complaint meant the district court was without original jurisdiction over the single, indivisible civil action before it, then the district court would have to dismiss the whole action rather than particular parties.

We also find it unconvincing to say that the definitional indivisibility theory applies in the context of diversity cases but not in the context of federal-question cases. The broad and general language of the statute does not permit this result. The contention is premised on the notion that the phrase "original jurisdiction of all civil actions" means different things in § 1331 and § 1332. It is implausible, however, to say that the identical phrase means one thing (original jurisdiction in all actions where at least one claim in the complaint meets the following requirements) in § 1331 and something else (original jurisdiction in all actions where every claim in the complaint meets the following requirements) in § 1332.

The contamination theory, as we have noted, can make some sense in the special context of the complete diversity requirement because the presence of nondiverse parties on both sides of a lawsuit eliminates the justification for providing a federal forum. The theory, however, makes little sense with respect to the amount-in-controversy requirement, which is meant to ensure that a dispute is sufficiently important to warrant federal-court attention. The presence of a single nondiverse party may eliminate the fear of bias with respect to all claims, but the presence of a claim that falls short of the minimum amount in controversy does nothing to reduce the importance of the claims that do meet this requirement.

* * *

We also reject the argument * * * that while the presence of additional claims over which the district court lacks jurisdiction does not mean the civil action is outside the purview of § 1367(a), the presence of additional parties does. The basis for this distinction is not altogether clear, and it is in considerable tension with statutory text. Section 1367(a) applies by its terms to any civil action of which the district courts have original jurisdiction, and the last sentence of § 1367(a) expressly contemplates that the court may have supplemental jurisdiction over additional parties. So it cannot be the case that the presence of those parties destroys the court's original jurisdiction, within the meaning of § 1367(a), over a civil action otherwise properly before it. Also, § 1367(b) expressly withholds supplemental jurisdiction in diversity cases over claims by plaintiffs joined as indispensable parties under Rule 19. If joinder of such parties were sufficient to deprive the district court of original jurisdiction over the civil action within the meaning of § 1367(a), this specific limitation on supplemental jurisdiction in § 1367(b) would be superfluous. The argument that the presence of additional parties removes the civil action from the scope of § 1367(a) also would mean that § 1367 left the *Finley* result undisturbed. *Finley*, after all, involved a Federal Tort Claims Act suit against a federal defendant and state-law claims against additional defendants not otherwise subject to federal jurisdiction. Yet all concede that one purpose of § 1367 was to change the result reached in *Finley*.

Finally, it is suggested that our interpretation of § 1367(a) creates an anomaly regarding the exceptions listed in § 1367(b): It is not immediately obvious why Congress would withhold supplemental jurisdiction over plaintiffs joined as parties "needed for just adjudication" under Rule 19 but would allow supplemental jurisdiction over plaintiffs permissively joined under Rule 20. The omission of Rule 20 plaintiffs from the list of exceptions in § 1367(b) may have been an "unintentional drafting gap," *Meritcare*, 166 F.3d, at 221, and n. 6. If that is the case, it is up to Congress rather than the courts to fix it. The omission may seem odd, but it is not absurd. An alternative explanation for the different treatment of Rules 19 and 20 is that Congress was concerned that extending supplemental jurisdiction to Rule 19 plaintiffs would allow circumvention of the complete diversity rule: A nondiverse plaintiff might be omitted intentionally from the original action, but joined later under Rule 19 as a necessary party. * * *

* * *

* * * [T]he threshold requirement of § 1367(a) is satisfied in cases, like those now before us, where some, but not all, of the plaintiffs in a diversity action allege a sufficient amount in controversy. We hold that § 1367 by its plain text overruled *Clark* and *Zahn* and authorized supplemental jurisdiction over all claims by diverse parties arising out of the same Article III case or controversy, subject only to enumerated exceptions not applicable in the cases now before us.

C

The proponents of the alternative view of § 1367 insist that the statute is at least ambiguous and that we should look to other interpretive tools, including the legislative history of § 1367, which supposedly demonstrate Congress did not intend § 1367 to overrule *Zahn*. We can reject this argument at the very outset simply because § 1367 is not ambiguous. * * *

Those who urge that the legislative history refutes our interpretation rely primarily on the House Judiciary Committee Report on the Judicial Improvements Act. H.R.Rep. No. 101–734 (1990) (House Report or Report). * * *

As we have repeatedly held, the authoritative statement is the statutory text, not the legislative history or any other extrinsic material. Extrinsic materials have a role in statutory interpretation only to the extent they shed a reliable light on the enacting Legislature's understanding of otherwise ambiguous terms. Not all extrinsic materials are reliable sources of insight into legislative understandings, however, and legislative history in particular is vulnerable to two serious criticisms. First, legislative history is itself often murky, ambiguous, and contradictory. Judicial investigation of legislative history has a tendency to become, to borrow Judge Leventhal's memorable phrase, an exercise in " 'looking over a crowd and picking out your friends.' " *See* Wald, Some Observations on the Use of Legislative History in the 1981 Supreme Court Term, 68 *Iowa L.Rev.* 195, 214 (1983). Second, judicial reliance on legislative materials like committee reports, which are not themselves subject to the requirements of Article I, may give unrepresentative committee members—or, worse yet, unelected staffers and lobbyists—both the power and the incentive to attempt strategic manipulations of legislative history to secure results they were unable to achieve through the statutory text. * * *

* * *

In sum, even if we believed resort to legislative history were appropriate in these cases—a point we do not concede—we would not give significant weight to the House Report. The distinguished jurists who drafted the Subcommittee Working Paper, along with three of the participants in the drafting of § 1367, agree that this provision, on its face, overrules *Zahn*. This accords with the best reading of the statute's text, and nothing in the legislative history indicates directly and explicitly that Congress understood the phrase "civil action of which the district courts have original jurisdiction" to exclude cases in which some but not all of the diversity plaintiffs meet the amount-in-controversy requirement.

* * *

D

Finally, we note that the Class Action Fairness Act (CAFA), Pub.L. 109–2, 119 Stat. 4, enacted this year, has no bearing on our analysis of these cases. Subject to certain limitations, the CAFA confers federal diversity jurisdiction over class actions where the aggregate amount in controversy exceeds $5 million. It abrogates the rule against aggregating claims, a rule this Court recognized in *Ben-Hur* and reaffirmed in *Zahn*. The CAFA, however, is not retroactive, and the views of the 2005 Congress are not relevant to our interpretation of a text enacted by Congress in 1990. The CAFA, moreover, does not moot the significance of our interpretation of § 1367, as many proposed exercises of supplemental jurisdiction, even in the class-action context, might not fall within the CAFA's ambit. The CAFA, then, has no impact, one way or the other, on our interpretation of § 1367.

* * *

The judgment of the Court of Appeals for the Eleventh Circuit is affirmed. The judgment of the Court of Appeals for the First Circuit is reversed, and the case is remanded for proceedings consistent with this opinion.

It is so ordered.

■ JUSTICE GINSBURG, with whom JUSTICE STEVENS, JUSTICE O'CONNOR, and JUSTICE BREYER join, dissenting.

These cases present the question whether Congress, by enacting 28 U.S.C. § 1367, overruled this Court's decisions in *Clark v. Paul Gray, Inc.*, 306 U.S. 583, 589 (1939) and *Zahn v. International Paper Co.*, 414 U.S. 291 (1973). *Clark* held that, when federal-court jurisdiction is predicated on a specified amount in controversy, each plaintiff joined in the litigation must independently meet the jurisdictional amount requirement. *Zahn* confirmed that in class actions governed by Federal Rule of Civil Procedure 23(b)(3), "[e]ach [class member] . . . must satisfy the jurisdictional amount, and any [class member] who does not must be dismissed from the case." 414 U.S., at 301.

Section 1367, all agree, was designed to overturn this Court's decision in *Finley v. United States*, 490 U.S. 545 (1989). * * *

What more § 1367 wrought is an issue on which courts of appeals have sharply divided. The Court today holds that § 1367, although prompted by *Finley*, a case in which original access to federal court was predicated on a federal question, notably enlarges federal diversity jurisdiction. The Court reads § 1367 to overrule *Clark* and *Zahn*, thereby allowing access to federal court by coplaintiffs or class members who do not meet the now in excess of $75,000 amount-in-controversy requirement, so long as at least one coplaintiff, or the named class representative, has a jurisdictionally sufficient claim.

The Court adopts a plausibly broad reading of § 1367, a measure that is hardly a model of the careful drafter's art. There is another plausible reading, however, one less disruptive of our jurisprudence regarding supplemental jurisdiction. If one reads § 1367(a) to instruct, as the statute's text suggests, that the district court must first have "original jurisdiction" over a "civil action" before supplemental jurisdiction can attach, then *Clark* and *Zahn* are preserved, and supplemental jurisdiction does not open the way for joinder of plaintiffs, or inclusion of class members, who do not independently meet the amount-in-controversy requirement. For the reasons that follow, I conclude that this narrower construction is the better reading of § 1367.

I

A

Section 1367, captioned "Supplemental jurisdiction," codifies court-recognized doctrines formerly labeled "pendent" and "ancillary" jurisdiction. Pendent jurisdiction involved the enlargement of federal-question litigation to include related state-law claims. Ancillary jurisdiction evolved primarily to protect defending parties, or others whose rights might be adversely affected if they could not air their claims in an ongoing federal-court action. Given jurisdiction over the principal action, federal courts entertained certain matters deemed ancillary regardless of the citizenship of the parties or the amount in controversy.

* * *

In sum, in federal-question cases before § 1367's enactment, the Court recognized pendent-claim jurisdiction, but not pendent-party jurisdiction. As to ancillary jurisdiction, the Court adhered to the limitation that in diversity cases, throughout the litigation, all plaintiffs must remain diverse from all defendants.

Although pendent jurisdiction and ancillary jurisdiction evolved discretely, the Court has recognized that they are "two species of the same generic problem: Under what circumstances may a federal court hear and decide a state-law claim arising between citizens of the same State?" *Id.*, at 370. Finley regarded that question as one properly addressed to Congress.

* * *

II

A

Section 1367, by its terms, operates only in civil actions "of which the district courts have original jurisdiction." The "original jurisdiction" relevant here is diversity-of-citizenship jurisdiction, conferred by § 1332. The character of that jurisdiction is the essential backdrop for comprehension of § 1367.

* * *

The statute today governing federal-court exercise of diversity jurisdiction in the generality of cases, § 1332, like all its predecessors, incorporates both a diverse-citizenship requirement and an amount-in-controversy specification. * * * This Court has long held that, in determining whether the amount-in-controversy requirement has been satisfied, a single plaintiff may aggregate two or more claims against a single defendant, even if the claims are unrelated. But in multiparty cases, including class actions, we have unyieldingly adhered to the nonaggregation rule stated in *Troy Bank* [*v. G.A. Whitehead & Co.*, 222 U.S. 39 (1911)].

This Court most recently addressed "[t]he meaning of [1332's] 'matter in controversy' language" in *Zahn*, 414 U.S., at 298. *Zahn*, like *Snyder* [*v. Harris*, 394 U.S. 332 (1969)], decided four years earlier, was a class action. In *Snyder,* no class member had a claim large enough to satisfy the jurisdictional amount. But in *Zahn*, the named plaintiffs had such claims. Nevertheless, the Court declined to depart from its "longstanding construction of the 'matter in controversy' requirement of § 1332." *Id.*, at 301. The *Zahn* Court stated:

> "Snyder invoked the well-established rule that each of several plaintiffs asserting separate and distinct claims must satisfy the jurisdictional-amount requirement if his claim is to survive a motion to dismiss. This rule plainly mandates not only that there may be no aggregation and that the entire case must be dismissed where none of the plaintiffs claims [meets the amount-in-controversy requirement] but also requires that any plaintiff without the jurisdictional amount must be dismissed from the case, even though others allege jurisdictionally sufficient claims." *Id.*, at 300.

The rule that each plaintiff must independently satisfy the amount-in-controversy requirement, unless Congress expressly orders otherwise, was thus the solidly established reading of § 1332 when Congress enacted the Judicial Improvements Act of 1990, which added § 1367 to Title 28.

B

* * *

The Court is unanimous in reading § 1367(a) to permit pendent-party jurisdiction in federal-question cases, and thus, to overrule *Finley*. The basic jurisdictional grant, § 1331, provides that "[t]he district courts shall have original jurisdiction of all civil actions arising under the Constitution, laws, or treaties of the United States." Since 1980, § 1331 has contained no amount-in-controversy requirement. Once there is a civil action presenting a qualifying claim arising under federal law, § 1331's sole requirement is met. District courts, we have held, may then adjudicate, additionally, state-law claims "deriv[ing] from a common nucleus of operative fact." *Gibbs*, 383 U.S., at 725. Section 1367(a) enlarges that category to include not only state-law claims against the defendant named in the federal claim, but also "[state-law] claims that involve the joinder or intervention of additional parties."

The Court divides, however, on the impact of § 1367(a) on diversity cases controlled by § 1332. Under the majority's reading, § 1367(a) permits the joinder of related claims cut loose from the nonaggregation rule that has long attended actions under § 1332. Only the claims specified in § 1367(b) would be excluded from § 1367(a)'s expansion of § 1332's grant of diversity jurisdiction. And because § 1367(b) contains no exception for joinder of plaintiffs under Rule 20 or class actions under Rule 23, the Court concludes, *Clark* and *Zahn* have been overruled.

The Court's reading is surely plausible, especially if one detaches § 1367(a) from its context and attempts no reconciliation with prior interpretations of § 1332's amount-in-controversy requirement. But § 1367(a)'s text, as the First Circuit held, can be read another way, one that would involve no rejection of *Clark* and *Zahn*.

As explained by the First Circuit in *Ortega*, and applied to class actions by the Tenth Circuit in *Leonhardt* [*v. Western Sugar Co.*, 160 F.3d 631, 641 (C.A.10 1998)], § 1367(a) addresses "civil action[s] of which the district courts have original jurisdiction," a formulation that, in diversity cases, is sensibly read to incorporate the rules on joinder and aggregation tightly tied to § 1332 at the time of § 1367's enactment. On this reading, a complaint must first meet that "original jurisdiction" measurement. If it does not, no supplemental jurisdiction is authorized. If it does, § 1367(a) authorizes "supplemental jurisdiction" over related claims. In other words, § 1367(a) would preserve undiminished, as part and parcel of § 1332 "original jurisdiction" determinations, both the "complete diversity" rule and the decisions restricting aggregation to arrive at the amount in controversy. * * * In contrast to the Court's construction of § 1367, which draws a sharp line between the diversity and amount-in-controversy components of § 1332, the interpretation presented here does not sever the two jurisdictional requirements.

The more restrained reading of § 1367 just outlined * * * would not discard entirely, as the Court does, the judicially developed doctrines of pendent and ancillary jurisdiction as they existed when Finley was decided. Instead, it would recognize § 1367 essentially as a codification of those doctrines, placing them under a single heading, but largely retaining their substance, with overriding Finley the only basic change: Supplemental jurisdiction, once the district court has original jurisdiction, would now include "claims that involve the joinder or intervention of additional parties." § 1367(a).

* * *

Nor does the more moderate reading assign different meanings to "original jurisdiction" in diversity and federal-question cases. As the First Circuit stated:

" '[O]riginal jurisdiction' in § 1367(a) has the same meaning in every case: [An] underlying statutory grant of original jurisdiction must be satisfied. What differs between federal question and diversity cases is not the meaning of 'original jurisdiction' but rather the [discrete] requirements of sections 1331 and 1332. Under § 1331, the sole issue is whether a federal question appears on the face of the plaintiff's well-pleaded complaint; the [citizenship] of the parties and the amounts they stand to recover [do not bear on that determination]. Section 1332, by

contrast, predicates original jurisdiction on the identity of the parties
(*i.e.*, [their] complete diversity) and their [satisfaction of the amount-in-
controversy specification]. [In short,] the 'original jurisdiction' language
in § 1367 operates differently in federal-question and diversity cases not
because the meaning of that term varies, but because the [jurisdiction-
granting] statutes are different." 370 F.3d, at 139–140.

What is the utility of § 1367(b) under my reading of § 1367(a)?
Section 1367(a) allows parties other than the plaintiff to assert reactive
claims once entertained under the heading ancillary jurisdiction. As
earlier observed, § 1367(b) stops plaintiffs from circumventing § 1332's
jurisdictional requirements by using another's claim as a hook to add a
claim that the plaintiff could not have brought in the first instance.
Kroger is the paradigm case. There, the Court held that ancillary
jurisdiction did not extend to a plaintiff's claim against a nondiverse
party who had been impleaded by the defendant under Rule 14. Section
1367(b), then, is corroborative of § 1367(a)'s coverage of claims formerly
called ancillary, but provides exceptions to ensure that accommodation
of added claims would not fundamentally alter "the jurisdictional
requirements of section 1332."

While § 1367's enigmatic text defies flawless interpretation, the
precedent-preservative reading, I am persuaded, better accords with the
historical and legal context of Congress' enactment of the supplemental
jurisdiction statute, and the established limits on pendent and ancillary
jurisdiction. It does not attribute to Congress a jurisdictional
enlargement broader than the one to which the legislators adverted,
and it follows the sound counsel that "close questions of [statutory]
construction should be resolved in favor of continuity and against
change," Shapiro, "Continuity and Change in Statutory Interpretation,"
67 *N.Y.U.L.Rev.* 921, 925 (1992).

* * *

For the reasons stated, I would hold that § 1367 does not overrule
Clark and *Zahn*. I would therefore affirm the judgment of the Court of
Appeals for the First Circuit and reverse the judgment of the Court of
Appeals for the Eleventh Circuit.

■ JUSTICE STEVENS, with whom JUSTICE BREYER joins, dissenting.

[Justice Stevens, joined by Justice Breyer, dissented in an opinion
focusing primarily on the legislative history of Section 1367. Justice
Stevens' dissent concluded as follows:

> After nearly 20 pages of complicated analysis, which
> explores subtle doctrinal nuances and coins various
> neologisms, the Court announces that § 1367 could not
> reasonably be read another way. That conclusion is difficult to
> accept. Given Justice GINSBURG's persuasive account of the
> statutory text and its jurisprudential backdrop, and given the

uncommonly clear legislative history, I am confident that the majority's interpretation of § 1367 is mistaken. I respectfully dissent.]

COMMENTS AND QUESTIONS CONCERNING
EXXON MOBIL CORP. V. ALLAPATTAH SERVICES, INC.

1.   Consider again the hypotheticals set forth prior to *Exxon v. Allapattah*. Prior to its decision in *Allapattah*, the Supreme Court had held that the federal district courts could exercise ancillary jurisdiction in *Moore v. New York Cotton Exchange* (Example A) and pendent jurisdiction in *Gibbs v. United Mine Workers* (Example B). Those outcomes did not change with the enactment of Section 1367 and the Court's decision in *Allapattah*.

Prior to *Allapattah*, the Supreme Court in *Zahn v. International Paper Co.* (Example D) had held that a district court could not hear the diversity claims of unnamed class members that did not satisfy the amount in controversy, even though the claim of the named plaintiff did. The Court in *Allapattah* held that Section 1367 changed this result and that class claims for less than the statutory amount in controversy could be heard so long as at least one class member satisfied the amount in controversy.

The Court in *Aldinger v. Howard* (Example C) refused to recognize pendent-party jurisdiction in an action in which a plaintiff brought a federal-question claim against her supervisor and attempted to include in that action a related state-law claim against the county for which she worked. (Example C). Should the enactment of Section 1367 overturn the result in *Aldinger*?

2.   In *Owen Equipment & Erection Co. v. Kroger*, 437 U.S. 365 (1978), the Supreme Court considered whether plaintiff Kroger could file a state-law claim (Claim #3 below) against a non-diverse party who had been brought into the action by a third-party complaint filed by the defendant (Claim #2 below). The claims are displayed in the graphic below.

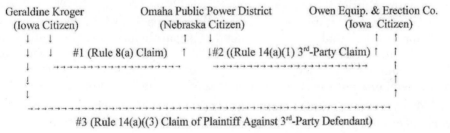

#3 (Rule 14(a)((3) Claim of Plaintiff Against 3ʳᵈ-Party Defendant)

The Supreme Court concluded that the court could not exercise ancillary jurisdiction over Kroger's state-law claim, even though it arose from the same nucleus of operative fact as did Kroger's original diversity claim against OPPD. Justice Stewart observed in his majority opinion:

> Complete diversity was destroyed just as surely as if she [Kroger] had sued Owen initially. In either situation, in the plain language of the statute, the "matter in controversy" could not be "between . . . citizens of different States."

* * *

> [N]either the convenience of litigants nor considerations of
> judicial economy can suffice to justify extension of the doctrine of
> ancillary jurisdiction to a plaintiff's cause of action against a
> citizen of the same State in a diversity case.

437 U.S. at 374, 377.

3.   What if plaintiff Kroger's original claim had been a federal-
question claim under Section 1331 rather than a diversity claim? Assume,
for example, that plaintiff's claim against the Omaha Public Power
Department (OPPD) arose under a federal workplace safety statute and
that OPPD then brought a third-party claim against (impleded) Owen
Equipment, asserting that Owen was liable for any damages for which
OPPD might be liable to Kroger. If Kroger then amended her complaint to
assert a claim against Owen, asserting that Owen was liable to her under
the federal workplace safety statute, would the district court have
jurisdiction to entertain that claim? What impact, if any, would Section
1367(b) have on Kroger's claim against Owen?

4.   In his opinion in Allapattah Justice Kennedy is not enthusiastic
about resorting to the legislative history of Section 1367, suggesting:
"[L]egislative history is itself often murky, ambiguous, and contradictory.
Judicial investigation of legislative history has a tendency to become, to
borrow Judge Leventhal's memorable phrase, an exercise in ' "looking over
a crowd and picking out your friends." ' " Do you agree?

5.   Although they differed as to whether Section 1367 legislatively
overruled *Zahn v. International Paper*, the Justices were unanimous in
Allapattah that Section 1367 overruled *Finley v. United States*. The *Finley*
Court held that pendent-party jurisdiction could not be exercised over
plaintiff's state-law claims against a municipality and a utility company
seeking damages for the death of her husband and child in an airplane
crash. However, the federal courts had exclusive jurisdiction over her claim
against the United States under the Federal Tort Claims Act. The Court's
decision that the state-law claims could not be heard in federal court
therefore meant that plaintiff must file separate lawsuits in state and
federal court. Thus there were strong policy reasons to statutorily vest the
federal courts with jurisdiction over pendent-party claims in actions such
as this and prevent the specific unfairness resulting from *Finley*.

6.   Justice Kennedy noted in *Allapattah*, "*Finley* held that in the
context of parties, in contrast to claims, 'we will not assume that the full
constitutional power has been congressionally authorized, and will not read
jurisdictional statutes broadly.' " Why the different treatment of pendent
parties and pendant claims?

What is the difference between a federal district court exercising
jurisdiction over a single state-law claim arising from the same nucleus of
operative fact as a federal claim over which the court has jurisdiction and
that court exercising supplemental jurisdiction over an entire class of
10,000 state-law claims?

7. While the justices in *Allapattah* analyzed the meaning of 28 U.S.C. §§ 1367(a) and 1367(b), the existence of jurisdiction under Section 1367 does not mean that a federal district court actually will exercise that jurisdiction to decide a particular case.

Section 1367(c) of Title 28 provides:

The district courts may decline to exercise supplemental jurisdiction over a claim under subsection (a) if—

(1) the claim raises a novel or complex issue of State law,

(2) the claim substantially predominates over the claim or claims over which the district court has original jurisdiction;

(3) the district court has dismissed all claims over which is has original jurisdiction, or

(4) in exceptional circumstances, there are other compelling reasons for declining jurisdiction.

Thus the party seeking a federal forum for a supplemental claim must convince the court that:

(1) the requirements of Section 1367(a) are met;

(2) if the district court's original jurisdiction is based solely on Section 1332 (diversity), none of the jurisdictional exceptions of Section 1367(b) apply; and

(3) none of the specific factors in Section 1367(c) or "other compelling reasons for declining jurisdiction" exist to cause the judge to decline to exercise supplemental jurisdiction.

8. The 10,000 Exxon dealers brought their action together as a class action, rather than bringing 10,000 separate civil actions. A federal class action must satisfy both constitutional due process requirements and the many more specific requirements set forth in Rule 23 of the Federal Rules of Civil Procedure. You will study these class action requirements in Chapter 7. For now, it is important to understand that:

(1) Subject-matter jurisdiction must exist for all actions— including class actions; and

(2) There are many additional requirements that also must be satisfied for a court to certify and entertain a class action.

9. In *Supreme Tribe of Ben Hur v. Cauble*, 255 U.S. 356 (1921), the Supreme Court held that only the state citizenship of named plaintiffs in a class action would be considered in determining whether there was complete diversity of citizenship under 28 U.S.C. § 1332. Thus, if the named class representatives are citizens of Oklahoma and the defendant is a citizen of Kansas, these representative plaintiffs would satisfy the diversity requirement of Section 1332—even if there were several hundred (or thousand) unnamed class members who were Kansas citizens. Could the jurisdictional question presented by the *Exxon* class action have been solved by considering only the amount in controversy of the named

plaintiffs—just as only the citizenship of the named plaintiffs was considered in *Supreme Tribe of Ben Hur*?

In footnote 3 of her *Allapattah* dissent, Justice Ginsburg noted: "Anomalously, in holding that each class member 'must satisfy the jurisdictional amount,' *Zahn v. International Paper Co.*, 414 U.S. 291, 301 (1973), the *Zahn* Court did not refer to *Supreme Tribe of Ben Hur v. Cauble*, 255 U.S. 356, 366 (1921), which established that in a class action, the citizenship of the named plaintiff is controlling."

10. Prior to its decision in *Zahn v. International Paper, Co.*, the Supreme Court decided *Snyder v. Harris*, 394 U.S. 332 (1969), in which class members attempted to aggregate their individual damages to satisfy the amount in controversy requirement of 28 U.S.C. § 1332(a). The Court held that, because no class member had a claim in excess of the jurisdictional minimum, the federal courts could not exercise subject-matter jurisdiction over these actions. Should this result change under Section 1367 and *Allapattah*?

11. As Justice Kennedy notes in the final section of his opinion, Congress explicitly allowed class members to aggregate their claims in the Class Action Fairness Act of 2005 ("CAFA"), Pub. L. 109–2, 119 Stat. 4 (2005). As we will see in Chapter 7, while class members are permitted to aggregate their claims under CAFA, those claims must be, in the aggregate, more than $5,000,000. 28 U.S.C. § 1332(d)(2). In addition, the CAFA statute requires only minimal, rather than complete, diversity of citizenship. *Id.* However, CAFA did not apply to *Allapattah*, because that class action was filed prior to CAFA's enactment. CAFA is, though, another instance in which Congress has broadened the federal judicial power entrusted to the federal district courts.

V. REMOVAL JURISDICTION

Plaintiff, a citizen of Washington, files a civil action seeking specific performance in Florida state court against a major corporation that is incorporated in North Carolina and has its principal place of business in New York. As counsel for the corporate defendant, your sense is that a Florida state court and jury will be sympathetic to the plaintiff. Is there a way to gain a more favorable forum in which to defend against plaintiff's claims?

One thing that you might consider is to remove the action from Florida state court to the federal district court encompassing the geographic area in which the state action is pending. As defense counsel, you may decide to do this for any number of reasons. You may believe that a federal judge and jury will be more sympathetic to your client, that you are likely to receive a trial sooner (or later) in federal court, or that removal to federal court will allow you to then transfer the action to a federal district court elsewhere in the United States.

This is what PepsiCo did in response to the civil action that John Leonard filed against it in Florida state court. PepsiCo initially removed the action from Florida state to federal court and then successfully moved to transfer the action to federal district court in New York—the state in which PepsiCo has its principal place of business.[14] When and how a defendant can remove a civil action from state to federal court is the subject of this section of this chapter.

A. REMOVAL OF CASES FROM STATE TO FEDERAL COURT

Section 1441(a) of Title 28 sets forth the basic requirements for removing a civil action from state to federal court:

> Except as otherwise expressly provided by Act of Congress, any civil action brought in a State court of which the district courts of the United States have original jurisdiction, may be removed by the defendant or the defendants, to the district court of the United States for the district and division embracing the place where such action is pending.

Thus the basic rule is that, if a federal court would have had jurisdiction over a matter filed in state court, a defendant can remove that action from state to federal court. However, there are several additional requirements that limit the ability of defendants to remove certain types of civil actions. Perhaps most significantly, 28 U.S.C. § 1441(b)(2) provides:

> A civil action otherwise removable solely on the basis of the jurisdiction under section 1332(a) of this title may not be removed if any of the parties in interest properly joined and served as defendants is a citizen of the State in which such action is brought.

If a New York plaintiff seeks $100,000 from a California defendant in an Ohio state court, the defendant could remove that action to federal court in Ohio. But if the New York plaintiff were to file the identical civil action against the California defendant in a California state court, the defendant could not remove the action to federal court (even though a California federal court could have exercised subject-matter jurisdiction over the action had it been filed in the first instance in that court).

The specific procedures that must be followed to remove an action from state to federal court are set forth in 28 U.S.C. § 1446. Section 1446(a) provides a straightforward removal procedure:

> A defendant or defendants desiring to remove any civil action from a State court shall file in the district court of the United States for the district or division within which such action is pending a notice of removal signed pursuant to Rule 11 of the Federal Rules of Civil Procedure and containing a short and plain statement of the grounds for removal, together

---

[14] *See Leonard v. PepsiCo, Inc.*, 88 F. Supp. 2d 116, 120–21 (S.D.N.Y. 1999).

with a copy of all process, pleadings, and orders served upon such defendant or defendants in such action.

The defendant does not make a motion or seek leave to remove a case from state to federal court. He simply files a notice of removal in the appropriate federal court.

Additional requirements for removal are set forth in Section 1446(b), most significantly:

(1) The notice of removal must be filed within 30 days after receipt by the defendant of the initial pleading or summons (28 U.S.C. § 1446(b)(1));

(2) If the action is removed solely under Section 1441(a), all defendants must join in or consent to the removal[15] (Section 1446(b)(2)(A)); and

(3) Except for certain diversity actions, if the action as originally filed is not removable, the notice of removal must be filed within 30 days after receipt by the defendant of the amended complaint or other paper "from which it may first be ascertained that the case is one which is or has become removable" (Section 1446(b)(3)).

Section 1446(c) contains specific requirements for the removal of diversity actions. Most importantly, Section 1446(c)(1) provides:

A case may not be removed under subsection (b)(3) on the basis of jurisdiction conferred by section 1332 more than 1 year after commencement of the action, unless the district court finds that the plaintiff has acted in bad faith in order to prevent a defendant from removing the action.

So, even if a defendant had not known that an action was removable as a federal diversity action, that action only can be removed within one year after the filing of the action in state court. However, if the plaintiff acted in bad faith in disguising the existence of diversity jurisdiction (for instance, by misrepresenting the amount in controversy or the citizenship of a party), the notice of removal can be filed outside the one-year period.

What if a state-court action contains a federal-question claim, as well as a state-law claim over which a federal court cannot exercise supplemental jurisdiction? Section 1441(c)(1) permits the removal of this entire action to federal court, but Section 1441(c)(2) requires that "the district court shall sever from the action all [state-law] claims [over which the court cannot exercise supplemental jurisdiction] * * * and shall remand the severed claims to the State court from which the

---

[15] The great bulk of actions removed to federal court are removed pursuant to Section 1441(a) of Title 28. There are, though, additional statutory provisions permitting the removal of specific types of cases such as certain civil rights cases and class actions initially commenced in state court. 28 U.S.C. §§ 1443; 1453.

action was removed." Thus the existence of claims over which a federal court cannot exercise subject-matter jurisdiction does not prevent the removal of an action to federal court, but the federal court must remand those claims over which it cannot exercise jurisdiction back to the state court.

If a defendant can remove an action by simply filing a notice of removal in federal court, is there any way by which the plaintiff can challenge the removal? The defendant is required by 28 U.S.C. § 1446(d) to give notice of the removal to all adverse parties and file a copy of the notice of removal with the state court. Section 1447(c) gives the plaintiff 30 days after the filing of the notice of removal to file with the federal court a motion to remand the action back to state court. However, Section 1447(c) also provides: "If at any time before final judgment it appears that the district court lacks subject matter jurisdiction, the case shall be remanded." As noted earlier in this chapter, federal subject-matter jurisdiction can be raised by any party or the court at any time.

Test your knowledge of federal removal procedure by determining which of the following cases can be removed from state to federal court.

    (1) Paul Plaintiff files an action in state court in Arizona. He then decides that the federal district court in Arizona may be a more favorable forum for his action. Assuming that his action arises under the laws of the United States and that the United States District Court for the District of Arizona could have exercised original jurisdiction over the action, can Paul remove it from Arizona state court to the United States District Court for the District of Arizona? *See* 28 U.S.C. § 1441(a).

    (2) Paula Plaintiff, a citizen of California, files a state-law contract action seeking $100,000 from Dean Defendant, a citizen of Arizona, in an Arizona state court. Assuming that the United States District Court for the District of Arizona could have exercised diversity jurisdiction over the action had it originally been filed in Arizona federal court, can Dean remove the action from state to federal court? *See* 28 U.S.C. § 1441(b)(2).

    (3) Paula Plaintiff, a citizen of California, files a state-law contract action in a Nevada state court seeking $250,000 from Dean Defendant, a citizen of Arizona, and Danielle Defendant, a citizen of New Mexico. Assuming that the United States District Court for the District of Nevada could have exercised diversity jurisdiction over the action had it originally been filed in Nevada federal court, can Dean and Danielle remove the action to federal court? Can Dean remove the claim against him if Danielle does not join in or consent to the removal of the action? *See* 28 U.S.C. § 1446(b)(2)(A).

(4) Paul Plaintiff, a citizen of Vermont, files an action in
Vermont state court asserting state-law assault and battery
claims against Daniel Detective, a local law enforcement officer
who is also a citizen of Vermont. Fifteen months after filing the
action, Paul amends his complaint to add a federal civil rights
claim against Detective. Can Detective remove the action to
the United States District Court for the District of Vermont?
See 28 U.S.C. § 1446(b)(3).

The plaintiff initially gets to choose the court in which to file his
lawsuit. In making this determination, plaintiff's counsel will choose
the court that she thinks will provide the most favorable forum for the
plaintiff. But if the forum chosen is a state court, the defendant may be
able to remove the action to a federal court that will be less hospitable
to the plaintiff. Are there ways a plaintiff can structure his lawsuit, and
decide whom to name as defendants, that will make it less likely that
the defendant can remove the action from state court? Think about this
as you read the following case.

B. *ROSE V. GIAMATTI*

Rose v. Giamatti

United States District Court, Southern District of Ohio, 1989
721 F.Supp. 906

MEMORANDUM AND ORDER

■ JOHN D. HOLSCHUH, DISTRICT JUDGE.

I. INTRODUCTION

This action by Peter Edward Rose against A. Bartlett Giamatti and
others, initially filed in the Court of Common Pleas of Hamilton County,
Ohio at Cincinnati, and removed to the United States District Court for
the Southern District of Ohio on July 3, 1989, was transferred forthwith
to the Eastern Division of this Court by an order issued by Judge Carl
B. Rubin and Judge Herman J. Weber, Judges of this Court sitting in
the Western Division at Cincinnati. In that transfer order, Judges
Rubin and Weber stated:

> Plaintiff is not just another litigant. He is instead a baseball
> figure of national reputation closely identified with the
> Cincinnati Reds and the City of Cincinnati. Under such
> circumstances, it would appear advisable that [this case] be
> transferred to a city of the Southern District of Ohio other than
> Cincinnati.

* * *

The Court emphasizes that the issues decided by this
Memorandum and Order are solely questions of law concerning the
jurisdiction of a United States district court when a case is removed

from a state court based upon diversity of citizenship of the parties to the controversy. The essential facts relative to these jurisdictional issues are not in dispute, and the merits of the controversy between plaintiff Rose and defendant Giamatti are not before the Court at this time. The fact that a judge of the Court of Common Pleas of Hamilton County, Ohio, where this action was commenced, issued a temporary restraining order against the defendants, while a relevant factor among all the circumstances, is clearly not dispositive of any of the jurisdictional issues confronting this Court. The sole question raised by the notice of removal and the motion to remand is whether, under applicable law, the federal court has jurisdiction over the subject matter of this action. For the reasons stated hereafter, I conclude that the action was properly removed to this Court, and that this Court does have jurisdiction over the action which I have a duty to recognize and to enforce.

II. PROCEDURAL HISTORY

Plaintiff, Peter Edward Rose, is the Field Manager of the Cincinnati Reds baseball team. In February of this year, then Commissioner of Baseball Peter V. Ueberroth and then Commissioner of Baseball-elect A. Bartlett Giamatti initiated an investigation regarding allegations that Rose wagered on major league baseball games. On February 23, 1989 Giamatti retained John M. Dowd as Special Counsel for the purpose of conducting the investigation. On May 9, 1989 Dowd submitted a report to Giamatti summarizing the evidence obtained during the investigation. Commissioner Giamatti ultimately scheduled a hearing concerning the allegations for June 26, 1989.

In an effort to prevent Commissioner Giamatti from conducting the June 26 hearing, Rose filed an action in the Court of Common Pleas of Hamilton County, Ohio, on June 19, 1989, seeking a temporary restraining order and preliminary injunction against the pending disciplinary proceedings. Named as defendants in that action were A. Bartlett Giamatti, Major League Baseball, and the Cincinnati Reds. The crux of the complaint is Rose's contention that he is being denied the right to a fair hearing on the gambling allegations by an unbiased decisionmaker. The complaint requests permanent injunctive relief, which, if granted, would prevent Commissioner Giamatti from ever conducting a hearing to determine whether Rose has engaged in gambling activities in violation of the Rules of Major League Baseball. Rose asks that the Court of Common Pleas of Hamilton County, Ohio determine whether he has wagered on major league baseball games, including those of the Cincinnati Reds.

Subsequent to a two-day evidentiary hearing, Common Pleas Court Judge Norbert Nadel issued a temporary restraining order on June 25, 1989. The order enjoined all defendants (1) from any involvement in deciding whether Rose should be disciplined or suspended from participation in baseball and (2) from terminating Rose's employment as Field Manager of the Cincinnati Reds, or interfering with his employment in response to any action taken by Giamatti, or in retaliation for Rose having filed the action. * * *

On July 3, 1989, defendant Giamatti filed a notice of removal of the action from the state court to the United States District Court for the Southern District of Ohio, Western Division at Cincinnati, contending that the federal court has diversity jurisdiction over this action. Defendants Cincinnati Reds and Major League Baseball consented to the removal of the action. * * *

On July 5, 1989, Rose filed a motion to remand this action to the Court of Common Pleas of Hamilton County, Ohio, asserting that there is a lack of complete diversity of citizenship between himself and the defendants, and that even if complete diversity exists, defendant Giamatti waived his right of removal by participating in the above-described proceedings in the state courts. * * *

III. DIVERSITY JURISDICTION

The United States district courts are courts of limited jurisdiction, and the federal statute permitting removal of cases filed in state court restricts the types of cases which may be removed from state court to federal court. The removal statute provides in pertinent part that "any civil action brought in a State court of which the district courts of the United States have original jurisdiction, may be removed by the defendant or the defendants to the district court of the United States for the district and division embracing the place where such action is pending." 28 U.S.C. § 1441(a). The statute also provides that except for a civil action founded on a claim arising under federal law, "[a]ny other such action shall be removable only if none of the parties in interest properly joined and served as defendants is a citizen of the State in which such action is brought." 28 U.S.C. § 1441(b).

Defendant Giamatti contends in his notice of removal that the district court has original jurisdiction of this action by virtue of 28 U.S.C. § 1332(a), which grants original jurisdiction to the district courts in civil actions where the amount in controversy exceeds $50,000 [now, $75,000] and the action is between citizens of different states. This jurisdiction of federal courts is commonly known as "diversity" jurisdiction. The reason for granting diversity jurisdiction to federal courts was stated many years ago by Chief Justice Marshall:

> However true the fact may be, that the tribunals of the states will administer justice as impartially as those of the nation, to parties of every description, it is not less true that the Constitution itself either entertains apprehensions on this subject, or views with such indulgence the possible fears and apprehensions of suitors, that it has established national tribunals for the decision of controversies between aliens and a citizen, or between citizens of different States.

Bank of the United States v. Deveaux, 5 Cranch 61, 87 (1809).[2] The diversity statute has historically been interpreted to require complete diversity of citizenship: ". . . diversity jurisdiction does not exist unless each defendant is a citizen of a different State from each plaintiff." *Owen Equipment & Erection Co. v. Kroger*, 437 U.S. 365, 373 (1978). If diversity of citizenship is found to exist among the parties to this action and none of the defendants in interest properly joined and served is a citizen of Ohio, then the action is properly removable from the state court. If the required diversity of citizenship does not exist, then the action is not properly removable and must be remanded to the state court.

With regard to the citizenship of the parties to this controversy, the complaint contains the following allegations concerning their identity and citizenship. Rose is alleged to be a resident of Hamilton County, Ohio. Commissioner Giamatti's residence is not stated in the complaint; in the notice of removal, however, he is alleged to be a citizen of the State of New York. Defendant Major League Baseball is alleged in the complaint to be an unincorporated association headquartered in New York and consisting of the two principal professional baseball leagues (National and American) and their twenty-six professional baseball clubs. The Cincinnati Reds, dba the Cincinnati Reds Baseball Club, is identified in the complaint as an Ohio limited partnership (hereinafter referred to in the singular as the "Cincinnati Reds").

* * *

In the present case, it appears from the allegations of the complaint that defendant Cincinnati Reds and defendant Major League Baseball are citizens of the same state as plaintiff Rose. Recognizing that diversity jurisdiction is not demonstrated on the face of the complaint, defendant Giamatti includes in his notice of removal a number of allegations in support of his contention that this Court has diversity jurisdiction over this action such that it is properly removable. First, with respect to the defendant identified as Major League Baseball, the notice asserts that defendant Major League Baseball is not a "juridical entity," but is only a trade name utilized by the professional baseball clubs of the American and National Leagues and thus has no citizenship for diversity purposes. Second, the notice asserts that any citizenship ascribed to Major League Baseball should be disregarded for purposes of removal, "since Major League Baseball is not a proper party to this action and is at most a nominal party against which no claim or cause of action has been asserted." Finally, the notice asserts that

---

[2]   In oral argument, counsel for the Commissioner argued that this case should be heard by a "national tribunal":

In the State Court in Cincinnati, I need not describe Mr. Rose's standing. He is a local hero, perhaps the first citizen of Cincinnati. And Commissioner Giamatti is viewed suspiciously as a foreigner from New York, trapped in an ivory tower, accused of bias by Mr. Rose. Your Honor, this is a textbook example of why diversity jurisdiction was created in the Federal Courts and why it exists to this very day.

Major League Baseball was "fraudulently joined" as a defendant for the purpose of attempting to defeat the removal jurisdiction of this Court. In a similar vein, the notice asserts that the defendant Cincinnati Reds is not a proper party to this action, is only a nominal party, and was fraudulently joined for the same purpose of defeating this Court's removal jurisdiction.

The issues framed by the notice of removal, the motion to remand, and the briefs of the parties are, accordingly, as follows:

1.   Is the named defendant, Major League Baseball, a legal entity which has a state of citizenship for diversity purposes?

2.   Can the citizenship of either Major League Baseball or the Cincinnati Reds be disregarded for diversity purposes?

3.   If diversity of citizenship among the parties properly joined in this action is found to exist, has defendant Giamatti nevertheless waived his right to remove this action to federal court?

The Court will address each of these issues in turn.

A. THE CITIZENSHIP OF DEFENDANT MAJOR LEAGUE BASEBALL

Rose asserts that Major League Baseball is an unincorporated association created by virtue of the execution of the "Major League Agreement," an agreement entered into by and between the National League of Professional Baseball Clubs and each of its twelve constituent member clubs, and the American League of Professional Baseball Clubs and each of its fourteen constituent member clubs. Rose argues that the Major League Agreement creates an unincorporated association which operates under the name Major League Baseball. * * * Commissioner Giamatti contends that Major League Baseball is merely a trade name and registered service mark under which the twenty-six major league professional baseball clubs do business with respect to certain commercial activities.

* * *

* * * The critical issue is whether the presence of the two major leagues and their twenty-six clubs, if before the Court as defendants in the form of an unincorporated association, would destroy the necessary diversity of citizenship. Inasmuch as under the Court's analysis which follows, the joinder as a defendant of the leagues and clubs as an unincorporated association doing business under the name Major League Baseball would not defeat the required diversity of citizenship, the Court, for purposes of this motion, will accept Rose's contention that the twenty-six major league professional baseball clubs joined together in the Major League Agreement to form an unincorporated association known as Major League Baseball, and that the unincorporated

association known as Major League Baseball is before this Court as a properly served defendant in this case.

It is undisputed that, for purposes of determining the citizenship of an unincorporated association, an unincorporated association has no citizenship of its own, but is a citizen of every state in which each of its constituent members is a citizen. As the Court of Appeals for the Sixth Circuit stated in *Sweeney v. Hiltebrant*, 373 F.2d 491, 492 (6th Cir.1967), affirming dismissal of the case for lack of jurisdiction:

> The district court found that no jurisdiction existed on the basis of diversity of citizenship since plaintiffs are citizens of Ohio, and the [defendant], a voluntary unincorporated association with Ohio members, must also be regarded as an Ohio citizen for diversity purposes. The court was correct in so holding.

* * *

The Cincinnati Reds Baseball Club, a citizen of Ohio, is one of the twenty-six major league baseball clubs which are members of the association doing business as Major League Baseball. Therefore, Major League Baseball is deemed to be a citizen of Ohio for diversity purposes. Because plaintiff Rose and the defendants Major League Baseball and the Cincinnati Reds are all citizens of Ohio, if either Major League Baseball or the Cincinnati Reds is a party properly joined in this action and whose citizenship, for diversity purposes, cannot be ignored, the lack of diversity of citizenship between plaintiff and all defendants would require the Court to conclude that the removal of the case to this Court was improper. Consequently, the Court must determine whether, as the Commissioner contends, the citizenship of these defendants should be ignored for the purpose of determining whether the removal of this case to this Court was proper.

B. DETERMINATION OF PROPER PARTIES TO THIS ACTION FROM "THE PRINCIPAL PURPOSE OF THE SUIT"

It is fundamental law that a plaintiff cannot confer jurisdiction upon the federal court, nor prevent a defendant from removing a case to the federal court on diversity grounds, by plaintiff's own determination as to who are proper plaintiffs and defendants to the action. As Justice Frankfurter said:

> Litigation is the pursuit of practical ends, not a game of chess. Whether the necessary "collision of interests," *Dawson v. Columbia Trust Co., supra* [197 U.S. 178], at 181 (1905), exists, is therefore not to be determined by mechanical rules. It must be ascertained from the "principal purpose of the suit," *East Tennessee, V. & G. R. v. Grayson*, 119 U.S. 240, 244 (1886), and the "primary and controlling matter in dispute," *Merchants' Cotton Press Co. v. Insurance Co.*, 151 U.S. 368, 385 (1894).

Indianapolis v. Chase National Bank, 314 U.S. 63, 69–70 (1941).

In considering whether diversity of citizenship exists with respect to the "principal purpose of the suit," certain doctrines are well established. First, a plaintiff cannot defeat a defendant's right of removal on the basis of diversity of citizenship by the "fraudulent joinder" of a non-diverse defendant against whom the plaintiff has no real cause of action.

> The joinder of a resident defendant against whom no cause of action is stated is a patent sham, *Parks v. New York Times Co.*, 5 Cir. [1962], 308 F.2d 474, and though a cause of action be stated, the joinder is similarly fraudulent if in fact no cause of action exists, *Lobato v. Pay Less Drug Stores, Inc.*, 10 Cir. [1958], 261 F.2d 406.

Dodd v. Fawcett Publications, Inc., 329 F.2d 82, 85 (10th Cir.1964). With respect to this doctrine, the Sixth Circuit has stated:

> In fraudulent joinder cases the underlying reason for removal is that there is no factual basis upon which it can be claimed that the resident defendant is jointly liable or where there is such liability there is no purpose to prosecute the action against the resident defendant in good faith. *Wilson v. Republic Iron & Steel Co.*, 257 U.S. 92. In such cases the assertion of the cause of action against the resident defendant is treated as a sham.

Brady v. Indemnity Ins. Co. of North America, 68 F.2d 302, 303 (6th Cir.1933). Other courts have held that the party opposing remand has the burden of establishing either that there is no possibility that the plaintiff can establish a valid cause of action under state law against the non-diverse defendant, or that there has been an outright fraud in the plaintiff's pleading of jurisdictional facts.

In many cases, removability may be determined from the original pleadings, and normally an allegation of a cause of action against the resident defendant will be sufficient to prevent removal. But when a defendant alleges that there has been fraudulent joinder, the court "may pierce the pleadings, consider the entire record, and determine the basis of joinder by any means available." *Dodd v. Fawcett Publications, Inc.*, 329 F.2d at 85.

Used in this sense, the term "fraudulent joinder" is a term of art and is not intended to impugn the integrity of a plaintiff or plaintiff's counsel. Although the doctrine of fraudulent joinder applies to situations in which there has been actual fraud committed in the plaintiff's pleading of jurisdictional facts for the purpose of defeating federal court jurisdiction, the Court emphasizes that there is no allegation of any fraud and no evidence of any fraud on the part of plaintiff or plaintiff's counsel in this case. To the contrary, plaintiff's counsel are highly distinguished attorneys of great integrity who have sincerely and vigorously argued that both the Cincinnati Reds and Major League Baseball are properly joined as defendants and whose citizenship cannot be ignored under any applicable rule of law.

Second, it is also a long-established doctrine that a federal court, in its determination of whether there is diversity of citizenship between the parties, must disregard nominal or formal parties to the action and determine jurisdiction based only upon the citizenship of the real parties to the controversy. *Navarro Savings Ass'n v. Lee*, 446 U.S. 458 (1980).

> Early in its history, [the Supreme Court] established that the "citizens' upon whose diversity a plaintiff grounds jurisdiction must be real and substantial parties to the controversy. *McNutt v. Bland*, 2 How. 9, 15 (1844). Thus a federal court must disregard nominal or formal parties and rest jurisdiction only upon the citizenship of real parties to the controversy.

Id. at 460–61. A real party in interest defendant is one who, by the substantive law, has the duty sought to be enforced or enjoined. In contrast to a "real party in interest," a formal or nominal party is one who, in a genuine legal sense, has no interest in the result of the suit, or no actual interest or control over the subject matter of the litigation.

While these related governing principles of federal court jurisdiction are clear and not in dispute, the parties strongly disagree as to their application in the present case. But, as Justice Frankfurter stated in the *Chase National Bank* case:

> As is true of many problems in the law, the answer is to be found not in legal learning but in the realities of the record.

Indianapolis v. Chase National Bank, 314 U.S. at 69. The Court turns, then, to the realities of the record in this case to determine the real parties to this controversy.

1.   Defendant Giamatti

It is apparent from the complaint that the actual controversy in this case is between Rose and Commissioner Giamatti. The complaint is replete with allegations of wrongdoing on the part of Giamatti. For example, Rose asserts that Giamatti and investigators hired by him attempted to bolster the credibility of witnesses against Rose, prejudged the truthfulness of certain testimony given as a part of the investigation, acted unreasonably in demanding information from Rose, improperly threatened him with refusing to cooperate in the investigation, requested that Rose step aside as the Reds' Field Manager without revealing to him the evidence which had been compiled concerning his alleged gambling activities, and otherwise acted improperly in violation of Giamatti's alleged duty to provide Rose with a fair and impartial hearing with respect to the allegations against him. The ultimate purpose of the action is to prevent Giamatti from

conducting any hearing because of his alleged improper conduct and
bias against Rose. * * *

The critical question now before the Court is whether, in this
controversy between Rose and Giamatti, there is "the necessary
collision of interests" between Rose on the one hand and the Cincinnati
Reds and Major League Baseball on the other hand so that the
citizenship of these defendants may not be disregarded by the Court. If
the necessary collision of interests exists, then the action was
improvidently removed and must be remanded to the state court. If,
however, the Cincinnati Reds and Major League Baseball were
fraudulently joined as parties or are only nominal parties in the
controversy, then diversity of citizenship is not defeated and Rose's
motion to remand this case to the Court of Common Pleas of Hamilton
County, Ohio must be denied.

2.   The Cincinnati Reds

Just as it is clear that the crux of the present controversy is
between Rose and Giamatti, it is equally clear that, in reality, there is
no controversy between Rose and the Cincinnati Reds. The complaint
explicitly asserts that Rose "alleges no wrongful conduct on the part of
the Reds." Despite this explicit assertion, Rose contends that "all
defendants herein owe Pete Rose the contractual duty to ensure that
the Commissioner adheres to the Major League Agreement and
discharges his duties in accordance with the Rules of Procedure. . . ." In
essence, Rose asserts that the Commissioner's rules of procedure
concerning fair disciplinary hearings are incorporated as a part of his
employment contract with the Cincinnati Reds, and that any action by
Commissioner Giamatti in violation of his own rules of procedure would
constitute a breach of Rose's contract with the Cincinnati Reds. * * *
Rose's claim against the Cincinnati Reds, involving no present wrongful
conduct on the part of the Reds, is for "anticipatory breach" of his
contract.

The Major League Agreement, which unquestionably is
incorporated as a part of Rose's contract with the Cincinnati Reds,
creates the office of Commissioner of Baseball and vests extraordinary
power in the Commissioner. The Commissioner has unlimited authority
to investigate any act, transaction or practice that is even suspected to
be "not in the best interests" of baseball. * * *

* * *

* * * [It] is apparent that "the Major League . . . Rules" which are
expressly incorporated into Rose's contract with the Cincinnati Reds are
the extensive rules of conduct formally adopted by the members of
Major League Baseball and not the procedural rules independently
promulgated by the Commissioner which govern only his own
proceedings. Furthermore, and of greater importance, there is nothing
in the Major League Agreement, the Major League Rules, or in Rose's

contract with the Cincinnati Reds which gives the Reds any right to prevent the Commissioner from holding a disciplinary hearing or to interfere with proceedings within the jurisdiction of the Commissioner. In fact, the parties are in agreement that the Cincinnati Reds has no such right.

Rose concedes that the Cincinnati Reds has done nothing that would be considered a breach of his contract at this time, nor does he allege that the Cincinnati Reds has taken any action that indicates an intention to refuse to perform its contract with him in the future so as to constitute an anticipatory breach of his contract under Ohio law. Rose's argument that any violation by Giamatti of the Commissioner's own procedural rules would somehow constitute an automatic breach of Rose's contract with the Cincinnati Reds is without legal basis.

It is undeniable that the Cincinnati Reds has, as a practical matter, an interest in the outcome of these proceedings, but not in the legal sense that requires its joinder as a defendant in this action. Rose's complaint specifically alleges that there has been no wrongdoing on the part of the Cincinnati Reds, and the Reds specifically states that it will comply with the terms and conditions of its contract with Rose; there is no real controversy between these parties. The Court concludes that, for the purpose of determining diversity of citizenship, the defendant Cincinnati Reds was, in a legal sense, fraudulently joined as a defendant and that it is, at best, a nominal party in this action. Consequently, the citizenship of the Cincinnati Reds as a defendant may be disregarded for the purpose of determining whether there is complete diversity of citizenship among the parties to this action. * * *

3.   Major League Baseball

If Major League Baseball were a typical unincorporated association, its jurisdictional status would be more easily determined. The reality, however, is that Major League Baseball is a unique organization. * * *

Given the background of the Major League Agreement and the unique manner in which the twenty-six major league baseball clubs have agreed to govern the conduct of players and others by a completely independent Commissioner, it is clear that Major League Baseball cannot be compared or equated with a typical unincorporated association engaged in any other business. As the court in [*Charles O. Finley & Co. v. Kuhn*, 569 F.2d 527 (7th Cir.), *cert denied*, 439 U.S. 876 (1978),] recognized:

> [B]aseball cannot be analogized to any other business or even to any other sport or entertainment. Baseball's relation to the federal antitrust laws has been characterized by the Supreme Court as an "exception," an "anomaly" and an "aberration." Baseball's management through a commissioner is equally an exception, anomaly and aberration * * * In no other sport or

business is there quite the same system, created for quite the
same reasons and with quite the same underlying policies.
Standards such as the best interests of baseball, the interests
of the morale of the players and the honor of the game, or
"sportsmanship which accepts the umpire's decision without
complaint," are not necessarily familiar to courts and obviously
require some expertise in their application. While it is true
that professional baseball selected as its first Commissioner a
federal judge, it intended only him and not the judiciary as a
whole to be its umpire and governor.

569 F.2d at 537.

The Commissioner's jurisdiction under the Major League
Agreement to investigate violations of Major League Rules, or any
activity he believes is "not in the best interests" of baseball, is exclusive.
The major leagues and the twenty-six major league clubs have
absolutely no control over such an investigation or the manner in which
the Commissioner conducts it. * * * What Rose challenges is
Commissioner Giamatti's conduct of the investigation and disciplinary
proceedings in his particular case. In short, Rose's controversy is not
with Major League Baseball, but is with the office of the Commissioner
of Baseball for the Commissioner's alleged failure to follow his own
procedural rules in conducting the investigation of Rose's alleged
gambling activities. Clearly, complete relief can be afforded with regard
to the primary relief sought in the complaint—preventing
Commissioner Giamatti from conducting a disciplinary hearing-without
the need for any order against Major League Baseball or its constituent
major league professional baseball clubs.

There is nothing in Rose's contract with the Cincinnati Reds or in
the Major League Agreement which gives to the Cincinnati Reds or any
other member of Major League Baseball any right, much less a duty, to
prevent the Commissioner from conducting hearings concerning
conduct "deemed by the Commissioner not to be in the best interests of
Baseball." * * *

* * *

The Court recognizes, of course, that in this case it was Major
League Baseball itself that placed the conduct of the Commissioner
beyond the scope of its control, and had Rose not agreed to this unique
delegation of absolute authority to the Commissioner, his claim against
Major League Baseball might have some substance. It is undisputed,
however, that the Major League Agreement, which deprives its
members of control over the Commissioner in disciplinary matters and
requires that its members "be finally and unappealably bound by [all
actions taken by the Commissioner under the authority of the
Agreement] and severally waive such right of recourse to the courts as
would otherwise have existed in their favor," is incorporated as a part of

Rose's contract with the Cincinnati Reds, and Rose necessarily has agreed to its terms and conditions.

* * *

The Court has examined the * * * authorities cited by Rose, as well as others, and concludes that none supports Rose's claims against Major League Baseball in this case. The controversy here, as stated, is between Rose and Commissioner Giamatti and not between Rose and the Cincinnati Reds or between Rose and Major League Baseball. Major League Baseball is, at best, a nominal party in this action. Therefore, the citizenship of Major League Baseball may be disregarded for diversity purposes.

IV. WAIVER OF RIGHT TO REMOVE

[Judge Holschuh concluded that the Commissioner's opposition to Rose's motion for a temporary restraining order, appeal of that order within the state courts, and taking discovery related to Rose's motion for a preliminary injunction did not constitute "clear and unequivocal action" evidencing an intention to waive his right to remove the action to federal court.]

V. CONCLUSION

In light of the foregoing analysis, the Court HOLDS that the controversy in this case is between plaintiff Rose and defendant Giamatti; that they are the real parties in interest in this case; that the Cincinnati Reds and Major League Baseball, are, at best, nominal parties in this controversy; and that, consequently, the citizenship of the Cincinnati Reds and Major League Baseball may be disregarded for diversity purposes. The Court determines that diversity of citizenship exists between Rose, a citizen of Ohio, and Commissioner Giamatti, a citizen of New York, and that the Court has diversity subject matter jurisdiction over this action. Defendant Giamatti is not a citizen of the State of Ohio and has not waived his right to remove this action, therefore, the action was properly removable from the Court of Common Pleas of Hamilton County, Ohio. Plaintiff Rose's motion to remand is DENIED.

The Court is aware that, in routine cases, appeals from interlocutory orders pursuant to 28 U.S.C. § 1292(b) are normally not viewed with favor by appellate courts. The instant case, however, is obviously not a routine case. Two district court judges sitting in Cincinnati transferred the case to the district court judges sitting in Columbus for the reason that the plaintiff is "a baseball figure of national reputation closely identified with the Cincinnati Reds and the City of Cincinnati" and, at the same time, expressed doubt regarding the removability of the case to the federal court. Accordingly, the Court CERTIFIES that this Order denying plaintiff Rose's motion to remand the case to the Court of Common Pleas of Hamilton County, Ohio involves a controlling question of law as to which there is substantial ground for difference of opinion and that an immediate appeal from this Order will materially advance the ultimate termination of the litigation. The Court, therefore, is certifying the case for an immediate appeal on the jurisdictional question to the United States Court of Appeals for the Sixth Circuit.

If plaintiff Rose desires to appeal the Court's ruling on the jurisdictional issue, he must file his application for appeal to the United States Court of Appeals for the Sixth Circuit within ten (10) days after the entry of this Memorandum and Order. 28 U.S.C. § 1292(b); Fed.R.App.P. 5. If Rose does not file his application within that time, a hearing on Rose's motion for a preliminary injunction will be held on Monday, August 14, 1989, at 9:00 a.m. In order to preserve the status quo until such time as an appeal is taken from this Memorandum and Order, or the hearing is held on Rose's motion for a preliminary injunction, if no appeal is taken, the restrictions on defendants' actions regarding plaintiff Rose, as agreed by the parties in the stipulation filed in this Court on July 5, 1989, shall remain in effect until August 14, 1989.

IT IS SO ORDERED.

COMMENTS AND QUESTIONS CONCERNING *ROSE V. GIAMATTI*

1.   What if individual major league baseball clubs, or Major League Baseball, had to approve any investigation of Pete Rose or a decision by Commissioner Giamatti to ban Rose from baseball? Would they then be proper parties to this action?

2.   How frequently will parties challenging federal jurisdiction be able to establish that a named party has been fraudulently joined or is simply a nominal party? How ready should judges be to permit discovery or hearings on such challenges?

3.   What if Rose had been seeking damages rather than an injunction? In *Frontier Airlines, Inc. v. United Air Lines, Inc.*, Judge Herman Finesilver refused to remand a removed action to state court, concluding:

> Defendants contend that the court may also disregard nominal resident defendants where complete relief may be afforded against non-resident defendants and disregard nominal resident defendants. *See Rose v. Giamatti*, 721 F.Supp. 906 (S.D.Ohio 1989). While we agree that in cases like *Rose*, where the relief sought is purely injunctive, this approach provides an avenue for determining whether joinder is fraudulent, the approach is not applicable to the matter at hand. Where a plaintiff seeks monetary damages against defendants alleged to be jointly and severally liable, the court may not disregard properly joined defendants simply because a non-resident defendant has the capital reserves to satisfy an entire judgment.

Frontier Airlines, Inc. v. United Air Lines, Inc., 758 F. Supp. 1399, 1404 (D. Colo. 1989).

4.   Judge Holschuh states, "Used in this sense, the term 'fraudulent joinder' is a term of art and is not intended to impugn the integrity of a plaintiff or plaintiff's counsel." But what if the argument for naming the Cincinnati Reds and Major League Baseball as defendants had not been as strong as it was in this case? *See* Federal Rule of Civil Procedure 11(b)(2) (requiring that claims be "warranted by existing law or by a nonfrivolous argument for extending, modifying, or reversing existing law or for establishing new law"). *See also* ABA Model Rule of Professional Conduct 3.1 (prohibiting a lawyer from bringing a proceeding or asserting an issue without a nonfrivolous legal and factual basis).

5.   Another way that parties may attempt to manipulate federal jurisdiction is to assign a claim or right to a person from another state to create diversity between this person and an adverse party. This is forbidden by 28 U.S.C. § 1359, which provides: "A district court shall not have jurisdiction of a civil action in which any party, by assignment or otherwise, has been improperly or collusively made or joined to invoke the jurisdiction of such court."

6.   Rose sought an injunction, which would be considered by a judge rather than a jury. Why could a Cincinnati judge not consider his request?

7.   Judge Holschuh certified his denial of Pete Rose's motion to remand this action to state court. Why did Rose need such a certification in order to appeal this order? As we will see in Chapter 15, the final judgment rule usually precludes federal appellate review before the district judge has entered final judgment in the district court. One of the exceptions to the final judgment rule is an interlocutory appeal pursuant to 28 U.S.C. § 1292(b), although such an appeal requires the approval of both the district judge and the court of appeals.

8.   Had Judge Holschuh remanded Pete Rose's action back to state court, how could Commissioner Giamatti have challenged that decision? *See* 28 U.S.C. § 1447(d).

9.   On August 11, 1989, Judge Holschuh entered an order enjoining Commissioner Giamatti from holding a hearing until after the Sixth Circuit had ruled on Pete Rose's application for a Section 1292(b) interlocutory appeal:

> In order to give the Court of Appeals for the Sixth Circuit an opportunity to rule on the jurisdictional issue raised by Rose's pending application for an appeal from this Court's Order of July 31, 1989, proceedings in this Court, except for discovery proceedings by the parties, are stayed until further order of this Court or the Court of Appeals for the Sixth Circuit and the defendant Giamatti is enjoined from conducting the disciplinary hearing scheduled for August 17, 1989 until further order of this Court or the Court of Appeals for the Sixth Circuit.

Rose v. Giamatti, 721 F. Supp. 924, 929 (S.D. Ohio 1989).

10. Pete Rose ultimately was banned from baseball. His major league records include most career base hits (4256). Rose also has been declared ineligible for election to the National Baseball Hall of Fame. Through his website Rose offers to sign and personalize copies of the "Pete Rose Banishment Document" and baseballs inscribed "I'm sorry I bet on baseball." http://www.peterose.com.

VI. CONCLUSION

Although other prerequisites to suit such as territorial jurisdiction and venue will be discussed in the next chapter, a mandatory requirement for any civil action is that the court have subject-matter jurisdiction over that action. Federal courts are courts of limited jurisdiction, so Congress must confer jurisdiction on those courts to hear specific types of cases within the Article III judicial power.

The major grants of federal subject-matter jurisdiction, or judicial power, over certain types of case are federal-question ("arising under") jurisdiction under 28 U.S.C. § 1331, diversity jurisdiction under 28 U.S.C. § 1332, supplemental jurisdiction under 28 U.S.C. § 1367, and the federal courts' power to hear actions removed from state court pursuant to 28 U.S.C. § 1441. While challenges to other prerequisites to suit can be waived by the parties to a civil action, an absence of subject-matter jurisdiction can be raised at any time, by any party or by the court itself. Counsel should not "wait until the last minute" to raise this question, however, but should ensure that a federal statute provides a jurisdictional basis for every action filed in the United States District Courts.

VII. CHAPTER ASSESSMENT

A. Multiple-Choice Questions. Answer the following questions, reviewing the sections of the chapter noted in connection with each question.

1. After her suspension from high school, an Indiana student files an action in Indiana federal district court. The student alleges that her first amendment rights were violated by the suspension. She seeks reinstatement and $50,000 in damages from the defendant school officials, who also are citizens of Indiana. The defendants answer the complaint, the parties engage in discovery, and, one week before trial, the defendants file a motion to dismiss because the district court does not have subject-matter jurisdiction over the action.

Should the court grant the motion to dismiss this action?

Review Section II and choose the best answer from the following choices:

(a) No, because the student's claim arises under federal law.

(b) No, because the defendants did not raise the lack of subject-matter jurisdiction in a timely manner.

(c) Yes, because there is not more than $75,000 in controversy.

(d) Yes, because the defendants are citizens of Indiana.

2. A critical expose is done about a TV newscaster by a rival TV network. The newscaster files an action in federal district court against the network. Both the newscaster and TV network are citizens of Illinois, and the newscaster seeks $75,000 in damages. As alleged in his complaint, the substance of the newscaster's claim is that the TV network "slandered the plaintiff in its broadcast, violating his rights under the common law of Illinois, and nothing in the first amendment to the United States Constitution protects such slanderous speech."

The TV network files a Rule 12(b)(1) motion to dismiss the action for lack of subject-matter jurisdiction.

Should the court grant the motion to dismiss?

Review Section II(A) and choose the best answer from the following choices:

(a) Yes, because the newscaster's claim does not arise under federal law.

(b) Yes, because the newscaster has not met the minimum amount in controversy for either a federal question or diversity action.

(c) No, because the network is likely to rely upon a first amendment defense in this action.

(d) No, because the complaint invokes the First Amendment.

3. A Tennessee gas station owner buys her gasoline from a corporation that is incorporated in Delaware and has its principal place of business in Texas. The contract between the owner and the corporation provides that the corporation will provide the owner with 50,000 gallons of gasoline per week. However, the corporation has informed the owner that it can no longer supply that amount of gasoline because of federal environmental restrictions on its production process.

The gas station owner files an action in federal district court against the corporation and the pipeline company that brings the gasoline to Tennessee. The owner seeks $200,000 from both the corporation and the pipeline company, which is a citizen of Tennessee. The defendant corporation files a motion to dismiss, asserting that the district court does not have subject-matter jurisdiction over this action.

Should the court grant the motion to dismiss?

Review Section III and choose the best answer from the following choices:

(a) The court should deny the motion, because the corporation is not a citizen of Tennessee.

(b) The court should deny the motion, because resolution of the action will require the court to apply the federal law upon which the corporation relies to excuse its non-compliance with the parties' contract.

(c) The court should grant the motion, because the minimum amount in controversy has not been met.

(d) The court should grant the motion, because there is no complete diversity between the parties.

4.   In the aftermath of a weekend brawl, a California citizen brings a tort action in federal district court seeking $75,000 in total damages from two others involved in the fight: a citizen of Nevada and a citizen of Colorado. The defendants file a Rule 12(b)(1) motion to dismiss for lack of subject-matter jurisdiction.

Should the court grant the motion to dismiss this action?

Review Section III and choose the best answer from the following choices:

(a) Yes, because the minimum amount in controversy requirement for a federal-question action is not satisfied.

(b) Yes, because the minimum amount in controversy requirement for a diversity action is not satisfied.

(c) No, because the complete diversity requirement of Article III is satisfied.

(d) No, because the defendants are citizens of different states.

5.   On April 1, 2014, Parker, a citizen of Ohio, filed an action in Massachusetts state court against Dennis, a citizen Massachusetts, and Danielle, a citizen of Tennessee. Parker sought $250,000 in damages on a state-law breach of contract claim.

On April 25, 2014, Danielle filed a notice of removal in the United States District Court for the District of Massachusetts. Dennis consented to the removal in writing.

Can Danielle remove the action?

Review Section V(A) and choose the best answer from the following choices:

(a) No, because Dennis is a citizen of Massachusetts.

(b) No, because the notice of removal was filed more than 21 days after the action was filed.

(c) Yes, because the federal court would have had original jurisdiction of the action.

(d) Yes, because Dennis has consented to the removal.

B.   Essay Questions. To test your understanding of this chapter's material, outline or write an answer to the following questions.

1.   A State-Law Claim in Federal Court?

Robotics, Inc., which is incorporated in Delaware with its principal place of business in New York, files an action in United States District Court for the Northern District of California against its chief competitor, Microchips, Inc. Microchips is incorporated in California with its principal place of business in Delaware. Robotics' action consists of two claims: (1) a federal antitrust claim seeking $35,000 in damages and (2) a claim brought under California's state antitrust statute seeking $35,000 in damages. Both claims challenge the same allegedly anticompetitive actions by Microchips.

The claim asserted under federal law has been recognized in several federal circuits, but this is the first instance in which such a claim has been asserted in California. The district court sua sponte dismisses the federal claim as untimely under the governing statute of limitations, but states in its dismissal order that the state antitrust claim was timely filed within the longer limitations period for such state claims.

Microchips then files a Rule 12(b)(1) motion to dismiss the state claim for lack of subject-matter jurisdiction.

(a)   Can the federal court entertain the state-law claim?

(b)   Must the court do so?

2.   "We're out of Here!"

A manufacturer is incorporated in Indiana, has its corporate offices in Illinois, and employs 1000 workers at three plants in Ohio. The company is sued in Ohio state court by a Pennsylvania consumer who asserts that she suffered $80,000 in damages when the company's product malfunctioned.

The consumer filed the action in a city in which the company has had significant troubles with its work force, and the company would prefer that the action be heard in a federal court in Illinois where it has its corporate offices.

(a)   How could the company attempt to move this action to federal court in Ohio?

(b)   Will the company be successful in its attempt to move the action to Illinois federal court?

CHAPTER 4

NOTICE, TERRITORIAL JURISDICTION, AND VENUE: "WHERE CAN WE FILE OUR ACTION?"

I. INTRODUCTION

As you learned in the prior chapter, a court must have the power to hear the particular type of case before it. But even though the action may be a federal-question or diversity case falling within the court's subject-matter jurisdiction, the court may not be able to adjudicate an action involving the particular parties in that action. In this chapter we will consider: the notice and service of process by which one learns that he or she has been named as a party to a lawsuit; the court's territorial, or personal, jurisdiction over the parties to a civil action; and the venue requirements that determine in which specific federal district court a particular civil action can be filed. Our focus thus will be upon not whether a particular type of action can be filed, but where and against whom.

II. NOTICE AND SERVICE OF PROCESS

Regardless of where an action is filed, all parties must receive notice of the action in order to respond to the claims asserted and otherwise participate in the action. The plaintiff initiates the action by filing the complaint, so the concern is to ensure that defendants and other persons named as parties receive notice of the claims against them.

Rule 4 of the Federal Rules of Civil Procedure requires that defendants receive notice of a civil action filed against them. Even without the very specific requirements of Rule 4, the United States Constitution requires that defendants be notified of a civil action. As Justice Jackson stated in *Mullane v. Central Hanover Trust*, 339 U.S. 306, 314 (1950), the Due Process Clause of the Fourteenth Amendment requires "notice reasonably calculated, under all the circumstances, to apprise interested parties of the pendency of the action and afford them an opportunity to present their objections." The Supreme Court's decision in *Mullane* follows.

A. *MULLANE V. CENTRAL HANOVER BANK & TRUST CO.*

Mullane v. Central Hanover Bank & Trust Co.

Supreme Court of the United States, 1950
339 U.S. 306

OPINION

■ MR. JUSTICE JACKSON delivered the opinion of the Court.

This controversy questions the constitutional sufficiency of notice to beneficiaries on judicial settlement of accounts by the trustee of a common trust fund established under the New York Banking Law, Consol.Laws, c. 2. The New York Court of Appeals considered and overruled objections that the statutory notice contravenes requirements of the Fourteenth Amendment and that by allowance of the account beneficiaries were deprived of property without due process of law. The case is here on appeal under 28 U.S.C. § 1257.

Common trust fund legislation is addressed to a problem appropriate for state action. Mounting overheads have made administration of small trusts undesirable to corporate trustees. In order that donors and testators of moderately sized trusts may not be denied the service of corporate fiduciaries, the District of Columbia and some thirty states other than New York have permitted pooling small trust estates into one fund for investment administration. The income, capital gains, losses and expenses of the collective trust are shared by the constituent trusts in proportion to their contribution. By this plan, diversification of risk and economy of management can be extended to those whose capital standing alone would not obtain such advantage.

Statutory authorization for the establishment of such common trust funds is provided in the New York Banking Law. Under this Act a trust company may, with approval of the State Banking Board, establish a common fund and, within prescribed limits, invest therein the assets of an unlimited number of estates, trusts or other funds of which it is trustee. Each participating trust shares ratably in the common fund, but exclusive management and control is in the trust company as trustee, and neither a fiduciary nor any beneficiary of a participating trust is deemed to have ownership in any particular asset or investment of this common fund. * * * Provisions are made for accountings twelve to fifteen months after the establishment of a fund and triennially thereafter. The decree in each such judicial settlement of accounts is made binding and conclusive as to any matter set forth in the account upon everyone having any interest in the common fund or in any participating estate, trust or fund.

In January, 1946, Central Hanover Bank and Trust Company established a common trust fund in accordance with these provisions, and in March, 1947, it petitioned the Surrogate's Court for settlement of its first account as common trustee. During the accounting period a total of 113 trusts, approximately half inter vivos [effective during the life of the trust's creator] and half testamentary [established in a will], participated in the common trust fund, the gross capital of which was nearly three million dollars. The record does not show the number or residence of the beneficiaries, but they were many and it is clear that some of them were not residents of the State of New York.

The only notice given beneficiaries of this specific application was by publication in a local newspaper in strict compliance with the minimum requirements of N.Y. Banking Law § 100–c(12): "After filing such petition (for judicial settlement of its account) the petitioner shall cause to be issued by the court in which the petition is filed and shall publish not less than once in each week for four successive weeks in a newspaper to be designated by the court a notice or citation addressed generally without naming them to all parties interested in such common trust fund and in such estates, trusts or funds mentioned in the petition, all of which may be described in the notice or citation only in the manner set forth in said petition and without setting forth the residence of any such decedent or donor of any such estate, trust or fund." Thus the only notice required, and the only one given, was by newspaper publication setting forth merely the name and address of the trust company, the name and the date of establishment of the common trust fund, and a list of all participating estates, trusts or funds.

At the time the first investment in the common fund was made on behalf of each participating estate, however, the trust company, pursuant to the requirements of § 100–c(9), had notified by mail each person of full age and sound mind whose name and address was then known to it and who was "entitled to share in the income therefrom * * * (or) * * * who would be entitled to share in the principal if the event upon which such estate, trust or fund will become distributable should have occurred at the time of sending such notice." Included in the notice was a copy of those provisions of the Act relating to the sending of the notice itself and to the judicial settlement of common trust fund accounts.

Upon the filing of the petition for the settlement of accounts, appellant was, by order of the court pursuant to § 100–c(12), appointed special guardian and attorney for all persons known or unknown not otherwise appearing who had or might thereafter have any interest in the income of the common trust fund; and appellee Vaughan was appointed to represent those similarly interested in the principal. There were no other appearances on behalf of any one interested in either interest or principal.

Appellant appeared specially, objecting that notice and the statutory provisions for notice to beneficiaries were inadequate to afford due process under the Fourteenth Amendment, and therefore that the court was without jurisdiction to render a final and binding decree.

Appellant's objections were entertained and overruled, the Surrogate [judge] holding that the notice required and given was sufficient. A final decree accepting the accounts has been entered, affirmed by the Appellate Division of the Supreme Court and by the Court of Appeals of the State of New York.

The effect of this decree, as held below, is to settle "all questions respecting the management of the common fund." We understand that every right which beneficiaries would otherwise have against the trust company, either as trustee of the common fund or as trustee of any individual trust, for improper management of the common trust fund during the period covered by the accounting is sealed and wholly terminated by the decree. * * *

We are met at the outset with a challenge to the power of the State—the right of its courts to adjudicate at all as against those beneficiaries who reside without the State of New York. It is contended that the proceeding is one in personam in that the decree affects neither title to nor possession of any res, but adjudges only personal rights of the beneficiaries to surcharge their trustee for negligence or breach of trust. Accordingly, it is said, under the strict doctrine of *Pennoyer v. Neff*, 95 U.S. 714, the Surrogate is without jurisdiction as to nonresidents upon whom personal service of process was not made.

* * *

* * * It is sufficient to observe that * * * the interest of each state in providing means to close trusts that exist by the grace of its laws and are administered under the supervision of its courts is so insistent and rooted in custom as to establish beyond doubt the right of its courts to determine the interests of all claimants, resident or nonresident, provided its procedure accords full opportunity to appear and be heard.

Quite different from the question of a state's power to discharge trustees is that of the opportunity it must give beneficiaries to contest. Many controversies have raged about the cryptic and abstract words of the Due Process Clause but there can be no doubt that at a minimum they require that deprivation of life, liberty or property by adjudication be preceded by notice and opportunity for hearing appropriate to the nature of the case.

In two ways this proceeding does or may deprive beneficiaries of property. It may cut off their rights to have the trustee answer for negligent or illegal impairments of their interests. Also, their interests are presumably subject to diminution in the proceeding by allowance of fees and expenses to one who, in their names but without their knowledge, may conduct a fruitless or uncompensatory contest. Certainly the proceeding is one in which they may be deprived of property rights and hence notice and hearing must measure up to the standards of due process.

Personal service of written notice within the jurisdiction is the classic form of notice always adequate in any type of proceeding. But the vital interest of the State in bringing any issues as to its fiduciaries to a final settlement can be served only if interests or claims of individuals who are outside of the State can somehow be determined. A construction of the Due Process Clause which would place impossible or impractical obstacles in the way could not be justified.

Against this interest of the State we must balance the individual interest sought to be protected by the Fourteenth Amendment. This is defined by our holding that "The fundamental requisite of due process of law is the opportunity to be heard." *Grannis v. Ordean*, 234 U.S. 385, 394. This right to be heard has little reality or worth unless one is informed that the matter is pending and can choose for himself whether to appear or default, acquiesce or contest.

* * *

An elementary and fundamental requirement of due process in any proceeding which is to be accorded finality is notice reasonably calculated, under all the circumstances, to apprise interested parties of the pendency of the action and afford them an opportunity to present their objections. The notice must be of such nature as reasonably to convey the required information, and it must afford a reasonable time for those interested to make their appearance. But if with due regard for the practicalities and peculiarities of the case these conditions are reasonably met the constitutional requirements are satisfied. * * *

But when notice is a person's due, process which is a mere gesture is not due process. The means employed must be such as one desirous of actually informing the absentee might reasonably adopt to accomplish it. The reasonableness and hence the constitutional validity of any chosen method may be defended on the ground that it is in itself reasonably certain to inform those affected, or, where conditions do not reasonably permit such notice, that the form chosen is not substantially less likely to bring home notice than other of the feasible and customary substitutes.

It would be idle to pretend that publication alone as prescribed here, is a reliable means of acquainting interested parties of the fact that their rights are before the courts. * * * Chance alone brings to the attention of even a local resident an advertisement in small type inserted in the back pages of a newspaper, and if he makes his home outside the area of the newspaper's normal circulation the odds that the information will never reach him are large indeed. The chance of actual notice is further reduced when as here the notice required does not even name those whose attention it is supposed to attract, and does not inform acquaintances who might call it to attention. In weighing its sufficiency on the basis of equivalence with actual notice we are unable to regard this as more than a feint.

Nor is publication here reinforced by steps likely to attract the parties' attention to the proceeding. It is true that publication traditionally has been acceptable as notification supplemental to other action which in itself may reasonably be expected to convey a warning. The ways [of] an owner with tangible property are such that he usually arranges means to learn of any direct attack upon his possessory or proprietary rights. Hence, libel of a ship, attachment of a chattel or entry upon real estate in the name of law may reasonably be expected to come promptly to the owner's attention. When the state within which the owner has located such property seizes it for some reason, publication or posting affords an additional measure of notification. A state may indulge the assumption that one who has left tangible property in the state either has abandoned it, in which case proceedings against it deprive him of nothing, or that he has left some caretaker under a duty to let him know that it is being jeopardized. As phrased long ago by Chief Justice Marshall in *The Mary*, 9 Cranch 126, 144, "It is the part of common prudence for all those who have any interest in (a thing), to guard that interest by persons who are in a situation to protect it."

In the case before us there is, of course, no abandonment. On the other hand these beneficiaries do have a resident fiduciary as caretaker of their interest in this property. But it is their caretaker who in the accounting becomes their adversary. Their trustee is released from giving notice of jeopardy, and no one else is expected to do so. Not even the special guardian is required or apparently expected to communicate with his ward and client, and, of course, if such a duty were merely transferred from the trustee to the guardian, economy would not be served and more likely the cost would be increased.

This Court has not hesitated to approve of resort to publication as a customary substitute in another class of cases where it is not reasonably possible or practicable to give more adequate warning. Thus it has been recognized that, in the case of persons missing or unknown, employment of an indirect and even a probably futile means of notification is all that the situation permits and creates no constitutional bar to a final decree foreclosing their rights.

Those beneficiaries represented by appellant whose interests or whereabouts could not with due diligence be ascertained come clearly within this category. As to them the statutory notice is sufficient. However great the odds that publication will never reach the eyes of such unknown parties, it is not in the typical case much more likely to fail than any of the choices open to legislators endeavoring to prescribe the best notice practicable.

Nor do we consider it unreasonable for the State to dispense with more certain notice to those beneficiaries whose interests are either conjectural or future or, although they could be discovered upon investigation, do not in due course of business come to knowledge of the common trustee. Whatever searches might be required in another situation under ordinary standards of diligence, in view of the character of the proceedings and the nature of the interests here involved we think them unnecessary. We recognize the practical difficulties and costs that would be attendant on frequent investigations into the status of great numbers of beneficiaries, many of whose interests in the common fund are so remote as to be ephemeral; and we have no doubt that such impracticable and extended searches are not required in the name of due process. The expense of keeping informed from day to day of substitutions among even current income beneficiaries and presumptive remaindermen, to say nothing of the far greater number of contingent beneficiaries, would impose a severe burden on the plan, and would likely dissipate its advantages. These are practical matters in which we should be reluctant to disturb the judgment of the state authorities.

Accordingly we overrule appellant's constitutional objections to published notice insofar as they are urged on behalf of any beneficiaries whose interests or addresses are unknown to the trustee.

As to known present beneficiaries of known place of residence, however, notice by publication stands on a different footing. Exceptions in the name of necessity do not sweep away the rule that within the limits of practicability notice must be such as is reasonably calculated to reach interested parties. Where the names and post office addresses of those affected by a proceeding are at hand, the reasons disappear for resort to means less likely than the mails to apprise them of its pendency.

The trustee has on its books the names and addresses of the income beneficiaries represented by appellant, and we find no tenable ground for dispensing with a serious effort to inform them personally of the accounting, at least by ordinary mail to the record addresses. Certainly sending them a copy of the statute months and perhaps years in advance does not answer this purpose. The trustee periodically remits their income to them, and we think that they might reasonably expect that with or apart from their remittances word might come to them personally that steps were being taken affecting their interests.

We need not weigh contentions that a requirement of personal service of citation on even the large number of known resident or nonresident beneficiaries would, by reasons of delay if not of expense, seriously interfere with the proper administration of the fund. Of course personal service even without the jurisdiction of the issuing authority serves the end of actual and personal notice, whatever power of compulsion it might lack. However, no such service is required under the circumstances. This type of trust presupposes a large number of small interests. The individual interest does not stand alone but is identical with that of a class. The rights of each in the integrity of the fund and the fidelity of the trustee are shared by many other beneficiaries. Therefore notice reasonably certain to reach most of those interested in objecting is likely to safeguard the interests of all, since any objections sustained would inure to the benefit of all. * * *

The statutory notice to known beneficiaries is inadequate, not because in fact it fails to reach everyone, but because under the circumstances it is not reasonably calculated to reach those who could easily be informed by other means at hand. However it may have been in former times, the mails today are recognized as an efficient and inexpensive means of communication. Moreover, the fact that the trust company has been able to give mailed notice to known beneficiaries at the time the common trust fund was established is persuasive that postal notification at the time of accounting would not seriously burden the plan.

In some situations the law requires greater precautions in its proceedings than the business world accepts for its own purposes. In few, if any, will it be satisfied with less. Certainly it is instructive, in determining the reasonableness of the impersonal broadcast notification here used, to ask whether it would satisfy a prudent man of business, counting his pennies but finding it in his interest to convey information to many persons whose names and addresses are in his files. We are not satisfied that it would. Publication may theoretically be available for all the world to see, but it is too much in our day to suppose that each or any individual beneficiary does or could examine all that is published to see if something may be tucked away in it that affects his property interests. We have before indicated in reference to notice by publication that, "Great caution should be used not to let fiction deny the fair play that can be secured only by a pretty close adhesion to fact." *McDonald v. Mabee*, 243 U.S. 90, 91.

We hold the notice of judicial settlement of accounts required by the New York Banking Law is incompatible with the requirements of the Fourteenth Amendment as a basis for adjudication depriving known persons whose whereabouts are also known of substantial property rights. Accordingly the judgment is reversed and the cause remanded for further proceedings not inconsistent with this opinion.

Reversed.

■ MR. JUSTICE DOUGLAS took no part in the consideration or decision of this case.

■ MR. JUSTICE BURTON, dissenting.

These common trusts are available only when the instruments creating the participating trusts permit participation in the common fund. Whether or not further notice to beneficiaries should supplement the notice and representation here provided is properly within the discretion of the State. The Federal Constitution does not require it here.

COMMENTS AND QUESTIONS CONCERNING
MULLANE V. CENTRAL HANOVER BANK & TRUST CO.

1.   The notice at issue in *Mullane* was publication in a newspaper for four successive weeks. Would such notice be more, or less, constitutionally sufficient today than it was at the time of that case? If something other than personal notice were attempted, could the notice be more targeted to likely beneficiaries than through notice in a local newspaper? How does Justice Jackson's comment about mail notice stand the test of time? Is it still the case that "[h]owever it may have been in former times, the mails today are recognized as an efficient and inexpensive means of communication"? If personal notification were attempted, would newspaper notice have been a useful supplement to such individual notice?

2.   The New York statute at issue in *Mullane* required that newspaper notice be "addressed generally without naming them to all parties interested in such common trust fund and in such estates, trusts or funds mentioned in the petition, all of which may be described in the notice or citation only in the manner set forth in said petition and without setting forth the residence of any such decedent or donor of any such estate, trust or fund." Will all trust beneficiaries realize that they are a beneficiary? Even if someone knows that she is a trust beneficiary, will she know that a trust listed in the newspaper is "her" trust? Why not include in the newspaper notice the names and addresses of those beneficiaries that the bank has?

3.   What was Mullane's role in this proceeding? Why did the Court nevertheless require that individual beneficiaries receive personal notice of the trust proceeding? Can the appointment of a guardian ever substitute for personal notice to everyone with an interest in a proceeding? Is it significant that it was Mullane who raised the constitutional due process challenge to the lack of personal notice in this case?

4.   What are the implications of the following statement by Justice Jackson:

> The individual interest does not stand alone but is identical with that of a class. The rights of each in the integrity of the fund and the fidelity of the trustee are shared by many other beneficiaries. Therefore notice reasonably certain to reach most of those interested in objecting is likely to safeguard the interests of all, since any objections sustained would inure to the benefit of all.

Would it be constitutional to send personal notice to 51% of the beneficiaries? Or must a reasonably diligent effort be made to notify all class members?

In Chapter 7, we will consider the differing notice requirements for a class action under Rule 23(c)(2) of the Federal Rules of Civil Procedure. *Compare* Rule 23(c)(2)(A) ("For any class certified under Rule 23(b)(1) or (b)(2), the court may direct appropriate notice to the class.") *with* Rule 23(c)(2)(B) ("For any class certified under Rule 23(b)(3), the court must direct to class members the best notice that is practicable under the circumstances, including individual notice to all members who can be identified through reasonable effort.").

5.   In what types of situations does Justice Jackson suggest that newspaper notification might satisfy the requirements of due process? If some beneficiaries cannot be located with due diligence, will an apparently futile attempt to notify them through newspaper ads be sufficient? Are there other beneficiaries to whom personal notice need not be sent? How much effort must the bank undertake to locate individual beneficiaries?

6.   Justice Jackson articulates a very practical due process standard: "[W]ithin the limits of practicability notice must be such as is reasonably calculated to reach interested parties." Would it have been practical to mail notices to all beneficiaries? If the beneficiaries owed money to the bank, is it likely that they would have received individual mail notices of this fact? *See* 339 U.S. at 320 ("Certainly it is instructive, in determining the reasonableness of the impersonal broadcast notification here used, to ask whether it would satisfy a prudent man of business, counting his pennies but finding it in his interest to convey information to many persons whose names and addresses are in his files.").

7.   Justice Burton's dissent, in its entirety, provides:

> These common trusts are available only when the instruments creating the participating trusts permit participation in the common fund. Whether or not further notice to beneficiaries should supplement the notice and representation here provided is properly within the discretion of the State. The Federal Constitution does not require it here.

What is Justice Burton suggesting as to why the Fourteenth Amendment Due Process Clause does not require additional notice in this action?

B. NOTICE AND SERVICE OF PROCESS UNDER RULE 4 OF THE FEDERAL RULES OF CIVIL PROCEDURE

Mullane makes it clear that parties with an interest in a civil action must receive notice of that action and be provided with an opportunity to respond to the claims asserted in the action. In the federal district courts, this notice is provided pursuant to Rule 4 of the Federal Rules of Civil Procedure.

Notice is provided in the federal district courts by the service of a summons and a copy of the complaint on the defendant or other party (such as a third-party defendant) against whom a claim is asserted in the action. The summons is the legal document that formally notifies a defendant of the lawsuit, informs him that "a failure to appear and defend will result in a default judgment against the defendant for the relief demanded in the complaint,"[1] and provides further details concerning the civil action and the name and address of the plaintiff's

---

[1]   Fed. R. Civ. P. 4(a)(1)(E).

attorney (or plaintiff, if she is not represented by an attorney).[2] Below is a copy of the federal summons form ("AO 440") used in United States District Courts.

[Case Caption]

SUMMONS IN A CIVIL ACTION

To: (*Defendant's name and address*)

A lawsuit has been filed against you.

Within 21 days after service of this summons on you (not counting the day you received it)—or 60 days if you are the United States or a United States agency, or an officer or employee of the United States described in Fed. R. Civ. P. 12(a)(2) or (3)—you must serve on the plaintiff an answer to the attached complaint or a motion under Rule 12 of the Federal Rules of Civil Procedure. The answer or motion must be served on the plaintiff or plaintiff's attorney, whose name and address are:

If you fail to respond, judgment by default will be entered against you for the relief demanded in the complaint. You also must file your answer or motion with the court.

CLERK OF COURT

Date:

Signature of Clerk or Deputy Clerk

Rule 4 provides different methods of service for different types of defendants. Rule 4(e) provides the basic means of service of process for individual defendants within a judicial district of the United States. Rule 4(e) provides several alternative methods for such service:

> Unless federal law provides otherwise, an individual— other than a minor, an incompetent person, or a person whose waiver has been filed—may be served in a judicial district of the United States by:
>
> (1) following state law for serving a summons in an action brought in courts of general jurisdiction in the state where the district court is located or where service is made; or
>
> (2) doing any of the following:
>
>> (A) delivering a copy of the summons and of the complaint to the individual personally;

---

[2] Fed. R. Civ. P. 4(a)(1).

(B) leaving a copy of each at the individual's dwelling or usual place of abode with someone of suitable age and discretion who resides there; or

(C) delivering a copy of each to an agent authorized by appointment or by law to receive service of process.[3]

Traditionally, service was effected by personally giving the defendant a copy of the summons and complaint, and, under Rule 4(e)(2)(A), this remains one of the ways in which service can be accomplished. Rule 4(e)(2)(B) also provides that service can be effected by leaving for the defendant a copy of the summons and complaint at the defendant's "usual place of abode" with "someone of suitable age and discretion who resides there." Thus the summons and complaint cannot be left with the mailman or anyone else who doesn't live at the dwelling or with the defendant's five-year-old son ("Could you please give this to your Mommy?"). But, rather than personally presenting the defendant with the summons and complaint, it could be left at the defendant's home with his or her spouse or partner—as long as they live there as well.

The final possible means of service under Rule 4(e)(2) is to give the summons and complaint to "an agent authorized by appointment or by law to receive service of process." Corporations and other businesses typically are required to appoint an agent for service of process in the states in which they do business, and service upon such an agent is considered service upon the organization in question.[4]

---

[3] Rule 4(e) specifically excludes from its coverage "a minor, an incompetent person, or a person whose waiver has been filed." Waiver of service of process is discussed in Section D, and Rule 4(g) provides the following specific provisions for service on a minor or incompetent person:

> A minor or an incompetent person in a judicial district of the United States must be served by following state law for serving a summons or like process on such a defendant in an action brought in the courts of general jurisdiction of the state where service is made. A minor or an incompetent person who is not within any judicial district of the United States must be served in the manner prescribed by Rule 4(f)(2)(A), (f)(2)(B), or (f)(3).

[4] Rule 4(h) lists additional ways by which a corporation, partnership or unincorporated association can be served. Rule 4(h) provides:

> Unless federal law provides otherwise or the defendant's waiver has been filed, a domestic or foreign corporation, or a partnership or other unincorporated association that is subject to suit under a common name, must be served:
>
> (1) in a judicial district of the United States:
>
>> (A) in the manner prescribed by Rule 4(e)(1) for serving an individual [pursuant to state law]; or
>>
>> (B) by delivering a copy of the summons and of the complaint to an officer, a managing or general agent, or any other agent authorized by appointment or by law to receive service of process and—if the agent is one authorized by statute and the statute so requires—by also mailing a copy of each to the defendant; or
>
> (2) at a place not within any judicial district of the United States, in any manner prescribed by Rule 4(f) for serving an individual, except personal delivery under (f)(2)(C)(i).

In addition to the possibilities delineated in Rule 4(e)(2), Rule 4(e)(1) authorizes federal service of process by "following state law for serving a summons in an action brought in courts of general jurisdiction in the state where the district court is located or where service is made." Thus, in *Keller Williams Realty, Inc. v. Lapeer*, CA No. 4:08–CV–1292, 2008 WL 2944601 (S.D. Tex. July 31, 2008), the court approved service of process by email pursuant to Rule 4(e)(2) and Rule 106(b) of the Texas Rules of Civil Procedure, which provides that, after unsuccessful mail or personal delivery, service is possible "in any other manner that the affidavit or other evidence before the court shows will be reasonably effective to give the defendant notice of the suit."

State law alternatives such as this, as well as the multiple possibilities under Rule 4 itself, have given parties a variety of ways in which to formally notify defendants about a civil action that has been filed against them. In an earlier era when the predominant way to serve defendants was to personally hand them a copy of the summons and complaint, crafty defendants resorted to creative stratagems to evade service of process. These evasive tactics were met by even more clever efforts to personally serve defendants. Consider the effort to serve Robert Vesco for alleged violations of the fraud provisions of the Securities and Exchange Act of 1934. After being rebuffed by a bolted door and armed bodyguards, the process server returned by taxi to Vesco's Nassau residence.

> There she threw a copy of the summons and complaint folded and tied with a blue ribbon over the fence and photographed the papers as they remained on the lawn in front of the house. The two guards immediately ran out to the gate, one armed with a stick and the other with a piece of pipe. One pulled open the door of the car and demanded that Miss Yohonn come out. The cab driver remonstrated with the guards and told them they could do nothing to Miss Yohonn while she was in his cab. When she told the guard that he had no right to touch the cab, he replied that she had no right to put anything on the property.[5]

Process servers also resorted to such stratagems as serving a defendant on a nonstop flight from Memphis to Dallas when the

---

When serving a corporation, partnership, or unincorporated association, counsel should be careful not to simply send a copy of the summons and complaint to "the corporation." *See* Advisory Committee Note to 1993 Amendment to Rule 4, 146 F.R.D. 401, 569 (1993) ("Care must be taken * * * to address the request [for waiver of service of process] to an individual officer or authorized agent of the corporation. It is not effective use of the Notice and Request procedure if the mail is sent undirected to the mail room of the organization.").

In addition to the specification in Rule 4(h) of these procedures for serving corporations, partnerships, and unincorporated associations, Rule 4(i) provides a separate procedure for serving the United States and its agencies, corporations, officers, and employees, while Rule 4(j) contains special rules by which a foreign, state, or local government must be served.

[5] *International Controls Corp. v. Vesco*, 593 F.2d 166, 177 (2d Cir. 1979) (which also describes the subsequent pursuit of the process server by Vesco's armed bodyguards).

airplane was over Arkansas and within the jurisdiction of the United States District Court for the Eastern District of Arkansas.[6] Because of the alternative means of service provided in Rule 4, the ability of federal courts to rely upon state service-of-process procedures pursuant to Rule 4(e)(1), and the possibility of service pursuant to electronic technology, these cat-and-mouse games are played much less frequently than in an earlier era.

In addition to the Rule 4 provisions governing service on defendants within the United States, Rule 4(f) contains specific requirements for serving an individual in a foreign country. These requirements are considered in Section D.

Figure 4-1 shows the different means of federal service of process.

FIGURE 4–1
SERVICE OF PROCESS METHODS UNDER FEDERAL RULE 4

Defendant Served	Federal Rule	Method(s) of Service
Individual within the United States	Rule 4(e)	state law service—Rule 4(e)(1); personal delivery—Rule 4(e)(2)(A); leaving papers at dwelling with someone of suitable age and discretion—Rule 4(e)(2)(B); or delivery to agent—Rule 4(e)(2)(C)
Individual Outside the United States	Rule 4(f)	pursuant to international agreement—Rule 4(f)(1); if no international agreement, by method reasonably calculated to give notice pursuant to (A) foreign law; (B) letter rogatory or letter of request; or (C) unless prohibited by foreign law, by personal delivery or mail from clerk requiring signed receipt—Rule 4(f)(2); or court order adopting other means not prohibited by international agreement—Rule 4(f)(3)

---

[6] *Grace v. MacArthur*, 170 F. Supp. 442 (E.D. Ark. 1959). This case was decided at a time when Rule 4 limited service to "anywhere within the territorial limits of the state in which the district court is held and, when a statute of the United States so provides, beyond the territorial limits of that state." Today, under Rule 4(k)(1)(A), state long-arm provisions can be used by a federal district court to serve defendants outside the state in which the court is located.

Minor or Incompetent Person	Rule 4(g)	pursuant to state law; or pursuant to Rule 4(f)(2)(A), 4(f)(2)(B), or 4(f)(3) if person is outside United States
Corporation, Partnership, or Unincorporated Association	Rule 4(h)	pursuant to Rule 4(e)(1)—Rule 4(h)(1)(A)); by delivery to officer or agent—Rule 4(h)(1)(B); or if outside United States, pursuant to Rule 4(f)(1); 4(f)(2)(A), (B), or (C)(ii); or 4(f)(3)—Rule 4(h)(2))
United States or U.S. Agencies, Corporations, Officers or Employees	Rule 4(i)	United States: delivery to U. S. Attorney, with copy to Attorney General and to nonparty agency or officer whose order is challenged—Rule 4(i)(1); U.S. Agency, Corporation, Officer or Employee: serve United States, with copy to agency, corporation, officer or employee sued—Rule 4(i)(2); or U.S. Officer or Employee: serve United States and officer or employee pursuant to Rule 4(e), (f), or (g)—Rule 4(i)(3)
Foreign, State, or Local Government	Rule 4(j)	Foreign State: pursuant to 28 U.S.C. § 1608; or State or Local Government: deliver papers to chief executive officer or serve pursuant to state law

C. WAIVER OF SERVICE OF PROCESS PURSUANT TO RULE 4(d)

Service of process pursuant to Rule 4 can be technical, time-consuming, and expensive. Rule 4(d), though, allows the parties to dispense with formal service of process. Rule 4(d)(1) provides:

> An individual, corporation, or association that is subject to service under Rule 4(e), (f), or (h) has a duty to avoid unnecessary expenses of serving the summons. The plaintiff may notify such a defendant that an action has been commenced and request that the defendant waive service of a summons.

Rule 4(d)(4) specifies the effect of a Rule 4(d) waiver of service of process: "When the plaintiff files a waiver, proof of service is not required and these rules apply as if a summons and complaint had been served at the time of filing the waiver."[7] Rule 4(d)(5) also specifically provides: "Waiving service of a summons does not waive any objection to personal jurisdiction or to venue." Thus a defendant can waive service of process, but later file a Rule 12(b)(2) motion to dismiss the action for lack of personal jurisdiction or a Rule 12(b)(3) motion to dismiss for improper venue.

The Federal Rules contain both a carrot and a stick to encourage defendants to waive service of process. Rules 4(d)(3) and 12(a)(1)(A)(ii) grant defendants who waive service additional time (typically 60 rather than the standard 21 days) to respond to the complaint.[8] In addition, Rule 4(d)(2) imposes upon a defendant located in the United States who, without good cause, fails to waive service: (A) the expenses of formal service and (B) the reasonable expenses of any motion required to collect these expenses of service.

Rule 4(d)(1) contains numerous requirements for requests to waive service, such as that the request be in writing, contain the name of the court where the complaint was filed, be accompanied by a copy of the complaint, and inform the defendant of the consequences of waiving and not waiving service. A form following Rule 4 within the Federal Rules of Civil Procedure illustrates the information that must be included in the notice of lawsuit and request for waiver of service contemplated by Rule 4(d)(1):

NOTICE OF A LAWSUIT AND REQUEST TO WAIVE SERVICE OF A SUMMONS

(CAPTION)

To: *(name of the defendant or—if the defendant is a corporation, partnership, or association—name of an officer or agent authorized to receive service)*

Why are you getting this?

A lawsuit has been filed against you, or the entity you represent, in this court under the number shown above. A copy of the complaint is attached.

---

[7]   The time of service can be significant, because Rule 4(m) provides that, except for service in a foreign country, "If a defendant is not served within 90 days after the complaint is filed, the court—on motion or on its own after notice to the plaintiff—must dismiss the action without prejudice against that defendant or order that service be made within a specified time." However, Rule 4(m) further provides that "if the plaintiff shows good cause for the failure, the court must extend the time for service for an appropriate period."

[8]   Defendants to whom the request for waiver of process is sent within the United States receive 60 days after the request was sent to respond to the complaint, while defendants sent the request outside any judicial district of the United States have 90 days after the request was sent in which to respond. F. R. Civ. P. 4(d)(3).

This is not a summons, or an official notice from the court. It is a request that, to avoid expenses, you waive formal service of a summons by signing and returning the enclosed waiver. To avoid these expenses, you must return the signed waiver within (*give at least 30 days or at least 60 days if the defendant is outside any judicial district of the United States*) from the date shown below, which is the date this notice was sent. Two copies of the waiver form are enclosed, along with a stamped, self-addressed envelope or other prepaid means for returning one copy. You may keep the other copy.

What happens next?

If you return the signed waiver, I will file it with the court. The action will then proceed as if you had been served on the date the waiver is filed, but no summons will be served on you and you will have 60 days from the date this notice is sent (see the date below) to answer the complaint (or 90 days if this notice is sent to you outside any judicial district of the United States).

If you do not return the signed waiver within the time indicated, I will arrange to have the summons and complaint served on you. And I will ask the court to require you, or the entity you represent, to pay the expenses of making service.

Please read the enclosed statement about the duty to avoid unnecessary expenses.

I certify that this request is being sent to you on the date below.

Date: _____

_____

(Signature of the attorney
or unrepresented party)

_____

(Printed name)

_____

(Address)

_____

(E-mail Address)

_____

(Telephone number)

_____

It generally is in the interest of all parties, and the court, that the defendant waive formal service of process. The typical response to a Notice of a Lawsuit and Request to Waive Service of Summons, therefore, is for the defendant to sign and return to the plaintiff a form waiving service—such as the second form that follows Rule 4 within the Federal Rules of Civil Procedure ("Waiver of the Service of Summons").

D. ELECTRONIC SERVICE OF PROCESS OUTSIDE THE UNITED STATES: *RIO PROPERTIES, INC. V. RIO INTERNATIONAL INTERLINK*

Rule 4(e) of the Federal Rules of Civil Procedure governs service upon most defendants in civil actions in the United States District Courts. However, Rule 4(e) only applies to defendants who are served within a judicial district of the United States.

Rule 4(f) of the Federal Rules of Civil Procedure sets forth the method by which defendants may be served in a foreign country. Rule 4(f) states:

> Unless federal law provides otherwise, an individual— other than a minor, an incompetent person, or a person whose waiver has been filed—may be served at a place not within any judicial district of the United States:
>
> > (1) by any internationally agreed means of service that is reasonably calculated to give notice, such as those authorized by the Hague Convention on the Service Abroad of Judicial and Extrajudicial Documents;
> >
> > (2) if there is no internationally agreed means, or if an international agreement allows but does not specify other means, by a method that is reasonably calculated to give notice:
> >
> > > (A) as prescribed by the foreign country's law for service in that country in an action in its courts of general jurisdiction;
> > >
> > > (B) as the foreign authority directs in response to a letter rogatory or letter of request; or
> > >
> > > (C) unless prohibited by the foreign country's law, by:
> > >
> > > > (i)   delivering a copy of the summons and of the complaint to the individual personally; or
> > > >
> > > > (ii) using any form of mail that the clerk addresses and sends to the individual and that requires a signed receipt; or
> >
> > (3) by other means not prohibited by international agreement, as the court orders.

If the defendant is to be served in a nation that has adopted the Hague Convention on the Service Abroad of Judicial and Extrajudicial Documents, the Supreme Court has held that "compliance with the Convention is mandatory in all cases to which it applies." *Volkswagenwerk Aktiengesellschaft v. Schlunk*, 486 U.S. 694, 705

(1988). In other situations, Rule 4(f)(2) provides specific possible means of service and Rule 4(f)(3) allows "other means not prohibited by international agreement, as the court orders." Just what type of service a court can adopt under Rule 4(f)(3) is at issue in the following case.

Rio Properties, Inc. v. International Interlink

United States Court of Appeals, Ninth Circuit, 2002
284 F.3d 1007

OPINION

■ TROTT, CIRCUIT JUDGE:

Las Vegas hotel and casino operator Rio Properties, Inc. ("RIO") sued Rio International Interlink ("RII"), a foreign Internet business entity, asserting various statutory and common law trademark infringement claims. The district court entered default judgment against RII for failing to comply with the court's discovery orders. RII now appeals the sufficiency of the service of process, effected via email and regular mail pursuant to Federal Rule of Civil Procedure 4(f)(3), the district court's exercise of personal jurisdiction, and ultimately, the entry of default judgment and the award of attorneys' fees and costs. We have jurisdiction pursuant to 28 U.S.C. § 1291, and we affirm the district court's decision.

BACKGROUND

RIO owns the RIO All Suite Casino Resort, the "Best Hotel Value in the World" according to Travel and Leisure Magazine, not to mention the "Best Overall Hotel in Las Vegas," according to the Zagat Survey of Resorts, Hotels and Spas. In addition to its elegant hotel, RIO's gambling empire consists of the Rio Race & Sports Book, which allows customers to wager on professional sports. To protect its exclusive rights in the "RIO" name, RIO registered numerous trademarks with the United States Patent and Trademark Office. When RIO sought to expand its presence onto the Internet, it registered the domain name, www.playrio.com. At that address, RIO operates a website that informs prospective customers about its hotel and allows those enticed by Lady Luck to make reservations.

RII is a Costa Rican entity that participates in an Internet sports gambling operation, doing business variously as Rio International Sportsbook, Rio Online Sportsbook, or Rio International Sports. RII enables its customers to wager on sporting events online or via a 1–800 telephone number. Far from a penny ante operation, RII grosses an estimated $3 million annually.

RIO became aware of RII's existence by virtue of RII's advertisement in the Football Betting Guide Preview. RIO later discovered, in the Nevada edition of the Daily Racing Form, another RII advertisement which invited customers to visit RII's website, www.riosports.com. RII also ran radio spots in Las Vegas as part of its comprehensive marketing strategy.

Upon learning of RII, RIO fired off an epistle demanding that RII cease and desist from operating the www.riosports.com website. Although RII did not formally respond, it promptly disabled the objectionable website. Apparently not ready to cash in its chips, RII soon activated the URL http://www.betrio.com to host an identical sports gambling operation. Perturbed, RIO filed the present action alleging various trademark infringement claims and seeking to enjoin RII from the continued use of the name "RIO."

To initiate suit, RIO attempted to locate RII in the United States for service of process. RIO discovered that RII claimed an address in Miami, Florida when it registered the allegedly infringing domain names. As it turned out, however, that address housed only RII's international courier, IEC, which was not authorized to accept service on RII's behalf. Nevertheless, IEC agreed to forward the summons and complaint to RII's Costa Rican courier.

After sending a copy of the summons and complaint through IEC, RIO received a telephone call from Los Angeles attorney John Carpenter ("Carpenter") inquiring about the lawsuit. Apparently, RII received the summons and complaint from IEC and subsequently consulted Carpenter about how to respond. Carpenter indicated that RII provided him with a partially illegible copy of the complaint and asked RIO to send him a complete copy. RIO agreed to resend the complaint and, in addition, asked Carpenter to accept service for RII; Carpenter politely declined. Carpenter did, however, request that RIO notify him upon successful completion of service of process on RII.

Thus thwarted in its attempt to serve RII in the United States, RIO investigated the possibility of serving RII in Costa Rica. Toward this end, RIO searched international directory databases looking for RII's address in Costa Rica. These efforts proved fruitless however; the investigator learned only that RII preferred communication through its email address, email@betrio.com, and received snail mail, including payment for its services, at the IEC address in Florida.

Unable to serve RII by conventional means, RIO filed an emergency motion for alternate service of process. RII opted not to respond to RIO's motion. The district court granted RIO's motion, and pursuant to Federal Rules of Civil Procedure 4(h)(2) and 4(f)(3), ordered service of process on RII through the mail to Carpenter and IEC and via RII's email address, email@betrio.com.

Court order in hand, RIO served RII by these court-sanctioned methods. RII filed a motion to dismiss for insufficient service of process and lack of personal jurisdiction. The parties fully briefed the issues, and the district court denied RII's motion without a hearing. RII then filed its answer, denying RIO's allegations and asserting twenty-two affirmative defenses.

As the case proceeded, RIO propounded discovery requests and interrogatories on RII. RIO granted RII two informal extensions of time in which to respond. Nonetheless, RII's eventual responses were almost entirely useless, consisting largely of the answer "N/A," ostensibly meaning "Not Applicable." After additional futile attempts to elicit good faith responses from RII, RIO brought a motion to compel discovery. In granting RIO's motion, the district court warned that in the event RII failed to comply, monetary sanctions would be an insufficient remedy and that "preclusive sanctions" would be awarded. When RII failed to comply with the district court's discovery order, RIO moved for terminating sanctions. Although RII belatedly complied, in part, with RIO's discovery request, the district court granted RIO's motion for sanctions and entered default judgment against RII. Citing RII's reprehensible conduct and bad faith, the district court additionally directed RII to pay reasonable attorneys' fees and costs to RIO in the amount of $88,761.50 and $7,859.52 respectively.

RII now appeals the sufficiency of the court-ordered service of process, the district court's exercise of personal jurisdiction as well as the propriety of the default judgment, and the award of attorneys' fees and costs.

DISCUSSION

I   ALTERNATIVE SERVICE OF PROCESS

A.   Applicability of Rule 4(f)(3)

We review for an abuse of discretion the district court's decision regarding the sufficiency of service of process. Federal Rule of Civil Procedure 4(h)(2) authorizes service of process on a foreign business entity in the manner prescribed by Rule 4(f) for individuals. The subsection of Rule 4(f) relevant to our decision, Rule 4(f)(3), permits service in a place not within any judicial district of the United States "by . . . means not prohibited by international agreement as may be directed by the court."

As obvious from its plain language, service under Rule 4(f)(3) must be (1) directed by the court; and (2) not prohibited by international agreement. No other limitations are evident from the text. In fact, as long as court-directed and not prohibited by an international agreement, service of process ordered under Rule 4(f)(3) may be accomplished in contravention of the laws of the foreign country. See *Mayoral-Amy v. BHI Corp.*, 180 F.R.D. 456, 459 n. 4 (S.D.Fla.1998). But see Fed.R.Civ.P. 4(f)(2) advisory committee notes (stating that under Rule 4(f)(2), "[s]ervice by methods that would violate foreign law is not generally authorized").

RII argues that Rule 4(f) should be read to create a hierarchy of preferred methods of service of process. RII's interpretation would require that a party attempt service of process by those methods enumerated in Rule 4(f)(2), including by diplomatic channels and letters rogatory, before petitioning the court for alternative relief under Rule 4(f)(3). We find no support for RII's position. No such requirement is found in the Rule's text, implied by its structure, or even hinted at in the advisory committee notes.

By all indications, court-directed service under Rule 4(f)(3) is as favored as service available under Rule 4(f)(1) or Rule 4(f)(2). Indeed, Rule 4(f)(3) is one of three separately numbered subsections in Rule 4(f), and each subsection is separated from the one previous merely by the simple conjunction "or." Rule 4(f)(3) is not subsumed within or in any way dominated by Rule 4(f)'s other subsections; it stands independently, on equal footing. Moreover, no language in Rules 4(f)(1) or 4(f)(2) indicates their primacy, and certainly Rule 4(f)(3) includes no qualifiers or limitations which indicate its availability only after attempting service of process by other means.

The advisory committee notes ("advisory notes") bolster our analysis. Beyond stating that service ordered under Rule 4(f)(3) must comport with constitutional notions of due process and must not be prohibited by international agreement, the advisory notes indicate the availability of alternate service of process under Rule 4(f)(3) without first attempting service by other means. Specifically, the advisory notes suggest that in cases of "urgency," Rule 4(f)(3) may allow the district court to order a "special method of service," even if other methods of service remain incomplete or unattempted.

Thus, examining the language and structure of Rule 4(f) and the accompanying advisory committee notes, we are left with the inevitable conclusion that service of process under Rule 4(f)(3) is neither a "last resort" nor "extraordinary relief." It is merely one means among several which enables service of process on an international defendant.

* * * [W]e hold that Rule 4(f)(3) is an equal means of effecting service of process under the Federal Rules of Civil Procedure, and we commit to the sound discretion of the district court the task of determining when the particularities and necessities of a given case require alternate service of process under Rule 4(f)(3).

Applying this proper construction of Rule 4(f)(3) and its predecessor, trial courts have authorized a wide variety of alternative methods of service including publication, ordinary mail, mail to the defendant's last known address, delivery to the defendant's attorney, telex, and most recently, email. See *SEC v. Tome*, 833 F.2d 1086, 1094 (2d Cir.1987) (condoning service of process by publication in the Int'l Herald Tribune); *Smith v. Islamic Emirate*, Nos. 01 Civ. 10132, 01 Civ. 10144, 2001 WL 1658211, at 2–3 (S.D.N.Y. Dec. 26, 2001) (authorizing service of process on terrorism impresario Osama bin Laden and al-Qaeda by publication); *Levin v. Ruby Trading Corp.*, 248 F.Supp. 537, 541–44 (S.D.N.Y.1965) (employing service by ordinary mail); *Int'l*

Controls Corp. v. Vesco, 593 F.2d 166, 176–78 (2d Cir.1979) (approving service by mail to last known address); *Forum Fin. Group*, 199 F.R.D. at 23–24 (authorizing service to defendant's attorney); *New Eng. Merchs. Nat'l Bank v. Iran Power Generation & Transmission Co.*, 495 F.Supp. 73, 80 (S.D.N.Y.1980) (allowing service by telex for Iranian defendants); *Broadfoot v. Diaz (In re Int'l Telemedia Assoc.)*, 245 B.R. 713, 719–20 (Bankr.N.D.Ga.2000) (authorizing service via email).

In this case, RIO attempted to serve RII by conventional means in the United States. Although RII claimed an address in Florida, that address housed only IEC, RII's international courier, which refused to accept service of process on RII's behalf. RII's attorney, Carpenter, who was specifically consulted in this matter, also declined to accept service of process. RIO's private investigator subsequently failed to discover RII's whereabouts in Costa Rica. Thus unable to serve RII, RIO brought an emergency motion to effectuate alternative service of process.

Contrary to RII's assertions, RIO need not have attempted every permissible means of service of process before petitioning the court for alternative relief. Instead, RIO needed only to demonstrate that the facts and circumstances of the present case necessitated the district court's intervention. Thus, when RIO presented the district court with its inability to serve an elusive international defendant, striving to evade service of process, the district court properly exercised its discretionary powers to craft alternate means of service. We expressly agree with the district court's handling of this case and its use of Rule 4(f)(3) to ensure the smooth functioning of our courts of law.

B. Reasonableness of the Court Ordered Methods of Service

Even if facially permitted by Rule 4(f)(3), a method of service of process must also comport with constitutional notions of due process. To meet this requirement, the method of service crafted by the district court must be "reasonably calculated, under all the circumstances, to apprise interested parties of the pendency of the action and afford them an opportunity to present their objections." *Mullane v. Cent. Hanover Bank & Trust Co.*, 339 U.S. 306, 314 (1950).

Without hesitation, we conclude that each alternative method of service of process ordered by the district court was constitutionally acceptable. In our view, each method of service was reasonably calculated, under these circumstances, to apprise RII of the pendency of the action and afford it an opportunity to respond.

In particular, service through IEC was appropriate because RII listed IEC's address as its own when registering the allegedly infringing domain name. The record also reflects that RII directed its customers to remit payment to IEC's address. Moreover, when RIO sent a copy of the summons and complaint to RII through IEC, RII received it. All told, this evidence indicates that RII relied heavily upon IEC to operate its business in the United States and that IEC could effectively pass information to RII in Costa Rica.

Service upon Carpenter was also appropriate because he had been specifically consulted by RII regarding this lawsuit. He knew of RII's legal positions, and it seems clear that he was in contact with RII in Costa Rica. Accordingly, service to Carpenter was also reasonably calculated in these circumstances to apprise RII of the pendency of the present action.

Finally, we turn to the district court's order authorizing service of process on RII by email at email@betrio.com. * * * Considering the facts presented by this case, we conclude not only that service of process by email was proper—that is, reasonably calculated to apprise RII of the pendency of the action and afford it an opportunity to respond—but in this case, it was the method of service most likely to reach RII.

To be sure, the Constitution does not require any particular means of service of process, only that the method selected be reasonably calculated to provide notice and an opportunity to respond. *See Mullane*, 339 U.S. at 314. In proper circumstances, this broad constitutional principle unshackles the federal courts from anachronistic methods of service and permits them entry into the technological renaissance. As noted by the court in *New England Merchants*, in granting permission to effect service of process via telex on Iranian defendants:

> Courts . . . cannot be blind to changes and advances in technology. No longer do we live in a world where communications are conducted solely by mail carried by fast sailing clipper . . . ships. Electronic communication via satellite can and does provide instantaneous transmission of notice and information. No longer must process be mailed to a defendant's door when he can receive complete notice at an electronic terminal inside his very office, even when the door is steel and bolted shut.

495 F.Supp. at 81. We agree wholeheartedly.

Although communication via email and over the Internet is comparatively new, such communication has been zealously embraced within the business community. RII particularly has embraced the modern e-business model and profited immensely from it. In fact, RII structured its business such that it could be contacted only via its email address. RII listed no easily discoverable street address in the United States or in Costa Rica. Rather, on its website and print media, RII designated its email address as its preferred contact information.

Unlike the Iranian officials in *New England Merchants*, RII had neither an office nor a door; it had only a computer terminal. If any method of communication is reasonably calculated to provide RII with notice, surely it is email—the method of communication which RII utilizes and prefers. In addition, email was the only court-ordered method of service aimed directly and instantly at RII, as opposed to methods of service effected through intermediaries like IEC and Carpenter. Indeed, when faced with an international e-business scofflaw, playing hide-and-seek with the federal court, email may be the only means of effecting service of process. Certainly in this case, it was a means reasonably calculated to apprise RII of the pendency of the lawsuit, and the Constitution requires nothing more.

Citing *WAWA, Inc. v. Christensen*, No. 99–1454, 1999 WL 557936, at 1 (E.D.Pa. July 29, 1999), RII contends that email is never an approved method of service under Rule 4. We disagree. In *WAWA*, the plaintiff attempted to serve the defendant via email absent a court order. Although RII is correct that a plaintiff may not generally resort to email service on his own initiative, in this case, as in *International Telemedia Associates*, email service was properly ordered by the district court using its discretion under Rule 4(f)(3).

Despite our endorsement of service of process by email in this case, we are cognizant of its limitations. In most instances, there is no way to confirm receipt of an email message. Limited use of electronic signatures could present problems in complying with the verification requirements of Rule 4(a) and Rule 11, and system compatibility problems may lead to controversies over whether an exhibit or attachment was actually received. Imprecise imaging technology may even make appending exhibits and attachments impossible in some circumstances. We note, however, that, except for the provisions recently introduced into Rule 5(b), email service is not available absent a Rule 4(f)(3) court decree. Accordingly, we leave it to the discretion of the district court to balance the limitations of email service against its benefits in any particular case. In our case, the district court performed the balancing test admirably, crafting methods of service reasonably calculated under the circumstances to apprise RII of the pendency of the action.

[The court of appeals then held that defendant RII was subject to personal jurisdiction pursuant to Nevada's long-arm statute and that the exercise of personal jurisdiction over RII did not violate its fourteenth amendment right to due process. Both of these topics are discussed in the next section of this chapter. Finally, the court held that the district court did not abuse its discretion by entering a Rule 37(b) default judgment against RII for its "willful and deliberate failure to comply with discovery orders" or by awarding attorneys' fees and costs to plaintiff Rio Properties, Inc.]

CONCLUSION

For the reasons delineated above, we affirm the district court's decision in all respects.

AFFIRMED.

COMMENTS AND QUESTIONS CONCERNING
RIO PROPERTIES, INC. V. INTERNATIONAL INTERLINK

1.   Judge Trott notes in his opinion: "Apparently, RII received the summons and complaint from IEC and subsequently consulted [attorney] Carpenter about how to respond." If Rio International actually received the complaint, why the further discussion of service of process? Isn't the purpose of service to notify a defendant of the civil action and provide it with a copy of the complaint? In footnote 8 of his opinion, Judge Trott ends his discussion of the appropriateness of email service by stating: "Notably, RII does not argue that it did not receive notice of the present lawsuit or that such notice was incomplete, delayed or in any way prejudicial to its ability to respond effectively and in a timely manner."

2.   Service in this case was ordered pursuant to Federal Rule of Civil Procedure 4(f)(3). The court of appeals states: "Rule 4(f)(3) is not subsumed within or in any way dominated by Rule 4(f)'s other subsections; it stands independently, on equal footing." However, Rule 4(f)(2) is only triggered "if there is no internationally agreed means, or if an international agreement allows but does not specify other means," while Rule 4(f)(3) only permits a court to order service "by other means not prohibited by international agreement."

3.   As the court points out, the Advisory Committee Note to the 1993 amendments to Rule 4 provides: "Service by methods that would violate foreign law is not generally authorized" pursuant to Rule 4(f). In what circumstances might service that violated foreign law be ordered by a United States court?

4.   Are there reasons why service upon RII via email was particularly appropriate in this case? After the initiation of a civil action pursuant to Rule 4, Rule 5 of the Federal Rules of Civil Procedure governs the service of additional pleadings and other papers. Rule 5(b)(2)(E) provides that such a pleading or paper can be filed by "sending it by electronic means if the person consented in writing—in which event service is complete upon transmission, but is not effective if the serving party learns that it did not reach the person to be served."

5.   The court cites various means of attempted service of process, often upon notorious individuals such as Osama bin Laden and Robert Vesco. While Rule 4(f)(3) provides for alternative service upon individuals "not within any judicial district of the United States," alternate service has been ordered within the United States. *See Kadic v. Karadzic*, 70 F.3d 232, 246 (2d Cir. 1995) (judge ordered service by delivering complaint "to a member of defendant's State Department security detail, who was ordered to hand the complaint to the defendant" in action against Radovan Karadzic for leading ethnic cleansing campaign during Bosnian civil war).

If service cannot be effected on the defendant, though, the civil action cannot proceed. *E.g., United States ex rel. Mayo v. Satan & his Staff*, 54 F.R.D. 282, 283 (W.D. Pa. 1971) ("We note that the plaintiff has failed to include with his complaint the required form of instructions for the United States Marshal for directions as to service of process.").

6.   After its motion to dismiss was denied, RII filed an answer with 22 affirmative defenses. Rule 8(c) provides for affirmative defenses. These are defenses that do not directly respond to the claims asserted in the complaint, but instead assert independent reasons why a civil action should be dismissed (such as, for instance, that the statute of limitations has run or that the claim is precluded because of a prior judgment).

Does it seem unusual that RII would assert 22 affirmative defenses? While students may receive additional points for spotting every conceivable issue on some law school exams, lawyers should be a bit more selective in asserting claims and defenses in an actual lawsuit. *See* Rule 11 of the Federal Rules of Civil Procedure; Model Rules of Professional Conduct Rule 3.1 (requiring lawyers to have a non-frivolous basis in law and in fact for litigation actions) and Rule 3.2 (requiring lawyers to make reasonable efforts, consistent with their clients' interests, to expedite litigation).

III. PERSONAL JURISDICTION

As you know from *Mullane v. Central Hanover Bank & Trust Co.*, 339 U.S. 306, 314 (1950), "An elementary and fundamental requirement of due process * * * is notice reasonably calculated, under all the circumstances, to apprise interested parties of the pendency of the action and afford them an opportunity to present their objections." In addition, as the Supreme Court stated in *International Shoe Co. v. Washington*, "[D]ue process requires * * * that * * * a defendant * * * have certain minimum contacts with it such that the maintenance of the suit does not offend 'traditional notions of fair play and substantial justice.'" 326 U.S. 310, 316 (1945), quoting *Milliken v. Meyer*, 311 U.S. 457, 463 (1940). This section of this chapter focuses on this additional requirement of due process—that the court has the power to exercise personal, or territorial, jurisdiction over the parties to the civil action.

Exercise of judicial power over plaintiffs presents no issue, because a plaintiff is assumed to have consented to the personal jurisdiction of the court by filing its civil action in that court. Similarly, courts have traditionally exercised personal jurisdiction over defendants who are residents of the forum state because of the court's power over persons present within the jurisdiction. To the extent that a person either consented to the court's jurisdiction, or was physically present within the jurisdiction of the court, that person traditionally has been held to be subject to the personal or territorial jurisdiction of the court.

Issues arose, though, as America entered the Twentieth Century, Americans became more mobile, and corporations and other non-natural persons sprouted across the country. One means by which states asserted jurisdiction over corporations was to require them to register with the state in order to do business within the state—

submitting themselves to the territorial jurisdiction of the state's courts through service upon the corporation's appointed agent.[9]

Another common situation in which states needed to assert jurisdiction over persons outside their territorial boundaries involved nonresidents who drove into a state, were involved in an automobile accident, and were sued within that state based upon that accident. Extending the concept of "consent" as a basis for personal jurisdiction, states enacted nonresident motorist statutes providing that driving on the roads of a state constituted appointment of a state official to receive process in any civil action stemming from a motor vehicle accident within the state.[10]

Whether based on consent or party presence within the state in which the civil action is filed, two separate requirements (in addition to notice) must be satisfied for the successful assertion of personal jurisdiction. For a state or federal court to exercise personal jurisdiction over the parties to an action it must be shown that both:

(1) A rule or statute authorizes the court to exercise personal jurisdiction over the parties; and

(2) The exercise of personal or territorial jurisdiction satisfies constitutional due process.

These requirements are considered in turn in the next subsections of this chapter.

A. A STATUTE OR RULE AUTHORIZING THE COURT TO EXERCISE PERSONAL JURISDICTION

Before a court can exercise personal or territorial jurisdiction over a party, there must be some authorization—by rule or statute— permitting the court to exercise judicial power over that person. Those rules and statutes now will be considered.

---

[9] *See Burnham v. Superior Court*, 495 U.S. 604, 617 (1990) ("States required, for example, that nonresident corporations appoint an in-state agent upon whom process could be served as a condition of transacting business within their borders.").

[10] *See* Miss. Code Ann. § 13–3–63:

   The acceptance by a nonresident of the rights and privileges conferred by the provisions of this section, as evidenced by his operating, either in person or by agent or employee, a motor vehicle upon any public street, road or highway of this state, * * * shall be deemed equivalent to an appointment by such nonresident of the Secretary of State of the State of Mississippi to be his true and lawful attorney, upon whom may be served all lawful processes or summonses in any action or proceeding against him, growing out of any accident or collision in which said nonresident may be involved while operating a motor vehicle on such street, road or highway, or elsewhere in this state, and said acceptance or operation shall be a signification of his agreement that any such process or summons against him which is so served shall be of the same legal force and validity as if served on him personally. * * *

Such a nonresident motorist statute, requiring that the state official provide actual notice to the nonresident motorist, was found to be constitutional under the Fourteenth Amendment Due Process Clause in *Hess v. Pawloski*, 274 U.S. 352 (1927).

1. LONG-ARM STATUTES

There must be an authorization, by statute or rule, for either a state or federal court to exercise personal or territorial jurisdiction over the parties to any lawsuit. There is an incentive for a state to attempt to exercise personal jurisdiction over non-residents, especially in civil actions brought by citizens of that state. States therefore initially enacted statutes construing the operation of a business or the driving of a motor vehicle within their state as "consent" to the exercise of personal jurisdiction over non-residents for claims arising from that party's actions within the state. Problems remained, however, in exercising jurisdiction over others not physically present within a state. As a result, states began to enact more comprehensive "long-arm" statutes to authorize their courts to exercise territorial jurisdiction over those not physically present within a state at the time of the filing of the civil action. Florida's long-arm statute, a portion of which is produced below, Fla. Stat. Ann. § 48.193, is typical of such state long-arm statutes:

> (1)(a) A person, whether or not a citizen or resident of this state, who personally or through an agent does any of the acts enumerated in this subsection thereby submits himself or herself and, if he or she is a natural person, his or her personal representative to the jurisdiction of the courts of this state for any cause of action arising from the doing of any of the following acts:
>
> 1. Operating, conducting, engaging in, or carrying on a business or business venture in this state or having an office or agency in this state.
>
> 2. Committing a tortious act within this state.
>
> 3. Owning, using, possessing, or holding a mortgage or other lien on any real property within this state.
>
> 4. Contracting to insure any person, property, or risk located within this state at the time of contracting.
>
> 5. With respect to a proceeding for alimony, child support, or division of property in connection with an action to dissolve a marriage or with respect to an independent action for support of dependents, maintaining a matrimonial domicile in this state at the time of the commencement of this action or, if the defendant resided in this state preceding the commencement of the action, whether cohabiting during that time or not. * * *
>
> 6. Causing injury to persons or property within this state arising out of an act or omission by the defendant outside this state, if, at or about the time of the injury, either:

a.   The defendant was engaged in solicitation or service activities within this state; or

b.   Products, materials, or things processed, serviced, or manufactured by the defendant anywhere were used or consumed within this state in the ordinary course of commerce, trade, or use.

7.   Breaching a contract in this state by failing to perform acts required by the contract to be performed in this state.

8.   With respect to a proceeding for paternity, engaging in the act of sexual intercourse within this state with respect to which a child may have been conceived.

9.   Entering into a contract [under which a person "agrees to submit to the jurisdiction of the courts of this state"].

States extended their long-arm jurisdiction throughout the twentieth century, and there was little incentive for state courts or legislatures to constrain the exercise of personal jurisdiction that might protect home-state plaintiffs in actions against out-of-state defendants.[11] Instead, many states either by statute or judicial interpretation have authorized the exercise of personal jurisdiction by state courts to the full extent permitted by state and federal

---

[11]   As recognized by Justice Brennan in *Burnham v. Superior Court of California*:

States have little incentive to limit rules such as transient jurisdiction that make it *easier* for their own citizens to sue out-of-state defendants. That States are more likely to expand their jurisdiction is illustrated by the adoption by many States of long-arm statutes extending the reach of personal jurisdiction to the limits established by the Federal Constitution. Out-of-staters do not vote in state elections or have a voice in state government.

495 U.S. 604, 639 n.14 (1990) (Brennan, J., concurring).

However, see McKinney's CPLR § 302(a)(2) and (3) (emphasis added):

As to a cause of action arising from any of the acts enumerated in this section, a court may exercise personal jurisdiction over any non-domiciliary, or his executor or administrator, who in person or through an agent:

2. commits a tortious act within the state, *except as to a cause of action for defamation of character arising from the act*; or

3. commits a tortious act without the state causing injury to person or property within the state, *except as to a cause of action for defamation of character arising from the act*, if he

(i) regularly does or solicits business, or engages in any other persistent course of conduct, or derives substantial revenue from goods used or consumed or services rendered, in the state, or

(ii) expects or should reasonably expect the act to have consequences in the state and derives substantial revenue from interstate or international commerce * * *.

Why does New York exempt from its long-arm statute causes of action for defamation of character arising from the acts specified in the statute?

constitutions.[12] Perhaps the prototypical such long-arm statute is California's, which provides:

> A court of this state may exercise jurisdiction on any basis not inconsistent with the Constitution of this state or of the United States.[13]

The territorial limits of effective service in the federal courts are set forth in Rule 4(k) of the Federal Rules of Civil Procedure. Rule 4(k)(1) states:

> Serving a summons or filing a waiver of service establishes personal jurisdiction over a defendant:
>
> (A) who is subject to the jurisdiction of a court of general jurisdiction in the state where the district court is located;
>
> (B) who is a party joined under Rule 14 or 19 and is served within a judicial district of the United States and not more than 100 miles from where the summons was issued; or
>
> (C) when authorized by a federal statute.

Most commonly, federal courts rely on Rule 4(k)(1)(A) and the reach of state courts of general jurisdiction in the state in which the federal court is located. Rule 4(k)(1)(B) and (C), though, authorize the expansion of personal jurisdiction in two additional ways. Rule 4(k)(1)(B) permits federal service to extend 100 miles beyond a state's boundaries if the party served has been brought into the action as a Rule 14 third-party defendant or as a Rule 19 required party. This "100 mile bulge" provision is used when the Rule 14 or 19 party is within 100 miles of the courthouse but cannot otherwise be reached pursuant to state process outside the forum state. There are, in addition, some federal statutes, such as the Federal Interpleader Act (28 U.S.C. § 2361), that authorize national service of process, and federal district courts can use those statutes for service pursuant to Rule 4(k)(1)(C).[14]

A long-arm statute such as California's collapses the personal jurisdiction analysis into a single question: Is the exercise of jurisdiction over a party constitutional under the applicable state constitution and

---

[12] As noted by the Supreme Court in *J. McIntyre Machinery, Ltd. v. Nicastro*, 131 S.Ct. 2780, 2800 n.8 (2011):

> State long-arm provisions allow the exercise of jurisdiction subject only to a due process limitation in Alabama, Arkansas, California, Colorado, Georgia, Illinois, Indiana, Iowa, Kansas, Kentucky, Louisiana, Maryland, Michigan, Minnesota, Missouri, Nevada, North Dakota, Oregon, Pennsylvania, Puerto Rico, South Carolina, South Dakota, Tennessee, Texas, Utah, Washington, and West Virginia.

[13] Cal. Civ. Proc. Code § 410.10 (West 2004).

[14] In addition, Rule 4(k)(2) provides for nationwide service of process when the defendant is not subject to the personal jurisdiction of any state but (1) has contacts with the United States that are sufficient for a federal court to exercise personal jurisdiction and (2) the claim asserted arises under federal law.

the Due Process Clause of the United States Constitution? Absent a long-arm statute such as California's, there are two distinct questions:

(1) Is the exercise of jurisdiction over the parties authorized by a statute or rule?

(2) Is the exercise of personal jurisdiction authorized by statute or rule constitutional?

Both of these questions must be answered in the affirmative for a court to exercise personal jurisdiction.

2. PROBLEMS IN INTERPRETING AND APPLYING LONG-ARM STATUTES

To the extent that a state long-arm statute extends to the full extent permitted by the Fourteenth Amendment, one might assume that the only question in applying that long-arm statute would be whether the attempted exercise of personal jurisdiction is constitutional. Depending on the state long-arm statute in question, though, that assumption may not be correct. Without determining whether the extension of personal jurisdiction would be constitutional, consider whether the state long-arm statutes in the cases below should be interpreted to cover the following two sets of claims.

a. *Crying over Spilt Milk in Missouri*

Bassett & Walker International, an international commodities broker headquartered in Toronto, purchases $5,000,000 of dairy products from Dairy Farmers of America ("DFA"), a Missouri cooperative, in about 80 transactions from 2009 to 2011. Bassett is not qualified to do business in Missouri, has no agents or employees in Missouri, and does not advertise in Missouri. Nor has any Bassett employee ever entered Missouri. The DFA agent who negotiated the purchases with Bassett in Toronto was headquartered in Michigan, although he spends three or four days each month in Missouri. The contracts he negotiated with Bassett were approved by DFA headquarters in Missouri.

DFA officials in Missouri extend a $400,000 line of credit to Bassett, which Bassett uses to buy 220,000 pounds of non-fat dry milk from DFA (with Bassett sending an email confirmation of the agreement to DFA headquarters in Missouri). The agreement provides that DFA will ship the milk from Colorado to Mexico; DFA manufactures no products in Missouri. Although Bassett was to send payment for the milk to Illinois, DFA brings a federal diversity action in Missouri claiming that Bassett failed to pay.

The Missouri long-arm statute authorizes jurisdiction for an action arising from the "transaction of any business within this state" or for the "making of any contract within this state," and this language has been interpreted to confer jurisdiction "to the extent allowed by the Due Process Clause."

Does this statute authorize personal jurisdiction over Basset in DFA's action?

b.   Rockets for Hezbollah

Several dozen Israeli families bring federal-question claims against the Lebanese Canadian Bank (LCB), which allegedly used a New York bank account to wire several million dollars to fund rocket attacks in Israel. LCB has no branches, offices, or employees in New York. Its sole contact with New York is through a corresponding bank account with American Express in New York, through which plaintiffs allege LCB transferred several million dollars through dozens of international wire transfers on behalf of the financial arm of Hezbollah. LCB allegedly knew that these wire transfers were used to finance the rocket attacks that killed or injured plaintiffs or their family members.

The New York long-arm statute provides for personal jurisdiction as to a cause of action "arising from" the acts of a non-domiciliary that "transacts any business within the state." Does this statute authorize jurisdiction over LCB in New York?

Having considered the types of statutes and rules that might authorize the exercise of personal jurisdiction outside the geographic boundaries of a state, we now turn to the limits imposed upon the exercise of personal jurisdiction by the Due Process Clause of the United States Constitution.

B.   THE CONSTITUTIONAL LIMITS OF PERSONAL JURISDICTION

Not only must there be a statute or rule authorizing a court to exercise personal jurisdiction over the defendants to a civil action, but the exercise of personal jurisdiction must comply with the Due Process Clause of the Fourteenth Amendment. This clause provides that "nor shall any State deprive any person of life, liberty, or property, without due process of law," while the Due Process Clause of the Fifth Amendment similarly prohibits the federal government from depriving any person of life, liberty, or property without due process of law. It is these due process requirements that are the subject of the cases that follow.

By filing its action in a particular court, the plaintiff thereby consents to that court's exercise of personal jurisdiction.[15] By their

---

[15] *Ins. Corp. of Ireland, Ltd. v. Compagnie des Bauxites de Guinee*, 456 U.S. 694, 703–04 (1982); *Adam v. Saenger*, 303 U.S. 59, 67–68 (1938) ("The plaintiff having, by his voluntary act in demanding justice from the defendant, submitted himself to the jurisdiction of the court, there is nothing arbitrary or unreasonable in treating him as being there for all purposes for which justice to the defendant requires his presence. It is the price which the state may exact as the condition of opening its courts to the plaintiff.").

domicile in a state, defendants, too, are subject to the personal jurisdiction of that state's courts.[16] Even non-residents traditionally have been found to be subject to personal jurisdiction if they are served with process while present within the forum state.[17]

In addition to personal jurisdiction based on presence, personal jurisdiction also can be obtained by the defendant's consent to the court's exercise of jurisdiction. This consent may be actual or implied. For instance, the parties may have entered into a contract containing a forum selection clause—by which they agree that any civil actions concerning the contract will be adjudicated by a particular court.[18] Or a state statute may provide that certain activity in the state by a person—such as driving a car—constitutes consent to personal jurisdiction in any action arising from that state activity.[19]

Clear cases of presence and consent provide relatively easy situations in which to determine the constitutionality of personal jurisdiction. As you will see in the cases that follow, determining the "due process of law" guaranteed by the Fourteenth Amendment can be much more difficult in other cases.

1.   THE CONSTITUTIONAL BEGINNINGS OF PERSONAL JURISDICTION: *PENNOYER V. NEFF*

Pennoyer v. Neff is a classic case that first-year law students have studied for over 100 years.[20] It also can be a difficult case for beginning law students. Your own understanding of the case will be heightened if you sort out the two separate civil actions that the case encompasses. As you read the Supreme Court opinion that follows, fill in the following blanks to keep these two actions distinct.

Case #1: _____ v. _____.

In what court was action filed?

Who received judgment in the action?

What happened after judgment was entered?

Case #2: _____ v. _____.

In what court was action filed?

Who received judgment in the action?

---

[16] *Milliken v. Meyer,* 311 U.S. 457 (1940).

[17] *Burham v. Superior Court,* 495 U.S. 604 (1990).

[18] As the Supreme Court held in *Atl. Marine Const. Co. v. U.S. Dist. Court for W. Dist. of Texas,* 134 S. Ct. 568, 581 (2013), "When the parties have agreed to a valid forum-selection clause, a district court should ordinarily transfer the case to the forum specified in that clause. Only under extraordinary circumstances unrelated to the convenience of the parties should a [28 U.S.C.] § 1404(a) motion be denied." *See also Carnival Cruise Lines, Inc. v. Shute,* 499 U.S. 585 (1991); *Nat'l Equip. Rental, Ltd. v. Szukhent,* 375 U.S. 311 (1964).

[19] *E.g., Hess v. Pawloski,* 274 U.S. 352 (1927).

[20] For the "underlying story" concerning *Pennoyer v. Neff* see Perdue, "Sin, Scandal, and Substantive Due Process: Personal Jurisdiction and *Pennoyer* Reconsidered," 62 *Wash. L. Rev.* 479 (1987).

What happened after judgment was entered?

Pennoyer v. Neff

Supreme Court of the United States, 1877
95 U.S. 714

OPINION

ERROR to the Circuit Court of the United States for the District of Oregon.

This action was brought by Neff against Pennoyer for the recovery of a tract of land situated in Multnomah County, Oregon. Pennoyer, in his answer, denied Neff's title and right to possession, and set up a title in himself.

By consent of parties, and in pursuance of their written stipulation filed in the case, the cause was tried by the court, and a special verdict given, upon which judgment was rendered in favor of Neff; whereupon Pennoyer sued out this writ of error.

The parties respectively claimed title as follows: Neff, under a patent issued to him by the United States, March 19, 1866; and Pennoyer, by virtue of a sale made by the sheriff of said county, under an execution sued out upon a judgment against Neff, rendered Feb. 19, 1866, by the Circuit Court for said county, in an action wherein he was defendant, and J. H. Mitchell was plaintiff. Neff was then a non-resident of Oregon.

In *Mitchell v. Neff*, jurisdiction of Neff was obtained by service of summons by publication. Pennoyer offered in evidence duly certified copies of the complaint, summons, order for publication of summons, affidavit of service by publication, and the judgment in that case; to the introduction of which papers the plaintiff objected, because, 1, said judgment is *in personam*, and appears to have been given without the appearance of the defendant in the action, or personal service of the summons upon him, and while he was a non-resident of the State, and is, therefore, void; 2, said judgment is not *in rem*, and, therefore, constitutes no basis of title in the defendant; 3, said copies of complaint, & c., do not show jurisdiction to give the judgment alleged, either *in rem* or *personam;* and, 4, it appears from said papers that no proof of service by publication was ever made, the affidavit thereof being made by the "editor" of the "Pacific Christian Advocate," and not by "the printer, or his foreman or principal clerk." The court admitted the evidence subject to the objections.

* * *

* * * [T]he complaint in said action was verified and filed on Nov. 3, 1865, and contained facts tending to prove that at that date said Mitchell had a cause of action against said Neff for services as an attorney, performed "between Jan. 1, 1862, and May 15, 1863." [T]he entry of judgment in said action contained the following averments:

> And it appearing to the court that the defendant was, at the time of the commencement of this action, and ever since has been, a non-resident of this State; and it further appearing that he has property in this State, and that defendant had notice of the pendency of this action by publication of the summons for six successive weeks in the "Pacific Christian Advocate," a weekly newspaper of general circulation published in Multnomah County, State of Oregon, the last issue of which was more than twenty days before the first day of this term.

* * *

■ MR. JUSTICE FIELD delivered the opinion of the court.

This is an action to recover the possession of a tract of land, of the alleged value of $15,000, situated in the State of Oregon. The plaintiff [Neff] asserts title to the premises by a patent of the United States issued to him in 1866, under the act of Congress of Sept. 27, 1850, usually known as the Donation Law of Oregon. The defendant [Pennoyer] claims to have acquired the premises under a sheriff's deed, made upon a sale of the property on execution issued upon a judgment recovered against the plaintiff in one of the circuit courts of the State. The case turns upon the validity of this judgment.

It appears from the record that the judgment was rendered in February, 1866, in favor of J. H. Mitchell, for less than $300, including costs, in an action brought by him upon a demand for services as an attorney; that, at the time the action was commenced and the judgment rendered, the defendant therein, the plaintiff here, was a non-resident of the State that he was not personally served with process, and did not appear therein; and that the judgment was entered upon his default in not answering the complaint, upon a constructive service of summons by publication.

The Code of Oregon provides for such service when an action is brought against a non-resident and absent defendant, who has property within the State. It also provides, where the action is for the recovery of money or damages, for the attachment of the property of the non-resident. And it also declares that no natural person is subject to the jurisdiction of a court of the State, "unless he appear in the court, or be found within the State, or be a resident thereof, or have property therein; and, in the last case, only to the extent of such property at the time the jurisdiction attached." Construing this latter provision to mean, that, in an action for money or damages where a defendant does not appear in the court, and is not found within the State, and is not a resident thereof, but has property therein, the jurisdiction of the court extends only over such property, the declaration expresses a principle of

general, if not universal, law. The authority of every tribunal is
necessarily restricted by the territorial limits of the State in which it is
established. Any attempt to exercise authority beyond those limits
would be deemed in every other forum, as has been said by this court,
[a]n illegitimate assumption of power, and be resisted as mere abuse. In
the case against the plaintiff, the property here in controversy sold
under the judgment rendered was not attached, nor in any way brought
under the jurisdiction of the court. Its first connection with the case was
caused by a levy of the execution. It was not, therefore, disposed of
pursuant to any adjudication, but only in enforcement of a personal
judgment, having no relation to the property, rendered against a non-
resident without service of process upon him in the action, or his
appearance therein. The court below did not consider that an
attachment of the property was essential to its jurisdiction or to the
validity of the sale, but held that the judgment was invalid from defects
in the affidavit upon which the order of publication was obtained, and
in the affidavit by which the publication was proved.

* * *

If * * * we were confined to the rulings of the court below upon the
defects in the affidavits mentioned, we should be unable to uphold its
decision. But it was also contended in that court, and is insisted upon
here, that the judgment in the State court against the plaintiff was void
for want of personal service of process on him, or of his appearance in
the action in which it was rendered and that the premises in
controversy could not be subjected to the payment of the demand of a
resident creditor except by a proceeding in rem; that is, by a direct
proceeding against the property for that purpose. If these positions are
sound, the ruling of the Circuit Court as to the invalidity of that
judgment must be sustained, notwithstanding our dissent from the
reasons upon which it was made. And that they are sound would seem
to follow from two well-established principles of public law respecting
the jurisdiction of an independent State over persons and property. * * *
[E]xcept as restrained and limited by [the Constitution], they possess
and exercise the authority of independent States, and the principles of
public law to which we have referred are applicable to them. One of
these principles is, that every State possesses exclusive jurisdiction and
sovereignty over persons and property within its territory. * * * The
other principle of public law referred to follows from the one mentioned;
that is, that no State can exercise direct jurisdiction and authority over
persons or property without its territory. The several States are of
equal dignity and authority, and the independence of one implies the
exclusion of power from all others. And so it is laid down by jurists, as
an elementary principle, that the laws of one State have no operation
outside of its territory, except so far as is allowed by comity; and that no
tribunal established by it can extend its process beyond that territory so
as to subject either persons or property to its decisions. "Any exertion of

authority of this sort beyond this limit," says Story, "is a mere nullity, and incapable of binding such persons or property in any other tribunals." Story, *Confl. Laws*, sect. 539.

But as contracts made in one State may be enforceable only in another State, and property may be held by non-residents, the exercise of the jurisdiction which every State is admitted to possess over persons and property within its own territory will often affect persons and property without it. To any influence exerted in this way by a State affecting persons resident or property situated elsewhere, no objection can be justly taken; whilst any direct exertion of authority upon them, in an attempt to give ex-territorial operation to its laws, or to enforce an ex-territorial jurisdiction by its tribunals, would be deemed an encroachment upon the independence of the State in which the persons are domiciled or the property is situated, and be resisted as usurpation.

Thus the State, through its tribunals, may compel persons domiciled within its limits to execute, in pursuance of their contracts respecting property elsewhere situated, instruments in such form and with such solemnities as to transfer the title, so far as such formalities can be complied with; and the exercise of this jurisdiction in no manner interferes with the supreme control over the property by the State within which it is situated.

So the State, through its tribunals, may subject property situated within its limits owned by non-residents to the payment of the demand of its own citizens against them; and the exercise of this jurisdiction in no respect infringes upon the sovereignty of the State where the owners are domiciled. Every State owes protection to its own citizens; and, when non-residents deal with them, it is a legitimate and just exercise of authority to hold and appropriate any property owned by such non-residents to satisfy the claims of its citizens. It is in virtue of the State's jurisdiction over the property of the non-resident situated within its limits that its tribunals can inquire into that non-resident's obligations to its own citizens, and the inquiry can then be carried only to the extent necessary to control the disposition of the property. If the non-resident have no property in the State, there is nothing upon which the tribunals can adjudicate.

* * *

* * * If, without personal service, judgments in personam, obtained ex parte against non-residents and absent parties, upon mere publication of process, which, in the great majority of cases, would never be seen by the parties interested, could be upheld and enforced, they would be the constant instruments of fraud and oppression. Judgments for all sorts of claims upon contracts and for torts, real or pretended, would be thus obtained, under which property would be seized, when the evidence of the transactions upon which they were founded, if they ever had any existence, had perished.

Substituted service by publication, or in any other authorized form, may be sufficient to inform parties of the object of proceedings taken where property is once brought under the control of the court by seizure or some equivalent act. The law assumes that property is always in the possession of its owner, in person or by agent; and it proceeds upon the theory that its seizure will inform him, not only that it is taken into the custody of the court, but that he must look to any proceedings authorized by law upon such seizure for its condemnation and sale. Such service may also be sufficient in cases where the object of the action is to reach and dispose of property in the State, or of some interest therein, by enforcing a contract or a lien respecting the same, or to partition it among different owners, or, when the public is a party, to condemn and appropriate it for a public purpose. In other words, such service may answer in all actions which are substantially proceedings in rem. But where the entire object of the action is to determine the personal rights and obligations of the defendants, that is, where the suit is merely in personam, constructive service in this form upon a non-resident is ineffectual for any purpose. * * *

The want of authority of the tribunals of a State to adjudicate upon the obligations of non-residents, where they have no property within its limits, is not denied by the court below: but the position is assumed, that, where they have property within the State, it is immaterial whether the property is in the first instance brought under the control of the court by attachment or some other equivalent act, and afterwards applied by its judgment to the satisfaction of demands against its owner; or such demands be first established in a personal action, and the property of the non-resident be afterwards seized and sold on execution. But the answer to this position has already been given in the statement, that the jurisdiction of the court to inquire into and determine his obligations at all is only incidental to its jurisdiction over the property. Its jurisdiction in that respect cannot be made to depend upon facts to be ascertained after it has tried the cause and rendered the judgment. If the judgment be previously void, it will not become valid by the subsequent discovery of property of the defendant, or by his subsequent acquisition of it. * * *

* * *

Since the adoption of the Fourteenth Amendment to the Federal Constitution, the validity of such judgments may be directly questioned, and their enforcement in the State resisted, on the ground that proceedings in a court of justice to determine the personal rights and obligations of parties over whom that court has no jurisdiction do not constitute due process of law. Whatever difficulty may be experienced in giving to those terms a definition which will embrace every permissible exertion of power affecting private rights, and exclude such as is forbidden, there can be no doubt of their meaning when applied to judicial proceedings. They then mean a course of legal proceedings according to those rules and principles which have been established in our systems of jurisprudence for the protection and enforcement of private rights. To give such proceedings any validity, there must be a tribunal competent by its constitution—that is, by the law of its creation—to pass upon the subject-matter of the suit; and, if that involves merely a determination of the personal liability of the defendant, he must be brought within its jurisdiction by service of process within the State, or his voluntary appearance.

Except in cases affecting the personal status of the plaintiff, and cases in which that mode of service may be considered to have been assented to in advance, as hereinafter mentioned, the substituted service of process by publication, allowed by the law of Oregon and by similar laws in other States, where actions are brought against non-residents, is effectual only where, in connection with process against the person for commencing the action, property in the State is brought under the control of the court, and subjected to its disposition by process adapted to that purpose, or where the judgment is sought as a means of reaching such property or affecting some interest therein; in other words, where the action is in the nature of a proceeding in rem. As stated by Cooley in his *Treatise on Constitutional Limitations*, 405, for any other purpose than to subject the property of a non-resident to valid claims against him in the State, "due process of law would require appearance or personal service before the defendant could be personally bound by any judgment rendered."

It is true that, in a strict sense, a proceeding in rem is one taken directly against property, and has for its object the disposition of the property, without reference to the title of individual claimants; but, in a larger and more general sense, the terms are applied to actions between parties, where the direct object is to reach and dispose of property owned by them, or of some interest therein. Such are cases commenced by attachment against the property of debtors, or instituted to partition real estate, foreclose a mortgage, or enforce a lien. So far as they affect property in the State, they are substantially proceedings in rem in the broader sense which we have mentioned.

* * *

It follows from the views expressed that the personal judgment recovered in the State court of Oregon against the plaintiff herein, then a non-resident of the State, was without any validity, and did not authorize a sale of the property in controversy.

To prevent any misapplication of the views expressed in this opinion, it is proper to observe that we do not mean to assert, by any thing we have said, that a State may not authorize proceedings to determine the status of one of its citizens towards a non-resident, which would be binding within the State, though made without service of process or personal notice to the non-resident. The jurisdiction which every State possesses to determine the civil status and capacities of all its inhabitants involves authority to prescribe the conditions on which proceedings affecting them may be commenced and carried on within its territory. The State, for example, has absolute right to prescribe the conditions upon which the marriage relation between its own citizens shall be created, and the causes for which it may be dissolved. One of the parties guilty of acts for which, by the law of the State, a dissolution may be granted, may have removed to a State where no dissolution is permitted. The complaining party would, therefore, fail if a divorce were sought in the State of the defendant; and if application could not be made to the tribunals of the complainant's domicile in such case, and proceedings be there instituted without personal service of process or personal notice to the offending party, the injured citizen would be without redress.

Neither do we mean to assert that a State may not require a non-resident entering into a partnership or association within its limits, or making contracts enforceable there, to appoint an agent or representative in the State to receive service of process and notice in legal proceedings instituted with respect to such partnership, association, or contracts, or to designate a place where such service may be made and notice given, and provide, upon their failure, to make such appointment or to designate such place that service may be made upon a public officer designated for that purpose, or in some other prescribed way, and that judgments rendered upon such service may not be binding upon the non-residents both within and without the State. As was said by the Court of Exchequer in *Vallee v. Dumergue*, 4 Exch. 290, "It is not contrary to natural justice that a man who has agreed to receive a particular mode of notification of legal proceedings should be bound by a judgment in which that particular mode of notification has been followed, even though he may not have actual notice of them." Nor do we doubt that a State, on creating corporations or other institutions for pecuniary or charitable purposes, may provide a mode in which their conduct may be investigated, their obligations enforced, or their charters revoked, which shall require other than personal service upon their officers or members. Parties becoming members of such corporations or institutions would hold their interest subject to the conditions prescribed by law.

In the present case, there is no feature of this kind, and, consequently, no consideration of what would be the effect of such legislation in enforcing the contract of a non-resident can arise. The question here respects only the validity of a money judgment rendered in one State, in an action upon a simple contract against the resident of another, without service of process upon him, or his appearance therein.

Judgment affirmed.

■ Mr. Justice Hunt dissenting.

I am compelled to dissent from the opinion and judgment of the court, and, deeming the question involved to be important, I take leave to record my views upon it.

The judgment of the court below was placed upon the ground that the provisions of the statute were not complied with. This is of comparatively little importance, as it affects the present case only. The judgment of this court is based upon the theory that the legislature had no power to pass the law in question; that the principle of the statute is vicious, and every proceeding under it void. It, therefore, affects all like cases, past and future, and in every State.

* * *

To say that a sovereign State has the power to ordain that the property of non-residents within its territory may be subjected to the payment of debts due to its citizens, if the property is levied upon at the commencement of a suit, but that it has not such power if the property is levied upon at the end of the suit, is a refinement and a depreciation of a great general principle that, in my judgment, cannot be sustained.

* * *

The question whether, in a suit commenced like the present one, a judgment can be obtained, which, if sued upon in another State, will be conclusive against the debtor, is not before us; nor does the question arise as to the faith and credit to be given in one State to a judgment recovered in another. The learning on that subject is not applicable. The point is simply whether land lying in the same State may be subjected to process at the end of a suit thus commenced.

It is here necessary only to maintain the principle laid down by Judge Cooley in his work on *Constitutional Limitations*, p. 404, and cited by Mr. Justice Field in *Galpin v. Page*, 3 Sawyer, 93, in these words:—

> The fact that process was not personally served is a conclusive objection to the judgment as a personal claim, unless the defendant caused his appearance to be entered in the attachment proceedings. Where a party has property in a State, and resides elsewhere, his property is justly subject to all valid claims that may exist against him there; but beyond this, due process of law would require appearance or personal service before the defendant could be personally bound by any judgment rendered.

The learned author does not make it a condition that there should be a preliminary seizure of the property by attachment; he lays down the rule that all a person's property in a State may be subjected to all valid claims there existing against him.

* * *

It is said that the case where a preliminary seizure has been made, and jurisdiction thereby conferred, differs from that where the property is seized at the end of the action, in this: in the first case, the property is supposed to be so near to its owner, that, if seizure is made of it, he will be aware of the fact, and have his opportunity to defend, and jurisdiction of the person is thus obtained. This, however, is matter of discretion and of judgment only. Such seizure is not in itself notice to the defendant, and it is not certain that he will by that means receive notice. Adopted as a means of communicating it, and although a very good means, it is not the only one, nor necessarily better than a publication of the pendency of the suit, made with an honest intention to reach the debtor. Who shall assume to say to the legislature, that if it authorizes a particular mode of giving notice to a debtor, its action may be sustained, but, if it adopts any or all others, its action is unconstitutional and void? The rule is universal, that modes, means, questions of expediency or necessity, are exclusively within the judgment of the legislature, and that the judiciary cannot review them. * * *

That a State can subject land within its limits belonging to non-resident owners to debts due to its own citizens as it can legislate upon all other local matters; that it can prescribe the mode and process by which it is to be reached,—seems to me very plain.

I am not willing to declare that a sovereign State cannot subject the land within its limits to the payment of debts due to its citizens, or that the power to do so depends upon the fact whether its statute shall authorize the property to be levied upon at the commencement of the suit or at its termination. This is a matter of detail, and I am of opinion, that if reasonable notice be given, with an opportunity to defend when appearance is made, the question of power will be fully satisfied.

COMMENTS AND QUESTIONS CONCERNING *PENNOYER V. NEFF*

1.   Return to the questions right before the *Pennoyer* opinion. Do you understand the two separate civil actions at issue in this litigation?

2.   In the civil action that the Supreme Court considers, Neff denominates the amount in controversy to be $15,000. At the time of this action, the jurisdictional minimum amount in controversy was only $500. 14AA C. Wright, A. Miller & E. Cooper, *Federal Practice and Procedure* § 3701, at 247 (4th ed. 2011).

3.   Justice Field states in his majority opinion:

So the State, through its tribunals, may subject property situated within its limits owned by non-residents to the payment of the demand of its own citizens against them; and the exercise of this jurisdiction in no respect infringes upon the sovereignty of the State where the owners are domiciled.

What, then, is the problem with what the Oregon state court did (or didn't do) in *Mitchell v. Neff?*

4.   In his dissent Justice Hunt argues that, for purposes of territorial jurisdiction, it makes no difference whether property of the defendant is attached at the beginning or at the end of a proceeding. What is the majority's response to this argument?

5.   Justice Field concludes that the constitutionality of specific notice depends on whether the action of which the defendant is being notified is an action "in rem" or "in personam." He states that service by publication "may answer in all actions which are substantially proceedings in rem. But where the entire object of the action is to determine the personal rights and obligations of the defendants, that is, where the suit is merely in personam, constructive service in this form upon a non-resident is ineffectual for any purpose." If the court is determining "the personal liability of the defendant, he must be brought within its jurisdiction by service of process within the State, or his voluntary appearance."

In an action "in personam," the court is asked to determine the legal rights and obligations of the parties with respect to one another. In a proceeding "in rem," though, the court determines the rights within a particular property or "res" of everyone—party to the action or not. In addition to actions determining the rights to real or personal property "against the world," in rem proceedings include divorce actions, bankruptcy determinations, and libel actions to determine rights in a ship. Why is it important in such cases to have a judgment that will bind the world and not just the parties to a particular civil action? Because an in rem judgment determines rights and obligations flowing from a res or property, the resulting judgment cannot exceed the value of that property. *See Shaffer v. Heitner*, 433 U.S. 186, 199 (1977) ("The effect of a judgment in such a case is limited to the property that supports jurisdiction and does not impose a personal liability on the property owner, since he is not before the court. In *Pennoyer's* terms, the owner is affected only 'indirectly' by an in rem judgment adverse to his interest in the property subject to the court's disposition.").

Because of the different scope of rights determined by in personam and in rem judgments, the captions of the different types of actions typically differ. An in personam action usually is styled *Smith v. Jones*, naming the parties whose rights and obligations will be adjudicated by the court in that action. Some in rem actions, though, such as a ship libel, are captioned with the name of the property, all rights to which will be determined by the court: *In re the Sloop John B.*

6.   Justice Field is particularly careful to note that the Court is not suggesting that states lack the power to adjudicate the status of its citizens toward a non-resident.

> To prevent any misapplication of the views expressed in this opinion, it is proper to observe that we do not mean to assert, by any thing we have said, that a State may not authorize proceedings to determine the status of one of its citizens towards a

non-resident, which would be binding within the State, though made without service of process or personal notice to the non-resident. The jurisdiction which every State possesses to determine the civil status and capacities of all its inhabitants involves authority to prescribe the conditions on which proceedings affecting them may be commenced and carried on within its territory. The State, for example, has absolute right to prescribe the conditions upon which the marriage relation between its own citizens shall be created, and the causes for which it may be dissolved.

A state court thus can dissolve a marriage even though one of the parties to the marriage may not be present within the state. However, in order to divide marital property, award alimony, or determine child support, personal jurisdiction must exist through the defendant's presence, consent, contract, or contacts with the state. *Vanderbilt v. Vanderbilt*, 354 U.S. 416 (1957). Thus the Supreme Court in *Burnham v. Superior Court*, 495 U.S. 604 (1990), *infra* p. 262, considered whether the husband in that action—which involved child custody as well as divorce—had subjected himself to the personal jurisdiction of the court by having been served while in the forum state.

7.   Upon what presumption did nineteenth century courts rely in upholding jurisdiction based upon publication once the defendant's property was seized by the court? Justice Field states:

Substituted service by publication, or in any other authorized form, may be sufficient to inform parties of the object of proceedings taken where property is once brought under the control of the court by seizure or some equivalent act. The law assumes that property is always in the possession of its owner, in person or by agent; and it proceeds upon the theory that its seizure will inform him, not only that it is taken into the custody of the court, but that he must look to any proceedings authorized by law upon such seizure for its condemnation and sale.

Is this a realistic assumption?

8.   Justice Field focuses on the power of state courts to exercise personal jurisdiction, rather than on defendants having to respond to actions in states in which they are not present: "The declaration expresses a principle of general, if not universal, law. The authority of every tribunal is necessarily restricted by the territorial limits of the State in which it is established. Any attempt to exercise authority beyond those limits would be deemed in every other forum, as has been said by this court, [a]n illegitimate assumption of power, and be resisted as mere abuse." Is this the appropriate focus?

9.   In his dissent, Justice Hunt states: "The rule is universal, that modes, means, questions of expediency or necessity, are exclusively within the judgment of the legislature, and that the judiciary cannot review them." But had the legal landscape changed in the decade before the Supreme Court's decision so as to affect such a "universal" rule?

254

NOTICE, TERRITORIAL JURISDICTION, AND VENUE: "WHERE CAN
WE FILE OUR ACTION?"

CHAPTER 4

2. THE MODERN FORMULATION OF PERSONAL JURISDICTION

Justice Field determined in *Pennoyer v. Neff* that "[t]o give such proceedings any validity, there must be a tribunal competent by its constitution—that is, by the law of its creation—to pass upon the subject-matter of the suit; and, if that involves merely a determination of the personal liability of the defendant, he must be brought within its jurisdiction by service of process within the State, or his voluntary appearance." 95 U.S. 714, 733.

Sometimes, though, personal jurisdiction is sought not over a natural person, but with respect to a corporation or other entity. How does a court determine whether such an entity is present within the jurisdiction and thus subject to the court's personal jurisdiction? This is the question presented to the Supreme Court in the next case, *International Shoe Co. v. Washington.*

To the extent that there is a situation in which it is "easy" to determine personal jurisdiction, that situation is presented by personal service upon the defendant while the defendant is within the forum state. That is what happened in *Burnham v. Superior Court*, which follows *International Shoe*. The cases that follow *Burnham* then work out the application of the *International Shoe* due process text in additional factual settings.

a. International Shoe Co. v. Washington

International Shoe Co. v. Washington

Supreme Court of the United States, 1945
326 U.S. 310

OPINION

■ MR. CHIEF JUSTICE STONE delivered the opinion of the Court.

The questions for decision are (1) whether, within the limitations of the due process clause of the Fourteenth Amendment, appellant, a Delaware corporation, has by its activities in the State of Washington rendered itself amenable to proceedings in the courts of that state to recover unpaid contributions to the state unemployment compensation fund exacted by state statutes, Washington Unemployment Compensation Act, Washington Revised Statutes, § 9998–103a through § 9998–123a, and (2) whether the state can exact those contributions consistently with the due process clause of the Fourteenth Amendment.

The statutes in question set up a comprehensive scheme of unemployment compensation, the costs of which are defrayed by contributions required to be made by employers to a state unemployment compensation fund. The contributions are a specified percentage of the wages payable annually by each employer for his employees' services in the state. The assessment and collection of the contributions and the fund are administered by respondents. Section 14(c) of the Act authorizes respondent Commissioner to issue an order and notice of assessment of delinquent contributions upon prescribed personal service of the notice upon the employer if found within the state, or, if not so found, by mailing the notice to the employer by registered mail at his last known address. That section also authorizes the Commissioner to collect the assessment by distraint if it is not paid within ten days after service of the notice. By §§ 14(e) and 6(b) the order of assessment may be administratively reviewed by an appeal tribunal within the office of unemployment upon petition of the employer, and this determination is by § 6(I) made subject to judicial review on questions of law by the state Superior Court, with further right of appeal in the state Supreme Court as in other civil cases.

In this case notice of assessment for the years in question was personally served upon a sales solicitor employed by appellant in the State of Washington, and a copy of the notice was mailed by registered mail to appellant at its address in St. Louis, Missouri. Appellant appeared specially before the office of unemployment and moved to set aside the order and notice of assessment on the ground that the service upon appellant's salesman was not proper service upon appellant; that appellant was not a corporation of the State of Washington and was not doing business within the state; that it had no agent within the state upon whom service could be made; and that appellant is not an employer and does not furnish employment within the meaning of the statute.

* * *

The facts as found by the appeal tribunal and accepted by the state Superior Court and Supreme Court, are not in dispute. Appellant is a Delaware corporation, having its principal place of business in St. Louis, Missouri, and is engaged in the manufacture and sale of shoes and other footwear. It maintains places of business in several states, other than Washington, at which its manufacturing is carried on and from which its merchandise is distributed interstate through several sales units or branches located outside the State of Washington.

Appellant has no office in Washington and makes no contracts either for sale or purchase of merchandise there. It maintains no stock of merchandise in that state and makes there no deliveries of goods in intrastate commerce. During the years from 1937 to 1940, now in question, appellant employed eleven to thirteen salesmen under direct supervision and control of sales managers located in St. Louis. These salesmen resided in Washington; their principal activities were confined to that state; and they were compensated by commissions based upon the amount of their sales. The commissions for each year totaled more than $31,000. Appellant supplies its salesmen with a line of samples, each consisting of one shoe of a pair, which they display to prospective purchasers. On occasion they rent permanent sample rooms, for exhibiting samples, in business buildings, or rent rooms in hotels or business buildings temporarily for that purpose. The cost of such rentals is reimbursed by appellant.

The authority of the salesmen is limited to exhibiting their samples and soliciting orders from prospective buyers, at prices and on terms fixed by appellant. The salesmen transmit the orders to appellant's office in St. Louis for acceptance or rejection, and when accepted the merchandise for filling the orders is shipped f.o.b. from points outside Washington to the purchasers within the state. All the merchandise shipped into Washington is invoiced at the place of shipment from which collections are made. No salesman has authority to enter into contracts or to make collections.

The Supreme Court of Washington was of opinion that the regular and systematic solicitation of orders in the state by appellant's salesmen, resulting in a continuous flow of appellant's product into the state, was sufficient to constitute doing business in the state so as to make appellant amenable to suit in its courts. But it was also of opinion that there were sufficient additional activities shown to bring the case within the rule frequently stated, that solicitation within a state by the agents of a foreign corporation plus some additional activities there are sufficient to render the corporation amenable to suit brought in the courts of the state to enforce an obligation arising out of its activities there. The court found such additional activities in the salesmen's display of samples sometimes in permanent display rooms, and the salesmen's residence within the state, continued over a period of years, all resulting in a substantial volume of merchandise regularly shipped by appellant to purchasers within the state. * * *

* * *

Appellant * * * insists that its activities within the state were not sufficient to manifest its "presence" there and that in its absence the state courts were without jurisdiction, that consequently it was a denial of due process for the state to subject appellant to suit. It refers to those cases in which it was said that the mere solicitation of orders for the purchase of goods within a state, to be accepted without the state and filled by shipment of the purchased goods interstate, does not render the corporation seller amenable to suit within the state. And appellant further argues that since it was not present within the state, it is a denial of due process to subject it to taxation or other money exaction. It thus denies the power of the state to lay the tax or to subject appellant to a suit for its collection.

Historically the jurisdiction of courts to render judgment in personam is grounded on their de facto power over the defendant's person. Hence his presence within the territorial jurisdiction of court was prerequisite to its rendition of a judgment personally binding him.

Pennoyer v. Neff, 95 U.S. 714, 733. But now that the capias ad respondendum has given way to personal service of summons or other form of notice, due process requires only that in order to subject a defendant to a judgment in personam, if he be not present within the territory of the forum, he have certain minimum contacts with it such that the maintenance of the suit does not offend "traditional notions of fair play and substantial justice." *Milliken v. Meyer*, 311 U.S. 457, 463.

Since the corporate personality is a fiction, although a fiction intended to be acted upon as though it were a fact, it is clear that unlike an individual its "presence" without, as well as within, the state of its origin can be manifested only by activities carried on in its behalf by those who are authorized to act for it. To say that the corporation is so far "present" there as to satisfy due process requirements, for purposes of taxation or the maintenance of suits against it in the courts of the state, is to beg the question to be decided. For the terms "present" or "presence" are used merely to symbolize those activities of the corporation's agent within the state which courts will deem to be sufficient to satisfy the demands of due process. L. Hand, J., in *Hutchinson v. Chase & Gilbert*, 2 Cir., 45 F.2d 139, 141. Those demands may be met by such contacts of the corporation with the state of the forum as make it reasonable, in the context of our federal system of government, to require the corporation to defend the particular suit which is brought there. An "estimate of the inconveniences" which would result to the corporation from a trial away from its "home" or principal place of business is relevant in this connection. *Hutchinson v. Chase & Gilbert*, supra, 45 F.2d 141.

"Presence" in the state in this sense has never been doubted when the activities of the corporation there have not only been continuous and systematic, but also give rise to the liabilities sued on, even though no consent to be sued or authorization to an agent to accept service of process has been given. Conversely it has been generally recognized that the casual presence of the corporate agent or even his conduct of single or isolated items of activities in a state in the corporation's behalf are not enough to subject it to suit on causes of action unconnected with the activities there. To require the corporation in such circumstances to defend the suit away from its home or other jurisdiction where it carries on more substantial activities has been thought to lay too great and unreasonable a burden on the corporation to comport with due process.

While it has been held in cases on which appellant relies that continuous activity of some sorts within a state is not enough to support the demand that the corporation be amenable to suits unrelated to that activity, there have been instances in which the continuous corporate operations within a state were thought so substantial and of such a nature as to justify suit against it on causes of action arising from dealings entirely distinct from those activities.

Finally, although the commission of some single or occasional acts of the corporate agent in a state sufficient to impose an obligation or liability on the corporation has not been thought to confer upon the state authority to enforce it, other such acts, because of their nature and quality and the circumstances of their commission, may be deemed sufficient to render the corporation liable to suit. True, some of the decisions holding the corporation amenable to suit have been supported by resort to the legal fiction that it has given its consent to service and suit, consent being implied from its presence in the state through the acts of its authorized agents. But more realistically it may be said that those authorized acts were of such a nature as to justify the fiction.

It is evident that the criteria by which we mark the boundary line between those activities which justify the subjection of a corporation to suit, and those which do not, cannot be simply mechanical or quantitative. The test is not merely, as has sometimes been suggested, whether the activity, which the corporation has seen fit to procure through its agents in another state, is a little more or a little less. Whether due process is satisfied must depend rather upon the quality and nature of the activity in relation to the fair and orderly administration of the laws which it was the purpose of the due process clause to insure. That clause does not contemplate that a state may make binding a judgment in personam against an individual or corporate defendant with which the state has no contacts, ties, or relations. Cf. *Pennoyer v. Neff, supra*.

But to the extent that a corporation exercises the privilege of conducting activities within a state, it enjoys the benefits and protection of the laws of that state. The exercise of that privilege may give rise to obligations; and, so far as those obligations arise out of or are connected with the activities within the state, a procedure which requires the corporation to respond to a suit brought to enforce them can, in most instances, hardly be said to be undue.

Applying these standards, the activities carried on in behalf of appellant in the State of Washington were neither irregular nor casual. They were systematic and continuous throughout the years in question. They resulted in a large volume of interstate business, in the course of which appellant received the benefits and protection of the laws of the state, including the right to resort to the courts for the enforcement of its rights. The obligation which is here sued upon arose out of those very activities. It is evident that these operations establish sufficient contacts or ties with the state of the forum to make it reasonable and just according to our traditional conception of fair play and substantial justice to permit the state to enforce the obligations which appellant has incurred there. Hence we cannot say that the maintenance of the present suit in the State of Washington involves an unreasonable or undue procedure.

We are likewise unable to conclude that the service of the process within the state upon an agent whose activities establish appellant's "presence" there was not sufficient notice of the suit, or that the suit was so unrelated to those activities as to make the agent an inappropriate vehicle for communicating the notice. It is enough that appellant has established such contacts with the state that the particular form of substituted service adopted there gives reasonable assurance that the notice will be actual. Nor can we say that the mailing of the notice of suit to appellant by registered mail at its home office was not reasonably calculated to apprise appellant of the suit.

Only a word need be said of appellant's liability for the demanded contributions of the state unemployment fund. The Supreme Court of Washington, construing and applying the statute, has held that it imposes a tax on the privilege of employing appellant's salesmen within the state measured by a percentage of the wages, here the commissions payable to the salesmen. This construction we accept for purposes of determining the constitutional validity of the statute. The right to employ labor has been deemed an appropriate subject of taxation in this country and England, both before and since the adoption of the Constitution. And such a tax imposed upon the employer for unemployment benefits is within the constitutional power of the states.

Appellant having rendered itself amenable to suit upon obligations arising out of the activities of its salesmen in Washington, the state may maintain the present suit in personam to collect the tax laid upon the exercise of the privilege of employing appellant's salesmen within the state. For Washington has made one of those activities, which taken together establish appellant's "presence" there for purposes of suit, the taxable event by which the state brings appellant within the reach of its taxing power. The state thus has constitutional power to lay the tax and to subject appellant to a suit to recover it. The activities which establish its "presence" subject it alike to taxation by the state and to suit to recover the tax.

Affirmed.

■ MR. JUSTICE JACKSON took no part in the consideration or decision of this case.

■ MR. JUSTICE BLACK delivered the following opinion.

* * *

Certainly appellant can not in the light of our past decisions meritoriously claim that notice by registered mail and by personal service on its sales solicitors in Washington did not meet the requirements of procedural due process. And the due process clause is not brought in issue any more by appellant's further conceptualistic contention that Washington could not levy a tax or bring suit against the corporation because it did not honor that State with its mystical "presence." For it is unthinkable that the vague due process clause was ever intended to prohibit a State from regulating or taxing a business carried on within its boundaries simply because this is done by agents of a corporation organized and having its headquarters elsewhere. To read this into the due process clause would in fact result in depriving a State's citizens of due process by taking from the State the power to protect them in their business dealings within its boundaries with representatives of a foreign corporation. * * *

The criteria adopted insofar as they can be identified read as follows: Due process does permit State courts to "enforce the obligations which appellant has incurred" if it be found "reasonable and just according to our traditional conception of fair play and substantial justice." And this in turn means that we will "permit" the State to act if upon an "estimate of the inconveniences" which would result to the corporation from a trial away from its "home" or principal place of business, we conclude that it is "reasonable" to subject it to suit in a State where it is doing business.

* * *

I believe that the Federal Constitution leaves to each State, without any "ifs" or "buts," a power to tax and to open the doors of its courts for its citizens to sue corporations whose agents do business in those States. Believing that the Constitution gave the States that power, I think it a judicial deprivation to condition its exercise upon this Court's notion of "fairplay," however appealing that term may be. Nor can I stretch the meaning of due process so far as to authorize this Court to deprive a State of the right to afford judicial protection to its citizens on the ground that it would be more "convenient" for the corporation to be sued somewhere else.

* * *

True, the State's power is here upheld. But the rule announced means that tomorrow's judgment may strike down a State or Federal enactment on the ground that it does not conform to this Court's idea of natural justice. I therefore find myself moved by the same fears that caused Mr. Justice Holmes to say in 1930:

> I have not yet adequately expressed the more than anxiety that I feel at the ever increasing scope given to the Fourteenth Amendment in cutting down what I believe to be the constitutional rights of the States. As the decisions now stand, I see hardly any limit but the sky to the invalidating of those rights if they happen to strike a majority of this Court as for any reason undesirable.

Baldwin v. Missouri, 281 U.S. 586, 595.

COMMENTS AND QUESTIONS CONCERNING
INTERNATIONAL SHOE CORP. V. WASHINGTON

1. The Court concluded that (1) International Shoe had minimum contacts with Washington; (2) those contacts were such that the maintenance of the suit did not offend "traditional notions of fair play and substantial justice;" and (3) the claim asserted against it arose from its forum contacts. What else is necessary for International Shoe to be subject to suit in Washington? *See Mullane v. Central Hanover Bank & Trust Co.,* 339 U.S. 306 (1950), *supra* p. 210. Was that showing made in this case?

2. Did the International Shoe Company receive notice of the proceeding brought against it by the State of Washington? Did International Shoe have an opportunity to challenge the assessment against it in state court? What is the due process problem?

3. How can International Shoe be subject to personal jurisdiction in Washington when it has no office, no merchandise, no contracts nor deliveries in that state, and St. Louis sales managers supervise its Washington salesmen and must accept or reject every purchase order?

4. If a person is not physically "present" within a jurisdiction, how is a court to obtain territorial jurisdiction over that person?

5. Is it realistic to presume that, by his actions within a state, a person has consented to the jurisdiction of that state's courts over him? Does Chief Justice Stone believe that this "legal fiction" must be continued to assert personal jurisdiction over defendants such as International Shoe? Or does he reformulate the test for determining personal jurisdiction over a defendant that is not physically present within the jurisdiction?

6. In this case, why is it not unfair to subject International Shoe to personal jurisdiction in Washington?

7. What if the claim against International Shoe did not arise from its contacts with Washington? Assume, for instance, that one of its salesmen, who lived and worked in Florida, brought a claim for unpaid wages against International Shoe in Washington state court. Would International Shoe be subject to personal jurisdiction on this claim in Washington? Reconsider your answer after reading *Daimler AG v. Bauman,* 134 S.Ct. 746 (2014), *infra* p. 281.

8. Why did Justice Black feel it necessary to write a separate opinion in this case? Reconsider his concern about the malleability of the "vague due process clause" after reading Justice Scalia's opinion in *Burnham v. Superior Court,* 495 U.S. 604, 623 (1990), *infra* p. 262 ("[T]he concurrence's proposed standard of 'contemporary notions of due process' * * * measures state-court jurisdiction not only against traditional doctrines in this country, including current state-court practice, but also against each Justice's subjective assessment of what is fair and just.").

9. For your next round of word games or trivia contests, why not use words and phrases from *International Shoe* such as "capias ad respondendum" and "distraint"? These terms are defined as follows:

Capias ad respondendum: A writ commanding the sheriff to take the defendant into custody to ensure that the defendant will appear in court.

Distraint: 1. The seizure of another's property to secure the performance of a duty, such as the payment of overdue rent. 2. The legal remedy authorizing such a seizure; the procedure by which the seizure is carried out.

Black's Law Dictionary (Bryan A. Garner, ed., 10th ed. 2014).

10. In *World-Wide Volkswagen Corp. v. Woodson*, 444 U.S. 286, 291–92 (1980), Justice White wrote for the Court:

The concept of minimum contacts * * * can be seen to perform two related, but distinguishable functions. It protects the defendant against the burdens of litigating in a distant or inconvenient forum. And it acts to ensure that the States, through their courts, do not reach out beyond the limits imposed on them by their status as coequal sovereigns in a federal system.

As you read the Supreme Court decisions that follow *International Shoe*, consider which of these functions is foremost in the mind of the justices.

b. Burnham v. Superior Court

Burnham v. Superior Court

Supreme Court of the United States, 1990
495 U.S. 604

OPINION

■ JUSTICE SCALIA announced the judgment of the Court and delivered an opinion in which THE CHIEF JUSTICE and JUSTICE KENNEDY join, and in which JUSTICE WHITE joins with respect to Parts I, II–A, II–B, and II–C.

The question presented is whether the Due Process Clause of the Fourteenth Amendment denies California courts jurisdiction over a nonresident, who was personally served with process while temporarily in that State, in a suit unrelated to his activities in the State.

I

Petitioner Dennis Burnham married Francie Burnham in 1976 in West Virginia. In 1977 the couple moved to New Jersey, where their two children were born. In July 1987 the Burnhams decided to separate. They agreed that Mrs. Burnham, who intended to move to California, would take custody of the children. Shortly before Mrs. Burnham departed for California that same month, she and petitioner agreed that she would file for divorce on grounds of "irreconcilable differences."

In October 1987, petitioner filed for divorce in New Jersey state court on grounds of "desertion." Petitioner did not, however, obtain an issuance of summons against his wife and did not attempt to serve her with process. Mrs. Burnham, after unsuccessfully demanding that petitioner adhere to their prior agreement to submit to an "irreconcilable differences" divorce, brought suit for divorce in California state court in early January 1988.

In late January, petitioner visited southern California on business, after which he went north to visit his children in the San Francisco Bay area, where his wife resided. He took the older child to San Francisco for the weekend. Upon returning the child to Mrs. Burnham's home on January 24, 1988, petitioner was served with a California court summons and a copy of Mrs. Burnham's divorce petition. He then returned to New Jersey.

Later that year, petitioner made a special appearance in the California Superior Court, moving to quash the service of process on the ground that the court lacked personal jurisdiction over him because his only contacts with California were a few short visits to the State for the purposes of conducting business and visiting his children. The Superior Court denied the motion, and the California Court of Appeal denied mandamus relief, rejecting petitioner's contention that the Due Process Clause prohibited California courts from asserting jurisdiction over him because he lacked "minimum contacts" with the State. The court held it to be "a valid jurisdictional predicate for in personam jurisdiction" that the "defendant [was] present in the forum state and personally served with process." We granted certiorari.

II

A

The proposition that the judgment of a court lacking jurisdiction is void traces back to the English Year Books, and was made settled law by Lord Coke in *Case of the Marshalsea*, 10 Coke Rep. 68b, 77a, 77 Eng.Rep. 1027, 1041 (K.B. 1612). Traditionally that proposition was embodied in the phrase coram non judice, "before a person not a judge"—meaning, in effect, that the proceeding in question was not a judicial proceeding because lawful judicial authority was not present, and could therefore not yield a judgment. American courts invalidated, or denied recognition to, judgments that violated this common-law principle long before the Fourteenth Amendment was adopted. In *Pennoyer v. Neff*, 95 U.S. 714, 732 (1878), we announced that the judgment of a court lacking personal jurisdiction violated the Due Process Clause of the Fourteenth Amendment as well.

To determine whether the assertion of personal jurisdiction is consistent with due process, we have long relied on the principles traditionally followed by American courts in marking out the territorial limits of each State's authority. That criterion was first announced in

Pennoyer v. Neff, in which we stated that due process "mean[s] a course of legal proceedings according to those rules and principles which have been established in our systems of jurisprudence for the protection and enforcement of private rights," *id.*, at 733, including the "well-established principles of public law respecting the jurisdiction of an independent State over persons and property," *id.*, at 722. In what has become the classic expression of the criterion, we said in *International Shoe Co. v. Washington*, 326 U.S. 310 (1945), that a state court's assertion of personal jurisdiction satisfies the Due Process Clause if it does not violate "'traditional notions of fair play and substantial justice.'" *Id.*, at 316, quoting *Milliken v. Meyer*, 311 U.S. 457, 463, (1940). Since *International Shoe*, we have only been called upon to decide whether these "traditional notions" permit States to exercise jurisdiction over absent defendants in a manner that deviates from the rules of jurisdiction applied in the 19th century. We have held such deviations permissible, but only with respect to suits arising out of the absent defendant's contacts with the State.[1] The question we must decide today is whether due process requires a similar connection between the litigation and the defendant's contacts with the State in cases where the defendant is physically present in the State at the time process is served upon him.

B

Among the most firmly established principles of personal jurisdiction in American tradition is that the courts of a State have jurisdiction over nonresidents who are physically present in the State. The view developed early that each State had the power to hale before its courts any individual who could be found within its borders, and that once having acquired jurisdiction over such a person by properly serving him with process, the State could retain jurisdiction to enter judgment against him, no matter how fleeting his visit. That view had antecedents in English common-law practice, which sometimes allowed "transitory" actions, arising out of events outside the country, to be maintained against seemingly nonresident defendants who were present in England. Justice Story believed the principle, which he traced to Roman origins, to be firmly grounded in English tradition:

---

[1] We have said that "[e]ven when the cause of action does not arise out of or relate to the foreign corporation's activities in the forum State, due process is not offended by a State's subjecting the corporation to its *in personam* jurisdiction when there are sufficient contacts between the State and the foreign corporation." *Helicopteros Nacionales de Colombia v. Hall*, 466 U.S., at 414. Our only holding supporting that statement, however, involved "regular service of summons upon [the corporation's] president while he was in [the forum State] acting in that capacity." See *Perkins v. Benguet Consolidated Mining Co.*, 342 U.S. 437, 440 (1952). It may be that whatever special rule exists permitting "continuous and systematic" contacts, *id.*, at 438, to support jurisdiction with respect to matters unrelated to activity in the forum applies *only* to corporations, which have never fitted comfortably in a jurisdictional regime based primarily upon "de facto power over the defendant's person." *International Shoe Co. v. Washington*, 326 U.S. 310, 316 (1945). We express no views on these matters—and, for simplicity's sake, omit reference to this aspect of "contacts"-based jurisdiction in our discussion.

"[B]y the common law[,] personal actions, being transitory, may be brought in any place, where the party defendant may be found," for "every nation may . . . rightfully exercise jurisdiction over all persons within its domains." J. Story, *Commentaries on the Conflict of Laws* § 554, 543 (1846).

* * *

Decisions in the courts of many States in the 19th and early 20th centuries held that personal service upon a physically present defendant sufficed to confer jurisdiction, without regard to whether the defendant was only briefly in the State or whether the cause of action was related to his activities there. * * * Although research has not revealed a case deciding the issue in every State's courts, that appears to be because the issue was so well settled that it went unlitigated. Opinions from the courts of other States announced the rule in dictum. Most States, moreover, had statutes or common-law rules that exempted from service of process individuals who were brought into the forum by force or fraud or who were there as a party or witness in unrelated judicial proceedings. These exceptions obviously rested upon the premise that service of process conferred jurisdiction. Particularly striking is the fact that, as far as we have been able to determine, not one American case from the period (or, for that matter, not one American case until 1978) held, or even suggested, that in-state personal service on an individual was insufficient to confer personal jurisdiction. * * *

* * *

C

Despite this formidable body of precedent, petitioner contends, in reliance on our decisions applying the *International Shoe* standard, that in the absence of "continuous and systematic" contacts with the forum a nonresident defendant can be subjected to judgment only as to matters that arise out of or relate to his contacts with the forum. This argument rests on a thorough misunderstanding of our cases.

The view of most courts in the 19th century was that a court simply could not exercise in personam jurisdiction over a nonresident who had not been personally served with process in the forum. *Pennoyer v. Neff*, while renowned for its statement of the principle that the Fourteenth Amendment prohibits such an exercise of jurisdiction, in fact set that forth only as dictum and decided the case (which involved a judgment rendered more than two years before the Fourteenth Amendment's ratification) under "well-established principles of public law." Those principles, embodied in the Due Process Clause, required (we said) that when proceedings "involv[e] merely a determination of the personal liability of the defendant, he must be brought within [the court's] jurisdiction by service of process within the State, or his voluntary appearance." We invoked that rule in a series of subsequent cases, as either a matter of due process or a "fundamental principl[e] of jurisprudence," *Wilson v. Seligman*, 144 U.S. 41, 46 (1892).

Later years, however, saw the weakening of the *Pennoyer* rule. In the late 19th and early 20th centuries, changes in the technology of transportation and communication, and the tremendous growth of interstate business activity, led to an "inevitable relaxation of the strict limits on state jurisdiction" over nonresident individuals and corporations. *Hanson v. Denckla*, 357 U.S. 235, 260 (1958) (Black, J., dissenting). States required, for example, that nonresident corporations appoint an in-state agent upon whom process could be served as a condition of transacting business within their borders, and provided in-state "substituted service" for nonresident motorists who caused injury in the State and left before personal service could be accomplished. We initially upheld these laws under the Due Process Clause on grounds that they complied with *Pennoyer*'s rigid requirement of either "consent," *see, e.g., Hess v. Pawloski*, [274 U.S. 352, 356 (1927)] or "presence." As many observed, however, the consent and presence were purely fictional. Our opinion in *International Shoe* cast those fictions aside and made explicit the underlying basis of these decisions: Due process does not necessarily require the States to adhere to the unbending territorial limits on jurisdiction set forth in *Pennoyer*. The validity of assertion of jurisdiction over a nonconsenting defendant who is not present in the forum depends upon whether "the quality and nature of [his] activity" in relation to the forum renders such jurisdiction consistent with " 'traditional notions of fair play and substantial justice.' " Subsequent cases have derived from the *International Shoe* standard the general rule that a State may dispense with in-forum personal service on nonresident defendants in suits arising out of their activities in the State. *See generally Helicopteros Nacionales de Colombia v. Hall*, 466 U.S., at 414–415. As *International Shoe* suggests, the defendant's litigation-related "minimum contacts" may take the place of physical presence as the basis for jurisdiction:

> Historically the jurisdiction of courts to render judgment in personam is grounded on their de facto power over the defendant's person. Hence his presence within the territorial jurisdiction of a court was prerequisite to its rendition of a judgment personally binding on him. *Pennoyer v. Neff*, 95 U.S. 714, 733. But now that the capias ad respondendum has given way to personal service of summons or other form of notice, due process requires only that in order to subject a defendant to a judgment in personam, if he be not present within the territory of the forum, he have certain minimum contacts with it such that the maintenance of the suit does not offend "traditional notions of fair play and substantial justice." 326 U.S., at 316 (citations omitted).

Nothing in *International Shoe* or the cases that have followed it, however, offers support for the very different proposition petitioner seeks to establish today: that a defendant's presence in the forum is not only unnecessary to validate novel, nontraditional assertions of jurisdiction, but is itself no longer sufficient to establish jurisdiction. That proposition is unfaithful to both elementary logic and the foundations of our due process jurisprudence. The distinction between what is needed to support novel procedures and what is needed to sustain traditional ones is fundamental, as we observed over a century ago:

> [A] process of law, which is not otherwise forbidden, must be taken to be due process of law, if it can show the sanction of settled usage both in England and in this country; but it by no means follows that nothing else can be due process of law. . . . [That which], in substance, has been immemorially the actual law of the land . . . therefor[e] is due process of law. But to hold that such a characteristic is essential to due process of law, would be to deny every quality of the law but its age, and to render it incapable of progress or improvement. It would be to stamp upon our jurisprudence the unchangeableness attributed to the laws of the Medes and Persians." *Hurtado v. California,* 110 U.S. 516, 528–529, (1884).

The short of the matter is that jurisdiction based on physical presence alone constitutes due process because it is one of the continuing traditions of our legal system that define the due process standard of "traditional notions of fair play and substantial justice." That standard was developed by analogy to "physical presence," and it would be perverse to say it could now be turned against that touchstone of jurisdiction.

D

Petitioner's strongest argument, though we ultimately reject it, relies upon our decision in *Shaffer v. Heitner,* 433 U.S. 186 (1977). In that case, a Delaware court hearing a shareholder's derivative suit against a corporation's directors secured jurisdiction quasi in rem by sequestering the out-of-state defendants' stock in the company, the situs of which was Delaware under Delaware law. Reasoning that Delaware's sequestration procedure was simply a mechanism to compel the absent defendants to appear in a suit to determine their personal rights and obligations, we concluded that the normal rules we had developed under *International Shoe* for jurisdiction over suits against absent defendants should apply—viz., Delaware could not hear the suit because the defendants' sole contact with the State (ownership of property there) was unrelated to the lawsuit.

It goes too far to say, as petitioner contends, that *Shaffer* compels the conclusion that a State lacks jurisdiction over an individual unless the litigation arises out of his activities in the State. *Shaffer,* like

NOTICE, TERRITORIAL JURISDICTION, AND VENUE: "WHERE CAN
WE FILE OUR ACTION?"

268

CHAPTER 4

International Shoe, involved jurisdiction over an absent defendant, and it stands for nothing more than the proposition that when the "minimum contact" that is a substitute for physical presence consists of property ownership it must, like other minimum contacts, be related to the litigation. Petitioner wrenches out of its context our statement in *Shaffer* that "all assertions of state-court jurisdiction must be evaluated according to the standards set forth in *International Shoe* and its progeny," 433 U.S., at 212. When read together with the two sentences that preceded it, the meaning of this statement becomes clear:

> The fiction that an assertion of jurisdiction over property is anything but an assertion of jurisdiction over the owner of the property supports an ancient form without substantial modern justification. Its continued acceptance would serve only to allow state-court jurisdiction that is fundamentally unfair to the defendant.

> We therefore conclude that all assertions of state-court jurisdiction must be evaluated according to the standards set forth in *International Shoe* and its progeny." *Ibid.* (emphasis added).

Shaffer was saying, in other words, not that all bases for the assertion of in personam jurisdiction (including, presumably, in-state service) must be treated alike and subjected to the "minimum contacts" analysis of *International Shoe*; but rather that quasi in rem jurisdiction, that fictional "ancient form," and in personam jurisdiction, are really one and the same and must be treated alike-leading to the conclusion that quasi in rem jurisdiction, i.e., that form of in personam jurisdiction based upon a "property ownership" contact and by definition unaccompanied by personal, in-state service, must satisfy the litigation-relatedness requirement of *International Shoe*. The logic of *Shaffer's* holding—which places all suits against absent nonresidents on the same constitutional footing, regardless of whether a separate Latin label is attached to one particular basis of contact—does not compel the conclusion that physically present defendants must be treated identically to absent ones. As we have demonstrated at length, our tradition has treated the two classes of defendants quite differently, and it is unreasonable to read *Shaffer* as casually obliterating that distinction. *International Shoe* confined its "minimum contacts" requirement to situations in which the defendant "be not present within the territory of the forum," and nothing in *Shaffer* expands that requirement beyond that.

It is fair to say, however, that while our holding today does not contradict *Shaffer*, our basic approach to the due process question is different. We have conducted no independent inquiry into the desirability or fairness of the prevailing in-state service rule, leaving that judgment to the legislatures that are free to amend it; for our purposes, its validation is its pedigree, as the phrase "traditional notions of fair play and substantial justice" makes clear. *Shaffer* did conduct such an independent inquiry, asserting that " 'traditional notions of fair play and substantial justice' can be as readily offended by the perpetuation of ancient forms that are no longer justified as by the adoption of new procedures that are inconsistent with the basic values of our constitutional heritage." 433 U.S., at 212. Perhaps that assertion can be sustained when the "perpetuation of ancient forms" is engaged in by only a very small minority of the States. Where, however, as in the present case, a jurisdictional principle is both firmly approved by tradition and still favored, it is impossible to imagine what standard we could appeal to for the judgment that it is "no longer justified." While in no way receding from or casting doubt upon the holding of *Shaffer* or any other case, we reaffirm today our time-honored approach. For new procedures, hitherto unknown, the Due Process Clause requires analysis to determine whether "traditional notions of fair play and substantial justice" have been offended. *International Shoe*, 326 U.S., at 316. But a doctrine of personal jurisdiction that dates back to the adoption of the Fourteenth Amendment and is still generally observed unquestionably meets that standard.

III

A few words in response to Justice BRENNAN's opinion concurring in the judgment: It insists that we apply "contemporary notions of due process" to determine the constitutionality of California's assertion of jurisdiction. But our analysis today comports with that prescription, at least if we give it the only sense allowed by our precedents. The "contemporary notions of due process" applicable to personal jurisdiction are the enduring "traditional notions of fair play and substantial justice" established as the test by *International Shoe*. By its very language, that test is satisfied if a state court adheres to jurisdictional rules that are generally applied and have always been applied in the United States.

But the concurrence's proposed standard of "contemporary notions of due process" requires more: It measures state-court jurisdiction not only against traditional doctrines in this country, including current state-court practice, but also against each Justice's subjective assessment of what is fair and just. Authority for that seductive standard is not to be found in any of our personal jurisdiction cases. It is, indeed, an outright break with the test of "traditional notions of fair play and substantial justice," which would have to be reformulated "our notions of fair play and substantial justice."

The subjectivity, and hence inadequacy, of this approach becomes apparent when the concurrence tries to explain why the assertion of jurisdiction in the present case meets its standard of continuing-American-tradition-plus-innate-fairness. Justice BRENNAN lists the "benefits" Mr. Burnham derived from the State of California—the fact that, during the few days he was there, "[h]is health and safety [were] guaranteed by the State's police, fire, and emergency medical services; he [was] free to travel on the State's roads and waterways; he likely enjoy[ed] the fruits of the State's economy." Three days' worth of these benefits strike us as powerfully inadequate to establish, as an abstract matter, that it is "fair" for California to decree the ownership of all Mr. Burnham's worldly goods acquired during the 10 years of his marriage, and the custody over his children. We daresay a contractual exchange swapping those benefits for that power would not survive the "unconscionability" provision of the Uniform Commercial Code. Even less persuasive are the other "fairness" factors alluded to by Justice BRENNAN. It would create "an asymmetry," we are told, if Burnham were permitted (as he is) to appear in California courts as a plaintiff, but were not compelled to appear in California courts as defendant; and travel being as easy as it is nowadays, and modern procedural devices being so convenient, it is no great hardship to appear in California courts. The problem with these assertions is that they justify the exercise of jurisdiction over everyone, whether or not he ever comes to California. The only "fairness" elements setting Mr. Burnham apart from the rest of the world are the three days' "benefits" referred to above—and even those, do not set him apart from many other people who have enjoyed three days in the Golden State (savoring the fruits of its economy, the availability of its roads and police services) but who were fortunate enough not to be served with process while they were there and thus are not (simply by reason of that savoring) subject to the general jurisdiction of California's courts. In other words, even if one agreed with Justice BRENNAN's conception of an equitable bargain, the "benefits" we have been discussing would explain why it is "fair" to assert general jurisdiction over Burnham-returned-to-New-Jersey-after-service only at the expense of proving that it is also "fair" to assert general jurisdiction over Burnham-returned-to-New-Jersey-without-service—which we know does not conform with "contemporary notions of due process."

There is, we must acknowledge, one factor mentioned by Justice BRENNAN that both relates distinctively to the assertion of jurisdiction on the basis of personal in-state service and is fully persuasive—namely, the fact that a defendant voluntarily present in a particular State has a "reasonable expectatio[n]" that he is subject to suit there. By formulating it as a "reasonable expectation" Justice BRENNAN makes that seem like a "fairness" factor; but in reality, of course, it is just tradition masquerading as "fairness." The only reason for charging Mr. Burnham with the reasonable expectation of being subject to suit is that the States of the Union assert adjudicatory jurisdiction over the person, and have always asserted adjudicatory jurisdiction over the person, by serving him with process during his temporary physical presence in their territory. That continuing tradition, which anyone entering California should have known about, renders it "fair" for Mr. Burnham, who voluntarily entered California, to be sued there for divorce—at least "fair" in the limited sense that he has no one but himself to blame. Justice BRENNAN's long journey is a circular one, leaving him, at the end of the day, in complete reliance upon the very factor he sought to avoid: The existence of a continuing tradition is not enough, fairness also must be considered; fairness exists here because there is a continuing tradition.

* * * [D]espite the fact that he manages to work the word "rule" into his formulation, Justice BRENNAN's approach does not establish a rule of law at all, but only a "totality of the circumstances" test, guaranteeing what traditional territorial rules of jurisdiction were designed precisely to avoid: uncertainty and litigation over the preliminary issue of the forum's competence. * * *

The difference between us and Justice BRENNAN has nothing to do with whether "further progress [is] to be made" in the "evolution of our legal system." It has to do with whether changes are to be adopted as progressive by the American people or decreed as progressive by the Justices of this Court. Nothing we say today prevents individual States from limiting or entirely abandoning the in-state-service basis of jurisdiction. And nothing prevents an overwhelming majority of them from doing so, with the consequence that the "traditional notions of fairness" that this Court applies may change. But the States have overwhelmingly declined to adopt such limitation or abandonment, evidently not considering it to be progress. The question is whether, armed with no authority other than individual Justices' perceptions of fairness that conflict with both past and current practice, this Court can compel the States to make such a change on the ground that "due process" requires it. We hold that it cannot.

Because the Due Process Clause does not prohibit the California courts from exercising jurisdiction over petitioner based on the fact of in-state service of process, the judgment is

Affirmed.

■ JUSTICE WHITE, concurring in part and concurring in the judgment.

I join Parts I, II–A, II–B, and II–C of Justice SCALIA's opinion and concur in the judgment of affirmance. The rule allowing jurisdiction to be obtained over a nonresident by personal service in the forum State, without more, has been and is so widely accepted throughout this country that I could not possibly strike it down, either on its face or as applied in this case, on the ground that it denies due process of law guaranteed by the Fourteenth Amendment. * * *

■ JUSTICE BRENNAN, with whom JUSTICE MARSHALL, JUSTICE BLACKMUN, and JUSTICE O'CONNOR join, concurring in the judgment.

I agree with Justice SCALIA that the Due Process Clause of the Fourteenth Amendment generally permits a state court to exercise jurisdiction over a defendant if he is served with process while voluntarily present in the forum State.[1] I do not perceive the need, however, to decide that a jurisdictional rule that " 'has been immemorially the actual law of the land,' " ante, at 2115, quoting *Hurtado v. California*, 110 U.S. 516, 528 (1884), automatically comports with due process simply by virtue of its "pedigree." Although I agree that history is an important factor in establishing whether a jurisdictional rule satisfies due process requirements, I cannot agree that it is the only factor such that all traditional rules of jurisdiction are, ipso facto, forever constitutional. Unlike Justice SCALIA, I would undertake an "independent inquiry into the . . . fairness of the prevailing in-state service rule." I therefore concur only in the judgment.

I

I believe that the approach adopted by Justice SCALIA's opinion today—reliance solely on historical pedigree—is foreclosed by our decisions in *International Shoe Co. v. Washington*, 326 U.S. 310 (1945), and *Shaffer v. Heitner*, 433 U.S. 186 (1977). In *International Shoe*, we held that a state court's assertion of personal jurisdiction does not violate the Due Process Clause if it is consistent with " 'traditional notions of fair play and substantial justice.' " 326 U.S., at 316, quoting *Milliken v. Meyer*, 311 U.S. 457, 463 (1940). In *Shaffer*, we stated that "all assertions of state-court jurisdiction must be evaluated according to the standards set forth in *International Shoe* and its progeny." 433 U.S., at 212. The critical insight of *Shaffer* is that all rules of jurisdiction, even ancient ones, must satisfy contemporary notions of due process. No longer were we content to limit our jurisdictional analysis to pronouncements that "[t]he foundation of jurisdiction is physical power," *McDonald v. Mabee*, 243 U.S. 90, 91 (1917), and that "every State possesses exclusive jurisdiction and sovereignty over persons and property within its territory." *Pennoyer v. Neff*, 95 U.S. 714, 722 (1878). While acknowledging that "history must be considered as supporting the proposition that jurisdiction based solely on the presence of property satisfie[d] the demands of due process," we found that this factor could not be "decisive." 433 U.S., at 211–212. We recognized that " '[t]raditional notions of fair play and substantial justice' can be as readily offended by the perpetuation of ancient forms that are no longer justified as by the adoption of new procedures that are inconsistent with the basic values of our constitutional heritage." *Id.*, at 212. I agree with this approach and continue to believe that "the minimum-contacts analysis developed in *International Shoe* . . . represents a far more sensible construct for the exercise of state-court jurisdiction than the patchwork of legal and factual fictions that has been generated from the decision in *Pennoyer v. Neff*." *Id.*, at 219 (BRENNAN, J., concurring in part and dissenting in part).

---

[1]   I use the term "transient jurisdiction" to refer to jurisdiction premised solely on the fact that a person is served with process while physically present in the forum State.

While our holding in *Shaffer* may have been limited to quasi in rem jurisdiction, our mode of analysis was not. Indeed, that we were willing in *Shaffer* to examine anew the appropriateness of the quasi in rem rule—until that time dutifully accepted by American courts for at least a century—demonstrates that we did not believe that the "pedigree" of a jurisdictional practice was dispositive in deciding whether it was consistent with due process. We later characterized *Shaffer* as "abandon[ing] the outworn rule of *Harris v. Balk*, 198 U.S. 215 (1905), that the interest of a creditor in a debt could be extinguished or otherwise affected by any State having transitory jurisdiction over the debtor." *World-Wide Volkswagen Corp. v. Woodson*, 444 U.S. 286, 296 (1980). If we could discard an "ancient form without substantial modern justification" in *Shaffer*, we can do so again. Lower courts, commentators, and the American Law Institute all have interpreted *International Shoe* and *Shaffer* to mean that every assertion of state-court jurisdiction, even one pursuant to a "traditional" rule such as transient jurisdiction, must comport with contemporary notions of due process. Notwithstanding the nimble gymnastics of Justice SCALIA's opinion today, it is not faithful to our decision in *Shaffer*.

II

Tradition, though alone not dispositive, is of course relevant to the question whether the rule of transient jurisdiction is consistent with due process. Tradition is salient not in the sense that practices of the past are automatically reasonable today; indeed, under such a standard, the legitimacy of transient jurisdiction would be called into question because the rule's historical "pedigree" is a matter of intense debate. The rule was a stranger to the common law and was rather weakly implanted in American jurisprudence "at the crucial time for present purposes: 1868, when the Fourteenth Amendment was adopted." For much of the 19th century, American courts did not uniformly recognize the concept of transient jurisdiction, and it appears that the transient rule did not receive wide currency until well after our decision in *Pennoyer v. Neff*, 95 U.S. 714 (1878).

Rather, I find the historical background relevant because, however murky the jurisprudential origins of transient jurisdiction, the fact that American courts have announced the rule for perhaps a century (first in dicta, more recently in holdings) provides a defendant voluntarily present in a particular State today "clear notice that [he] is subject to suit" in the forum. *World-Wide Volkswagen Corp. v. Woodson*, 444 U.S., at 297. Regardless of whether Justice Story's account of the rule's genesis is mythical, our common understanding now, fortified by a century of judicial practice, is that jurisdiction is often a function of geography. The transient rule is consistent with reasonable expectations and is entitled to a strong presumption that it comports with due process. "If I visit another State, . . . I knowingly assume some risk that the State will exercise its power over my property or my person while there. My contact with the State, though minimal, gives rise to predictable risks." *Shaffer*, 433 U.S., at 218 (STEVENS, J., concurring in judgment). Thus, proposed revisions to the *Restatement (Second) of Conflict of Laws* § 28, p. 39 (1986), provide that "[a] state has power to exercise judicial jurisdiction over an individual who is present within its territory unless the individual's relationship to the state is so attenuated as to make the exercise of such jurisdiction unreasonable."[11]

By visiting the forum State, a transient defendant actually "avail[s]" himself, *Burger King*, of significant benefits provided by the State. His health and safety are guaranteed by the State's police, fire, and emergency medical services; he is free to travel on the State's roads and waterways; he likely enjoys the fruits of the State's economy as well. Moreover, the Privileges and Immunities Clause of Article IV prevents a state government from discriminating against a transient defendant by denying him the protections of its law or the right of access to its courts. Subject only to the doctrine of forum non conveniens, an out-of-state plaintiff may use state courts in all circumstances in which those courts would be available to state citizens. Without transient jurisdiction, an asymmetry would arise: A transient would have the full benefit of the power of the forum State's courts as a plaintiff while retaining immunity from their authority as a defendant.

The potential burdens on a transient defendant are slight. " '[M]odern transportation and communications have made it much less burdensome for a party sued to defend himself' " in a State outside his place of residence. *Burger King*, supra, 471 U.S., at 474, quoting *McGee v. International Life Ins. Co.*, 355 U.S. 220, 223 (1957). That the defendant has already journeyed at least once before to the forum—as evidenced by the fact that he was served with process there—is an indication that suit in the forum likely would not be prohibitively inconvenient. Finally, any burdens that do arise can be ameliorated by a variety of procedural devices.[13] For these reasons, as a rule the exercise of personal jurisdiction over a defendant based on his voluntary presence in the forum will satisfy the requirements of due process.

----

[11] As the *Restatement* suggests, there may be cases in which a defendant's involuntary or unknowing presence in a State does not support the exercise of personal jurisdiction over him. The facts of the instant case do not require us to determine the outer limits of the transient jurisdiction rule.

[13] For example, in the federal system, a transient defendant can avoid protracted litigation of a spurious suit through a motion to dismiss for failure to state a claim or though a motion for summary judgment. Fed. Rules Civ. Proc. 12(b)(6) and 56. He can use relatively inexpensive methods of discovery, such as oral deposition by telephone (Rule 30(b)[4]), deposition upon written questions (Rule 31), interrogatories (Rule 33), and requests for admission (Rule 36), while enjoying protection from harassment (Rule 26(c)), and possibly obtaining costs and attorney's fees for some of the work involved (Rules 37(a)[5], (b)–(d)). Moreover, a change of venue may be possible. 28 U.S.C. § 1404. In state court, many of the same procedural protections are available, as is the doctrine of forum non conveniens, under which the suit may be dismissed.

In this case, it is undisputed that petitioner was served with process while voluntarily and knowingly in the State of California. I therefore concur in the judgment.

■ JUSTICE STEVENS, concurring in the judgment.

As I explained in my separate writing, I did not join the Court's opinion in *Shaffer v. Heitner*, 433 U.S. 186 (1977), because I was concerned by its unnecessarily broad reach. The same concern prevents me from joining either Justice SCALIA's or Justice BRENNAN's opinion in this case. For me, it is sufficient to note that the historical evidence and consensus identified by Justice SCALIA, the considerations of fairness identified by Justice BRENNAN, and the common sense displayed by Justice WHITE, all combine to demonstrate that this is, indeed, a very easy case.* Accordingly, I agree that the judgment should be affirmed.

COMMENTS AND QUESTIONS CONCERNING
BURNHAM V. SUPERIOR COURT

1.   In reciting the facts of this case, Justice Scalia states: "Later that year, petitioner made a special appearance in the California Superior Court, moving to quash the service of process on the ground that the court lacked personal jurisdiction over him because his only contacts with California were a few short visits to the State for the purposes of conducting business and visiting his children."

A "special appearance" is entered in some state courts when an attorney intends to challenge the personal jurisdiction of the court, but does not want to subject her client to the court's jurisdiction by the very act of appearing on the client's behalf in the lawsuit. In the federal courts, special appearances are no longer necessary, and an attorney can appear on behalf of her client without risking that her appearance itself will subject her client to the personal jurisdiction of the court. *In re Hijazi*, 589 F.3d 401, 413 (7th Cir. 2009); *S.E.C. v. Ross*, 504 F.3d 1130, 1149 (9th Cir. 2007).

2.   Why does the California court need to establish personal jurisdiction over Dennis Burnham in order to dissolve the Burnham's marriage? Consider the Court's statement in *Pennoyer v. Neff*: "The State * * * has absolute right to prescribe the conditions upon which the marriage relation between its own citizens shall be created, and the causes for which it may be dissolved." U.S. at 734–35.

3.   How is *Burnham* different from the other due process actions involving personal jurisdiction that had been decided by the Supreme Court after *International Shoe*?

4.   Justice Scalia observed in the first footnote to his opinion:

We have said that "[e]ven when the cause of action does not arise out of or relate to the foreign corporation's activities in the

---

*   Perhaps the adage about hard cases making bad law should be revised to cover easy cases.

NOTICE, TERRITORIAL JURISDICTION, AND VENUE: "WHERE CAN
WE FILE OUR ACTION?"

276

CHAPTER 4

forum State, due process is not offended by a State's subjecting the corporation to its in personam jurisdiction when there are sufficient contacts between the State and the foreign corporation." *Helicopteros Nacionales de Colombia v. Hall*, 466 U.S., at 414. Our only holding supporting that statement, however, involved "regular service of summons upon [the corporation's] president while he was in [the forum State] acting in that capacity." *See Perkins v. Benguet Consolidated Mining Co.*, 342 U.S. 437, 440 (1952). It may be that whatever special rule exists permitting "continuous and systematic" contacts, *id.*, at 438, to support jurisdiction with respect to matters unrelated to activity in the forum applies only to corporations, which have never fitted comfortably in a jurisdictional regime based primarily upon "de facto power over the defendant's person." *International Shoe Co. v. Washington*, 326 U.S. 310, 316 (1945). We express no views on these matters—and, for simplicity's sake, omit reference to this aspect of "contacts"-based jurisdiction in our discussion.

The Supreme Court revisited such general jurisdiction in *Goodyear Dunlop Tires Operations, S.A. v. Brown,* 131 S.Ct. 2846, 2857 (2011), concluding that the defendants' "attenuated connections to the State fall far short of the 'the continuous and systematic general business contacts' necessary to empower North Carolina to entertain suit against them on claims unrelated to anything that connects them to the State. *Helicopteros,* 466 U.S., at 416."

5.   In portions of his opinion not included in the text, Justice Scalia cited many state cases—from both the 19th and 20th centuries—upholding the legality of personal jurisdiction based upon service of a defendant within the court's jurisdiction. What is the significance of these cases?

6.   Who has the better of the debate between Justice Scalia and Justice Brennan as to whether "contemporary notions of due process" or "traditional notions of due process" control in a case such as this? Do you agree with Justice Scalia's characterization of Justice Brennan's concurrence: "The existence of a continuing tradition is not enough, fairness also must be considered; fairness exists here because there is a continuing tradition"?

7.   Justice Scalia criticizes Justice Brennan's analysis as establishing "only a 'totality of the circumstances' test." What is the difficulty with such a test? Is it really possible to have a more definite test to determine whether a person has been afforded due process?

8.   What if a defendant has been brought into a jurisdiction against his will? Should service upon the defendant in such situations result in personal jurisdiction? Section 82 of the *Restatement (Second) of Conflict of Laws* provides: "A state will not exercise judicial jurisdiction, which has been obtained by fraud or unlawful force, over a defendant or his property." *See Wyman v. Newhouse*, 93 F.2d 313, 314 (2d Cir. 1937) (court did not acquire jurisdiction over defendant, because he was served after being fraudulently induced to travel to Florida by plaintiff's statements that she had to see him

before she left the United States due to her mother's illness in Ireland); *Bowman v. Neblett*, 24 S.W.2d 697 (Mo. Ct. App. 1930) (improper service because defendant was fraudulently induced into jurisdiction by police officers who arrested him and told him that he must go to that jurisdiction to answer criminal charges). *See also Fitzgerald & Mallory Const. Co. v. Fitzgerald*, 137 U.S. 98, 105 (1890) ("If a person is induced by false representations to come within the jurisdiction of a court for the purpose of obtaining service of process upon him, and process is there served, it is such an abuse that the court will, on motion, set the process aside").

9.   Why didn't Justice White join in part II(D) or part III of Justice Scalia's opinion?

10.   In his opinion, Justice Brennan states: "Thus, proposed revisions to the *Restatement (Second) of Conflict of Laws* § 28, p. 39 (1986), provide that '[a] state has power to exercise judicial jurisdiction over an individual who is present within its territory unless the individual's relationship to the state is so attenuated as to make the exercise of such jurisdiction unreasonable.'" However, the current version of Section 28 of the *Restatement (Second) of Conflict of Laws* provides: "A state has power to exercise judicial jurisdiction over an individual who is present within its territory, whether permanently or temporarily," while comment a to that section in part provides:

> The rule that physical presence is a basis of judicial jurisdiction may result at times in a defendant being compelled to stand suit in a state to which he has no relationship other than the fact that he was served with process while passing through that state's territory. It can also be contended that the rule is inconsistent with the basic principle of reasonableness which underlies the field of judicial jurisdiction (see § 24). In any event, the rule's potentialities for hardship, are mitigated by the fact that the court may refuse to exercise its jurisdiction under the rules of §§ 82–84.

Restatement (Second) of Conflict of Laws § 28 cmt. a (1971).

11.   Do you agree with Justice Stevens that "[p]erhaps the adage about hard cases making bad law should be revised to cover easy cases"?

c.   *Personal Jurisdiction Involving Property*

The Supreme Court's doctrine concerning personal jurisdiction over persons (individual and corporate) evolved from *Pennoyer v. Neff* to *International Shoe*. Attempts were made to convince the Court to similarly modify the application of personal jurisdiction over property— whether in actions to determine rights in the property itself or to use that property to indirectly gain personal jurisdiction over the owner of that property. As recounted in the notes that follow, those efforts were only partially successful.

1.   Justice Scalia states in his majority opinion in *Burnham v. Superior Court*:

Petitioner's strongest argument, though we ultimately reject it, relies upon our decision in *Shaffer v. Heitner*, 433 U.S. 186 (1977). In that case, a Delaware court hearing a shareholder's derivative suit against a corporation's directors secured jurisdiction quasi in rem by sequestering the out-of-state defendants' stock in the company, the situs of which was Delaware under Delaware law. Reasoning that Delaware's sequestration procedure was simply a mechanism to compel the absent defendants to appear in a suit to determine their personal rights and obligations, we concluded that the normal rules we had developed under *International Shoe* for jurisdiction over suits against absent defendants should apply—viz., Delaware could not hear the suit because the defendants' sole contact with the State (ownership of property there) was unrelated to the lawsuit.

495 U.S. at 619–20. While the Court held that an *International Shoe* minimum contacts analysis should be applied in a quasi in rem situation such as was presented in *Shaffer*, the *Burnham* majority did not find such an analysis necessary when a non-resident was served with process while voluntarily within the forum state.

2.   There are three types of personal or territorial jurisdiction by which a court constitutionally can assert its power over a party to a civil action:

In personam: The "entire object of the action is to determine the personal rights and obligations of the defendants." *Pennoyer v. Neff*, 95 U.S. 714, 727 (1877). The court traditionally obtained personal jurisdiction over the defendant through service upon the defendant while present in the jurisdiction or based upon the express or implied consent of the defendant to the court's jurisdiction. Since the Supreme Court's decision in *International Shoe Co. v. Washington*, 326 U.S. 310 (1945), in personam jurisdiction has been upheld based upon service pursuant to a state long-arm provision and satisfaction of the *International Shoe* minimum contacts test.

In rem: Rather than determining the rights of parties in relation to one another, the court is asked to determine all rights involving a particular property or "res" present within the court's jurisdiction. In addition to determining rights to real or personal property, in rem actions include proceedings such as a divorce, bankruptcy determination, and maritime libel action. "The effect of a judgment in such a case is limited to the property that supports jurisdiction and does not impose a personal liability on the property owner, since he is not before the court." *Shaffer v. Heitner*, 433 U.S. 186, 199 (1977).

Quasi in rem: While property within the jurisdiction is attached, the attachment is not to permit the court to determine all rights to the property vis-a-vis the world, as is the case with an in rem adjudication. Instead, quasi in rem jurisdiction is used to indirectly gain personal jurisdiction over the defendant, himself.

In *Shaffer v. Heitner* the Supreme Court held that, in such cases, the minimum contacts standards of *International Shoe* applied—and the Court then struck down an attempt to assert personal jurisdiction in Delaware over defendants with no actual Delaware contacts. The attempted personal jurisdiction was based solely upon the attachment of shares of stock considered by Delaware law to be constructively held in that state but unrelated to the claims asserted in the civil action. In the event, though, that the underlying claim is related to the property, the *International Shoe* standards may well be satisfied. *Shaffer v. Heitner*, 433 U.S. 186, 207 (1977) ("[W]hen claims to the property itself are the source of the underlying controversy between the plaintiff and the defendant, it would be unusual for the State where the property is located not to have jurisdiction."

3.   Prior to *Shaffer v. Heitner*, plaintiffs' lawyers used quasi in rem jurisdiction to obtain personal jurisdiction over defendants who otherwise were beyond the territorial jurisdiction of the court. Perhaps the most creative use of quasi in rem jurisdiction occurred in *Harris v. Balk*, 195 U.S. 215 (1905). In his majority opinion in *Shaffer*, 433 U.S. at 200–201, Justice Marshall described this case as follows:

> Epstein, a resident of Maryland, had a claim against Balk, a resident of North Carolina. Harris, another North Carolina resident, owed money to Balk. When Harris happened to visit Maryland, Epstein garnished his debt to Balk. Harris did not contest the debt to Balk and paid it to Epstein's North Carolina attorney. When Balk later sued Harris in North Carolina, this Court held that the Full Faith and Credit Clause, U.S. Const., Art. IV, § 1, required that Harris' payment to Epstein be treated as a discharge of his debt to Balk. This Court reasoned that the debt Harris owed Balk was an intangible form of property belonging to Balk, and that the location of that property traveled with the debtor. By obtaining personal jurisdiction over Harris, Epstein had "arrested" his debt to Balk and brought it into the Maryland court. Under the structure established by *Pennoyer*, Epstein was then entitled to proceed against that debt to vindicate his claim against Balk, even though Balk himself was not subject to the jurisdiction of a Maryland tribunal.

4.   In *Shaffer v. Heitner*, the Court applied the requirements of *International Shoe* to quasi in rem proceedings, "[r]easoning that Delaware's sequestration procedure was simply a mechanism to compel

the absent defendants to appear in a suit to determine their personal rights and obligations." *Burnham v. Superior Court*, 495 U.S. 604, 620 (1990). As Justice White noted in his majority opinion in *World-Wide Volkswagen Corp. v. Woodson*, 444 U.S. 286, 296 (1980), "We recently abandoned the outworn rule of *Harris v. Balk*, 198 U.S. 215 (1905), that the interest of a creditor in a debt could be extinguished or otherwise affected by any State having transitory jurisdiction over the debtor."

5.   Justice Marshall in *Shaffer v. Heitner* not only "abandoned" *Harris v. Balk*, but also noted the impact of *International Shoe* upon some aspects of *Pennoyer v. Neff*:

> [T]he relationship among the defendant, the forum, and the litigation, rather than the mutually exclusive sovereignty of the States on which the rules of *Pennoyer* rest, became the central concern of the inquiry into personal jurisdiction. The immediate effect of this departure from *Pennoyer*'s conceptual apparatus was to increase the ability of the state courts to obtain personal jurisdiction over nonresident defendants.
>
> No equally dramatic change has occurred in the law governing jurisdiction in rem. There have, however, been intimations that the collapse of the in personam wing of *Pennoyer* has not left that decision unweakened as a foundation for in rem jurisdiction. Well-reasoned lower court opinions have questioned the proposition that the presence of property in a State gives that State jurisdiction to adjudicate rights to the property regardless of the relationship of the underlying dispute and the property owner to the forum. The overwhelming majority of commentators have also rejected *Pennoyer*'s premise that a proceeding "against" property is not a proceeding against the owners of that property. Accordingly, they urge that the "traditional notions of fair play and substantial justice" that govern a State's power to adjudicate in personam should also govern its power to adjudicate personal rights to property located in the State.
>
> * * *
>
> It is clear, therefore, that the law of state-court jurisdiction no longer stands securely on the foundation established in *Pennoyer*. We think that the time is ripe to consider whether the standard of fairness and substantial justice set forth in *International Shoe* should be held to govern actions in rem as well as in personam.

Shaffer v. Heitner, 433 U.S. 186, 204–06 (1977). This is, indeed, just what the Court did in *Shaffer*, although it would not extend the *International Shoe* test in a similar fashion to transient jurisdiction in *Burnham v. Superior Court*.

d. *General Jurisdiction:* Daimler AG v. Bauman

Until now, the cases that you have read have involved actions arising from the defendant's contacts with the judicial forum—instances of specific (personal) jurisdiction. Claims that do not arise from the defendant's forum contacts require a court to assert general (personal) jurisdiction. As you will see in the next case, such general jurisdiction may be difficult to establish.

Daimler AG v. Bauman

Supreme Court of the United States, 2014
134 S.Ct. 746

OPINION

■ JUSTICE GINSBURG delivered the opinion of the Court.

This case concerns the authority of a court in the United States to entertain a claim brought by foreign plaintiffs against a foreign defendant based on events occurring entirely outside the United States. The litigation commenced in 2004, when twenty-two Argentinian residents filed a complaint in the United States District Court for the Northern District of California against DaimlerChrysler Aktiengesellschaft (Daimler), a German public stock company, headquartered in Stuttgart, that manufactures Mercedes-Benz vehicles in Germany. The complaint alleged that during Argentina's 1976–1983 "Dirty War," Daimler's Argentinian subsidiary, Mercedes-Benz Argentina (MB Argentina) collaborated with state security forces to kidnap, detain, torture, and kill certain MB Argentina workers, among them, plaintiffs or persons closely related to plaintiffs. Damages for the alleged human-rights violations were sought from Daimler under the laws of the United States, California, and Argentina. Jurisdiction over the lawsuit was predicated on the California contacts of Mercedes-Benz USA, LLC (MBUSA), a subsidiary of Daimler incorporated in Delaware with its principal place of business in New Jersey. MBUSA distributes Daimler-manufactured vehicles to independent dealerships throughout the United States, including California.

The question presented is whether the Due Process Clause of the Fourteenth Amendment precludes the District Court from exercising jurisdiction over Daimler in this case, given the absence of any California connection to the atrocities, perpetrators, or victims described in the complaint. Plaintiffs invoked the court's general or all-purpose jurisdiction. California, they urge, is a place where Daimler may be sued on any and all claims against it, wherever in the world the claims may arise. For example, as plaintiffs' counsel affirmed, under the proffered jurisdictional theory, if a Daimler-manufactured vehicle overturned in Poland, injuring a Polish driver and passenger, the injured parties could maintain a design defect suit in California.

Exercises of personal jurisdiction so exorbitant, we hold, are barred by due process constraints on the assertion of adjudicatory authority.

In *Goodyear Dunlop Tires Operations, S.A. v. Brown*, 564 U.S. ___ (2011), we addressed the distinction between general or all-purpose jurisdiction, and specific or conduct-linked jurisdiction. As to the former, we held that a court may assert jurisdiction over a foreign corporation "to hear any and all claims against [it]" only when the corporation's affiliations with the State in which suit is brought are so constant and pervasive "as to render [it] essentially at home in the forum State." *Id.*, at ___. Instructed by *Goodyear*, we conclude Daimler is not "at home" in California, and cannot be sued there for injuries plaintiffs attribute to MB Argentina's conduct in Argentina.

I

In 2004, plaintiffs (respondents here) filed suit in the United States District Court for the Northern District of California, alleging that MB Argentina collaborated with Argentinian state security forces to kidnap, detain, torture, and kill plaintiffs and their relatives during the military dictatorship in place there from 1976 through 1983, a period known as Argentina's "Dirty War." Based on those allegations, plaintiffs asserted claims under the Alien Tort Statute, 28 U.S.C. § 1350, and the Torture Victim Protection Act of 1991, 106 Stat. 73, note following 28 U.S.C. § 1350, as well as claims for wrongful death and intentional infliction of emotional distress under the laws of California and Argentina. The incidents recounted in the complaint center on MB Argentina's plant in Gonzalez Catan, Argentina; no part of MB Argentina's alleged collaboration with Argentinian authorities took place in California or anywhere else in the United States.

Plaintiffs' operative complaint names only one corporate defendant: Daimler, the petitioner here. Plaintiffs seek to hold Daimler vicariously liable for MB Argentina's alleged malfeasance. Daimler is a German *Aktiengesellschaft* (public stock company) that manufactures Mercedes-Benz vehicles in Germany and has its headquarters in Stuttgart. At times relevant to this case, MB Argentina was a subsidiary wholly owned by Daimler's predecessor in interest.

Daimler moved to dismiss the action for want of personal jurisdiction. Opposing the motion, plaintiffs submitted declarations and exhibits purporting to demonstrate the presence of Daimler itself in California. Alternatively, plaintiffs maintained that jurisdiction over Daimler could be founded on the California contacts of MBUSA, a distinct corporate entity that, according to plaintiffs, should be treated as Daimler's agent for jurisdictional purposes.

MBUSA, an indirect subsidiary of Daimler, is a Delaware limited liability corporation. MBUSA serves as Daimler's exclusive importer and distributor in the United States, purchasing Mercedes-Benz automobiles from Daimler in Germany, then importing those vehicles, and ultimately distributing them to independent dealerships located throughout the Nation. Although MBUSA's principal place of business is in New Jersey, MBUSA has multiple California-based facilities, including a regional office in Costa Mesa, a Vehicle Preparation Center in Carson, and a Classic Center in Irvine. According to the record developed below, MBUSA is the largest supplier of luxury vehicles to the California market. In particular, over 10% of all sales of new vehicles in the United States take place in California, and MBUSA's California sales account for 2.4% of Daimler's worldwide sales.

The relationship between Daimler and MBUSA is delineated in a General Distributor Agreement, which sets forth requirements for MBUSA's distribution of Mercedes-Benz vehicles in the United States. That agreement established MBUSA as an "independent contracto[r]" that "buy[s] and sell[s] [vehicles] . . . as an independent business for [its] own account." The agreement "does not make [MBUSA] . . . a general or special agent, partner, joint venturer or employee of DAIMLERCHRYSLER or any DaimlerChrysler Group Company"; MBUSA "ha[s] no authority to make binding obligations for or act on behalf of DAIMLERCHRYSLER or any DaimlerChrysler Group Company."

After allowing jurisdictional discovery on plaintiffs' agency allegations, the District Court granted Daimler's motion to dismiss. Daimler's own affiliations with California, the court first determined, were insufficient to support the exercise of all-purpose jurisdiction over the corporation. Next, the court declined to attribute MBUSA's California contacts to Daimler on an agency theory, concluding that plaintiffs failed to demonstrate that MBUSA acted as Daimler's agent.

* * *

We granted certiorari to decide whether, consistent with the Due Process Clause of the Fourteenth Amendment, Daimler is amenable to suit in California courts for claims involving only foreign plaintiffs and conduct occurring entirely abroad.

II

Federal courts ordinarily follow state law in determining the bounds of their jurisdiction over persons. See Fed. Rule Civ. Proc. 4(k)(1)(A) (service of process is effective to establish personal jurisdiction over a defendant "who is subject to the jurisdiction of a court of general jurisdiction in the state where the district court is located"). Under California's long-arm statute, California state courts may exercise personal jurisdiction "on any basis not inconsistent with the Constitution of this state or of the United States." Cal. Civ. Proc. Code Ann. § 410.10. California's long-arm statute allows the exercise of personal jurisdiction to the full extent permissible under the U.S. Constitution. We therefore inquire whether the Ninth Circuit's holding comports with the limits imposed by federal due process.

III

In *Pennoyer v. Neff*, 95 U.S. 714 (1878), decided shortly after the enactment of the Fourteenth Amendment, the Court held that a tribunal's jurisdiction over persons reaches no farther than the geographic bounds of the forum. In time, however, that strict territorial approach yielded to a less rigid understanding, spurred by "changes in the technology of transportation and communication, and the tremendous growth of interstate business activity." *Burnham v. Superior Court*, 495 U.S. 604, 617 (1990) (opinion of SCALIA, J.).

"The canonical opinion in this area remains *International Shoe [Co. v. Washington]*, 326 U.S. 310 [(1945)], in which we held that a State may authorize its courts to exercise personal jurisdiction over an out-of-state defendant if the defendant has 'certain minimum contacts with [the State] such that the maintenance of the suit does not offend "traditional notions of fair play and substantial justice." ' " *Goodyear*, 564 U.S., at ___ (quoting *International Shoe*, 326 U.S., at 316). Following *International Shoe*, "the relationship among the defendant, the forum, and the litigation, rather than the mutually exclusive sovereignty of the States on which the rules of *Pennoyer* rest, became the central concern of the inquiry into personal jurisdiction." *Shaffer*, 433 U.S., at 204.

International Shoe's conception of "fair play and substantial justice" presaged the development of two categories of personal jurisdiction. The first category is represented by *International Shoe* itself, a case in which the in-state activities of the corporate defendant "ha[d] not only been continuous and systematic, but also g[a]ve rise to the liabilities sued on." 326 U.S., at 317. *International Shoe* recognized, as well, that "the commission of some single or occasional acts of the corporate agent in a state" may sometimes be enough to subject the corporation to jurisdiction in that State's tribunals with respect to suits relating to that in-state activity. *Id.*, at 318. Adjudicatory authority of this order, in which the suit "aris[es] out of or relate[s] to the defendant's contacts with the forum," *Helicopteros Nacionales de Colombia, S.A. v. Hall*, 466 U.S. 408, 414, n. 8 (1984), is today called "specific jurisdiction."

International Shoe distinguished between, on the one hand, exercises of specific jurisdiction, as just described, and on the other, situations where a foreign corporation's "continuous corporate operations within a state [are] so substantial and of such a nature as to justify suit against it on causes of action arising from dealings entirely distinct from those activities." 326 U.S., at 318. As we have since explained, "[a] court may assert general jurisdiction over foreign (sister-state or foreign-country) corporations to hear any and all claims against them when their affiliations with the State are so 'continuous and systematic' as to render them essentially at home in the forum State."

Goodyear, 564 U.S., at ___; see *id.,* at ___; *Helicopteros,* 466 U.S., at 414, n. 9.

Since *International Shoe,* "specific jurisdiction has become the centerpiece of modern jurisdiction theory, while general jurisdiction [has played] a reduced role." *Goodyear,* 564 U.S., at ___ (quoting Twitchell, "The Myth of General Jurisdiction," 101 *Harv. L.Rev.* 610, 628 (1988)). *International Shoe*'s momentous departure from *Pennoyer*'s rigidly territorial focus, we have noted, unleashed a rapid expansion of tribunals' ability to hear claims against out-of-state defendants when the episode-in-suit occurred in the forum or the defendant purposefully availed itself of the forum. * * *

Our post-*International Shoe* opinions on general jurisdiction, by comparison, are few. "[The Court's] 1952 decision in *Perkins v. Benguet Consol. Mining Co.* remains the textbook case of general jurisdiction appropriately exercised over a foreign corporation that has not consented to suit in the forum." *Goodyear,* 564 U.S., at ___. The defendant in *Perkins,* Benguet, was a company incorporated under the laws of the Philippines, where it operated gold and silver mines. Benguet ceased its mining operations during the Japanese occupation of the Philippines in World War II; its president moved to Ohio, where he kept an office, maintained the company's files, and oversaw the company's activities. *Perkins v. Benguet Consol. Mining Co.,* 342 U.S. 437, 448 (1952). The plaintiff, an Ohio resident, sued Benguet on a claim that neither arose in Ohio nor related to the corporation's activities in that State. We held that the Ohio courts could exercise general jurisdiction over Benguet without offending due process. That was so, we later noted, because "Ohio was the corporation's principal, if temporary, place of business." *Keeton v. Hustler Magazine, Inc.,* 465 U.S. 770, 780, n. 11 (1984).

The next case on point, *Helicopteros,* 466 U.S. 408, arose from a helicopter crash in Peru. Four U.S. citizens perished in that accident; their survivors and representatives brought suit in Texas state court against the helicopter's owner and operator, a Colombian corporation. That company's contacts with Texas were confined to "sending its chief executive officer to Houston for a contract-negotiation session; accepting into its New York bank account checks drawn on a Houston bank; purchasing helicopters, equipment, and training services from [a Texas-based helicopter company] for substantial sums; and sending personnel to [Texas] for training." *Id.,* at 416. Notably, those contacts bore no apparent relationship to the accident that gave rise to the suit. We held that the company's Texas connections did not resemble the "continuous and systematic general business contacts . . . found to exist in *Perkins.*" *Ibid.* "[M]ere purchases, even if occurring at regular intervals," we clarified, "are not enough to warrant a State's assertion of *in personam* jurisdiction over a nonresident corporation in a cause of action not related to those purchase transactions." *Id.,* at 418.

Most recently, in *Goodyear*, we answered the question: "Are foreign subsidiaries of a United States parent corporation amenable to suit in state court on claims unrelated to any activity of the subsidiaries in the forum State?" 564 U.S., at ___. That case arose from a bus accident outside Paris that killed two boys from North Carolina. The boys' parents brought a wrongful-death suit in North Carolina state court alleging that the bus's tire was defectively manufactured. The complaint named as defendants not only The Goodyear Tire and Rubber Company (Goodyear), an Ohio corporation, but also Goodyear's Turkish, French, and Luxembourgian subsidiaries. Those foreign subsidiaries, which manufactured tires for sale in Europe and Asia, lacked any affiliation with North Carolina. A small percentage of tires manufactured by the foreign subsidiaries were distributed in North Carolina, however, and on that ground, the North Carolina Court of Appeals held the subsidiaries amenable to the general jurisdiction of North Carolina courts.

We reversed, observing that the North Carolina court's analysis "elided the essential difference between case-specific and all-purpose (general) jurisdiction." *Id.,* at ___. Although the placement of a product into the stream of commerce "may bolster an affiliation germane to *specific* jurisdiction," we explained, such contacts "do not warrant a determination that, based on those ties, the forum has *general* jurisdiction over a defendant." *Id.,* at ___. As *International Shoe* itself teaches, a corporation's "continuous activity of some sorts within a state is not enough to support the demand that the corporation be amenable to suits unrelated to that activity." 326 U.S., at 318. Because Goodyear's foreign subsidiaries were "in no sense at home in North Carolina," we held, those subsidiaries could not be required to submit to the general jurisdiction of that State's courts. 564 U.S., at ___.

As is evident from *Perkins, Helicopteros,* and *Goodyear*, general and specific jurisdiction have followed markedly different trajectories post-*International Shoe*. Specific jurisdiction has been cut loose from *Pennoyer*'s sway, but we have declined to stretch general jurisdiction beyond limits traditionally recognized. As this Court has increasingly trained on the "relationship among the defendant, the forum, and the litigation," *Shaffer,* 433 U.S., at 204, *i.e.,* specific jurisdiction, general jurisdiction has come to occupy a less dominant place in the contemporary scheme.

IV

With this background, we turn directly to the question whether Daimler's affiliations with California are sufficient to subject it to the general (all-purpose) personal jurisdiction of that State's courts. In the proceedings below, the parties agreed on, or failed to contest, certain points we now take as given. Plaintiffs have never attempted to fit this case into the *specific* jurisdiction category. Nor did plaintiffs challenge on appeal the District Court's holding that Daimler's own contacts with

California were, by themselves, too sporadic to justify the exercise of general jurisdiction. While plaintiffs ultimately persuaded the Ninth Circuit to impute MBUSA's California contacts to Daimler on an agency theory, at no point have they maintained that MBUSA is an alter ego of Daimler.

Daimler, on the other hand, failed to object below to plaintiffs' assertion that the California courts could exercise all-purpose jurisdiction over MBUSA. We will assume then, for purposes of this decision only, that MBUSA qualifies as at home in California.

A

In sustaining the exercise of general jurisdiction over Daimler, the Ninth Circuit relied on an agency theory, determining that MBUSA acted as Daimler's agent for jurisdictional purposes and then attributing MBUSA's California contacts to Daimler. The Ninth Circuit's agency analysis derived from Circuit precedent considering principally whether the subsidiary "performs services that are sufficiently important to the foreign corporation that if it did not have a representative to perform them, the corporation's own officials would undertake to perform substantially similar services." 644 F.3d, at 920 (quoting *Doe v. Unocal Corp.,* 248 F.3d 915, 928 (C.A.9 2001)).

This Court has not yet addressed whether a foreign corporation may be subjected to a court's general jurisdiction based on the contacts of its in-state subsidiary. Daimler argues, and several Courts of Appeals have held, that a subsidiary's jurisdictional contacts can be imputed to its parent only when the former is so dominated by the latter as to be its alter ego. The Ninth Circuit adopted a less rigorous test based on what it described as an "agency" relationship. Agencies, we note, come in many sizes and shapes: "One may be an agent for some business purposes and not others so that the fact that one may be an agent for one purpose does not make him or her an agent for every purpose." 2A C. J. S., *Agency* § 43, p. 367 (2013). A subsidiary, for example, might be its parent's agent for claims arising in the place where the subsidiary operates, yet not its agent regarding claims arising elsewhere. The Court of Appeals did not advert to that prospect. But we need not pass judgment on invocation of an agency theory in the context of general jurisdiction, for in no event can the appeals court's analysis be sustained.

The Ninth Circuit's agency finding rested primarily on its observation that MBUSA's services were "important" to Daimler, as gauged by Daimler's hypothetical readiness to perform those services itself if MBUSA did not exist. Formulated this way, the inquiry into importance stacks the deck, for it will always yield a pro-jurisdiction answer: "Anything a corporation does through an independent contractor, subsidiary, or distributor is presumably something that the corporation would do 'by other means' if the independent contractor, subsidiary, or distributor did not exist." 676 F.3d, at 777 (O'Scannlain,

J., dissenting from denial of rehearing en banc). The Ninth Circuit's agency theory thus appears to subject foreign corporations to general jurisdiction whenever they have an in-state subsidiary or affiliate, an outcome that would sweep beyond even the "sprawling view of general jurisdiction" we rejected in *Goodyear*. 564 U.S., at ___.

B

Even if we were to assume that MBUSA is at home in California, and further to assume MBUSA's contacts are imputable to Daimler, there would still be no basis to subject Daimler to general jurisdiction in California, for Daimler's slim contacts with the State hardly render it at home there.

Goodyear made clear that only a limited set of affiliations with a forum will render a defendant amenable to all-purpose jurisdiction there. "For an individual, the paradigm forum for the exercise of general jurisdiction is the individual's domicile; for a corporation, it is an equivalent place, one in which the corporation is fairly regarded as at home." 564 U.S., at ___, (citing Brilmayer et al., "A General Look at General Jurisdiction," 66 *Texas L.Rev.* 721, 728 (1988)). With respect to a corporation, the place of incorporation and principal place of business are "paradig[m] . . . bases for general jurisdiction." *Id.*, at 735. See also Twitchell, 101 *Harv. L.Rev.*, at 633. Those affiliations have the virtue of being unique—that is, each ordinarily indicates only one place—as well as easily ascertainable. Cf. *Hertz Corp. v. Friend,* 559 U.S. 77, 94 (2010) ("Simple jurisdictional rules . . . promote greater predictability."). These bases afford plaintiffs recourse to at least one clear and certain forum in which a corporate defendant may be sued on any and all claims.

Goodyear did not hold that a corporation may be subject to general jurisdiction *only* in a forum where it is incorporated or has its principal place of business; it simply typed those places paradigm all-purpose forums. Plaintiffs would have us look beyond the exemplar bases *Goodyear* identified, and approve the exercise of general jurisdiction in every State in which a corporation "engages in a substantial, continuous, and systematic course of business." That formulation, we hold, is unacceptably grasping.

As noted, the words "continuous and systematic" were used in *International Shoe* to describe instances in which the exercise of *specific* jurisdiction would be appropriate. See 326 U.S., at 317 (jurisdiction can be asserted where a corporation's in-state activities are not only "continuous and systematic, but also give rise to the liabilities sued on"). Turning to all-purpose jurisdiction, in contrast, *International Shoe* speaks of "instances in which the continuous corporate operations within a state [are] so substantial and of such a nature as to justify suit . . . *on causes of action arising from dealings entirely distinct from those activities.*" *Id.,* at 318. Accordingly, the inquiry under *Goodyear* is not whether a foreign corporation's in-forum contacts can be said to be in some sense "continuous and systematic," it is whether that corporation's "affiliations with the State are so 'continuous and systematic' as to render [it] essentially at home in the forum State." 564 U.S., at ___.[19]

Here, neither Daimler nor MBUSA is incorporated in California, nor does either entity have its principal place of business there. If Daimler's California activities sufficed to allow adjudication of this Argentina-rooted case in California, the same global reach would presumably be available in every other State in which MBUSA's sales are sizable. Such exorbitant exercises of all-purpose jurisdiction would scarcely permit out-of-state defendants "to structure their primary conduct with some minimum assurance as to where that conduct will and will not render them liable to suit." *Burger King Corp.*, 471 U.S., at 472.

It was therefore error for the Ninth Circuit to conclude that Daimler, even with MBUSA's contacts attributed to it, was at home in California, and hence subject to suit there on claims by foreign plaintiffs having nothing to do with anything that occurred or had its principal impact in California.[20]

C

Finally, the transnational context of this dispute bears attention. The Court of Appeals emphasized, as supportive of the exercise of general jurisdiction, plaintiffs' assertion of claims under the Alien Tort Statute (ATS) and the Torture Victim Protection Act of 1991 (TVPA). Recent decisions of this Court, however, have rendered plaintiffs' ATS and TVPA claims infirm. See *Kiobel v. Royal Dutch Petroleum Co.*, 569 U.S. ___, ___ (2013) (presumption against extraterritorial application

---

[19] We do not foreclose the possibility that in an exceptional case, *see, e.g., Perkins*, a corporation's operations in a forum other than its formal place of incorporation or principal place of business may be so substantial and of such a nature as to render the corporation at home in that State. But this case presents no occasion to explore that question, because Daimler's activities in California plainly do not approach that level. It is one thing to hold a corporation answerable for operations in the forum State, quite another to expose it to suit on claims having no connection whatever to the forum State.

[20] To clarify in light of Justice SOTOMAYOR's opinion concurring in the judgment, the general jurisdiction inquiry does not "focu[s] solely on the magnitude of the defendant's in-state contacts." General jurisdiction instead calls for an appraisal of a corporation's activities in their entirety, nationwide and worldwide. A corporation that operates in many places can scarcely be deemed at home in all of them. Otherwise, "at home" would be synonymous with "doing business" tests framed before specific jurisdiction evolved in the United States. Nothing in *International Shoe* and its progeny suggests that "a particular quantum of local activity" should give a State authority over a "far larger quantum of . . . activity" having no connection to any in-state activity. Feder, *supra,* at 694.

Justice SOTOMAYOR would reach the same result, but for a different reason. Rather than concluding that Daimler is not at home in California, Justice SOTOMAYOR would hold that the exercise of general jurisdiction over Daimler would be unreasonable "in the unique circumstances of this case." In other words, she favors a resolution fit for this day and case only. True, a multipronged reasonableness check was articulated in *Asahi*, 480 U.S., at 113–114, but not as a free-floating test. Instead, the check was to be essayed when *specific* jurisdiction is at issue. First, a court is to determine whether the connection between the forum and the episode-in-suit could justify the exercise of specific jurisdiction. Then, in a second step, the court is to consider several additional factors to assess the reasonableness of entertaining the case. When a corporation is genuinely at home in the forum State, however, any second-step inquiry would be superfluous.

controls claims under the ATS); *Mohamad v. Palestinian Authority,* 566 U.S. ___, ___ (2012) (only natural persons are subject to liability under the TVPA).

The Ninth Circuit, moreover, paid little heed to the risks to international comity its expansive view of general jurisdiction posed. Other nations do not share the uninhibited approach to personal jurisdiction advanced by the Court of Appeals in this case. In the European Union, for example, a corporation may generally be sued in the nation in which it is "domiciled," a term defined to refer only to the location of the corporation's "statutory seat," "central administration," or "principal place of business." European Parliament and Council Reg. 1215/2012, Arts. 4(1), and 63(1), 2012 O.J. (L. 351) 7, 18. The Solicitor General informs us, in this regard, that "foreign governments' objections to some domestic courts' expansive views of general jurisdiction have in the past impeded negotiations of international agreements on the reciprocal recognition and enforcement of judgments." U.S. Brief 2 (citing Juenger, "The American Law of General Jurisdiction," 2001 *U. Chi. Legal Forum* 141, 161–162). See also U.S. Brief 2 (expressing concern that unpredictable applications of general jurisdiction based on activities of U.S.-based subsidiaries could discourage foreign investors). Considerations of international rapport thus reinforce our determination that subjecting Daimler to the general jurisdiction of courts in California would not accord with the "fair play and substantial justice" due process demands. *International Shoe,* 326 U.S., at 316 (quoting *Milliken v. Meyer,* 311 U.S. 457, 463 (1940)).

* * *

For the reasons stated, the judgment of the United States Court of Appeals for the Ninth Circuit is

Reversed.

■ JUSTICE SOTOMAYOR, concurring in the judgment.

I agree with the Court's conclusion that the Due Process Clause prohibits the exercise of personal jurisdiction over Daimler in light of the unique circumstances of this case. I concur only in the judgment, however, because I cannot agree with the path the Court takes to arrive at that result.

The Court acknowledges that Mercedes-Benz USA, LLC (MBUSA), Daimler's wholly owned subsidiary, has considerable contacts with California. It has multiple facilities in the State, including a regional headquarters. Each year, it distributes in California tens of thousands of cars, the sale of which generated billions of dollars in the year this suit was brought. And it provides service and sales support to customers throughout the State. Daimler has conceded that California courts may exercise general jurisdiction over MBUSA on the basis of these contacts, and the Court assumes that MBUSA's contacts may be attributed to Daimler for the purpose of deciding whether Daimler is also subject to general jurisdiction.

* * * [T]he Court does not dispute that the presence of multiple offices, the direct distribution of thousands of products accounting for billions of dollars in sales, and continuous interaction with customers throughout a State would be enough to support the exercise of general jurisdiction over some businesses. Daimler is just not one of those businesses, the Court concludes, because its California contacts must be viewed in the context of its extensive "nationwide and worldwide" operations. In recent years, Americans have grown accustomed to the concept of multinational corporations that are supposedly "too big to fail"; today the Court deems Daimler "too big for general jurisdiction."

* * * [T]he Court's focus on Daimler's operations outside of California ignores the lodestar of our personal jurisdiction jurisprudence: A State may subject a defendant to the burden of suit if the defendant has sufficiently taken advantage of the State's laws and protections through its contacts in the State; whether the defendant has contacts elsewhere is immaterial.

* * * The Court can and should decide this case on the * * * ground that, no matter how extensive Daimler's contacts with California, that State's exercise of jurisdiction would be unreasonable given that the case involves foreign plaintiffs suing a foreign defendant based on foreign conduct, and given that a more appropriate forum is available. Because I would reverse the judgment below on this ground, I concur in the judgment only.

I

I begin with the point on which the majority and I agree: The Ninth Circuit's decision should be reversed.

Our personal jurisdiction precedents call for a two-part analysis. The contacts prong asks whether the defendant has sufficient contacts with the forum State to support personal jurisdiction; the reasonableness prong asks whether the exercise of jurisdiction would be unreasonable under the circumstances. As the majority points out, all of the cases in which we have applied the reasonableness prong have involved specific as opposed to general jurisdiction. Whether the reasonableness prong should apply in the general jurisdiction context is therefore a question we have never decided, and it is one on which I can appreciate the arguments on both sides. But it would be imprudent to decide that question in this case given that respondents have failed to argue against the application of the reasonableness prong during the entire 8-year history of this litigation. As a result, I would decide this case under the reasonableness prong without foreclosing future consideration of whether that prong should be limited to the specific jurisdiction context.

* * *

II

[Justice Sotomayor asserted that the parties had not litigated below and the Court's grant of certiorari did not extend to the question of whether, if MBUSA's contacts could be attributed to Daimler, those contacts were sufficient to subject Daimler to personal jurisdiction in California.]

III

While the majority's decisional process is problematic enough, I fear that process leads it to an even more troubling result.

A

Until today, our precedents had established a straightforward test for general jurisdiction: Does the defendant have "continuous corporate operations within a state" that are "so substantial and of such a nature as to justify suit against it on causes of action arising from dealings entirely distinct from those activities"? *International Shoe Co. v. Washington,* 326 U.S. 310, 318 (1945). In every case where we have applied this test, we have focused solely on the magnitude of the defendant's in-state contacts, not the relative magnitude of those contacts in comparison to the defendant's contacts with other States.

* * *

This approach follows from the touchstone principle of due process in this field, the concept of reciprocal fairness. When a corporation chooses to invoke the benefits and protections of a State in which it operates, the State acquires the authority to subject the company to suit in its courts. The majority's focus on the extent of a corporate defendant's out-of-forum contacts is untethered from this rationale. After all, the degree to which a company intentionally benefits from a forum State depends on its interactions with that State, not its interactions elsewhere. * * *

Had the majority applied our settled approach, it would have had little trouble concluding that Daimler's California contacts rise to the requisite level, given the majority's assumption that MBUSA's contacts may be attributed to Daimler and given Daimler's concession that those contacts render MBUSA "at home" in California. * * *

* * *

B

The majority today concludes otherwise. Referring to the "continuous and systematic" contacts inquiry that has been taught to generations of first-year law students as "unacceptably grasping," the majority announces the new rule that in order for a foreign defendant to be subject to general jurisdiction, it must not only possess continuous and systematic contacts with a forum State, but those contacts must also surpass some unspecified level when viewed in comparison to the company's "nationwide and worldwide" activities.

Neither of the majority's two rationales for this proportionality requirement is persuasive. First, the majority suggests that its approach is necessary for the sake of predictability. Permitting general jurisdiction in every State where a corporation has continuous and substantial contacts, the majority asserts, would "scarcely permit out-of-state defendants 'to structure their primary conduct with some minimum assurance as to where that conduct will and will not render them liable to suit.'" *Ante,* at 762 (quoting *Burger King Corp.,* 471 U.S., at 472). But there is nothing unpredictable about a rule that instructs multinational corporations that if they engage in continuous and substantial contacts with more than one State, they will be subject to general jurisdiction in each one. The majority may not favor that rule as a matter of policy, but such disagreement does not render an otherwise routine test unpredictable.

* * *

The majority's approach will also lead to greater unpredictability by radically expanding the scope of jurisdictional discovery. Rather than ascertaining the extent of a corporate defendant's forum-state contacts alone, courts will now have to identify the extent of a company's contacts in every other forum where it does business in order to compare them against the company's in-state contacts. That considerable burden runs headlong into the majority's recitation of the familiar principle that "'[s]imple jurisdictional rules ... promote greater predictability.'" *Ante,* at 760–761 (quoting *Hertz Corp. v. Friend,* 559 U.S. 77, 94 (2010)).

Absent the predictability rationale, the majority's sole remaining justification for its proportionality approach is its unadorned concern for the consequences. "If Daimler's California activities sufficed to allow adjudication of this Argentina-rooted case in California," the majority laments, "the same global reach would presumably be available in every other State in which MBUSA's sales are sizable."

The majority characterizes this result as "exorbitant," but in reality it is an inevitable consequence of the rule of due process we set forth nearly 70 years ago, that there are "instances in which [a company's] continuous corporate operations within a state" are "so substantial and of such a nature as to justify suit against it on causes of action arising from dealings entirely distinct from those activities," *International Shoe,* 326 U.S., at 318. In the era of *International Shoe,* it was rare for a corporation to have such substantial nationwide contacts that it would be subject to general jurisdiction in a large number of States. Today, that circumstance is less rare. But that is as it should be. What has changed since *International Shoe* is not the due process principle of fundamental fairness but rather the nature of the global economy. Just as it was fair to say in the 1940's that an out-of-state company could enjoy the benefits of a forum State enough to make it "essentially at home" in the State, it is fair to say today that a multinational conglomerate can enjoy such extensive benefits in multiple forum States that it is "essentially at home" in each one.

In any event, to the extent the majority is concerned with the modern-day consequences of *International Shoe*'s conception of personal jurisdiction, there remain other judicial doctrines available to mitigate any resulting unfairness to large corporate defendants. Here, for instance, the reasonableness prong may afford petitioner relief. In other cases, a defendant can assert the doctrine of *forum non conveniens* if a given State is a highly inconvenient place to litigate a dispute. See *Gulf Oil Corp. v. Gilbert,* 330 U.S. 501, 508–509 (1947). In still other cases, the federal change of venue statute can provide protection. See 28 U.S.C. § 1404(a) (permitting transfers to other districts "[f]or the convenience of parties and witnesses" and "in the interests of justice"). And to the degree that the majority worries these doctrines are not enough to protect the economic interests of multinational businesses (or that our longstanding approach to general jurisdiction poses "risks to international comity,"), the task of weighing those policy concerns belongs ultimately to legislators, who may amend state and federal long-arm statutes in accordance with the democratic process. Unfortunately, the majority short circuits that process by enshrining today's narrow rule of general jurisdiction as a matter of constitutional law.

C

The majority's concern for the consequences of its decision should have led it the other way, because the rule that it adopts will produce deep injustice in at least four respects.

First, the majority's approach unduly curtails the States' sovereign authority to adjudicate disputes against corporate defendants who have engaged in continuous and substantial business operations within their boundaries. * * * Put simply, the majority's rule defines the Due Process Clause so narrowly and arbitrarily as to contravene the States' sovereign prerogative to subject to judgment defendants who have manifested an unqualified "intention to benefit from and thus an intention to submit to the[ir] laws," *J. McIntyre,* 564 U.S., at ___.

Second, the proportionality approach will treat small businesses unfairly in comparison to national and multinational conglomerates. Whereas a larger company will often be immunized from general jurisdiction in a State on account of its extensive contacts outside the forum, a small business will not be. * * *

Third, the majority's approach creates the incongruous result that an individual defendant whose only contact with a forum State is a one-time visit will be subject to general jurisdiction if served with process during that visit, *Burnham v. Superior Court*, 495 U.S. 604 (1990), but a large corporation that owns property, employs workers, and does billions of dollars' worth of business in the State will not be, simply because the corporation has similar contacts elsewhere (though the visiting individual surely does as well).

Finally, it should be obvious that the ultimate effect of the majority's approach will be to shift the risk of loss from multinational corporations to the individuals harmed by their actions. Under the majority's rule, for example, a parent whose child is maimed due to the negligence of a foreign hotel owned by a multinational conglomerate will be unable to hold the hotel to account in a single U.S. court, even if the hotel company has a massive presence in multiple States. Similarly, a U.S. business that enters into a contract in a foreign country to sell its products to a multinational company there may be unable to seek relief in any U.S. court if the multinational company breaches the contract, even if that company has considerable operations in numerous U.S. forums.[12] Indeed, the majority's approach would preclude the plaintiffs in these examples from seeking recourse anywhere in the United States even if no other judicial system was available to provide relief. I cannot agree with the majority's conclusion that the Due Process Clause requires these results.

The Court rules against respondents today on a ground that no court has considered in the history of this case, that this Court did not grant certiorari to decide, and that Daimler raised only in a footnote of its brief. In doing so, the Court adopts a new rule of constitutional law that is unmoored from decades of precedent. Because I would reverse the Ninth Circuit's decision on the narrower ground that the exercise of jurisdiction over Daimler would be unreasonable in any event, I respectfully concur in the judgment only.

COMMENTS AND QUESTIONS CONCERNING *DAIMLER AG V. BAUMAN*

1. Sometimes you have a good sense of how a case will be decided by just reading the first sentence of the court's opinion. Consider this opening sentence: "This case concerns the authority of a court in the United States to entertain a claim brought by foreign plaintiffs against a foreign defendant based on events occurring entirely outside the United States."

2. What does it mean that "Plaintiffs seek to hold Daimler vicariously liable for MB Argentina's alleged malfeasance"?

3. Why should the United States courts be open to non-U.S. citizens to sue one another concerning matters that occurred outside the United

---

[12] The present case and the examples posited involve foreign corporate defendants, but the principle announced by the majority would apply equally to preclude general jurisdiction over a U.S. company that is incorporated and has its principal place of business in another U.S. State. Under the majority's rule, for example, a General Motors autoworker who retires to Florida would be unable to sue GM in that State for disabilities that develop from the retiree's labor at a Michigan parts plant, even though GM undertakes considerable business operations in Florida.

States? Do the names of the two statutes upon which plaintiffs brought suit suggest an answer?

4.   Why the different treatment of specific and general jurisdiction in determining whether the Due Process Clause has been satisfied? In *J. McIntyre Mach., Ltd. v. Nicastro*, decided the same day as the Supreme Court's other recent general jurisdiction case, *Goodyear Dunlop Tires Operations, S.A. v. Brown*, 131 S.Ct. 2846 (2011), the Court addressed the difference between general and specific jurisdiction as follows:

> Citizenship or domicile—or, by analogy, incorporation or principal place of business for corporations—also indicates general submission to a State's powers. Each of these examples reveals circumstances, or a course of conduct, from which it is proper to infer an intention to benefit from and thus an intention to submit to the laws of the forum State. These examples support exercise of the general jurisdiction of the State's courts and allow the State to resolve both matters that originate within the State and those based on activities and events elsewhere. By contrast, those who live or operate primarily outside a State have a due process right not to be subjected to judgment in its courts as a general matter.

131 S.Ct. 2780, 2787 (2011).

5.   Why is it to a plaintiff's advantage to establish that its claims arise from the defendant's' forum contacts rather than rely upon the doctrine of general (personal) jurisdiction?

6.   What is the significance of the "transnational context" of this action? Would courts in the United States be in a stronger position to assert jurisdiction over a foreign defendant if the action were brought by citizens of the United States? *But cf. Goodyear Dunlop Tires Operations, S.A. v. Brown*, 131 S.Ct. 2846 (2011) (foreign subsidiaries of United States corporation not subject to general jurisdiction in action challenging subsidiaries' actions outside the United States brought by North Carolina citizens in North Carolina state court).

7.   In an opinion in which all nine justices agreed on the outcome and eight joined in a single opinion, what caused Justice Sotomayor to write a separate concurrence? Might she have been concerned about footnote 19 of the majority opinion? ("We do not foreclose the possibility that in an exceptional case, *see, e.g., Perkins*, a corporation's operations in a forum other than its formal place of incorporation or principal place of business may be so substantial and of such a nature as to render the corporation at home in that State."). How "exceptional" must a case be to justify a finding of general jurisdiction outside a corporation's state of incorporation or principal place of business?

e. *Due Process in the Stream of Commerce:* J. Mcintyre Machinery, Ltd. v. Nicastro

J. McIntyre Machinery, Ltd. v. Nicastro

Supreme Court of the United States, 2011
131 S.Ct. 2780

OPINION

■ JUSTICE KENNEDY announced the judgment of the Court and delivered an opinion, in which THE CHIEF JUSTICE, JUSTICE SCALIA, and JUSTICE THOMAS join.

Whether a person or entity is subject to the jurisdiction of a state court despite not having been present in the State either at the time of suit or at the time of the alleged injury, and despite not having consented to the exercise of jurisdiction, is a question that arises with great frequency in the routine course of litigation. The rules and standards for determining when a State does or does not have jurisdiction over an absent party have been unclear because of decades-old questions left open in *Asahi Metal Industry Co. v. Superior Court*, 480 U.S. 102 (1987).

Here, the Supreme Court of New Jersey, relying in part on *Asahi*, held that New Jersey's courts can exercise jurisdiction over a foreign manufacturer of a product so long as the manufacturer "knows or reasonably should know that its products are distributed through a nationwide distribution system that might lead to those products being sold in any of the fifty states." Applying that test, the court concluded that a British manufacturer of scrap metal machines was subject to jurisdiction in New Jersey, even though at no time had it advertised in, sent goods to, or in any relevant sense targeted the State.

That decision cannot be sustained. Although the New Jersey Supreme Court issued an extensive opinion with careful attention to this Court's cases and to its own precedent, the "stream of commerce" metaphor carried the decision far afield. Due process protects the defendant's right not to be coerced except by lawful judicial power. As a general rule, the exercise of judicial power is not lawful unless the defendant "purposefully avails itself of the privilege of conducting activities within the forum State, thus invoking the benefits and protections of its laws." *Hanson v. Denckla*, 357 U.S. 235, 253 (1958). There may be exceptions, say, for instance, in cases involving an intentional tort. But the general rule is applicable in this products-liability case, and the so-called "stream-of-commerce" doctrine cannot displace it.

This case arises from a products-liability suit filed in New Jersey state court. Robert Nicastro seriously injured his hand while using a metal-shearing machine manufactured by J. McIntyre Machinery, Ltd. (J. McIntyre). The accident occurred in New Jersey, but the machine was manufactured in England, where J. McIntyre is incorporated and operates. The question here is whether the New Jersey courts have jurisdiction over J. McIntyre, notwithstanding the fact that the company at no time either marketed goods in the State or shipped them there. Nicastro was a plaintiff in the New Jersey trial court and is the respondent here; J. McIntyre was a defendant and is now the petitioner.

At oral argument in this Court, Nicastro's counsel stressed three primary facts in defense of New Jersey's assertion of jurisdiction over J. McIntyre.

First, an independent company agreed to sell J. McIntyre's machines in the United States. J. McIntyre itself did not sell its machines to buyers in this country beyond the U.S. distributor, and there is no allegation that the distributor was under J. McIntyre's control.

Second, J. McIntyre officials attended annual conventions for the scrap recycling industry to advertise J. McIntyre's machines alongside the distributor. The conventions took place in various States, but never in New Jersey.

Third, no more than four machines (the record suggests only one), including the machine that caused the injuries that are the basis for this suit, ended up in New Jersey.

In addition to these facts emphasized by petitioner, the New Jersey Supreme Court noted that J. McIntyre held both United States and European patents on its recycling technology. It also noted that the U.S. distributor "structured [its] advertising and sales efforts in accordance with" J. McIntyre's "direction and guidance whenever possible," and that "at least some of the machines were sold on consignment to" the distributor.

In light of these facts, the New Jersey Supreme Court concluded that New Jersey courts could exercise jurisdiction over petitioner without contravention of the Due Process Clause. Jurisdiction was proper, in that court's view, because the injury occurred in New Jersey; because petitioner knew or reasonably should have known "that its products are distributed through a nationwide distribution system that might lead to those products being sold in any of the fifty states"; and because petitioner failed to "take some reasonable step to prevent the distribution of its products in this State."

Both the New Jersey Supreme Court's holding and its account of what it called "[t]he stream-of-commerce doctrine of jurisdiction," were incorrect, however. This Court's *Asahi* decision may be responsible in part for that court's error regarding the stream of commerce, and this case presents an opportunity to provide greater clarity.

II

The Due Process Clause protects an individual's right to be deprived of life, liberty, or property only by the exercise of lawful power. This is no less true with respect to the power of a sovereign to resolve disputes through judicial process than with respect to the power of a sovereign to prescribe rules of conduct for those within its sphere. As a general rule, neither statute nor judicial decree may bind strangers to the State.

A court may subject a defendant to judgment only when the defendant has sufficient contacts with the sovereign "such that the maintenance of the suit does not offend 'traditional notions of fair play and substantial justice.'" *International Shoe Co. v. Washington*, 326 U.S. 310, 316 (1945) (quoting *Milliken v. Meyer*, 311 U.S. 457, 463 (1940)). Freeform notions of fundamental fairness divorced from traditional practice cannot transform a judgment rendered in the absence of authority into law. As a general rule, the sovereign's exercise of power requires some act by which the defendant "purposefully avails itself of the privilege of conducting activities within the forum State, thus invoking the benefits and protections of its laws," *Hanson*, 357 U.S., at 253, though in some cases, as with an intentional tort, the defendant might well fall within the State's authority by reason of his attempt to obstruct its laws. In products-liability cases like this one, it is the defendant's purposeful availment that makes jurisdiction consistent with "traditional notions of fair play and substantial justice."

A person may submit to a State's authority in a number of ways. There is, of course, explicit consent. Presence within a State at the time suit commences through service of process is another example. Citizenship or domicile—or, by analogy, incorporation or principal place of business for corporations—also indicates general submission to a State's powers. Each of these examples reveals circumstances, or a course of conduct, from which it is proper to infer an intention to benefit from and thus an intention to submit to the laws of the forum State. These examples support exercise of the general jurisdiction of the State's courts and allow the State to resolve both matters that originate within the State and those based on activities and events elsewhere. By contrast, those who live or operate primarily outside a State have a due process right not to be subjected to judgment in its courts as a general matter.

There is also a more limited form of submission to a State's authority for disputes that "arise out of or are connected with the activities within the state." *International Shoe Co.*, supra, at 319. Where a defendant "purposefully avails itself of the privilege of conducting activities within the forum State, thus invoking the benefits and protections of its laws," *Hanson*, supra, at 253, it submits to the judicial power of an otherwise foreign sovereign to the extent that power is exercised in connection with the defendant's activities touching on the State. In other words, submission through contact with and activity directed at a sovereign may justify specific jurisdiction "in a suit arising out of or related to the defendant's contacts with the forum." *Helicopteros*, supra, at 414, n. 8.

The imprecision arising from *Asahi*, for the most part, results from its statement of the relation between jurisdiction and the "stream of commerce." The stream of commerce, like other metaphors, has its deficiencies as well as its utility. It refers to the movement of goods from manufacturers through distributors to consumers, yet beyond that descriptive purpose its meaning is far from exact. This Court has stated that a defendant's placing goods into the stream of commerce "with the expectation that they will be purchased by consumers within the forum State" may indicate purposeful availment. *World-Wide Volkswagen Corp. v. Woodson*, 444 U.S. 286, 298 (1980). But that statement does not amend the general rule of personal jurisdiction. It merely observes that a defendant may in an appropriate case be subject to jurisdiction without entering the forum—itself an unexceptional proposition—as where manufacturers or distributors "seek to serve" a given State's market. The principal inquiry in cases of this sort is whether the defendant's activities manifest an intention to submit to the power of a sovereign. In other words, the defendant must "purposefully avai[l] itself of the privilege of conducting activities within the forum State, thus invoking the benefits and protections of its laws." *Hanson*, supra, at 253. Sometimes a defendant does so by sending its goods rather than its agents. The defendant's transmission of goods permits the exercise of jurisdiction only where the defendant can be said to have targeted the forum; as a general rule, it is not enough that the defendant might have predicted that its goods will reach the forum State.

In *Asahi*, an opinion by Justice Brennan for four Justices outlined a different approach. It discarded the central concept of sovereign authority in favor of considerations of fairness and foreseeability. As that concurrence contended, "jurisdiction premised on the placement of a product into the stream of commerce [without more] is consistent with the Due Process Clause," for "[a]s long as a participant in this process is aware that the final product is being marketed in the forum State, the possibility of a lawsuit there cannot come as a surprise." 480 U.S., at 117 (opinion concurring in part and concurring in judgment). It was the premise of the concurring opinion that the defendant's ability to anticipate suit renders the assertion of jurisdiction fair. In this way, the opinion made foreseeability the touchstone of jurisdiction.

The standard set forth in Justice Brennan's concurrence was rejected in an opinion written by Justice O'Connor; but the relevant part of that opinion, too, commanded the assent of only four Justices, not a majority of the Court. That opinion stated: "The 'substantial connection' between the defendant and the forum State necessary for a finding of minimum contacts must come about by an action of the defendant purposefully directed toward the forum State. The placement of a product into the stream of commerce, without more, is not an act of the defendant purposefully directed toward the forum State."

Since *Asahi* was decided, the courts have sought to reconcile the competing opinions. But Justice Brennan's concurrence, advocating a rule based on general notions of fairness and foreseeability, is inconsistent with the premises of lawful judicial power. This Court's precedents make clear that it is the defendant's actions, not his expectations, that empower a State's courts to subject him to judgment.

The conclusion that jurisdiction is in the first instance a question of authority rather than fairness explains, for example, why the principal opinion in *Burnham* "conducted no independent inquiry into the desirability or fairness" of the rule that service of process within a State suffices to establish jurisdiction over an otherwise foreign defendant. 495 U.S., at 621. As that opinion explained, "[t]he view developed early that each State had the power to hale before its courts any individual who could be found within its borders." *Id.*, at 610. Furthermore, were general fairness considerations the touchstone of jurisdiction, a lack of purposeful availment might be excused where carefully crafted judicial procedures could otherwise protect the defendant's interests, or where the plaintiff would suffer substantial hardship if forced to litigate in a foreign forum. That such considerations have not been deemed controlling is instructive.

Two principles are implicit in the foregoing. First, personal jurisdiction requires a forum-by-forum, or sovereign-by-sovereign, analysis. The question is whether a defendant has followed a course of conduct directed at the society or economy existing within the jurisdiction of a given sovereign, so that the sovereign has the power to subject the defendant to judgment concerning that conduct. Personal jurisdiction, of course, restricts "judicial power not as a matter of sovereignty, but as a matter of individual liberty," for due process protects the individual's right to be subject only to lawful power. *Insurance Corp.*, 456 U.S., at 702. But whether a judicial judgment is lawful depends on whether the sovereign has authority to render it.

The second principle is a corollary of the first. Because the United States is a distinct sovereign, a defendant may in principle be subject to the jurisdiction of the courts of the United States but not of any particular State. This is consistent with the premises and unique genius of our Constitution. Ours is "a legal system unprecedented in form and design, establishing two orders of government, each with its own direct relationship, its own privity, its own set of mutual rights and obligations to the people who sustain it and are governed by it." *U.S. Term Limits, Inc. v. Thornton*, 514 U.S. 779, 838 (1995) (KENNEDY, J., concurring). For jurisdiction, a litigant may have the requisite relationship with the United States Government but not with the government of any individual State. That would be an exceptional case, however. If the defendant is a domestic domiciliary, the courts of its home State are available and can exercise general jurisdiction. And if another State were to assert jurisdiction in an inappropriate case, it would upset the federal balance, which posits that each State has a sovereignty that is not subject to unlawful intrusion by other States. Furthermore, foreign corporations will often target or concentrate on particular States, subjecting them to specific jurisdiction in those forums.

It must be remembered, however, that although this case and *Asahi* both involve foreign manufacturers, the undesirable consequences of Justice Brennan's approach are no less significant for domestic producers. The owner of a small Florida farm might sell crops to a large nearby distributor, for example, who might then distribute them to grocers across the country. If foreseeability were the controlling criterion, the farmer could be sued in Alaska or any number of other States' courts without ever leaving town. And the issue of foreseeability may itself be contested so that significant expenses are incurred just on the preliminary issue of jurisdiction. Jurisdictional rules should avoid these costs whenever possible.

The conclusion that the authority to subject a defendant to judgment depends on purposeful availment, consistent with Justice O'Connor's opinion in *Asahi*, does not by itself resolve many difficult questions of jurisdiction that will arise in particular cases. The defendant's conduct and the economic realities of the market the defendant seeks to serve will differ across cases, and judicial exposition will, in common-law fashion, clarify the contours of that principle.

III

In this case, petitioner directed marketing and sales efforts at the United States. It may be that, assuming it were otherwise empowered to legislate on the subject, the Congress could authorize the exercise of jurisdiction in appropriate courts. That circumstance is not presented in this case, however, and it is neither necessary nor appropriate to address here any constitutional concerns that might be attendant to that exercise of power. Nor is it necessary to determine what substantive law might apply were Congress to authorize jurisdiction in a federal court in New Jersey. A sovereign's legislative authority to regulate conduct may present considerations different from those presented by its authority to subject a defendant to judgment in its courts. Here the question concerns the authority of a New Jersey state court to exercise jurisdiction, so it is petitioner's purposeful contacts with New Jersey, not with the United States, that alone are relevant.

Respondent has not established that J. McIntyre engaged in conduct purposefully directed at New Jersey. Recall that respondent's claim of jurisdiction centers on three facts: The distributor agreed to sell J. McIntyre's machines in the United States; J. McIntyre officials attended trade shows in several States but not in New Jersey; and up to four machines ended up in New Jersey. The British manufacturer had no office in New Jersey; it neither paid taxes nor owned property there; and it neither advertised in, nor sent any employees to, the State. Indeed, after discovery the trial court found that the "defendant does not have a single contact with New Jersey short of the machine in question ending up in this state." These facts may reveal an intent to serve the U.S. market, but they do not show that J. McIntyre purposefully availed itself of the New Jersey market.

* * *

Due process protects petitioner's right to be subject only to lawful authority. At no time did petitioner engage in any activities in New Jersey that reveal an intent to invoke or benefit from the protection of its laws. New Jersey is without power to adjudge the rights and liabilities of J. McIntyre, and its exercise of jurisdiction would violate due process. The contrary judgment of the New Jersey Supreme Court is

Reversed.

■ JUSTICE BREYER, with whom JUSTICE ALITO joins, concurring in the judgment.

The Supreme Court of New Jersey adopted a broad understanding of the scope of personal jurisdiction based on its view that "[t]he increasingly fast-paced globalization of the world economy has removed national borders as barriers to trade." I do not doubt that there have been many recent changes in commerce and communication, many of which are not anticipated by our precedents. But this case does not present any of those issues. So I think it unwise to announce a rule of broad applicability without full consideration of the modern-day consequences.

In my view, the outcome of this case is determined by our precedents. Based on the facts found by the New Jersey courts, respondent Robert Nicastro failed to meet his burden to demonstrate that it was constitutionally proper to exercise jurisdiction over petitioner J. McIntyre Machinery, Ltd. (British Manufacturer), a British firm that manufactures scrap-metal machines in Great Britain and sells them through an independent distributor in the United States (American Distributor). On that basis, I agree with the plurality that the contrary judgment of the Supreme Court of New Jersey should be reversed.

I

In asserting jurisdiction over the British Manufacturer, the Supreme Court of New Jersey relied most heavily on three primary facts as providing constitutionally sufficient "contacts" with New Jersey, thereby making it fundamentally fair to hale the British Manufacturer before its courts: (1) The American Distributor on one occasion sold and shipped one machine to a New Jersey customer, namely, Mr. Nicastro's employer, Mr. Curcio; (2) the British Manufacturer permitted, indeed wanted, its independent American Distributor to sell its machines to anyone in America willing to buy them; and (3) representatives of the British Manufacturer attended trade shows in "such cities as Chicago, Las Vegas, New Orleans, Orlando, San Diego, and San Francisco." In my view, these facts do not provide contacts between the British firm and the State of New Jersey constitutionally sufficient to support New Jersey's assertion of jurisdiction in this case.

None of our precedents finds that a single isolated sale, even if accompanied by the kind of sales effort indicated here, is sufficient. Rather, this Court's previous holdings suggest the contrary. The Court has held that a single sale to a customer who takes an accident-causing product to a different State (where the accident takes place) is not a sufficient basis for asserting jurisdiction. *See World-Wide Volkswagen Corp. v. Woodson*, 444 U.S. 286 (1980). And the Court, in separate opinions, has strongly suggested that a single sale of a product in a State does not constitute an adequate basis for asserting jurisdiction over an out-of-state defendant, even if that defendant places his goods in the stream of commerce, fully aware (and hoping) that such a sale will take place. *See Asahi Metal Industry Co. v. Superior Court*, 480 U.S. 102, 111, 112 (1987) (opinion of O'Connor, J.) (requiring "something more" than simply placing "a product into the stream of commerce," even if defendant is "awar[e]" that the stream "may or will sweep the product into the forum State"); *id.*, at 117 (Brennan, J., concurring in part and concurring in judgment) (jurisdiction should lie where a sale in a State is part of "the regular and anticipated flow" of commerce into the State, but not where that sale is only an "edd[y]," i.e., an isolated occurrence); *id.*, at 122 (Stevens, J., concurring in part and concurring in judgment) (indicating that "the volume, the value, and the hazardous character" of a good may affect the jurisdictional inquiry and emphasizing Asahi's "regular course of dealing").

Here, the relevant facts found by the New Jersey Supreme Court show no "regular . . . flow" or "regular course" of sales in New Jersey; and there is no "something more," such as special state-related design, advertising, advice, marketing, or anything else. Mr. Nicastro, who here bears the burden of proving jurisdiction, has shown no specific effort by the British Manufacturer to sell in New Jersey. He has introduced no list of potential New Jersey customers who might, for example, have regularly attended trade shows. And he has not otherwise shown that the British Manufacturer "purposefully avail[ed] itself of the privilege of conducting activities" within New Jersey, or that it delivered its goods in the stream of commerce "with the expectation that they will be purchased" by New Jersey users. *World-Wide Volkswagen*, supra, at 297–298.

There may well have been other facts that Mr. Nicastro could have demonstrated in support of jurisdiction. And the dissent considers some of those facts. But the plaintiff bears the burden of establishing jurisdiction, and here I would take the facts precisely as the New Jersey Supreme Court stated them.

Accordingly, on the record present here, resolving this case requires no more than adhering to our precedents.

II

I would not go further. Because the incident at issue in this case does not implicate modern concerns, and because the factual record leaves many open questions, this is an unsuitable vehicle for making broad pronouncements that refashion basic jurisdictional rules.

A

The plurality seems to state strict rules that limit jurisdiction where a defendant does not "inten[d] to submit to the power of a sovereign" and cannot "be said to have targeted the forum." But what do those standards mean when a company targets the world by selling products from its Web site? And does it matter if, instead of shipping the products directly, a company consigns the products through an intermediary (say, Amazon.com) who then receives and fulfills the orders? And what if the company markets its products through popup advertisements that it knows will be viewed in a forum? Those issues have serious commercial consequences but are totally absent in this case.

B

But though I do not agree with the plurality's seemingly strict no-jurisdiction rule, I am not persuaded by the absolute approach adopted by the New Jersey Supreme Court and urged by respondent and his amici. Under that view, a producer is subject to jurisdiction for a products-liability action so long as it "knows or reasonably should know that its products are distributed through a nationwide distribution system that *might* lead to those products being sold in any of the fifty states." 201 N.J., at 76–77. In the context of this case, I cannot agree.

For one thing, to adopt this view would abandon the heretofore accepted inquiry of whether, focusing upon the relationship between "the defendant, the *forum*, and the litigation," it is fair, in light of the defendant's contacts with that forum, to subject the defendant to suit there. *Shaffer v. Heitner*, 433 U.S. 186, 204 (1977) (emphasis added). It would ordinarily rest jurisdiction instead upon no more than the occurrence of a product-based accident in the forum State. But this Court has rejected the notion that a defendant's amenability to suit "travel[s] with the chattel." *World-Wide Volkswagen*, 444 U.S., at 296.

For another, I cannot reconcile so automatic a rule with the constitutional demand for "minimum contacts" and "purposefu[l]

NOTICE, TERRITORIAL JURISDICTION, AND VENUE: "WHERE CAN
WE FILE OUR ACTION?"

306

CHAPTER 4

avail[ment]," each of which rest upon a particular notion of defendant-focused fairness. A rule like the New Jersey Supreme Court's would permit every State to assert jurisdiction in a products-liability suit against any domestic manufacturer who sells its products (made anywhere in the United States) to a national distributor, no matter how large or small the manufacturer, no matter how distant the forum, and no matter how few the number of items that end up in the particular forum at issue. What might appear fair in the case of a large manufacturer which specifically seeks, or expects, an equal-sized distributor to sell its product in a distant State might seem unfair in the case of a small manufacturer (say, an Appalachian potter) who sells his product (cups and saucers) exclusively to a large distributor, who resells a single item (a coffee mug) to a buyer from a distant State (Hawaii). I know too little about the range of these or in-between possibilities to abandon in favor of the more absolute rule what has previously been this Court's less absolute approach.

Further, the fact that the defendant is a foreign, rather than a domestic, manufacturer makes the basic fairness of an absolute rule yet more uncertain. I am again less certain than is the New Jersey Supreme Court that the nature of international commerce has changed so significantly as to require a new approach to personal jurisdiction.

It may be that a larger firm can readily "alleviate the risk of burdensome litigation by procuring insurance, passing the expected costs on to customers, or, if the risks are too great, severing its connection with the State." *World-Wide Volkswagen, supra*, at 297. But manufacturers come in many shapes and sizes. It may be fundamentally unfair to require a small Egyptian shirt maker, a Brazilian manufacturing cooperative, or a Kenyan coffee farmer, selling its products through international distributors, to respond to products-liability tort suits in virtually every State in the United States, even those in respect to which the foreign firm has no connection at all but the sale of a single (allegedly defective) good. And a rule like the New Jersey Supreme Court suggests would require every product manufacturer, large or small, selling to American distributors to understand not only the tort law of every State, but also the wide variance in the way courts within different States apply that law.

C

At a minimum, I would not work such a change to the law in the way either the plurality or the New Jersey Supreme Court suggests without a better understanding of the relevant contemporary commercial circumstances. Insofar as such considerations are relevant to any change in present law, they might be presented in a case (unlike the present one) in which the Solicitor General participates.

This case presents no such occasion, and so I again reiterate that I would adhere strictly to our precedents and the limited facts found by the New Jersey Supreme Court. And on those grounds, I do not think we can find jurisdiction in this case. Accordingly, though I agree with the plurality as to the outcome of this case, I concur only in the judgment of that opinion and not its reasoning.

■ JUSTICE GINSBURG, with whom JUSTICE SOTOMAYOR and JUSTICE KAGAN join, dissenting.

A foreign industrialist seeks to develop a market in the United States for machines it manufactures. It hopes to derive substantial revenue from sales it makes to United States purchasers. Where in the United States buyers reside does not matter to this manufacturer. Its goal is simply to sell as much as it can, wherever it can. It excludes no region or State from the market it wishes to reach. But, all things considered, it prefers to avoid products liability litigation in the United States. To that end, it engages a U.S. distributor to ship its machines stateside. Has it succeeded in escaping personal jurisdiction in a State where one of its products is sold and causes injury or even death to a local user?

Under this Court's pathmarking precedent in *International Shoe Co. v. Washington*, 326 U.S. 310 (1945), and subsequent decisions, one would expect the answer to be unequivocally, "No." But instead, six Justices of this Court, in divergent opinions, tell us that the manufacturer has avoided the jurisdiction of our state courts, except perhaps in States where its products are sold in sizeable quantities. Inconceivable as it may have seemed yesterday, the splintered majority today "turn[s] the clock back to the days before modern long-arm statutes when a manufacturer, to avoid being haled into court where a user is injured, need only Pilate-like wash its hands of a product by having independent distributors market it." Weintraub, "A Map Out of the Personal Jurisdiction Labyrinth," 28 *U.C. Davis L.Rev.* 531, 555 (1995).

I

On October 11, 2001, a three-ton metal shearing machine severed four fingers on Robert Nicastro's right hand. Alleging that the machine was a dangerous product defectively made, Nicastro sought compensation from the machine's manufacturer, J. McIntyre Machinery Ltd. (McIntyre UK). Established in 1872 as a United Kingdom corporation, and headquartered in Nottingham, England, McIntyre UK "designs, develops and manufactures a complete range of equipment for metal recycling." The company's product line, as advertised on McIntyre UK's Web site, includes "metal shears, balers, cable and can recycling equipment, furnaces, casting equipment and . . . the world's best aluminium dross processing and cooling system." McIntyre UK holds both United States and European patents on its technology.

The machine that injured Nicastro, a "McIntyre Model 640 Shear," sold in the United States for $24,900 in 1995 and features a "massive cutting capacity." According to McIntyre UK's product brochure, the machine is "use[d] throughout the [w]orld." McIntyre UK represented in the brochure that, by "incorporat[ing] off-the-shelf hydraulic parts from suppliers with international sales outlets," the 640 Shear's design guarantees serviceability "wherever [its customers] may be based." The instruction manual advises "owner[s] and operators of a 640 Shear [to] make themselves aware of [applicable health and safety regulations]," including "the American National Standards Institute Regulations (USA) for the use of Scrap Metal Processing Equipment."

Nicastro operated the 640 Shear in the course of his employment at Curcio Scrap Metal (CSM) in Saddle Brook, New Jersey. * * *

CSM's owner, Frank Curcio, "first heard of [McIntyre UK's] machine while attending an Institute of Scrap Metal Industries [(ISRI)] convention in Las Vegas in 1994 or 1995, where [McIntyre UK] was an exhibitor." * * *

McIntyre UK representatives attended every ISRI convention from 1990 through 2005. These annual expositions were held in diverse venues across the United States; in addition to Las Vegas, conventions were held 1990–2005 in New Orleans, Orlando, San Antonio, and San Francisco. McIntyre UK's president, Michael Pownall, regularly attended ISRI conventions. He attended ISRI's Las Vegas convention the year CSM's owner first learned of, and saw, the 640 Shear. McIntyre UK exhibited its products at ISRI trade shows, the company acknowledged, hoping to reach "anyone interested in the machine from anywhere in the United States."

* * *

From at least 1995 until 2001, McIntyre UK retained an Ohio-based company, McIntyre Machinery America, Ltd. (McIntyre America), "as its exclusive distributor for the entire United States." Though similarly named, the two companies were separate and independent entities with "no commonality of ownership or management." In invoices and other written communications, McIntyre America described itself as McIntyre UK's national distributor, "America's Link" to "Quality Metal Processing Equipment" from England.

In a November 23, 1999 letter to McIntyre America, McIntyre UK's president spoke plainly about the manufacturer's objective in authorizing the exclusive distributorship: "All we wish to do is sell our products in the [United] States—and get paid!" Notably, McIntyre America was concerned about U.S. litigation involving McIntyre UK products, in which the distributor had been named as a defendant. McIntyre UK counseled McIntyre America to respond personally to the litigation, but reassured its distributor that "the product was built and designed by McIntyre Machinery in the UK and the buck stops here—if there's something wrong with the machine." Answering jurisdictional interrogatories, McIntyre UK stated that it had been named as a defendant in lawsuits in Illinois, Kentucky, Massachusetts, and West

Virginia. And in correspondence with McIntyre America, McIntyre UK noted that the manufacturer had products liability insurance coverage.

* * *

In sum, McIntyre UK's regular attendance and exhibitions at ISRI conventions was surely a purposeful step to reach customers for its products "anywhere in the United States." At least as purposeful was McIntyre UK's engagement of McIntyre America as the conduit for sales of McIntyre UK's machines to buyers "throughout the United States." Given McIntyre UK's endeavors to reach and profit from the United States market as a whole, Nicastro's suit, I would hold, has been brought in a forum entirely appropriate for the adjudication of his claim. He alleges that McIntyre UK's shear machine was defectively designed or manufactured and, as a result, caused injury to him at his workplace. The machine arrived in Nicastro's New Jersey workplace not randomly or fortuitously, but as a result of the U.S. connections and distribution system that McIntyre UK deliberately arranged.[2] On what sensible view of the allocation of adjudicatory authority could the place of Nicastro's injury within the United States be deemed off limits for his products liability claim against a foreign manufacturer who targeted the United States (including all the States that constitute the Nation) as the territory it sought to develop?

II

A few points on which there should be no genuine debate bear statement at the outset. First, all agree, McIntyre UK surely is not subject to general (all-purpose) jurisdiction in New Jersey courts, for that foreign-country corporation is hardly "at home" in New Jersey. *See Goodyear Dunlop Tires Operations, S.A. v. Brown*. The question, rather, is one of specific jurisdiction, which turns on an "affiliatio[n] between the forum and the underlying controversy." *Goodyear Dunlop*, at 2851 (quoting von Mehren & Trautman, "Jurisdiction to Adjudicate: A Suggested Analysis," 79 *Harv. L.Rev.* 1121, 1136 (1966) (hereinafter von Mehren & Trautman).

Second, no issue of the fair and reasonable allocation of adjudicatory authority among States of the United States is present in this case. New Jersey's exercise of personal jurisdiction over a foreign manufacturer whose dangerous product caused a workplace injury in New Jersey does not tread on the domain, or diminish the sovereignty, of any sister State. Indeed, among States of the United States, the State

---

[2] McIntyre UK resisted Nicastro's efforts to determine whether other McIntyre machines had been sold to New Jersey customers. McIntyre did allow that McIntyre America "may have resold products it purchased from [McIntyre UK] to a buyer in New Jersey," but said it kept no record of the ultimate destination of machines it shipped to its distributor. A private investigator engaged by Nicastro found at least one McIntyre UK machine, of unspecified type, in use in New Jersey. But McIntyre UK objected that the investigator's report was "unsworn and based upon hearsay." Moreover, McIntyre UK maintained, no evidence showed that the machine the investigator found in New Jersey had been "sold into [that State]."

NOTICE, TERRITORIAL JURISDICTION, AND VENUE: "WHERE CAN
WE FILE OUR ACTION?"

310

CHAPTER 4

in which the injury occurred would seem most suitable for litigation of a products liability tort claim.

Third, the constitutional limits on a state court's adjudicatory authority derive from considerations of due process, not state sovereignty. As the Court clarified in *Insurance Corp. of Ireland v. Compagnie des Bauxites de Guinee*, 456 U.S. 694 (1982):

> The restriction on state sovereign power described in *World-Wide Volkswagen Corp.* . . . must be seen as ultimately a function of the individual liberty interest preserved by the Due Process Clause. That Clause is the only source of the personal jurisdiction requirement and the Clause itself makes no mention of federalism concerns. Furthermore, if the federalism concept operated as an independent restriction on the sovereign power of the court, it would not be possible to waive the personal jurisdiction requirement: Individual actions cannot change the powers of sovereignty, although the individual can subject himself to powers from which he may otherwise be protected. *Id.*, at 703, n. 10.

Finally, in *International Shoe* itself, and decisions thereafter, the Court has made plain that legal fictions, notably "presence" and "implied consent," should be discarded, for they conceal the actual bases on which jurisdiction rests. *See* 326 U.S., at 316, 318. "[T]he relationship among the defendant, the forum, and the litigation" determines whether due process permits the exercise of personal jurisdiction over a defendant, *Shaffer*, 433 U.S., at 204, and "fictions of implied consent" or "corporate presence" do not advance the proper inquiry, *id.*, at 202. See also *Burnham v. Superior Court*, 495 U.S. 604, 618 (1990) (plurality opinion) (*International Shoe* "cast . . . aside" fictions of "consent" and "presence").

Whatever the state of academic debate over the role of consent in modern jurisdictional doctrines, the plurality's notion that consent is the animating concept draws no support from controlling decisions of this Court. Quite the contrary, the Court has explained, a forum can exercise jurisdiction when its contacts with the controversy are sufficient; invocation of a fictitious consent, the Court has repeatedly said, is unnecessary and unhelpful. See, e.g., *Burger King Corp. v. Rudzewicz*, 471 U.S. 462, 472 (1985) (Due Process Clause permits "forum . . . to assert specific jurisdiction over an out-of-state defendant who has not consented to suit there"); *McGee v. International Life Ins. Co.*, 355 U.S. 220, 222 (1957) ("[T]his Court [has] abandoned 'consent,' 'doing business,' and 'presence' as the standard for measuring the extent of state judicial power over [out-of-state] corporations.").

III

This case is illustrative of marketing arrangements for sales in the United States common in today's commercial world. A foreign-country manufacturer engages a U.S. company to promote and distribute the manufacturer's products, not in any particular State, but anywhere and everywhere in the United States the distributor can attract purchasers. The product proves defective and injures a user in the State where the user lives or works. Often, as here, the manufacturer will have liability insurance covering personal injuries caused by its products.

When industrial accidents happen, a long-arm statute in the State where the injury occurs generally permits assertion of jurisdiction, upon giving proper notice, over the foreign manufacturer. For example, the State's statute might provide, as does New York's long-arm statute, for the "exercise [of] personal jurisdiction over any non-domiciliary . . . who . . .

> commits a tortious act without the state causing injury to person or property within the state, . . . if he . . . expects or should reasonably expect the act to have consequences in the state and derives substantial revenue from interstate or international commerce." N.Y. Civ. Prac. Law Ann. § 302(a)(3)(ii).

Or, the State might simply provide, as New Jersey does, for the exercise of jurisdiction "consistent with due process of law." N.J. Ct. Rule 4:4–4(b)(1) (2011).

The modern approach to jurisdiction over corporations and other legal entities, ushered in by *International Shoe*, gave prime place to reason and fairness. Is it not fair and reasonable, given the mode of trading of which this case is an example, to require the international seller to defend at the place its products cause injury? Do not litigational convenience and choice-of-law considerations point in that direction? On what measure of reason and fairness can it be considered undue to require McIntyre UK to defend in New Jersey as an incident of its efforts to develop a market for its industrial machines anywhere and everywhere in the United States?[12] Is not the burden on McIntyre UK to defend in New Jersey fair, i.e., a reasonable cost of transacting business internationally, in comparison to the burden on Nicastro to go to Nottingham, England to gain recompense for an injury he sustained using McIntyre's product at his workplace in Saddle Brook, New Jersey?

McIntyre UK dealt with the United States as a single market. Like most foreign manufacturers, it was concerned not with the prospect of suit in State X as opposed to State Y, but rather with its subjection to

---

[12] The plurality suggests that the Due Process Clause might permit a federal district court in New Jersey, sitting in diversity and applying New Jersey law, to adjudicate McIntyre UK's liability to Nicastro. In other words, McIntyre UK might be compelled to bear the burden of traveling to New Jersey and defending itself there under New Jersey's products liability law, but would be entitled to federal adjudication of Nicastro's state-law claim. I see no basis in the Due Process Clause for such a curious limitation.

suit anywhere in the United States. As a McIntyre UK officer wrote in an e-mail to McIntyre America: "American law—who needs it?!" * * *

In sum, McIntyre UK, by engaging McIntyre America to promote and sell its machines in the United States, "purposefully availed itself" of the United States market nationwide, not a market in a single State or a discrete collection of States. McIntyre UK thereby availed itself of the market of all States in which its products were sold by its exclusive distributor. "Th[e] 'purposeful availment' requirement," this Court has explained, simply "ensures that a defendant will not be haled into a jurisdiction solely as a result of 'random,' 'fortuitous,' or 'attenuated' contacts." *Burger King*, 471 U.S., at 475. Adjudicatory authority is appropriately exercised where "actions by the defendant *himself*" give rise to the affiliation with the forum. How could McIntyre UK not have intended, by its actions targeting a national market, to sell products in the fourth largest destination for imports among all States of the United States and the largest scrap metal market?

Courts, both state and federal, confronting facts similar to those here, have rightly rejected the conclusion that a manufacturer selling its products across the USA may evade jurisdiction in any and all States, including the State where its defective product is distributed and causes injury. They have held, instead, that it would undermine principles of fundamental fairness to insulate the foreign manufacturer from accountability in court at the place within the United States where the manufacturer's products caused injury.

IV

A

While this Court has not considered in any prior case the now-prevalent pattern presented here—a foreign-country manufacturer enlisting a U.S. distributor to develop a market in the United States for the manufacturer's products—none of the Court's decisions tug against the judgment made by the New Jersey Supreme Court. McIntyre contends otherwise, citing *World-Wide Volkswagen,* and *Asahi Metal Industry Co. v. Superior Court*, 480 U.S. 102 (1987).

* * *

Notably, the foreign manufacturer of the Audi in *World-Wide Volkswagen* did not object to the jurisdiction of the Oklahoma courts and the U.S. importer abandoned its initially stated objection. And most relevant here, the Court's opinion indicates that an objection to jurisdiction by the manufacturer or national distributor would have been unavailing. To reiterate, the Court said in *World-Wide Volkswagen* that, when a manufacturer or distributor aims to sell its product to customers in several States, it is reasonable "to subject it to suit in [any] one of those States if its allegedly defective [product] has there been the source of injury." *Id.*, at 297.

* * *

* * * Asahi, unlike McIntyre UK, did not itself seek out customers in the United States, it engaged no distributor to promote its wares here, it appeared at no tradeshows in the United States, and, of course, it had no Web site advertising its products to the world. Moreover, Asahi was a component-part manufacturer with "little control over the final destination of its products once they were delivered into the stream of commerce." It was important to the Court in Asahi that "those who use Asahi components in their final products, and sell those products in California, [would be] subject to the application of California tort law." 480 U.S., at 115 (majority opinion). To hold that *Asahi* controls this case would, to put it bluntly, be dead wrong.[15]

B

The Court's judgment also puts United States plaintiffs at a disadvantage in comparison to similarly situated complainants elsewhere in the world. Of particular note, within the European Union, in which the United Kingdom is a participant, the jurisdiction New Jersey would have exercised is not at all exceptional. The European Regulation on Jurisdiction and the Recognition and Enforcement of Judgments provides for the exercise of specific jurisdiction "in matters relating to tort . . . in the courts for the place where the harmful event occurred." Council Reg. 44/2001, Art. 5, 2001 O.J. (L.12) 4. The European Court of Justice has interpreted this prescription to authorize jurisdiction either where the harmful act occurred or at the place of injury.

V

The commentators who gave names to what we now call "general jurisdiction" and "specific jurisdiction" anticipated that when the latter achieves its full growth, considerations of litigational convenience and the respective situations of the parties would determine when it is appropriate to subject a defendant to trial in the plaintiff's community. *See* von Mehren & Trautman 1166–1179. Litigational considerations include "the convenience of witnesses and the ease of ascertaining the governing law." *Id.,* at 1168–1169. As to the parties, courts would differently appraise two situations: (1) cases involving a substantially local plaintiff, like Nicastro, injured by the activity of a defendant engaged in interstate or international trade; and (2) cases in which the defendant is a natural or legal person whose economic activities and legal involvements are largely home-based, i.e., entities without designs

---

[15] The plurality notes the low volume of sales in New Jersey. A $24,900 shearing machine, however, is unlikely to sell in bulk worldwide, much less in any given State. By dollar value, the price of a single machine represents a significant sale. Had a manufacturer sold in New Jersey $24,900 worth of flannel shirts, *see Nelson v. Park Industries, Inc.,* 717 F.2d 1120 (C.A.7 1983), cigarette lighters, *see Oswalt v. Scripto, Inc.,* 616 F.2d 191 (C.A.5 1980), or wire-rope splices, *see Hedrick v. Daiko Shoji Co.,* 715 F.2d 1355 (C.A.9 1983), the Court would presumably find the defendant amenable to suit in that State.

to gain substantial revenue from sales in distant markets. *See id.*, at 1167–1169. As the attached appendix of illustrative cases indicates, courts presented with von Mehren and Trautman's first scenario—a local plaintiff injured by the activity of a manufacturer seeking to exploit a multistate or global market—have repeatedly confirmed that jurisdiction is appropriately exercised by courts of the place where the product was sold and caused injury.

* * *

For the reasons stated, I would hold McIntyre UK answerable in New Jersey for the harm Nicastro suffered at his workplace in that State using McIntyre UK's shearing machine. While I dissent from the Court's judgment, I take heart that the plurality opinion does not speak for the Court, for that opinion would take a giant step away from the "notions of fair play and substantial justice" underlying *International Shoe*.

[The appendix containing twelve federal and state "[i]llustrative cases upholding exercise of personal jurisdiction over an alien or out-of-state corporation that, through a distributor, targeted a national market, including any and all States" is omitted.]

COMMENTS AND QUESTIONS CONCERNING *J. MCINTYRE MACHINERY, LTD. V. NICASTRO*

1. In the first paragraph of his plurality opinion, Justice Kennedy states: "The rules and standards for determining when a State does or does not have jurisdiction over an absent party have been unclear because of decades-old questions left open in *Asahi Metal Industry Co. v. Superior Court*, 480 U.S. 102 (1987)." Are those questions answered in the three opinions in *McIntyre*?

2. In his opinion, Justice Kennedy criticizes Justice Brennan's *Asahi* opinion: "Justice Brennan's concurrence, advocating a rule based on general notions of fairness and foreseeability, is inconsistent with the premises of lawful judicial power. This Court's precedents make clear that it is the defendant's actions, not his expectations, that empower a State's courts to subject him to judgment."

Justice Ginsburg responds:

[T]he constitutional limits on a state court's adjudicatory authority derive from considerations of due process, not state sovereignty. As the Court clarified in *Insurance Corp. of Ireland v. Compagnie des Bauxites de Guinee*, 456 U.S. 694 (1982):

The restriction on state sovereign power described in *World-Wide Volkswagen Corp.* . . . must be seen as ultimately a function of the individual liberty interest preserved by the Due Process Clause. That Clause is the only source of the personal jurisdiction requirement and the Clause itself makes no mention of federalism concerns. Furthermore, if the federalism concept operated as an independent restriction on the sovereign power of the court, it would not be possible to waive the personal jurisdiction requirement: Individual actions cannot change the powers of sovereignty, although the individual can subject himself to powers from which he may otherwise be protected. *Id.*, at 703, n. 10.

With which justice do you agree?

3. What difference does it make whether due process clause protections are based on the limitations of state judicial power or personal liberty interests? Justice Ginsburg notes in her dissent: "The Court's judgment also puts United States plaintiffs at a disadvantage in comparison to similarly situated complainants elsewhere in the world," because those injured in the European Union can bring tort actions "in the courts for the place where the harmful event occurred." Is this fact relevant to whether New Jersey has the power to entertain an action against McIntyre? Is it relevant to whether subjecting McIntyre to suit in New Jersey would be constitutionally unfair to that company?

4. Justice Kennedy recognizes an exception to the "purposeful availment" test for intentional torts:

As a general rule, the exercise of judicial power is not lawful unless the defendant "purposefully avails itself of the privilege of conducting activities within the forum State, thus invoking the benefits and protections of its laws." *Hanson v. Denckla*, 357 U.S. 235, 253 (1958). There may be exceptions, say, for instance, in cases involving an intentional tort.

Why the exception for intentional torts? Consider, for example, a New Hampshire man who has never visited Vermont. He shoots across the New Hampshire border and wounds a Maryland citizen in Vermont. Why should Vermont be able to exercise personal jurisdiction over the shooter in a civil action filed by the Maryland citizen?

5. The Ninth Circuit Court of Appeals upheld alternate email service upon a Costa Rican defendant in *Rio Properties, Inc. v. Rio Int'l Interlink*, 284 F.3d 1007 (9th Cir. 2002), *supra* p. 227. Having upheld email service, the court then concluded that the defendant was subject to service under Nevada's long-arm statute and that personal jurisdiction was constitutional. In upholding the constitutionality of personal jurisdiction, the court concluded that defendant had purposefully availed itself of the Nevada market by "an insistent marketing campaign directed toward Nevada," 284 F.3d at 1020, that plaintiff's claim arose from those forum contacts ("RII specifically competed with RIO in Nevada by targeting Nevada consumers in radio and print media."), 284 F. 3d at 1021, and that, defendant having targeted plaintiff in Nevada and the Nevada market, the exercise of jurisdiction in Nevada "comports with traditional notions of fair play and substantial justice" and was thus reasonable. *Id.*

6. Justice Kennedy states in his plurality opinion: "At no time did petitioner engage in any activities in New Jersey that reveal an intent to invoke or benefit from the protection of its laws." Are most foreign

manufacturers likely to target particular states for their products, as opposed to availing themselves more generally of the United States market? After reading the plurality opinion in *McIntyre*, is there less reason for foreign manufacturers to think about specific state markets— and more reason to instruct distributors to target markets more generally in the United States?

7. In his concurrence, Justice Breyer offers the following hypothetical:

> What might appear fair in the case of a large manufacturer which specifically seeks, or expects, an equal-sized distributor to sell its product in a distant State might seem unfair in the case of a small manufacturer (say, an Appalachian potter) who sells his product (cups and saucers) exclusively to a large distributor, who resells a single item (a coffee mug) to a buyer from a distant State (Hawaii).

Is McIntyre Machinery positioned similarly to an Appalachian potter, with one of its coffee cups having been sold within a distant state? Regardless of the rigidity of the test adopted by the New Jersey Supreme Court, is it constitutionally unfair—under Justice Breyer's approach—to subject McIntyre to suit in New Jersey concerning its "three-ton metal shearing machine" which "sold in the United States for $24,900 in 1995 and features a 'massive cutting capacity' "?

8. What does Justice Breyer mean in his statement that "the fact that the defendant is a foreign, rather than a domestic, manufacturer makes the basic fairness of an absolute rule yet more uncertain"? Should a foreign defendant receive more or fewer due process protections in United States courts?

9. Why does Justice Ginsburg's opinion contain so many facts?

10. What is the answer to Justice Ginsburg's question: "On what sensible view of the allocation of adjudicatory authority could the place of Nicastro's injury within the United States be deemed off limits for his products liability claim against a foreign manufacturer who targeted the United States (including all the States that constitute the Nation) as the territory it sought to develop?"

11. Justice Kennedy notes in his plurality opinion:

> It may be that, assuming it were otherwise empowered to legislate on the subject, the Congress could authorize the exercise of jurisdiction in appropriate courts. That circumstance is not presented in this case, however, and it is neither necessary nor appropriate to address here any constitutional concerns that might be attendant to that exercise of power. Here the question concerns the authority of a New Jersey state court to exercise jurisdiction, so it is petitioner's purposeful contacts with New Jersey, not with the United States, that alone are relevant.

Had Congress enacted a federal products liability statute, personal jurisdiction might have been asserted pursuant to Federal Rule of Civil

Procedure 4(k)(2). Rule 4(k)(2) authorizes reliance on national contacts, rather than those with any particular state, and provides:

> For a claim that arises under federal law, serving a summons or filing a waiver of service establishes personal jurisdiction over a defendant if:
>
> > (A) the defendant is not subject to jurisdiction in any state's courts of general jurisdiction; and
> >
> > (B) exercising jurisdiction is consistent with the United States Constitution and laws.

The Advisory Committee Note to the 1993 amendment to Rule 4 explained the reach of Rule 4(k)(2) as follows:

> This narrow extension of the federal reach applies only if a claim is made against the defendant under federal law. It does not establish personal jurisdiction if the only claims are those arising under state law or the law of another country, even though there might be diversity or alienage subject matter jurisdiction as to such claims. If, however, personal jurisdiction is established under this paragraph with respect to a federal claim, then 28 U.S.C. § 1367(a) provides supplemental jurisdiction over related claims against that defendant, subject to the court's discretion to decline exercise of supplemental jurisdiction under 28 U.S.C. § 1367(c).

146 F.R.D. 401, 572 (1993).

f.   A Bit More on Personal Jurisdiction

As you know, courts can exercise personal or territorial jurisdiction over parties on several bases. State domicile and presence are a traditional basis for asserting personal jurisdiction. For non-natural persons, presence may be more difficult to determine, and the Supreme Court has formulated tests for both general and specific jurisdiction— depending on whether the claims asserted arise from the defendant's forum contacts. Consent, either explicit or implied, is another traditional basis for personal jurisdiction, and jurisdiction in rem remains another way in which to achieve territorial jurisdiction. However, in *Shaffer v. Heitner* the Supreme Court held that such jurisdiction must be tested under the contacts and fairness standards of *International Shoe*.

Figure 4–2 illustrates the bases for asserting personal jurisdiction, as well as the Supreme Court opinions recognizing these particular jurisdictional tests.[21]

---

[21] The Supreme Court summarized the various bases for personal jurisdiction in *J. McIntyre Machinery, Ltd. v. Nicastro*, 131 S.Ct. 2780, 2787–88 (2011):

> A person may submit to a State's authority in a number of ways. There is, of course, explicit consent. *E.g., Insurance Corp. of Ireland v. Compagnie des Bauxites de Guinee*, 456 U.S. 694, 703 (1982). Presence within a State at the time suit commences through service of process is another example. *See Burnham, supra.*

FIGURE 4–2
BASES OF PERSONAL OR TERRITORIAL JURISDICTION

State Domicile	Transient (Tag) Jurisdiction during Voluntary State Presence	Specific Jurisdiction (State Contacts from which Claim Arises)	General Jurisdiction (if claim doesn't arise from forum contacts)	Contractual Consent to Jurisdiction	Implied Consent to Jurisdiction	Property Attached (In Rem jurisdiction)
Milliken v. Meyer, 311 U.S. 457 (1940)	*Burnham v. Superior Court*, 495 U.S. 604 (1990)	*Int'l Shoe v. Washington*, 326 U.S. 310 (1945)	*Daimler AG v. Bauman*, 134 S.Ct. 746 (2011)	*Nat'l Equip. Rental v. Szukhent*, 375 U.S. 311 (1964)	*Hess v. Pawloski*, 274 U.S. 352 (1927)	*Shaffer v. Heitner*, 433 U.S. 186 (1977)

Test your knowledge of these principals by determining whether personal jurisdiction is constitutionally asserted in the following situations.

(1) Plaintiff filed a California state court action seeking insurance proceeds. She served defendant insurance company at its principal place of business in Texas pursuant to California's long-arm statute. The insured had received the life insurance policy in California and had mailed regular premium payments from his home in California to the defendant in Texas. The company never had an office or employees in California, never solicited insurance business in California, and had no policies in California other than the one on which the plaintiff sought payment.

Is the assertion of personal jurisdiction over the defendant by the California court constitutional? *See McGee v. International Life Insurance Co.*, 355 U.S. 220 (1957).

(2) A wife and husband lived for more than ten years in New York, where their two children were born and raised. The couple separated, and the wife moved to California. She then flew to New York to sign a

---

Citizenship or domicile—or, by analogy, incorporation or principal place of business for corporations—also indicates general submission to a State's powers. *Goodyear Dunlop Tires Operations, S.A. v. Brown.* Each of these examples reveals circumstances, or a course of conduct, from which it is proper to infer an intention to benefit from and thus an intention to submit to the laws of the forum State. *Cf. Burger King Corp. v. Rudzewicz*, 471 U.S. 462, 476 (1985). These examples support exercise of the general jurisdiction of the State's courts and allow the State to resolve both matters that originate within the State and those based on activities and events elsewhere. *Helicopteros Nacionales de Colombia, S.A. v. Hall*, 466 U.S. 408, 414, and n. 9 (1984). By contrast, those who live or operate primarily outside a State have a due process right not to be subjected to judgment in its courts as a general matter.

There is also a more limited form of submission to a State's authority for disputes that "arise out of or are connected with the activities within the state." *International Shoe Co., supra*, at 319. Where a defendant "purposefully avails itself of the privilege of conducting activities *within* the forum State, thus invoking the benefits and protections of its laws," *Hanson, supra*, at 253, it submits to the judicial power of an otherwise foreign sovereign to the extent that power is exercised in connection with the defendant's activities touching on the State. In other words, submission through contact with and activity directed at a sovereign may justify specific jurisdiction "in a suit arising out of or related to the defendant's contacts with the forum." *Helicopteros, supra*, at 414, n. 8; *see also Goodyear, post*, at 2850–2851.

written separation agreement, later incorporating the agreement into a divorce decree that she obtained in Haiti (using a power of attorney signed by her husband). The wife returned to California, where the two minor children ultimately joined her. She then sought to establish the Haitian divorce decree as a California judgment and to modify that decree to provide her with full custody of the children and an increased amount of child support.

The husband moved to quash service of the California court, arguing that he was not a resident of California and had insufficient contacts with California to support personal jurisdiction. The wife argued that her husband purposefully availed himself of the benefits of California, because his children lived there nine months of the year and he had bought a one-way plane ticket for his daughter to fly to California to live with her mother.

Should the court grant the husband's motion to quash service, because it cannot constitutionally exercise personal jurisdiction over him? *See Kulko v. Kulko*, 436 U.S. 84 (1978).

(3) A Michigan resident entered into a franchise agreement with a Florida corporation that franchises over 3000 restaurants across the United States. In order to ensure national uniformity of service, the franchiser closely regulated the operations of all franchisees. The franchise agreement provided that the agreement was governed by Florida law and that all franchisee fees and notices were to be sent to the franchiser's headquarters in Florida. Day-to-day supervision of franchisees, though, was conducted by ten regional offices. The Michigan franchisee negotiated with both Florida headquarters and the Michigan regional office in securing the initial franchise agreement and concerning the later termination of that agreement by the franchiser.

The franchiser alleged that the Michigan franchisee violated the franchise agreement by not paying the required franchise fees and sued the franchisee in a federal diversity action in Florida. The franchisee was served pursuant to Florida's long-arm statute, which extended personal jurisdiction to persons who breach a contract in Florida "by failing to perform acts required by the contract to be performed in this state" so long as the action arises from the alleged contractual breach.

Should the Florida court quash service on the Michigan defendant? *See Burger King Corp. v. Rudzewicz*, 471 U.S. 462, 476 (1985).

(4) Plaintiff was an entertainer who lived and worked in California. Defendants wrote and edited in Florida an article for a national newspaper headquartered in Florida. The article stated that plaintiff drank so heavily that she was unable to fulfill her professional obligations. The plaintiff filed a libel action against defendants in California, serving them in Florida pursuant to California's long-arm statute.

The writer of the article asserted that, although he visited California for work, he had written the article in Florida, where he has his home and office. In writing this article, though, he had telephone conversations with individuals in California. The newspaper editor asserted that he had only been in California twice in his life—neither time in connection with this story. The defendant newspaper, which did not challenge personal jurisdiction, sold 5,000,000 copies nationally each week, 600,000 of which were in California.

Should the court grant the defendants' motion to quash service of process upon them? *See Calder v. Jones*, 465 U.S. 783 (1984).

IV. VENUE, TRANSFER, AND FORUM NON CONVENIENS

Subject-matter jurisdiction determines what types of cases a court can hear, while personal jurisdiction limits the particular parties over which a court can exercise its judicial power. But, in addition to subject-matter jurisdiction and personal jurisdiction, a court must have venue over a specific action to consider that case. Both state and federal courts have venue rules that allocate cases to specific courts within those judicial systems, based upon the nexus between the case, the parties, and specific courts.[22] In this section we consider the statutory venue rules applicable in the federal courts, as well as the circumstances under which a federal district court can transfer an action to another federal district court or dismiss that action under the doctrine of forum non conveniens.

A. VENUE IN THE FEDERAL DISTRICT COURTS

Although there are specific venue requirements for a few specific federal actions, venue is determined in most cases by the general venue rule set forth in 28 U.S.C. § 1391. Section 1391(b) provides:

A civil action may be brought in

(1) a judicial district in which any defendant resides, if all defendants are residents of the State in which the district is located;

(2) a judicial district in which a substantial part of the events or omissions giving rise to the claim occurred, or a substantial part of property that is the subject of the action is situated; or

(3) if there is no district in which an action may otherwise be brought as provided in this section, any judicial district in which any defendant is subject to the court's personal jurisdiction with respect to such action.

---

[22] As defined in 28 U.S.C. § 1390(a), "the term 'venue' refers to the geographic specification of the proper court or courts for the litigation of a civil action that is within the subject-matter jurisdiction of the district courts in general * * *."

So, while a plaintiff may be able to obtain personal jurisdiction over a defendant in many federal district courts, the Section 1391 venue requirements may limit the courts in which an action can be filed. Assume, for example, that John Jones resides in Tennessee and has a contract dispute with Sally Smith, a resident of Lexington, Kentucky, concerning the sale of his Knoxville, Tennessee home to Sally. Sally would like to file a federal diversity action against John, seeking the $150,000 in damages that she alleges he has caused her. Sally knows that, while he lives and works in Knoxville, John frequently visits his children in Georgia and attends business conferences in Atlanta.

Because Sally and John are citizens of different states and the amount in controversy is more than the jurisdictional minimum under 28 U.S.C. § 1332(a), federal subject-matter jurisdiction under Section 1332 would exist in any one of the 94 United States district courts across the nation.

However, Sally's action would have to be filed in a state in which John is subject to personal jurisdiction. Such states would include Tennessee (his domicile) and may well include Kentucky (depending on his contacts with that state stemming from the contractual negotiations with Sally) and Georgia (depending on whether he has sufficient contacts with that state through his personal and business travels to that state). Pursuant to *Burnham v. Superior Court*, 495 U.S. 604 (1990), personal jurisdiction might be constitutionally asserted in other states if John were served with process in a state while voluntarily present in that state.

Venue is focused on individual federal district courts, rather than entire states, and, in this case, will further limit the courts that might entertain this action. Consider the possibilities:

- **Section 1391(a)(1)** provides for venue in "a judicial district in which any defendant resides, if all defendants are residents of the State in which the district is located." Section 1391(c)(1) defines "residency" for a natural person as "the judicial district in which that person is domiciled." For John this would be the Eastern District of Tennessee, and, because he will be the only defendant, all defendants "are residents of the State in which the district is located."

- **Section 1391(b)(2)** additionally provides for venue in "a judicial district in which a substantial part of the events or omissions giving rise to the claim occurred, or a substantial part of property that is the subject of the action is situated." Depending upon how the negotiations over the property were structured, it is likely that a "substantial part of the events or omissions giving rise to [Sally's] claim occurred" in Lexington, Kentucky (within the Eastern District of Kentucky) and Knoxville, Tennessee (within the Eastern District of Tennessee). The "property that is the subject of the action is situated" in Knoxville, but this does not add an additional venue choice because venue already is available in the Eastern District of Tennessee under Section 1391(a)(1) or possibly the first portion of Section 1391(b)(2).

- **Section 1391(b)(3)** is not applicable in this situation because it only applies "if there is no district in which an action may otherwise be brought as provided in this section," and there are one or more venue possibilities under Sections 1391(b)(1) and (2). In the event that there were no possibilities under Sections 1391(b)(1) or (2), venue would be possible in "any judicial district in which any defendant is subject to the court's personal jurisdiction with respect to such action" pursuant to the "fall back" provision of 28 U.S.C. § 1391(b)(3).

Thus subject-matter jurisdiction for Sally's action would exist in every federal district court and personal jurisdiction may exist in several states. However, the only district in which venue may exist is the United States District Court for the Eastern District of Tennessee and, possibly, the United States District Court for the Eastern District of Kentucky (depending upon the manner in which the property sales contract was negotiated).

The forum possibilities are shown in Figure 4–3.[23]

FIGURE 4–3
POSSIBLE JUDICIAL FORUMS FOR SALLY'S ACTION AGAINST JOHN

	Subject-Matter Jurisdiction	Personal Jurisdiction	Venue
Governing Law	28 U.S.C. § 1332 Diversity of Citizenship	*International Shoe* minimum contacts test	28 U.S.C. § 1391(b)
Test for a Federal Action	diverse citizenship and minimum amount in controversy	minimum contacts; suit arises from contacts; suit does not offend "traditional notions of fair play and	district in which any defendant resides (if all defendants are residents of that state); or district in which a substantial part of events/omissions giving rise to claim occurred or substantial

---

[23] This chart illustrates not only possible forum possibilities in the federal courts, but state court possibilities as well. Lawyers should always consider both federal and state possibilities before filing any action or deciding how to respond to any action or claim filed by another party.

		substantial justice"	part of property that is subject of claim is situated; or, if no other venue, district in which any defendant is subject to personal jurisdiction
Possible Federal Forums	all 94 federal district courts	federal courts in Tennessee, Kentucky, and perhaps Georgia	Eastern District of Tennessee; Eastern District of Kentucky
Possible State Forums	all States Courts of General Jurisdiction	state courts in Tennessee, Kentucky, and perhaps Georgia	statutes or rules in Tennessee, Kentucky, and Georgia will determine which courts in those states could hear action.

While Section 1391(b) applies to civil actions involving both natural and non-natural persons, there may be more venue choices under Section 1391 in a civil action against a corporation or other non-natural person. This is because, for venue purposes, 28 U.S.C. Section 1391(c)(1) broadly defines the residence of defendant corporations and other non-natural persons with the capacity to sue or be sued. Section 1391(c)(2) states:

> [A]n entity with the capacity to sue and be sued in its common name under applicable law, whether or not incorporated, shall be deemed to reside, if a defendant, in any judicial district in which such defendant is subject to the court's personal jurisdiction with respect to the civil action in question * * *.

Consider, therefore, a civil action such as the one that John Leonard filed against PepsiCo, Inc.[24] Pursuant to 28 U.S.C. § 1391(b)(1), PepsiCo could be sued in "a judicial district in which [it, as the sole defendant,] resides." The Section 1391(c)(2) definition of residence for a corporate defendant means that it resides, for venue purposes, "in any judicial district in which [it] is subject to the court's personal jurisdiction with respect to the civil action in question." PepsiCo is a major corporation that has availed itself of the national marketplace—not only in the sale of its products but by advertising those products through national media campaigns. Therefore it would be subject to personal jurisdiction in any state with which it has minimum contacts and from which a plaintiff's claim arose. With

---

[24] The federal venue statutes were amended significantly in 2012, but assume for the purposes of this illustration that the current statutory provisions were in existence at the time of the *PepsiCo* litigation in the 1990s.

respect to venue in the federal courts, venue pursuant to 28 U.S.C. § 1391(b)(1) would exist in all federal district courts in which PepsiCo is subject to personal jurisdiction. Thus, with such a national corporate defendant, a plaintiff should have multiple districts in which to bring suit and in which there would be subject-matter jurisdiction, personal jurisdiction, and venue.[25]

B. CHANGE OF VENUE IN THE FEDERAL COURTS

Even though the requirements of Section 1391 are met and venue exists in a particular federal district court, there may be another federal court that could more appropriately resolve the action. Section 1404(a) of Title 28 permits a change of venue from one federal district court to another, providing:

> For the convenience of parties and witnesses, in the interest of justice, a district court may transfer any civil action to any other district or division where it might have been brought or to any district or division to which all parties have consented.

John Leonard initially filed his civil action against PepsiCo, Inc. in Florida state court, and PepsiCo then removed the action to the United States District Court for the Southern District of Florida.[26] Once removed to federal court, the action was transferred to the United States District Court for the Southern District of New York pursuant to 28 U.S.C. § 1404(a).[27] Can you think of why such a transfer might have enhanced "the convenience of parties and witnesses" and been "in the interest of justice"?

Transfers within the federal district courts also are possible under 28 U.S.C. Section 1406(a). This statute provides:

> The district court of a district in which is filed a case laying venue in the wrong division or district shall dismiss, or if it be in the interest of justice, transfer such case to any district or division in which it could have been brought.

A civil action can be dismissed for improper venue pursuant to Federal Rule of Civil Procedure 12(b)(3). However, the statute of limitations governing the claims asserted may run before a dismissed action can be refiled in the appropriate court. This problem can be avoided if, instead of being dismissed, the action is transferred to a court with proper venue. Although Section 1406 does not explicitly so provide, the Supreme Court has held that civil actions can be

---

[25] However, if the basis of personal jurisdiction against a corporate defendant is general rather than specific personal jurisdiction, the states in which the corporation may be subject to personal jurisdiction may be limited to that corporation's states of incorporation and principal place of business. *Daimler AG v. Bauman*, 134 S.Ct. 746 (2014), *supra* p. 281.

[26] See *Leonard v. PepsiCo, Inc.*, 88 F.Supp. 2d 116, 120 (S.D.N.Y. 1999).

[27] *Id.*

transferred pursuant to 28 U.S.C. § 1406 when not only venue but personal jurisdiction is not present in the district court in which the action originally was filed.[28]

While plaintiffs' counsel can choose the forum in the first instance, they must do so with the understanding that defense counsel may move to transfer a federal civil action to another federal district court.[29] Just because an action can be heard in federal court does not mean that any particular United States District Court must decide that action.

C. FORUM NON CONVENIENS DISMISSALS: *PIPER AIRCRAFT CO. V. REYNO*

Sections 1404 and 1406 permit a federal district court to transfer an action to another district court within the federal judicial system. But what if the more appropriate forum is not one to which the action can be transferred? For instance, what if the action is filed in a state or federal court in the United States but a significantly more appropriate forum exists in a foreign country? In such circumstances the United States court might enter a forum non conveniens dismissal, with the expectation that the plaintiff will refile its action in the foreign forum.[30]

Because of 28 U.S.C. §§ 1404 and 1406, forum non conveniens dismissals are not necessary to move an action from one federal district court to another. The following case describes the process and standards that apply when transfer is not possible and a forum non conveniens dismissal may be in order.

Piper Aircraft Co. v. Reyno
Supreme Court of the United States, 1981
454 U.S. 235

OPINION

■ JUSTICE MARSHALL delivered the opinion of the Court.

These cases arise out of an air crash that took place in Scotland. Respondent, acting as representative of the estates of several Scottish citizens killed in the accident, brought wrongful-death actions against petitioners that were ultimately transferred to the United States District Court for the Middle District of Pennsylvania. Petitioners moved to dismiss on the ground of forum non conveniens. After noting that an alternative forum existed in Scotland, the District Court

---

[28] *Goldlawr, Inc. v. Heiman*, 369 U.S. 463 (1962).

[29] Or, if the action initially is filed in state court, defense counsel may be able to remove the action to federal court under 28 U.S.C. § 1441. *See* Chapter 3, *supra* pp. 186–204.

[30] Forum non conveniens dismissals also can be entered by state courts that determine that a significantly more convenient forum exists in another state. Because there is no mechanism for one state court to transfer an action to a court in another state, the first court simply dismisses the action. The plaintiff then must refile that action in the more appropriate state court.

granted their motions. The United States Court of Appeals for the Third Circuit reversed. The Court of Appeals based its decision, at least in part, on the ground that dismissal is automatically barred where the law of the alternative forum is less favorable to the plaintiff than the law of the forum chosen by the plaintiff. Because we conclude that the possibility of an unfavorable change in law should not, by itself, bar dismissal, and because we conclude that the District Court did not otherwise abuse its discretion, we reverse.

I

A

In July 1976, a small commercial aircraft crashed in the Scottish highlands during the course of a charter flight from Blackpool to Perth. The pilot and five passengers were killed instantly. The decedents were all Scottish subjects and residents, as are their heirs and next of kin. There were no eyewitnesses to the accident. At the time of the crash the plane was subject to Scottish air traffic control.

The aircraft, a twin-engine Piper Aztec, was manufactured in Pennsylvania by petitioner Piper Aircraft Co. (Piper). The propellers were manufactured in Ohio by petitioner Hartzell Propeller, Inc. (Hartzell). At the time of the crash the aircraft was registered in Great Britain and was owned and maintained by Air Navigation and Trading Co., Ltd. (Air Navigation). It was operated by McDonald Aviation, Ltd. (McDonald), a Scottish air taxi service. Both Air Navigation and McDonald were organized in the United Kingdom. The wreckage of the plane is now in a hangar in Farnsborough, England.

The British Department of Trade investigated the accident shortly after it occurred. A preliminary report found that the plane crashed after developing a spin, and suggested that mechanical failure in the plane or the propeller was responsible. At Hartzell's request, this report was reviewed by a three-member Review Board, which held a 9-day adversary hearing attended by all interested parties. The Review Board found no evidence of defective equipment and indicated that pilot error may have contributed to the accident. The pilot, who had obtained his commercial pilot's license only three months earlier, was flying over high ground at an altitude considerably lower than the minimum height required by his company's operations manual.

In July 1977, a California probate court appointed respondent Gaynell Reyno administratrix of the estates of the five passengers. Reyno is not related to and does not know any of the decedents or their survivors; she was a legal secretary to the attorney who filed this lawsuit. Several days after her appointment, Reyno commenced separate wrongful-death actions against Piper and Hartzell in the Superior Court of California, claiming negligence and strict liability. Air Navigation, McDonald, and the estate of the pilot are not parties to this litigation. The survivors of the five passengers whose estates are represented by Reyno filed a separate action in the United Kingdom against Air Navigation, McDonald, and the pilot's estate. Reyno candidly admits that the action against Piper and Hartzell was filed in the United States because its laws regarding liability, capacity to sue, and damages are more favorable to her position than are those of Scotland. Scottish law does not recognize strict liability in tort. Moreover, it permits wrongful-death actions only when brought by a decedent's relatives. The relatives may sue only for "loss of support and society."

On petitioners' motion, the suit was removed to the United States District Court for the Central District of California. Piper then moved for transfer to the United States District Court for the Middle District of Pennsylvania, pursuant to 28 U.S.C. § 1404(a). Hartzell moved to dismiss for lack of personal jurisdiction, or in the alternative, to transfer.[5] In December 1977, the District Court quashed service on Hartzell and transferred the case to the Middle District of Pennsylvania. Respondent then properly served process on Hartzell.

B

In May 1978, after the suit had been transferred, both Hartzell and Piper moved to dismiss the action on the ground of forum non conveniens. The District Court granted these motions in October 1979. It relied on the balancing test set forth by this Court in *Gulf Oil Corp. v. Gilbert*, 330 U.S. 501 (1947), and its companion case, *Koster v. Lumbermens Mut. Cas. Co.*, 330 U.S. 518 (1947). In those decisions, the Court stated that a plaintiff's choice of forum should rarely be disturbed. However, when an alternative forum has jurisdiction to hear the case, and when trial in the chosen forum would "establish . . . oppressiveness and vexation to a defendant . . . out of all proportion to plaintiff's convenience," or when the "chosen forum [is] inappropriate because of considerations affecting the court's own administrative and legal problems," the court may, in the exercise of its sound discretion, dismiss the case. *Koster*, supra, at 524. To guide trial court discretion, the Court provided a list of "private interest factors" affecting the convenience of the litigants, and a list of "public interest factors" affecting the convenience of the forum. *Gilbert*, supra, 330 U.S. at 508–509.[6]

---

[5]   The District Court concluded that it could not assert personal jurisdiction over Hartzell consistent with due process. However, it decided not to dismiss Hartzell because the corporation would be amenable to process in Pennsylvania.

[6]   The factors pertaining to the private interests of the litigants included the "relative ease of access to sources of proof; availability of compulsory process for attendance of unwilling, and the cost of obtaining attendance of willing, witnesses; possibility of view of premises, if view would be appropriate to the action; and all other practical problems that make trial of a case easy, expeditious and inexpensive." *Gilbert*, 330 U.S., at 508. The public factors bearing on the question included the administrative difficulties flowing from court congestion; the "local interest in having localized controversies decided at home"; the interest in having the trial of a diversity case in a forum that is at home with the law that must govern the action; the avoidance of unnecessary problems in conflict of laws, or in the application of

After describing our decisions in *Gilbert* and *Koster*, the District Court analyzed the facts of these cases. It began by observing that an alternative forum existed in Scotland; Piper and Hartzell had agreed to submit to the jurisdiction of the Scottish courts and to waive any statute of limitations defense that might be available. It then stated that plaintiff's choice of forum was entitled to little weight. The court recognized that a plaintiff's choice ordinarily deserves substantial deference. It noted, however, that Reyno "is a representative of foreign citizens and residents seeking a forum in the United States because of the more liberal rules concerning products liability law," and that "the courts have been less solicitous when the plaintiff is not an American citizen or resident, and particularly when the foreign citizens seek to benefit from the more liberal tort rules provided for the protection of citizens and residents of the United States."

The District Court next examined several factors relating to the private interests of the litigants, and determined that these factors strongly pointed towards Scotland as the appropriate forum. Although evidence concerning the design, manufacture, and testing of the plane and propeller is located in the United States, the connections with Scotland are otherwise "overwhelming." The real parties in interest are citizens of Scotland, as were all the decedents. Witnesses who could testify regarding the maintenance of the aircraft, the training of the pilot, and the investigation of the accident—all essential to the defense—are in Great Britain. Moreover, all witnesses to damages are located in Scotland. Trial would be aided by familiarity with Scottish topography, and by easy access to the wreckage.

The District Court reasoned that because crucial witnesses and evidence were beyond the reach of compulsory process, and because the defendants would not be able to implead potential Scottish third-party defendants, it would be "unfair to make Piper and Hartzell proceed to trial in this forum." The survivors had brought separate actions in Scotland against the pilot, McDonald, and Air Navigation. "[I]t would be fairer to all parties and less costly if the entire case was presented to one jury with available testimony from all relevant witnesses." Although the court recognized that if trial were held in the United States, Piper and Hartzell could file indemnity or contribution actions against the Scottish defendants, it believed that there was a significant risk of inconsistent verdicts.[7]

The District Court concluded that the relevant public interests also pointed strongly towards dismissal. The court determined that Pennsylvania law would apply to Piper and Scottish law to Hartzell if

---

foreign law; and the unfairness of burdening citizens in an unrelated forum with jury duty. *Id.*, at 509.

[7]   The District Court explained that inconsistent verdicts might result if petitioners were held liable on the basis of strict liability here, and then required to prove negligence in an indemnity action in Scotland. Moreover, even if the same standard of liability applied, there was a danger that different juries would find different facts and produce inconsistent results.

the case were tried in the Middle District of Pennsylvania.[8] As a result, "trial in this forum would be hopelessly complex and confusing for a jury." In addition, the court noted that it was unfamiliar with Scottish law and thus would have to rely upon experts from that country. The court also found that the trial would be enormously costly and time-consuming; that it would be unfair to burden citizens with jury duty when the Middle District of Pennsylvania has little connection with the controversy; and that Scotland has a substantial interest in the outcome of the litigation.

In opposing the motions to dismiss, respondent contended that dismissal would be unfair because Scottish law was less favorable. The District Court explicitly rejected this claim. It reasoned that the possibility that dismissal might lead to an unfavorable change in the law did not deserve significant weight; any deficiency in the foreign law was a "matter to be dealt with in the foreign forum."

C

On appeal, the United States Court of Appeals for the Third Circuit reversed and remanded for trial. The decision to reverse appears to be based on two alternative grounds. First, the Court held that the District Court abused its discretion in conducting the *Gilbert* analysis. Second, the Court held that dismissal is never appropriate where the law of the alternative forum is less favorable to the plaintiff.

* * *

We granted certiorari in these cases to consider the questions they raise concerning the proper application of the doctrine of forum non conveniens.

II

The Court of Appeals erred in holding that plaintiffs may defeat a motion to dismiss on the ground of forum non conveniens merely by showing that the substantive law that would be applied in the alternative forum is less favorable to the plaintiffs than that of the present forum. The possibility of a change in substantive law should ordinarily not be given conclusive or even substantial weight in the forum non conveniens inquiry.

---

[8]   Under *Klaxon v. Stentor Electric Mfg. Co.*, 313 U.S. 487 (1941), a court ordinarily must apply the choice-of-law rules of the State in which it sits. However, where a case is transferred pursuant to 28 U.S.C. § 1404(a), it must apply the choice-of-law rules of the State from which the case was transferred. *Van Dusen v. Barrack*, 376 U.S. 612 (1946). Relying on these two cases, the District Court concluded that California choice-of-law rules would apply to Piper, and Pennsylvania choice-of-law rules would apply to Hartzell. It further concluded that California applied a "governmental interests" analysis in resolving choice-of-law problems, and that Pennsylvania employed a "significant contacts" analysis. The court used the "governmental interests" analysis to determine that Pennsylvania liability rules would apply to Piper, and the "significant contacts" analysis to determine that Scottish liability rules would apply to Hartzell.

We expressly rejected the position adopted by the Court of Appeals in our decision in *Canada Malting Co. v. Paterson Steamships, Ltd.*, 285 U.S. 413 (1932). That case arose out of a collision between two vessels in American waters. The Canadian owners of cargo lost in the accident sued the Canadian owners of one of the vessels in Federal District Court. The cargo owners chose an American court in large part because the relevant American liability rules were more favorable than the Canadian rules. The District Court dismissed on grounds of forum non conveniens. The plaintiffs argued that dismissal was inappropriate because Canadian laws were less favorable to them. This Court nonetheless affirmed:

> We have no occasion to enquire by what law the rights of the parties are governed, as we are of the opinion that under any view of that question, it lay within the discretion of the District Court to decline to assume jurisdiction over the controversy.... "[T]he court will not take cognizance of the case if justice would be as well done by remitting the parties to their home forum." *Id.*, at 419–420, quoting *Charter Shipping Co. v. Bowring, Jones & Tidy*, 281 U.S. 515, 517 (1930).

The Court further stated that "[t]here was no basis for the contention that the District Court abused its discretion." 285 U.S., at 423.

It is true that *Canada Malting* was decided before *Gilbert*, and that the doctrine of forum non conveniens was not fully crystallized until our decision in that case.[13] However, *Gilbert* in no way affects the validity of *Canada Malting*. Indeed, by holding that the central focus of the forum non conveniens inquiry is convenience, *Gilbert* implicitly recognized that dismissal may not be barred solely because of the possibility of an unfavorable change in law. Under Gilbert, dismissal will ordinarily be appropriate where trial in the plaintiff's chosen forum imposes a heavy burden on the defendant or the court, and where the plaintiff is unable to offer any specific reasons of convenience supporting his choice. If substantial weight were given to the possibility of an unfavorable change in law, however, dismissal might be barred even where trial in the chosen forum was plainly inconvenient.

---

[13] The doctrine of forum non conveniens has a long history. It originated in Scotland and became part of the common law of many States. The doctrine was also frequently applied in federal admiralty actions. In *Williams v. Green Bay & Western R. Co.*, 326 U.S. 549 (1946), the Court first indicated that motions to dismiss on grounds of forum non conveniens could be made in federal diversity actions. The doctrine became firmly established when *Gilbert* and *Koster* were decided one year later.

In previous forum non conveniens decisions, the Court has left unresolved the question whether under *Erie R. Co. v. Tompkins*, 304 U.S. 64 (1938), state or federal law of forum non conveniens applies in a diversity case. The Court did not decide this issue because the same result would have been reached in each case under federal or state law. The lower courts in these cases reached the same conclusion: Pennsylvania and California law on forum non conveniens dismissals are virtually identical to federal law. Thus, here also, we need not resolve the *Erie* question.

The Court of Appeals' decision is inconsistent with this Court's earlier forum non conveniens decisions in another respect. Those decisions have repeatedly emphasized the need to retain flexibility. In *Gilbert*, the Court refused to identify specific circumstances "which will justify or require either grant or denial of remedy." 330 U.S., at 508. Similarly, in *Koster*, the Court rejected the contention that where a trial would involve inquiry into the internal affairs of a foreign corporation, dismissal was always appropriate. "That is one, but only one, factor which may show convenience." 330 U.S., at 527. And in *Williams v. Green Bay & Western R. Co.*, 326 U.S. 549, 557 (1946), we stated that we would not lay down a rigid rule to govern discretion, and that "[e]ach case turns on its facts." If central emphasis were placed on any one factor, the forum non conveniens doctrine would lose much of the very flexibility that makes it so valuable.

In fact, if conclusive or substantial weight were given to the possibility of a change in law, the forum non conveniens doctrine would become virtually useless. Jurisdiction and venue requirements are often easily satisfied. As a result, many plaintiffs are able to choose from among several forums. Ordinarily, these plaintiffs will select that forum whose choice-of-law rules are most advantageous. Thus, if the possibility of an unfavorable change in substantive law is given substantial weight in the forum non conveniens inquiry, dismissal would rarely be proper.

* * *

The Court of Appeals' approach is not only inconsistent with the purpose of the forum non conveniens doctrine, but also poses substantial practical problems. If the possibility of a change in law were given substantial weight, deciding motions to dismiss on the ground of forum non conveniens would become quite difficult. Choice-of-law analysis would become extremely important, and the courts would frequently be required to interpret the law of foreign jurisdictions. First, the trial court would have to determine what law would apply if the case were tried in the chosen forum, and what law would apply if the case were tried in the alternative forum. It would then have to compare the rights, remedies, and procedures available under the law that would be applied in each forum. Dismissal would be appropriate only if the court concluded that the law applied by the alternative forum is as favorable to the plaintiff as that of the chosen forum. The doctrine of forum non conveniens, however, is designed in part to help courts avoid conducting complex exercises in comparative law. As we stated in *Gilbert*, the public interest factors point towards dismissal where the court would be required to "untangle problems in conflict of laws, and in law foreign to itself." 330 U.S., at 509.

Upholding the decision of the Court of Appeals would result in other practical problems. At least where the foreign plaintiff named an

American manufacturer as defendant,[17] a court could not dismiss the case on grounds of forum non conveniens where dismissal might lead to an unfavorable change in law. The American courts, which are already extremely attractive to foreign plaintiffs,[18] would become even more attractive. The flow of litigation into the United States would increase and further congest already crowded courts.

The Court of Appeals based its decision, at least in part, on an analogy between dismissals on grounds of forum non conveniens and transfers between federal courts pursuant to § 1404(a). In *Van Dusen v. Barrack*, 376 U.S. 612 (1964), this Court ruled that a § 1404(a) transfer should not result in a change in the applicable law. Relying on dictum in an earlier Third Circuit opinion interpreting *Van Dusen*, the court below held that that principle is also applicable to a dismissal on forum non conveniens grounds. However, § 1404(a) transfers are different than dismissals on the ground of forum non conveniens.

Congress enacted § 1404(a) to permit change of venue between federal courts. Although the statute was drafted in accordance with the doctrine of forum non conveniens, it was intended to be a revision rather than a codification of the common law. District courts were given more discretion to transfer under § 1404(a) than they had to dismiss on grounds of forum non conveniens.

The reasoning employed in *Van Dusen v. Barrack* is simply inapplicable to dismissals on grounds of forum non conveniens. That case did not discuss the common-law doctrine. Rather, it focused on "the construction and application" of § 1404(a). Emphasizing the remedial purpose of the statute, *Barrack* concluded that Congress could not have intended a transfer to be accompanied by a change in law. The statute was designed as a "federal housekeeping measure," allowing easy change of venue within a unified federal system. The Court feared that if a change in venue were accompanied by a change in law, forum-shopping parties would take unfair advantage of the relaxed standards

---

[17] In fact, the defendant might not even have to be American. A foreign plaintiff seeking damages for an accident that occurred abroad might be able to obtain service of process on a foreign defendant who does business in the United States. Under the Court of Appeals' holding, dismissal would be barred if the law in the alternative forum were less favorable to the plaintiff—even though none of the parties are American, and even though there is absolutely no nexus between the subject-matter of the litigation and the United States.

[18] First, all but 6 of the 50 American States—Delaware, Massachusetts, Michigan, North Carolina, Virginia, and Wyoming—offer strict liability. Rules roughly equivalent to American strict liability are effective in France, Belgium, and Luxembourg. West Germany and Japan have a strict liability statute for pharmaceuticals. However, strict liability remains primarily an American innovation. Second, the tort plaintiff may choose, at least potentially, from among 50 jurisdictions if he decides to file suit in the United States. Each of these jurisdictions applies its own set of malleable choice-of-law rules. Third, jury trials are almost always available in the United States, while they are never provided in civil law jurisdictions. Even in the United Kingdom, most civil actions are not tried before a jury. Fourth, unlike most foreign jurisdictions, American courts allow contingent attorney's fees, and do not tax losing parties with their opponents' attorney's fees. Fifth, discovery is more extensive in American than in foreign courts.

for transfer. The rule was necessary to ensure the just and efficient operation of the statute.

We do not hold that the possibility of an unfavorable change in law should never be a relevant consideration in a forum non conveniens inquiry. Of course, if the remedy provided by the alternative forum is so clearly inadequate or unsatisfactory that it is no remedy at all, the unfavorable change in law may be given substantial weight; the district court may conclude that dismissal would not be in the interests of justice. In these cases, however, the remedies that would be provided by the Scottish courts do not fall within this category. Although the relatives of the decedents may not be able to rely on a strict liability theory, and although their potential damages award may be smaller, there is no danger that they will be deprived of any remedy or treated unfairly.

III

The Court of Appeals also erred in rejecting the District Court's *Gilbert* analysis. The Court of Appeals stated that more weight should have been given to the plaintiff's choice of forum, and criticized the District Court's analysis of the private and public interests. However, the District Court's decision regarding the deference due plaintiff's choice of forum was appropriate. Furthermore, we do not believe that the District Court abused its discretion in weighing the private and public interests.

A

The District Court acknowledged that there is ordinarily a strong presumption in favor of the plaintiff's choice of forum, which may be overcome only when the private and public interest factors clearly point towards trial in the alternative forum. It held, however, that the presumption applies with less force when the plaintiff or real parties in interest are foreign.

The District Court's distinction between resident or citizen plaintiffs and foreign plaintiffs is fully justified. In *Koster*, the Court indicated that a plaintiff's choice of forum is entitled to greater deference when the plaintiff has chosen the home forum. When the home forum has been chosen, it is reasonable to assume that this choice is convenient. When the plaintiff is foreign, however, this assumption is much less reasonable. Because the central purpose of any forum non conveniens inquiry is to ensure that the trial is convenient, a foreign plaintiff's choice deserves less deference.

B

The forum non conveniens determination is committed to the sound discretion of the trial court. It may be reversed only when there has been a clear abuse of discretion; where the court has considered all relevant public and private interest factors, and where its balancing of these factors is reasonable, its decision deserves substantial deference.

Here, the Court of Appeals expressly acknowledged that the standard of review was one of abuse of discretion. In examining the District Court's analysis of the public and private interests, however, the Court of Appeals seems to have lost sight of this rule, and substituted its own judgment for that of the District Court.

(1)

In analyzing the private interest factors, the District Court stated that the connections with Scotland are "overwhelming." This characterization may be somewhat exaggerated. Particularly with respect to the question of relative ease of access to sources of proof, the private interests point in both directions. As respondent emphasizes, records concerning the design, manufacture, and testing of the propeller and plane are located in the United States. She would have greater access to sources of proof relevant to her strict liability and negligence theories if trial were held here.[25] However, the District Court did not act unreasonably in concluding that fewer evidentiary problems would be posed if the trial were held in Scotland. A large proportion of the relevant evidence is located in Great Britain.

The Court of Appeals found that the problems of proof could not be given any weight because Piper and Hartzell failed to describe with specificity the evidence they would not be able to obtain if trial were held in the United States. It suggested that defendants seeking forum non conveniens dismissal must submit affidavits identifying the witnesses they would call and the testimony these witnesses would provide if the trial were held in the alternative forum. Such detail is not necessary. Piper and Hartzell have moved for dismissal precisely because many crucial witnesses are located beyond the reach of compulsory process, and thus are difficult to identify or interview. Requiring extensive investigation would defeat the purpose of their motion. Of course, defendants must provide enough information to enable the District Court to balance the parties' interests. Our examination of the record convinces us that sufficient information was provided here. Both Piper and Hartzell submitted affidavits describing the evidentiary problems they would face if the trial were held in the United States.

The District Court correctly concluded that the problems posed by the inability to implead potential third-party defendants clearly supported holding the trial in Scotland. Joinder of the pilot's estate, Air Navigation, and McDonald is crucial to the presentation of petitioners' defense. If Piper and Hartzell can show that the accident was caused not by a design defect, but rather by the negligence of the pilot, the plane's owners, or the charter company, they will be relieved of all liability. It is true, of course, that if Hartzell and Piper were found

---

[25] In the future, where similar problems are presented, district courts might dismiss subject to the condition that defendant corporations agree to provide the records relevant to the plaintiff's claims.

liable after a trial in the United States, they could institute an action for indemnity or contribution against these parties in Scotland. It would be far more convenient, however, to resolve all claims in one trial. The Court of Appeals rejected this argument. Forcing petitioners to rely on actions for indemnity or contributions would be "burdensome" but not "unfair." Finding that trial in the plaintiff's chosen forum would be burdensome, however, is sufficient to support dismissal on grounds of forum non conveniens.

(2)

The District Court's review of the factors relating to the public interest was also reasonable. On the basis of its choice-of-law analysis, it concluded that if the case were tried in the Middle District of Pennsylvania, Pennsylvania law would apply to Piper and Scottish law to Hartzell. It stated that a trial involving two sets of laws would be confusing to the jury. It also noted its own lack of familiarity with Scottish law. Consideration of these problems was clearly appropriate under *Gilbert*; in that case we explicitly held that the need to apply foreign law pointed towards dismissal. The Court of Appeals found that the District Court's choice-of-law analysis was incorrect, and that American law would apply to both Hartzell and Piper. Thus, lack of familiarity with foreign law would not be a problem. Even if the Court of Appeals' conclusion is correct, however, all other public interest factors favored trial in Scotland.

Scotland has a very strong interest in this litigation. The accident occurred in its airspace. All of the decedents were Scottish. Apart from Piper and Hartzell, all potential plaintiffs and defendants are either Scottish or English. As we stated in *Gilbert*, there is "a local interest in having localized controversies decided at home." Respondent argues that American citizens have an interest in ensuring that American manufacturers are deterred from producing defective products, and that additional deterrence might be obtained if Piper and Hartzell were tried in the United States, where they could be sued on the basis of both negligence and strict liability. However, the incremental deterrence that would be gained if this trial were held in an American court is likely to be insignificant. The American interest in this accident is simply not sufficient to justify the enormous commitment of judicial time and resources that would inevitably be required if the case were to be tried here.

IV

The Court of Appeals erred in holding that the possibility of an unfavorable change in law bars dismissal on the ground of forum non conveniens. It also erred in rejecting the District Court's Gilbert analysis. The District Court properly decided that the presumption in favor of the respondent's forum choice applied with less than maximum force because the real parties in interest are foreign. It did not act unreasonably in deciding that the private interests pointed towards trial in Scotland. Nor did it act unreasonably in deciding that the public interests favored trial in Scotland. Thus, the judgment of the Court of Appeals is

Reversed.

■ JUSTICE POWELL took no part in the decision of these cases.

■ JUSTICE O'CONNOR took no part in the consideration or decision of these cases.

■ JUSTICE WHITE, concurring in part and dissenting in part.

I join Parts I and II of the Court's opinion. However, like Justice BRENNAN and Justice STEVENS, I would not proceed to deal with the issues addressed in Part III. To that extent, I am in dissent.

■ JUSTICE STEVENS, with whom JUSTICE BRENNAN joins, dissenting.

In No. 80–848, only one question is presented for review to this Court:

> Whether, in an action in federal district court brought by foreign plaintiffs against American defendants, the plaintiffs may defeat a motion to dismiss on the ground of forum non conveniens merely by showing that the substantive law that would be applied if the case were litigated in the district court is more favorable to them than the law that would be applied by the courts of their own nation.

In No. 80–883, the Court limited its grant of certiorari to the same question:

> Must a motion to dismiss on grounds of forum non conveniens be denied whenever the law of the alternate forum is less favorable to recovery than that which would be applied by the district court?

I agree that this question should be answered in the negative. Having decided that question, I would simply remand the case to the Court of Appeals for further consideration of the question whether the District Court correctly decided that Pennsylvania was not a convenient forum in which to litigate a claim against a Pennsylvania company that a plane was defectively designed and manufactured in Pennsylvania.

COMMENTS AND QUESTIONS CONCERNING *PIPER AIRCRAFT CO. V. REYNO*

1. *Piper* provides an excellent review of potential procedural moves on the civil procedure chess board. Trace the steps taken by the parties that led to the defendants' presentation of their forum non conveniens motion to a federal district court in Pennsylvania. Why didn't defendants simply file their forum non conveniens motion in Superior Court in California? Why not file that motion in the United States District Court for the Central District of California?

2. Why might a judicial forum in the United States be particularly attractive to foreign plaintiffs? Consider Justice Marshall's list of some of the reasons for the comparative attractiveness of U.S. courts:

> First, all but 6 of the 50 American States—Delaware, Massachusetts, Michigan, North Carolina, Virginia, and Wyoming—offer strict liability. Rules roughly equivalent to American strict liability are effective in France, Belgium, and Luxembourg. West Germany and Japan have a strict liability statute for pharmaceuticals. However, strict liability remains primarily an American innovation. Second, the tort plaintiff may choose, at least potentially, from among 50 jurisdictions if he decides to file suit in the United States. Each of these jurisdictions applies its own set of malleable choice-of-law rules. Third, jury trials are almost always available in the United States, while they are never provided in civil law jurisdictions. Even in the United Kingdom, most civil actions are not tried before a jury. Fourth, unlike most foreign jurisdictions, American courts allow contingent attorney's fees, and do not tax losing parties with their opponents' attorney's fees. Fifth, discovery is more extensive in American than in foreign courts.

3. The Supreme Court in *Van Dusen v. Barrack* referred to plaintiffs' "venue privilege conferred by federal statutes." 376 U.S. 612, 627 (1964). Why are plaintiffs granted such a "venue privilege"? Why should foreign plaintiffs receive less deference concerning the forum in which they have chosen to file their action?

> In *Koster*, the Court indicated that a plaintiff's choice of forum is entitled to greater deference when the plaintiff has chosen the home forum. When the home forum has been chosen, it is reasonable to assume that this choice is convenient. When the plaintiff is foreign, however, this assumption is much less reasonable. Because the central purpose of any forum non conveniens inquiry is to ensure that the trial is convenient, a foreign plaintiff's choice deserves less deference.

Piper Aircraft Co. v. Reyno, 454 U.S. at 255–56.

4. The Supreme Court concluded that the "alternative forum" in Scotland was a sufficient basis upon which to dismiss this action. However, the potential damages in a Scottish action were significantly less than what might have been awarded in the United States, and the claims were not pursued in Scotland. Clermont, "The Story of *Piper*: Forum Matters," in *Civil Procedure Stories* 199, 222 (K. Clermont ed., 2nd ed. 2008).

5. Justice Marshall's *Piper* opinion characterizes "the central focus of the forum non conveniens inquiry [as] convenience," continuing that, "[u]nder *Gilbert*, dismissal will ordinarily be appropriate where trial in the plaintiff's chosen forum imposes a heavy burden on the defendant or the court, and where the plaintiff is unable to offer any specific reasons of convenience supporting his choice." So is dismissal appropriate only when plaintiff has chosen a forum that places a "heavy burden on the defendant

or the court" (*i.e.*, chosen an abusive forum) or can dismissal be ordered simply because there is a more convenient forum available?

6.   Perhaps the answer to the prior question is not as significant as it might seem at first glance. One way to read the outcome in *Piper* is as a vindication of trial-court discretion. Consider the implications for appellate review of this portion of the Court's opinion:

> The Court of Appeals' decision is inconsistent with this Court's earlier forum non conveniens decisions in another respect. Those decisions have repeatedly emphasized the need to retain flexibility. In *Gilbert*, the Court refused to identify specific circumstances "which will justify or require either grant or denial of remedy." 330 U.S., at 508. Similarly, in *Koster*, the Court rejected the contention that where a trial would involve inquiry into the internal affairs of a foreign corporation, dismissal was always appropriate. "That is one, but only one, factor which may show convenience." 330 U.S., at 527. And in *Williams v. Green Bay & Western R. Co.*, 326 U.S. 549, 557 (1946), we stated that we would not lay down a rigid rule to govern discretion, and that "[e]ach case turns on its facts." If central emphasis were placed on any one factor, the forum non conveniens doctrine would lose much of the very flexibility that makes it so valuable.

7.   Justice Marshall states: "Scotland has a very strong interest in this litigation." Isn't a major part of that interest, though, that its citizens be afforded the fullest possible relief for their damages? When coupled with the interest of the United States in ensuring that American manufacturers produce safe products, don't the *Gilbert* "public interest factors" suggest trial in the United States (which was plaintiff's chosen forum)?

8.   Justice Marshall, recognizing that the plaintiff will not have access to all of the evidence available in the United States if these claims must be maintained in Scotland, suggests in footnote 25 of his opinion:

> In the future, where similar problems are presented, district courts might dismiss subject to the condition that defendant corporations agree to provide the records relevant to the plaintiff's claims.

Using such conditional dismissals, courts can ensure, or even create, an adequate alternate forum, conditioning dismissals on, for instance, defendants' waiver of any statute of limitations defense in the alternative forum or the provision of certain discovery to a plaintiff in that forum.

9.   Justice Marshall raises, but does not resolve, the following question in footnote 13 of his opinion:

> In previous forum non conveniens decisions, the Court has left unresolved the question whether under *Erie R. Co. v. Tompkins*, 304 U.S. 64 (1938), state or federal law of forum non conveniens applies in a diversity case. The Court did not decide this issue because the same result would have been reached in each case under federal or state law. The lower courts in these cases reached the same conclusion: Pennsylvania and California

law on forum non conveniens dismissals are virtually identical to federal law. Thus, here also, we need not resolve the *Erie* question.

The *Erie Railroad* doctrine is considered in the next chapter of the text.

10. What is the status of Justice Marshall's opinion in *Piper*? Two justices (O'Connor and Powell) did not participate in the decision of these cases. Justices White, Stevens, and Brennan either dissented from Justice Marshall's opinion or did not join in Part III of that opinion reviewing the application of the *Gilbert* factors to these cases. Does Justice Stevens' dissent suggest his likely disposition of the question of "whether the District Court correctly decided that Pennsylvania was not a convenient forum in which to litigate a claim against a Pennsylvania company that a plane was defectively designed and manufactured in Pennsylvania"?

D. HAVING ONE'S CAKE AND EATING IT, TOO: *FERENS V. JOHN DEERE CO.*

Ferens v. John Deere Co.
Supreme Court of the United States, 1990
494 U.S. 516

OPINION

■ JUSTICE KENNEDY delivered the opinion of the Court.

Section 1404(a) of Title 28 states: "For the convenience of parties and witnesses, in the interest of justice, a district court may transfer any civil action to any other district or division where it might have been brought." In *Van Dusen v. Barrack*, 376 U.S. 612 (1964), we held that, following a transfer under § 1404(a) initiated by a defendant, the transferee court must follow the choice-of-law rules that prevailed in the transferor court. We now decide that, when a plaintiff moves for the transfer, the same rule applies.

I

Albert Ferens lost his right hand when, the allegation is, it became caught in his combine harvester, manufactured by Deere & Company. The accident occurred while Ferens was working with the combine on his farm in Pennsylvania. For reasons not explained in the record, Ferens delayed filing a tort suit, and Pennsylvania's 2-year limitations period expired. In the third year, he and his wife sued Deere in the United States District Court for the Western District of Pennsylvania, raising contract and warranty claims as to which the Pennsylvania limitations period had not yet run. The District Court had diversity jurisdiction, as Ferens and his wife are Pennsylvania residents, and Deere is incorporated in Delaware with its principal place of business in Illinois.

Not to be deprived of a tort action, the Ferenses in the same year filed a second diversity suit against Deere in the United States District Court for the Southern District of Mississippi, alleging negligence and products liability. Diversity jurisdiction and venue were proper. The Ferenses sued Deere in the District Court in Mississippi because they knew that, under *Klaxon Co. v. Stentor Electric Mfg. Co.*, 313 U.S. 487, 496 (1941), the federal court in the exercise of diversity jurisdiction must apply the same choice-of-law rules that Mississippi state courts would apply if they were deciding the case. A Mississippi court would rule that Pennsylvania substantive law controls the personal injury claim but that Mississippi's own law governs the limitation period.

Although Mississippi has a borrowing statute which, on its face, would seem to enable its courts to apply statutes of limitations from other jurisdictions, the State Supreme Court has said that the borrowing statute "only applies where a nonresident [defendant] in whose favor the statute has accrued afterwards moves into this state." *Louisiana & Mississippi R. Transfer Co. v. Long*, 159 Miss. 654, 667 (1930). The borrowing statute would not apply to the Ferenses' action because, as the parties agree, Deere was a corporate resident of Mississippi before the cause of action accrued. The Mississippi courts, as a result, would apply Mississippi's 6-year statute of limitations to the tort claim arising under Pennsylvania law and the tort action would not be time barred under the Mississippi statute.

The issue now before us arose when the Ferenses took their forum shopping a step further: having chosen the federal court in Mississippi to take advantage of the State's limitations period, they next moved, under § 1404(a), to transfer the action to the federal court in Pennsylvania on the ground that Pennsylvania was a more convenient forum. The Ferenses acted on the assumption that, after the transfer, the choice-of-law rules in the Mississippi forum, including a rule requiring application of the Mississippi statute of limitations, would continue to govern the suit.

Deere put up no opposition, and the District Court in Mississippi granted the § 1404(a) motion. The court accepted the Ferenses' arguments that they resided in Pennsylvania; that the accident occurred there; that the claim had no connection to Mississippi; that a substantial number of witnesses resided in the Western District of Pennsylvania but none resided in Mississippi; that most of the documentary evidence was located in the Western District of Pennsylvania but none was located in Mississippi; and that the warranty action pending in the Western District of Pennsylvania presented common questions of law and fact.

The District Court in Pennsylvania consolidated the transferred tort action with the Ferenses' pending warranty action but declined to honor the Mississippi statute of limitations as the District Court in Mississippi would have done. It ruled instead that, because the

Ferenses had moved for transfer as plaintiffs, the rule in *Van Dusen* did not apply. Invoking the 2-year limitations period set by Pennsylvania law, the District Court dismissed their tort action.

The Court of Appeals for the Third Circuit affirmed, but not, at first, on grounds that the Ferenses had lost their entitlement to Mississippi choice-of-law rules by invoking § 1404(a). The Court of Appeals relied at the outset on the separate theory that applying Mississippi's statute of limitations would violate due process because Mississippi had no legitimate interest in the case. We vacated this decision and remanded in light of *Sun Oil Co. v. Wortman*, 486 U.S. 717 (1988), in which we held that a State may choose to apply its own statute of limitations to claims governed by the substantive laws of another State without violating either the Full Faith and Credit Clause or the Due Process Clause. On remand, the Court of Appeals again affirmed, this time confronting the *Van Dusen* question and ruling that a transferor court's choice-of-law rules do not apply after a transfer under § 1404(a) on a motion by a plaintiff. We granted certiorari.

II

Section 1404(a) states only that a district court may transfer venue for the convenience of the parties and witnesses when in the interest of justice. It says nothing about choice of law and nothing about affording plaintiffs different treatment from defendants. We touched upon these issues in *Van Dusen*, but left open the question presented in this case. In *Van Dusen*, an airplane flying from Boston to Philadelphia crashed into Boston Harbor soon after takeoff. The personal representatives of the accident victims brought more than 100 actions in the District Court for the District of Massachusetts and more than 40 actions in the District Court for the Eastern District of Pennsylvania. When the defendants moved to transfer the actions brought in Pennsylvania to the federal court in Massachusetts, a number of the Pennsylvania plaintiffs objected because they lacked capacity under Massachusetts law to sue as representatives of the decedents. The plaintiffs also averred that the transfer would deprive them of the benefits of Pennsylvania's choice-of-law rules because the transferee forum would apply to their wrongful-death claims a different substantive rule. The plaintiffs obtained from the Court of Appeals a writ of mandamus ordering the District Court to vacate the transfer.

We reversed. After considering issues not related to the present dispute, we held that the Court of Appeals erred in its assumption that Massachusetts law would govern the action following transfer. The legislative history of § 1404(a) showed that Congress had enacted the statute because broad venue provisions in federal Acts often resulted in inconvenient forums and that Congress had decided to respond to this problem by permitting transfer to a convenient federal court under § 1404(a). We said:

This legislative background supports the view that § 1404(a) was not designed to narrow the plaintiff's venue privilege or to defeat the state-law advantages that might accrue from the exercise of this venue privilege but rather the provision was simply to counteract the inconveniences that flowed from the venue statutes by permitting transfer to a convenient federal court. The legislative history of § 1404(a) certainly does not justify the rather startling conclusion that one might "get a change of a law as a bonus for a change of venue." Indeed, an interpretation accepting such a rule would go far to frustrate the remedial purposes of § 1404(a). If a change in the law were in the offing, the parties might well regard the section primarily as a forum-shopping instrument. And, more importantly, courts would at least be reluctant to grant transfers, despite considerations of convenience, if to do so might conceivably prejudice the claim of a plaintiff who initially selected a permissible forum. We believe, therefore, that both the history and purposes of § 1404(a) indicate that it should be regarded as a federal judicial housekeeping measure, dealing with the placement of litigation in the federal courts and generally intended, on the basis of convenience and fairness, simply to authorize a change of courtrooms." *Id.*, at 635–637.

We thus held that the law applicable to a diversity case does not change upon a transfer initiated by a defendant.

III

The quoted part of *Van Dusen* reveals three independent reasons for our decision. First, § 1404(a) should not deprive parties of state-law advantages that exist absent diversity jurisdiction. Second, § 1404(a) should not create or multiply opportunities for forum shopping. Third, the decision to transfer venue under § 1404(a) should turn on considerations of convenience and the interest of justice rather than on the possible prejudice resulting from a change of law. Although commentators have questioned whether the scant legislative history of § 1404(a) compels reliance on these three policies, we find it prudent to consider them in deciding whether the rule in *Van Dusen* applies to transfers initiated by plaintiffs. We decide that, in addition to other considerations, these policies require a transferee forum to apply the law of the transferor court, regardless of who initiates the transfer. A transfer under § 1404(a), in other words, does not change the law applicable to a diversity case.

A

The policy that § 1404(a) should not deprive parties of state-law advantages, although perhaps discernible in the legislative history, has its real foundation in *Erie R. Co. v. Tompkins*, 304 U.S. 64 (1938). The *Erie* rule remains a vital expression of the federal system and the concomitant integrity of the separate States. We explained *Erie* in *Guaranty Trust Co. v. York*, 326 U.S. 99, 109, (1945), as follows:

> In essence, the intent of [the *Erie*] decision was to insure that, in all cases where a federal court is exercising jurisdiction solely because of the diversity of citizenship of the parties, the outcome of the litigation in the federal court should be substantially the same, so far as legal rules determine the outcome of a litigation, as it would be if tried in a State court. The nub of the policy that underlies *Erie R. Co. v. Tompkins* is that for the same transaction the accident of a suit by a non-resident litigant in a federal court instead of in a State court a block away should not lead to a substantially different result.

In *Hanna v. Plumer*, 380 U.S. 460, 473 (1965), we held that Congress has the power to prescribe procedural rules that differ from state-law rules even at the expense of altering the outcome of litigation. This case does not involve a conflict. As in *Van Dusen*, our interpretation of § 1404(a) is in full accord with the *Erie* rule.

The *Erie* policy had a clear implication for *Van Dusen*. The existence of diversity jurisdiction gave the defendants the opportunity to make a motion to transfer venue under § 1404(a), and if the applicable law were to change after transfer, the plaintiff's venue privilege and resulting state-law advantages could be defeated at the defendant's option. To allow the transfer and at the same time preserve the plaintiff's state-law advantages, we held that the choice-of-law rules should not change following a transfer initiated by a defendant.

Transfers initiated by a plaintiff involve some different considerations, but lead to the same result. Applying the transferor law, of course, will not deprive the plaintiff of any state-law advantages. A defendant, in one sense, also will lose no legal advantage if the transferor law controls after a transfer initiated by the plaintiff; the same law, after all, would have applied if the plaintiff had not made the motion. In another sense, however, a defendant may lose a nonlegal advantage. Deere, for example, would lose whatever advantage inheres in not having to litigate in Pennsylvania, or, put another way, in forcing the Ferenses to litigate in Mississippi or not at all.

We, nonetheless, find the advantage that the defendant loses slight. A plaintiff always can sue in the favorable state court or sue in diversity and not seek a transfer. By asking for application of the Mississippi statute of limitations following a transfer to Pennsylvania on grounds of convenience, the Ferenses are seeking to deprive Deere only of the advantage of using against them the inconvenience of litigating in Mississippi. The text of § 1404(a) may not say anything about choice of law, but we think it not the purpose of the section to protect a party's ability to use inconvenience as a shield to discourage or hinder litigation otherwise proper. The section exists to eliminate inconvenience without altering permissible choices under the venue statutes. This interpretation should come as little surprise. As in our previous cases, we think that "[t]o construe § 1404(a) this way merely carries out its design to protect litigants, witnesses and the public against unnecessary inconvenience and expense, not to provide a shelter for ... proceedings in costly and inconvenient forums." *Continental Grain Co. v. Barge FBL*, 364 U.S. 19, 27 (1960). By creating an opportunity to have venue transferred between courts in different States on the basis of convenience, an option that does not exist absent federal jurisdiction, Congress, with respect to diversity, retained the *Erie* policy while diminishing the incidents of inconvenience.

Applying the transferee law, by contrast, would undermine the *Erie* rule in a serious way. It would mean that initiating a transfer under § 1404(a) changes the state law applicable to a diversity case. We have held, in an isolated circumstance, that § 1404(a) may pre-empt state law. *See Stewart Organization, Inc. v. Ricoh Corp.*, 487 U.S. 22 (1988) (holding that federal law determines the validity of a forum selection clause). In general, however, we have seen § 1404(a) as a housekeeping measure that should not alter the state law governing a case under *Erie*. The Mississippi statute of limitations, which everyone agrees would have applied if the Ferenses had not moved for a transfer, should continue to apply in this case.

In any event, defendants in the position of Deere would not fare much better if we required application of the transferee law instead of the transferor law. True, if the transferee law were to apply, some plaintiffs would not sue these defendants for fear that they would have no choice but to litigate in an inconvenient forum. But applying the transferee law would not discourage all plaintiffs from suing. Some plaintiffs would prefer to litigate in an inconvenient forum with favorable law than to litigate in a convenient forum with unfavorable law or not to litigate at all. The Ferenses, no doubt, would have abided by their initial choice of the District Court in Mississippi had they known that the District Court in Pennsylvania would dismiss their action. If we were to rule for Deere in this case, we would accomplish little more than discouraging the occasional motions by plaintiffs to transfer inconvenient cases. Other plaintiffs would sue in an inconvenient forum with the expectation that the defendants themselves would seek transfer to a convenient forum, resulting in application of the transferor law under *Van Dusen*. In this case, for example, Deere might have moved for a transfer if the Ferenses had not.

B

Van Dusen also sought to fashion a rule that would not create opportunities for forum shopping. Some commentators have seen this policy as the most important rationale of *Van Dusen*, but few attempt to explain the harm of forum shopping when the plaintiff initiates a transfer. An opportunity for forum shopping exists whenever a party has a choice of forums that will apply different laws. The *Van Dusen* policy against forum shopping simply requires us to interpret § 1404(a) in a way that does not create an opportunity for obtaining a more favorable law by selecting a forum through a transfer of venue. In the *Van Dusen* case itself, this meant that we could not allow defendants to use a transfer to change the law.

No interpretation of § 1404(a), however, will create comparable opportunities for forum shopping by a plaintiff because, even without § 1404(a), a plaintiff already has the option of shopping for a forum with the most favorable law. The Ferenses, for example, had an opportunity for forum shopping in the state courts because both the Mississippi and Pennsylvania courts had jurisdiction and because they each would have applied a different statute of limitations. Diversity jurisdiction did not eliminate these forum shopping opportunities; instead, under *Erie*, the federal courts had to replicate them. Applying the transferor law would not give a plaintiff an opportunity to use a transfer to obtain a law that he could not obtain through his initial forum selection. If it does make selection of the most favorable law more convenient, it does no more than recognize a forum shopping choice that already exists. This fact does not require us to apply the transferee law. Section 1404(a), to reiterate, exists to make venue convenient and should not allow the defendant to use inconvenience to discourage plaintiffs from exercising the opportunities that they already have.

Applying the transferee law, by contrast, might create opportunities for forum shopping in an indirect way. The advantage to Mississippi's personal injury lawyers that resulted from the State's then applicable 6-year statute of limitations has not escaped us; Mississippi's long limitation period no doubt drew plaintiffs to the State. Although *Sun Oil* held that the federal courts have little interest in a State's decision to create a long statute of limitations or to apply its statute of limitations to claims governed by foreign law, we should recognize the consequences of our interpretation of § 1404(a). Applying the transferee law, to the extent that it discourages plaintiff-initiated transfers, might give States incentives to enact similar laws to bring in out-of-state business that would not be moved at the instance of the plaintiff.

C

Van Dusen also made clear that the decision to transfer venue under § 1404(a) should turn on considerations of convenience rather than on the possibility of prejudice resulting from a change in the applicable law. See 376 U.S., at 636; *Piper Aircraft Co. v. Reyno*, 454 U.S. 235, 253–254, and n. 20 (1981). We reasoned in *Van Dusen* that, if the law changed following a transfer initiated by the defendant, a district court "would at least be reluctant to grant transfers, despite considerations of convenience, if to do so might conceivably prejudice the claim of a plaintiff." 376 U.S., at 636. The court, to determine the prejudice, might have to make an elaborate survey of the law, including statutes of limitations, burdens of proof, presumptions, and the like. This would turn what is supposed to be a statute for convenience of the courts into one expending extensive judicial time and resources. Because this difficult task is contrary to the purpose of the statute, in *Van Dusen* we made it unnecessary by ruling that a transfer of venue by the defendant does not result in a change of law. This same policy requires application of the transferor law when a plaintiff initiates a transfer.

If the law were to change following a transfer initiated by a plaintiff, a district court in a similar fashion would be at least reluctant to grant a transfer that would prejudice the defendant. Hardship might occur because plaintiffs may find as many opportunities to exploit application of the transferee law as they would find opportunities for exploiting application of the transferor law. If the transferee law were to apply, moreover, the plaintiff simply would not move to transfer unless the benefits of convenience outweighed the loss of favorable law.

Some might think that a plaintiff should pay the price for choosing an inconvenient forum by being put to a choice of law versus forum. But this assumes that § 1404(a) is for the benefit only of the moving party. By the statute's own terms, it is not. Section 1404(a) also exists for the benefit of the witnesses and the interest of justice, which must include the convenience of the court. Litigation in an inconvenient forum does not harm the plaintiff alone. As Justice Jackson said:

> Administrative difficulties follow for courts when litigation is piled up in congested centers instead of being handled at its origin. Jury duty is a burden that ought not to be imposed upon the people of a community which has no relation to the litigation. In cases which touch the affairs of many persons, there is reason for holding the trial in their view and reach rather than in remote parts of the country where they can learn of it by report only. There is a local interest in having localized controversies decided at home. There is an appropriateness too, in having the trial of a diversity case in a forum that is at home with the state law that must govern the case, rather than having a court in some other forum untangle problems in conflicts of laws, and in law foreign to itself. *Gulf Oil Corp. v. Gilbert*, 330 U.S. 501, 508–509 (1947).

The desire to take a punitive view of the plaintiff's actions should not obscure the systemic costs of litigating in an inconvenient place.

D

This case involves some considerations to which we perhaps did not give sufficient attention in *Van Dusen*. Foresight and judicial economy now seem to favor the simple rule that the law does not change following a transfer of venue under § 1404(a). Affording transfers initiated by plaintiffs different treatment from transfers initiated by defendants may seem quite workable in this case, but the simplicity is an illusion. If we were to hold that the transferee law applies following a § 1404(a) motion by a plaintiff, cases such as this would not arise in the future. Although applying the transferee law, no doubt, would catch the Ferenses by surprise, in the future no plaintiffs in their position would move for a change of venue.

Other cases, however, would produce undesirable complications. The rule would leave unclear which law should apply when both a defendant and a plaintiff move for a transfer of venue or when the court transfers venue on its own motion. The rule also might require variation in certain situations, such as when the plaintiff moves for a transfer following a removal from state court by the defendant, or when only one of several plaintiffs requests the transfer, or when circumstances change through no fault of the plaintiff making a once convenient forum inconvenient. True, we could reserve any consideration of these questions for a later day. But we have a duty, in deciding this case, to consider whether our decision will create litigation and uncertainty. On the basis of these considerations, we again conclude that the transferor law should apply regardless of who makes the § 1404(a) motion.

IV

Some may object that a district court in Pennsylvania should not have to apply a Mississippi statute of limitations to a Pennsylvania cause of action. This point, although understandable, should have little to do with the outcome of this case. Congress gave the Ferenses the power to seek a transfer in § 1404(a), and our decision in *Van Dusen* already could require a district court in Pennsylvania to apply the Mississippi statute of limitations to Pennsylvania claims. Our rule may seem too generous because it allows the Ferenses to have both their choice of law and their choice of forum, or even to reward the Ferenses for conduct that seems manipulative. We nonetheless see no alternative rule that would produce a more acceptable result. Deciding that the transferee law should apply, in effect, would tell the Ferenses that they should have continued to litigate their warranty action in Pennsylvania and their tort action in Mississippi. Some might find this preferable, but we do not. We have made quite clear that "[t]o permit a situation in which two cases involving precisely the same issues are simultaneously pending in different District Courts leads to the wastefulness of time, energy and money that § 1404(a) was designed to prevent." *Continental Grain*, 364 U.S., at 26.

From a substantive standpoint, two further objections give us pause but do not persuade us to change our rule. First, one might ask why we require the Ferenses to file in the District Court in Mississippi at all. Efficiency might seem to dictate a rule allowing plaintiffs in the Ferenses' position not to file in an inconvenient forum and then to return to a convenient forum though a transfer of venue, but instead simply to file in the convenient forum and ask for the law of the inconvenient forum to apply. Although our rule may invoke certain formality, one must remember that § 1404(a) does not provide for an automatic transfer of venue. The section, instead, permits a transfer only when convenient and "in the interest of justice." Plaintiffs in the position of the Ferenses must go to the distant forum because they have no guarantee, until the court there examines the facts, that they may obtain a transfer. No one has contested the justice of transferring this particular case, but the option remains open to defendants in future cases. Although a court cannot ignore the systemic costs of inconvenience, it may consider the course that the litigation already has taken in determining the interest of justice.

Second, one might contend that, because no per se rule requiring a court to apply either the transferor law or the transferee law will seem appropriate in all circumstances, we should develop more sophisticated federal choice-of-law rules for diversity actions involving transfers. To a large extent, however, state conflicts-of-law rules already ensure that appropriate laws will apply to diversity cases. Federal law, as a general matter, does not interfere with these rules. In addition, even if more elaborate federal choice-of-law rules would not run afoul of *Klaxon* and *Erie*, we believe that applying the law of the transferor forum effects the appropriate balance between fairness and simplicity.

For the foregoing reasons, we conclude that Mississippi's statute of limitations should govern the Ferenses' action. We reverse and remand for proceedings consistent with this opinion.

It is so ordered.

■ JUSTICE SCALIA, with whom JUSTICE BRENNAN, JUSTICE MARSHALL, and JUSTICE BLACKMUN join, dissenting.

Plaintiffs, having filed this diversity action in Federal District Court in Mississippi, successfully moved for a transfer of venue to the District Court in Pennsylvania where their warranty action was then pending. The question we must decide is which State's choice-of-law principles will govern the case now that it is to be litigated in that court.

The Rules of Decision Act, first placed in the Judicial Code by the Judiciary Act of 1789, currently provides:

> The laws of the several states, except where the Constitution or treaties of the United States or Acts of Congress otherwise require or provide, shall be regarded as rules of decision in civil actions in the courts of the United States, in cases where they apply." 28 U.S.C. 1652 (1982 ed.).

In *Erie R. Co. v. Tompkins*, 304 U.S. 64 (1938), we held that the Act requires a federal court to apply, in diversity cases, the law of the State in which it sits, both statutory law and common law established by the courts. Three years later, in *Klaxon Co. v. Stentor Electric Mfg. Co.*, 313

U.S. 487, 494 (1941), we considered "whether in diversity cases the federal courts must follow conflict of laws rules prevailing in the states in which they sit." We answered the question in the affirmative, reasoning that, were the rule otherwise, "the accident of diversity of citizenship would constantly disturb equal administration of justice in coordinate state and federal courts sitting side by side," a state of affairs that "would do violence to the principle of uniformity within a state, upon which the *Tompkins* decision is based." *Id.*, at 496. Although the venue provision of § 1404(a) was enacted after *Klaxon*, we have repeatedly reaffirmed *Klaxon* since then.

The question we must answer today is whether 28 U.S.C. § 1404(a) and the policies underlying *Klaxon*—namely, uniformity within a State and the avoidance of forum shopping—produce a result different from *Klaxon* when the suit in question was not filed in the federal court initially, but was transferred there under § 1404(a) on plaintiff's motion. In *Van Dusen v. Barrack*, 376 U.S. 612 (1964), we held that a result different from *Klaxon* is produced when a suit has been transferred under § 1404(a) on defendant's motion. Our reasons were two. First, we thought it highly unlikely that Congress, in enacting § 1404(a), meant to provide defendants with a device by which to manipulate the substantive rules that would be applied. That conclusion rested upon the fact that the law grants the plaintiff the advantage of choosing the venue in which his action will be tried, with whatever state-law advantages accompany that choice. A defensive use of § 1404(a) in order to deprive the plaintiff of this "venue privilege" would allow the defendant to " 'get a change of law as a bonus for a change of venue,' " and would permit the defendant to engage in forum shopping among States, a privilege that the *Klaxon* regime reserved for plaintiffs. Second, we concluded that the policies of *Erie* and *Klaxon* would be undermined by application of the transferee court's choice-of-law principles in the case of a defendant-initiated transfer, because then "the 'accident' of federal diversity jurisdiction" would enable the defendant "to utilize a transfer to achieve a result in federal court which could not have been achieved in the courts of the State where the action was filed." The goal of *Erie* and *Klaxon*, we reasoned, was to prevent "forum shopping" as between state and federal systems; the plaintiff makes a choice of forum law by filing the complaint, and that choice must be honored in federal court, just as it would have been honored in state court, where the defendant would not have been able to transfer the case to another State.

We left open in *Van Dusen* the question presented today, viz., whether "the same considerations would govern" if a plaintiff sought a § 1404(a) transfer. In my view, neither of those considerations is served—and indeed both are positively defeated—by a departure from *Klaxon* in that context. First, just as it is unlikely that Congress, in enacting § 1404(a), meant to provide the defendant with a vehicle by which to manipulate in his favor the substantive law to be applied in a diversity case, so too is it unlikely that Congress meant to provide the plaintiff with a vehicle by which to appropriate the law of a distant and inconvenient forum in which he does not intend to litigate, and to carry that prize back to the State in which he wishes to try the case. Second, application of the transferor court's law in this context would encourage forum shopping between federal and state courts in the same jurisdiction on the basis of differential substantive law. It is true, of course, that the plaintiffs here did not select the Mississippi federal court in preference to the Mississippi state courts because of any differential substantive law; the former, like the latter, would have applied Mississippi choice-of-law rules and thus the Mississippi statute of limitations. But one must be blind to reality to say that it is the Mississippi federal court in which these plaintiffs have chosen to sue. That was merely a way station en route to suit in the Pennsylvania federal court. The plaintiffs were seeking to achieve exactly what *Klaxon* was designed to prevent: the use of a Pennsylvania federal court instead of a Pennsylvania state court in order to obtain application of a different substantive law. Our decision in *Van Dusen* compromised "the principle of uniformity within a state," *Klaxon, supra*, 313 U.S., at 496, only in the abstract, but today's decision compromises it precisely in the respect that matters—i.e., insofar as it bears upon the plaintiff's choice between a state and a federal forum. The significant federal judicial policy expressed in *Erie* and *Klaxon* is reduced to a laughingstock if it can so readily be evaded through filing-and-transfer.

* * *

The Court expresses concern that if normal *Erie-Klaxon* principles were applied a district judge might be reluctant to order a transfer, even when faced with the prospect of a trial that would be manifestly inconvenient to the parties, for fear that in doing so he would be ordering what is tantamount to a dismissal on the merits. But where the plaintiff himself has moved for a transfer, surely the principle of volenti non fit injuria suffices to allay that concern. The Court asserts that in some cases it is the defendant who will be prejudiced by a transfer-induced change in the applicable law. That seems likely to be quite rare, since it assumes that the plaintiff has gone to the trouble of bringing the suit in a less convenient forum, where the law is less favorable to him. But where the defendant is disadvantaged by a plaintiff-initiated transfer, I do not see how it can reasonably be said that he has been "prejudiced," since the plaintiff could have brought the suit in the "plaintiff's-law forum" with the law more favorable to him (and the more convenient forum) in the first place. Prejudice to the defendant, it seems to me, occurs only when the plaintiff is enabled to have his cake and eat it too—to litigate in the more convenient forum that he desires, but with the law of the distant forum that he desires.

The Court suggests that applying the choice-of-law rules of the forum court to a transferred case ignores the interest of the federal courts themselves in avoiding the "systemic costs of litigating in an inconvenient place," citing Justice Jackson's eloquent remarks on that subject in *Gulf Oil Corp. v. Gilbert*, 330 U.S. 501, 508–509 (1947). The point, apparently, is that these systemic costs will increase because the change in law attendant to transfer will not only deter the plaintiff from moving to transfer but will also deter the court from ordering sua sponte a transfer that will harm the plaintiff's case. Justice Jackson's remarks were addressed, however, not to the operation of § 1404(a), but to "those rather rare cases where the doctrine [of forum non conveniens] should be applied." 330 U.S., at 509. Where the systemic costs are that severe, transfer ordinarily will occur whether the plaintiff moves for it or not; the district judge can be expected to order it sua sponte. I do not think that the prospect of depriving the plaintiff of favorable law will any more deter a district judge from transferring[1] than it would have deterred a district judge, under the prior regime, from ordering a dismissal sua sponte pursuant to the doctrine of forum non conveniens. In fact the deterrence to sua sponte transfer will be considerably less, since transfer involves no risk of statute-of-limitations bars to refiling.

Thus, it seems to me that a proper calculation of systemic costs would go as follows: Saved by the Court's rule will be the incremental cost of trying in forums that are inconvenient (but not so inconvenient as to prompt the court's sua sponte transfer) those suits that are now filed in such forums for choice-of-law purposes. But incurred by the Court's rule will be the costs of considering and effecting transfer, not only in those suits but in the indeterminate number of additional suits that will be filed in inconvenient forums now that filing-and-transfer is an approved form of shopping for law; plus the costs attending the necessity for transferee courts to figure out the choice-of-law rules (and probably the substantive law) of distant States much more often than our *Van Dusen* decision would require. It should be noted that the file-and-transfer ploy sanctioned by the Court today will be available not merely to achieve the relatively rare (and generally unneeded) benefit of a longer statute of limitations, but also to bring home to the desired state of litigation all sorts of favorable choice-of-law rules regarding substantive liability—in an era when the diversity among the States in choice-of-law principles has become kaleidoscopic.

The Court points out, apparently to deprecate the prospect that filing-and-transfer will become a regular litigation strategy, that there

---

[1] The prospective transferor court would not be deterred at all, of course, if we simply extended the *Van Dusen* rule to court-initiated transfers. In my view that would be inappropriate, however, since court-initiated transfer, like plaintiff-initiated transfer, does not confer upon the defendant the advantage of forum shopping for law, *Van Dusen v. Barrack*, 376 U.S. 612, 636, (1964), and does not enable the defendant "to utilize a transfer to achieve a result in federal court which could not have been achieved in the courts of the State where the action was filed," *id.*, at 638.

is "no guarantee" that a plaintiff will be accorded a transfer; that while "[n]o one has contested the justice of transferring this particular case," that option "remains open to defendants in future cases"; and that "[a]lthough a court cannot ignore the systemic costs of inconvenience, it may consider the course that the litigation already has taken in determining the interest of justice." I am not sure what this means—except that it plainly does not mean what it must mean to foreclose the filing-and-transfer option, namely, that transfer can be denied because the plaintiff was law shopping. The whole theory of the Court's opinion is that it is not in accord with the policy of § 1404(a) to deprive the plaintiff of the "state-law advantages" to which his "venue privilege" entitles him. The Court explicitly repudiates "[t]he desire to take a punitive view of the plaintiff's actions," and to make him "pay the price for choosing an inconvenient forum by being put to a choice of law versus forum." Thus, all the Court is saying by its "no guarantee" language is that the plaintiff must be careful to choose a really inconvenient forum if he wants to be sure about getting a transfer. That will often not be difficult. In sum, it seems to me quite likely that today's decision will cost the federal courts more time than it will save them.

Thus, even as an exercise in giving the most extensive possible scope to the policies of § 1404(a), the Court's opinion seems to me unsuccessful. But as I indicated by beginning this opinion with the Rules of Decision Act, that should not be the object of the exercise at all. The Court and I reach different results largely because we approach the question from different directions. For the Court, this case involves an "interpretation of § 1404(a)," and the central issue is whether *Klaxon* stands in the way of the policies of that statute. For me, the case involves an interpretation of the Rules of Decision Act, and the central issue is whether § 1404(a) alters the "principle of uniformity within a state" which *Klaxon* says that Act embodies. I think my approach preferable, not only because the Rules of Decision Act does, and § 1404(a) does not, address the specific subject of which law to apply, but also because, as the Court acknowledges, our jurisprudence under that statute is "a vital expression of the federal system and the concomitant integrity of the separate States." To ask, as in effect the Court does, whether *Erie* gets in the way of § 1404(a), rather than whether § 1404(a) requires adjustment of *Erie*, seems to me the expression of a mistaken sense of priorities.

For the foregoing reasons, I respectfully dissent.

COMMENTS AND QUESTIONS CONCERNING
FERENS V. JOHN DEERE CO.

1.   In the first sentence of his opinion, Justice Kennedy quotes 28 U.S.C. § 1404(a) as it read at the time of the *Ferens* decision. As a result of

the Federal Courts Jurisdiction and Venue Clarification Act of 2011, Pub. L. 112–63, 125 Stat. 758 (2011), Section 1404(a) now provides:

> For the convenience of the parties and witnesses, in the interest of justice, a district court may transfer any civil action to any other district or division where it might have been brought *or to any district or division to which all parties have consented.* (Emphasis added.)

The House of Representatives report explained this amendment as follows:

> In addition to the existing authority to transfer a civil action to a district or division ["]where it might have been brought," the proposed amendment to subsection 1404(a) would permit an action to be transferred to any district or division to which all parties have consented, even if the action could not have been brought in that district or division originally. Under the proposed amendment, such transfers would only be possible where all parties agreed and only if the court found it to be for the convenience of the parties and witnesses and in the interest of justice.

H.R. Rep. No. 112–10, at 24 (2011).

2.   Which is the more significant litigation advantage in this case—applying the Mississippi statute of limitations or being able to litigate the action in Pennsylvania? Are the Ferenses "seeking to deprive Deere only of the advantage of using against them the inconvenience of litigating in Mississippi"? Is more than party convenience at issue? *See* Why The Forum Matters, Section E, *infra* p. 354.

3.   Is the motion to transfer this action to Pennsylvania (where the Ferenses lived and the accident occurred) a more problematic example of forum-shopping than filing the action initially in Mississippi (which apparently had no connection with the action)? How could the action be filed in Mississippi in the first instance?

4.   Does *Ferens* preclude future arguments that, on the facts of a particular case, it would not be "in the interest of justice" for the purposes of Section 1404(a) to permit a plaintiff to file an action in one district and then move to transfer the action to another district? The Supreme Court "will not apply the *Van Dusen* rule when a transfer stems from enforcement of a forum-selection clause: The court in the contractually selected venue should not apply the law of the transferor venue to which the parties waived their right [through their contractual forum selection clause]." *Atl. Marine Const. Co. v. U.S. Dist. Court for W. Dist. of Texas*, 134 S. Ct. 568, 583 (2013).

5.   The *Erie Railroad* doctrine is discussed in Chapter 5, *infra.* The aspect of that doctrine most relevant to *Ferens* provides that a federal district court hearing a diversity action must apply the same choice-of-law rules as would a state court sitting in the same state. *Klaxton Co. v. Stentor Electric Mfg. Co.*, 313 U.S. 487 (1941). A state court in Mississippi would apply Mississippi's choice of law rule that, in turn, required the application

of Mississippi's six-year statute of limitations. A federal district court in Mississippi also must apply that six-year limitations period. *Erie* thus creates uniformity between state courts and federal courts hearing diversity actions in the same state ("vertical uniformity"), which may result in less uniformity among different federal courts ("horizontal uniformity").

6.   In his dissent Justice Scalia asserts: "Prejudice to the defendant, it seems to me, occurs only when the plaintiff is enabled to have his cake and eat it too—to litigate in the more convenient forum that he desires, but with the law of the distant forum that he desires." Do you agree with Justice Scalia? Would there be a cost to not permitting plaintiffs "to litigate * * * with the law of the distant forum that he desires" in the transferee forum? Professor Kermit Roosevelt has observed, "We are used to the idea that plaintiffs go to a forum in order to get its law, but we are less used to the idea that they can order it for takeout." "Choice of Law in Federal Courts: From *Erie* and *Klaxon* to CAFA and *Shady Grove*," 106 *Nw.U.L.Rev.* 1, 29 (2012).

7.   Justice Scalia is concerned that "today's decision will cost the federal courts more time than it will save them." Would there be more or less forum shopping if parties were to " ' "get a change of law as a bonus for a change of venue" ' "? 494 U.S. at 522, quoting *Van Dusen v. Barrack*, 376 U.S. 612, 636 (1964), quoting *Wells v. Simonds Abrasive Co.*, 345 U.S. 514, 522 (1953) (Jackson, J., dissenting). Moreover, is the purpose of the venue statutes to save judicial time—or to site actions in districts that are most convenient for the parties, their witnesses, and the court?

E. WHY THE FORUM MATTERS

There are many reasons why some possible judicial forums may be better than others.[31] The most important factors and advantages will depend on the circumstances of a given case. Some of the factors that are generally worth considering include:

---

[31] Justice Marshall in his plurality opinion in *Piper Aircraft Co. v. Reyno*, listed some of the major reasons why a foreign plaintiff might prefer to bring suit in the United States:

> First, all but 6 of the 50 American States—Delaware, Massachusetts, Michigan, North Carolina, Virginia, and Wyoming—offer strict liability. Rules roughly equivalent to American strict liability are effective in France, Belgium, and Luxembourg. West Germany and Japan have a strict liability statute for pharmaceuticals. However, strict liability remains primarily an American innovation. Second, the tort plaintiff may choose, at least potentially, from among 50 jurisdictions if he decides to file suit in the United States. Each of these jurisdictions applies its own set of malleable choice-of-law rules. Third, jury trials are almost always available in the United States, while they are never provided in civil law jurisdictions. Even in the United Kingdom, most civil actions are not tried before a jury. Fourth, unlike most foreign jurisdictions, American courts allow contingent attorney's fees, and do not tax losing parties with their opponents' attorney's fees. Fifth, discovery is more extensive in American than in foreign courts.

454 U.S. 235, 252 (1981). While there will not be as much variation among courts in this country as between courts in this country and many foreign courts, differences concerning some of these variables may make one domestic court significantly more attractive than others. *See* R. Casad, *Jurisdiction and Forum Selection* (2d ed. 2005); Rothschild, "Forum Shopping," *Litigation*, Spring 1998, at 40.

- Likely judges (elected vs. appointed; general quality of the bench; general background, outlook, and experience of different benches);

- Likely jury pool (federal jurors are typically drawn from a larger geographic area, while state jurors may be drawn from a single large city);

- Likely delay in pretrial and post-trial rulings and in getting a case to trial (judicial delay typically favors defendants, while plaintiffs usually are more likely to need a settlement or judgment sooner);

- Likely length of appellate process;

- Possibility of interlocutory appeal (not normally available in federal courts, but may be possible in state court);

- Law clerks and staff support for judges (federal judges have law clerks to help with legal research, many state trial judges do not);

- Different law (substantive, procedural, and evidentiary) that may apply in different forums (from one circuit to another within federal courts; between state and federal courts; or between different state courts);

- Convenience of the courts for client, attorneys, and witnesses; and

- Enforceability of judgment ultimately obtained.

Because the chances of success are more or less likely in different courts,[32] a significant part of lawyers' pretrial strategy is to ensure the most favorable forum for their clients and the least favorable forum for opposing parties. Not only do plaintiffs' lawyers research particular judges and jurisdictions, but defense counsel consider the possibility of removing cases from state to federal court, transferring actions within court systems, or filing a declaratory judgment to initiate the litigation and choose the initial forum.[33]

If parties are engaged in business dealings, their contract can include a forum selection clause to choose, in advance, the forum in which any disputes involving their contract will be resolved. The forum matters, and good lawyers will do their best—both during litigation and before a dispute ever arises—to ensure the most favorable forum for their clients.

---

[32] Justice Breyer in his concurrence in *J. McIntyre Machinery, Ltd. v. Nicastro*, 131 S.Ct. 2780, 2794 (2011), cited the following study: Dept. of Justice, Bureau of Justice Statistics Bulletin, *Tort Trials and Verdicts in Large Counties*, 2001, p. 11 (reporting percentage of plaintiff winners in tort trials among 46 populous counties, ranging from 17.9% (Worcester, Mass.) to 69.1% (Milwaukee, Wis.)).

[33] As was done by PepsiCo, Inc., in the *Leonard v. PepsiCo, Inc.* litigation. *See* 88 F.Supp. 2d 116, 120 (S.D.N.Y. 1999).

V. CONCLUSION

Even if a court has subject-matter jurisdiction, there also must be notice and service of process, personal jurisdiction, and venue before a court can consider a civil action. These prerequisites to suit must be met in each case, and they present different litigation possibilities in all cases. Taking creative advantage of these possibilities should enable the lawyer to gain the most favorable forum, and litigation result, for her client in each and every case.

VI. CHAPTER ASSESSMENT

A. Multiple-Choice Questions. Answer the following questions, reviewing the sections of the chapter noted in connection with each question.

1.   A Delaware citizen is driving across the country and decides to visit Missouri, in which state she has never been. In driving from St. Louis to Kansas City, she hits a pedestrian, injuring him badly. She therefore cancels the remainder of her trip and drives home to Delaware.

After learning about the accident through the media, the driver's lender, incorporated and with its principal place of business in Arkansas, brings a civil action against the driver in Missouri state court. This action seeks $100,000 in damages, the amount that the lender alleges the driver owes on a loan that the lender made to the driver.

Missouri's long-arm statute in part provides:

> Any person or firm, whether or not a citizen or resident of this state * * *, who in person or through an agent does any of the acts enumerated in this section, thereby submits such person * * * to the jurisdiction of the courts of this state as to any cause of action arising from the doing of any of such acts: [including] the commission of a tortious act within this state.

Is the driver subject to the jurisdiction of a Missouri state court in the lender's action pursuant to Missouri's long-arm statute?

Review Section III(A) and choose the best answer from the following choices:

(a) No, because the driver is not a citizen or resident of Missouri.

(b) No, because the cause of action asserted by the lender does not arise from the driver's actions within Missouri.

(c) Yes, because the driver has committed a tortious act within Missouri.

(d) Yes, because the driver utilized a Missouri highway and received other benefits from Missouri in her trip across that state.

2. A citizen of Missouri travels to South Carolina to attend a football game between the University of Missouri and the University of South Carolina. While at the game, the Missouri fan gets into a fight with a citizen of South Carolina. After the fight, the South Carolina fan disappears into the crowd.

Upon returning to Missouri, the Missourian files a tort action in Missouri state court against the South Carolinian. When the Missourian learns that the South Carolinian will be in Kansas City, Kansas, he asks some of his friends to meet the South Carolinian, throw him into a car, and drive him to Kansas City, Missouri. The friends do this, and, upon their arrival in Kansas City, Missouri, one of these individuals serves the South Carolinian with the summons and complaint from the Missouri state action.

The South Carolinian, who has never been to Missouri except for the time that he was served there, files a motion to dismiss the Missouri state-court action for lack of personal jurisdiction.

Should the court grant the motion to dismiss?

Review Section III(B)(2)(b) and choose the best answer from the following choices:

(a) Yes, because the South Carolinian has no minimum contacts with Missouri.

(b) Yes, because the South Carolinian was not voluntarily in Missouri when served.

(c) No, because the South Carolinian was served with process while within Missouri.

(d) No, because the South Carolinian reasonably should have foreseen that he would be sued in Missouri.

3. A manufacturer produces thermostats at its factory in Maine. It sells these thermostats to three other manufacturing companies in New Jersey, Pennsylvania, and Georgia. These three companies incorporate the thermostats into microwave ovens that they sell in the eastern United States. A consumer buys a microwave manufactured by one of the three companies from a department store in Delaware. The consumer then moves to California, soon after which the thermostat and microwave malfunction—resulting in a fire that destroys his California house.

The consumer files a civil action in California state court against the thermostat manufacturer, and the manufacturer is served at its Maine headquarters pursuant to the state long-arm statute (which extends to the limits of constitutional due process). The manufacturer files a motion to dismiss for lack of personal jurisdiction, attaching to it an affidavit stating that the thermostat is a new, unique product and the company is not aware that any of its thermostats (other than the one that allegedly malfunctioned) have been sold in, or otherwise reached, California.

Should the court grant the motion to dismiss?

Review Section III(B)(2)(e) and choose the best answer from the following choices:

(a) The court should grant the motion, because the manufacturer has no physical presence in California.

(b) The court should grant the motion, because the manufacturer did not purposefully avail itself of the California market.

(c) The court should deny the motion, because it was foreseeable that a thermostat might malfunction in California.

(d) The court should deny the motion, because California's long-arm statute extends to the limits of constitutional due process.

4.   An oil drilling company is incorporated in Delaware, but has no physical presence in that state. Its offices, other buildings, employees, oil fields, and drilling equipment are all in New Mexico.

A company employee, who is a citizen of Arizona, is seriously injured when one of the company's oil wells explodes. One of the many witnesses who were involved in the explosion and fire stated to the local media, "I can't believe that the company didn't take better care of that well. The well is visible from the corporate offices and all of the company's other structures, but no one knew how to stop the blaze."

The injured employee files a diversity action against the company in the United States District Court for the District of Delaware. The company, the only defendant in the action, responds to the complaint by filing a motion to transfer the action to the United States District Court for the District of New Mexico.

Should the court grant the motion to transfer?

Review Section IV(A) and (B) and choose the best answer from the following choices:

(a) Yes, because the convenience of the parties and witnesses and the interest of justice favors such a transfer.

(b) Yes, because venue is not proper in the District of Delaware.

(c) No, because the action was filed in a district court that does not have proper venue.

(d) No, because the court must respect the forum chosen by the plaintiff.

5.   Two Canadian terrorists plant a bomb on a Canadian plane flying from Toronto to Vancouver. The bomb detonates, the plane crashes, and over 100 lives are lost. The family of one of the passengers, a United States citizen who had lived in Miami, Florida, consults you about filing a civil action seeking damages against the terrorists in the

United States District Court for the Southern District of Florida. A state long-arm statute permits state courts to exercise personal jurisdiction over non-residents to the limits of the United States Constitution.

Should this civil action be filed in the United States District Court for the Southern District of Florida?

Review Section IV(A), (B), and (C) and choose the best answer from the following choices:

(a) Yes, because the long-arm statute permits the United States District Court for the Southern District of Florida to hear this suit even if the defendants have never visited Florida and have no minimum contacts with that state.

(b) Yes, because Federal Rule of Civil Procedure 4(k)(2) extends the jurisdiction of a federal district court to entertain state-law claims such as this.

(c) No, because there would not be proper venue in an action against the terrorists in the United States District Court for the Southern District of Florida.

(d) No, because, whether or not there is proper venue in the United States District Court for the Southern District of Florida, that court should transfer any case filed in that district to a court in Canada pursuant to either 28 U.S.C. §§ 1404 or 1406.

B. Essay Questions. To test your understanding of this chapter's material, outline or write an answer to the following questions.

1. Election Night Tricks?

Disc Discjockey hosts a local radio talk show in Manchester, New Hampshire. Although Disc would love to go big time, his show is produced in Manchester and only can be heard by a few thousand people in the area immediately surrounding Manchester.

People in Manchester are still talking about Disc's 2015 Halloween show. Among his guests on that show were Paulene LePue, a political activist from Portland, Maine, and Charles McCarthy, a Vermont mayor. The show was sponsored by Puritan Prunes, a California company that buys its prunes from local growers in the Western United States.

During the Halloween show, LePue sharply criticized Molly Maguire, a New Hampshire elected official, stating that "Molly symbolizes everything that's wrong with New Hampshire and she makes me glad I've never been to New Hampshire before tonight and that I'll be leaving New Hampshire immediately after this broadcast and returning to Maine." During this same broadcast McCarthy says, "It's Halloween tonight, a great time to play tricks on Democrats and their ilk." Randy Menace, a juvenile delinquent in Reno, Nevada, hears this statement on a special radio receiver that he has built from stolen car parts and, as a result, firebombs the headquarters of the Reno Democratic Party. Another unfortunate result of Disc's broadcast is that several people in and around Manchester order Puritan Prunes from the California headquarters of Puritan Prunes. The prunes shipped to these individuals had been purchased by Puritan from Farmer Jones of Provo, Utah and had been treated by Jones with an insecticide that made several people in Manchester quite ill.

(a) Assuming that it would have subject-matter jurisdiction under 28 U.S.C. § 1332, could the United States District Court for the District of New Hampshire entertain a slander action brought against LePue by Molly Maguire?

(b) Assuming that McCarthy has never been to Nevada and has no ties to Nevada other than those described in this question, would a state court in Nevada have personal jurisdiction over McCarthy in a lawsuit brought against him by the Reno Democratic Party?

(c) Assume that Farmer Jones has never been out of the state of Utah and sold the bad prunes to Puritan Prunes in Utah, knowing that Puritan markets prunes throughout the United States. Would Farmer Jones be subject to personal jurisdiction in New Hampshire state court in actions brought against him by the New Hampshire citizens who became sick after eating the prunes?

2.   Can We Get There from Here?

A Georgia doctor prescribes a drug for one of her patients, who is also a citizen of Georgia. The patient purchases the drug at a local pharmacy, and, soon after taking the drug, suffers serious brain injury. The drug was manufactured by a company that is incorporated in Delaware and has its corporate offices and manufacturing operations in New York.

The patient brings a products liability action seeking $10,000,000 from the company in state court in New Mexico. New Mexico is the tenth largest state market for the drug in question, with the company selling $10,000,000 of the drug in New Mexico. The company sells its drug through 50 state representatives in each of the 50 states, which representatives deal directly with the company's headquarters and manufacturing facilities in New York and with physicians in their individual states.

Pursuant to state rules modeled on the Federal Rules of Civil Procedure, the defendant drug company files a motion to (1) dismiss the New Mexico action because of lack of personal jurisdiction or, in the alternative, (2) transfer the action to the United States District Court for the Western District of New York (in which the company is headquartered and has its manufacturing facilities).

Should the court grant this motion in whole or in part?

CHAPTER 5

THE LAW APPLIED IN FEDERAL COURT: *"ERIE* CHOICES FOR THE FEDERAL JUDGE."

I. INTRODUCTION

Imagine that you have been retained by John Leonard, a citizen of Washington, who would like to file a civil action against PepsiCo, Inc., which is incorporated in North Carolina and has its principal place of business in New York. You and Mr. Leonard would like to assert claims for specific performance, contract breach, fraud, and violations of state laws prohibiting deceptive practices and false advertising. Because PepsiCo has a major national presence, it is likely that it will be subject to personal jurisdiction in several state courts (including North Carolina, where it is incorporated, New York, where it has its principal place of business, and Washington, the state in which John Leonard viewed the television commercial in which PepsiCo allegedly promised to provide a Harrier jet in return for 7,000,000 "Pepsi Points"[1]).

Assume that, after considering the relative advantages and disadvantages of the different state courts, you determine that the most advantageous forum for your client is New York (for reasons of convenience and perhaps because of the New York deceptive practices and false advertising statutes).[2] However, because the parties are citizens of different states and there is more than the statutory minimum amount in controversy, Leonard could bring his claims as a diversity action in federal court under 28 U.S.C. § 1332(a). If he does so, will a federal court apply the same law as would a New York state court if it heard the action? For instance:

- Will a federal court apply the same state deceptive practices statutes as would a New York state court?

- Will a federal court apply the same common law of contracts and specific performance as would a New York state court?

---

[1] Amended Complaint at ¶ 13, *Leonard v. Pepsico, Inc.*, No. 96 Civ. 9069 (S.D.N.Y. Mar. 8, 1999), 1999 WL 33932389.

[2] Leonard's actual action was filed in state court in Florida, but removed to federal court by PepsiCo pursuant to 28 U.S.C. § 1441 and then transferred to the United States District Court for the Southern District of New York pursuant to 28 U.S.C. § 1404(a). *Leonard v. PepsiCo, Inc.*, 88 F.Supp. 2d 116, 120 (S.D.N.Y. 1999).

- Will a federal court apply the Federal Rules of Civil Procedure if they differ from the procedural law that would be applied by a New York state court?

- Will a federal court apply the same procedural law as would be applied by a New York state court on matters not covered by the Federal Rules of Civil Procedure?

Differences in such laws can make a judicial forum significantly more attractive to plaintiffs or defendants. This chapter discusses how such potential differences between state and federal court are handled when state-law claims are filed in a United States District Court pursuant to 28 U.S.C. § 1332.

II. *ERIE RAILROAD* AND STATE LAW IN THE FEDERAL COURTS

In 1938 President Franklin Roosevelt founded the March of Dimes, heavyweight boxing champion Joe Louis defeated Max Schmeling, Germany annexed Austria, and British Prime Minister Neville Chamberlain declared "Peace for our time." This was also a watershed year for the United States federal courts and American civil procedure. For in 1938 the Federal Rules of Civil Procedure became effective and the Supreme Court decided the case of *Erie Railroad Co. v. Tompkins*. This chapter considers *Erie*, "one of the most famous cases in American law, unusually important and also unusually puzzling,"[3] and the law stemming from this 1938 decision.

A. *ERIE RAILROAD V. TOMPKINS*

As part of the Judiciary Act of 1789, Congress enacted the Rules of Decision Act, 28 U.S.C. § 1652, which now provides:

The laws of the several states, except where the Constitution or treaties of the United States or Acts of Congress otherwise require or provide, shall be regarded as rules of decision in civil actions in the courts of the United States, in cases where they apply.

As you read *Erie Railroad*, consider the following questions.

- What, if any, ambiguity is there in this statutory provision?

- What is the practical impact of the application of this statutory provision by the federal courts?

- Would the federal courts have the constitutional power to ignore state law in diversity actions in the absence of such a statutory direction?

---

[3] Purcell, "The Story of *Erie*: How Litigants, Lawyers, Judges, Politics, and Social Change Reshape the Law," in *Civil Procedure Stories* 21, 21 (K. Clermont ed., 2nd ed. 2008).

Erie Railroad v. Tompkins

United States Supreme Court, 1938
304 U.S. 64

OPINION

■ MR. JUSTICE BRANDEIS delivered the opinion of the Court.

The question for decision is whether the oft-challenged doctrine of *Swift v. Tyson* shall now be disapproved.

Tompkins, a citizen of Pennsylvania, was injured on a dark night by a passing freight train of the Erie Railroad Company while walking along its right of way at Hughestown in that state. He claimed that the accident occurred through negligence in the operation, or maintenance, of the train; that he was rightfully on the premises as licensee because on a commonly used beaten footpath which ran for a short distance alongside the tracks; and that he was struck by something which looked like a door projecting from one of the moving cars. To enforce that claim he brought an action in the federal court for Southern New York, which had jurisdiction because the company is a corporation of that state. It denied liability; and the case was tried by a jury.

The Erie insisted that its duty to Tompkins was no greater than that owed to a trespasser. It contended, among other things, that its duty to Tompkins, and hence its liability, should be determined in accordance with the Pennsylvania law; that under the law of Pennsylvania, as declared by its highest court, persons who use pathways along the railroad right of way—that is, a longitudinal pathway as distinguished from a crossing—are to be deemed trespassers; and that the railroad is not liable for injuries to undiscovered trespassers resulting from its negligence, unless it be wanton or willful. Tompkins denied that any such rule had been established by the decisions of the Pennsylvania courts; and contended that, since there was no statute of the state on the subject, the railroad's duty and liability is to be determined in federal courts as a matter of general law.

The trial judge refused to rule that the applicable law precluded recovery. The jury brought in a verdict of $30,000; and the judgment entered thereon was affirmed by the Circuit Court of Appeals, which held that it was unnecessary to consider whether the law of Pennsylvania was as contended, because the question was one not of local, but of general, law, and that "upon questions of general law the federal courts are free, in absence of a local statute, to exercise their independent judgment as to what the law is; and it is well settled that the question of the responsibility of a railroad for injuries caused by its servants is one of general law. * * * Where the public has made open and notorious use of a railroad right of way for a long period of time and without objection, the company owes to persons on such permissive pathway a duty of care in the operation of its trains. * * * It is likewise generally recognized law that a jury may find that negligence exists toward a pedestrian using a permissive path on the railroad right of way if he is hit by some object projecting from the side of the train."

The Erie had contended that application of the Pennsylvania rule was required, among other things, by section 34 of the Federal Judiciary Act of September 24, 1789, c. 20, 28 U.S.C. § 725 [now 28 U.S.C. § 1652], which provides: "The laws of the several States, except where the Constitution, treaties, or statutes of the United States otherwise require or provide, shall be regarded as rules of decision in trials at common law, in the courts of the United States, in cases where they apply."

Because of the importance of the question whether the federal court was free to disregard the alleged rule of the Pennsylvania common law, we granted certiorari.

First. *Swift v. Tyson*, 16 Pet. 1, 18, held that federal courts exercising jurisdiction on the ground of diversity of citizenship need not, in matters of general jurisprudence, apply the unwritten law of the state as declared by its highest court; that they are free to exercise an independent judgment as to what the common law of the state is—or should be; and that, as there stated by Mr. Justice Story, "the true interpretation of the 34th section limited its application to state laws, strictly local, that is to say, to the positive statutes of the state, and the construction thereof adopted by the local tribunals, and to rights and titles to things having a permanent locality, such as the rights and titles to real estate, and other matters immovable and intra-territorial in their nature and character. It never has been supposed by us, that the section did apply, or was designed to apply, to questions of a more general nature, not at all dependent upon local statutes or local usages of a fixed and permanent operation, as, for example, to the construction of ordinary contracts or other written instruments, and especially to questions of general commercial law, where the state tribunals are called upon to perform the like functions as ourselves, that is, to ascertain, upon general reasoning and legal analogies, what is the true exposition of the contract or instrument, or what is the just rule furnished by the principles of commercial law to govern the case."

The Court in applying the rule of section 34 to equity cases, in *Mason v. United States*, 260 U.S. 545, 559, said: "The statute, however, is merely declarative of the rule which would exist in the absence of the statute." The federal courts assumed, in the broad field of "general law," the power to declare rules of decision which Congress was confessedly without power to enact as statutes. Doubt was repeatedly expressed as to the correctness of the construction given section 34, and as to the soundness of the rule which it introduced. But it was the more recent research of a competent scholar, who examined the original document, which established that the construction given to it by the Court was erroneous; and that the purpose of the section was merely to make certain that, in all matters except those in which some federal law is controlling, the federal courts exercising jurisdiction in diversity of citizenship cases would apply as their rules of decision the law of the state, unwritten as well as written.[5]

Criticism of the doctrine became widespread after the decision of *Black & White Taxicab & Transfer Co. v. Brown & Yellow Taxicab & Transfer Co.*, 276 U.S. 518. There, Brown & Yellow, a Kentucky corporation owned by Kentuckians, and the Louisville & Nashville Railroad, also a Kentucky corporation, wished that the former should have the exclusive privilege of soliciting passenger and baggage transportation at the Bowling Green, Ky., Railroad station; and that the Black & White, a competing Kentucky corporation, should be prevented from interfering with that privilege. Knowing that such a contract would be void under the common law of Kentucky, it was arranged that the Brown & Yellow reincorporate under the law of Tennessee, and that the contract with the railroad should be executed there. The suit was then brought by the Tennessee corporation in the federal court for Western Kentucky to enjoin competition by the Black & White; an injunction issued by the District Court was sustained by the Court of Appeals; and this Court, citing many decisions in which the doctrine of *Swift & Tyson* had been applied, affirmed the decree.

Second. Experience in applying the doctrine of *Swift v. Tyson*, had revealed its defects, political and social; and the benefits expected to flow from the rule did not accrue. Persistence of state courts in their own opinions on questions of common law prevented uniformity; and the impossibility of discovering a satisfactory line of demarcation between the province of general law and that of local law developed a new well of uncertainties.

On the other hand, the mischievous results of the doctrine had become apparent. Diversity of citizenship jurisdiction was conferred in order to prevent apprehended discrimination in state courts against those not citizens of the state. *Swift v. Tyson* introduced grave discrimination by noncitizens against citizens. It made rights enjoyed under the unwritten "general law" vary according to whether enforcement was sought in the state or in the federal court; and the privilege of selecting the court in which the right should be determined was conferred upon the noncitizen. Thus, the doctrine rendered impossible equal protection of the law. In attempting to promote uniformity of law throughout the United States, the doctrine had prevented uniformity in the administration of the law of the state.

The discrimination resulting became in practice far-reaching. This resulted in part from the broad province accorded to the so-called "general law" as to which federal courts exercised an independent

---

[5]   Charles Warren, New Light on the History of the Federal Judiciary Act of 1789 (1923) 37 *Harv.L.Rev.* 49, 51–52, 81–88, 108.

judgment. In addition to questions of purely commercial law, "general law" was held to include the obligations under contracts entered into and to be performed within the state, the extent to which a carrier operating within a state may stipulate for exemption from liability for his own negligence or that of his employee; the liability for torts committed within the state upon persons resident or property located there, even where the question of liability depended upon the scope of a property right conferred by the state; and the right to exemplary or punitive damages. Furthermore, state decisions construing local deeds, mineral conveyances, and even devises of real estate, were disregarded.

In part the discrimination resulted from the wide range of persons held entitled to avail themselves of the federal rule by resort to the diversity of citizenship jurisdiction. Through this jurisdiction individual citizens willing to remove from their own state and become citizens of another might avail themselves of the federal rule. And, without even change of residence, a corporate citizen of the state could avail itself of the federal rule by reincorporating under the laws of another state, as was done in the *Taxicab* Case.

The injustice and confusion incident to the doctrine of *Swift v. Tyson* have been repeatedly urged as reasons for abolishing or limiting diversity of citizenship jurisdiction. Other legislative relief has been proposed. If only a question of statutory construction were involved, we should not be prepared to abandon a doctrine so widely applied throughout nearly a century. But the unconstitutionality of the course pursued has now been made clear, and compels us to do so.

Third. Except in matters governed by the Federal Constitution or by acts of Congress, the law to be applied in any case is the law of the state. And whether the law of the state shall be declared by its Legislature in a statute or by its highest court in a decision is not a matter of federal concern. There is no federal general common law. Congress has no power to declare substantive rules of common law applicable in a state whether they be local in their nature or "general," be they commercial law or a part of the law of torts. And no clause in the Constitution purports to confer such a power upon the federal courts. As stated by Mr. Justice Field when protesting in *Baltimore & Ohio R.R. Co. v. Baugh*, 149 U.S. 368, 401, against ignoring the Ohio common law of fellow-servant liability: "I am aware that what has been termed the general law of the country—which is often little less than what the judge advancing the doctrine thinks at the time should be the general law on a particular subject—has been often advanced in judicial opinions of this court to control a conflicting law of a state. I admit that learned judges have fallen into the habit of repeating this doctrine as a convenient mode of brushing aside the law of a state in conflict with their views. And I confess that, moved and governed by the authority of the great names of those judges, I have, myself, in many instances, unhesitatingly and confidently, but I think now erroneously, repeated the same doctrine. But, notwithstanding the great names which may be cited in favor of the doctrine, and notwithstanding the frequency with which the doctrine has been reiterated, there stands, as a perpetual protest against its repetition, the constitution of the United States, which recognizes and preserves the autonomy and independence of the states,—independence in their legislative and independence in their judicial departments. Supervision over either the legislative or the judicial action of the states is in no case permissible except as to matters by the constitution specifically authorized or delegated to the United States. Any interference with either, except as thus permitted, is an invasion of the authority of the state, and, to that extent, a denial of its independence."

The fallacy underlying the rule declared in *Swift v. Tyson* is made clear by Mr. Justice Holmes. The doctrine rests upon the assumption that there is "a transcendental body of law outside of any particular State but obligatory within it unless and until changed by statute," that federal courts have the power to use their judgment as to what the rules of common law are; and that in the federal courts "the parties are entitled to an independent judgment on matters of general law":

> But law in the sense in which courts speak of it today does not exist without some definite authority behind it. The common law so far as it is enforced in a State, whether called common law or not, is not the common law generally but the law of that State existing by the authority of that State without regard to what it may have been in England or anywhere else. * * *

> The authority and only authority is the State, and if that be so, the voice adopted by the State as its own (whether it be of its Legislature or of its Supreme Court) should utter the last word.

Thus the doctrine of *Swift v. Tyson* is, as Mr. Justice Holmes said, "an unconstitutional assumption of powers by the Courts of the United States which no lapse of time or respectable array of opinion should make us hesitate to correct." In disapproving that doctrine we do not hold unconstitutional section 34 of the Federal Judiciary Act of 1789 or any other act of Congress. We merely declare that in applying the doctrine this Court and the lower courts have invaded rights which in our opinion are reserved by the Constitution to the several states.

Fourth. The defendant contended that by the common law of Pennsylvania as declared by its highest court in *Falchetti v. Pennsylvania R. Co.*, 307 Pa. 203, 160 A. 859, the only duty owed to the plaintiff was to refrain from willful or wanton injury. The plaintiff denied that such is the Pennsylvania law. In support of their respective contentions the parties discussed and cited many decisions of the Supreme Court of the state. The Circuit Court of Appeals ruled that the question of liability is one of general law; and on that ground declined to decide the issue of state law. As we hold this was error, the judgment is reversed and the case remanded to it for further proceedings in conformity with our opinion.

Reversed.

■ MR. JUSTICE CARDOZO took no part in the consideration or decision of this case.

■ MR. JUSTICE BUTLER (dissenting).

* * *

No constitutional question was suggested or argued below or here. And as a general rule, this Court will not consider any question not raised below and presented by the petition. Here it does not decide either of the questions presented, but, changing the rule of decision in force since the foundation of the government, remands the case to be adjudged according to a standard never before deemed permissible.

* * *

While amendments to section 34 have from time to time been suggested, the section stands as originally enacted. Evidently Congress has intended throughout the years that the rule of decision as construed should continue to govern federal courts in trials at common law. * * *

* * *

* * * Against the protest of those joining in this opinion, the Court declines to assign the case for reargument. It may not justly be assumed that the labor and argument of counsel for the parties would not disclose the right conclusion and aid the Court in the statement of reasons to support it. Indeed, it would have been appropriate to give Congress opportunity to be heard before devesting it of power to prescribe rules of decision to be followed in the courts of the United States.

* * *

■ MR. JUSTICE MCREYNOLDS, concurs in this opinion.

■ MR. JUSTICE REED (concurring in part).

I concur in the conclusion reached in this case, in the disapproval of the doctrine of *Swift v. Tyson*, and in the reasoning of the majority opinion, except in so far as it relies upon the unconstitutionality of the "course pursued" by the federal courts.

The "doctrine of *Swift v. Tyson*," as I understand it, is that the words "the laws," as used in section 34, line 1, of the Federal Judiciary Act of September 24, 1789, 28 U.S.C.A. § 725, do not include[ ] in their meaning "the decisions of the local tribunals." Mr. Justice Story, in deciding that point, said, "Undoubtedly, the decisions of the local tribunals upon such subjects are entitled to, and will receive, the most deliberate attention and respect of this court; but they cannot furnish positive rules, or conclusive authority, by which our own judgments are to be bound up and governed."

To decide the case now before us and to "disapprove" the doctrine of *Swift v. Tyson* requires only that we say that the words "the laws" include in their meaning the decisions of the local tribunals. As the majority opinion shows, by its reference to Mr. Warren's researches and the first quotation from Mr. Justice Holmes, that this Court is now of the view that "laws" includes "decisions," it is unnecessary to go further and declare that the "course pursued" was "unconstitutional," instead of merely erroneous.

The "unconstitutional" course referred to in the majority opinion is apparently the ruling in *Swift v. Tyson* that the supposed omission of Congress to legislate as to the effect of decisions leaves federal courts free to interpret general law for themselves. I am not at all sure whether, in the absence of federal statutory direction, federal courts would be compelled to follow state decisions. There was sufficient doubt about the matter in 1789 to induce the first Congress to legislate. No former opinions of this Court have passed upon it. Mr. Justice Holmes evidently saw nothing "unconstitutional" which required the overruling of *Swift v. Tyson*, for he said in the very opinion quoted by the majority, "I should leave *Swift v. Tyson* undisturbed, as I indicated in *Kuhn v. Fairmont Coal Co.*, but I would not allow it to spread the assumed dominion into new fields." *Black & White Taxicab Co. v. Brown & Yellow Taxicab Co.*, 276 U.S. 518, 535. If the opinion commits this Court to the position that the Congress is without power to declare what rules of substantive law shall govern the federal courts, that conclusion also seems questionable. The line between procedural and substantive law is hazy, but no one doubts federal power over procedure. The Judiciary Article, 3, and the "necessary and proper" clause of article 1, § 8, may fully authorize legislation, such as this section of the Judiciary Act.

In this Court, stare decisis, in statutory construction, is a useful rule, not an inexorable command. It seems preferable to overturn an established construction of an act of Congress, rather than, in the circumstances of this case, to interpret the Constitution.

There is no occasion to discuss further the range or soundness of these few phrases of the opinion. It is sufficient now to call attention to them and express my own non-acquiescence.

COMMENTS AND QUESTIONS CONCERNING *ERIE RAILROAD V. TOMPKINS*

1.   Why did his lawyers file Harry Tompkins' action in federal, rather than state, court? Why was the action filed in the Southern District of New York rather than in a federal court in Pennsylvania (Tompkins' home state and the state of the accident)?

2. What if the Pennsylvania trespass/negligence rule had been contained in a state statute? Would there be any question that a federal court would have to apply that statute in a diversity action? Is it too much to expect states to enact their law legislatively if they want the federal courts to apply that law?

3. Is it significant that *Swift v. Tyson* articulated the doctrine of general federal common law in the context of a commercial dispute? Why might nationally uniform rules of commercial law have been particularly significant at the time of *Swift*?

4. Justice Brandeis relies upon "the * * * recent research of a competent scholar, who examined the original document [containing the Judiciary Act of 1789], which established that the construction given to it by the Court was erroneous; and that the purpose of the section was merely to make certain that, in all matters except those in which some federal law is controlling, the federal courts exercising jurisdiction in diversity of citizenship cases would apply as their rules of decision the law of the state, unwritten as well as written." 304 U.S. at 72–73.

What, though, if Professor Warren's research had been mistaken? *See* Pollak, "In Praise of Friendly," 133 *U. Pa. L. Rev.* 39, 48 n.33 (1984) ("It now appears that Charles Warren's research on § 34 was not as conclusive as Justice Reed and Brandeis supposed. *See* Friendly, 'In Praise of Erie— and the New Federal Common Law,' 39 *N.Y.U.L.REV.* 383, 388–390 (1964); *see also* Fletcher, 'The General Common Law and Section 34 of the Judiciary Act of 1789: The Example of Marine Insurance,' 97 *HARV.L.REV.* 1513 (1984).").

The document upon which Professor Warren relied in concluding that "the laws" in Section 34 of the Judiciary Act of 1789 included both statutory and common law is set forth below.

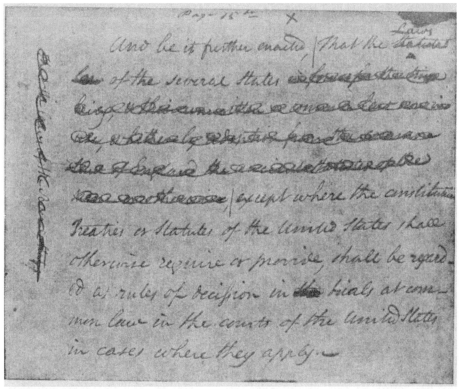

Warren, "New Light on the History of the Federal Judiciary Act of 1789," 37 *Harv.L.Rev.* 49, 87 (1923).

Is there more than one possible interpretation of this statute?

5.   Trace the pre-litigation moves in *Black & White Taxicab & Transfer Co. v. Brown & Yellow Taxicab & Transfer Co.*, 276 U.S. 518 (1928). Does the possibility of re-incorporation in another state to gain a federal judicial forum indicate that the Rules of Decision Act was being incorrectly interpreted? What if Brown & Yellow Taxicab had incorporated in Tennessee to gain a more favorable judge, a less geographically-concentrated jury, or a faster trial and appellate process than could be obtained in state court? *Cf. Ferens v. John Deere Co.* 494 U.S. 516 (1990), *supra* p. 339; *Piper Aircraft v. Reyno*, 454 U.S. 235 (1981), *supra* p. 325.

Prior to the 1958 amendment that added subsection (c) to 28 U.S.C. § 1332, corporations were only considered to be citizens of the state in which they were incorporated. 13F C. Wright, A. Miller & E. Cooper, *Federal Practice and Procedure* § 3624, at 38 (3d ed. 2009). Thus a local corporation could manipulate the availability of federal diversity jurisdiction ("make a federal case" out of a state-law dispute) simply by reincorporating in another state as did Brown & Yellow Taxicab. In his law school case book, then Professor Felix Frankfurter included excerpts from a pamphlet entitled *Why Corporations Leave Home*, printed and distributed by The Corporation Trust Company, which furnished "service to attorneys in the formation of corporations under the laws of Delaware and other states and serving as statutory resident agent for corporations whose principal business offices are maintained outside the state of incorporation." F. Frankfurter & H. Shulman, *Cases on Federal Jurisdiction and Procedure* 197 n.2 (2d ed. 1937).

6. Justice Brandeis observes, "*Swift v. Tyson* introduced grave discrimination by noncitizens against citizens. It made rights enjoyed under the unwritten 'general law' vary according to whether enforcement was sought in the state or in the federal court; and the privilege of selecting the court in which the right should be determined was conferred upon the noncitizen." 304 U.S. at 74–75. If the parties are diverse and the Section 1332(a) amount in controversy requirement is satisfied, though, why can't the defendant remove the action to federal court to gain any advantages of a federal forum? *See* 28 U.S.C. § 1441(b)(2). What if the basis of federal jurisdiction is not 28 U.S.C. § 1332(a), but the Class Action Fairness Act of 2005? *See* 28 U.S.C. §§ 1332(d)(2); 1453(b).

7. Justice Brandeis states that "the doctrine [of *Swift v. Tyson*] rendered impossible equal protection of the law. In attempting to promote uniformity of law throughout the United States, the doctrine had prevented uniformity in the administration of the law of the state." In 1938 the Equal Protection Clause of the Fourteenth Amendment was the sole basis upon which to premise an equal protection challenge, but that provision only prohibits states, and not the federal government, from "den[ying] to any person within its jurisdiction the equal protection of the laws." So Brandeis must have been speaking more generally in referring to "equal protection of the law." But, to the extent state citizens are treated the same whether they are litigants in the state or federal courts of that state (vertical uniformity), won't this create a lack of uniformity for parties in federal diversity actions in different states (forfeiting horizontal uniformity)? Not only lack of uniformity within a state, but lack of uniformity among different states, can create perceived unfairness for litigants and those attempting to comply with state and federal law.

8. Near the end of his opinion, Justice Brandeis states that "the doctrine of *Swift v. Tyson* is, as Mr. Justice Holmes said, 'an unconstitutional assumption of powers by the Courts of the United States which no lapse of time or respectable array of opinion should make us hesitate to correct.'" However, the next two sentences of his opinion provide: "In disapproving that doctrine we do not hold unconstitutional section 34 of the Federal Judiciary Act of 1789 or any other act of Congress. We merely declare that in applying the doctrine this Court and the lower courts have invaded rights which in our opinion are reserved by the Constitution to the several states." How can the Court conclude that *Swift* is "an unconstitutional assumption of powers" and yet not hold Section 34 unconstitutional?

9. As a legal realist, why would Justice Brandeis have difficulty conceiving of law as a "brooding omnipresence in the sky"? *Southern Pacific Co. v. Jenson*, 244 U.S. 205, 222 (1917) (Holmes, J., dissenting). Does Justice Brandeis believe that common law judges actually make the law or simply discover "a transcendental body of law outside of any particular State but obligatory within it unless and until changed by statute"? 304

U.S. at 79, quoting *Black and White Taxicab & Transfer Co. v. Brown and Yellow Taxicab & Transfer Co.*, 276 U.S. 518, 533 (1928) (Holmes, J., dissenting). *See also Sosa v. Alvarez-Machain*, 542 U.S. 692, 725 (2004) ("Now, however, in most cases where a court is asked to state or formulate a common law principle in a new context, there is a general understanding that the law is not so much found or discovered as it is either made or created."). However, to the extent that Justice Story was correct that federal judges, pursuant to *Swift v. Tyson*, merely discovered the law, establishing federal general common law would be less of an intrusion on states and state courts.

10. In his concurrence, Justice Reed suggests that the Court simply could rest its decision to disavow *Swift v. Tyson* on a different interpretation of the Rules of Decision Act: "To decide the case now before us and to 'disapprove' the doctrine of *Swift v. Tyson* requires only that we say that the words 'the laws' include in their meaning the decisions of the local tribunals." Why does Justice Brandeis and the majority say more? What are the advantages of the more restrictive approach urged by Justice Reed?

11. Do you agree with Justice Butler that the Court should have more deliberately structured the argument in this case and given notice of its intention to reconsider *Swift v. Tyson*? *See* 28 U.S.C. § 2403 ("In any action, suit or proceeding in a court of the United States to which the United States or any agency, officer or employee thereof is not a party, wherein the constitutionality of any Act of Congress affecting the public interest is drawn in question, the court shall certify such fact to the Attorney General, and shall permit the United States to intervene for presentation of evidence, if evidence is otherwise admissible in the case, and for argument on the question of constitutionality.").

12. The briefing and argument of *Erie* was not a textbook model of how important issues should be presented to and decided by the Supreme Court. The actions of the lawyers outside the courtroom raised a few questions as well. Consider the following description of an effort to settle Harry Tompkins' claim before the argument of his case in the Supreme Court.

> As the date for the argument in the Supreme Court grew near, the railroad apparently made one last effort to end the case through the back door. While Tompkins' lawyers were sitting in their offices at 32 Broadway, the railroad had apparently sent an emissary to the plaintiff. A man in Tompkins' hometown who owned a local gas station went to Tompkins' house with the message that the railroad would drop its petition for certiorari if he would accept a settlement of $22,000 [over $350,000 in today's dollars]. Danzig and Nemeroff reacted with a fitting countermove. They sent for Tompkins, and secreted him in a hotel near Masapequa, Long Island, where he could be protected from the enticements of the railroad. There he stayed for several weeks, until the "danger" of early settlement had passed. Both Nemeroff

and Danzig were sure that the judgment was as good as won, with interest and costs.

Rizzi, "Erie Memoirs Reveal Drama, Tragedy," *Harv. L. Rec.*, Sept. 24, 1976, at 2, 12.[4]

Ethics and professional responsibility are the subject of a separate course that you will take later in law school. In that course you will study the ABA's Model Rules of Professional Conduct, which have been adopted in most states to cover attorney conduct. However, think about the following questions and whether the attorneys' actions in *Erie* raise any ethical concerns.

- Who decides whether to accept a settlement offer—the client or that client's lawyer? *See* Model Rule of Professional Conduct 1.2(a); Comment 2 to Model Rule of Professional Conduct 1.4.

- Was it appropriate for Erie's lawyers to communicate the settlement offer to Harry Tompkins rather than to his lawyers? *See* Model Rule of Professional Conduct 4.2.

- Is such communication with another party who is represented by counsel appropriate if that party initiates or consents to the communication? *See* Comment 3 to Model Rule of Professional Conduct 4.2.

- Is such communication with another party who is represented by counsel appropriate if a lawyer does not directly contact that party but communicates through a third party? *See* Comment 4 to Model Rule of Professional Conduct 4.2.

After the Supreme Court's decision, the United States Court of Appeals for the Second Circuit applied Pennsylvania's common law of tort, holding that "where the complaint sets forth no cause of action and no amendment to correct its deficiencies can properly be granted, this court may direct that judgment be entered for the defendant. * * * The judgment is reversed and the cause remanded with directions to enter judgment for the defendant." *Tompkins v. Erie Railroad*, 98 F.2d 49, 52 (2d Cir. 1938).

Harry Tompkins struggled economically for the rest of his life.[5] A historical marker in Hughestown, Pennsylvania states:

In a landmark decision, the U.S. Supreme Court ruled in 1938 that, in cases between citizens of different states, federal courts must apply state common law, not federal "general common

---

[4]   Although the participants had somewhat differing recollections of a settlement offer or offers from Erie, there is agreement "that a settlement offer was made, that it came through one of Tompkins' acquaintances in Hughestown, that Tompkins' lawyers were confident of victory and dissuaded their client from accepting, and that for approximately two weeks his lawyers hid Tompkins away from the railroad at a location near [attorney] Nemeroff's home on Long Island." Purcell, "The Story of *Erie*: How Litigants, Lawyers, Judges, Politics, and Social Change Reshape the Law," in *Civil Procedure Stories* 21, 43 n.62 (K. Clermont ed., 2nd ed. 2008).

[5]   Purcell, *supra* note 4, at 64.

law." Under Pennsylvania common law, Harry Tompkins of Hughestown lost his case against the Erie Railroad, a New York State company. Tompkins had been struck by an unsecured door of a passing train and severely injured near this spot on July 27, 1934.[6]

B. *GUARANTY TRUST CO. V. YORK*, 326 U.S. 99 (1945)

In 1939 Felix Frankfurter assumed the seat on the Supreme Court formerly held by Benjamin Cardozo. Immediately before his appointment to the Court, Frankfurter had been a professor at Harvard Law School, with particular expertise in the areas of constitutional law and federal jurisdiction. In the second edition of his casebook on federal jurisdiction and procedure, the case of *Swift v. Tyson* was footnoted with the following quotation from John Chipman Gray's *The Nature and Sources of the Law* 253 (2d ed. 1921):

> Among the causes which led to the decision in *Swift v. Tyson*, the chief seems to have been the character and position of Judge Story. He was then by far the oldest judge in commission on the bench; he was a man of great learning, and of reputation for learning greater even than the learning itself; he was occupied at the time in writing a book on bills of exchange, which would, of itself, lead him to dogmatize on the subject; he had had great success in extending the jurisdiction of the Admiralty; he was fond of glittering generalities; and he was possessed by a restless vanity. All these things conspired to produce the result.

F. Frankfurter & H. Shulman, *Cases on Federal Jurisdiction and Procedure* 189 n.1 (2d ed. 1937).

> Several years later, as an associate justice on the Supreme Court, Frankfurter wrote for the Court in *Guaranty Trust Co. v. York*, 326 U.S. 99, 101–02 (1945):

> In overruling *Swift v. Tyson, Erie R. Co. v. Tompkins* did not merely overrule a venerable case. It overruled a particular way of looking at law which dominated the judicial process long after its inadequacies had been laid bare. Law was conceived as a "brooding omnipresence" of Reason, of which decisions were merely evidence and not themselves the controlling formulations. Accordingly, federal courts deemed themselves free to ascertain what Reason, and therefore Law, required wholly independent of authoritatively declared State law, even in cases where a legal right as the basis for relief was created by State authority and could not be created by federal

---

[6] Website of Pennsylvania Historical and Museum Commission, http://www.portal.state. pa.us/portal/server.pt/community/pennsylvania_historical_marker_program/2539/search_for_historical_markers/300886 (last visited Oct. 18, 2015).

authority and the case got into a federal court merely because it was "between Citizens of different States" under Art. III, § 2 of the Constitution of the United States.

The Supreme Court in *Guaranty Trust* held that a federal court hearing a matter in equity as a diversity action must apply a state statute of limitations that would have barred the action had it been filed in state court. Justice Frankfurter characterized the case before the Court as follows:

> And so this case reduces itself to the narrow question whether, when no recovery could be had in a State court because the action is barred by the statute of limitations, a federal court in equity can take cognizance of the suit because there is diversity of citizenship between the parties. Is the outlawry, according to State law, of a claim created by the States a matter of "substantive rights" to be respected by a federal court of equity when that court's jurisdiction is dependent on the fact that there is a State-created right, or is such statute of "a mere remedial character" which a federal court may disregard?

326 U.S. at 107.

Frankfurter continued:

> Here we are dealing with a right to recover derived not from the United States but from one of the States. When, because the plaintiff happens to be a nonresident, such a right is enforceable in a federal as well as in a State court, the forms and mode of enforcing the right may at times, naturally enough, vary because the two judicial systems are not identic. But since a federal court adjudicating a state-created right solely because of the diversity of citizenship of the parties is for that purpose, in effect, only another court of the State, it cannot afford recovery if the right to recover is made unavailable by the State nor can it substantially affect the enforcement of the right as given by the State.

> And so the question is not whether a statute of limitations is deemed a matter of "procedure" in some sense. The question is whether such a statute concerns merely the manner and the means by which a right to recover, as recognized by the State, is enforced, or whether such statutory limitation is a matter of substance in the aspect that alone is relevant to our problem, namely, does it significantly affect the result of a litigation for a federal court to disregard a law of a State that would be controlling in an action upon the same claim by the same parties in a State court?

> * * * In essence, the intent of [*Erie*] was to insure that, in all cases where a federal court is exercising jurisdiction solely

because of the diversity of citizenship of the parties, the outcome of the litigation in the federal court should be substantially the same, so far as legal rules determine the outcome of a litigation, as it would be if tried in a State court. The nub of the policy that underlies *Erie R. Co. v. Tompkins* is that for the same transaction the accident of a suit by a non-resident litigant in a federal court instead of in a State court a block away, should not lead to a substantially different result. And so, putting to one side abstractions regarding "substance" and "procedure", we have held that in diversity cases the federal courts must follow the law of the State as to burden of proof, *Cities Service Oil Co. v. Dunlap*, 308 U.S. 208, as to conflict of laws, *Klaxon Co. v. Stentor Co.*, 313 U.S. 487, as to contributory negligence, *Palmer v. Hoffman*, 318 U.S. 109, 117.

326 U.S. at 108–110.

Applying this test to the case before it, Frankfurter concluded, 326 U.S. at 110, "Plainly enough, a statute that would completely bar recovery in a suit if brought in a State court bears on a State-created right vitally and not merely formally or negligibly. As to consequences that so intimately affect recovery or non-recovery a federal court in a diversity case should follow State law."

The question before the Court was less troublesome in some respects because the state law at issue was a statute of limitations, rather than state common law. As Justice Frankfurter acknowledged in his opinion, "But even before *Erie R. Co. v. Tompkins*, federal courts relied on statutes of limitations of the States in which they sat. In suits at law State limitations statutes were held to be 'rules of decision' within § 34 of the Judiciary Act of 1789 and as such applied in 'trials at common law'." 326 U.S. at 110–11.

In his *Guaranty Trust* opinion, Justice Frankfurter explained the historic basis for federal diversity jurisdiction and the impact of that historic purpose on the application of state law in federal diversity actions:

The Framers of the Constitution, according to Marshall, entertained "apprehensions" lest distant suitors be subjected to local bias in State courts, or, at least, viewed with "indulgence the possible fears and apprehensions" of such suitors. And so Congress afforded out-of-State litigants another tribunal, not another body of law. The operation of a double system of conflicting laws in the same State is plainly hostile to the reign of law. Certainly, the fortuitous circumstance of residence out of a State of one of the parties to a litigation ought not to give rise to a discrimination against others equally concerned but locally resident. The source of substantive rights enforced by a federal court under diversity jurisdiction, it cannot be said too often, is the law of the States. Whenever that law is authoritatively declared by a State, whether its voice be the legislature or its highest court, such law ought to govern in litigation founded on that law, whether the forum of application is a State or a federal court and whether the remedies be sought at law or may be had in equity.

Guaranty Trust Co. v. York, 326 U.S. 99, 111–12 (1945).

As you read the next two cases, *Byrd v. Blue Ridge Rural Electric Cooperative*, 356 U.S. 525 (1958), and *Hanna v. Plumer*, 380 U.S. 460 (1965), consider whether these decisions are consistent with Justice Frankfurter's "outcome determinative" test based upon his conclusions that federal diversity jurisdiction "afforded out-of-State litigants another tribunal, not another body of law" and that "the outcome of the litigation in the federal court should be substantially the same, so far as legal rules determine the outcome of a litigation, as it would be if tried in a State court."

C. *BYRD V. BLUE RIDGE RURAL ELECTRIC COOPERATIVE, INC.*

In determining whether to apply state or federal law in a diversity action, is the only relevant question whether the application of state law would result in a different outcome in the federal court? Consider the following case.

Byrd v. Blue Ridge Rural Electric Cooperative, Inc.

Supreme Court of the United States, 1958
356 U.S. 525

OPINION

■ MR. JUSTICE BRENNAN delivered the opinion of the Court.

This case was brought in the District Court for the Western District of South Carolina. Jurisdiction was based on diversity of citizenship. The petitioner, a resident of North Carolina, sued respondent, a South Carolina corporation, for damages for injuries allegedly caused by the respondent's negligence. He had judgment on a jury verdict. The Court of Appeals for the Fourth Circuit reversed and directed the entry of judgment for the respondent. We granted certiorari, and subsequently ordered reargument.

The respondent is in the business of selling electric power to subscribers in rural sections of South Carolina. The petitioner was employed as a lineman in the construction crew of a construction contractor. The contractor, R. H. Bouligny, Inc., held a contract with the respondent in the amount of $334,300 for the building of some 24 miles of new power lines, the reconversion to higher capacities of about 88 miles of existing lines, and the construction of 2 new substations and a breaker station. The petitioner was injured while connecting power lines to one of the new substations.

One of respondent's affirmative defenses was that under the South Carolina Workmen's Compensation Act, the petitioner—because the work contracted to be done by his employer was work of the kind also done by the respondent's own construction and maintenance crews— had the status of a statutory employee of the respondent and was therefore barred from suing the respondent at law because obliged to accept statutory compensation benefits as the exclusive remedy for his injuries. Two questions concerning this defense are before us: (1) whether the Court of Appeals erred in directing judgment for respondent without a remand to give petitioner an opportunity to introduce further evidence; and (2) whether petitioner, state practice notwithstanding, is entitled to a jury determination of the factual issues raised by this defense.

I.

[Justice Brennan concluded that the court of appeals erred in directing judgment for Blue Ridge without allowing Byrd to offer evidence in the District Court as to whether he was a statutory employee and therefore barred from bringing a civil action:

> [T]he petitioner [Byrd] is entitled to have the question determined in the trial court. This would be necessary even if petitioner offered no proof of his own. Although the respondent's evidence was sufficient to withstand the motion [to strike Blue Ridge's affirmative defense] under the meaning given the statute by the Court of Appeals, it presented a fact question, which, in the circumstances of this case to be discussed *infra*, is properly to be decided by a jury. This is clear not only because of the issue of the credibility of the manager's vital testimony, but also because, even should the jury resolve that issue as did the Court of Appeals, the jury on the entire record—consistent with the view of the South Carolina cases that this question is in each case largely one of degree and of fact—might reasonably reach an opposite conclusion from the Court of Appeals as to the ultimate fact whether the respondent was a statutory employer.]

II.

A question is also presented as to whether on remand the factual issue is to be decided by the judge or by the jury. The respondent argues on the basis of the decision of the Supreme Court of South Carolina in *Adams v. Davison-Paxon Co.* that the issue of immunity should be decided by the judge and not by the jury. That was a negligence action brought in the state trial court against a store owner by an employee of an independent contractor who operated the store's millinery department. The trial judge denied the store owner's motion for a directed verdict made upon the ground that § 72–111 barred the plaintiff's action. The jury returned a verdict for the plaintiff. The South Carolina Supreme Court reversed, holding that it was for the judge and not the jury to decide on the evidence whether the owner was a statutory employer, and that the store owner had sustained his defense. The court rested its holding on decisions involving judicial review of the Industrial Commission and said:

> Thus the trial court should have in this case resolved the conflicts in the evidence and determined the fact of whether (the independent contractor) was performing a part of the "trade, business or occupation" of the department store-appellant and, therefore, whether (the employee's) remedy is exclusively under the Workmen's Compensation Law.

The respondent argues that this state-court decision governs the present diversity case and "divests the jury of its normal function" to decide the disputed fact question of the respondent's immunity under § 72–111. This is to contend that the federal court is bound under *Erie R. Co. v. Tompkins* to follow the state court's holding to secure uniform enforcement of the immunity created by the State.

First. It was decided in *Erie R. Co. v. Tompkins* that the federal courts in diversity cases must respect the definition of state-created rights and obligations by the state courts. We must, therefore, first examine the rule in *Adams v. Davison-Paxon Co.* to determine whether it is bound up with these rights and obligations in such a way that its application in the federal court is required.

The Workmen's Compensation Act is administered in South Carolina by its Industrial Commission. The South Carolina courts hold that, on judicial review of actions of the Commission under § 72–111, the question whether the claim of an injured workman is within the Commission's jurisdiction is a matter of law for decision by the court, which makes its own findings of fact relating to that jurisdiction. The South Carolina Supreme Court states no reasons in *Adams v. Davison-Paxon Co.* why, although the jury decides all other factual issues raised by the cause of action and defenses, the jury is displaced as to the factual issue raised by the affirmative defense under § 72–111. * * * A State may, of course, distribute the functions of its judicial machinery as it sees fit. The decisions relied upon, however, furnish no reason for selecting the judge rather than the jury to decide this single affirmative defense in the negligence action. They simply reflect a policy that administrative determination of "jurisdictional facts" should not be final but subject to judicial review. The conclusion is inescapable that the *Adams* holding is grounded in the practical consideration that the question had theretofore come before the South Carolina courts from the Industrial Commission and the courts had become accustomed to deciding the factual issue of immunity without the aid of juries. We find nothing to suggest that this rule was announced as an integral part of the special relationship created by the statute. Thus the requirement appears to be merely a form and mode of enforcing the immunity, *Guaranty Trust Co. of New York v. York*, 326 U.S. 99, and not a rule intended to be bound up with the definition of the rights and obligations of the parties. The situation is therefore not analogous to that in *Dice v. Akron, C. & Y.R. Co.*, 342 U.S. 359, where this Court held that the right to trial by jury is so substantial a part of the cause of action created by the Federal Employers' Liability Act, 45 U.S.C.A. § 51 et seq. that the Ohio courts could not apply, in an action under that statute, the Ohio rule that the question of fraudulent release was for determination by a judge rather than by a jury.

Second. But cases following *Erie* have evinced a broader policy to the effect that the federal courts should conform as near as may be—in the absence of other considerations—to state rules even of form and mode where the state rules may bear substantially on the question whether the litigation would come out one way in the federal court and another way in the state court if the federal court failed to apply a particular local rule. *E.g., Guaranty Trust Co. of New York v. York, supra; Bernhardt v. Polygraphic Co.*, 350 U.S. 198. Concededly the nature of the tribunal which tries issues may be important in the enforcement of the parcel of rights making up a cause of action or defense, and bear significantly upon achievement of uniform enforcement of the right. It may well be that in the instant personal-injury case the outcome would be substantially affected by whether the issue of immunity is decided by a judge or a jury. Therefore, were "outcome" the only consideration, a strong case might appear for saying that the federal court should follow the state practice.

But there are affirmative countervailing considerations at work here. The federal system is an independent system for administering justice to litigants who properly invoke its jurisdiction. An essential characteristic of that system is the manner in which, in civil common-law actions, it distributes trial functions between judge and jury and, under the influence—if not the command[10]—of the Seventh Amendment, assigns the decisions of disputed questions of fact to the jury. The policy of uniform enforcement of state-created rights and obligations, *see, e.g., Guaranty Trust Co. of New York v. York, supra*, cannot in every case exact compliance with a state rule[12]—not bound up with rights and obligations—which disrupts the federal system of allocating functions between judge and jury. *Herron v. Southern Pacific Co.*, 283 U.S. 91. Thus the inquiry here is whether the federal policy favoring jury decisions of disputed fact questions should yield to the

---

[10] Our conclusion makes unnecessary the consideration of—and we intimate no view upon—the constitutional question whether the right of jury trial protected in federal courts by the Seventh Amendment embraces the factual issue of statutory immunity when asserted, as here, as an affirmative defense in a common-law negligence action.

[12] This Court held in *Sibbach v. Wilson & Co.*, 312 U.S. 1, 655, that Federal Rules of Civil Procedure 35 should prevail over a contrary state rule.

state rule in the interest of furthering the objective that the litigation should not come out one way in the federal court and another way in the state court.

We think that in the circumstances of this case the federal court should not follow the state rule. It cannot be gainsaid that there is a strong federal policy against allowing state rules to disrupt the judge-jury relationship in the federal courts. In *Herron v. Southern Pacific Co.*, supra, the trial judge in a personal-injury negligence action brought in the District Court for Arizona on diversity grounds directed a verdict for the defendant when it appeared as a matter of law that the plaintiff was guilty of contributory negligence. The federal judge refused to be bound by a provision of the Arizona Constitution which made the jury the sole arbiter of the question of contributory negligence. This Court sustained the action of the trial judge, holding that "state laws cannot alter the essential character or function of a federal court" because that function "is not in any sense a local matter, and state statutes which would interfere with the appropriate performance of that function are not binding upon the federal court under either the Conformity Act or the 'Rules of Decision' Act." *Id.*, 283 U.S. at page 94. Perhaps even more clearly in light of the influence of the Seventh Amendment, the function assigned to the jury "is an essential factor in the process for which the Federal Constitution provides." *Id.*, 283 U.S. at page 95. Concededly the *Herron* case was decided before *Erie R. Co. v. Tompkins*, but even when *Swift v. Tyson*, 16 Pet. 1, was governing law and allowed federal courts sitting in diversity cases to disregard state decisional law, it was never thought that state statutes or constitutions were similarly to be disregarded. Yet *Herron* held that state statutes and constitutional provisions could not disrupt or alter the essential character or function of a federal court.

Third. We have discussed the problem upon the assumption that the outcome of the litigation may be substantially affected by whether the issue of immunity is decided by a judge or a jury. But clearly there is not present here the certainty that a different result would follow, *cf. Guaranty Trust Co. of New York v. York*, supra, or even the strong possibility that this would be the case, *cf. Bernhardt v. Polygraphic Co.*, supra. There are factors present here which might reduce that possibility. The trial judge in the federal system has powers denied the judges of many States to comment on the weight of evidence and credibility of witnesses, and discretion to grant a new trial if the verdict appears to him to be against the weight of the evidence. We do not think the likelihood of a different result is so strong as to require the federal practice of jury determination of disputed factual issues to yield to the state rule in the interest of uniformity of outcome.[15]

---

[15] *Stoner v. New York Life Ins. Co.*, 311 U.S. 464, is not contrary. It was there held that the federal court should follow the state rule defining the evidence sufficient to raise a jury question whether the state-created right was established. But the state rule did not have the

The Court of Appeals did not consider other grounds of appeal raised by the respondent because the ground taken disposed of the case. We accordingly remand the case to the Court of Appeals for the decision of the other questions, with instructions that, if not made unnecessary by the decision of such questions, the Court of Appeals shall remand the case to the District Court for a new trial of such issues as the Court of Appeals may direct.

Reversed and remanded.

■ MR. JUSTICE WHITTAKER concurring in part and dissenting in part.

* * *

* * * It is urged by respondent that, from the colloquy between the district judge and counsel, which, as stated, as set forth in substance in Mr. Justice FRANKFURTER'S dissenting opinion, it appears that petitioner had "rested," and thus had waived his right to adduce rebuttal evidence upon the issue of respondent's jurisdictional defense, before the district judge sustained his motion to strike that defense and the supporting evidence. But my analysis of the record convinces me that petitioner, in fact, never did so. For this reason I believe that so much of the judgment of the Court of Appeals as directed the District Court to enter judgment for respondent deprives petitioner of his right to adduce rebuttal evidence upon the issue of respondent's prima facie established jurisdictional defense, and, therefore, cannot stand.

But the Court's opinion proceeds to discuss and determine the question whether, upon remand to the District Court, if such becomes necessary, the jurisdictional issue is to be determined by the judge or by the jury—a question which, to my mind, is premature, not now properly before us, and is one we need not and should not now reach for or decide. The Court, although premising its conclusion "upon the assumption that the outcome of the litigation may be substantially affected by whether the issue of immunity is decided by a judge or a jury," holds that the issue is to be determined by a jury—not by the judge. I cannot agree to this conclusion for the following reasons.

* * *

It * * * seems to be settled under the South Carolina Workmen's Compensation Law, and the decisions of the highest court of that State construing it, that the question whether exclusive jurisdiction, in cases like this, is vested in its Industrial Commission or in its courts of general jurisdiction is one for decision by the court, not by a jury. The Federal District Court, in this diversity case, is bound to follow the

---

effect of nullifying the function of the federal judge to control a jury submission as did the Arizona constitutional provision which was denied effect in *Herron*. The South Carolina rule here involved affects the jury function as the Arizona provision affected the function of the judge: The rule entirely displaces the jury without regard to the sufficiency of the evidence to support a jury finding of immunity.

substantive South Carolina law that would be applied if the trial were to be held in a South Carolina court, in which State the Federal District Court sits. *Erie R. Co. v. Tompkins*, 304 U.S. 64. A Federal District Court sitting in South Carolina may not legally reach a substantially different result than would have been reached upon a trial of the same case "in a State court a block away." *Guaranty Trust Co. v. York*, 326 U.S. 99, 109.

The Court's opinion states: "Concededly the nature of the tribunal which tries issues may be important in the enforcement of the parcel of rights making up a cause of action or defense, and bear significantly upon achievement of uniform enforcement of the right. It may well be that in the instant personal-injury case the outcome would be substantially affected by whether the issue of immunity is decided by a judge or a jury." And the Court premises its conclusion "upon the assumption that the outcome of the litigation may be substantially affected by whether the issue of immunity is decided by a judge or a jury." Upon that premise, the Court's conclusion, to my mind, is contrary to our cases. "Here (as in *Guaranty Trust Co. of New York v. York*, *supra*) we are dealing with a right to recover derived not from the United States but from one of the States. When, because the plaintiff happens to be a non-resident, such a right is enforceable in a federal as well as in a State court, the forms and mode of enforcing the right may at times, naturally enough, vary because the two judicial systems are not identic. But since a federal court adjudicating a state-created right solely because of the diversity of citizenship of the parties is for that purpose, in effect, only another court of the State, it cannot afford recovery if the right to recover is made unavailable by the State nor can it substantially affect the enforcement of the right as given by the State." *Guaranty Trust Co. v. York*, *supra*, 326 U.S. at pages 108–109.

* * *

Inasmuch as the law of South Carolina, as construed by its highest court, requires its courts—not juries—to determine whether jurisdiction over the subject matter of cases like this is vested in its Industrial Commission, and inasmuch as the Court's opinion concedes "that in the instant personal-injury case the outcome would be substantially affected by whether the issue of immunity is decided by a judge or a jury," it follows that in this diversity case the jurisdictional issue must be determined by the judge—not by the jury. Insofar as the Court holds that the question of jurisdiction should be determined by the jury, I think the Court departs from its past decisions. I therefore respectfully dissent from part II of the opinion of the Court.

■ MR. JUSTICE FRANKFURTER, whom MR. JUSTICE HARLAN joins, dissenting.

* * *

The construction of the state law by the Court of Appeals is clearly supported by the decisions of the Supreme Court of South Carolina, and so we need not rest on the usual respect to be accorded to a reading of a local statute by a Federal Court of Appeals. It is clear from the state cases that a determination as to whether a defendant is an "employer" for purposes of § 72–111 will depend upon the entire circumstances of the relationship between such defendant and the work being done on its behalf; no single factor is determinative. Both the approach of the Court of Appeals and the conclusions that it reached from the evidence in this case are entirely consistent with prior declarations of South Carolina law by the highest court of that State.

* * *

It is apparent that petitioner had no intention of introducing any evidence on the issue of whether respondent was his statutory employer and that he was prepared to—and did—submit the issue to the court on that basis. Clearly petitioner cannot be said to have relied upon, and thus to have been misled by, the court's erroneous construction of the law, for it was before the court had disclosed its view of the law that petitioner made apparent his willingness to submit the issue to it on the basis of respondent's evidence. If petitioner could have cast any doubt on that evidence or could have brought in any other matter relevant to the issue, it was his duty to bring it forward before the issue was submitted to the court. For counsel to withhold evidence on an issue submitted for decision until after that issue has been resolved against him would be an abuse of the judicial process that this Court surely should not countenance, however strong the philanthropic appeal in a particular case. Nor does it appear that petitioner had any such "game" in mind. He gave not the slightest indication of an intention to introduce any additional evidence, no matter how the court might decide the issue. It seems equally clear that, had the trial court decided the issue—on any construction—in favor of the respondent, the petitioner was prepared to rely solely upon his right of appeal.

We are not to read the record as though we are making an independent examination of the trial proceedings. We are sitting in judgment on the Court of Appeals' review of the record. That court, including Chief Judge Parker and Judge Soper, two of the most experienced and esteemed circuit judges in the federal judiciary, interpreted the record as it did in light of its knowledge of local practice and of the ways of local lawyers. In ordering judgment entered for respondent, it necessarily concluded, as a result of its critical examination of the record, that petitioner's counsel chose to have the issue decided on the basis of the record as it then stood. The determination of the Court of Appeals can properly be reversed only if it is found that it was baseless. Even granting that the record is susceptible of two interpretations, it is to disregard the relationship of this Court to the Courts of Appeals, especially as to their function in appeals in diversity cases, to substitute our view for theirs.

The order of the Court of Appeals that the District Court enter judgment for the respondent is amply sustained on either theory as to whether or not the issue was one for the court to decide. If the question is for the court, the Court of Appeals has satisfactorily resolved it in accordance with state decisions. And if, on the other hand, the issue is such that it would have to be submitted to the jury if there were any crucial facts in controversy, both the District Court and the Court of Appeals agreed that there was no conflict as to the relevant evidence—not, at any rate, if such inconsistency as existed was resolved in favor of petitioner. According to the governing view of South Carolina law, as given us by the Court of Appeals, that evidence would clearly have required the District Court to grant a directed verdict to the respondent. Accordingly, I would affirm the judgment.

■ MR. JUSTICE HARLAN, dissenting.

* * * I do not perceive how any further evidence which might be adduced by petitioner could change the result reached by the Court of Appeals. In any event, in the circumstances disclosed by the record before us, we should at the very least require petitioner to make some showing here of the character of the further evidence he expects to introduce before we disturb the judgment below.

COMMENTS AND QUESTIONS CONCERNING
BYRD V. BLUE RIDGE RURAL ELECTRIC COOPERATIVE, INC.

1. What are the two reasons why the court of appeals could not direct entry of judgment for Blue Ridge on its affirmative defense that Byrd was a statutory employee who could not bring a civil action?

2. Justice Brennan describes the *Erie* question in this case as "whether petitioner, state practice notwithstanding, is entitled to a jury determination of the factual issues raised by this defense." Under what circumstances should "state practice" control in a United States District Court? Is it clear that, under the *Guaranty Trust* outcome determinative test, a jury resolution of the statutory employee question would be different than an adjudication by a judge?

3. If plaintiffs are entitled to a jury trial in federal court, but not state court, won't plaintiffs be encouraged to forum shop?

4. Justice Brennan recognizes a "broader policy to the effect that the federal courts should conform as near as may be—in the absence of other considerations—to state rules even of form and mode where the state rules may bear substantially on the question whether the litigation would come

out one way in the federal court and another way in the state court if the federal court failed to apply a particular local rule." Having endorsed such an "outcome determinative" test, however, Justice Brennan concludes that "there is not present here the certainty that a different result would follow, *cf. Guaranty Trust Co. of New York v. York, supra*, or even the strong possibility that this would be the case, cf. *Bernhardt v. Polygraphic Co., supra*."

Would the lawyers involved in this action agree that a plaintiff would gain no advantage from a jury determination of the statutory question? Might this, in fact, be a reason why Byrd's lawyer filed the action in federal court?

5.   What does Justice Brennan mean that "in spite of [a] difference in procedure, the federal court enforcing a state-created right in a diversity case is, as we said in *Guaranty Trust Co. of New York v. York*, 326 U.S. 99, 108, in substance 'only another court of the State' "?

6.   Do you agree with Justice Brennan that "there are affirmative countervailing considerations at work here" that make it appropriate to have a jury, rather than judge, decide the relevant question—even though the difference between judge and jury might be outcome determinative? Justice Brennan describes the test to resolve conflicts between state and federal rules as follows: "Thus the inquiry here is whether the federal policy favoring jury decisions of disputed fact questions should yield to the state rule in the interest of furthering the objective that the litigation should not come out one way in the federal court and another way in the state court." However, regardless of the outcome determinative character of the rules in question, "state statutes and constitutional provisions [can] not disrupt or alter the essential character or function of a federal court."

7.   Justice Brennan, in footnote 10, is careful to note that his opinion is not based upon a conclusion that the Seventh Amendment requires a jury trial in *Byrd*:

> Our conclusion makes unnecessary the consideration of—and we intimate no view upon—the constitutional question whether the right of jury trial protected in federal courts by the Seventh Amendment embraces the factual issue of statutory immunity when asserted, as here, as an affirmative defense in a common-law negligence action.

Although Justice Brennan professes that the Seventh Amendment played no role in the Court's resolution of this case, wouldn't this looming constitutional question push the Court to find a jury to be an "essential characteristic of [the federal judicial] system"? The Seventh Amendment right to jury trial is considered in Chapter 12, *infra* p. 895.

8.   Justice Brennan cites *Dice v. Akron, Canton & Youngstown R.R.*, 342 U.S. 359 (1952), which poses the "reverse *Erie*" situation, in which a state court has jurisdiction over a federal claim—and may be required to apply additional federal law that is an integral part of that federal claim. The Court in *Byrd* rejected Blue Ridge's argument that, consistent with

state law, a federal judge, rather than a jury, should determine the validity
of the statutory employee defense:

> We find nothing to suggest that this [non-jury] rule was
> announced as an integral part of the special relationship created
> by the statute. Thus the requirement appears to be merely a form
> and mode of enforcing the immunity, *Guaranty Trust Co. v. York*,
> 326 U.S. 99, and not a rule intended to be bound up with the
> definition of the rights and obligations of the parties. The
> situation is therefore not analogous to that in *Dice v. Akron, C. &
> Y. R. Co.*, where this Court held that the right to trial by jury is so
> substantial a part of the cause of action created by the Federal
> Employers' Liability Act, 45 U.S.C.A. § 51 et seq. that the Ohio
> courts could not apply, in an action under that statute, the Ohio
> rule that the question of fraudulent release was for determination
> by a judge rather than by a jury.

9.   In footnote 12 of his opinion, Justice Brennan suggests that, as
was the case in *Sibbach v. Wilson*, a Federal Rule of Civil Procedure can
trump a "contrary state rule." The Court deals directly with conflicts
between a Federal Rule and a "contrary state rule" in *Hanna v. Plumer*,
380 U.S. 460 (1965), *infra* p. 389.

10. In both *Byrd* and *Erie* the state supreme court had definitively
determined the state law that would be applied in a state-court action.
Judge Jerome Frank characterized the role of the federal judge in such
situations as simply "to play the rule of ventriloquist's dummy to the courts
of some particular state." *Richardson v. Commissioner of Internal Revenue*,
126 F.2d 562, 567 (2d Cir. 1942).

But what if a state supreme court has not spoken so clearly? Judge
Henry Friendly described the role of the federal court in such a situation as
follows: "Our principal task, in this diversity of citizenship case, is to
determine what the New York courts would think the California courts
would think on an issue about which neither has thought." *Nolan v.
Transocean Air Lines*, 276 F.2d 280, 281 (2d Cir. 1960), *judgment set aside*,
365 U.S. 293 (1961).

When the state supreme court has not definitively addressed the state-
law issue, the Supreme Court has concluded:

> The highest state court is the final authority on state law, but it is
> still the duty of the federal courts, where the state law supplies
> the rule of decision, to ascertain and apply that law even though it
> has not been expounded by the highest court of the State. An
> intermediate state court in declaring and applying the state law is
> acting as an organ of the State and its determination, in the
> absence of more convincing evidence of what the state law is,
> should be followed by a federal court in deciding a state question.

Fidelity Union Trust Co. v. Field, 311 U.S. 169, 177–78 (1940). *See also
West v. Am. Tel. & Tel. Co.*, 311 U.S. 223, 237 (1940) ("Where an
intermediate appellate state court rests its considered judgment upon the
rule of law which it announces, that is a datum for ascertaining state law

which is not to be disregarded by a federal court unless it is convinced by other persuasive data that the highest court of the state would decide otherwise.").

Rather than require the federal court to attempt to predict how a state supreme court might decide an issue of state law, most state supreme courts will consider questions of law certified to them by a federal court. *See Arizonans for Official English v. Arizona*, 520 U.S. 43, 76 (1997) ("Certification procedure * * * allows a federal court faced with a novel state-law question to put the question directly to the State's highest court, reducing the delay, cutting the cost, and increasing the assurance of gaining an authoritative response. Most States have adopted certification procedures.").

D. WHEN A FEDERAL RULE IS A "FEDERAL RULE": *HANNA V. PLUMER*

The question in *Erie Railroad* was whether state common law should displace "federal general common law." In *Erie* and the cases that followed, federal common law may have governed commercial law (*Erie*), statute of limitations periods (*Guaranty Trust*), or whether the parties were entitled to a jury (*Byrd*). But what if the question is not whether state law should displace federal common law, but federal law that has been adopted as a Federal Rule of Civil Procedure? Does it make a difference whether the effort is to displace a federal rule or a Federal Rule? Consider the following case.

Hanna v. Plumer

Supreme Court of the United States, 1965
380 U.S. 460

OPINION

■ MR. CHIEF JUSTICE WARREN delivered the opinion of the Court.

The question to be decided is whether, in a civil action where the jurisdiction of the United States district court is based upon diversity of citizenship between the parties, service of process shall be made in the manner prescribed by state law or that set forth in Rule 4(d)(1) of the Federal Rules of Civil Procedure.

On February 6, 1963, petitioner, a citizen of Ohio, filed her complaint in the District Court for the District of Massachusetts, claiming damages in excess of $10,000 [at that time the minimum amount in controversy under 28 U.S.C. § 1332(a)] for personal injuries resulting from an automobile accident in South Carolina, allegedly caused by the negligence of one Louise Plumer Osgood, a Massachusetts citizen deceased at the time of the filing of the complaint. Respondent, Mrs. Osgood's executor and also a Massachusetts citizen, was named as defendant. On February 8, service was made by leaving copies of the summons and the complaint with respondent's wife at his residence, concededly in compliance with Rule 4(d)(1) [the relevant portion of which is now in Rule 4(e)(2)(B)], which provides:

> The summons and complaint shall be served together. The plaintiff shall furnish the person making service with such copies as are necessary. Service shall be made as follows:
>
> > (1) Upon an individual other than an infant or an incompetent person, by delivering a copy of the summons and of the complaint to him personally or by leaving copies thereof at his dwelling house or usual place of abode with some person of suitable age and discretion then residing therein * * *.

Respondent filed his answer on February 26, alleging, inter alia, that the action could not be maintained because it had been brought "contrary to and in violation of the provisions of Massachusetts General Laws (Ter.Ed.) Chapter 197, Section 9." That section provides:

> Except as provided in this chapter, an executor or administrator shall not be held to answer to an action by a creditor of the deceased which is not commenced within one year from the time of his giving bond for the performance of his trust, or to such an action which is commenced within said year unless before the expiration thereof the writ in such action has been served by delivery in hand upon such executor or administrator or service thereof accepted by him or a notice stating the name of the estate, the name and address of the creditor, the amount of the claim and the court in which the action has been brought has been filed in the proper registry of probate. * * *

On October 17, 1963, the District Court granted respondent's motion for summary judgment, citing *Ragan v. Merchants Transfer & Warehouse Co.*, 337 U.S. 530, and *Guaranty Trust Co. of New York v. York*, 326 U.S. 99, in support of its conclusion that the adequacy of the service was to be measured by § 9, with which, the court held, petitioner had not complied. On appeal, petitioner admitted noncompliance with § 9, but argued that Rule 4(d)(1) defines the method by which service of process is to be effected in diversity actions. The Court of Appeals for the First Circuit, finding that "(r)elatively recent amendments (to § 9) evince a clear legislative purpose to require personal notification within the year," concluded that the conflict of state and federal rules was over "a substantive rather than a procedural matter," and unanimously affirmed. Because of the threat to the goal of uniformity of federal procedure posed by the decision below, we granted certiorari.

We conclude that the adoption of Rule 4(d)(1), designed to control service of process in diversity actions, neither exceeded the congressional mandate embodied in the Rules Enabling Act nor transgressed constitutional bounds, and that the Rule is therefore the standard against which the District Court should have measured the adequacy of the service. Accordingly, we reverse the decision of the Court of Appeals.

The Rules Enabling Act, 28 U.S.C. § 2072, provides, in pertinent part:

> The Supreme Court shall have the power to prescribe, by general rules, the forms of process, writs, pleadings, and motions, and the practice and procedure of the district courts of the United States in civil actions.

> Such rules shall not abridge, enlarge or modify any substantive right and shall preserve the right of trial by jury * * *.

Under the cases construing the scope of the Enabling Act, Rule 4(d)(1) clearly passes muster. Prescribing the manner in which a defendant is to be notified that a suit has been instituted against him, it relates to the "practice and procedure of the district courts."

"The test must be whether a rule really regulates procedure,—the judicial process for enforcing rights and duties recognized by substantive law and for justly administering remedy and redress for disregard or infraction of them." *Sibbach v. Wilson & Co.*, 312 U.S. 1, 14.

In *Mississippi Pub. Corp. v. Murphree*, 326 U.S. 438, this Court upheld Rule 4(f), which permits service of a summons anywhere within the State (and not merely the district) in which a district court sits:

> We think that Rule 4(f) is in harmony with the Enabling Act * * *. Undoubtedly most alterations of the rules of practice and procedure may and often do affect the rights of litigants. Congress' prohibition of any alteration of substantive rights of litigants was obviously not addressed to such incidental effects as necessarily attend the adoption of the prescribed new rules of procedure upon the rights of litigants who, agreeably to rules of practice and procedure, have been brought before a court authorized to determine their rights. *Sibbach v. Wilson & Co.*, 312 U.S. 1, 11–14. The fact that the application of Rule 4(f) will operate to subject petitioner's rights to adjudication by the district court for northern Mississippi will undoubtedly affect those rights. But it does not operate to abridge, enlarge or modify the rules of decision by which that court will adjudicate its rights. *Id.*, at 445–446.

Thus were there no conflicting state procedure, Rule 4(d)(1) would clearly control. However, respondent, focusing on the contrary Massachusetts rule, calls to the Court's attention another line of cases, a line which—like the Federal Rules—had its birth in 1938. *Erie R. Co. v. Tompkins*, 304 U.S. 64, overruling *Swift v. Tyson*, 16 Pet. 1, held that federal courts sitting in diversity cases, when deciding questions of "substantive" law, are bound by state court decisions as well as state statutes. The broad command of *Erie* was therefore identical to that of the Enabling Act: federal courts are to apply state substantive law and federal procedural law. However, as subsequent cases sharpened the distinction between substance and procedure, the line of cases following *Erie* diverged markedly from the line construing the Enabling Act. *Guaranty Trust Co. v. York*, 326 U.S. 99, made it clear that *Erie*-type problems were not to be solved by reference to any traditional or common-sense substance-procedure distinction:

> And so the question is not whether a statute of limitations is deemed a matter of "procedure" in some sense. The question is * * * does it significantly affect the result of a litigation for a federal court to disregard a law of a State that would be controlling in an action upon the same claim by the same parties in a State court? 326 U.S., at 109.

Respondent, by placing primary reliance on *York* and *Ragan*, suggests that the *Erie* doctrine acts as a check on the Federal Rules of Civil Procedure, that despite the clear command of Rule 4(d)(1), Erie and its progeny demand the application of the Massachusetts rule. Reduced to essentials, the argument is: (1) *Erie*, as refined in *York*, demands that federal courts apply state law whenever application of federal law in its stead will alter the outcome of the case. (2) In this case, a determination that the Massachusetts service requirements obtain will result in immediate victory for respondent. If, on the other hand, it should be held that Rule 4(d)(1) is applicable, the litigation will continue, with possible victory for petitioner. (3) Therefore, *Erie* demands application of the Massachusetts rule. The syllogism possesses an appealing simplicity, but is for several reasons invalid.

In the first place, it is doubtful that, even if there were no Federal Rule making it clear that in-hand service is not required in diversity actions, the *Erie* rule would have obligated the District Court to follow the Massachusetts procedure. "Outcome-determination" analysis was never intended to serve as a talisman. *Byrd v. Blue Ridge Rural Elec. Cooperative*, 356 U.S. 525, 537. Indeed, the message of *York* itself is that choices between state and federal law are to be made not by application of any automatic, "litmus paper" criterion, but rather by reference to the policies underlying the *Erie* rule. *Guaranty Trust Co. v. York*, supra, 326 U.S. at 108–112.

The *Erie* rule is rooted in part in a realization that it would be unfair for the character of result of a litigation materially to differ because the suit had been brought in a federal court.

> Diversity of citizenship jurisdiction was conferred in order to prevent apprehended discrimination in state courts against those not citizens of the state. *Swift v. Tyson* (16 Pet. 1) introduced grave discrimination by noncitizens against citizens. It made rights enjoyed under the unwritten "general

law" vary according to whether enforcement was sought in the state or in the federal court; and the privilege of selecting the court in which the right should be determined was conferred upon the noncitizen. Thus, the doctrine rendered impossible equal protection of the law. *Erie R. Co. v. Tompkins, supra,* 304 U.S. at 74–75.

The decision was also in part a reaction to the practice of "forum-shopping" which had grown up in response to the rule of *Swift v. Tyson.* That the *York* test was an attempt to effectuate these policies is demonstrated by the fact that the opinion framed the inquiry in terms of "substantial" variations between state and federal litigation. Not only are nonsubstantial, or trivial, variations not likely to raise the sort of equal protection problems which troubled the Court in *Erie*; they are also unlikely to influence the choice of a forum. The "outcome-determination" test therefore cannot be read without reference to the twin aims of the Erie rule: discouragement of forum-shopping and avoidance of inequitable administration of the laws.[9]

The difference between the conclusion that the Massachusetts rule is applicable, and the conclusion that it is not, is of course at this point "outcome-determinative" in the sense that if we hold the state rule to apply, respondent prevails, whereas if we hold that Rule 4(d)(1) governs, the litigation will continue. But in this sense every procedural variation is "outcome-determinative." For example, having brought suit in a federal court, a plaintiff cannot then insist on the right to file subsequent pleadings in accord with the time limits applicable in state courts, even though enforcement of the federal timetable will, if he continues to insist that he must meet only the state time limit, result in determination of the controversy against him. So it is here. Though choice of the federal or state rule will at this point have a marked effect upon the outcome of the litigation, the difference between the two rules would be of scant, if any, relevance to the choice of a forum. Petitioner, in choosing her forum, was not presented with a situation where

---

[9]   The Court of Appeals seemed to frame the inquiry in terms of how "important" § 9 is to the State. In support of its suggestion that § 9 serves some interest the State regards as vital to its citizens, the court noted that something like § 9 has been on the books in Massachusetts a long time, that § 9 has been amended a number of times and that § 9 is designed to make sure that executors receive actual notice. The apparent lack of relation among these three observations is not surprising, because it is not clear to what sort of question the Court of Appeals was addressing itself. One cannot meaningfully ask how important something is without first asking "important for what purpose?" *Erie* and its progeny make clear that when a federal court sitting in a diversity case is faced with a question of whether or not to apply state law, the importance of a state rule is indeed relevant, but only in the context of asking whether application of the rule would make so important a difference to the character or result of the litigation that failure to enforce it would unfairly discriminate against citizens of the forum State, or whether application of the rule would have so important an effect upon the fortunes of one or both of the litigants that failure to enforce it would be likely to cause a plaintiff to choose the federal court.

application of the state rule would wholly bar recovery;[10] rather, adherence to the state rule would have resulted only in altering the way in which process was served.[11] Moreover, it is difficult to argue that permitting service of defendant's wife to take the place of inhand service of defendant himself alters the mode of enforcement of state-created rights in a fashion sufficiently "substantial" to raise the sort of equal protection problems to which the *Erie* opinion alluded.

There is, however, a more fundamental flaw in respondent's syllogism: the incorrect assumption that the rule of *Erie R. Co. v. Tompkins* constitutes the appropriate test of the validity and therefore the applicability of a Federal Rule of Civil Procedure. The *Erie* rule has never been invoked to void a Federal Rule. It is true that there have been cases where this Court has held applicable a state rule in the face of an argument that the situation was governed by one of the Federal Rules. But the holding of each such case was not that Erie commanded displacement of a Federal Rule by an inconsistent state rule, but rather that the scope of the Federal Rule was not as broad as the losing party urged, and therefore, there being no Federal Rule which covered the point in dispute, Erie commanded the enforcement of state law.

> Respondent contends in the first place that the charge was correct because of the fact that Rule 8(c) of the Rules of Civil Procedure makes contributory negligence an affirmative defense. We do not agree. Rule 8(c) covers only the manner of pleading. The question of the burden of establishing contributory negligence is a question of local law which federal courts in diversity of citizenship cases (*Erie R. Co. v. Tompkins*, 304 U.S. 64) must apply. *Palmer v. Hoffman*, 318 U.S. 109, 117.

(Here, of course, the clash is unavoidable; Rule 4(d)(1) says— implicitly, but with unmistakable clarity—that inhand service is not required in federal courts.) At the same time, in cases adjudicating the validity of Federal Rules, we have not applied the *York* rule or other refinements of *Erie*, but have to this day continued to decide questions concerning the scope of the Enabling Act and the constitutionality of specific Federal Rules in light of the distinction set forth in *Sibbach*. E.g., *Schlagenhauf v. Holder*, 379 U.S. 104.

---

[10] *See Guaranty Trust Co. of New York v. York, supra*, 326 U.S. at 108–109; *Ragan v. Merchants Transfer & Warehouse Co.*, supra, 337 U.S. at 532; *Woods v. Interstate Realty Co.*, *supra*, note 5, 337 U.S. at 538.

Similarly, a federal court's refusal to enforce the New Jersey rule involved in *Cohen v. Beneficial Indus. Loan Corp.*, 337 U.S. 541, requiring the posting of security by plaintiffs in stockholders' derivative actions, might well impel a stockholder to choose to bring suit in the federal, rather than the state, court.

[11] Cf. *Monarch Insurance Co. of Ohio v. Spach*, 281 F.2d 401, 412 (C.A.5th Cir. 1960). We cannot seriously entertain the thought that one suing an estate would be led to choose the federal court because of a belief that adherence to Rule 4(d)(1) is less likely to give the executor actual notice than § 9, and therefore more likely to produce a default judgment. Rule 4(d)(1) is well designed to give actual notice, as it did in this case.

Nor has the development of two separate lines of cases been inadvertent. The line between "substance" and "procedure" shifts as the legal context changes. "Each implies different variables depending upon the particular problem for which it is used." *Guaranty Trust Co. v. York, supra*, 326 U.S. at 108. It is true that both the Enabling Act and the *Erie* rule say, roughly, that federal courts are to apply state "substantive" law and federal "procedural" law, but from that it need not follow that the tests are identical. For they were designed to control very different sorts of decisions. When a situation is covered by one of the Federal Rules, the question facing the court is a far cry from the typical, relatively unguided *Erie* Choice: the court has been instructed to apply the Federal Rule, and can refuse to do so only if the Advisory Committee, this Court, and Congress erred in their prima facie judgment that the Rule in question transgresses neither the terms of the Enabling Act nor constitutional restrictions.

We are reminded by the *Erie* opinion that neither Congress nor the federal courts can, under the guise of formulating rules of decision for federal courts, fashion rules which are not supported by a grant of federal authority contained in Article I or some other section of the Constitution; in such areas state law must govern because there can be no other law. But the opinion in *Erie*, which involved no Federal Rule and dealt with a question which was "substantive" in every traditional sense (whether the railroad owed a duty of care to Tompkins as a trespasser or a licensee), surely neither said nor implied that measures like Rule 4(d)(1) are unconstitutional. For the constitutional provision for a federal court system (augmented by the Necessary and Proper Clause) carries with it congressional power to make rules governing the practice and pleading in those courts, which in turn includes a power to regulate matters which, though falling within the uncertain area between substance and procedure, are rationally capable of classification as either. *Cf. M'Culloch v. State of Maryland*, 4 Wheat. 316, 421. Neither *York* nor the cases following it ever suggested that the rule there laid down for coping with situations where no Federal Rule applies is coextensive with the limitation on Congress to which *Erie* had adverted. Although this Court has never before been confronted with a case where the applicable Federal Rule is in direct collision with the law of the relevant State,[15] courts of appeals faced with such clashes have rightly discerned the implications of our decisions.

One of the shaping purposes of the Federal Rules is to bring about uniformity in the federal courts by getting away from local rules. This is especially true of matters which relate

---

[15] In *Sibbach v. Wilson & Co.* the law of the forum State (Illinois) forbade the sort of order authorized by Rule 35. However, *Sibbach* was decided before *Klaxon Co. v. Stentor Electric Mfg. Co.*, and the *Sibbach* opinion makes clear that the Court was proceeding on the assumption that if the law of any State was relevant, it was the law of the State where the tort occurred (Indiana), which, like Rule 35, made provision for such orders. 312 U.S., at 6–7, 10–11.

to the administration of legal proceedings, an area in which federal courts have traditionally exerted strong inherent power, completely aside from the powers Congress expressly conferred in the Rules. The purpose of the *Erie* doctrine, even as extended in *York* and *Ragan*, was never to bottle up federal courts with "outcome-determinative" and "integral-relations" stoppers—when there are "affirmative countervailing (federal) considerations" and when there is a Congressional mandate (the Rules) supported by constitutional authority. *Lumbermen's Mutual Casualty Co. v. Wright*, 322 F.2d 759, 764 (C.A.5th Cir. 1963).

Erie and its offspring cast no doubt on the long-recognized power of Congress to prescribe housekeeping rules for federal courts even though some of those rules will inevitably differ from comparable state rules. "When, because the plaintiff happens to be a non-resident, such a right is enforceable in a federal as well as in a State court, the forms and mode of enforcing the right may at times, naturally enough, vary because the two judicial systems are not identic." *Guaranty Trust Co. of New York v. York*, supra, 326 U.S. at 108. Thus, though a court, in measuring a Federal Rule against the standards contained in the Enabling Act and the Constitution, need not wholly blind itself to the degree to which the Rule makes the character and result of the federal litigation stray from the course it would follow in state courts, it cannot be forgotten that the *Erie* rule, and the guidelines suggested in *York*, were created to serve another purpose altogether. To hold that a Federal Rule of Civil Procedure must cease to function whenever it alters the mode of enforcing state-created rights would be to disembowel either the Constitution's grant of power over federal procedure or Congress' attempt to exercise that power in the Enabling Act. Rule 4(d)(1) is valid and controls the instant case.

Reversed.

■ MR. JUSTICE BLACK concurs in the result.

■ MR. JUSTICE HARLAN, concurring.

It is unquestionably true that up to now *Erie* and the cases following it have not succeeded in articulating a workable doctrine governing choice of law in diversity actions. I respect the Court's effort to clarify the situation in today's opinion. However, in doing so I think it has misconceived the constitutional premises of *Erie* and has failed to deal adequately with those past decisions upon which the courts below relied.

Erie was something more than an opinion which worried about "forum-shopping and avoidance of inequitable administration of the laws," although to be sure these were important elements of the decision. I have always regarded that decision as one of the modern cornerstones of our federalism, expressing policies that profoundly touch the allocation of judicial power between the state and federal systems. *Erie* recognized that there should not be two conflicting systems of law controlling the primary activity of citizens, for such alternative governing authority must necessarily give rise to a debilitating uncertainty in the planning of everyday affairs.[1] And it recognized that the scheme of our Constitution envisions an allocation of law-making functions between state and federal legislative processes which is undercut if the federal judiciary can make substantive law affecting state affairs beyond the bounds of congressional legislative powers in this regard. Thus, in diversity cases *Erie* commands that it be the state law governing primary private activity which prevails.

The shorthand formulations which have appeared in some past decisions are prone to carry untoward results that frequently arise from oversimplification. The Court is quite right in stating that the "outcome-determinative" test of *Guaranty Trust Co. v. York*, if taken literally, proves too much, for any rule, no matter how clearly "procedural," can affect the outcome of litigation if it is not obeyed. In turning from the "outcome" test of *York* back to the unadorned forum-shopping rationale of *Erie*, however, the Court falls prey to like oversimplification, for a simple forum-shopping rule also proves too much; litigants often choose a federal forum merely to obtain what they consider the advantages of the Federal Rules of Civil Procedure or to try their cases before a supposedly more favorable judge. To my mind the proper line of approach in determining whether to apply a state or a federal rule, whether "substantive" or "procedural," is to stay close to basic principles by inquiring if the choice of rule would substantially affect those primary decisions respecting human conduct which our constitutional system leaves to state regulation.[2] If so, *Erie* and the Constitution require that the state rule prevail, even in the face of a conflicting federal rule.

The Court weakens, if indeed it does not submerge, this basic principle by finding, in effect, a grant of substantive legislative power in the constitutional provision for a federal court system (compare *Swift v. Tyson*, 16 Pet. 1), and through it, setting up the Federal Rules as a body of law inviolate.

> (T)he constitutional provision for a federal court system * * * carries with it congressional power * * * to regulate matters which, though falling within the uncertain area between substance and procedure, are rationally capable of classification as either.

---

[1] Since the rules involved in the present case are parallel rather than conflicting, this first rationale does not come into play here.

[2] See Hart and Wechsler, *The Federal Court and the Federal System* 678. *Byrd v. Blue Ridge Rural Elec. Coop., Inc.*, 356 U.S. 525, 536–540, indicated that state procedures would apply if the State had manifested a particularly strong interest in their employment. *Compare Dice v. Akron, C. & Y.R. Co.*, 342 U.S. 359. However, this approach may not be of constitutional proportions.

So long as a reasonable man could characterize any duly adopted federal rule as "procedural," the Court, unless I misapprehend what is said, would have it apply no matter how seriously it frustrated a State's substantive regulation of the primary conduct and affairs of its citizens. Since the members of the Advisory Committee, the Judicial Conference, and this Court who formulated the Federal Rules are presumably reasonable men, it follows that the integrity of the Federal Rules is absolute. Whereas the unadulterated outcome and forum-shopping tests may err too far toward honoring state rules, I submit that the Court's "arguably procedural, ergo constitutional" test moves too fast and far in the other direction.

The courts below relied upon this Court's decisions in *Ragan v. Merchants Transfer & Warehouse Co.*, 337 U.S. 530, and *Cohen v. Beneficial Indus. Loan Corp.*, 337 U.S. 541. Those cases deserve more attention than this Court has given them, particularly *Ragan* which, if still good law, would in my opinion call for affirmance of the result reached by the Court of Appeals. Further, a discussion of these two cases will serve to illuminate the "diversity" thesis I am advocating.

In *Ragan* a Kansas statute of limitations provided that an action was deemed commenced when service was made on the defendant. Despite Federal Rule 3 which provides that an action commences with the filing of the complaint, the Court held that for purposes of the Kansas statute of limitations a diversity tort action commenced only when service was made upon the defendant. The effect of this holding was that although the plaintiff had filed his federal complaint within the state period of limitations, his action was barred because the federal marshal did not serve a summons on the defendant until after the limitations period had run. I think that the decision was wrong. At most, application of the Federal Rule would have meant that potential Kansas tort defendants would have to defer for a few days the satisfaction of knowing that they had not been sued within the limitations period. The choice of the Federal Rule would have had no effect on the primary stages of private activity from which torts arise, and only the most minimal effect on behavior following the commission of the tort. In such circumstances the interest of the federal system in proceeding under its own rules should have prevailed.

Cohen v. Beneficial Indus. Loan Corp. held that a federal diversity court must apply a state statute requiring a small stockholder in a stockholder derivative suit to post a bond securing payment of defense costs as a condition to prosecuting an action. Such a statute is not "outcome determinative"; the plaintiff can win with or without it. The Court now rationalizes the case on the ground that the statute might affect the plaintiff's choice of forum, but as has been pointed out, a simple forum-shopping test proves too much. The proper view of *Cohen* is in my opinion, that the statute was meant to inhibit small stockholders from instituting "strike suits," and thus it was designed and could be expected to have a substantial impact on private primary activity. Anyone who was at the trial bar during the period when *Cohen* arose can appreciate the strong state policy reflected in the statute. I think it wholly legitimate to view Federal Rule 23 as not purporting to deal with the problem. But even had the Federal Rules purported to do so, and in so doing provided a substantially less effective deterrent to strike suits, I think the state rule should still have prevailed. That is where I believe the Court's view differs from mine; for the Court attributes such overriding force to the Federal Rules that it is hard to think of a case where a conflicting state rule would be allowed to operate, even though the state rule reflected policy considerations which, under *Erie*, would lie within the realm of state legislative authority.

It remains to apply what has been said to the present case. The Massachusetts rule provides that an executor need not answer suits unless in-hand service was made upon him or notice of the action was filed in the proper registry of probate within one year of his giving bond. The evident intent of this statute is to permit an executor to distribute the estate which he is administering without fear that further liabilities may be outstanding for which he could be held personally liable. If the Federal District Court in Massachusetts applies Rule 4(d)(1) of the Federal Rules of Civil Procedure instead of the Massachusetts service rule, what effect would that have on the speed and assurance with which estates are distributed? As I see it, the effect would not be substantial. It would mean simply that an executor would have to check at his own house or the federal courthouse as well as the registry of probate before he could distribute the estate with impunity. As this does not seem enough to give rise to any real impingement on the vitality of the state policy which the Massachusetts rule is intended to serve, I concur in the judgment of the Court.

COMMENTS AND QUESTIONS CONCERNING *HANNA V. PLUMER*

1.   Chief Justice Warren summarizes Plumer's argument as follows:

Reduced to essentials, the argument is: (1) *Erie*, as refined in *York*, demands that federal courts apply state law whenever application of federal law in its stead will alter the outcome of the case. (2) In this case, a determination that the Massachusetts service requirements obtain will result in immediate victory for respondent. If, on the other hand, it should be held that Rule 4(d)(1) is applicable, the litigation will continue, with possible victory for petitioner. (3) Therefore, *Erie* demands application of the Massachusetts rule. The syllogism possesses an appealing simplicity, but is for several reasons invalid.

Why does Chief Justice Warren and the Court not accept this argument?

THE LAW APPLIED IN FEDERAL COURT: "ERIE CHOICES FOR THE

2.   Is Massachusetts' interest in personal service upon an executor particularly strong in this case? Although process was left with Plumer's wife, rather than personally given to Plumer, did he receive actual notice of the civil action?

3.   In an initial footnote to his opinion, Chief Justice Warren notes:

> Section 9 is in part a statute of limitations, providing that an executor need not "answer to an action * * * which is not commenced within one year from the time of his giving bond * * *." This part of the statute, the purpose of which is to speed the settlement of estates, is not involved in this case, since the action clearly was timely commenced.

Hanna v. Plumer, 380 U.S. 460, 463 n.1 (1965).

What, though, if the one-year state limitations period had not been met? Would a federal court be required to apply that state period in a diversity action?

4.   How does *Hanna* differ from *Erie*, *Guaranty Trust*, and *Byrd*, in which the question was whether state law should displace federal common law? Why is *Hanna* even considered within the line of *Erie* cases? Isn't it quite different to suggest that state law displace a properly adopted Federal Rule of Civil Procedure, as opposed to federal common law?

5.   Chief Justice Warren states in his opinion:

> Under the cases construing the scope of the [Rules] Enabling Act, Rule 4(d)(1) clearly passes muster. Prescribing the manner in which a defendant is to be notified that a suit has been instituted against him, it relates to the "practice and procedure of the district courts."

> "The test must be whether a rule really regulates procedure,—the judicial process for enforcing rights and duties recognized by substantive law and for justly administering remedy and redress for disregard or infraction of them." *Sibbach v. Wilson & Co.*, 312 U.S. 1, 14.

What is the likelihood that any Federal Rule will not be seen as "really regulat[ing] procedure"? Is Justice Harlan correct that, under this "arguably procedural, ergo constitutional" test, "the integrity of the Federal Rules is absolute"?

6.   Is the procedure by which a Federal Rule of Civil Procedure is adopted significant in determining whether such a rule can be displaced by state law?

As you learned in Section II(A) of Chapter 2, *supra* pp. 48–50, the creation of the Federal Rules was authorized by Congress with its 1934 passage of the Rules Enabling Act, 28 U.S.C. §§ 2071–2077. Initially, proposed Rules are considered by the Advisory Committee on Civil Rules, which publishes drafts of the proposed Rules that it may pursue. Based on the comments received to such drafts from members of the bench, bar, and general public, the Advisory Committee may decide to submit a proposed Rule or Rule amendment to the standing Committee on Rules of Practice and Procedure, which independently reviews any proposals and may, in turn, recommend a proposed Rule or amendment to the Judicial Conference (the policy-making body of the United States Courts). The Judicial Conference then may decide to recommend proposals to the Supreme Court, which can promulgate proposed Rules and Rules amendments by May 1 of each year. If Congress does not act by December 1 of that year to reject, modify, or defer the Supreme Court's proposed Rules, they become effective. *See* Administrative Office of the United States Courts, "How the Rulemaking Process Works," http://www.uscourts.gov/RulesAndPolicies/ rules/about-rulemaking/how-rulemaking-process-works.aspx.

Should a rule that has become a Federal Rule of Civil Procedure through this process be entitled to greater deference than "federal general common law"?

7.   Chief Justice Warren suggests that "every procedural variation" can be "outcome-determinative."

> For example, having brought suit in a federal court, a plaintiff cannot then insist on the right to file subsequent pleadings in accord with the time limits applicable in state courts, even though enforcement of the federal timetable will, if he continues to insist that he must meet only the state time limit, result in determination of the controversy against him. So it is here. Though choice of the federal or state rule will at this point have a marked effect upon the outcome of the litigation, the difference between the two rules would be of scant, if any, relevance to the choice of a forum.

Professor John Hart Ely has analyzed Chief Justice Warren's *Hanna* opinion as follows:

> The Court * * * suggested by its examples that a federal court may adhere to its own rules in diversity cases insofar, but only insofar, as they are neither materially more or less difficult for the burdened party to comply with than their state counterparts, nor likely to generate an outcome different from that which would result were the case litigated in the state court system and the state rules followed.
>
>   Thus, state rules controlling such things as burden of proof, presumptions, and sufficiency of evidence should be followed where they differ from the federal court's usual practice; but those regulating such matters as the form of pleadings, order of proof, time limits on responsive pleadings, and the method by which an adversary is given notice can ordinarily be disregarded, though of course there is no reason that they must.

Ely, "The Irrepressible Myth of *Erie*," 87 *Harv. L. Rev.* 693, 714–16 (1974).

8.   Another way to think about the possibility of different federal and state rules leading to forum shopping would be to consider the attorney's conversation with her client at the outset of the legal representation. In a case such as *Hanna*, is it likely that the attorney would say something like this to her client:

In thinking about whether it's best to file your action in federal or state court, I've decided not to worry about the possible state and federal judges or juries, the case backlogs, the distance to the state and federal courthouses, or the appellate structures in the state and federal courts.

Instead, we should file your action in federal court because, if we do, Mrs. Plumer may not give the process to Mr. Plumer.

9.   Does Chief Justice Warren believe that this case is controlled by *Erie*? Is the test different when it is a **F**ederal **R**ule, rather than just a federal rule, that is at issue?

10.   Justice Harlan concurred in the Court's unanimous decision in *Hanna*. His concurrence harks back to the majority opinion of Justice Brandeis in *Erie*:

> *Erie* was something more than an opinion which worried about "forum-shopping and avoidance of inequitable administration of the laws," although to be sure these were important elements of the decision. I have always regarded that decision as one of the modern cornerstones of our federalism, expressing policies that profoundly touch the allocation of judicial power between the state and federal systems.

Is Justice Harlan concerned that the Court may have moved too far in endorsing the displacement of state law by either federal rules or Federal Rules?

11.   Justice Harlan also uses his concurrence to offer his own test for the application of federal or state law in a diversity action:

> To my mind the proper line of approach in determining whether to apply a state or a federal rule, whether "substantive" or "procedural," is to stay close to basic principles by inquiring if the choice of rule would substantially affect those primary decisions respecting human conduct which our constitutional system leaves to state regulation. If so, *Erie* and the Constitution require that the state rule prevail, even in the face of a conflicting federal rule.

See also Ely, "The Irrepressible Myth of *Erie*," 87 *Harv. L. Rev.* 693, 725 (1974) ("The most helpful way, it seems to me, of defining a substantive rule—or more particularly a substantive right, which is what the [Rules Enabling] Act refers to—is as a right granted for one or more nonprocedural reasons, for some purpose or purposes not having to do with the fairness or efficiency of the litigation process.").

12.   Although there have been few cases such as *Hanna* in which the Supreme Court has resolved a direct conflict between state law and a Federal Rule of Civil Procedure, in several cases the Court has interpreted a Federal Rule narrowly—concluding that there is no conflicting law and that state law should be applied. *E.g.*, *Walker v. Armco Steel Corp.*, 446 U.S. 740 (1980) (state law, rather than Rule 3 of the Federal Rules of Civil Procedure, applies to determine when federal diversity action is

commenced); *Ragan v. Merchants Transfer & Warehouse Co.*, 337 U.S. 530 (1949) (same).

13. Figure 5–1 diagrams one way to conceptualize the *Erie-Hanna* decision-making process.

FIGURE 5–1
***ERIE RAILROAD* FLOWCHART**[7]

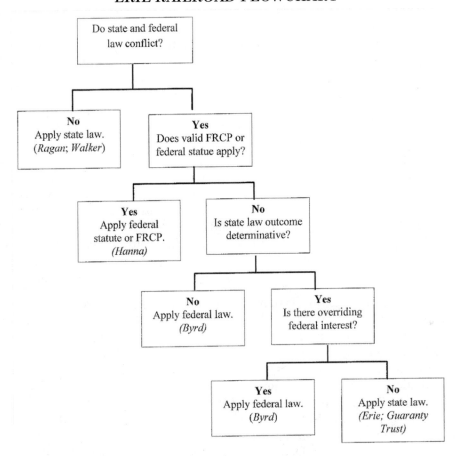

E. COLLISIONS, CONFLICTS, AND SENSITIVITY TO IMPORTANT STATE INTERESTS: *GASPERINI V. CENTER FOR HUMANITIES, INC.*

In *Erie* and *Hanna* the Court had to determine whether to apply state or federal law when those laws were in conflict. What, though, if the conflict between the state and federal law is not so clear? Consider the different approaches of Justices Ginsburg, Stevens, and Scalia in the following case.

---

[7]   This flowchart is based upon the "three question inquiry" suggested by Dean Erwin Chemerinsky in *Federal Jurisdiction* 341–42 (6th ed. 2012). *See also* Ely, "The Irrepressible Myth of *Erie*," 87 *Harv. L. Rev.* 693 (1974).

Gasperini v. Center for Humanities, Inc.

Supreme Court of the United States, 1996
518 U.S. 415

OPINION

■ JUSTICE GINSBURG delivered the opinion of the Court.

Under the law of New York, appellate courts are empowered to
review the size of jury verdicts and to order new trials when the jury's
award "deviates materially from what would be reasonable
compensation." N.Y. Civ. Prac. Law and Rules (CPLR) § 5501(c). Under
the Seventh Amendment, which governs proceedings in federal court,
but not in state court, "the right of trial by jury shall be preserved, and
no fact tried by a jury, shall be otherwise re-examined in any Court of
the United States, than according to the rules of the common law." The
compatibility of these provisions, in an action based on New York law
but tried in federal court by reason of the parties' diverse citizenship, is
the issue we confront in this case. We hold that New York's law
controlling compensation awards for excessiveness or inadequacy can be
given effect, without detriment to the Seventh Amendment, if the
review standard set out in CPLR § 5501(c) is applied by the federal trial
court judge, with appellate control of the trial court's ruling limited to
review for "abuse of discretion."

I

Petitioner William Gasperini, a journalist for CBS News and the
Christian Science Monitor, began reporting on events in Central
America in 1984. He earned his living primarily in radio and print
media and only occasionally sold his photographic work. During the
course of his seven-year stint in Central America, Gasperini took over
5,000 slide transparencies, depicting active war zones, political leaders,
and scenes from daily life. In 1990, Gasperini agreed to supply his
original color transparencies to The Center for Humanities, Inc.
(Center) for use in an educational videotape, *Conflict in Central
America*. Gasperini selected 300 of his slides for the Center; its
videotape included 110 of them. The Center agreed to return the
original transparencies, but upon the completion of the project, it could
not find them.

Gasperini commenced suit in the United States District Court for
the Southern District of New York, invoking the court's diversity
jurisdiction pursuant to 28 U.S.C. § 1332. He alleged several state-law
claims for relief, including breach of contract, conversion, and
negligence. The Center conceded liability for the lost transparencies
and the issue of damages was tried before a jury.

At trial, Gasperini's expert witness testified that the "industry
standard" within the photographic publishing community valued a lost
transparency at $1,500. This industry standard, the expert explained,
represented the average license fee a commercial photograph could earn

over the full course of the photographer's copyright, i.e., in Gasperini's case, his lifetime plus 50 years. Gasperini estimated that his earnings from photography totaled just over $10,000 for the period from 1984 through 1993. He also testified that he intended to produce a book containing his best photographs from Central America.

After a three-day trial, the jury awarded Gasperini $450,000 in compensatory damages. This sum, the jury foreperson announced, "is [$]1500 each, for 300 slides." Moving for a new trial under Federal Rule of Civil Procedure 59, the Center attacked the verdict on various grounds, including excessiveness. Without comment, the District Court denied the motion.

The Court of Appeals for the Second Circuit vacated the judgment entered on the jury's verdict. Mindful that New York law governed the controversy, the Court of Appeals endeavored to apply CPLR § 5501(c), which instructs that, when a jury returns an itemized verdict, as the jury did in this case, the New York Appellate Division "shall determine that an award is excessive or inadequate if it deviates materially from what would be reasonable compensation." The Second Circuit's application of § 5501(c) as a check on the size of the jury's verdict followed Circuit precedent * * *. Surveying Appellate Division decisions that reviewed damage awards for lost transparencies, the Second Circuit concluded that testimony on industry standard alone was insufficient to justify a verdict; prime among other factors warranting consideration were the uniqueness of the slides' subject matter and the photographer's earning level.

Guided by Appellate Division rulings, the Second Circuit held that the $450,000 verdict "materially deviates from what is reasonable compensation." Some of Gasperini's transparencies, the Second Circuit recognized, were unique, notably those capturing combat situations in which Gasperini was the only photographer present. But others "depicted either generic scenes or events at which other professional photojournalists were present." No more than 50 slides merited a $1,500 award, the court concluded, after "[g]iving Gasperini every benefit of the doubt." Absent evidence showing significant earnings from photographic endeavors or concrete plans to publish a book, the court further determined, any damage award above $100 each for the remaining slides would be excessive. Remittiturs "presen[t] difficult problems for appellate courts," the Second Circuit acknowledged, for court of appeals judges review the evidence from "a cold paper record." Nevertheless, the Second Circuit set aside the $450,000 verdict and ordered a new trial, unless Gasperini agreed to an award of $100,000.

This case presents an important question regarding the standard a federal court uses to measure the alleged excessiveness of a jury's verdict in an action for damages based on state law. We therefore granted certiorari.

II

Before 1986, state and federal courts in New York generally invoked the same judge-made formulation in responding to excessiveness attacks on jury verdicts: courts would not disturb an award unless the amount was so exorbitant that it "shocked the conscience of the court." * * *

In both state and federal courts, trial judges made the excessiveness assessment in the first instance, and appellate judges ordinarily deferred to the trial court's judgment.

In 1986, as part of a series of tort reform measures, New York codified a standard for judicial review of the size of jury awards. Placed in CPLR § 5501(c), the prescription reads:

> In reviewing a money judgment . . . in which it is contended that the award is excessive or inadequate and that a new trial should have been granted unless a stipulation is entered to a different award, the appellate division shall determine that an award is excessive or inadequate if it deviates materially from what would be reasonable compensation."

As stated in Legislative Findings and Declarations accompanying New York's adoption of the "deviates materially" formulation, the lawmakers found the "shock the conscience" test an insufficient check on damage awards; the legislature therefore installed a standard "invit[ing] more careful appellate scrutiny." At the same time, the legislature instructed the Appellate Division, in amended § 5522, to state the reasons for the court's rulings on the size of verdicts, and the factors the court considered in complying with § 5501(c). In his signing statement, then-Governor Mario Cuomo emphasized that the CPLR amendments were meant to rachet up the review standard: "This will assure greater scrutiny of the amount of verdicts and promote greater stability in the tort system and greater fairness for similarly situated defendants throughout the State."

New York state-court opinions confirm that § 5501(c)'s "deviates materially" standard calls for closer surveillance than "shock the conscience" oversight.

Although phrased as a direction to New York's intermediate appellate courts, § 5501(c)'s "deviates materially" standard, as construed by New York's courts, instructs state trial judges as well. Application of § 5501(c) at the trial level is key to this case.

To determine whether an award "deviates materially from what would be reasonable compensation," New York state courts look to awards approved in similar cases. Under New York's former "shock the conscience" test, courts also referred to analogous cases. The "deviates materially" standard, however, in design and operation, influences outcomes by tightening the range of tolerable awards.

III

In cases like Gasperini's, in which New York law governs the claims for relief, does New York law also supply the test for federal-court review of the size of the verdict? The Center answers yes. The "deviates materially" standard, it argues, is a substantive standard that must be applied by federal appellate courts in diversity cases. The Second Circuit agreed. Gasperini, emphasizing that § 5501(c) trains on the New York Appellate Division, characterizes the provision as procedural, an allocation of decisionmaking authority regarding damages, not a hard cap on the amount recoverable. Correctly comprehended, Gasperini urges, § 5501(c)'s direction to the Appellate Division cannot be given effect by federal appellate courts without violating the Seventh Amendment's Re-examination Clause.

As the parties' arguments suggest, CPLR § 5501(c), appraised under *Erie R. Co. v. Tompkins*, 304 U.S. 64 (1938), and decisions in *Erie*'s path, is both "substantive" and "procedural": "substantive" in that § 5501(c)'s "deviates materially" standard controls how much a plaintiff can be awarded; "procedural" in that § 5501(c) assigns decisionmaking authority to New York's Appellate Division. Parallel application of § 5501(c) at the federal appellate level would be out of sync with the federal system's division of trial and appellate court functions, an allocation weighted by the Seventh Amendment. The dispositive question, therefore, is whether federal courts can give effect to the substantive thrust of § 5501(c) without untoward alteration of the federal scheme for the trial and decision of civil cases.

A

Federal diversity jurisdiction provides an alternative forum for the adjudication of state-created rights, but it does not carry with it generation of rules of substantive law. As *Erie* read the Rules of Decision Act: "Except in matters governed by the Federal Constitution or by Acts of Congress, the law to be applied in any case is the law of the State." 304 U.S., at 78. Under the *Erie* doctrine, federal courts sitting in diversity apply state substantive law and federal procedural law.

Classification of a law as "substantive" or "procedural" for Erie purposes is sometimes a challenging endeavor.[7] *Guaranty Trust Co. v.*

---

[7] Concerning matters covered by the Federal Rules of Civil Procedure, the characterization question is usually unproblematic: It is settled that if the Rule in point is consonant with the Rules Enabling Act, 28 U.S.C. § 2072, and the Constitution, the Federal Rule applies regardless of contrary state law. See *Hanna v. Plumer*, 380 U.S. 460, 469–474 (1965); *Burlington Northern R. Co. v. Woods*, 480 U.S. 1, 4–5 (1987). Federal courts have interpreted the Federal Rules, however, with sensitivity to important state interests and regulatory policies. See, e.g., *Walker v. Armco Steel Corp.*, 446 U.S. 740, 750–752 (1980) (reaffirming decision in *Ragan v. Merchants Transfer & Warehouse Co.*, 337 U.S. 530 (1949)), that state law rather than Rule 3 determines when a diversity action commences for the purposes of tolling the state statute of limitations; Rule 3 makes no reference to the tolling of state limitations, the Court observed, and accordingly found no "direct conflict"); *S.A. Healy Co. v. Milwaukee Metropolitan Sewerage Dist.*, 60 F.3d 305, 310–312 (C.A.7 1995) (state

York, 326 U.S. 99 (1945), an early interpretation of *Erie*, propounded an "outcome-determination" test: "[D]oes it significantly affect the result of a litigation for a federal court to disregard a law of a State that would be controlling in an action upon the same claim by the same parties in a State court?" 326 U.S., at 109. Ordering application of a state statute of limitations to an equity proceeding in federal court, the Court said in *Guaranty Trust*: "[W]here a federal court is exercising jurisdiction solely because of the diversity of citizenship of the parties, the outcome of the litigation in the federal court should be substantially the same, so far as legal rules determine the outcome of a litigation, as it would be if tried in a State court." *Ibid.*; *see also Ragan v. Merchants Transfer & Warehouse Co.*, 337 U.S. 530, 533 (1949) (when local law that creates the cause of action qualifies it, "federal court must follow suit," for "a different measure of the cause of action in one court than in the other [would transgress] the principle of *Erie*"). A later pathmarking case, qualifying *Guaranty Trust*, explained that the "outcome-determination" test must not be applied mechanically to sweep in all manner of variations; instead, its application must be guided by "the twin aims of the *Erie* rule: discouragement of forum-shopping and avoidance of inequitable administration of the laws." *Hanna v. Plumer*, 380 U.S. 460, 468 (1965).

Informed by these decisions, we address the question whether New York's "deviates materially" standard, codified in CPLR § 5501(c), is outcome affective in this sense: Would "application of the [standard] . . . have so important an effect upon the fortunes of one or both of the litigants that failure to [apply] it would [unfairly discriminate against citizens of the forum State, or] be likely to cause a plaintiff to choose the federal court"? *Id.*, at 468, n. 9.[8]

We start from a point the parties do not debate. Gasperini acknowledges that a statutory cap on damages would supply substantive law for *Erie* purposes. Although CPLR § 5501(c) is less readily classified, it was designed to provide an analogous control.

New York's Legislature codified in § 5501(c) a new standard, one that requires closer court review than the common-law "shock the conscience" test. More rigorous comparative evaluations attend application of § 5501(c)'s "deviates materially" standard. To foster predictability, the legislature required the reviewing court, when overturning a verdict under § 5501(c), to state its reasons, including the factors it considered relevant. We think it a fair conclusion that CPLR

---

provision for offers of settlement by plaintiffs is compatible with Federal Rule 68, which is limited to offers by defendants).

[8]   *Hanna* keyed the question to *Erie*'s "twin aims"; in full, *Hanna* instructed federal courts to ask "whether application of the [State's] rule would make so important a difference to the character or result of the litigation that failure to enforce it would unfairly discriminate against citizens of the forum State, or whether application of the rule would have so important an effect upon the fortunes of one or both of the litigants that failure to enforce it would be likely to cause a plaintiff to choose the federal court." 380 U.S., at 468, n. 9.

§ 5501(c) differs from a statutory cap principally "in that the maximum amount recoverable is not set forth by statute, but rather is determined by case law." Brief for City of New York as Amicus Curiae 11. In sum, § 5501(c) contains a procedural instruction, but the State's objective is manifestly substantive.

It thus appears that if federal courts ignore the change in the New York standard and persist in applying the "shock the conscience" test to damage awards on claims governed by New York law, " 'substantial' variations between state and federal [money judgments]" may be expected. *See Hanna*, 380 U.S., at 467–468. We therefore agree with the Second Circuit that New York's check on excessive damages implicates what we have called *Erie's* "twin aims."[12] Just as the *Erie* principle precludes a federal court from giving a state-created claim "longer life . . . than [the claim] would have had in the state court," *Ragan*, 337 U.S., at 533–534, so *Erie* precludes a recovery in federal court significantly larger than the recovery that would have been tolerated in state court.

B

CPLR § 5501(c), as earlier noted, is phrased as a direction to the New York Appellate Division. Acting essentially as a surrogate for a New York appellate forum, the Court of Appeals reviewed Gasperini's award to determine if it "deviate[d] materially" from damage awards the Appellate Division permitted in similar circumstances. The Court of Appeals performed this task without benefit of an opinion from the District Court, which had denied "without comment" the Center's Rule 59 motion. Concentrating on the authority § 5501(c) gives to the Appellate Division, Gasperini urges that the provision shifts fact-finding responsibility from the jury and the trial judge to the appellate court. Assigning such responsibility to an appellate court, he maintains, is incompatible with the Seventh Amendment's Reexamination Clause, and therefore, Gasperini concludes, § 5501(c) cannot be given effect in federal court. Although we reach a different conclusion than Gasperini, we agree that the Second Circuit did not attend to "[a]n essential characteristic of [the federal court] system," *Byrd v. Blue Ridge Rural Elec. Cooperative, Inc.*, 356 U.S. 525, 537, (1958), when it used § 5501(c) as "the standard for [federal] appellate review."

That "essential characteristic" was described in *Byrd*, a diversity suit for negligence in which a pivotal issue of fact would have been tried by a judge were the case in state court. The *Byrd* Court held that, despite the state practice, the plaintiff was entitled to a jury trial in federal court. In so ruling, the Court said that the *Guaranty Trust*

---

[12] For rights that are state created, state law governs the amount properly awarded as punitive damages, subject to an ultimate federal constitutional check for exorbitancy. *See BMW of North America, Inc. v. Gore*, 517 U.S. 559, 568 (1996); *Browning-Ferris Industries of Vt., Inc. v. Kelco Disposal, Inc.*, 492 U.S. 257, 278–279 (1989). An evenhanded approach would require federal-court deference to endeavors like New York's to control compensatory damages for excessiveness.

"outcome-determination" test was an insufficient guide in cases presenting countervailing federal interests. The Court described the countervailing federal interests present in *Byrd* this way:

> The federal system is an independent system for administering justice to litigants who properly invoke its jurisdiction. An essential characteristic of that system is the manner in which, in civil common-law actions, it distributes trial functions between judge and jury and, under the influence—if not the command—of the Seventh Amendment, assigns the decisions of disputed questions of fact to the jury.

The Seventh Amendment, which governs proceedings in federal court, but not in state court, bears not only on the allocation of trial functions between judge and jury, the issue in *Byrd*; it also controls the allocation of authority to review verdicts, the issue of concern here. The Amendment reads:

> In Suits at common law, where the value in controversy shall exceed twenty dollars, the right of trial by jury shall be preserved, and no fact tried by a jury, shall be otherwise re-examined in any Court of the United States, than according to the rules of the common law.

Byrd involved the first Clause of the Amendment, the "trial by jury" Clause. This case involves the second, the "Reexamination" Clause. In keeping with the historic understanding, the Reexamination Clause does not inhibit the authority of trial judges to grant new trials "for any of the reasons for which new trials have heretofore been granted in actions at law in the courts of the United States." Fed. Rule Civ. Proc. 59(a). That authority is large. "The trial judge in the federal system," we have reaffirmed, "has . . . discretion to grant a new trial if the verdict appears to [the judge] to be against the weight of the evidence." *Byrd*, 356 U.S., at 540. This discretion includes overturning verdicts for excessiveness and ordering a new trial without qualification, or conditioned on the verdict winner's refusal to agree to a reduction (remittitur). *See Dimick v. Schiedt*, 293 U.S. 474, 486–487 (1935) (recognizing that remittitur withstands Seventh Amendment attack, but rejecting additur as unconstitutional).

In contrast, appellate review of a federal trial court's denial of a motion to set aside a jury's verdict as excessive is a relatively late, and less secure, development. Such review was once deemed inconsonant with the Seventh Amendment's Reexamination Clause. * * *

Before today, we have not "expressly [held] that the Seventh Amendment allows appellate review of a district court's denial of a motion to set aside an award as excessive." *Browning-Ferris Industries of Vt., Inc. v. Kelco Disposal, Inc.*, 492 U.S. 257, 279, n. 25 (1989). But in successive reminders that the question was worthy of this Court's attention, we noted, without disapproval, that courts of appeals engage in review of district court excessiveness determinations, applying "abuse of discretion" as their standard. We noted the Circuit decisions in point, and, in *Browning-Ferris*, we again referred to appellate court abuse-of-discretion review:

> [T]he role of the district court is to determine whether the jury's verdict is within the confines set by state law, and to determine, by reference to federal standards developed under Rule 59, whether a new trial or remittitur should be ordered. The court of appeals should then review the district court's determination under an abuse-of-discretion standard. 492 U.S., at 279.

As the Second Circuit explained, appellate review for abuse of discretion is reconcilable with the Seventh Amendment as a control necessary and proper to the fair administration of justice: "We must give the benefit of every doubt to the judgment of the trial judge; but surely there must be an upper limit, and whether that has been surpassed is not a question of fact with respect to which reasonable men may differ, but a question of law." *Dagnello v. Long Island R. Co.*, 289 F.2d 797, 806 (C.A.2 1961) (quoted in *Grunenthal*, 393 U.S., at 159). All other Circuits agree. We now approve this line of decisions, and thus make explicit what Justice Stewart thought implicit in our *Grunenthal* disposition: "[N]othing in the Seventh Amendment ... precludes appellate review of the trial judge's denial of a motion to set aside [a jury verdict] as excessive." 393 U.S., at 164 (Stewart, J., dissenting).[20]

C

In *Byrd*, the Court faced a one-or-the-other choice: trial by judge as in state court, or trial by jury according to the federal practice.[21] In the case before us, a choice of that order is not required, for the principal state and federal interests can be accommodated. The Second Circuit correctly recognized that when New York substantive law governs a claim for relief, New York law and decisions guide the allowable damages. But that court did not take into account the characteristic of

---

[20] If the meaning of the Seventh Amendment were fixed at 1791, our civil juries would remain, as they unquestionably were at common law, "twelve good men and true," 3 W. Blackstone, *Commentaries* 349. *But see Colgrove v. Battin*, 413 U.S. 149, 160 (1973) (six-member jury for civil trials satisfies Seventh Amendment's guarantee). Procedures we have regarded as compatible with the Seventh Amendment, although not in conformity with practice at common law when the Amendment was adopted, include new trials restricted to the determination of damages, *Gasoline Products Co. v. Champlin Refining Co.*, 283 U.S. 494 (1931), and Federal Rule of Civil Procedure 50(b)'s motion for judgment as a matter of law, *see* 9A Charles A. Wright & Arthur R. Miller, & Mary Kay Kane, *Federal Practice and Procedure* § 2522, pp. 244–246 (2d ed.1995). *See also Parklane Hosiery Co. v. Shore*, 439 U.S. 322, 335–337 (1979) (issue preclusion absent mutuality of parties does not violate Seventh Amendment, although common law as it existed in 1791 permitted issue preclusion only when there was mutuality).

[21] The two-trial rule posited by Justice SCALIA, surely would be incompatible with the existence of "[t]he federal system [as] an independent system for administering justice," *Byrd v. Blue Ridge Rural Elec. Cooperative, Inc.*, 356 U.S. 525, 537 (1958). We discern no disagreement on such examples among the many federal judges who have considered this case.

the federal court system that caused us to reaffirm: "The proper role of
the trial and appellate courts in the federal system in reviewing the size
of jury verdicts is ... a matter of federal law." *Donovan v. Penn
Shipping Co.*, 429 U.S. 648, 649 (1977) (*per curiam*); *see also Browning-
Ferris*, 492 U.S., at 279 ("[T]he role of the district court is to determine
whether the jury's verdict is within the confines set by state law. . . .
The court of appeals should then review the district court's
determination under an abuse-of-discretion standard.").

New York's dominant interest can be respected, without disrupting
the federal system, once it is recognized that the federal district court is
capable of performing the checking function, i.e., that court can apply
the State's "deviates materially" standard in line with New York case
law evolving under CPLR § 5501(c).[22] We recall, in this regard, that the
"deviates materially" standard serves as the guide to be applied in trial
as well as appellate courts in New York.

Within the federal system, practical reasons combine with Seventh
Amendment constraints to lodge in the district court, not the court of
appeals, primary responsibility for application of § 5501(c)'s "deviates
materially" check. Trial judges have the "unique opportunity to consider
the evidence in the living courtroom context," *Taylor v. Washington
Terminal Co.*, 409 F.2d 145, 148 (C.A.D.C.1969), while appellate judges
see only the "cold paper record," 66 F.3d, at 431.

District court applications of the "deviates materially" standard
would be subject to appellate review under the standard the Circuits
now employ when inadequacy or excessiveness is asserted on appeal:
abuse of discretion. In light of *Erie*'s doctrine, the federal appeals court
must be guided by the damage-control standard state law supplies,[23]
but as the Second Circuit itself has said: "If we reverse, it must be
because of an abuse of discretion. . . . The very nature of the problem

---

[22] Justice SCALIA finds in Federal Rule of Civil Procedure 59 a "federal standard" for
new trial motions in " 'direct collision' " with, and " 'leaving no room for the operation of,' " a
state law like CPLR § 5501(c). The relevant prescription, Rule 59(a), has remained unchanged
since the adoption of the Federal Rules by this Court in 1937. Rule 59(a) is as encompassing as
it is uncontroversial. It is indeed "Hornbook" law that a most usual ground for a Rule 59
motion is that "the damages are excessive." See C. Wright, *Law of Federal Courts* 676–677
(5th ed.1994). Whether damages are excessive for the claim-in-suit must be governed by some
law. And there is no candidate for that governance other than the law that gives rise to the
claim for relief—here, the law of New York. See 28 U.S.C. § 2072(a) and (b) ("Supreme Court
shall have the power to prescribe general rules of . . . procedure"; "[s]uch rules shall not
abridge, enlarge or modify any substantive right"); *Browning-Ferris*, 492 U.S., at 279
("standard of excessiveness" is a "matte[r] of state, and not federal, common law"); see also R.
Fallon, D. Meltzer, & D. Shapiro, *Hart and Wechsler's The Federal Courts and the Federal
System* 729–730 (4th ed.1996) (observing that Court "has continued since [*Hanna v. Plumer*,
380 U.S. 460 (1965),] to interpret the federal rules to avoid conflict with important state
regulatory policies," citing *Walker v. Armco Steel Corp.*, 446 U.S. 740 (1980)).

[23] If liability and damage-control rules are split apart here, as Justice SCALIA says they
must be to save the Seventh Amendment, then Gasperini's claim and others like it would be
governed by a most curious "law." The sphinx-like, damage-determining law he would apply to
this controversy has a state forepart, but a federal hindquarter. The beast may not be brutish,
but there is little judgment in its creation.

counsels restraint. . . . We must give the benefit of every doubt to the judgment of the trial judge." *Dagnello*, 289 F.2d, at 806.

IV

It does not appear that the District Court checked the jury's verdict against the relevant New York decisions demanding more than "industry standard" testimony to support an award of the size the jury returned in this case. As the Court of Appeals recognized, the uniqueness of the photographs and the plaintiff's earnings as photographer—past and reasonably projected—are factors relevant to appraisal of the award. Accordingly, we vacate the judgment of the Court of Appeals and instruct that court to remand the case to the District Court so that the trial judge, revisiting his ruling on the new trial motion, may test the jury's verdict against CPLR § 5501(c)'s "deviates materially" standard.

It is so ordered.

■ JUSTICE STEVENS, dissenting.

While I agree with most of the reasoning in the Court's opinion, I disagree with its disposition of the case. I would affirm the judgment of the Court of Appeals. I would also reject the suggestion that the Seventh Amendment limits the power of a federal appellate court sitting in diversity to decide whether a jury's award of damages exceeds a limit established by state law.

I

The Court correctly explains why the 1986 enactment of § 5501(c) of the N.Y. Civ. Prac. Law and Rules changed the substantive law of the State. A state-law ceiling on allowable damages, whether fixed by a dollar limit or by a standard that forbids any award that "deviates materially from what would be reasonable compensation," is a substantive rule of decision that federal courts must apply in diversity cases governed by New York law.

I recognize that state rules of appellate procedure do not necessarily bind federal appellate courts. The majority persuasively shows, however, that New York has not merely adopted a new procedure for allocating the decisionmaking function between trial and appellate courts. Instead, New York courts have held that all jury awards, not only those reviewed on appeal, must conform to the requirement that they not "deviat[e] materially" from amounts awarded in like cases. That New York has chosen to tie its damages ceiling to awards traditionally recovered in similar cases, rather than to a legislatively determined but inflexible monetary sum, is none of our concern.

Given the nature of the state-law command, the Court of Appeals for the Second Circuit correctly concluded in *Consorti v. Armstrong World Industries, Inc.*, 64 F.3d 781, superseded, 72 F.3d 1003 (1995),

that New York's excessiveness standard applies in federal court in
diversity cases controlled by New York law. *Consorti* erred in basing
that conclusion in part on the fact that a New York statute requires
that State's appellate division to apply the standard, but it was
nevertheless faithful to the Rules of Decisions Act, as construed in *Erie
R. Co. v. Tompkins*, 304 U.S. 64 (1938), in holding that a state-law
limitation on the size of a judgment could not be ignored.[1] Similarly, the
Court of Appeals correctly followed *Consorti* in this case and considered
whether the damages awarded materially deviated from damages
awarded in similar cases. I endorse both opinions in these respects.

Although the majority agrees with the Court of Appeals that New
York law establishes the size of the damages that may be awarded, it
chooses to vacate and remand. The majority holds that a federal court of
appeals should review for abuse of discretion a district court's decision
to deny a motion for new trial based on a jury's excessive award. As a
result, it concludes that the District Court should be given the
opportunity to apply in the first instance the "deviates materially"
standard that New York law imposes.

The District Court had its opportunity to consider the propriety of
the jury's award, and it erred. The Court of Appeals has now corrected
that error after "drawing all reasonable inferences in favor of"
petitioner. As there is no reason to suppose that the Court of Appeals
has reached a conclusion with which the District Court could
permissibly disagree on remand, I would not require the District Court
to repeat a task that has already been well-performed by the reviewing
court. I therefore would affirm the judgment of the Court of Appeals.

II

Although I have addressed the question presented as if our decision
in *Erie* alone controlled its outcome, petitioner argues that the second
clause of the Seventh Amendment, which states that "no fact tried by
jury, shall be otherwise re-examined in any Court of the United States,
than according to the rules of the common law," bars the procedure
followed by the Court of Appeals. There is no merit to that position.

Early cases do state that the Reexamination Clause prohibits
appellate review of excessive jury awards, but they do not foreclose the
practice altogether. Indeed, for the last 30 years, we have consistently
reserved the question whether the Constitution permits such review,

---

[1] Because there is no conceivable conflict between Federal Rule of Civil Procedure 59
and the application of the New York damages limit, this case is controlled by *Erie* and the
Rules of Decision Act, rather than by the Rules Enabling Act's limitation on federal procedural
rules that conflict with state substantive rights. The Rule does state that new trials may be
granted "for any of the reasons for which new trials have heretofore been granted in actions at
law in the courts of the United States," but that hardly constitutes a command that federal
courts must always substitute federal limits on the size of judgments for those set by the
several States in cases founded upon state-law causes of action. Even at the time of the Rule's
adoption, federal courts were bound to apply state statutory law in such cases.

and, in the meantime, every Court of Appeals has agreed that the Seventh Amendment establishes no bar.

Taking the question to be an open one, I start with certain basic principles. It is well settled that jury verdicts are not binding on either trial judges or appellate courts if they are unauthorized by law. A verdict may be insupportable as a matter of law either because of deficiencies in the evidence or because an award of damages is larger than permitted by law. If an award is excessive as a matter of law—in a diversity case if it is larger than applicable state law permits—a trial judge has a duty to set it aside. A failure to do so is an error of law that the court of appeals has a duty to correct on appeal.

These principles are sufficiently well established that no Seventh Amendment issue would arise if an appellate court ordered a new trial because a jury award exceeded a monetary cap on allowable damages. That New York has chosen to define its legal limit in less mathematical terms does not require a different constitutional conclusion.

* * *

Here, New York has prescribed an objective, legal limitation on damages. If an appellate court may reverse a jury's damages award when its own conscience has been shocked, or its sense of justice outraged, it may surely follow a sovereign's command that it do so when a jury has materially deviated from awards granted by other juries. If anything, the New York standard, though less deferential, is more certain.

III

For the reasons set forth above, I agree with the majority that the Reexamination Clause does not bar federal appellate courts from reviewing jury awards for excessiveness. I confess to some surprise, however, at its conclusion that " 'the influence—if not the command—of the Seventh Amendment,' " ante, at 2222 (quoting *Byrd v. Blue Ridge Rural Elec. Cooperative, Inc.*, 356 U.S. 525, 537 (1958)) requires federal courts of appeals to review district court applications of state-law excessiveness standards for an "abuse of discretion." Ante, at 2225.

The majority's persuasive demonstration that New York law sets forth a substantive limitation on the size of jury awards seems to refute the contention that New York has merely asked appellate courts to reexamine facts. The majority's analysis would thus seem to undermine the conclusion that the Reexamination Clause is relevant to this case.

Certainly, our decision in *Byrd* does not make the Clause relevant. There, we considered only whether the Seventh Amendment's first clause should influence our decision to give effect to a state-law rule denying the right to a jury altogether. That holding in no way requires us to consult the Amendment's second clause to determine the standard of review for a district court's application of state substantive law.

My disagreement is tempered, however, because the majority carefully avoids defining too strictly the abuse-of-discretion standard it announces. To the extent that the majority relies only on "practical reasons" for its conclusion that the Court of Appeals should give some weight to the District Court's assessment in determining whether state substantive law has been properly applied, I do not disagree with its analysis.

As a matter of federal-court administration, we have recognized in other contexts the need for according some deference to the lower court's resolution of legal, yet fact-intensive, questions. Indeed, it is a familiar, if somewhat circular, maxim that deems an error of law an abuse of discretion.

In the end, therefore, my disagreement with the label that the majority attaches to the standard of appellate review should not obscure the far more fundamental point on which we agree. Whatever influence the Seventh Amendment may be said to exert, *Erie* requires federal appellate courts sitting in diversity to apply "the damage-control standard state law supplies."

IV

Because I would affirm the judgment of the Court of Appeals, and because I do not agree that the Seventh Amendment in any respect influences the proper analysis of the question presented, I respectfully dissent.

■ JUSTICE SCALIA, with whom the CHIEF JUSTICE and JUSTICE THOMAS join, dissenting.

Today the Court overrules a longstanding and well-reasoned line of precedent that has for years prohibited federal appellate courts from reviewing refusals by district courts to set aside civil jury awards as contrary to the weight of the evidence. One reason is given for overruling these cases: that the Courts of Appeals have, for some time now, decided to ignore them. Such unreasoned capitulation to the nullification of what was long regarded as a core component of the Bill of Rights—the Seventh Amendment's prohibition on appellate reexamination of civil jury awards—is wrong. It is not for us, much less for the Courts of Appeals, to decide that the Seventh Amendment's restriction on federal-court review of jury findings has outlived its usefulness.

The Court also holds today that a state practice that relates to the division of duties between state judges and juries must be followed by federal courts in diversity cases. On this issue, too, our prior cases are directly to the contrary.

As I would reverse the judgment of the Court of Appeals, I respectfully dissent.

I

* * *

A

Granting appellate courts authority to decide whether an award is "excessive or inadequate" in the manner of CPLR § 5501(c) may reflect a sound understanding of the capacities of modern juries and trial judges. That is to say, the people of the State of New York may well be correct that such a rule contributes to a more just legal system. But the practice of federal appellate reexamination of facts found by a jury is precisely what the People of the several States considered not to be good legal policy in 1791. Indeed, so fearful were they of such a practice that they constitutionally prohibited it by means of the Seventh Amendment.

That Amendment was Congress's response to one of the principal objections to the proposed Constitution raised by the Anti-Federalists during the ratification debates: its failure to ensure the right to trial by jury in civil actions in federal court. The desire for an explicit constitutional guarantee against reexamination of jury findings was explained by Justice Story, sitting as Circuit Justice in 1812, as having been specifically prompted by Article III's conferral of "appellate Jurisdiction, both as to Law and Fact" upon the Supreme Court. "[O]ne of the most powerful objections urged against [the Constitution]," he recounted, was that this authority "would enable that court, with or without a new jury, to re-examine the whole facts, which had been settled by a previous jury." *United States v. Wonson*, 28 F.Cas. 745, 750 (No. 16,750) (C.C.Mass.).

The second clause of the Amendment responded to that concern by providing that "[i]n [s]uits at common law . . . no fact tried by a jury, shall be otherwise re-examined in any Court of the United States, than according to the rules of the common law." The Reexamination Clause put to rest "apprehensions" of "new trials by the appellate courts," *Wonson*, 28 F.Cas., at 750, by adopting, in broad fashion, "the rules of the common law" to govern federal-court interference with jury determinations. * * * It quite plainly barred reviewing courts from entertaining claims that the jury's verdict was contrary to the evidence.

* * *

C

The Court, as is its wont of late, all but ignores the relevant history. * * * That our earlier cases are so poorly recounted is not surprising, however, given the scant analysis devoted to the conclusion that "appellate review for abuse of discretion is reconcilable with the Seventh Amendment."

* * *

In the last analysis, the Court frankly abandons any pretense at faithfulness to the common law, suggesting that "the meaning" of the Reexamination Clause was not "fixed at 1791," contrary to the view that all our prior discussions of the Reexamination Clause have adopted. The Court believes we can ignore the very explicit command that "no fact tried by a jury shall be otherwise reexamined in any Court of the United States, than according to the rules of the common law" because, after all, we have not insisted that juries be all male, or consist of 12 jurors, as they were at common law. This is a desperate analogy, since there is of course no comparison between the specificity of the command of the Reexamination Clause and the specificity of the command that there be a "jury." The footnote abandonment of our traditional view of the Reexamination Clause is a major step indeed.

II

The Court's holding that federal courts of appeals may review district-court denials of motions for new trials for error of fact is not the only novel aspect of today's decision. The Court also directs that the case be remanded to the District Court, so that it may "test the jury's verdict against CPLR § 5501(c)'s 'deviates materially' standard." This disposition contradicts the principle that "[t]he proper role of the trial and appellate courts in the federal system in reviewing the size of jury verdicts is . . . a matter of federal law." *Donovan v. Penn Shipping Co.*, 429 U.S. 648, 649 (1977) (per curiam).

The Court acknowledges that state procedural rules cannot, as a general matter, be permitted to interfere with the allocation of functions in the federal court system. Indeed, it is at least partly for this reason that the Court rejects direct application of § 5501(c) at the appellate level as inconsistent with an " 'essential characteristic' " of the federal court system—by which the Court presumably means abuse-of-discretion review of denials of motions for new trials. But the scope of the Court's concern is oddly circumscribed. The "essential characteristic" of the federal jury, and, more specifically, the role of the federal trial court in reviewing jury judgments, apparently counts for little. The Court approves the "accommodat[ion]" achieved by having district courts review jury verdicts under the "deviates materially" standard, because it regards that as a means of giving effect to the State's purposes "without disrupting the federal system." But changing the standard by which trial judges review jury verdicts does disrupt the federal system, and is plainly inconsistent with the "strong federal policy against allowing state rules to disrupt the judge-jury relationship in federal court." *Byrd v. Blue Ridge Rural Elec. Cooperative, Inc.*, 356 U.S. 525, 538 (1958). The Court's opinion does not even acknowledge, let alone address, this dislocation.

* * *

* * * It seems to me quite wrong to regard [Section 5501(c)] as a "substantive" rule for *Erie* purposes. The "analog[y]" to "a statutory cap on damages" fails utterly. There is an absolutely fundamental distinction between a rule of law such as that, which would ordinarily be imposed upon the jury in the trial court's instructions, and a rule of review, which simply determines how closely the jury verdict will be scrutinized for compliance with the instructions. A tighter standard for reviewing jury determinations can no more plausibly be called a "substantive" disposition than can a tighter appellate standard for reviewing trial-court determinations. The one, like the other, provides additional assurance that the law has been complied with; but the other, like the one, leaves the law unchanged.

The Court commits the classic *Erie* mistake of regarding whatever changes the outcome as substantive. That is not the only factor to be considered. See *Byrd*, supra, at 537 ("[W]ere 'outcome' the only consideration, a strong case might appear for saying that the federal court should follow the state practice. But there are affirmative countervailing considerations at work here"). Outcome determination "was never intended to serve as a talisman," *Hanna v. Plumer*, 380 U.S. 460, 466–467 (1965), and does not have the power to convert the most classic elements of the process of assuring that the law is observed into the substantive law itself. The right to have a jury make the findings of fact, for example, is generally thought to favor plaintiffs, and that advantage is often thought significant enough to be the basis for forum selection. But no one would argue that *Erie* confers a right to a jury in federal court wherever state courts would provide it; or that, were it not for the Seventh Amendment, *Erie* would require federal courts to dispense with the jury whenever state courts do so.

In any event, the Court exaggerates the difference that the state standard will make. It concludes that different outcomes are likely to ensue depending on whether the law being applied is the state "deviates materially" standard of § 5501(c) or the "shocks the conscience" standard. Of course it is not the federal appellate standard but the federal district-court standard for granting new trials that must be compared with the New York standard to determine whether substantially different results will obtain—and it is far from clear that the district-court standard ought to be "shocks the conscience." * * * In sum, it is at least highly questionable whether the consistent outcome differential claimed by the Court even exists. What seems to me far more likely to produce forum shopping is the consistent difference between the state and federal appellate standards, which the Court leaves untouched. Under the Court's disposition, the Second Circuit reviews only for abuse of discretion, whereas New York's appellate courts engage in a de novo review for material deviation, giving the defendant a double shot at getting the damages award set aside. The only result that would produce the conformity the Court erroneously believes *Erie* requires is the one adopted by the Second Circuit and rejected by the Court: de novo federal appellate review under the § 5501(c) standard.

To say that application of § 5501(c) in place of the federal standard will not consistently produce disparate results is not to suggest that the decision the Court has made today is not a momentous one. The principle that the state standard governs is of great importance, since it bears the potential to destroy the uniformity of federal practice and the integrity of the federal court system. Under the Court's view, a state rule that directed courts "to determine that an award is excessive or inadequate if it deviates in any degree from the proper measure of compensation" would have to be applied in federal courts, effectively requiring federal judges to determine the amount of damages de novo, and effectively taking the matter away from the jury entirely. Or consider a state rule that allowed the defendant a second trial on damages, with judgment ultimately in the amount of the lesser of two jury awards. Under the reasoning of the Court's opinion, even such a rule as that would have to be applied in the federal courts.

The foregoing describes why I think the Court's *Erie* analysis is flawed. But in my view, one does not even reach the *Erie* question in this case. The standard to be applied by a district court in ruling on a motion for a new trial is set forth in Rule 59 of the Federal Rules of Civil Procedure, which provides that "[a] new trial may be granted . . . for any of the reasons for which new trials have heretofore been granted in actions at law in the courts of the United States." That is undeniably a federal standard. Federal District Courts in the Second Circuit have interpreted that standard to permit the granting of new trials where " 'it is quite clear that the jury has reached a seriously erroneous result" and letting the verdict stand would result in a " 'miscarriage of justice.' " Assuming (as we have no reason to question) that this is a correct interpretation of what Rule 59 requires, it is undeniable that the Federal Rule is " 'sufficiently broad' to cause a 'direct collision' with the state law or, implicitly, to 'control the issue' before the court, thereby leaving no room for the operation of that law." *Burlington Northern R. Co. v. Woods*, 480 U.S. 1, 4–5 (1987). It is simply not possible to give controlling effect both to the federal standard and the state standard in reviewing the jury's award. That being so, the court has no choice but to apply the Federal Rule, which is an exercise of what we have called Congress's "power to regulate matters which, though falling within the uncertain area between substance and procedure, are rationally capable of classification as either," *Hanna*, 380 U.S., at 472.

There is no small irony in the Court's declaration today that appellate review of refusals to grant new trials for error of fact is "a control necessary and proper to the fair administration of justice." It is objection to precisely that sort of "control" by federal appellate judges that gave birth to the Reexamination Clause of the Seventh

Amendment. Alas, those who drew the Amendment, and the citizens who approved it, did not envision an age in which the Constitution means whatever this Court thinks it ought to mean—or indeed, whatever the courts of appeals have recently thought it ought to mean.

When there is added to the revision of the Seventh Amendment the Court's precedent-setting disregard of Congress's instructions in Rule 59, one must conclude that this is a bad day for the Constitution's distinctive Article III courts in general, and for the role of the jury in those courts in particular. I respectfully dissent.

COMMENTS AND QUESTIONS CONCERNING
GASPERINI V. CENTER FOR HUMANITIES, INC.

1. Does this case present a difficult *Erie* question if the New York statute is truly a "damages ceiling" as asserted by Justice Stevens in his dissent?

2. The Supreme Court rejected an argument that state law should apply in *Byrd v. Blue Ridge*, forsaking (at least direct) reliance on the Seventh Amendment right to jury trial in reaching its conclusion. In *Gasperini*, the Court confronted the Seventh Amendment Reexamination Clause, concluding that state law nevertheless applied. Are these two decisions inconsistent concerning the application of state law in the face of these Seventh Amendment clauses?

3. Is the application of different rules in state and federal court likely to lead to forum shopping in cases such as *Gasperini*? Is the New York statute one that could totally eliminate a cause of action (such as a state statute of limitations) or a more amorphous standard the impact of which is difficult to predict when filing a complaint? Will plaintiffs' lawyers be more concerned with the standard of review applied in challenges to plaintiffs' verdicts or with the judge or judges who will exercise that review?

4. In addition to a "pure *Erie*" question, *Gasperini* presents a potential conflict between Section 5501(c) of New York state law and Rule 59 of the Federal Rules of Civil Procedure. Rule 59(a)(1)(A) provides that federal courts may grant a new trial "for any reason for which a new trial has heretofore been granted in an action at law in federal court."

Justice Scalia concludes that there is a "direct collision" between Section 5501(c) and Rule 59, while Justice Stevens asserts that "there is no conceivable conflict between Federal Rule of Civil Procedure 59 and the application of the New York damages limit."

In footnote 7 of her majority opinion, Justice Ginsburg steers a middle course:

> It is settled that if the Rule in point is consonant with the Rules Enabling Act, 28 U.S.C. § 2072, and the Constitution, the Federal Rule applies regardless of contrary state law. See *Hanna v. Plumer*, 380 U.S. 460, 469–474 (1965); *Burlington Northern R. Co. v. Woods*, 480 U.S. 1, 4–5 (1987). Federal courts have interpreted

the Federal Rules, however, with sensitivity to important state interests and regulatory policies.

Is there any practical difference between concluding that there is no conflict between the state and federal law (so that the state law applies) and narrowly interpreting the Federal Rule in order to avoid a conflict?

5.   The Second Circuit in *Gasperini* applied the doctrine of remittur— a form of conditional new trial order. Based upon its finding of an excessive verdict, the Court of Appeals ordered a new trial—unless plaintiff Gasperini agreed to accept a reduced judgment (a remittur) of $100,000.

Remittitur is the counterpart to additur, in which the trial judge orders a new trial unless the defendant agrees to accept a judgment with damages greater than those awarded by the jury. As you will see in Chapter 13, *infra* p. 1022, the Supreme Court has upheld the constitutionality of remittitur, but not additur, in the federal courts. *Dimick v. Schiedt*, 293 U.S. 474 (1935). How can the two types of conditional new trial orders be distinguished under the Seventh Amendment?

6.   Once the Court determines that New York law must be applied by the federal courts in diversity cases such as this, the question arises as to just how that should be done. Is it the duty of the Supreme Court to redesign the federal courts to create a state-federal hybrid that will withstand challenge under *Erie* and be true to the Rules of Decision Act? Doesn't CPLR § 5501(c) require New York appellate, rather than trial, courts to apply the "deviates materially" standard?

If your professor gives extra credit, sketch the "sphinx-like, damage-determining law * * * [with] a state forepart, but a federal hindquarter" that Justice Ginsburg in footnote 23 of her opinion asserts that Justice Scalia suggests the Court create.

7.   In footnote 21 of her opinion, Justice Ginsburg notes: "The two-trial rule posited by Justice SCALIA, surely would be incompatible with the existence of '[t]he federal system [as] an independent system for administering justice,' *Byrd v. Blue Ridge Rural Elec. Cooperative, Inc.*, 356 U.S. 525, 537 (1958)." What are the essential elements of such a system? Does it make the Supreme Court's task easier that the New York standard applies in both New York appellate and trial courts?

8.   As you will see in Chapter 12, the Seventh Amendment Right to Jury Trial and Reexamination Clauses are different from other amendments to the federal constitution in that they preserve rights available as of the adoption of the Seventh Amendment in 1791. The interpretation of these clauses requires historical examination not necessary in the application of other Bill of Rights amendments. Thus Justice Ginsburg feels the need to include in footnote 20 of her majority opinion examples of modern federal procedures affecting juries that were not established in 1791 but have been found to be constitutional.

F. "WAD[ING] INTO *ERIE*'S MURKY WATERS": *SHADY GROVE ORTHOPEDIC ASSOCIATES, P.A. V. ALLSTATE INSURANCE CO.*

A majority of the Supreme Court held in *Gasperini* that a provision of the New York Civil Practice Law and Rules should be applied by federal courts in diversity actions. As the following case illustrates, though, not all provisions of New York's Civil Practice Law have fared as well in the Supreme Court.

Shady Grove Orthopedic Associates, P.A. v. Allstate Insurance Co.

Supreme Court of the United States, 2010
559 U.S. 393

OPINION

■ JUSTICE SCALIA announced the judgment of the Court and delivered the opinion of the Court with respect to Parts I and II–A, an opinion with respect to Parts II–B and II–D, in which THE CHIEF JUSTICE, JUSTICE THOMAS, and JUSTICE SOTOMAYOR join, and an opinion with respect to Part II–C, in which THE CHIEF JUSTICE and JUSTICE THOMAS join.

New York law prohibits class actions in suits seeking penalties or statutory minimum damages. We consider whether this precludes a federal district court sitting in diversity from entertaining a class action under Federal Rule of Civil Procedure 23.

I

The petitioner's complaint alleged the following: Shady Grove Orthopedic Associates, P. A., provided medical care to Sonia E. Galvez for injuries she suffered in an automobile accident. As partial payment for that care, Galvez assigned to Shady Grove her rights to insurance benefits under a policy issued in New York by Allstate Insurance Co. Shady Grove tendered a claim for the assigned benefits to Allstate, which under New York law had 30 days to pay the claim or deny it. Allstate apparently paid, but not on time, and it refused to pay the statutory interest that accrued on the overdue benefits (at two percent per month).

Shady Grove filed this diversity suit in the Eastern District of New York to recover the unpaid statutory interest. Alleging that Allstate routinely refuses to pay interest on overdue benefits, Shady Grove sought relief on behalf of itself and a class of all others to whom Allstate owes interest. The District Court dismissed the suit for lack of jurisdiction. It reasoned that N.Y. Civ. Prac. Law Ann. § 901(b), which precludes a suit to recover a "penalty" from proceeding as a class action, applies in diversity suits in federal court, despite Federal Rule of Civil

Procedure 23. Concluding that statutory interest is a "penalty" under New York law, it held that § 901(b) prohibited the proposed class action. And, since Shady Grove conceded that its individual claim (worth roughly $500) fell far short of the amount-in-controversy requirement for individual suits under 28 U.S.C. § 1332(a), the suit did not belong in federal court.[2]

The Second Circuit affirmed. The court did not dispute that a federal rule adopted in compliance with the Rules Enabling Act, 28 U.S.C. § 2072, would control if it conflicted with § 901(b). But there was no conflict because (as we will describe in more detail below) the Second Circuit concluded that Rule 23 and § 901(b) address different issues. Finding no federal rule on point, the Court of Appeals held that § 901(b) is "substantive" within the meaning of *Erie R. Co. v. Tompkins*, 304 U.S. 64 (1938), and thus must be applied by federal courts sitting in diversity.

We granted certiorari.

II

The framework for our decision is familiar. We must first determine whether Rule 23 answers the question in dispute. If it does, it governs—New York's law notwithstanding—unless it exceeds statutory authorization or Congress's rulemaking power. We do not wade into *Erie*'s murky waters unless the federal rule is inapplicable or invalid.

A

The question in dispute is whether Shady Grove's suit may proceed as a class action. Rule 23 provides an answer. It states that "[a] class action may be maintained" if two conditions are met: The suit must satisfy the criteria set forth in subdivision (a) (i.e., numerosity, commonality, typicality, and adequacy of representation), and it also must fit into one of the three categories described in subdivision (b). By its terms this creates a categorical rule entitling a plaintiff whose suit meets the specified criteria to pursue his claim as a class action. (The Federal Rules regularly use "may" to confer categorical permission, see, e.g., Fed. Rules Civ. Proc. 8(d)(2)–(3), 14(a)(1), 18(a)–(b), 20(a)(1)–(2), 27(a)(1), 30(a)(1), as do federal statutes that establish procedural entitlements, see, e.g., 29 U.S.C. 626(c)(1); 42 U.S.C. § 2000e–5(f)(1).) Thus, Rule 23 provides a one-size-fits-all formula for deciding the class-action question. Because § 901(b) attempts to answer the same question—i.e., it states that Shady Grove's suit "may *not* be maintained as a class action" because of the relief it seeks—it cannot apply in diversity suits unless Rule 23 is ultra vires.

---

[2]   Shady Grove had asserted jurisdiction under 28 U.S.C. § 1332(d)(2), which relaxes, for class actions seeking at least $5 million, the rule against aggregating separate claims for calculation of the amount in controversy. *See Exxon Mobil Corp. v. Allapattah Services, Inc.*, 545 U.S. 546, 571 (2005).

The Second Circuit believed that § 901(b) and Rule 23 do not conflict because they address different issues. Rule 23, it said, concerns only the criteria for determining whether a given class can and should be certified; section 901(b), on the other hand, addresses an antecedent question: whether the particular type of claim is eligible for class treatment in the first place—a question on which Rule 23 is silent. Allstate embraces this analysis.

We disagree. To begin with, the line between eligibility and certifiability is entirely artificial. Both are preconditions for maintaining a class action. Allstate suggests that eligibility must depend on the "particular cause of action" asserted, instead of some other attribute of the suit. But that is not so. Congress could, for example, provide that only claims involving more than a certain number of plaintiffs are "eligible" for class treatment in federal court. In other words, relabeling Rule 23(a)'s prerequisites "eligibility criteria" would obviate Allstate's objection—a sure sign that its eligibility-certifiability distinction is made-to-order.

There is no reason, in any event, to read Rule 23 as addressing only whether claims made eligible for class treatment by some other law should be certified as class actions. Allstate asserts that Rule 23 neither explicitly nor implicitly empowers a federal court "to certify a class in each and every case" where the Rule's criteria are met. But that is exactly what Rule 23 does: It says that if the prescribed preconditions are satisfied "[a] class action may be maintained"—not "a class action may be permitted." Courts do not maintain actions; litigants do. The discretion suggested by Rule 23's "may" is discretion residing in the plaintiff: He may bring his claim in a class action if he wishes. And like the rest of the Federal Rules of Civil Procedure, Rule 23 automatically applies "in all civil actions and proceedings in the United States district courts," Fed. Rule Civ. Proc. 1.

Allstate points out that Congress has carved out some federal claims from Rule 23's reach, see, e.g., 8 U.S.C. § 1252(e)(1)(B)—which shows, Allstate contends, that Rule 23 does not authorize class actions for all claims, but rather leaves room for laws like § 901(b). But Congress, unlike New York, has ultimate authority over the Federal Rules of Civil Procedure; it can create exceptions to an individual rule as it sees fit—either by directly amending the rule or by enacting a separate statute overriding it in certain instances. The fact that Congress has created specific exceptions to Rule 23 hardly proves that the Rule does not apply generally. In fact, it proves the opposite. If Rule 23 did not authorize class actions across the board, the statutory exceptions would be unnecessary.

Allstate next suggests that the structure of § 901 shows that Rule 23 addresses only certifiability. * * * [But] Rule 23 permits all class actions that meet its requirements, and a State cannot limit that permission by structuring one part of its statute to track Rule 23 and

enacting another part that imposes additional requirements. Both of
§ 901's subsections undeniably answer the same question as Rule 23:
whether a class action may proceed for a given suit.

The dissent argues that § 901(b) has nothing to do with whether
Shady Grove may maintain its suit as a class action, but affects only the
remedy it may obtain if it wins. Whereas "Rule 23 governs procedural
aspects of class litigation" by "prescrib[ing] the considerations relevant
to class certification and postcertification proceedings," § 901(b)
addresses only "the size of a monetary award a class plaintiff may
pursue." Accordingly, the dissent says, Rule 23 and New York's law may
coexist in peace.

We need not decide whether a state law that limits the remedies
available in an existing class action would conflict with Rule 23; that is
not what § 901(b) does. By its terms, the provision precludes a plaintiff
from "maintain[ing]" a class action seeking statutory penalties. Unlike
a law that sets a ceiling on damages (or puts other remedies out of
reach) in properly filed class actions, § 901(b) says nothing about what
remedies a court may award; it prevents the class actions it covers from
coming into existence at all. Consequently, a court bound by § 901(b)
could not certify a class action seeking both statutory penalties and
other remedies even if it announces in advance that it will refuse to
award the penalties in the event the plaintiffs prevail; to do so would
violate the statute's clear prohibition on "maintain[ing]" such suits as
class actions.

The dissent asserts that a plaintiff can avoid § 901(b)'s barrier by
omitting from his complaint (or removing) a request for statutory
penalties. Even assuming all statutory penalties are waivable, the fact
that a complaint omitting them could be brought as a class action would
not at all prove that § 901(b) is addressed only to remedies. If the state
law instead banned class actions for fraud claims, a would-be class-
action plaintiff could drop the fraud counts from his complaint and
proceed with the remainder in a class action. Yet that would not mean
the law provides no remedy for fraud; the ban would affect only the
procedural means by which the remedy may be pursued. In short,
although the dissent correctly abandons Allstate's eligibility-
certifiability distinction, the alternative it offers fares no better.

The dissent all but admits that the literal terms of § 901(b) address
the same subject as Rule 23—i.e., whether a class action may be
maintained—but insists the provision's purpose is to restrict only
remedies. * * * Unlike Rule 23, designed to further procedural fairness
and efficiency, § 901(b) (we are told) "responds to an entirely different
concern": the fear that allowing statutory damages to be awarded on a
class-wide basis would "produce overkill." The dissent reaches this
conclusion on the basis of (1) constituent concern recorded in the law's
bill jacket; (2) a commentary suggesting that the Legislature
"apparently fear[ed]" that combining class actions and statutory

penalties "could result in annihilating punishment of the defendant"; (3) a remark by the Governor in his signing statement that § 901(b) " 'provides a controlled remedy," and (4) a state court's statement that the final text of § 901(b) " 'was the result of a compromise among competing interests.' "

This evidence of the New York Legislature's purpose is pretty sparse. But even accepting the dissent's account of the Legislature's objective at face value, it cannot override the statute's clear text. Even if its aim is to restrict the remedy a plaintiff can obtain, § 901(b) achieves that end by limiting a plaintiff's power to maintain a class action. The manner in which the law "could have been written" has no bearing; what matters is the law the Legislature did enact. We cannot rewrite that to reflect our perception of legislative purpose.[6] The dissent's concern for state prerogatives is frustrated rather than furthered by revising state laws when a potential conflict with a Federal Rule arises; the state-friendly approach would be to accept the law as written and test the validity of the Federal Rule.

The dissent's approach of determining whether state and federal rules conflict based on the subjective intentions of the state legislature is an enterprise destined to produce "confusion worse confounded," *Sibbach v. Wilson & Co.*, 312 U.S. 1, 14, (1941). It would mean, to begin with, that one State's statute could survive pre-emption (and accordingly affect the procedures in federal court) while another State's identical law would not, merely because its authors had different aspirations. It would also mean that district courts would have to discern, in every diversity case, the purpose behind any putatively pre-empted state procedural rule, even if its text squarely conflicts with federal law. That task will often prove arduous. Many laws further more than one aim, and the aim of others may be impossible to discern. Moreover, to the extent the dissent's purpose-driven approach depends on its characterization of § 901(b)'s aims as substantive, it would apply to many state rules ostensibly addressed to procedure. Pleading standards, for example, often embody policy preferences about the types of claims that should succeed—as do rules governing summary judgment, pretrial discovery, and the admissibility of certain evidence. * * *

---

[6] Our decision in *Walker v. Armco Steel Corp.*, 446 U.S. 740 (1980), discussed by the dissent, is not to the contrary. There we held that Rule 3 (which provides that a federal civil action is " 'commenced' " by filing a complaint in federal court) did not displace a state law providing that " '[a]n action shall be deemed commenced, within the meaning of this article [the statute of limitations], as to each defendant, at the date of the summons which is served on him. . . .' " 446 U.S. at 743, n.4. Rule 3, we explained, "governs the date from which various timing requirements of the Federal Rules begin to run, but does not affect state statutes of limitations" or tolling rules, which it did not "purpor[t] to displace." 446 U.S. at 751, 750. The texts were therefore not in conflict. While our opinion observed that the State's actual-service rule was (in the State's judgment) an "integral part of the several policies served by the statute of limitations," *id.* at 751, nothing in our decision suggested that a federal court may resolve an obvious conflict between the texts of state and federal rules by resorting to the state law's ostensible objectives.

THE LAW APPLIED IN FEDERAL COURT: "ERIE CHOICES FOR THE
FEDERAL JUDGE."

428   CHAPTER 5

But while the dissent does indeed artificially narrow the scope of § 901(b) by finding that it pursues only substantive policies, that is not the central difficulty of the dissent's position. The central difficulty is that even artificial narrowing cannot render § 901(b) compatible with Rule 23. Whatever the policies they pursue, they flatly contradict each other. Allstate asserts (and the dissent implies) that we can (and must) interpret Rule 23 in a manner that avoids overstepping its authorizing statute.[7] If the Rule were susceptible of two meanings—one that would violate 2072(b) and another that would not—we would agree. But it is not. Rule 23 unambiguously authorizes any plaintiff, in any federal civil proceeding, to maintain a class action if the Rule's prerequisites are met. We cannot contort its text, even to avert a collision with state law that might render it invalid. What the dissent's approach achieves is not the avoiding of a "conflict between Rule 23 and § 901(b)," but rather the invalidation of Rule 23 (pursuant to § 2072(b) of the Rules Enabling Act) to the extent that it conflicts with the substantive policies of § 901. There is no other way to reach the dissent's destination. We must therefore confront head-on whether Rule 23 falls within the statutory authorization.

B

Erie involved the constitutional power of federal courts to supplant state law with judge-made rules. In that context, it made no difference whether the rule was technically one of substance or procedure; the touchstone was whether it "significantly affect[s] the result of a litigation." *Guaranty Trust Co. v. York*, 326 U.S. 99, 109 (1945). That is not the test for either the constitutionality or the statutory validity of a Federal Rule of Procedure. Congress has undoubted power to supplant state law, and undoubted power to prescribe rules for the courts it has created, so long as those rules regulate matters "rationally capable of classification" as procedure. *Hanna*, 380 U.S. at 472. In the Rules Enabling Act, Congress authorized this Court to promulgate rules of procedure subject to its review, 28 U.S.C. § 2072(a), but with the limitation that those rules "shall not abridge, enlarge or modify any substantive right," § 2072(b).

---

[7]   The dissent also suggests that we should read the Federal Rules " 'with sensitivity to important state interests' " and " 'to avoid conflict with important state regulatory policies.' " Post at 1463 (quoting *Gasperini v. Center for Humanities, Inc.*, 518 U.S. 415, 427, n. 7, 438, n. 22 (1996)). The search for state interests and policies that are "important" is just as standardless as the "important or substantial" criterion we rejected in *Sibbach v. Wilson & Co.*, 312 U.S. 1, 13–14 (1941), to define the state-created rights a Federal Rule may not abridge.

If all the dissent means is that we should read an ambiguous Federal Rule to avoid "substantial variations [in outcomes] between state and federal litigation," *Semtek Int'l Inc. v. Lockheed Martin Corp.*, 531 U.S. 497, 504 (2001), we entirely agree. We should do so not to avoid doubt as to the Rule's validity—since a Federal Rule that fails *Erie*'s forum-shopping test is not ipso facto invalid—but because it is reasonable to assume that "Congress is just as concerned as we have been to avoid significant differences between state and federal courts in adjudicating claims," *Stewart Organization, Inc. v. Ricoh Corp.*, 487 U.S. 22, 37–38 (1988) (Scalia, J., dissenting). The assumption is irrelevant here, however, because there is only one reasonable reading of Rule 23.

We have long held that this limitation means that the Rule must "really regulat[e] procedure,—the judicial process for enforcing rights and duties recognized by substantive law and for justly administering remedy and redress for disregard or infraction of them," *Sibbach*, 312 U.S. at 14. The test is not whether the rule affects a litigant's substantive rights; most procedural rules do. *Mississippi Publishing Corp. v. Murphree*, 326 U.S. 438, 445 (1946). What matters is what the rule itself regulates: If it governs only "the manner and the means" by which the litigants' rights are "enforced," it is valid; if it alters "the rules of decision by which [the] court will adjudicate [those] rights," it is not. *Id.* at 446.

Applying that test, we have rejected every statutory challenge to a Federal Rule that has come before us. We have found to be in compliance with § 2072(b) rules prescribing methods for serving process, *see id.* at 445–446 (Fed. Rule Civ. Proc. 4(f)); *Hanna, supra* at 463–465 (Fed. Rule Civ. Proc. 4(d)(1)), and requiring litigants whose mental or physical condition is in dispute to submit to examinations, see *Sibbach, supra* at 14–16 (Fed. Rule Civ. Proc. 35); *Schlagenhauf v. Holder*, 379 U.S. 104, 113–114 (1964) (same). Likewise, we have upheld rules authorizing imposition of sanctions upon those who file frivolous appeals, *see Burlington, supra* at 8 (Fed. Rule App. Proc. 38), or who sign court papers without a reasonable inquiry into the facts asserted, *see Business Guides, Inc. v. Chromatic Communications Enterprises, Inc.*, 498 U.S. 533, 551–554 (1991) (Fed. Rule Civ. Proc. 11). Each of these rules had some practical effect on the parties' rights, but each undeniably regulated only the process for enforcing those rights; none altered the rights themselves, the available remedies, or the rules of decision by which the court adjudicated either.

Applying that criterion, we think it obvious that rules allowing multiple claims (and claims by or against multiple parties) to be litigated together are also valid. *See, e.g.*, Fed. Rules Civ. Proc. 18 (joinder of claims), 20 (joinder of parties), 42(a) (consolidation of actions). Such rules neither change plaintiffs' separate entitlements to relief nor abridge defendants' rights; they alter only how the claims are processed. For the same reason, Rule 23—at least insofar as it allows willing plaintiffs to join their separate claims against the same defendants in a class action—falls within § 2072(b)'s authorization. A class action, no less than traditional joinder (of which it is a species), merely enables a federal court to adjudicate claims of multiple parties at once, instead of in separate suits. And like traditional joinder, it leaves the parties' legal rights and duties intact and the rules of decision unchanged.

Allstate contends that the authorization of class actions is not substantively neutral: Allowing Shady Grove to sue on behalf of a class "transform[s][the] dispute over a five *hundred* dollar penalty into a dispute over a five *million* dollar penalty." Allstate's aggregate liability, however, does not depend on whether the suit proceeds as a class action. Each of the 1,000-plus members of the putative class could (as Allstate acknowledges) bring a freestanding suit asserting his individual claim. It is undoubtedly true that some plaintiffs who would not bring individual suits for the relatively small sums involved will choose to join a class action. That has no bearing, however, on Allstate's or the plaintiffs' legal rights. The likelihood that some (even many) plaintiffs will be induced to sue by the availability of a class action is just the sort of "incidental effec[t]" we have long held does not violate § 2072(b), *Mississippi Publishing, supra* at 445.

Allstate argues that Rule 23 violates § 2072(b) because the state law it displaces, § 901(b), creates a right that the Federal Rule abridges—namely, a "substantive right . . . not to be subjected to aggregated class-action liability" in a single suit. To begin with, we doubt that that is so. Nothing in the text of § 901(b) (which is to be found in New York's procedural code) confines it to claims under New York law; and of course New York has no power to alter substantive rights and duties created by other sovereigns. As we have said, the consequence of excluding certain class actions may be to cap the damages a defendant can face in a single suit, but the law itself alters only procedure. In that respect, § 901(b) is no different from a state law forbidding simple joinder. As a fallback argument, Allstate argues that even if § 901(b) is a procedural provision, it was enacted "for substantive reasons." Its end was not to improve "the conduct of the litigation process itself" but to alter "the outcome of that process."

The fundamental difficulty with both these arguments is that the substantive nature of New York's law, or its substantive purpose, *makes no difference.* A Federal Rule of Procedure is not valid in some jurisdictions and invalid in others—or valid in some cases and invalid in others—depending upon whether its effect is to frustrate a state substantive law (or a state procedural law enacted for substantive purposes). * * *

                              * * *

In sum, it is not the substantive or procedural nature or purpose of the affected state law that matters, but the substantive or procedural nature of the Federal Rule. We have held since *Sibbach*, and reaffirmed repeatedly, that the validity of a Federal Rule depends entirely upon whether it regulates procedure. If it does, it is authorized by § 2072 and is valid in all jurisdictions, with respect to all claims, regardless of its incidental effect upon state-created rights.

C

A few words in response to the concurrence. We understand it to accept the framework we apply—which requires first, determining whether the federal and state rules can be reconciled (because they answer different questions), and second, if they cannot, determining whether the Federal Rule runs afoul of § 2072(b). The concurrence agrees with us that Rule 23 and § 901(b) conflict, and departs from us only with respect to the second part of the test, i.e., whether application of the Federal Rule violates § 2072(b). Like us, it answers no, but for a reason different from ours.

The concurrence would decide this case on the basis, not that Rule 23 is procedural, but that the state law it displaces is procedural, in the sense that it does not "function as a part of the State's definition of substantive rights and remedies." A state procedural rule is not preempted, according to the concurrence, so long as it is "so bound up with," or "sufficiently intertwined with," a substantive state-law right or remedy "that it defines the scope of that substantive right or remedy."

This analysis squarely conflicts with *Sibbach*, which established the rule we apply. The concurrence contends that *Sibbach* did not rule out its approach, but that is not so. Recognizing the impracticability of a test that turns on the idiosyncrasies of state law, *Sibbach* adopted and applied a rule with a single criterion: whether the Federal Rule "really regulates procedure." 312 U.S. at 14. That the concurrence's approach would have yielded the same result in *Sibbach* proves nothing; what matters is the rule we did apply, and that rule leaves no room for special exemptions based on the function or purpose of a particular state rule. * * *

In reality, the concurrence seeks not to apply *Sibbach*, but to overrule it (or, what is the same, to rewrite it). Its approach, the concurrence insists, gives short shrift to the statutory text forbidding the Federal Rules from "abridg[ing], enlarg[ing], or modify[ing] any substantive right." § 2072(b). There is something to that. It is possible to understand how it can be determined whether a Federal Rule "enlarges" substantive rights without consulting State law: If the Rule creates a substantive right, even one that duplicates some state-created rights, it establishes a new federal right. But it is hard to understand how it can be determined whether a Federal Rule "abridges" or "modifies" substantive rights without knowing what state-created rights would obtain if the Federal Rule did not exist. *Sibbach*'s exclusive focus on the challenged Federal Rule—driven by the very real concern that Federal Rules which vary from State to State would be chaos—is hard to square with § 2072(b)'s terms.

Sibbach has been settled law, however, for nearly seven decades. Setting aside any precedent requires a "special justification" beyond a bare belief that it was wrong. *Patterson v. McLean Credit Union*, 491 U.S. 164, 172 (1989). And a party seeking to overturn a statutory precedent bears an even greater burden, since Congress remains free to correct us, *ibid.*, and adhering to our precedent enables it do so, *see, e.g., Finley v. United States*, 490 U.S. 545, 556 (1989); 28 U.S.C. § 1367; *Exxon Mobil Corp. v. Allapattah Services, Inc.*, 545 U.S. 546, 558 (2005).

We do Congress no service by presenting it a moving target. In all events, Allstate has not even asked us to overrule *Sibbach*, let alone carried its burden of persuading us to do so. Why we should cast aside our decades-old decision escapes us, especially since (as the concurrence explains) that would not affect the result.

* * *

D

We must acknowledge the reality that keeping the federal-court door open to class actions that cannot proceed in state court will produce forum shopping. That is unacceptable when it comes as the consequence of judge-made rules created to fill supposed "gaps" in positive federal law. For where neither the Constitution, a treaty, nor a statute provides the rule of decision or authorizes a federal court to supply one, "state law must govern because there can be no other law." [*Hanna v. Plumer*, 380 U.S. 460, 471–72 (1965).] But divergence from state law, with the attendant consequence of forum shopping, is the inevitable (indeed, one might say the intended) result of a uniform system of federal procedure. Congress itself has created the possibility that the same case may follow a different course if filed in federal instead of state court. The short of the matter is that a Federal Rule governing procedure is valid whether or not it alters the outcome of the case in a way that induces forum shopping. To hold otherwise would be to "disembowel either the Constitution's grant of power over federal procedure" or Congress's exercise of it.

* * *

The judgment of the Court of Appeals is reversed, and the case is remanded for further proceedings.

It is so ordered.

■ JUSTICE STEVENS, concurring in part and concurring in the judgment.

The New York law at issue, N.Y. Civ. Prac. Law Ann. § 901(b), is a procedural rule that is not part of New York's substantive law. Accordingly, I agree with Justice SCALIA that Federal Rule of Civil Procedure 23 must apply in this case and join Parts I and II–A of the Court's opinion. But I also agree with Justice GINSBURG that there are some state procedural rules that federal courts must apply in diversity cases because they function as a part of the State's definition of substantive rights and remedies.

I

It is a long-recognized principle that federal courts sitting in diversity "apply state substantive law and federal procedural law." *Hanna v. Plumer*, 380 U.S. 460, 465 (1965). This principle is governed by a statutory framework, and the way that it is administered varies depending upon whether there is a federal rule addressed to the matter.

If no federal rule applies, a federal court must follow the Rules of Decision Act, 28 U.S.C. § 1652, and make the "relatively unguided *Erie* choice," *Hanna*, 380 U.S. at 471, to determine whether the state law is the "rule of decision." But when a situation is covered by a federal rule, the Rules of Decision Act inquiry by its own terms does not apply. Instead, the Rules Enabling Act (Enabling Act) controls. See 28 U.S.C. § 2072.

That does not mean, however, that the federal rule always governs. Congress has provided for a system of uniform federal rules, under which federal courts sitting in diversity operate as "an independent system for administering justice to litigants who properly invoke its jurisdiction," *Byrd v. Blue Ridge Rural Elec. Cooperative, Inc.*, 356 U.S. 525, 537 (1958), and not as state-court clones that assume all aspects of state tribunals but are managed by Article III judges. But while Congress may have the constitutional power to prescribe procedural rules that interfere with state substantive law in any number of respects, that is not what Congress has done. Instead, it has provided in the Enabling Act that although "[t]he Supreme Court" may "prescribe general rules of practice and procedure," § 2072(a), those rules "shall not abridge, enlarge or modify any substantive right," § 2072(b). Therefore, "[w]hen a situation is covered by one of the Federal Rules, . . . the court has been instructed to apply the Federal Rule" unless doing so would violate the Act or the Constitution. *Hanna*, 380 U.S. at 471.

Although the Enabling Act and the Rules of Decision Act "say, roughly, that federal courts are to apply state 'substantive' law and federal 'procedural' law," the inquiries are not the same. *Ibid.* The Enabling Act does not invite federal courts to engage in the "relatively unguided *Erie* choice," but instead instructs only that federal rules cannot "abridge, enlarge or modify any substantive right," § 2072(b). The Enabling Act's limitation does not mean that federal rules cannot displace state policy judgments; it means only that federal rules cannot displace a State's definition of its own rights or remedies. See *Sibbach v. Wilson & Co.*, 312 U.S. 1, 13–14 (1941) (reasoning that "the phrase 'substantive rights' " embraces only those state rights that are sought to be enforced in the judicial proceedings).

Congress has thus struck a balance: "[H]ousekeeping rules for federal courts" will generally apply in diversity cases, notwithstanding that some federal rules "will inevitably differ" from state rules. *Hanna*, 380 U.S. at 473. But not every federal "rul[e] of practice or procedure," § 2072(a), will displace state law. To the contrary, federal rules must be interpreted with some degree of "sensitivity to important state interests and regulatory policies," *Gasperini v. Center for Humanities, Inc.*, 518 U.S. 415, 427, n. 7 (1996), and applied to diversity cases against the background of Congress' command that such rules not alter substantive rights and with consideration of "the degree to which the Rule makes the character and result of the federal litigation stray from the course it would follow in state courts," *Hanna*, 380 U.S. at 473. This can be a tricky balance to implement.

It is important to observe that the balance Congress has struck turns, in part, on the nature of the state law that is being displaced by a federal rule. And in my view, the application of that balance does not necessarily turn on whether the state law at issue takes the form of what is traditionally described as substantive or procedural. Rather, it turns on whether the state law actually is part of a State's framework of substantive rights or remedies. See § 2072(b).

Applying this balance, therefore, requires careful interpretation of the state and federal provisions at issue. "The line between procedural and substantive law is hazy," *Erie R. Co. v. Tompkins*, 304 U.S. 64, 92 (1938) (Reed, J., concurring), and matters of procedure and matters of substance are not "mutually exclusive categories with easily ascertainable contents," *Sibbach*, 312 U.S. at 17 (Frankfurter, J., dissenting). Rather, "[r]ules which lawyers call procedural do not always exhaust their effect by regulating procedure," *Cohen v. Beneficial Industrial Loan Corp.*, 337 U.S. 541, 555 (1949), and in some situations, "procedure and substance are so interwoven that rational separation becomes well-nigh impossible," *id.* at 559 (Rutledge, J., dissenting). A "state procedural rule, though undeniably 'procedural' in the ordinary sense of the term," may exist "to influence substantive outcomes," *S.A. Healy Co. v. Milwaukee Metropolitan Sewerage Dist.*, 60 F.3d 305, 310 (C.A.7 1995) (Posner, J.), and may in some instances become so bound up with the state-created right or remedy that it defines the scope of that substantive right or remedy. Such laws, for example, may be seemingly procedural rules that make it significantly more difficult to bring or to prove a claim, thus serving to limit the scope of that claim. See, e.g., *Cohen*, 337 U.S. at 555 (state "procedure" that required plaintiffs to post bond before suing); *Guaranty Trust Co.*, 326 U.S. 99 (state statute of limitations). Such "procedural rules" may also define the amount of recovery. See, e.g., *Gasperini*, 518 U.S. at 427 (state procedure for examining jury verdicts as means of capping the available remedy).

In our federalist system, Congress has not mandated that federal courts dictate to state legislatures the form that their substantive law must take. And were federal courts to ignore those portions of substantive state law that operate as procedural devices, it could in many instances limit the ways that sovereign States may define their rights and remedies. When a State chooses to use a traditionally procedural vehicle as a means of defining the scope of substantive rights or remedies, federal courts must recognize and respect that choice. Cf. *Ragan v. Merchants Transfer & Warehouse Co.*, 337 U.S. 530, 533 (1949) ("Since th[e] cause of action is created by local law, the measure of it is to be found only in local law. . . . Where local law qualifies or abridges it, the federal court must follow suit").

II

When both a federal rule and a state law appear to govern a question before a federal court sitting in diversity, our precedents have set out a two-step framework for federal courts to negotiate this thorny area. At both steps of the inquiry, there is a critical question about what the state law and the federal rule mean.

The court must first determine whether the scope of the federal rule is " 'sufficiently broad' " to " 'control the issue' " before the court, "thereby leaving no room for the operation" of seemingly conflicting state law. See *Burlington Northern R. Co. v. Woods*, 480 U.S. 1, 4–5 (1987); *Walker v. Armco Steel Corp.*, 446 U.S. 740, 749–750, and n. 9 (1980). If the federal rule does not apply or can operate alongside the state rule, then there is no "Ac[t] of Congress" governing that particular question, 28 U.S.C. § 1652, and the court must engage in the traditional Rules of Decision Act inquiry under *Erie* and its progeny. * * *

If, on the other hand, the federal rule is "sufficiently broad to control the issue before the Court," such that there is a "direct collision," *Walker*, 446 U.S. at 749–750, the court must decide whether application of the federal rule "represents a valid exercise" of the "rulemaking authority . . . bestowed on this Court by the Rules Enabling Act." *Burlington Northern R. Co.*, 480 U.S. at 5. That Act requires, inter alia, that federal rules "not abridge, enlarge or modify any substantive right." 28 U.S.C. § 2072(b). * * *

* * *

Justice SCALIA believes that the sole Enabling Act question is whether the federal rule "really regulates procedure," which means, apparently, whether it regulates "the manner and the means by which the litigants' rights are enforced." I respectfully disagree. This interpretation of the Enabling Act is consonant with the Act's first limitation to "general rules of practice and procedure," § 2072(a). But it ignores the second limitation that such rules also "not abridge, enlarge or modify *any* substantive right," § 2072(b), and in so doing ignores the balance that Congress struck between uniform rules of federal procedure and respect for a State's construction of its own rights and remedies. It also ignores the separation-of-powers presumption and federalism presumption that counsel against judicially created rules displacing state substantive law.

Although the plurality appears to agree with much of my interpretation of § 2072, it nonetheless rejects that approach for two reasons, both of which are mistaken. First, Justice SCALIA worries that if federal courts inquire into the effect of federal rules on state law, it will enmesh federal courts in difficult determinations about whether application of a given rule would displace a state determination about substantive rights. I do not see why an Enabling Act inquiry that looks to state law necessarily is more taxing than Justice SCALIA's. But in any event, that inquiry is what the Enabling Act requires: While it may not be easy to decide what is actually a "substantive right," "the designations substantive and procedural become important, for the Enabling Act has made them so." Ely, [The Irrepressible Myth of Erie, 87 *Harv. L.Rev.* 693, 723 (1974)]. * * *

Second, the plurality argues that its interpretation of the Enabling Act is dictated by this Court's decision in *Sibbach*, which applied a Federal Rule about when parties must submit to medical examinations. But the plurality misreads that opinion. * * * To understand *Sibbach*, it is first necessary to understand the issue that was before the Court. The petitioner raised only the facial question whether "Rules 35 and 37 [of the Federal Rules of Civil Procedure] are . . . within the mandate of Congress to this court" and not the specific question of "the obligation of federal courts to apply the substantive law of a state." The Court, therefore, had no occasion to consider whether the particular application of the Federal Rules in question would offend the Enabling Act.

Nor, in *Sibbach*, was any further analysis necessary to the resolution of the case because the matter at issue, requiring medical exams for litigants, did not pertain to "substantive rights" under the Enabling Act. * * * [W]e held that "the phrase 'substantive rights'" embraces only state rights, such as the tort law in that case, that are sought to be enforced in the judicial proceedings. If the Federal Rule had in fact displaced a state rule that was sufficiently intertwined with a state right or remedy, then perhaps the Enabling Act analysis would have been different. * * *

III

Justice GINSBURG views the basic issue in this case as whether and how to apply a federal rule that dictates an answer to a traditionally procedural question (whether to join plaintiffs together as a class), when a state law that "defines the dimensions" of a state-created claim dictates the opposite answer. As explained above, I readily acknowledge that if a federal rule displaces a state rule that is " 'procedural' in the ordinary sense of the term," but sufficiently interwoven with the scope of a substantive right or remedy, there would be an Enabling Act problem, and the federal rule would have to give way. In my view, however, this is not such a case.

Rule 23 Controls Class Certification

When the District Court in the case before us was asked to certify a class action, Federal Rule of Civil Procedure 23 squarely governed the determination whether the court should do so. That is the explicit function of Rule 23. Rule 23, therefore, must apply unless its application would abridge, enlarge, or modify New York rights or remedies.

Notwithstanding the plain language of Rule 23, I understand the dissent to find that Rule 23 does *not* govern the question of class certification in this matter because New York has made a substantive judgment that such a class should not be certified, as a means of proscribing damages. Although * * * I do not accept the dissent's view of § 901(b), I also do not see how the dissent's interpretation of Rule 23 follows from that view. I agree with Justice Ginsburg that courts should "avoi[d] immoderate interpretations of the Federal Rules that would trench on state prerogatives" and should in some instances "interpre[t] the federal rules to avoid conflict with important state regulatory policies." But that is not what the dissent has done. Simply because a rule should be read in light of federalism concerns, it does not follow that courts may rewrite the rule.

At bottom, the dissent's interpretation of Rule 23 seems to be that Rule 23 covers only those cases in which its application would create no *Erie* problem. The dissent would apply the Rules of Decision Act inquiry under *Erie* even to cases in which there is a governing federal rule, and thus the Act, by its own terms, does not apply. But "[w]hen a situation is covered by one of the Federal Rules, the question facing the court is a far cry from the typical, relatively unguided *Erie* choice." *Hanna,* 380 U.S. at 471. The question is only whether the Enabling Act is satisfied. Although it reflects a laudable concern to protect "state regulatory policies," Justice GINSBURG's approach would, in my view, work an end run around Congress' system of uniform federal rules, and our decision in *Hanna.* * * *

Applying Rule 23 Does Not Violate the Enabling Act

As I have explained, in considering whether to certify a class action such as this one, a federal court must inquire whether doing so would abridge, enlarge, or modify New York's rights or remedies, and thereby violate the Enabling Act. * * * Faced with a federal rule that dictates an answer to a traditionally procedural question and that displaces a state rule, one can often argue that the state rule was *really* some part of the State's definition of its rights or remedies.

In my view, however, the bar for finding an Enabling Act problem is a high one. The mere fact that a state law is designed as a procedural rule suggests it reflects a judgment about how state courts ought to operate and not a judgment about the scope of state-created rights and remedies. And for the purposes of operating a federal court system, there are costs involved in attempting to discover the true nature of a state procedural rule and allowing such a rule to operate alongside a federal rule that appears to govern the same question. The mere possibility that a federal rule would alter a state-created right is not sufficient. There must be little doubt.

* * *

The legislative history of § 901 thus reveals a classically procedural calibration of making it easier to litigate claims in New York courts (under any source of law) only when it is necessary to do so, and not making it *too* easy when the class tool is not required. This is the same sort of calculation that might go into setting filing fees or deadlines for briefs. There is of course a difference of degree between those examples and class certification, but not a difference of kind; the class vehicle may have a greater practical effect on who brings lawsuits than do low filing fees, but that does not transform it into a damages "proscription" or "limitation."

The difference of degree is relevant to the forum shopping considerations that are part of the Rules of Decision Act or *Erie* inquiry. If the applicable federal rule did not govern the particular question at issue (or could be fairly read not to do so), then those considerations would matter, for precisely the reasons given by the dissent. But that is not *this* case. As the Court explained in *Hanna,* it is an "incorrect assumption that the rule of *Erie R. Co. v. Tompkins* constitutes the appropriate test of . . . the applicability of a Federal Rule of Civil Procedure." "It is true that both the Enabling Act and the *Erie* rule say, roughly, that federal courts are to apply state 'substantive' law and federal 'procedural' law," but the tests are different and reflect the fact that "they were designed to control very different sorts of decisions."

Because Rule 23 governs class certification, the only decision is whether certifying a class in this diversity case would "abridge, enlarge or modify" New York's substantive rights or remedies. * * * [W]e should respect the plain textual reading of § 901(b), a rule in New York's procedural code about when to certify class actions brought under any source of law, and respect Congress' decision that Rule 23 governs class certification in federal courts. In order to displace a federal rule, there must be more than just a possibility that the state rule is different than it appears.

Accordingly, I concur in part and concur in the judgment.

■ JUSTICE GINSBURG, with whom JUSTICE KENNEDY, JUSTICE BREYER, and JUSTICE ALITO join, dissenting.

The Court today approves Shady Grove's attempt to transform a $500 case into a $5,000,000 award, although the State creating the right to recover has proscribed this alchemy. If Shady Grove had filed suit in New York state court, the 2% interest payment authorized as a penalty for overdue benefits would, by Shady Grove's own measure, amount to no more than $500. By instead filing in federal court based on the parties' diverse citizenship and requesting class certification, Shady Grove hopes to recover, for the class, statutory damages of more than $5,000,000. The New York Legislature has barred this remedy, instructing that, unless specifically permitted, "an action to recover a penalty, or minimum measure of recovery created or imposed by statute may not be maintained as a class action." N.Y. Civ. Prac. Law Ann. (CPLR) § 901(b). The Court nevertheless holds that Federal Rule of Civil Procedure 23, which prescribes procedures for the conduct of class actions in federal courts, preempts the application of § 901(b) in diversity suits.

The Court reads Rule 23 relentlessly to override New York's restriction on the availability of statutory damages. Our decisions, however, caution us to ask, before undermining state legislation: Is this conflict really necessary? Had the Court engaged in that inquiry, it would not have read Rule 23 to collide with New York's legitimate interest in keeping certain monetary awards reasonably bounded. I would continue to interpret Federal Rules with awareness of, and sensitivity to, important state regulatory policies. Because today's judgment radically departs from that course, I dissent.

I

* * *

B

In our prior decisions in point, many of them not mentioned in the Court's opinion, we have avoided immoderate interpretations of the Federal Rules that would trench on state prerogatives without serving any countervailing federal interest. "Application of the *Hanna* analysis," we have said, "is premised on a 'direct collision' between the Federal Rule and the state law." *Walker v. Armco Steel Corp.*, 446 U.S. 740, 749–750 (1980) (quoting *Hanna*, 380 U.S. at 472). To displace state law, a Federal Rule, "when fairly construed," must be " 'sufficiently broad' " so as "to 'control the issue' before the court, thereby leaving *no room* for the operation of that law." *Burlington Northern R. Co. v. Woods*, 480 U.S. 1, 4–5 (1987) (quoting *Walker*, 446 U.S. at 749–750, and n. 9); *cf. Stewart Organization, Inc. v. Ricoh Corp.*, 487 U.S. 22, 37–38 (1988) (SCALIA, J., dissenting) ("[I]n deciding whether a federal . . . Rule of Procedure encompasses a particular issue, a broad reading that would create significant disuniformity between state and federal courts should be avoided if the text permits.").

In pre-*Hanna* decisions, the Court vigilantly read the Federal Rules to avoid conflict with state laws. In *Palmer v. Hoffman*, 318 U.S. 109, 117 (1943), for example, the Court read Federal Rule 8(c), which lists affirmative defenses, to control only the manner of pleading the listed defenses in diversity cases; as to the burden of proof in such cases, *Palmer* held, state law controls.

Six years later, in *Ragan v. Merchants Transfer & Warehouse Co.*, 337 U.S. 530 (1949), the Court ruled that state law determines when a diversity suit commences for purposes of tolling the state limitations period. Although Federal Rule 3 specified that "[a] civil action is commenced by filing a complaint with the court," we held that the Rule did not displace a state law that tied an action's commencement to service of the summons. The "cause of action [wa]s created by local law," the Court explained, therefore "the measure of it [wa]s to be found only in local law."

Similarly in *Cohen v. Beneficial Industrial Loan Corp.,* 337 U.S. 541 (1949), the Court held applicable in a diversity action a state statute requiring plaintiffs, as a prerequisite to pursuit of a stockholder's derivative action, to post a bond as security for costs. At the time of the litigation, Rule 23, now Rule 23.1, addressed a plaintiff's institution of a derivative action in federal court. Although the Federal Rule specified prerequisites to a stockholder's maintenance of a derivative action, the Court found no conflict between the Rule and the state statute in question; the requirements of both could be enforced, the Court observed. Burdensome as the security-for-costs requirement may be, *Cohen* made plain, suitors could not escape the upfront outlay by resorting to the federal court's diversity jurisdiction.

In all of these cases, the Court stated in *Hanna,* "the scope of the Federal Rule was not as broad as the losing party urged, and therefore, there being no Federal Rule which covered the point in dispute, *Erie* commanded the enforcement of state law." In *Hanna* itself, the Court found the clash "unavoidable"; the petitioner had effected service of process as prescribed by Federal Rule 4(d)(1), but that "how-to" method did not satisfy the special Massachusetts law applicable to service on an executor or administrator. Even as it rejected the Massachusetts prescription in favor of the federal procedure, however, "[t]he majority in Hanna recognized . . . that federal rules . . . must be interpreted by the courts applying them, and that the process of interpretation can and should reflect an awareness of legitimate state interests." R. Fallon, J. Manning, D. Meltzer, & D. Shapiro, Hart and Wechsler's *The Federal Courts and the Federal System* 593 (6th ed. 2009).

Following *Hanna,* we continued to "interpre[t] the federal rules to avoid conflict with important state regulatory policies." *Hart & Wechsler* 593. In *Walker,* the Court took up the question whether *Ragan* should be overruled; we held, once again, that Federal Rule 3 does not directly conflict with state rules governing the time when an action commences for purposes of tolling a limitations period. * * *

We were similarly attentive to a State's regulatory policy in *Gasperini.* That diversity case concerned the standard for determining when the large size of a jury verdict warrants a new trial. Federal and state courts alike had generally employed a "shock the conscience" test in reviewing jury awards for excessiveness. Federal courts did so pursuant to Federal Rule 59(a) which, as worded at the time of *Gasperini,* instructed that a trial court could grant a new trial "for any of the reasons for which new trials have heretofore been granted in actions at law in the courts of the United States." In an effort to provide greater control, New York prescribed procedures under which jury verdicts would be examined to determine whether they "deviate[d] materially from what would be reasonable compensation." This Court held that Rule 59(a) did not inhibit federal-court accommodation of New York's invigorated test.

Most recently, in *Semtek*, we addressed the claim-preclusive effect of a federal-court judgment dismissing a diversity action on the basis of a California statute of limitations. The case came to us after the same plaintiff renewed the same fray against the same defendant in a Maryland state court. (Plaintiff chose Maryland because that State's limitations period had not yet run.) We held that Federal Rule 41(b), which provided that an involuntary dismissal "operate[d] as an adjudication on the merits," did not bar maintenance of the renewed action in Maryland. To hold that Rule 41(b) precluded the Maryland courts from entertaining the case, we said, "would arguably violate the jurisdictional limitation of the Rules Enabling Act" and "would in many cases violate [*Erie*'s] federalism principle."

In sum, both before and after *Hanna,* the above-described decisions show, federal courts have been cautioned by this Court to "interpre[t] the Federal Rules . . . with sensitivity to important state interests," *Gasperini,* 518 U.S. at 427, n. 7, and a will "to avoid conflict with important state regulatory policies," *id.* at 438, n. 22. The Court veers away from that approach—and conspicuously, its most recent reiteration in *Gasperini*—in favor of a mechanical reading of Federal Rules, insensitive to state interests and productive of discord.

C

Our decisions instruct over and over again that, in the adjudication of diversity cases, state interests—whether advanced in a statute, *e.g., Cohen,* or a procedural rule, *e.g., Gasperini*—warrant our respectful consideration. Yet today, the Court gives no quarter to New York's limitation on statutory damages and requires the lower courts to thwart the regulatory policy at stake: To prevent excessive damages, New York's law controls the penalty to which a defendant may be exposed in a single suit. * * *

* * *

* * * Section 901(a) allows courts leeway in deciding whether to certify a class, but § 901(b) rejects the use of the class mechanism to pursue the particular remedy of statutory damages. The limitation was not designed with the fair conduct or efficiency of litigation in mind. Indeed, suits seeking statutory damages are arguably *best* suited to the class device because individual proof of actual damages is unnecessary. New York's decision instead to block class-action proceedings for statutory damages therefore makes scant sense, except as a means to a manifestly substantive end: Limiting a defendant's liability in a single lawsuit in order to prevent the exorbitant inflation of penalties—

remedies the New York Legislature created with individual suits in mind.

D

Shady Grove contends—and the Court today agrees—that Rule 23 unavoidably preempts New York's prohibition on the recovery of statutory damages in class actions. The Federal Rule, the Court emphasizes, states that Shady Grove's suit "may be" maintained as a class action, which conflicts with § 901(b)'s instruction that it "may not" so proceed. Accordingly, the Court insists, § 901(b) "cannot apply in diversity suits unless Rule 23 is ultra vires." Concluding that Rule 23 does not violate the Rules Enabling Act, the Court holds that the federal provision controls Shady Grove's ability to seek, on behalf of a class, a statutory penalty of over $5,000,000.

* * *

* * * Rule 23 describes a method of enforcing a claim for relief, while § 901(b) defines the dimensions of the claim itself. In this regard, it is immaterial that § 901(b) bars statutory penalties in wholesale, rather than retail, fashion. The New York Legislature could have embedded the limitation in every provision creating a cause of action for which a penalty is authorized; § 901(b) operates as shorthand to the same effect. It is as much a part of the delineation of the claim for relief as it would be were it included claim by claim in the New York Code.

* * *

Suppose, for example, that a State, wishing to cap damages in class actions at $1,000,000, enacted a statute providing that "a suit to recover more than $1,000,000 may not be maintained as a class action." Under the Court's reasoning—which attributes dispositive significance to the words "may not be maintained"—Rule 23 would preempt this provision, nevermind that Congress, by authorizing the promulgation of rules of procedure for federal courts, surely did not intend to displace state-created ceilings on damages. * * *

The absence of an inevitable collision between Rule 23 and § 901(b) becomes evident once it is comprehended that a federal court sitting in diversity can accord due respect to both state and federal prescriptions. Plaintiffs seeking to vindicate claims for which the State has provided a statutory penalty may pursue relief through a class action if they forgo statutory damages and instead seek actual damages or injunctive or declaratory relief; any putative class member who objects can opt out and pursue actual damages, if available, and the statutory penalty in an individual action. In this manner, the Second Circuit explained, "Rule 23's procedural requirements for class actions can be applied along with the substantive requirement of CPLR 901(b)." In sum, while phrased as responsive to the question whether certain class actions may begin, § 901(b) is unmistakably aimed at controlling how those actions must end. On that remedial issue, Rule 23 is silent.

* * *

By finding a conflict without considering whether Rule 23 rationally should be read to avoid any collision, the Court unwisely and unnecessarily retreats from the federalism principles undergirding *Erie*. Had the Court reflected on the respect for state regulatory interests endorsed in our decisions, it would have found no cause to interpret Rule 23 so woodenly—and every reason not to do so.

II

Because I perceive no unavoidable conflict between Rule 23 and § 901(b), I would decide this case by inquiring "whether application of the [state] rule would have so important an effect upon the fortunes of one or both of the litigants that failure to [apply] it would be likely to cause a plaintiff to choose the federal court." *Hanna*, 380 U.S. at 468, n. 9. See *Gasperini*, 518 U.S. at 428.

* * *

* * * Shady Grove's effort to characterize § 901(b) as simply "procedural" cannot successfully elide this fundamental norm: When no federal law or rule is dispositive of an issue, and a state statute is outcome affective in the sense our cases on *Erie* (pre and post-*Hanna*) develop, the Rules of Decision Act commands application of the State's law in diversity suits. As this case starkly demonstrates, if federal courts exercising diversity jurisdiction are compelled by Rule 23 to award statutory penalties in class actions while New York courts are bound by § 901(b)'s proscription, "substantial variations between state and federal [money judgments] may be expected." *Gasperini*, 518 U.S. at 430 (quoting *Hanna*, 380 U.S. at 467–468). The "variation" here is indeed "substantial." Shady Grove seeks class relief that is *ten thousand times* greater than the individual remedy available to it in state court. As the plurality acknowledges, forum shopping will undoubtedly result if a plaintiff need only file in federal instead of state court to seek a massive monetary award explicitly barred by state law. The "accident of diversity of citizenship," *Klaxon Co. v. Stentor Elec. Mfg. Co.*, 313 U.S. 487, 496 (1941), should not subject a defendant to such augmented liability.

It is beyond debate that "a statutory cap on damages would supply substantive law for *Erie* purposes." *Gasperini*, 518 U.S. at 428. See also *id.* at 439–440 2211 (STEVENS, J., dissenting) ("A state-law ceiling on allowable damages . . . is a substantive rule of decision that federal courts must apply in diversity cases governed by New York law."); *id.* at 464 (SCALIA, J., dissenting) ("State substantive law controls what injuries are compensable and in what amount."). In *Gasperini*, we determined that New York's standard for measuring the alleged excessiveness of a jury verdict was designed to provide a control analogous to a damages cap. The statute was framed as "a procedural instruction," we noted, "but the State's objective [wa]s manifestly substantive."

Gasperini's observations apply with full force in this case. By barring the recovery of statutory damages in a class action, § 901(b) controls a defendant's maximum liability in a suit seeking such a remedy. The remedial provision could have been written as an explicit cap: "In any class action seeking statutory damages, relief is limited to the amount the named plaintiff would have recovered in an individual suit." That New York's Legislature used other words to express the very same meaning should be inconsequential.

We have long recognized the impropriety of displacing, in a diversity action, state-law limitations on state-created remedies. Just as *Erie* precludes a federal court from entering a deficiency judgment when a State has "authoritatively announced that [such] judgments cannot be secured within its borders," *Angel v. Bullington,* 330 U.S. 183, 191 (1947), so too *Erie* should prevent a federal court from awarding statutory penalties aggregated through a class action when New York prohibits this recovery. In sum, because "New York substantive law governs [this] claim for relief, New York law . . . guide[s] the allowable damages." *Gasperini,* 518 U.S. at 437.

III

The Court's erosion of *Erie*'s federalism grounding impels me to point out the large irony in today's judgment. Shady Grove is able to pursue its claim in federal court only by virtue of the recent enactment of the Class Action Fairness Act of 2005 (CAFA), 28 U.S.C. § 1332(d). In CAFA, Congress opened federal-court doors to state-law-based class actions so long as there is minimal diversity, at least 100 class members, and at least $5,000,000 in controversy. By providing a federal forum, Congress sought to check what it considered to be the overreadiness of some state courts to certify class actions. In other words, Congress envisioned fewer—not more—class actions overall. Congress surely never anticipated that CAFA would make federal courts a mecca for suits of the kind Shady Grove has launched: class actions seeking state-created penalties for claims arising under state law—claims that would be barred from class treatment in the State's own courts.[7]

* * *

I would continue to approach *Erie* questions in a manner mindful of the purposes underlying the Rules of Decision Act and the Rules Enabling Act, faithful to precedent, and respectful of important state

---

[7] It remains open to Congress, of course, to exclude from federal-court jurisdiction under the Class Action Fairness Act of 2005, 28 U.S.C. § 1332(d), claims that could not be maintained as a class action in state court.

interests. I would therefore hold that the New York Legislature's limitation on the recovery of statutory damages applies in this case, and would affirm the Second Circuit's judgment.

COMMENTS AND QUESTIONS CONCERNING *SHADY GROVE ORTHOPEDIC ASSOCIATES, P.A. V. ALLSTATE INS. CO.*

1. At the outset of his opinion, Justice Scalia describes the test for challenges to the Federal Rules as follows:

> The framework for our decision is familiar. We must first determine whether Rule 23 answers the question in dispute. If it does, it governs—New York's law notwithstanding—unless it exceeds statutory authorization or Congress's rulemaking power. We do not wade into *Erie*'s murky waters unless the federal rule is inapplicable or invalid.

His opinion concludes:

> The short of the matter is that a Federal Rule governing procedure is valid whether or not it alters the outcome of the case in a way that induces forum shopping. To hold otherwise would be to "disembowel either the Constitution's grant of power over federal procedure" or Congress's exercise of it.

Is the task as easy, and mechanical, as Justice Scalia suggests, or has Justice Scalia interpreted Rule 23 too "woodenly" as Justice Ginsburg states in her dissent?

2. Justice Scalia asserts that "the substantive nature of New York's law, or its substantive purpose, *makes no difference.* A Federal Rule of Procedure is not valid in some jurisdictions and invalid in others—or valid in some cases and invalid in others—depending upon whether its effect is to frustrate a state substantive law (or a state procedural law enacted for substantive purposes)." But, as Justice Stevens notes in his concurrence, "This interpretation of the Enabling Act is consonant with the Act's first limitation to 'general rules of practice and procedure.' But it ignores the second limitation that such rules also 'not abridge, enlarge or modify *any* substantive right,' and in so doing ignores the balance that Congress struck between uniform rules of federal procedure and respect for a State's construction of its own rights and remedies." Does this mean that the courts must determine the validity of each Federal Rule with respect to each state law with which it may conflict?

3. In *Shady Grove*, Justices Scalia and Ginsburg switched their roles in *Gasperini* (in which Justice Ginsburg wrote the majority opinion and Justice Scalia dissented). In both cases, though, Justice Scalia argued that federal law should control and Justice Ginsburg would have applied state law. Although she dissents in *Shady Grove*, Justice Ginsburg notes in footnote 2 of her dissent that "a majority of this Court, it bears emphasis, agrees that Federal Rules should be read with moderation in diversity suits to accommodate important state concerns." Why did Justice Ginsburg believe it necessary to emphasize this point?

4.   Doesn't *Shady Grove* illustrate the very forum shopping that *Erie* was meant to avoid? Are there other cases in which the Supreme Court was faced with a greater potential for forum shopping than in *Shady Grove*, with the opportunity for exponentially greater damage awards in federal than in state court?

5.   In reaching the conclusion that Rule 23 "really regulates procedure" and does not "abridge, enlarge or modify any substantive right," Justice Scalia asserts:

> A class action, no less than traditional joinder (of which it is a species), merely enables a federal court to adjudicate claims of multiple parties at once, instead of in separate suits. And like traditional joinder, it leaves the parties' legal rights and duties intact and the rules of decision unchanged.

What about "negative value class actions" such as this that involve potential individual damage awards so small that the underlying claims will not be pursued unless they can be asserted within a class action? As Justice Scalia notes, "Allstate contends that the authorization of class actions is not substantively neutral: Allowing Shady Grove to sue on behalf of a class 'transform[s] [the] dispute over a five *hundred* dollar penalty into a dispute over a five *million* dollar penalty.'"

Think about which of these views paints a more accurate picture of the realities of class action litigation, which are discussed in Chapter 7.

6.   Justice Ginsburg asserts a "large irony in today's judgment" because Shady Grove was able to use the Class Action Fairness Act of 2005 ("CAFA") to seek certification of a class action in federal court that could not be certified in state court. CAFA relaxed federal statutory jurisdictional requirements in 28 U.S.C. § 1332(d), permitting federal courts to exercise jurisdiction over certain class actions with only minimal diversity between the parties if there is more than $5,000,000 total in controversy and there are at least 100 members in the class. 28 U.S.C. §§ 1332(d)(2); 1332(d)(5)(B). Justice Ginsburg notes that CAFA was intended to protect defendants, by allowing them to remove class actions from state courts and state judges personifying an " 'I never met a class action I didn't like' approach to class certification." 559 U.S. at 459. In *Shady Grove*, though, CAFA was used by the plaintiff to gain a much more favorable federal forum than that presented in state court.

7.   Justice Ginsburg asserts that the Court's job is to "interpret Federal Rules with awareness of, and sensitivity to, important state regulatory policies," while Justices Scalia and Stevens accuse her of "rewriting" Rule 23 to avoid a conflict between state and federal law. Who is right, and where is the boundary between these two schools of judicial interpretation?

G.   APPLYING *ERIE* AND *HANNA* IN PRACTICE

The case of *Leonard v. PepsiCo* originally was filed in Florida state court, then removed to the United States District Court for the

Southern District of Florida.[8] Plaintiff John Leonard's common law claims were for specific performance, breach of contract, and fraud, and he asserted additional statutory claims for false advertising and deceptive practices. Even under *Swift v. Tyson*, the state statutory claims would have been considered the "laws of the several states" that "shall be regarded as rules of decision in civil actions in the courts of the United States" under the Rules of Decision Act, 28 U.S.C. § 1652.

But what about the state common law claims for specific performance, breach of contract, and fraud? Judge Kimba Wood wrote in her opinion in *Leonard v. PepsiCo, Inc.*:

> The parties disagree concerning whether the Court should apply the law of the state of New York or of some other state in evaluating whether defendant's promotional campaign constituted an offer. Because the action was transferred from Florida, the choice of law rules of Florida, the transferor state, apply. *See Ferens v. John Deere Co.*, 494 U.S. 516, 523–33 (1990). Under Florida law, the choice of law in a contract case is determined by the place "where the last act necessary to complete the contract is done."[9]

However, Judge Wood also concluded that she need not resolve the choice of law question, because "resolution of this issue requires consideration of principles of contract law that are not limited to the law of any one state. * * * [T]he questions presented by this case implicate questions of contract law 'deeply ingrained in the common law of England and the States of the Union.' "[10]

What if there had been differing state contract law that required resolution of the conflict of law question? The United States District Court for the Southern District of Florida, when "adjudicating a state-created right solely because of the diversity of citizenship of the parties[,] is for that purpose, in effect, only another court of the State." *Guaranty Trust Co. v. York*, 326 U.S. 99, 108 (1945). Thus, had it not transferred the *Leonard* case to the Southern District of New York, the federal court in the Southern District of Florida should have applied the same law as a Florida state court.

However, this does not necessarily mean that the Florida courts, state or federal, would have applied Florida contract law. If the action had remained in Florida state court, the state court would have had to determine just what state contract law to apply—in an action between a Washington plaintiff and a corporation incorporated in North Carolina with its principal place of business in New York concerning a contract that may have been reached in any one of several states.[11] State courts

---

[8]   *See Leonard v. PepsiCo, Inc.*, 88 F.Supp. 2d 116, 120 (S.D.N.Y. 1999).

[9]   *Id.* at 122.

[10] *Id.*, quoting Plaintiff's Memorandum, at 8.

[11] *See Leonard v. PepsiCo, Inc.*, 88 F.Supp. 2d 116, 122 (S.D.N.Y. 1999).

apply "choice-of-law" rules to determine which state's law to apply when a civil action involves parties and events involving more than one state.

Choice of law also can be a question for a federal court hearing a diversity action involving parties and underlying facts from several states. This issue was presented to the Supreme Court in *Klaxon Co. v. Stentor Electric Mfr. Co.*, 313 U.S. 487, 494 (1941) ("The principal question in this case is whether in diversity cases the federal courts must follow conflict of law rules prevailing in the states in which they sit."). The *Klaxon* Court answered this question in the affirmative:

> The conflict of laws rules to be applied by the federal court in Delaware must conform to those prevailing in Delaware's state courts. Otherwise the accident of diversity of citizenship would constantly disturb equal administration of justice in coordinate state and federal courts sitting side by side. Any other ruling would do violence to the principle of uniformity within a state upon which the *Tompkins* decision is based. Whatever lack of uniformity this may produce between federal courts in different states is attributable to our federal system, which leaves to a state, within the limits permitted by the Constitution, the right to pursue local policies diverging from those of its neighbors. It is not for the federal courts to thwart such local policies by enforcing an independent "general law" of conflict of laws. * * * And the proper function of the Delaware federal court is to ascertain what the state law is, not what it ought to be.

313 U.S. at 496–97.

Figure 5–2 illustrates the manner in which the governing contract law would have been determined in *Leonard v. PepsiCo* if there had been differences in such contract law among the states. Because of *Ferens v. John Deere Co.*, 494 U.S. 516 (1990), the U.S. District Court for the Southern District of New York had to apply the same law as would the U.S. District Court for the Southern District of Florida (from which the action was transferred). Because of *Erie Railroad Co. v. Tompkins*, 304 U.S. 64 (1938), and *Klaxon Co. v. Stentor Electric Mfr. Co.*, 313 U.S. 487 (1941), the U.S. District Court for the Southern District of Florida had to apply the same choice-of-law rule as would a Florida state court. And, under governing Florida state law, a Florida state court would have had to apply the contract law of the state "where the last act necessary to complete the contract is done." *Jemco, Inc. v. United Parcel Service, Inc.*, 400 So. 2d 499, 500 (Fla. Dist. Ct. Appl. 1981).

Do you suspect that everyone in *Leonard v. PepsiCo* was pleased that the relevant contract law in that case was "not limited to the law of any one state" and that the court therefore did not have to conduct this conflicts or choice-of-law analysis?

FIGURE 5–2
KLAXON v. STENTOR FLOWCHART TO DETERMINE
GOVERNING STATE LAW IN *LEONARD v. PEPSICO, INC.*

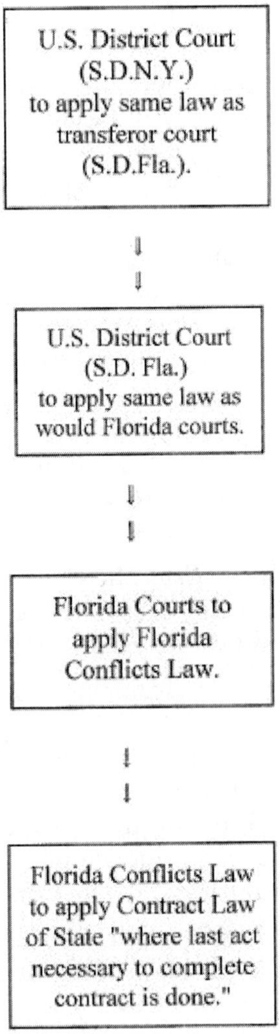

```
┌─────────────────────┐
│  U.S. District Court │
│      (S.D.N.Y.)      │
│  to apply same law as│
│   transferor court   │
│      (S.D.Fla.).     │
└─────────────────────┘
           ⇓
           ⇓
┌─────────────────────┐
│  U.S. District Court │
│      (S.D. Fla.)     │
│  to apply same law as│
│ would Florida courts.│
└─────────────────────┘
           ⇓
           ⇓
┌─────────────────────┐
│   Florida Courts to  │
│    apply Florida     │
│    Conflicts Law.    │
└─────────────────────┘
           ↓
           ↓
┌─────────────────────┐
│ Florida Conflicts Law│
│ to apply Contract Law│
│ of State "where last act│
│ necessary to complete│
│   contract is done." │
└─────────────────────┘
```

III. FEDERAL COMMON LAW

Justice Brandeis famously stated in *Erie Railroad*, "There is no federal general common law." 304 U.S. at 78. However, the same day that the Court announced its decision in *Erie*, it also decided *Hinderlider v. La Plata River & Cherry Creek Ditch Co.* 304 U.S. 92 (1938). Writing for a unanimous court, Justice Brandeis stated in *Hinderlider*, 304 U.S. at 110, "[W]hether the water of an interstate stream must be apportioned between the two States is a question of 'federal common law' upon which neither the statutes nor the decisions of either State can be conclusive." Is this inconsistent with Justice

Brandeis' opinion in *Erie Railroad*? What federal common law is left
after the *Erie* and *Hanna* lines of cases?

In *City of Milwaukee v. Illinois & Michigan*, 451 U.S. 304 (1981),
the Supreme Court held that federal environmental legislation
preempted the federal common law of nuisance that otherwise might
have been available in that action. In his dissent, Justice Blackmun
outlined the areas in which the Court had recognized federal common
law even after its decision in *Erie Railroad*:

> It is well settled that a body of federal common law has
> survived the decision in *Erie R. Co. v. Tompkins*, 304 U.S. 64
> (1938). *Erie* made clear that federal courts, as courts of limited
> jurisdiction, lack general power to formulate and impose their
> own rules of decision. The Court, however, did not there upset,
> nor has it since disturbed, a deeply rooted, more specialized
> federal common law that has arisen to effectuate federal
> interests embodied either in the Constitution or an Act of
> Congress. Chief among the federal interests served by this
> common law are the resolution of interstate disputes and the
> implementation of national statutory or regulatory policies.

> Both before and after *Erie*, the Court has fashioned federal
> law where the interstate nature of a controversy renders
> inappropriate the law of either State. * * *

> Long before the 1972 decision in *Illinois v. Milwaukee*,
> federal common law enunciated by this Court assured each
> State the right to be free from unreasonable interference with
> its natural environment and resources when the interference
> stems from another State or its citizens. The right to such
> federal protection is a consequence of each State's entry into
> the Union and its commitment to the Constitution. * * *

> This Court also has applied federal common law where
> federally created substantive rights and obligations are at
> stake. Thus, the Court has been called upon to pronounce
> common law that will fill the interstices of a pervasively
> federal framework, or avoid subjecting relevant federal
> interests to the inconsistencies in the laws of several States.
> *Textile Workers v. Lincoln Mills*, 353 U.S. 448, 456–457 (1957);
> *United States v. Standard Oil Co.*, 332 U.S. 301, 305 (1947);
> *Clearfield Trust Co. v. United States*, 318 U.S. 363, 366–367
> (1943); *D'Oench, Duhme & Co. v. Federal Deposit Ins. Corp.*,
> 315 U.S. 447 (1942). If the federal interest is sufficiently
> strong, federal common law may be drawn upon in settling
> disputes even though the statute or Constitution alone
> provides no precise answer to the question posed. *See, e.g.,*
> *Textile Workers v. Lincoln Mills*, 353 U.S., at 458; *Clearfield*
> *Trust Co. v. United States*, 318 U.S., at 368–370. *See generally*
> *United States v. Little Lake Misere Land Co.*, 412 U.S. 580, 593

(1973) ("the inevitable incompleteness presented by all legislation means that interstitial federal law-making is a basic responsibility of the federal courts").

City of Milwaukee v. Illinois & Michigan, 451 U.S. 304, 334–36 (1981) (Blackmun, J., dissenting).

Two of the cases cited by Justice Blackmun, *Clearfield Trust* and *Lincoln Mills*, are particularly instructive. In *Clearfield Trust Co. v. United States*, 318 U.S. 363 (1943), the Supreme Court held that federal common law, rather than state law, applied to determine the rights and duties of the United States concerning a federal paycheck. The Court stated:

> The issuance of commercial paper by the United States is on a vast scale and transactions in that paper from issuance to payment will commonly occur in several states. The application of state law, even without the conflict of laws rules of the forum, would subject the rights and duties of the United States to exceptional uncertainty. It would lead to great diversity in results by making identical transactions subject to the vagaries of the laws of the several states. The desirability of a uniform rule is plain.

318 U.S. at 367. *But see Bank of America v. Parnell*, 352 U.S. 29, 33 (1956) (State law applied in action concerning title to government bonds because "[t]he present litigation is purely between private parties and does not touch the rights and duties of the United States.").

In *Textile Workers v. Lincoln Mills*, 353 U.S. 448, 451 (1957), the Court held that Section 301 of the Labor Management Relations Act of 1947 authorized the federal courts to "fashion a body of federal law for the enforcement of * * * collective bargaining agreements." Justice Douglas explained the manner in which federal courts could create federal common law in this context:

> We conclude that the substantive law to apply in suits under § 301(a) is federal law, which the courts must fashion from the policy of our national labor laws. The Labor Management Relations Act expressly furnishes some substantive law. It points out what the parties may or may not do in certain situations. Other problems will lie in the penumbra of express statutory mandates. Some will lack express statutory sanction but will be solved by looking at the policy of the legislation and fashioning a remedy that will effectuate that policy. The range of judicial inventiveness will be determined by the nature of the problem.* * *

> It is not uncommon for federal courts to fashion federal law where federal rights are concerned. Congress has indicated by § 301(a) the purpose to follow that course here. There is no constitutional difficulty. Article III, § 2, extends the judicial

power to cases "arising under * * * the Laws of the United States * * *." The power of Congress to regulate these labor-management controversies under the Commerce Clause is plain. A case or controversy arising under § 301(a) is, therefore, one within the purview of judicial power as defined in Article III.

353 U.S. at 456–57.

More recently, in *Boyle v. United Technologies Corp.*, 487 U.S. 500 (1988), the Supreme Court held that a contractor providing military equipment to the United States could not be held liable for an alleged design defect under state tort law. Justice Scalia explained that "we have held that a few areas, involving 'uniquely federal interests,' are so committed by the Constitution and laws of the United States to federal control that state law is pre-empted and replaced, where necessary, by federal law of a content prescribed (absent explicit statutory directive) by the courts—so-called 'federal common law.'" 487 U.S. at 504. The Court found that this was an area for the creation of federal common law, because "the liability of independent contractors performing work for the Federal Government, like the liability of federal officials, is an area of uniquely federal interest," 487 U.S. at 505 n.1, and a "'significant conflict' exists between an identifiable 'federal policy or interest and the [operation] of state law,' [*Wallis v. Pan American Petroleum Corp.*, 384 U.S. 63, 68 (1966)], or the application of state law would 'frustrate specific objectives' of federal legislation, *Kimbell Foods*, 440 U.S., at 728." *Boyle v. United Technologies Corp.*, 487 U.S. 500, 507 (1988).

So, while *Erie* ended the era of federal **general** common law, specialized federal common law persists in areas of uniquely federal concern. Congressional action may invite the creation of specialized federal common law, when, for instance, Congress leaves openings in a federal statutory scheme for judicially-created law as it did in *Lincoln Mills*. Or a federal statutory scheme may occupy the field, thus preempting the possibility of common law, as was the case in *City of Milwaukee v. Illinois & Michigan*. Despite the Supreme Court's deference to States and state law in *Erie* and its progeny, federal courts can still craft common law in specialized areas of uniquely federal interest.

IV. CONCLUSION

In contrast to your other first-year courses, Civil Procedure focuses on the procedural law applied in the United States District Courts. Even when this law is clear, though, federal judges must make difficult decisions as to the substantive law to apply to resolve tort, contract, and other issues presented to them. If the action has been filed pursuant to Section 1332 diversity jurisdiction and there is no applicable Federal

Rule of Civil Procedure, *Erie Railroad* and its progeny should guide the federal judge's choice of law. Most important for the judge to remember in choosing the applicable substantive law is the admonition of Justice Brandeis in *Erie Railroad* that there "is no federal general common law."

V. CHAPTER ASSESSMENT

A. Multiple-Choice Questions. Answer the following questions, reviewing the sections of the chapter noted in connection with each question.

1. A New Mexico citizen buys a ticket on a bus from Los Angeles, California to his home in Santa Fe, New Mexico. As the bus travels through Arizona, the driver falls asleep, the bus crashes, and the passenger is seriously injured.

In considering where to file an action against the bus company, the passenger's attorney determines that a New Mexico state court is likely to apply New Mexico's common law of torts, which is not as favorable to plaintiffs as the attorney would prefer. The attorney then files the passenger's action against the bus company, a citizen of New York and Delaware, in federal court in New Mexico.

What law should the New Mexico federal judge apply to determine the bus company's liability?

Review Section II(A) and choose the best answer from the following choices:

(a) Federal common law, because the bus was traveling in interstate commerce.

(b) Federal common law, because the accident occurred in Arizona and the action was filed in New Mexico.

(c) Arizona common law, because the accident occurred in Arizona.

(d) New Mexico common law, because this is the law that a New Mexico state court would apply.

2. A retailer brings a federal diversity action against a wholesaler in the United States District Court for the Northern District of Georgia. In its complaint, the retailer alleges that the wholesaler has broken the parties' contract by not providing all the products specified in the contract.

After the filing of the complaint and answer, the parties have a discovery conference with the district judge. The wholesaler asserts that it is entitled to 50 interrogatories, because parties are entitled to 50 interrogatories in the Georgia state courts and this is a federal diversity action. The retailer responds that the wholesaler is only

454 THE LAW APPLIED IN FEDERAL COURT: "ERIE CHOICES FOR THE FEDERAL JUDGE."

CHAPTER 5

entitled to 25 interrogatories as a matter of right, because that is the number specified in Rule 33 of the Federal Rules of Civil Procedure.

Should the federal district court apply the federal rule, limiting the wholesaler to 25 interrogatories as a matter of right, or the state rule, allowing the wholesaler 50 interrogatories?

Review Section II(D) and choose the best answer from the following choices as to which rule the court should apply.

(a) The federal rule, because the outcome is not likely to be different if the federal, rather than the state, rule is applied in this case.

(b) The federal rule, because Federal Rule of Civil Procedure 33 regulates procedure in the federal courts and does not abridge, enlarge or modify any substantive right.

(c) The state rule, because Georgia has a significant substantive interest in its rule in this case.

(d) The state rule, because the federal court has little interest in the application of its interrogatory rule in this case.

3. An Alabama citizen purchases a fence that is to be made from treated lumber, but the fence rots within a few years. The purchaser files a federal diversity action against the company that made the fence, which company is a citizen of Tennessee.

The purchaser's action is brought as a class action in Alabama federal court and seeks $10,000,000 on behalf of 10,000 asserted class members. The action is brought under an Alabama deceptive practices act that creates a private right of action for defrauded consumers. However, that state act also provides that only the state attorney general can bring class actions under the act.

The company files a motion to strike the class claims, arguing that class claims cannot be brought under the Alabama statute by a private party. The purchaser asserts that he is entitled to bring a class action under Rule 23 of the Federal Rules of Civil Procedure.

Should the judge dismiss the class claims brought by the purchaser?

Review Section II(F) and choose the best answer from the following choices.

(a) The court should dismiss the class claims, because the Alabama law has a substantive purpose and effect in restricting private class actions.

(b) The court should dismiss the class claims, because permitting a federal class action will be outcome determinative and result in plaintiff forum shopping.

(c)   The court should not dismiss the class claims, because Rule 23 regulates procedure in the federal courts and does not abridge, enlarge or modify any substantive right.

(d)   The court should not dismiss the class claims, because a Federal Rule of Civil Procedure preempts any conflicting state law.

4.   A Montana man and an Idaho woman are injured in a bus crash in California. They bring a diversity action in Oregon federal court against the bus company, which is incorporated and has its principal place of business in Oregon.

There is no governing state or federal statute establishing the tort law that should be applied in this action. What tort law should the Oregon federal court apply?

Review Section II(G) and choose the best answer from the following choices.

(a)   Federal common law, because there is no applicable state statute on point.

(b)   The common law of Oregon, because the action was filed in the United States District Court for the District of Oregon.

(c)   The state common law that an Oregon state court would select in such a case by applying Oregon's choice-of-law rules.

(d)   The state common law as determined by applying federal choice-of-law rules.

5.   The Columbia River forms a portion of the boundary between the states of Washington and Oregon. After a severe drought, a Washington vineyard brings suit in the United States District Court for the District of Oregon against an Oregon vineyard. The Washington vineyard alleges that the Oregon vineyard illegally diverted water from the Columbia River, depriving the Washington vineyard of sufficient water to support its grapes. In this diversity action the Washington vineyard seeks $10,000,000 in damages and an injunction against the Oregon vineyard's diversion of water from the interstate river.

The Oregon vineyard files a motion to dismiss, asserting that the diversion of water is legal under Oregon law. The Washington vineyard opposes the motion to dismiss. It argues that federal common law, rather than state law, applies in this action involving rights in an interstate river and that the actions of the Oregon vineyard violate this federal common law.

Should the federal district court apply state law or federal common law to this dispute?

Review Section III and choose the best answer from the following choices.

(a)   State law, because, after *Erie Railroad*, there is no federal common law.

(b)   State law, because federal common law would abridge a substantive right.

(c)   Federal common law, because federal common law would not abridge a substantive right.

(d)   Federal common law, because of the interstate nature of the dispute.

B.   Essay Questions. To test your understanding of this chapter's material, outline or write an answer to the following questions.

1.   True Lies.

After printing an editorial calling a local merchant a "bald-faced liar," *The Morning News* is sued by the merchant. The merchant, a citizen of Arkansas, brings his action against the *News* (which is headquartered, written, produced, and incorporated in Tennessee) in the United States District Court for the Western District of Tennessee.

In its answer, the *News* asserts truth as an affirmative defense to the merchant's libel claim. At the parties' Rule 16(e) final pretrial conference, the *News* asserts that federal common law entitles it to a jury instruction that the burden of persuasion is on the plaintiff to show that the alleged libel is not true. The merchant's lawyer objects to this proposed instruction, offering both Arkansas and Tennessee case law holding that the burden of persuasion is on the *News* to prove that the asserted libel was true. The merchant's lawyer further argues that *Erie Railroad v. Tompkins* requires the judge to follow these state court precedents and apply them in this action.

You are the law clerk to the federal district judge who must decide on which party to place the burden of persuasion concerning the truthfulness of the editorial. What advice would you give the judge as to the impact of *Erie Railroad* on the question of the placement of the burden of persuasion at trial?

2.   When Is a Counterclaim Really Compulsory?

Two drivers, Kentucky (a citizen of Kentucky) and Tennessee (a citizen of Tennessee) are in a traffic accident in Johnson City, Tennessee, in which accident they both suffer significant injuries. Tennessee files a federal diversity action under 28 U.S.C. Section 1332 in the Eastern District of Tennessee against Kentucky. Kentucky's answer to the complaint simply denies Tennessee's allegations of negligence, and a jury ultimately returns a verdict for Kentucky on Tennessee's negligence claim.

Kentucky then files her own federal diversity action against Tennessee seeking damages for her injuries in this accident. Tennessee answers the complaint and files a Rule 12(c) motion for judgment on the pleadings, asserting that any claim Kentucky had arising from the accident was a compulsory counterclaim that had to have been asserted in Tennessee's initial action pursuant to Rule 13(a) of the Federal Rules of Civil Procedure.

Rule 13.01 of the Tennessee Rules of Civil Procedure in part provides: "A pleading shall state as a counterclaim any claim, other than a tort claim, which at the time of serving the pleading the pleader has against any opposing party, if it arises out of the transaction or occurrence that is the subject matter of the opposing party's claim and does not require for its adjudication the presence of third parties of whom the court cannot acquire jurisdiction."

Kentucky argues in opposition to Tennessee's motion for judgment on the pleadings that, because the first action was a federal diversity action, the federal judge should have applied Rule 13.01 of the Tennessee Rules of Civil Procedure rather than Rule 13(a) of the Federal Rules of Civil Procedure. Kentucky asserts that the claim that Tennessee now seeks to bar is a tort claim, which, under Tennessee Rule 13.01, did not have to be asserted as a compulsory counterclaim in the first action.

Should the judge grant Tennessee's motion for judgment on the pleadings?

CHAPTER 6

PARTY AND CLAIM JOINDER: "WHO CAN WE SUE ABOUT WHAT?"

I. INTRODUCTION

The second sentence of Rule 1 of the Federal Rules of Civil Procedure states that the Federal Rules "should be construed, administered, and employed by the court and the parties to secure the just, speedy, and inexpensive determination of every action and proceeding." As a practical matter, it is not possible to achieve justice, speed, and efficiency with mathematical precision in most cases. Judges and lawyers, though, do attempt to achieve rough justice, reasonable speed, and the relatively inexpensive determination of disputes through our state and federal systems of civil procedure.

The focus of this chapter is on some of the practical ways by which lawyers attempt to use the Federal Rules to achieve the relief desired by their clients in United States District Courts. When is it practical for parties to bring their claims in a single civil action, for a party to bring multiple claims in one action, or for a property holder to bring together in one action all those who claim this property? When might a person's interests be prejudiced by the determination of an action in which that person cannot intervene? These are the sometimes legally complex, and often factually intricate, questions that we consider in this chapter.

II. PARTY JOINDER

One of the ways to further justice, speed, and efficiency is to permit several plaintiffs to bring their claims in a single action, rather than require each plaintiff to file a separate action. Similar efficiencies can be achieved by permitting a plaintiff to file one action against several defendants, rather than requiring the filing of a series of separate actions. As we will see in this section, some plaintiffs may have the discretion under Rule 20 to join with other plaintiffs or to file claims against several defendants in a single action. In other situations, Rule 19 actually may require such party joinder.

A. PERMISSIVE PARTY JOINDER

Rule 20(a) of the Federal Rules of Civil Procedure authorizes the permissive joinder of both plaintiffs and defendants. Rule 20(a)(1) allows persons to join in one action as plaintiffs if:

> (A) they assert any right to relief jointly, severally, or in the alternative with respect to or arising out of the same transaction, occurrence, or series of transactions or occurrences; and
>
> (B) any question of law or fact common to all plaintiffs will arise in the action.

Similarly, Rule 20(a)(2) provides for the permissive joinder of defendants:

> Persons—as well as a vessel, cargo, or other property subject to admiralty process in rem—may be joined in one action as defendants if:
>
> (A) any right to relief is asserted against them jointly, severally, or in the alternative with respect to or arising out of the same transaction, occurrence, or series of transactions or occurrences; and
>
> (B) any question of law or fact common to all defendants will arise in the action.

Must co-plaintiffs or co-defendants seek or defend against identical relief in order to join as co-parties in an action? No, Rule 20(a)(3) specifically states:

> Neither a plaintiff nor a defendant need be interested in obtaining or defending against all the relief demanded. The court may grant judgment to one or more plaintiffs according to their rights, and against one or more defendants according to their liabilities.

Does the fact that multiple plaintiffs or defendants can be joined in a single civil action mean that there must be a single trial to determine the rights of all parties? No, Rule 20(b) provides: "The court may issue orders—including an order for separate trials—to protect a party against embarrassment, delay, expense, or other prejudice that arises from including a person against whom the party asserts no claim and who asserts no claim against the property."[1]

If the requirements of Rule 20 are met, must the court hear the claims asserted in that action? Not necessarily, because a federal court only can hear an action if (1) the claims are authorized by the Federal Rules and (2) federal subject-matter jurisdiction exists over those claims.

---

[1]   Rule 42(b) also authorizes the court to order separate trials of issues or claims within a single civil action:

> For convenience, to avoid prejudice, or to expedite and economize, the court may order a separate trial of one or more separate issues, claims, crossclaims, counterclaims, or third-party claims. When ordering a separate trial, the court must preserve any federal right to a jury trial.

In addition, Rule 21 states that "the court may at any time, on just terms, add or drop a party. The court may also sever any claim against a party."

Assume that several plaintiffs bring federal civil rights claims against a defendant. A federal district court could hear these claims if the requirements of Rule 20(a)(1)(A) and (B) are satisfied and (as is presumably the case) the civil rights claims raise federal questions over which the court can exercise subject-matter jurisdiction under 28 U.S.C. § 1331 or another jurisdictional statute such as 28 U.S.C. § 1343.

However, if the claims don't raise federal questions, but are asserted under the court's diversity jurisdiction, the court could not hear the claims of plaintiffs who are from the same state as the defendant—even though Rule 20(a)(1) is satisfied.

Whether Rule 20(a) is met in a particular case can be a very fact-intensive determination. This can be seen from the following case, which also illustrates the permissive joinder—and misjoinder—of parties under Rules 20 and 21.

Baughman v. Lee County, Mississippi

United States District Court, Northern District of Mississippi, 2008
554 F.Supp.2d 652

ORDER

■ MICHAEL P. MILLS, CHIEF JUDGE.

This cause comes before the court on the motion of defendant Lee County, Mississippi to sever, pursuant to Fed.R.Civ.P. 21. Plaintiffs Melanie Baughman et al have responded in opposition to the motion, and the court, having considered the memoranda and submissions of the parties, concludes that the motion is well taken and should be granted.

This is, inter alia, a 42 U.S.C. § 1983 action involving twenty-seven plaintiffs, each of whom alleges that he or she was unnecessarily strip-searched at the Lee County Jail, in violation of his or her Constitutional rights. A party seeking joinder of claimants under Rule 20 must establish (1) a right to relief arising out of the same transaction or occurrence, or series of transactions or occurrences, and (2) some question of law or fact common to all persons seeking to be joined. In deciding whether claims should be severed pursuant to Rule 21, this court determines (1) whether the claims arise out of the same transaction or occurrence; (2) whether the claims present some common questions of law or fact; (3) whether settlement of the claims or judicial economy would be facilitated; (4) whether prejudice would be avoided if severance were granted; and (5) whether different witnesses and documentary proof are required for separate claims. See *McFarland v. State Farm Fire & Cas. Co.*, 2006 WL 2577852 (S.D.Miss.2006), citing *Morris v. Northrop Grumman Corp.*, 37 F.Supp.2d 556, 580 (S.D.N.Y.1999).

In analyzing the joinder issues in this case, the court finds persuasive the reasoning of Magistrate Judge Robert H. Walker in *McFarland*, a Hurricane Katrina case in which hundreds of plaintiffs sought to join together to assert insurance fraud and other claims against State Farm. This case, like *McFarland*, involves plaintiffs who assert what are superficially similar claims but which will require different fact witnesses and individualized proof regarding damages. This lawsuit does not arise from a single incident in which large numbers of inmates were strip-searched at the same time. To the contrary, the complaint alleges a series of allegedly unlawful strip searches which took place between 2005 and 2007, and each incident will require individualized proof regarding the circumstances and nature of the strip search in question. Moreover, each plaintiff alleges that he or she suffered emotional distress damages as a result of being strip searched, and federal law requires that, to recover emotional distress damages, a § 1983 plaintiff must demonstrate a "specific discernable injury to [his] emotional state" resulting from a constitutional violation, proven with evidence regarding the "nature and extent" of the harm. *Patterson v. P.H.P. Healthcare Corp.*, 90 F.3d 927, 938–40 (5th Cir.1996).

The foregoing considerations make it clear that, as in *McFarland*, the similarity between the claims of the various plaintiffs in this case is more illusory than real. As noted by Judge Walker in *McFarland*:

The Court concludes that the Plaintiffs should be required to file separate complaints. Although there may be some common issues of law and fact, the Court finds that the Plaintiffs have not met the same transaction or occurrence prong of Rule 20(a). In a superficial sense, the hurricane was a common occurrence; however, the storm was vastly different in its effect depending on the specific geographic location of each particular home. Although Plaintiffs each held basically the same standard homeowner's policy, each insurance contract is a separate transaction. . . . Likewise, any alleged negligent or fraudulent misrepresentations by insurance agents constitute separate transactions or occurrences.

McFarland, at *1. In the court's view, Judge Walker's observations apply equally to the claims of the plaintiffs in this case.

In opposing severance, plaintiffs' primary argument is that it would be costly in time and money to try these lawsuits individually. However, it is not a goal of the federal judiciary to implement justice on the cheap by compromising the basic integrity of the judicial process. The court has little doubt that a jury would find it impossible to give plaintiffs' claims the individual attention and scrutiny which they deserve if they were joined together in the manner sought. Differing facts among the claimants would likely far exceed common facts. Mississippi state courts have, in recent years, moved away from the "herd justice" approach once prevailing in those courts. There is little doubt that plaintiffs would be unable to maintain these mass-joined claims in Mississippi state court. No valid reason dictates that Mississippi federal courts should be any less attentive to ensuring that juries are not overwhelmed by mass-joined actions such as the present one. Defendant's motion to sever should be granted.

Having granted defendant's motion to sever, this court will follow Judge Walker's approach in *McFarland* to implement this severance. It is therefore ordered that:

(1) All plaintiffs' claims in Civil Action No. 1:07cv239 shall be severed into individual actions, one for each plaintiff, and the Clerk shall assign a new civil action number for each severed claim.

(2) The Clerk shall copy the pleadings and exhibits from Civil Action No. 1:07cv239, which shall then be included as part of the record for each severed action. Each of the previous filings will be deemed filed in the new cases as of the dates shown on the docket sheet for Civil Action No. 1:07 cv239.

(3) The current case, No. 1:07cv239, shall be closed upon the individual cases being severed and replaced by the new filings.

(4) Within (30) days of this Order, Plaintiffs shall file an amended complaint and filing fee in each new civil action.

(5) All pre-discovery disclosure of case information or other cooperative discovery devices provided for by the Uniform Local Rules of the United States District Courts of Mississippi 26.1(A) and Federal Rules of Civil Procedure 26(a)(1) which have not been previously furnished by the parties shall be disclosed pursuant to said rules. Should the court find that common questions of law or fact exist in separate cases, the court may then order those cases consolidated as provided in Fed.R.Civ.P. 42(a).

(6) All severed cases shall remain assigned to United States District Judge Michael P. Mills and United States Magistrate Judge S. Allan Alexander.

COMMENTS AND QUESTIONS CONCERNING *BAUGHMAN V. LEE COUNTY, MISSISSIPPI*

1. Why would claimants want to bring their claims in a single action? Why would the defendant county oppose their efforts to do so?

2. Plaintiffs unsuccessfully sought reconsideration of Judge Mills's severance order. *Baughman v. Lee County*, Civ. A. 1:07CV239, 2008 WL 2229805 (N.D.Miss May 27, 2008). Judge Mills characterized the motion as follows: "Plaintiffs' primary argument in seeking reconsideration relates not to this court's legal analysis regarding joinder, but rather is a lament

regarding the financial viability of filing twenty-seven separate causes of action." *Id.* at 1.

The judge continued, *id.* at 1–2:

> The language of the plaintiffs' motion for reconsideration leads this court to suspect that this entire lawsuit was filed to intimidate both defendants and this court with the prospect of large and unwieldy litigation, in order to have this court shrink from applying the rules of joinder and to intimidate defendants into paying a quick settlement. * * *
>
> Faced with the sudden prospect of litigating less lucrative lawsuits, counsel for plaintiffs now seek to be cut loose, to allow their twenty-seven clients to fend for themselves *in forma pauperis.* * * *
>
> Counsel overlook the fact that their withdrawal from this case can only come with the permission of this court. Counsel elected to file this lawsuit, and they must now accept the consequences of having done so. * * *
>
> * * *
>
> It appears that, at this juncture, the parties' efforts should be directed towards an orderly resolution of this litigation, given counsel's surprising representation that these claims are not viable individually. The court remains of the view that these claims must proceed individually or not at all, and plaintiffs' motion to reconsider is therefore denied.

Rule 1.16(b)(5) of the Mississippi Rules of Professional Conduct, modeled on and identical to Rule 1.6(b)(5) of the ABA Model Rules of Professional Conduct, permits a lawyer to withdraw from representation if "the representation will result in an unreasonable financial burden on the lawyer." However, this ability to withdraw is subject to Mississippi Rule 1.16(c), which provides: "When ordered to do so by a tribunal, a lawyer shall continue representation notwithstanding good cause for terminating the representation."

If Judge Mills believed that this action "was filed to intimidate both defendants and this court," were there other actions that he could take?

3.   Assuming that the plaintiffs do not seek relief "with respect to or arising out of the same transaction [or] occurrence," is it possible that the relief they seek arises out of the same "**series** of transactions or occurrences" under Rule 20(a)(1)(A)?

Section 24(2) of the *Restatement (Second) of Judgments* (1982), which we will consider in the discussion of respect for judgments in Chapter 14, provides:

> What factual grouping constitutes a "transaction", and what grouping constitute a "series", are to be determined pragmatically, giving weight to such considerations as whether the facts are related in time, space, origin, or motivation, whether they form a

convenient trial unit, and whether their treatment as a unit conforms to the parties' expectations or business understanding or usage.

Even if not all of the 27 alleged strip searches were part of the same "series of transactions or occurrences," isn't it likely that at least some of these were part of the same series of transactions? Is it possible, for instance, that the searches conducted in 2007, or those conducted by a specific deputy sheriff, or those subject to a specific set of rules or policies might be considered one series of occurrences?

4.   Judge Mills states: "The court has little doubt that a jury would find it impossible to give plaintiffs' claims the individual attention and scrutiny which they deserve if they were joined together in the manner sought." But aren't the plaintiffs, who sought to bring their claims together, the best judge of whether the jury will be able to better consider their claims individually or joined in a single action?

5.   In addition to joining in a single action with co-plaintiffs under Rule 20(a)(1), a plaintiff may want to sue more than one defendant in the same action pursuant to Rule 20(a)(2). In *Deskovic v. City of Peekskill*, 673 F.Supp.2d 154 (S.D.N.Y. 2009), the plaintiff filed a civil rights action against a city, county, several police officers, and various public officials after serving 16 years in prison for a crime that he did not commit. One of the defendants was a corrections officer, whom plaintiff alleged had sexually abused him 14 years after his conviction. In granting a motion to sever the corrections officer from the action against the other defendants, the district judge stated:

> [T]he connection between Tweed's misconduct and the remaining Defendants' misconduct is too attenuated, factually and temporally, to support a causal connection. * * * Whereas the claims against Tweed allegedly occurred "[t]hroughout the . . . years [Plaintiff] was incarcerated at Elmira Correctional Facility, and on multiple occasions on or subsequent to September 18, 2004," Plaintiff's claims against the other Defendants relate to conduct that occurred years earlier, in late 1989 through 1990. * * * And Plaintiff's claims against Tweed center around Tweed's alleged acts of touching Plaintiff inappropriately during pat-down frisks while Plaintiff was incarcerated, while Plaintiff's claims against the other Defendants center around alleged misconduct that led to his arrest, prosecution, and conviction for a crime he did not commit. * * *
>
> Put simply, there are no allegations that Tweed was personally involved in the other Defendants' misconduct, or that the other Defendants were personally involved in Tweed's alleged misconduct. In the absence of a connection between Defendants' alleged misconduct, the mere allegation that Plaintiff was injured by all Defendants "is not sufficient [by itself] to join unrelated parties as defendants in the same lawsuit pursuant to Rule 20(a)." *Pergo, Inc. v. Alloc, Inc.*, 262 F.Supp.2d 122, 128 (S.D.N.Y. 2003)

(concluding that allegations that two defendants that infringed plaintiff's patent in an identical way were insufficient to meet the "transaction or occurrence" standard because there was nothing, such as a cooperative or collusive relationship, connecting defendants' conduct).

Deskovic v. City of Peekskill, 673 F. Supp. 2d 154, 166–67 (S.D.N.Y. 2009).

The *Deskovic* judge held that not only was Rule 20(a)(2)(A) not met, but that the claims against the corrections officer and the other defendants did not share any common question of law or fact as required by Rule 20(a)(2)(B). *Id.* at 169–71. The judge therefore severed the claims against the corrections officer from plaintiff's other claims pursuant to Rule 21. *Id.* at 172.

B. MANDATORY PARTY JOINDER

While Rule 20 authorizes permissive party joinder, Rule 19 is the Federal Rule of Civil Procedure that requires mandatory party joinder. Prior to the amendment of Rule 19 in 2007, parties who had to be joined if feasible were classified as "necessary" parties, while "indispensable" parties were those necessary parties without whose joinder a civil action could not proceed. Now Rule 19(a) refers to certain parties as "required," while Rule 19(b) considers whether a civil action can proceed if a required party cannot be joined.

1. IS A PERSON A "REQUIRED PARTY" WHOM RULE 19(a) REQUIRES TO BE JOINED?

The caption of Rule 19(a) refers to "Persons Required to be Joined if Feasible." Rule 19(a)(1) provides:

A person who is subject to service of process and whose joinder will not deprive the court of subject-matter jurisdiction must be joined as a party if:

(A) in that person's absence, the court cannot accord complete relief among existing parties; or

(B) that person claims an interest relating to the subject of the action and is so situated that disposing of the action in the person's absence may:

(i) as a practical matter impair or impede the person's ability to protect the interest; or

(ii) leave an existing party subject to a substantial risk of incurring double, multiple, or otherwise inconsistent obligations because of the interest.

Assume that the court determines that someone is, in fact, a person "required to be joined if feasible" under Rule 19(a). The court then must determine whether it is "feasible" to join that person. For instance, it would not be feasible to join a person as a party if joinder would destroy complete diversity of citizenship under 28 U.S.C. § 1332(a). If it is, though, feasible to join the person, joinder will be ordered. But, if not, the court must answer a third question—posed in Rule 19(b): "whether, in equity and good conscience, the action should proceed among the existing parties or should be dismissed."

2.   IF A REQUIRED PARTY CANNOT BE JOINED, CAN THE ACTION PROCEED?

Assume that an Ohio citizen brings a diversity action against a Michigan defendant challenging the defendant's title to property. If another Ohio citizen alleges that she is co-owner of the property, she normally should be joined as a defendant under Rule 19(a). However, such joinder would destroy the complete diversity of citizenship required by 28 U.S.C. § 1332(a).

Thus the second Ohio citizen, although a required party, cannot be joined as a party pursuant to Rule 19. But what is the consequence of the inability to join this person as a party? Rule 19(b) directs the court to consider a series of factors in determining whether the action can go forward in that person's absence.

Rule 19(b) provides:

> If a person who is required to be joined if feasible cannot be joined, the court must determine whether, in equity and good conscience, the action should proceed among the existing parties or should be dismissed. The factors for the court to consider include:
>
>> (1) the extent to which a judgment rendered in the person's absence might prejudice that person or the existing parties;
>>
>> (2) the extent to which any prejudice could be lessened or avoided by:
>>
>>> (A) protective provisions in the judgment;
>>>
>>> (B) shaping the relief; or
>>>
>>> (C) other measures;
>>
>> (3) whether a judgment rendered in the person's absence would be adequate; and
>>
>> (4) whether the plaintiff would have an adequate remedy if the action were dismissed for nonjoinder.

Figure 6–1 sets forth the questions that must be answered in applying Rule 19 to determine whether a third person must be joined to a civil action.

FIGURE 6–1
REQUIRED JOINDER PURSUANT TO RULE 19

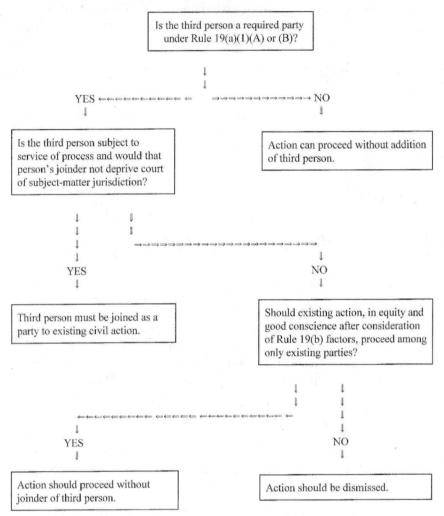

3.   *REPUBLIC OF THE PHILIPPINES V. PIMENTEL*

Consider the manner in which the Supreme Court applies the Rule 19(b) factors in the following case.

Republic of the Philippines v. Pimentel

Supreme Court of the United States, 2008
553 U.S. 851

■ JUSTICE KENNEDY delivered the opinion of the Court.

This case turns on the interpretation and proper application of Rule 19 of the Federal Rules of Civil Procedure and requires us to address the Rule's operation in the context of foreign sovereign immunity.

This interpleader action was commenced to determine the ownership of property allegedly stolen by Ferdinand Marcos when he was the President of the Republic of the Philippines. Two entities named in the suit invoked sovereign immunity. They are the Republic of the Philippines and the Philippine Presidential Commission on Good Governance, referred to in turn as the Republic and the Commission. They were dismissed, but the interpleader action proceeded to judgment over their objection. Together with two parties who remained in the suit, the Republic and the Commission now insist it was error to allow the litigation to proceed. Under Rule 19, they contend, the action should have been dismissed once it became clear they could not be joined as parties without their consent.

The United States Court of Appeals for the Ninth Circuit, agreeing with the District Court, held the action could proceed without the Republic and the Commission as parties. Among the reasons the Court of Appeals gave was that the absent, sovereign entities would not prevail on their claims. We conclude the Court of Appeals gave insufficient weight to the foreign sovereign status of the Republic and the Commission, and that the court further erred in reaching and discounting the merits of their claims.

I

* * *

B

In 1972, Ferdinand Marcos, then President of the Republic, incorporated Arelma, S.A. (Arelma), under Panamanian law. Around the same time, Arelma opened a brokerage account with Merrill Lynch, Pierce, Fenner & Smith Inc. (Merrill Lynch) in New York, in which it deposited $2 million. As of the year 2000, the account had grown to approximately $35 million.

Alleged crimes and misfeasance by Marcos during his presidency became the subject of worldwide attention and protest. A class action by and on behalf of some 9,539 of his human rights victims was filed against Marcos and his estate, among others. The class action was tried in the United States District Court for the District of Hawaii and resulted in a nearly $2 billion judgment for the class. We refer to that litigation as the *Pimentel* case and to its class members as the *Pimentel* class. In a related action, the Estate of Roger Roxas and Golden Budha *[sic]* Corporation (the Roxas claimants) claim a right to execute against the assets to satisfy their own judgment against Marcos' widow, Imelda Marcos.

The *Pimentel* class claims a right to enforce its judgment by attaching the Arelma assets held by Merrill Lynch. The Republic and the Commission claim a right to the assets under a 1955 Philippine law providing that property derived from the misuse of public office is forfeited to the Republic from the moment of misappropriation. After Marcos fled the Philippines in 1986, the Commission was created to recover any property he wrongfully took. Almost immediately the Commission asked the Swiss Government for assistance in recovering assets—including shares in Arelma—that Marcos had moved to Switzerland. In compliance the Swiss Government froze certain assets and, in 1990, that freeze was upheld by the Swiss Federal Supreme Court. In 1991, the Commission asked the Sandiganbayan, a Philippine court of special jurisdiction over corruption cases, to declare forfeited to the Republic any property Marcos had obtained through misuse of his office. That litigation is still pending in the Sandiganbayan.

The Swiss assets were transferred to an escrow account set up by the Commission at the Philippine National Bank (PNB), pending the Sandiganbayan's decision as to their rightful owner. The Republic and the Commission requested that Merrill Lynch follow the same course and transfer the Arelma assets to an escrow account at PNB. Merrill Lynch did not do so. Facing claims from various Marcos creditors, including the *Pimentel* class, Merrill Lynch instead filed an interpleader action under 28 U.S.C. § 1335. The named defendants in the interpleader action were, among others, the Republic and the Commission, Arelma, PNB, and the *Pimentel* class (the respondents here).

The *Pimentel* case had been tried as a class action before Judge Manuel Real of the United States District Court for the Central District of California, who was sitting by designation in the District of Hawaii after the Judicial Panel on Multidistrict Litigation consolidated the various human rights complaints against Marcos in that court. Judge Real directed Merrill Lynch to file the interpleader action in the District of Hawaii, and he presided over the matter.

After being named as defendants in the interpleader action, the Republic and the Commission asserted sovereign immunity under the Foreign Sovereign Immunities Act of 1976 (FSIA), 28 U.S.C. § 1604. They moved to dismiss pursuant to Rule 19(b), based on the premise that the action could not proceed without them. Arelma and PNB also moved to dismiss pursuant to Rule 19(b). Without addressing whether they were entitled to sovereign immunity, Judge Real initially rejected the request by the Republic and the Commission to dismiss the interpleader action. They appealed, and the Court of Appeals reversed. It held the Republic and the Commission are entitled to sovereign immunity and that under Rule 19(a) they are required parties (or "necessary" parties under the old terminology). The Court of Appeals entered a stay pending the outcome of the litigation in the Sandiganbayan over the Marcos assets.

After concluding that the pending litigation in the Sandiganbayan could not determine entitlement to the Arelma assets, Judge Real vacated the stay, allowed the action to proceed, and awarded the assets to the *Pimentel* class. A week later, in the case initiated before the Sandiganbayan in 1991, the Republic asked that court to declare the Arelma assets forfeited, arguing the matter was ripe for decision. The Sandiganbayan has not yet ruled.

In the interpleader case the Republic, the Commission, Arelma, and PNB appealed the District Court's judgment in favor of the *Pimentel* claimants. This time the Court of Appeals affirmed. Dismissal of the interpleader suit, it held, was not warranted under Rule 19(b) because, though the Republic and the Commission were required ("necessary") parties under Rule 19(a), their claim had so little likelihood of success on the merits that the interpleader action could proceed without them. One of the reasons the court gave was that any action commenced by the Republic and the Commission to recover the assets would be barred by New York's 6-year statute of limitations for claims involving the misappropriation of public property. The court thus found it unnecessary to consider whether any prejudice to the Republic and the Commission might be lessened by some form of judgment or interim decree in the interpleader action. The court also considered the failure of the Republic and the Commission to obtain a judgment in the Sandiganbayan—despite the Arelma share certificates having been located and held in escrow at the PNB since 1997–1998—to be an equitable consideration counseling against dismissal of the interpleader suit. The court further found it relevant that allowing the interpleader case to proceed would serve the interests of the *Pimentel* class, which, at this point, likely has no other available forum in which to enforce its judgment against property belonging to Marcos.

This Court granted certiorari.

* * *

III

We turn to the question whether the interpleader action could proceed in the District Court without the Republic and the Commission as parties.

Subdivision (a) of Rule 19 states the principles that determine when persons or entities must be joined in a suit. The Rule instructs that nonjoinder even of a required person does not always result in dismissal. Subdivision (a) opens by noting that it addresses joinder "if Feasible." Where joinder is not feasible, the question whether the action should proceed turns on the factors outlined in subdivision (b). The considerations set forth in subdivision (b) are nonexclusive, as made clear by the introductory statement that "[t]he factors for the court to consider include." The general direction is whether "in equity and good conscience, the action should proceed among the existing parties or should be dismissed." The design of the Rule, then, indicates that the determination whether to proceed will turn upon factors that are case specific, which is consistent with a Rule based on equitable considerations. This is also consistent with the fact that the determination of who may, or must, be parties to a suit has consequences for the persons and entities affected by the judgment; for the judicial system and its interest in the integrity of its processes and the respect accorded to its decrees; and for society and its concern for the fair and prompt resolution of disputes. For these reasons, the issue of joinder can be complex, and determinations are case specific.

Under the earlier Rules the term "indispensable party" might have implied a certain rigidity that would be in tension with this case-specific approach. The word "indispensable" had an unforgiving connotation that did not fit easily with a system that permits actions to proceed even when some persons who otherwise should be parties to the action cannot be joined. As the Court noted in *Provident Bank,* the use of "indispensable" in Rule 19 created the "verbal anomaly" of an "indispensable person who turns out to be dispensable after all." 390 U.S., at 117, n. 12. Though the text has changed, the new Rule 19 has the same design and, to some extent, the same tension. Required persons may turn out not to be required for the action to proceed after all.

In all events it is clear that multiple factors must bear on the decision whether to proceed without a required person. This decision "must be based on factors varying with the different cases, some such factors being substantive, some procedural, some compelling by themselves, and some subject to balancing against opposing interests." *Id.,* at 119.

IV

We turn to Rule 19 as it relates to this case. The application of subdivision (a) of Rule 19 is not contested. The Republic and the Commission are required entities because "[w]ithout [them] as parties in this interpleader action, their interests in the subject matter are not protected." *In re Republic of Philippines,* 309 F.3d, at 1152; see Fed. Rule Civ. Proc. 19(a)(1)(B)(i). All parties appear to concede this. The disagreement instead centers around the application of subdivision (b), which addresses whether the action may proceed without the Republic and the Commission, given that the Rule requires them to be parties.

* * *

The Court of Appeals erred in not giving the necessary weight to the absent entities' assertion of sovereign immunity. The court in effect decided the merits of the Republic and the Commission's claims to the Arelma assets. Once it was recognized that those claims were not frivolous, it was error for the Court of Appeals to address them on their merits when the required entities had been granted sovereign immunity. The court's consideration of the merits was itself an infringement on foreign sovereign immunity; and, in any event, its analysis was flawed. We discuss these errors first in the context of how they affected the Court of Appeals' analysis under the first factor of Rule 19(b). We then explain that the outcome suggested by the first factor is confirmed by our analysis under the other provisions of Rule 19(b). The action may not proceed.

A

As to the first Rule 19(b) factor—the extent to which a judgment rendered in the person's absence might prejudice that person or the existing parties, Fed. Rule Civ. Proc. 19(b)(1)—the judgment of the Court of Appeals is incorrect.

In considering whether the Republic and the Commission would be prejudiced if the action were to proceed in their absence, the Court of Appeals gave insufficient weight to their sovereign status. The doctrine of foreign sovereign immunity has been recognized since early in the history of our Nation. * * *

The privilege is codified by federal statute. FSIA, 28 U.S.C. §§ 1330, 1602–1611, provides that "a foreign state shall be immune from the jurisdiction of the courts of the United States and of the States except as provided in sections 1605 to 1607," absent existing international agreements to the contrary. § 1604. * * * Immunity in this case, then, is uncontested; and pursuant to the Court of Appeals' earlier ruling on the issue, the District Court dismissed the Republic and the Commission from the action on this ground.

The District Court and the Court of Appeals failed to give full effect to sovereign immunity when they held the action could proceed without the Republic and the Commission. Giving full effect to sovereign immunity promotes the comity interests that have contributed to the development of the immunity doctrine.

Comity and dignity interests take concrete form in this case. The claims of the Republic and the Commission arise from events of historical and political significance for the Republic and its people. The Republic and the Commission have a unique interest in resolving the ownership of or claims to the Arelma assets and in determining if, and how, the assets should be used to compensate those persons who suffered grievous injury under Marcos. There is a comity interest in allowing a foreign state to use its own courts for a dispute if it has a right to do so. The dignity of a foreign state is not enhanced if other nations bypass its courts without right or good cause. Then, too, there is the more specific affront that could result to the Republic and the Commission if property they claim is seized by the decree of a foreign court.

* * *

The Court of Appeals * * * erred in undertaking to rule on the merits of the Republic and the Commission's claims. There may be cases where the person who is not joined asserts a claim that is frivolous. In that instance a court may have leeway under both Rule 19(a)(1), defining required parties, and Rule 19(b), addressing when a suit may go forward nonetheless, to disregard the frivolous claim. Here, the claims of the absent entities are not frivolous; and the Court of Appeals should not have proceeded on the premise that those claims would be determined against the sovereign entities that asserted immunity.

The Court of Appeals determined that the claims of the Republic and the Commission as to the assets would not succeed because a suit would be time barred in New York. This is not necessarily so. If the Sandiganbayan rules that the Republic owns the assets or stock of Arelma because Marcos did not own them and the property was forfeited to the Republic under Philippine law, then New York misappropriation rules might not be the applicable law. * * * Or the Republic and the Commission might bring an action either in state or federal court to enforce the Sandiganbayan's judgment. * * * Merrill Lynch makes arguments why these actions would not succeed, to which the Republic, the Commission, and the United States respond. We need not seek to predict the outcomes. It suffices that the claims would not be frivolous.

* * * Rule 19 cannot be applied in a vacuum, and it may require some preliminary assessment of the merits of certain claims. For example, the Rule directs a court, in determining who is a required person, to consider whether complete relief can be afforded in their absence. See Fed. Rule Civ. Proc. 19(a)(1)(A). Likewise, in the Rule 19(b) inquiry, a court must examine, to some extent, the claims presented and the interests likely to be asserted both by the joined parties and the absent entities or persons. Here, however, it was improper to issue a definitive holding regarding a nonfrivolous, substantive claim made by an absent, required entity that was entitled by its sovereign status to immunity from suit. * * *

As explained above, the decision to proceed in the absence of the Republic and the Commission ignored the substantial prejudice those entities likely would incur. This most directly implicates Rule 19(b)'s first factor, which directs consideration of prejudice both to absent persons and those who are parties. We have discussed the absent entities. As to existing parties, we do not discount the *Pimentel* class' interest in recovering damages it was awarded pursuant to a judgment. Furthermore, combating public corruption is a significant international policy. The policy is manifested in treaties providing for international cooperation in recovering forfeited assets. This policy does support the interest of the *Pimentel* class in recovering damages awarded to it. But it also underscores the important comity concerns implicated by the

Republic and the Commission in asserting foreign sovereign immunity. The error is not that the District Court and the Court of Appeals gave too much weight to the interest of the *Pimentel* class, but that it did not accord proper weight to the compelling claim of sovereign immunity.

Based on these considerations we conclude the District Court and the Court of Appeals gave insufficient weight to the likely prejudice to the Republic and the Commission should the interpleader proceed in their absence.

B

As to the second Rule 19(b) factor—the extent to which any prejudice could be lessened or avoided by relief or measures alternative to dismissal, Fed. Rule Civ. Proc. 19(b)(2)—there is no substantial argument to allow the action to proceed. No alternative remedies or forms of relief have been proposed to us or appear to be available. *See* 7 C. Wright, A. Miller, & M. Kane, *Federal Practice and Procedure* § 1608, pp. 106–110 (3d ed.2001) (collecting cases using alternative forms of relief, including the granting of money damages rather than specific performance, the use of declaratory judgment, and the direction that payment be withheld pending suits against the absent party). If the Marcos estate did not own the assets, or if the Republic owns them now, the claim of the *Pimentel* class likely fails; and in all events, if there are equally valid but competing claims, that too would require adjudication in a case where the Republic and the Commission are parties.

C

As to the third Rule 19(b) factor—whether a judgment rendered without the absent party would be adequate, Fed. Rule Civ. Proc. 19(b)(3)—the Court of Appeals understood "adequacy" to refer to satisfaction of the *Pimentel* class' claims. But adequacy refers to the "public stake in settling disputes by wholes, whenever possible." *Provident Bank,* 390 U.S., at 111. This "social interest in the efficient administration of justice and the avoidance of multiple litigation" is an interest that has "traditionally been thought to support compulsory joinder of absent and potentially adverse claimants." *Illinois Brick Co.,* 431 U.S., at 737–738. Going forward with the action without the Republic and the Commission would not further the public interest in settling the dispute as a whole because the Republic and the Commission would not be bound by the judgment in an action where they were not parties.

D

As to the fourth Rule 19(b) factor—whether the plaintiff would have an adequate remedy if the action were dismissed for nonjoinder, Fed. Rule Civ. Proc. 19(b)(4)—the Court of Appeals made much of what it considered the tort victims' lack of an alternative forum should this action be dismissed. This seems to assume the plaintiff in this interpleader action was the *Pimentel* class. It is Merrill Lynch, however, that has the statutory status of plaintiff as the stakeholder in the interpleader action.

It is true that, in an interpleader action, the stakeholder is often neutral as to the outcome, while other parties press claims in the manner of a plaintiff. That is insufficient, though, to overcome the statement in the interpleader statute that the stakeholder is the plaintiff. See 28 U.S.C. § 1335(a) (conditioning jurisdiction in part upon whether "the plaintiff has deposited such money or property" at issue with the district court or has "given bond payable to the clerk of the court in such amount and with such surety as the court or judge may deem proper"). We do not ignore that, in context, the *Pimentel* class (and indeed all interpleader claimants) are to some extent comparable to the plaintiffs in noninterpleader cases. Their interests are not irrelevant to the Rule 19(b) equitable balance; but the other provisions of the Rule are the relevant ones to consult.

Merrill Lynch, as the stakeholder, makes the point that if the action is dismissed it loses the benefit of a judgment allowing it to disburse the assets and be done with the matter. Dismissal of the action, it urges, leaves it without an adequate remedy, for it "could potentially be forced . . . to defend lawsuits by the various claimants in different jurisdictions, possibly leading to inconsistent judgments." A dismissal of the action on the ground of nonjoinder, however, will protect Merrill Lynch in some respects. That disposition will not provide Merrill Lynch with a judgment determining the party entitled to the assets, but it likely would provide Merrill Lynch with an effective defense against piecemeal litigation and inconsistent, conflicting judgments. As matters presently stand, in any later suit against it Merrill Lynch may seek to join the Republic and the Commission and have the action dismissed under Rule 19(b) should they again assert sovereign immunity. Dismissal for nonjoinder to some extent will serve the purpose of interpleader, which is to prevent a stakeholder from having to pay two or more parties for one claim.

Any prejudice to Merrill Lynch in this regard is outweighed by prejudice to the absent entities invoking sovereign immunity. Dismissal under Rule 19(b) will mean, in some instances, that plaintiffs will be left without a forum for definitive resolution of their claims. But that result is contemplated under the doctrine of foreign sovereign immunity.

V

The Court of Appeals' failure to give sufficient weight to the likely prejudice to the Republic and the Commission should the interpleader proceed in their absence would, in the usual course, warrant reversal and remand for further proceedings. In this case, however, that error and our further analysis under the additional provisions of Rule 19(b) lead us to conclude the action must be dismissed. This leaves the *Pimentel* class, which has waited for years now to be compensated for grievous wrongs, with no immediate way to recover on its judgment against Marcos. And it leaves Merrill Lynch, the stakeholder, without a judgment.

The balance of equities may change in due course. One relevant change may occur if it appears that the Sandiganbayan cannot or will not issue its ruling within a reasonable period of time. Other changes could result when and if there is a ruling. If the Sandiganbayan rules that the Republic and the Commission have no right to the assets, their claims in some later interpleader suit would be less substantial than they are now. If the ruling is that the Republic and the Commission own the assets, then they may seek to enforce a judgment in our courts; or consent to become parties in an interpleader suit, where their claims could be considered; or file in some other forum if they can obtain jurisdiction over the relevant persons. We do note that if Merrill Lynch, or other parties, elect to commence further litigation in light of changed circumstances, it would not be necessary to file the new action in the District Court where this action arose, provided venue and jurisdictional requirements are satisfied elsewhere. The present action, however, may not proceed.

* * *

The judgment of the Court of Appeals for the Ninth Circuit is reversed, and the case is remanded with instructions to order the District Court to dismiss the interpleader action.

It is so ordered.

■ JUSTICE STEVENS, concurring in part and dissenting in part.

While I join Part II of the Court's opinion holding that we have jurisdiction to review the Court of Appeals' decision and agree that we should not affirm the Court of Appeals' judgment on the merits of its analysis under Rule 19 of the Federal Rules of Civil Procedure, I believe the appropriate disposition of this case is to reverse and remand for further proceedings. The District Court and the Ninth Circuit erred by concluding that the New York statute of limitations provides a virtually insuperable obstacle to petitioners' recovery of the Arelma, S. A., assets, and I therefore agree that this Court should reverse. I would not, however, give near-dispositive effect to the Republic of the Philippines (Republic) and the Philippine Presidential Commission on Good Governance's (Commission) status as sovereign entities, as the Court does in ordering outright dismissal of the case.

In my judgment, the Court of Appeals should either order the District Judge to stay further proceedings pending a reasonably prompt decision of the Sandiganbayan or order the case reassigned to a different District Judge to conduct further proceedings. There is, of course, a risk of unfairness in conducting such proceedings without the participation of petitioners. But it is a risk that they can avoid by waiving their sovereign immunity, and the record provides a basis for believing that they would do so if the case proceeded before a different judge.

* * *

It appears * * * that the District Judge summoned an attorney representing Merrill Lynch to a meeting in chambers in Los Angeles on September 11, 2000, after learning that the Republic and the Commission sought to obtain the Arelma funds from Merrill Lynch. During these proceedings, the District Judge directed Merrill Lynch to file an interpleader action before him in the District of Hawaii and to deposit the Arelma funds with the court, despite the attorney's argument that New York would likely be the more appropriate forum. Merrill Lynch filed the interpleader on September 14, 2000, and the District Judge sealed the file, making it difficult for other parties to determine the status of the proceedings. These actions bespeak a level of personal involvement and desire to control the Marcos proceedings that create at least a colorable basis for the Republic and the Commission's concern about the District Judge's impartiality.

* * *

In sum, I am persuaded that the Court's judgment today represents a more "inflexible approach" than the Rule contemplates. *Provident,* 390 U.S., at 107. All parties have an interest in the prompt resolution of the disposition of the Arelma assets. A remand would allow a new judge to handle the matter in an expeditious fashion rather than requiring a brand new proceeding. The Court suggests that Merrill Lynch may file in another District Court—presumably in New York—if it seeks to commence further litigation. While this solution would put the matter before another District Judge, it requires the initiation of a new proceeding that may unnecessarily delay the final resolution.

Accordingly, I respectfully dissent.

■ JUSTICE SOUTER, concurring in part and dissenting in part.

I join all but Parts IV–B and V of the Court's opinion. I differ as to relief because a conclusion of the matter pending before the Sandiganbayan may simplify the issues raised in this case and render one disposition or another more clearly correct. I would therefore vacate the judgment and remand for a stay of proceedings for a reasonable time to await a decree of the Philippine court. If it should appear later that no such decree can be expected, the Court of Appeals could decide on the next step in light of the Court's opinion. For reasons given by Justice STEVENS, I would order that any further proceedings in the District Court be held before a judge fresh to the case.

COMMENTS AND QUESTIONS CONCERNING
REPUBLIC OF THE PHILIPPINES V. PIMENTEL

1.   This case was filed as an interpleader action, in which someone (in this case, Merrill Lynch) holding property claimed by others joins those claimants to determine the rights of all parties in a single civil action. By permitting a determination of the rights of all claimants in a single action, an interpleader action protects the property holder from the possibility of multiple liability that might occur if the claimants' rights were determined in successive actions. Interpleader is the subject of the next section of this text.

2.   Justice Kennedy mentions that "various human rights complaints against [President] Marcos" were consolidated in the District of Hawaii by the Judicial Panel on Multidistrict Litigation. The multidistrict litigation statute in part provides: "When civil actions involving one or more common questions of fact are pending in different districts, such actions may be transferred to any district for coordinated or consolidated pretrial proceedings." 28 U.S.C. § 1407. These transfers are for the "convenience of parties and witnesses and [to] promote the just and efficient conduct of such actions," and the actions are to be transferred back to their original districts at the conclusion of the consolidated pretrial proceedings.

3.   At several points in his opinion, Justice Kennedy refers to the "comity" that United States courts afford to other nations. He notes:

> There is a comity interest in allowing a foreign state to use its own courts for a dispute if it has a right to do so. The dignity of a foreign state is not enhanced if other nations bypass its courts without right or good cause. Then, too, there is the more specific affront that could result to the Republic and the Commission if property they claim is seized by the decree of a foreign court.

"Comity" refers to judicial deference to another nation that is not compelled by statute or treaty.

> "Comity," in the legal sense, is neither a matter of absolute obligation, on the one hand, nor of mere courtesy and good will, upon the other. But it is the recognition which one nation allows within its territory to the legislative, executive, or judicial acts of another nation, having due regard both to international duty and convenience, and to the rights of its own citizens, or of other persons who are under the protection of its laws.

Hilton v. Guyot, 159 U.S. 113, 163–64 (1895).

4.   The Republic of the Philippines and the Commission both were dismissed from the interpleader action after they asserted sovereign immunity. As we will see in Chapter 14, they could not be bound by the interpleader action to which they were no longer a party. So how have the lower courts not properly respected the sovereignty of the Philippines and the Commission?

5.   Justice Kennedy describes the outcome for the parties after dismissal of this action: "This leaves the *Pimentel* class, which has waited

for years now to be compensated for grievous wrongs, with no immediate way to recover on its judgment against Marcos. And it leaves Merrill Lynch, the stakeholder, without a judgment." Is there any hope for a resolution of this litigation?

6.   As we will see in Chapter 12, judicial recusal within the federal courts is governed by 28 U.S.C. §§ 144 and 455. Section 144 requires a judge to recuse upon the filing of "a timely and sufficient affidavit that the judge before whom the matter is pending has a personal bias or prejudice either against him or in favor of any adverse party," while Section 455(a) requires disqualification "in any proceeding in which his impartiality might reasonably be questioned." How do these standards differ? Are they met in this case?

7.   Rule 19(b) requires a district judge to determine, "in equity and good conscience," whether this action should go forward without the Philippines and the Commission as parties. Is the Supreme Court the appropriate court to conduct this Rule 19(b) balancing in the first instance?

8.   A Missouri jewelry store and an Iowa shopping center entered into a lease, one term of which was that the shopping center would lease space to no more than two other full-line jewelry stores. The shopping center leased space to two other full-line jewelers, and then entered into a lease with an Iowa company which opened a third full-line jewelry store.

The Missouri jewelry store brought an action in Missouri federal court against the shopping center, seeking to enforce the lease agreement and obtain an injunction precluding the operation of the third full-line jewelry store. The Iowa jeweler was not subject to the personal jurisdiction of the Missouri court, and the shopping center argued that the action must be dismissed because the Iowa store could not be joined.

Is the Iowa jewelry store a required party under Rule 19(a)? If so, should the action proceed in the absence of the Iowa jeweler? *See Helzberg's Diamond Shops, Inc. v. Valley W. Des Moines Shopping Ctr., Inc.*, 564 F.2d 816 (8th Cir. 1977).

III. INTERPLEADER

What if a person has custody of property that he or she knows belongs to others—but is not sure to just whom? For instance, assume that a bank has funds to which there may be several claimants. The bank will be concerned that it may be successfully sued by one claimant, only to later be sued by another claimant for the same property. As we will see in Chapter 14, because the second claimant was not a party to the first action, that claimant is not bound by the first judgment. Thus the bank could be ordered to provide the property to the second claimant in the second action—even though it already gave the property to the first claimant pursuant to an order of the first court.

In order to protect itself from multiple judgments, the bank will want to bring all potential claimants together in a single civil action so that the court can determine the rightful owner of the property. The bank then can provide the property to that claimant, without worrying that another claimant will sue the bank later for the same property. Interpleader is the procedural device that allows a stakeholder, such as a bank, to bring together in a single action all potential claimants and obtain a judicial declaration as to which claimant(s) the property should be given. An example of the use of this procedural device is provided in the case that you just read, *Republic of the Philippines v. Pimentel*, in which Merrill Lynch filed a Section 1335 interpleader action seeking a judicial determination as to which defendants were entitled to the funds held by Merrill Lynch.

As the Supreme Court notes in *State Farm Fire and Casualty Co. v. Tashire*, which follows, federal statutes provided for interpleader actions well before the 1938 adoption of the Federal Rules of Civil Procedure. The current federal interpleader statute is codified at 28 U.S.C. §§ 1335, 1397, and 2361. Section 1397 provides for venue for an interpleader action "in the judicial district in which one or more of the claimants reside," while Section 2361 provides for national service of process in such actions.

Section 1335 of Title 28 authorizes statutory interpleader and provides:

> The district courts shall have original jurisdiction of any civil action of interpleader or in the nature of interpleader filed by any person, firm, or corporation, association, or society having in his or its custody or possession money or property of the value of $500 or more, or having issued a note, bond, certificate, policy of insurance, or other instrument of value or amount of $500 or more, or providing for the delivery or payment or the loan of money or property of such amount or value, or being under any obligation written or unwritten to the amount of $500 or more, if

> (1) two or more adverse claimants, of diverse citizenship as defined in subjection (a) or (d) of section 1332 of this title, are claiming or may claim to be entitled to such money or property, or to any one or more of the benefits arising by virtue of any note, bond, certificate, policy or other instrument, or arising by virtue of any such obligation; and if (2) the plaintiff has deposited such money or property or has paid the amount of or the loan or other value of such instrument or the amount due under such obligation into the registry of the court, there to abide the judgment of the court, or has given bond payable to the clerk of the court in such amount and with such surety as the court or judge may deem proper, conditioned upon the compliance by the plaintiff with the future order or judgment of the court with respect to the subject matter of the controversy.

Section 1335 thus requires "two or more adverse claimants, of diverse citizenship as defined in subjection (a) or (d) of section 1332 of this title." So there must be at least one claimant who is a citizen of a state different than another claimant—but Section 1335 does not require "complete diversity" as is necessary in a Section 1332 diversity action. In addition, while Section 1335 incorporates the definition of diverse citizenship from Section 1332, it does not incorporate Section 1332(a)'s minimum amount in controversy requirement. Under Section 1335, the requirement for statutory interpleader is only $500.

In addition to federal statutory interpleader, interpleader is possible under Rule 22 of the Federal Rules of Civil Procedure. Rule 22(a) provides:

(a) Grounds.

(1) *By a Plaintiff.* Persons with claims that may expose a plaintiff to double or multiple liability may be joined as defendants and required to interplead. Joinder for interpleader is proper even though:

(A) the claims of the several claimants, or the titles on which their claims depend, lack a common origin or are adverse and independent rather than identical; or

(B) the plaintiff denies liability in whole or in part to any or all of the claimants.

(2) *By a Defendant.* A defendant exposed to similar liability may seek interpleader through a crossclaim or counterclaim.

Because an interpleader action can be filed under either the federal interpleader statute or Rule 22, Rule 22(b) provides:

This rule supplements—and does not limit—the joinder of parties allowed by Rule 20. The remedy this rule provides is in addition to—and does not supersede or limit—the remedy provided by 28 U.S.C. §§ 1335, 1397, and 2361. An action under those statutes must be conducted under these rules.

Some of the requirements for Rule 22 interpleader differ from those for statutory interpleader, providing alternative ways in which to bring an interpleader action in federal court. Most significantly, there must be an independent basis for federal subject matter jurisdiction under Rule 22, which means that the minimal diversity between claimants that is sufficient for a Section 1335 statutory interpleader action will not suffice for a Rule 22 action. On the other hand, if a statutory interpleader action is not possible because all claimants are citizens of the same state, an interpleader action still may be possible under Rule 22 if none of the claimants are citizens of the same state as the stakeholder and more than $75,000 is in controversy.

Figure 6–2 illustrates the options for filing an interpleader action under either the federal interpleader statute or Rule 22—or both!

- In Case No. 1, there is no diversity between the claimants, so statutory interpleader is not possible. However, because there is complete diversity between the stakeholder and the claimants and more than $75,000 is in controversy, the action could be filed in federal court pursuant to Rule 22.

- In Case No. 2, there is not complete diversity between the stakeholder and the claimants, so a Rule 22 action is not possible. However, because there is minimal diversity among the claimants and at least $500 is in controversy, jurisdiction for a Section 1335 interpleader action exists.

- In Case No. 3, not only is there not complete diversity between the stakeholder and the claimants, but the amount in controversy is not more than $75,000. Thus the diversity requirements of 28 U.S.C. § 1332(a) are not met. But there would be jurisdiction to file an action under the federal interpleader statute, because there is minimal diversity among the claimants and at least $500 in controversy as required by Section 1335(a).

- In Case No. 4, there is complete diversity between the stakeholder and the claimants and more than $75,000 in controversy, so a Rule 22 interpleader action could be filed. Because there is also minimal diversity between the claimants and at least $500 in controversy, a statutory interpleader action also could be filed.

FIGURE 6–2
SUBJECT-MATTER JURISDICTION FOR
INTERPLEADER ACTIONS

Case No.	Stakeholder Citizenship	Claimant #1 Citizenship	Claimant #2 Citizenship	Claimant #3 Citizenship	Amount in Controversy	Interpleader Action
1	Ohio	Indiana	Indiana	Indiana	> $75,000	Rule 22
2	Ohio	Ohio	Indiana	Indiana	> $75,000	Section 1335
3	Ohio	Ohio	Indiana	Indiana	<= $75,000 but >= $500	Section 1335
4	Ohio	Michigan	Indiana	Indiana	> $75,000	Both Rule 22 & Sec. 1335

In addition to the different jurisdictional bases for a statutory or Rule 22 interpleader action, these actions also differ as to venue and service of process. Figure 6–3 compares the major attributes of statutory and Rule 22 interpleader.

FIGURE 6–3
FEDERAL INTERPLEADER: INTERPLEADER UNDER
RULE 22 AND 28 U.S.C. §§ 1335, 1397 and 2361[2]

Procedural Prerequisite	Rule 22 Interpleader	Statutory Interpleader
Subject-Matter Jurisdiction	28 U.S.C. § 1331 (federal question); § 1332 (complete diversity and more than $75,000 in controversy); or other jurisdictional statute	28 U.S.C. § 1335 (minimal diversity among claimants and property claim of at least $500 at issue)
Venue	28 U.S.C. § 1391(b) (district in which any defendant resides, if all defendants are residents of that State; where substantial part of events/ omissions giving rise to claim occurred or substantial part of property subject of action is situated; or, if no other district, district in which any defendant is subject to personal jurisdiction)	28 U.S.C. § 1397 (district in which any claimant resides)
Service of Process	Rule 4 of the Federal Rules of Civil Procedure	28 U.S.C. § 2361 (nationwide service of process)

The following case illustrates how interpleader works in practice in the federal courts.

State Farm Fire & Casualty Co. v. Tashire

Supreme Court of the United States, 1967
386 U.S. 523

■ MR. JUSTICE FORTAS delivered the opinion of the Court.

Early one September morning in 1964, a Greyhound bus proceeding northward through Shasta County, California, collided with a southbound pickup truck. Two of the passengers aboard the bus were killed. Thirty-three others were injured, as were the bus driver, the driver of the truck and its lone passenger. One of the dead and 10 of the injured passengers were Canadians; the rest of the individuals involved were citizens of five American States. The ensuing litigation led to the

---

[2] Rule 22 and the Federal Interpleader Statute are not mutually exclusive, and an interpleader action can be filed pursuant to both of these sets of rules.

present case, which raises important questions concerning administration of the interpleader remedy in the federal courts.

The litigation began when four of the injured passengers filed suit in California state courts, seeking damages in excess of $1,000,000. Named as defendants were Greyhound Lines, Inc., a California corporation; Theron Nauta, the bus driver; Ellis Clark, who drove the truck; and Kenneth Glasgow, the passenger in the truck who was apparently its owner as well. Each of the individual defendants was a citizen and resident of Oregon. Before these cases could come to trial and before other suits were filed in California or elsewhere, petitioner State Farm Fire & Casualty Company, an Illinois corporation, brought this action in the nature of interpleader in the United States District Court for the District of Oregon.

In its complaint State Farm asserted that at the time of the Shasta County collision it had in force an insurance policy with respect to Ellis Clark, driver of the truck, providing for bodily injury liability up to $10,000 per person and $20,000 per occurrence and for legal representation of Clark in actions covered by the policy. It asserted that actions already filed in California and others which it anticipated would be filed far exceeded in aggregate damages sought the amount of its maximum liability under the policy. Accordingly, it paid into court the sum of $20,000 and asked the court (1) to require all claimants to establish their claims against Clark and his insurer in this single proceeding and in no other, and (2) to discharge State Farm from all further obligations under its policy—including its duty to defend Clark in lawsuits arising from the accident. Alternatively, State Farm expressed its conviction that the policy issued to Clark excluded from coverage accidents resulting from his operation of a truck which belonged to another and was being used in the business of another. The complaint, therefore, requested that the court decree that the insurer owed no duty to Clark and was not liable on the policy, and it asked the court to refund the $20,000 deposit.

Joined as defendants were Clark, Glasgow, Nauta, Greyhound Lines, and each of the prospective claimants. Jurisdiction was predicated upon 28 U.S.C. § 1335, the federal interpleader statute, and upon general diversity, of citizenship, there being diversity between two or more of the claimants to the fund and between State Farm and all of the named defendants.

An order issued, requiring the defendants to show cause why they should not be restrained from filing or prosecuting "any proceeding in any state or United States Court affecting the property or obligation involved in this interpleader action, and specifically against the plaintiff and the defendant Ellis D. Clark." Personal service was effected on each of the American defendants, and registered mail was employed to reach the 11 Canadian claimants. Defendants Nauta, Greyhound, and several of the injured passengers responded, contending that the policy did cover this accident and advancing various arguments for the position that interpleader was either impermissible or inappropriate in the present circumstances. Greyhound, however, soon switched sides and moved that the court broaden any injunction to include Nauta and Greyhound among those who could not be sued except within the confines of the interpleader proceeding.

When a temporary injunction along the lines sought by State Farm was issued by the United States District Court for the District of Oregon, the present respondents moved to dismiss the action and, in the alternative, for a change of venue—to the Northern District of California, in which district the collision had occurred. After a hearing, the court declined to dissolve the temporary injunction, but continued the motion for a change of venue. The injunction was later broadened to include the protection sought by Greyhound, but modified to permit the filing—although not the prosecution—of suits. The injunction, therefore, provided that all suits against Clark, State Farm, Greyhound, and Nauta be prosecuted in the interpleader proceeding.

On interlocutory appeal,[2] the Court of Appeals for the Ninth Circuit reversed. The court found it unnecessary to reach respondents' contentions relating to service of process and the scope of the injunction, for it concluded that interpleader was not available in the circumstances of this case. It held that in States like Oregon which do not permit "direct action" suits against insurance companies until judgments are obtained against the insured, the insurance companies may not invoke federal interpleader until the claims against the insured, the alleged tortfeasor, have been reduced to judgment. Until that is done, said the court, claimants with unliquidated tort claims are not "claimants" within the meaning of § 1335, nor are they "(p)ersons having claims against the plaintiff" within the meaning of Rule 22 of the Federal Rules of Civil Procedure. In accord with that view, it directed dissolution of the temporary injunction and dismissal of the action. Because the Court of Appeals' decision on this point conflicts with those of other federal courts, and concerns a matter of significance to the administration of federal interpleader, we granted certiorari. Although we reverse the decision of the Court of Appeals upon the jurisdictional question, we direct a substantial modification of the District Court's injunction for reasons which will appear.

I.

Before considering the issues presented by the petition for certiorari, we find it necessary to dispose of a question neither raised by the parties nor passed upon by the courts below. Since the matter concerns our jurisdiction, we raise it on our own motion. The interpleader statute, 28 U.S.C. § 1335, applies where there are "Two or

---

[2]   28 U.S.C. § 1292(a)(1).

more adverse claimants, of diverse citizenship * * *." This provision has been uniformly construed to require only "minimal diversity," that is, diversity of citizenship between two or more claimants, without regard to the circumstance that other rival claimants may be co-citizens. The language of the statute, the legislative purpose broadly to remedy the problems posed by multiple claimants to a single fund, and the consistent judicial interpretation tacitly accepted by Congress, persuade us that the statute requires no more. There remains, however, the question whether such a statutory construction is consistent with Article III of our Constitution, which extends the federal judicial power to "Controversies * * * between citizens of different States * * * and between a State, or the Citizens thereof, and foreign States, Citizens or Subjects." In *Strawbridge v. Curtiss*, 3 Cranch 267 (1806), this Court held that the diversity of citizenship statute required 'complete diversity': where co-citizens appeared on both sides of a dispute, jurisdiction was lost. But Chief Justice Marshall there purported to construe only "The words of the act of congress," not the Constitution itself. And in a variety of contexts this Court and the lower courts have concluded that Article III poses no obstacle to the legislative extension of federal jurisdiction, founded on diversity, so long as any two adverse parties are not co-citizens. Accordingly, we conclude that the present case is properly in the federal courts.

II.

We do not agree with the Court of Appeals that, in the absence of a state law or contractual provision for "direct action" suits against the insurance company, the company must wait until persons asserting claims against its insured have reduced those claims to judgment before seeking to invoke the benefits of federal interpleader. * * *

Considerations of judicial administration demonstrate the soundness of this view which, in any event, seems compelled by the language of the present statute, which is remedial and to be liberally construed. Were an insurance company required to await reduction of claims to judgment, the first claimant to obtain such a judgment or to negotiate a settlement might appropriate all or a disproportionate slice of the fund before his fellow claimants were able to establish their claims. The difficulties such a race to judgment pose for the insurer, and the unfairness which may result to some claimants, were among the principal evils the interpleader device was intended to remedy.

III.

The fact that State Farm had properly invoked the interpleader jurisdiction under § 1335 did not, however, entitle it to an order both enjoining prosecution of suits against it outside the confines of the interpleader proceeding and also extending such protection to its insured, the alleged tortfeasor. Still less was Greyhound Lines entitled to have that order expanded so as to protect itself and its driver, also alleged to be tortfeasors, from suits brought by its passengers in various state or federal courts. Here, the scope of the litigation, in terms of parties and claims, was vastly more extensive than the confines of the "fund," the deposited proceeds of the insurance policy. In these circumstances, the mere existence of such a fund cannot, by use of interpleader, be employed to accomplish purposes that exceed the needs of orderly contest with respect to the fund.

There are situations, of a type not present here, where the effect of interpleader is to confine the total litigation to a single forum and proceeding. One such case is where a stakeholder, faced with rival claims to the fund itself, acknowledges—or denies—his liability to one or the other of the claimants. In this situation, the fund itself is the target of the claimants. It marks the outer limits of the controversy. It is, therefore, reasonable and sensible that interpleader, in discharge of its office to protect the fund, should also protect the stakeholder from vexatious and multiple litigation. In this context, the suits sought to be enjoined are squarely within the language of 28 U.S.C. § 2361, which provides in part:

> In any civil action of interpleader or in the nature of interpleader under section 1335 of this title, a district court may issue its process for all claimants and enter its order restraining them from instituting or prosecuting any proceeding in any State or United States court affecting the property, instrument or obligation involved in the interpleader action * * *.

But the present case is another matter. Here, an accident has happened. Thirty-five passengers or their representatives have claims which they wish to press against a variety of defendants: the bus company, its driver, the owner of the truck, and the truck driver. The circumstance that one of the prospective defendants happens to have an insurance policy is a fortuitous event which should not of itself shape the nature of the ensuing litigation. For example, a resident of California, injured in California aboard a bus owned by a California corporation should not be forced to sue that corporation anywhere but in California simply because another prospective defendant carried an insurance policy. And an insurance company whose maximum interest in the case cannot exceed $20,000 and who in fact asserts that it has no interest at all, should not be allowed to determine that dozens of tort plaintiffs must be compelled to press their claims—even those claims which are not against the insured and which in no event could be satisfied out of the meager insurance fund—in a single forum of the insurance company's choosing. There is nothing in the statutory scheme, and very little in the judicial and academic commentary upon that scheme, which requires that the tail be allowed to wag the dog in this fashion.

State Farm's interest in this case, which is the fulcrum of the interpleader procedure, is confined to its $20,000 fund. That interest receives full vindication when the court restrains claimants from seeking to enforce against the insurance company any judgment obtained against its insured, except in the interpleader proceeding itself. To the extent that the District Court sought to control claimants' lawsuits against the insured and other alleged tortfeasors, it exceeded the powers granted to it by the statutory scheme.

We recognize, of course, that our view of interpleader means that it cannot be used to solve all the vexing problems of multiparty litigation arising out of a mass tort. But interpleader was never intended to perform such a function, to be an all-purpose "bill of peace." Had it been so intended, careful provision would necessarily have been made to insure that a party with little or no interest in the outcome of a complex controversy should not strip truly interested parties of substantial rights—such as the right to choose the forum in which to establish their claims, subject to generally applicable rules of jurisdiction, venue, service of process, removal, and change of venue. None of the legislative and academic sponsors of a modern federal interpleader device viewed their accomplishment as a "bill of peace," capable of sweeping dozens of lawsuits out of the various state and federal courts in which they were brought and into a single interpleader proceeding. * * *

In light of the evidence that federal interpleader was not intended to serve the function of a "bill of peace" in the context of multiparty litigation arising out of a mass tort, of the anomalous power which such a construction of the statute would give the stakeholder, and of the thrust of the statute and the purpose it was intended to serve, we hold that the interpleader statute did not authorize the injunction entered in the present case. Upon remand, the injunction is to be modified consistently with this opinion.

IV.

The judgment of the Court of Appeals is reversed, and the case is remanded to the United States District Court for proceedings consistent with this opinion.

It is so ordered.

Judgment of Court of Appeals reversed and case remanded to the District Court.

■ MR. JUSTICE DOUGLAS, dissenting.

[Justice Douglas concluded that the litigants in this action were not "claimants" within the meaning of 28 U.S.C. § 1335: "[U]nder this insurance policy as enforced in California and in Oregon a 'claimant' against the insured can become a 'claimant' against the insurer only after final judgment against the insured or after a consensual written agreement of the insurer, a litigant, and the insured."]

COMMENTS AND QUESTIONS CONCERNING
STATE FARM FIRE & CASUALTY CO. V. TASHIRE

1.   Is it significant that 11 of the injured passengers were from Canada? Would this have created difficulties for the filing of a traditional civil action?

2.   Why was the initial action brought in state court, rather than in federal court?

3.   In this case an interlocutory appeal was taken pursuant to 28 U.S.C. § 1292(a)(1). As we will see in Chapter 15, Section 1292(a) interlocutory appeals are exceptions to the general rule that appeals only can be taken from the "final judgments" of federal district courts.

4.   Why does the Court find it necessary to raise the question of its own jurisdiction, when none of the parties raised this question? Having raised this question, isn't the Court's holding in *Strawbridge v. Curtiss* that complete diversity is required for subject-matter jurisdiction under the federal diversity statute, 28 U.S.C. § 1332, dispositive?

5.   Why can't the interpleader court enjoin all litigation stemming from the accident?

6.   Justice Fortas notes: "We recognize, of course, that our view of interpleader means that it cannot be used to solve all the vexing problems of multiparty litigation arising out of a mass tort. But interpleader was never intended to perform such a function, to be an all-purpose 'bill of peace.'"

In what other ways has Congress attempted to facilitate the more efficient resolution of complex litigation?

IV. INTERVENTION

Joinder under Rules 19 and 20 is a means by which a party can, or must, add another party to a civil action that he or she has filed. But sometimes a party with an interest in a legal action is not initially included in that action and therefore attempts to join the action. Rule 24 allows persons not initially included in an action to intervene, or join, in an action. The operation of Rule 24 intervention is the subject of the following opinion.

As you read this opinion, consider how the intervenor satisfied the "4 Is" necessary to establish a right to intervene under Rule 24(a)(2):

(1) an **Interest** in the property or transaction that is the subject of the action;

(2) **Impairment** of the person's interest if the motion to intervene is not granted;

(3) **Inadequacy** of the existing parties to protect the interest of the person seeking intervention; and

(4) the motion to intervene is filed **In Time**.

A. THE RULE 24 INTERVENTION REQUIREMENTS

Rule 24 permits a person to intervene in a federal civil action. The following opinion illustrates how the Rule 24 requirements are applied in practice.

Windsor v. United States

United States District Court, Southern District of New York, 2011
797 F.Supp. 2d 320

MEMORANDUM AND ORDER

■ JAMES C. FRANCIS IV, UNITED STATES MAGISTRATE JUDGE.

Plaintiff Edith Schlain Windsor brings this action challenging the constitutionality of Section 3 of the Defense of Marriage Act ("DOMA"), 1 U.S.C. § 7. The Bipartisan Legal Advisory Group of the United States House of Representatives ("BLAG") has filed a motion to intervene as a party defendant pursuant to Rule 24 of the Federal Rules of Civil Procedure. For the reasons that follow, the motion is granted.

Background

Ms. Windsor and Thea Clara Spyer were married in 2007 following a 40-year engagement. In 2009, Ms. Spyer passed away. Although their marriage was recognized by New York State, DOMA prevented the federal government, and, in particular, the Internal Revenue Service ("IRS"), from treating them as a married couple. As a result, Ms. Spyer's estate was required to pay $363,053 in federal tax that would have been waived by the estate tax marital deduction had the IRS recognized their marriage. Ms. Windsor, the executor of Ms. Spyer's estate, filed a Claim for Refund with the IRS, seeking return of the $363,053; her request was denied on the ground that DOMA restricts the definition of "spouse" to "a person of the opposite sex."

Ms. Windsor filed this action on November 9, 2010, arguing that the IRS's refusal to apply the estate tax marital deduction to her wife's estate—and by extension DOMA itself—discriminated against her on the basis of her sexual orientation in violation of the equal protection clause of the Fifth Amendment to the United States Constitution. The Department of Justice (the "DOJ") appeared on behalf of the defendant, the United States of America, and an amended complaint was filed on February 2, 2011. Soon thereafter, however, the Department of Justice gave notice to the plaintiff and this Court that it would "cease defending the constitutionality" of Section 3 of DOMA because

> the Attorney General and President have concluded: that heightened scrutiny is the appropriate standard of review for classifications based on sexual orientation; [and] that, consistent with that standard, Section 3 of DOMA may not be constitutionally applied to same-sex couples whose marriages are legally recognized under state law. . . .

The DOJ also notified Representative John A. Boehner, Speaker of the United States House of Representatives, of its change in position and expressed its "interest in providing Congress a full and fair opportunity to participate in [this] litigation" while still "remain[ing] parties to the case and continu[ing] to represent the interests of the United States throughout the litigation." On March 9, 2011, BLAG decided to seek approval to intervene in this litigation to defend the constitutionality of Section 3 of DOMA. Neither the plaintiff nor the DOJ opposes BLAG's intervention; however, the DOJ asks that BLAG's involvement be limited to making substantive arguments in defense of Section 3 of DOMA while the DOJ continues to file all procedural notices. BLAG does not acquiesce in this request, which it contends would relegate it to the status of amicus curiae.

Discussion

A.   Intervention

BLAG seeks intervention pursuant to Rule 24 of the Federal Rules of Civil Procedure, which states in relevant part:

(a)   Intervention of Right. On timely motion, the court must permit anyone to intervene who:

> (1)   is given an unconditional right to intervene by a federal statute; or

> (2)   claims an interest relating to the property or transaction that is the subject of the action, and is so situated that disposing of the action may as a practical matter impair or impede the movant's ability to protect its interest, unless existing parties adequately represent that interest.

(b)   Permissive Intervention.

> (1)   In General. On timely motion, the court may permit anyone to intervene who:

>> (A)   is given a conditional right to intervene by a federal statute. . . .

BLAG first argues that its intervention is appropriate pursuant to subsection (a)(1), or, in the alternative, subsection (b)(1)(A), because it is authorized by 28 U.S.C. § 2403(a). However, that statute only authorizes "the United States to intervene" in an action where "the United States or any agency, officer or employee thereof is not a party." 28 U.S.C. § 2403(a). Here, the United States of America is already a party to the litigation, and thus the statute does not authorize BLAG's intervention, either permissively or as of right.[2]

---

[2]   Although there is a statute that contemplates intervention by the Senate in defense of the constitutionality of statutes, see 2 U.S.C. §§ 288a–288n, and federal law requires the Attorney General to notify both houses of Congress when it intends not to defend the constitutionality of any statute, see 28 U.S.C. § 530D, there is no statute explicitly authorizing

BLAG also seeks to intervene pursuant to subsection (a)(2) of Rule 24 of the Federal Rules of Civil Procedure. Such intervention is appropriate where:

> (1) the motion is timely; (2) the applicant asserts an interest relating to the property or transaction that is the subject of the action; (3) the applicant is so situated that without intervention, disposition of the action may, as a practical matter, impair or impede the applicant's ability to protect its interest; and (4) the applicant's interest is not adequately represented by the other parties.

United States v. New York State Board of Elections, 312 Fed.Appx. 353, 354 (2d Cir.2008) (quoting *MasterCard International Inc. v. Visa International Service Association, Inc.*, 471 F.3d 377, 389 (2d Cir. 2006)). Although failure to satisfy any of these requirements justifies denial of the motion, courts apply them in a " 'flexible and discretionary' " way, considering " 'all four factors as a whole rather than focusing narrowly on any one of the criteria.' " *Cole Mechanical Corp. v. National Grange Mutual Insurance Co.*, No. 06 Civ. 2875, 2007 WL 2593000, at *2 (S.D.N.Y. Sept. 7, 2007) (quoting *Tachiona ex rel. Tachiona v. Mugabe*, 186 F.Supp.2d 383, 394 (S.D.N.Y.2002) ("*Tachiona I*")).

BLAG has fulfilled all four prerequisites. First, the DOJ does not dispute that this motion is timely, and there is no evidence of delay in its filing. Second, BLAG has a cognizable interest in defending the enforceability of statutes the House has passed when the President declines to enforce them. See *Barnes v. Kline*, 759 F.2d 21, 23 n. 3 (D.C.Cir.1985) (noting district court allowed BLAG's intervention pursuant to Rule 24(a)(2) to challenge presidential "pocket veto" of legislation passed by House), *vacated on other grounds sub nom. Burke v. Barnes*, 479 U.S. 361 (1987). In recognition of this interest, courts have permitted Congress to intervene as a full party in numerous cases where the Executive Branch declines to enforce a statute that is alleged to be unconstitutional, although they have often neglected to explain their rationale for doing so. Third, BLAG may be unable to advance its arguments regarding the constitutionality of Section 3 of DOMA in any forum should it be denied intervention here and should the statute subsequently be declared unconstitutional in the course of this litigation. Finally, BLAG's interests are not currently being adequately represented in this action, particularly in light of the " 'minimal' " burden for demonstrating inadequacy of representation. The DOJ has made clear that it will not defend the constitutionality of Section 3 of DOMA in any way, while such a defense is precisely what BLAG wishes to undertake here. Therefore, intervention pursuant to Rule 24(a)(2) of the Federal Rules of Civil Procedure is justified.

---

intervention by the House (or any subgroup or representative thereof) to defend the constitutionality of a statute.

The DOJ asks that BLAG be permitted to appear in this action only for the limited purpose of "present[ing] arguments in support of the constitutionality of Section 3" of DOMA, while the DOJ would continue to file all procedural motions, including notices of appeal and petitions for certiorari, that are necessary "to ensure that this Court can consider arguments on both sides of the constitutional issue." As established above, however, BLAG is entitled to intervene in this action as a party defendant, which enables it to make such procedural motions on its own. See *INS v. Chadha*, 462 U.S. 919, 930 n. 5, 939 (1983) (finding House to be "proper petitioner" for certiorari following its intervention to defend constitutionality of statute that executive agency had declined to defend). * * * The DOJ continues to represent a party to the present litigation and may certainly file any petitions or appeals that it chooses. However, there is no good precedent for preventing BLAG from intervening as a full party. Therefore, the DOJ's request that BLAG's participation be circumscribed is denied.

B. Standing

The DOJ's desire to remain the sole defendant for procedural purposes appears premised on the contention that BLAG does not have standing to intervene in this action as a party "any more than citizens with a generalized grievance would have standing to do so" because "Congress's interest in the constitutional validity of a law does not confer standing." This characterization is incorrect. The Second Circuit does not require intervenors to establish independent Article III standing as long as there is an ongoing case or controversy between the existing parties to the litigation. Therefore, BLAG has standing to intervene in this litigation to defend the constitutionality of Section 3 of DOMA.

C. Pleading Requirements

Rule 24(c) of the Federal Rules of Civil Procedure requires all intervenors to submit a pleading setting out "the claim or defense for which intervention is sought." "Where, however, the position of the movant is apparent from other filings and where the opposing party will not be prejudiced, Rule 24(c) permits a degree of flexibility with technical requirements." *Tachiona I*, 186 F.Supp.2d at 393 n. 8; see also *Official Committee of Asbestos Claimants of G-I Holding, Inc. v. Heyman*, No. 01 Civ. 8539, 2003 WL 22790916, at *4 (S.D.N.Y. Nov. 25, 2003) (allowing intervenor to adopt "claims already asserted" by plaintiff where no prejudice would be caused to either party).

BLAG asks this Court to waive its obligation to file an answer, arguing that its motion to intervene is sufficient to put the plaintiff on notice of its intent to "defend[ ] Section [3 of DOMA] on equal protection grounds." The DOJ does not oppose this request. Waiver of the pleading requirement is justified here because BLAG's position on the subject matter of the litigation is clearly articulated in its motion papers. Furthermore, the plaintiff appears to have waived the DOJ's obligation to file an answer, and the parties are preparing to make cross-motions for summary judgment. Therefore, BLAG is not required to file an answer at this time.

Conclusion

For the reasons set forth above, BLAG's motion to intervene as a party defendant is granted.

SO ORDERED.

COMMENTS AND QUESTIONS CONCERNING *WINDSOR V. UNITED STATES*

1.   In a subsequent 2013 decision in this case, the Supreme Court declared that the Defense of Marriage Act's definition of "marriage" (as "only a legal union between one man and one woman") and "spouse" (as "refer[ing] only to a person of the opposite sex who is a husband or a wife") violated the Fifth Amendment to the United States Constitution. *United States v. Windsor*, 133 S.Ct. 2675 (2013).

2.   Although the Bipartisan Legal Advisory Group intervened in this action as a defendant, Rule 24 also permits non-parties to intervene as plaintiffs. *Nissei Sangyo Am., Ltd. v. United States*, 31 F.3d 435, 438 (7th Cir. 1994). However, if diversity of citizenship is the basis for the court's subject-matter jurisdiction, Rule 24 intervention that would destroy complete diversity may not be permitted. *See* 28 U.S.C. § 1367(b) ("In any civil action of which the district courts have original jurisdiction founded solely on section 1332 of this title, the district courts shall not have supplemental jurisdiction * * * over claims by plaintiffs against persons made parties under Rule * * * 24 * * * or over claims by persons * * * seeking to intervene as plaintiffs under Rule 24 * * *, when exercising supplemental jurisdiction over such claims would be inconsistent with the jurisdictional requirements of section 1332.").

3.   Rule 24(a)(2) does not permit intervention if "existing parties adequately represent [the prospective intervenor's] interest." Why was this not an issue in this case? Would BLAG have been permitted to intervene had the Department of Justice decided to defend the Defense of Marriage Act?

4.   Magistrate Judge Francis found that BLAG had a right to intervene pursuant to Rule 24(a). However, if he had not done so, might BLAG have sought permissive intervention under Rule 24(b)(1)(B) by showing that it had "a claim or defense that shares with the main action a common question of law or fact"? Would BLAG have been able to satisfy this requirement?

5.   What is an amicus curiae? Why did BLAG want to intervene as a party rather than participate as an amicus curiae?

6.   Article III of the Constitution requires that a party bringing a federal action must have standing to sue. As the Supreme Court noted in *Steel Co. v. Citizens for a Better Environment*, 523 U.S. 83, 103–104 (1998), a "triad of injury in fact, causation, and redressability constitutes the core

of Article III's case-or-controversy requirement, and the party invoking federal jurisdiction bears the burden of establishing its existence." Although Magistrate Judge Francis concluded that an intervenor need not itself have standing in order to intervene in an existing case or controversy, there is a split in the federal courts of appeal as to whether this is necessary. *City of Chicago v. Fed. Emergency Mgmt. Agency*, 660 F.3d 980, 984–85 (7th Cir. 2011).

7.   About a month before Judge Francis' decision, the law firm of King & Spalding withdrew from representation of BLAG one week after having agreed to represent it in this action. As a result, former Solicitor General Paul Clement, who had been representing BLAG in this action, left King & Spalding to join another law firm so he could continue to represent BLAG. Rule 1.16(c)(4) of the New York Rules of Professional Conduct provides that "a lawyer may withdraw from representing a client when * * * withdrawal can be accomplished without material adverse effect on the interests of the client." However, in many jurisdictions (including New York), counsel may be required to obtain the permission of the court to withdraw from a matter pending before a tribunal. *See id.* at Rule 1.16(d); ABA Model Rule of Professional Conduct 1.16(c).

8.   As you will see in the next case, *Martin v. Wilks*, whether a person is granted the right to intervene pursuant to Rule 24 not only has implications for that person's ability to participate in that action, but also determines whether that person will be considered bound by the judgment with respect to future litigation.

B. WHY INTERVENTION MATTERS: *MARTIN V. WILKS*

Martin v. Wilks

Supreme Court of the United States, 1989
490 U.S. 755

■ CHIEF JUSTICE REHNQUIST delivered the opinion of the Court.

A group of white firefighters sued the city of Birmingham, Alabama (City), and the Jefferson County Personnel Board (Board) alleging that they were being denied promotions in favor of less qualified black firefighters. They claimed that the City and the Board were making promotion decisions on the basis of race in reliance on certain consent decrees, and that these decisions constituted impermissible racial discrimination in violation of the Constitution and federal statutes. The District Court held that the white firefighters were precluded from challenging employment decisions taken pursuant to the decrees, even though these firefighters had not been parties to the proceedings in which the decrees were entered. We think this holding contravenes the general rule that a person cannot be deprived of his legal rights in a proceeding to which he is not a party.

The litigation in which the consent decrees were entered began in 1974, when the Ensley Branch of the National Association for the

Advancement of Colored People and seven black individuals filed separate class-action complaints against the City and the Board. They alleged that both had engaged in racially discriminatory hiring and promotion practices in various public service jobs in violation of Title VII of the Civil Rights Act of 1964, 42 U.S.C. § 2000e *et seq.,* and other federal law. After a bench trial on some issues, but before judgment, the parties entered into two consent decrees, one between the black individuals and the City and the other between them and the Board. These proposed decrees set forth an extensive remedial scheme, including long-term and interim annual goals for the hiring of blacks as firefighters. The decrees also provided for goals for promotion of blacks within the fire department.

The District Court entered an order provisionally approving the decrees and directing publication of notice of the upcoming fairness hearings. Notice of the hearings, with a reference to the general nature of the decrees, was published in two local newspapers. At that hearing, the Birmingham Firefighters Association (BFA) appeared and filed objections as *amicus curiae.* After the hearing, but before final approval of the decrees, the BFA and two of its members also moved to intervene on the ground that the decrees would adversely affect their rights. The District Court denied the motions as untimely and approved the decrees. Seven white firefighters, all members of the BFA, then filed a complaint against the City and the Board seeking injunctive relief against enforcement of the decrees. The seven argued that the decrees would operate to illegally discriminate against them; the District Court denied relief.

Both the denial of intervention and the denial of injunctive relief were affirmed on appeal. The District Court had not abused its discretion in refusing to let the BFA intervene, thought the Eleventh Circuit, in part because the firefighters could "institut[e] an independent Title VII suit, asserting specific violations of their rights." And, for the same reason, petitioners had not adequately shown the potential for irreparable harm from the operation of the decrees necessary to obtain injunctive relief.

A new group of white firefighters, the *Wilks* respondents, then brought suit against the City and the Board in District Court. They too alleged that, because of their race, they were being denied promotions in favor of less qualified blacks in violation of federal law. The Board and the City admitted to making race-conscious employment decisions, but argued that the decisions were unassailable because they were made pursuant to the consent decrees. A group of black individuals, the *Martin* petitioners, were allowed to intervene in their individual capacities to defend the decrees.

The defendants moved to dismiss the reverse discrimination cases as impermissible collateral attacks on the consent decrees. The District Court denied the motions, ruling that the decrees would provide a defense to claims of discrimination for employment decisions "mandated" by the decrees, leaving the principal issue for trial whether the challenged promotions were indeed required by the decrees. After trial the District Court granted the motion to dismiss. The court concluded that "if in fact the City was required to [make promotions of blacks] by the consent decree, then they would not be guilty of [illegal] racial discrimination" and that the defendants had "establish[ed] that the promotions of the black individuals . . . were in fact required by the terms of the consent decree."

On appeal, the Eleventh Circuit reversed. It held that, "[b]ecause . . . [the *Wilks* respondents] were neither parties nor privies to the consent decrees, . . . their independent claims of unlawful discrimination are not precluded." The court explicitly rejected the doctrine of "impermissible collateral attack" espoused by other Courts of Appeals to immunize parties to a consent decree from charges of discrimination by nonparties for actions taken pursuant to the decree. Although it recognized a "strong public policy in favor of voluntary affirmative action plans," the panel acknowledged that this interest "must yield to the policy against requiring third parties to submit to bargains in which their interests were either ignored or sacrificed." The court remanded the case for trial of the discrimination claims, suggesting that the operative law for judging the consent decrees was that governing voluntary affirmative-action plans.[1]

We granted certiorari and now affirm the Eleventh Circuit's judgment. All agree that "[i]t is a principle of general application in Anglo-American jurisprudence that one is not bound by a judgment *in personam* in a litigation in which he is not designated as a party or to which he has not been made a party by service of process." *Hansberry v. Lee,* 311 U.S. 32, 40 (1940). This rule is part of our "deep-rooted historic tradition that everyone should have his own day in court." 18 C. Wright, A. Miller, & E. Cooper, *Federal Practice and Procedure* § 4449, p. 417 (1981) (hereafter 18 Wright). A judgment or decree among parties to a lawsuit resolves issues as among them, but it does not conclude the rights of strangers to those proceedings.[2]

---

[1] Judge Anderson, dissenting, "agree[d] with the opinion for the court that these plaintiffs [the *Wilks* respondents] were not parties to the prior litigation which resulted in the consent decree, and that the instant plaintiffs are not bound by the consent decree and should be free on remand to challenge the consent decree prospectively and test its validity against the recent Supreme Court precedent." He distinguished, however, between claims for prospective relief and claims for backpay, the latter being barred, in his opinion, by the City's good-faith reliance on the decrees.

[2] We have recognized an exception to the general rule when, in certain limited circumstances, a person, although not a party, has his interests adequately represented by someone with the same interests who is a party. *See Hansberry v. Lee,* 311 U.S. 32, 41–42 (1940) ("class" or "representative" suits); Fed.Rule Civ.Proc. 23 (same); *Montana v. United States,* 440 U.S. 147, 154–155 (1979) (control of litigation on behalf of one of the parties in the litigation). Additionally, where a special remedial scheme exists expressly foreclosing successive litigation by nonlitigants, as for example in bankruptcy or probate, legal proceedings may terminate preexisting rights if the scheme is otherwise consistent with due process. *See NLRB v. Bildisco & Bildisco,* 465 U.S. 513, 529–530, n. 10 (1984) ("[P]roof of

Petitioners argue that, because respondents failed to timely intervene in the initial proceedings, their current challenge to actions taken under the consent decree constitutes an impermissible "collateral attack." They argue that respondents were aware that the underlying suit might affect them, and if they chose to pass up an opportunity to intervene, they should not be permitted to later litigate the issues in a new action. The position has sufficient appeal to have commanded the approval of the great majority of the Federal Courts of Appeals, but we agree with the contrary view expressed by the Court of Appeals for the Eleventh Circuit in these cases. We begin with the words of Justice Brandeis in *Chase National Bank v. Norwalk,* 291 U.S. 431 (1934):

> "The law does not impose upon any person absolutely entitled to a hearing the burden of voluntary intervention in a suit to which he is a stranger. . . . Unless duly summoned to appear in a legal proceeding, a person not a privy may rest assured that a judgment recovered therein will not affect his legal rights."
> *Id.,* at 441.

While these words were written before the adoption of the Federal Rules of Civil Procedure, we think the Rules incorporate the same principle; a party seeking a judgment binding on another cannot obligate that person to intervene; he must be joined. Against the background of permissive intervention set forth in *Chase National Bank,* the drafters cast Rule 24, governing intervention, in permissive terms. *See* Fed.Rule Civ.Proc. 24(a) (intervention as of right) ("Upon timely application anyone shall be permitted to intervene"); Fed.Rule Civ.Proc. 24(b) (permissive intervention) ("Upon timely application anyone may be permitted to intervene"). They determined that the concern for finality and completeness of judgments would be "better [served] by mandatory joinder procedures." 18 Wright § 4452, p. 453. Accordingly, Rule 19(a) provides for mandatory joinder in circumstances where a judgment rendered in the absence of a person may "leave . . . persons already parties subject to a substantial risk of incurring . . . inconsistent obligations. . . ." Rule 19(b) sets forth the factors to be considered by a court in deciding whether to allow an action to proceed in the absence of an interested party.

Joinder as a party, rather than knowledge of a lawsuit and an opportunity to intervene, is the method by which potential parties are subjected to the jurisdiction of the court and bound by a judgment or decree. The parties to a lawsuit presumably know better than anyone else the nature and scope of relief sought in the action, and at whose expense such relief might be granted. It makes sense, therefore, to place on them a burden of bringing in additional parties where such a step is indicated, rather than placing on potential additional parties a duty to

claim must be presented to the Bankruptcy Court . . . or be lost"); *Tulsa Professional Collection Services, Inc. v. Pope,* 485 U.S. 478 (1988) (nonclaim statute terminating unsubmitted claims against the estate). Neither of these exceptions, however, applies in these cases.

intervene when they acquire knowledge of the lawsuit. The linchpin of the "impermissible collateral attack" doctrine—the attribution of preclusive effect to a failure to intervene—is therefore quite inconsistent with Rule 19 and Rule 24.

* * *

Petitioners contend that a different result should be reached because the need to join affected parties will be burdensome and ultimately discouraging to civil rights litigation. Potential adverse claimants may be numerous and difficult to identify; if they are not joined, the possibility for inconsistent judgments exists. Judicial resources will be needlessly consumed in relitigation of the same question.

Even if we were wholly persuaded by these arguments as a matter of policy, acceptance of them would require a rewriting rather than an interpretation of the relevant Rules. But we are not persuaded that their acceptance would lead to a more satisfactory method of handling cases like these. It must be remembered that the alternatives are a duty to intervene based on knowledge, on the one hand, and some form of joinder, as the Rules presently provide, on the other. No one can seriously contend that an employer might successfully defend against a Title VII claim by one group of employees on the ground that its actions were required by an earlier decree entered in a suit brought against it by another, if the later group did not have adequate notice or knowledge of the earlier suit.

* * *

Nor do we think that the system of joinder called for by the Rules is likely to produce more relitigation of issues than the converse rule. The breadth of a lawsuit and concomitant relief may be at least partially shaped in advance through Rule 19 to avoid needless clashes with future litigation. And even under a regime of mandatory intervention, parties who did not have adequate knowledge of the suit would relitigate issues. Additional questions about the adequacy and timeliness of knowledge would inevitably crop up. We think that the system of joinder presently contemplated by the Rules best serves the many interests involved in the run of litigated cases, including cases like the present ones.

Petitioners also urge that the congressional policy favoring voluntary settlement of employment discrimination claims * * * also supports the "impermissible collateral attack" doctrine. But once again it is essential to note just what is meant by "voluntary settlement." A voluntary settlement in the form of a consent decree between one group of employees and their employer cannot possibly "settle," voluntarily or otherwise, the conflicting claims of another group of employees who do not join in the agreement. This is true even if the second group of employees is a party to the litigation:

> "[P]arties who choose to resolve litigation through settlement may not dispose of the claims of a third party . . . without that party's agreement. A court's approval of a consent decree between some of the parties therefore cannot dispose of the valid claims of nonconsenting intervenors." *Firefighters v. Cleveland,* 478 U.S. 501, 529 (1986).

Insofar as the argument is bottomed on the idea that it may be easier to settle claims among a disparate group of affected persons if they are all before the court, joinder bids fair to accomplish that result as well as a regime of mandatory intervention.

For the foregoing reasons we affirm the decision of the Court of Appeals for the Eleventh Circuit. That court remanded the case for trial of the reverse discrimination claims. Petitioners point to language in the District Court's findings of fact and conclusions of law which suggests that respondents will not prevail on the merits. We agree with the view of the Court of Appeals, however, that the proceedings in the District Court may have been affected by the mistaken view that respondents' claims on the merits were barred to the extent they were inconsistent with the consent decree.

Affirmed.

■ JUSTICE STEVENS, with whom JUSTICE BRENNAN, JUSTICE MARSHALL, and JUSTICE BLACKMUN join, dissenting.

As a matter of law there is a vast difference between persons who are actual parties to litigation and persons who merely have the kind of interest that may as a practical matter be impaired by the outcome of a case. Persons in the first category have a right to participate in a trial and to appeal from an adverse judgment; depending on whether they win or lose, their legal rights may be enhanced or impaired. Persons in the latter category have a right to intervene in the action in a timely fashion, or they may be joined as parties against their will. But if they remain on the sidelines, they may be harmed as a practical matter even though their legal rights are unaffected. One of the disadvantages of sideline-sitting is that the bystander has no right to appeal from a judgment no matter how harmful it may be.

In these cases the Court quite rightly concludes that the white firefighters who brought the second series of Title VII cases could not be deprived of their legal rights in the first series of cases because they had neither intervened nor been joined as parties. The consent decrees obviously could not deprive them of any contractual rights, such as seniority, or accrued vacation pay, or of any other legal rights, such as the right to have their employer comply with federal statutes like Title VII. There is no reason, however, why the consent decrees might not produce changes in conditions at the white firefighters' place of employment that, as a practical matter, may have a serious effect on their opportunities for employment or promotion even though they are not bound by the decrees in any legal sense. The fact that one of the effects of a decree is to curtail the job opportunities of nonparties does not mean that the nonparties have been deprived of legal rights or that they have standing to appeal from that decree without becoming parties.

Persons who have no right to appeal from a final judgment—either because the time to appeal has elapsed or because they never became parties to the case—may nevertheless collaterally attack a judgment on certain narrow grounds. If the court had no jurisdiction over the subject matter, or if the judgment is the product of corruption, duress, fraud, collusion, or mistake, under limited circumstances it may be set aside in an appropriate collateral proceeding. *See Restatement (Second) of Judgments* §§ 69–72 (1982). This rule not only applies to parties to the original action, but also allows interested third parties collaterally to attack judgments. In both civil and criminal cases, however, the grounds that may be invoked to support a collateral attack are much more limited than those that may be asserted as error on direct appeal. Thus, a person who can foresee that a lawsuit is likely to have a practical impact on his interests may pay a heavy price if he elects to sit on the sidelines instead of intervening and taking the risk that his legal rights will be impaired.

In these cases there is no dispute about the fact that respondents are not parties to the consent decrees. It follows as a matter of course that they are not bound by those decrees. Those judgments could not, and did not, deprive them of any legal rights. The judgments did, however, have a practical impact on respondents' opportunities for advancement in their profession. For that reason, respondents had standing to challenge the validity of the decrees, but the grounds that they may advance in support of a collateral challenge are much more limited than would be allowed if they were parties prosecuting a direct appeal.

* * *

In its decision approving the consent decrees, the District Court first noted "that there is no contention or suggestion that the settlements are fraudulent or collusive." The court then explained why it was satisfied that the affirmative-action goals and quotas set forth in the decrees were "well within the limits upheld as permissible" in *Steelworkers v. Weber,* 443 U.S. 193 (1979), and other cases. It pointed out that the decrees "do not preclude the hiring or promotion of whites and males even for a temporary period of time," and that the City's commitment to promote blacks and whites to the position of fire lieutenant at the same rate was temporary and was subject both to the availability of qualified candidates and "to the caveat that the decree is not to be interpreted as requiring the hiring or promotion of a person who is not qualified or of a person who is demonstrably less qualified according to a job-related selection procedure." It further found that the record provided "more than ample reason" to conclude that the City would eventually be held liable for discrimination against blacks at high-level positions in the fire and police departments.[12] * * *

* * *

* * * [I]t is absolutely clear that the court did not hold that respondents were bound by the decree. * * * Indeed, respondents, the Court of Appeals, and the majority opinion all fail to draw attention to any point in these cases' long history at which the judge may have given the impression that any nonparty was legally bound by the consent decree.[20]

* * *

Hence, there is no basis for collaterally attacking the judgment as collusive, fraudulent, or transparently invalid. Moreover, respondents do not claim—nor has there been any showing of—mistake, duress, or lack of jurisdiction. Instead, respondents are left to argue that somewhat different relief would have been more appropriate than the relief that was actually granted. Although this sort of issue may provide the basis for a direct appeal, it cannot, and should not, serve to open the door to relitigation of a settled judgment.

* * *

There is nothing unusual about the fact that litigation between adverse parties may, as a practical matter, seriously impair the

---

[12] In approving the decree, the District Court expressed confidence that the United States and the black firefighters brought suit in good faith and that there was a strong evidentiary basis for their complaints. It observed:

"Employment statistics for Birmingham's police and fire departments as of July 21, 1981, certainly lend support to the claim made in this litigation against the City— that, notwithstanding this court's directions in 1977 with respect to certifications by the Personnel Board for the entry-level police officer and firefighters positions and despite the City's adoption of a 'fair hiring ordinance' and of affirmative action plans, the effects of past discrimination against blacks persist. According to those figures, 79 of the 480 police officers are black, 3 of the 131 police sergeants are black, and none of the 40 police lieutenants and captains are black. In the fire department, 42 of the 453 firefighters are black, and none of the 140 lieutenants, captains, and battalion chiefs are black."

The evidence of discrimination presented at the 1979 trial is described in greater detail in the United States' 100-page, post-trial brief, which is reprinted in the Joint Appendix.

[20] In *Provident Tradesmens Bank & Trust Co. v. Patterson*, 390 U.S., at 114, we expressly did not decide whether a litigant might "be bound by [a] previous decision because, although technically a nonparty, he had purposely bypassed an adequate opportunity to intervene." Today, the Court answers this question, at least in the limited context of the instant dispute, holding that "[j]oinder as a party [under Federal Rule of Civil Procedure 19], rather than knowledge of a lawsuit and an opportunity to intervene [under Federal Rule of Civil Procedure 24], is the method by which potential parties are subjected to the jurisdiction of the court and bound by a judgment or decree." Because I conclude that the District Court did not hold that respondents were bound by the consent decrees, I do not reach this issue.

interests of third persons who elect to sit on the sidelines. Indeed, in complex litigation this Court has squarely held that a sideline-sitter may be bound as firmly as an actual party if he had adequate notice and a fair opportunity to intervene and if the judicial interest in finality is sufficiently strong. *See Penn-Central Merger and N & W Inclusion Cases,* 389 U.S. 486, 505–506 (1968).

There is no need, however, to go that far in order to agree with the District Court's eminently sensible view that compliance with the terms of a valid decree remedying violations of Title VII cannot itself violate that statute or the Equal Protection Clause. The city of Birmingham, in entering into and complying with this decree, has made a substantial step toward the eradication of the long history of pervasive racial discrimination that has plagued its fire department. The District Court, after conducting a trial and carefully considering respondents' arguments, concluded that this effort is lawful and should go forward. Because respondents have thus already had their day in court and have failed to carry their burden, I would vacate the judgment of the Court of Appeals and remand for further proceedings consistent with this opinion.

COMMENTS AND QUESTIONS CONCERNING *MARTIN V. WILKS*

1.   Although the litigation involving the Birmingham firefighters had been pending for 15 years when the Supreme Court decided *Martin v. Wilks* in 1989, that litigation continued for another two decades thereafter. This included modification of the consent decree; holding the Personnel Board in civil contempt; placing the Board in receivership and judicial appointment of board members when board positions came open; enactment of a state statute increasing the Board from three to seven members; and, in 2008, a final district court order that "explained that the Board had 'complied with its Consent Decree in good faith,' had 'demonstrated a good faith commitment to continued compliance with federal law,' and had 'implemented policies, practices, and procedures which make it unlikely that the Board will repeat its former violations . . . , making it unnecessary for this Court to provide further judicial supervision.'" *Birmingham Fire Fighters Ass'n 117 v. City Of Birmingham*, 603 F.3d 1248, 1253 n.1 (11th Cir. 2010).

In a 2010 decision involving this litigation, the Court of Appeals noted:

As District Judge Smith observed in his September 2008 opinion, the case's thirty-year tenure in the federal-court system has solidified its Dickensian nature. *See United States v. Jefferson County, Ala.*, No. 2:75–cv–666 at 11 (N.D.Ala. Sept. 12, 2008); *see also* Charles Dickens, *Bleak House* 4–5 (Pollard & Moss 1884) ("[The case] drones on. This . . . suit has, in course of time, become so complicated that no man alive knows what it means. . . . Innumerable children have been born into the cause; innumerable young people have married into it; innumerable old people have died out of it. Scores of persons have deliriously found themselves

made parties . . . without knowing how or why. . . . [It] still drags
its dreary length before the court. . . .").

Birmingham Fire Fighters Ass'n 117 v. City Of Birmingham, 603 F.3d
1248, 1251 n.1 (11th Cir. 2010).

2. Justice Rehnquist states "the general rule [is] that a person
cannot be deprived of his legal rights in a proceeding to which he is not a
party." The white firefighters bringing this action were not parties to the
action that resulted in the consent degrees, so why did the Supreme Court
even consider the case? Is it significant, or surprising, that other federal
courts of appeal had adopted an "impermissible collateral attack" doctrine?

3. Is it significant that the Birmingham Firefighters Association
participated in the action that resulted in the consent decrees? Wasn't BFA
representing the individual firefighters in this action? *See Taylor v.
Sturgell*, 553 U.S. 880, 900 (2008) ("A party's representation of a nonparty
is 'adequate' for preclusion purposes only if, at a minimum: (1) the interests
of the nonparty and her representative are aligned; and (2) either the party
understood herself to be acting in a representative capacity or the original
court took care to protect the interests of the nonparty. In addition,
adequate representation sometimes requires (3) notice of the original suit
to the persons alleged to have been represented.").

4. Note Chief Justice Rehnquist's statement concerning the
relationship between the ability to intervene in an action and the ability to
later challenge actions taken pursuant to a consent judgment in the first
action: "The District Court had not abused its discretion in refusing to let
the BFA intervene, thought the Eleventh Circuit, in part because the
firefighters could 'institut[e] an independent Title VII suit, asserting
specific violations of their rights.' " Thus, just as one who intervenes will be
bound by the judgment in that action, the denial of a motion to intervene
may highlight the ability of that person to file an independent action.

5. When the actions taken by the Board and City pursuant to the
consent decree were challenged, the Martin petitioners were permitted to
intervene to defend the consent decree and the actions of the Board and
City. By granting these petitioners the right to intervene, was the district
judge stating, in effect, that their interests would not be adequately
protected by the Board and the City?

6. Justice Stevens writes in his dissent:

The consent decrees obviously could not deprive [the firefighters]
of any contractual rights, such as seniority, or accrued vacation
pay, or of any other legal rights, such as the right to have their
employer comply with federal statutes like Title VII. There is no
reason, however, why the consent decrees might not produce
changes in conditions at the white firefighters' place of
employment that, as a practical matter, may have a serious effect
on their opportunities for employment or promotion even though
they are not bound by the decrees in any legal sense.

506 PARTY AND CLAIM JOINDER: "WHO CAN WE SUE ABOUT WHAT?" CHAPTER 6

In footnote 1 of his opinion, Chief Justice Rehnquist notes a similar distinction made by Court of Appeals Judge R. Lanier Anderson with respect to the binding effect of different types of relief in the consent decree: "[Judge Anderson] distinguished * * * between claims for prospective relief and claims for backpay, the latter being barred, in his opinion, by the City's good-faith reliance on the decrees." Does this mean that firefighters who were not parties to the first action can be bound by some aspects of the consent decrees but not others?

7.   What is the basis for the following two preclusion exceptions that Chief Justice Rehnquist recognizes in the second footnote to his opinion:

> We have recognized an exception to the general rule when, in certain limited circumstances, a person, although not a party, has his interests adequately represented by someone with the same interests who is a party. *See Hansberry v. Lee*, 311 U.S. 32, 41–42 (1940) ("class" or "representative" suits); Fed.Rule Civ.Proc. 23 (same); *Montana v. United States*, 440 U.S. 147, 154–155 (1979) (control of litigation on behalf of one of the parties in the litigation). Additionally, where a special remedial scheme exists expressly foreclosing successive litigation by nonlitigants, as for example in bankruptcy or probate, legal proceedings may terminate preexisting rights if the scheme is otherwise consistent with due process. *See NLRB v. Bildisco & Bildisco*, 465 U.S. 513, 529–530, n. 10 (1984) ("[P]roof of claim must be presented to the Bankruptcy Court . . . or be lost"); *Tulsa Professional Collection Services, Inc. v. Pope*, 485 U.S. 478 (1988) (nonclaim statute terminating unsubmitted claims against the estate). Neither of these exceptions, however, applies in these cases.

As a practical matter, why does it make sense to bind non-parties in this very limited number of situations? What protections exist in these situations for the non-party? Should non-parties in cases such as *Martin v. Wilks*, in which a consent decree is challenged by members of a group of similarly-situated individuals, also be bound by a prior judgment?

8.   In response to the Supreme Court's decision in *Martin v. Wilks* and other civil rights cases, Congress enacted the Civil Rights Act of 1991, adding Section 2000e–2(n) to Title 42. Pub.L. 102–166, § 108, 105 Stat. 1071, 1076 (1991).

Section 2000e–2(n) of Title 42 provides another, limited exception to the general rule that a person who is not a party to an action cannot be bound by the judgment in that action. Section 2000e–2(n) concerns the "resolution of challenges to employment practices implementing litigated or consent judgments or orders" and provides:

> (1)(A) Notwithstanding any other provision of law, and except as provided in paragraph (2), an employment practice that implements and is within the scope of a litigated or consent judgment or order that resolves a claim of employment discrimination under the Constitution or Federal civil rights laws

may not be challenged under the circumstances described in subparagraph (B).

(B) A practice described in subparagraph (A) may not be challenged in a claim under the Constitution or Federal civil rights laws—

(i)   by a person who, prior to the entry of the judgment or order described in subparagraph (A), had—

(I)   actual notice of the proposed judgment or order sufficient to apprise such person that such judgment or order might adversely affect the interests and legal rights of such person and that an opportunity was available to present objections to such judgment or order by a future date certain; and

(II) a reasonable opportunity to present objections to such judgment or order; or

(ii) by a person whose interests were adequately represented by another person who had previously challenged the judgment or order on the same legal grounds and with a similar factual situation, unless there has been an intervening change in law or fact.

While Congress thus gave preclusive effect to certain consent decrees and litigated judgments in employment discrimination actions such as *Martin v. Wilks*, the Civil Rights Act of 1991 provides that it does not change some specific preexisting law. Section 2000e–2(n)(2) of Title 42 provides:

(2)   Nothing in this subsection shall be construed to—

(A) alter the standards for intervention under rule 24 of the Federal Rules of Civil Procedure or apply to the rights of parties who have successfully intervened pursuant to such rule in the proceeding in which the parties intervened;

(B) apply to the rights of parties to the action in which a litigated or consent judgment or order was entered, or of members of a class represented or sought to be represented in such action, or of members of a group on whose behalf relief was sought in such action by the Federal Government;

(C) prevent challenges to a litigated or consent judgment or order on the ground that such judgment or order was obtained through collusion or fraud, or is transparently invalid or was entered by a court lacking subject matter jurisdiction; or

(D) authorize or permit the denial to any person of the due process of law required by the Constitution.

9.   Why should potential class members be able to "wait and see" how things come out in an action—reserving the right to file a separate action raising the same issues adjudicated in the first action? In most cases the claimant can choose whether, when, where, with and against whom, and

how to assert a claim. What is the proper balance between such claimant autonomy and systemic efficiency?

10. In his opinion Chief Justice Rehnquist states: "No one can seriously contend that an employer might successfully defend against a Title VII claim by one group of employees on the ground that its actions were required by an earlier decree entered in a suit brought against it by another, if the later group did not have adequate notice or knowledge of the earlier suit." But what if the other group did have adequate notice? What if these persons also were represented in the first action by an association such as the Birmingham Firefighters Association? Are there additional ways in which the district court could enhance the binding effect of the consent decree?

11. Justice Stevens writes in his dissent:

> Persons who have no right to appeal from a final judgment— either because the time to appeal has elapsed or because they never became parties to the case—may nevertheless collaterally attack a judgment on certain narrow grounds. If the court had no jurisdiction over the subject matter, or if the judgment is the product of corruption, duress, fraud, collusion, or mistake, under limited circumstances it may be set aside in an appropriate collateral proceeding.

In Chapter 14 we explore situations in which a party asserts that it is not bound by a judgment because the court did not have subject-matter jurisdiction. *See Lemkin v. Hahn, Loeser & Parks*, 2011 WL 2555378 (S.D. Ohio), *infra* p. 1058.

V. RULE 18 CLAIM JOINDER

At common law, claims had to be asserted with the proper procedural form of action, and claims sounding in different forms of action (*e.g.*, trespass and case) could not be joined in the same legal action. While the forms of action were abolished by the 19th Century procedural codes, these state codes retained some of the rigidity of the common law.[3]

One of the innovations of the Federal Rules of Civil Procedure was the liberalization of claim joinder. Rule 18(a) is very direct, and very liberal, with respect to the joinder of claims against a single opposing party. It provides:

> A party asserting a claim, counterclaim, crossclaim, or third-party claim may join, as independent or alternative claims, as many claims as it has against an opposing party.

Assume, for instance, that a worker is to receive weekly payment from her employer, but does not. The employer also has bumped the worker's car in the parking lot. Rule 18 would permit the worker to

---

[3]   6A C. Wright, A. Miller & M. Kane, *Federal Practice & Procedure* § 1581 (3d ed. 2010) ("History of Joinder of Claims").

bring two unrelated claims against the employer in the same action: (1) one for the wages owed and (2) a separate tort claim for damages to her car. However, civil litigation is rarely that simple, and counsel always must remember the following three qualifications to Rule 18 claim joinder.

A. FEDERAL SUBJECT-MATTER JURISDICTION MUST EXIST FOR EACH CLAIM

Does satisfaction of the (minimal) requirements of Rule 18 mean that a federal court must hear this action? Not necessarily. Rule 82 provides that the Federal Rules of Civil Procedure "do not extend or limit the jurisdiction of the district courts or the venue of actions in those courts." So a federal district cannot hear these claims unless they satisfy the requirements for federal subject-matter jurisdiction.

In the above hypothetical there does not appear to be a federal question presented by either claim, and it is unlikely that either of the worker's claims would involve more than $75,000 and thus satisfy the amount in controversy requirement of 28 U.S.C. § 1332(a) (even if the worker and employer are citizens of different states). Only if an action is authorized by the Federal Rules of Civil Procedure **and** the action falls within the subject-matter jurisdiction of the federal courts can the action be heard in a United States District Court.

In order to satisfy 28 U.S.C. § 1332(a), though, a single plaintiff can aggregate the amount in controversy stemming from separate claims against a single defendant—even if those claims are unrelated. So if the plaintiff's claims in the hypothetical were each for $60,000, the minimum amount in controversy requirement would be satisfied.

In addition, if federal jurisdiction exists with respect to at least one of the claims, Section 1367 of Title 28 may supply the jurisdictional basis for related state-law claims. But Section 1367 provides that supplemental jurisdiction will only exist if the state law claim is so related to the federal claim that the federal and state claims "form part of the same case or controversy under Article III of the United States Constitution."

B. SATISFACTION OF RULE 18 AND FEDERAL SUBJECT-MATTER JURISDICTION DOESN'T NECESSARILY MEAN THAT THE CLAIMS WILL BE TRIED TOGETHER

Assume that the worker's claims satisfy the requirements for subject-matter jurisdiction (she is a citizen of a state different than that of her employer, she earned more than $75,000 per week, and she had a very expensive car). Does this mean that the federal court will hear both claims in a single trial? Not necessarily.

Rule 42(b) provides:

> For convenience, to avoid prejudice, or to expedite and economize, the court may order a separate trial of one or more separate issues, claims, crossclaims, counterclaims, or third-party claims. When ordering a separate trial, the court must preserve any federal right to a jury trial.[4]

A federal judge would determine whether it would be more convenient to try both claims in one trial or if a single trial would result in inconvenience, prejudice, or inefficiencies. The court has discretion to try together or separately claims that have been brought in a single civil action pursuant to Rule 18.[5]

C. JOINDER THAT IS PERMISSIVE UNDER RULE 18 MAY BE MANDATORY UNDER COMMON LAW CLAIM PRECLUSION

The operative verb in Rule 18(a) is "may." That Rule thus does not require a claimant (plaintiff or defendant) to join multiple claims against an opposing party in a single civil action. However, as we will see in Chapter 14, to the extent that these multiple claims arise from the same transaction or occurrence, the common law doctrine of claim preclusion may require that all claims be raised in the same action. *See Restatement (Second) of Judgments* §§ 17–19; 24.

VI. CONCLUSION

As noted at the beginning of this chapter, Rule 1 of the Federal Rules of Civil Procedure envisions the "just, speedy, and inexpensive determination of every action." One of the ways in which the multiple claims of individual parties, and the claims of multiple parties, can be so resolved is by consolidating claims and parties within a single action. In structuring her action, the lawyer therefore must be sure to consider whether she may, or must, bring multiple parties and claims together in that single action.

---

[4] While Rule 42(b) allows a district court to order separate trials of issues or claims that may have been brought in a single action, Rule 42(a) gives the court discretion to consolidate the trial of matters involving a common question even though those matters have been asserted in separate actions:

> If actions before the court involve a common question of law or fact, the court may:
>> (1) join for hearing or trial any or all matters at issue in the actions;
>> (2) consolidate the actions; or
>> (3) issue any other orders to avoid unnecessary cost or delay.

[5] As Professor Edson Sunderland, a member of the Advisory Committee that drafted the Federal Rules, stated:

> [The Federal Rules] proceed upon the theory that no inconvenience can result from the joinder of any two or more matters in the pleadings, but only from trying two or more matters together which have little or nothing in common. They therefore permit the joinder of practically anything, and the court is allowed in its discretion to make an order for the separate trial of any matters which can be more conveniently tried that way.

Sunderland, "The New Federal Rules," 45 *W.Va.L.Quarterly* 5, 13 (1938).

VII. CHAPTER ASSESSMENT

A. Multiple-Choice Questions. Answer the following questions, reviewing the sections of the chapter noted in connection with each question.

1. Due to improper maintenance, a plane operated by an airline company had to be removed from service, resulting in a flight cancellation for the 37 passengers on that flight. In addition, because the plane had to be withheld from service for the remainder of the day, another 17 passengers on 4 other routes could not reach their destinations on schedule.

Passengers from the four flights contact a lawyer seeking to file claims against the airline. Assuming that the prerequisites to suit otherwise are satisfied, can (or must) these claims be filed against the airline in a single federal civil action?

Review Section II and choose the best answer from the following choices:

(a) Plaintiffs may join their claims together in a single federal action.

(b) Plaintiffs must join their claims together in a single federal action.

(c) Plaintiffs cannot join their claims together in a single federal action.

(d) Plaintiffs may join their claims together in a single federal action, but the court is not required to try their claims together in a single trial.

2. Four citizens of State A own lake-front property in State A. In between these four properties is a lot owned by a citizen of State B. The four State A citizens file a federal diversity action against a company that is incorporated and has its principal place of business in State B. Plaintiffs in this diversity action claim that discharges from the company have resulted in pollution of their property. They seek extensive changes in this company's manufacturing processes, which the company contends will lead to more, rather than less, pollution discharge onto their properties. The State B lot owner does not join the civil action.

Soon after the filing of the complaint, the company files a Rule 12(b)(7) motion to dismiss the action due to the failure to join the State B landowner as a required party plaintiff.

Review Section II and choose the best answer from the following choices:

(a) The State B landowner need not be joined to the action.

(b) The State B landowner must be joined to the action.

(c)   The State B landowner cannot be joined to the action, and the action should be dismissed.

(d)   The State B landowner cannot be joined to the action, and the action should proceed among the existing parties.

3.   An insured man dies with a $10,000 insurance policy naming "my wife" as his beneficiary. The insurance company is headquartered in Delaware with its principal place of business in New Jersey. The company is contacted by both the insured's wife at the time of his death and his wife at the time that the insurance policy was written. The insurance company is concerned that, if it pays either the first wife, a citizen of California, or the second wife, a citizen of Nevada, the other claimant will bring suit against the company.

Review Section III and choose the best answer from the following choices:

(a)   The company can file an interpleader action in federal court pursuant to the federal interpleader statute.

(b)   The company can file an interpleader action in federal court pursuant to Rule 22 of the Federal Rules of Civil Procedure.

(c)   The company can file an interpleader action in federal court pursuant to both the federal interpleader statute and Rule 22.

(d)   The company can file an interpleader action in federal court pursuant to neither the federal interpleader statute nor Rule 22.

4.   A local grocery store is sued in federal court by the store's unionized employees. The employees assert violations of federal food and labor laws. The store is a franchise of a national grocery corporation, which supplies 50 other franchise groceries across the country. These franchise stores are all treated in the same manner by the national corporation, and they are expected to adopt the food and labor policies specified by the national corporation.

The national grocery corporation is not named as a defendant in the federal action, but seeks to intervene as a defendant in that action. The national corporation argues in its motion to intervene that its motion should be granted because "an adverse judgment in this action could be much more damaging, financially and otherwise, to the national corporation than to a single local grocery franchise."

Review Section IV and choose the best answer from the following choices:

(a)   The corporation has the right to intervene.

(b)   The corporation does not have the right to intervene.

(c)   The corporation can only be permitted to intervene if the existing parties agree to such intervention.

(d)   The corporation can only be permitted to intervene if it is given such a right by a federal statute.

5.   A car and a truck are in an accident, which results in the destruction of the car and serious injury to the car's driver. The driver of the car (a citizen of Tennessee) brings a federal diversity action against the trucking company (incorporated and with its principal place of business in Kentucky), which results in a $100,000 judgment for the driver's personal injuries.

The driver then brings a second federal diversity action against the trucking company, seeking $50,000 in damages due to the destruction of the car and $20,000 for the destruction of a painting that was in the front seat of the car.

Review Section V and choose the best answer from the following choices:

(a) The Federal Rules permit these two claims to be brought together in the second action.

(b) The Federal Rules require these two claims to be brought together in the second action.

(c) The Federal Rules do not permit these two claims to be brought together in the second action.

(d) The Federal Rules permit these two claims to be brought together in the second action, but the court must dismiss the second action.

B.   Essay Questions. To test your understanding of this chapter's material, outline or write an answer to the following questions.

1.   Whose Money Is This Anyway?

Two brothers, Gopher (a citizen of Minnesota) and Badger (a citizen of Wisconsin) open an account in a bank incorporated, and with its principal place of business, in Wisconsin. Gopher brings a federal diversity action against the bank. In this action Gopher alleges that, although he presented the bank with a notarized document in which Badger gave his rights in the account to Gopher, the bank refused to pay Gopher the $150,000 in the account. In its answer in the federal action, the bank asserts that Badger has told the bank that he still retains a one-half interest in the account.

(a) Should Badger be joined as a party to Gopher's action if feasible?

(b) Is it feasible to join Badger to this action?

(c) If Badger cannot be joined as a party to Gopher's action, should Gopher's action continue without Badger?

(d) Is there a way for the bank to receive a judicial determination as to the ownership rights of both Gopher and Badger to the account?

2.   We Want Our Painting Back!

Several decades ago, the parents of Alex and Alyssa loaned a painting valued at $500,000 to a museum in a nearby state. The parents are now deceased, and Alyssa recently learned that the museum was no longer displaying the painting. She filed a diversity action in federal court against the museum. Alyssa is a citizen of Georgia, and the museum is a citizen of North Carolina. Alyssa asserts three claims in her complaint:

(1) a claim seeking the return of the painting to her, because the museum has violated the terms of the contract with her parents by not displaying the painting;

(2) a claim seeking $50,000 in damages, because the museum has violated the terms of the contract with her parents by not properly caring for the painting; and

(3) a claim seeking return of another painting—valued at $50,000—that Alyssa owns, because the museum has not invited local schools to special showings of the painting as provided in the contract by which the museum borrowed the painting from Alyssa.

Alex, a citizen of Georgia, learns about Alyssa's civil action against the museum and seeks to intervene as a plaintiff in Alyssa's action, claiming that the painting should be returned to her, rather than to Alyssa.

(a) Can the court hear Alyssa's second claim (for $50,000 in damages, because the museum has violated the terms of the contract with Alyssa's parents by not properly caring for the painting)?

(b) Can the court hear Alyssa's third claim (seeking the return of Alyssa's painting valued at $50,000)?

(c) Can Alex intervene as a plaintiff in Alyssa's action against the museum?

(d) Could Alex intervene as a plaintiff in Alyssa's action if she were a citizen of North Carolina?

CHAPTER 7

CLASS ACTIONS: "IF TWO'S A COUPLE AND THREE'S A CROWD, WHAT'S A CLASS?"

I. INTRODUCTION

As you have seen from the discussion of party joinder, claim joinder, intervention, and interpleader in the previous chapter, there are reasons why different people may want to bring their claims in a single civil action. If a company has polluted the stream that flows along my backyard and the backyards of my neighbors, we may want to bring a single civil action to challenge the company's actions. Litigation can be expensive, and by bringing one action, the property owners can share the expenses of an attorney and other litigation costs. By banding together in this fashion, plaintiffs also may have more power to gain relief from the company—both in the civil action and beyond. A class action is the procedural device that, in the words of Rule 23(a), allows one or more members of a class of people to "sue or be sued as representative parties on behalf of all members" of that class.

There also can be advantages to the judicial system from allowing people to aggregate individual claims into a single civil action. As the second sentence of Rule 1 of the Federal Rules of Civil Procedure provides, the Rules "should be construed, administered, and employed by the court and the parties to secure the just, speedy, and inexpensive determination of every action and proceeding." Class actions can further all three of the goals of Rule 1: justice, speed, and efficiency.

If the goal of the civil justice system is to facilitate the vindication of civil injuries, class actions can be the procedural vehicle for achieving such justice. There are situations in which people are injured, but the amount of injury is so small that there is no economic incentive to pursue an individual civil action to attempt to right the alleged wrong. For instance, if a credit card company illegally rounded up consumer interest charges to the nearest dollar, it would be infeasible as a practical matter for a single consumer to take on the burden, economically and personally, to bring an action against the company. But if millions of consumers suffered the same alleged injury and could aggregate their claims, the injury might be redressed and the challenged conduct ended. Thus justice for consumers in such a situation might be achieved by a negative value class action—an action that, because of the small amount at issue for any individual, would never be brought unless many individual claims could be aggregated into a class action.[1]

When hundreds, thousands, or millions of people sustain an injury, the resulting claims may be resolved with greater speed through a class action. There are many procedural requirements for a class action, and satisfying all these requirements may delay the resolution of any particular claim. However, aggregate adjudication or settlement of a great number of claims may more quickly resolve the entirety of the many disputes.

In addition to resolving a great number of related claims in a more just and speedy fashion, a class action may lessen the expense of bringing hundreds or thousands of individual claims. If an attorney provides representation for an entire class of claimants, the expense to any single claimant will be significantly less than if each person had to pay his or her own attorney to handle claims individually. There also may be a great savings for the court system if a single judge can conclude the claims of thousands of individuals, rather than require many judges to handle many individual actions. The goals of Rule 1— justice, speed, and efficiency—all may be furthered by class action treatment of claims in appropriate situations.

The question then becomes, in what situations is class action treatment appropriate? Similar to deciding whether personal jurisdiction is appropriate, separate determinations must be made as to whether constitutional, statutory, and rule requirements have been satisfied. Initially, the lawyer must decide whether a class action comports with constitutional due process. Then specific statutory requirements must be met for a class action to be heard in federal court. These federal requirements are considered in the next section of this chapter. But even if constitutional and statutory requirements are met, a class action only can be certified in federal court if the requirements of Rule 23 of the Federal Rules of Civil Procedure are met. These requirements are discussed in Section III of this chapter.

Class actions permit the assertion of claims that otherwise would not, as a practical matter, be brought absent the possibility of class action treatment. There is thus robust legal and political debate about the appropriate use of class actions, some of which is evident in the following opinions. Class actions place attorneys in a unique position, typically representing individual class members whom they have never met, and these litigation realities also are considered in this chapter. Finally, Section V of this chapter discusses the increasing use of private

---

[1] Certification of a class action also might prevent a civil action from becoming moot before final judgment can be rendered. Assume, for instance, that a high school senior wants to challenge his school's policy forbidding students from bringing same-sex partners to the high school prom. If he graduates from high school before the court rules, his action could be dismissed as moot. However, by certifying the case as a class action, the mootness problem would be solved if the class that is certified contains additional students (some of whom will not graduate until after the court can rule).

contracts to preclude class actions—in both the courts and in private arbitration.

While entire treatises and textbooks are written on class actions, this chapter should give you a sense of the general contours of, and debate concerning, federal class action law and practice.

II. CONSTITUTIONAL AND STATUTORY CLASS ACTION REQUIREMENTS

In order for a court to entertain a class action, constitutional due process and class action requirements imposed by statute and rule must be met. These separate sets of class action requirements are considered in turn.

A. THE CONSTITUTIONAL REQUIREMENTS OF ADEQUATE REPRESENTATION AND NOTICE

The Due Process Clause of the Fourteenth Amendment of the United States Constitution provides that no State shall "deprive any person of life, liberty, or property, without due process of law." The Supreme Court has interpreted this to mean (1) that individuals cannot be bound by a class-action judgment unless they were adequately represented in that action and, (2) with respect to most class actions, that class members received notice of the action and an opportunity to participate in or opt out of that action.

1. ADEQUACY OF REPRESENTATION: *HANSBERRY V. LEE*

In contrast to the parties in individual litigation, most class members in class actions do not themselves participate in those class actions. Regardless of the state or federal rules governing a class action, one must be either a participant in the action himself or be adequately represented by a party to the action. While Federal Rule of Civil Procedure 23(a)(4) requires that the representative parties "fairly and adequately protect the interests of the class," the Due Process Clauses of the Fifth and Fourteenth Amendments also have been held to require adequacy of representation. The leading case imposing such a constitutional requirement follows.

Hansberry v. Lee
United States Supreme Court, 1940
311 U.S. 32

OPINION

■ MR. JUSTICE STONE delivered the opinion of the Court.

The question is whether the Supreme Court of Illinois, by its adjudication that petitioners in this case are bound by a judgment rendered in an earlier litigation to which they were not parties, has deprived them of the due process of law guaranteed by the Fourteenth Amendment.

Respondents brought this suit in the Circuit Court of Cook County, Illinois, to enjoin the breach by petitioners of an agreement restricting the use of land within a described area of the City of Chicago, which was alleged to have been entered into by some five hundred of the land owners. The agreement stipulated that for a specified period no part of the land should be "sold, leased to or permitted to be occupied by any person of the colored race", and provided that it should not be effective unless signed by the "owners of 95 per centum of the frontage" within the described area. The bill of complaint set up that the owners of 95 per cent of the frontage had signed; that respondents are owners of land within the restricted area who have either signed the agreement or acquired their land from others who did sign and that petitioners Hansberry, who are Negroes, have, with the alleged aid of the other petitioners and with knowledge of the agreement, acquired and are occupying land in the restricted area formerly belonging to an owner who had signed the agreement.

To the defense that the agreement had never become effective because owners of 95 per cent of the frontage had not signed it, respondents pleaded that that issue was res judicata by the decree in an earlier suit. *Burke v. Kleiman*, 277 Ill.App. 519. To this petitioners pleaded, by way of rejoinder, that they were not parties to that suit or bound by its decree, and that denial of their right to litigate, in the present suit, the issue of performance of the condition precedent to the validity of the agreement would be a denial of due process of law guaranteed by the Fourteenth Amendment. It does not appear, nor is it contended that any of petitioners is the successor in interest to or in privity with any of the parties in the earlier suit.

The circuit court, after a trial on the merits, found that owners of only about 54 per cent of the frontage had signed the agreement, and that the only support of the judgment in the *Burke* case was a false and fraudulent stipulation of the parties that 95 per cent had signed. But it ruled that the issue of performance of the condition precedent to the validity of the agreement was res judicata as alleged and entered a decree for respondents. The Supreme Court of Illinois affirmed. We granted certiorari to resolve the constitutional question.

The Supreme Court of Illinois, upon an examination of the record in *Burke v. Kleiman*, found that that suit, in the Superior Court of Cook County, was brought by a landowner in the restricted area to enforce the agreement which had been signed by her predecessor in title, in behalf of herself and other property owners in like situation, against four named individuals who had acquired or asserted an interest in a plot of land formerly owned by another signer of the agreement; that upon stipulation of the parties in that suit that the agreement had been signed by owners of 95 per cent of all the frontage, the court had adjudged that the agreement was in force, that it was a covenant running with the land and binding all the land within the described area in the hands of the parties to the agreement and those claiming under them including defendants, and had entered its decree restraining the breach of the agreement by the defendants and those claiming under them, and that the appellate court had affirmed the decree. It found that the stipulation was untrue but held, contrary to the trial court, that it was not fraudulent or collusive. It also appears from the record in *Burke v. Kleiman* that the case was tried on an agreed statement of facts which raised only a single issue, whether by reason of changes in the restricted area, the agreement had ceased to be enforcible in equity.

From this the Supreme Court of Illinois concluded in the present case that *Burke v. Kleiman* was a "class" or ' "representative" suit and that in such a suit "where the remedy is pursued by a plaintiff who has the right to represent the class to which he belongs, other members of the class are bound by the results in the case unless it is reversed or set aside on direct proceedings"; that petitioners in the present suit were members of the class represented by the plaintiffs in the earlier suit and consequently were bound by its decree which had rendered the issue of performance of the condition precedent to the restrictive agreement res judicata, so far as petitioners are concerned. The court thought that the circumstance that the stipulation in the earlier suit that owners of 95 per cent of the frontage had signed the agreement was contrary to the fact as found in the present suit did not militate against this conclusion since the court in the earlier suit had jurisdiction to determine the fact as between the parties before it and that its determination, because of the representative character of the suit, even though erroneous, was binding on petitioners until set aside by a direct attack on the first judgment.

State courts are free to attach such descriptive labels to litigations before them as they may choose and to attribute to them such consequences as they think appropriate under state constitutions and laws, subject only to the requirements of the Constitution of the United States. But when the judgment of a state court, ascribing to the judgment of another court the binding force and effect of res judicata, is challenged for want of due process it becomes the duty of this Court to examine the course of procedure in both litigations to ascertain whether the litigant whose rights have thus been adjudicated has been afforded such notice and opportunity to be heard as are requisite to the due process which the Constitution prescribes.

It is a principle of general application in Anglo-American jurisprudence that one is not bound by a judgment in personam in a litigation in which he is not designated as a party or to which he has not been made a party by service of process. *Pennoyer v. Neff*, 95 U.S.

714. A judgment rendered in such circumstances is not entitled to the full faith and credit which the Constitution and statute of the United States, R.S. s 905, 28 U.S.C. s 687 [now 28 U.S.C. § 1738], prescribe, *Pennoyer v. Neff,* and judicial action enforcing it against the person or property of the absent party is not that due process which the Fifth and Fourteenth Amendments requires.

To these general rules there is a recognized exception that, to an extent not precisely defined by judicial opinion, the judgment in a "class" or "representative" suit, to which some members of the class are parties, may bind members of the class or those represented who were not made parties to it.

The class suit was an invention of equity to enable it to proceed to a decree in suits where the number of those interested in the subject of the litigation is so great that their joinder as parties in conformity to the usual rules of procedure is impracticable. Courts are not infrequently called upon to proceed with causes in which the number of those interested in the litigation is so great as to make difficult or impossible the joinder of all because some are not within the jurisdiction or because their whereabouts is unknown or where if all were made parties to the suit its continued abatement by the death of some would prevent or unduly delay a decree. In such cases where the interests of those not joined are of the same class as the interests of those who are, and where it is considered that the latter fairly represent the former in the prosecution of the litigation of the issues in which all have a common interest, the court will proceed to a decree.

It is evident that the considerations which may induce a court thus to proceed, despite a technical defect of parties, may differ from those which must be taken into account in determining whether the absent parties are bound by the decree or, if it is adjudged that they are, in ascertaining whether such an adjudication satisfies the requirements of due process and of full faith and credit. Nevertheless there is scope within the framework of the Constitution for holding in appropriate cases that a judgment rendered in a class suit is res judicata as to members of the class who are not formal parties to the suit. Here, as elsewhere, the Fourteenth Amendment does not compel state courts or legislatures to adopt any particular rule for establishing the conclusiveness of judgments in class suits; nor does it compel the adoption of the particular rules thought by this court to be appropriate for the federal courts. With a proper regard for divergent local institutions and interests, this Court is justified in saying that there has been a failure of due process only in those cases where it cannot be said that the procedure adopted, fairly insures the protection of the interests of absent parties who are to be bound by it.

It is familiar doctrine of the federal courts that members of a class not present as parties to the litigation may be bound by the judgment where they are in fact adequately represented by parties who are present, or where they actually participate in the conduct of the litigation in which members of the class are present as parties, or where the interest of the members of the class, some of whom are present as parties, is joint, or where for any other reason the relationship between the parties present and those who are absent is such as legally to entitle the former to stand in judgment for the latter.

In all such cases, so far as it can be said that the members of the class who are present are, by generally recognized rules of law, entitled to stand in judgment for those who are not, we may assume for present purposes that such procedure affords a protection to the parties who are represented though absent, which would satisfy the requirements of due process and full faith and credit. Nor do we find it necessary for the decision of this case to say that, when the only circumstance defining the class is that the determination of the rights of its members turns upon a single issue of fact or law, a state could not constitutionally adopt a procedure whereby some of the members of the class could stand in judgment for all, provided that the procedure were so devised and applied as to insure that those present are of the same class as those absent and that the litigation is so conducted as to insure the full and fair consideration of the common issue. We decide only that the procedure and the course of litigation sustained here by the plea of res judicata do not satisfy these requirements.

The restrictive agreement did not purport to create a joint obligation or liability. I[f] valid and effective its promises were the several obligations of the signers and those claiming under them. The promises ran severally to every other signer. It is plain that in such circumstances all those alleged to be bound by the agreement would not constitute a single class in any litigation brought to enforce it. Those who sought to secure its benefits by enforcing it could not be said to be in the same class with or represent those whose interest was in resisting performance, for the agreement by its terms imposes obligations and confers rights on the owner of each plot of land who signs it. If those who thus seek to secure the benefits of the agreement were rightly regarded by the state Supreme Court as constituting a class, it is evident that those signers or their successors who are interested in challenging the validity of the agreement and resisting its performance are not of the same class in the sense that their interests are identical so that any group who had elected to enforce rights conferred by the agreement could be said to be acting in the interest of any others who were free to deny its obligation.

Because of the dual and potentially conflicting interests of those who are putative parties to the agreement in compelling or resisting its performance, it is impossible to say, solely because they are parties to it, that any two of them are of the same class. Nor without more, and with the due regard for the protection of the rights of absent parties which due process exacts, can some be permitted to stand in judgment for all.

It is one thing to say that some members of a class may represent other members in a litigation where the sole and common interest of the class in the litigation, is either to assert a common right or to challenge an asserted obligation. It is quite another to hold that all those who are free alternatively either to assert rights or to challenge them are of a single class, so that any group merely because it is of the class so constituted, may be deemed adequately to represent any others of the class in litigating their interests in either alternative. Such a selection of representatives for purposes of litigation, whose substantial interests are not necessarily or even probably the same as those whom they are deemed to represent, does not afford that protection to absent parties which due process requires. The doctrine of representation of absent parties in a class suit has not hitherto been thought to go so far. * * *

The plaintiffs in the *Burke* case sought to compel performance of the agreement in behalf of themselves and all others similarly situated. They did not designate the defendants in the suit as a class or seek any injunction or other relief against others than the named defendants, and the decree which was entered did not purport to bind others. In seeking to enforce the agreement the plaintiffs in that suit were not representing the petitioners here whose substantial interest is in resisting performance. The defendants in the first suit were not treated by the pleadings or decree as representing others or as foreclosing by their defense the rights of others, and even though nominal defendants, it does not appear that their interest in defeating the contract outweighed their interest in establishing its validity. For a court in this situation to ascribe to either the plaintiffs or defendants the performance of such functions on behalf of petitioners here, is to attribute to them a power that it cannot be said that they had assumed to exercise, and a responsibility which, in view of their dual interests it does not appear that they could rightly discharge.

Reversed.

■ MR. JUSTICE MCREYNOLDS, MR. JUSTICE ROBERTS and MR. JUSTICE REED concur in the result.

QUESTIONS AND COMMENTS CONCERNING *HANSBERRY V. LEE*

1.   There were two separate Illinois state court actions at issue in *Hansberry*. The first of these actions, *Burke v. Kleiman*, was filed by Olive Burke against Isaac Kleiman and others to prevent the rental of an apartment in Washington Park to Dr. James Hall. Olive Burke brought her action on behalf of herself and other neighborhood property owners, and, based upon a stipulation that more than 95% of the property owners had signed the restrictive covenant, the court entered judgment upholding the covenant. This judgment then was affirmed by the Illinois Supreme Court.

When the Hansberrys later purchased their home in Washington Park, Anna Lee and others living near the Hansberry's new home brought an action in Cook County Circuit Court. Among the defendants were Carl and Nannie Hansberry (wife of Carl Hansberry) and James Burke (Olive Burke's husband, who was the real estate broker who sold the Hansberrys their new home). Judge George Bristow held that the defendants were included in the plaintiff class in *Burke v. Kleiman*, in which the court concluded that 95% of the property owners had signed the restrictive covenant and entered judgment for Lee and the other plaintiffs. The Illinois Supreme Court affirmed this judgment, stating: "The principle of res judicata [or claim preclusion] covers wrong as well as right decisions, for the fundamental reason that there must be an end to litigation." *Lee v. Hansberry*, 372 Ill. 369, 373–74 (1939). This is the decision that is considered by the United States Supreme Court in *Hansberry v. Lee*.

For much more of the background, context, and significance of *Hansberry* see Kamp, "The History Behind *Hansberry v. Lee*," 20 *U. C. Davis L. Rev.* 481 (1987); Tidmarsh, "The Story of *Hansberry*: The Rise of the Modern Class Action," in *Civil Procedure Stories* 233 (K. Clermont ed., 2nd ed. 2008).

2.   How does the United States Supreme Court obtain jurisdiction over this case, which involves two Illinois civil actions and the Illinois law of respect for judgments?

3.   Justice Stone states as a "principle of general application in Anglo-American jurisprudence that one is not bound by a judgment in personam in a litigation in which he is not designated as a party or to which he has not been made a party by service of process." Where have we seen that principle first enunciated? Although this may be a "principle of general application," what is the "recognized exception" to this principle noted by Justice Stone?

4.   Justice Stone refers to *Burke v. Kleiman* as a "'class' or 'representative' suit." Does this description summarize the major holding of the case: in order to be a constitutional "class" or "representative" suit, the class representative must actually and adequately represent the other class members? Why was that not the case in this particular litigation?

5.   Is there any way in which the Hansberrys could have been bound by a valid and final judgment on the merits in *Burke v. Kleiman*?

6.   The Illinois Supreme Court held that, even though the stipulation in the first case (*Burke v. Kleiman*) that 95% of the landowners had signed the restrictive covenant was untrue, it still bound the parties in the second action (*Hansberry v. Lee*). If bound to this conclusion in a second action, do class members have any way in which to challenge such an erroneous finding or conclusion?

7.   It was not until 1948 that the Supreme Court held in *Shelley v. Kraemer*, 334 U.S. 1 (1948), that it was a violation of Fourteenth Amendment equal protection for a state court to enforce a racially restrictive covenant.

8.   Loraine Hansberry was the daughter of defendants Carl and Nannie Hansberry. Her play, *A Raisin in the Sun*, was based upon the litigation that culminated in *Hansberry v. Lee*, and it was the first play written by an African-American woman to be produced on Broadway. Loraine Hansberry had this to say about *Hansberry v. Lee*:

> My father * * * spent a small personal fortune, his considerable talents, and many years of his life fighting, in association with the NAACP attorneys, Chicago's "restrictive covenants" in one of this nation's ugliest ghettoes.
>
> That fight also required that our family occupy the disputed property in a hellishly hostile "white neighborhood" in which literally howling mobs surrounded our house. * * * My memories of this "correct" way of fighting white supremacy in America include being spat at, cursed and pummeled in the daily trek to and from school. And I also remember my desperate and courageous mother, patrolling our household all night with a loaded German lugar, doggedly guarding her four children, while my father fought the respectable part of the battle in the Washington court.

L. Hansberry, *To Be Young, Gifted and Black: Lorraine Hansberry in Her Own Words* 20–21 (adapted by R. Nemeroff 1969).

2.   NOTICE AND OPPORTUNITY TO PARTICIPATE IN, OR OPT OUT OF, THE CLASS

Hansberry v. Lee requires that, in order to be bound by a class-action judgment, a class member must be adequately represented in the class action. In addition to this constitutional due process requirement recognized in *Hansberry*, Federal Rule of Civil Procedure 23(a)(4) requires that, in a federal class action, "the representative parties will fairly and adequately protect the interests of the class."

Are there additional constitutional protections that must be afforded the members of a plaintiffs' class action?[2] In *Phillips Petroleum Co. v. Shutts*, 472 U.S. 797 (1985), the Supreme Court held that, in addition to the constitutional requirement that class members be adequately represented in the action:

(1)   the plaintiff must receive notice;

(2)   plus an opportunity to be heard and participate in the litigation, whether in person or through counsel; and

(3)   be provided with an opportunity to remove himself from the class by executing and returning an "opt out" or "request for exclusion" form to the court.

---

[2]   Defendant class actions also are possible, but these are much rarer creatures than plaintiff class actions. In defendant class actions, the same constitutional and Rule 23 protections apply as in the plaintiff classes in *Hansberry* and *Shutts*.

472 U.S. at 812. Apart from this constitutional requirement, Rule 23(c)(2)(B) requires such notice in Rule 23(b)(3) class actions, in which class certification is sought because common questions of law or fact predominate over questions affecting only individual class members.

While the holding of *Shutts* is clear, defendant Phillips Petroleum made a novel argument that the Supreme Court did not accept. Phillips argued that, because members of the plaintiff class stood to lose their claims if the class action was unsuccessful, the Due Process Clause required that class members without minimum contacts with the forum state could not be bound by the class judgment unless they had "opted in" to the action. Why are a plaintiff's, as opposed to a defendant's, forum contacts not an issue in non-class actions? What would the implications be if the Supreme Court had accepted defendants' argument in *Shutts*?

In rejecting Phillips' argument that class members without minimum state contacts could not be bound through an "opt out" procedure, the Supreme Court reasoned as follows:

> Because States place fewer burdens upon absent class plaintiffs than they do upon absent defendants in nonclass suits, the Due Process Clause need not and does not afford the former as much protection from state-court jurisdiction as it does the latter. The Fourteenth Amendment does protect "persons," not "defendants," however, so absent plaintiffs as well as absent defendants are entitled to some protection from the jurisdiction of a forum State which seeks to adjudicate their claims. In this case we hold that a forum State may exercise jurisdiction over the claim of an absent class-action plaintiff, even though that plaintiff may not possess the minimum contacts with the forum which would support personal jurisdiction over a defendant. If the forum State wishes to bind an absent plaintiff concerning a claim for money damages or similar relief at law, it must provide minimal procedural due process protection. The plaintiff must receive notice plus an opportunity to be heard and participate in the litigation, whether in person or through counsel. The notice must be the best practicable, "reasonably calculated, under all the circumstances, to apprise interested parties of the pendency of the action and afford them an opportunity to present their objections." *Mullane*, 339 U.S., at 314–315. The notice should describe the action and the plaintiffs' rights in it. Additionally, we hold that due process requires at a minimum that an absent plaintiff be provided with an opportunity to remove himself from the class by executing and returning an "opt out" or "request for exclusion" form to the court. Finally, the Due Process Clause of course requires that the named

plaintiff at all times adequately represent the interests of the absent class members. *Hansberry*, 311 U.S., at 42–43, 45.

We reject petitioner's contention that the Due Process Clause of the Fourteenth Amendment requires that absent plaintiffs affirmatively "opt in" to the class, rather than be deemed members of the class if they do not "opt out." * * *

We think that the procedure followed by Kansas, where a fully descriptive notice is sent first-class mail to each class member, with an explanation of the right to "opt out," satisfies due process. Requiring a plaintiff to affirmatively request inclusion would probably impede the prosecution of those class actions involving an aggregation of small individual claims, where a large number of claims are required to make it economical to bring suit. * * *

In this case over 3,400 members of the potential class did "opt out," which belies the contention that "opt out" procedures result in guaranteed jurisdiction by inertia. Another 1,500 were excluded because the notice and "opt out" form was undeliverable. We think that such results show that the "opt out" procedure provided by Kansas is by no means pro forma, and that the Constitution does not require more to protect what must be the somewhat rare species of class member who is unwilling to execute an "opt out" form, but whose claim is nonetheless so important that he cannot be presumed to consent to being a member of the class by his failure to do so. * * *

We therefore hold that the protection afforded the plaintiff class members by the Kansas statute satisfies the Due Process Clause. The interests of the absent plaintiffs are sufficiently protected by the forum State when those plaintiffs are provided with a request for exclusion that can be returned within a reasonable time to the court. Both the Kansas trial court and the Supreme Court of Kansas held that the class received adequate representation, and no party disputes that conclusion here. We conclude that the Kansas court properly asserted personal jurisdiction over the absent plaintiffs and their claims against petitioner.

Phillips Petroleum Co. v. Shutts, 472 U.S. 797, 811–14 (1985).

In addition to the constitutional due process requirement that class members receive notice, an opportunity to participate in the class action, and the opportunity to opt out of the class action, Rule 23(c)(2)(B) requires that the same notice and opportunities to participate and opt out be provided in Rule 23(b)(3) class actions.

B. SUBJECT-MATTER JURISDICTION FOR FEDERAL CLASS ACTIONS

As with any civil action, a class action only can be entertained by a federal court if there is a statutory grant of subject-matter jurisdiction for the court to entertain that action. This requirement is easily met for class actions raising federal questions, with 28 U.S.C. § 1331 providing the basis of subject-matter jurisdiction (with no required minimum amount in controversy) just as it does with respect to individual federal question actions. Things become a bit more complicated with respect to federal diversity actions, which typically require more than $75,000 in controversy and complete diversity among the parties.

1. Complete Diversity. In a brief opinion by Chief Justice John Marshall, the Supreme Court held in *Strawbridge v. Curtiss*, 7 U.S. 267 (1806), that complete diversity was required under the federal diversity statute. Thus none of the plaintiffs in a diversity action can be a citizen of the same state as any defendant. If, for instance, 50 Massachusetts citizens and 1 Pennsylvania citizen sued 50 Ohio citizens and 1 Pennsylvania citizen, there would not be the complete diversity required by 28 U.S.C. § 1332(a). However, as the Supreme Court noted in *State Farm Fire & Cas. Co. v. Tashire*, 386 U.S. 523, 531 (1967), *Strawbridge* construed only the federal diversity statute and not the Article III constitutional judicial power. Thus "Article III poses no obstacle to the legislative extension of federal jurisdiction, founded on diversity, so long as any two adverse parties are not co-citizens." *Id.*

If the complete diversity requirement of *Strawbridge v. Curtiss* were employed inflexibly to class actions, it would be difficult to obtain federal diversity jurisdiction over many large nationwide class actions. However, the Court in *Supreme Tribe of Ben Hur v. Cauble*, 255 U.S. 356 (1921), upheld diversity jurisdiction in a class action brought by non-Indiana citizens against an Indiana association—even though there were many Indiana citizens in the class. By not naming as a class representative a citizen of the same state as that of any defendant, the Court held that the diversity required by Section 1332(a) was satisfied. So, in the hypothetical in the prior paragraph, diversity could be created for a class action merely by not naming the citizen of Pennsylvania as a representative plaintiff.

2. Amount in Controversy. Having thus addressed the question of diversity of citizenship, an issue still exists in many class actions as to the satisfaction of the $75,000 + minimum amount in controversy required by 28 U.S.C. § 1332(a). In fact, many class actions are filed because no single individual has suffered major losses, but many hundreds or thousands of individuals have been injured. Assume, for instance, an action in which a class of 100,000 consumers allege that they all suffered injury of $100 due to a merchant's refusal to honor certificates mailed to them. While none of the individual class members suffered damages of more than $75,000, the **total** damages alleged by the class is quite a bit more than $75,000. Such class actions were considered by the Supreme Court in *Snyder v. Harris*, 394 U.S. 332 (1969), in which the Court held that Section 1332(a) did not permit class members to aggregate their individual damages to satisfy the required amount in controversy.

Several years later, the Court considered a class action in which the four named class representatives asserted claims for more than the required amount in controversy, but attempted to represent a class containing persons who could not themselves satisfy the minimum amount in controversy. *Zahn v. International Paper Co.* 414 U.S. 291 (1973). Over a dissent by Justices Brennan, Douglas, and Marshall that the Court should follow the path it took in *Supreme Tribe of Ben Hur* and consider only the representative parties in determining satisfaction of the amount in controversy, the Court held that every class member individually must satisfy the amount in controversy under 28 U.S.C. § 1332(a).

3. **Supplemental Jurisdiction.** As you learned in Chapter 3, Congress in 1990 extended federal statutory jurisdiction to recognize supplemental jurisdiction in 28 U.S.C. § 1367. The Supreme Court considered the extent to which Section 1367 modified subject-matter jurisdiction over diversity class actions in *Exxon Mobil Corp. v. Allapattah Services, Inc.*, 545 U.S. 546 (2005), *supra* p. 168. Specifically, the Court held that Section 1367 overruled its decision in *Zahn v. International Paper Co.*, requiring that every member of a class must individually satisfy the amount in controversy requirement of Section 1332(a) for there to be subject-matter jurisdiction over the action. The *Allapattah* Court concluded, 545 U.S. at 566–67, "We hold that § 1367 by its plain text overruled * * * *Zahn* and authorized supplemental jurisdiction over all claims by diverse parties arising out of the same Article III case or controversy, subject only to enumerated exceptions [in 28 U.S.C. § 1367(b)] not applicable in the cases now before us."

4. **Class Action Fairness Act of 2005.** Not only did Congress expand federal subject-matter jurisdiction over class actions with the enactment of the supplemental jurisdiction statute, 28 U.S.C. § 1367, but it further expanded such jurisdiction in the Class Action Fairness Act of 2005, Pub. L. 109–2, 119 Stat. 12 (codified in 28 U.S.C. §§ 1332(d), 1453, 1711–15). Even after the enactment of the Section 1367 supplemental jurisdiction statute, federal diversity jurisdiction would not permit a federal court to hear a class action in which 100,000 consumers alleged they each suffered $100 in damages. While such a class alleges total damages of $10,000,000, no single class member alleges damages in excess of $75,000. By enacting the Class Action Fairness Act ("CAFA"), Congress provided a statutory basis for a federal district court to hear such an action—either as filed originally by the plaintiffs in federal court pursuant to 28 U.S.C. § 1332(d) or

upon removal by a defendant from state to federal court pursuant to 28 U.S.C. § 1453. CAFA provides an additional jurisdictional basis of federal subject-matter jurisdiction over a class action, and actions that satisfy the requirements of CAFA also may satisfy the jurisdictional requirements for a class action of 28 U.S.C. §§ 1331 or 1332 (providing more than one basis for a federal court to consider the proposed class action).

Congress enacted CAFA due to its perception of "numerous problems with our current class action system."[3] Congress was particularly concerned with class action practice in state courts:

> A mounting stack of evidence reviewed by the [Senate Judiciary] Committee demonstrates that abuses are undermining the rights of both plaintiffs and defendants. One key reason for these problems is that most class actions are currently adjudicated in state courts, where the governing rules are applied inconsistently (frequently in a manner that contravenes basic fairness and due process considerations) and where there is often inadequate supervision over litigation procedures and proposed settlements. The problem of inconsistent and inadequate judicial involvement is exacerbated in class actions because the lawyers who bring the lawsuits effectively control the litigation; their clients—the injured class members—typically are not consulted about what they wish to achieve in the litigation and how they wish it to proceed. * * *

> To make matters worse, current law enables lawyers to "game" the procedural rules and keep nationwide or multi-state class actions in state courts whose judges have reputations for readily certifying classes and approving settlements without regard to class member interests. * * * Finally, many state courts freely issue rulings in class action cases that have nationwide ramifications, sometimes overturning well-established laws and policies of other jurisdictions.[4]

To counter perceived difficulties with state-court class actions, Congress enacted CAFA. Not only did CAFA create a federal forum for many class actions that otherwise would be filed in state court, but it permitted a defendant to remove state class actions to federal court. In addition, removal of a class action pursuant to CAFA was made easier than removal of other cases to federal court. 28 U.S.C. § 1453.

In order for a class action to be heard in federal court pursuant to the Class Action Fairness Act, there must be:

---

[3] S. Rep. No. 109–14, at 4 (2005).

[4] *Id.*

(1) a plaintiffs' class action involving at least 100 class members (28 U.S.C. § 1332(d)(5)(B));

(2) the total matter in controversy (for all class members) must "exceed[ ] the sum or value of $5,000,000, exclusive of interest and costs" (28 U.S.C. § 1332(d)(2)); and

(3) at least one plaintiff class member must be a citizen of a state different from that of any defendant—thus minimal, rather than complete, diversity is required (28 U.S.C. § 1332(d)(2)(A)).[5]

Thus all it takes to establish federal subject-matter jurisdiction under CAFA is a 100-member class action with more than $5,000,000 total in controversy and minimal diversity between the plaintiffs and defendant(s). However, in enacting CAFA Congress recognized that there would be cases in which these requirements would be met that most appropriately should be heard in state, rather than federal, court. Section 1332(d)(4)(A), CAFA's "local controversy exception," requires district courts to decline to exercise jurisdiction even though the jurisdictional requirements of CAFA are met. The CAFA Senate report gives an example of one such situation in which district courts are not permitted to exercise subject matter jurisdiction:

A class action is brought in Florida state court against a Florida funeral home regarding alleged wrongdoing in burial practices. Nearly all the plaintiffs live in Florida (about 90 percent). The suit is brought against the cemetery, a Florida corporation, and an out-of-state parent company that was involved in supervising the cemetery. No other class action suits have been filed against the cemetery. This is precisely the type of case for which the Local Controversy Exception was developed. Although there is one out-of-state defendant (the parent company), the controversy is at its core a local one, and the Florida state court where it was brought has a strong interest in resolving the dispute. Thus, this case would remain in state court.[6]

In addition to situations in which district courts "**shall** decline" jurisdiction under 28 U.S.C. § 1332(d)(4), CAFA provides that district courts "**may**, in the interests of justice and looking at the totality of the circumstances," decline to exercise jurisdiction under CAFA even though the requirements of that Act have been met. 28 U.S.C.

---

[5] Minimum diversity sufficient to support jurisdiction under CAFA is also possible if at least one member of the plaintiff class is a foreign state or foreign citizen and a defendant is a citizen of a state, 28 U.S.C. § 1332(d)(2)(B), or at least one member of the plaintiff class is a citizen of a state and a defendant is a foreign state or foreign citizen. 28 U.S.C. § 1332(d)(2)(C).

[6] S. Rep. No. 109–14, at 41 (2005). In addition to Section 1332(d)(4)(A)'s local controversy exception, 28 U.S.C. § 1332(d)(4)(B) provides that a district court shall decline jurisdiction over actions in which "two-thirds or more of the members of all proposed plaintiff classes in the aggregate, and the primary defendants, are citizens of the State in which the action was originally filed."

§ 1332(d)(3). Such discretionary dismissals may be appropriate in actions in which "greater than one-third but less than two-thirds of the members of all proposed plaintiff classes in the aggregate and the primary defendants are citizens of the State in which the action was originally filed." This section of CAFA specifies the factors a district court is to consider in determining whether, in its discretion, it should decline to exercise its subject-matter jurisdiction under CAFA.

Thus not only must all class actions comply with constitutional due process, but there must be a statutory basis for subject-matter jurisdiction for a class action to be considered by a federal court. As we'll see in the next section of this chapter, class actions also must comply with governing procedural rules or statutes. In the federal courts, the governing provision is Rule 23 of the Federal Rules of Civil Procedure.

III. THE REQUIREMENTS OF RULE 23

In addition to meeting the constitutional and statutory requirements for a class action, the action must satisfy the requirements of Rule 23 of the Federal Rules of Civil Procedure or, if the class action is in a state court, that state's class action statutes or rules.[7] Some of the requirements of Rule 23 are the same or similar to the requirements imposed by the Due Process Clause. Thus Rule 23(a)(4) requires that "the representative parties will fairly and adequately protect the interests of the class," just as does the Due Process Clause as interpreted in *Hansberry v. Lee*. In addition, Rule 23(c)(2)(B) requires that class members in Rule 23(b)(3) class actions receive the type of notice contemplated by the Supreme Court in *Phillips Petroleum Co. v. Shutts*. These and other Rule 23 requirements are considered in this section of this chapter.

A. THE RULE 23(a) AND 23(b) REQUIREMENTS

The case that follows, *Wal-Mart Stores, Inc. v. Dukes*, applies and interprets the prerequisites for a class action (set forth in Rule 23(a)) and the different types of class actions (delineated in Rule 23(b)). Initially, Rule 23(a) sets forth the prerequisites for all federal class actions:

> One or more members of a class may sue or be sued as representative parties on behalf of all members only if:
>
> > (1) the class is so numerous that joinder of all members is impracticable;
> >
> > (2) there are questions of law or fact common to the class;

---

[7] The procedural rules in many states mirror the Federal Rules of Civil Procedure and, in particular, Federal Rule of Civil Procedure 23.

(3) the claims or defenses of the representative parties are typical of the claims or defenses of the class; and

(4) the representative parties will fairly and adequately protect the interests of the class.

These requirements of numerosity (Rule 23(a)(1)), commonality (Rule 23(a)(2)), typicality (Rule 23(a)(3)), and adequacy (Rule 23(a)(4)) are discussed in the materials that follow.[8]

Once the named class representatives have established that the class satisfies all four of the Rule 23(a) requirements, those representatives must show that the proposed class action also satisfies the requirements for one or more of the four class actions specified in Rule 23(b). Rule 23(b) provides:

A class action may be maintained if Rule 23(a) is satisfied and if:

(1) prosecuting separate actions by or against individual class members would create a risk of:

(A) inconsistent or varying adjudications with respect to individual class members that would establish incompatible standards of conduct for the party opposing the class, or

(B) adjudications with respect to individual class members that, as a practical matter, would be dispositive of the interests of the other members not parties to the individual adjudications or would substantially impair or impede their ability to protect their interests; or

(2) the party opposing the class has acted or refused to act on grounds that apply generally to the class, so that final injunctive relief or corresponding declaratory relief is appropriate respecting the class as a whole; or

(3) the court finds that the questions of law or fact common to class members predominate over any questions affecting only individual members, and that a class action is superior to other available methods for fairly and efficiently adjudicating the controversy. * * *

---

[8] Although not listed as a Rule 23(a) class certification requirement, some courts have recognized an implicit requirement of "ascertainability" for class certification, so that membership of persons within the class can be determined by an objective standard. Thus in *Astiana v. Ben and Jerry's Homemade, Inc.*, No. C 10–4387 PJH, 2014 WL 60097 (N.D.Cal. Jan. 7, 2014), Judge Phyllis Hamilton denied a class certification motion, in part, because plaintiff had not identified an ascertainable class. Plaintiff's proposed class was brought on behalf of those who had purchased Ben and Jerry's products that had been made with synthetic alkalized cocoa yet were labeled "all natural." While 1 of 15 suppliers to Ben and Jerry's used a synthetic alkalizing agent, there was no way to determine which consumers had purchased this rather than ice cream made with "all natural" alkalizing agents.

These different types of class actions authorized by Rule 23(b) now will be considered in turn.

1. Rule 23(b)(1) Class Actions. The Advisory Committee Note to the 1966 Amendment to Rule 23 explains the rationale for the two types of Rule 23(b)(1) class actions:

> The difficulties which would be likely to arise if resort were had to separate actions by or against the individual members of the class here furnish the reasons for, and the principal key to, the propriety and value of utilizing the class-action device. The considerations stated under clauses (A) and (B) are comparable to certain of the elements which define the persons whose joinder in an action is desirable as stated in Rule 19(a).

Advisory Committee Note to 1966 Amendment to Rule 23, 39 F.R.D. 69, 100 (1966) [hereinafter *1966 Advisory Committee Note*].

Class actions can be certified pursuant to Rule 23(b)(1)(A) if "prosecuting separate actions by or against individual class members would create a risk of inconsistent or varying adjudications with respect to individual class members that would establish incompatible standards of conduct for the party opposing the class." Such a situation might arise, for instance, if different groups seek inconsistent government action to regulate the water level in a river or lake. Farmers may want a greater flow of water, environmentalists a different level, and canoers still another level of water flow, and the government defendant cannot, as a practical matter, comply with different judgments seeking different water levels. But if all those with an interest in the matter can be brought into a single class action, the defendant would not be faced with the "incompatible standards of conduct" that otherwise could result. As the Advisory Committee noted concerning the 1966 amendment to Rule 23, "Separate actions by individuals against a municipality to declare a bond issue invalid or condition or limit it, to prevent or limit the making of a particular appropriation or to compel or invalidate an assessment, might create a risk of inconsistent or varying determinations. * * * Actions by or against a class provide a ready and fair means of achieving unitary adjudication." *1966 Advisory Committee Note*, 39 F.R.D. at 100.

The second category of Rule 23(b)(1) class actions are provided by Rule 23(b)(1)(B) and involves situations in which "prosecuting separate actions by or against individual class members would create a risk of * * * adjudications with respect to individual class members that, as a practical matter, would be dispositive of the interests of the other members not parties to the individual adjudications or would substantially impair or impede their ability to protect their interests." In a Rule 23(b)(1)(B) class action, it is those seeking relief, rather than the person opposing those claims, who will be prejudiced if claims are determined individually rather than in a class action. For instance, "actions by shareholders to compel the declaration of a dividend, the proper recognition and handling of redemption or pre-emption rights, or the like (or actions by the corporation for corresponding declarations of rights), should ordinarily be conducted as class actions * * *." *1966 Advisory Committee Note*, 39 F.R.D. at 101.

A Rule 23(b)(1)(B) class action also might be appropriate if claimants seek more in total damages from a defendant than that defendant has available to satisfy all such claims. In this situation, those who first obtain judgments against the defendant may obtain full satisfaction of their judgments, while there may be no funds left to satisfy later judgments. In such "limited fund" situations, a Rule 23(b)(1)(B) class action in which the recoveries of all claimants are pro-rated may be appropriate in order to avoid "adjudications with respect to individual class members that, as a practical matter, would be dispositive of the interests of the other members not parties to the individual adjudications." Neither Rule 23(b)(1)(A) or (B) class actions usually involve classes seeking money—unless there is not enough money to satisfy all claims and a Rule 23(b)(1)(B) limited-fund class action is appropriate.

2. Rule 23(b)(2) Class Actions. Nor can money be the main relief sought in a Rule 23(b)(2) class action, which action may be available if "the party opposing the class has acted or refused to act on grounds that generally apply to the class, so that final injunctive relief or corresponding declaratory relief is appropriate respecting the class as a whole." While not limited to such cases, Rule 23(b)(2) class actions are typically seen in civil rights challenges to governmental action such as, for instance, an action brought to restructure a state prison system. In such a case, the state government "has acted or refused to act on grounds that generally apply to the class," and final injunctive relief "is appropriate respecting the class as a whole." The Advisory Committee Note to the 1966 Amendment to Rule 23 provides that Rule 23(b)(2) "does not extend to cases in which the appropriate final relief relates exclusively or predominantly to money damages." This statement had been read to mean that monetary relief that is merely incidental to class-wide injunctive or declaratory relief could be awarded in a (b)(2) class. *E.g., Allison v. Citgo Petroleum Corp.*, 151 F.3d 402, 415 (5th Cir. 1998). However, the Supreme Court in *Wal-Mart Stores, Inc. v. Dukes*, 131 S. Ct. 2541, 2557–61 (2011), left open the question whether even "incidental" monetary relief can be awarded under Rule 23(b)(2).

3. Rule 23(b)(3) Class Actions. The 1966 amendment to Rule 23 led to a great increase in federal class actions—especially Rule 23(b)(3) class actions, referred to prior to 1966 as "spurious" class actions. *Amchem Products, Inc. v. Windsor*, 521 U.S. 591, 615 (1997) ("Rule 23(b)(3) 'opt-out' class actions superseded the former 'spurious' class action, so characterized because it generally functioned as a permissive joinder ('opt-in') device."). The 1966 Advisory Committee noted:

> [C]lass-action treatment is not as clearly called for [under Rule 23(b)(3)] as in [Rule (b)(1) and (b)(2) class actions], but it may nevertheless be convenient and desirable depending upon the particular facts. Subdivision (b)(3) encompasses those cases in which a class action would achieve economies of time, effort, and expense, and promote uniformity of decision as to persons similarly situated, without sacrificing procedural fairness or bringing about other undesirable results.

1966 Advisory Committee Note, 39 F.R.D. at 102–103.

To certify a class action under Rule 23(b)(3), that Rule requires the court to find that "the questions of law or fact common to class members predominate over any questions affecting only individual members, and that a class action is superior to other available methods for fairly and efficiently adjudicating the controversy." Thus, to obtain Rule 23(b)(3) certification, the class must satisfy both the predominance and superiority tests of that Rule.

In making its findings as to predominance and superiority, Rule 23(b)(3) itself provides:

> The matters pertinent to these findings include:
>
> (A) the class members' interests in individually controlling the prosecution or defense of separate actions;
>
> (B) the extent and nature of any litigation concerning the controversy already begun by or against class members;
>
> (C) the desirability or undesirability of concentrating the litigation of the claims in the particular forum; and
>
> (D) the likely difficulties in managing a class action.

These matters are usually more relevant to the Rule 23(b)(3) question of superiority, rather than predominance, with a key factor in many superiority determinations the Rule 23(b)(3)(D) question of "likely difficulties in managing a class action." Just as an action with fragmented, individual questions may not satisfy the 23(b)(3) predominance requirement, such an action also may present "likely difficulties in managing a class action" that preclude the action from satisfying the 23(b)(3) superiority requirement. Thus mass tort actions do not often lend themselves to class treatment. "A 'mass accident' resulting in injuries to numerous persons is ordinarily not appropriate for a class action because of the likelihood that significant questions, not only of damages but of liability and defenses of liability, would be present, affecting the individuals in different ways. In these circumstances an action conducted nominally as a class action would degenerate in practice into multiple lawsuits separately tried." *1966 Advisory Committee Note*, 39 F.R.D. at 103.

4. Why It Matters Under Which Provision of Rule 23(b) a Class Is Certified. While a class action must satisfy all four of the Rule 23(a) prerequisites, it only need fit within one of the four types of class actions specified in Rule 23(b). In many cases the requirements of Rule 23(b)(3) may be easier to satisfy than those of Rule 23(b)(1) or (b)(2). As the Supreme Court noted in *Wal-Mart Stores, Inc. v. Dukes*, 131 S.Ct. 2541, 2558 (2011), the Rule 23(b)(3) class action

> allows class certification in a much wider set of circumstances but with greater procedural protections. Its only prerequisites are that "the questions of law or fact common to class members predominate over any questions affecting only individual members, and that a class action is superior to other available methods for fairly and efficiently adjudicating the controversy." Rule 23(b)(3). And unlike (b)(1) and (b)(2) classes, the (b)(3) class is not mandatory; class members are entitled to receive "the best notice that is practicable under the circumstances" and to withdraw from the class at their option. *See* Rule 23(c)(2)(B).

Yet plaintiffs' lawyers typically seek certification under Rule 23(b)(1) or (b)(2).[9] Why is this the case? While Rule 23(b)(3) class actions are possible in many situations in which (b)(1) or (b)(2) class actions are not, certification under Rule 23(b)(3) requires that class members receive notice, an opportunity to participate in the class action, and an opportunity to opt out of that action.

Not only must notice be provided to all class members, but "the [class action] plaintiff must pay for the cost of notice as part of the ordinary burden of financing his own suit." *Eisen v. Carlisle & Jacquelin*, 417 U.S. 156, 179 (1974). The effort to notify thousands, or hundreds of thousands, of class members can complicate the action in many ways, while the up-front cost of such notice can be both a major financial burden and deterrent to bringing Rule 23(b)(3) class actions. So plaintiffs' lawyers typically seek class certification under Rule 23(b)(1) or (2) to avoid notice costs and the focus on class members' opting out of the class that typically are involved in Rule 23(b)(3) class actions.

B. RULE 23 APPLIED AND INTERPRETED

Rule 23(a)(2) requires that any class action present "questions of law or fact common to the class." Traditionally this was not a requirement that presented any difficulties for class certification. Things changed, though, with the Supreme Court's decision in *Wal-Mart Stores, Inc. v. Dukes*. In reading *Wal-Mart*, consider how the

---

[9] However, unless it is a limited-fund class action that fits within Rule 23(b)(1)(B), a class action seeking monetary relief (even back pay) typically must be filed under Rule 23(b)(3).

majority opinion has made class actions more difficult to certify in the federal courts.

Wal-Mart Stores, Inc. v. Dukes

United States Supreme Court, 2011
564 U.S. 338

OPINION

■ SCALIA, J., delivered the opinion of the Court, in which ROBERTS, C.J., and KENNEDY, THOMAS, and ALITO, JJ., joined, and in which GINSBURG, BREYER, SOTOMAYOR, and KAGAN, JJ., joined as to Parts I and III. GINSBURG, J., filed an opinion concurring in part and dissenting in part, in which BREYER, SOTOMAYOR, and KAGAN, JJ., joined.

We are presented with one of the most expansive class actions ever. The District Court and the Court of Appeals approved the certification of a class comprising about one and a half million plaintiffs, current and former female employees of petitioner Wal-Mart who allege that the discretion exercised by their local supervisors over pay and promotion matters violates Title VII by discriminating against women. In addition to injunctive and declaratory relief, the plaintiffs seek an award of backpay. We consider whether the certification of the plaintiff class was consistent with Federal Rules of Civil Procedure 23(a) and (b)(2).

I

A

Petitioner Wal-Mart is the Nation's largest private employer. It operates four types of retail stores throughout the country: Discount Stores, Supercenters, Neighborhood Markets, and Sam's Clubs. Those stores are divided into seven nationwide divisions, which in turn comprise 41 regions of 80 to 85 stores apiece. Each store has between 40 and 53 separate departments and 80 to 500 staff positions. In all, Wal-Mart operates approximately 3,400 stores and employs more than one million people.

Pay and promotion decisions at Wal-Mart are generally committed to local managers' broad discretion, which is exercised "in a largely subjective manner." Local store managers may increase the wages of hourly employees (within limits) with only limited corporate oversight. As for salaried employees, such as store managers and their deputies, higher corporate authorities have discretion to set their pay within preestablished ranges.

Promotions work in a similar fashion. Wal-Mart permits store managers to apply their own subjective criteria when selecting candidates as "support managers," which is the first step on the path to management. Admission to Wal-Mart's management training program, however, does require that a candidate meet certain objective criteria, including an above-average performance rating, at least one year's tenure in the applicant's current position, and a willingness to relocate. But except for those requirements, regional and district managers have discretion to use their own judgment when selecting candidates for management training. Promotion to higher office—e.g., assistant manager, co-manager, or store manager—is similarly at the discretion of the employee's superiors after prescribed objective factors are satisfied.

B

The named plaintiffs in this lawsuit, representing the 1.5 million members of the certified class, are three current or former Wal-Mart employees who allege that the company discriminated against them on the basis of their sex by denying them equal pay or promotions, in violation of Title VII of the Civil Rights Act of 1964, 78 Stat. 253, as amended, 42 U.S.C. § 2000e–1 et seq.

Betty Dukes began working at a Pittsburgh, California, Wal-Mart in 1994. She started as a cashier, but later sought and received a promotion to customer service manager. After a series of disciplinary violations, however, Dukes was demoted back to cashier and then to greeter. Dukes concedes she violated company policy, but contends that the disciplinary actions were in fact retaliation for invoking internal complaint procedures and that male employees have not been disciplined for similar infractions. Dukes also claims two male greeters in the Pittsburgh store are paid more than she is.

Christine Kwapnoski has worked at Sam's Club stores in Missouri and California for most of her adult life. She has held a number of positions, including a supervisory position. She claims that a male manager yelled at her frequently and screamed at female employees, but not at men. The manager in question "told her to 'doll up,' to wear some makeup, and to dress a little better."

The final named plaintiff, Edith Arana, worked at a Wal-Mart store in Duarte, California, from 1995 to 2001. In 2000, she approached the store manager on more than one occasion about management training, but was brushed off. Arana concluded she was being denied opportunity for advancement because of her sex. She initiated internal complaint procedures, whereupon she was told to apply directly to the district manager if she thought her store manager was being unfair. Arana, however, decided against that and never applied for management training again. In 2001, she was fired for failure to comply with Wal-Mart's timekeeping policy.

These plaintiffs, respondents here, do not allege that Wal-Mart has any express corporate policy against the advancement of women. Rather, they claim that their local managers' discretion over pay and promotions is exercised disproportionately in favor of men, leading to an unlawful disparate impact on female employees, see 42 U.S.C. § 2000e–2(k). And, respondents say, because Wal-Mart is aware of this effect, its refusal to cabin its managers' authority amounts to disparate treatment, see § 2000e–2(a). Their complaint seeks injunctive and declaratory relief, punitive damages, and backpay. It does not ask for compensatory damages.

Importantly for our purposes, respondents claim that the discrimination to which they have been subjected is common to all Wal-Mart's female employees. The basic theory of their case is that a strong and uniform "corporate culture" permits bias against women to infect, perhaps subconsciously, the discretionary decisionmaking of each one of Wal-Mart's thousands of managers—thereby making every woman at the company the victim of one common discriminatory practice. Respondents therefore wish to litigate the Title VII claims of all female employees at Wal-Mart's stores in a nationwide class action.

C

Class certification is governed by Federal Rule of Civil Procedure 23. Under Rule 23(a), the party seeking certification must demonstrate, first, that:

"(1) the class is so numerous that joinder of all members is impracticable,

"(2) there are questions of law or fact common to the class,

"(3) the claims or defenses of the representative parties are typical of the claims or defenses of the class, and

"(4) the representative parties will fairly and adequately protect the interests of the class"

Second, the proposed class must satisfy at least one of the three requirements listed in Rule 23(b). Respondents rely on Rule 23(b)(2), which applies when "the party opposing the class has acted or refused to act on grounds that apply generally to the class, so that final injunctive relief or corresponding declaratory relief is appropriate respecting the class as a whole."

Invoking these provisions, respondents moved the District Court to certify a plaintiff class consisting of " '[a]ll women employed at any Wal-Mart domestic retail store at any time since December 26, 1998, who have been or may be subjected to Wal-Mart's challenged pay and management track promotions policies and practices.' " As evidence that there were indeed "questions of law or fact common to" all the women of Wal-Mart, as Rule 23(a)(2) requires, respondents relied chiefly on three forms of proof: statistical evidence about pay and promotion disparities between men and women at the company, anecdotal reports of discrimination from about 120 of Wal-Mart's female employees, and the testimony of a sociologist, Dr. William Bielby, who conducted a "social framework analysis" of Wal-Mart's "culture" and personnel practices, and concluded that the company was "vulnerable" to gender discrimination.

540

CLASS ACTIONS: "IF TWO'S A COUPLE AND THREE'S A CROWD,
WHAT'S A CLASS?"

CHAPTER 7

Wal-Mart unsuccessfully moved to strike much of this evidence. It also offered its own countervailing statistical and other proof in an effort to defeat Rule 23(a)'s requirements of commonality, typicality, and adequate representation. Wal-Mart further contended that respondents' monetary claims for backpay could not be certified under Rule 23(b)(2), first because that Rule refers only to injunctive and declaratory relief, and second because the backpay claims could not be manageably tried as a class without depriving Wal-Mart of its right to present certain statutory defenses. With one limitation not relevant here, the District Court granted respondents' motion and certified their proposed class.

D

A divided en banc Court of Appeals substantially affirmed the District Court's certification order. The majority concluded that respondents' evidence of commonality was sufficient to "raise the common question whether Wal-Mart's female employees nationwide were subjected to a single set of corporate policies (not merely a number of independent discriminatory acts) that may have worked to unlawfully discriminate against them in violation of Title VII." It also agreed with the District Court that the named plaintiffs' claims were sufficiently typical of the class as a whole to satisfy Rule 23(a)(3), and that they could serve as adequate class representatives, see Rule 23(a)(4). With respect to the Rule 23(b)(2) question, the Ninth Circuit held that respondents' backpay claims could be certified as part of a (b)(2) class because they did not "predominat[e]" over the requests for declaratory and injunctive relief, meaning they were not "superior in strength, influence, or authority" to the nonmonetary claims.[4]

Finally, the Court of Appeals determined that the action could be manageably tried as a class action because the District Court could adopt the approach the Ninth Circuit approved in *Hilao v. Estate of Marcos*, 103 F.3d 767, 782–787 (1996). There compensatory damages for some 9,541 class members were calculated by selecting 137 claims at random, referring those claims to a special master for valuation, and then extrapolating the validity and value of the untested claims from the sample set. The Court of Appeals "s[aw] no reason why a similar procedure to that used in *Hilao* could not be employed in this case." It would allow Wal-Mart "to present individual defenses in the randomly selected 'sample cases,' thus revealing the approximate percentage of

---

[4] To enable that result, the Court of Appeals trimmed the (b)(2) class in two ways: First, it remanded that part of the certification order which included respondents' punitive-damages claim in the (b)(2) class, so that the District Court might consider whether that might cause the monetary relief to predominate. Second, it accepted in part Wal-Mart's argument that since class members whom it no longer employed had no standing to seek injunctive or declaratory relief, as to them monetary claims must predominate. It excluded from the certified class "those putative class members who were no longer Wal-Mart employees at the time Plaintiffs' complaint was filed."

class members whose unequal pay or nonpromotion was due to something other than gender discrimination."

We granted certiorari.

II

The class action is "an exception to the usual rule that litigation is conducted by and on behalf of the individual named parties only." *Califano v. Yamasaki*, 442 U.S. 682, 700–701 (1979). In order to justify a departure from that rule, "a class representative must be part of the class and 'possess the same interest and suffer the same injury' as the class members." *East Tex. Motor Freight System, Inc. v. Rodriguez*, 431 U.S. 395, 403 (1977) (quoting *Schlesinger v. Reservists Comm. to Stop the War*, 418 U.S. 208, 216 (1974)). Rule 23(a) ensures that the named ·plaintiffs are appropriate representatives of the class whose claims they wish to litigate. The Rule's four requirements—numerosity, commonality, typicality, and adequate representation—"effectively 'limit the class claims to those fairly encompassed by the named plaintiff's claims.'" *General Telephone Co. of Southwest v. Falcon*, 457 U.S. 147, 156 (1982) (quoting *General Telephone Co. of Northwest v. EEOC*, 446 U.S. 318, 330 (1980)).

A

The crux of this case is commonality—the rule requiring a plaintiff to show that "there are questions of law or fact common to the class." Rule 23(a)(2). That language is easy to misread, since "[a]ny competently crafted class complaint literally raises common 'questions.'" Nagareda, "Class Certification in the Age of Aggregate Proof," 84 *N.Y.U.L.Rev.* 97, 131–132 (2009). For example: Do all of us plaintiffs indeed work for Wal-Mart? Do our managers have discretion over pay? Is that an unlawful employment practice? What remedies should we get? Reciting these questions is not sufficient to obtain class certification. Commonality requires the plaintiff to demonstrate that the class members "have suffered the same injury," *Falcon*, supra, at 157. This does not mean merely that they have all suffered a violation of the same provision of law. Title VII, for example, can be violated in many ways—by intentional discrimination, or by hiring and promotion criteria that result in disparate impact, and by the use of these practices on the part of many different superiors in a single company. Quite obviously, the mere claim by employees of the same company that they have suffered a Title VII injury, or even a disparate-impact Title VII injury, gives no cause to believe that all their claims can productively be litigated at once. Their claims must depend upon a common contention—for example, the assertion of discriminatory bias on the part of the same supervisor. That common contention, moreover, must be of such a nature that it is capable of classwide resolution—which means that determination of its truth or falsity will resolve an issue that is central to the validity of each one of the claims in one stroke.

"What matters to class certification . . . is not the raising of common 'questions'—even in droves—but, rather the capacity of a classwide proceeding to generate common answers apt to drive the resolution of the litigation. Dissimilarities within the proposed class are what have the potential to impede the generation of common answers." Nagareda, *supra*, at 132.

Rule 23 does not set forth a mere pleading standard. A party seeking class certification must affirmatively demonstrate his compliance with the Rule—that is, he must be prepared to prove that there are in fact sufficiently numerous parties, common questions of law or fact, etc. We recognized in *Falcon* that "sometimes it may be necessary for the court to probe behind the pleadings before coming to rest on the certification question," 457 U.S., at 160, and that certification is proper only if "the trial court is satisfied, after a rigorous analysis, that the prerequisites of Rule 23(a) have been satisfied," *id.*, at 161. Frequently that "rigorous analysis" will entail some overlap with the merits of the plaintiff's underlying claim. That cannot be helped. "'[T]he class determination generally involves considerations that are enmeshed in the factual and legal issues comprising the plaintiff's cause of action.'" *Falcon, supra,* at 160 (quoting *Coopers & Lybrand v. Livesay*, 437 U.S. 463, 469 (1978)).[6] Nor is there anything unusual about that consequence: The necessity of touching aspects of the merits in order to resolve preliminary matters, e.g., jurisdiction and venue, is a familiar feature of litigation.

In this case, proof of commonality necessarily overlaps with respondents' merits contention that Wal-Mart engages in a pattern or practice of discrimination. That is so because, in resolving an individual's Title VII claim, the crux of the inquiry is "the reason for a particular employment decision," *Cooper v. Federal Reserve Bank of*

---

[6]   A statement in one of our prior cases, *Eisen v. Carlisle & Jacquelin*, 417 U.S. 156, 177 (1974), is sometimes mistakenly cited to the contrary: "We find nothing in either the language or history of Rule 23 that gives a court any authority to conduct a preliminary inquiry into the merits of a suit in order to determine whether it may be maintained as a class action." But in that case, the judge had conducted a preliminary inquiry into the merits of a suit, not in order to determine the propriety of certification under Rules 23(a) and (b) (he had already done that), but in order to shift the cost of notice required by Rule 23(c)(2) from the plaintiff to the defendants. To the extent the quoted statement goes beyond the permissibility of a merits inquiry for any other pretrial purpose, it is the purest dictum and is contradicted by our other cases.

Perhaps the most common example of considering a merits question at the Rule 23 stage arises in class-action suits for securities fraud. Rule 23(b)(3)'s requirement that "questions of law or fact common to class members predominate over any questions affecting only individual members" would often be an insuperable barrier to class certification, since each of the individual investors would have to prove reliance on the alleged misrepresentation. But the problem dissipates if the plaintiffs can establish the applicability of the so-called "fraud on the market" presumption, which says that all traders who purchase stock in an efficient market are presumed to have relied on the accuracy of a company's public statements. To invoke this presumption, the plaintiffs seeking 23(b)(3) certification must prove that their shares were traded on an efficient market, *Erica P. John Fund, Inc. v. Halliburton Co.*, 563 U.S. ___, ___, (2011), an issue they will surely have to prove again at trial in order to make out their case on the merits.

Richmond, 467 U.S. 867, 876 (1984). Here respondents wish to sue about literally millions of employment decisions at once. Without some glue holding the alleged reasons for all those decisions together, it will be impossible to say that examination of all the class members' claims for relief will produce a common answer to the crucial question why was I disfavored.

B

This Court's opinion in *Falcon* describes how the commonality issue must be approached. There an employee who claimed that he was deliberately denied a promotion on account of race obtained certification of a class comprising all employees wrongfully denied promotions and all applicants wrongfully denied jobs. 457 U.S., at 152. We rejected that composite class for lack of commonality and typicality, explaining:

> "Conceptually, there is a wide gap between (a) an individual's claim that he has been denied a promotion [or higher pay] on discriminatory grounds, and his otherwise unsupported allegation that the company has a policy of discrimination, and (b) the existence of a class of persons who have suffered the same injury as that individual, such that the individual's claim and the class claim will share common questions of law or fact and that the individual's claim will be typical of the class claims." *Id.*, at 157–158.

Falcon suggested two ways in which that conceptual gap might be bridged. First, if the employer "used a biased testing procedure to evaluate both applicants for employment and incumbent employees, a class action on behalf of every applicant or employee who might have been prejudiced by the test clearly would satisfy the commonality and typicality requirements of Rule 23(a)." *Id.*, at 159, n. 15. Second, "[s]ignificant proof that an employer operated under a general policy of discrimination conceivably could justify a class of both applicants and employees if the discrimination manifested itself in hiring and promotion practices in the same general fashion, such as through entirely subjective decisionmaking processes." *Ibid.* We think that statement precisely describes respondents' burden in this case. The first manner of bridging the gap obviously has no application here; Wal-Mart has no testing procedure or other companywide evaluation method that can be charged with bias. The whole point of permitting discretionary decisionmaking is to avoid evaluating employees under a common standard.

The second manner of bridging the gap requires "significant proof" that Wal-Mart "operated under a general policy of discrimination." That is entirely absent here. Wal-Mart's announced policy forbids sex discrimination, and as the District Court recognized the company imposes penalties for denials of equal employment opportunity. The only evidence of a "general policy of discrimination" respondents produced was the testimony of Dr. William Bielby, their sociological expert. Relying on "social framework" analysis, Bielby testified that Wal-Mart has a "strong corporate culture," that makes it " 'vulnerable' " to "gender bias." He could not, however, "determine with any specificity how regularly stereotypes play a meaningful role in employment decisions at Wal-Mart. At his deposition . . . Dr. Bielby conceded that he could not calculate whether 0.5 percent or 95 percent of the employment decisions at Wal-Mart might be determined by stereotyped thinking." The parties dispute whether Bielby's testimony even met the standards for the admission of expert testimony under Federal Rule of Civil Procedure 702 and our *Daubert* case, see *Daubert v. Merrell Dow Pharmaceuticals, Inc.*, 509 U.S. 579 (1993). The District Court concluded that Daubert did not apply to expert testimony at the certification stage of class-action proceedings. We doubt that is so, but even if properly considered, Bielby's testimony does nothing to advance respondents' case. "[W]hether 0.5 percent or 95 percent of the employment decisions at Wal-Mart might be determined by stereotyped thinking" is the essential question on which respondents' theory of commonality depends. If Bielby admittedly has no answer to that question, we can safely disregard what he has to say. It is worlds away from "significant proof" that Wal-Mart "operated under a general policy of discrimination."

C

The only corporate policy that the plaintiffs' evidence convincingly establishes is Wal-Mart's "policy" of allowing discretion by local supervisors over employment matters. On its face, of course, that is just the opposite of a uniform employment practice that would provide the commonality needed for a class action; it is a policy against having uniform employment practices. It is also a very common and presumptively reasonable way of doing business—one that we have said "should itself raise no inference of discriminatory conduct," *Watson v. Fort Worth Bank & Trust*, 487 U.S. 977, 990 (1988).

* * *

Respondents have not identified a common mode of exercising discretion that pervades the entire company—aside from their reliance on Dr. Bielby's social frameworks analysis that we have rejected. In a company of Wal-Mart's size and geographical scope, it is quite unbelievable that all managers would exercise their discretion in a common way without some common direction. Respondents attempt to make that showing by means of statistical and anecdotal evidence, but their evidence falls well short.

The statistical evidence consists primarily of regression analyses performed by Dr. Richard Drogin, a statistician, and Dr. Marc Bendick, a labor economist. Drogin conducted his analysis region-by-region, comparing the number of women promoted into management positions with the percentage of women in the available pool of hourly workers.

After considering regional and national data, Drogin concluded that "there are statistically significant disparities between men and women at Wal-Mart . . . [and] these disparities . . . can be explained only by gender discrimination." Bendick compared work-force data from Wal-Mart and competitive retailers and concluded that Wal-Mart "promotes a lower percentage of women than its competitors."

Even if they are taken at face value, these studies are insufficient to establish that respondents' theory can be proved on a classwide basis. In *Falcon*, we held that one named plaintiff's experience of discrimination was insufficient to infer that "discriminatory treatment is typical of [the employer's employment] practices." 457 U.S., at 158. A similar failure of inference arises here. As Judge Ikuta observed in her dissent, "[i]nformation about disparities at the regional and national level does not establish the existence of disparities at individual stores, let alone raise the inference that a company-wide policy of discrimination is implemented by discretionary decisions at the store and district level." A regional pay disparity, for example, may be attributable to only a small set of Wal-Mart stores, and cannot by itself establish the uniform, store-by-store disparity upon which the plaintiffs' theory of commonality depends.

* * *

Respondents' anecdotal evidence suffers from the same defects, and in addition is too weak to raise any inference that all the individual, discretionary personnel decisions are discriminatory. In *Teamsters v. United States*, 431 U.S. 324 (1977), in addition to substantial statistical evidence of company-wide discrimination, the Government (as plaintiff) produced about 40 specific accounts of racial discrimination from particular individuals. That number was significant because the company involved had only 6,472 employees, of whom 571 were minorities, and the class itself consisted of around 334 persons. The 40 anecdotes thus represented roughly one account for every eight members of the class. Moreover, the Court of Appeals noted that the anecdotes came from individuals "spread throughout" the company who "for the most part" worked at the company's operational centers that employed the largest numbers of the class members. Here, by contrast, respondents filed some 120 affidavits reporting experiences of discrimination—about 1 for every 12,500 class members—relating to only some 235 out of Wal-Mart's 3,400 stores. More than half of these reports are concentrated in only six States (Alabama, California, Florida, Missouri, Texas, and Wisconsin); half of all States have only one or two anecdotes; and 14 States have no anecdotes about Wal-Mart's operations at all. Even if every single one of these accounts is true, that would not demonstrate that the entire company "operate [s] under a general policy of discrimination," *Falcon*, supra, at 159, n. 15, which is what respondents must show to certify a companywide class.

* * *

In sum, we agree with Chief Judge Kozinski that the members of the class:

> "held a multitude of different jobs, at different levels of Wal-Mart's hierarchy, for variable lengths of time, in 3,400 stores, sprinkled across 50 states, with a kaleidoscope of supervisors (male and female), subject to a variety of regional policies that all differed. . . . Some thrived while others did poorly. They have little in common but their sex and this lawsuit." 603 F.3d, at 652 (dissenting opinion).

III

We also conclude that respondents' claims for backpay were improperly certified under Federal Rule of Civil Procedure 23(b)(2). Our opinion in *Ticor Title Ins. Co. v. Brown*, 511 U.S. 117, 121 (1994) (per curiam) expressed serious doubt about whether claims for monetary relief may be certified under that provision. We now hold that they may not, at least where (as here) the monetary relief is not incidental to the injunctive or declaratory relief.

A

Rule 23(b)(2) allows class treatment when "the party opposing the class has acted or refused to act on grounds that apply generally to the class, so that final injunctive relief or corresponding declaratory relief is appropriate respecting the class as a whole." One possible reading of this provision is that it applies only to requests for such injunctive or declaratory relief and does not authorize the class certification of monetary claims at all. We need not reach that broader question in this case, because we think that, at a minimum, claims for individualized relief (like the backpay at issue here) do not satisfy the Rule. The key to the (b)(2) class is "the indivisible nature of the injunctive or declaratory remedy warranted—the notion that the conduct is such that it can be enjoined or declared unlawful only as to all of the class members or as to none of them." Nagareda, 84 *N.Y.U.L.Rev.*, at 132. In other words, Rule 23(b)(2) applies only when a single injunction or declaratory judgment would provide relief to each member of the class. It does not authorize class certification when each individual class member would be entitled to a different injunction or declaratory judgment against the defendant. Similarly, it does not authorize class certification when each class member would be entitled to an individualized award of monetary damages.

* * *

Permitting the combination of individualized and classwide relief in a (b)(2) class is also inconsistent with the structure of Rule 23(b). Classes certified under (b)(1) and (b)(2) share the most traditional justifications for class treatment—that individual adjudications would be impossible or unworkable, as in a (b)(1) class, or that the relief sought must perforce affect the entire class at once, as in a (b)(2) class. For that reason these are also mandatory classes: The Rule provides no opportunity for (b)(1) or (b)(2) class members to opt out, and does not even oblige the District Court to afford them notice of the action. Rule 23(b)(3), by contrast, is an "adventuresome innovation" of the 1966 amendments, *Amchem*, 521 U.S., at 614, framed for situations "in which 'class-action treatment is not as clearly called for'," id., at 615 (quoting Advisory Committee's Notes, 28 U.S.C.App., p. 697 (1994 ed.)). It allows class certification in a much wider set of circumstances but with greater procedural protections. Its only prerequisites are that "the questions of law or fact common to class members predominate over any questions affecting only individual members, and that a class action is superior to other available methods for fairly and efficiently adjudicating the controversy." Rule 23(b)(3). And unlike (b)(1) and (b)(2) classes, the (b)(3) class is not mandatory; class members are entitled to receive "the best notice that is practicable under the circumstances" and to withdraw from the class at their option. See Rule 23(c)(2)(B).

Given that structure, we think it clear that individualized monetary claims belong in Rule 23(b)(3). The procedural protections attending the (b)(3) class—predominance, superiority, mandatory notice, and the right to opt out—are missing from (b)(2) not because the Rule considers them unnecessary, but because it considers them unnecessary *to a (b)(2) class*. When a class seeks an indivisible injunction benefitting all its members at once, there is no reason to undertake a case-specific inquiry into whether class issues predominate or whether class action is a superior method of adjudicating the dispute. Predominance and superiority are self-evident. But with respect to each class member's individualized claim for money, that is not so—which is precisely why (b)(3) requires the judge to make findings about predominance and superiority before allowing the class. Similarly, (b)(2) does not require that class members be given notice and opt-out rights, presumably because it is thought (rightly or wrongly) that notice has no purpose when the class is mandatory, and that depriving people of their right to sue in this manner complies with the Due Process Clause. In the context of a class action predominantly for money damages we have held that absence of notice and opt-out violates due process. *See Phillips Petroleum Co. v. Shutts*, 472 U.S. 797, 812 (1985). While we have never held that to be so where the monetary claims do not predominate, the serious possibility that it may be so provides an additional reason not to read Rule 23(b)(2) to include the monetary claims here.

B

Against that conclusion, respondents argue that their claims for backpay were appropriately certified as part of a class under Rule 23(b)(2) because those claims do not "predominate" over their requests for injunctive and declaratory relief. They rely upon the Advisory

Committee's statement that Rule 23(b)(2) "does not extend to cases in which the appropriate final relief relates exclusively or predominantly to money damages." 39 F.R.D., at 102. The negative implication, they argue, is that it does extend to cases in which the appropriate final relief relates only partially and nonpredominantly to money damages. Of course it is the Rule itself, not the Advisory Committee's description of it, that governs. And a mere negative inference does not in our view suffice to establish a disposition that has no basis in the Rule's text, and that does obvious violence to the Rule's structural features. The mere "predominance" of a proper (b)(2) injunctive claim does nothing to justify elimination of Rule 23(b)(3)'s procedural protections: It neither establishes the superiority of class adjudication over individual adjudication nor cures the notice and opt-out problems. We fail to see why the Rule should be read to nullify these protections whenever a plaintiff class, at its option, combines its monetary claims with a request—even a "predominating request"—for an injunction.

Respondents' predominance test, moreover, creates perverse incentives for class representatives to place at risk potentially valid claims for monetary relief. In this case, for example, the named plaintiffs declined to include employees' claims for compensatory damages in their complaint. That strategy of including only backpay claims made it more likely that monetary relief would not "predominate." But it also created the possibility (if the predominance test were correct) that individual class members' compensatory-damages claims would be precluded by litigation they had no power to hold themselves apart from. If it were determined, for example, that a particular class member is not entitled to backpay because her denial of increased pay or a promotion was not the product of discrimination, that employee might be collaterally estopped from independently seeking compensatory damages based on that same denial. That possibility underscores the need for plaintiffs with individual monetary claims to decide for themselves whether to tie their fates to the class representatives' or go it alone—a choice Rule 23(b)(2) does not ensure that they have.

* * *

Finally, respondents argue that their backpay claims are appropriate for a (b)(2) class action because a backpay award is equitable in nature. The latter may be true, but it is irrelevant. The Rule does not speak of "equitable" remedies generally but of injunctions and declaratory judgments. As Title VII itself makes pellucidly clear, backpay is neither. *See* 42 U.S.C. § 2000e–5(g)(2)(B)(I) and (ii) (distinguishing between declaratory and injunctive relief and the payment of "backpay," *see* § 2000e–5(g)(2)(A)).

C

* * *

Contrary to the Ninth Circuit's view, Wal-Mart is entitled to individualized determinations of each employee's eligibility for backpay. Title VII includes a detailed remedial scheme. If a plaintiff prevails in showing that an employer has discriminated against him in violation of the statute, the court "may enjoin the respondent from engaging in such unlawful employment practice, and order such affirmative action as may be appropriate, [including] reinstatement or hiring of employees, with or without backpay . . . or any other equitable relief as the court deems appropriate." § 2000e–5(g)(1). But if the employer can show that it took an adverse employment action against an employee for any reason other than discrimination, the court cannot order the "hiring, reinstatement, or promotion of an individual as an employee, or the payment to him of any backpay." § 2000e–5(g)(2)(A).

* * *

The Court of Appeals believed that it was possible to replace such proceedings [to determine each individual's right to particular relief] with Trial by Formula. A sample set of the class members would be selected, as to whom liability for sex discrimination and the backpay owing as a result would be determined in depositions supervised by a master. The percentage of claims determined to be valid would then be applied to the entire remaining class, and the number of (presumptively) valid claims thus derived would be multiplied by the average backpay award in the sample set to arrive at the entire class recovery—without further individualized proceedings. We disapprove that novel project. Because the Rules Enabling Act forbids interpreting Rule 23 to "abridge, enlarge or modify any substantive right," 28 U.S.C. § 2072(b); *see Ortiz*, 527 U.S., at 845, a class cannot be certified on the premise that Wal-Mart will not be entitled to litigate its statutory defenses to individual claims. And because the necessity of· that litigation will prevent backpay from being "incidental" to the classwide injunction, respondents' class could not be certified even assuming, arguendo, that "incidental" monetary relief can be awarded to a 23(b)(2) class.

* * *

The judgment of the Court of Appeals is

Reversed.

■ JUSTICE GINSBURG, with whom JUSTICE BREYER, JUSTICE SOTOMAYOR, and JUSTICE KAGAN join, concurring in part and dissenting in part.

The class in this case, I agree with the Court, should not have been certified under Federal Rule of Civil Procedure 23(b)(2). The plaintiffs,

CLASS ACTIONS: "IF TWO'S A COUPLE AND THREE'S A CROWD,
WHAT'S A CLASS?"

550

CHAPTER 7

alleging discrimination in violation of Title VII, 42 U.S.C. § 2000e et seq., seek monetary relief that is not merely incidental to any injunctive or declaratory relief that might be available. A putative class of this type may be certifiable under Rule 23(b)(3), if the plaintiffs show that common class questions "predominate" over issues affecting individuals—e.g., qualification for, and the amount of, backpay or compensatory damages—and that a class action is "superior" to other modes of adjudication.

Whether the class the plaintiffs describe meets the specific requirements of Rule 23(b)(3) is not before the Court, and I would reserve that matter for consideration and decision on remand. The Court, however, disqualifies the class at the starting gate, holding that the plaintiffs cannot cross the "commonality" line set by Rule 23(a)(2). In so ruling, the Court imports into the Rule 23(a) determination concerns properly addressed in a Rule 23(b)(3) assessment.

I

A

Rule 23(a)(2) establishes a preliminary requirement for maintaining a class action: "[T]here are questions of law or fact common to the class." The Rule "does not require that all questions of law or fact raised in the litigation be common," 1 H. Newberg & A. Conte, *Newberg on Class Actions* § 3.10, pp. 3–48 to 3–49 (3d ed.1992); indeed, "[e]ven a single question of law or fact common to the members of the class will satisfy the commonality requirement," Nagareda, "The Preexistence Principle and the Structure of the Class Action," 103 *Colum. L.Rev.* 149, 176, n. 110 (2003). *See* Advisory Committee's 1937 Notes on Fed. Rule Civ. Proc. 23, 28 U.S.C.App., p. 138 (citing with approval cases in which "there was only a question of law or fact common to" the class members).

A "question" is ordinarily understood to be "[a] subject or point open to controversy." *American Heritage Dictionary* 1483 (3d ed.1992). *See also Black's Law Dictionary* 1366 (9th ed.2009) (defining "question of fact" as "[a] disputed issue to be resolved . . . [at] trial" and "question of law" as "[a]n issue to be decided by the judge"). Thus, a "question" "common to the class" must be a dispute, either of fact or of law, the resolution of which will advance the determination of the class members' claims.

B

The District Court, recognizing that "one significant issue common to the class may be sufficient to warrant certification," found that the plaintiffs easily met that test. Absent an error of law or an abuse of discretion, an appellate tribunal has no warrant to upset the District Court's finding of commonality. *See Califano v. Yamasaki*, 442 U.S. 682, 703 (1979) ("[M]ost issues arising under Rule 23 . . . [are] committed in the first instance to the discretion of the district court.").

The District Court certified a class of "[a]ll women employed at any Wal-Mart domestic retail store at any time since December 26, 1998." The named plaintiffs, led by Betty Dukes, propose to litigate, on behalf of the class, allegations that Wal-Mart discriminates on the basis of gender in pay and promotions. They allege that the company "[r]eli[es] on gender stereotypes in making employment decisions such as . . . promotion[s][and] pay." Wal-Mart permits those prejudices to infect personnel decisions, the plaintiffs contend, by leaving pay and promotions in the hands of "a nearly all male managerial workforce" using "arbitrary and subjective criteria." Further alleged barriers to the advancement of female employees include the company's requirement, "as a condition of promotion to management jobs, that employees be willing to relocate." Absent instruction otherwise, there is a risk that managers will act on the familiar assumption that women, because of their services to husband and children, are less mobile than men.

Women fill 70 percent of the hourly jobs in the retailer's stores but make up only "33 percent of management employees." "[T]he higher one looks in the organization the lower the percentage of women." The plaintiffs' "largely uncontested descriptive statistics" also show that women working in the company's stores "are paid less than men in every region" and "that the salary gap widens over time even for men and women hired into the same jobs at the same time." cf. Ledbetter v. Goodyear Tire & Rubber Co., 550 U.S. 618, 643 (2007) (GINSBURG, J., dissenting).

The District Court identified "systems for . . . promoting in-store employees" that were "sufficiently similar across regions and stores" to conclude that "the manner in which these systems affect the class raises issues that are common to all class members." The selection of employees for promotion to in-store management "is fairly characterized as a 'tap on the shoulder' process," in which managers have discretion about whose shoulders to tap. Vacancies are not regularly posted; from among those employees satisfying minimum qualifications, managers choose whom to promote on the basis of their own subjective impressions.

Wal-Mart's compensation policies also operate uniformly across stores, the District Court found. The retailer leaves open a $2 band for every position's hourly pay rate. Wal-Mart provides no standards or criteria for setting wages within that band, and thus does nothing to counter unconscious bias on the part of supervisors.

Wal-Mart's supervisors do not make their discretionary decisions in a vacuum. The District Court reviewed means Wal-Mart used to maintain a "carefully constructed . . . corporate culture," such as frequent meetings to reinforce the common way of thinking, regular transfers of managers between stores to ensure uniformity throughout the company, monitoring of stores "on a close and constant basis," and "Wal-Mart TV," "broadcas[t] . . . into all stores."

The plaintiffs' evidence, including class members' tales of their own experiences, suggests that gender bias suffused Wal-Mart's company culture. Among illustrations, senior management often refer to female associates as "little Janie Qs." One manager told an employee that "[m]en are here to make a career and women aren't." A committee of female Wal-Mart executives concluded that "[s]tereotypes limit the opportunities offered to women."

Finally, the plaintiffs presented an expert's appraisal to show that the pay and promotions disparities at Wal-Mart "can be explained only by gender discrimination and not by . . . neutral variables." Using regression analyses, their expert, Richard Drogin, controlled for factors including, inter alia, job performance, length of time with the company, and the store where an employee worked. The results, the District Court found, were sufficient to raise an "inference of discrimination."

C

The District Court's identification of a common question, whether Wal-Mart's pay and promotions policies gave rise to unlawful discrimination, was hardly infirm. The practice of delegating to supervisors large discretion to make personnel decisions, uncontrolled by formal standards, has long been known to have the potential to produce disparate effects. Managers, like all humankind, may be prey to biases of which they are unaware.[6] The risk of discrimination is heightened when those managers are predominantly of one sex, and are steeped in a corporate culture that perpetuates gender stereotypes.

* * *

We have held that "discretionary employment practices" can give rise to Title VII claims, not only when such practices are motivated by discriminatory intent but also when they produce discriminatory results. *See Watson v. Fort Worth Bank & Trust*, 487 U.S. 977, 988, 991 (1988). In *Watson*, as here, an employer had given its managers large authority over promotions. An employee sued the bank under Title VII, alleging that the "discretionary promotion system" caused a discriminatory effect based on race. Four different supervisors had declined, on separate occasions, to promote the employee. Their reasons were subjective and unknown. The employer, we noted "had not developed precise and formal criteria for evaluating candidates"; "[i]t relied instead on the subjective judgment of supervisors."

---

[6] An example vividly illustrates how subjective decisionmaking can be a vehicle for discrimination. Performing in symphony orchestras was long a male preserve. Goldin and Rouse, *Orchestrating Impartiality: The Impact of "Blind" Auditions on Female Musicians*, 90 Am. Econ. Rev. 715, 715–716 (2000). In the 1970's orchestras began hiring musicians through auditions open to all comers. *Id.*, at 716. Reviewers were to judge applicants solely on their musical abilities, yet subconscious bias led some reviewers to disfavor women. Orchestras that permitted reviewers to see the applicants hired far fewer female musicians than orchestras that conducted blind auditions, in which candidates played behind opaque screens. *Id.*, at 738.

Aware of "the problem of subconscious stereotypes and prejudices," we held that the employer's "undisciplined system of subjective decisionmaking" was an "employment practic[e]" that "may be analyzed under the disparate impact approach." *Id.*, at 990–991.

The plaintiffs' allegations state claims of gender discrimination in the form of biased decisionmaking in both pay and promotions. The evidence reviewed by the District Court adequately demonstrated that resolving those claims would necessitate examination of particular policies and practices alleged to affect, adversely and globally, women employed at Wal-Mart's stores. Rule 23(a)(2), setting a necessary but not a sufficient criterion for class-action certification, demands nothing further.

II

A

The Court gives no credence to the key dispute common to the class: whether Wal-Mart's discretionary pay and promotion policies are discriminatory. * * * "What matters," the Court asserts, "is not the raising of common 'questions,' " but whether there are "[d]issimilarities within the proposed class" that "have the potential to impede the generation of common answers." (quoting Nagareda, "Class Certification in the Age of Aggregate Proof," 84 *N.Y.U.L.Rev.* 97, 132 (2009)).

The Court blends Rule 23(a)(2)'s threshold criterion with the more demanding criteria of Rule 23(b)(3), and thereby elevates the (a)(2) inquiry so that it is no longer "easily satisfied," 5 J. Moore et al., *Moore's Federal Practice* § 23.23[2], p. 23–72 (3d ed.2011). Rule 23(b)(3) certification requires, in addition to the four 23(a) findings, determinations that "questions of law or fact common to class members predominate over any questions affecting only individual members" and that "a class action is superior to other available methods for . . . adjudicating the controversy."

The Court's emphasis on differences between class members mimics the Rule 23(b)(3) inquiry into whether common questions "predominate" over individual issues. And by asking whether the individual differences "impede" common adjudication, the Court duplicates 23(b)(3)'s question whether "a class action is superior" to other modes of adjudication. * * * "The Rule 23(b)(3) predominance inquiry" is meant to "tes[t] whether proposed classes are sufficiently cohesive to warrant adjudication by representation." *Amchem Products, Inc. v. Windsor*, 521 U.S. 591, 623 (1997). If courts must conduct a "dissimilarities" analysis at the Rule 23(a)(2) stage, no mission remains for Rule 23(b)(3).

Because Rule 23(a) is also a prerequisite for Rule 23(b)(1) and Rule 23(b)(2) classes, the Court's "dissimilarities" position is far reaching. Individual differences should not bar a Rule 23(b)(1) or Rule 23(b)(2) class, so long as the Rule 23(a) threshold is met. For example, in *Franks v. Bowman Transp. Co.*, 424 U.S. 747 (1976), a Rule 23(b)(2) class of African-American truckdrivers complained that the defendant had discriminatorily refused to hire black applicants. We recognized that the "qualification[s] and performance" of individual class members might vary. *Id.*, at 772. "Generalizations concerning such individually applicable evidence," we cautioned, "cannot serve as a justification for the denial of [injunctive] relief to the entire class." *Ibid.*

B

The "dissimilarities" approach leads the Court to train its attention on what distinguishes individual class members, rather than on what unites them. Given the lack of standards for pay and promotions, the majority says, "demonstrating the invalidity of one manager's use of discretion will do nothing to demonstrate the invalidity of another's."

Wal-Mart's delegation of discretion over pay and promotions is a policy uniform throughout all stores. The very nature of discretion is that people will exercise it in various ways. A system of delegated discretion, *Watson* held, is a practice actionable under Title VII when it produces discriminatory outcomes. A finding that Wal-Mart's pay and promotions practices in fact violate the law would be the first step in the usual order of proof for plaintiffs seeking individual remedies for company-wide discrimination. That each individual employee's unique circumstances will ultimately determine whether she is entitled to backpay or damages, should not factor into the Rule 23(a)(2) determination.

* * *

The Court errs in importing a "dissimilarities" notion suited to Rule 23(b)(3) into the Rule 23(a) commonality inquiry. I therefore cannot join Part II of the Court's opinion.

COMMENTS AND QUESTIONS CONCERNING
WAL-MART STORES, INC. V. DUKES

1.   The court's ultimate judgment, rather than its reasoning, is crucial for litigants and most lawyers. Lawyers therefore often read the final page of an opinion first—to see whether their client has prevailed on the motion or other matter before the court. Sometimes, though, the court's framing of a case in the first sentence or two of an opinion will make it easy to predict the court's ultimate ruling. So it is in this case, in which Justice Scalia's opinion for the Court begins:

> We are presented with one of the most expansive class actions ever. The District Court and the Court of Appeals approved the certification of a class comprising about one and a half million plaintiffs, current and former female employees of petitioner Wal-Mart who allege that the discretion exercised by

their local supervisors over pay and promotion matters violates Title VII by discriminating against women.

2.   Because the majority concludes that the class did not satisfy the Rule 23(a)(2) requirement of commonality, it does not consider the additional Rule 23(a) requirements of numerosity, typicality, and adequacy of representation. Rule 23(a)(1) requires a "class so numerous that joinder of all members is impracticable," making numerosity the easiest Rule 23(a) requirement to satisfy. "As a general guideline * * * a class that encompasses fewer than 20 members will likely not be certified absent other indications of impracticability of joinder, while a class of 40 or more members raises a presumption of impracticability of joinder based on numbers alone." *Newberg on Class Actions* § 3:12 (5th ed. 2013).

3.   The Rule 23(a)(2) commonality requirement focuses on the characteristics of the class itself ("questions of law or fact common to the class"), while Rule 23(a)(3) asks whether "the claims or defenses of the representative parties are typical of the claims or defenses of the class." Could there be situations in which there are one or more common questions of law or fact that satisfy Rule 23(a)(2), but the claims or defenses of the representative parties are not typical of the claims or defenses of the class? Why is it important that the named plaintiffs assert claims that are typical of those asserted in the class?

4.   The Rule 23(a)(4) requirement of adequacy of representation is frequently contested in class certifications determinations. Rule 23(a)(4) requires that "the representative parties will fairly and adequately protect the interests of the class." As the United States Court of Appeals for the Third Circuit has noted, "This [Rule 23(a)(4)] requirement encompasses two distinct inquiries designed to protect the interests of absentee class members: 'it considers whether the named plaintiffs' interests are sufficiently aligned with the absentees', and it tests the qualifications of the counsel to represent the class.'" *In re Community Bank of Northern Virginia*, 418 F.3d 277, 303 (3d Cir. 2005), quoting *In re General Motors Corp. Pick-Up Truck Fuel Tank Products Liability Litigation*, 55 F.3rd 768, 800 (3rd Cir. 1995).

As the Supreme Court held in *Hansberry v. Lee*, 311 U.S. 32 (1940), *supra* p. 517, constitutional due process also imposes a requirement that named class representatives adequately represent the remaining members of the class—who typically will not actively participate in the civil action. Thus there can be no conflicts of interest between the class representatives and the other class members under the requirements of both the United States Constitution and Rule 23(a)(4).

5.   Not only does Rule 23(a)(4) preclude conflicts between the named class representatives and the remainder of the class, but that provision precludes conflicts between class counsel and the class. For instance, an attorney would be inadequate as class counsel if she or a close family member were a member of the class. In such a situation, the attorney is likely to have a conflict that could cause her to subordinate the best interest of the class to her own interests or those of her family.

In addition to preventing conflicts between the attorney and the class, Rule 23(a)(4) is to insure that the attorney has the experience, ability, and resources to adequately represent the class. Some of the factors that a court should consider in determining the adequacy of counsel are set forth in Federal Rule of Civil Procedure 23(g)(1)(A), which requires the court to consider:

(i)   the work counsel has done in identifying or investigating potential claims in the action;

(ii) counsel's experience in handling class actions, other complex litigation, and the types of claims asserted in the action;

(iii) counsel's knowledge of the applicable law; and

(iv) the resources that counsel will commit to representing the class.

Whether it involves the adequacy of the representative parties or of counsel, why is adequacy such a concern in class action litigation? Consider the three named plaintiffs who represented the 1,500,000 women in the *Dukes* class. Why were these women chosen as class representatives? How do their work histories impact their representation of the other women in the class? When a class contains members who are differentially situated or seek somewhat different relief, Rule 23(c)(5) provides that "a class may be divided into subclasses that are each treated as a class under this rule."

6.   What was the evidence of Wal-Mart's discrimination upon which plaintiffs relied? How would the evidence have differed if the three class representatives were merely suing on their own behalf?

7.   In *Daubert v. Merrell Dow Pharmaceuticals, Inc.*, 509 U.S. 579 (1993), the Supreme Court concluded that "the Rules of Evidence— especially Rule 702—do assign to the trial judge the task of ensuring that an expert's testimony both rests on a reliable foundation and is relevant to the task at hand." 509 U.S. at 597. Wal-Mart argued that the trial judge should exercise a similar screening role in determining the admissibility of expert testimony in connection with a motion for class certification. The district judge concluded that *Daubert* did not apply in such a situation. Although the Supreme Court did not address this ruling, Justice Scalia stated for the majority: "We doubt that is so."

8.   In what circumstances should an appellate court overturn a trial court's determination that Rule 23 requirements have or have not been met?

9.   In section III of its opinion, a unanimous Court determined that class actions seeking backpay that is not incidental to class-wide injunctive or declaratory relief must be filed under Rule 23(b)(3) rather than Rule 23(b)(2). Why did the Court reach this conclusion? What is the significance of this conclusion for plaintiffs?

This portion of the majority opinion, in which all justices joined, reasoned as follows:

The procedural protections attending the (b)(3) class— predominance, superiority, mandatory notice, and the right to opt out—are missing from (b)(2) not because the Rule considers them unnecessary, but because it considers them unnecessary *to a (b)(2) class*. When a class seeks an indivisible injunction benefitting all its members at once, there is no reason to undertake a case-specific inquiry into whether class issues predominate or whether class action is a superior method of adjudicating the dispute. Predominance and superiority are self-evident. But with respect to each class member's individualized claim for money, that is not so—which is precisely why (b)(3) requires the judge to make findings about predominance and superiority before allowing the class.

The practical import of this conclusion is that plaintiffs seeking significant monetary relief must comply with all the additional procedural requirements of Rule 23(b)(3)—including the need to provide and pay for class notice at the outset of the case.

10. All nine members of the Supreme Court agreed that the class in this case had not been properly certified pursuant to Rule 23(b)(2). Why, then, did the Court consider the interpretation of the common question requirement of Rule 23(a)(2)?

11. Rule 23(a)(2) requires as a prerequisite for any class action "questions of law or fact common to the class," while, in Rule 23(b)(3) class actions, "questions of law or fact common to class members [must] predominate over any questions affecting only individual members." What is the role of the Rule 23(b)(3) predominance requirement if Rule 23(a)(2) is interpreted to require a "common contention of such a nature that it is capable of classwide resolution—which means that determination of its truth or falsity will resolve an issue that is central to the validity of each one of the claims in one stroke."

12. On remand to the United States District Court for the Northern District of California, Judge Charles Breyer, brother of Justice Stephen Breyer, considered a motion to certify a reformulated class in *Dukes* consisting of 150,000 women who worked in Wal-Mart's "California Regions." Judge Breyer denied certification of this new class, concluding:

> Plaintiffs' proposed class suffers from the same problems identified by the Supreme Court, but on a somewhat smaller scale. Indeed, it is revealing that there is no particular logic to the precise scope of the class Plaintiffs now propose. They picked three corporate regions covering a smaller area than the rejected national class, but nothing in Plaintiffs' evidence shows that those three regions are actually different from any other Wal-Mart regions along any relevant dimension. Rather than identify an employment practice and define a class around it, Plaintiffs continue to challenge the discretionary decisions of hundreds of decision makers, while arbitrarily confining their proposed class to corporate regions that include stores in California, among other states. Accordingly, the Court DENIES their motion for class certification. This Order does not consider whether Plaintiffs

themselves were victims of discrimination as alleged in their complaint; those individual claims shall proceed in this litigation.

Dukes v. Wal-Mart Stores, Inc., 964 F.Supp.2d 1115, 1127 (N.D. Cal. 2013).

C. CONSTITUTIONAL, STATUTORY, AND RULE 23 FEDERAL CLASS ACTION REQUIREMENTS

Figure 7–1 illustrates the constitutional, statutory, and Rule 23 requirements for a federal class action. Use it as a checklist to test the validity of class actions filed in the federal courts.

FIGURE 7–1
PREREQUISITES FOR A FEDERAL CLASS ACTION

NOTICE (required in all cases)	JURISDICTION (one or more must be satisfied)	RULE 23(a) (all four must be satisfied)	RULE 23(b) (one or more must be satisfied)
Constitutional Due Process Clause requires notice to all class members in most cases (*Hansberry v. Lee*)	Section 1331 Federal Question: same as with non-class actions; class action must arise under the Constitution, laws, or treaties of the United States	Rule 23(a)(1) Numerosity: class "so numerous that joinder of all members is impracticable" (typically, more than 40 class members)	Rule 23(b)(1)(A): separate actions would risk inconsistent or varying adjudications establishing incompatible standards for party opposing class
Rule 23(c)(2)(B) requires notice in all Rule 23(b)(3) class actions	Section 1332(a) Diversity: (1) only citizenship of named representatives is considered for complete diversity; (2) under Section 1367, at least one class member must satisfy minimum amount in controversy	Rule 23(a)(2) Commonality: common question of law or fact capable of classwide resolution so its determination will resolve a central issue "in one stroke." *Wal-Mart v. Dukes*	Rule 23(b)(1)(B): separate actions would risk adjudications dispositive of interests of non-parties or substantially impair or impede their ability to protect their interests

Rule 23(c)(2)(A) authorizes court to direct notice in Rule 23(b)(1) and (2) class actions	Section 1332(d) Class Action Fairness Act: more than $5 million total in controversy; at least 100 class members; and minimal diversity	Rule 23(a)(3) Typicality: claims or defenses of class representatives "are typical of the claims or defenses of the class"	Rule 23(b)(2): party opposing class has acted or refused to act on classwide basis justifying classwide declaratory or injunctive relief
Rule 23(e)(1) requires notice to all class members before settlement of certified class		Rule 23(a)(4) Adequacy: class representatives and counsel "will fairly and adequately protect the interests of the class"	Rule 23(b)(3): (1) common questions of law or fact predominate and (2) class action is superior method of resolving controversy

IV. THE SETTLEMENT OF CLASS ACTIONS

Most civil litigation, federal and state, is resolved well before trial.[10] So few cases are now resolved by trial that the American Bar Association and others have expressed concern about the "Vanishing Trial."[11] When civil actions are resolved by party settlement, the parties simply file a stipulation pursuant to Rule 41(a)(1)(A)(ii) of the Federal Rules of Civil Procedure. In virtually all cases, such a party stipulation is sufficient to dismiss the action from the court's docket—without any order or other action by the judge.

But the dismissal of a class action is not so easy. As part of the major amendment of Rule 23 in 1966, Rule 23(e) was added to provide,

---

[10] For the 12 month period that ended on December 31, 2014, only 1.1% of the civil actions, other than land condemnation cases, that were terminated in the federal courts reached trial. Director, Admin. Office of the U.S. Courts, *Judicial Business of the United States Courts* (Table C–4) (2014). In a major study of trial trends in 22 state courts, civil jury trials as a percentage of total civil dispositions decreased from about 1.8% in 1976 to 0.6% in 2002, while bench trials decreased from 34% to 15%. Considering just torts, contract, and real property rights cases, the percentage of jury trials per total dispositions was 1.3% in 2002, while the percentage of bench trials was 4.3%. Ostrom et al., "Examining Trial Trends in State Courts: 1976–2002," 1 *J. Emp. Legal Studies* 755, 768–771 (2004). *See also* Eisenberg et al., "Litigation Outcomes in State and Federal Courts: A Statistical Portrait," 19 *Seattle U. Law Rev.* 433, 444 (1996); Grossman et al., "Measuring the Pace of Civil Litigation in Federal and State Trial Courts," 65 *Judicature* 86, 106 (Table 6) (1981).

[11] *See generally* Galanter, "A World Without Trials?," 2006 *J. Disp. Res.* 7; Symposium, "The Vanishing Trial," 1 *J. Emp. Legal Studies* 459 (2004).

at that time, that a "class action shall not be dismissed or compromised without the approval of the court, and notice of the proposed dismissal or compromise shall be given to all members of the class in such manner as the court directs." Advisory Committee Note to 1966 Amendment to Rule 23, 39 F.R.D. 69, 98 (1966). Why can't the parties themselves simply dismiss a class action—just as they can dismiss virtually any other civil action?

In traditional civil litigation, someone chooses and retains an attorney, speaks with her about the desired relief, and contracts to pay an agreed-upon attorney's fee. The lawyer consults with the client about how the client's objectives may be accomplished and keeps the client reasonably informed about the status of the matter. Indeed, the lawyer is required to do this by Rule 1.4 of the ABA Model Rules of Professional Conduct. In addition, Rule 1.2(a) of the Model Rules requires a lawyer to abide by her client's decision whether or not to settle a matter.

However, these conventions and constraints do not typically apply to class actions, in which class counsel may represent thousands of individuals whom the lawyer will never meet and with whom the lawyer may never communicate after an initial class notice. Class actions move the focus from individual plaintiffs to class counsel, from individual relief to class relief and attorneys' fees, and from adjudication to settlement. Because of these changes, and the significant changes in the attorney-client relationship, additional procedural protections for class members have been built into the Federal Rules of Civil Procedure. Most of these procedures, contained within Rule 23, require the active involvement of the judge in supervising the class action and class counsel.

As you have seen, there are four Rule 23(a) prerequisites for any class action, and the class action must satisfy one of the three subsections of Rule 23(b). Rule 23(c)(1) requires a certification order defining the class, while Rule 23(c)(2) requires entry of notice in a (b)(3) class and permits such notice in (b)(1) and (b)(2) classes. Rule 23(g) and (h) were added to Rule 23 in 2003, and deal, respectively, with the appointment of class counsel and attorney's fees and costs.

Rule 23(e) also was greatly expanded in 2003 to deal with settlement, voluntary dismissal, and compromise of certified class actions. A careful reading of Rule 23(e) suggests the concerns motivating the creation and expansion of that subdivision of Rule 23. Rule 23(e) provides:

> The claims, issues, or defenses of a certified class may be settled, voluntarily dismissed, or compromised only with the court's approval. The following procedures apply to a proposed settlement, voluntary dismissal, or compromise:

(1) The court must direct notice in a reasonable manner to all class members who would be bound by the proposal.

(2) If the proposal would bind class members, the court may approve it only after a hearing and on finding that it is fair, reasonable, and adequate.

(3) The parties seeking approval must file a statement identifying any agreement made in connection with the proposal.

(4) If the class action was previously certified under Rule 23(b)(3), the court may refuse to approve a settlement unless it affords a new opportunity to request exclusion to individual class members who had an earlier opportunity to request exclusion but did not do so.

(5) Any class member may object to the proposal if it requires court approval under this subdivision (e); the objection may be withdrawn only with the court's approval.

Test your reading of Rule 23(e) by answering the following questions.

1. At what stage of a class action does Rule 23(e) require court approval of a dismissal of the class action?

2. Who must be notified of the dismissal of a certified class action?

3. What procedures must a judge follow in dismissing a certified class action?

4. What standard should the judge apply in determining whether to dismiss a certified class action?

5. With what sorts of agreements concerning the proposed dismissal will the judge be concerned?

6. Are there any class members who may not be bound by the proposed settlement?

7. Why can objections to a proposed settlement only be withdrawn with court approval?

Which brings us back to the question of why class actions, and the settlement of class actions, are treated differently than other civil actions. Consider this question as you read the opinions in the following case.

A. *AMCHEM PRODUCTS, INC. V. WINDSOR*

Amchem Products, Inc. v. Windsor
Supreme Court of the United States, 1997
521 U.S. 591

OPINION

■ JUSTICE GINSBURG delivered the opinion of the Court.

This case concerns the legitimacy under Rule 23 of the Federal Rules of Civil Procedure of a class-action certification sought to achieve global settlement of current and future asbestos-related claims. The class proposed for certification potentially encompasses hundreds of thousands, perhaps millions, of individuals tied together by this commonality: Each was, or some day may be, adversely affected by past exposure to asbestos products manufactured by one or more of 20 companies. Those companies, defendants in the lower courts, are petitioners here.

The United States District Court for the Eastern District of Pennsylvania certified the class for settlement only, finding that the proposed settlement was fair and that representation and notice had been adequate. That court enjoined class members from separately pursuing asbestos-related personal-injury suits in any court, federal or state, pending the issuance of a final order. The Court of Appeals for the Third Circuit vacated the District Court's orders, holding that the class certification failed to satisfy Rule 23's requirements in several critical respects. We affirm the Court of Appeals' judgment.

I

A

The settlement-class certification we confront evolved in response to an asbestos-litigation crisis. A United States Judicial Conference Ad Hoc Committee on Asbestos Litigation, appointed by THE CHIEF JUSTICE in September 1990, described facets of the problem in a 1991 report:

> "[This] is a tale of danger known in the 1930s, exposure inflicted upon millions of Americans in the 1940s and 1950s, injuries that began to take their toll in the 1960s, and a flood of lawsuits beginning in the 1970s. On the basis of past and current filing data, and because of a latency period that may last as long as 40 years for some asbestos related diseases, a continuing stream of claims can be expected. The final toll of asbestos related injuries is unknown. Predictions have been made of 200,000 asbestos disease deaths before the year 2000 and as many as 265,000 by the year 2015.

> "The most objectionable aspects of asbestos litigation can be briefly summarized: dockets in both federal and state courts

continue to grow; long delays are routine; trials are too long; the same issues are litigated over and over; transaction costs exceed the victims' recovery by nearly two to one; exhaustion of assets threatens and distorts the process; and future claimants may lose altogether." *Report of The Judicial Conference Ad Hoc Committee on Asbestos Litigation* 2–3 (Mar.1991).

Real reform, the report concluded, required federal legislation creating a national asbestos dispute-resolution scheme. As recommended by the Ad Hoc Committee, the Judicial Conference of the United States urged Congress to act. To this date, no congressional response has emerged.

In the face of legislative inaction, the federal courts—lacking authority to replace state tort systems with a national toxic tort compensation regime—endeavored to work with the procedural tools available to improve management of federal asbestos litigation. Eight federal judges, experienced in the superintendence of asbestos cases, urged the Judicial Panel on Multidistrict Litigation (MDL Panel), to consolidate in a single district all asbestos complaints then pending in federal courts. Accepting the recommendation, the MDL Panel transferred all asbestos cases then filed, but not yet on trial in federal courts to a single district, the United States District Court for the Eastern District of Pennsylvania; pursuant to the transfer order, the collected cases were consolidated for pretrial proceedings before Judge Weiner. The order aggregated pending cases only; no authority resides in the MDL Panel to license for consolidated proceedings claims not yet filed.

B

After the consolidation, attorneys for plaintiffs and defendants formed separate steering committees and began settlement negotiations. Ronald L. Motley and Gene Locks—later appointed, along with Motley's law partner Joseph F. Rice, to represent the plaintiff class in this action—cochaired the Plaintiffs' Steering Committee. Counsel for the Center for Claims Resolution (CCR), the consortium of 20 former asbestos manufacturers now before us as petitioners, participated in the Defendants' Steering Committee.[2] Although the MDL Panel order collected, transferred, and consolidated only cases already commenced in federal courts, settlement negotiations included efforts to find a "means of resolving . . . future cases."

* * *

To that end, CCR counsel approached the lawyers who had headed the Plaintiffs' Steering Committee in the unsuccessful negotiations, and a new round of negotiations began; that round yielded the mass settlement agreement now in controversy. At the time, the former

---

[2]   * * * All of the CCR petitioners stopped manufacturing asbestos products around 1975.

heads of the Plaintiffs' Steering Committee represented thousands of plaintiffs with then-pending asbestos-related claims—claimants the parties to this suit call "inventory" plaintiffs. CCR indicated in these discussions that it would resist settlement of inventory cases absent "some kind of protection for the future."

Settlement talks thus concentrated on devising an administrative scheme for disposition of asbestos claims not yet in litigation. In these negotiations, counsel for masses of inventory plaintiffs endeavored to represent the interests of the anticipated future claimants, although those lawyers then had no attorney-client relationship with such claimants.

Once negotiations seemed likely to produce an agreement purporting to bind potential plaintiffs, CCR agreed to settle, through separate agreements, the claims of plaintiffs who had already filed asbestos-related lawsuits. In one such agreement, CCR defendants promised to pay more than $200 million to gain release of the claims of numerous inventory plaintiffs. After settling the inventory claims, CCR, together with the plaintiffs' lawyers CCR had approached, launched this case, exclusively involving persons outside the MDL Panel's province—plaintiffs without already pending lawsuits.[3]

C

The class action thus instituted was not intended to be litigated. Rather, within the space of a single day, January 15, 1993, the settling parties—CCR defendants and the representatives of the plaintiff class described below—presented to the District Court a complaint, an answer, a proposed settlement agreement, and a joint motion for conditional class certification.[4]

The complaint identified nine lead plaintiffs, designating them and members of their families as representatives of a class comprising all persons who had not filed an asbestos-related lawsuit against a CCR defendant as of the date the class action commenced, but who (1) had been exposed—occupationally or through the occupational exposure of a spouse or household member—to asbestos or products containing asbestos attributable to a CCR defendant, or (2) whose spouse or family member had been so exposed. Untold numbers of individuals may fall within this description. All named plaintiffs alleged that they or a member of their family had been exposed to asbestos-containing products of CCR defendants. More than half of the named plaintiffs alleged that they or their family members had already suffered various

---

[3]   It is basic to comprehension of this proceeding to notice that no transferred case is included in the settlement at issue, and no case covered by the settlement existed as a civil action at the time of the MDL Panel transfer.

[4]   Also on the same day, the CCR defendants filed a third-party action against their insurers, seeking a declaratory judgment holding the insurers liable for the costs of the settlement. The insurance litigation, upon which implementation of the settlement is conditioned, is still pending in the District Court.

physical injuries as a result of the exposure. The others alleged that they had not yet manifested any asbestos-related condition. The complaint delineated no subclasses; all named plaintiffs were designated as representatives of the class as a whole.

The complaint invoked the District Court's diversity jurisdiction and asserted various state-law claims for relief, including (1) negligent failure to warn, (2) strict liability, (3) breach of express and implied warranty, (4) negligent infliction of emotional distress, (5) enhanced risk of disease, (6) medical monitoring, and (7) civil conspiracy. Each plaintiff requested unspecified damages in excess of $100,000. CCR defendants' answer denied the principal allegations of the complaint and asserted 11 affirmative defenses.

A stipulation of settlement accompanied the pleadings; it proposed to settle, and to preclude nearly all class members from litigating against CCR companies, all claims not filed before January 15, 1993, involving compensation for present and future asbestos-related personal injury or death. An exhaustive document exceeding 100 pages, the stipulation presents in detail an administrative mechanism and a schedule of payments to compensate class members who meet defined asbestos-exposure and medical requirements. The stipulation describes four categories of compensable disease: mesothelioma; lung cancer; certain "other cancers" (colon-rectal, laryngeal, esophageal, and stomach cancer); and "non-malignant conditions" (asbestosis and bilateral pleural thickening). Persons with "exceptional" medical claims—claims that do not fall within the four described diagnostic categories—may in some instances qualify for compensation, but the settlement caps the number of "exceptional" claims CCR must cover.

For each qualifying disease category, the stipulation specifies the range of damages CCR will pay to qualifying claimants. Payments under the settlement are not adjustable for inflation. Mesothelioma claimants—the most highly compensated category—are scheduled to receive between $20,000 and $200,000. The stipulation provides that CCR is to propose the level of compensation within the prescribed ranges; it also establishes procedures to resolve disputes over medical diagnoses and levels of compensation.

Compensation above the fixed ranges may be obtained for "extraordinary" claims. But the settlement places both numerical caps and dollar limits on such claims. The settlement also imposes "case flow maximums," which cap the number of claims payable for each disease in a given year.

Class members are to receive no compensation for certain kinds of claims, even if otherwise applicable state law recognizes such claims. Claims that garner no compensation under the settlement include claims by family members of asbestos-exposed individuals for loss of consortium, and claims by so-called "exposure-only" plaintiffs for increased risk of cancer, fear of future asbestos-related injury, and medical monitoring. * * * Defendants forgo defenses to liability, including statute of limitations pleas.

Class members, in the main, are bound by the settlement in perpetuity, while CCR defendants may choose to withdraw from the settlement after ten years. A small number of class members—only a few per year—may reject the settlement and pursue their claims in court. Those permitted to exercise this option, however, may not assert any punitive damages claim or any claim for increased risk of cancer. Aspects of the administration of the settlement are to be monitored by the AFL-CIO and class counsel. Class counsel are to receive attorneys' fees in an amount to be approved by the District Court.

D

On January 29, 1993, as requested by the settling parties, the District Court conditionally certified, under Federal Rule of Civil Procedure 23(b)(3), an encompassing opt-out class. The certified class included persons occupationally exposed to defendants' asbestos products, and members of their families, who had not filed suit as of January 15. Judge Weiner appointed Locks, Motley, and Rice as class counsel, noting that "[t]he Court may in the future appoint additional counsel if it is deemed necessary and advisable." At no stage of the proceedings, however, were additional counsel in fact appointed. Nor was the class ever divided into subclasses. In a separate order, Judge Weiner assigned to Judge Reed, also of the Eastern District of Pennsylvania, "the task of conducting fairness proceedings and of determining whether the proposed settlement is fair to the class." Various class members raised objections to the settlement stipulation, and Judge Weiner granted the objectors full rights to participate in the subsequent proceedings.

In preliminary rulings, Judge Reed held that the District Court had subject-matter jurisdiction, and he approved the settling parties' elaborate plan for giving notice to the class. The court-approved notice informed recipients that they could exclude themselves from the class, if they so chose, within a three-month opt-out period.

Objectors raised numerous challenges to the settlement. They urged that the settlement unfairly disadvantaged those without currently compensable conditions in that it failed to adjust for inflation or to account for changes, over time, in medical understanding. They maintained that compensation levels were intolerably low in comparison to awards available in tort litigation or payments received by the inventory plaintiffs. And they objected to the absence of any compensation for certain claims, for example, medical monitoring, compensable under the tort law of several States. Rejecting these and all other objections, Judge Reed concluded that the settlement terms were fair and had been negotiated without collusion. He also found that adequate notice had been given to class members, and that final class certification under Rule 23(b)(3) was appropriate.

* * *

Strenuous objections had been asserted regarding the adequacy of representation, a Rule 23(a)(4) requirement. Objectors maintained that class counsel and class representatives had disqualifying conflicts of interests. In particular, objectors urged, claimants whose injuries had become manifest and claimants without manifest injuries should not have common counsel and should not be aggregated in a single class. Furthermore, objectors argued, lawyers representing inventory plaintiffs should not represent the newly formed class.

Satisfied that class counsel had ably negotiated the settlement in the best interests of all concerned, and that the named parties served as adequate representatives, the District Court rejected these objections. * * *

The objectors appealed. The United States Court of Appeals for the Third Circuit vacated the certification, holding that the requirements of Rule 23 had not been satisfied.

* * *

IV

We granted review to decide the role settlement may play, under existing Rule 23, in determining the propriety of class certification. The Third Circuit's opinion stated that each of the requirements of Rule 23(a) and (b)(3) "must be satisfied without taking into account the settlement." That statement, petitioners urge, is incorrect.

We agree with petitioners to this limited extent: Settlement is relevant to a class certification. The Third Circuit's opinion bears modification in that respect. But, as we earlier observed, the Court of Appeals in fact did not ignore the settlement; instead, that court homed in on settlement terms in explaining why it found the absentees' interests inadequately represented. The Third Circuit's close inspection of the settlement in that regard was altogether proper.

Confronted with a request for settlement-only class certification, a district court need not inquire whether the case, if tried, would present intractable management problems, *see* Fed. Rule Civ. Proc. 23(b)(3)(D), for the proposal is that there be no trial. But other specifications of the Rule—those designed to protect absentees by blocking unwarranted or overbroad class definitions—demand undiluted, even heightened, attention in the settlement context. Such attention is of vital importance, for a court asked to certify a settlement class will lack the opportunity, present when a case is litigated, to adjust the class, informed by the proceedings as they unfold. *See* Rule 23(c), (d).[16]

---

[16] Portions of the opinion dissenting in part appear to assume that settlement counts only one way—in favor of certification. To the extent that is the dissent's meaning, we disagree. Settlement, though a relevant factor, does not inevitably signal that class-action certification should be granted more readily than it would be were the case to be litigated. For

And, of overriding importance, courts must be mindful that the Rule as now composed sets the requirements they are bound to enforce. Federal Rules take effect after an extensive deliberative process involving many reviewers: a Rules Advisory Committee, public commenters, the Judicial Conference, this Court, the Congress. *See* 28 U.S.C. §§ 2073, 2074. The text of a rule thus proposed and reviewed limits judicial inventiveness. Courts are not free to amend a rule outside the process Congress ordered, a process properly tuned to the instruction that rules of procedure "shall not abridge . . . any substantive right." § 2072(b).

* * * Th[e] prescription [of Rule 23(e)] was designed to function as an additional requirement, not a superseding direction, for the "class action" to which Rule 23(e) refers is one qualified for certification under Rule 23(a) and (b). Subdivisions (a) and (b) focus court attention on whether a proposed class has sufficient unity so that absent members can fairly be bound by decisions of class representatives. That dominant concern persists when settlement, rather than trial, is proposed.

The safeguards provided by the Rule 23(a) and (b) class-qualifying criteria, we emphasize, are not impractical impediments—checks shorn of utility—in the settlement-class context. First, the standards set for the protection of absent class members serve to inhibit appraisals of the chancellor's foot kind—class certifications dependent upon the court's gestalt judgment or overarching impression of the settlement's fairness.

Second, if a fairness inquiry under Rule 23(e) controlled certification, eclipsing Rule 23(a) and (b), and permitting class designation despite the impossibility of litigation, both class counsel and court would be disarmed. Class counsel confined to settlement negotiations could not use the threat of litigation to press for a better offer, and the court would face a bargain proffered for its approval without benefit of adversarial investigation.

Federal courts, in any case, lack authority to substitute for Rule 23's certification criteria a standard never adopted—that if a settlement is "fair," then certification is proper. Applying to this case criteria the rulemakers set, we conclude that the Third Circuit's appraisal is essentially correct. Although that court should have acknowledged that settlement is a factor in the calculus, a remand is not warranted on that account. The Court of Appeals' opinion amply demonstrates why—with or without a settlement on the table—the sprawling class the District Court certified does not satisfy Rule 23's requirements.

A

We address first the requirement of Rule 23(b)(3) that "[common] questions of law or fact . . . predominate over any questions affecting only individual members." The District Court concluded that

---

reasons the Third Circuit aired, proposed settlement classes sometimes warrant more, not less, caution on the question of certification.

predominance was satisfied based on two factors: class members' shared experience of asbestos exposure and their common "interest in receiving prompt and fair compensation for their claims, while minimizing the risks and transaction costs inherent in the asbestos litigation process as it occurs presently in the tort system." The settling parties also contend that the settlement's fairness is a common question, predominating over disparate legal issues that might be pivotal in litigation but become irrelevant under the settlement.

The predominance requirement stated in Rule 23(b)(3), we hold, is not met by the factors on which the District Court relied. The benefits asbestos-exposed persons might gain from the establishment of a grand-scale compensation scheme is a matter fit for legislative consideration, but it is not pertinent to the predominance inquiry. That inquiry trains on the legal or factual questions that qualify each class member's case as a genuine controversy, questions that preexist any settlement.

The Rule 23(b)(3) predominance inquiry tests whether proposed classes are sufficiently cohesive to warrant adjudication by representation.[19] The inquiry appropriate under Rule 23(e), on the other hand, protects unnamed class members "from unjust or unfair settlements affecting their rights when the representatives become fainthearted before the action is adjudicated or are able to secure satisfaction of their individual claims by a compromise." *See* 7B *Wright, Miller, & Kane* § 1797, at 340–341. But it is not the mission of Rule 23(e) to assure the class cohesion that legitimizes representative action in the first place. If a common interest in a fair compromise could satisfy the predominance requirement of Rule 23(b)(3), that vital prescription would be stripped of any meaning in the settlement context.

The District Court also relied upon this commonality: "The members of the class have all been exposed to asbestos products supplied by the defendants. . . ." Even if Rule 23(a)'s commonality requirement may be satisfied by that shared experience, the predominance criterion is far more demanding. Given the greater number of questions peculiar to the several categories of class members, and to individuals within each category, and the significance of those uncommon questions, any overarching dispute about the health consequences of asbestos exposure cannot satisfy the Rule 23(b)(3) predominance standard.

The Third Circuit highlighted the disparate questions undermining class cohesion in this case:

> "Class members were exposed to different asbestos-containing products, for different amounts of time, in different ways, and

---

[19] This case, we note, involves no "limited fund" capable of supporting class treatment under Rule 23(b)(1)(B), which does not have a predominance requirement. The settling parties sought to proceed exclusively under Rule 23(b)(3).

over different periods. Some class members suffer no physical injury or have only asymptomatic pleural changes, while others suffer from lung cancer, disabling asbestosis, or from mesothelioma. . . . Each has a different history of cigarette smoking, a factor that complicates the causation inquiry.

"The [exposure-only] plaintiffs especially share little in common, either with each other or with the presently injured class members. It is unclear whether they will contract asbestos-related disease and, if so, what disease each will suffer. They will also incur different medical expenses because their monitoring and treatment will depend on singular circumstances and individual medical histories."

Differences in state law, the Court of Appeals observed, compound these disparities.

No settlement class called to our attention is as sprawling as this one. Predominance is a test readily met in certain cases alleging consumer or securities fraud or violations of the antitrust laws. Even mass tort cases arising from a common cause or disaster may, depending upon the circumstances, satisfy the predominance requirement. The Advisory Committee for the 1966 revision of Rule 23, it is true, noted that "mass accident" cases are likely to present "significant questions, not only of damages but of liability and defenses of liability, . . . affecting the individuals in different ways." *Adv. Comm. Notes*, 28 U.S.C.App., p. 697. And the Committee advised that such cases are "ordinarily not appropriate" for class treatment. *Ibid.* But the text of the Rule does not categorically exclude mass tort cases from class certification, and District Courts, since the late 1970's, have been certifying such cases in increasing number. The Committee's warning, however, continues to call for caution when individual stakes are high and disparities among class members great. As the Third Circuit's opinion makes plain, the certification in this case does not follow the counsel of caution. That certification cannot be upheld, for it rests on a conception of Rule 23(b)(3)'s predominance requirement irreconcilable with the Rule's design.

B

Nor can the class approved by the District Court satisfy Rule 23(a)(4)'s requirement that the named parties "will fairly and adequately protect the interests of the class." The adequacy inquiry under Rule 23(a)(4) serves to uncover conflicts of interest between named parties and the class they seek to represent. "[A] class representative must be part of the class and 'possess the same interest and suffer the same injury' as the class members." *East Tex. Motor Freight System, Inc. v. Rodriguez*, 431 U.S. 395, 403, (1977) (quoting *Schlesinger v. Reservists Comm. to Stop the War*, 418 U.S. 208, 216, (1974)).

As the Third Circuit pointed out, named parties with diverse medical conditions sought to act on behalf of a single giant class rather than on behalf of discrete subclasses. In significant respects, the interests of those within the single class are not aligned. Most saliently, for the currently injured, the critical goal is generous immediate payments. That goal tugs against the interest of exposure-only plaintiffs in ensuring an ample, inflation-protected fund for the future.

The disparity between the currently injured and expossure-only categories of plaintiffs, and the diversity within each category are not made insignificant by the District Court's finding that petitioners' assets suffice to pay claims under the settlement. Although this is not a "limited fund" case certified under Rule 23(b)(1)(B), the terms of the settlement reflect essential allocation decisions designed to confine compensation and to limit defendants' liability. For example, as earlier described, the settlement includes no adjustment for inflation; only a few claimants per year can opt out at the back end; and loss-of-consortium claims are extinguished with no compensation.

The settling parties, in sum, achieved a global compromise with no structural assurance of fair and adequate representation for the diverse groups and individuals affected. Although the named parties alleged a range of complaints, each served generally as representative for the whole, not for a separate constituency. * * *

The Third Circuit found no assurance here—either in the terms of the settlement or in the structure of the negotiations—that the named plaintiffs operated under a proper understanding of their representational responsibilities. That assessment, we conclude, is on the mark.

C

Impediments to the provision of adequate notice, the Third Circuit emphasized, rendered highly problematic any endeavor to tie to a settlement class persons with no perceptible asbestos-related disease at the time of the settlement. Many persons in the exposure-only category, the Court of Appeals stressed, may not even know of their exposure, or realize the extent of the harm they may incur. Even if they fully appreciate the significance of class notice, those without current afflictions may not have the information or foresight needed to decide, intelligently, whether to stay in or opt out.

Family members of asbestos-exposed individuals may themselves fall prey to disease or may ultimately have ripe claims for loss of consortium. Yet large numbers of people in this category—future spouses and children of asbestos victims—could not be alerted to their class membership. And current spouses and children of the occupationally exposed may know nothing of that exposure.

Because we have concluded that the class in this case cannot satisfy the requirements of common issue predominance and adequacy of representation, we need not rule, definitively, on the notice given here. In accord with the Third Circuit, however, we recognize the gravity of the question whether class action notice sufficient under the Constitution and Rule 23 could ever be given to legions so unselfconscious and amorphous.

V

The argument is sensibly made that a nationwide administrative claims processing regime would provide the most secure, fair, and efficient means of compensating victims of asbestos exposure. Congress, however, has not adopted such a solution. And Rule 23, which must be interpreted with fidelity to the Rules Enabling Act and applied with the interests of absent class members in close view, cannot carry the large load CCR, class counsel, and the District Court heaped upon it. As this case exemplifies, the rulemakers' prescriptions for class actions may be endangered by "those who embrace [Rule 23] too enthusiastically just as [they are by] those who approach [the Rule] with distaste." C. Wright, *Law of Federal Courts* 508 (5th ed.1994).

* * *

For the reasons stated, the judgment of the Court of Appeals for the Third Circuit is

Affirmed.

■ JUSTICE O'CONNOR took no part in the consideration or decision of this case.

■ JUSTICE BREYER, with whom JUSTICE STEVENS joins, concurring in part and dissenting in part.

Although I agree with the Court's basic holding that "[s]ettlement is relevant to a class certification," I find several problems in its approach that lead me to a different conclusion. First, I believe that the need for settlement in this mass tort case, with hundreds of thousands of lawsuits, is greater than the Court's opinion suggests. Second, I would give more weight than would the majority to settlement-related issues for purposes of determining whether common issues predominate. Third, I am uncertain about the Court's determination of adequacy of representation, and do not believe it appropriate for this Court to second-guess the District Court on the matter without first having the Court of Appeals consider it. Fourth, I am uncertain about the tenor of an opinion that seems to suggest the settlement is unfair. And fifth, in the absence of further review by the Court of Appeals, I cannot accept the majority's suggestions that "notice" is inadequate.

These difficulties flow from the majority's review of what are highly fact-based, complex, and difficult matters, matters that are inappropriate for initial review before this Court. The law gives broad leeway to district courts in making class certification decisions, and their judgments are to be reviewed by the court of appeals only for abuse of discretion. Indeed, the District Court's certification decision rests upon more than 300 findings of fact reached after five weeks of comprehensive hearings. Accordingly, I do not believe that we should in effect set aside the findings of the District Court. That court is far more familiar with the issues and litigants than is a court of appeals or are we, and therefore has "broad power and discretion . . . with respect to matters involving the certification" of class actions. *Reiter v. Sonotone Corp.*, 442 U.S. 330, 345 (1979).

I do not believe that we can rely upon the Court of Appeals' review of the District Court record, for that review, and its ultimate conclusions, are infected by a legal error. There is no evidence that the Court of Appeals at any point considered the settlement as something that would help the class meet Rule 23. I find, moreover, the fact-related issues presented here sufficiently close to warrant further detailed appellate court review under the correct legal standard. * * *

II

The issues in this case are complicated and difficult. The District Court might have been correct. Or not. Subclasses might be appropriate. Or not. I cannot tell. And I do not believe that this Court should be in the business of trying to make these fact-based determinations. That is a job suited to the district courts in the first instance, and the courts of appeals on review. But there is no reason in this case to believe that the Court of Appeals conducted its prior review with an understanding that the settlement could have constituted a reasonably strong factor in favor of class certification. For this reason, I would provide the courts below with an opportunity to analyze the factual questions involved in certification by vacating the judgment, and remanding the case for further proceedings.

COMMENTS AND QUESTIONS CONCERNING *AMCHEM PRODUCTS, INC. V. WINDSOR*

1.   The pending asbestos cases were transferred to Judge Weiner in the Eastern District of Pennsylvania for consolidated pretrial proceedings under the Multidistrict Litigation Act, 28 U.S.C. § 1407. This act permits the consolidation of civil actions "involving one or more common questions of fact [that] are pending in different districts" in a single United States District Court. 28 U.S.C. § 1407(a). Such transfers are only for "coordinated or consolidated pretrial proceedings" (which can include settlement), and the actions must be transferred back to their original districts for trial at the conclusion of the pretrial proceedings. *Id.*

2.   How could there be diversity of citizenship in an action with "hundreds of thousands, perhaps millions" of class members? Isn't it inevitable that some of these plaintiff class members will be citizens of the same states as the defendants?

3.   In their settlement agreement, the lawyers attempted to settle claims that did not yet exist (although the class members had been exposed

to asbestos). If this had not been a class action, would there have been difficulties with identifying and notifying individual plaintiffs? With obtaining an individual plaintiff's consent to settle a claim that did not yet exist?

4.   In his opinion, Justice Breyer notes that the Court of Appeals reversed a district court certification decision that "rests upon more than 300 findings of fact reached after five weeks of comprehensive hearings." Is this the proper role of an appellate court? Who are the Court of Appeals and the Supreme Court attempting to protect? If the parties have agreed to settle this litigation, why should the courts stop them? Weren't class members adequately protected by the three-month period in which they could opt out of the settlement?

5.   Rule 23(c)(5) provides: "When appropriate, a class may be divided into subclasses that are each treated as a class under this rule." How might Rule 23(c)(5) subclasses have been used by plaintiffs in this action?

6.   Did the plaintiffs satisfy the Rule 23(a)(2) commonality requirement as that requirement was later interpreted in *Wal-Mart Stores, Inc. v. Dukes*?

7.   Why does Justice Ginsburg suggest that this class is more difficult to certify than a tort action in which the plaintiffs' damages stem from a single accident?

8.   Why shouldn't the district court approve a proposed settlement that is "fair, reasonable, and adequate" within the meaning of Rule 23(e)(2)? Why the additional focus on the requirements of Rules 23(a) and (b)?

9.   What aspects of the settlement may have been disadvantageous to class members (especially those whose injuries had not yet manifested)?

10.   Rule 23(f) was added to Rule 23 in 1988, authorizing a court of appeals to "permit an appeal from an order granting or denying class-action certification under [Rule 23] if a petition for permission to appeal is filed with the circuit clerk within 14 days after the order is entered." However, Rule 23(f) further provides: "An appeal does not stay proceedings in the district court unless the district judge or the court of appeals so orders."

11.   Two years after its decision in *Amchem* the Supreme Court was presented with another appeal from an asbestos class settlement in *Ortiz v. Fibreboard Corp.*, 527 U.S. 815 (1999). The Court reversed the court of appeals' affirmance of the district court's certification of a Rule 23(b)(1)(B) limited fund class and approval of the settlement of 186,000 potential future asbestos claims for $1.535 billion. The Court reasoned: "Assuming, *arguendo*, that a mandatory, limited fund rationale could under some circumstances be applied to a settlement class of tort claimants, it would be essential that the fund be shown to be limited independently of the agreement of the parties to the action, and equally essential under Rules 23(a) and (b)(1)(B) that the class include all those with claims unsatisfied at the time of the settlement negotiations, with intraclass conflicts addressed by recognizing independently represented subclasses." 527 U.S. at 848.

As they had in *Amchem*, Justices Breyer and Stevens dissented. In his dissent Justice Breyer stated, "I believe our Court should allow a district court full authority to exercise every bit of discretionary power that the law provides. And, in doing so, the Court should prove extremely reluctant to overturn a fact-specific or circumstance-specific exercise of that discretion, where a court of appeals has found it lawful." 527 U.S. at 868.

12. Rule 1 of the Federal Rules of Civil Procedure admonishes counsel and judges that the Federal Rules are to be construed, administered, and employed "to secure the just, speedy, and inexpensive determination of every action and proceeding." Would the proposed settlement in *Amchem* or the case-by-case litigation of asbestos cases do a better job of insuring justice, speed, and efficiency?

Consider Justice Breyer's quote from the district court in *Amchem*:

> The inadequate tort system has demonstrated that the lawyers are well paid for their services but the victims are not receiving speedy and reasonably inexpensive resolution of their claims. Rather, the victims' recoveries are delayed, excessively reduced by transaction costs and relegated to the impersonal group trials and mass consolidations. The sickest of victims often go uncompensated for years while valuable funds go to others who remain unimpaired by their mild asbestos disease. Indeed, these unimpaired victims have, in many states, been forced to assert their claims prematurely or risk giving up all rights to future compensation for any future lung cancer or mesothelioma. The plan which this Court approves today will correct that unfair result for the class members and the . . . defendants.

521 U.S. at 639, quoting 157 F.R.D. at 335.

According to the website of the Asbestos Products Liability Litigation of the Judicial Panel on Multidistrict Litigation in the Eastern District of Pennsylvania, between August 1, 2006, and April 30, 2015, 186,603 cases were transferred into that MDL from across the country and 185,175 of those cases were terminated in the Eastern District of Pennsylvania. *Asbestos Products Liability Litigation (No. VI)* MDL 875 (E.D.Pa. 2014), https://www.paed.uscourts.gov/documents/MDL/MDL875/MDL–875.Vapr 30.2015.pdf.

After the Supreme Court's rejection of the settlements in *Amchem* and *Ortiz*, bankruptcy increasingly has been used to resolve significant mass tort disputes. R. Nagareda, *Mass Torts in a World of Settlement* 167 (2007). *See also* McKenzie, "Toward A Bankruptcy Model for Nonclass Aggregate Litigation," 87 N.Y.U. L. Rev. 960 (2012); Hensler, "As Time Goes By: Asbestos Litigation After *Amchem* and *Ortiz*," 80 *Tex. L. Rev.* 1899 (2002).

B. COUPON SETTLEMENTS

Have you seen tee shirts with proclamations such as this: "My Parents went to Las Vegas and All I Got was This Crummy T-Shirt"? After some class action settlements, class members might want to buy tee shirts stating: "My Lawyers got Millions of Dollars and All I got were some Crummy Coupons."

In addition to the tightening of judicial supervision over class action settlements through the 2003 amendment of Rule 23, Congress included settlement protections for class members in the Class Action Fairness Act of 2005. 28 U.S.C. §§ 1332(d), 1453, 1711–15. Congress was specifically concerned about "coupon settlements," in which class members receive coupons, rather than cash, in return for settling a class action. In enacting this portion of the Class Action Fairness Act, Congress was particularly concerned about situations in which a defendant might "buy off" the class cheaply while providing class counsel with sizable attorneys' fees.

> New section 28 U.S.C. 1712 is aimed at situations in which plaintiffs' lawyers negotiate settlements under which class members receive nothing but essentially valueless coupons, while the class counsel receive substantial attorneys' fees. For example, in a recent settlement of a class action against a video rental chain, customers received coupons toward video rentals and purchases, while the plaintiffs' class counsel were paid $9.25 million in fees and expenses. One commentator observed that "the real winners in the settlement are the lawyers who sued the company," who will be paid "in cash, not coupons."

S.Rep. No. 109–14, at 30 (2005) (citing *Scott v. Blockbuster Inc.*, No. DI62–535 (Jefferson County, Texas, 2001), and "Judge OKs Blockbuster Plan On Fees," *Associated Press*, Jan. 11, 2002)).

Section 1712(a) of Title 28 provides that, in calculating the recovery upon which the attorney for the class will be compensated, only the value of coupons actually redeemed, rather than all those provided in settlement, are to be counted. Courts are given authority to receive expert testimony concerning the actual value of coupons redeemed by class members, 28 U.S.C. § 1712(d), and judges are required to determine that any coupon settlement is "fair, reasonable, and adequate for class members," 28 U.S.C. § 1712(e), just as courts are required to find with respect to the settlement of any class action under Rule 23(e)(2).

If they're lucky, class members will receive settlements containing not only coupons, but enough cash to buy a new tee shirt. Even if the class receives no cash in the settlement, though, CAFA ensures that class counsel's attorneys' fees will be based on the actual value of the settlement received by members of the class.

C. THE LAWYER'S ROLE IN CLASS ACTIONS AND CLASS ACTION SETTLEMENTS

While the potential conflict between class counsel and class members has been vividly illustrated in proposed settlements with handsome fees for counsel but only coupons for the class, coupon settlements are not the only situation in which there is potential for conflicting interests between class counsel and the class. The American Bar Association's Model Rules of Professional Conduct are the basis for the rules of professional conduct adopted in individual states to govern lawyers practicing before judicial tribunals in those states. The Pennsylvania Rules of Professional Conduct, 204 Pa. Code § 81.4 (2015), would govern lawyers in *Amchem Products, Inc. v. Windsor*, so these are the Rules used to illustrate lawyers' ethical duties in this portion of this chapter.

1. Client Solicitation. Initially, there are ethical limitations on an attorney's ability to directly contact prospective clients. Such issues can arise in class actions with respect to the solicitation of class members, often as lawyers jockey to add clients as they seek appointment as class counsel pursuant to Rule 23(g) of the Federal Rules of Civil Procedure. Pennsylvania Rule of Professional Conduct 7.3(a) provides:

> A lawyer shall not solicit in-person or by intermediary professional employment from a person with whom the lawyer has no family or prior professional relationship when a significant motive for the lawyer's doing so is the lawyer's pecuniary gain, unless the person contacted is a lawyer or has a family, close personal, or prior professional relationship with the lawyer. The term "solicit" includes contact in-person by telephone or by real-time electronic communication, but, subject to the requirements of Rule 7.1 and Rule 7.3(b), does not include written communications, which may include targeted, direct mail advertisements.

Despite the general authority given attorneys by Rule 7.3(a) to contact clients other than through in-person contact, Pennsylvania Rule 7.3(b)(1) restricts an attorney's ability to contact a client even by writing or through the media if "the lawyer knows or reasonably should know that the physical, emotional or mental state of the person is such that the person could not exercise reasonable judgment in employing a lawyer." The United States Supreme Court has rejected a first amendment challenge to a Florida bar rule prohibiting even written communications concerning a personal injury or wrongful death action within 30 days of an accident or disaster.[12]

---

[12] *Florida Bar v. Went For It, Inc.*, 515 U.S. 618 (1995). *See also* 49 U.S.C. § 1136(g)(2) (prohibiting unsolicited communication concerning a personal injury or wrongful death action with those injured in an air crash or their families within 45 days of the crash).

2.   Client Loyalty. Rule 1.7(a) of the Pennsylvania Rules of Professional Conduct provides that, with limited exceptions, "a lawyer shall not represent a client if the representation involves a concurrent conflict of interest." Such conflicts include situations in which "the representation of one client will be directly adverse to another client" and "there is a significant risk that the representation of one or more clients will be materially limited by the lawyer's responsibilities to another client * * * or by a personal interest of the lawyer." *Id.* As Comment 1 to Rule 1.7 of the Pennsylvania Rules states, "Loyalty and independent judgment are essential elements in the lawyer's relationship to a client."

A conflict between class counsel and the class may arise, for instance, if defense counsel were to offer the attorney generous fees— but on the condition that she recommend that the class settle for only coupons of questionable value. Conflicts of interest within a class arise in actions such as *Amchem*, in which the interest of some class members is in maximizing current recovery while other class members desire to preserve settlement funds for future needs. An attorney cannot represent both sets of class members pursuant to ethical rules such as Pennsylvania Rule 1.7, nor is such representation appropriate under Federal Rule of Civil Procedure 23.[13]

A conflict also may arise if class counsel is placed in a position to allocate settlement proceeds among individual class members. Pennsylvania Rule of Professional Conduct 1.8(g) provides: "A lawyer who represents two or more clients shall not participate in making an aggregate settlement of the claims of or against the clients, * * * unless each client gives informed consent." Comment 13 to this Rule, though, recognizes the difficulty of applying this proscription within class actions. It thus explains: "Lawyers representing a class of plaintiffs or defendants * * * may not have a full client-lawyer relationship with each member of the class; nevertheless, such lawyers must comply with applicable rules regulating notification of class members and other procedural requirements designed to ensure adequate protection of the entire class." Among the procedural requirements governing class actions is Rule 23(c)(2)(B)'s requirement that members of a Rule 23(b)(3) class must receive "the best notice that is practicable under the circumstances, including individual notice to all members who can be identified through reasonable effort," the authorization of such notice in

---

[13]   In appointing counsel under Rule 23(g)(1)(B), the court is to consider "counsel's ability to fairly and adequately represent the interests of the class." As noted by the Advisory Committee to the 2003 amendment to Rule 23:

> The rule thus establishes the obligation of class counsel, an obligation that may be different from the customary obligations of counsel to individual clients. Appointment as class counsel means that the primary obligation of counsel is to the class rather than to any individual members of it.

Advisory Committee Note to 2003 Amendment to Rule 23, 215 F.R.D. 258, 226 (2003).

Rule 23(b)(1) and (2) class actions, and the Rule 23(e) provisions for judicial approval of the settlement of certified class actions.

3. Attorneys' Fees. Rule 1.5 of the ABA Model Rules of Professional Conduct provides the ethical framework for attorneys' fee awards and agreements. Rule 1.5(a) of the Pennsylvania Code of Professional Conduct provides that a lawyer "shall not enter into an agreement for, charge, or collect an illegal or clearly excessive fee." Rule 1.5(a) also lists a series of factors to be considered in determining a fee's propriety:

(1) whether the fee is fixed or contingent;

(2) the time and labor required, the novelty and difficulty of the questions involved, and the skill requisite to perform the legal service properly;

(3) the likelihood, if apparent to the client, that the acceptance of the particular employment will preclude other employment by the lawyer;

(4) the fee customarily charged in the locality for similar legal services;

(5) the amount involved and the results obtained;

(6) the time limitations imposed by the client or by the circumstances;

(7) the nature and length of the professional relationship with the client; and

(8) the experience, reputation, and ability of the lawyer or lawyers performing the services.

There is no hierarchy among the Rule 1.5 factors, which can make the application of these factors in individual cases challenging. When counsel seeks fees for the representation of a class, the challenges can be multiplied exponentially.

Most attorneys are paid pursuant to a retainer agreement into which they enter with their clients. Under the "American Rule," clients pay their own attorneys (in contrast to the "English Rule" applicable in most other common law countries, under which the losing party in civil litigation pays the fees of both parties). However, some state and federal statutes, such as federal civil rights laws, provide that the attorneys' fees of a prevailing plaintiff must be paid by the losing defendant. Why would Congress or a state legislature adopt such an exception to the American Rule?

In class actions there is another basis upon which to compensate class counsel. To the extent that a class action results in the creation of a "common fund" from which to compensate plaintiff class members, the courts have held that it is appropriate to charge that fund with an amount to compensate the class attorneys whose work has created the common fund.

Thus, while defense lawyers typically are compensated on an hourly basis pursuant to retainer agreements with their clients, plaintiffs' class counsel may be compensated pursuant to a client retainer agreement, a fee-shifting statute providing for the award of attorneys' fees to a prevailing party, or from a common fund the attorney has created on behalf of the class by prevailing against the defendant. All such fees are subject to judicial scrutiny pursuant to Rule 23(e) and (h) and must be consistent with governing ethical requirements such as Rule 1.5 of the Pennsylvania Code of Professional Conduct.

There are two basic approaches to determine the amount of attorneys' fees that successful class counsel should receive. The first, and simplest, approach is to apply a standard percentage rate to the total monetary recovery. A typical contingency percentage in tort actions is 33%, with plaintiff's counsel receiving one-third of the total settlement or award after litigation costs (such as the costs of travel, expert witnesses, and court fees) have been subtracted from the total. Thus, if the total recovery is $1,000,000 and there are $100,000 in costs, plaintiff's lawyer would receive $300,000 under a one-third contingency fee.

Attorneys' fees of $300,000 for a $1,000,000 recovery may be quite appropriate, but what if the class recovery were $1,000,000,000 rather than $1,000,000? In that situation, a one-third attorney fee may exceed $300,000,000, which might be considered "clearly excessive" for the purposes of Pennsylvania Rule 1.5(a). Attorneys' fees of this amount may be particularly suspect in a class action, because the class members have not individually agreed to such a fee. In this situation a more appropriate method of calculating attorneys' fees might be the "lodestar" approach.

The lodestar method of determining attorneys' fees was developed by the United States Court of Appeals for the Third Circuit in *Lindy Brothers Builders, Inc. v. American Radiator & Standard Sanitary Corp.*, 487 F.2d 161 (3rd Cir. 1973). In this case the Third Circuit determined the time spent by class counsel and then multiplied those hours by the attorney's normal billing rate. Then, having established this "lodestar" figure, that amount was subject to adjustment for such factors as the contingent nature of success and the quality of the attorney's work. Other courts have adopted tests with many more factors, such as those included in ABA Model Rule of Professional Conduct 1.5. *See*, most significantly, *Johnson v. Georgia Highway Express, Inc.*, 488 F.2d 714 (5th Cir. 1974) (adopting 12-part test, including such factors as time and labor required, novelty and difficulty of questions, skill required, the customary fee, whether fee is fixed or contingent, the amount involved and results obtained, and awards in similar cases).

The *Manual for Complex Litigation, Fourth* (2004), created by the Federal Judicial Center as a resource for judges and lawyers involved in class actions and other complex litigation, notes that a "number of courts favor the lodestar as a backup or cross-check on the percentage method when fees might be excessive." *Id.* at § 14.121. In determining the propriety of attorneys' fees requested in a proposed class action settlement, the fee motion must be served on all parties and directed in a reasonable manner to class members, who may object to the proposed fees at a hearing or otherwise. Federal Rule of Civil Procedure 23(e) and (h). But it is the judge who ultimately determines the appropriateness of the fees sought by class counsel.

Especially because so much attorney work on class actions takes place outside the presence of the judge, class action practice requires a great deal of professionalism on behalf of all counsel. "The added demands and burdens of complex litigation place a premium on attorney professionalism, and the judge should encourage counsel to act responsibly." *Manual for Complex Litigation, Fourth* § 10.21 (2004). The *Manual* also stresses that "[e]ven when stakes are high, counsel should avoid unnecessary contentiousness and limit the controversy to material issues genuinely in dispute." *Id.*, citing Model Rule of Professional Conduct 3.2 requiring lawyers to attempt to expedite litigation while protecting the interests of their clients.

D. WHAT'S A REASONABLE FEE?

Test your understanding of the rules governing attorneys' fees by determining how the court should rule on the motion for fees in the following situation.

Linda Lawyer practices law in a small Pennsylvania city with two friends with whom she graduated from law school five years ago. The law firm is engaged in a general practice, with Linda primarily representing individuals in family matters. One of her clients, Thomas Teacher, asked Linda to represent him and some of his fellow teachers in a federal civil rights action against the local school district, which Thomas believes discriminates against teachers with respect to its family leave policies. Although Linda had not handled prior civil rights actions, she agreed to represent Thomas in this case, which she ultimately was successful in having certified as a class action on behalf of the 475 teachers in the school district.

After extensive pretrial proceedings and trial, the court entered an injunction prohibiting the school district from requiring extensive documentation from teachers seeking parental leave, eliminating a requirement that teachers seek leave at least six months before the expected birth of their children, and guaranteeing teachers the right to return to their prior positions after their leaves. In addition, the court ordered the school district to reassign 12 teachers to positions that they had lost as a result of parental leaves, pay each of these teachers $10,000 in back pay, and provide a total of $200,000 in damages to the class.

Linda had agreed to represent the class for a contingency fee of 30% of the class recovery. In her state domestic relations practice, her usual billing rate is $125 per hour, although she has learned that the hourly rates for the school district lawyers in this litigation ranged from $200 to $300 per hour. Linda does not have detailed time records, although she is confident that she spent more than 1500 hours on this case over its three year duration.

Linda files a motion pursuant to Rule 23(h) of the Federal Rules of Civil Procedure seeking $375,000 in fees, which she calculated by multiplying the 1500 hours she believes she worked on the case by the average hourly rate charged by defense counsel for their work on the same action.

Should the court grant Linda's motion?

V. CONTRACTING OUT OF CLASS ACTIONS

Despite Rule 1's exhortation that the Federal Rules of Civil Procedure should be construed, administered, and employed "to secure the just, speedy, and inexpensive determination of every action and proceeding," modern civil litigation is all too often quite slow and expensive. In response to the pace and cost of formal litigation, alternative methods of dispute resolution have been developed—both as alternatives to the filing of civil actions and as ways in which to resolve civil actions actually filed. Such forms of "alternative dispute resolution," or ADR, have become increasingly popular in recent decades.

Indeed, most civil litigation traditionally has been resolved by the most popular alternative to formal adjudication by a judge or jury—in settlements negotiated and agreed to by the parties and their counsel. Many judges, in fact, encourage and facilitate settlement, through settlement conferences with counsel and parties or by requiring counsel to themselves meet and discuss settlement. Indeed, most disputes are resolved without the filing of a civil action.[14]

The parties also may decide to use a third party (other than a judge) to help them resolve their dispute. The parties themselves may agree upon mediation, or the judicial system in which they have filed an

---

[14] One study found that 1000 grievances resulted in 718 informal complaints to the offending party, 449 disputes (in which the complaints were rebuffed), 103 situations in which lawyers were retained, and 50 court filings. Trubek et al., "The Costs of Ordinary Litigation," 31 *UCLA L. Rev.* 72, 86–87 (1983). Thus only 5% of grievances resulted in the filing of litigation.

action may require them to engage in mediation. In the mediation process, the parties present their cases to the mediator, who goes back and forth between the parties in an effort to bring them together in an acceptable settlement. The mediator has no authority to bind the parties, however, and it is up to the parties as to whether, and on what terms, they will settle their dispute.

A more formal alternative dispute resolution device than mediation is arbitration. In arbitration, the arbitrator is given the power to resolve the parties' dispute. The arbitrator is chosen by the parties, often because she or he has familiarity with the type of dispute in question. The parties present evidence to the arbitrator, just as they would to a judge if the action were heard in a courtroom. If the parties have themselves chosen arbitration (rather than having been required to engage in arbitration by the court), they typically will have flexibility as to when and where the arbitration will be heard. Arbitrations are typically private, which makes them especially attractive in certain types of cases, such as divorce or child custody proceedings or in commercial disputes involving confidential business information.

Especially because it may not involve significant discovery, arbitration traditionally has been considered less expensive and significantly faster than civil litigation. The parties also typically have much greater control over the process, being able to themselves set the time for arbitration proceedings, choose an arbitrator with expertise in the relevant area (such as, for instance, for disputes arising within the construction industry), set the procedural rules governing the arbitration (permitting, for instance, hearsay to be offered in the arbitration), and resolve their dispute in private. Thus construction contracts, union agreements, and commercial sales contracts often include arbitration clauses providing that arbitration, rather than civil litigation in a court of law, will be used to resolve any disputes between the parties.

In contrast with mediation, the arbitrator renders an actual decision at the conclusion of the arbitration proceedings. Under the Federal Arbitration Act, 9 U.S.C. §§ 1–15, both an agreement to arbitrate and the arbitration award are generally judicially enforceable. 9 U.S.C. §§ 2; 9. The Act has been held to establish "a liberal federal policy favoring arbitration agreements"[15] requiring the courts to "rigorously enforce agreements to arbitrate."[16]

One of the major advantages of private arbitration is that the parties themselves choose to arbitrate and choose the arbitration format. But what if the parties who contractually choose a specific type of arbitration do not have equal bargaining power? What if, for instance, the arbitration clause was written by a major international

---

[15] *Moses H. Cone Mem'l Hosp. v. Mercury Constr. Corp.*, 460 U.S. 1, 24 (1983).
[16] *Dean Witter Reynolds, Inc. v. Byrd*, 470 U.S. 213, 221 (1985).

corporation and the consumer must agree to waive the right to file a civil action in order to receive goods or services from the corporation? What if the consumer must not only agree to waive the ability to bring a civil action, but must also waive the possibility of a class action in any arbitration that might be filed?

The majority and dissenting justices in the following case disagree as to just how to approach these issues. Their disagreement may stem, at least in part, from their view of class actions and the importance of class actions in enforcing substantive rights that will not otherwise be enforced. Congress in the Class Action Fairness Act created an additional forum in the federal courts for the litigation of many class actions. In the case that follows, the Supreme Court upheld a private party contract that not only required contractual disputes to be arbitrated rather than litigated, but also prohibited class treatment of the parties' dispute in the resulting arbitration.

American Express Co. v. Italian Colors Restaurant

Supreme Court of the United States, 2013
133 S.Ct. 2304

OPINION

■ JUSTICE SCALIA delivered the opinion of the Court.

We consider whether a contractual waiver of class arbitration is enforceable under the Federal Arbitration Act when the plaintiff's cost of individually arbitrating a federal statutory claim exceeds the potential recovery.

I

Respondents are merchants who accept American Express cards. Their agreement with petitioners—American Express and a wholly owned subsidiary—contains a clause that requires all disputes between the parties to be resolved by arbitration. The agreement also provides that "[t]here shall be no right or authority for any Claims to be arbitrated on a class action basis."

Respondents brought a class action against petitioners for violations of the federal antitrust laws. According to respondents, American Express used its monopoly power in the market for charge cards to force merchants to accept credit cards at rates approximately 30% higher than the fees for competing credit cards. This tying arrangement, respondents said, violated § 1 of the Sherman Act. They sought treble damages for the class under § 4 of the Clayton Act.

Petitioners moved to compel individual arbitration under the Federal Arbitration Act (FAA), 9 U.S.C. § 1 et seq. In resisting the motion, respondents submitted a declaration from an economist who estimated that the cost of an expert analysis necessary to prove the antitrust claims would be "at least several hundred thousand dollars, and might exceed $1 million," while the maximum recovery for an individual plaintiff would be $12,850, or $38,549 when trebled. The District Court granted the motion and dismissed the lawsuits. The Court of Appeals reversed and remanded for further proceedings. It held that because respondents had established that "they would incur prohibitive costs if compelled to arbitrate under the class action waiver," the waiver was unenforceable and the arbitration could not proceed.

We granted certiorari, vacated the judgment, and remanded for further consideration in light of *Stolt-Nielsen S.A. v. AnimalFeeds Int'l Corp.*, 559 U.S. 662 (2010), which held that a party may not be compelled to submit to class arbitration absent an agreement to do so. The Court of Appeals stood by its reversal, stating that its earlier ruling did not compel class arbitration. It then sua sponte reconsidered its ruling in light of *AT & T Mobility LLC v. Concepcion*, 563 U.S. ___ (2011), which held that the FAA pre-empted a state law barring enforcement of a class-arbitration waiver. Finding *AT & T Mobility* inapplicable because it addressed pre-emption, the Court of Appeals reversed for the third time. It then denied rehearing en banc with five judges dissenting. We granted certiorari to consider the question "[w]hether the Federal Arbitration Act permits courts . . . to invalidate arbitration agreements on the ground that they do not permit class arbitration of a federal-law claim."

II

Congress enacted the FAA in response to widespread judicial hostility to arbitration. See *AT & T Mobility*, supra, at ___. As relevant here, the Act provides:

> "A written provision in any maritime transaction or contract evidencing a transaction involving commerce to settle by arbitration a controversy thereafter arising out of such contract or transaction . . . shall be valid, irrevocable, and enforceable, save upon such grounds as exist at law or in equity for the revocation of any contract." 9 U.S.C. § 2.

This text reflects the overarching principle that arbitration is a matter of contract. And consistent with that text, courts must "rigorously enforce" arbitration agreements according to their terms, *Dean Witter Reynolds Inc. v. Byrd*, 470 U.S. 213, 221 (1985), including terms that "specify with whom [the parties] choose to arbitrate their disputes," *Stolt-Nielsen*, supra, at 683, and "the rules under which that arbitration will be conducted," *Volt Information Sciences, Inc. v. Board of Trustees of Leland Stanford Junior Univ.*, 489 U.S. 468, 479 (1989). That holds true for claims that allege a violation of a federal statute, unless the FAA's mandate has been " 'overridden by a contrary congressional command.' "*CompuCredit Corp. v. Greenwood*, 565 U.S. ___, ___ (2012) (quoting *Shearson/American Express Inc. v. McMahon*, 482 U.S. 220, 226 (1987)).

III

No contrary congressional command requires us to reject the waiver of class arbitration here. Respondents argue that requiring them to litigate their claims individually—as they contracted to do—would contravene the policies of the antitrust laws. But the antitrust laws do not guarantee an affordable procedural path to the vindication of every claim. Congress has taken some measures to facilitate the litigation of antitrust claims—for example, it enacted a multiplied-damages remedy. *See* 15 U.S.C. § 15 (treble damages). In enacting such measures, Congress has told us that it is willing to go, in certain respects, beyond the normal limits of law in advancing its goals of deterring and remedying unlawful trade practice. But to say that Congress must have intended whatever departures from those normal limits advance antitrust goals is simply irrational. "[N]o legislation pursues its purposes at all costs." *Rodriguez v. United States*, 480 U.S. 522, 525–526 (1987) (per curiam).

The antitrust laws do not "evinc[e] an intention to preclude a waiver" of class-action procedure. *Mitsubishi Motors Corp. v. Soler Chrysler-Plymouth, Inc.*, 473 U.S. 614, 628 (1985). The Sherman and Clayton Acts make no mention of class actions. In fact, they were enacted decades before the advent of Federal Rule of Civil Procedure 23, which was "designed to allow an exception to the usual rule that litigation is conducted by and on behalf of the individual named parties only." *Califano v. Yamasaki*, 442 U.S. 682, 700–701 (1979). The parties here agreed to arbitrate pursuant to that "usual rule," and it would be remarkable for a court to erase that expectation.

Nor does congressional approval of Rule 23 establish an entitlement to class proceedings for the vindication of statutory rights. To begin with, it is likely that such an entitlement, invalidating private arbitration agreements denying class adjudication, would be an "abridg[ment]" or "modif[ication]" of a "substantive right" forbidden to the Rules, *see* 28 U.S.C. § 2072(b). But there is no evidence of such an entitlement in any event. The Rule imposes stringent requirements for certification that in practice exclude most claims. And we have specifically rejected the assertion that one of those requirements (the class-notice requirement) must be dispensed with because the "prohibitively high cost" of compliance would "frustrate [plaintiff's] attempt to vindicate the policies underlying the antitrust" laws. *Eisen v. Carlisle & Jacquelin*, 417 U.S. 156, 166–168, 175–176 (1974). One might respond, perhaps, that federal law secures a nonwaivable opportunity to vindicate federal policies by satisfying the procedural strictures of Rule 23 or invoking some other informal class mechanism in arbitration. But we have already rejected that proposition in *AT & T Mobility*, 563 U.S., at ___.

IV

Our finding of no "contrary congressional command" does not end the case. Respondents invoke a judge-made exception to the FAA which, they say, serves to harmonize competing federal policies by allowing courts to invalidate agreements that prevent the "effective vindication" of a federal statutory right. Enforcing the waiver of class arbitration bars effective vindication, respondents contend, because they have no economic incentive to pursue their antitrust claims individually in arbitration.

The "effective vindication" exception to which respondents allude originated as dictum in *Mitsubishi Motors*, where we expressed a willingness to invalidate, on "public policy" grounds, arbitration agreements that "operat[e] . . . as a prospective waiver of a party's right to pursue statutory remedies." 473 U.S., at 637, n. 19. Dismissing concerns that the arbitral forum was inadequate, we said that "so long as the prospective litigant effectively may vindicate its statutory cause of action in the arbitral forum, the statute will continue to serve both its remedial and deterrent function." *Id.*, at 637. Subsequent cases have similarly asserted the existence of an "effective vindication" exception, *see, e.g.,* *14 Penn Plaza LLC v. Pyett*, 556 U.S. 247, 273–274 (2009); *Gilmer v. Interstate/Johnson Lane Corp.*, 500 U.S. 20, 28 (1991), but have similarly declined to apply it to invalidate the arbitration agreement at issue.

And we do so again here. As we have described, the exception finds its origin in the desire to prevent "prospective waiver of a party's right to pursue statutory remedies," *Mitsubishi Motors, supra,* at 637, n. 19. That would certainly cover a provision in an arbitration agreement forbidding the assertion of certain statutory rights. And it would perhaps cover filing and administrative fees attached to arbitration that are so high as to make access to the forum impracticable. *See Green Tree Financial Corp.-Ala. v. Randolph*, 531 U.S. 79, 90 (2000). But the fact that it is not worth the expense involved in proving a statutory remedy does not constitute the elimination of the right to pursue that remedy. The class-action waiver merely limits arbitration to the two contracting parties. It no more eliminates those parties' right to pursue their statutory remedy than did federal law before its adoption of the class action for legal relief in 1938. Or, to put it differently, the individual suit that was considered adequate to assure "effective vindication" of a federal right before adoption of class-action procedures did not suddenly become "ineffective vindication" upon their adoption.

* * *

Truth to tell, our decision in *AT & T Mobility* all but resolves this case. There we invalidated a law conditioning enforcement of arbitration on the availability of class procedure because that law "interfere [d] with fundamental attributes of arbitration." 563 U.S., at

___. "[T]he switch from bilateral to class arbitration," we said, "sacrifices the principal advantage of arbitration—its informality—and makes the process slower, more costly, and more likely to generate procedural morass than final judgment." *Id.*, at ___. We specifically rejected the argument that class arbitration was necessary to prosecute claims "that might otherwise slip through the legal system." *Id.*, at ___.[5]

The regime established by the Court of Appeals' decision would require—before a plaintiff can be held to contractually agreed bilateral arbitration—that a federal court determine (and the parties litigate) the legal requirements for success on the merits claim-by-claim and theory-by-theory, the evidence necessary to meet those requirements, the cost of developing that evidence, and the damages that would be recovered in the event of success. Such a preliminary litigating hurdle would undoubtedly destroy the prospect of speedy resolution that arbitration in general and bilateral arbitration in particular was meant to secure. The FAA does not sanction such a judicially created superstructure.

The judgment of the Court of Appeals is reversed.

It is so ordered.

■ JUSTICE SOTOMAYOR took no part in the consideration or decision of this case.

■ JUSTICE THOMAS, concurring.

I join the Court's opinion in full. I write separately to note that the result here is also required by the plain meaning of the Federal Arbitration Act. In *AT & T Mobility LLC v. Concepcion*, 563 U.S. ___ (2011), I explained that "the FAA requires that an agreement to arbitrate be enforced unless a party successfully challenges the formation of the arbitration agreement, such as by proving fraud or duress." *Id.*, at ___ (concurring opinion). In this case, Italian Colors makes two arguments to support its conclusion that the arbitration agreement should not be enforced. First, it contends that enforcing the arbitration agreement "would contravene the policies of the antitrust laws." Second, it contends that a court may "invalidate agreements that prevent the 'effective vindication' of a federal statutory right." Neither argument "concern[s] whether the contract was properly made," *Concepcion, supra*, at ___ (THOMAS, J., concurring). Because Italian Colors has not furnished "grounds . . . for the revocation of any contract," 9 U.S.C. § 2, the arbitration agreement must be enforced. Italian Colors voluntarily entered into a contract containing a bilateral

---

[5]   In dismissing *AT & T Mobility* as a case involving pre-emption and not the effective-vindication exception, the dissent ignores what that case established—that the FAA's command to enforce arbitration agreements trumps any interest in ensuring the prosecution of low-value claims. The latter interest, we said, is "unrelated" to the FAA. 563 U.S., at ___. Accordingly, the FAA does, contrary to the dissent's assertion, favor the absence of litigation when that is the consequence of a class-action waiver, since its " 'principal purpose' " is the enforcement of arbitration agreements according to their terms. 563 U.S., at ___ (quoting *Volt Information Sciences, Inc. v. Board of Trustees of Leland Stanford Junior Univ.*, 489 U.S. 468, 487 (1989)).

arbitration provision. It cannot now escape its obligations merely because the claim it wishes to bring might be economically infeasible.

■ JUSTICE KAGAN, with whom JUSTICE GINSBURG and JUSTICE BREYER join, dissenting.

Here is the nutshell version of this case, unfortunately obscured in the Court's decision. The owner of a small restaurant (Italian Colors) thinks that American Express (Amex) has used its monopoly power to force merchants to accept a form contract violating the antitrust laws. The restaurateur wants to challenge the allegedly unlawful provision (imposing a tying arrangement), but the same contract's arbitration clause prevents him from doing so. That term imposes a variety of procedural bars that would make pursuit of the antitrust claim a fool's errand. So if the arbitration clause is enforceable, Amex has insulated itself from antitrust liability—even if it has in fact violated the law. The monopolist gets to use its monopoly power to insist on a contract effectively depriving its victims of all legal recourse.

And here is the nutshell version of today's opinion, admirably flaunted rather than camouflaged: Too darn bad.

That answer is a betrayal of our precedents, and of federal statutes like the antitrust laws. Our decisions have developed a mechanism—called the effective-vindication rule—to prevent arbitration clauses from choking off a plaintiff's ability to enforce congressionally created rights. That doctrine bars applying such a clause when (but only when) it operates to confer immunity from potentially meritorious federal claims. In so doing, the rule reconciles the Federal Arbitration Act (FAA) with all the rest of federal law—and indeed, promotes the most fundamental purposes of the FAA itself. As applied here, the rule would ensure that Amex's arbitration clause does not foreclose Italian Colors from vindicating its right to redress antitrust harm.

* * * Because the Court today prevents the effective vindication of federal statutory rights, I respectfully dissent.

I

Start with an uncontroversial proposition: We would refuse to enforce an exculpatory clause insulating a company from antitrust liability—say, "Merchants may bring no Sherman Act claims"—even if that clause were contained in an arbitration agreement. Congress created the Sherman Act's private cause of action not solely to compensate individuals, but to promote "the public interest in vigilant enforcement of the antitrust laws." *Lawlor v. National Screen Service Corp.*, 349 U.S. 322, 329 (1955). Accordingly, courts will not enforce a prospective waiver of the right to gain redress for an antitrust injury, whether in an arbitration agreement or any other contract. *See Mitsubishi Motors Corp. v. Soler Chrysler-Plymouth, Inc.*, 473 U.S. 614, 637, and n. 19 (1985). The same rule applies to other important federal statutory rights. *See 14 Penn Plaza LLC v. Pyett*, 556 U.S. 247, 273

(2009) (Age Discrimination in Employment Act); *Brooklyn Savings Bank v. O'Neil*, 324 U.S. 697, 704 (1945) (Fair Labor Standards Act). But its necessity is nowhere more evident than in the antitrust context. Without the rule, a company could use its monopoly power to protect its monopoly power, by coercing agreement to contractual terms eliminating its antitrust liability.

If the rule were limited to baldly exculpatory provisions, however, a monopolist could devise numerous ways around it. Consider several alternatives that a party drafting an arbitration agreement could adopt to avoid antitrust liability, each of which would have the identical effect. On the front end: The agreement might set outlandish filing fees or establish an absurd (*e.g.*, one-day) statute of limitations, thus preventing a claimant from gaining access to the arbitral forum. On the back end: The agreement might remove the arbitrator's authority to grant meaningful relief, so that a judgment gets the claimant nothing worthwhile. And in the middle: The agreement might block the claimant from presenting the kind of proof that is necessary to establish the defendant's liability—say, by prohibiting any economic testimony (good luck proving an antitrust claim without that!). Or else the agreement might appoint as an arbitrator an obviously biased person—say, the CEO of Amex. The possibilities are endless—all less direct than an express exculpatory clause, but no less fatal. So the rule against prospective waivers of federal rights can work only if it applies not just to a contract clause explicitly barring a claim, but to others that operate to do so.

And sure enough, our cases establish this proposition: An arbitration clause will not be enforced if it prevents the effective vindication of federal statutory rights, however it achieves that result. The rule originated in *Mitsubishi*, where we held that claims brought under the Sherman Act and other federal laws are generally subject to arbitration. By agreeing to arbitrate such a claim, we explained, "a party does not forgo the substantive rights afforded by the statute; it only submits to their resolution in an arbitral, rather than a judicial, forum." *Ibid.* But crucial to our decision was a limiting principle, designed to safeguard federal rights: An arbitration clause will be enforced only "so long as the prospective litigant effectively may vindicate its statutory cause of action in the arbitral forum." *Id.*, at 637. If an arbitration provision "operated . . . as a prospective waiver of a party's right to pursue statutory remedies," we emphasized, we would "condemn[ ]" it. *Id.*, at 637, n. 19. Similarly, we stated that such a clause should be "set [ ] aside" if "proceedings in the contractual forum will be so gravely difficult" that the claimant "will for all practical purposes be deprived of his day in court." *Id.*, at 632. And in the decades since *Mitsubishi*, we have repeated its admonition time and again, instructing courts not to enforce an arbitration agreement that effectively (even if not explicitly) forecloses a plaintiff from remedying the violation of a federal statutory right. *See Gilmer v. Interstate/Johnson Lane Corp.*, 500 U.S. 20, 28 (1991); *Vimar Seguros y Reaseguros, S.A. v. M/V Sky Reefer*, 515 U.S. 528, 540 (1995); *14 Penn Plaza*, 556 U.S., at 266, 273–274.

Our decision in *Green Tree Financial Corp.-Ala. v. Randolph*, 531 U.S. 79 (2000), confirmed that this principle applies when an agreement thwarts federal law by making arbitration prohibitively expensive. The plaintiff there (seeking relief under the Truth in Lending Act) argued that an arbitration agreement was unenforceable because it "create[d] a risk" that she would have to "bear prohibitive arbitration costs" in the form of high filing and administrative fees. We rejected that contention, but not because we doubted that such fees could prevent the effective vindication of statutory rights. To the contrary, we invoked our rule from *Mitsubishi*, making clear that it applied to the case before us. Indeed, we added a burden of proof: "[W]here, as here," we held, a party asserting a federal right "seeks to invalidate an arbitration agreement on the ground that arbitration would be prohibitively expensive, that party bears the burden of showing the likelihood of incurring such costs." *Id.*, at 92. Randolph, we found, had failed to meet that burden: The evidence she offered was "too speculative." *Id.*, at 91. But even as we dismissed Randolph's suit, we reminded courts to protect against arbitration agreements that make federal claims too costly to bring.

Applied as our precedents direct, the effective-vindication rule furthers the purposes not just of laws like the Sherman Act, but of the FAA itself. That statute reflects a federal policy favoring actual arbitration—that is, arbitration as a streamlined "method of resolving disputes," not as a foolproof way of killing off valid claims. *Rodriguez de Quijas v. Shearson/American Express, Inc.*, 490 U.S. 477, 481 (1989). Put otherwise: What the FAA prefers to litigation is arbitration, not de facto immunity. The effective-vindication rule furthers the statute's goals by ensuring that arbitration remains a real, not faux, method of dispute resolution. With the rule, companies have good reason to adopt arbitral procedures that facilitate efficient and accurate handling of complaints. Without it, companies have every incentive to draft their agreements to extract backdoor waivers of statutory rights, making arbitration unavailable or pointless. So down one road: More arbitration, better enforcement of federal statutes. And down the other: Less arbitration, poorer enforcement of federal statutes. Which would you prefer? Or still more aptly: Which do you think Congress would?

* * *

And this is just the kind of case the rule was meant to address. Italian Colors, as I have noted, alleges that Amex used its market power to impose a tying arrangement in violation of the Sherman Act. The antitrust laws, all parties agree, provide the restaurant with a cause of action and give it the chance to recover treble damages. Here, that would mean Italian Colors could take home up to $38,549. But a problem looms. As this case comes to us, the evidence shows that Italian Colors cannot prevail in arbitration without an economic analysis defining the relevant markets, establishing Amex's monopoly power, showing anticompetitive effects, and measuring damages. And that expert report would cost between several hundred thousand and one million dollars. So the expense involved in proving the claim in arbitration is ten times what Italian Colors could hope to gain, even in a best-case scenario. That counts as a "prohibitive" cost, in Randolph's terminology, if anything does. No rational actor would bring a claim worth tens of thousands of dollars if doing so meant incurring costs in the hundreds of thousands.

An arbitration agreement could manage such a mismatch in many ways, but Amex's disdains them all. As the Court makes clear, the contract expressly prohibits class arbitration. But that is only part of the problem. The agreement also disallows any kind of joinder or consolidation of claims or parties. And more: Its confidentiality provision prevents Italian Colors from informally arranging with other merchants to produce a common expert report. And still more: The agreement precludes any shifting of costs to Amex, even if Italian Colors prevails. And beyond all that: Amex refused to enter into any stipulations that would obviate or mitigate the need for the economic analysis. In short, the agreement as applied in this case cuts off not just class arbitration, but any avenue for sharing, shifting, or shrinking necessary costs. Amex has put Italian Colors to this choice: Spend way, way, way more money than your claim is worth, or relinquish your Sherman Act rights.

* * *

II

* * *

The Court today mistakes what this case is about. To a hammer, everything looks like a nail. And to a Court bent on diminishing the usefulness of Rule 23, everything looks like a class action, ready to be dismantled. So the Court does not consider that Amex's agreement bars not just class actions, but "other forms of cost-sharing . . . that could provide effective vindication." In short, the Court does not consider—and does not decide—Italian Colors's (and similarly situated litigants') actual argument about why the effective-vindication rule precludes this agreement's enforcement.

As a result, Amex's contract will succeed in depriving Italian Colors of any effective opportunity to challenge monopolistic conduct allegedly in violation of the Sherman Act. The FAA, the majority says, so requires. Do not be fooled. Only the Court so requires; the FAA was never meant to produce this outcome. The FAA conceived of arbitration as a "method of resolving disputes"—a way of using tailored and streamlined procedures to facilitate redress of injuries. *Rodriguez de Quijas*, 490 U.S., at 481. In the hands of today's majority, arbitration threatens to become more nearly the opposite—a mechanism easily made to block the vindication of meritorious federal claims and insulate wrongdoers from liability. The Court thus undermines the FAA no less than it does the Sherman Act and other federal statutes providing rights of action. I respectfully dissent.

COMMENTS AND QUESTIONS CONCERNING *AMERICAN EXPRESS CO. V. ITALIAN COLORS RESTAURANT*

1. If American Express can contractually preclude effective challenge from restaurants such as Italian Colors, are there other ways in which its actions can be challenged? *See United States v. Am. Exp. Co.*, 88 F.Supp.3d 143, 152 (E.D.N.Y. 2015) ("[T]he court concludes that Plaintiffs have proven by a preponderance of the evidence that the challenged restraints constitute an unlawful restraint on trade under Section 1 of the Sherman Act.").

2. Justice Scalia asserts in *Italian Colors Restaurant* that the outcome in that case was presaged, if not predetermined, by the Court's earlier decision in *AT & T Mobility LLC v. Concepcion*, 563 U.S. 333 (2011) ("Truth to tell, our decision in *AT & T Mobility* all but resolves this case."). In *Concepcion* the Supreme Court held that the Federal Arbitration Act preempted California law making unenforceable contract terms waiving the right to arbitrate claims collectively.

3. Writing for the majority in *Concepcion*, Justice Scalia rebutted the dissent's argument in that case that the consumer claims against AT & T were unlikely to be addressed unless they could be brought as a collective arbitration proceeding:

> [T]he arbitration agreement provides that AT & T will pay claimants a minimum of $7,500 and twice their attorney's fees if they obtain an arbitration award greater than AT & T's last settlement offer. The District Court found this scheme sufficient to provide incentive for the individual prosecution of meritorious claims that are not immediately settled, and the Ninth Circuit admitted that aggrieved customers who filed claims would be "essentially guarantee[d]" to be made whole. Indeed, the District Court concluded that the Concepcions were *better off* under their arbitration agreement with AT & T than they would have been as participants in a class action, which "could take months, if not years, and which may merely yield an opportunity to submit a claim for recovery of a small percentage of a few dollars."

AT & T Mobility LLC v. Concepcion, 563 U.S. 333, 352 (2011). Would California law still have been preempted in *Concepcion* if the parties' dispute resolution clause had not provided the above advantages to consumers?

4. Despite the above statement in *Concepcion* that consumers were able to effectively vindicate their contractual rights through individual arbitrations, Justice Scalia stated in footnote 5 of his opinion in *Italian Colors Restaurant* that *Concepcion* established that

> the FAA's command to enforce arbitration agreements trumps any interest in ensuring the prosecution of low-value claims. The latter interest, we said, is "unrelated" to the FAA. Accordingly, the FAA does * * * favor the absence of litigation when that is the consequence of a class-action waiver, since its " 'principal purpose' " is the enforcement of arbitration agreements according to their terms. 563 U.S., at ___ (quoting *Volt Information Sciences, Inc. v. Board of Trustees of Leland Stanford Junior Univ.*, 489 U.S. 468, 487 (1989)).

So, in deciding whether to uphold contractual terms prohibiting collective or class claims, is it relevant that those claims are not likely to be enforced individually?

5. What's the common thread tying together the majority opinions in *Concepcion* and *Italian Colors Restaurant*?

6. In her dissent, Justice Kagan states: "To a hammer, everything looks like a nail. And to a Court bent on diminishing the usefulness of Rule 23, everything looks like a class action, ready to be dismantled." Is the Court embarked on a mission to dismantle Rule 23?

VI. CONCLUSION

Class actions are a procedural device that may be used to further "the just, speedy, and inexpensive determination" of civil actions as contemplated by Rule 1 of the Federal Rules of Civil Procedure. They can be a way to achieve resolution of disputes that, by themselves, would not justify the filing of a civil action. They also can quickly become unwieldy and result in potential conflicts of interest between lawyers and clients and among class members. For these reasons, class actions are treated differently—at class certification, during pretrial proceedings, in the event of settlement, and with respect to appeal.

Well before the advent of modern class action practice, individual civil actions were used to achieve significant relief and structural change. Most notably, *Brown v. Board of Education* was not a class action. But class actions are now part of the legal landscape, and today's lawyers need to understand the special advantages and challenges of class actions as they represent clients in contemporary civil litigation.

VII. CHAPTER ASSESSMENT

A. Multiple-Choice Questions. Answer the following questions, reviewing the sections of the chapter noted in connection with each question.

1.   A woman suffered a minor heart attack after taking a new drug for three years. She filed a lawsuit in the Nevada state courts on behalf of "all those who, as a result of taking this drug, suffered a nonfatal heart attack, stroke, or other coronary illness." Pursuant to a class action rule identical to Federal Rule of Civil Procedure 23, the state judge certified a nationwide class as requested by the woman. Notice was sent to the 10,000 individuals identified through medical records as likely class members. The defendants ultimately settled this lawsuit in 2012, with individual damages calculated under a "point system" that factors in such things as the severity of the coronary attack, age, and expected earning capacity of the class member.

After taking this same drug for only six months, a man suffered a massive heart attack in 2014 that hospitalized him for three months. He had not received notice of the class action, but filed a 2015 lawsuit of his own in the Iowa state courts. The defendants in this action are the same as in the class action, and they assert that the man is bound by the class action settlement. The defendants argue that, while the man is entitled to a monetary payment calculated under the point system agreed to in the class action settlement, he cannot bring a new lawsuit against these same defendants.

Review Section II(A) and choose the best answer from the following choices:

(a)   Because the man was not taking the drug at the time the class action was settled and thus was not included in the class as defined in that case, he is not bound by that class settlement.

(b)   Even if all requirements of the Nevada class action rule were satisfied in the first case, the Due Process Clause of the Fourteenth Amendment guaranteed all members of the Nevada class a right to notice and an opportunity to be heard in that case.

(c)   The adequacy of the woman as a class representative would be relevant in determining compliance with both the Nevada rule and the Due Process Clause of the Fourteenth Amendment.

(d)   All of the above answers are correct.

2.   A homeowner had a mortgage for several years with a mortgage company before learning that the company had added a monthly "servicing fee" that was lumped into the total amount shown as interest on his statements. He asked his sister, a lawyer, about this, and she replied, "Even though I just graduated six months ago from law school, this sounds pretty illegal to me under Arizona law."

The lawyer then filed a federal diversity action in the United States District Court for the District of Arizona on behalf of her brother, who is a citizen of Arizona, against the company (a citizen of Delaware and New York). The lawyer seeks certification of a class of "all Arizona citizens who had similar charges applied to their mortgages without proper disclosure as required by Arizona law." The complaint's prayer for relief seeks $80,000 for each of the estimated 15,000 class members.

Review Section II(A) and III and choose the best answer from the following choices:

(a) The class action requirements of numerosity, commonality, typicality, and adequacy of representation are met in this case.

(b) Even if all the requirements of Federal Rule of Civil Procedure 23 are met, the homeowner must satisfy constitutional due process requirements as well.

(c) Because it appears likely that the homeowner will prevail on the merits of his claim, the district court should certify this case as a class action.

(d) All of the above answers are correct.

3. A citizen of Missouri filed a diversity class action in federal district court against a cable television company, claiming that the company violated her cable contract by dropping her favorite show from her television cable package. She sued on behalf of all 10,000 national subscribers to the cable service of this company, which is a citizen of New York and Massachusetts. The plaintiff is the international president of a fan club for the television show in question, and this has turned into a quite profitable career for her. She is the only named class representative, and she seeks $100,000 in damages for the alleged breach of contract.

Review Section II(B) and choose the best answer from the following choices:

(a) The federal district court will not be able to exercise subject-matter jurisdiction over this action if any member of the class is a citizen of Massachusetts or New York.

(b) The federal district court will not be able to exercise subject-matter jurisdiction over this action unless all of the class members have suffered more than $75,000 in damages.

(c) The federal district court should be able to exercise subject-matter jurisdiction over this action, but the class representative and the class must satisfy all four Rule 23(a) requirements.

(d) The federal district court should be able to exercise subject matter-jurisdiction over this action, but the class must also satisfy all three of the requirements of Rule 23(b).

4. A recent ice storm brought down power lines throughout Colorado, causing many homes to lose power. A Denver hotel has its own generator, however, and therefore never lost power. Many individuals who had lost power wanted to stay at the hotel, and the motel added a $75.00 "storm surcharge" to its normal $185.00 per night

rates. Because Denver shelters were full throughout the storm, many people stayed at the hotel during the storm.

A lawyer brings a federal class action on behalf of the 497 individuals who were charged the "storm surcharge," alleging that the surcharge violated a federal law prohibiting businesses from "profiting unfairly from a natural disaster that disrupts interstate commerce."

Review Section IV(A) and (B) and choose the best answer from the following choices:

(a) A fluid recovery under which the next 497 people who stay at the hotel would receive a $75 per night discount on their hotel rooms would be the best way to settle this lawsuit.

(b) If a portion of the settlement included "$75.00 off" coupons for the class members' next stay at the hotel, a portion of the attorneys' fees can be based upon the number of coupons redeemed.

(c) Class members will have to be notified that they have the right to opt out of this class, and this notice must be paid by the hotel.

(d) If plaintiff's lawyer and defense counsel are in agreement about a proposed settlement, the court need not hold a settlement hearing before approving the proposed settlement.

5. A citizen of Wyoming financed his new home with a 3% mortgage from a corporation incorporated in Delaware with its principal place of business in Illinois. However, after one year he was informed that his mortgage had "reset" to a rate of 10%. Because he is an attorney, the borrower brings a federal class action, seeking $80,000 in damages. The class that he seeks to represent includes himself and "the 90 other individuals who financed their homes through this corporation and, like plaintiff, were not told that their initial interest rate could be increased." The complaint is based on state contract law and consumer statutes and states that the losses suffered by class members "range from $2000 to $100,000."

In its answer, the corporation asserts that the plaintiff and all other class members had agreed to arbitrate, rather than litigate, any claims that they might have with their mortgages. The corporation files a motion for summary judgment based on this arbitration agreement, although the plaintiff responds that, because the clause prohibits class arbitration claims and most of the claims are only for a few thousand dollars, the clause is illegal under state law and should not be enforced.

Review Section II, III, and V and choose the best answer from the following choices:

(a) Even though the arbitration clause would, as a practical matter, prevent the effective vindication of the class members' rights, that clause should be enforced.

(b) Assuming that the arbitration clause is not enforced, the plaintiff should be able to fairly and adequately protect the interests of the proposed class.

(c) Assuming that the arbitration clause is not enforced and the requirements of Rule 23(a) are met, this action should be certified as a class pursuant to Rule 23(b)(2).

(d) If there is more than $5,000,000 in controversy, the federal court may have jurisdiction over this lawsuit pursuant to the Class Action Fairness Act of 2005.

B. Essay Questions. To test your understanding of this chapter's material, outline or write an answer to the following questions.

1. Should the Class Be Certified?

Motor Cars, Inc. imports from Canada the Rapid Car—a car that has become very popular in recent years. There have been problems with the ignition system on the most recent version of the car. These problems have resulted in car owners not being able to start their cars, cars stalling at high speeds, and 25 highway accidents and 12 deaths resulting from stalled cars.

On several occasions Oliver Owner has not been able to start his car, and he has retained attorney Lucy Lawyer to represent him in a class action filed in federal court in Oliver's home state of Tennessee. The civil action is filed as a damage action against Motor Cars, Inc. "on behalf of the 21,000 United States citizens—from all 50 states and the District of Columbia—who bought Rapid Cars imported to the United States by Motor Cars, Inc., which is incorporated in Delaware and has its principal place of business in California."

Oliver is one of three named class representatives in this action, and seeks $75,000 in damages. The other two named class representatives are Carli Colorado (a citizen of Colorado who seeks $50,000) and James Tucson (a citizen of Arizona, who was badly injured in a crash and seeks $500,000 in damages). Lawyer is quite excited about the action, because this is the first class action that she has had the opportunity to file since her graduation from law school five years ago. All three named plaintiffs assert products liability claims, although Oliver asserts an additional contract claim based on the allegation that Motor Cars did not responded to his repeated requests to fix or replace his car.

The three named plaintiffs move to certify their case as a class action. Should the court grant that motion?

2. Should the Settlement Be Approved?

As his first case after leaving the local prosecutor's office, Attorney filed a class action against an Internet gaming company that promised "six months of free games for a one-time payment of $10." Those who signed up for this offer later became angry when they realized that they were not able to play all the games offered by the company, but only short, elementary versions of those games. Attorney filed the class action "on behalf of the more than 100,000 consumers whose rights under federal consumer protection law have been violated by the Company's actions." The attorney named as the class representative her secretary, who signed up for this gaming service two weeks before the action was filed in federal court. The complaint seeks $100 per class member, an injunction against further violations of federal consumer law, and attorneys' fees.

Lawyer, the general counsel of the gaming company, was a classmate of Attorney, and she is able to work out a settlement with Attorney. Lawyer and Attorney present their settlement to the judge, seeking court approval. The settlement contains an agreement by the gaming company not to violate federal law in the future; to provide the company's newest game to any class member who requests a copy; and to pay $1,000,000 in fees to Attorney. When the judge asks about notice, counsel respond that they plan to place statements on the company's web site and create public service announcements rather than send individualized notice.

Should the judge approve the settlement?

CHAPTER 8

THE RELIEF SOUGHT: "THE CLIENT'S BOTTOM LINE."

I. INTRODUCTION

While lawyers may be rightly proud of their pleadings and procedural victories in the course of litigation, clients are most concerned about the relief that ultimately is, or is not, recovered as a result of a civil action. In crafting her civil action, the lawyer should begin with a determination of just what relief her client most prefers—and build her litigation strategy around that preference. Rule 1.2(a) of the ABA's Model Rules of Professional Conduct requires a lawyer to (1) abide by her client's decisions concerning litigation objectives and (2) consult with her client as to the means used to obtain those objectives.

There is an entire law school course in remedies. This chapter merely highlights the major types of relief that may be available to a party in a civil action: provisional relief before final judgment; damages; injunctions; declaratory judgments; attorneys' fees and costs. Even after obtaining a favorable judgment, further proceedings may be necessary to reduce that judgment (a mere piece of paper) into dollars and cents (which is the ultimate relief sought in most civil actions). Rule 69(a) of the Federal Rules of Civil Procedure provides: "A money judgment is enforced by a writ of execution, unless the court directs otherwise."[1]

The sections of this chapter that follow provide an overview of the major types of relief available to parties in a federal civil action.

II. PROVISIONAL RELIEF

Civil litigation takes time, and the parties' positions and real-world facts may change to one party's detriment in the time that it takes to secure a final judgment in state or federal court. To protect its position in litigation, and gain the full relief ultimately awarded in a final judgment, a plaintiff may seek provisional relief before achieving final judgment on a claim. Consider the following case.[2]

---

[1] Rule 70 provides for the enforcement of a judgment that requires a party to convey land, deliver a deed or other document, or perform another specific act and also recognizes the court's power to hold in contempt a party who does not comply with a judgment.

[2] For the history, context, and implications of the Supreme Court's decision in *Connecticut v. Doehr*, see Bone, "The Story of *Connecticut v. Doehr*: Balancing Costs and Benefits in Defining Procedural Rights," in *Civil Procedure Stories* 159 (K. Clermont ed., 2nd ed. 2008).

Connecticut v. Doehr

Supreme Court of the United States, 1991
501 U.S. 1

■ JUSTICE WHITE delivered an opinion, Parts I, II, and III of which are the opinion of the Court. THE CHIEF JUSTICE, JUSTICE BLACKMUN, JUSTICE KENNEDY, and JUSTICE SOUTER join Parts I, II, and III of this opinion, and JUSTICE SCALIA joins Parts I and III.

This case requires us to determine whether a state statute that authorizes prejudgment attachment of real estate without prior notice or hearing, without a showing of extraordinary circumstances, and without a requirement that the person seeking the attachment post a bond, satisfies the Due Process Clause of the Fourteenth Amendment. We hold that, as applied to this case, it does not.

I

On March 15, 1988, petitioner John F. DiGiovanni submitted an application to the Connecticut Superior Court for an attachment in the amount of $75,000 on respondent Brian K. Doehr's home in Meriden, Connecticut. DiGiovanni took this step in conjunction with a civil action for assault and battery that he was seeking to institute against Doehr in the same court. The suit did not involve Doehr's real estate, nor did DiGiovanni have any pre-existing interest either in Doehr's home or any of his other property.

Connecticut law authorizes prejudgment attachment of real estate without affording prior notice or the opportunity for a prior hearing to the individual whose property is subject to the attachment. The State's prejudgment remedy statute provides, in relevant part:

> The court or a judge of the court may allow the prejudgment remedy to be issued by an attorney without hearing as provided in sections 52–278c and 52–278d upon verification by oath of the plaintiff or of some competent affiant, that there is probable cause to sustain the validity of the plaintiff's claims and (1) that the prejudgment remedy requested is for an attachment of real property. . . ." Conn.Gen.Stat. § 52–278e (1991).

The statute does not require the plaintiff to post a bond to insure the payment of damages that the defendant may suffer should the attachment prove wrongfully issued or the claim prove unsuccessful.

As required, DiGiovanni submitted an affidavit in support of his application. In five one-sentence paragraphs, DiGiovanni stated that the facts set forth in his previously submitted complaint were true; that "I was willfully, wantonly and maliciously assaulted by the defendant, Brian K. Doehr"; that "[s]aid assault and battery broke my left wrist and further caused an ecchymosis to my right eye, as well as other injuries"; and that "I have further expended sums of money for medical care and treatment." The affidavit concluded with the statement, "In my opinion, the foregoing facts are sufficient to show that there is probable cause that judgment will be rendered for the plaintiff."

On the strength of these submissions the Superior Court Judge, by an order dated March 17, found "probable cause to sustain the validity of the plaintiff's claim" and ordered the attachment on Doehr's home "to the value of $75,000." The sheriff attached the property four days later, on March 21. Only after this did Doehr receive notice of the attachment. He also had yet to be served with the complaint, which is ordinarily necessary for an action to commence in Connecticut. As the statute further required, the attachment notice informed Doehr that he had the right to a hearing: (1) to claim that no probable cause existed to sustain the claim; (2) to request that the attachment be vacated, modified, or dismissed or that a bond be substituted; or (3) to claim that some portion of the property was exempt from execution. Conn.Gen.Stat. § 52–278e(b) (1991).

Rather than pursue these options, Doehr filed suit against DiGiovanni in Federal District Court, claiming that § 52–278e(a)(1) was unconstitutional under the Due Process Clause of the Fourteenth Amendment. The District Court upheld the statute and granted summary judgment in favor of DiGiovanni. On appeal, a divided panel of the United States Court of Appeals for the Second Circuit reversed. *Pinsky v. Duncan*, 898 F.2d 852 (1990).[3] Judge Pratt, who wrote the opinion for the court, concluded that the Connecticut statute violated due process in permitting ex parte attachment absent a showing of extraordinary circumstances. "The rule to be derived from *Sniadach v. Family Finance Corp. of Bay View*, 395 U.S. 337 (1969) and its progeny, therefore, is not that postattachment hearings are generally acceptable provided that plaintiff files a factual affidavit and that a judicial officer supervises the process, but that a prior hearing may be postponed where exceptional circumstances justify such a delay, and where sufficient additional safeguards are present." *Id.*, at 855. This conclusion was deemed to be consistent with our decision in *Mitchell v. W.T. Grant Co.*, 416 U.S. 600 (1974), because the absence of a preattachment hearing was approved in that case based on the presence of extraordinary circumstances.

A further reason to invalidate the statute, the court ruled, was the highly factual nature of the issues in this case. In *Mitchell*, there were "uncomplicated matters that len[t] themselves to documentary proof" and "[t]he nature of the issues at stake minimize[d] the risk that the writ [would] be wrongfully issued by a judge." Similarly, in *Mathews v. Eldridge*, 424 U.S. 319, 343–344 (1976), where an evidentiary hearing was not required prior to the termination of disability benefits, the

---

[3]   The Court of Appeals invited Connecticut to intervene pursuant to 28 U.S.C. § 2403(b) after oral argument. The State elected to intervene in the appeal and has fully participated in the proceedings before this Court.

determination of disability was "sharply focused and easily documented." Judge Pratt observed that in contrast the present case involved the fact-specific event of a fist fight and the issue of assault. He doubted that the judge could reliably determine probable cause when presented with only the plaintiff's version of the altercation. "Because the risk of a wrongful attachment is considerable under these circumstances, we conclude that dispensing with notice and opportunity for a hearing until after the attachment, without a showing of extraordinary circumstances, violates the requirements of due process." Judge Pratt went on to conclude that in his view, the statute was also constitutionally infirm for its failure to require the plaintiff to post a bond for the protection of the defendant in the event the attachment was ultimately found to have been improvident.

Judge Mahoney was also of the opinion that the statutory provision for attaching real property in civil actions, without a prior hearing and in the absence of extraordinary circumstances, was unconstitutional. He disagreed with Judge Pratt's opinion that a bond was constitutionally required. Judge Newman dissented from the holding that a hearing prior to attachment was constitutionally required and, like Judge Mahoney, disagreed with Judge Pratt on the necessity for a bond.

The dissent's conclusion accorded with the views of the Connecticut Supreme Court, which had previously upheld § 52–278e(b) in *Fermont Division, Dynamics Corp. of America v. Smith*, 178 Conn. 393 (1979). We granted certiorari to resolve the conflict of authority.

II

With this case we return to the question of what process must be afforded by a state statute enabling an individual to enlist the aid of the State to deprive another of his or her property by means of the prejudgment attachment or similar procedure. Our cases reflect the numerous variations this type of remedy can entail. In *Sniadach v. Family Finance Corp. of Bay View*, 395 U.S. 337 (1969), the Court struck down a Wisconsin statute that permitted a creditor to effect prejudgment garnishment of wages without notice and prior hearing to the wage earner. In *Fuentes v. Shevin*, 407 U.S. 67 (1972), the Court likewise found a due process violation in state replevin provisions that permitted vendors to have goods seized through an ex parte application to a court clerk and the posting of a bond. Conversely, the Court upheld a Louisiana ex parte procedure allowing a lienholder to have disputed goods sequestered in *Mitchell v. W.T. Grant Co. Mitchell*, however, carefully noted that Fuentes was decided against "a factual and legal background sufficiently different . . . that it does not require the invalidation of the Louisiana sequestration statute." Id., 416 U.S., at 615. Those differences included Louisiana's provision of an immediate postdeprivation hearing along with the option of damages; the requirement that a judge rather than a clerk determine that there is a clear showing of entitlement to the writ; the necessity for a detailed affidavit; and an emphasis on the lienholder's interest in preventing waste or alienation of the encumbered property. Id., at 615–618. In *North Georgia Finishing, Inc. v. Di-Chem, Inc.*, 419 U.S. 601, (1975), the Court again invalidated an ex parte garnishment statute that not only failed to provide for notice and prior hearing but also failed to require a bond, a detailed affidavit setting out the claim, the determination of a neutral magistrate, or a prompt postdeprivation hearing.

These cases "underscore the truism that ' "[d]ue process," unlike some legal rules, is not a technical conception with a fixed content unrelated to time, place and circumstances.' " *Mathews v. Eldridge*, supra, 424 U.S., at 334 (quoting *Cafeteria & Restaurant Workers v. McElroy*, 367 U.S. 886, 895 (1961)). In *Mathews*, we drew upon our prejudgment remedy decisions to determine what process is due when the government itself seeks to effect a deprivation on its own initiative. That analysis resulted in the now familiar threefold inquiry requiring consideration of "the private interest that will be affected by the official action"; "the risk of an erroneous deprivation of such interest through the procedures used, and the probable value, if any, of additional or substitute safeguards"; and lastly "the Government's interest, including the function involved and the fiscal and administrative burdens that the additional or substitute procedural requirement would entail." Id., at 335.

Here the inquiry is similar, but the focus is different. Prejudgment remedy statutes ordinarily apply to disputes between private parties rather than between an individual and the government. Such enactments are designed to enable one of the parties to "make use of state procedures with the overt, significant assistance of state officials," and they undoubtedly involve state action "substantial enough to implicate the Due Process Clause." *Tulsa Professional Collection Services, Inc. v. Pope*, 485 U.S. 478, 486 (1988). Nonetheless, any burden that increasing procedural safeguards entails primarily affects not the government, but the party seeking control of the other's property. For this type of case, therefore, the relevant inquiry requires, as in Mathews, first, consideration of the private interest that will be affected by the prejudgment measure; second, an examination of the risk of erroneous deprivation through the procedures under attack and the probable value of additional or alternative safeguards; and third, in contrast to *Mathews*, principal attention to the interest of the party seeking the prejudgment remedy, with, nonetheless, due regard for any ancillary interest the government may have in providing the procedure or forgoing the added burden of providing greater protections.

We now consider the *Mathews* factors in determining the adequacy of the procedures before us, first with regard to the safeguards of notice and a prior hearing, and then in relation to the protection of a bond.

III

We agree with the Court of Appeals that the property interests that attachment affects are significant. For a property owner like Doehr, attachment ordinarily clouds title; impairs the ability to sell or otherwise alienate the property; taints any credit rating; reduces the chance of obtaining a home equity loan or additional mortgage; and can even place an existing mortgage in technical default where there is an insecurity clause. Nor does Connecticut deny that any of these consequences occurs.

* * *

We also agree with the Court of Appeals that the risk of erroneous deprivation that the State permits here is substantial. By definition, attachment statutes premise a deprivation of property on one ultimate factual contingency—the award of damages to the plaintiff which the defendant may not be able to satisfy. For attachments before judgment, Connecticut mandates that this determination be made by means of a procedural inquiry that asks whether "there is probable cause to sustain the validity of the plaintiff's claim." Conn.Gen.Stat. § 52–278e(a) (1991). The statute elsewhere defines the validity of the claim in terms of the likelihood "that judgment will be rendered in the matter in favor of the plaintiff." Conn.Gen.Stat. § 52–278c(a)(2) (1991). What probable cause means in this context, however, remains obscure. The State initially took the position, as did the dissent below, that the statute requires a plaintiff to show the objective likelihood of the suit's success. Doehr, citing ambiguous state cases, reads the provision as requiring no more than that a plaintiff demonstrate a subjective good-faith belief that the suit will succeed. At oral argument, the State shifted its position to argue that the statute requires something akin to the plaintiff stating a claim with sufficient facts to survive a motion to dismiss.

We need not resolve this confusion since the statute presents too great a risk of erroneous deprivation under any of these interpretations. If the statute demands inquiry into the sufficiency of the complaint, or, still less, the plaintiff's good-faith belief that the complaint is sufficient, requirement of a complaint and a factual affidavit would permit a court to make these minimal determinations. But neither inquiry adequately reduces the risk of erroneous deprivation. Permitting a court to authorize attachment merely because the plaintiff believes the defendant is liable, or because the plaintiff can make out a facially valid complaint, would permit the deprivation of the defendant's property when the claim would fail to convince a jury, when it rested on factual allegations that were sufficient to state a cause of action but which the defendant would dispute, or in the case of a mere good-faith standard, even when the complaint failed to state a claim upon which relief could be granted. The potential for unwarranted attachment in these situations is self-evident and too great to satisfy the requirements of due process absent any countervailing consideration.

* * *

What safeguards the State does afford do not adequately reduce this risk. Connecticut points out that the statute also provides an "expeditiou[s]" postattachment adversary hearing, § 52–278e(c); notice for such a hearing, § 52–278e(b); judicial review of an adverse decision, § 52–278l(a); and a double damages action if the original suit is commenced without probable cause, § 52–568(a)(1). Similar considerations were present in *Mitchell*, where we upheld Louisiana's sequestration statute despite the lack of predeprivation notice and hearing. But in *Mitchell*, the plaintiff had a vendor's lien to protect, the risk of error was minimal because the likelihood of recovery involved uncomplicated matters that lent themselves to documentary proof, and the plaintiff was required to put up a bond. None of these factors diminishing the need for a predeprivation hearing is present in this case. It is true that a later hearing might negate the presence of probable cause, but this would not cure the temporary deprivation that an earlier hearing might have prevented. "The Fourteenth Amendment draws no bright lines around three-day, 10-day or 50-day deprivations of property. Any significant taking of property by the State is within the purview of the Due Process Clause." *Fuentes*, 407 U.S., at 86.

Finally, we conclude that the interests in favor of an ex parte attachment, particularly the interests of the plaintiff, are too minimal to supply such a consideration here. The plaintiff had no existing interest in Doehr's real estate when he sought the attachment. His only interest in attaching the property was to ensure the availability of assets to satisfy his judgment if he prevailed on the merits of his action. Yet there was no allegation that Doehr was about to transfer or encumber his real estate or take any other action during the pendency of the action that would render his real estate unavailable to satisfy a judgment. Our cases have recognized such a properly supported claim would be an exigent circumstance permitting postponing any notice or hearing until after the attachment is effected. See *Mitchell*, supra, 416 U.S., at 609; *Fuentes*, supra, 407 U.S., at 90–92; *Sniadach*, 395 U.S., at 339. Absent such allegations, however, the plaintiff's interest in attaching the property does not justify the burdening of Doehr's ownership rights without a hearing to determine the likelihood of recovery.

No interest the government may have affects the analysis. The State's substantive interest in protecting any rights of the plaintiff cannot be any more weighty than those rights themselves. Here the plaintiff's interest is de minimis. Moreover, the State cannot seriously plead additional financial or administrative burdens involving predeprivation hearings when it already claims to provide an immediate post-deprivation hearing.

* * *

IV

A

Although a majority of the Court does not reach the issue, Justices MARSHALL, STEVENS, O'CONNOR, and I deem it appropriate to consider whether due process also requires the plaintiff to post a bond or other security in addition to requiring a hearing or showing of some exigency.

As noted, the impairments to property rights that attachments effect merit due process protection. Several consequences can be severe, such as the default of a homeowner's mortgage. In the present context, it need only be added that we have repeatedly recognized the utility of a bond in protecting property rights affected by the mistaken award of prejudgment remedies. *Di-Chem*, 419 U.S., at 610, 611 (Powell, J., concurring in judgment); *id.*, at 619 (BLACKMUN, J., dissenting); *Mitchell*, 416 U.S., at 606, n. 8.

Without a bond, at the time of attachment, the danger that these property rights may be wrongfully deprived remains unacceptably high even with such safeguards as a hearing or exigency requirement. The need for a bond is especially apparent where extraordinary circumstances justify an attachment with no more than the plaintiff's ex parte assertion of a claim. We have already discussed how due process tolerates, and the States generally permit, the otherwise impermissible chance of erroneously depriving the defendant in such situations in light of the heightened interest of the plaintiff. Until a postattachment hearing, however, a defendant has no protection against damages sustained where no extraordinary circumstance in fact existed or the plaintiff's likelihood of recovery was nil. Such protection is what a bond can supply. Both the Court and its individual Members have repeatedly found the requirement of a bond to play an essential role in reducing what would have been too great a degree of risk in precisely this type of circumstance.

But the need for a bond does not end here. A defendant's property rights remain at undue risk even when there has been an adversarial hearing to determine the plaintiff's likelihood of recovery. At best, a court's initial assessment of each party's case cannot produce more than an educated prediction as to who will win. This is especially true when, as here, the nature of the claim makes any accurate prediction elusive. In consequence, even a full hearing under a proper probable-cause standard would not prevent many defendants from having title to their homes impaired during the pendency of suits that never result in the contingency that ultimately justifies such impairment, namely, an award to the plaintiff. Attachment measures currently on the books reflect this concern. All but a handful of States require a plaintiff's bond despite also affording a hearing either before, or (for the vast majority, only under extraordinary circumstances) soon after, an attachment takes place. Bonds have been a similarly common feature of other prejudgment remedy procedures that we have considered, whether or not these procedures also included a hearing.

The State stresses its double damages remedy for suits that are commenced without probable cause. This remedy, however, fails to make up for the lack of a bond. As an initial matter, the meaning of "probable cause" in this provision is no more clear here than it was in the attachment provision itself. Should the term mean the plaintiff's good faith or the facial adequacy of the complaint, the remedy is clearly insufficient. A defendant who was deprived where there was little or no likelihood that the plaintiff would obtain a judgment could nonetheless recover only by proving some type of fraud or malice or by showing that the plaintiff had failed to state a claim. Problems persist even if the plaintiff's ultimate failure permits recovery. At best a defendant must await a decision on the merits of the plaintiff's complaint, even assuming that a § 52–568(a)(1) action may be brought as a counterclaim. Settlement, under Connecticut law, precludes seeking the damages remedy, a fact that encourages the use of attachments as a tactical device to pressure an opponent to capitulate. An attorney's advice that there is probable cause to commence an action constitutes a complete defense, even if the advice was unsound or erroneous. Finally, there is no guarantee that the original plaintiff will have adequate assets to satisfy an award that the defendant may win.

Nor is there any appreciable interest against a bond requirement. Section 52–278e(a)(1) does not require a plaintiff to show exigent circumstances nor any pre-existing interest in the property facing attachment. A party must show more than the mere existence of a claim before subjecting an opponent to prejudgment proceedings that carry a significant risk of erroneous deprivation. See *Mitchell*, supra, 416 U.S., at 604–609; *Fuentes*, supra, 407 U.S., at 90–92; *Sniadach*, 395 U.S., at 339.

B

Our foregoing discussion compels the four of us to consider whether a bond excuses the need for a hearing or other safeguards altogether. If a bond is needed to augment the protections afforded by preattachment and postattachment hearings, it arguably follows that a bond renders these safeguards unnecessary. That conclusion is unconvincing, however, for it ignores certain harms that bonds could not undo but that hearings would prevent. The law concerning attachments has rarely, if ever, required defendants to suffer an encumbered title until the case is concluded without any prior opportunity to show that the attachment was unwarranted. Our cases have repeatedly emphasized the importance of providing a prompt postdeprivation hearing at the very least. Every State but one, moreover, expressly requires a preattachment or postattachment hearing to determine the propriety of an attachment.

The necessity for at least a prompt postattachment hearing is self-evident because the right to be compensated at the end of the case, if the plaintiff loses, for all provable injuries caused by the attachment is inadequate to redress the harm inflicted, harm that could have been avoided had an early hearing been held. An individual with an immediate need or opportunity to sell a property can neither do so, nor otherwise satisfy that need or recreate the opportunity. The same applies to a parent in need of a home equity loan for a child's education, an entrepreneur seeking to start a business on the strength of an otherwise strong credit rating, or simply a homeowner who might face the disruption of having a mortgage placed in technical default. The extent of these harms, moreover, grows with the length of the suit. Here, oral argument indicated that civil suits in Connecticut commonly take up to four to seven years for completion. Many state attachment statutes require that the amount of a bond be anywhere from the equivalent to twice the amount the plaintiff seeks. These amounts bear no relation to the harm the defendant might suffer even assuming that money damages can make up for the foregoing disruptions. It should be clear, however, that such an assumption is fundamentally flawed. Reliance on a bond does not sufficiently account for the harms that flow from an erroneous attachment to excuse a State from reducing that risk by means of a timely hearing.

If a bond cannot serve to dispense with a hearing immediately after attachment, neither is it sufficient basis for not providing a preattachment hearing in the absence of exigent circumstances even if in any event a hearing would be provided a few days later. The reasons are the same: a wrongful attachment can inflict injury that will not fully be redressed by recovery on the bond after a prompt postattachment hearing determines that the attachment was invalid.

Once more, history and contemporary practices support our conclusion. Historically, attachments would not issue without a showing of extraordinary circumstances even though a plaintiff bond was almost invariably required in addition. Likewise, all but eight States currently require the posting of a bond. Out of this 42-State majority, all but one requires a preattachment hearing, a showing of some exigency, or both, and all but one expressly require a postattachment hearing when an attachment has been issued ex parte. This testimony underscores the point that neither a hearing nor an extraordinary circumstance limitation eliminates the need for a bond, no more than a bond allows waiver of these other protections. To reconcile the interests of the defendant and the plaintiff accurately, due process generally requires all of the above.

V

Because Connecticut's prejudgment remedy provision violates the requirements of due process by authorizing prejudgment attachment without prior notice or a hearing, the judgment of the Court of Appeals is affirmed, and the case is remanded to that court for further proceedings consistent with this opinion.

It is so ordered.

■ CHIEF JUSTICE REHNQUIST, with whom JUSTICE BLACKMUN joins, concurring in part and concurring in the judgment.

I agree with the Court that the Connecticut attachment statute, "as applied to this case," fails to satisfy the Due Process Clause of the Fourteenth Amendment. I therefore join Parts I, II, and III of its opinion. Unfortunately, the remainder of the opinion does not confine itself to the facts of this case, but enters upon a lengthy disquisition as to what combination of safeguards are required to satisfy due process in hypothetical cases not before the Court. I therefore do not join Part IV.

* * *

Today's holding is a significant development in the law; the only cases dealing with real property cited in the Court's opinion, *Peralta v. Heights Medical Center, Inc.*, 485 U.S. 80, 85 (1988), and *Hodge v. Muscatine County*, 196 U.S. 276, 281 (1905), arose out of lien foreclosure sales in which the question was whether the owner was entitled to proper notice. The change is dramatically reflected when we compare today's decision with the almost casual statement of Justice Holmes, writing for a unanimous Court in *Coffin Brothers & Co. v. Bennett*, 277 U.S. 29, 31 (1928):

> [N]othing is more common than to allow parties alleging themselves to be creditors to establish in advance by attachment a lien dependent for its effect upon the result of the suit.

The only protection accorded to the debtor in that case was the right to contest his liability in a postdeprivation proceeding.

It is both unwise and unnecessary, I believe, for the plurality to proceed, as it does in Part IV, from its decision of the case before it to discuss abstract and hypothetical situations not before it. This is especially so where we are dealing with the Due Process Clause which, as the Court recognizes, " ' "unlike some legal rules, is not a technical conception with a fixed content unrelated to time, place and circumstances." ' " And it is even more true in a case involving constitutional limits on the methods by which the States may transfer or create interests in real property; in other areas of the law, dicta may do little damage, but those who insure titles or write title opinions often do not enjoy the luxury of distinguishing between dicta and holding.

* * *

■ [JUSTICE SCALIA concurred in the judgment and in parts I and III of the opinion.]

COMMENTS AND QUESTIONS CONCERNING *CONNECTICUT V. DOEHR*

1.   Why did John DiGiovanni seek prejudgment attachment of Brian Doehr's house? Whether or not it is attached prior to the conclusion of his assault and battery action, won't the house be available to satisfy any judgment that is ultimately obtained in that action?

2.   Why didn't Doehr challenge Connecticut's prejudgment attachment procedure in Connecticut state court?

3.   How did the State of Connecticut intervene in this action? Section 2403(b) of Title 28 in part provides:

> In any action, suit, or proceeding in a court of the United States to which a State or any agency, officer, or employee thereof is not a party, wherein the constitutionality of any statute of that State affecting the public interest is drawn in question, the court shall certify such fact to the attorney general of the State, and shall permit the State to intervene for presentation of evidence, if evidence is otherwise admissible in the case, and for argument on the question of constitutionality.

Federal Rule of Civil Procedure 24(a) provides for intervention of right in federal actions, extending the right to intervene to those who are "given an unconditional right to intervene by a federal statute."

4.   What sort of "extraordinary circumstances" might justify prejudgment seizure of property without a prior hearing?

5.   Why does the Court conclude that there is a great risk of error under the Connecticut prejudgement attachment statute in cases such as this?

6.   The Connecticut statute provided for an expedited postattachment adversary hearing, notice of such hearing, judicial review of any adverse decision, and a double damages action if the original suit was commenced without probable cause. Isn't this case therefore similar to *Mitchell v. W. T. Grant*, in which the Court upheld Louisiana's prejudgment attachment statute?

7.   What if DiGiovanni had sought an attachment in connection with an action involving Doehr's house (for instance, an action for specific performance in which DiGiovanni was seeking to enforce a sales contract for the house)?

8.   An attachment to the Court's opinion showed: "Only Washington, Connecticut, and Rhode Island authorize attachments without a prior hearing in situations that do not involve any purportedly heightened threat to the plaintiff's interests. Even those States permit ex parte deprivations only in certain types of cases." 501 U.S. at 18. What should be the significance of such facts for the Supreme Court in deciding this case?

9. Only Justices Marshall, Stevens, and O'Connor joined Justice White in part IV of the opinion concerning Connecticut's failure to require attachment bonds. Why don't the other justices join in this part of the opinion? What is the precedential value of this portion of the opinion?

10. Why do Chief Justice Rehnquist and Justice Blackmun, who concur in the judgment, write a separate concurring opinion?

III. DAMAGES

While provisional remedies such as prejudgment attachment may be sought in some cases, those provisional remedies are only a prelude to the final resolution of a civil action by motion, trial, or settlement. This is the point at which final relief is sought, and the classic relief that plaintiffs seek is the legal remedy of damages. However, there are several different types of damages that a plaintiff (or a defendant on a counterclaim) can seek. We initially consider these different types of damages and then explore individual damage remedies more closely.

A. DIFFERENT TYPES OF DAMAGES

There are several different types of damages that a plaintiff, or a defendant on a counterclaim, can seek.

- **Compensatory Damages** are to compensate or "make whole" an injured party.

- **Punitive Damages** are not to compensate the injured party, but to punish a wrongdoer who has acted willfully or recklessly and deter such conduct by others; Punitive damages are in addition to compensatory damages and typically are awarded to the injured party (even though it may have received full compensatory damages).

- **Statutory Damages** may be provided in a statute that specifies that a specific amount of damages are to be awarded if that statute is violated.

- **Liquidated Damages** can be set by the parties themselves; Thus a construction contract may provide that the builder will pay $10,000 for each day beyond a certain date that the construction remains uncompleted.

- **Nominal Damages** may be awarded in a situation in which the injured party's loss is difficult to measure but a statute or other legal duty has been breached;[3] Although a plaintiff may be awarded nominal damages of only $1.00, such a judgment establishes that the defendant has acted

---

[3] *Carey v. Piphus*, 435 U.S. 247, 266 (1978) ("Because the right to procedural due process is 'absolute' in the sense that it does not depend upon the merits of a claimant's substantive assertions, and because of the importance to organized society that procedural due process be observed, we believe that the denial of procedural due process should be actionable for nominal damages without proof of actual injury.").

illegally and, under certain statutes, may entitle the plaintiff to an award of attorneys' fees significantly greater than the nominal damages recovered.[4]

The next subsections of this chapter more closely consider compensatory and punitive damages.

B. COMPENSATORY DAMAGES: ARE THERE SOME THINGS IN LIFE THAT MONEY JUST CAN'T BUY?

Damages typically are described as monetary compensation that is sufficient to "make the plaintiff whole." Is this always possible? Consider the following case.

Boan v. Blackwell
Supreme Court of South Carolina, 2001
343 S.C. 498

OPINION
ON WRIT OF CERTIORARI TO THE COURT OF APPEALS

■ PLEICONES, JUSTICE:

We granted certiorari to the Court of Appeals to consider the jury charge in this automobile negligence case. We now hold that "loss of enjoyment of life" and "pain and suffering" are separately compensable elements of damages, and overrule *Boan v. Blackwell, supra*, and *Stroud v. Stroud*, 299 S.C. 394 (Ct.App.1989), to the extent they hold otherwise. Accordingly, we affirm the decision of the Court of Appeals as modified.

Petitioners admitted liability, and the only issue for the jury was the amount of damages to be awarded to respondent. In the course of charging the jury on damages, the trial judge stated:

> In determining the amount of compensation for personal injuries, it is proper to take into consideration past and present aspects of that injury. This would include, as I have told you, **physical and mental pain and suffering endured**, expenses incurred for necessary medical treatment, loss of time and income which resulted from the impairment of the ability to work, **the loss of enjoyment of life suffered as a result of the injury**, and any other losses which are reflected by the character of the injury. Now in this connection, I charge you that mental pain and suffering, sometimes called mental distress, is a proper element of actual damages where it is the natural and proximate consequence of a negligent act committed by another.

---

[4] However, "When a plaintiff recovers only nominal damages because of his failure to prove an essential element of his claim for monetary relief, the only reasonable fee is usually no fee at all." *Farrar v. Hobby*, 506 U.S. 103, 115 (1992).

Now an injured party may also recover for such future damages as it is reasonably certain will of necessity result from the injury received. The principal underlying compensation for future damages is that only one action can be brought, and, therefore, only one recovery had. It is proper to include in the estimate of future damages compensation for pain and suffering which will with reasonable certainty result. (emphasis added).

Petitioners objected to the charge, stating, "[Y]ou charged on both lost enjoyment of life and pain and suffering. Our courts have indicated that that is basically the same element of damages, and we don't believe they should be able to recover for it twice." The trial judge declined to act on petitioners' objection.

On appeal, the Court of Appeals held the single reference to "loss of enjoyment of life" in the damages charge "simply indicated to the jury what it could consider when assessing damages for pain and suffering." The court acknowledged its holding in *Stroud v. Stroud* that loss of enjoyment of life is merely a component of pain and suffering and not a separately compensable element of damages. After reviewing the entire charge in this case, however, the court found no violation of *Stroud* and consequently held there was no reversible error.

We granted certiorari, and now hold that where there is evidence of "loss of enjoyment of life," South Carolina juries should be charged that this loss is a compensable element, separate and apart from pain and suffering, of a damages award. Although this Court has never directly decided this issue, we have acknowledged "loss of enjoyment of life" as a basis for a damages award in previous cases. *See Young v. Warr*, 252 S.C. 179 (1969) (paraplegic's loss of social and business activities is compensable intangible injury); *Cabler v. L.V. Hart, Inc.*, 251 S.C. 576 (1968) (proper to consider how pain, suffering, and disability "decrease and diminish the joys and pleasures of a normal life" in awarding damages).

In *Stroud v. Stroud* the Court of Appeals held, "[l]oss of enjoyment of life is not a separate species of damage deserving a distinct award, but instead is only an element of general damages for pain and suffering." We disagree, and find more persuasive the decisions of the United States District Court for the district of South Carolina which permit a separate recovery for loss of enjoyment of life. *See McNeill v. United States*, 519 F.Supp. 283 (D.S.C.1981); *see also, e.g., Schumacher v. Cooper*, 850 F.Supp. 438 (D.S.C.1994); *Bates v. Merritt Seafood, Inc.*, 663 F.Supp. 915 (D.S.C.1987); *Kapuschinsky v. United States*, 259 F.Supp. 1 (D.S.C.1966).

An award for pain and suffering compensates the injured person for the physical discomfort and the emotional response to the sensation of pain caused by the injury itself. Separate damages are given for mental anguish where the evidence shows, for example, that the injured person suffered shock, fright, emotional upset, and/or humiliation as the result of the defendant's negligence.

On the other hand, damages for "loss of enjoyment of life" compensate for the limitations, resulting from the defendant's negligence, on the injured person's ability to participate in and derive pleasure from the normal activities of daily life, or for the individual's inability to pursue his talents, recreational interests, hobbies, or avocations.[1] *See Overstreet v. Shoney's, Inc.,* 4 S.W.3d 694 (Tenn.Ct.App.1999); *Sawyer v. Midelfort,* 227 Wis.2d 124 (1999); *K.M. Leasing, Inc. v. Butler,* 749 So.2d 310 (Miss.Ct.App.1999). For example, an award for the diminishment of pleasure resulting from the loss of use of one of the senses, or for a paraplegic's loss of the ability to participate in certain physical activities, falls under the rubric of hedonic damages. In our view, "loss of enjoyment of life" damages compensate the individual not only for the subjective knowledge that one can no longer enjoy all of life's pursuits, but also for the objective loss of the ability to engage in these activities.

We hold that, where supported by the evidence, the jury shall be charged that the injured person is entitled to recover damages for loss of enjoyment of life. In our view, a separate charge on hedonic damages will minimize the risk that a jury will under-or over-compensate an injured person for her noneconomic losses. While there are cases in which it is difficult to segregate the various components of these types of damages, we conclude that a separate charge will clarify for the jurors the issues they should consider in awarding money for injuries which are not readily reducible to specific amounts. In situations where the differences may be difficult to discern, defendants may request the submission of a special interrogatory. *See* Rule 49, SCRCP.

We agree with the Court of Appeals that there was no error in the charge given in this trial. Accordingly, the decision of the Court of Appeals is

AFFIRMED AS MODIFIED.

■ TOAL, C.J., MOORE, WALLER and BURNETT, JJ., concur.

COMMENTS AND QUESTIONS CONCERNING *BOAN V. BLACKWELL*

1. *Boan v. Blackwell* has not been followed uniformly by other state courts and legislatures, which have refused to recognize hedonic damages. *E.g.,* Alaska Stat. § 09.55.549(c) (2013) (excluding in medical malpractice actions separate hedonic damages "that attempt to compensate for the pleasure of being alive"); *Kemp v. Pfizer, Inc.,* 947 F.Supp. 1139, 1146

---

[1] It is for this reason that "loss of enjoyment of life" damages are sometimes referred to as "hedonic damages." *See, e.g.,* Crowe, "The Semantical Bifurcation of Noneconomic Loss: Should Hedonic Damages Be Recognized Independently of Pain and Suffering Damage?" 74 *Iowa L.Rev.* 1275 (1990).

(E.D.Mich. 1996) (hedonic damages not recoverable under Michigan Wrongful Death Act).

2.   The Nevada Supreme Court has described the different state approaches to hedonic damages as follows:

> While the majority of jurisdictions recognize hedonic loss as a recoverable element of damages, the jurisdictions differ as to how hedonic loss should be presented and awarded. In particular, jurisdictions disagree as to whether an expert should be permitted to testify concerning the value of hedonic loss. Some jurisdictions will not permit an expert to testify concerning the value of a person's life on the grounds that the loss is subjective, that the damages are incapable of being accurately measured or that the methods used by experts to measure hedonic losses are unreliable. Other courts permit experts, such as economists, to testify concerning the value of hedonic loss, recognizing that the jury is ultimately responsible for computing damages and that expert testimony will often assist the jury in making its determination.

Banks ex rel. Banks v. Sunrise Hosp., 120 Nev. 822, 836–37 (2004). While some state courts have recognized hedonic damages, some commentators have been quite critical of such damages. Posner et al., "Measuring Damages for Lost Enjoyment of Life: The View from the Bench and the Jury Box," 27 *Law & Hum. Behav.* 53 (2003); Kuiper, Note, "The Courts, *Daubert*, and Willingness-to-Pay: The Doubtful Future of Hedonic Damages Testimony under the Federal Rules of Evidence," 1996 *U. Ill. L. Rev.* 1197.

3.   As the court notes in *Boan*, courts confronted with requests for hedonic damages attempt to apportion total damages so that the plaintiff's recovery neither overcounts nor undercounts that individual's total loss. Consider the way in which this might happen in an action not based on personal injury.

> In this case * * * the only hedonic loss is caused by the lack of a job. The back pay award fully compensates the class for any hedonic damage. Once the class is awarded back pay, the past lost ability to enjoy life is fully restored, since the class has received the object which caused the deprivation. For example, in the personal injury context, a plaintiff who has lost an arm may have a claim for hedonic damages. However, if the arm was restored to him, his claim for hedonic damages would disappear, since he could no longer claim that he cannot enjoy the more subjective pleasures of life to the fullest. Similarly here, the plaintiff class has been made whole by an award of back pay. To allow hedonic damages on top of the back pay would be equivalent to a double recovery.

Mister v. Illinois Cent. Gulf R. Co., 790 F. Supp. 1411, 1421 (S.D. Ill. 1992).

Do you agree?

4.   One way around the difficulties of proving specific damages is to set the amount of damages before the legal dispute even arises. Such statutory damages can be created by Congress or a state legislature, by

specifying in a statute the amount of damages the injured party will receive in the event a statute is violated. Thus the federal Truth in Lending Act, 15 U.S.C. § 1640(a)(2)(A)(i); (ii), provides for recoveries of "twice the amount of any finance charge in connection with the transaction, [or] * * * 25 per centum of the total amount of monthly payments under the lease, except that the liability under this subparagraph shall not be less than $200 nor greater than $2000." The parties, themselves, also can agree in the contract itself to a specific amount of liquidated damages for breach of the contract.

5.   The court mentions the possibility of a "special interrogatory." As part of your consideration of discovery in Chapter 10, you will study Rule 33 interrogatories, by which a party can ask written questions of another party during the discovery period prior to trial. The court in *Boan*, though, refers to jury interrogatories available under Rule 49 of the Federal Rules of Civil Procedure and South Carolina Rules of Civil Procedure. Rule 49 permits a court to require a jury to answer specific questions (interrogatories) on individual issues of fact in an action (for instance, "Was the plaintiff in the crosswalk when she was struck by defendant's car?"). Such special jury interrogatories can be used in a complex case to focus the jury on the specific questions that it is to decide, rather than lump individual issues together into a general verdict that may approximate a form of "rough justice."

6.   As you may have learned in your contracts course, under the English case of *Hadley v. Baxendale*, plaintiffs typically are not entitled to remote consequential damages that the parties reasonably would not have contemplated in reaching the contract that was breached.

> In *Hadley v. Baxendale*, 156 Eng. Rep. 145 (Ex. 1854) plaintiff's mill was brought to a standstill when a shaft broke. The broken shaft was sent to a manufacturer to serve as a model for a new one. Due to the neglect of a common carrier, wholly unaware of the mill closure, the broken shaft was delayed en route to the manufacturer, thereby prolonging the mill shutdown. Plaintiffs brought suit against the carrier to recover the loss of profit during the prolonged closure. Reversing the judgment in the lower court, the Court of Appeal ordered a new trial finding the jury should not have taken lost profit into account in fixing damages. During the course of the opinion Alderson, B. set forth a standard for limiting recovery of damages in contract:

>> Where two parties have made a contract which one of them has broken, the damages which the other party ought to receive in respect of such breach of contract should be such as may fairly and reasonably be considered either arising naturally, *i.e.*, according to the usual course of things, from such breach of contract itself, or such as may reasonably be supposed to have been in the contemplation of both parties, at the time they made the contract, as the probable result of the breach of it.

Phillips Petroleum Int'l (UK) Ltd. v. Sentry Refining, Inc., Society of Maritime Arbitrators, Inc. No. 1883, WL 825048 (S.M.A.A.S), 8 (1983).

7.   In addition to hedonic and consequential damages, compensatory damages can be subdivided into special and general damages. General damages are damages that are assumed to flow naturally from the injury asserted. In an action seeking redress due to a car accident, general damages would include monetary relief for the plaintiff's pain and suffering or damaged car, while medical expenses are considered special damages (because they are not the necessary consequence of such an accident). *Restatement (Second) of Torts* § 904 cmt. b (1979). The significance of this for civil litigation is that Rule 9(g) of the Federal Rules of Civil Procedure requires: "If an item of special damage is claimed, it must be specifically stated." While it may be difficult to differentiate general from specific damages in some actions, Rule 9(g) typically will be considered to have been satisfied if the complaint provides sufficient information for the opposing party to formulate its response. 5A C. Wright & A. Miller, *Federal Practice and Procedure* § 1311 (3rd ed. 2004).

C. PUNITIVE DAMAGES

Compensatory damages are to compensate or make whole the injured plaintiff, but damage awards serve other purposes as well. In particular, punitive damages are to deter others from taking the same action (or inaction) that the defendant took in a particular case and to punish the defendant. As the Supreme Court discusses in the following case, there are constitutional limits to such punitive damage awards.

Philip Morris USA v. Williams
Supreme Court of the United States, 2007
549 U.S. 346

■ JUSTICE BREYER delivered the opinion of the Court.

The question we address today concerns a large state-court punitive damages award. We are asked whether the Constitution's Due Process Clause permits a jury to base that award in part upon its desire to *punish* the defendant for harming persons who are not before the court (*e.g.,* victims whom the parties do not represent). We hold that such an award would amount to a taking of "property" from the defendant without due process.

I

This lawsuit arises out of the death of Jesse Williams, a heavy cigarette smoker. Respondent, Williams' widow, represents his estate in this state lawsuit for negligence and deceit against Philip Morris, the manufacturer of Marlboro, the brand that Williams favored. A jury found that Williams' death was caused by smoking; that Williams smoked in significant part because he thought it was safe to do so; and that Philip Morris knowingly and falsely led him to believe that this was so. The jury ultimately found that Philip Morris was negligent (as was Williams) and that Philip Morris had engaged in deceit. In respect to deceit, the claim at issue here, it awarded compensatory damages of about $821,000 (about $21,000 economic and $800,000 noneconomic) along with $79.5 million in punitive damages.

The trial judge subsequently found the $79.5 million punitive damages award "excessive," see, *e.g., BMW of North America, Inc. v. Gore*, 517 U.S. 559 (1996), and reduced it to $32 million. Both sides appealed. The Oregon Court of Appeals rejected Philip Morris' arguments and restored the $79.5 million jury award. Subsequently, Philip Morris sought review in the Oregon Supreme Court (which denied review) and then here. We remanded the case in light of *State Farm Mut. Automobile Ins. Co. v. Campbell*, 538 U.S. 408 (2003). The Oregon Court of Appeals adhered to its original views. And Philip Morris sought, and this time obtained, review in the Oregon Supreme Court.

Philip Morris then made two arguments relevant here. First, it said that the trial court should have accepted, but did not accept, a proposed "punitive damages" instruction that specified the jury could not seek to punish Philip Morris for injury to other persons not before the court. In particular, Philip Morris pointed out that the plaintiff's attorney had told the jury to "think about how many other Jesse Williams in the last 40 years in the State of Oregon there have been. . . . In Oregon, how many people do we see outside, driving home . . . smoking cigarettes? . . . [C]igarettes . . . are going to kill ten [of every hundred]. [And] the market share of Marlboros [*i.e.*, Philip Morris] is one-third [*i.e.*, one of every three killed]." In light of this argument, Philip Morris asked the trial court to tell the jury that "you may consider the extent of harm suffered by others in determining what [the] reasonable relationship is" between any punitive award and "the harm caused to Jesse Williams" by Philip Morris' misconduct, "[but] you are not to punish the defendant for the impact of its alleged misconduct on other persons, who may bring lawsuits of their own in which other juries can resolve their claims. . . ." The judge rejected this proposal and instead told the jury that "[p]unitive damages are awarded against a defendant to punish misconduct and to deter misconduct," and "are not intended to compensate the plaintiff or anyone else for damages caused by the defendant's conduct." In Philip Morris' view, the result was a significant likelihood that a portion of the $79.5 million award represented punishment for its having harmed others, a punishment that the Due Process Clause would here forbid.

Second, Philip Morris pointed to the roughly 100-to-1 ratio the $79.5 million punitive damages award bears to $821,000 in compensatory damages. Philip Morris noted that this Court in *BMW* emphasized the constitutional need for punitive damages awards to reflect (1) the "reprehensibility" of the defendant's conduct, (2) a "reasonable relationship" to the harm the plaintiff (or related victim) suffered, and (3) the presence (or absence) of "sanctions," *e.g.*, criminal penalties, that state law provided for comparable conduct, 517 U.S., at 575–585. And in *State Farm*, this Court said that the longstanding historical practice of setting punitive damages at two, three, or four times the size of compensatory damages, while "not binding," is "instructive," and that "[s]ingle-digit multipliers are more likely to comport with due process." 538 U.S., at 425. Philip Morris claimed that, in light of this case law, the punitive award was "grossly excessive."

The Oregon Supreme Court rejected these and other Philip Morris arguments. In particular, it rejected Philip Morris' claim that the Constitution prohibits a state jury "from using punitive damages to punish a defendant for harm to nonparties." And in light of Philip Morris' reprehensible conduct, it found that the $79.5 million award was not "grossly excessive."

Philip Morris then sought certiorari. It asked us to consider, among other things, (1) its claim that Oregon had unconstitutionally permitted it to be punished for harming nonparty victims; and (2) whether Oregon had in effect disregarded "the constitutional requirement that punitive damages be reasonably related to the plaintiff's harm." We granted certiorari limited to these two questions.

For reasons we shall set forth, we consider only the first of these questions. We vacate the Oregon Supreme Court's judgment, and we remand the case for further proceedings.

II

This Court has long made clear that "[p]unitive damages may properly be imposed to further a State's legitimate interests in punishing unlawful conduct and deterring its repetition." *BMW, supra,* at 568. At the same time, we have emphasized the need to avoid an arbitrary determination of an award's amount. Unless a State insists upon proper standards that will cabin the jury's discretionary authority, its punitive damages system may deprive a defendant of "fair notice . . . of the severity of the penalty that a State may impose," *BMW, supra,* at 574; it may threaten "arbitrary punishments," *i.e.,* punishments that reflect not an "application of law" but "a decisionmaker's caprice," *State Farm, supra,* at 416, 418; and, where the amounts are sufficiently large, it may impose one State's (or one jury's) "policy choice," say, as to the conditions under which (or even whether) certain products can be sold, upon "neighboring States" with different public policies, *BMW, supra,* at 571–572.

For these and similar reasons, this Court has found that the Constitution imposes certain limits, in respect both to procedures for awarding punitive damages and to amounts forbidden as "grossly excessive." See *Honda Motor Co. v. Oberg,* 512 U.S. 415, 432 (1994) (requiring judicial review of the size of punitive awards); *Cooper*

Industries, Inc. v. Leatherman Tool Group, Inc., 532 U.S. 424, 443 (2001) (review must be *de novo*); *BMW, supra,* at 574–585 (excessiveness decision depends upon the reprehensibility of the defendant's conduct, whether the award bears a reasonable relationship to the actual and potential harm caused by the defendant to the plaintiff, and the difference between the award and sanctions "authorized or imposed in comparable cases"); *State Farm, supra,* at 425 (excessiveness more likely where ratio exceeds single digits). Because we shall not decide whether the award here at issue is "grossly excessive," we need now only consider the Constitution's procedural limitations.

III

In our view, the Constitution's Due Process Clause forbids a State to use a punitive damages award to punish a defendant for injury that it inflicts upon nonparties or those whom they directly represent, *i.e.,* injury that it inflicts upon those who are, essentially, strangers to the litigation. For one thing, the Due Process Clause prohibits a State from punishing an individual without first providing that individual with "an opportunity to present every available defense." *Lindsey v. Normet,* 405 U.S. 56, 66 (1972). Yet a defendant threatened with punishment for injuring a nonparty victim has no opportunity to defend against the charge, by showing, for example in a case such as this, that the other victim was not entitled to damages because he or she knew that smoking was dangerous or did not rely upon the defendant's statements to the contrary.

For another, to permit punishment for injuring a nonparty victim would add a near standardless dimension to the punitive damages equation. How many such victims are there? How seriously were they injured? Under what circumstances did injury occur? The trial will not likely answer such questions as to nonparty victims. The jury will be left to speculate. And the fundamental due process concerns to which our punitive damages cases refer—risks of arbitrariness, uncertainty, and lack of notice—will be magnified.

Finally, we can find no authority supporting the use of punitive damages awards for the purpose of punishing a defendant for harming others. We have said that it may be appropriate to consider the reasonableness of a punitive damages award in light of the *potential* harm the defendant's conduct could have caused. But we have made clear that the potential harm at issue was harm potentially caused *the plaintiff.* See *State Farm, supra,* at 424 ("[W]e have been reluctant to identify concrete constitutional limits on the ratio between harm, or potential harm, *to the plaintiff* and the punitive damages award" (emphasis added)). * * *

Respondent argues that she is free to show harm to other victims because it is relevant to a different part of the punitive damages constitutional equation, namely, reprehensibility. That is to say, harm to others shows more reprehensible conduct. Philip Morris, in turn, does not deny that a plaintiff may show harm to others in order to demonstrate reprehensibility. Nor do we. Evidence of actual harm to nonparties can help to show that the conduct that harmed the plaintiff also posed a substantial risk of harm to the general public, and so was particularly reprehensible—although counsel may argue in a particular case that conduct resulting in no harm to others nonetheless posed a grave risk to the public, or the converse. Yet for the reasons given above, a jury may not go further than this and use a punitive damages verdict to punish a defendant directly on account of harms it is alleged to have visited on nonparties.

Given the risks of unfairness that we have mentioned, it is constitutionally important for a court to provide assurance that the jury will ask the right question, not the wrong one. And given the risks of arbitrariness, the concern for adequate notice, and the risk that punitive damages awards can, in practice, impose one State's (or one jury's) policies (*e.g.*, banning cigarettes) upon other States—all of which accompany awards that, today, may be many times the size of such awards in the 18th and 19th centuries—it is particularly important that States avoid procedure that unnecessarily deprives juries of proper legal guidance. We therefore conclude that the Due Process Clause requires States to provide assurance that juries are not asking the wrong question, *i.e.*, seeking, not simply to determine reprehensibility, but also to punish for harm caused strangers.

IV

Respondent suggests as well that the Oregon Supreme Court, in essence, agreed with us, that it did not authorize punitive damages awards based upon punishment for harm caused to nonparties. We concede that one might read some portions of the Oregon Supreme Court's opinion as focusing only upon reprehensibility. But the Oregon court's opinion elsewhere makes clear that that court held more than these few phrases might suggest.

The instruction that Philip Morris said the trial court should have given distinguishes between using harm to others as part of the "reasonable relationship" equation (which it would allow) and using it directly as a basis for punishment. The instruction asked the trial court to tell the jury that "you *may* consider the extent of harm suffered by others *in determining what [the] reasonable relationship is*" between Philip Morris' punishable misconduct and harm caused to Jesse Williams, "*[but] you are not to punish the defendant for the impact of its alleged misconduct on other persons, who may bring lawsuits of their own* in which other juries can resolve their claims. . . ." (emphasis added). And as the Oregon Supreme Court explicitly recognized, Philip Morris argued that the Constitution "prohibits the state, acting through a civil jury, from using punitive damages to punish a defendant for harm to nonparties."

The court rejected that claim. In doing so, it pointed out (1) that this Court in *State Farm* had held only that a jury could not base its award upon "dissimilar" acts of a defendant. It added (2) that "[i]f a jury cannot punish for the conduct, then it is difficult to see why it may consider it at all." And it stated (3) that "[i]t is unclear to us how a jury could 'consider' harm to others, yet withhold that consideration from the punishment calculus."

The Oregon court's first statement is correct. We did not previously hold explicitly that a jury may not punish for the harm caused others. But we do so hold now. We do not agree with the Oregon court's second statement. We have explained why we believe the Due Process Clause prohibits a State's inflicting punishment for harm caused strangers to the litigation. At the same time we recognize that conduct that risks harm to many is likely more reprehensible than conduct that risks harm to only a few. And a jury consequently may take this fact into account in determining reprehensibility.

The Oregon court's third statement raises a practical problem. How can we know whether a jury, in taking account of harm caused others under the rubric of reprehensibility, also seeks to *punish* the defendant for having caused injury to others? Our answer is that state courts cannot authorize procedures that create an unreasonable and unnecessary risk of any such confusion occurring. In particular, we believe that where the risk of that misunderstanding is a significant one—because, for instance, of the sort of evidence that was introduced at trial or the kinds of argument the plaintiff made to the jury—a court, upon request, must protect against that risk. Although the States have some flexibility to determine what *kind* of procedures they will implement, federal constitutional law obligates them to provide *some* form of protection in appropriate cases.

V

As the preceding discussion makes clear, we believe that the Oregon Supreme Court applied the wrong constitutional standard when considering Philip Morris' appeal. We remand this case so that the Oregon Supreme Court can apply the standard we have set forth. Because the application of this standard may lead to the need for a new trial, or a change in the level of the punitive damages award, we shall not consider whether the award is constitutionally "grossly excessive." We vacate the Oregon Supreme Court's judgment and remand the case for further proceedings not inconsistent with this opinion.

It is so ordered.

■ JUSTICE STEVENS, dissenting.

The Due Process Clause of the Fourteenth Amendment imposes both substantive and procedural constraints on the power of the States to impose punitive damages on tortfeasors. I remain firmly convinced that the cases announcing those constraints were correctly decided. In my view the Oregon Supreme Court faithfully applied the reasoning in those opinions to the egregious facts disclosed by this record. I agree with Justice GINSBURG's explanation of why no procedural error even arguably justifying reversal occurred at the trial in this case.

Of greater importance to me, however, is the Court's imposition of a novel limit on the State's power to impose punishment in civil litigation. Unlike the Court, I see no reason why an interest in punishing a wrongdoer "for harming persons who are not before the court," should not be taken into consideration when assessing the appropriate sanction for reprehensible conduct.

Whereas compensatory damages are measured by the harm the defendant has caused the plaintiff, punitive damages are a sanction for the public harm the defendant's conduct has caused or threatened. There is little difference between the justification for a criminal sanction, such as a fine or a term of imprisonment, and an award of punitive damages. In our early history either type of sanction might have been imposed in litigation prosecuted by a private citizen. And while in neither context would the sanction typically include a pecuniary award measured by the harm that the conduct had caused to any third parties, in both contexts the harm to third parties would surely be a relevant factor to consider in evaluating the reprehensibility of the defendant's wrongdoing. We have never held otherwise.

In the case before us, evidence attesting to the possible harm the defendant's extensive deceitful conduct caused other Oregonians was properly presented to the jury. No evidence was offered to establish an appropriate measure of damages to compensate such third parties for their injuries, and no one argued that the punitive damages award would serve any such purpose. To award compensatory damages to remedy such third-party harm might well constitute a taking of property from the defendant without due process. But a punitive damages award, instead of serving a compensatory purpose, serves the entirely different purposes of retribution and deterrence that underlie every criminal sanction. This justification for punitive damages has even greater salience when, as in this case, the award is payable in whole or in part to the State rather than to the private litigant.[1]

While apparently recognizing the novelty of its holding, the majority relies on a distinction between taking third-party harm into account in order to assess the reprehensibility of the defendant's conduct—which is permitted—and doing so in order to punish the

---

[1]   The Court's holding in *Browning-Ferris Industries of Vt., Inc. v. Kelco Disposal, Inc.*, 492 U.S. 257 (1989), distinguished, for the purposes of appellate review under the Excessive Fines Clause of the Eighth Amendment, between criminal sanctions and civil fines awarded entirely to the plaintiff. The fact that part of the award in this case is payable to the State lends further support to my conclusion that it should be treated as the functional equivalent of a criminal sanction. I continue to agree with Justice O'Connor and those scholars who have concluded that the Excessive Fines Clause is applicable to punitive damages awards regardless of who receives the ultimate payout.

defendant "directly"—which is forbidden. This nuance eludes me. When a jury increases a punitive damages award because injuries to third parties enhanced the reprehensibility of the defendant's conduct, the jury is by definition punishing the defendant—directly—for third-party harm. A murderer who kills his victim by throwing a bomb that injures dozens of bystanders should be punished more severely than one who harms no one other than his intended victim. Similarly, there is no reason why the measure of the appropriate punishment for engaging in a campaign of deceit in distributing a poisonous and addictive substance to thousands of cigarette smokers statewide should not include consideration of the harm to those "bystanders" as well as the harm to the individual plaintiff. The Court endorses a contrary conclusion without providing us with any reasoned justification.

It is far too late in the day to argue that the Due Process Clause merely guarantees fair procedure and imposes no substantive limits on a State's lawmaking power. It remains true, however, that the Court should be "reluctant to expand the concept of substantive due process because guideposts for responsible decisionmaking in this unchartered area are scarce and open-ended." *Collins v. Harker Heights,* 503 U.S. 115, 125 (1992). Judicial restraint counsels us to "exercise the utmost care whenever we are asked to break new ground in this field." *Ibid.* Today the majority ignores that sound advice when it announces its new rule of substantive law.

Essentially for the reasons stated in the opinion of the Supreme Court of Oregon, I would affirm its judgment.

■ JUSTICE THOMAS, dissenting.

I join Justice GINSBURG's dissent in full. I write separately to reiterate my view that " 'the Constitution does not constrain the size of punitive damages awards.' " *State Farm Mut. Automobile Ins. Co. v. Campbell,* 538 U.S. 408, 429–430 (2003) (THOMAS, J., dissenting) (quoting *Cooper Industries, Inc. v. Leatherman Tool Group, Inc.,* 532 U.S. 424, 443 (2001) (THOMAS, J., concurring)). It matters not that the Court styles today's holding as "procedural" because the "procedural" rule is simply a confusing implementation of the substantive due process regime this Court has created for punitive damages. See *Pacific Mut. Life Ins. Co. v. Haslip,* 499 U.S. 1, 26–27 (1991) (SCALIA, J., concurring in judgment) ("In 1868 . . . punitive damages were undoubtedly an established part of the American common law of torts. It is . . . clear that no particular procedures were deemed necessary to circumscribe a jury's discretion regarding the award of such damages, or their amount"). Today's opinion proves once again that this Court's punitive damages jurisprudence is "insusceptible of principled application." *BMW of North America, Inc. v. Gore,* 517 U.S. 559, 599 (1996) (SCALIA, J., joined by THOMAS, J., dissenting).

■ JUSTICE GINSBURG, with whom JUSTICE SCALIA and JUSTICE THOMAS join, dissenting.

The purpose of punitive damages, it can hardly be denied, is not to compensate, but to punish. Punish for what? Not for harm actually caused "strangers to the litigation," the Court states, but for the *reprehensibility* of defendant's conduct. "[C]onduct that risks harm to many," the Court observes, "is likely more reprehensible than conduct that risks harm to only a few." The Court thus conveys that, when punitive damages are at issue, a jury is properly instructed to consider the extent of harm suffered by others as a measure of reprehensibility, but not to mete out punishment for injuries in fact sustained by nonparties. The Oregon courts did not rule otherwise. They have endeavored to follow our decisions, most recently in *BMW of North America, Inc. v. Gore,* 517 U.S. 559 (1996), and *State Farm Mut. Automobile Ins. Co. v. Campbell,* 538 U.S. 408 (2003), and have "deprive[d] [no jury] of proper legal guidance." Vacation of the Oregon Supreme Court's judgment, I am convinced, is unwarranted.

The right question regarding reprehensibility, the Court acknowledges, would train on "the harm that Philip Morris was prepared to inflict on the smoking public at large." *Ibid.* (quoting 340 Or. 35, 51 (2006)). The Court identifies no evidence introduced and no charge delivered inconsistent with that inquiry.

The Court's order vacating the Oregon Supreme Court's judgment is all the more inexplicable considering that Philip Morris did not preserve any objection to the charges in fact delivered to the jury, to the evidence introduced at trial, or to opposing counsel's argument. The sole objection Philip Morris preserved was to the trial court's refusal to give defendant's requested charge number 34. The proposed instruction read in pertinent part:

> If you determine that some amount of punitive damages should be imposed on the defendant, it will then be your task to set an amount that is appropriate. This should be such amount as you believe is necessary to achieve the objectives of deterrence and punishment. While there is no set formula to be applied in reaching an appropriate amount, I will now advise you of some of the factors that you may wish to consider in this connection.

> (1) The size of any punishment should bear a reasonable relationship to the harm caused to Jesse Williams by the defendant's punishable misconduct. Although you may consider the extent of harm suffered by others in determining what that reasonable relationship is, you are not to punish the defendant for the impact of its alleged misconduct on other persons, who may bring lawsuits of their own in which other juries can resolve their claims and award punitive damages for those harms, as such other juries see fit.

. . . . .

(2) The size of the punishment may appropriately reflect the degree of reprehensibility of the defendant's conduct—that is, how far the defendant has departed from accepted societal norms of conduct."

Under that charge, just what use could the jury properly make of "the extent of harm suffered by others"? The answer slips from my grasp. A judge seeking to enlighten rather than confuse surely would resist delivering the requested charge.

The Court ventures no opinion on the propriety of the charge proposed by Philip Morris, though Philip Morris preserved no other objection to the trial proceedings. Rather than addressing the one objection Philip Morris properly preserved, the Court reaches outside the bounds of the case as postured when the trial court entered its judgment. I would accord more respectful treatment to the proceedings and dispositions of state courts that sought diligently to adhere to our changing, less than crystalline precedent.

* * *

For the reasons stated, and in light of the abundant evidence of "the potential harm [Philip Morris'] conduct could have caused," I would affirm the decision of the Oregon Supreme Court.

COMMENTS AND QUESTIONS CONCERNING
PHILIP MORRIS USA V. WILLIAMS

1.   Justice Breyer states the issue in this case as "whether the Constitution's Due Process Clause permits a jury to base [its] award in part upon its desire to *punish* the defendant for harming persons who are not before the court (*e.g.,* victims whom the parties do not represent)." Are there ways in which all of the victims could have been heard in a single action? Consider the increasing difficulty of bringing the claims of all potential plaintiffs in a single class action, as discussed in the previous chapter.

2.   Before reaching the question of punitive damages, what might account for the significant difference between the amount of economic damages ($21,000) and noneconomic damages ($800,000) recovered in this action?

3.   Philip Morris challenged the constitutionality of the punitive damages award because it was almost 100 times larger than the compensatory damages awarded by the jury. While not reaching this question, the Court noted that "in *State Farm,* this Court said that the longstanding historical practice of setting punitive damages at two, three, or four times the size of compensatory damages, while 'not binding,' is 'instructive,' and that '[s]ingle-digit multipliers are more likely to comport with due process.' "

4.   If the purpose of punitive damages is to punish and deter, what is the problem with basing such damages on injuries done to non-parties? While Justice Stevens concedes in his dissent that there would be constitutional problems with calculating compensatory damages based on injuries to parties not before the court, he notes that punitive damages present a different question—especially when a significant portion of those damages do not even go to the plaintiff.

5.   Does the Court suggest that a plaintiff can introduce evidence of harm to non-parties other than as a basis upon which to calculate damages against the defendant? Are juries capable of making fine distinctions as to the purposes for which they can and cannot consider harm to non-parties? Recognizing that this may be difficult for juries in some cases, the majority states that "where the risk of that misunderstanding is a significant one—because, for instance, of the sort of evidence that was introduced at trial or the kinds of argument the plaintiff made to the jury—a court, upon request, must protect against that risk." What sort of protections might a court invoke in such situations?

6.   What brought Justices Ginsburg, Thomas, and Scalia together in the same dissent?

7.   After the Supreme Court's decision in *Williams*, the original punitive damages judgment was upheld by the Oregon Supreme Court because the jury instruction Philip Morris offered at trial did not correctly state the law of Oregon. *Williams v. Philip Morris Inc.* 344 Or. 45 (2008). However, Oregon's "split recovery" statute provided that 60% of any punitive damages recovered in a private action was to go to Oregon's Criminal Injuries Compensation Account. *Williams v. RJ Reynolds Tobacco Co.*, 351 Or. 368 (2011). Do such statutes make sense in a case such as *Williams* in which the State has not participated in the civil action leading to the punitive damages judgment?

IV. INJUNCTIONS

There are some situations in which an after-the-fact monetary remedy will not be sufficient to make a person whole. If, for instance, a developer is about to tear down a historic building, a plaintiff may seek an injunction from the court ordering the developer not to destroy the building.

Equitable relief such as the injunction developed in the English Court of Chancery, as that court competed with the English common law courts—which could only award legal relief such as damages. The chancery court also awarded specific performance; because land was considered unique, the court of equity could specifically order the landowner to sell real property rather than award damages for a contract breach. Additional equitable remedies included, and include today, reformation and rescission of contracts; an accounting (when damages are uncertain); and the imposition of a constructive trust over property owned by the defendant.

Law and equity have been merged in the federal courts, and equitable and legal relief can be sought in a single action in a single federal district court. Rule 2 of the Federal Rules of Civil Procedure thus states: "There is one form of action—the civil action."

The distinction between law and equity is still significant, though, because litigants only can receive equitable relief if legal relief (typically, damages) would be inadequate. If damages or other relief that could be provided by an English common law court were sufficient, relief was not available in chancery. Even after the merger of law and equity in federal (and most state) courts, an equitable remedy such as an injunction cannot be awarded if damages would adequately remedy the alleged wrong. In addition, as we will see in Chapter 12, the Seventh Amendment to the United States Constitution only preserves the right to jury trial in "Suits at common law, where the value in controversy shall exceed twenty dollars." Thus a plaintiff seeking an injunction in federal court will not be entitled to a jury on that claim.

Rule 65 of the Federal Rules of Civil Procedure governs injunctions and restraining orders (injunctions of short duration) issued by the federal courts. Rule 65(d) provides that all injunctions and restraining orders must specify the reasons why the order is being issued and the act or acts required or restrained. This Rule also provides that the order only binds parties or those aligned with parties who receive actual notice of the order.

Three different types of injunctions and retraining orders are recognized by Rule 65. These types of court orders are differentiated by the duration of the order. A **permanent injunction** is a court order that permanently orders a party to take or refrain from taking a specific action. Thus a court might permanently enjoin a developer from destroying a historic building.

However, a permanent injunction only can issue after the court has fully heard the parties on the merits of their claims and considered the appropriateness of a permanent injunction. Rule 65(a) therefore contemplates a **preliminary injunction**, which requires notice to the adverse party but can issue before the matter has been fully heard on the merits. The impact of a preliminary injunction is to preserve the status quo (stop any planned destruction, in our example) until the court can fully hear the matter.

Sometimes, however, it may be impractical even to give notice to the adverse party if the challenged action or inaction is to be halted before irreparable damage can occur. If, for instance, bulldozers are about to destroy a historic building, those challenging the action may need emergency action from the court. Rule 65(b) provides that a **temporary restraining order** (or TRO) can be issued without written or oral notice to the adverse party if:

(A) specific facts in an affidavit or a verified complaint clearly show that immediate and irreparable injury, loss, or damage will result to the movant before the adverse party can be heard in opposition; and

(B) the movant's attorney certifies in writing any efforts made to give notice and the reasons why it should not be required.

If a temporary restraining order issues without notice to the adverse party, it can only extend for 14 days, although Rule 65(b)(2) permits the court, during that 14-day period, to extend the TRO for an additional 14 days. As with any injunction, the violation of the terms of a temporary restraining order can be punished as contempt of court.

Figure 8–1 shows the major differences between permanent injunctions, preliminary injunctions, and temporary restraining orders.

FIGURE 8–1
INJUNCTIONS AND RESTRAINING ORDERS

Type of Injunction	Governing Rule	Notice Required	Injunction Duration
Permanent Injunction	Rule 65	yes	indefinite
Preliminary Injunction	Rule 65(a)	yes	until trial on merits
Temporary Restraining Order	Rule 65(b)	not required if movant certifies it will suffer "immediate and irreparable injury, loss, or damage" before adverse party can be heard	14 days + possible 14 day extension

The classic equitable remedy is the civil injunction. An injunction may be appropriate in situations in which money damages or other legal relief would be an inadequate remedy. For instance, if the acts challenged allegedly caused environmental degradation (such as killing whales), an injunction might be the only way to prevent further illegal harm. In a dispute involving complex facts and law, waiting until the court can determine whether to issue a permanent injunction could result in continued degradation, only later found to have been illegal.

Such a dispute seems like just the situation that the preliminary injunction is designed to address. So why did the Supreme Court hold that the district court improperly issued a preliminary injunction in the following case?

Winter v. Natural Resources Defense Council, Inc.

Supreme Court of the United States, 2008
555 U.S. 7

■ CHIEF JUSTICE ROBERTS delivered the opinion of the Court.

"To be prepared for war is one of the most effectual means of preserving peace." So said George Washington in his first Annual Address to Congress, 218 years ago. One of the most important ways the Navy prepares for war is through integrated training exercises at sea. These exercises include training in the use of modern sonar to detect and track enemy submarines, something the Navy has done for the past 40 years. The plaintiffs, respondents here, complained that the Navy's sonar-training program harmed marine mammals, and that the Navy should have prepared an environmental impact statement before commencing its latest round of training exercises. The Court of Appeals upheld a preliminary injunction imposing restrictions on the Navy's sonar training, even though that court acknowledged that "the record contains no evidence that marine mammals have been harmed" by the Navy's exercises.

The Court of Appeals was wrong, and its decision is reversed.

I

* * *

Antisubmarine warfare is currently the Pacific Fleet's top war-fighting priority. Modern diesel-electric submarines pose a significant threat to Navy vessels because they can operate almost silently, making them extremely difficult to detect and track. Potential adversaries of the United States possess at least 300 of these submarines.

The most effective technology for identifying submerged diesel-electric submarines within their torpedo range is active sonar, which involves emitting pulses of sound underwater and then receiving the acoustic waves that echo off the target. * * * This case concerns the Navy's use of "mid-frequency active" (MFA) sonar, which transmits sound waves at frequencies between 1 kHz and 10 kHz.

* * *

The waters off the coast of southern California (SOCAL) are an ideal location for conducting integrated training exercises, as this is the only area on the west coast that is relatively close to land, air, and sea bases, as well as amphibious landing areas. At issue in this case are the Composite Training Unit Exercises and the Joint Tactical Force Exercises, in which individual naval units (ships, submarines, and aircraft) train together as members of a strike group. * * *

Sharing the waters in the SOCAL operating area are at least 37 species of marine mammals, including dolphins, whales, and sea lions. The parties strongly dispute the extent to which the Navy's training activities will harm those animals or disrupt their behavioral patterns. The Navy emphasizes that it has used MFA sonar during training exercises in SOCAL for 40 years, without a single documented sonar-related injury to any marine mammal. The Navy asserts that, at most, MFA sonar may cause temporary hearing loss or brief disruptions of marine mammals' behavioral patterns.

* * *

II

The procedural history of this case is rather complicated. The Marine Mammal Protection Act of 1972 (MMPA), 86 Stat. 1027, generally prohibits any individual from "taking" a marine mammal, defined as harassing, hunting, capturing, or killing it. 16 U.S.C. §§ 1362(13), 1372(a). The Secretary of Defense may "exempt any action or category of actions" from the MMPA if such actions are "necessary for national defense." § 1371(f)(1). In January 2007, the Deputy Secretary of Defense—acting for the Secretary—granted the Navy a 2-year exemption from the MMPA for the training exercises at issue in this case. The exemption was conditioned on the Navy adopting several mitigation procedures, including: (1) training lookouts and officers to watch for marine mammals; (2) requiring at least five lookouts with binoculars on each vessel to watch for anomalies on the water surface (including marine mammals); (3) requiring aircraft and sonar operators to report detected marine mammals in the vicinity of the training exercises; (4) requiring reduction of active sonar transmission levels by 6 dB if a marine mammal is detected within 1,000 yards of the bow of the vessel, or by 10 dB if detected within 500 yards; (5) requiring complete shutdown of active sonar transmission if a marine mammal is detected within 200 yards of the vessel; (6) requiring active sonar to be operated at the "lowest practicable level"; and (7) adopting coordination and reporting procedures.

The National Environmental Policy Act of 1969 (NEPA), 83 Stat. 852, requires federal agencies "to the fullest extent possible" to prepare an environmental impact statement (EIS) for "every . . . major Federal actio[n] significantly affecting the quality of the human environment." 42 U.S.C. § 4332(2)(C). An agency is not required to prepare a full EIS if it determines—based on a shorter environmental assessment (EA)—that the proposed action will not have a significant impact on the environment. 40 CFR §§ 1508.9(a), 1508.13.

In February 2007, the Navy issued an EA concluding that the 14 SOCAL training exercises scheduled through January 2009 would not have a significant impact on the environment. * * *

* * *

Shortly after the Navy released its EA, the plaintiffs sued the Navy, seeking declaratory and injunctive relief on the grounds that the Navy's SOCAL training exercises violated NEPA, the Endangered Species Act of 1973 (ESA), and the Coastal Zone Management Act of 1972 (CZMA). The District Court granted plaintiffs' motion for a preliminary injunction and prohibited the Navy from using MFA sonar during its remaining training exercises. The court held that plaintiffs had "demonstrated a probability of success" on their claims under NEPA and the CZMA. The court also determined that equitable relief was appropriate because, under Ninth Circuit precedent, plaintiffs had established at least a " 'possibility' " of irreparable harm to the environment. Based on scientific studies, declarations from experts, and other evidence in the record, the District Court concluded that there was in fact a "near certainty" of irreparable injury to the environment, and that this injury outweighed any possible harm to the Navy.

The Navy filed an emergency appeal, and the Ninth Circuit stayed the injunction pending appeal. After hearing oral argument, the Court of Appeals agreed with the District Court that preliminary injunctive relief was appropriate. The appellate court concluded, however, that a blanket injunction prohibiting the Navy from using MFA sonar in SOCAL was overbroad, and remanded the case to the District Court "to narrow its injunction so as to provide mitigation conditions under which the Navy may conduct its training exercises."

On remand, the District Court entered a new preliminary injunction allowing the Navy to use MFA sonar only as long as it implemented the following mitigation measures (in addition to the measures the Navy had adopted pursuant to its MMPA exemption): (1) imposing a 12 nautical mile "exclusion zone" from the coastline; (2) using lookouts to conduct additional monitoring for marine mammals; (3) restricting the use of "helicopter-dipping" sonar; (4) limiting the use of MFA sonar in geographic "choke points"; (5) shutting down MFA sonar when a marine mammal is spotted within 2,200 yards of a vessel; and (6) powering down MFA sonar by 6 dB during significant surface ducting conditions, in which sound travels further than it otherwise would due to temperature differences in adjacent layers of water. The Navy filed a notice of appeal, challenging only the last two restrictions.

The Navy then sought relief from the Executive Branch. The President, pursuant to 16 U.S.C. § 1456(c)(1)(B), granted the Navy an exemption from the CZMA. Section 1456(c)(1)(B) permits such exemptions if the activity in question is "in the paramount interest of the United States." The President determined that continuation of the exercises as limited by the Navy was "essential to national security." He concluded that compliance with the District Court's injunction would "undermine the Navy's ability to conduct realistic training exercises that are necessary to ensure the combat effectiveness of . . . strike groups."

Simultaneously, the Council on Environmental Quality (CEQ) authorized the Navy to implement "alternative arrangements" to NEPA compliance in light of "emergency circumstances." See 40 CFR § 1506.11. The CEQ determined that alternative arrangements were appropriate because the District Court's injunction "create[s] a significant and unreasonable risk that Strike Groups will not be able to train and be certified as fully mission capable." Under the alternative arrangements, the Navy would be permitted to conduct its training exercises under the mitigation procedures adopted in conjunction with the exemption from the MMPA. The CEQ also imposed additional notice, research, and reporting requirements.

In light of these actions, the Navy then moved to vacate the District Court's injunction with respect to the 2,200-yard shutdown zone and the restrictions on training in surface ducting conditions. The District Court refused to do so, and the Court of Appeals affirmed. The Ninth Circuit held that there was a serious question regarding whether the CEQ's interpretation of the "emergency circumstances" regulation was lawful. Specifically, the court questioned whether there was a true "emergency" in this case, given that the Navy has been on notice of its obligation to comply with NEPA from the moment it first planned the SOCAL training exercises. The Court of Appeals concluded that the preliminary injunction was entirely predictable in light of the parties' litigation history. The court also held that plaintiffs had established a likelihood of success on their claim that the Navy was required to prepare a full EIS for the SOCAL training exercises. The Ninth Circuit agreed with the District Court's holding that the Navy's EA—which resulted in a finding of no significant environmental impact—was "cursory, unsupported by cited evidence, or unconvincing."

The Court of Appeals further determined that plaintiffs had carried their burden of establishing a "possibility" of irreparable injury. Even under the Navy's own figures, the court concluded, the training exercises would cause 564 physical injuries to marine mammals, as well as 170,000 disturbances of marine mammals' behavior. Lastly, the Court of Appeals held that the balance of hardships and consideration of the public interest weighed in favor of the plaintiffs. The court emphasized that the negative impact on the Navy's training exercises was "speculative," since the Navy has never before operated under the procedures required by the District Court. In particular, the court determined that: (1) The 2,200-yard shutdown zone imposed by the District Court was unlikely to affect the Navy's operations, because the Navy often shuts down its MFA sonar systems during the course of training exercises; and (2) the power-down requirement during significant surface ducting conditions was not unreasonable because such conditions are rare, and the Navy has previously certified strike groups that had not trained under such conditions. The Ninth Circuit concluded that the District Court's preliminary injunction struck a proper balance between the competing interests at stake.

We granted certiorari, and now reverse and vacate the injunction.

III

A

A plaintiff seeking a preliminary injunction must establish that he is likely to succeed on the merits, that he is likely to suffer irreparable harm in the absence of preliminary relief, that the balance of equities tips in his favor, and that an injunction is in the public interest.

The District Court and the Ninth Circuit concluded that plaintiffs have shown a likelihood of success on the merits of their NEPA claim. The Navy strongly disputes this determination, arguing that plaintiffs' likelihood of success is low because the CEQ reasonably concluded that "emergency circumstances" justified alternative arrangements to NEPA compliance. * * *

The District Court and the Ninth Circuit also held that when a plaintiff demonstrates a strong likelihood of prevailing on the merits, a preliminary injunction may be entered based only on a "possibility" of irreparable harm. The lower courts held that plaintiffs had met this standard because the scientific studies, declarations, and other evidence in the record established to "a near certainty" that the Navy's training exercises would cause irreparable harm to the environment.

The Navy challenges these holdings, arguing that plaintiffs must demonstrate a likelihood of irreparable injury—not just a possibility—in order to obtain preliminary relief. On the facts of this case, the Navy contends that plaintiffs' alleged injuries are too speculative to give rise to irreparable injury, given that ever since the Navy's training program began 40 years ago, there has been no documented case of sonar-related injury to marine mammals in SOCAL. And even if MFA sonar does cause a limited number of injuries to individual *marine mammals,* the Navy asserts that plaintiffs have failed to offer evidence of species-level harm that would adversely affect *their* scientific, recreational, and ecological interests. For their part, plaintiffs assert that they would prevail under any formulation of the irreparable injury standard, because the District Court found that they had established a "near certainty" of irreparable harm.

We agree with the Navy that the Ninth Circuit's "possibility" standard is too lenient. Our frequently reiterated standard requires plaintiffs seeking preliminary relief to demonstrate that irreparable injury is *likely* in the absence of an injunction . . . Issuing a preliminary injunction based only on a possibility of irreparable harm is inconsistent with our characterization of injunctive relief as an extraordinary remedy that may only be awarded upon a clear showing that the plaintiff is entitled to such relief.

* * *

It is not clear that articulating the incorrect standard affected the Ninth Circuit's analysis of irreparable harm. Although the court referred to the "possibility" standard, and cited Circuit precedent along the same lines, it affirmed the District Court's conclusion that plaintiffs had established a " 'near certainty' "of irreparable harm. At the same time, however, the nature of the District Court's conclusion is itself unclear. The District Court originally found irreparable harm from sonar-training exercises generally. But by the time of the District Court's final decision, the Navy challenged only two of six restrictions imposed by the court. The District Court did not reconsider the likelihood of irreparable harm in light of the four restrictions not challenged by the Navy. * * *

We also find it pertinent that this is not a case in which the defendant is conducting a new type of activity with completely unknown effects on the environment. When the Government conducts an activity, "NEPA itself does not mandate particular results." *Robertson v. Methow Valley Citizens Council,* 490 U.S. 332, 350 (1989). Instead, NEPA imposes only procedural requirements to "ensur[e] that the agency, in reaching its decision, will have available, and will carefully consider, detailed information concerning significant environmental impacts." *Id.,* at 349. Part of the harm NEPA attempts to prevent in requiring an EIS is that, without one, there may be little if any information about prospective environmental harms and potential mitigating measures. Here, in contrast, the plaintiffs are seeking to enjoin—or substantially restrict—training exercises that have been taking place in SOCAL for the last 40 years. And the latest series of exercises were not approved until after the defendant took a "hard look at environmental consequences."

As explained in the next section, even if plaintiffs have shown irreparable injury from the Navy's training exercises, any such injury is outweighed by the public interest and the Navy's interest in effective, realistic training of its sailors. A proper consideration of these factors alone requires denial of the requested injunctive relief. For the same reason, we do not address the lower courts' holding that plaintiffs have also established a likelihood of success on the merits.

B

A preliminary injunction is an extraordinary remedy never awarded as of right. In each case, courts "must balance the competing claims of injury and must consider the effect on each party of the granting or withholding of the requested relief." *Amoco Production Co.,* 480 U.S., at 542, "In exercising their sound discretion, courts of equity should pay particular regard for the public consequences in employing the extraordinary remedy of injunction." *Romero-Barcelo,* 456 U.S., at 312; see also *Railroad Comm'n of Tex. v. Pullman Co.,* 312 U.S. 496,

500 (1941). In this case, the District Court and the Ninth Circuit significantly understated the burden the preliminary injunction would impose on the Navy's ability to conduct realistic training exercises, and the injunction's consequent adverse impact on the public interest in national defense.

This case involves "complex, subtle, and professional decisions as to the composition, training, equipping, and control of a military force," which are "essentially professional military judgments." *Gilligan v. Morgan,* 413 U.S. 1, 10 (1973). We "give great deference to the professional judgment of military authorities concerning the relative importance of a particular military interest." *Goldman v. Weinberger,* 475 U.S. 503, 507 (1986). As the Court emphasized just last Term, "neither the Members of this Court nor most federal judges begin the day with briefings that may describe new and serious threats to our Nation and its people." *Boumediene v. Bush,* 553 U.S. 723, 797 (2008).

* * * Captain Martin May—the Third Fleet's Assistant Chief of Staff for Training and Readiness—emphasized that the use of MFA sonar is "mission-critical." He described the ability to operate MFA sonar as a "highly perishable skill" that must be repeatedly practiced under realistic conditions. During training exercises, MFA sonar operators learn how to avoid sound-reducing "clutter" from ocean floor topography and environmental conditions; they also learn how to avoid interference and how to coordinate their efforts with other sonar operators in the strike group. Several Navy officers emphasized that realistic training cannot be accomplished under the two challenged restrictions imposed by the District Court—the 2,200-yard shutdown zone and the requirement that the Navy power down its sonar systems during significant surface ducting conditions. We accept these officers' assertions that the use of MFA sonar under realistic conditions during training exercises is of the utmost importance to the Navy and the Nation.

These interests must be weighed against the possible harm to the ecological, scientific, and recreational interests that are legitimately before this Court. Plaintiffs have submitted declarations asserting that they take whale watching trips, observe marine mammals underwater, conduct scientific research on marine mammals, and photograph these animals in their natural habitats. Plaintiffs contend that the Navy's use of MFA sonar will injure marine mammals or alter their behavioral patterns, impairing plaintiffs' ability to study and observe the animals.

While we do not question the seriousness of these interests, we conclude that the balance of equities and consideration of the overall public interest in this case tip strongly in favor of the Navy. For the plaintiffs, the most serious possible injury would be harm to an unknown number of the marine mammals that they study and observe. In contrast, forcing the Navy to deploy an inadequately trained antisubmarine force jeopardizes the safety of the fleet. Active sonar is the only reliable technology for detecting and tracking enemy diesel-electric submarines, and the President—the Commander in Chief—has determined that training with active sonar is "essential to national security."

The public interest in conducting training exercises with active sonar under realistic conditions plainly outweighs the interests advanced by the plaintiffs. Of course, military interests do not always trump other considerations, and we have not held that they do. In this case, however, the proper determination of where the public interest lies does not strike us as a close question.

C

1.   Despite the importance of assessing the balance of equities and the public interest in determining whether to grant a preliminary injunction, the District Court addressed these considerations in only a cursory fashion. * * * The subsequent Ninth Circuit panel framed its opinion as reviewing the District Court's exercise of discretion, but that discretion was barely exercised here.

* * *

* * * The lower courts failed properly to defer to senior Navy officers' specific, predictive judgments about how the preliminary injunction would reduce the effectiveness of the Navy's SOCAL training exercises.

2.   The preliminary injunction requires the Navy to shut down its MFA sonar if a marine mammal is detected within 2,200 yards of a sonar-emitting vessel. The Ninth Circuit stated that the 2,200-yard shutdown zone would not be overly burdensome because sightings of marine mammals during training exercises are relatively rare. But regardless of the frequency of marine mammal sightings, the injunction will greatly increase the size of the shutdown zone. Pursuant to its exemption from the MMPA, the Navy agreed to reduce the power of its MFA sonar at 1,000 yards and 500 yards, and to completely turn off the system at 200 yards. The District Court's injunction does not include a graduated power-down, instead requiring a total shutdown of MFA sonar if a marine mammal is detected within 2,200 yards of a sonar-emitting vessel. * * *

The lower courts did not give sufficient weight to the views of several top Navy officers, who emphasized that because training scenarios can take several days to develop, each additional shutdown can result in the loss of several days' worth of training. * * * Even if there is a low likelihood of a marine mammal sighting, the preliminary injunction would clearly increase the number of disruptive sonar shutdowns the Navy is forced to perform during its SOCAL training exercises.

* * *

3.   The Court of Appeals also concluded that the Navy's training exercises would not be significantly affected by the requirement that it power down MFA sonar by 6 dB during significant surface ducting conditions. Again, we think the Ninth Circuit understated the burden this requirement would impose on the Navy's ability to conduct realistic training exercises.

Surface ducting is a phenomenon in which relatively little sound energy penetrates beyond a narrow layer near the surface of the water. When surface ducting occurs, active sonar becomes more useful near the surface but less useful at greater depths. Diesel-electric submariners are trained to take advantage of these distortions to avoid being detected by sonar.

The Ninth Circuit determined that the power-down requirement during surface ducting conditions was unlikely to affect certification of the Navy's strike groups because surface ducting occurs relatively rarely, and the Navy has previously certified strike groups that did not train under such conditions. This reasoning is backwards. Given that surface ducting is both rare and unpredictable, it is especially important for the Navy to be able to train under these conditions when they occur. * * *

4.   The District Court acknowledged that " 'the imposition of these mitigation measures will require the Navy to alter and adapt the way it conducts antisubmarine warfare training—a substantial challenge. Nevertheless, evidence presented to the Court reflects that the Navy has employed mitigation measures in the past, without sacrificing training objectives.' "Apparently no good deed goes unpunished. The fact that the Navy has taken measures in the past to address concerns about marine mammals—or, for that matter, has elected not to challenge four additional restrictions imposed by the District Court in this case—hardly means that other, more intrusive restrictions pose no threat to preparedness for war.

The Court of Appeals concluded its opinion by stating that "the Navy may return to the district court to request relief on an emergency basis" if the preliminary injunction "actually result[s] in an inability to train and certify sufficient naval forces to provide for the national defense." This is cold comfort to the Navy. The Navy contends that the injunction will hinder efforts to train sonar operators under realistic conditions, ultimately leaving strike groups more vulnerable to enemy submarines. Unlike the Ninth Circuit, we do not think the Navy is required to wait until the injunction "actually result[s] in an inability to train . . . sufficient naval forces to provide for the national defense" before seeking its dissolution. By then it may be too late.

IV

As noted above, we do not address the underlying merits of plaintiffs' claims. While we have authority to proceed to such a decision at this point, doing so is not necessary here. In addition, reaching the merits is complicated by the fact that the lower courts addressed only one of several issues raised, and plaintiffs have largely chosen not to defend the decision below on that ground.

At the same time, what we have said makes clear that it would be an abuse of discretion to enter a permanent injunction, after final decision on the merits, along the same lines as the preliminary injunction. An injunction is a matter of equitable discretion; it does not follow from success on the merits as a matter of course. *Romero-Barcelo,* 456 U.S., at 313 ("[A] federal judge sitting as chancellor is not mechanically obligated to grant an injunction for every violation of law").

The factors examined above—the balance of equities and consideration of the public interest—are pertinent in assessing the propriety of any injunctive relief, preliminary or permanent. See *Amoco Production Co.,* 480 U.S., at 546, n. 12 ("The standard for a preliminary injunction is essentially the same as for a permanent injunction with the exception that the plaintiff must show a likelihood of success on the merits rather than actual success"). Given that the ultimate legal claim is that the Navy must prepare an EIS, not that it must cease sonar training, there is no basis for enjoining such training in a manner credibly alleged to pose a serious threat to national security. This is particularly true in light of the fact that the training has been going on for 40 years with no documented episode of harm to a marine mammal. A court concluding that the Navy is required to prepare an EIS has many remedial tools at its disposal, including declaratory relief or an injunction tailored to the preparation of an EIS rather than the Navy's training in the interim. See, *e.g., Steffel v. Thompson,* 415 U.S. 452, 466 (1974) ("Congress plainly intended declaratory relief to act as an alternative to the strong medicine of the injunction"). In the meantime, we see no basis for jeopardizing national security, as the present injunction does. Plaintiffs confirmed at oral argument that the preliminary injunction was "the whole ball game," and our analysis of the propriety of preliminary relief is applicable to any permanent injunction as well.

* * *

President Theodore Roosevelt explained that "the only way in which a navy can ever be made efficient is by practice at sea, under all the conditions which would have to be met if war existed." We do not discount the importance of plaintiffs' ecological, scientific, and recreational interests in marine mammals. Those interests, however, are plainly outweighed by the Navy's need to conduct realistic training exercises to ensure that it is able to neutralize the threat posed by enemy submarines. The District Court abused its discretion by imposing a 2,200-yard shutdown zone and by requiring the Navy to power down its MFA sonar during significant surface ducting conditions. The judgment of the Court of Appeals is reversed, and the preliminary injunction is vacated to the extent it has been challenged by the Navy.

It is so ordered.

■ JUSTICE BREYER, with whom JUSTICE STEVENS joins as to Part I, concurring in part and dissenting in part.

As of December 2006, the United States Navy planned to engage in a series of 14 antisubmarine warfare training exercises off the southern California coast. The Natural Resources Defense Council, Inc., and others (hereinafter NRDC) brought this case in Federal District Court claiming that the National Environmental Policy Act of 1969 (NEPA) requires the Navy to prepare an environmental impact statement (EIS) (assessing the impact of the exercises on marine mammals) prior to its engaging in the exercises. As the case reaches us, the District Court has found that the NRDC will likely prevail on its demand for an EIS; the Navy has agreed to prepare an EIS; the District Court has forbidden the Navy to proceed with the exercises unless it adopts six mitigating measures; and the Navy has agreed to adopt all but two of those measures.

The controversy between the parties now concerns the two measures that the Navy is unwilling to adopt. The first concerns the "shutdown zone," a circle with a ship at the center within which the Navy must try to spot marine mammals and shut down its sonar if one is found. The controverted condition would enlarge the radius of that circle from about one-tenth of a mile (200 yards) to one and one-quarter miles (2,200 yards). The second concerns special ocean conditions called "surface ducting conditions." The controverted condition would require the Navy, when it encounters any such condition, to diminish the sonar's power by 75%. The Court of Appeals affirmed the District Court order that contained these two conditions.

I

* * *

* * * [S]everal features of this case lead me to conclude that the record, as now before us, lacks adequate support for an injunction imposing the two controverted requirements. *First,* the evidence of need for the two special conditions is weak or uncertain. * * *

* * *

Given the uncertainty the figures create in respect to the harm caused by the Navy's original training plans, it would seem important to have before us at least some estimate of the harm likely avoided by the Navy's decision not to contest here *four of the six mitigating conditions* that the District Court ordered. Without such evidence, it is difficult to assess the *relevant* harm—that is, the environmental harm likely caused by the Navy's exercises with the four uncontested mitigation measures (but without the two contested mitigation measures) in place.

Second, the Navy has filed multiple affidavits from Navy officials explaining in detail the seriousness of the harm that the delay associated with completion of this EIS (approximately one year) would create in respect to the Navy's ability to maintain an adequate national defense. Taken by themselves, those affidavits make a strong case for the proposition that insistence upon the two additional mitigating conditions would seriously interfere with necessary defense training.

* * *

Third, and particularly important in my view, the District Court did not explain *why* it rejected the Navy's affidavit-supported contentions. * * *

* * *

While a District Court is often free simply to state its conclusion in summary fashion, in this instance neither that conclusion, nor anything else I have found in the District Court's opinion, answers the Navy's documented claims that the two extra conditions the District Court imposed will, in effect, seriously interfere with its ability to carry out necessary training exercises.

* * *

Fourth, the Court of Appeals sought, through its own thorough examination of the record, to supply the missing explanations. But those explanations are not sufficient. In respect to the surface ducting conditions, the Court of Appeals rejected the Navy's contentions on the ground that those conditions are "rar[e]," and the Navy has certified trainings that did not involve any encounter with those conditions. I am not certain, however, why the rarity of the condition supports the District Court's conclusion. Rarity argues as strongly for training when the condition is encountered as it argues for the contrary.

* * *

Fifth, when the Court of Appeals first heard this case following the District Court's imposition of a broad, absolute injunction, it held that any injunction must be crafted so that the Navy could continue its training exercises. Noting that the Navy had, in the past, been able to use mitigation measures to "reduce the harmful effects of its active sonar," it "vacate[d] the stay and remand[ed] this matter to the district court to narrow its injunction so as to provide mitigation conditions *under which the Navy may conduct its training exercises.*" For the reasons just stated, neither the District Court nor the Court of Appeals has explained why we should reject the Navy's assertions that it cannot effectively conduct its training exercises under the mitigation conditions imposed by the District Court.

I would thus vacate the preliminary injunction imposed by the District Court to the extent it has been challenged by the Navy. Neither the District Court nor the Court of Appeals has adequately explained its conclusion that the balance of the equities tips in favor of plaintiffs. Nor do those parts of the record to which the parties have pointed supply the missing explanation.

II

Nonetheless, as the Court of Appeals held when it first considered this case, the Navy's past use of mitigation conditions makes clear that the Navy can effectively train under *some* mitigation conditions. In the ordinary course, I would remand so the District Court could, pursuant to the Court of Appeals' direction, set forth mitigation conditions that will protect the marine wildlife while also enabling the Navy to carry out its exercises. But, at this point, the Navy has informed us that this set of exercises will be complete by January, at the latest, and an EIS will likely be complete at that point, as well. Thus, by the time the District Court would have an opportunity to impose new conditions, the case could very well be moot.

In February of this year, the Court of Appeals stayed the injunction imposed by the District Court—*but only pending this Court's resolution of the case.* The Court of Appeals concluded that "[i]n light of the short time before the Navy is to commence its next exercise, the importance of the Navy's mission to provide for the national defense and the representation by the Chief of Naval Operations that the district court's preliminary injunction in its current form will 'unacceptably risk' effective training and strike group certification and thereby interfere with his statutory responsibility . . . to 'organiz[e], train[ ], and equip[ ] the Navy,' " interim relief was appropriate, and the court then modified the two mitigation conditions at issue.

With respect to the 2,200-yard shutdown zone, it required the Navy to suspend its use of the sonar if a marine mammal is detected within 2,200 yards, *except* when sonar is being used at a "critical point in the exercise," in which case the amount by which the Navy must power down is proportional to the mammal's proximity to the sonar. With respect to surface ducting, the Navy is only required to shut down sonar altogether when a marine mammal is detected within 500 meters and the amount by which it is otherwise required to power down is again proportional to the mammal's proximity to the sonar source. The court believed these conditions would permit the Navy to go forward with its imminently planned exercises while at the same time minimizing the harm to marine wildlife.

In my view, the modified conditions imposed by the Court of Appeals in its February stay order reflect the best equitable conditions that can be created in the short time available before the exercises are complete and the EIS is ready. The Navy has been training under these conditions since February, so allowing them to remain in place will, in effect, maintain what has become the status quo. Therefore, I would modify the Court of Appeals' February 29, 2008, order so that the provisional conditions it contains remain in place until the Navy's completion of an acceptable EIS.

■ JUSTICE GINSBURG, with whom JUSTICE SOUTER joins, dissenting.

The central question in this action under the National Environmental Policy Act of 1969 (NEPA) was whether the Navy must prepare an environmental impact statement (EIS). The Navy does not challenge its obligation to do so, and it represents that the EIS will be complete in January 2009—one month after the instant exercises conclude. If the Navy had completed the EIS before taking action, as NEPA instructs, the parties and the public could have benefited from the environmental analysis—and the Navy's training could have proceeded without interruption. Instead, the Navy acted first, and thus thwarted the very purpose an EIS is intended to serve. To justify its course, the Navy sought dispensation not from Congress, but from an executive council that lacks authority to countermand or revise NEPA's requirements. I would hold that, in imposing manageable measures to mitigate harm until completion of the EIS, the District Court conscientiously balanced the equities and did not abuse its discretion.

* * *

III

A

Flexibility is a hallmark of equity jurisdiction. "The essence of equity jurisdiction has been the power of the Chancellor to do equity and to mould each decree to the necessities of the particular case. Flexibility rather than rigidity has distinguished it." *Weinberger v. Romero-Barcelo,* 456 U.S. 305, 312 (1982) (quoting *Hecht Co. v. Bowles,* 321 U.S. 321, 329 (1944)). Consistent with equity's character, courts do not insist that litigants uniformly show a particular, predetermined quantum of probable success or injury before awarding equitable relief. Instead, courts have evaluated claims for equitable relief on a "sliding scale," sometimes awarding relief based on a lower likelihood of harm when the likelihood of success is very high. This Court has never rejected that formulation, and I do not believe it does so today.

Equity's flexibility is important in the NEPA context. Because an EIS is the tool for *uncovering* environmental harm, environmental plaintiffs may often rely more heavily on their probability of success than the likelihood of harm. The Court is correct that relief is not warranted "simply to prevent the possibility of some remote future injury." "However, the injury need not have been inflicted when application is made or be certain to occur; a strong threat of irreparable injury before trial is an adequate basis." Wright & Miller, *supra*, § 2948.1, at 155–156. I agree with the District Court that NRDC made the required showing here.

B

The Navy's own EA predicted substantial and irreparable harm to marine mammals. Sonar is linked to mass strandings of marine mammals, hemorrhaging around the brain and ears, acute spongiotic changes in the central nervous system, and lesions in vital organs. As the Ninth Circuit noted, the EA predicts that the Navy's "use of MFA sonar in the SOCAL exercises will result in 564 instances of physical injury including permanent hearing loss (Level A harassment) and nearly 170,000 behavioral disturbances (Level B harassment), more than 8,000 of which would also involve temporary hearing loss." Within those totals, "the EA predicts 436 Level A harassments of Cuvier's beaked whales. According to [the National Oceanic and Atmospheric Administration (NOAA)], as few as 1,121 may exist in California, Oregon and Washington combined. Likewise, the EA predicts 1,092 Level B harassments of bottlenose dolphins, of which only 5,271 may exist in the California Coastal and Offshore stocks."

* * *

In light of the likely, substantial harm to the environment, NRDC's almost inevitable success on the merits of its claim that NEPA required the Navy to prepare an EIS, the history of this litigation, and the public interest, I cannot agree that the mitigation measures the District Court imposed signal an abuse of discretion. Cf. *Amoco Production Co. v. Gambell*, 480 U.S. 531, 545, (1987) ("Environmental injury, by its nature, can seldom be adequately remedied by money damages and is often permanent or at least of long duration, *i.e.*, irreparable. If such injury is sufficiently likely, therefore, the balance of harms will usually favor the issuance of an injunction to protect the environment.").

For the reasons stated, I would affirm the judgment of the Ninth Circuit.

COMMENTS AND QUESTIONS CONCERNING *WINTER V. NATURAL RESOURCES DEFENSE COUNCIL*

1.   As discussed in Chapter 15, appeals to the United States Courts of Appeal typically cannot be taken until a United States District Court has entered final judgment. 28 U.S.C. § 1291. However, in this case the Secretary of the Navy appealed a preliminary injunction entered prior to final judgment. Why is there a statutory exception to the final judgment rule in actions such as this? *See* 28 U.S.C. § 1292(a)(1) (granting federal courts of appeal jurisdiction to consider "[i]nterlocutory orders of the

district courts of the United States * * * granting, continuing, modifying, refusing or dissolving injunctions, or refusing to dissolve or modify injunctions, except where a direct review may be had in the Supreme Court").

2.	The test for a preliminary injunction is set forth by Chief Justice Roberts and requires that the plaintiff must establish that

- he is likely to succeed on the merits;
- he is likely to suffer irreparable harm in the absence of preliminary relief;
- the balance of equities tips in his favor; and
- an injunction is in the public interest.

Which prongs of this test did these plaintiffs not establish?

3.	Note the impact of time upon the plaintiffs' request for a preliminary injunction. Plaintiffs claimed that they would suffer irreparable injury unless the district court entered a preliminary injunction, while the Navy filed an emergency appeal in the Ninth Circuit seeking review of the initial district court injunction and later argued that "emergency circumstances" justified alternative arrangements to NEPA compliance. Couldn't some of these "emergencies" have been anticipated?

4.	What showing could the plaintiffs make in this case to overcome the conclusion of the President that some of the conditions imposed upon the Navy by the district court were inconsistent with the national security of the United States?

5.	Rule 65(a)(2) in part provides: "Before or after beginning the hearing on a motion for a preliminary injunction, the court may advance the trial on the merits and consolidate it with the hearing." This was not done in this case, and the Supreme Court majority states that "we do not address the underlying merits of plaintiffs' claims." Nevertheless, the Court notes that "it would be an abuse of discretion to enter a permanent injunction, after final decision on the merits, along the same lines as the preliminary injunction." How can this be?

6.	In her dissent Justice Ginsburg quotes language from *Amoco Production Co. v. Village of Gambell,* 480 U.S. 531, 545 (1987), suggesting that injunctions are particularly appropriate in actions alleging environmental damage: "Environmental injury, by its nature, can seldom be adequately remedied by money damages and is often permanent or at least of long duration, *i.e.,* irreparable. If such injury is sufficiently likely, therefore, the balance of harms will usually favor the issuance of an injunction to protect the environment." Why is the majority unconvinced?

7.	Background concerning the mass stranding of whales, other environmental challenges facing whales, and the history of *Winter v. Natural Resources Defense Council* are related in J. Horwitz, *War of the Whales: A True Story* (2014).

V. DECLARATORY JUDGMENTS

In some cases, the relief that will be most helpful to a party will not be a court order requiring another person to take, or not take, certain action. Instead, the appropriate relief may be a declaration of the legal rights and obligations of the parties. Declaratory judgments are authorized by 28 U.S.C. § 2201. Section 2201(a) provides that, except for certain tax and other specific exceptions:

> In a case of actual controversy within its jurisdiction * * *, any court of the United States, upon the filing of an appropriate pleading, may declare the rights and other legal relations of any interested party seeking such declaration, whether or not further relief is or could be sought. Any such declaration shall have the force and effect of a final judgment or decree and shall be reviewable as such.

Rule 57 of the Federal Rules of Civil Procedure states that the Federal Rules "govern the procedure for obtaining a declaratory judgment under 28 U.S.C. § 2201."

In what sort of situations might a party want a declaratory judgment? One typical situation occurs when someone has been sued and there is a question as to whether someone else is liable to defend that action or satisfy any judgment obtained in the action. The person being sued might file a declaratory judgment action, or assert a Rule 14 claim for a declaratory judgment, against the insurance company to obtain a binding determination of that company's liability in the initial action. Or the insurance company might file its own declaratory judgment action seeking such a judicial declaration.

The initial action involving John Leonard and PepsiCo was a declaratory judgment action filed by PepsiCo in the United States District Court for the Southern District of New York. *PepsiCo, Inc. v. Leonard*, No. 96 Civ. 5320 (filed July 18, 1996). The complaint set forth the basics of the PepsiCo television commercial and the resulting dispute between PepsiCo and Leonard and then alleged in the complaint's sole count:

> 19. Leonard has made a demand for a "new Harrier jet" from PepsiCo, and has alleged that PepsiCo's refusal to provide such a jet constitutes a breach of contract, fraud and deception and unfair business practices.

> 20. Leonard now threatens to institute litigation against PepsiCo unless it furnishes Leonard with a "new Harrier jet."

> 21. PepsiCo is not obligated to provide Leonard with a jet and has refused to comply with this demand.

> 22. A live and actual controversy exists between the parties.

> 23. By reason of the foregoing, PepsiCo is entitled [to] a judgment declaring: (1) Leonard's claims are frivolous and

without merit as he has no legal or factual basis under any applicable law to assert claims against PepsiCo; and (2) PepsiCo has no further obligation to Leonard.

Following this simple statement of PepsiCo's claim was the complaint's prayer for relief, which stated in its entirety:

PRAYER FOR RELIEF

WHEREFORE, Plaintiff PepsiCo prays that this Court enter judgment that:

1. Defendant Leonard has no valid claim against PepsiCo for breach of contract, fraud, unfair or deceptive business practices, or any other alleged violation of applicable law; and

2. Plaintiff PepsiCo be awarded its reasonable attorneys' fees and costs incurred in connection with the disposition of defendant Leonard's frivolous claims, and such other and further relief as the Court deems just and proper.

So PepsiCo sought not only a declaratory judgment, but also attorneys' fees and costs—which are the subject of the next section of this chapter.

VI. ATTORNEYS' FEES AND COSTS

In addition to legal, equitable, or declaratory relief on the merits, plaintiffs typically seek payment by the defendant of plaintiffs' attorneys' fees and costs. Federal Rule of Civil Procedure 54(d)(1) provides: "Unless a federal statute, these rules, or a court order provides otherwise, costs—other than attorney's fees—should be allowed to the prevailing party."[5] The good news is that either a plaintiff or a defendant can recover its costs in a federal civil action in which it prevails. The bad news is that "costs" are defined quite narrowly. Section 1920 of Title 28 limits the costs that can be recovered pursuant to Rule 54 to such items as court fees, the fees for copies of documents, and transcripts "necessarily obtained for use in the case."[6]

The major expense of initiating civil litigation is not the cost of court filing fees or deposition transcripts offered in that litigation, but the fees charged by an attorney to bring the civil action. Lawyers are ethically prohibited from charging an unreasonable fee, with the reasonableness of the fees to be determined by a consideration of factors such as the following:

(1) whether the fee is fixed or contingent;

---

[5] Rule 54(d)(1), though, continues: "But costs against the United States, its officers, and its agencies may be imposed only to the extent allowed by law."

[6] However, specific costs and fees can be shifted under other provisions of the Federal Rules of Civil Procedure. *See* Fed. R. Civ. P. 11, 16(f), 26(g), 37, 41(d), and 68.

(2) the time and labor required, the novelty and difficulty of the questions involved, and the skill requisite to perform the legal service properly;

(3) the likelihood, if apparent to the client, that the acceptance of the particular employment will preclude other employment by the lawyer;

(4) the fee customarily charged in the locality for similar legal services;

(5) the amount involved and the results obtained;

(6) the time limitations imposed by the client or by the circumstances;

(7) the nature and length of the professional relationship with the client; and

(8) the experience, reputation, and ability of the lawyer or lawyers performing the services.[7]

Thus, as an attorney determines what her fee will be in a particular matter, these are the factors that she should consider.

Attorneys' fees are not routinely recoverable as costs under Rule 54, and the "American Rule" provides that each party bears the costs of its own attorney. This common law presumption is contrary to the "English Rule," under which the losing party must pay not only its own attorneys' fees but the attorneys' fees of the prevailing party. However, federal statutes allow prevailing plaintiffs to recover attorneys' fees from the defendant in certain types of actions. *Alyeska Pipeline Service Co. v. Wilderness Society*, 421 U.S. 240, 260 n.33 (1975). How to determine a "reasonable fee" is the subject of the following case.

A. WHAT'S A "REASONABLE FEE"?: *PERDUE V. KENNY A. EX REL. WINN.*

Perdue v. Kenny A. ex rel. Winn

Supreme Court of the United States, 2010
559 U.S. 542

■ JUSTICE ALITO delivered the opinion of the Court.

This case presents the question whether the calculation of an attorney's fee, under federal fee-shifting statutes, based on the "lodestar," i.e., the number of hours worked multiplied by the prevailing hourly rates, may be increased due to superior performance and results. We have stated in previous cases that such an increase is permitted in

---

[7]   These are the factors set forth in Rule 1.5 of the Pennsylvania Rules of Professional Conduct, which were considered in Chapter 7, *supra* pp. 579–581, in connection with attorneys' fees in class actions. The eight listed factors are identical to those in Rule 1.5 of the ABA Model Rules of Professional Conduct, although factor 8 in Model Rule 1.5 is factor 1 in Pennsylvania Rule 1.5.

extraordinary circumstances, and we reaffirm that rule. But as we have also said in prior cases, there is a strong presumption that the lodestar is sufficient; factors subsumed in the lodestar calculation cannot be used as a ground for increasing an award above the lodestar; and a party seeking fees has the burden of identifying a factor that the lodestar does not adequately take into account and proving with specificity that an enhanced fee is justified. Because the District Court did not apply these standards, we reverse the decision below and remand for further proceedings consistent with this opinion.

I

A

Respondents (plaintiffs below) are children in the Georgia foster-care system and their next friends. They filed this class action on behalf of 3,000 children in foster care and named as defendants the Governor of Georgia and various state officials (petitioners in this case). Claiming that deficiencies in the foster-care system in two counties near Atlanta violated their federal and state constitutional and statutory rights, respondents sought injunctive and declaratory relief, as well as attorney's fees and expenses.

The United States District Court for the Northern District of Georgia eventually referred the case to mediation, where the parties entered into a consent decree, which the District Court approved. The consent decree resolved all pending issues other than the fees that respondents' attorneys were entitled to receive under 42 U.S.C. § 1988.

B

Respondents submitted a request for more than $14 million in attorney's fees. Half of that amount was based on their calculation of the lodestar—roughly 30,000 hours multiplied by hourly rates of $200 to $495 for attorneys and $75 to $150 for non attorneys. In support of their fee request, respondents submitted affidavits asserting that these rates were within the range of prevailing market rates for legal services in the relevant market.

The other half of the amount that respondents sought represented a fee enhancement for superior work and results. Affidavits submitted in support of this request claimed that the lodestar amount "would be generally insufficient to induce lawyers of comparable skill, judgment, professional representation and experience" to litigate this case. Petitioners objected to the fee request, contending that some of the proposed hourly rates were too high, that the hours claimed were excessive, and that the enhancement would duplicate factors that were reflected in the lodestar amount.

The District Court awarded fees of approximately $10.5 million. The District Court found that the hourly rates proposed by respondents were "fair and reasonable," but that some of the entries on counsel's billing records were vague and that the hours claimed for many of the billing categories were excessive. The court therefore cut the non-travel hours by 15% and halved the hourly rate for travel hours. This resulted in a lodestar calculation of approximately $6 million.

The court then enhanced this award by 75%, concluding that the lodestar calculation did not take into account "(1) the fact that class counsel were required to advance case expenses of $1.7 million over a three-year period with no on[-]going reimbursement, (2) the fact that class counsel were not paid on an on-going basis as the work was being performed, and (3) the fact that class counsel's ability to recover a fee and expense reimbursement were completely contingent on the outcome of the case." The court stated that respondents' attorneys had exhibited "a higher degree of skill, commitment, dedication, and professionalism ... than the Court has seen displayed by the attorneys in any other case during its 27 years on the bench." The court also commented that the results obtained were " 'extraordinary' " and added that "[a]fter 58 years as a practicing attorney and federal judge, the Court is unaware of any other case in which a plaintiff class has achieved such a favorable result on such a comprehensive scale." The enhancement resulted in an additional $4.5 million fee award.

Relying on prior Circuit precedent, a panel of the Eleventh Circuit affirmed. The panel held that the District Court had not abused its discretion by failing to make a larger reduction in the number of hours for which respondents' attorneys sought reimbursement, but the panel commented that it "would have cut the billable hours more if we were deciding the matter in the first instance" and added that the hourly rates approved by the District Court also "appear[ed] to be on the generous side." On the question of the enhancement, however, the panel splintered, with each judge writing a separate opinion.

Judge Carnes concluded that binding Eleventh Circuit precedent required that the decision of the District Court be affirmed, but he opined that the reasoning in our opinions suggested that no enhancement should be allowed in this case. He concluded that the quality of the attorneys' performance was "adequately accounted for 'either in determining the reasonable number of hours expended on the litigation or in setting the reasonable hourly rates.' " He found that an enhancement could not be justified based on delay in the recovery of attorney's fees and reimbursable expenses because such delay is a routine feature of cases brought under 42 U.S.C. § 1983. And he reasoned that the District Court had contravened our holding in *Burlington v. Dague*, 505 U.S. 557 (1992), when it relied on " 'the fact that class counsel's compensation was totally contingent upon prevailing in this action.' "

Judge Wilson concurred in the judgment but disagreed with Judge Carnes' view that Eleventh Circuit precedent is inconsistent with our decisions. Judge Hill also concurred in the judgment but expressed no view about the correctness of the prior Circuit precedent.

* * *

II

The general rule in our legal system is that each party must pay its own attorney's fees and expenses, see *Hensley v. Eckerhart*, 461 U.S. 424, 429, (1983), but Congress enacted 42 U.S.C. § 1988 in order to ensure that federal rights are adequately enforced. Section 1988 provides that a prevailing party in certain civil rights actions may recover "a reasonable attorney's fee as part of the costs." Unfortunately, the statute does not explain what Congress meant by a "reasonable" fee, and therefore the task of identifying an appropriate methodology for determining a "reasonable" fee was left for the courts.

One possible method was set out in *Johnson v. Georgia Highway Express, Inc.*, 488 F.2d 714, 717–719 (C.A.5 1974), which listed 12 factors that a court should consider in determining a reasonable fee.[4] This method, however, "gave very little actual guidance to district courts. Setting attorney's fees by reference to a series of sometimes subjective factors placed unlimited discretion in trial judges and produced disparate results." *Delaware Valley I*, [478 U.S.] at 563.

An alternative, the lodestar approach, was pioneered by the Third Circuit in *Lindy Bros. Builders, Inc. of Philadelphia v. American Radiator & Standard Sanitary Corp.*, 487 F.2d 161 (1973), *appeal after remand*, 540 F.2d 102 (1976), and "achieved dominance in the federal courts" after our decision in *Hensley*. *Gisbrecht v. Barnhart*, 535 U.S. 789, 801 (2002). "Since that time, '[t]he "lodestar" figure has, as its name suggests, become the guiding light of our fee-shifting jurisprudence.'" *Ibid.* (quoting *Dague, supra*, at 562).

Although the lodestar method is not perfect, it has several important virtues. First, in accordance with our understanding of the aim of fee-shifting statutes, the lodestar looks to "the prevailing market rates in the relevant community." *Blum v. Stenson*, 465 U.S. 886, 895 (1984). Developed after the practice of hourly billing had become widespread, the lodestar method produces an award that roughly approximates the fee that the prevailing attorney would have received if he or she had been representing a paying client who was billed by the hour in a comparable case. Second, the lodestar method is readily administrable, and unlike the *Johnson* approach, the lodestar calculation is "objective," *Hensley, supra*, at 433, and thus cabins the

---

4   These factors were: "(1) the time and labor required; (2) the novelty and difficulty of the questions; (3) the skill requisite to perform the legal service properly; (4) the preclusion of employment by the attorney due to the acceptance of the case; (5) the customary fee; (6) whether the fee is fixed or contingent; (7) time limitations imposed by the client or the circumstances; (8) the amount involved and the results obtained; (9) the experience, reputation, and ability of the attorneys; (10) the 'undesirability' of the case; (11) the nature and length of the professional relationship with the client; and (12) awards in similar cases." *Hensley v. Eckerhart*, 461 U.S. 424, 430, n. 3 (1983).

discretion of trial judges, permits meaningful judicial review, and produces reasonably predictable results.

III

Our prior decisions concerning the federal fee-shifting statutes have established six important rules that lead to our decision in this case.

First, a "reasonable" fee is a fee that is sufficient to induce a capable attorney to undertake the representation of a meritorious civil rights case. Section 1988's aim is to enforce the covered civil rights statutes, not to provide "a form of economic relief to improve the financial lot of attorneys." *Delaware Valley I, supra*, at 565.

Second, the lodestar method yields a fee that is presumptively sufficient to achieve this objective. Indeed, we have said that the presumption is a "strong" one. *Dague, supra*, at 562, *Delaware Valley I, supra*, at 565.

Third, although we have never sustained an enhancement of a lodestar amount for performance, we have repeatedly said that enhancements may be awarded in "'rare'" and "'exceptional'" circumstances. *Delaware Valley I, supra*, at 565; *Blum, supra*, at 897; *Hensley*, 461 U.S., at 435.

Fourth, we have noted that "the lodestar figure includes most, if not all, of the relevant factors constituting a 'reasonable' attorney's fee," *Delaware Valley I, supra*, at 566, and have held that an enhancement may not be awarded based on a factor that is subsumed in the lodestar calculation. We have thus held that the novelty and complexity of a case generally may not be used as a ground for an enhancement because these factors "presumably [are] fully reflected in the number of billable hours recorded by counsel." We have also held that the quality of an attorney's performance generally should not be used to adjust the lodestar "[b]ecause considerations concerning the quality of a prevailing party's counsel's representation normally are reflected in the reasonable hourly rate." *Delaware Valley I, supra*, at 566.

Fifth, the burden of proving that an enhancement is necessary must be borne by the fee applicant. *Dague, supra*, at 561; *Blum*, 465 U.S., at 901–902.

Finally, a fee applicant seeking an enhancement must produce "specific evidence" that supports the award. *Id.*, at 899, 901 (An enhancement must be based on "evidence that enhancement was necessary to provide fair and reasonable compensation"). This requirement is essential if the lodestar method is to realize one of its chief virtues, *i.e.*, providing a calculation that is objective and capable of being reviewed on appeal.

IV

A

In light of what we have said in prior cases, we reject any contention that a fee determined by the lodestar method may not be enhanced in any situation. The lodestar method was never intended to be conclusive in all circumstances. Instead, there is a "strong presumption" that the lodestar figure is reasonable, but that presumption may be overcome in those rare circumstances in which the lodestar does not adequately take into account a factor that may properly be considered in determining a reasonable fee.

B

In this case, we are asked to decide whether either the quality of an attorney's performance or the results obtained are factors that may properly provide a basis for an enhancement. We treat these two factors as one. When a plaintiff's attorney achieves results that are more favorable than would have been predicted based on the governing law and the available evidence, the outcome may be attributable to superior performance and commitment of resources by plaintiff's counsel. Or the outcome may result from inferior performance by defense counsel, unanticipated defense concessions, unexpectedly favorable rulings by the court, an unexpectedly sympathetic jury, or simple luck. Since none of these latter causes can justify an enhanced award, superior results are relevant only to the extent it can be shown that they are the result of superior attorney performance. Thus, we need only consider whether superior attorney performance can justify an enhancement. And in light of the principles derived from our prior cases, we inquire whether there are circumstances in which superior attorney performance is not adequately taken into account in the lodestar calculation. We conclude that there are a few such circumstances but that these circumstances are indeed "rare" and "exceptional," and require specific evidence that the lodestar fee would not have been "adequate to attract competent counsel."

First, an enhancement may be appropriate where the method used in determining the hourly rate employed in the lodestar calculation does not adequately measure the attorney's true market value, as demonstrated in part during the litigation. This may occur if the hourly rate is determined by a formula that takes into account only a single factor (such as years since admission to the bar) or perhaps only a few similar factors. In such a case, an enhancement may be appropriate so that an attorney is compensated at the rate that the attorney would receive in cases not governed by the federal fee-shifting statutes. But in order to provide a calculation that is objective and reviewable, the trial judge should adjust the attorney's hourly rate in accordance with specific proof linking the attorney's ability to a prevailing market rate.

Second, an enhancement may be appropriate if the attorney's performance includes an extraordinary outlay of expenses and the litigation is exceptionally protracted. As Judge Carnes noted below, when an attorney agrees to represent a civil rights plaintiff who cannot afford to pay the attorney, the attorney presumably understands that no reimbursement is likely to be received until the successful resolution of the case, and therefore enhancements to compensate for delay in reimbursement for expenses must be reserved for unusual cases. In such exceptional cases, however, an enhancement may be allowed, but the amount of the enhancement must be calculated using a method that is reasonable, objective, and capable of being reviewed on appeal, such as by applying a standard rate of interest to the qualifying outlays of expenses.

Third, there may be extraordinary circumstances in which an attorney's performance involves exceptional delay in the payment of fees. An attorney who expects to be compensated under § 1988 presumably understands that payment of fees will generally not come until the end of the case, if at all. Compensation for this delay is generally made "either by basing the award on current rates or by adjusting the fee based on historical rates to reflect its present value." *Missouri v. Jenkins*, 491 U.S. 274, 282, (1989). But we do not rule out the possibility that an enhancement may be appropriate where an attorney assumes these costs in the face of unanticipated delay, particularly where the delay is unjustifiably caused by the defense. In such a case, however, the enhancement should be calculated by applying a method similar to that described above in connection with exceptional delay in obtaining reimbursement for expenses.

* * *

We are told that, under an increasingly popular arrangement, attorneys are paid at a reduced hourly rate but receive a bonus if certain specified results are obtained, and this practice is analogized to the award of an enhancement such as the one in this case. The analogy, however, is flawed. An attorney who agrees, at the outset of the representation, to a reduced hourly rate in exchange for the opportunity to earn a performance bonus is in a position far different from an attorney in a § 1988 case who is compensated at the full prevailing rate and then seeks a performance enhancement in addition to the lodestar amount after the litigation has concluded. Reliance on these comparisons for the purposes of administering enhancements, therefore, is not appropriate.

V

In the present case, the District Court did not provide proper justification for the large enhancement that it awarded. The court increased the lodestar award by 75% but, as far as the court's opinion reveals, this figure appears to have been essentially arbitrary. Why, for example, did the court grant a 75% enhancement instead of the 100% increase that respondents sought? And why 75% rather than 50% or 25% or 10%?

The District Court commented that the enhancement was the "minimum enhancement of the lodestar necessary to reasonably compensate [respondents'] counsel." But the effect of the enhancement was to increase the top rate for the attorneys to more than $866 per hour, and the District Court did not point to anything in the record that shows that this is an appropriate figure for the relevant market.

The District Court pointed to the fact that respondents' counsel had to make extraordinary outlays for expenses and had to wait for reimbursement, but the court did not calculate the amount of the enhancement that is attributable to this factor. Similarly, the District Court noted that respondents' counsel did not receive fees on an ongoing basis while the case was pending, but the court did not sufficiently link this factor to proof in the record that the delay here was outside the normal range expected by attorneys who rely on § 1988 for the payment of their fees or quantify the disparity. Nor did the court provide a calculation of the cost to counsel of any extraordinary and unwarranted delay. And the court's reliance on the contingency of the outcome contravenes our holding in *Dague*.

Finally, insofar as the District Court relied on a comparison of the performance of counsel in this case with the performance of counsel in unnamed prior cases, the District Court did not employ a methodology that permitted meaningful appellate review. Needless to say, we do not question the sincerity of the District Court's observations, and we are in no position to assess their accuracy. But when a trial judge awards an enhancement on an impressionistic basis, a major purpose of the lodestar method—providing an objective and reviewable basis for fees—is undermined.

Determining a "reasonable attorney's fee" is a matter that is committed to the sound discretion of a trial judge, see 42 U.S.C. § 1988 (permitting court, "in its discretion," to award fees), but the judge's discretion is not unlimited. It is essential that the judge provide a reasonably specific explanation for all aspects of a fee determination, including any award of an enhancement. Unless such an explanation is given, adequate appellate review is not feasible, and without such review, widely disparate awards may be made, and awards may be influenced (or at least, may appear to be influenced) by a judge's subjective opinion regarding particular attorneys or the importance of the case. In addition, in future cases, defendants contemplating the possibility of settlement will have no way to estimate the likelihood of having to pay a potentially huge enhancement.

Section 1988 serves an important public purpose by making it possible for persons without means to bring suit to vindicate their rights. But unjustified enhancements that serve only to enrich attorneys are not consistent with the statute's aim.[8] In many cases, attorney's fees awarded under § 1988 are not paid by the individuals responsible for the constitutional or statutory violations on which the judgment is based. Instead, the fees are paid in effect by state and local taxpayers, and because state and local governments have limited budgets, money that is used to pay attorney's fees is money that cannot be used for programs that provide vital public services.

* * *

For all these reasons, the judgment of the Court of Appeals is reversed, and the case is remanded for proceedings consistent with this opinion.

It is so ordered.

■ JUSTICE KENNEDY, concurring.

If one were to ask an attorney or a judge to name the significant cases of his or her career, it would be unsurprising to find the list includes a case then being argued or just decided. When immersed in a case, lawyers and judges find within it a fascination, an intricacy, an importance that transcends what the detached observer sees. So the pending or just completed case will often seem extraordinary to its participants. That is the dynamic of the adversary system, the system that so well serves the law.

It is proper for the Court today to reject the proposition that all enhancements are barred; still, it must be understood that extraordinary cases are presented only in the rarest circumstances.

With these comments, I join in full the opinion of the Court.

■ JUSTICE THOMAS, concurring.

[In his concurrence Judge Thomas noted that the Court had never sustained an enhancement of a fee calculated under the lodestar method and that "the lodestar calculation will in virtually every case already reflect all indicia of attorney performance relevant to a fee award."]

■ JUSTICE BREYER, with whom JUSTICE STEVENS, JUSTICE GINSBURG, and JUSTICE SOTOMAYOR join, concurring in part and dissenting in part.

We granted certiorari in this case to consider "whether the calculation of an attorney's fee" that is "based on the 'lodestar,'" can "ever be enhanced based solely on [the] quality of [the lawyers']

---

[8]   Justice BREYER's opinion dramatically illustrates the danger of allowing a trial judge to award a huge enhancement not supported by any discernible methodology. That approach would retain the $4.5 million enhancement here so that respondents' attorneys would earn as much as the attorneys at some of the richest law firms in the country. These fees would be paid by the taxpayers of Georgia, where the annual per capita income is less than $34,000, and the annual salaries of attorneys employed by the State range from $48,000 for entry-level lawyers to $118,000 for the highest paid division chief. Section 1988 was enacted to ensure that civil rights plaintiffs are adequately represented, not to provide such a windfall.

performance and [the] results obtained." The Court answers that question in the affirmative. As our prior precedents make clear, the lodestar calculation "does not end the [fee] inquiry" because there "remain other considerations that may lead the district court to adjust the fee upward." *Hensley v. Eckerhart*, 461 U.S. 424, 434 (1983). For that reason, "[t]he lodestar method was never intended to be conclusive in all circumstances." Instead, as the Court today reaffirms, when "superior attorney performance," leads to "exceptional success an enhanced award may be justified," *Hensley supra*, at 435. I agree with that conclusion.

Where the majority and I part ways is with respect to a question that is not presented, but that the Court obliquely, and in my view inappropriately, appears to consider nonetheless—namely, whether the lower courts correctly determined in this case that exceptional circumstances justify a lodestar enhancement. I would not reach that issue, which lies beyond the narrow question that we agreed to consider. Nor do I believe that this Court, which is twice removed from the litigation underlying the fee determination, is properly suited to resolve the fact-intensive inquiry that 42 U.S.C. § 1988 demands. But even were I to engage in that inquiry, I would hold that the District Court did not abuse its discretion in awarding an enhancement. And I would therefore affirm the judgment of the Court of Appeals.

As the Court explains, the basic question that must be resolved when considering an enhancement to the lodestar is whether the lodestar calculation "adequately measure[s]" an attorney's "value," as "demonstrated" by his performance "during the litigation." While I understand the need for answering that question through the application of standards, I also believe that the answer inevitably involves an element of judgment. Moreover, when reviewing a district court's answer to that question, an appellate court must inevitably give weight to the fact that a district court is better situated to provide that answer. For it is the district judge, and only the district judge, who will have read all of the motions filed in the case, witnessed the proceedings, and been able to evaluate the attorneys' overall performance in light of the objectives, context, legal difficulty, and practical obstacles present in the case. In a word, the district judge will have observed the attorney's true "value, as demonstrated . . . during the litigation." * * *

This case well illustrates why our tiered and functionally specialized judicial system places the task of determining an attorney's fee award primarily in the district court's hands. The plaintiffs' lawyers spent eight years investigating the underlying facts, developing the initial complaint, conducting court proceedings, and working out final relief. The District Court's docket, with over 600 entries, consists of more than 18,000 pages. Transcripts of hearings and depositions, along with other documents, have produced a record that fills 20 large boxes. Neither we, nor an appellate panel, can easily read that entire record.

Nor should we attempt to second-guess a district judge who is aware of the many intangible matters that the written page cannot reflect.

My own review of this expansive record cannot possibly be exhaustive. But those portions of the record I have reviewed lead me to conclude, like the Court of Appeals, that the District Judge did not abuse his discretion when awarding an enhanced fee. I reach this conclusion based on four considerations.

First, the record indicates that the lawyers' objective in this case was unusually important and fully consistent with the central objectives of the basic federal civil-rights statute, 42 U.S.C. § 1983. Moreover, the problem the attorneys faced demanded an exceptionally high degree of skill and effort. Specifically, these lawyers and their clients sought to have the State of Georgia reform its entire foster-care system—a system that much in the record describes as well below the level of minimal constitutional acceptability. * * *

* * *

Second, the course of the lawsuit was lengthy and arduous. The plaintiffs and their lawyers began with factual investigations beyond those which the child advocate had already conducted. They then filed suit. And the State met the plaintiffs' efforts with a host of complex procedural, as well as substantive, objections. * * *

* * * All told, in opposing the plaintiffs' efforts to have the foster-care system reformed, the State spent $2.4 million on outside counsel (who, because they charge the State reduced rates, worked significantly more hours than that figure alone indicates) and tapped its own law department for an additional 5,200 hours of work.

Third, in the face of this opposition, the results obtained by the plaintiffs' attorneys appear to have been exceptional. The 47-page consent decree negotiated over the course of the mediation sets forth 31 specific steps that the State will take in order to address the specific deficiencies of the sort that I described above. And it establishes a reporting and oversight mechanism that is backed up by the District Court's enforcement authority. As a result of the decree, the State agreed to comprehensive reforms of its foster-care system, to the benefit of children in many different communities. And informed observers have described the decree as having brought about significant positive results.

Fourth and finally, the District Judge, who supervised these proceedings, who saw the plaintiffs amass, process, compile, and convincingly present vast amounts of factual information, who witnessed their defeat of numerous state procedural and substantive motions, and who was in a position to evaluate the ultimate mediation effort, said:

1. the "mediation effort in this case went far beyond anything that this Court has seen in any previous case;"

2. "based on its personal observation of plaintiffs' counsel's performance throughout this litigation, the Court finds that ... counsel brought a higher degree of skill, commitment, dedication, and professionalism to this litigation than the Court has seen displayed by the attorneys in any other case during its 27 years on the bench;"

3. the Consent Decree "provided extraordinary benefits to the plaintiff class. . . ." "[T]he settlement achieved by plaintiffs' counsel is comprehensive in its scope and detailed in its coverage. . . . After 58 years as a practicing attorney and federal judge, the Court is unaware of any other case in which a plaintiff class has achieved such a favorable result on such a comprehensive scale."

Based on these observations and on its assessment of the attorneys' performance during the course of the litigation, the District Court concluded that "the evidence establishes that the quality of service rendered by class counsel ... was far superior to what consumers of legal services in the legal marketplace ... could reasonably expect to receive for the rates used in the lodestar calculation."

On the basis of what I have read, I believe that assessment was correct. I recognize that the ordinary lodestar calculation yields a large fee award. But by my assessment, the lodestar calculation in this case translates to an average hourly fee per attorney of $249. (The majority's reference to an hourly fee of $866 refers to the rate associated with the single highest paid of the 17 attorneys under the enhanced fee, not the average hourly rate under the lodestar. The lay reader should also bear in mind that a lawyer's "fee" is substantially greater than his "profit," given that attorneys must sometimes cover case-specific costs (which in this case exceeded $800,000) and also must cover routine overhead expenses, which typically consume 40% of their fees.)

At $249 per hour, the lodestar would compensate this group of attorneys—whom the District Court described as extraordinary—at a rate lower than the average rate charged by attorneys practicing law in the State of Georgia, where the average hourly rate is $268. * * * By comparison, the District Court's enhanced award—a special one-time adjustment unique to this exceptional case—would compensate these attorneys, on this one occasion, at an average hourly rate of $435, which is comparable to the rates charged by the Nation's leading law firms on average on every occasion. Thus, it would appear that the enhanced award is wholly consistent with the purpose of § 1988, which was enacted to ensure that "counsel for prevailing parties [are] paid as is traditional with attorneys compensated by a fee-paying client."

In any event, the circumstances I have listed likely make this a "rare" or "exceptional" case warranting an enhanced fee award. And they certainly make clear that it was neither unreasonable nor an abuse of discretion for the District Court to reach that conclusion. Indeed, if the facts and circumstances that I have described are even roughly correct, then it is fair to ask: If this is not an exceptional case, what is?

* * *

* * * [T]he majority and I do disagree in this respect: I would not disturb the judgment below. "A request for attorney's fees should not result in a second major litigation." *Hensley*, 461 U.S., at 437. Nor should it lead to years of protracted appellate review. We did not grant certiorari in this case to consider the fact-intensive dispute over whether this is, in fact, an exceptional case that merits a lodestar enhancement. The District Court has already resolved that question and the Court of Appeals affirmed its judgment, having found no abuse of discretion. I would have been content to resolve no more than the question presented. But, even were I to follow the Court's inclination to say more, I would hold that the principles upon which we agree—including the applicability of abuse-of-discretion review to a District Court's fee determination—require us to affirm the judgment below.

COMMENTS AND QUESTIONS CONCERNING
PERDUE V. KENNY A. EX REL. WINN.

1.   After remand from the Supreme Court, the defendants paid $8.14 million to cover the lodestar and expense amounts initially awarded by the district court plus post-judgment interest. District Judge Marvin Shoob denied plaintiffs' motion for additional fees, concluding: "Notwithstanding the truly outstanding performance of plaintiffs' counsel in this case and the resulting benefit to the plaintiff class, the evidence in the record does not support the award of an enhancement under [the Supreme Court's] newly established guidelines." *Kenny A. ex rel. Winn v. Deal*, No. 1:02 CV–1686–MHS, slip op. at 28 (N.D. Ga. July 19, 2011).

2.   Is the Supreme Court uniquely qualified to do the numerical and other calculations necessary to consider the reasonableness of an attorneys' fee award? Isn't the awarding of attorneys' fees a matter best left to the discretion of a district judge who has seen the work product of the attorney seeking fees and is familiar with the local bar? On the other hand, isn't it appropriate for the Supreme Court to set forth general principles to guide the lower federal courts? Might the Court have granted certiorari because of the 75% lodestar enhancement without further calculation to support such a significant and "round number" enhancement?

3.   Consider, also, the difficulty with appellate review of attorneys' fees awards if the district judge does not make specific factual findings to support all aspects of the fee calculations. As the Court noted:

[I]nsofar as the District Court relied on a comparison of the performance of counsel in this case with the performance of counsel in unnamed prior cases, the District Court did not employ a methodology that permitted meaningful appellate review. * * * [W]hen a trial judge awards an enhancement on an impressionistic basis, a major purpose of the lodestar method—providing an objective and reviewable basis for fees—is undermined.

4. The Supreme Court has favored the lodestar method of calculating attorneys' fees over the multi-factor analysis recognized by the United States Court of Appeals for the 11th Circuit in *Johnson v. Georgia Highway Express*. What problems does the Court have with the *Johnson* test? Are there any reasons to favor that test over a lodestar calculation?

5. Isn't there some circularity in the Court's reasoning? To the extent that courts award legal fees at a certain level, doesn't this become a benchmark for reasonable fees in future cases? On the other hand, to the extent that attorneys' fee calculations are based on a state's per capita income or the average salaries of attorneys working for the state, won't likely attorneys' fees be suppressed in many states? Would it be a "windfall" to award prevailing attorneys in a complex action with 3000 class members and issues of great public significance "as much as the attorneys at some of the richest law firms in the country"?

6. Was it ethical for class counsel to advance $1.5 million in costs on behalf of the plaintiff class? Georgia Rule of Professional Responsibility 1.8(e) provides:

A lawyer shall not provide financial assistance to a client in connection with pending or contemplated litigation, except that:

1. a lawyer may advance court costs and expenses of litigation, the repayment of which may be contingent on the outcome of the matter; or

2. a lawyer representing a client unable to pay court costs and expenses of litigation may pay those costs and expenses on behalf of the client.

While identical in substance, this Georgia provision is slightly different in wording than ABA Model Rule of Professional Conduct 1.8(e). What if lawyers were not permitted to advance court costs and expenses in an action such as this? Why do state rules of professional conduct generally prohibit lawyers from providing financial assistance to a client in connection with litigation?

7. Not only might a plaintiff pay her lawyer on an hourly basis, but many plaintiffs enter into contingent fee agreements with their attorneys. Under such a representation contract, the attorneys' fee is only due if the plaintiff prevails by way of judgment or settlement and, if the plaintiff is unsuccessful, she owes her attorney nothing in fees.

While such contingent fee agreements are common in personal injury actions, contingent fees typically are prohibited for the representation of defendants in criminal actions or as payment in a domestic relations matter that is contingent on securing a divorce or on the amount of alimony or support awarded. ABA Model Rule of Professional Conduct 1.5(d). *See also Restatement (Third) of Law Governing Lawyers* § 35 (2000). Why the prohibition on contingent fees in such situations?

8.   Another way litigation can be supported is through third-party litigation financing. By agreeing to handle a civil action on a contingent fee basis, the lawyer, in effect, invests in the outcome of that action and will only receive a fee if her client is successful. In third-party (or alternative) litigation finance, a non-party provides financing to a party in return for a share in any recovery in the action. *E.g.*, Steinitz & Field, "A Model Litigation Finance Contract," 99 *Iowa L. Rev.* 711 (2014); Abrams & Chen, "A Market for Justice: A First Empirical Look at Third Party Litigation Funding," 15 *U. Penn. J. Bus. L.* 1075 (2013); Appelbaum, "Taking Sides in a Divorce, Chasing Profit," *N.Y. Times*, Dec. 5, 2010, § 1, at 1 (firm providing funding for parties in domestic relations actions in return for share of lawsuit proceeds).

Because Rule 5.4(a) of the ABA Model Rules of Professional Conduct prohibits lawyers from sharing fees with non-lawyers, third-party financing is provided directly to the parties themselves. Nevertheless, lawyers need to be aware of the ethical issues that may arise for lawyers due to third-party litigation finance. ABA Commission on Ethics 20/20, *White Paper on Alternative Litigation Financing* (2012) (lawyers must exercise independent professional judgment on behalf of clients, protect confidential and privileged matters, and ensure that they competently advise clients concerning such financing).

B. FEES FOR THE ATTORNEY VS. RELIEF FOR THE CLIENT

Under 42 U.S.C. § 1988, the Civil Rights Attorney's Fees Awards Act of 1976, prevailing plaintiffs in specified civil rights actions are entitled to recover their attorneys' fees from the defendant. Assume that a legal aid organization that represents only individuals who cannot pay for private counsel brings a class action against the State of Idaho seeking injunctive relief concerning the State's provision of services to disabled children. As the trial date approaches, the State offers a settlement providing all the injunctive relief plaintiffs seek, but requiring plaintiffs' counsel to waive his right to attorneys' fees.

Plaintiffs' counsel initially refuses to agree to the settlement, but then determines that his duty to his clients requires him to accept the settlement. He argues, though, that the district court should strike the settlement provision requiring waiver of attorneys' fees, permitting plaintiffs to recover their attorneys' fees pursuant to 42 U.S.C. § 1988. Rule 2.1 of the Idaho Rules of Professional Conduct provides, in part: "In representing a client, a lawyer shall exercise independent professional judgment and render candid advice." In addition, Rule 1.7(b) of these same Rules of Professional Conduct provides that, absent appropriate client consent, "a lawyer shall not represent a client if the representation involves * * * a significant risk that the representation * * * will be materially limited by * * * the personal interests of the lawyer."

When the case ultimately reached the Supreme Court, Justice Stevens posed the controlling issue as follows:

> The defect, if any, in the negotiated fee waiver must be traced not to the rules of ethics but to the Fees Act. Following this tack, respondents argue that the statute must be construed to forbid a fee waiver that is the product of "coercion." They submit that a "coercive waiver" results when the defendant in a civil rights action (1) offers a settlement on the merits of equal or greater value than that which plaintiffs could reasonably expect to achieve at trial but (2) conditions the offer on a waiver of plaintiffs' statutory eligibility for attorney's fees. Such an offer, they claim, exploits the ethical obligation of plaintiffs' counsel to recommend settlement in order to avoid defendant's statutory liability for its opponents' fees and costs.

Evans v. Jeff D., 475 U.S. 717, 728–29 (1986).

While the majority concluded that the district court did not abuse its discretion in approving the settlement, including the fee waiver, Justice Brennan argued in dissent:

> Ultimately, enforcement of the laws is what really counts. It was with this in mind that Congress enacted the Civil Rights Attorney's Fees Awards Act of 1976, 42 U.S.C. § 1988. Congress authorized fee shifting to improve enforcement of civil rights legislation by making it easier for victims of civil rights violations to find lawyers willing to take their cases. Because today's decision will make it more difficult for civil rights plaintiffs to obtain legal assistance, a result plainly contrary to Congress' purpose, I dissent.

475 U.S. at 743.

Do you agree with Justice Brennan? Or should defendants be able to offer such settlements in order to define their total settlement liability (rather than agreeing that plaintiffs can petition the court for an undetermined amount of attorneys' fees after the case is settled)? Is there a way for plaintiffs' counsel to avoid such fee waivers after *Jeff D.*?

C. COST-SHIFTING UNDER RULE 68

Rule 68(a) of the Federal Rules of Civil Procedure provides:

> At least 14 days before the date set for trial, a party defending against a claim may serve on an opposing party an offer to allow judgment on specified terms, with the costs then

accrued. If, within 14 days after being served, the opposing party serves written notice accepting the offer, either party may then file the offer and notice of acceptance, plus proof of service. The clerk must then enter judgment.

Thus far Rule 68 does not seem particularly revolutionary. A Rule 68 offer of judgment, in fact, sounds very much like a settlement offer that a defendant could make in any action. Note, though, that the offer must include both any recovery on the merits plus "the costs then accrued." The Supreme observed in *Marek v. Chesny*, 473 U.S. 1, 6 (1985):

> If an offer recites that costs are included or specifies an amount for costs, and the plaintiff accepts the offer, the judgment will necessarily include costs; if the offer does not state that costs are included and an amount for costs is not specified, the court will be obliged by the terms of the Rule to include in its judgment an additional amount which in its discretion * * * it determines to be sufficient to cover the costs.

In many cases Rule 68 will only encompass court fees, fees for copies "necessarily obtained for use in the case," and other fees specified in 28 U.S.C. § 1920. However, pursuant to the Civil Rights Attorney's Fees Awards Act of 1976, 42 U.S.C. § 1988, prevailing plaintiffs may recover "a reasonable attorney's fee as part of the costs." So, if an offer of judgment is made under Rule 68, it must include entitlement to filing fees and Section 1920 costs and it also might carry with it entitlement to attorneys' fees under 42 U.S.C. § 1988 *if* those fees are considered to be part of the costs in that type of civil rights action.

What gives Rule 68 its real bite in settlement negotiations is Section (d) of that Rule, which describes the consequences of an offer of judgment that is not accepted. Rule 68(d) provides:

> If the judgment that the offeree [usually, the plaintiff] finally obtains is not more favorable than the unaccepted offer, the offeree must pay the costs incurred after the offer was made.

Assume that the defendant made a Rule 68 offer of judgment for $100,000 14 days before trial and the plaintiff did not accept that offer. If the plaintiff later recovered only $10,000 at trial and had $20,000 in pre-offer costs, Rule 68(d) requires the plaintiff to pay defendant's costs incurred after the offer of judgment. Perhaps during trial the defendant offered deposition transcripts as evidence; pursuant to 28 U.S.C. § 1920 and Rule 54, plaintiff would have to pay those costs.

This doesn't sound like a real incentive for a plaintiff to seriously consider acceptance of a pretrial offer of judgment. However, in *Marek v. Chesny*, 473 U.S. 1 (1985), the Supreme Court held that in such a situation the plaintiff cannot recover any of its *own* attorneys' fees after the offer of judgment—even though the plaintiff ultimately prevailed at trial (but for an amount less than the offer of judgment). This is the serious potential consequence of Rule 68. As the Supreme Court stated in *Marek v. Chesney,* "Rule 68 will require plaintiffs to 'think very hard' about whether continued litigation is worthwhile." 473 U.S. at 11.

Test your understanding of Rule 68 by considering the following factual scenarios.

(1) In the above hypothetical, the plaintiff cannot recover his post-offer costs (including "a reasonable attorney's fee as part of the costs" pursuant to 42 U.S.C. § 1988). However, Rule 68(d) provides: "If the judgment that the offeree finally obtains is not more favorable than the unaccepted offer, the offeree must pay the costs incurred after the offer was made." Why, then, doesn't the plaintiff have to pay the attorneys' fees that the defendant incurred after the Rule 68 offer was made?

"[T]he term 'costs' in Rule 68 was intended to refer to all costs properly awardable under the relevant substantive statute or other authority." *Merek v. Chesny,* 473 U.S. 1, 9 (1985). Because defendants typically cannot recover attorneys' fees as costs under 42 U.S.C. § 1988, defendants' attorneys fees generally cannot be shifted to the plaintiff under Rule 68. *Stanczyk v. City of New York,* 752 F.3d 273, 281 (2d Cir. 2014).

(2) What if, after the plaintiff did not accept a Rule 68 pretrial offer of judgment, the defendant prevails at trial? Even though the Rule 68 offer was more favorable for the plaintiff than the trial outcome (the defendant having prevailed at trial), the Supreme Court has held that Rule 68 cost-shifting is not triggered because the plaintiff did not obtain a judgment at trial. *Delta Airlines, Inc. v. August,* 450 U.S. 346 (1981). If the plaintiff were to recover $1 at trial, costs would shift, but if the plaintiff loses the case at trial, he need not worry about Rule 68.

(3) Assume that, two months before trial, defendant makes a Rule 68 offer of judgment for $10,000 to plaintiff. The offer is not accepted by the plaintiff, so defendant makes a second offer of judgment one month before trial for $20,000. The plaintiff does not accept this second offer either, and then recovers $15,000 at trial. Costs would shift in this situation pursuant to Rule 68(b), which provides that a party may make multiple Rule 68 offers of judgment.

(4) In a bifurcated trial, the court determines that the defendant is liable to the plaintiff. Fifteen days before the date of the hearing on damages, the defendant serves a Rule 68 offer of judgment for $50,000 on the plaintiff. The offer is not accepted and the court then determines the amount of damages to be $30,000. Rule 68(c) authorizes offers of judgment after determination of liability, so long as the offer is served at least 14 days before the date set to determine the extent of liability.

Figure 8–2 includes the four questions that must be answered to determine whether costs must be shifted under Rule 68. If all four questions are answered "yes," then:

(1) The claimant (typically the plaintiff) must pay the offeror's post-offer costs (which usually do not include attorney's fees); and

(2) The claimant cannot recover from the opposing party its own post-offer costs (which may include attorneys' fees if a statute provides that prevailing plaintiffs recover their attorneys' fees).

FIGURE 8–2
RULE 68 OFFERS OF JUDGMENT

	Yes	No
1) Was offer of judgment made 14 or more days before trial or a liability hearing?		
2) Was offer not accepted by claimant?		
3) Did claimant recover a judgment (so *Delta Airlines* does not apply)?		
4) Was ultimate judgment not more favorable than unaccepted offer?		
If answer to questions 1, 2, 3, and 4 is "yes," then:	(A) Offeree (claimant) must pay Offeror's (defendant's) post-offer "costs" (which typically don't include attorneys' fees); and	(B) Offeree (claimant) cannot recover its own costs (which may include attorneys' fees) incurred after offer was made.

VII. THE RELIEF SOUGHT IN *LEONARD V. PEPSICO, INC.*

In many cases, plaintiffs seek several different types of relief. This was the case in *Leonard v. PepsiCo, Inc.*, in which the demand for relief sought specific remedies tailored to each count of the amended complaint (with the six counts based on, respectively, specific performance, breach of contract, fraud, deceptive acts and practices under New York law, false advertising under New York law, and deceptive acts and practices under Washington law).[8] The *Leonard* demand for relief provided:

WHEREFORE, Leonard demands judgment against PepsiCo as follows:

a)   on Claim I, directing PepsiCo to deliver a Harrier jet to Leonard;

b)   on Claim II, an award of damages in an amount to be determined at trial;

c)   on Claim III, an award of actual and punitive damages in amounts to be determined at trial;

d)   on Claim IV, an award of damages in an amount to be determined at trial, an award of treble damages, and his attorneys' fees and costs herein;

e)   on Claim V, an award of damages in an amount to be determined at trial, an award of treble damages, and his attorneys' fees and costs herein;

f)   on Claim VI, an award of damages in an amount to be determined at trial, an award of treble damages, and his attorneys' fees and costs herein; and

g)   such other and further relief as the Court deems just.

So a single civil action may seek multiple types of relief, and the complaint or counterclaim should be specific as to what relief is sought in connection with each claim asserted.

VIII. CONCLUSION

The lawyer's job is to represent her client in civil litigation in an effort to obtain the relief that the client desires. As this chapter discusses, there are many types of relief that may be available to the client. The lawyer must determine at the outset of the legal representation just what is desired by the client and then craft a civil action to obtain that relief. While the attorney will focus on the civil action, for the client that action is simply a means to secure the remedy it seeks to redress a perceived legal wrong.

IX. CHAPTER ASSESSMENT

A.   Multiple-Choice Questions. Answer the following questions, reviewing the sections of the chapter noted in connection with each question.

---

8   This was in John Leonard's action against PepsiCo., which was filed initially in Florida state court, removed to federal court in Florida, and then transferred under 28 U.S.C. § 1404(a) to the United States District Court for the Southern District of New York. Prior to Leonard's action, PepsiCo had filed its own declaratory judgment action in the Southern District of New York. Judge Kimba Wood resolved both cases in the opinion set forth in Chapter 1 of this text, *supra* p. 29.

1.   A consumer buys a big-screen television set from an electronics store, using his car as collateral for the purchase. After two years of payments, the consumer loses his job. When he falls behind on his television payments, the store files a contract action against him, seeking payment of the total amount due on the television (as provided in the parties' sales contract). Simultaneous with the filing of the state civil action, the store files a replevin action asking the sheriff to seize the consumer's car immediately and, pursuant to state statute, hold a hearing on the merits of the contract action in two weeks. Without notice to the consumer, the sheriff seizes his car.

Review Section II and choose the best answer from the following choices:

(a)   Because the consumer was not given notice of the seizure, the seizure of his car was unconstitutional.

(b)   Because the consumer had not paid his television loan, rather than his car loan, the seizure of his car was unconstitutional.

(c)   Because the consumer was provided with the opportunity of a full hearing after the seizure of his car, the seizure of his car was constitutional.

(d)   Because the deprivation of the consumer's car was only for two weeks before the opportunity for a full hearing, the seizure of his car was constitutional.

2.   A woman was driving her car when it lost power and crashed into a guardrail. The woman was not badly hurt, but her doctor's bills and personal injury damages totaled $25,000. At her state court trial against the manufacturer of the car, there is uncontested evidence that similar power losses occurred to 15 other drivers, but the manufacturer did not recall the cars in question nor take other remedial action. The jury returned a verdict of $25,000 in compensatory damages plus $200,000 in punitive damages—one-half of which went to the woman and the other one-half to a state fund to compensate those injured by uninsured drivers.

Review Section III(C) and choose the best answer from the following choices:

(a)   Because the punitive damages awarded were for more than the injuries the woman suffered, the damage award is unconstitutional.

(b)   Because a portion of the damages awarded went to the State, rather than to the woman, the damage award is unconstitutional.

(c)   Because the punitive damages awarded were not more than ten times the amount of the compensatory damages, the damage award is constitutional.

(d)   Because the punitive damages were awarded after a full trial, the damage award is constitutional.

3. A chef owns and runs a small restaurant on Main Street that makes a disproportionate amount of its annual profits on the fall weekends when the local college team plays its home games. At its monthly meeting in January, the city council decides that, during next fall's football season, public parking areas for those visiting Main Street businesses will be closed to encourage people to gather on campus. The chef calculates that such a plan will cost her restaurant over $100,000, and her lawyer is aware of no legal basis for the city council to take this action. The chef's lawyer therefore suggests that a federal action be filed against the city council and a preliminary injunction be sought immediately.

Review Section IV and choose the best answer from the following choices:

(a) Because damages should be sufficient to redress any injury that the chef might suffer, the court should not issue a preliminary injunction.

(b) Because the chef cannot show that she is likely to suffer irreparable harm in the absence of preliminary relief, the court should not issue a preliminary injunction.

(c) Because the chef is likely to succeed on the merits of this action, the court should issue a preliminary injunction.

(d) Because the issuance of an injunction would be in the public interest, the court should issue a preliminary injunction.

4. A citizen of Colorado is injured in an accident while driving her neighbor's car. Her passenger is badly injured and brings a state court action against the driver seeking $150,000 in damages. The driver asks her insurance company to defend her in this state court action and to assume responsibility for any resulting damage award up to the limits of her insurance policy. The driver's insurance company, which is incorporated and has its principal place of business in California, asserts that its policy does not cover the accident because the driver was improperly driving her neighbor's car. The driver then brings a federal diversity action against the insurance company, seeking a declaratory judgment that she is covered under the terms of her insurance policy.

Review Section V and choose the best answer from the following choices:

(a) Because the personal injury action was filed in state court, the federal court cannot issue a declaration of the parties' rights under the insurance contract.

(b) Because there is no actual controversy between the parties, the federal court cannot issue a declaration of the parties' rights under the insurance contract.

(c) Because there is diversity jurisdiction and an actual controversy between the parties, the federal court can issue a declaration of the parties' rights under the insurance contract.

(d) Because a declaratory judgment by the federal court might expedite the state action, the federal court can issue a declaration of the parties' rights under the insurance contract.

5. A protester is injured by a police officer after a protest march through town. The protester files a federal civil rights action against the officer. Ten days after the action is filed, the officer serves on the protester an offer of judgment to allow the protester to take judgment against the officer in the amount of $5000. The protester does not accept the offer of judgment, and, 30 days later, the officer serves on the protester another offer of judgment, this time for $7000. This offer also is not accepted by the protester, and after the completion of discovery, a third offer of judgment is served by the officer on the protester in the amount of $15,000.

The protester does not respond to this third offer of judgment, and trial begins 20 days later. After trial the jury returns a verdict for $12,000.

Review Section VI(C) and choose the best answer from the following choices:

(a) Because the officer has served three separate offers of judgment, the protester can recover his full costs and attorneys' fees for the entire action.

(b) Because the protester did not recover more than the third offer of judgment, the protester can recover none of his costs and attorneys' fees in this action.

(c) Because the protester did not recover more than the third offer of judgment, the protester can recover none of his costs and attorneys' fees incurred after the third offer was made.

(d) Because the protester did not recover more than the third offer of judgment, the protester can recover none of his costs and attorney's fees incurred after the third offer was made and also must pay the officer's attorneys' fees incurred after the third offer.

B. Essay Questions. To test your understanding of this chapter's material, outline or write an answer to the following questions.

1. Stop the Presses!

Media watchdog organization No Secrets obtains classified information concerning United States counterintelligence efforts, including the identities of over 50 individual around the world who have been paid to gather intelligence for the United States. The group initially attempts to confirm the authenticity of the information and translate it from several other languages into English.

Within one hour of learning about this apparent theft of intelligence data, the United States files a civil action asking a federal district court to order the return of the data to the United States and forbid No Secrets from sharing, publishing, or disseminating the information.

(a) Can the United States obtain such injunctive relief without providing notice to No Secrets? If so, what must it show to obtain such a retraining order? What would be the contours of the relief that it might obtain in such a situation?

(b) If a temporary retraining order is granted without notice to No Secrets, what must the United States show in order to obtain a preliminary injunction? Is it likely to be able to make such a showing?

(c) How is the district court likely to craft any permanent injunction that it might issue to prevent the sharing, publishing, or disseminating of this information?

See New York Times Co. v. United States, 403 U.S. 713 (1971) (per curiam) (Pentagon Papers litigation).

2. "A Reasonable Attorney's Fee as Part of the Costs."[9]

After other attorneys refuse to take the case, Audrey Attorney agrees to represent the parents of several girls who allege that their daughters have been discriminated against with respect to the high school basketball team. While the state champion boys practice and play in the "big gym," the girls practice and play in an older, smaller gym in a building near the high school where the big gym is located.

The school board vigorously contests the federal administrative complaint and federal civil rights action filed by Attorney. Attorney, who has never filed a federal civil rights action before, must devote a great percentage of her practice time to this action, having to turn down several potential clients. She also attends several continuing legal education programs to come up to speed on the relevant law.

After two years the action reaches trial, which results in an injunction requiring the school district to provide the same support and opportunities to the girls' basketball team as provided to the boys' basketball team. Attorney expended 2500 hours in the underlying administrative and judicial proceedings to secure this judgment.

Attorney's representation contract with the parents provides that they will pay $125 per hour, which is one-half of the rate Attorney normally charges her commercial clients. Because the action is subject to 42 U.S.C. § 1988, the Civil Rights Attorney's Fees Awards Act of 1976, Attorney plans to ask the district court to award her fees pursuant to that Act.

---

[9]   42 U.S.C. § 1988.

(a) What method would you use to calculate the hourly rate that the court should apply?

(b) For what number of hours should the court permit Attorney to receive payment?

(c) Should the district court enhance or reduce the fees to be awarded in this action for any reason? If so, for what reasons and by how much?

(d) What additional facts would you like to know to either support or oppose Attorney's fee application to the court?

CHAPTER 9

RESPONSES TO THE COMPLAINT: "HOW DO WE RESPOND TO THIS?"

I. INTRODUCTION

Until now, we have focused on the decisions made by the plaintiff and his counsel in advancing his claims—whether to file the action in state or federal court, how to draft the complaint, and how to satisfy prerequisites to suit such as subject-matter jurisdiction, personal jurisdiction, and venue. This chapter addresses the options that the defendant and defense counsel have in responding to the complaint and the civil action initiated by the plaintiff.

Initially, the chapter describes the defenses available to the defendant under Rule 12 of the Federal Rules of Civil Procedure. The chapter then discusses the manner in which those defenses can be asserted in a Rule 12 preanswer motion or in the answer. Finally, the chapter considers the defendant's ability to file additional claims, such as counterclaims, cross-claims, and third-party claims.

II. THE POSSIBLE DEFENSES

There are many possible responses that a defendant might make to a civil action. Those defenses are set forth in Rule 12 of the Federal Rules of Civil Procedure. Once the lawyer has identified the defenses that are appropriate in a particular civil action, she must decide whether to assert those defenses in a preanswer motion or in the defendant's answer to the complaint. For now, though, let's consider the potential defenses.

A. RULE 12(b) DEFENSES TO THE ACTION

Turn back to Section II(B) of Chapter 1, in which the Rule 12 prerequisites to suit are discussed. These potential defenses include:

- **Subject-Matter Jurisdiction (Rule 12(b)(1)).** Does the federal court have subject-matter jurisdiction, or judicial power, to hear the civil action? Not only must the judicial power set forth in Article III of the Constitution encompass the civil action in question, but Congress must have enacted a statute to authorize the exercise of that judicial power in such an action. As you know from Chapter 3, the great majority of federal civil actions are federal-question actions under 28 U.S.C. § 1331 or diversity actions under 28 U.S.C. § 1332.

- **Personal Jurisdiction (Rule 12(b)(2)).** In addition to federal subject-matter jurisdiction, the district court also must have personal or territorial jurisdiction over the action. This requires both that a statute or rule (such as Federal Rule of Civil Procedure 4(e), (f), or (k)) authorizes personal jurisdiction over the defendants and that the exercise of such jurisdiction is constitutional under the Due Process Clause of the Fifth or Fourteenth Amendments to the United States Constitution.

- **Venue (Rule 12(b)(3)).** Venue rules or statutes such as 28 U.S.C. § 1391 allocate civil actions to specific districts within a judicial system. Even when both subject-matter and personal jurisdiction exist in several United States District Courts, federal venue statutes or the parties' contract may further limit the federal courts that can hear the action.

- **Process (Rule 12(b)(4)).** Judicial process consists of the plaintiff's complaint and the summons that is directed to each defendant to notify that defendant that it has been named as a defendant in a federal civil action. Federal Rule of Civil Procedure 4(a) and (b) specify the process that must be used to bring individual defendants into a federal civil action.

- **Service of Process (Rule 12(b)(5)).** Not only must the summons and complaint (which constitute civil process) be properly prepared, but that process must be properly served upon each defendant. Federal Rule of Civil Procedure 4(c) and (e)–(j) specify the manner in which process must be served or delivered to each type of defendant. In order to save the time and money necessitated by formal service of process, Rule 4(d) permits a defendant to waive formal service of process and accept less formal notice that it has been sued and of the claims that have been brought against it.

- **Joinder of Required Parties Under Rule 19 (Rule 12(b)(7)).** As we saw in Chapter 6, Rule 19 of the Federal Rules of Civil Procedure may require that an action be dismissed if it is not possible to join a required party indispensable to the resolution of the civil action. Rule 12(b)(7) provides the procedural route for dismissing such actions.

- **Statement of a Claim upon Which Relief Can Be Granted (Rule 12(b)(6)).** Apart from the procedural requirements of Rule 12(b)(1)–(5) and (7), Rule 12(b)(6) provides that a federal civil action can be dismissed if the complaint fails to "state a claim upon which relief can be granted." The best pled civil action will be for naught, if the complaint does not set forth a valid claim under the law of torts, contracts, property, or other substantive law upon which that claim is premised. If, taking all of the factual allegations of the complaint to be true, those allegations do not make out a valid claim for relief, the civil action can be dismissed prior to trial under Rule 12(b)(6) of the Federal Rules of Civil Procedure. Rule 12(b)(6) recognizes a "So what?" defense that may lead to the early dismissal of a civil action. By asserting this defense, the defendant (or plaintiff seeking the dismissal of a counterclaim) is asserting, in effect: "So what if all you allege is true? It still doesn't make out a sufficient legal claim against me!"

B. ADDITIONAL DEFENSES TO THE ACTION

The Rule 12(b) defenses are procedural defenses that can be asserted to gain the dismissal of a civil action at the very outset of the case. In addition to the seven defenses set forth in Rule 12(b), defense counsel should consider asserting additional defenses in every civil action. As one might imagine, a very common defense is simply that the version of the facts set forth in the complaint is not true. As we will see in our discussion of the answer, Rule 8(b) contains specific requirements concerning the manner in which such denials should be alleged.

In addition to Rule 8(b) denials or admissions, Rule 8(c) authorizes the defendant to set forth various affirmative defenses. Take a moment to look at the list of affirmative defenses set forth in Rule 8(c). You will be familiar with some of these affirmative defenses already from your torts and contracts classes, for they include such common defenses as assumption of risk, contributory negligence, fraud, release, and statute of limitations. Think of these Rule 8(c) affirmative defenses as "Yes, but . . ." defenses: "Yes, you've alleged I have done certain things, but I am not liable to you for an independent reason." Thus if, for example, the plaintiff properly pleads a good tort claim against the defendant, the defendant may nevertheless not be liable to the plaintiff because the plaintiff himself engaged in contributory negligence or allowed the statute of limitations to run before filing his lawsuit. Rule 8(c)(1) refers to an "avoidance or affirmative defense," and the word "avoidance" gives a good sense of the practical effect of affirmative defenses.

There also may be specific requirements that must be satisfied prior to the filing of specific types of claims. For instance, an administrative complaint must be filed before commencing certain types of discrimination actions or actions challenging governmental action. In addition, each of the United States District Courts has adopted local rules of court pursuant to Federal Rule of Civil Procedure 83(a) that must be "consistent with—but not duplicate" federal statutes and the Federal Rules of Civil Procedure. Such rules may specify, for instance, the precise format for all documents filed with that particular federal court.

Once all of the relevant defenses have been identified, defense counsel must decide whether to assert those defenses in (1) a preanswer motion or (2) in the defendant's answer. These two responses to the complaint are considered in the following two sections.

III. PREANSWER MOTIONS

In determining whether to assert defenses in a preanswer motion or in the answer to the complaint, counsel should act consistently with her overall litigation strategy. Rule 11(b) extends the requirements of Rule 11 to every "pleading, written motion, or other paper," and Rule 11(b)(4) states that, by presenting an answer to the court, defense counsel certifies that "the denials of factual contentions are warranted on the evidence or, if specifically so identified, are reasonably based on belief or a lack of information." This section of the chapter considers the assertion of threshold defenses in a motion filed before the defendant's answer, while the next section considers the filing of an answer.

A. THE RULE 12(b) MOTION TO DISMISS

Looking at Rule 12(b), you'll see that it not only lists seven threshold defenses, but also prescribes how to present those defenses in a civil action. Initially, Rule 12(b) states, "Every defense to a claim for relief in any pleading must be asserted in the responsive pleading if one is required." Thus if a defendant has a defense to a claim set forth in the complaint, the defendant must assert that defense in its answer (which is the Rule 7(a) pleading that is responsive to the complaint).

However, Rule 12(b) also states that a party may assert the Rule 12(b)(1)–(7) defenses in a motion "made before pleading if a responsive pleading is allowed." Rule 7(a) sets forth the responsive pleadings that are allowed. These include an answer to a complaint, to a counterclaim "designated as a counterclaim," to a crossclaim, to a third-party complaint, and, "if the court orders one, a reply to an answer." The overwhelming majority of responsive pleadings are answers to the complaint.

Rule 12(b) states that the 12(b)(1)–(7) defenses "may" be asserted by a motion "made before pleading if a responsive pleading is allowed." Why would defense counsel file a Rule 12(b) motion to dismiss including one or more of the Rule 12(b) defenses before filing an answer? If the motion to dismiss is successful, the court will dismiss the claim in question or, in many cases, the entire civil action. Particularly if the relevant facts are not in dispute, a Rule 12(b) motion to dismiss may provide a good way to test the legal sufficiency of the complaint and, hopefully, lead to the dismissal of at least some of the plaintiff's claims. Thus defendants assert the Rule 12(b) defenses in a preanswer motion in most cases.[1]

Prior to its abrogation in 2015, the Federal Rules of Civil Procedure contained an Appendix of Forms with illustrative forms relevant to the Rules. Form 40 of these Forms, which follows, illustrates the typical simplicity of a motion to dismiss.

United States District Court

for the

<_____> DISTRICT OF <_____>

\<Name(s) of plaintiff(s)>,	)
Plaintiff(s)	)
v.	)
\<Name(s) of defendant(s)>,	) Civil Action No. \<Number>
Defendant(s)	)

MOTION TO DISMISS UNDER RULE 12(b) FOR LACK OF JURISDICTION, IMPROPER VENUE, INSUFFICIENT SERVICE OF PROCESS, OR FAILURE TO STATE A CLAIM

The defendant moves to dismiss the action because:

1.   the amount in controversy is less than the sum or value specified by 28 U.S.C. § 1332;

2.   the defendant is not subject to the personal jurisdiction of this court;

3.   venue is improper (this defendant does not reside in this district and no part of the events or omissions giving rise to the claim occurred in the district);

4.   the defendant has not been properly served, as shown by the attached affidavits of <_____>; or

5.   the complaint fails to state a claim upon which relief can be granted.

---

[1]   Counsel should realize, though, that Rule 15(a)(1)(B) gives the plaintiff the right to amend its complaint "as a matter of course within * * * 21 days after service of a motion under Rule 12(b), (e), or (f)." So, if the plaintiff, consistent with Rule 11, can amend the complaint to address the issues raised in the motion to dismiss, plaintiff will have the right to do so (in an attempt to avoid dismissal of the action).

Date: <Date>   <Signature   of   the   attorney   or
                                unrepresented party>

_____

<Printed name>

<Address>

<E-mail address>

<Telephone number>

_____

Rule 5(a)(1)(D) provides that the motion to dismiss must be served on every party to the civil action, which Rule 5(b) provides is typically accomplished by sending the pleading by mail or electronically to each party's attorney. Rule 5(d)(1) additionally requires that the motion be filed with the court, accompanied by a certificate from the moving party's attorney that the motion has been served on the other parties.

In considering a Rule 12(b) motion to dismiss, the allegations of the complaint are to be construed in favor of the party opposing dismissal. As the leading civil procedure treatise has said about a Rule 12(b)(6) motion to dismiss for failure to state a claim upon which relief can be granted, "(1) the complaint is construed in the light most favorable to the plaintiff, (2) its allegations are taken as true, and (3) all reasonable inferences that can be drawn from the pleading are drawn in favor of the pleader." 5B C. Wright & A. Miller, *Federal Practice and Procedure* § 1357, at 417 (3rd ed. 2004). However, under the factual plausibility standard recognized in *Bell Atlantic Corp. v. Twombly*, the facts asserted must "be enough to raise a right to relief above the speculative level." 550 U.S. 544, 555 (2007).

In ruling on a Rule 12(b) motion to dismiss or a Rule 12(c) motion for judgment on the pleadings, the court is only to consider the complaint (if the motion is to dismiss the complaint) or the complaint and the answer (if the motion is for judgment on the pleadings). However, Rule 12(d) provides: "If, on a motion under Rule 12(b)(6) or 12(c), matters outside the pleadings are presented to and not excluded by the court, the motion must be treated as one for summary judgment under Rule 56. All parties must be given a reasonable opportunity to present all the material that is pertinent to the motion." Indeed, it is possible to file a motion to dismiss or, in the alternative, for summary judgment. By such a motion dismissal is sought under Rule 12(b), but if the judge believes that factual issues preclude dismissal on such basis, he can consider the additional material submitted by the parties and treat the motion as one for summary judgment under Rule 56.

B. OTHER PREANSWER MOTIONS

In addition to the motion to dismiss pursuant to Rule 12(b), there are other preanswer motions that the defendant can make to obtain an early dismissal of the civil action. Rule 12(c) provides for a motion for judgment on the pleadings. In contrast to a 12(b)(6) motion to dismiss for failure to state a claim, either the plaintiff or the defendant can file a motion for judgment on the pleadings. In ruling upon a Rule 12(c) motion, the court is to consider as true the well-pled allegations in the pleading (complaint or answer) of the party opposing judgment.[2] This motion is infrequently filed. Rarely would an answer entitle a plaintiff to judgment on the pleadings, while the defenses raised in a motion for judgment on the pleadings are typically the same as those that would be raised in support of a defendant's Rule 12(b)(6) motion to dismiss. The Rule 12(c) motion, though, may be filed in situations in which the defendant was unable to prepare a motion to dismiss before the time for the filing of defendant's answer.

Rule 12(e) provides for a motion for a more definite statement. This motion, too, must be filed before the answer, and Rule 12(e) provides that it should be filed in response to a pleading (typically, the complaint) that is "so vague or ambiguous that the party cannot reasonably prepare a response." This motion is rarely filed, because the party opposing a vague or ambiguous pleading usually can get clarification concerning that pleading through the discovery process.

Finally, the Rule 12(f) motion to strike permits any party to ask the court to "strike from a pleading an insufficient defense or any redundant, immaterial, impertinent, or scandalous matter." While rarely filed, this motion can be useful to a plaintiff seeking an early judicial determination as to the sufficiency of specific defenses in the answer. As for moving to strike "redundant, immaterial, impertinent, or scandalous matter," this material typically reflects poorly on the party making such allegations, and lawyers may not bother with a Rule 12(f) motion to strike (or, if appropriate, they may file a Rule 12 motion to dismiss the entire complaint).

While Rule 12 sets forth the most common preanswer motions, there are other motions that the defendant may file that are not restricted to the preanswer stage of litigation. For instance, prior to filing the answer counsel might file a motion to transfer the action to another district court, a motion to remove an action from state to federal court or to remand a removed action back to state court, or a motion to stay discovery pending a ruling on another preanswer motion. These are motions that usually can be filed even after the answer is filed.

---

[2] *Nat'l Metropolitan Bank v. United States*, 323 U.S. 454, 456–57 (1945); *Beal v. Missouri Pacific R.R. Corp.*, 312 U.S. 45, 51 (1941).

C. CONSOLIDATION AND WAIVER OF RULE 12(b) DEFENSES

The final sentence of Rule 12(b) provides: "No defense or objection is waived by joining it with one or more other defenses or objections in a responsive pleading or in a motion." In addition, Rule 12(g)(1) provides that a "motion under this rule may be joined with any other motion allowed by this rule." Thus a defendant can file a preanswer motion to dismiss because of lack of subject-matter jurisdiction (Rule 12(b)(1)), personal jurisdiction (Rule 12(b)(2)), and insufficient service of process (Rule 12(b)(5)).

Not only does Rule 12 permit the consolidation of Rule 12(b) defenses, but Rule 12(g)(2) states: "Except as provided in Rule 12(h)(2) or (3), a party that makes a motion under this rule must not make another motion under this rule raising a defense or objection that was available to the party but omitted from its earlier motion." So, not only **may** Rule 12 defenses be consolidated in a single preanswer motion, but if a preanswer motion is filed, that single motion **must** contain certain Rule 12 defenses or they will be considered waived.

Rule 12(h) categorizes the Rule 12(b) defenses as to the circumstances under which they will be considered waived. Certain Rule 12(b) defenses are treated as personal to the plaintiff and therefore are rather easily waived. These defenses are lack of personal jurisdiction (Rule 12(b)(2)), improper venue (Rule 12(b)(3)), insufficient process (Rule 12(b)(4)), and insufficient service of process (Rule 12(b)(5)). Rule 12(h)(1) provides that any of these personal defenses will be considered waived by:

(A) omitting it from a motion in the circumstances described in Rule 12(g)(2); or

(B) failing to either:

(i)   make it by motion under this rule; or

(ii) include it in a responsive pleading or in an amendment allowed by Rule 15(a)(1) as a matter of course.

So each of these four defenses can be waived in either of two ways: (A) if a Rule 12 motion is actually made but does not include that defense or (B) if the defense is not raised in a preanswer motion or in the answer to the complaint.

Rule 12(h)(2) gives a higher level of protection to three other Rule 12 defenses by providing:

Failure to state a claim upon which relief can be granted, to join a person required by Rule 19(b), or to state a legal defense to a claim may be raised:

(A) in any pleading allowed or ordered under Rule 7(a);

(B) by a motion under Rule 12(c); or

(C) at trial.

Thus these three defenses can not only be raised prior to trial, but can be raised for the first time at the trial itself.

Finally, Rule 12(h)(3) gives a very special status to the defense of lack of subject-matter jurisdiction. The court cannot entertain an action if it does not have subject-matter jurisdiction over that action. Rule 12(h)(3) therefore states: "If the court determines at any time that it lacks subject-matter jurisdiction, the court must dismiss the action."

The circumstances under which Rule 12(b) defenses are waived are set forth in Figure 9–1.

FIGURE 9–1
WAIVER OF RULE 12(b) DEFENSES

Defense	Subject-Matter Jurisdiction	Personal Jurisdiction	Venue	Insufficiency of Process or Service of Process	Failure to State a Claim	Failure to Join an Indispensable Party
Rule 12 Provision	12(b)(1)	12(b)(2)	12(b)(3)	12(b)(4)–(5)	12(b)(6)	12(b)(7)
Rule 12(h)(1)		Defense Waived if Omitted from Answer or Rule 12 Motion.	Defense Waived if Omitted from Answer or Rule 12 Motion.	Defense Waived if Omitted from Answer or Rule 12 Motion.		
Rule 12(h)(2)					Defense Can be Raised up to Time of Trial.	Defense Can be Raised up to Time of Trial.
Rule 12(h)(3)	Defense Never Waived.					

IV. THE ANSWER

Typically the defendant's best defenses are presented to the court in a motion to dismiss. The hope, and plan, is that the court will grant such a motion and dismiss the action. However, what if the motion is not granted? Or what if a motion to dismiss is not filed? In that event the defendant is required to file an answer to the plaintiff's complaint.

A. TIME TO SERVE THE ANSWER

Rule 12(a)(1) sets the time to serve a responsive pleading, such as an answer to the complaint. This Rule provides that most defendants must serve their answers "within 21 days after being served with the summons and complaint." Rule 12(a)(2) and (3), though, allow 60 days after service for the response of the United States and its agencies, officers, or employees.

However, Rule 4(d) permits defendants who are competent adults, corporations or associations to waive service of process by an individual and agree to simply receive notice of the action and the complaint "by first-class mail or other reliable means." In return for waiving formal service of process, Rule 12(a)(1)(A)(ii) provides that the time to respond to the complaint is extended to "60 days after the request for a waiver was sent, or * * * 90 days after it was sent to the defendant outside any judicial district of the United States."

So, if no preanswer motion is filed, the defendant must file its answer:

- 21 days after service (if it does not waive formal service);
- 60 days after service (if the defendant is the United States or its agency, officer, or employee);
- 60 days after a request to waive service (if the defendant waives formal service); or
- 90 days (if the defendant has waived service and was served outside the United States).

If a motion to dismiss is filed and denied, Rule 12(a)(4)(A) states that, unless the court sets a different time, the answer "must be served within 14 days after notice of the court's action."

B. DENIALS AND AFFIRMATIVE DEFENSES

While Rule 12(a) establishes the time by which the answer must be filed, Rule 8(b) includes specific directives as to just how the answer should be pled. One of the major purposes of pleading rules is to narrow the differences between the parties and focus them and the court on the areas of factual and legal controversy. Rule 8(b) contains several requirements intended to further this purpose by requiring the defendant to respond in its answer to the specific allegations of the complaint.

Rule 8(b)(1) provides that, in "responding to a pleading, a party must:

(A) state in short and plain terms its defenses to each claim asserted against it; and

(B) admit or deny the allegations asserted against it by an opposing party."

The consequence for not responding to each of the allegations of the complaint is set forth in Rule 8(b)(6), which provides: "An allegation— other than one relating to the amount of damages—is admitted if a responsive pleading is required and the allegation is not denied."

But what if a party does not have sufficient information to admit or deny the allegations made against it by another party? Rule 8(b)(5) addresses this fairly common situation, providing: "A party that lacks knowledge or information sufficient to form a belief about the truth of an allegation must so state, and the statement has the effect of a denial."

An example of a Rule 8(b)(5) response is provided in paragraph 8 of PepsiCo's answer in *Leonard v. PepsiCo, Inc.*:

> 8. Defendant is without information sufficient to form a belief as to the truth of the allegations in paragraph 8 of the Complaint, except that defendant denies that the commercial plaintiff saw was broadcast in the state of Florida.

¶ 8 of Answer in *Leonard v. PepsiCo, Inc.*, No. 96 Civ. 9069 (KMW) (March 8, 1999). While PepsiCo did not have information sufficient to admit or deny the rest of plaintiff's allegations, it did specifically deny the portion of plaintiff's allegations that it believed to be false (presumably based on knowledge that the television commercial was not broadcast in Florida).

Rule 8(b) also contains three additional requirements concerning the denials in the answer.

> Rule 8(b)(2) provides: "A denial must fairly respond to the substance of the allegation."

> Rule 8(b)(3) provides: "A party that intends in good faith to deny all the allegations of a pleading—including the jurisdictional grounds—may do so by a general denial. A party that does not intend to deny all the allegations must either specifically deny designated allegations or generally deny all except those specifically admitted."

> Rule 8(b)(4) provides: "A party that intends in good faith to deny only part of an allegation must admit the part that is true and deny the rest."

Not only must the defendant in its answer address the allegations of the complaint quite specifically, but Rule 8(c) requires that the defendant include in its answer any "avoidance or affirmative defense" that the defendant intends to assert in the action.[3] Rule 8(c) provides that "a party must affirmatively state any avoidance or affirmative defense" such as contributory negligence, fraud, release, statute of frauds, or statute of limitations in a responsive pleading (such as the answer). If the affirmative defense is initially omitted from the answer, it may be possible to amend the answer as a matter of course pursuant to Rule 15(a) or with the opposing party's written consent pursuant to

---

[3] Affirmative **defenses** are asserted to defeat the claims asserted against a defendant in the complaint. As you will see in the next section of this chapter, the defendant also may be able, or required, to assert affirmative **claims** of its own as counterclaims, crossclaims, or third-party claims that seek relief from other parties to the action.

Rule 15(b). As with the amendment of complaints and other pleadings, in considering whether to grant a motion to amend the answer Rule 15(a)(2) provides that the court "should freely give leave [to amend] when justice so requires."

While Rule 8(c) does not specify the consequence for failure to include an affirmative defense in the answer (at the time of its filing or through later amendment), "It is a frequently stated proposition of virtually universal acceptance by the federal courts that a failure to plead an affirmative defense as required by Federal Rule 8(c) results in the waiver of that defense and its exclusion from the case." 5A. C. Wright & A. Miller, *Federal Practice and Procedure* § 1278, at 644–45 (3d ed. 2004). Consider the consequences of the defendant's assertion of only general denials and failure to include an affirmative defense in its answer in the following case.

Leleck v. Triple G Express, Inc.

United States District Court, E.D. Louisiana., 2002
2002 WL 441337

OPINION

■ PORTEOUS, DISTRICT J.

Before the Court is a Motion for Summary Judgment filed on behalf of the defendants, Triple G Express, Inc. and Select Insurance Company. The parties waived oral argument and the matter was taken under submission. The Court, having considered the arguments of the parties, the Court record, the law and applicable jurisprudence, is fully advised in the premises and ready to rule.

ORDER AND REASONS

I. BACKGROUND:

On or about September 3, 1998, the plaintiff, Mark Leleck, was traveling north on Interstate 59 in St. Tammany Parish when his vehicle left the highway and struck a bridge piling causing the alleged injuries forming the basis of this lawsuit. The plaintiffs allege that a tractor-trailer driven by Curtis Downs crossed the center line into Mark Leleck's lane of travel, causing Leleck to run-off of the road and collide with the bridge piling.

As a result of this accident, suit was filed by the plaintiffs on May 21, 1999 against Triple G Express, Inc. ("Triple G") alleging that Triple G is vicariously liable for Curtis Downs' alleged torts based on the theory of *respondeat superior*.

II. LEGAL ANALYSIS:

A. Law on Summary Judgment

The Federal Rules of Civil Procedure provide that summary judgment should be granted only "if the pleadings, depositions, answers to interrogatories, and admissions on file, together with the affidavits, if any, show that there is no genuine issue as to any material fact and that the moving party is entitled to a judgment as a matter of law." FED. R. CIV. P. 56(c). The party moving for summary judgment bears the initial responsibility of informing the district court of the basis for its motion, and identifying those portions of the record which it believes demonstrate the absence of a genuine issue of material fact. When the moving party has carried its burden under Rule 56(c), its opponent must do more than simply show that there is some metaphysical doubt as to the material facts. The nonmoving party must come forward with "specific facts showing that there is a *genuine issue for trial.*" *Matsushita Elec. Indus. Co. v. Zenith Radio Corp.,* 475 U.S. 574, 587 (1986) (emphasis supplied).

Thus, where the record taken as a whole could not lead a rational trier of fact to find for the nonmoving party, there is no "genuine issue for trial." *Matsushita Elec. Indus. Co.,* 475 U.S. at 588. Finally, the Court notes that substantive law determines the materiality of facts and only "facts that might affect the outcome of the suit under the governing law will properly preclude the entry of summary judgment." *Anderson v. Liberty Lobby, Inc.,* 477 U.S. 242, 248 (1986).

B.   The Defendants are Estopped from Denying Agency.

The defendants base their motion on the allegation that there was no employer/employee relationship between Triple G and the driver of the vehicle in the alleged accident, Curtis Downs. The defendants argue that if there was no employer/employee relationship, than Triple G cannot be vicariously liable under a theory of *respondeat superior.* In support of this argument, the defendants cite and explain Interstate Commerce Commission regulations and numerous cases that have determined whether an employer/employee relationship exists. However, the defendants are raising this defense of lack of agency or of a master-servant relationship for the first time in this Court through this motion.

This suit was filed on May 21, 1999. In their answer to this suit, the defendants asserted general denials and did not assert any affirmative defenses regarding the status or relationship of the parties. On October 12, 1999, Triple G, in its Answers to Interrogatories, specifically admitted that "Triple G Express, Inc. employed Curtis Downs at the time of the alleged incident in question of this litigation." In addition, in response to plaintiffs' Interrogatory No. 6 "Was your employee/driver acting in the course and scope of your business or employment at the time of the accident; . . . ," Triple G answered: "Yes. Triple G Express, Inc. was the contract employer of Curtis Downs at the time of the accident. . . ."

On June 22, 2001, more than two years after the filing of the lawsuit, the defendants attempted to amend and supplement their answers to interrogatories. These attempted amended and supplemental answers deny liability for this matter on behalf of the defendants because the answers allege that Curtis Downs was an independent contractor and not an employee. However, the defendants cannot avoid liability through amending answers to interrogatories over one and a half years later.

This case is analogous to *Zielinski v. Philadelphia Piers, Inc.,* 139 F.Supp. 408 (E.D.Pa.1956). The plaintiff in *Zielinski* was injured when the fork lift that he was driving collided with another fork lift. The plaintiff sued the company that he believed employed the driver of the fork lift with which he collided. Through the answer to the complaint and answers to the interrogatories, the defendant admitted that the employee involved in the collision was in fact their employee. More than four years after the accident, the defendant filed a summary judgment alleging that, through newly discovered facts, the evidence showed that the employee in question was not their employee, and therefore they could not be vicariously liable for his actions. The Court did not allow the defendant to make this argument because the statute of limitations had run, and a suit against another party was time-barred. In its reasoning, the Court stated:

> [T]he plaintiff through the careless pleading, if it was careless pleading, of the defendant was deprived of a chance to recover for the serious injuries he had suffered. There is reason for requiring from a defendant, in such a case as this, a prompt and certain statement of the relation to the individual whose negligence causes injury to a plaintiff. The employment of such a person, his, and his immediate employer's relation to the work in question, are matters nearly always unknown to the injured person. Whether the immediate actor is working on his own account, or is agent for a third person, and who that third person is, and also the latter's relations to the work, depend so often upon private contracts that the injured party is at a loss to know who, in fact, is at fault.

> Under the circumstances of this case, principles of equity require that the defendant be estopped from denying agency because, otherwise, its inaccurate statements and statements in the record, which it knew (or had the means of knowing within its control) were inaccurate, will have deprived plaintiff of his right of action.

Zielinski at 413. (Footnotes Omitted.)

As in *Zielinski,* if a summary judgment in favor of the defendants was entered in this matter, the plaintiffs would be unable to file suit against another party because it would be time-barred. Therefore, principles of equity require that the defendants be estopped from denying agency.

In addition to their response to the Motion for Summary Judgment filed by the defendants, the plaintiffs filed a Motion for Summary Judgment requesting that this Court find that Triple G is in fact vicariously liable for the actions of Curtis Downs. In a memorandum entitled Opposition to Plaintiffs' Motion for Summary Judgment and Reply Memorandum in Support of Defendants Motion for Summary Judgment, the defendants failed to address the argument that they are estopped from denying vicarious liability because they have previously admitted to the fact the Curtis Downs was their employee. Instead, the defendants further argue the Interstate Commerce Commission regulations and the cases which interpret employer/employee relationships. Based on the above referenced cases and the pleadings submitted by the parties, the Court GRANTS the Motion for Summary Judgment filed by the plaintiffs and DENIES the Motion for Summary Judgment filed by the defendants. The defendants are estopped from denying an employer/employee relationship between Curtis Downs and Triple G because it was previously admitted as fact and remained fact until after the time limitations had run.

COMMENTS AND QUESTIONS CONCERNING
LELECK V. TRIPLE G EXPRESS, INC.

1.   The defendants offered regulations and other authorities to establish that Curtis Downs was not their employee or agent. Why did the court conclude that defendants nevertheless were estopped from denying agency?

2.   Why does Rule 8(c)(1) require that in "responding to a pleading, a party must affirmatively state any avoidance or affirmative defense"? Would lack of agency have been an affirmative defense in this action?

3.   The portion of the opinion in *Zielinski v. Philadelphia Piers, Inc.* quoted in *Leleck* refers to "careless pleading" by the defendant in *Zielinski*. Paragraph 5 of Zielinkski's complaint stated that "a motor-driven vehicle known as a fork lift or chisel, owned, operated and controlled by the defendant, its agents, servants and employees, was so negligently and carelessly managed * * * that the same * * * did come into contact with the plaintiff causing him to sustain the injuries more fully hereinafter set forth." The defendant's answer stated that "Defendant * * * denies the averments of paragraph 5 * * *." 139 F. Supp. at 409.

Why did the court in *Zielinkski* hold this to be an ineffective denial?

4.   In neither *Zielinski* nor *Leleck* did the defendant include an affirmative defense denying agency in its answer. In which case was the defendant's pleading more misleading? What other factors should the court consider in deciding whether to permit the defendants to amend their answers?

5.   Compare the result in *Leleck* with the decision in *Beeck v. Aquaslide*, 562 F.2d 537 (8th Cir. 1977), that you read in Chapter 2's discussion of amendment of the pleadings, *supra* p. 105. The *Beeck* Court of

Appeals affirmed a district court order permitting the defendant to amend its answer, filed within the statute of limitations period, to deny manufacture of the allegedly defective product after the statute of limitations had run.

6.   Does the "plausibility" pleading requirement of *Twombly* and *Iqbal*, *supra* pp. 77–93, apply to affirmative defenses? *See* Janssen, "The Odd State of *Twiqbal* Plausibility in Pleading Affirmative Defenses," 70 *Wash. & Lee L.Rev.* 1573 (2013). *Compare* Pelikan, Note, "Plausible Defenses: Historical, Plain Meaning, and Public Policy Arguments for Applying *Iqbal* and *Twombly* to Affirmative Defenses," 96 *Minn. L. Rev.* 1828, 1855 (2012), *with* Gambol, Note, "The *Twombly* Standard and Affirmative Defenses: What Is Good for the Goose Is Not Always Good for the Gander," 79 *Fordham L. Rev.* 2173, 2174 (2011).

C. THE ANSWER IN *LEONARD V. PEPSICO*

As an example of an answer in a federal civil action, consider the answer filed by PepsiCo in response to John Leonard's complaint in the United States District Court for the Southern District of New York. Note both the focus of the answer's responses on the specific allegations of Leonard's complaint and PepsiCo's assertion of a series of affirmative defenses to Leonard's claims.

**John D.R. Leonard, Plaintiff v.
Pepsico, Inc., Defendant**

No. 96–Civ–9069 (KMW)
March 1, 1999

Answer

Defendant PepsiCo, Inc. ("PepsiCo"), hereby answers the allegations in the Complaint filed by plaintiff, John D.R. Leonard ("Leonard"), as follows:

Jurisdiction and Venue

1.   Defendant admits the allegations in paragraph 1 of the Complaint.

2.   Defendant admits Leonard is a resident of Seattle[,] Washington. Defendant is without sufficient knowledge to form a belief as the remaining allegations in paragraph 2 of the Complaint.

3.   Defendant denies that it is doing business in the State of Florida and admits the remaining allegations in paragraph 3 of the Complaint.

Factual Allegations

4.   Defendant admits it is a corporation engaged in the business of producing and distributing soft drinks worldwide, but denies that it is "primarily engaged" in that business. Defendant denies the second sentence of paragraph 4 of the Complaint.

5. Defendant admits that its "Pepsi Stuff" advertising campaign involves the exchange of "Pepsi Points" for merchandise, but denies the remaining allegations in paragraph 5 of the Complaint.

6. Defendant admits the allegations in the first three sentences of paragraph 6 of the Complaint[.] Defendant denies the allegations in the last sentence of paragraph 6 of the Complaint.

7. Defendant denies the allegations in paragraph 7 of the Complaint.

8. Defendant is without information sufficient to form a belief as to the truth of the allegations in paragraph 8 of the Complaint, except that defendant denies that the commercial plaintiff saw was broadcast in the state of Florida.

9. Defendant denies the allegations in paragraph 9 of the Complaint.

10. Defendant denies the allegations in the [first] sentence of paragraph 10 of the Complaint. Defendant is without information sufficient to form a belief as to the truth of the allegations in the last sentence of paragraph 10 of the Complaint.

11. Defendant admits the allegations in paragraph 11 of the Complaint except that defendant denies that there was anything "surprising . . ." about its refusal to process plaintiff's request for a Harrier jet.

12. Defendant admits the allegations in paragraph 12 of the Complaint.

* * *

Count I

17. Defendant hereby incorporates by reference paragraphs 1–16 herein.

18. Defendant denies the allegations in paragraph 18 of the Complaint.

* * *

The prayer for relief after paragraph 22 is not an allegation to which an answer is required. To the extent an answer is required, Defendant denies the allegations in this paragraph.

Count II

23. Defendant hereby incorporates by reference paragraphs 1–16 herein.

24. Defendant denies the allegations in paragraph 24 of the Complaint.

25. Defendant denies the allegations in paragraph 25 of the Complaint.

26. Defendant denies the allegations in paragraph 26 of the Complaint.

27. Defendant denies the allegations in paragraph 27 of the Complaint.

The prayer for relief after paragraph 27 is not an allegation to which an answer is required. To the extent an answer is required, defendant denies the allegations in this paragraph.

* * *

Demand for Jury Trial

45. The jury demand in paragraph [45] is not an allegation to which an answer is required. To the extent an answer is required, defendant denies the allegations in this paragraph.[4]

First Affirmative Defense

46. Plaintiff's Complaint fails to state a claim upon which the requested relief could be granted.

47. The alleged "offer" of a Harrier jet was rescinded, revoked and/or cancelled before plaintiff's alleged acceptance.

* * *

Fourth Affirmative Defense

49. The alleged "contract" is illegal and therefore void.

Fifth Affirmative Defense

50. The alleged "contract" is impossible to perform and is therefore unenforceable.

* * *

Eighth Affirmative Defense

53. The alleged "contract" on which plaintiff is suing is unenforceable because it does not comply with the Statute of Frauds or U.C.C. § 2.201.

WHEREFORE, defendant requests the following relief:

(1) Plaintiff's Complaint be dismissed with prejudice and that plaintiff takes nothing by its Complaint;

(2) Judgment be entered in favor of defendant and against plaintiff for all claims set forth in the Complaint;

(3) Defendant be awarded its costs of this suit and reasonable attorney's fees and expenses; and

(4) Defendant be granted such other and further relief as this Court may deem just and proper under the circumstances.

[Attorney Signature Lines]

V. COUNTERCLAIMS, CROSSCLAIMS AND THIRD-PARTY CLAIMS

The defendant must respond to the complaint by way of a preanswer motion or answer. However, the defendant does not have to

---

[4]   [In the event that PepsiCo, itself, desired trial by jury on any of the parties' claims, Rule 38(b) would have permitted the inclusion of such a jury demand in PepsiCo's answer.]

only defend against the plaintiff's claims, but may assert affirmative claims of its own. As we'll see in this section, the defendant can assert permissive counterclaims against the plaintiff, crossclaims against any codefendants, or third-party claims against another person who may be liable to the defendant for all or part of the plaintiff's claims against the defendant. The defendant also must assert any compulsory counterclaims against the plaintiff or forfeit such claims. We will consider those claims in turn.

A. COUNTERCLAIMS, CROSSCLAIMS AND THIRD-PARTY CLAIMS UNDER THE FEDERAL RULES

In order for plaintiff to assert a claim in a civil action, there must be both authorization for that claim under the Federal Rules of Civil Procedure and constitutional and statutory authorization for the exercise of federal subject-matter jurisdiction over that claim. Rule 8(a) authorizes such claims, while subject-matter jurisdiction is typically provided by Article III of the Constitution and statutes such as 28 U.S.C. §§ 1331 or 1332.

A similar analysis is necessary concerning counterclaims, crossclaims, and third-party claims. Initially we consider what claims are authorized by the Federal Rules. Then, in the next subsection, we consider the constitutional and statutory bases for such claims. Figure 9–2 illustrates the counterclaims, crossclaims, and third-party claims that are discussed below.

FIGURE 9–2
CLAIMS IN A CIVIL ACTION

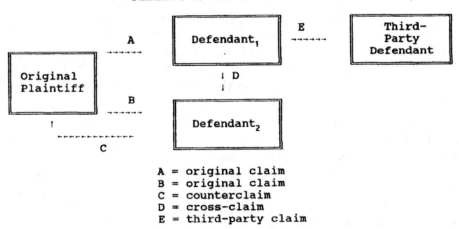

A = original claim
B = original claim
C = counterclaim
D = cross-claim
E = third-party claim

1. **Counterclaims.** Assume that, as a result of a car crash, the two drivers Able and Baker are both injured. Able, a citizen of Minnesota, brings a diversity action against Baker, a citizen of South Dakota, in federal district court. In his complaint, Able alleges $150,000 in injuries to himself and damages to his car. Baker plans to deny his

own negligence, believing that it was Able's negligence that caused the accident.

Rather than having to file a separate action against Able, Rule 13 permits Baker to bring any claim stemming from the accident as a counterclaim in the action that Able has filed. Indeed, Rule 13(a) requires Baker to bring his claim as a counterclaim in Able's action. Rule 13(a) of the Federal Rules provides for **compulsory** counterclaims, while Rule 13(b) permits the assertion of non-compulsory, or **permissive**, counterclaims.

Rule 13(a)(1) provides that, with quite limited exceptions,[5] a pleading such as the answer "must state as a counterclaim any claim that—at the time of its service—the pleader has against an opposing party if the claim:

> (A) arises out of the transaction or occurrence that is the subject matter of the opposing party's claim; and

> (B) does not require adding another party over whom the court cannot acquire jurisdiction."

In the Able-Baker action, Rule 13(a)(1) would require Baker to include in his answer his claim for damages against Able stemming from the accident. This claim must be asserted as a counterclaim because it (A) arises out of the same accident that is the subject of Able's claim against Baker and (B) does not require the addition of any other person to the action as a party over whom the court cannot acquire jurisdiction. Rule 13(h) further provides that persons other than the original parties to the action can be named in the counterclaim pursuant to the requirements of Rules 19 and 20.

Rule 13(a) compulsory counterclaims are an exception to the general rule that parties are able to choose the forum in which to assert their claims. As the Supreme Court recognized in *Baker v. Gold Seal Liquors, Inc.*, 417 U.S. 467, 469 n.1 (1974), "A counterclaim which is compulsory but is not brought is thereafter barred." In Figure 9–2, claim "C" is an example of a counterclaim.

What if Baker had a potential claim against Able that had nothing to do with the car accident that is the subject of Able's federal action? Assume, for instance, that Baker had done some work on Able's house, for which Able had never paid Baker. Rule 13(b) would permit Baker to include in his complaint a permissive counterclaim for these damages. Indeed, Rule 13(b) has no limit on the counterclaims that can be asserted in a federal action, providing that a "pleading may state as a

---

[5]   The two exceptions to the Rule 13(a)(1) compulsory counterclaim rule are set forth in Rule 13(a)(2). Claims that otherwise would have to be asserted as compulsory counterclaims need not be asserted by a defendant if (1) at the time the action was filed the defendant's claim already was the subject of another lawsuit or (2) the plaintiff sued by attachment or for other reasons has not obtained personal jurisdiction over the defendant, itself, and the defendant has not asserted any other counterclaim.

counterclaim against an opposing party any claim that is not compulsory."

There are, however, two significant caveats to Rule 13(b)'s wide-open authorization of counterclaims:

- In addition to authorization for a permissive counterclaim under Rule 13(b), federal subject-matter jurisdiction must also exist over that claim. As we'll see in Subsection B, *infra* p. 698, a federal court would not be able to consider a permissive state-law counterclaim unrelated to Able's initial claims if Baker sought no more than $75,000 on that counterclaim.

- Moreover, even if there were subject-matter jurisdiction to entertain a permissive counterclaim, the court might not try that counterclaim with plaintiff's claims, instead ordering a separate trial on the counterclaim pursuant to Rule 42(b).

Finally, whether defendant's counterclaim is compulsory or permissive, Rule 7(a)(3) includes within its list of pleadings "an answer to a counterclaim designated as a counterclaim." The defendant should be sure to explicitly designate in its answer any claim for affirmative relief as a counterclaim, so that the plaintiff will be required to file an answer to that counterclaim setting forth its responses to defendant's counterclaim allegations.

2. Crossclaims. Not only may the defendant have claims to affirmatively assert against the plaintiff, but it may have claims arising out of the subject matter of plaintiff's original claims against a coparty (in the case of a defendant, against a codefendant). Rule 13(g) authorizes crossclaims, stating:

> A pleading may state as a crossclaim any claim by one party against a coparty if the claim arises out of the transaction or occurrence that is the subject matter of the original action or of a counterclaim, or if the claim relates to any property that is the subject matter of the original action.

Assume that Able sued both Baker, the driver of the second car, and the rental company that had rented Baker the car. In its answer, the rental company might: (1) respond to the allegations of Able's complaint (denying the liability of the company to Able); (2) assert a counterclaim against Able (seeking compensation for the damages to its car); and (3) file a crossclaim against Baker, alleging that his negligence was at least partially responsible for the damage to the company's car.

In this example, the company asserts a crossclaim seeking compensation for damages that it has suffered due to Baker's actions in the accident (the subject matter of plaintiff's original action). However, the last sentence of Rule 13(g) provides that a crossclaim "may include a claim that the coparty is or may be liable to the crossclaimant for all or part of a claim asserted in the action against the crossclaimant." Thus the company can not only file a crossclaim seeking damages for its own injuries, but also can file a crossclaim asserting that, if the company is liable for Able's injuries, Baker, in turn, is liable to the company for all or part of any claim that Able successfully asserts against the company.

Claim D in Figure 9–2 illustrates a Rule 13(g) crossclaim brought by one defendant against a codefendant. In contrast to Rule 13(a) compulsory counterclaims, all Rule 13(g) crossclaims are permissive.

As later discussed in Subsection B, not only must there be authorization for a crossclaim under the Rules (in this case, Rule 13(g)), but subject-matter jurisdiction also must extend to that crossclaim. Rule 13(g), though, only authorizes crossclaims that arise "out of the transaction or occurrence that is the subject matter of the original action or of a counterclaim, or if the claim relates to any property that is the subject matter of the original action." Thus, if a crossclaim satisfies the requirements of Rule 13(g), it also should satisfy the requirements of supplemental jurisdiction under 28 U.S.C. § 1367.

Finally, as is the case with Rule 13(a) and (b) counterclaims, Rule 13(h) authorizes the naming of persons other than the original parties in the crossclaim if the requirements of Rules 19 and 20 are satisfied.

3.   Third-Party Claims. Imagine that, in the accident between Able and Baker, a pedestrian had run out in front of Baker, causing him to swerve and collide with Able. In this situation, Baker may want to implead the pedestrian as a party in the action—asserting that, if he, Baker, is liable to Able, the pedestrian then is liable to Baker for any damages for which Baker is liable to Able. Such impleader, or third-party practice, is authorized by Rule 14 of the Federal Rules of Civil Procedure. Claim E in Figure 9–2 is a third-party claim asserted by the defendant (or third-party plaintiff) against the third-party defendant.

Rule 14(a)(1) provides:

> A defending party may, as third-party plaintiff, serve a summons and complaint on a nonparty who is or may be liable to it for all or part of the claim against it. But the third-party plaintiff must, by motion, obtain the court's leave if it files the third-party complaint more than 14 days after serving its original answer.

As is the case with Rule 13(g) crossclaims, the third-party claims authorized by Rule 14(a) are permissive and "may" be brought. Thus the defendant can decide to withhold its claim against the person who may be liable to indemnify it for any damages awarded against the defendant in the original civil action. The defendant may, for instance, want to choose a different forum in which to assert that claim, rather than file its indemnity claim in the forum that the plaintiff has chosen.

On the other hand, it usually is more efficient to try related claims in a single action. In addition, the defendant may be subject to inconsistent judgments if two actions are separately litigated. In the first action, the judge or jury may conclude that the defendant was liable and order defendant to pay damages to the plaintiff. In a second action seeking indemnity, the defendant (third-party plaintiff) may lose its claim against the third-party defendant (who is not bound by the first action) due to an inconsistent factual finding. By bringing all claims into a single action through a Rule 14(a) third-party claim, such inconsistent outcomes should be avoided.

As with Rule 13(g) crossclaims, supplemental subject-matter jurisdiction under 28 U.S.C. § 1367 extends to third-party claims (which must, by definition, relate directly to the plaintiff's original claim). Also as with Rule 13(g) crossclaims, the court might try the third-party claim separately pursuant to Rule 42(b).

In contrast to counterclaims and crossclaims, which are simply included as part of the answer, Rule 14 third-party claims require the filing of a separate complaint against the third-party defendant. Form 16 of the former Appendix of Forms to the Federal Rules of Civil Procedure is illustrative of how a third-party complaint might be drafted.

UNITED STATES DISTRICT COURT

for the

<_____> DISTRICT OF <_____>

<Name(s) of plaintiff(s)>,	)
Plaintiff(s)	)
v.	)
<Name(s) of defendant(s)>,	) Civil Action No. <Number>
Defendant(s)	)
v.	)
<Name(s) of third-party defendant(s)>,	)
Third-Party Defendant(s)	

THIRD-PARTY COMPLAINT

1. Plaintiff <Name of plaintiff> has filed against defendant <Name of defendant> a complaint, a copy of which is attached.

2. <State grounds entitling (defendant's name) to recover from (third-party defendant's name) for (all or an identified share) of any judgment for (plaintiff's name) against (defendant's name).>

Therefore, the defendant demands judgment against <third-party defendant's name> for <all or an identified share> of sums that may be adjudged against the defendant in the plaintiff's favor.

Date: <Date>   <Signature   of   the   attorney   or
                                 unrepresented party>

_____

<Printed name>

<Address>

<E-mail address>

<Telephone number>

_____

Rule 14 not only authorizes third-party claims, but specifies the manner in which the third-party defendant is to respond to such claims. Rule 14(a)(2) provides that the third-party defendant is to assert its defenses pursuant to Rule 12; must assert any compulsory counterclaims against the third-party plaintiff pursuant to Rule 13(a); and may assert any permissive counterclaims pursuant to Rule 13(b) or crossclaims pursuant to Rule 13(g). Rule 14(a)(3) provides for claims by the original plaintiff against the third-party defendant (to which the defendant must assert Rule 12 defenses and Rule 13(a) compulsory counterclaims and may assert any Rule 13(b) permissive counterclaims and Rule 13(g) crossclaims). As discussed in the next section of this chapter, though, any of these claims will fail if there is no subject-matter jurisdiction to support them.

B. JURISDICTION OVER COUNTERCLAIMS, CROSSCLAIMS AND THIRD-PARTY CLAIMS

Rule 82 of the Federal Rules of Civil Procedure provides that those rules "do not extend or limit the jurisdiction of the district courts or the venue of actions in those courts." Thus not only must a claim be authorized by the Federal Rules, but there must be a constitutional and statutory basis for the exercise of subject-matter jurisdiction over that claim. See how this requirement plays out in the following cases.

1. *OWEN EQUIPMENT & ERECTION CO. V. KROGER*

As you read this case, be sure to keep track of the claims in question. As shown in Figure 9–3, the initial claim was filed by Geraldine Kroger, as administratrix of her deceased husband's estate, against the Omaha Public Power District (Claim #1). In response to this claim, the Power District filed a Rule 14(a) third-party claim against Owen Equipment & Erection Company (Claim #2). Once Owen was a party to the action, Kroger filed her own claim against Owen (Claim

#3). Then the fun began, leading to this opinion and dissent in the United States Supreme Court. This case was decided before the 1990 adoption of the supplemental jurisdiction statute, 28 U.S.C. § 1367, at a time when the federal courts applied the doctrines of pendent and ancillary jurisdiction. As you read the opinions, consider what, if any, difference Section 1367 would have made in the justices' reasoning.

FIGURE 9–3
CLAIMS IN *OWEN EQUIPMENT AND ERECTION COMPANY v. KROGER*

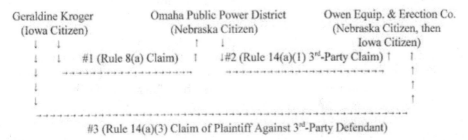

Owen Equipment and Erection Company v. Kroger

Supreme Court of the United States, 1978
437 U.S. 365

OPINION

■ MR. JUSTICE STEWART delivered the opinion of the Court.

In an action in which federal jurisdiction is based on diversity of citizenship, may the plaintiff assert a claim against a third-party defendant when there is no independent basis for federal jurisdiction over that claim? The Court of Appeals for the Eighth Circuit held in this case that such a claim is within the ancillary jurisdiction of the federal courts. We granted certiorari, because this decision conflicts with several recent decisions of other Courts of Appeals.

I

On January 18, 1972, James Kroger was electrocuted when the boom of a steel crane next to which he was walking came too close to a high-tension electric power line. The respondent (his widow, who is the administratrix of his estate) filed a wrongful-death action in the United States District Court for the District of Nebraska against the Omaha Public Power District (OPPD). Her complaint alleged that OPPD's negligent construction, maintenance, and operation of the power line had caused Kroger's death. Federal jurisdiction was based on diversity of citizenship, since the respondent was a citizen of Iowa and OPPD was a Nebraska corporation.

OPPD then filed a third-party complaint pursuant to Fed.Rule Civ.Proc. 14(a) against the petitioner, Owen Equipment and Erection Co. (Owen), alleging that the crane was owned and operated by Owen, and that Owen's negligence had been the proximate cause of Kroger's death.[3] OPPD later moved for summary judgment on the respondent's complaint against it. While this motion was pending, the respondent was granted leave to file an amended complaint naming Owen as an additional defendant. Thereafter, the District Court granted OPPD's motion for summary judgment in an unreported opinion. The case thus went to trial between the respondent and the petitioner alone.

The respondent's amended complaint alleged that Owen was "a Nebraska corporation with its principal place of business in Nebraska." Owen's answer admitted that it was "a corporation organized and existing under the laws of the State of Nebraska," and denied every other allegation of the complaint. On the third day of trial, however, it was disclosed that the petitioner's principal place of business was in Iowa, not Nebraska,[5] and that the petitioner and the respondent were thus both citizens of Iowa. The petitioner then moved to dismiss the complaint for lack of jurisdiction. The District Court reserved decision on the motion, and the jury thereafter returned a verdict in favor of the respondent. In an unreported opinion issued after the trial, the District Court denied the petitioner's motion to dismiss the complaint.

The judgment was affirmed on appeal. The Court of Appeals held that under this Court's decision in *Mine Workers v. Gibbs*, 383 U.S. 715, the District Court had jurisdictional power, in its discretion, to adjudicate the respondent's claim against the petitioner because that claim arose from the "core of 'operative facts' giving rise to both [respondent's] claim against OPPD and OPPD's claim against Owen." It further held that the District Court had properly exercised its discretion in proceeding to decide the case even after summary judgment had been granted to OPPD, because the petitioner had concealed its Iowa citizenship from the respondent. Rehearing en banc was denied by an equally divided court.

II

It is undisputed that there was no independent basis of federal jurisdiction over the respondent's state-law tort action against the petitioner, since both are citizens of Iowa. And although Fed.Rule

---

[3] Under Rule 14(a), a third-party defendant may not be impleaded merely because he may be liable to the *plaintiff*. While the third-party complaint in this case alleged merely that Owen's negligence caused Kroger's death, and the basis of Owen's alleged liability *to OPPD* is nowhere spelled out, OPPD evidently relied upon the state common-law right of contribution among joint tortfeasors. The petitioner has never challenged the propriety of the third-party complaint as such.

[5] The problem apparently was one of geography. Although the Missouri River generally marks the boundary between Iowa and Nebraska, Carter Lake, Iowa, where the accident occurred and where Owen had its main office, lies west of the river, adjacent to Omaha, Neb. Apparently the river once avulsed at one of its bends, cutting Carter Lake off from the rest of Iowa.

Civ.Proc. 14(a) permits a plaintiff to assert a claim against a third-party defendant, it does not purport to say whether or not such a claim requires an independent basis of federal jurisdiction. Indeed, it could not determine that question, since it is axiomatic that the Federal Rules of Civil Procedure do not create or withdraw federal jurisdiction.[7]

In affirming the District Court's judgment, the Court of Appeals relied upon the doctrine of ancillary jurisdiction, whose contours it believed were defined by this Court's holding in *Mine Workers v. Gibb.* The *Gibbs* case differed from this one in that it involved pendent jurisdiction, which concerns the resolution of a plaintiff's federal-and state-law claims against a single defendant in one action. By contrast, in this case there was no claim based upon substantive federal law, but rather state-law tort claims against two different defendants. Nonetheless, the Court of Appeals was correct in perceiving that *Gibbs* and this case are two species of the same generic problem: Under what circumstances may a federal court hear and decide a state-law claim arising between citizens of the same State? But we believe that the Court of Appeals failed to understand the scope of the doctrine of the *Gibbs* case.

The plaintiff in *Gibbs* alleged that the defendant union had violated the common law of Tennessee as well as the federal prohibition of secondary boycotts. This Court held that, although the parties were not of diverse citizenship, the District Court properly entertained the state-law claim as pendent to the federal claim. The crucial holding was stated as follows:

"Pendent jurisdiction, in the sense of judicial *power*, exists whenever there is a claim 'arising under [the] Constitution, the Laws of the United States, and Treaties made, or which shall be made, under their Authority . . . ,' U.S.Const., Art. III, § 2, and the relationship between that claim and the state claim permits the conclusion that the entire action before the court comprises but one constitutional 'case.' . . . The state and federal claims must derive from a common nucleus of operative fact. But if, considered without regard to their federal or state character, a plaintiff's claims are such that he would ordinarily be expected to try them all in one judicial proceeding, then, assuming substantiality of the federal issues, there is *power* in federal courts to hear the whole." 383 U.S., at 725.[9]

It is apparent that *Gibbs* delineated the constitutional limits of federal judicial power. But even if it be assumed that the District Court in the present case had constitutional power to decide the respondent's

---

[7] Fed.Rule Civ.Proc. 82; see *Snyder v. Harris*, 394 U.S. 332; *Sibbach v. Wilson & Co.*, 312 U.S. 1, 10.

[9] The Court further noted that even when such power exists, its exercise remains a matter of discretion based upon "considerations of judicial economy, convenience and fairness to litigants," 383 U.S., at 726, and held that the District Court had not abused its discretion in retaining jurisdiction of the state-law claim.

lawsuit against the petitioner, it does not follow that the decision of the Court of Appeals was correct. Constitutional power is merely the first hurdle that must be overcome in determining that a federal court has jurisdiction over a particular controversy. For the jurisdiction of the federal courts is limited not only by the provisions of Art. III of the Constitution, but also by Acts of Congress.

That statutory law as well as the Constitution may limit a federal court's jurisdiction over nonfederal claims is well illustrated by two recent decisions of this Court, *Aldinger v. Howard*, 427 U.S. 1, and *Zahn v. International Paper Co.*, 414 U.S. 291. In *Aldinger* the Court held that a Federal District Court lacked jurisdiction over a state-law claim against a county, even if that claim was alleged to be pendent to one against county officials under 42 U.S.C. § 1983. In *Zahn* the Court held that in a diversity class action under Fed.Rule Civ.Proc. 23(b)(3), the claim of each member of the plaintiff class must independently satisfy the minimum jurisdictional amount set by 28 U.S.C. § 1332(a), and rejected the argument that jurisdiction existed over those claims that involved $10,000 or less [Section 1332 required more than $10,000 in controversy at the time of *Zahn*] as ancillary to those that involved more. In each case, despite the fact that federal and nonfederal claims arose from a "common nucleus of operative fact," the Court held that the statute conferring jurisdiction over the federal claim did not allow the exercise of jurisdiction over the nonfederal claim.

The *Aldinger* and *Zahn* cases thus make clear that a finding that federal and nonfederal claims arise from a "common nucleus of operative fact," the test of *Gibbs*, does not end the inquiry into whether a federal court has power to hear the nonfederal claims along with the federal ones. Beyond this constitutional minimum, there must be an examination of the posture in which the nonfederal claim is asserted and of the specific statute that confers jurisdiction over the federal claim, in order to determine whether "Congress in [that statute] has . . . expressly or by implication negated" the exercise of jurisdiction over the particular nonfederal claim. *Aldinger v. Howard, supra*, 427 U.S., at 18.

III

The relevant statute in this case, 28 U.S.C. § 1332(a)(1), confers upon federal courts jurisdiction over "civil actions where the matter in controversy exceeds the sum or value of $10,000 . . . and is between . . . citizens of different States." This statute and its predecessors have consistently been held to require complete diversity of citizenship. That is, diversity jurisdiction does not exist unless *each* defendant is a citizen of a different State from *each* plaintiff. Over the years Congress has repeatedly re-enacted or amended the statute conferring diversity jurisdiction, leaving intact this rule of complete diversity. Whatever may have been the original purposes of diversity-of-citizenship jurisdiction, this subsequent history clearly demonstrates a congressional mandate that diversity jurisdiction is not to be available when any plaintiff is a citizen of the same State as any defendant.

Thus it is clear that the respondent could not originally have brought suit in federal court naming Owen and OPPD as codefendants, since citizens of Iowa would have been on both sides of the litigation. Yet the identical lawsuit resulted when she amended her complaint. Complete diversity was destroyed just as surely as if she had sued Owen initially. In either situation, in the plain language of the statute, the "matter in controversy" could not be "between . . . citizens of different States."

It is a fundamental precept that federal courts are courts of limited jurisdiction. The limits upon federal jurisdiction, whether imposed by the Constitution or by Congress, must be neither disregarded nor evaded. Yet under the reasoning of the Court of Appeals in this case, a plaintiff could defeat the statutory requirement of complete diversity by the simple expedient of suing only those defendants who were of diverse citizenship and waiting for them to implead nondiverse defendants. If, as the Court of Appeals thought, a "common nucleus of operative fact" were the only requirement for ancillary jurisdiction in a diversity case, there would be no principled reason why the respondent in this case could not have joined her cause of action against Owen in her original complaint as ancillary to her claim against OPPD. Congress' requirement of complete diversity would thus have been evaded completely.

It is true, as the Court of Appeals noted, that the exercise of ancillary jurisdiction over nonfederal claims has often been upheld in situations involving impleader, cross-claims or counterclaims.[18] But in determining whether jurisdiction over a nonfederal claim exists, the context in which the nonfederal claim is asserted is crucial. And the claim here arises in a setting quite different from the kinds of nonfederal claims that have been viewed in other cases as falling within the ancillary jurisdiction of the federal courts.

First, the nonfederal claim in this case was simply not ancillary to the federal one in the same sense that, for example, the impleader by a defendant of a third-party defendant always is. A third-party complaint depends at least in part upon the resolution of the primary lawsuit. Its relation to the original complaint is thus not mere factual similarity but logical dependence. The respondent's claim against the petitioner,

---

[18] The ancillary jurisdiction of the federal courts derives originally from cases such as *Freeman v. Howe*, 24 How. 450, which held that when federal jurisdiction "effectively controls the property or fund under dispute, other claimants thereto should be allowed to intervene in order to protect their interests, without regard to jurisdiction." *Aldinger v. Howard*, 427 U.S., at 11. More recently, it has been said to include cases that involve multiparty practice, such as compulsory counterclaims, *e. g., Moore v. New York Cotton Exchange*, 270 U.S. 593; impleader, *e. g., H. L. Peterson Co. v. Applewhite*, 383 F.2d 430, 433 (CA5); cross-claims, *e. g., LASA Per L'Industria Del Marmo Soc. Per Azioni v. Alexander*, 414 F.2d 143 (CA6); or intervention as of right, *e. g., Phelps v. Oaks*, 117 U.S. 236, 241.

however, was entirely separate from her original claim against OPPD, since the petitioner's liability to her depended not at all upon whether or not OPPD was also liable. Far from being an ancillary and dependent claim, it was a new and independent one.

Second, the nonfederal claim here was asserted by the plaintiff, who voluntarily chose to bring suit upon a state-law claim in a federal court. By contrast, ancillary jurisdiction typically involves claims by a defending party haled into court against his will, or by another person whose rights might be irretrievably lost unless he could assert them in an ongoing action in a federal court. A plaintiff cannot complain if ancillary jurisdiction does not encompass all of his possible claims in a case such as this one, since it is he who has chosen the federal rather than the state forum and must thus accept its limitations. "[T]he efficiency plaintiff seeks so avidly is available without question in the state courts." *Kenrose Mfg. Co. v. Fred Whitaker Co.*, 512 F.2d 890, 894 (CA4).

It is not unreasonable to assume that, in generally requiring complete diversity, Congress did not intend to confine the jurisdiction of federal courts so inflexibly that they are unable to protect legal rights or effectively to resolve an entire, logically entwined lawsuit. Those practical needs are the basis of the doctrine of ancillary jurisdiction. But neither the convenience of litigants nor considerations of judicial economy can suffice to justify extension of the doctrine of ancillary jurisdiction to a plaintiff's cause of action against a citizen of the same State in a diversity case. Congress has established the basic rule that diversity jurisdiction exists under 28 U.S.C. § 1332 only when there is complete diversity of citizenship. "The policy of the statute calls for its strict construction." *Healy v. Ratta*, 292 U.S. 263, 270; *Snyder v. Harris*, 394 U.S., at 340. To allow the requirement of complete diversity to be circumvented as it was in this case would simply flout the congressional command.

Accordingly, the judgment of the Court of Appeals is reversed.

It is so ordered.

■ MR. JUSTICE WHITE, with whom MR. JUSTICE BRENNAN joins, dissenting.

The Court today states that "[i]t is not unreasonable to assume that, in generally requiring complete diversity, Congress did not intend to confine the jurisdiction of federal courts so inflexibly that they are unable . . . effectively to resolve an entire, logically entwined lawsuit." In spite of this recognition, the majority goes on to hold that in diversity suits federal courts do not have the jurisdictional power to entertain a claim asserted by a plaintiff against a third-party defendant, no matter how entwined it is with the matter already before the court, unless there is an independent basis for jurisdiction over that claim. Because I find no support for such a requirement in either Art. III of the

Constitution or in any statutory law, I dissent from the Court's "unnecessarily grudging" approach.

* * *

In *Mine Workers v. Gibbs*, 383 U.S. 715, 725 (1966), we held that once a claim has been stated that is of sufficient substance to confer subject-matter jurisdiction on the federal district court, the court has judicial power to consider a nonfederal claim if it and the federal claim are derived from "a common nucleus of operative fact." Although the specific facts of that case concerned a state claim that was said to be pendent to a federal-question claim, the Court's language and reasoning were broad enough to cover the instant factual situation: "[I]f, considered without regard to their federal or state character, a plaintiff's claims are such that he would ordinarily be expected to try them all in one judicial proceeding, then, assuming substantiality of the federal issues, there is *power* in federal courts to hear the whole." *Ibid.* In the present case, Mrs. Kroger's claim against Owen and her claim against OPPD derived from a common nucleus of fact; this is necessarily so because in order for a plaintiff to assert a claim against a third-party defendant, Fed.Rule Civ.Proc. 14(a) requires that it "aris[e] out of the transaction or occurrence that is the subject matter of the plaintiff's claim against the third-party plaintiff. . . ." Furthermore, the substantiality of the claim Mrs. Kroger asserted against OPPD is unquestioned. Accordingly, as far as Art. III of the Constitution is concerned, the District Court had power to entertain Mrs. Kroger's claim against Owen.

The majority correctly points out, however, that the analysis cannot stop here. As *Aldinger v. Howard*, 427 U.S. 1 (1976), teaches, the jurisdictional power of the federal courts may be limited by Congress, as well as by the Constitution. In *Aldinger*, although the plaintiff's state claim against Spokane County was closely connected with her 42 U.S.C. § 1983 claim against the county treasurer, the Court held that the District Court did not have pendent jurisdiction over the state claim, for, under the Court's precedents at that time, it was thought that Congress had specifically determined not to confer on the federal courts jurisdiction over civil rights claims against cities and counties. That being so, the Court refused to allow "the federal courts to fashion a jurisdictional doctrine under the general language of Art. III enabling them to circumvent this exclusion. . . ." 427 U.S., at 16.

In the present case, the only indication of congressional intent that the Court can find is that contained in the diversity jurisdictional statute, 28 U.S.C. § 1332(a), which states that "district courts shall have original jurisdiction of all civil actions where the matter in controversy exceeds the sum or value of $10,000 . . . and is between . . . citizens of different States. . . ." Because this statute has been interpreted as requiring complete diversity of citizenship between each plaintiff and each defendant, *Strawbridge v. Curtiss*, 3 Cranch 267 (1806), the Court holds that the District Court did not have ancillary jurisdiction over Mrs. Kroger's claim against Owen. In so holding, the Court unnecessarily expands the scope of the complete-diversity requirement while substantially limiting the doctrine of ancillary jurisdiction.

The complete-diversity requirement, of course, could be viewed as meaning that in a diversity case, a federal district court may adjudicate only those claims that are between parties of different States. Thus, in order for a defendant to implead a third-party defendant, there would have to be diversity of citizenship; the same would also be true for cross-claims between defendants and for a third-party defendant's claim against a plaintiff. Even the majority, however, refuses to read the complete-diversity requirement so broadly; it recognizes with seeming approval the exercise of ancillary jurisdiction over nonfederal claims in situations involving impleader, cross-claims, and counterclaims. Given the Court's willingness to recognize ancillary jurisdiction in these contexts, despite the requirements of § 1332(a), I see no justification for the Court's refusal to approve the District Court's exercise of ancillary jurisdiction in the present case.

It is significant that a plaintiff who asserts a claim against a third-party defendant is not seeking to add a new party to the lawsuit. In the present case, for example, Owen had already been brought into the suit by OPPD, and, that having been done, Mrs. Kroger merely sought to assert against Owen a claim arising out of the same transaction that was already before the court. * * *

Because in the instant case Mrs. Kroger merely sought to assert a claim against someone already a party to the suit, considerations of judicial economy, convenience, and fairness to the litigants—the factors relied upon in *Gibbs*—support the recognition of ancillary jurisdiction here. Already before the court was the whole question of the cause of Mr. Kroger's death. Mrs. Kroger initially contended that OPPD was responsible; OPPD in turn contended that Owen's negligence had been the proximate cause of Mr. Kroger's death. In spite of the fact that the question of Owen's negligence was already before the District Court, the majority requires Mrs. Kroger to bring a separate action in state court in order to assert that very claim. Even if the Iowa statute of limitations will still permit such a suit, considerations of judicial economy are certainly not served by requiring such duplicative litigation.

The majority, however, brushes aside such considerations of convenience, judicial economy, and fairness because it concludes that recognizing ancillary jurisdiction over a plaintiff's claim against a third-party defendant would permit the plaintiff to circumvent the complete-diversity requirement and thereby "flout the congressional command." Since the plaintiff in such a case does not bring the third-party defendant into the suit, however, there is no occasion for deliberate circumvention of the diversity requirement, absent collusion with the defendant. In the case of such collusion, of which there is absolutely no indication here, the court can dismiss the action under the authority of 28 U.S.C. § 1359.[6] In the absence of such collusion, there is no reason to adopt an absolute rule prohibiting the plaintiff from asserting those claims that he may properly assert against the third-party defendant pursuant to Fed.Rule Civ.Proc. 14(a). * * * Since the plaintiff has no control over the defendant's decision to implead a third party, the fact that he could not have originally sued that party in federal court should be irrelevant. Moreover, the fact that a plaintiff in some cases may be able to foresee the subsequent chain of events leading to the impleader does not seem to me to be a sufficient reason to declare that a district court does not have the *power* to exercise ancillary jurisdiction over the plaintiff's claims against the third-party defendant.

We have previously noted that "[s]ubsequent decisions of this Court indicate that *Strawbridge* is not to be given an expansive reading." *State Farm Fire & Cas. Co. v. Tashire*, 386 U.S. 523, 531 n. 6 (1967). In light of this teaching, it seems to me appropriate to view § 1332 as requiring complete diversity only between the plaintiff and those parties he actually brings into the suit. Beyond that, I would hold that in a diversity case the District Court has power, both constitutional and statutory, to entertain all claims among the parties arising from the same nucleus of operative fact as the plaintiff's original, jurisdiction-conferring claim against the defendant. Accordingly, I dissent from the Court's disposition of the present case.

COMMENTS AND QUESTIONS CONCERNING *OWEN EQUIPMENT AND ERECTION CO. V. KROGER*

1. The first sentence of Federal Rule of Civil Procedure 14(a)(3) provides: "The plaintiff may assert against the third-party defendant any claim arising out of the transaction or occurrence that is the subject matter of the plaintiff's claim against the third-party plaintiff." Both Kroger's claim against the Omaha Public Power District and her claim against Owen Equipment arose from the death of Kroger's husband. So why does the Supreme Court conclude that the district cannot hear Kroger's claim against Owen?

2. Owen Equipment waited until the third day of trial to move to dismiss Kroger's claim against it. Was this a timely motion? Should the motion be granted if Owen had deliberately delayed its filing?

3. Justice Stewart explains the confusion over Owen's citizenship in footnote 5 of his opinion:

---

[6] Section 1359 states: "A district court shall not have jurisdiction of a civil action in which any party, by assignment or otherwise, has been improperly or collusively made or joined to invoke the jurisdiction of such court."

The problem apparently was one of geography. Although the Missouri River generally marks the boundary between Iowa and Nebraska, Carter Lake, Iowa, where the accident occurred and where Owen had its main office, lies west of the river, adjacent to Omaha, Neb. Apparently the river once avulsed at one of its bends, cutting Carter Lake off from the rest of Iowa.

The Missouri River created a similar issue in the case of *Durfee v. Duke*, which you will read in Chapter 14, *infra* p. 1106. In *Durfee* the question was how land had crossed the Missouri River to the Missouri side of the River and whether this meant the land was now in Missouri rather than in Nebraska. So, although there may be little left of Nebraska if the Missouri River keeps shifting, we owe a debt to the Cornhusker State for its contributions to civil procedure jurisprudence.

4. *Owen* was decided before the 1990 enactment of the supplemental jurisdiction statute, 28 U.S.C. § 1367. As you will remember from Chapter 3, *supra* pp. 165–186, Section 1367(a) generally provides:

[I]n any civil action of which the district courts have original jurisdiction, the district courts shall have supplemental jurisdiction over all other claims that are so related to claims in the action within such original jurisdiction that they form part of the same case or controversy under Article III of the United States Constitution. Such supplemental jurisdiction shall include claims that involve the joinder or intervention of additional parties.

Had it existed at the time of *Owen*, would Kroger's claim against Owen fall within Section 1367(a)?

5. The supplemental jurisdiction statute extends beyond Section 1367(a). Section 1367(b) takes back some of the supplemental jurisdiction bestowed by Section 1367(a). Section 1367(b) provides:

In any civil action of which the district courts have original jurisdiction founded solely on section 1332 of this title, the district courts shall not have supplemental jurisdiction under subsection (a) over claims by plaintiffs against persons made parties under Rule 14, 19, 20, or 24 of the Federal Rules of Civil Procedure * * *, when exercising supplemental jurisdiction over such claims would be inconsistent with the jurisdictional requirements of section 1332.

Even if Kroger's claim against Owen would fall within Section 1367(a), does it also fall within Section 1367(b)—so that there is no statutory authorization of subject-matter jurisdiction over that claim?

6. In order for a federal district court to exercise subject-matter jurisdiction over a claim, that claim must:

• be authorized by the Federal Rules of Civil Procedure;

• be within the statutory subject-matter jurisdiction authorized by Congress; and

- be within the scope of the Article III judicial power of the United States Constitution.

Which of these three requirements did Kroger's claim against Owen not meet?

7.   The majority recognizes that ancillary subject-matter jurisdiction (what we today call supplemental jurisdiction) provides a jurisdictional base permitting a federal court to hear impleader claims under Rule 14(a), compulsory counterclaims under Rule 13(a), crossclaims under Rule 13(g), and intervention as of right under Rule 24(a). How do these claims differ from the claim that Kroger attempted to assert against Owen? How do the parties asserting these claims differ from the status of Kroger in her civil action? Had it not been dismissed for other reasons, was there subject-matter jurisdiction over OPPD's claim against Owen when Owen was presumed to be a citizen of Nebraska?

8.   Why didn't the district judge rule on Owen's motion to dismiss before submitting Kroger's claim against Owen to the jury? If the motion was well-taken, there would not have been any reason for the jury to even consider Kroger's claim.

9.   The third-party claim that OPPD filed against Owen was dismissed prior to trial, leaving only Kroger's claim against Owen for trial. Even if the supplemental jurisdiction statute had been in effect at that time and provided a basis for jurisdiction over Kroger's claim, is it clear that the district court should have heard that claim? *See* 28 U.S.C. § 1367(c).

10.   After the Supreme Court held that the district court had no subject-matter jurisdiction over Kroger's claim against Owen, Kroger filed an action against Owen in state court. The state court held that the statute of limitations had not run on Kroger's claim because of Iowa's tolling statute. Owen's insurer then paid $234,756 to settle the claim—the same amount that Kroger had recovered in her federal district court judgment. Oakley, "The Story of *Owen Equipment v. Kroger*: A Change in the Weather of Federal Jurisdiction," in *Civil Procedure Stories* 81, 117 (K. Clermont ed., 2nd ed. 2008).

2.   SUBJECT-MATTER JURISDICTION UNDER SECTION 1367: *JOBE V. ALLIANCE COLLECTION SERVICE*

The Supreme Court, ruling prior to the enactment of the supplemental jurisdiction statute, held that the district court could not entertain Kroger's claim against Owen Equipment. As the following case illustrates, Section 1367 has not cured all such jurisdictional problems.

Jobe v. Alliance Collection Service

United States District Court, Northern District of Mississippi, 2012
2012 WL 3985182

MEMORANDUM OPINION

■ SHARION AYCOCK, DISTRICT JUDGE.

Presently before the Court is Plaintiff's Motion to Dismiss Defendant's Counterclaim. For the reasons set forth below, the motion is GRANTED.

FACTUAL BACKGROUND

On September 12, 2011, Plaintiff Misty Jobe initiated the instant action against Defendant Alliance Collection Services, seeking to remedy Defendant's alleged violation of the Fair Debt Collection Practices Act, 15 U.S.C. § 1962, et seq. (FDCPA). Defendant, in turn, filed a counterclaim on October 21, 2011, attempting to collect on Plaintiff's underlying credit obligation. Plaintiff thereafter filed a Rule 12(b)(1) Motion to Dismiss asserting this Court does not have supplemental jurisdiction over Defendant's counterclaim on November 10, 2011.

MOTION TO DISMISS STANDARD

Federal courts are courts of limited jurisdiction. Without an explicit Congressional conferral of jurisdiction, the federal courts have no power to adjudicate claims. Parties may therefore challenge the district court's jurisdiction to hear a claim under Federal Rule of Civil Procedure 12(b)(1). The court must consider a motion to dismiss for want of subject matter jurisdiction before hearing any other claim because if lacking, the court has no power to issue a ruling.

DISCUSSION

Federal Rule of Civil Procedure 13 defines two possible categories of counterclaims, compulsory and permissive. Compulsory counterclaims "arise out of the transaction or occurrence that is the subject matter of the opposing party's claim." Such claims are unique in that they fall within the jurisdiction of federal courts even if they would normally be a matter for state court consideration. *Plant v. Blazer Fin. Servs., Inc., of Georgia*, 598 F.2d 1357, 1359 (5th Cir.1979). The court applies the "logical relationship" test to determine whether a counterclaim is compulsory, inquiring into whether "the counterclaim arises from the same 'aggregate of operative facts,'" or, whether the "aggregate core of facts upon which the claims rests activates additional legal rights, otherwise dormant, in the defendant." *Plant*, 598 F.2d at 1361 (quoting *Revere Copper & Brass, Inc. v. Aetna Cas. & Sur. Co.*, 426 F.2d 709, 715 (5th Cir. 1970)).

Permissive counterclaims, on the other hand, do "not aris[e] out of the transaction or occurrence that is the subject matter of the opposing party's claims." Such permissive counterclaims can nonetheless be brought so long as there exists an independent source of jurisdiction, or, in the alternative, the exercise of supplemental jurisdiction under 28 U.S.C. § 1367 would be proper. *Plant*, 598 F.2d at 1359. Section 1367 provides that "district courts shall have supplemental jurisdiction over all other claims that are so related to claims in the action within such original jurisdiction that they form part of the same case or controversy under Article III of the United States Constitution." 28 U.S.C. § 1367(a). However, a court may deny to exercise supplement jurisdiction if: (i) the claim raises a novel or complex issue of state law, (ii) the claim substantially predominates over the claim or claims over which the district court has original jurisdiction, [iii] the district court has dismissed all claims over which it has original jurisdiction, or (iv) in exceptional circumstances, there are other compelling reasons for declining jurisdiction. 28 U.S.C. § 1367(c).

Because finding the counterclaim to be compulsive would cut short the court's analysis, that question is addressed first. Plaintiff argues, and this Court finds persuasive, that "the counterclaim does not arise from the same aggregate of operative facts, as Plaintiff's claim is for unfair debt collection practices, which is separate and distinct from the breach of contract action Defendant brings."

Although the Fifth Circuit has not directly addressed the question of whether an action to collect on an underlying loan transaction arises from the same aggregate of operative facts as does an FDCPA claim based on the creditor's attempt to make good on that loan, at least two district courts in our Circuit have confronted this question. Those courts both held that such a counterclaim does not arise from the same aggregate of operative facts, and thus fails to meet the "logical relationship test." *See Barcena v. TAM Fin. Corp.*, 2007 WL 1452587, *3 (W.D.Tex. May 8, 2007), *Hurtado v. TAM Fin. Corp.*, 2007 WL 1746884, * 2 (W .D. Tex. June 5, 2007).

These holdings are additionally widely supported by various other courts. In *Hart* [*v. Clayton-Parker and Assoc. Inc.*, 869 F.Supp. 774 (D.Ariz.1994)], for instance, the court also found the facts giving rise to the FDCPA violation and those of the underlying defense to be too discrete. The court in Hart concluded that the plaintiff's claim turned exclusively on the content of defendant's demand for payments, rendering inapposite any consideration of the validity of the actual debt. Moreover, the defendant's counterclaim required broad proof of facts regarding state contract law.

In spite of this, Defendant, here, argues that the Fifth Circuit's holding in *Plant v. Blazer Financial Services, Inc.*, controls the instant dispute. 598 F.2d 1357, 1357 (5th Cir.1979). In *Plant*, the court considered an admittedly similar situation in which a plaintiff filed suit under the Truth in Lending Act (TILA), and the defendant subsequently counterclaimed for the underlying debt obligation. There, the court determined that the two claims arose from the same "aggregate of operative facts" and thus met the "logical relationship test." As such, the counterclaim for the underlying debt was indeed compulsory.

This Court, however, finds Defendant's reliance on *Plant* misplaced for two reasons. First, the actual text of the court's opinion in *Plant* fails to support its extension from the TILA to the FDCPA. In *Plant*, the court stated, "[a]pplying the logical relationship test to the counterclaim in this case clearly suggests its compulsory character because a single aggregate of operative facts, the loan transaction, gave rise to both plaintiff's and defendant's claim." This is not the case in the situation at bar, however. In regard to an FDCPA claim, the claims arise from two factually distinct scenarios: the loan transaction, as in *Plant*, and the methods employed to actually collect on that loan, as here. Second, contrary to Defendant's assertion that the TILA is a consumer protection statute "just like" the FDCPA, there are distinct policy differences in the TILA and the FDCPA that support their dichotomous treatment. Violations of the TILA, on one hand, turn directly on the factual circumstances of entering into the loan and allow, in some circumstances, for a plaintiff to dissolve the transaction, while violations of the FDCPA do not in any way implicate the consummation of the loan transaction.

* * *

[T]his Court finds that the two factual scenarios are too attenuated to arise from the same aggregate of operative facts. Thus, the Defendant's counterclaim for the underlying debt obligation is permissive, rather than compulsory.

As a permissive claim, Defendant's counterclaim can only be heard in federal court if there is an independent source of jurisdiction. Defendant does not contend that its counterclaim is justiciable under 28 U.S.C. § 1331 or § 1332, but merely asserts that jurisdiction should be granted under § 1367. Under § 1367, the court is empowered to hear claims that form part of the same case or controversy as a validly plead federal claim. Supplemental jurisdiction under § 1367, however, is discretionary and the court need not hear the claim if "there are . . . compelling reasons for declining jurisdiction." 28 U.S.C. § 1367(c)(4). As have a number of other district courts that have confronted the issue, this Court finds that significant countervailing policy considerations exist here and the exercise of supplemental jurisdiction would be improper. As stated in *Sparrow* [*v. Mazda Amer. Credit*, 385 F.Supp.2d 1063 (E.D.Cal.2005)], a primary purpose of the FDCPA is to protect individuals from unfair collection practices regardless of whether the debt is owed and allowing a counterclaim might have a significant chilling effect on the number of litigants under the FDCPA. Therefore, the Court finds that the exercise of § 1367 supplemental jurisdiction would be improper in the case at hand.

CONCLUSION

Because Defendant's counterclaim for the underlying debt obligation is permissive rather than compulsory and the Court declines to exercise § 1367 Supplemental Jurisdiction, the Plaintiff's Motion to Dismiss is hereby GRANTED.

SO ORDERED.

COMMENTS AND QUESTIONS CONCERNING *JOBE V. ALLIANCE COLLECTION SERVICE*

1. Why does it matter whether Alliance's counterclaim is permissive or mandatory?

2. If the counterclaim is not compulsory, can the court nevertheless exercise subject-matter jurisdiction over that counterclaim?

3. On the jurisdictional question, what is the basis for subject-matter jurisdiction over Jobe's initial claim against Alliance Collection Service? How can the court have jurisdiction over that claim but not over Alliance's counterclaim?

4. What distinction does the court draw between counterclaims under the Fair Debt Collection Practices Act and the Truth in Lending Act? Do you agree that only claims under the Truth in Lending Act present compulsory counterclaims?

5. If supplemental jurisdiction extended to the counterclaim in this action, does that mean that the district court would necessarily decide that counterclaim?

6. Defendants may have other strategic reasons for asserting a counterclaim than just to set off or defeat individual claims filed against them. In *Heaven v. Trust Company Bank*, 118 F.3d 735 (11th Cir. 1997), the plaintiff filed a class action alleging violations of the Consumer Leasing Act. The defendant bank counterclaimed, asserting that class members had defaulted on their leases and made false statements in their lease applications. The United States Court of Appeals for the Eleventh Circuit upheld the district court's denial of class certification based on conclusions that the counterclaims were compulsory and would require individual defenses by class members—thus making class-wide treatment under Rule 23 inappropriate.

VI. CONCLUSION

Although the defendant often will have an idea that a lawsuit is coming its way, it is the plaintiff and the plaintiff's lawyer who decide when and where to file the action, what claims to assert, and how to structure the lawsuit. When defense counsel are presented with the plaintiff's complaint, they need to consider both defensive and offensive responses. They must follow the specific requirements of Rules 8 and 12, filing a preanswer motion or an answer that specifically addresses the allegations of the complaint. In addition, they should consider affirmative claims that the defendant can assert: as counterclaims, crossclaims, and third-party claims. With respect to such claims, counsel must ensure that not only is each claim authorized by the Federal Rules of Civil Procedure, but that there is also a constitutional and statutory basis for the exercise of federal subject-matter jurisdiction.

If the complaint is not dismissed at the preanswer stage, the action will proceed to disclosure and discovery. These are the subjects of the next chapter of this text.

VII. CHAPTER ASSESSMENT

A. Multiple-Choice Questions. Answer the following questions, reviewing the sections of the chapter noted in connection with each question.

1. A manufacturer, incorporated in Delaware with its principal place of business in California, sells screws to another manufacturer in California that uses the screws in building solar panels that are sold to California construction companies. One of these solar panels is resold over the Internet to a citizen of Maine. This Maine homeowner uses the panel on her house in Maine, but it malfunctions causing the house to burn down.

The homeowner files a federal diversity action against the screw manufacturer and others. The manufacturer does not file any preanswer motions, but includes in its answer the defense of lack of personal jurisdiction. The parties then engage in 18 months of discovery. At a pretrial conference with the judge one week before the trial date, the manufacturer asks for a continuance of the trial so that it can file a motion for judgment on the pleadings.

Review Section III(B) and choose the best answer from the following choices:

(a) Because a motion for judgment on the pleadings can be filed at any time after the filing of the answer, the court should entertain the motion.

(b) Because the court cannot proceed if it does not have personal jurisdiction over the defendant, the court should entertain the motion.

(c) Because lack of personal jurisdiction was not asserted in a preanswer motion, the court should not entertain the motion.

(d) Because consideration of the motion for judgment on the pleadings would delay trial, the court should not entertain the motion.

2. A buyer contracts with a department store to buy a washing machine, which is delivered and installed in the buyer's house. When the washing machine stops working, the buyer stops paying the loan to the store that he used to purchase the machine. The store then files a federal diversity action against the buyer.

After being served with the summons and complaint, the buyer files a motion to dismiss pursuant to Rule 12(b)(3), asserting improper venue. The court denies the motion. Thirty days later, the buyer files another motion to dismiss asserting both (1) lack of subject-matter jurisdiction and (2) lack of personal jurisdiction.

Review Section III(C) and choose the best answer from the following choices:

(a) Because the buyer has filed a prior motion to dismiss, he has waived his right to file a second motion to dismiss.

(b) Because the buyer has filed a prior motion to dismiss, he has waived his right to file a second motion to dismiss asserting personal jurisdiction but not his right to raise lack of subject-matter jurisdiction.

(c) Because Buyer has filed a prior motion to dismiss, he has waived his right to file a second motion to dismiss asserting subject-matter jurisdiction but not his right to raise lack of personal jurisdiction.

(d) Because they both implicate the United States Constitution, the buyer can assert both lack of personal jurisdiction and lack of subject-matter jurisdiction in a second motion to dismiss.

3. An employee applies for a promotion from her employer, a large office supply store. The promotion is given to another individual with significantly less experience than the employee. The employee says nothing about this, but several years later files a federal discrimination action in federal court against her employer. In her complaint, the employee does not refer to the statute of limitations, which is also not raised in her employer's answer. After a year of discovery and pretrial proceedings, the action is set for trial. At the pretrial conference one week before trial, the employer asks the judge to dismiss the action because the employee has not complied with the statute of limitations.

Review Section IV(B) and choose the best answer from the following choices:

(a) Because the employer did not assert the statute of limitations as an affirmative defense in its answer, the employer has waived this defense.

(b) Because the court cannot entertain the action if the statute of limitations has run, the employer properly asserted that defense at the pretrial conference.

(c) Because the employee did not affirmatively state in her complaint that the statute of limitations had not run, the employer properly asserted that defense at the pretrial conference.

(d) Because the statute of limitations cannot defeat a federal question claim, the employer properly asserted that defense at the pretrial conference.

4.   While on vacation in South Carolina, a citizen of Georgia slips and falls at a store incorporated and with its principal place of business in South Carolina. Due to complications from the fall, the shopper is hospitalized and has several operations. After her recovery the shopper brings a federal diversity action seeking $110,000 from the store, alleging that the store was negligent in not keeping its floors clean and dry. In its answer the store asserts a counterclaim designated as such, seeking $2500 in damages because the shopper had not paid her charges from a prior trip to the store. The shopper's attorney files a motion to dismiss this counterclaim.

Review Section V and choose the best answer from the following choices:

(a)   Because the counterclaim is compulsory, the court should deny the motion to dismiss the counterclaim.

(b)   Because the counterclaim cannot be challenged by a motion to dismiss, the court should deny the motion to dismiss the counterclaim.

(c)   Because a counterclaim that does not arise out of the transaction or occurrence that is the subject matter of the complaint cannot be asserted under the Federal Rules, the court should grant the motion to dismiss the counterclaim.

(d)   Because the counterclaim does not seek more than $75,000, the court should grant the motion to dismiss the counterclaim.

5.   An employee drives a delivery truck for her employer and hits a pedestrian with her truck. The pedestrian, a citizen of Ohio, files a federal diversity action seeking $150,000 from the employee, a citizen of Kentucky. Fifteen days after filing her answer to the pedestrian's complaint, the employee decides that she would like to seek indemnification from her employer, because the delivery truck that the employee was asked to drive was not properly maintained. The employer is incorporated and has its principal place of business in Kentucky.

Review Section V and choose the best answer from the following choices:

(a)   The employee cannot assert a third-party claim against her employer without leave of court, because the employee filed her answer more than 14 days ago.

(b)   The employee cannot assert a third-party claim against her employer, because the employee and employer are both citizens of Kentucky,

(c)   The employee has the right to assert a third-party claim against her employer in the employee's answer.

(d)   The employee can assert a third-party claim against her employer in a separate federal action.

B.   Essay Questions. To test your understanding of this chapter's material, outline or write an answer to the following questions.

1.   How Should Defendant Respond?

Plaintiff was injured in a recent environmental protest and has filed a federal civil rights action in federal district court against the local parks department and one of its officers. Below are six allegations from the plaintiff's complaint. You represent the defendant officer and have decided not to file a preanswer motion. Draft the specific language with which you would respond to the following allegations of the complaint.

　　　1.   Plaintiff is a life-long citizen of New York City, has taught kindergarten for over 30 years, and recently was awarded the "Citizen of the Year Award" from her college alumnae association.

　　　2.   Defendant officer is a person of impaired character, having fathered two children out of wedlock and been expelled from his children's baseball games.

　　　3.   Although it was another officer who hit Plaintiff on January 14, that officer reported to the Defendant, who encouraged, knew of, and condoned the beating.

　　　4.   After Plaintiff was hit by Defendant, the Defendant either fraudulently or mistakenly denied the incident when asked by others about it.

　　　5.   Plaintiff has suffered $150,000 in damages and demands $150,000 from the defendant.

　　　6.   Plaintiff demands a trial by jury.

2.   Follow the Bouncing Claims!

A grocery store incorporated and with its principal place of business in Tennessee lost power during a storm and had to discard several hundred thousand dollars worth of meats and frozen foods. The grocery brought a federal action against the wholesaler that sold it the spoiled meat and the wholesaler's sales manager. The grocery's complaint asserts two claims against the wholesaler: (1) a claim for $110,000 for reimbursement for meat that spoiled as a result of the blizzard and (2) a claim for $70,000 in connection with some meat that had spoiled six months before the blizzard.

In addition to these two claims against the wholesaler, the grocery's complaint asserts a third claim against the wholesaler's sales manager. This claim seeks $120,000 based on the assertion that the manager sent meat to the grocery that was not fresh. The sales manager is a citizen of North Carolina and the wholesaler is incorporated and has its principal place of business in North Carolina.

In response to the complaint, these other claims are filed:

The sales manager files a claim against the wholesaler, asserting that, if the sales manager is liable to the store, then the wholesaler (as the manager's employer) is required to indemnify the manager.

The wholesaler files a claim against the local utility company (a Tennessee citizen), asserting that, if the grocery prevails against the wholesaler, then the utility company is secondarily liable to the wholesaler for $50,000 of the meat that spoiled.

The Tennessee utility company files a claim against the grocery, claiming that the grocery caused $175,000 in damage to utility equipment by tampering with that equipment during the blizzard in an effort to restore power to the store.

Disregarding any questions of personal jurisdiction or venue, discuss whether the federal district court can hear the following claims and explain the basis for your answers.

(a) The grocery's claim against the wholesaler for $70,000 concerning meat that spoiled six months before the blizzard.

(b) The grocery's claim against the sales manager.

(c) The sales manager's claim against the wholesaler.

(d) The wholesaler's claim against the utility company.

(e) The utility company's claim against the grocery.

CHAPTER 10

DISCLOSURE AND DISCOVERY: "LET'S SEE WHAT THE OTHER SIDE'S GOT."

I. INTRODUCTION

The complaint and answer and any other pleadings define the parties' claims and defenses in their civil action. The parties, themselves, will have much of the information supporting their claims and defenses, and much additional information can be gathered informally from public sources or will be voluntarily provided by non-parties. However, it is likely that others will have relevant information that they will not voluntarily provide. Rules 26 through 37 of the Federal Rules of Civil Procedure therefore create a formal process by which a party to a civil action can obtain such information from others.

Rule 26(b)(1) provides the parameters of the discovery to which parties are entitled, specifying that parties "may obtain discovery regarding any nonprivileged matter that is relevant to any party's claim or defense and proportional to the needs of the case * * *." This chapter explores (1) pretrial disclosures that must be automatically provided by the parties; (2) the Rule 26(b)(1) scope of discovery to which parties are entitled; (3) the methods by which such discovery can be sought (including depositions, interrogatories, document requests, examinations, and requests for admissions); (4) discovery planning; and (5) the means by which the courts monitor appropriate discovery conduct. However, before considering discovery scope, discovery methods, and the court's intervention in the discovery process, the next section addresses the manner by which certain information must automatically be provided before it is even requested by another party to the action. Discussion of the formal information exchange process thus begins with consideration of Rule 26(a) disclosures.

II. RULE 26(a) REQUIRED DISCLOSURES

Rule 26(a) of the Federal Rules of Civil Procedure provides for three different types of mandatory disclosures:

- Rule 26(a)(1) **initial disclosures** (that Rule 26(a)(1)(C) requires to be made "at or within 14 days after the parties' Rule 26(f) conference unless a different time is set by stipulation or court order * * * ");

- Rule 26(a)(2) **expert disclosures** (that Rule 26(a)(2)(D)(i) typically requires to be made "at least 90 days before the date set for trial or for the case to be ready for trial" unless there is a stipulation or court order to the contrary); and

- Rule 26(a)(3) **pretrial disclosures** (that Rule 26(a)(3)(B) requires to be made "at least 30 days before trial" unless the court orders otherwise).

These pretrial disclosures will be considered in turn in the following subsections of this chapter.

A. RULE 26(a)(1) INITIAL DISCLOSURES

1. THE RULE 26(a)(1) INITIAL DISCLOSURE REQUIREMENT

Rules 27 through 36 of the Federal Rules of Civil Procedure create specific devices by which a party can request discovery from others. However, some basic information, like grits at some Southern restaurants, is provided without a request. Rule 26(a)(1)(A) provides that, unless there is a party stipulation or court order to the contrary, the following information must automatically be provided by each party to the other parties to that action:[1]

(i) the name and, if known, the address and telephone number of each individual likely to have discoverable information—along with the subjects of that information—that the disclosing party may use to support its claims or defenses, unless the use would be solely for impeachment;

(ii) a copy—or a description by category and location—of all documents, electronically stored information, and tangible things that the disclosing party has in its possession, custody, or control and may use to support its claims or defenses, unless the use would be solely for impeachment;

(iii) a computation of each category of damages claimed by the disclosing party—who must also make available for inspection and copying as under Rule 34 the documents or other evidentiary material, unless privileged or protected from disclosure, on which each computation is based, including materials bearing on the nature and extent of injuries suffered; and

(iv) for inspection and copying as under Rule 34, any insurance agreement under which an insurance business may be liable to satisfy all or part of a possible judgment in the

---

[1] Rule 26(a)(1)(B), though, exempts from the 26(a)(1) initial disclosure requirement certain specific types of cases such as actions for review on an administrative record, petitions for habeas corpus, and actions to enforce or quash administrative subpoenas or to enforce an arbitration award. Federal Rule of Civil Procedure 26(b)(1)(B)(i); (iii); (v); and (ix).

action or to indemnify or reimburse for payments made to satisfy the judgment.

Rule 26(a)(1)(C) requires that these initial disclosures be provided "at or within 14 days after the parties' Rule 26(f) conference unless a different time is set by stipulation or court order * * *." Rule 26(f) requires that the parties confer concerning discovery and submit a joint discovery plan to the court within 14 days after this conference. In most cases, all parties also must submit their Rule 26(a)(1) initial disclosures to the other parties within this 14 day period.

2. WHAT INFORMATION MUST BE DISCLOSED?

In order to test your understanding of the types of information that must be automatically disclosed pursuant to Rule 26(a)(1), consider whether the following information must be disclosed within 14 days after the parties' Rule 26(f) pretrial conference.

(A) A pedestrian files a federal diversity action against the driver of the car that hit him while he was crossing the street. The police report indicates that one bystander who saw the accident stated that the pedestrian was in the cross-walk when hit by the car, while a second bystander stated that the pedestrian was outside the cross-walk. Must either of these bystanders be disclosed by the pedestrian? Must either of them be disclosed by the driver?

(B) In his complaint the pedestrian alleges that, as a result of the accident, he can no longer walk without a cane or other assistance. One of the driver's neighbors told the driver that she recently saw the pedestrian at a wedding reception, where he was a great hit because of his acrobatic moves on the dance floor. Must the driver disclose the name of the neighbor at this time?

(C) One of the two bystanders to the accident took a photograph at the time of the accident, and the photograph may indicate whether the pedestrian was inside or outside the crosswalk when he was hit. Must the pedestrian or the driver disclose this photograph? What if the photograph was taken automatically by a city camera posted alongside the traffic light at this intersection?

(D) The pedestrian had just left an antique store before the accident. He was carrying with him an antique vase and an appraisal stating the value of the vase, which was destroyed in the accident. Must the pedestrian disclose the appraisal? What about his doctors' bills due to the accident?

(E) Must the driver provide a copy of the driver's auto insurance policy to the pedestrian? Must the driver provide a financial statement showing his income and net worth?

B. RULE 26(a)(2) EXPERT DISCLOSURES

Following the Rule 26(a)(1) initial disclosures, parties are required to disclose specific information concerning expert testimony that may be offered at trial. Expert testimony is treated separately in the Federal Rules of Civil Procedure for several reasons. It typically involves complex subject matter that only can be rebutted by additional expert evidence. Such expert testimony also is paid for by the party presenting the evidence, in contrast to other trial testimony. Finally, expert evidence often is crucial to the outcome of the action. For these reasons, expert testimony is separately addressed in the Federal Rules, and Rule 26(a)(2) requires the disclosure of such testimony before trial.

If a party may present expert testimony at trial, the individuals who will present such evidence must be disclosed prior to trial pursuant to Rule 26(a)(2). If there is not a party stipulation or court order setting another time for disclosure, expert disclosures are to be made "at least 90 days before the date set for trial or for the case to be ready for trial." However, if the expert testimony will be offered solely to rebut or contradict other expert testimony, the party who will offer such rebuttal testimony has until 30 days after the other party's disclosure to make its own disclosure.

As will be discussed in Section IV, *infra*, the specific information that must be provided depends on the circumstances under which the expert may be testifying at trial. Most experts are described in Rule 26(a)(2)(B) as witnesses who are "retained or specially employed to provide expert testimony in the case or one whose duties as the party's employee regularly involve giving expert testimony." The majority of such experts are retained specifically to provide testimony in a particular legal action. However, Rule 26(a)(2)(B) also extends to experts "whose duties as the party's employee regularly involve giving expert testimony," such as, for instance, an employee of an insurance company whose job is to investigate the cause of fires.

With respect to either of these types of experts, Rule 26(a)(2)(B) requires that the party who may offer the expert testimony provide a written report containing the following items:

    (i)   a complete statement of all opinions the witness will express and the basis and reasons for them;

    (ii)   the facts or data considered by the witness in forming them;

    (iii) any exhibits that will be used to summarize or support them;

    (iv) the witness's qualifications, including a list of all publications authored in the previous ten years;

(v) a list of all other cases in which, during the previous four years, the witness testified as an expert at trial or by deposition; and

(vi) a statement of the compensation to be paid for the study and testimony in the case.

Such written reports are only required concerning experts who are "retained or specifically employed to provide expert testimony in the case or * * * whose duties as the party's employee regularly involve giving expert testimony." Under what other circumstances might an expert testify? The classic example of an expert who is not retained or is not a party employee is the emergency room physician who examined a party soon after an accident and who may be able to offer expert testimony concerning the party's condition at that time. Because such experts are not being compensated for their time (either pursuant to a retainer or as a party's employee), the required Rule 26(b) expert disclosure is much less comprehensive than the written report required from other testifying experts. These non-retained, non-employee experts are not required to provide a written report, but Rule 26(a)(2)(C) merely requires disclosure of:

(i)   the subject matter on which the witness is expected to present evidence under Federal Rule of Evidence 702, 703, or 705; and

(ii) a summary of the facts and opinions to which the witness is expected to testify.

As with other discovery, Rule 26(e) requires supplementation of information concerning experts who are required to provide a Rule 26(a)(2)(B) written report. Rule 26(e)(2) provides that a party's duty to supplement "extends both to information included in the report and to information given during the expert's deposition."

C. RULE 26(a)(3) PRETRIAL DISCLOSURES

The third type of pretrial disclosure required by Rule 26(a) is the Rule 26(a)(3) pretrial disclosure. These disclosures are to be made at the end of the pretrial period, in contrast to the Rule 26(a)(1) initial disclosures which come at the outset of the action. Rule 26(a)(3)(A) provides:

In addition to the disclosures required by Rule 26(a)(1) and (2), a party must provide to the other parties and promptly file the following information about the evidence that it may present at trial other than solely for impeachment:

(i)   the name and, if not previously provided, the address and telephone number of each witness— separately identifying those the party expects to present and those it may call if the need arises;

(ii) the designation of those witnesses whose testimony the party expects to present by deposition and, if not taken stenographically, a transcript of the pertinent parts of the deposition; and

(iii) an identification of each document or other exhibit, including summaries of other evidence— separately identifying those items the party expects to offer and those it may offer if the need arises.

The pretrial stages of the action having been completed, the parties are now required to disclose to the other parties and the court the witnesses they may call at trial and the deposition testimony and exhibits that may be offered at trial. The court can set the time for these pretrial disclosures, although Rule 26(a)(3)(B) provides that, absent a court order to the contrary, such disclosure must be made at least 30 days before trial. Rule 26(a)(3)(B) also provides that, unless the court orders otherwise, objections to deposition testimony and exhibits proposed to be offered by other parties must be made within 14 days after their disclosure under that same rule.

Figure 10–1 illustrates the initial disclosures, expert disclosures, and pretrial disclosures required by Rule 26(a).

FIGURE 10–1
RULE 26(a) DISCLOSURES

Rule 26(a) Provision	Material to be Disclosed	Can Stipulation Supersede Rule?	Can Court Supersede Rule?	When Disclosure is Required
Rule 26(a)(1)(A)(i) Initial Disclosures	Names, Addresses, and Phone Numbers of Persons with Supportive Discoverable Information	Yes	Yes	Unless Otherwise Stipulated or Ordered or Party Objects, Within 14 Days After Rule 26(f) Conference
Rule 26(a)(1)(A)(ii) Initial Disclosures	Copies or a Description of Relevant Supportive Documents/ESI/Things	Yes	Yes	
Rule 26(a)(1)(A)(iii) Initial Disclosures	Computation of Damages by Disclosing Party	Yes	Yes	
Rule 26(a)(1)(A)(iv) Initial Disclosures	Insurance Agreements	Yes	Yes	
Rule 26(a)(2)(A) Expert Disclosures	Identities of Experts	No	No	Unless Otherwise Stipulated or Directed by the Court, at Least 90 Days Before Trial
Rule 26(a)(2)(B) Expert Disclosures	Expert Reports	Yes	Yes	

Rule 26(a)(3)(A)(i) Pretrial Disclosures	Identification of Trial Witnesses	No	No	Unless Otherwise Directed by the Court, at Least 30 Days Before Trial
Rule 26(a)(3)(A)(ii) Pretrial Disclosures	Designation of Depositions for Trial	No	No	
Rule 26(a)(3)(A)(iii) Pretrial Disclosures	Identification of Trial Exhibits	No	No	

III. DISCOVERY SCOPE AND LIMITS

While Rule 26(a) provides for required pretrial disclosures, Rule 26(b) sets forth the scope, and limits, of party-initiated discovery. Rule 26(b)(1), as amended in 2015, provides:

> Unless otherwise limited by court order, the scope of discovery is as follows: Parties may obtain discovery regarding any nonprivileged matter that is relevant to any party's claim or defense and proportional to the needs of the case, considering the importance of the issues at stake in the action, the amount in controversy, the parties' relative access to relevant information, the parties' resources, the importance of the discovery in resolving the issues, and whether the burden or expense of the proposed discovery outweighs its likely benefit. Information within this scope of discovery need not be admissible in evidence to be discoverable.

Thus, to be discoverable, information must be:

- **Relevant** to any party's claim or defense;
- **Proportional** to the needs of the case; and
- **Nonprivileged**.

These three requirements will be considered in turn.

A. RELEVANCE

1. THE RULE 26(b)(1) RELEVANCE STANDARD

Rule 26(b)(1) requires that, to be discoverable, information must be relevant. Prior to 2015, Rule 26(b)(1) permitted a party to obtain, on a showing of good cause, "discovery of any matter relevant to the subject matter involved in the action." However, Rule 26(b)(1) now only permits discovery concerning matters "relevant to any party's claim or defense."

But just what sort of information is "relevant to any party's claim or defense"? Rule 401 of the Federal Rules of Evidence defines "relevant evidence" to be evidence having "any tendency to make the existence of any fact that is of consequence to the determination of the action more probable or less probable than it would be without the evidence." This does not mean that a single bit of evidence only will be considered relevant if it, by itself, establishes a particular aspect of a claim or defense. "A brick is not a wall." *McCormick on Evidence* § 185, at 278 (J. Strong ed. 5th ed. 2000).

There is a different standard for Rule 26(a)(1) initial disclosures than for discovery under Rule 26(b)(1). While discovery is permitted concerning matters "relevant to any party's claim or defense," Rule 26(a)(1) initial disclosures are required concerning only matters that support the claims or defenses of the party making the disclosures. Why the different standards? What difference do they make in practice?

Finally, while relevance is one of the Rule 26(b)(1) requirements for discoverability, the final sentence of Rule 26(b)(1) provides: "Information within this scope of discovery need not be admissible in evidence to be discoverable." Why should a party be entitled to discovery concerning information that is not even admissible at trial? What purpose might such inadmissible discovery serve?

2. **WHAT INFORMATION IS "RELEVANT TO ANY PARTY'S CLAIM OR DEFENSE"?**

While information must be relevant to a party's claim or defense to be discoverable in the federal courts, relevance requires a very fact-based determination in the context of each individual civil action. Should the discovery sought in the following cases be considered relevant for the purposes of Rule 26(b)(1)?

(a) Plaintiff alleges in her complaint that, as a result of a slip-and-fall at the defendant airport, she suffered back and other injuries that impaired her ability to work and enjoy life. After viewing an on-line photo of plaintiff which showed her holding a small dog, defendants sought production of her entire social media account, including all the private pages of that account. Is this material relevant for the purposes of Rule 26(b)(1)? *See Tompkins v. Detroit Metro. Airport*, 278 F.R.D. 387 (E.D. Mich. 2012).

(b) Plaintiff brings an action claiming that architectural barriers that she encountered as a guest at the defendant motel violated the Americans with Disabilities Act, 42 U.S.C. § 12181 *et seq.* Plaintiff seeks to conduct a full-site inspection of the property. Should such an inspection be required? *See Wiele v. Zenith Arizona, Inc.*, 278 F.R.D. 477 (D. Ariz. 2012).

(c) Beneficiaries bring an action seeking payment under life insurance policies. Defendants answer that they are not required to pay because the decedent, in seeking insurance, concealed material facts pertaining to his health, previous illnesses, and prior treatment by physicians. At his deposition, one of the decedent's treating physicians was asked, "Doctor, have you heard that [the decedent] did consult any other doctors besides yourself?" Should an objection to the question as seeking inadmissible hearsay be sustained? *See Lowe's of Roanoke, Inc. v. Jefferson Standard Life Ins. Co.*, 219 F. Supp. 181 (S.D.N.Y. 1963).

B. PROPORTIONALITY

1. THE RULE 26(b)(1) PROPORTIONALITY STANDARD

Rule 26(b)(1) not only limits discovery to relevant information, but to information that is "proportional to the needs of the case." Discovery proportionality was first introduced into Rule 26 in 1983. The 1983 Advisory Committee noted that "many cases in public policy spheres, such as employment practices, free speech, and other matters, may have importance far beyond the monetary amount involved. The court must apply the standards in an even-handed manner that will prevent use of discovery to wage a war of attrition or as a device to coerce a party, whether financially weak or affluent." 97 F.R.D. 165, 218 (1983).

The 2015 amendment to Rule 26(b)(1) moved the proportionality requirement to the beginning of that Rule. The factors to be considered in determining whether proposed discovery is proportional to the needs of the case were also moved forward in Rule 26(b)(1). These proportionality factors include:

- the importance of the issues at stake in the action;
- the amount in controversy;
- the parties' relative access to relevant information;
- the parties' resources;
- the importance of the discovery in resolving the issues; and
- whether the burden or expense of the proposed discovery outweighs its likely benefit.

The Advisory Committee Note to the 2015 amendments to Rule 26, 305 F.R.D. 457, 551 (2015), suggests the difficulty in implementing this proportionality standard in practice:

> The parties may begin discovery without a full appreciation of the factors that bear on proportionality. A party requesting discovery, for example, may have little information about the burden or expense of responding. A party requested to provide discovery may have little information about the importance of the discovery in resolving the issues as understood by the requesting party.

So how can these difficulties be resolved? The same Advisory Committee Note continues:

> Many of these uncertainties should be addressed and reduced in the parties' Rule 26(f) conference and in scheduling and pretrial conferences with the court. But if the parties continue to disagree, the discovery dispute could be brought before the court and the parties' responsibilities would remain as they have been since 1983. A party claiming undue burden or expense ordinarily has far better information—perhaps the only information—with respect to that part of the determination. A party claiming that a request is important to resolve the issues should be able to explain the ways in which the underlying information bears on the issues as that party understands them. The court's responsibility, using all the information provided by the parties, is to consider these and all the other factors in reaching a case-specific determination of the appropriate scope of discovery.

Id.

2. WHAT INFORMATION IS PROPORTIONAL TO THE NEEDS OF THE CASE?

Consider the following cases and apply the Rule 26(b)(1) factors to determine whether the proportionality requirement of that Rule has been met.

(a) Plaintiff brings claims against her insurance company for breach of contract, breach of the covenant of good faith and fair dealing, and violation of a state unfair practices act. The insurance company contracted with a claims review company and denied the plaintiff's insurance claim in reliance upon the opinion of a non-treating physician working for the claims review company. Plaintiff seeks in discovery all other medical reviews from the past three years involving Nevada auto accident claimants prepared by (1) the physician who reviewed her injuries and (2) any other physician retained by the claims review company to review claims for the defendant insurance company. Is plaintiff entitled to this discovery? *See Abueg v. State Farm Mut. Auto. Ins. Co.*, 2014 WL 5503114 (D. Nev. Oct. 30, 2014).

(b) Plaintiff company brings an action alleging illegal restraint of trade and other claims against several defendants. One of the defendants, which is also a third-party plaintiff, seeks to redepose the senior vice-president and general counsel of the third-party defendant. This individual was deposed seven years ago in the same action for less than four hours, and the third-party defendant's recent amended third-party answer has added a claim about which this person was not questioned in his earlier deposition. Should this new deposition go forward? *See Tri-Star Pictures, Inc. v. Unger*, 171 F.R.D. 94 (S.D.N.Y. 1997).

(c) In their class action complaint plaintiffs alleged that defendants discriminated against women with respect to evaluation, compensation, and promotion, and they sought the production of eight years of computerized employment data relevant to their class claims. The defendants sought to limit some of the data produced by types of employees and time period, estimating that it would take 90–150 hours to produce the information sought and an additional 40–80 hours to perform a quality check on that data. Should defendants be required to produce all of the information sought? *See Chen-Oster v. Goldman, Sachs & Co.*, 285 F.R.D. 294 (S.D.N.Y. 2012).

C. PRIVILEGE

For matter to be discoverable under Rule 26(b)(1), it must not only be relevant and proportional to the needs of the case, but it also must not be privileged. Privileges developed at common law because of the belief that the protection of certain communications was more important than the benefit to civil adjudications from considering such communications. While statements by a husband to his wife or by a patient to her doctor may be relevant to a judicial proceeding, such statements are typically protected in order to encourage full and free communication between spouses and between patients and their doctors.

The privileges applied in the federal courts are not defined in the Federal Rules of Civil Procedure or the Federal Rules of Evidence. Federal Rule of Evidence 501 instead provides:

> The common law—as interpreted by United States courts in the light of reason and experience—governs a claim of privilege unless any of the following provides otherwise:
>
> •   the United States Constitution;
>
> •   a federal statute; or
>
> •   rules prescribed by the Supreme Court.
>
> But in a civil case, state law governs privilege regarding a claim or defense for which state law supplies the rule of decision.

What privilege law does Federal Rule of Evidence 501 require a federal court to apply in a diversity action? In a federal civil rights action? Consider the manner in which the Supreme Court relied upon "reason and experience" to determine the scope of the attorney-client privilege within the federal courts in the following federal action.

Upjohn Co. v. United States

Supreme Court of the United States, 1981
449 U.S. 383

■ JUSTICE REHNQUIST delivered the opinion of the Court.

We granted certiorari in this case to address important questions concerning the scope of the attorney-client privilege in the corporate context and the applicability of the work-product doctrine in proceedings to enforce tax summonses. With respect to the privilege question the parties and various *amici* have described our task as one of choosing between two "tests" which have gained adherents in the courts of appeals. We are acutely aware, however, that we sit to decide concrete cases and not abstract propositions of law. We decline to lay down a broad rule or series of rules to govern all conceivable future questions in this area, even were we able to do so. We can and do, however, conclude that the attorney-client privilege protects the communications involved in this case from compelled disclosure and that the work-product doctrine does apply in tax summons enforcement proceedings.

I

Petitioner Upjohn Co. manufactures and sells pharmaceuticals here and abroad. In January 1976 independent accountants conducting an audit of one of Upjohn's foreign subsidiaries discovered that the subsidiary made payments to or for the benefit of foreign government officials in order to secure government business. The accountants so informed petitioner Mr. Gerard Thomas, Upjohn's Vice President, Secretary, and General Counsel. Thomas is a member of the Michigan and New York Bars, and has been Upjohn's General Counsel for 20 years. He consulted with outside counsel and R. T. Parfet, Jr., Upjohn's Chairman of the Board. It was decided that the company would conduct an internal investigation of what were termed "questionable payments." As part of this investigation the attorneys prepared a letter containing a questionnaire which was sent to "All Foreign General and Area Managers" over the Chairman's signature. The letter began by noting recent disclosures that several American companies made "possibly illegal" payments to foreign government officials and emphasized that the management needed full information concerning any such payments made by Upjohn. The letter indicated that the Chairman had asked Thomas, identified as "the company's General Counsel," "to conduct an investigation for the purpose of determining the nature and magnitude of any payments made by the Upjohn Company or any of its subsidiaries to any employee or official of a foreign government." The questionnaire sought detailed information concerning such payments.

Managers were instructed to treat the investigation as "highly confidential" and not to discuss it with anyone other than Upjohn employees who might be helpful in providing the requested information. Responses were to be sent directly to Thomas. Thomas and outside counsel also interviewed the recipients of the questionnaire and some 33 other Upjohn officers or employees as part of the investigation.

On March 26, 1976, the company voluntarily submitted a preliminary report to the Securities and Exchange Commission on Form 8–K disclosing certain questionable payments. A copy of the report was simultaneously submitted to the Internal Revenue Service, which immediately began an investigation to determine the tax consequences of the payments. Special agents conducting the investigation were given lists by Upjohn of all those interviewed and all who had responded to the questionnaire. On November 23, 1976, the Service issued a summons pursuant to 26 U.S.C. § 7602 demanding production of:

> "All files relative to the investigation conducted under the supervision of Gerard Thomas to identify payments to employees of foreign governments and any political contributions made by the Upjohn Company or any of its affiliates since January 1, 1971 and to determine whether any funds of the Upjohn Company had been improperly accounted for on the corporate books during the same period.

> "The records should include but not be limited to written questionnaires sent to managers of the Upjohn Company's foreign affiliates, and memorandums or notes of the interviews conducted in the United States and abroad with officers and employees of the Upjohn Company and its subsidiaries."

The company declined to produce the documents specified in the second paragraph on the grounds that they were protected from disclosure by the attorney-client privilege and constituted the work product of attorneys prepared in anticipation of litigation. On August 31, 1977, the United States filed a petition seeking enforcement of the summons under 26 U.S.C. §§ 7402(b) and 7604(a) in the United States District Court for the Western District of Michigan. That court adopted the recommendation of a Magistrate who concluded that the summons should be enforced. Petitioners appealed to the Court of Appeals for the Sixth Circuit which rejected the Magistrate's finding of a waiver of the attorney-client privilege, but agreed that the privilege did not apply "[t]o the extent that the communications were made by officers and agents not responsible for directing Upjohn's actions in response to legal advice . . . for the simple reason that the communications were not the 'client's.' " The court reasoned that accepting petitioners' claim for a broader application of the privilege would encourage upper-echelon management to ignore unpleasant facts and create too broad a "zone of silence." Noting that Upjohn's counsel had interviewed officials such as the Chairman and President, the Court of Appeals remanded to the

District Court so that a determination of who was within the "control group" could be made. In a concluding footnote the court stated that the work-product doctrine "is not applicable to administrative summonses issued under 26 U.S.C. § 7602."

II

Federal Rule of Evidence 501 provides that "the privilege of a witness . . . shall be governed by the principles of the common law as they may be interpreted by the courts of the United States in light of reason and experience." The attorney-client privilege is the oldest of the privileges for confidential communications known to the common law. 8 J. Wigmore, Evidence § 2290 (McNaughton rev. 1961). Its purpose is to encourage full and frank communication between attorneys and their clients and thereby promote broader public interests in the observance of law and administration of justice. The privilege recognizes that sound legal advice or advocacy serves public ends and that such advice or advocacy depends upon the lawyer's being fully informed by the client. As we stated last Term in *Trammel v. United States,* 445 U.S. 40, 51 (1980): "The lawyer-client privilege rests on the need for the advocate and counselor to know all that relates to the client's reasons for seeking representation if the professional mission is to be carried out." And in *Fisher v. United States,* 425 U.S. 391, 403 (1976), we recognized the purpose of the privilege to be "to encourage clients to make full disclosure to their attorneys." This rationale for the privilege has long been recognized by the Court. Admittedly complications in the application of the privilege arise when the client is a corporation, which in theory is an artificial creature of the law, and not an individual; but this Court has assumed that the privilege applies when the client is a corporation and the Government does not contest the general proposition.

* * *

* * * [T]he fact that the privilege exists to protect not only the giving of professional advice to those who can act on it but also the giving of information to the lawyer to enable him to give sound and informed advice. The first step in the resolution of any legal problem is ascertaining the factual background and sifting through the facts with an eye to the legally relevant. See ABA Code of Professional Responsibility, Ethical Consideration 4–1:

> "A lawyer should be fully informed of all the facts of the matter he is handling in order for his client to obtain the full advantage of our legal system. It is for the lawyer in the exercise of his independent professional judgment to separate the relevant and important from the irrelevant and unimportant. The observance of the ethical obligation of a lawyer to hold inviolate the confidences and secrets of his client not only facilitates the full development of facts essential

to proper representation of the client but also encourages laymen to seek early legal assistance."

See also Hickman v. Taylor, 329 U.S. 495, 511 (1947).

In the case of the individual client the provider of information and the person who acts on the lawyer's advice are one and the same. In the corporate context, however, it will frequently be employees beyond the control group as defined by the court below—"officers and agents . . . responsible for directing [the company's] actions in response to legal advice"—who will possess the information needed by the corporation's lawyers. Middle-level—and indeed lower-level—employees can, by actions within the scope of their employment, embroil the corporation in serious legal difficulties, and it is only natural that these employees would have the relevant information needed by corporate counsel if he is adequately to advise the client with respect to such actual or potential difficulties. This fact was noted in *Diversified Industries, Inc. v. Meredith,* 572 F.2d 596 (C.A.8 1977) (en banc):

> "In a corporation, it may be necessary to glean information relevant to a legal problem from middle management or non-managerial personnel as well as from top executives. The attorney dealing with a complex legal problem 'is thus faced with a "Hobson's choice". If he interviews employees not having "the very highest authority", their communications to him will not be privileged. If, on the other hand, he interviews *only* those employees with "the very highest authority", he may find it extremely difficult, if not impossible, to determine what happened.'" *Id.,* at 608–609 (quoting Weinschel, Corporate Employee Interviews and the Attorney-Client Privilege, 12 B.C. Ind. & Com. L. Rev. 873, 876 (1971)).

The control group test adopted by the court below thus frustrates the very purpose of the privilege by discouraging the communication of relevant information by employees of the client to attorneys seeking to render legal advice to the client corporation. The attorney's advice will also frequently be more significant to noncontrol group members than to those who officially sanction the advice, and the control group test makes it more difficult to convey full and frank legal advice to the employees who will put into effect the client corporation's policy.

The narrow scope given the attorney-client privilege by the court below not only makes it difficult for corporate attorneys to formulate sound advice when their client is faced with a specific legal problem but also threatens to limit the valuable efforts of corporate counsel to ensure their client's compliance with the law. In light of the vast and complicated array of regulatory legislation confronting the modern corporation, corporations unlike most individuals "constantly go to lawyers to find out how to obey the law," Burnham, The Attorney-Client Privilege in the Corporate Arena, 24 Bus. Law. 901, 913 (1969), particularly since compliance with the law in this area is hardly an instinctive matter. The test adopted by the court below is difficult to apply in practice, though no abstractly formulated and unvarying "test" will necessarily enable courts to decide questions such as this with mathematical precision. But if the purpose of the attorney-client privilege is to be served, the attorney and client must be able to predict with some degree of certainty whether particular discussions will be protected. * * *

The communications at issue were made by Upjohn employees to counsel for Upjohn acting as such, at the direction of corporate superiors in order to secure legal advice from counsel. As the Magistrate found, "Mr. Thomas consulted with the Chairman of the Board and outside counsel and thereafter conducted a factual investigation to determine the nature and extent of the questionable payments *and to be in a position to give legal advice to the company with respect to the payments.*" (Emphasis supplied.) Information, not available from upper-echelon management, was needed to supply a basis for legal advice concerning compliance with securities and tax laws, foreign laws, currency regulations, duties to shareholders, and potential litigation in each of these areas. The communications concerned matters within the scope of the employees' corporate duties, and the employees themselves were sufficiently aware that they were being questioned in order that the corporation could obtain legal advice. The questionnaire identified Thomas as "the company's General Counsel" and referred in its opening sentence to the possible illegality of payments such as the ones on which information was sought. A statement of policy accompanying the questionnaire clearly indicated the legal implications of the investigation. The policy statement was issued "in order that there be no uncertainty in the future as to the policy with respect to the practices which are the subject of this investigation." It began "Upjohn will comply with all laws and regulations," and stated that commissions or payments "will not be used as a subterfuge for bribes or illegal payments" and that all payments must be "proper and legal." Any future agreements with foreign distributors or agents were to be approved "by a company attorney" and any questions concerning the policy were to be referred "to the company's General Counsel." This statement was issued to Upjohn employees worldwide, so that even those interviewees not receiving a questionnaire were aware of the legal implications of the interviews. Pursuant to explicit instructions from the Chairman of the Board, the communications were considered "highly confidential" when made and have been kept confidential by the company. Consistent with the underlying purposes of the attorney-client privilege, these communications must be protected against compelled disclosure.

The Court of Appeals declined to extend the attorney-client privilege beyond the limits of the control group test for fear that doing so would entail severe burdens on discovery and create a broad "zone of silence" over corporate affairs. Application of the attorney-client privilege to communications such as those involved here, however, puts the adversary in no worse position than if the communications had never taken place. The privilege only protects disclosure of communications; it does not protect disclosure of the underlying facts by those who communicated with the attorney:

> "[T]he protection of the privilege extends only to *communications* and not to facts. A fact is one thing and a communication concerning that fact is an entirely different thing. The client cannot be compelled to answer the question, 'What did you say or write to the attorney?' but may not refuse to disclose any relevant fact within his knowledge merely because he incorporated a statement of such fact into his communication to his attorney." *Philadelphia v. Westinghouse Electric Corp.,* 205 F.Supp. 830, 831 (E.D.Pa.1962).

See also Diversified Industries, 572 F.2d, at 611; *State ex rel. Dudek v. Circuit Court,* 34 Wis.2d 559, 580, 150 N.W.2d 387, 399 (1967) ("the courts have noted that a party cannot conceal a fact merely by revealing it to his lawyer"). Here the Government was free to question the employees who communicated with Thomas and outside counsel. Upjohn has provided the IRS with a list of such employees, and the IRS has already interviewed some 25 of them. While it would probably be more convenient for the Government to secure the results of petitioner's internal investigation by simply subpoenaing the questionnaires and notes taken by petitioner's attorneys, such considerations of convenience do not overcome the policies served by the attorney-client privilege. As Justice Jackson noted in his concurring opinion in *Hickman v. Taylor,* 329 U.S., at 516: "Discovery was hardly intended to enable a learned profession to perform its function . . . on wits borrowed from the adversary."

Needless to say, we decide only the case before us, and do not undertake to draft a set of rules which should govern challenges to investigatory subpoenas. Any such approach would violate the spirit of Federal Rule of Evidence 501. While such a "case-by-case" basis may to some slight extent undermine desirable certainty in the boundaries of the attorney-client privilege, it obeys the spirit of the Rules. At the same time we conclude that the narrow "control group test" sanctioned by the Court of Appeals in this case cannot, consistent with "the principles of the common law as . . . interpreted . . . in the light of reason and experience," Fed. Rule Evid. 501, govern the development of the law in this area.

[The Court then held that the court of appeals had been incorrect in concluding that the attorney work-product doctrine was inapplicable to non-attorney-client communications in a tax summons enforcement proceeding such as this.]

Accordingly, the judgment of the Court of Appeals is reversed, and the case remanded for further proceedings.

It is so ordered.

■ CHIEF JUSTICE BURGER, concurring in part and concurring in the judgment.

I join in Parts I and III of the opinion of the Court and in the judgment. As to Part II, I agree fully with the Court's rejection of the so-called "control group" test, its reasons for doing so, and its ultimate holding that the communications at issue are privileged. As the Court states, however, "if the purpose of the attorney-client privilege is to be served, the attorney and client must be able to predict with some degree of certainty whether particular discussions will be protected." For this very reason, I believe that we should articulate a standard that will govern similar cases and afford guidance to corporations, counsel advising them, and federal courts.

The Court properly relies on a variety of factors in concluding that the communications now before us are privileged. Because of the great importance of the issue, in my view the Court should make clear now that, as a general rule, a communication is privileged at least when, as here, an employee or former employee speaks at the direction of the management with an attorney regarding conduct or proposed conduct within the scope of employment. The attorney must be one authorized by the management to inquire into the subject and must be seeking information to assist counsel in performing any of the following functions: (a) evaluating whether the employee's conduct has bound or would bind the corporation; (b) assessing the legal consequences, if any, of that conduct; or (c) formulating appropriate legal responses to actions that have been or may be taken by others with regard to that conduct. Other communications between employees and corporate counsel may indeed be privileged—as the petitioners and several *amici* have suggested in their proposed formulations—but the need for certainty does not compel us now to prescribe all the details of the privilege in this case.

Nevertheless, to say we should not reach all facets of the privilege does not mean that we should neglect our duty to provide guidance in a case that squarely presents the question in a traditional adversary context. Indeed, because Federal Rule of Evidence 501 provides that the law of privileges "shall be governed by the principles of the common law as they may be interpreted by the courts of the United States in the light of reason and experience," this Court has a special duty to clarify aspects of the law of privileges properly before us. Simply asserting that this failure "may to some slight extent undermine desirable certainty," neither minimizes the consequences of continuing uncertainty and confusion nor harmonizes the inherent dissonance of acknowledging that uncertainty while declining to clarify it within the frame of issues presented.

COMMENTS AND QUESTIONS CONCERNING
UPJOHN CO. V. UNITED STATES

1.   Judge Charles Wyzanski's frequently cited recitation of the requirements of the attorney-client privilege provides:

> The privilege applies only if (1) the asserted holder of the privilege is or sought to become a client; (2) the person to whom the communication was made (a) is a member of the bar of a court, or his subordinate and (b) in connection with this communication is acting as a lawyer; (3) the communication relates to a fact of which the attorney was informed (a) by his client (b) without the presence of strangers (c) for the purpose of securing primarily either (i) an opinion on law or (ii) legal services or (iii) assistance in some legal proceeding, and not (d) for the purpose of committing a crime or tort; and (4) the privilege has been (a) claimed and (b) not waived by the client.

United States v. United Shoe Mach. Corp., 89 F.Supp. 357, 358–59 (D.Mass. 1950). The satisfaction of which of these requirements was at issue in *Upjohn?*

2.   Seven of the individuals interviewed in this case had terminated their employment with Upjohn at the time they were interviewed. 449 U.S. at 394 n.3. Because the lower courts had not addressed the issue, the Supreme Court did not consider whether the attorney-client privilege applied to communications by these former employees concerning activities during their period of employment. *Id.* Should the attorney-client privilege be recognized in connection with attorney interviews of former corporate employees? *See generally* Section of Litigation, American Bar Association, *Ex Parte Contacts with Former Employees* (2002); Becker, "Discovery of Information and Documents from a Litigant's Former Employees: Synergy and Synthesis of Civil Rules, Ethical Standards, Privilege Doctrines, and Common Law Principles," 81 *Neb. L. Rev.* 868 (2003).

3.   Once the Supreme Court decides that Upjohn's questionnaires are privileged, what should the lawyers for the United States do?

4.   Consider some of the things that Upjohn did in order to ensure that its questionnaires would be considered protected:

    (a) Upjohn's general counsel was in charge of the investigation;

    (b) The Upjohn officials to whom the general counsel's questionnaire was sent were general and area managers, rather than lower level employees;

    (c) Upjohn officials were instructed to treat the investigation as "highly confidential" and not to discuss it with anyone other than employees who might be helpful in providing the requested information;

    (d) Responses were to be sent directly to Upjohn's general counsel;

(e) The information sought was needed to permit the general counsel to give legal advice to Upjohn;

(f) The communications concerned matters within the scope of the employees' corporate duties, and the employees were aware that they were being questioned so that the corporation could obtain legal advice; and

(g) The questionnaire responses were kept confidential by Upjohn.

5. Will the attorney-client privilege recognized in *Upjohn* lead corporate employees to freely confide in corporate attorneys? Are corporate employees primarily concerned about possible actions that may be taken against their employer or about sanctions that may be imposed against them by members of the corporate control group? *See* D. Luban, *Lawyers and Justice* 224–25 (1988). For a study of the operation of the attorney-client privilege in the corporate setting *see* Alexander, "The Corporate Attorney-Client Privilege: A Study of the Participants," 63 *St. John's L. Rev.* 191 (1988).

6. When an attorney conducts an investigation on behalf of a corporation, what should she tell corporate employees about whom she represents? Need employees be warned at the outset of the interview that the attorney's primary allegiance is to the corporation? *See* ABA Model Rules of Professional Conduct Rule 1.13(d).

7. As with any privilege, the attorney-client privilege can be waived. Does a waiver occur if privileged documents are included within non-privileged documents produced in discovery? Rule 16(b)(3)(B)(iv) lists among the matters that a pretrial scheduling order may include "any agreements the parties reach for asserting claims of privilege or of protection as trial-preparation material after information is produced, including agreements reached under Federal Rule of Evidence 502."

In addition, Rule 26(f)(3)(D) states that the parties' discovery plan is to consider "any issues about claims of privilege or of protection as trial-preparation material, including—if the parties agree on a procedure to assert these claims after production—whether to ask the court to include their agreement in an order under Federal Rule of Evidence 502." While Federal Rule of Evidence 502(e) provides that an "agreement on the effect of disclosure in a federal proceeding is binding only on the parties to the agreement," Rule 502(d) provides: "A federal court may order that the privilege or protection is not waived by disclosure connected with the litigation pending before the court—in which event the disclosure is also not a waiver in any other federal or state proceeding." So, in order to obtain maximum protection for privileged and protected material, parties should seek to have their agreements on this subject incorporated into a court order.

8. In recommending amendments to Rule 26(f), the Advisory Committee on the Federal Rules of Civil Procedure in 2006 described some of the ways in which counsel attempt to prevent inadvertent waiver of privilege:

They may agree that the responding party will provide certain requested materials for initial examination without waiving any privilege or protection—sometimes known as a "quick peek." The requesting party then designates the documents it wishes to have actually produced. This designation is the Rule 34 request. The responding party then responds in the usual course, screening only those documents actually requested for formal production and asserting privilege claims as provided in Rule 26(b)(5)(A). On other occasions, parties enter agreements—sometimes called "clawback agreements"—that production without intent to waive privilege or protection should not be a waiver so long as the responding party identifies the documents mistakenly produced, and that the documents should be returned under those circumstances.

234 F.R.D. 219, 324 (2006).

9. Rule 26(b)(5)(B) deals with situations in which information (electronic or otherwise) that is arguably protected as privileged or work product is mistakenly produced in discovery:

> If information is produced in discovery that is subject to a claim of privilege or of protection as trial-preparation material, the party making the claim may notify any party that received the information of the claim and the basis for it. After being notified, a party must promptly return, sequester, or destroy the specified information and any copies it has; must not use or disclose the information until the claim is resolved; must take reasonable steps to retrieve the information if the party disclosed it before being notified; and may promptly present the information to the court under seal for a determination of the claim. The producing party must preserve the information until the claim is resolved.

10. Hopefully, counsel will realize that material is privileged before producing it to other parties. Once counsel decides that information sought in discovery is privileged, she must assert the privilege. Rule 26(b)(5)(A) prescribes the manner in which a claim of privilege or trial preparation protection must be asserted:

> When a party withholds information otherwise discoverable by claiming that the information is privileged or subject to protection as trial preparation material, the party must:
>
> (i) expressly make the claim; and
>
> (ii) describe the nature of the documents, communications, or tangible things not produced or disclosed—and do so in a manner that, without revealing information itself privileged or protected, will enable other parties to assess the claim.

While the detail with which an objection must be asserted under Rule 26(b)(5)(A) will vary from case to case, claims of privilege and work-product protection must be expressly asserted. "To withhold materials without such notice is contrary to the rule, subjects the party to sanctions under Rule

37(b)(2), and may be viewed as a waiver of the privilege or protection."
Advisory Committee Note to 1993 Amendment to Rule 26, 146 F.R.D. 401,
639 (1993).

D. ATTORNEY WORK-PRODUCT

Although not mentioned in Rule 26(b)(1)'s general statement of
discovery scope and limits, discovery is also limited by the attorney
work-product doctrine. This protection was recognized by the Supreme
Court in its 1947 decision in *Hickman v. Taylor*. That decision, and the
1970 inclusion of that protection in Rule 26(b)(3) of the Federal Rules of
Civil Procedure, are considered in the two subsections that follows.

1. *HICKMAN V. TAYLOR*

Hickman v. Taylor

Supreme Court of the United States, 1947
329 U.S. 495

OPINION

■ MR. JUSTICE MURPHY delivered the opinion of the Court.

This case presents an important problem under the Federal Rules
of Civil Procedure as to the extent to which a party may inquire into
oral and written statements of witnesses, or other information, secured
by an adverse party's counsel in the course of preparation for possible
litigation after a claim has arisen. Examination into a person's files and
records, including those resulting from the professional activities of an
attorney, must be judged with care. It is not without reason that
various safeguards have been established to preclude unwarranted
excursions into the privacy of a man's work. At the same time, public
policy supports reasonable and necessary inquiries. Properly to balance
these competing interests is a delicate and difficult task.

On February 7, 1943, the tug "J. M. Taylor" sank while engaged in
helping to tow a car float of the Baltimore & Ohio Railroad across the
Delaware River at Philadelphia. The accident was apparently unusual
in nature, the cause of it still being unknown. Five of the nine crew
members were drowned. Three days later the tug owners and the
underwriters employed a law firm, of which respondent Fortenbaugh is
a member, to defend them against potential suits by representatives of
the deceased crew members and to sue the railroad for damages to the
tug.

A public hearing was held on March 4, 1943, before the United
States Steamboat Inspectors, at which the four survivors were
examined. This testimony was recorded and made available to all
interested parties. Shortly thereafter, Fortenbaugh privately
interviewed the survivors and took statements from them with an eye
toward the anticipated litigation; the survivors signed these statements

on March 29. Fortenbaugh also interviewed other persons believed to have some information relating to the accident and in some cases he made memoranda of what they told him. At the time when Fortenbaugh secured the statements of the survivors, representatives of two of the deceased crew members had been in communication with him. Ultimately claims were presented by representatives of all five of the deceased; four of the claims, however, were settled without litigation. The fifth claimant, petitioner herein, brought suit in a federal court under the Jones Act on November 26, 1943, naming as defendants the two tug owners, individually and as partners, and the railroad.

One year later, petitioner filed 39 interrogatories directed to the tug owners. The 38th interrogatory read: "State whether any statements of the members of the crews of the Tugs 'J. M. Taylor' and 'Philadelphia' or of any other vessel were taken in connection with the towing of the car float and the sinking of the Tug 'John M. Taylor.' Attach hereto exact copies of all such statements if in writing, and if oral, set forth in detail the exact provisions of any such oral statements or reports."

Supplemental interrogatories asked whether any oral or written statements, records, reports or other memoranda had been made concerning any matter relative to the towing operation, the sinking of the tug, the salvaging and repair of the tug, and the death of the deceased. If the answer was in the affirmative, the tug owners were then requested to set forth the nature of all such records, reports, statements or other memoranda.

The tug owners, through Fortenbaugh, answered all of the interrogatories except No. 38 and the supplemental ones just described. While admitting that statements of the survivors had been taken, they declined to summarize or set forth the contents. They did so on the ground that such requests called "for privileged matter obtained in preparation for litigation" and constituted "an attempt to obtain indirectly counsel's private files." It was claimed that answering these requests "would involve practically turning over not only the complete files, but also the telephone records and, almost, the thoughts of counsel."

* * * The District Court for the Eastern District of Pennsylvania, sitting en banc, held that the requested matters were not privileged. The court then decreed that the tug owners and Fortenbaugh, as counsel and agent for the tug owners, forthwith "Answer plaintiff's 38th interrogatory and supplementary interrogatories; produce all written statements of witnesses obtained by Mr. Fortenbaugh, as counsel and agent for Defendants; state in substance any fact concerning this case which Defendants learned through oral statements made by witnesses to Mr. Fortenbaugh whether or not included in his private memoranda and produce Mr. Fortenbaugh's memoranda containing statements of fact by witnesses or to submit these memoranda to the Court for

742   DISCLOSURE AND DISCOVERY: "LET'S SEE WHAT THE OTHER
SIDE'S GOT."
       CHAPTER 10

determination of those portions which should be revealed to Plaintiff." Upon their refusal, the court adjudged them in contempt and ordered them imprisoned until they complied.

The Third Circuit Court of Appeals, also sitting en banc, reversed the judgment of the District Court. It held that the information here sought was part of the "work product of the lawyer" and hence privileged from discovery under the Federal Rules of Civil Procedure. The importance of the problem, which has engendered a great divergence of views among district courts, led us to grant certiorari.

The pre-trial deposition-discovery mechanism established by Rules 26 to 37 is one of the most significant innovations of the Federal Rules of Civil Procedure. Under the prior federal practice, the pre-trial functions of notice-giving, issue-formulation and fact-revelation were performed primarily and inadequately by the pleadings. Inquiry into the issues and the facts before trial was narrowly confined and was often cumbersome in method. The new rules, however, restrict the pleadings to the task of general notice-giving and invest the deposition-discovery process with a vital role in the preparation for trial. The various instruments of discovery now serve (1) as a device, along with the pre-trial hearing under Rule 16, to narrow and clarify the basic issues between the parties, and (2) as a device for ascertaining the facts, or information as to the existence or whereabouts of facts, relative to those issues. Thus civil trials in the federal courts no longer need be carried on in the dark. The way is now clear, consistent with recognized privileges, for the parties to obtain the fullest possible knowledge of the issues and facts before trial.

[The Court then noted that neither Rule 33 nor Rule 34 of the Federal Rules of Civil Procedure could be used to obtain information from attorney Fortenbaugh, because Rule 33 interrogatories and Rule 34 requests for production only can be directed to a party. The Court suggested that Hickman should have attempted to take Fortenbaugh's deposition and seek the documents in question by means of a Rule 45 subpoena *duces tecum*.]

But, under the circumstances, we deem it unnecessary and unwise to rest our decision upon this procedural irregularity, an irregularity which is not strongly urged upon us and which was disregarded in the two courts below. It matters little at this late stage whether Fortenbaugh fails to answer interrogatories filed under Rule 26 or under Rule 33 or whether he refuses to produce the memoranda and statements pursuant to a subpoena under Rule 45 or a court order under Rule 34. The deposition-discovery rules create integrated procedural devices. And the basic question at stake is whether any of those devices may be used to inquire into materials collected by an adverse party's counsel in the course of preparation for possible litigation. The fact that the petitioner may have used the wrong method does not destroy the main thrust of his attempt. Nor does it relieve us of

the responsibility of dealing with the problem raised by that attempt.
* * *

In urging that he has a right to inquire into the materials secured and prepared by Fortenbaugh, petitioner emphasizes that the deposition-discovery portions of the Federal Rules of Civil Procedure are designed to enable the parties to discover the true facts and to compel their disclosure wherever they may be found. It is said that inquiry may be made under these rules, epitomized by Rule 26, as to any relevant matter which is not privileged; and since the discovery provisions are to be applied as broadly and liberally as possible, the privilege limitation must be restricted to its narrowest bounds. On the premise that the attorney-client privilege is the one involved in this case, petitioner argues that it must be strictly confined to confidential communications made by a client to his attorney. And since the materials here in issue were secured by Fortenbaugh from third persons rather than from his clients, the tug owners, the conclusion is reached that these materials are proper subjects for discovery under Rule 26.

As additional support for this result, petitioner claims that to prohibit discovery under these circumstances would give a corporate defendant a tremendous advantage in a suit by an individual plaintiff. Thus in a suit by an injured employee against a railroad or in a suit by an insured person against an insurance company the corporate defendant could pull a dark veil of secrecy over all the pertinent facts it can collect after the claim arises merely on the assertion that such facts were gathered by its large staff of attorneys and claim agents. At the same time, the individual plaintiff, who often has direct knowledge of the matter in issue and has no counsel until some time after his claim arises could be compelled to disclose all the intimate details of his case. By endowing with immunity from disclosure all that a lawyer discovers in the course of his duties, it is said, the rights of individual litigants in such cases are drained of vitality and the lawsuit becomes more of a battle of deception than a search for truth.

But framing the problem in terms of assisting individual plaintiffs in their suits against corporate defendants is unsatisfactory. Discovery concededly may work to the disadvantage as well as to the advantage of individual plaintiffs. Discovery, in other words, is not a one-way proposition. It is available in all types of cases at the behest of any party, individual or corporate, plaintiff or defendant. The problem thus far transcends the situation confronting this petitioner. And we must view that problem in light of the limitless situations where the particular kind of discovery sought by petitioner might be used.

We agree, of course, that the deposition-discovery rules are to be accorded a broad and liberal treatment. No longer can the time-honored cry of "fishing expedition" serve to preclude a party from inquiring into the facts underlying his opponent's case. Mutual knowledge of all the

744

DISCLOSURE AND DISCOVERY: "LET'S SEE WHAT THE OTHER
SIDE'S GOT."

CHAPTER 10

relevant facts gathered by both parties is essential to proper litigation. To that end, either party may compel the other to disgorge whatever facts he has in his possession. The deposition-discovery procedure simply advances the stage at which the disclosure can be compelled from the time of trial to the period preceding it, thus reducing the possibility of surprise. But discovery, like all matters of procedure, has ultimate and necessary boundaries. * * * [A]s Rule 26(b) provides, * * * limitations come into existence when the inquiry touches upon the irrelevant or encroaches upon the recognized domains of privilege.

We also agree that the memoranda, statements and mental impressions in issue in this case fall outside the scope of the attorney-client privilege and hence are not protected from discovery on that basis. It is unnecessary here to delineate the content and scope of that privilege as recognized in the federal courts. For present purposes, it suffices to note that the protective cloak of this privilege does not extend to information which an attorney secures from a witness while acting for his client in anticipation of litigation. Nor does this privilege concern the memoranda, briefs, communications and other writings prepared by counsel for his own use in prosecuting his client's case; and it is equally unrelated to writings which reflect an attorney's mental impressions, conclusions, opinions or legal theories.

But the impropriety of invoking that privilege does not provide an answer to the problem before us. Petitioner has made more than an ordinary request for relevant, nonprivileged facts in the possession of his adversaries or their counsel. He has sought discovery as of right of oral and written statements of witnesses whose identity is well known and whose availability to petitioner appears unimpaired. He has sought production of these matters after making the most searching inquiries of his opponents as to the circumstances surrounding the fatal accident, which inquiries were sworn to have been answered to the best of their information and belief. Interrogatories were directed toward all the events prior to, during and subsequent to the sinking of the tug. Full and honest answers to such broad inquiries would necessarily have included all pertinent information gleaned by Fortenbaugh through his interviews with the witnesses. Petitioner makes no suggestion, and we cannot assume, that the tug owners or Fortenbaugh were incomplete or dishonest in the framing of their answers. In addition, petitioner was free to examine the public testimony of the witnesses taken before the United States Steamboat Inspectors. We are thus dealing with an attempt to secure the production of written statements and mental impressions contained in the files and mind of the attorney Fortenbaugh without any showing of necessity or any indication or claim that denial of such production would unduly prejudice the preparation of petitioner's case or cause him any hardship or injustice. For aught that appears, the essence of what petitioner seeks either has been revealed to him already through the interrogatories or is readily available to him direct from the witnesses for the asking.

* * *

In our opinion, neither Rule 26 nor any other rule dealing with discovery contemplates production under such circumstances. That is not because the subject matter is privileged or irrelevant, as those concepts are used in these rules. Here is simply an attempt, without purported necessity or justification, to secure written statements, private memoranda and personal recollections prepared or formed by an adverse party's counsel in the course of his legal duties. As such, it falls outside the arena of discovery and contravenes the public policy underlying the orderly prosecution and defense of legal claims. Not even the most liberal of discovery theories can justify unwarranted inquiries into the files and the mental impressions of an attorney.

Historically, a lawyer is an officer of the court and is bound to work for the advancement of justice while faithfully protecting the rightful interests of his clients. In performing his various duties, however, it is essential that a lawyer work with a certain degree of privacy, free from unnecessary intrusion by opposing parties and their counsel. Proper preparation of a client's case demands that he assemble information, sift what he considers to be the relevant from the irrelevant facts, prepare his legal theories and plan his strategy without undue and needless interference. That is the historical and the necessary way in which lawyers act within the framework of our system of jurisprudence to promote justice and to protect their clients' interests. This work is reflected, of course, in interviews, statements, memoranda, correspondence, briefs, mental impressions, personal beliefs, and countless other tangible and intangible ways—aptly though roughly termed by the Circuit Court of Appeals in this case as the "work product of the lawyer." Were such materials open to opposing counsel on mere demand, much of what is now put down in writing would remain unwritten. An attorney's thoughts, heretofore inviolate, would not be his own. Inefficiency, unfairness and sharp practices would inevitably develop in the giving of legal advice and in the preparation of cases for trial. The effect on the legal profession would be demoralizing. And the interests of the clients and the cause of justice would be poorly served.

We do not mean to say that all written materials obtained or prepared by an adversary's counsel with an eye toward litigation are necessarily free from discovery in all cases. Where relevant and non-privileged facts remain hidden in an attorney's file and where production of those facts is essential to the preparation of one's case, discovery may properly be had. Such written statements and documents might, under certain circumstances, be admissible in evidence or give clues as to the existence or location of relevant facts. Or they might be useful for purposes of impeachment or corroboration. And production might be justified where the witnesses are no longer available or can be reached only with difficulty. Were production of written statements and documents to be precluded under such circumstances, the liberal ideals of the deposition-discovery portions of the Federal Rules of Civil Procedure would be stripped of much of their meaning. But the general policy against invading the privacy of an attorney's course of preparation is so well recognized and so essential to an orderly working of our system of legal procedure that a burden rests on the one who would invade that privacy to establish adequate reasons to justify production through a subpoena or court order. That burden, we believe, is necessarily implicit in the rules as now constituted.

Rule 30(b), as presently written [now, Rule 26(c)], gives the trial judge the requisite discretion to make a judgment as to whether discovery should be allowed as to written statements secured from witnesses. But in the instant case there was no room for that discretion to operate in favor of the petitioner. No attempt was made to establish any reason why Fortenbaugh should be forced to produce the written statements. There was only a naked, general demand for these materials as of right and a finding by the District Court that no recognizable privilege was involved. That was insufficient to justify discovery under these circumstances and the court should have sustained the refusal of the tug owners and Fortenbaugh to produce.

But as to oral statements made by witnesses to Fortenbaugh, whether presently in the form of his mental impressions or memoranda, we do not believe that any showing of necessity can be made under the circumstances of this case so as to justify production. Under ordinary conditions, forcing an attorney to repeat or write out all that witnesses have told him and to deliver the account to his adversary gives rise to grave dangers of inaccuracy and untrustworthiness. No legitimate purpose is served by such production. The practice forces the attorney to testify as to what he remembers or what he saw fit to write down regarding witnesses' remarks. Such testimony could not qualify as evidence; and to use it for impeachment or corroborative purposes would make the attorney much less an officer of the court and much more an ordinary witness. The standards of the profession would thereby suffer.

Denial of production of this nature does not mean that any material, non-privileged facts can be hidden from the petitioner in this case. He need not be unduly hindered in the preparation of his case, in the discovery of facts or in his anticipation of his opponent's position. Searching interrogatories directed to Fortenbaugh and the tug owners, production of written documents and statements upon a proper showing and direct interviews with the witnesses themselves all serve to reveal the facts in Fortenbaugh's possession to the fullest possible extent consistent with public policy. Petitioner's counsel frankly admits that he wants the oral statements only to help prepare himself to examine witnesses and to make sure that he has overlooked nothing. That is insufficient under the circumstances to permit him an exception to the policy underlying the privacy of Fortenbaugh's professional activities. If there should be a rare situation justifying production of these matters, petitioner's case is not of that type.

* * * When Rule 26 and the other discovery rules were adopted, this Court and the members of the bar in general certainly did not believe or contemplate that all the files and mental processes of lawyers were thereby opened to the free scrutiny of their adversaries. And we refuse to interpret the rules at this time so as to reach so harsh and unwarranted a result.

We therefore affirm the judgment of the Circuit Court of Appeals.

Affirmed.

■ MR. JUSTICE JACKSON, concurring.

The narrow question in this case concerns only one of thirty-nine interrogatories which defendants and their counsel refused to answer. As there was persistence in refusal after the court ordered them to answer it, counsel and clients were committed to jail by the district court until they should purge themselves of contempt.

* * *

The primary effect of the practice advocated here would be on the legal profession itself. But it too often is overlooked that the lawyer and the law office are indispensable parts of our administration of justice. Law-abiding people can go nowhere else to learn the ever changing and constantly multiplying rules by which they must behave and to obtain redress for their wrongs. The welfare and tone of the legal profession is therefore of prime consequence to society, which would feel the consequences of such a practice as petitioner urges secondarily but certainly.

"Discovery" is one of the working tools of the legal profession. It traces back to the equity bill of discovery in English Chancery practice and seems to have had a forerunner in Continental practice. *See* Ragland, Discovery Before Trial (1932) 13–16. Since 1848 when the draftsmen of New York's Code of Procedure recognized the importance of a better system of discovery, the impetus to extend and expand discovery, as well as the opposition to it, has come from within the Bar itself. It happens in this case that it is the plaintiff's attorney who demands such unprecedented latitude of discovery and, strangely enough, *amicus* briefs in his support have been filed by several labor unions representing plaintiffs as a class. It is the history of the movement for broader discovery, however, that in actual experience the chief opposition to its extension has come from lawyers who specialize in representing plaintiffs, because defendants have made liberal use of it to force plaintiffs to disclose their cases in advance. *See* Report of the

Commission on the Administration of Justice in New York State (1934)
330–31; Ragland, Discovery Before Trial (1932) 35–36. Discovery is a
two-edged sword and we cannot decide this problem on any doctrine of
extending help to one class of litigants.

* * *

To consider first the most extreme aspect of the requirement in
litigation here, we find it calls upon counsel, if he has had any
conversations with any of the crews of the vessels in question or of any
other, to "set forth in detail the exact provision of any such oral
statements or reports." Thus the demand is not for the production of a
transcript in existence but calls for the creation of a written statement
not in being. But the statement by counsel of what a witness told him is
not evidence when written. Plaintiff could not introduce it to prove his
case. What, then, is the purpose sought to be served by demanding this
of adverse counsel?

Counsel for the petitioner candidly said on argument that he
wanted this information to help prepare himself to examine witnesses,
to make sure he overlooked nothing. He bases his claim to it in his brief
on the view that the Rules were to do away with the old situation where
a lawsuit developed into "a battle of wits between counsel." But a
common law trial is and always should be an adversary proceeding.
Discovery was hardly intended to enable a learned profession to
perform its functions either without wits or on wits borrowed from the
adversary.

The real purpose and the probable effect of the practice ordered by
the district court would be to put trials on a level even lower than a
"battle of wits." I can conceive of no practice more demoralizing to the
Bar than to require a lawyer to write out and deliver to his adversary
an account of what witnesses have told him. Even if his recollection
were perfect, the statement would be his language, permeated with his
inferences. Every one who has tried it knows that it is almost
impossible so fairly to record the expressions and emphasis of a witness
that when he testifies in the environment of the court and under the
influence of the leading question there will not be departures in some
respects. Whenever the testimony of the witness would differ from the
"exact" statement the lawyer had delivered, the lawyer's statement
would be whipped out to impeach the witness. Counsel producing his
adversary's "inexact" statement could lose nothing by saying, "Here is a
contradiction, gentlemen of the jury. I do not know whether it is my
adversary or his witness who is not telling the truth, but one is not." Of
course, if this practice were adopted, that scene would be repeated over
and over again. The lawyer who delivers such statements often would
find himself branded a deceiver afraid to take the stand to support his
own version of the witness's conversation with him, or else he will have

SECTION III DISCOVERY SCOPE AND LIMITS **749**

to go on the stand to defend his own credibility—perhaps against that of his chief witness, or possibly even his client.

Every lawyer dislikes to take the witness stand and will do so only for grave reasons. This is partly because it is not his role; he is almost invariably a poor witness. But he steps out of professional character to do it. He regrets it; the profession discourages it. But the practice advocated here is one which would force him to be a witness, not as to what he has seen or done but as to other witnesses' stories, and not because he wants to do so but in self-defense.

And what is the lawyer to do who has interviewed one whom he believes to be a biased, lying or hostile witness to get his unfavorable statements and know what to meet? He must record and deliver such statements even though he would not vouch for the credibility of the witness by calling him. Perhaps the other side would not want to call him either, but the attorney is open to the charge of suppressing evidence at the trial if he fails to call such a hostile witness even though he never regarded him as reliable or truthful.

Having been supplied the names of the witnesses, petitioner's lawyer gives no reason why he cannot interview them himself. If an employee-witness refuses to tell his story, he, too, may be examined under the Rules. He may be compelled on discovery, as fully as on the trial, to disclose his version of the facts. But that is his own disclosure—it can be used to impeach him if he contradicts it and such a deposition is not useful to promote an unseemly disagreement between the witness and the counsel in the case.

* * *

The question remains as to signed statements or those written by witnesses. Such statements are not evidence for the defendant. *Palmer v. Hoffman,* 318 U.S. 109. Nor should I think they ordinarily could be evidence for the plaintiff. But such a statement might be useful for impeachment of the witness who signed it, if he is called and if he departs from the statement. There might be circumstances, too, where impossibility or difficulty of access to the witness or his refusal to respond to requests for information or other facts would show that the interests of justice require that such statements be made available. Production of such statements are governed by Rule 34 and on "showing good cause therefor" the court may order their inspection, copying or photographing. No such application has here been made; the demand is made on the basis of right, not on showing of cause.

I agree to the affirmance of the judgment of the Circuit Court of Appeals which reversed the district court.

■ MR. JUSTICE FRANKFURTER joins in this opinion.

COMMENTS AND QUESTIONS CONCERNING *HICKMAN V. TAYLOR*

1.   After the Supreme Court's ruling in *Hickman v. Taylor,* the case
was tried and resulted in a $5000 verdict for Hickman's estate. At the trial
Fortenbaugh offered the witness statements that he had refused to provide
in discovery, but the court sustained plaintiff's objection to this evidence.
Coady, "Dredging the Depths of *Hickman v. Taylor,*" *Harv. L. Rec.,* May 6,
1977, at 2.

2.   What was really at stake in this action? Why would the defendant
tug owners and attorney Fortenbaugh litigate the discovery issue in this
case all the way to the United States Supreme Court? Both the Eastern
District of Pennsylvania and the United States Court of Appeals for the
Third Circuit decided this case en banc, and the American Bar Association
participated as *amicus curiae* in the Supreme Court and the lower federal
courts.

3.   Why were Fortenbaugh's interviews not protected by the attorney-
client privilege? What if the survivors he interviewed had been ordered to
talk to Fortenbaugh by the tug owners? What if the survivors were
themselves co-owners of the tug?

4.   Would this case have been decided differently if the surviving
crew members had not given public testimony? What if they not only gave
no public testimony but, after their interviews with Fortenbaugh, they
refused to talk with plaintiff's counsel?

5.   Could the plaintiff obtain the information he sought directly from
the witnesses from whom Fortenbaugh had taken statements? Why did
plaintiff nevertheless want the statements taken by Fortenbaugh?

6.   The Supreme Court in *Hickman v. Taylor* establishes a hierarchy
of attorney work-product protections. Consider the degree of protection
given the following under *Hickman:* written statements taken from a
witness at the time of an interview; memoranda prepared by an attorney
contemporaneously with witness interviews; and the current mental
impressions and recollections of an attorney concerning a witness.

7.   Why did Justice Jackson write a concurring opinion in *Hickman v.
Taylor*? He served as chief Allied prosecutor at the Nuremberg War Crimes
Trials, observing firsthand the abuses of a legal system in which an
attorney's primary loyalty was not to his client. Even prior to his service at
Nuremberg, Jackson had written eloquently about the role of the lawyer,
and, in particular, of the "country lawyer," in protecting individual rights
within our legal system:

> [T]his vanishing country lawyer left his mark on his times, and he
> was worth knowing. * * * Once enlisted for a client, he took his
> obligation seriously. He insisted on complete control of the
> litigation—he was no mere hired hand. But he gave every power
> and resource to the cause. He identified himself with the client's
> cause fully, sometimes too fully. He would fight the adverse party
> and fight his counsel, fight every hostile witness, and fight the
> court, fight public sentiment, fight any obstacle to his client's

success. He never quit. * * * He moved for new trials, he appealed; and if he lost out in the end, he joined the client at the tavern in damning the judge—which is the last rite in closing an unsuccessful case, and I have officiated at many. * * * The law to him was like a religion, and its practice was more than a means of support; it was a mission. He was not always popular in his community, but he was respected. Unpopular minorities and individuals often found in him their only mediator and advocate. He was too independent to court the populace—he thought of himself as a leader and lawgiver, not as a mouthpiece.

Jackson, "Tribute to Country Lawyers: A Review," 30 *A.B.A.J.* 136, 139 (1944).

8.   In his opinion Justice Murphy states: "Mutual knowledge of all the relevant facts gathered by both parties is essential to proper litigation." Is this a self-evident proposition? Why is discovery in criminal cases, in which life and liberty are at stake, much more limited than in civil actions? Why have other countries not followed the United States in providing expansive civil discovery? Is the presumption underlying the Supreme Court's statement in *Hickman v. Taylor* one of the reasons for current problems with discovery abuse?

9.   Professor Geoffrey Hazard has stated that "broad discovery is * * * not a mere procedural rule. Rather it has become, at least for our era, a procedural institution perhaps of virtually constitutional foundation." Hazard, "From Whom No Secrets Are Hid," 76 *Tex. L. Rev.* 1665, 1694 (1998). Should we attempt to turn back the clock to an earlier era in which discovery played a less dominant role? Would it be possible?

2.   THE WORK-PRODUCT DOCTRINE UNDER RULE 26(b)(3)

In 1970, well after the Supreme Court's decision in *Hickman v. Taylor,* Rule 26(b)(3) was added to the Federal Rules of Civil Procedure to protect trial preparation materials from discovery. Rule 26(b)(3)(A) provides:

> Ordinarily, a party may not discover documents and tangible things that are prepared in anticipation of litigation or for trial by or for another party or its representative (including the other party's attorney, consultant, surety, indemnitor, insurer, or agent). But, subject to Rule 26(b)(4) [concerning discovery of expert witnesses], those materials may be discovered if:
>
> > (i) they are otherwise discoverable under Rule 26(b)(1); and
> >
> > (ii) the party shows that it has substantial need for the materials to prepare its case and cannot, without undue hardship, obtain their substantial equivalent by other means.

Rule 26(b)(3) applies only to "documents and tangible things." The Advisory Committee's Note to the 1970 amendments to Rule 26 explained this restriction as follows:

> Rules 33 and 36 have been revised in order to permit discovery calling for opinions, contentions, and admissions relating not only to fact but also to the application of law to fact. Under those rules, a party and his attorney or other representative may be required to disclose, to some extent, mental impressions, opinions, or conclusions. But documents or parts of documents containing these matters are protected against discovery by this subdivision. Even though a party may ultimately have to disclose in response to interrogatories or requests to admit, he is entitled to keep confidential documents containing such matters prepared for internal use.

48 F.R.D. 487, 502 (1970). Despite the limitation of Rule 26(b)(3) to "documents and tangible things," *Hickman* itself continues to protect unrecorded attorney work-product. Special Project, "The Work Product Doctrine," 68 *Cornell L. Rev.* 760, 841 (1983).

Rule 26(b)(3)(B) mirrors *Hickman* in providing the very highest protection for core attorney work-product, stating: "If the court orders discovery of those [trial preparation materials described in Rule 26(b)(3)(A)], it must protect against disclosure of the mental impressions, conclusions, opinions, or legal theories of a party's attorney or other representative concerning the litigation." However, Rule 26(b)(3)(C) gives an explicit right for persons to obtain their own witness statements: "Any party or other person may, on request and without the required showing, obtain the person's own previous statement about the action or its subject matter."

While *Hickman v. Taylor* involved work-product created by an attorney, the protections of Rule 26(b)(3) extend beyond attorneys to other party representatives, including consultants, sureties, indemnitors, insurers, and agents. This is a recognition that the representation of most parties in modern litigation involves persons other than their attorneys.

COMMENTS AND QUESTIONS CONCERNING RULE 26(b)(3) WORK-PRODUCT

1. Must a specific legal claim have arisen at the time that a document was created in order for that document to have been "prepared in anticipation of litigation" for the purposes of Rule 26(b)(3)? In *In re Sealed Case*, 146 F.3d 881, 884 (D.C.Cir. 1998), the court stated: "For a document to meet this [Rule 26(b)(3)] standard, the lawyer must at least have had a subjective belief that litigation was a real possibility, and that belief must have been objectively reasonable." The court concluded that, in the case before it, this standard was met even though no specific claim was pending at the time the document in question was created.

2.   In processing insurance claims, business activity at some point may shift from general claims investigation and evaluation to efforts undertaken in anticipation of litigation. In *Lett v. State Farm Fire and Casualty Co.*, 115 F.R.D. 501 (N.D.Ga. 1987), the court held that Rule 26(b)(3) applied to documents created after a claim was assigned to an investigative unit because of suspicion of plaintiffs' involvement in a fire; It also appeared that the claim would be denied if the information in the file was confirmed to be true. The court concluded that plaintiffs could not show the substantial need and undue hardship necessary to overcome the work-product protection. The insurer's bad faith that plaintiffs needed to establish was to be determined as of the date of trial, and plaintiffs had neither identified facts known exclusively by defendants nor shown that they could not obtain the facts necessary to support their claims by deposing the individuals who wrote the reports they sought to discover.

3.   Rule 26(b)(3)(C) permits any person to obtain "the person's own previous statement about the action or its subject matter." Doesn't this provision circumvent some of the protections established by *Hickman v. Taylor*? Under this Rule, could the plaintiff in *Hickman* merely have asked those who had given statements to attorney Fortenbaugh to request copies of their statements from the defendant? Consider the definition of "statement" contained in Rule 26(b)(3)(C) and the protections that Rule 26(b)(3)(B) requires to be given to "the mental impressions, conclusions, opinions, or legal theories of a party's attorney or other representative concerning the litigation."

4.   Are there circumstances in which a party can depose opposing counsel concerning the investigation undertaken prior to the filing of suit? The plaintiff in *Brown v. Hart, Schaffner & Marx,* 96 F.R.D. 64 (N.D.Ill. 1982), brought a shareholders' derivative action. Although Rule 23.1 of the Federal Rules of Civil Procedure requires that the complaint in such an action be verified, plaintiff's deposition revealed that she had not "even the vaguest notion of whether or not a factual basis existed for any of the grave charges she had made against the [defendant] directors." 96 F.R.D. at 66. Instead, plaintiff left any investigation to her attorneys (who also represented her in five other derivative actions). The defendants sought to depose her attorneys to ascertain the nature and extent of any investigation conducted prior to the filing and verification of the complaint.

The court rejected plaintiff's assertion of attorney-client privilege, because her lack of information indicated that she could not have communicated any relevant information to her attorneys. Nor did the court believe that the work-product doctrine precluded the discovery sought; plaintiff made no showing that the documents requested had been prepared in anticipation of litigation, and the defendants established their substantial need for the information sought and their inability to obtain that information by other means. The court stressed that it was the purpose of Rule 23.1 to discourage "strike suits," which it described as "a particularly repugnant species of blackmail. Such lawsuits are the base work of rapacious jackals whose declared concern for the corporate well-being camouflages their unwholesome appetite for corporate dollars." 96 F.R.D. at 67.

5.   In other circumstances as well, the work-product doctrine may not preclude the deposition of attorney-employees concerning non-privileged, pre-litigation facts. In *United States v. Philip Morris*, 209 F.R.D. 13 (D.D.C. 2002), the court refused to quash the depositions of defendant's senior vice president, general counsel, and three in-house counsel because the depositions sought were not of trial or litigation counsel and would not expose the defendant's litigation strategy in the pending case. 209 F.R.D. at 17. Judge Gladys Kessler noted that to preclude these depositions "would allow Defendants to immunize themselves from discovery on key issues, by knowingly and strategically placing persons who happen to be attorneys in positions where they perform critical business, marketing, public relations, research, scientific and development duties." 209 F.R.D. at 19. In reaching her decision, Judge Kessler distinguished the decision in *Shelton v. American Motors Corp.*, 805 F.2d 1323, 1327 (8th Cir. 1986), which had precluded the deposition of trial counsel unless "(1) no other means exist to obtain the information than to depose opposing counsel * * *; (2) the information sought is relevant and nonprivileged; and (3) the information is crucial to the preparation of the case."

IV. EXPERT DISCOVERY

Because of the important role that expert witnesses play in civil litigation, Rule 26(a)(2) requires that the identity of experts (and, in most cases, written expert reports) must be provided before trial. Section II(B), *supra*. For similar reasons, there are specific provisions in Rule 26(b)(4) regulating discovery of expert witnesses, their reports, and their communications.

A. RULE 26(b)(4) EXPERT DISCOVERY AND PROTECTIONS

Initially, Rule 26(b)(4)(A) establishes the right of parties to take the deposition of those who have been identified as potential expert witnesses at trial:

> A party may depose any person who has been identified as an expert whose opinions may be presented at trial. If Rule 26(a)(2)(B) requires a report from the expert, the deposition may be conducted only after the report is provided.

While Rule 26(b)(4)(A) provides a right to depose expert witnesses who will testify at trial, Rule 26(b)(4)(D) severely limits the ability of parties to obtain discovery from experts who have been retained by other parties but who will not testify at trial. This section provides:

> Ordinarily, a party may not, by interrogatories or deposition, discover facts known or opinions held by an expert who has been retained or specially employed by another party in anticipation of litigation or to prepare for trial and who is

not expected to be called as a witness at trial. But a party may do so only:

> (i)   as provided in Rule 35(b); or

> (ii) on showing exceptional circumstances under which it is impracticable for the party to obtain facts or opinions on the same subject by other means.

The first possibility for obtaining discovery of a retained, non-testifying expert arises under the Rule 35(b) provisions for physical and mental examinations. Under Rule 35 a party can seek an order requiring an individual whose mental or physical condition is in controversy to submit himself to a physical or mental examination. In seeking such an examination, the party must show good cause for the examination and specify the person who will perform the examination. But what if the examining doctor or other expert reaches conclusions that are unfavorable to the party who sought the exam (if, for instance, a doctor examines the plaintiff at the request of the defendant but substantiates all of plaintiff's allegations of injury)? In this situation, the defendant may decide not to call the doctor as a trial witness, so that the plaintiff has no right to depose the doctor pursuant to Rule 26(b)(4)(A). Nevertheless, the plaintiff will be able to obtain a copy of the doctor's written report pursuant to Rule 35(b)(1) or, if the plaintiff can show exceptional circumstances, even obtain the deposition of the doctor pursuant to Rule 26(b)(4)(D).

Rule 26(b)(4)(D) describes the "exceptional circumstances" that can provide a basis for discovery of a non-testifying expert as occurring when "it is impracticable for the party [seeking discovery] to obtain facts or opinions on the same subject by other means." Imagine, for example, a party retaining all of the available experts on a subject—thus precluding other parties from calling experts of their own. One party might retain all the experts in a particular geographic area (leaving no one to testify to the medical standard of care in a case arising in a small community), or a party might retain all the national experts in a specialty with few true experts. Whether this has been done to preclude other parties from retaining their own experts or not, these are the types of situations in which a court might authorize a party to obtain discovery from one of the retained experts who will not be offered at trial.

Not only does Rule 26(b)(4) set forth the procedures for obtaining expert discovery, but that subsection also protects drafts of expert reports, as well as disclosures and communications between experts and the attorneys who have retained them. By classifying reports, disclosures, and attorney-expert communications as within the Rule 26(b)(3) trial preparation protections, both experts and their attorneys have greater freedom in preparing expert testimony for trial.

Rule 26(b)(4)(B) provides: "Rules 26(b)(3)(A) and (B) protect drafts of any report or disclosure required under Rule 26(a)(2), regardless of the form in which the draft is recorded." Expert witnesses typically work through preliminary drafts in preparing the written report required by Rule 26(a)(2), and they typically communicate with the attorneys who have retained them as they develop their reports and trial testimony. Therefore Rule 26(b)(4)(C) provides:

> Rules 26(b)(3)(A) and (B) protect communications between the party's attorney and any witness required to provide a report under Rule 26(a)(2)(B), regardless of the form of the communications, except to the extent that the communications:
>
> > (i)   relate to compensation for the expert's study or testimony;
> >
> > (ii) identify facts or data that the party's attorney provided and that the expert considered in forming the opinions to be expressed; or
> >
> > (iii) identify assumptions that the party's attorney provided and that the expert relied on in forming the opinions to be expressed.

All three of these exceptions to the protection of expert-attorney communications are to allow a party to obtain specific information with which to cross-examine the expert in a deposition or at trial. The fact that an expert is being compensated by a party can be used by other parties to suggest that expert's bias. If the expert, in reaching her opinions, considered data or assumptions given to her by the attorney who retained her, other parties might be able to use this to undermining the expert's ultimate conclusions.

While the complexity of expert testimony makes pretrial discovery of that testimony essential, experts differ from other witnesses because they are usually paid for their testimony. Rule 26(b)(4)(E) therefore prevents parties from attempting to obtain expert discovery "for free." This provision requires payment to the expert for her time in responding to discovery and payment to the party who initially paid the expert to develop her facts and opinions. Rule 26(b)(4)(E) provides:

> Unless manifest injustice would result, the court must require that the party seeking discovery:
>
> > (i)   pay the expert a reasonable fee for time spent in responding to discovery under Rule 26(b)(4)(A) or (D); and
> >
> > (ii) for discovery under (D), also pay the other party a fair portion of the fees and expenses it reasonably incurred in obtaining the expert's facts and opinions.

So, even if a party has a right to depose another party's expert witness, that discovery will cost the examining party. In order to obtain discovery from either a testifying or non-testifying expert, the party must pay the expert a reasonable fee for her time in responding to that discovery (typically the time for her deposition testimony). In addition, if the discovery is sought from a retained expert who will not testify at trial, the party seeking the discovery must pay the party who retained the expert a reasonable portion of the fees and expenses it incurred to enable the expert to develop her facts and opinions.

Assume, for instance, that a plaintiff retains an expert to conduct a major study, pays the expert $50,000 to conduct this study, but then decides not to have that expert testify at trial. Even if the defendant satisfies Rule 26(b)(4)(D)(ii) by convincing the court that there are "exceptional circumstances under which it is impracticable for the [defendant] to obtain facts or opinions on the same subject by other means," the defendant will have to (1) pay the expert a reasonable fee for taking her deposition and (2) pay the plaintiff a reasonable portion of the $50,000 that it paid the expert to develop her facts and opinions.

Figure 10–2 illustrates the discovery that parties may obtain from expert witnesses under the Federal Rules.

FIGURE 10–2
DISCLOSURE AND DISCOVERY CONCERNING
TESTIFYING EXPERTS ("T") AND RETAINED BUT
NON-TESTIFYING EXPERTS ("N")

Type of Expert	Subject to Disclosure?	Subject to Discovery?	Written Report Required?	Draft Reports Protected?	Attorney Communications Protected?	Must Pay Expert for Discovery?	Must Pay other Party?
T	Yes—Rule 26(a)(2)	Yes—Rule 26(b)(4)(A)	Yes—Rule 26(a)(2)(B)	Yes—Rule 26(b)(4)(B)	Yes—Rule 26(b)(4)(C), except for pay or material given by attorney	Yes—Rule 26(b)(4)(E)	No
N	No	Only under Rule 35(b) or if exceptional circumstances —Rule 26(b)(4)(D)	No—unless otherwise stipulated or ordered by court— Rule 26(a)(2)(B)	Yes—Rule 26(b)(4)(B)	Yes—Rule 26(b)(4)(C), except for pay or material given by attorney	Yes—Rule 26(b)(4)(E)	Yes—Rule 26(b)(4)(E)

B. QUESTIONS CONCERNING DISCOVERY FROM RETAINED AND NON-RETAINED EXPERTS

Test your knowledge of the expert disclosure and discovery rules by analyzing the following fact pattern.

Elaine Engineer has a Ph.D. in civil engineering and has designed bridges across the country. She was fishing alongside a rural highway bridge, when the bridge sagged and collapsed. Engineer was the only person to see the bridge collapse, and she was fascinated to watch some of the classic bridge design defects that she had studied for so many years lead to the collapse of this bridge. She was quoted in a local paper as stating, "It was difficult to imagine that so many design errors could have been included in a single bridge."

County Government brings a federal diversity action against DesignCo, which designed and built the bridge, seeking damages due to the bridge's collapse. County Government would like to call Elaine Engineer as a witness at trial and also retains Dr. Buddy Bridges as an expert. However, some of Bridges's opinions cause County's attorneys to decide not to call him as a witness at trial. As a new attorney in the firm representing County Government, you are asked about the disclosure and discovery obligations of the County.

(1) Must the County disclose to DesignCo the identity of Engineer? Of Bridges?

(2) Must the County provide DesignCo with a written report from Engineer? From Bridges?

(3) If the County is not required to provide a written report from Engineer, must it provide DesignCo with any other information concerning Engineer? From Bridges?

(4) Does DesignCo has a right to depose Engineer? To depose Bridges?

(5) If DesignCo takes the deposition of Engineer, must it pay Engineer or the County for such discovery? What if it takes the deposition of Bridges?

As you work out your answers to this question, it may be helpful to fill out the following chart to guide your analysis.

Person	Expert or Fact Witness?	Required Disclosure of Witness?	Is Report Required?	Is Other Discovery Required?	Is there a Right to Depose?	Must Witness or County be Paid for Deposition?
Engineer						
Bridges						

V. DISCOVERY CONFERENCES, ORDERS, AND PLANNING

Disclosure and discovery can be both extremely expensive and extremely time consuming. In some cases, discovery becomes an end in itself, rather than a means to better-tried actions or better-informed case settlements. Even if discovery is not abused, it may cause corporate general counsels to comment, "We gave our attorneys an unlimited litigation budget—and they exceeded it!"

Efforts to contain and focus discovery have taken several forms. Amendments to the Federal Rules of Civil Procedure have limited both the scope of civil discovery (to "nonprivileged matter that is relevant to any party's claim or defense and proportional to the needs of the case") and the number of certain discovery devices (i.e., interrogatories and depositions) that can be used without party stipulation or court order. As discussed in Section VII, infra, judges have become increasingly involved in superintending discovery and imposing sanctions against those who violate discovery rules and orders.

A more proactive approach to discovery control has been the increasing focus in recent years on discovery planning. Counsel are required by Rule 26(f) to confer with one another in an attempt to reach agreement on a proposed discovery plan. This proposed plan is then presented to the court and, upon its adoption, governs the sequence, timing, and amount of discovery to be undertaken by all parties in the case. In order to channel all formal discovery into the discovery planning process, Rule 26(d)(1) provides: "A party may not seek discovery from any source before the parties have conferred as required by Rule 26(f), except in a proceeding exempted from initial disclosure under Rule 26(a)(1)(B), or when authorized by these rules, by stipulation, or by court order."[2]

Except in cases exempted from initial disclosures by Rule 26(a)(1)(B) or when the court orders otherwise, Rule 26(f)(1) requires that "the parties must confer as soon as practicable—and in any event at least 21 days before a scheduling conference is to be held or a scheduling order is due under Rule 16(b)." Rule 26(f)(2) requires the parties, through their counsel, to confer on several things at their discovery conference: "In conferring, the parties must consider the nature and basis of their claims and defenses and the possibilities for promptly settling or resolving the case; make or arrange for the disclosures required by Rule 26(a)(1); discuss any issues about preserving discoverable information; and develop a proposed discovery plan." Rule 26(f)(2) also requires the parties to submit their proposed plan to the court within 14 days after their discovery conference.

Rule 26(f)(3) lists six separate matters on which the parties must focus in their proposed discovery plan:

> (A) what changes should be made in the timing, form, or requirement for disclosures under Rule 26(a), including a statement of when initial disclosures were made or will be made;
>
> (B) the subjects on which discovery may be needed, when discovery should be completed, and whether discovery should be conducted in phases or be limited to or focused on particular issues;

---

[2]   Most significantly, Rule 26(d)(2) provides an exception to this limitation for Rule 34 requests, which can be delivered to a party more than 21 days after that party has been served (or, by that party, to the plaintiff)—even if this is before the parties' Rule 26(f) discovery conference. In calculating the time to respond to such early requests, they are considered to have been served at the initial Rule 26(f) conference. The Advisory Committee Note to the 2015 Amendments to Rule 26 explained: "This relaxation of the discovery moratorium is designed to facilitate focused discussion during the Rule 26(f) conference. Discussion at the conference may produce changes in the requests." 305 F.R.D. 457, 556 (2015).

(C) any issues about disclosure, discovery, or preservation of electronically stored information, including the form or forms in which it should be produced;

(D) any issues about claims of privilege or of protection as trial-preparation materials, including—if the parties agree on a procedure to assert these claims after production—whether to ask the court to include their agreement in an order under Federal Rule of Evidence 502;

(E) what changes should be made in the limitations on discovery imposed under these rules or by local rule, and what other limitations should be imposed; and

(F) any other orders that the court should issue under Rule 26(c) or under Rule 16(b) and (c).

One of the advantages of the Rule 26(f) discovery planning process is that the parties are permitted to propose to the court a discovery plan that works best for them and their particular civil action. Thus Rule 26(f)(3)(A) explicitly invites the parties to suggest "what changes should be made in the timing, form, or requirement for disclosures under Rule 26(a)," while Rule 26(f)(3)(E) asks for the parties' views on "what changes should be made in the limitations on discovery imposed under these rules or by local rule, and what other limitations should be imposed." Thus, working together cooperatively with other counsel, an attorney should be able to tailor the discovery in most cases to the specific needs of each case.

In many cases, local rules or orders of court provide further details governing the contents and format of Rule 26(f) discovery plans. Former Form 52 of the Appendix of Forms to the Federal Rules of Civil Procedure provides a helpful template for a Rule 26(f) plan:

United States District Court

for the

<_____> District of <_____>

<Name(s) of plaintiff(s)>,   )

)

            Plaintiff(s)   )

)

            v.   )   Civil Action No. <Number>

)

<Name(s) of defendant(s)>,   )

)

)

Defendant(s)   )

)

)

REPORT OF THE PARTIES' PLANNING MEETING

1.   The following persons participated in a Rule 26(f) conference on <Date> by <State the method of conferring>:

2.   Initial Disclosures. The parties [have completed] [will complete by <Date>] the initial disclosures required by Rule 26(a)(1).

3.   Discovery Plan. The parties propose this discovery plan:

<Use separate paragraphs or subparagraphs if the parties disagree.>

(a)   Discovery will be needed on these subjects: <Describe>

(b)   Disclosure or discovery of electronically stored information should be handled as follows: <Briefly describe the parties' proposals, including the form or forms for production. >

(c)   The parties have agreed to an order regarding claims of privilege or of protection as trial-protection material asserted after production, as follows: <Briefly describe the provisions of the proposed order. >

(d)   <Dates for commencing and completing discovery, including discovery to be commenced or completed before other discovery.>

(e)   <Maximum number of interrogatories by each party to another party, along with the dates the answers are due.>

(f)   <Maximum number of requests for admission, along with the dates responses are due.>

(g)   <Maximum number of depositions by each party.>

(h)   <Limits on the length of depositions, in hours.>

(i)   <Dates for exchanging reports of expert witnesses.>

(j)   <Dates for supplementations under Rule 26(e).>

4.   Other Items:

(a)   <A date if the parties ask to meet with the court before a scheduling order.>

(b)   <Requested dates for pretrial conferences.>

(c)   <Final dates for the plaintiff to amend pleadings or to join parties.>

(d)   <Final dates for the defendant to amend pleadings or to join parties.>

(e)   <Final dates to file dispositive motions.>

(f)   <State the prospects for settlement.>

(g)   <Identify any alternative dispute resolution procedure that may enhance settlement prospects.>

(h)   <Final dates for submitting Rule 26(a)(3) witness lists, designations of witnesses whose testimony will be presented by deposition, and exhibit lists.>

(i)   <Final dates to file objections under Rule 26(a)(3).>

(j)   <Suggested trial date and estimate of trial length.>

(k)   <Other matters.>

Date: <Date>   <Signature of the attorney or unrepresented party>

<Printed name>

<Address>

<E-mail address>

<Telephone number>

Date: <Date>   <Signature of the attorney or unrepresented party>

<Printed name>

<Address>

<E-mail address>

<Telephone number>

The role of the court in overseeing discovery is reinforced by Rule 16. Rule 16(b)(3)(A) lists among the mandatory contents of the required Rule 16 scheduling order a limitation on the time to complete discovery, while Rule 16(b)(3)(B) provides that the scheduling order may, *inter alia*:

(i)   modify the timing of disclosures under Rules 26(a) and 26(e)(1);

(ii)   modify the extent of discovery;

(iii) provide for disclosure, discovery, or preservation of electronically stored information; [and]

(iv) include any agreements the parties reach for asserting claims of privilege or of protection as trial-preparation material after information is provided.

In addition, Rule 16(c)(2)(F) specifies that a subject for pretrial conferences is "controlling and scheduling discovery, including orders affecting disclosures and discovery under Rule 26 and Rules 29 through 37."

Because the judge should have the parties' proposed discovery plan before entering the Rule 16 scheduling order, disclosure and discovery in the action can be tailored to the needs of the parties and their case. While Rule 26(f) requires the parties and their counsel to invest a great amount of effort in planning discovery, that front-end investment of time should save the parties, and the court, time later in the case as disclosure and discovery proceed among the parties pursuant to the discovery plan.

Figure 10–3 shows the pretrial deadlines in a civil action, including the relationship of the deadlines for the parties' discovery conference, initial disclosures, submission of the proposed discovery plan, and entry of the Rule 16 pretrial order. The deadlines for the Rule 26(f) discovery conference and Rule 26(a) disclosures can be altered by court order in a particular action.

FIGURE 10–3 PRETRIAL DEADLINES		
PRETRIAL ACTION	**TIME LIMIT**	**GOVERNING RULE**
Filing Complaint	varies	Statutes of Limitations
Serving Defendant	within 90 days after filing complaint	Rule 4(m)
Scheduling Order	within earlier of 90 days after any defendant has been served or 60 days after any defendant has appeared	Rule 16(b)(2)
Party Discovery Conference	at least 21 days before scheduling conference or order	Rule 26(f)(1)
Initial Disclosures	at or within 14 days after Rule 26(f) conference	Rule 26(a)(1)(C)
Submission of Written Discovery Plan to Court	within 14 days after Rule 26(f) conference	Rule 26(f)(2)

VI. DISCOVERY DEVICES

While Rule 26(b) sets forth the scope of and limits on discovery under the Federal Rules of Civil Procedure, those Rules also recognize several specific means by which discovery within the scope of Rule 26(b) can be obtained. This section will describe these different discovery devices.

Figure 10–4 illustrates the manner in which the Rule 26(b) discovery scope and limitations govern discovery under all of the Rule 27–36 discovery devices.

FIGURE 10–4
DISCOVERY SCOPE AND SPECIFIC DISCOVERY DEVICES

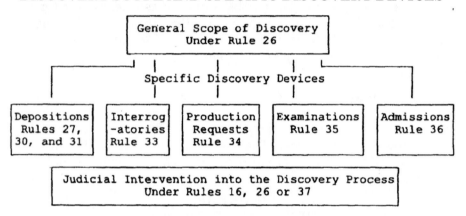

In addition to the Rules noted in Figure 10–4, Rules 16 (governing pretrial conferences and orders) and 45 (providing for subpoenas to obtain non-party documents and testimony) also are used to obtain formal pretrial discovery. Local rules of court and the orders of individual judges also govern specific aspects of some discovery, and additional information may be obtained informally without resort to the Federal Rules. However, Figure 10–4 illustrates the major rules governing civil discovery in the federal courts. The next subsections of this chapter consider the individual discovery devices in turn.

A. INTERROGATORIES

1. THE GOVERNING LAW

Rule 33 interrogatories are the most common, and least expensive, form of civil discovery. An interrogatory is simply a written question asked by one party of another party to the civil action. Rule 33(a)(2) provides that interrogatories "may relate to any matter that may be inquired into under Rule 26(b)." Although some of the basic, background information relevant to an action should be provided in Rule 26(a) disclosures, Rule 33 interrogatories allow parties to ask questions to further develop relevant facts. Rule 26(a)(1)(A)(i) and (ii) disclosures only require a party to identify individuals and documents that the disclosing party "may use to support its claims or defenses." Usually of much more interest to opposing parties is information that is not supportive of the claims or defenses of their opponents—and this information can be sought with Rule 33 interrogatories.

In a diversity action stemming from an automobile accident, interrogatories such as the following might be asked:

"At the time of the accident, who was the owner of the car that defendant was driving?"

"Was the defendant given a traffic ticket for the collision on December 1, 2015, that injured the plaintiff?"

"Has the defendant ever taken a course in driver's education? If so, what grade did the defendant receive in this course?"

These sample interrogatories ask for objective information which should elicit rather straightforward answers. Rule 33(b)(2) gives a party 30 days after being served with interrogatories to respond to those interrogatories. Thus the defendant will be able to think carefully about his interrogatory answers and discuss his answers with his attorney. Interrogatories therefore can't be used to "catch a party off guard" (as may be possible with deposition questioning), but are best framed as relatively simple questions intended to elicit relatively straightforward answers.

In addition to interrogatories such as these, parties can ask "contention interrogatories" that seek a party's opinions or contentions in the action. Rule 33(a)(2) provides:

> An interrogatory is not objectionable merely because it asks for an opinion or contention that relates to fact or the application of law to fact, but the court may order that the interrogatory need not be answered until designated discovery is complete, or until a pretrial conference or some other time.

Possible contention interrogatories in an action involving an automobile accident might be:

"Upon what facts do you rely in support of the contention in your answer that the plaintiff was contributorily negligent for the accident of December 1, 2015?"

"Is it your contention that the plaintiff was contributorily negligent with respect to the December 1, 2015, accident because he was not within the crosswalk at the time of the accident?"

If the contention interrogatories are asked at the beginning of discovery, the responding party may not yet have determined or fully formed its contentions in the action. Thus Rule 33(a)(2) authorizes the court to extend the time by which such interrogatories must be answered.

Rule 33(b)(3) provides that each "interrogatory must, to the extent it is not objected to, be answered separately and fully in writing under oath." Thus the responding party may decide not to answer certain interrogatories because they are objectionable. Rule 33(b)(4) provides that the "grounds for objecting to an interrogatory must be stated with specificity. Any ground not stated in a timely objection is waived unless the court, for good cause, excuses the failure." For instance, if an interrogatory seeks information that is not relevant to any party's claim or defense, is privileged, or is not proportional to the needs of the case, the responding party may assert an objection because the interrogatory seeks information outside the Rule 26(b)(1) scope of discovery.

Interrogatories can be quickly written, yet require an extensive amount of time to properly answer. As discussed in Section VII(A), *infra*, a Rule 26(c) protective order can be sought in response to interrogatories or other discovery to protect the responding party "from annoyance, embarrassment, oppression, or undue burden or expense."

Rule 33 itself, though, provides a way for a party to shift the burden of ascertaining an interrogatory answer from the responding party to the party seeking the information. Rule 33(d) provides:

> If the answer to an interrogatory may be determined by examining, auditing, compiling, abstracting, or summarizing a party's business records (including electronically stored information), and if the burden of deriving or ascertaining the answer will be substantially the same for either party, the responding party may answer by:
>
> > (1) specifying the records that must be reviewed, in sufficient detail to enable the interrogating party to locate and identify them as readily as the responding party could; and
> >
> > (2) giving the interrogating party a reasonable opportunity to examine and audit the records and to make copies, compilations, abstracts, or summaries.

Assume that the plaintiff in an employment discrimination action seeks information that only can be gleaned from a mass of employment files involving hundreds, or thousands, of other employees. In that case, the employer might rely on Rule 33(d) and permit the plaintiff's counsel to examine its records to answer plaintiff's own interrogatories. While such a response might shift the burden of determining the interrogatory answer to the plaintiff, can you think of reasons why the defendant might not utilize the Rule 33(d) option to produce business records in such a situation?

Unless the parties stipulate or the court orders to the contrary, Rule 33(a)(1) limits parties to "no more than 25 written interrogatories, including all discrete subparts." Rule 33(a)(1) and the courts recognize, though, that it may be appropriate to grant the parties a larger number of interrogatories in appropriate cases.

2.   INTERROGATORY QUESTIONS

1.   Plaintiff's counsel has no objection to defendant's interrogatories, but needs more time to answer them. Can the parties

stipulate to an extension of the 30 day period for answering the interrogatories? *See* Rule 33(b)(2). What if the case is set for trial next week? *See* Rule 29.

2.   Other than providing other parties with information prior to trial, can interrogatory answers be used at trial? *See* Rule 33(c).

3.   In applying the 25-interrogatory limitation of Rule 33(a)(1), should each of the following interrogatories count for one, or more, of that 25 interrogatory limit?

—For the person answering these interrogatories, please state the following:

(a)   that person's name;

(b)   that person's job position or title;

(c)   any prior positions that that person has held with the defendant company; and

(d)   the dates during which that person held each of the positions listed in response to subsections (b) and (c).

—With respect to the accident of November 30, 2015, please state the following:

(a)   the names, addresses, and phone numbers of any witnesses to that accident (other than the parties to this action);

(b)   the owner of the car that the defendant was driving at the time of the accident;

(c)   the identification of any documents describing or mentioning the accident of November 30, 2015; and

(d)   whether you contend that the plaintiff's negligence contributed to that accident and, if so, what actions on the plaintiff's part were contributorily negligent.

4.   A defendant corporation receives the following interrogatory:

From March 31, 2015, through December 31, 2015, who in the defendant's Human Resources Department was responsible for insuring that all employees were aware of their eligibility to enroll in the retirement plan offered by defendant?

Neither defense counsel nor the employees of the defendant with whom counsel are working are aware of the answer to this question. Can the defendant respond to the interrogatory that its representatives are unaware of the answer to this question? What about interrogatories seeking details concerning the creation of the retirement plan in 1946? *See* Rule 33(b)(1)(B).

5.   Plaintiff's counsel would like to obtain basic information from someone who has not been named as a party to the civil action that she

has brought. Can she use a Rule 33 interrogatory to obtain this information? Are there other ways in which the information can be obtained from a non-party? Can the plaintiff name the third person as a party to the action so that interrogatories can be used?

B. DEPOSITIONS

1. THE GOVERNING LAW

While Rule 33 interrogatory answers are typically reviewed by the responding party's counsel before being served on other parties, Rule 30 depositions permit parties to directly ask oral questions of both parties and non-parties to the civil action. Under Rule 30(a), leave of court is usually not necessary before a deposition is taken. However, Rule 30(a)(2) provides that leave of court or party stipulation is necessary if (1) the parties on one side of a case seek to take more than 10 depositions, (2) the proposed deponent already has been deposed, (3) the deposition is set before the parties have held their Rule 26(f) discovery conference (unless the party seeking the deposition certifies that the deponent is expected to leave the United States or be unavailable for examination), or (4) the deponent is in prison.

Rule 30(b)(1) requires that the party taking a deposition "must give reasonable written notice to every other party," which notice must state the time and place of the deposition. In order to be sure that the time of deposition is acceptable to all parties, the attorneys typically work out deposition schedules—often as part of their Rule 26(f) discovery plan. While just a deposition notice is sufficient to take the deposition of parties to the action, the party seeking the deposition of a non-party must use a Rule 45 subpoena in addition to a deposition notice. If documents are sought in connection with the deposition, the deposition notice may be accompanied by a Rule 34 request to produce the documents (if the deponent is a party to the action) or a Rule 45(a)(1)(C) subpoena *duces tecum* (from the Latin for "bring with you") to require a non-party to bring documents to the deposition).

Rule 30(b)(3)(A) requires the party noticing the deposition to state the method by which deposition testimony will be recorded: "by audio, audiovisual, or stenographic means." Rule 30(b)(4) permits depositions to be taken "by telephone or other remote means," although face-to-face depositions with the examining attorney in the same room with the deponent are typically used for depositions of important witnesses or those involving crucial testimony.

Sometimes the party seeking deposition testimony will not know which people, within an organization or corporation, have the information that the party seeks. If the party notices a specific corporate official for a deposition, that official may say (quite truthfully) that the deposition questions are not within her area of knowledge or responsibility—requiring the deposition of other officials until the right person is located.

Rather than proceeding from one official to the next in such a situation, the party instead might take a deposition pursuant to Rule 30(b)(6). Rule 30(b)(6), in part, provides:

> In its notice or subpoena, a party may name as the deponent a public or private corporation, partnership, an association, a governmental agency, or other entity and must describe with reasonable particularity the matters for examination. The named organization must then designate one or more officers, directors, or managing agents, or designate other persons who consent to testify on its behalf; and it may set out the matters on which each person designated will testify. * * *

Use of Rule 30(b)(6) can avoid the need for useless preliminary depositions, especially because Rule 30(b)(6) provides that the "persons designated must testify about information known or reasonably available to the organization." So the organization must designate individuals who truly can provide the information that the deposing party seeks.

However, the deposing party may not want to rely on another party to designate those whom it will depose, and the final sentence of Rule 30(b)(6) provides: "This paragraph (6) does not preclude a deposition by any other procedure allowed by these rules." The deposing party is thus not required to rely on Rule 30(b)(6) and can still choose the specific individuals whom it will depose. In fact, a deponent's lack of knowledge about a specific matter may be quite helpful in certain situations. For example, plaintiff's counsel in an employment discrimination action may be quite pleased to hear the CEO of the defendant company testify that she does not have any real knowledge about the company's antidiscrimination policies or duties.

So what does a deposition look like? Very much like a court proceeding, with the examining attorney asking questions of the deponent, and the deponent's attorney being present to object to improper questions. The deponent's attorney and counsel for the parties may ask a few questions of their own at the end of the deposing attorney's questioning. A court reporter takes down the testimony and/or a camera operator preserves the testimony audiovisually. The deposition does not take place in a courtroom, but in a conference room (often at the offices of one of the attorneys). An even more significant difference from trial testimony is that there is no judge present at the deposition.

This does not mean, however, that objections aren't raised to deposition questions. Rule 30(c)(2) explains deposition objection procedure:

An objection at the time of the examination—whether to evidence, to a party's conduct, to the officer's qualifications, to the manner of taking the deposition, or to any other aspect of the deposition—must be noted on the record, but the examination still proceeds; the testimony is taken subject to any objection.[3]

Thus the colloquy surrounding a deposition objection might be something like this:

Defendant's Attorney:	Mr. Plaintiff, what is your height?
Plaintiff's Attorney:	Objection. The question is not relevant to any claim or defense in this action. However, because this is a deposition, you can answer.
Plaintiff:	I am six feet three inches tall.

What, though, if a deposition question improperly seeks privileged information? The final sentence of Rule 30(c)(2) provides: "A person may instruct a deponent not to answer only when necessary to preserve a privilege, to enforce a limitation ordered by the court, or to present a motion under Rule 30(d)(3)." The objection to a deposition question seeking privileged information therefore might look something like this:

Defendant's Attorney:	Mr. Plaintiff, what did you tell your attorney about whether you were speeding right before the accident?
Plaintiff's Attorney:	Objection. The question seeks information protected by the attorney-client privilege. I instruct my client not to answer the question.

While the plaintiff cannot be asked what she told her attorney, it would be proper for an attorney simply to ask the plaintiff "Were you speeding right before the accident?"—assuming that this question is relevant to a claim or defense in the action.

Rule 30(c)(2) also limits the form of any objections raised during a deposition, providing: "An objection must be stated concisely in a nonargumentative and nonsuggestive manner." Thus an appropriate objection might be: "Objection. The question seeks irrelevant information." Contrast this objection with an improper "speaking" objection such as this: "Objection. The question has been asked and

---

[3]   Rule 32 governs the use of depositions at trial. This Rule generally provides that, in order to preserve an objection for trial, it must be made to matters occurring at the deposition that could be corrected at that time. Rule 32(d)(3)(B) provides:

An objection to an error or irregularity at an oral examination is waived if:

(i)   it relates to the manner of taking the deposition, the form of a question or answer, the oath or affirmation, a party's conduct, or other matters that might have been corrected at that time; and

(ii) it is not timely made during the deposition.

answered repeatedly, and plaintiff has said that he doesn't know the answer. But you may answer, Ms. Plaintiff, if you know."

As with interrogatories, the Federal Rules limit the deposition discovery that can be sought without a stipulation or court order raising Rule 30's default limits. As previously mentioned, Rule 30(a)(2)(A)(i) limits each side in a case (all plaintiffs, all defendants, or all third-party defendants) to no more than 10 depositions—unless there is a party stipulation or court order permitting more depositions.

In addition, Rule 30(d)(1) provides: "Unless otherwise stipulated or ordered by the court, a deposition is limited to 1 day of 7 hours." However, this Rule continues: "The court must allow additional time consistent with Rule 26(b)(1) and (2) if needed to fairly examine the deponent or if the deponent, another person, or any other circumstance impedes or delays the examination."

Because there is no judge present during the deposition, Rule 30(d)(3)(A) provides: "At any time during a deposition, the deponent or a party may move to terminate or limit it on the ground that it is being conducted in bad faith or in a manner that unreasonably annoys, embarrasses, or oppresses the deponent or party." This provision of Rule 30 also permits the objecting attorney to demand that the deposition be suspended so that that party can seek an order from the court terminating or limiting the deposition.

2.   DEPOSITION QUESTIONS

1.   Why does Rule 30(c)(2) provide that, except for the limited exceptions noted in that Rule, "[a]n objection at the time of the examination * * * must be noted on the record, but the examination still proceeds"?

2.   In what situations might a party decide to record a deposition audiovisually, rather than simply have a stenographic transcription made of the deposition?

3.   During counsel's deposition of an important witness, opposing counsel repeatedly interjects long objections and discusses, on the record, issues such as the length of the deposition lunch break, whether documents discussed by the deponent are legible, and the relevance of specific deposition questions and answers. Six hours of deposition time have elapsed, and the examining attorney still has many important areas to cover. What should she do? *See* Rule 30(d).

4.   During a deposition, the examining attorney phrases her questions so as to suggest the answers to those questions. Opposing counsel makes no objection to the questions or the resulting testimony. If the deposition testimony is later offered at trial, can opposing counsel object to its admission? *See* Rule 32(d)(3)(B).

5.   During that same deposition, the examining attorney elicits a great deal of testimony that is not relevant to any party's claims or

defenses or to any issues in the action. Opposing counsel do not object to this deposition testimony. If this portion of the deposition is offered at trial, can opposing counsel object to its admission? *See* Rule 32(d)(3)(A).

6. Defense counsel notices the deposition of a witness to the parties' automobile crash. The witness is not a party, and after the accident, the witness moved to another city, where the deposition is scheduled. Both defense counsel and plaintiff's counsel travel to this city, but the witness was not served with a deposition subpoena and, consequently, does not attend. Does plaintiff's counsel have any recourse in this situation? *See* Rule 30(g).

C. PRODUCTION REQUESTS

1. THE GOVERNING LAW

Pretrial discovery can be used to obtain a person's answers to questions, either verbally (at a Rule 30 deposition) or in writing (in answer to a Rule 33 interrogatory). Even more powerful evidence, though, may be records prepared before the litigation, photographs taken contemporaneously with the events at issue, and physical objects such as the car that was involved in the accident. Rule 34 permits a party to obtain such documents and things from another party to the action, while Rule 45 can be used to compel a non-party to produce such evidence as well.

Rule 34(a) provides:

> A party may serve on any other party a request within the scope of Rule 26(b):
>
>> (1) to produce and permit the requesting party or its representative to inspect, copy, test, or sample the following items in the responding party's possession, custody, or control:
>>
>>> (A) any designated documents or electronically stored information—including writings, drawings, graphs, charts, photographs, sound recordings, images, and other data or data compilations—stored in any medium from which information can be obtained either directly or, if necessary, after translation by the responding party into a reasonably usable form; or
>>>
>>> (B) any designated tangible things.

In addition, Rule 34(a)(2) permits parties to request entry onto land or other property. If the plaintiff was injured while on defendant's property, Rule 34(a)(2) permits the plaintiff to seek entry onto the property to "inspect, measure, survey, photograph, test, or sample the property or any designated object or operation on it."

In contrast to the numerical limitations on interrogatories and depositions, the Federal Rules contain no limitation on the number of production requests. However, just as can a respondent to any discovery request, a party from whom Rule 34 production is sought can file a Rule 26(c) motion for a protective order that the material sought need not be produced or any production be limited due to the "annoyance, embarrassment, oppression, or undue burden or expense" that would result were the requested production provided.

Pursuant to Rule 34(b)(1), production requests:

> (A) must describe with reasonable particularity each item or category of items to be inspected;

> (B) must specify a reasonable time, place, and manner for the inspection and for performing the related acts; and

> (C) may specify the form or forms in which electronically stored information is to be produced.

Rule 34(b)(2)(A) provides that a written response to a Rule 34 request must be served within 30 days after service of the request. Rule 34(b)(2)(B) further provides that the response must state either that inspection will be permitted or set forth a specific objection to the request. If the requesting party has not specified the form for the production of any electronically stored information, or if the responding party objects to the form requested, the responding party must state the form or form in which it will produce the electronically-stored information.

A great deal of focus in recent years has been on the production of electronically stored information, and Rule 34(b)(2)(E) contains specific provisions for such productions:

> Unless otherwise stipulated or ordered by the court, these procedures apply to producing documents or electronically stored information:

> (i) A party must produce documents as they are kept in the usual course of business or must organize and label them to correspond to the categories in the request;

> (ii) If a request does not specify a form for producing electronically stored information, a party must produce it in a form or forms in which it is ordinarily maintained or in a reasonably usable form or forms; and

> (iii) A party need not produce the same electronically stored information in more than one form.

The discovery of electronically stored information (ESI) will be considered in more depth in Section VII(B) of this chapter. For now, be sure to note that Rule 34 encompasses ESI as well as hard copies of documents, but that Rule 34(b)(2)(E) permits the parties to stipulate or the court to order a different method for producing electronically stored information. Such methods are described in the parties' Rule 26(f) discovery plans, and Rule 16(b)(3)(B)(iii) explicitly provides that the court's scheduling order may "provide for disclosure, discovery, or preservation of electronically stored information."

Rule 26(d)(1) generally provides that discovery cannot be sought until after the parties' Rule 26(f) discovery conference. However, the 2015 amendments to the Federal Rules created a specific exemption for early Rule 34 requests, with Rule 26(d)(2)(A) providing:

> More than 21 days after the summons and complaint are served on a party, a request under Rule 34 may be delivered:
>
> (i)   to that party by any other party, and
>
> (ii) by that party to any plaintiff or to any other party that has been served.

For calculating the 30 day period for responding to an early Rule 34 request, Rule 26(d)(2)(B) provides that the request "is considered to have been served at the first Rule 26(f) conference." By permitting the service of Rule 34 requests before the discovery conference, and granting the parties 30 days after that conference in which to respond, such requests can be discussed, and perhaps narrowed, at that conference.

2.   PRODUCTION QUESTIONS

1.   A shopper falls at a grocery store, contending that she tripped on a broken tile that had become slippery due to a nearby leaking faucet. After filing a federal diversity action against the grocery store, plaintiff's counsel would like to examine the site of the fall. How should counsel attempt to obtain access to this portion of the store?

2.   Must a party responding to a Rule 34 request permit the requesting party to inspect the originals of the documents sought? The 2015 amendment to Rule 34(b)(2)(B) made explicit what was common practice before that amendment: "The responding party may state that it will produce copies of documents or of electronically stored information instead of permitting inspection." What are the advantages and disadvantages of producing copies of documents rather than the documents themselves?

3.   The plaintiff asks for specific relevant documents in a Rule 34 request, but the defendant's Rule 34 response states that it "has no responsive documents." During trial, defense counsel offer a document falling within the Rule 34 request and inform the judge and plaintiff's counsel that their client "just located this document." Should the judge admit the document? What will the judge ask before deciding on the admission of the document? If the document is admitted, are there other actions that the judge might take? *See* Rule 37(c)(1).

4. In complex cases involving thousands of documents, the parties may establish a joint document depository. These provide a central location for storage of relevant documents and spare parties the expense of duplicative copying of every potentially relevant document. Computerized document retrieval systems often are developed to speed access to documents in these depositories. *See* Sugarman, "Coordinating Complex Discovery," *Litigation,* Fall 1988, at 41, 42–43. Discovery in the breast implant products liability litigation was put on CD-ROM computer disks, with a single disk containing 15,000 pages of discovery selling for $25.00. DeBenedictis, "Implant Documents on CD-ROMs," *A.B.A.J.*, July 1993, at 24. *See generally Manual for Complex Litigation, Fourth* § 11.444 (2004).

D. PHYSICAL AND MENTAL EXAMINATIONS

1. THE GOVERNING LAW

Sometimes the evidence sought in discovery cannot be provided in an interrogatory answer or learned in a deposition, but involves the physical or mental state of a party himself. Rule 35(a)(1) provides: "The court where the action is pending may order a party whose mental or physical condition—including blood group—is in controversy to submit to a physical or mental examination by a suitably licensed or certified examiner." Rule 35(a)(2) contains further requirements for obtaining a court order for a physical or mental examination:

The order:

(A) may be made only on motion for good cause and on notice to all parties and the person to be examined; and

(B) must specify the time, place, manner, conditions, and scope of the examination, as well as the person or persons who will perform it.

Unlike the other discovery devices, physical or mental examinations only can be obtained by agreement of the parties or upon court order if (1) the condition of the party to be examined is "in controversy;" (2) there is "good cause" for the examination; (3) all parties have been notified; and (4) the court order specifies the time, place, manner, conditions, and scope of the examination and the person who will perform the examination. Rule 35 examinations are the only discovery device that requires a court order, but it is the device with the greatest potential for impinging on an individual's personal privacy. Indeed, Rule 35 examinations are the only discovery device that can result in a court order to remove your clothes!

In what situations is the physical or mental condition of a party "in controversy"? The easiest cases are those in which a plaintiff alleges that he was injured due to the actions of the defendant. In this situation, he has placed his condition in controversy, and it should not be difficult for the defendant to show good cause for a court-ordered examination.

However, the Supreme Court has held that a Rule 35 examination can be obtained in situations in which a party has not himself put his condition in controversy. In *Schlagenhauf v. Holder*, 379 U.S. 104, 114 (1963), the Court held that "Rule 35, as applied to either plaintiffs or defendants to an action, is free of constitutional difficulty and is within the scope of the Enabling Act." The Court, though, further concluded that Rule 35 examinations "are only to be ordered upon a discriminating application by the district judge of the limitations prescribed by the Rule." 379 U.S. at 121. Thus, because the district judge had not carefully considered the Rule 35 request but had instead ordered nine separate examinations of the defendant, the Supreme Court remanded the case for the district judge to reconsider the order for examinations.

Rule 35 not only provides the possibility of obtaining a court order requiring a party to submit to a physical or mental examination, but also requires an exchange of medical reports in certain circumstances. Initially, Rule 35(b)(1) requires the party who sought the examination order, on request, to provide the party examined with a copy of the examiner's written report (including, pursuant to Rule 35(b)(2), diagnoses, conclusions, and the results of any tests), as well as copies of "like reports of all earlier examinations of the same condition."

However, Rule 35(b)(3) provides that, by providing a report of the examination, the party who requested the examination is entitled to receive "from the party against whom the examination order was issued like reports of all earlier or later examinations of the same condition." Thus there is a full exchange of relevant examination reports, and Rule 35(b)(4) provides that by "requesting and obtaining the examiner's report, or by deposing the examiner, the party examined waives any privilege it may have—in that action or any other action involving the same controversy—concerning testimony about all examinations of the same condition."

While Rule 35 permits parties to seek court orders for physical or mental examinations, such examinations are typically worked out by counsel (especially because examinations often will be sought of multiple parties). In the event that examinations are arranged by party agreement, counsel should not overlook the fact that Rule 35(b)(6) provides that the waiver and reciprocity provisions of Rule 35(b) apply "to an examination made by the parties' agreement, unless the agreement states otherwise."

2.   PHYSICAL AND MENTAL EXAMINATION QUESTIONS

1.   Rule 35 examinations only can be ordered of parties to a civil action—with one exception. The final sentence of Rule 35(a)(1) provides: "The court has the same authority to order a party to produce for

examination a person who is in its custody or under its legal control." In what situations might an examination of such a non-party be ordered?

2.   A mother brings suit on behalf of her minor child against her landlord, claiming that exposure to lead paint in their apartment caused the child's learning disabilities. The landlord seeks not only physical and mental examinations of the child but also IQ and other testing of the mother and her other children. Must these non-parties submit to such examinations? *Compare Anderson v. Seigel*, 680 N.Y.S.2d 587 (1998) (yes) *with Monica W. v. Milevoi*, 685 N.Y.S.2d 231 (1999) (no).

3.   Why should more than one examiner examine a party? Federal Rule of Evidence 706 allows the court to appoint its own experts. Rather than selecting separate examiners, why shouldn't the parties agree on a single expert to examine parties under Rule 35 of the Federal Rules of Civil Procedure?

4.   Rule 35 originally only provided for physical or mental examination by a physician. What other types of "suitably licensed or certified" examiners might examine a party under Rule 35 today? Why the requirement that the examiner be "suitably licensed or certified?"

E. ADMISSION REQUESTS

1. THE GOVERNING LAW

Rule 36 is an unusual discovery device, because Rule 36 admission requests do not ask the responding party to provide any information. Instead, an admission request simply asks the responding party to admit the truth of the matter set forth in the request. In contrast to the other discovery devices, which often result in the discovery of new information that leads to expanded discovery or pleadings, Rule 36 admission requests typically constrain the scope of the action by resolving otherwise disputed issues in the litigation. Admitted Rule 36 requests take contested issues out of an action, rather than expand the issues within the case.

Rule 36(a)(1) provides:

A party may serve on any other party a written request to admit, for purposes of the pending action only, the truth of any matters within the scope of Rule 26(b)(1) relating to:

(A) facts, the application of law to fact, or opinions about either; and

(B) the genuineness of any described documents.

Prior to the 2015 abrogation of the forms that accompanied the Federal Rules of Civil Procedure, Form 51 of the Appendix of Forms illustrated the general format for Rule 36 requests:

REQUEST FOR ADMISSIONS UNDER RULE 36

(Caption—See Form 1.)

The plaintiff _name_ asks the defendant _name_ to respond within 30 days to these requests by admitting, for purposes of this action only and subject to objections to admissibility at trial:

1. The genuineness of the following documents, copies of which [are attached] [are or have been furnished or made available for inspection and copying].

(List each document.)

2. The truth of each of the following statements:

(List each statement.)

(Date and sign—See Form 2.)

———————

Rule 36(a)(3) gives the responding party 30 days after service to answer or object to admission requests, although the parties may stipulate to, or the court may order, a shorter or longer response time. Rule 36(a)(4) contains several specific requirements for answers to admission requests:

> If a matter is not admitted, the answer must specifically deny it or state in detail why the answering party cannot truthfully admit or deny it. A denial must fairly respond to the substance of the matter; and when good faith requires that a party qualify an answer or deny only a part of a matter, the answer must specify the part admitted and qualify or deny the rest. The answering party may assert lack of knowledge or information as a reason for failing to admit or deny only if the party states that it has made reasonable inquiry and that the information it knows or can readily obtain is insufficient to enable it to admit or deny.

A responding party can do more than admit or deny particular admission requests. It also can object that a request is not within the Rule 26(b)(1) scope of discovery or for other reasons. Rule 36(a)(5) provides: "The grounds for objecting to a request must be stated. A party must not object solely on the ground that the request presents a genuine issue for trial."

A party's failure to respond to Rule 36 admission requests has a quite different impact than failure to respond to other discovery devices. Interrogatories, production requests, and deposition questions are only effective if information is provided in response to the discovery request. The party serving Rule 36 requests, though, may be content if there is no response to those requests. Rule 36(a)(3) provides that a "matter is admitted unless, within 30 days after being served, the party to whom

the request is directed serves on the requesting party a written answer
or objection addressed to the matter and signed by the party or its
attorney."

Admission requests therefore may be one of the few areas of civil
litigation in which "no news is good news." However, Rule 36(b)
anticipates that there will be situations in which a party (or, more
likely, the party's attorney) has inadvertently overlooked admission
requests or for other reasons should be relieved from the binding effect
of Rule 36 admissions due to a nonresponse to the requests. Rule 36(b)
provides:

> A matter admitted under this rule is conclusively
> established unless the court, on motion, permits the admission
> to be withdrawn or amended. Subject to Rule 16(e) [concerning
> final pretrial conferences and orders], the court may permit
> withdrawal or amendment if it would promote the presentation
> of the merits of the action and if the court is not persuaded
> that it would prejudice the requesting party in maintaining or
> defending the action on the merits. An admission under this
> rule is not an admission for any other purposes and cannot be
> used against the party in any other proceeding.

The Federal Rules also contain a special sanctions provision for
when a party fails to admit the truth of a fact or the authenticity of a
document and the requesting party later proves the matter to be true or
the document genuine. Rule 37(c)(2) provides:

> If a party fails to admit what is requested under Rule 36
> and if the requesting party later proves a document to be
> genuine or the matter true, the requesting party may move
> that the party who failed to admit pay the reasonable
> expenses, including attorney's fees, incurred in making that
> proof. The court must so order unless:
>
> (A) the request was held objectionable under Rule
> 36(a);
>
> (B) the admission sought was of no substantial
> importance;
>
> (C) the party failing to admit had a reasonable
> ground to believe that it might prevail on the matter; or
>
> (D) there was other good reason for the failure to
> admit.

In order to avoid the payment of such expenses, or the need to seek
amendment or withdrawal of admission requests, counsel must focus on
all Rule 36 admission requests at the time that they are served.

2. ADMISSION QUESTIONS

1.   The plaintiff in a diversity action alleging negligence serves an admission request upon the defendant, asking the defendant to admit that she was "exceeding the speed limit at the time of the accident." The defendant denies the request, and the action goes to trial. After trial the jury returns a verdict for $500,000 for the plaintiff. The jury also answers a Rule 49(b) interrogatory finding that the defendant was "exceeding the speed limit at the time of the accident." Should the plaintiff be able to recover from the defendant the cost of proving at trial that the defendant was speeding?

2.   The plaintiff serves upon the defendant a Rule 36 request asking that the defendant admit the genuineness of a specified document, a copy of which is attached to the Rule 36 request. The defendant denies that the document is authentic. The document is not offered at trial by either party. After the plaintiff prevails at trial, should the defendant be sanctioned for failure to admit the genuineness of the document?

3.   In a federal diversity action, the defendant serves on plaintiff's counsel a Rule 36 request, seeking an admission that the plaintiff had not had her brakes checked within three years before the accident. The assistant to plaintiff's counsel mislays this admission request. Two months later, and three months before the scheduled date for trial, plaintiff's counsel sees these admission requests for the first time. She files a motion to withdraw this particular admission. Should the court grant that motion?

4.   A bank is sued in two separate federal actions by different consumers who contend that the bank violated federal law by the manner in which it advertised the interest that it pays on savings accounts. In the first case the bank admits a Rule 36 admission request concerning how it calculates interest. That admission is submitted to the jury, and the jury returns a verdict for the plaintiff. The plaintiff in the second action asks the court to include in the parties' final pretrial order a finding, based upon this admission in the first action, that the defendant calculated interest in this fashion. Should the judge include that finding in the pretrial order for the second action?

F.   THE DUTY TO SUPPLEMENT DISCLOSURES AND DISCOVERY RESPONSES

Regardless of the device through which discovery is requested and provided, counsel must remember the duty to supplement disclosures and discovery responses imposed by Rule 26(e). Rule 26(e)(1) provides:

> A party who has made a disclosure under Rule 26(a)—or who has responded to an interrogatory, request for production, or request for admission—must supplement or correct its disclosure or response:

(A) in a timely manner if the party learns that in some material respect the disclosure or response is incomplete or incorrect, and if the additional or corrective information has not otherwise been made known to the other parties during the discovery process or in writing; or

(B) as ordered by the court.[4]

The Rule 26(e) duty to supplement may arise if counsel discovers that a prior discovery response or disclosure was materially incorrect or incomplete at the time that it was provided. The Rule 26(e) duty to supplement also applies if the facts underlying a disclosure or discovery response have changed materially since the information was provided. "The obligation to supplement disclosures and discovery responses applies whenever a party learns that its prior disclosures or responses are in some material respect incomplete or incorrect." Advisory Committee Note to 1993 Amendment to Rule 26, 146 F.R.D. 401, 641 (1993).

Failure to supplement materially incomplete or incorrect disclosures or discovery responses is a serious matter. Indeed, Rule 37(c)(1) subjects a party to the same sanctions that are provided for failure to provide disclosures or discovery. The party will not be allowed to use at trial the information not provided "unless the failure was substantially justified or is harmless," and additional sanctions may be as severe as dismissing an action or rendering a default judgment against the party who did not supplement its disclosures or discovery responses.

G. INCORPORATING INDIVIDUAL DISCOVERY DEVICES INTO A DISCOVERY PLAN

Knowing the individual discovery devices does not suggest how those specific means of obtaining discovery should be coordinated in a comprehensive and cost-effective discovery plan. In developing a discovery plan, counsel must consider the interests of her client (who must fund the discovery), of the other parties to the action (who have their own interests in the contemplated discovery), and the judge (who must approve the final discovery plan). Counsel also should remember that Rule 26(d)(3) provides:

---

[4] The Rule 26(e)(1) duty to supplement does not apply to deposition testimony. As the Advisory Committee noted concerning the 1993 amendment to Rule 26(e):

> [T]he obligation to supplement responses to formal discovery requests * * * [does not apply] ordinarily to deposition testimony. However, with respect to experts from whom a written report is required under [Rule 26(a)(2)(B)], changes in the opinions expressed by the expert whether in the report or at a subsequent deposition are subject to a duty of supplemental disclosure [now, under Rule 26(e)(2)].

146 F.R.D. 401, 641 (1993).

> Unless the parties stipulate or the court orders otherwise for the parties' and witnesses' convenience and in the interests of justice:
>
> (A) methods of discovery may be used in any sequence; and
>
> (B) discovery by one party does not require any other party to delay its discovery."

Assume that you represent the defendant driver in a federal diversity action stemming from a car crash. The plaintiff driver alleges in his complaint that your client drove through a red light and crashed into his car. He alleges that his car, valued at $45,000 was destroyed in the crash and that he suffered severe injuries resulting in $200,000 in pain and suffering damages, $45,000 in medical bills, and permanent damage to his left arm.

Develop the outline of a discovery plan that you would propose for the defendant driver in this action. In your plan, consider:

- the role that interrogatories, depositions, production requests, examinations, and admission requests will play in your plan;

- the sequence in which you will you use these various discovery devices;

- the likely responses of the plaintiff to your discovery requests;

- the likely discovery that plaintiff's counsel will seek and discovery devices that plaintiff will utilize, as well as your responses to these discovery requests;

- any agreements that you will seek with other counsel to modify discovery deadlines or other aspects of discovery; and

- the information that you will seek to obtain informally without resort to the Federal Rules.

As you develop your discovery plan, Figure 10–5 may help you organize your planning.

FIGURE 10–5
DISCOVERY DEVICES IN THE FEDERAL COURTS

Discovery Device	Numerical Limitation	Can be used Against	Requirements
Rule 30 Deposition	10 per side	by Notice: other parties; by Subpoena: any person	within Scope of Rule 26(b)(1): relevant to claim or defense; non-privileged; proportional to case

Rule 33 Interrogatory	25 per party	only other parties	Rule 26(b)(1) Scope
Rule 34 Request for Documents/ Things	no limit in Federal Rules	only other parties, but documents can be sought from non-parties with Rule 45 subpoena	Rule 26(b)(1) Scope
Rule 35 Examinations	no limit in Federal Rules	only other parties or person in party custody or control	Rule 26(b)(1) Scope; condition examined "in controversy" and "good cause"
Rule 36 Admissions	no limit in Federal Rules	only other parties	Rule 26(b)(1) Scope

VII. JUDICIAL INVOLVEMENT IN THE DISCOVERY PROCESS

Discovery in civil actions initially was structured so that the parties and their counsel would conduct their discovery with each other and, once discovery was complete, the judge would try the action. In recent decades, though, federal judges have become much more involved in the civil pretrial process. Recent amendments to the Federal Rules emphasize the judge's role in Rule 16 scheduling and pretrial conferences and in Rule 26(f) discovery planning.

The Rules still contemplate that, after the Rule 16 scheduling order has been entered, the parties themselves will conduct the discovery contemplated by that order without involvement by the judge. However, the Rules permit parties to call upon the judge to resolve discovery disputes through either Rule 26(c) motions for a protective order or Rule 37(a) motions to compel. If a person has been nonresponsive to discovery requests or has failed to comply with a discovery order, the court can sanction that person. This judicial pretrial involvement— through the entry of discovery orders or the award of fees or sanctions— is the subject of the sections that follow.

A. RULE 26(c) PROTECTIVE ORDERS AND RULE 37(a) MOTIONS TO COMPEL

Figure 10–6 illustrates the possible responses to a discovery request (or the Rule 26(a) duty to disclose information). Ideally, the person from whom information is sought will provide the discovery sought or disclosure required. If so, there is no dispute for the court to consider, and the discovery and pretrial processes continue.

FIGURE 10–6
DISCOVERY RESPONSES AND INTERVENTION BY THE COURT

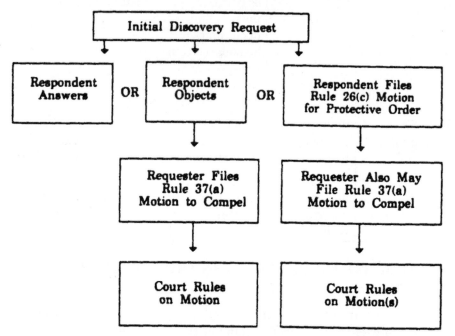

However, the person from whom discovery or disclosure is sought may object to providing that information. In that situation, he can state his objection to providing the discovery or disclosure. Typically, though, the court will not consider such objections on its own, so the requesting party will be without the information sought. In order to bring the court into the dispute, the requesting party must do two things:

(1) Pursuant to Rule 37(a)(1), "in good faith [confer or attempt to confer] with the person or party failing to make disclosure or discovery in an effort to obtain it without court action;" and

(2) if the effort to obtain the information without court intervention is unsuccessful, file a Rule 37(a)(1) motion for an order to compel the disclosure or discovery.

The court's ruling on this Rule 37(a) motion to compel should resolve the dispute concerning the right of the party seeking this information to obtain that information. The person opposing the release of this information may not, though, want to wait for another party to file a motion to compel. Adopting the strategy that "the best defense is a good offense," this person may choose to file a Rule 26(c) motion for a protective order. A motion for a protective order typically is filed because the information sought falls outside the Rule 26(b)(1) scope of discovery. For instance, the motion may assert that the discovery sought is not relevant to any party's claim or defense, is privileged, or is not proportional to the needs of the case.

As is the case with a Rule 37(a) motion to compel, Rule 26(c) requires a motion for a protective order to be preceded by a good faith attempt "to confer with other affected parties in an effort to resolve the dispute without court action." As is also the case with a motion to compel, the motion for a protective order must include a certification of this effort to resolve the dispute without initially seeking judicial resolution of that dispute.

If a Rule 26(c) motion for a protective order is filed, the party seeking the information can (1) oppose that motion or (2) both oppose that motion and file its own motion to compel. In either situation, the judge's ruling on the motion(s) should resolve the party's right to the discovery or disclosure that it seeks.

In many cases the judge will simply (1) determine that a party has a right to obtain the information (by granting a motion to compel and/or denying a motion for a protective order) or (2) determine that the party is not entitled to the information (by granting a motion for a protective order and/or denying a motion to compel). However, in some cases the judge may decide that the party seeking the information is entitled to some of the information but is not entitled to other parts of the information sought.

Rule 26(c) suggests the many different ways in which a judge can resolve a discovery dispute by ruling on a motion for a protective order. This Rule allows a court to, for good cause, "issue an order to protect a party or person from annoyance, embarrassment, oppression, or undue burden or expense." Among the eight specific types of relief listed in Rule 26(c) are orders:

(A) forbidding the disclosure or discovery;

(B) specifying terms, including time and place, for the disclosure or discovery;

(C) prescribing a discovery method other than the one selected by the party seeking discovery;

(D) forbidding inquiry into certain matters, or limiting the scope of disclosure or discovery to certain matters;

(E) designating the persons who may be present while the discovery is conducted;

(F) requiring that a deposition be sealed and opened only on court order; * * *

A person who successfully seeks a Rule 26(c) protective order or a Rule 37(a) order compelling discovery will generally also receive from the losing party the reasonable expenses incurred in obtaining that order. Rule 37(a)(5)(A) provides:

> If the motion [to compel] is granted—or if the disclosure or requested discovery is provided after the motion was filed—the court must, after giving an opportunity to be heard, require the

party or deponent whose conduct necessitated the motion, the party or attorney advising that conduct, or both to pay the movant's reasonable expenses incurred in making the motion, including attorney's fees. But the court must not order this payment if:

> (i)   the movant filed the motion before attempting in good faith to obtain the disclosure or discovery without court action;

> (ii) the opposing party's nondisclosure, response, or objection was substantially justified; or

> (iii) other circumstances make an award of expenses unjust.

While Rule 37(a)(5)(A) specifically addresses the award of attorneys' fees in connection with a Rule 37 motion to compel disclosure or discovery, Rule 26(c)(3) makes Rule 37(a)(5) applicable to successful motions for protective orders as well.

B. JUDICIAL SANCTIONS FOR DISCOVERY ABUSE

Rules 26(c)(3) and 37(a)(5) provide that those who succeed on motions for a protective order or to compel discovery usually will recover the reasonable attorneys' fees they incurred in connection with those motions. But what if the person from whom disclosure or discovery is sought totally fails to disclose information, provide discovery, or refuses to comply with a court order to provide disclosure or discovery? In these circumstances, other parties may be able to recover not only the costs of their disclosure or discovery motions but the court may, in addition, award sanctions against the nonresponding or noncompliant person.

1. JUDICIAL SANCTIONS FOR DISCOVERY ABUSE

As illustrated in Figure 10–7, discovery sanctions can be awarded under Rule 37(b) (for failure to comply with an order to provide disclosures) or Rule 37(d) (for a party's failure to attend its own deposition, serve answers to interrogatories, or respond to an inspection request).[5]

---

[5]   In addition to these two routes to discovery sanctions shown in Figure 10–7, Rule 37(c) provides sanctions for failure to provide a Rule 26(a) disclosure, supplement a disclosure or discovery response as required by Rule 26(e), or fail to properly admit a Rule 36 admission request.

FIGURE 10–7
RULE 37 SANCTIONS

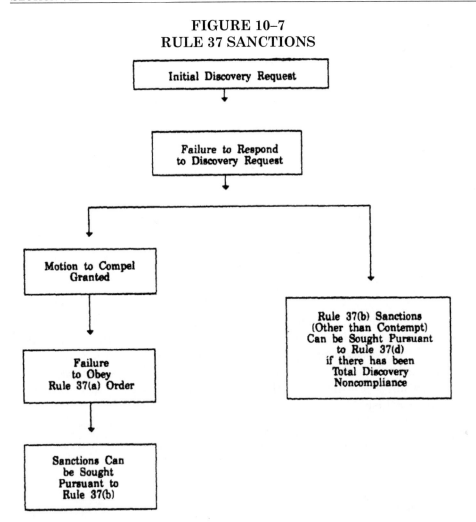

Rule 37(b) provides the surest, and most common, way to discovery sanctions—invoked against a party who has failed to obey a court order. When a person successfully obtains a Rule 26(c) protective order or Rule 37(a) order compelling discovery production, the opposing party normally must pay the expenses of that motion. However, there is usually a two-step process to the award of sanctions. First, the court orders a person to provide discovery pursuant to Rule 26(f), Rule 35, or Rule 37(a). Then, if the person against whom the order was entered still does not provide the information, this failure to comply with the order may result in Rule 37(b) sanctions. This is illustrated in the initial column of Figure 10–7.

Rule 37(b) sanctions are discretionary, and Rule 37(b)(2)(A) provides that these sanctions may include:

(i)   directing that the matters embraced in the order or other designated facts be taken as established for purposes of the action, as the prevailing party claims;

(ii) prohibiting the disobedient party from supporting or opposing designated claims or defenses, or from introducing designated matters in evidence;

(iii) striking pleadings in whole or in part;

(iv) staying further proceedings until the order is obeyed;

(v) dismissing the action or proceeding in whole or in part;

(vi) rendering a default judgment against the disobedient party; or

(vii) treating as contempt of court the failure to obey any order except an order to submit to a physical or mental examination.

In addition to these sanctions, Rule 37(b)(2)(C) adds the following: "Instead of or in addition to the orders above, the court must order the disobedient party, the attorney advising that party, or both to pay the reasonable expenses, including attorney's fees, caused by the failure, unless the failure was substantially justified or other circumstances make an award of expenses unjust." So, while the Rule 37(b)(2)(A) sanctions are discretionary, those who caused the failure to obey the order "must" pay the reasonable expenses of the failure, unless it was "substantially justified or other circumstances makes an award of expenses unjust."

In addition to the award of sanctions for failure to obey a court order, Rule 37(d) gives district courts the discretion to award sanctions for serious noncompliance with discovery obligations that does not involve the failure to obey a court order. Rule 37(d)(1)(A) provides that all of the sanctions listed in Rule 37(b)(2)(A), other than contempt, may be awarded if:

(i) a party or a party's officer, director, or managing agent—or a person designated under Rule 30(b)(6) or 31(a)(4)—fails after being served with proper notice, to appear for that person's deposition; or

(ii) a party, after being properly served with interrogatories under Rule 33 or a request for inspection under Rule 34, fails to serve its answers, objections, or written response.

As with the award of sanctions under Rule 37(b), Rule 37(d)(3) provides: "Instead of or in addition to [sanctions awarded pursuant to Rule 37(d)], the court must require the party failing to act, the attorney advising that party, or both to pay the reasonable expenses, including attorney's fees, caused by the failure, unless the failure was substantially justified or other circumstances make an award of expenses unjust."

This route to sanctions is illustrated in the right-hand column of Figure 10–7. The types of situations in which sanctions might be awarded pursuant to Rule 37(d) involve clear failure to comply with the discovery rules: a party fails to appear for her deposition after being served with proper notice, a party fails to respond to properly-served interrogatories, or a party fails to respond to a properly-served request for production. Rule 37(d) sanctions are not for situations in which a party answers some interrogatories but not others or produces some documents but not all. Nevertheless, courts are not required to award sanctions in such circumstances, and many judges first will order a party to produce discovery pursuant to Rule 37(a) before invoking the quite serious sanctions permissible under Rule 37(b).

Whether or not a judge ultimately dismisses an action for failure to provide discovery responses, such failure is a serious matter. In this regard, Rule 37(d)(2) cautions: "A failure described in Rule 37(d)(1)(A) is not excused on the ground that the discovery sought was objectionable, unless the party failing to act has a pending motion for a protective order under Rule 26(c)."

All of the Rule 37(b) sanctions can be awarded for a Rule 37(d) discovery failure except for the Rule 37(b)(2)(A)(vii) sanction of contempt. Why is contempt a possible sanction under Rule 37(b) but not under Rule 37(d)?

2. SANCTIONS FOR FAILURE TO PRESERVE ELECTRONICALLY STORED INFORMATION

Because of the unique complexity, volume, and expense of preserving and producing electronically stored information, it is treated separately under the discovery provisions of the Federal Rules. A continuing concern with electronic data is that the holders of such information will be required to expend vast sums to preserve the data and will be subject to huge penalties if data relevant to a civil action is unintentionally destroyed. As amended in 2015, Rule 37(e) deals with both of these concerns, providing:

> If electronically stored information that should have been preserved in the anticipation or conduct of litigation is lost because a party failed to take reasonable steps to preserve it, and it cannot be restored or replaced through additional discovery, the court:
>
> (1) upon finding prejudice to another party from loss of the information, may order measures no greater than necessary to cure the prejudice; or
>
> (2) only upon finding that the party acted with the intent to deprive another party of the information's use in the litigation may:

(A) presume that the lost information was unfavorable to the party;

(B) instruct the jury that it may or must presume the information was unfavorable to the party; or

(C) dismiss the action or enter a default judgment.

Parties therefore only can be subject to sanctions for the destruction of electronically stored information (ESI) if (1) that information should have been preserved in anticipation or conduct of litigation; (2) the information is lost because the party failed to take reasonable steps to preserve it; (3) the information cannot be restored or replaced through additional discovery; (4) another party has been prejudiced due to the loss of the information; and (5) the sanction awarded by the court is "no greater than necessary to cure the prejudice." Even if all of these Rule 37(e) requirements are met, the court is not required to order any sanction but, instead, "*may* order measures no greater than necessary to cure the prejudice."

Not only is Rule 37(e)(1) a unique sanctions provision for the loss of ESI, but Rule 37(e)(2) contains an even stricter requirement—a finding that the party acted with the intent to deprive another party of the information's use in the litigation—for imposing the following sanctions: (A) a presumption that the lost information was unfavorable to the party; (B) in a jury action, an instruction to the jury that it may, or must, presume that the lost information was unfavorable to the party; or (C) dismissal of the action or entry of a default judgment.

Although the case that follows was decided before the 2015 amendment of Rule 37(e), it illustrates the complexities of actions involving electronically stored information.

3.   FAILURE TO PRESERVE ELECTRONICALLY STORED INFORMATION: *FEDERICO V. LINCOLN MILITARY HOUSING, LLC*

In thinking about discovery battles over the preservation and destruction of electronically stored information, one imagines a battle involving corporate parties with vast information technology departments, thousands of computers, and sophisticated hardware and software. However, virtually everyone in the United States today possesses electronically stored information of some sort. If you're a party to a civil action, and your ESI fits within the Rule 26(b)(1) scope of discovery, you, too, can be required to produce that ESI pursuant to Rule 34 of the Federal Rules of Civil Procedure. And, if you haven't properly preserved the electronically stored information, you may be subject to Rule 37(e) sanctions.

Federico v. Lincoln Military Housing, LLC

United States District Court, Eastern District of Virginia, 2014
2014 WL 7447937

OPINION AND ORDER

■ DOUGLAS E. MILLER, UNITED STATES MAGISTRATE JUDGE.

In these consolidated claims for personal injury and property damage allegedly arising from mold in military housing, contentious discovery disputes have produced 28 contested motions, including several motions for sanctions and reciprocal requests for costs and fees related to the parties' alleged non-compliance. The Court resolved most of the previous disputes from the bench, or in brief written orders entered after oral argument. This Memorandum Order resolves the most contentious and expensive disagreement involving the Defendants' requests for Plaintiffs' electronic media, including text messages, email and social media posts.

In the sixteen consolidated cases, eight military families filed suit with allegations primarily against Defendant Lincoln Military Housing, LLC ("Lincoln"), a contractor engaged by the United States Military to manage government-owned housing used by active duty military. The Plaintiffs allege various illnesses and property damage they experienced were caused by Lincoln's failure to maintain the properties, or properly remediate the properties after mold was discovered. Lincoln, and the other Defendants alleged to be responsible for the deficient response, deny liability.

I. FACTUAL BACKGROUND

Even before suit was filed, Lincoln was aware that some of the Plaintiffs were very active users of email and social media. Lincoln's attorneys had visited Plaintiffs' publically available Facebook pages, as well as Facebook groups and other pages set up specifically to deal with the issue of mold and mold-related injuries. As a result, in January 2012 defense counsel sent a preservation letter to the first identified Plaintiff, Shelley Federico, roughly three months after she moved out of the subject housing. The letter, directed to her counsel, outlined Defendants' requests that she preserve and eventually produce electronic media. Among other things, the letter purported to require Ms. Federico to preserve:

1. Internet and web browser history files.

2. Potentially relevant texts and email messages.

3. Social media postings concerning their claims in the lawsuit and claimed damages.

4. Any photo or video images of the subject properties.

The four-page letter also demanded that Ms. Federico and her counsel make a written response confirming their receipt of the letters, their understanding of the obligations they impose, and that they "have imaged their computers and related devices." Thereafter, as suits commenced discovery was permitted but the District Court limited discovery to issues involving liability which were then set for a consolidated trial in October, 2014. Defendants served interrogatories and requests for production seeking all of this material from each Plaintiff.

Although the detailed preservation letter should have signaled to Plaintiffs' counsel the seriousness with which Defendants would pursue electronic discovery, their initial response included almost no production of electronic records. In fact, most of the Plaintiffs produced no electronic media of any kind. Those that did, produced only a few printed copies of emails, but no original emails, no social media posts and no text messages.

On June 4, 2014, the Court held the first hearing on discovery disputes, which came on Plaintiffs' motions for Protective Orders seeking relief from Defendants' requests for production, and certain subpoenas. For unrelated scheduling purposes, many of the Plaintiffs were present in court at the hearing. In response to Defense counsel's description of the meager production, Plaintiffs' counsel made a familiar assertion, advising the Court that he had not withheld anything, but had produced all electronic media which had been provided to him by his clients. He then noted that his clients were "heavy users of email" and that he perceived they did "not quite understand how comprehensive [their production] had to be." The Court admonished the assembled Plaintiffs to turn over related material to their attorney and permit counsel to determine whether it was relevant. The Court also advised the Plaintiffs that there could be consequences if materials were not provided as required by the Rules. The Court also retained under advisement Lincoln's request for costs and fees associated with the lack of production.

Despite the Court's guidance, the Plaintiffs produced few additional emails, but continued to communicate with counsel concerning their ongoing efforts to search for electronic media and produce additional responsive material. * * * On June 25, 2014, the Court held a second previously scheduled hearing and reviewed additional arguments on compliance. Defendants again expressed their disbelief that Plaintiffs' production was complete, particularly with regard to their extensive use of social media. Plaintiffs seemed to concede the point, with their counsel stating they had engaged an outside vendor, Sensei Enterprises, to provide estimates and design a search protocol for electronic media. Later the Plaintiffs received a cost estimate for Sensei's work to perform "email and social media recovery" from Plaintiffs' accounts. The proposal described costs which were then estimated to be $22,450.00, and Plaintiffs requested that the Defendants agree to bear this cost of electronic production. The Court did not order a forensic exam nor allocate the expected cost to the Defendants, as it perceived that additional production by a thorough self-directed search would yield sufficient results.

On July 10, 2014, Plaintiffs requested an emergency hearing in an effort to extend the Court's previously imposed deadline for production of electronic records. * * * After hearing Plaintiffs' arguments and Defendants' response, the Court declined to extend the deadline and advised Plaintiffs' counsel that if Plaintiffs were unable to produce any more responsive documents, they were required to advise the Court and Defendants of the nature of any search they had performed. * * *

The Court was reluctant to allocate responsibility for the contractor's estimated cost of reviewing the Plaintiffs' various email accounts and social media noting that the electronic data should be available to the individual Plaintiffs. The Court provided the following direction to the parties:

> This data is available to them and they should be able to get it, and it's crazy to have to pay somebody $22,000.00 to do what they should be able to do within a matter of an hour or an hour and a half of looking through their own files. And if they are unwilling to do that, then I will entertain a request for sanctions. And those sanctions may include the cost of having a professional engaged to produce them. * * *

The Plaintiffs failed to meet the July 17 production deadline, but they did produce letters describing their search criteria . . . * * *

On July 31, 2014, Defendants filed their Motion for Sanctions. The supporting brief argued that Plaintiffs' failure to produce texts, email, and other electronic media had severely compromised Defendants' ability to proceed with depositions and prepare for trial. The motion sought only one sanction, dismissal of Plaintiffs' claims for failure to comply. * * * Relevant to this dispute, Plaintiffs proffered at that hearing that they had engaged their IT consultant, who was working to search and produce relevant records, primarily from social media. The consultant was present and described the ongoing process for searching and processing the Facebook records using previously agreed upon search terms. He stated that the process of analyzing the records had produced 4.2 million "artifacts" from the parties' various Facebook accounts * * *.

At the hearing, the Court noted that the information sought was discoverable and had not been timely produced despite the Court's order. Nevertheless, the undersigned expressed skepticism that the material eventually produced would yield much that was relevant to the liability phase of the trial. As a result, the Court deferred any ruling until after the consultant's production * * *.

In September, Plaintiffs produced the results of their consultant's search, including over 5,000 records from social media. Almost

794   DISCLOSURE AND DISCOVERY: "LET'S SEE WHAT THE OTHER SIDE'S GOT."

CHAPTER 10

immediately thereafter, Defendants began deposing Plaintiffs and other witnesses. In November, the parties filed supplemental briefing on the outstanding issue of sanctions relating to production of electronic media. Defendants' briefing argues that the September production, combined with other records already produced, is still inadequate and that the relevance of the material which was produced demonstrates the severe consequences flowing from data which Defendants contend is missing, lost or destroyed. Plaintiffs responded and argued the exact opposite. They claim that the material already produced-over 5,500 Facebook posts and over 1,300 emails—includes almost all of the discoverable electronic evidence, and demonstrates the minimal relevance of the electronic media to the liability issues which will be contested in the April trial. In addition, Plaintiffs contend that any material omitted resulted from their clients' inexperience in managing electronic production and not from bad faith or intentional destruction of evidence. Combined, the parties' briefing and exhibits on this motion alone totals 2,233 pages. Again, the only sanction Defendants specifically request is dismissal, but their brief also refers more generally to "those sanctions [the Court] deems appropriate against Plaintiffs and their counsel."

After reviewing the parties' briefing, exhibits, and the five-month history of the discovery disputes over this and other evidence, the Court, for the reasons that follow, declines to impose any further sanction against Plaintiffs beyond the $29,000 expense associated with their expert's production of the Facebook records, but will award a portion of the reasonable attorney's fees associated with the original motion to compel.

II. STANDARD OF REVIEW

Defendants' request for sanctions implicates the Court's authority to police discovery noncompliance under three separate, but overlapping standards. First, as nearly all of the electronic production occurred after Defendants' first Motion to Compel, Rule 37(a) provides a means to reallocate the costs of that compelled production. * * * The plain language of Rule 37(a) permits monetary sanctions, including fees and reasonable expenses, if the non-disclosure is not substantially justified, and the movant attempts in good faith to resolve the dispute without court action.

Second, extensive additional production occurred after the expired deadlines set by the Court's initial orders on the Motion to Compel. As a result, the sanction remedies under Rule 37(b) and (c) apply. The Fourth Circuit has established a four-part test to help decide whether to impose sanctions for discovery violations. The court must determine (1) whether the noncomplying party acted in bad faith, (2) the amount of prejudice that noncompliance caused the adversary, (3) the need for deterrence of the particular sort of non-compliance, and (4) whether less drastic sanctions would have been effective. *Belk v. Charlotte-*

Mecklenberg Bd. Of Educ., 269 F.3d 305, 348 (4th Cir.2001). While all four factors are relevant to the Court's exercise of discretion, a finding of bad faith is not a necessary precursor to imposing attorney's fees and costs incurred as a result of a party's failure to comply with discovery. However, because the information sought is almost entirely electronically stored, the sanctions request is subject to Rule 37(e) which bars sanctions under the Rules for failing to provide information lost "as a result of the routine, good-faith operation of an electronic information system," absent exceptional circumstances [the standard under Rule 37(e) until it was amended in 2015].

The third standard relates to Defendants' claim of spoliation. Because they also alleged the Plaintiffs destroyed or irretrievably lost relevant evidence, their sanction request implicates the Court's inherent power to remedy spoliation of evidence. *Silvestri v. Gen. Motors Corp.*, 271 F.3d 583, 590 (4th Cir.2001). In this Circuit, to prove that spoliation of evidence warrants sanction, the party seeking the sanction must show:

(1) The party having control over the evidence had an obligation to preserve it when it was destroyed or altered;

(2) The destruction or loss was accompanied by a "culpable state of mind;" and

(3) The evidence that was destroyed or altered was "relevant" to the claims or defenses of the party that sought the discovery.

Goodman v. Praxair Svcs., Inc., 632 F.Supp.2d 494, 509 (D.Md.2009). A party's duty to preserve evidence "arises not only during litigation but also extends to that period before the litigation when a party reasonably should know that the evidence may be relevant to anticipated litigation." *Silvestri*, 271 F.3d at 591. A party breaches this duty when it fails to act reasonably to preserve material evidence. *Victor Stanley, Inc. v. Creative Pipe, Inc.*, 269 F.R.D. 497, 525 (D.Md.2010). The right to impose sanctions for spoliation derives from the Court's inherent power to control the judicial process in litigation, but it is limited to that necessary to redress conduct "which abuses the judicial process." *Silvestri.* 271 F.3d at 590 (quoting *Chambers v. NASCO. Inc.* 501 U.S. 32, 45–46 (1991)).

The Court's power to remedy spoliation includes a variety of sanctions from dismissal or default judgment to the preclusion of evidence or imposition of an adverse inference. But the harsh sanction of dismissal or default requires a showing of "bad faith" or other "like action" unless the spoliation was so prejudicial that it prevents the non-spoliating party from maintaining his case. *Silvestri.* 271 F.3d at 593 (quoting *Cole v. Keller Indus., Inc.*, 132 F.3d 1044, 1047 (4th Cir.1998)). While sanctions for spoliation require some showing of fault, assessments of the level of culpability primarily inform selection of an appropriate sanction, not whether spoliation has occurred in the first instance.

III. ANALYSIS

The Defendants' motion primarily seeks dismissal, the harshest sanction reserved for either severe misconduct or the loss of evidence central to their defense. Indeed, where dismissal is ordered, it usually follows the intentional bad faith destruction of evidence which was central to the issues in dispute. *See, e.g., Hosch v. BAE Svs. Info. Solutions, Inc.*, 2014 WL 1681694, at *1 (E.D.Va. Apr.24, 2014) (dismissing employment retaliation case with prejudice where the plaintiff permanently deleted all data on an iPhone and a Blackberry after a Court Order and two days before turning them over for examination); *Taylor v. Mitre Corp.*, 2013 WL 588763, at *1 (E.D.Va. Feb.13, 2013) (dismissing employment claims where the plaintiff previously smashed a work computer with a sledge hammer and ran specialized programs to delete information on his laptop in direct response to an Order to surrender the laptop). As set forth in greater detail below, no category of Plaintiffs' electronic evidence in this case is so central to the defense that its loss would deprive the Defendants of their ability to defend. In addition, Defendants have failed to establish that any Plaintiff deliberately destroyed evidence known to be relevant, or otherwise acted in bad faith. * * *

* * * [V]iewing the discovery record as a whole, the consistency of the records which were produced supports Plaintiffs' claim that any missing information was likely cumulative, and not lost due to any party's culpable conduct. As a result, Defendants cannot demonstrate either prerequisite for the ultimate sanction of dismissal for spoliation or failure to comply with a Court Order under Rule 37(b) or (c).

Nevertheless, nearly all of the electronic production occurred after the motion to compel. The parties' depositions demonstrate they were either initially poorly instructed or deliberately dilatory in their obligations to search for and produce responsive media. Accordingly, despite the marginal relevance of the electronic media which was produced, the costs of insuring a complete production, including the $29,000 fee for the production, will remain with the Plaintiffs. In addition, the Court will award, under Rule 37(a), a portion of the attorney's fees incurred in preparing and arguing the original motion to compel, following an opportunity to evaluate the circumstances which affect such an order under Rule 37(a)(5)(A)(iii).

A.   No sanction is warranted for text messages lost as a result of good faith operation of Plaintiffs' smart phones.

Although not central to their argument, Defendants contend that sanctions are warranted for Plaintiffs' failure to produce text messages, despite evidence that several of the Plaintiffs communicated by text during the relevant time period. Plaintiffs do not dispute that they have failed to produce text messages, but argue that their text messages would not be relevant to any contested issue, and were irretrievably lost prior to any of them being made aware that they would be specifically sought in discovery. After evaluating the extensive production of other electronic media and under the facts of this case, the Court does not find Plaintiffs' loss of access to their text messages to have been in bad faith. As a result, sanctions for their loss are precluded under Rule 37(e) * * *.

* * *

* * * Here, because Plaintiffs did not have a duty to take the steps necessary to preserve text message content at a time when any relevant content could have been preserved, the Court finds that Defendants have not established the elements of spoliation and therefore, sanctions are not warranted.

B. Plaintiffs' nearly complete production of emails does not warrant sanction, given the volume of materials which were produced and their marginal relevance.

* * *

With regard to the two accounts specifically addressed in Defendants' motion, the Court does not find any failure to produce email content warrants sanctions. The unused account named militarymoldwarriors@gmail.com contained no responsive email. * * * Contrary to their argument, Defendants' own forensic examiner did not state or imply that evidence was spoliated. He only stated that the password reset (undertaken as a result of a Plaintiff's inability to recall creating the account) prevented him from identifying when the account had earlier been accessed. Given that the Plaintiffs' had no memory of the account, which was located on a third party server, accessing it would be a necessary step to locating responsive, non-privileged email. In fact, a sworn declaration by Plaintiffs' paralegal established that after she reset the password, the original 2012 emails related to the setup of the account had never been opened, and the only other emails in the account related to the 2014 original password reset. This hardly constitutes evidence that emails or other data had been deliberately or even negligently destroyed. In addition, the Defendants have not identified a single email originating from this account. Given the volume of electronic media already produced, this is more than sufficient evidence to corroborate the Plaintiffs' position that the militarymoldwarriors account went unused after it was created despite its suggestive title.

With regard to Mr. Sulligan's account titled jrsywild@gmail.com, the Plaintiffs concede both that it may contain responsive email and they have been unable to produce them. * * * [Mr. Sulligan's] declaration authorizes the Defendant to obtain access to his email content directly, subject to the terms of a previously entered Protective Order. The Defendants did not respond to this suggestion, but it appears they have not undertaken their own subpoena or other direct inquiry to Google despite the Sulligans' permission.

After reviewing Mr. Sulligan's declaration, and the other email already produced, the Court does not find that his inability to produce email from this particular account warrants sanction. * * * Under these circumstances, and given the cumulative nature of any material likely to be found, the Defendants' ability to separately subpoena Mr. Sulligan's account subject to the terms of the Protective Order is an adequate remedy.

Finally, in contrast to those cases where sanctions have been imposed for the loss of electronic messages, Plaintiffs here did not act in bad faith or intentionally delete email to avoid their discovery. * * * The Defendants' evidence does not establish that they did so. Accordingly, the Court will not award sanctions for failing to produce additional email.

C. Plaintiffs' Facebook production, though delayed, does not demonstrate bad faith or prejudice sufficient to warrant severe sanctions.

The bulk of Defendants' briefing is devoted to argument regarding the insufficiency of Plaintiffs' production of social media posts, particularly from Facebook. This dispute originated even before the lawsuit when Defendants discovered that several of the Plaintiffs were prolific posters on Facebook. Not only were several of the Plaintiffs' Facebook profiles public, but certain Plaintiffs created and/or posted to special interest pages, including "Families Affected by Military Housing Mold," "the Truth About Lincoln Military Housing in Hampton Roads," and "Victims of Toxic Mold." As a result, Defendants were justifiably troubled by Plaintiffs' initial production which included no Facebook posts at all.

After engaging expert assistance, however, Plaintiffs eventually produced 5,527 Facebook records, including records from every Plaintiff with a Facebook account. These records were identified by search terms provided by Defendants and were produced directly to the Defendants without preliminary review by Plaintiffs' counsel subject to the terms of an Agreed Protective Order. At present, the Plaintiffs have incurred the fees for retaining expert assistance, retrieving, and producing the material.

The Defendants argue these records are "highly relevant" and demonstrate both the necessity of their vigorous motions practice, and the likelihood that additional relevant records have been lost or destroyed. Plaintiffs concede the discoverability of the material, but argue its relevance is minimal, and that it is largely, if not entirely, cumulative of other evidence already produced. After reviewing the

Defendants' argument, including approximately 200 separately numbered Facebook posts attached as exhibits to the sanctions motion, the Court agrees with the Plaintiffs. * * * Accordingly, as explained in greater detail below, the Court does not find the production warrants sanction under Rule 37(b) or (c), nor do any small gaps in production warrant relief for spoliation.

The Defendants' supplemental brief and accompanying exhibits attempt to show the relevance of the Facebook production in three general areas. Defendants argue that the records are relevant to show 1) the condition of the Plaintiffs' homes during the time of their tenancy, 2) the deficiencies in Plaintiffs' production of other records, and 3) the Plaintiffs' motivation for suit, or demonstrations of ill-will against Lincoln. In each of these three areas, the Defendants have overstated the importance of the Plaintiffs' individual use of social media to the liability issues to be contested.

i. Condition of the home.

Several Facebook posts have been identified by the Defendants as relevant because they demonstrate the condition of the Plaintiffs' home during the time of their tenancy. * * * After reviewing the materials selected by the Defendants to support their motion, however, the undersigned finds that the posts do little to shed light on relevant conditions in any of the family homes.

Most of the posts identified in this category either relate specifically to a Plaintiff's complaint of mold damage or depict unaffected areas of the home as background for photos or descriptions of routine family life. To the extent any of the photographs demonstrate mold damage, they appear to be entirely cumulative of other photographs already produced or already in Lincoln's possession. The other photos or descriptions of the residences do not document any particular defect but mostly show family situations with the home as backdrop. * * * Far more relevant than these innocuous depictions of family life are pictures and descriptions of black mold in vents, under floors, and behind walls. These mold-related posts are clearly relevant and discoverable, but they are also almost entirely cumulative of other discovery * * *. As a result, the already incurred cost of producing them must be considered under the proportionality mandate of Federal Rule 26(b)(2)(B) and (C) [now, Rule 26(b)(1)].

ii. Deficiencies in other discovery.

A number of the selected Facebook posts are identified by Defendants as demonstrating deficiencies in the Plaintiffs' prior production. In some cases this is because a photo or image was produced in the Facebook production which had not been produced in prior discovery. In most cases, however, the allegedly omitted image is completely irrelevant and was only produced in the Facebook production due to the extremely broad nature of the search terms and the Plaintiffs' agreement to disclose every record produced by the search.

* * *

[Some] posts are identified as demonstrating the deficiencies involved posts between Plaintiffs which had been produced by only one. As set out by Plaintiffs' forensic expert, there are a variety of reasons why posts might appear in one place and not in another, including specifically where a user comments on another's post. The comment is not recorded on the Facebook data of the original commenter.

* * * If Defendants came into possession of a document or image they believe was discoverable, it certainly mitigates any prejudice that Defendants may have suffered. Thus, even assuming that either of these scenarios presents a deficient discovery production, the lack of prejudice steers the Court away from imposing sanctions. * * * As set forth elsewhere, the Defendants provided over 5,000 social media posts from 16 different accounts. That production was obtained through a retained forensic consultant who produced records directly to the requesting party. Moreover, the belatedness of any production was already mitigated after the trial on liability was continued, and the Court extended the discovery cutoffs. Finally, the vast majority of posts in this category are irrelevant, and were produced solely because they were selected in the protocol devised by the Defendants to obtain the broadest possible response.

iii. Motivation for suit or ill-will against Lincoln.

By far, the largest number of selected posts described in Defendants' motion are relevant to the Defendants' contention that Plaintiffs' bear ill-will or animosity toward Lincoln as evidenced by their public posts condemning the company and its response to their Complaint. Were that issue in dispute, the treasure trove of electronic evidence obtained through Facebook certainly answers the question definitively. But the Plaintiffs have not made a secret of their ill-will towards Lincoln, which is amply documented in other evidence, videotapes, news reports, email and correspondence. The identified Facebook posts, intended for a sympathetic audience, merely amplify any particular Plaintiff's previously demonstrated unhappiness—sometimes through the use of more colorful language—but shed little new light on this established fact. Most importantly, they do not suggest that additional relevant evidence has been lost.

* * *

While the Defendants' rightly fault Plaintiffs' for their admittedly lackluster initial production, the Court does not find their efforts demonstrate bad faith, or even any lesser standard of culpability necessary to impose sanctions. Indeed, if any data was lost as a result of the delay, the loss was minimal, and likely incidental to automatic deletion or some other unrelated change in the parties' use of media. It does not follow that any person intentionally, or even negligently failed to preserve evidence they knew to be relevant. Instead, where electronic data is concerned, "the more logical inference is that the party was disorganized, or distracted, or technically challenged, or over-extended," or all of these. *In re Ethicon, Inc. Pelvic Repair Systems Prod. Liab. Litis.* 299 F.R.D. 502, 518 (S.D.W.Va.2014).

D. Proportionality requirements of Rule 26(b)(2)(C) [now, Rule 26(b)(1)] require the Court to consider costs to the Plaintiff in evaluating any sanction under Rule 37(b) or (c).

In their several briefs since the Facebook production, the Defendants have highlighted a post made by Ms. Federico on the date contractors opened the wall of her Lincoln-managed apartment on October 13, 2011. When workers discovered black mold on the back of the drywall, Ms. Federico posted a picture of the mold on Facebook, commenting "black mold in the walls! Gotta love base housing." Later in the same post, Ms. Federico responded to a friend's inquiry on her timeline for repairs by posting "urn, yeah, about that . . . Duces [sic] I'm moving out!"). Defendants argue this post undermines Ms. Federico's complaint in which she alleged that when her wall was opened up she became ill with severe headaches, dizziness, and "projectile vomiting."

The Plaintiffs see no inconsistency. They point out that the photographs in the post had previously been produced. With regard to Ms. Federico's comments, they argue that her Complaint did not disclose the exact timeline of her illness and that interrogatory answers later clarified the timing in a way not inconsistent with her posts. In response to this contention, Defendants cite several other references from discovery during which Ms. Federico variously describes the timing of her illness.

The foregoing exchange, which the parties even more elaborately briefed, illustrates the difficulty the Court will inevitably face in trying to achieve the proportionality required by Rule 26(b)(2)(C) [now, Rule 26(b)(1)] in electronic discovery of social media. The Defendants correctly note that this post is potentially relevant to Ms. Federico's credibility. To the extent she made prior statements suggesting she was "immediately" incapacitated or being exposed to the mold, her ability to post what defense counsel describes as "sassy" descriptions of the circumstances may undermine her credibility. But having already produced the photographs and other documents related to the work being performed, it is difficult for the Plaintiff or her attorney to understand in advance how describing these already disclosed facts in a Facebook post might have independent significance. This is especially so where, as here, the parties do not agree on the existence of any previous inconsistency in her description.

This potential problem can be mitigated when a thorough self-directed search allows the Court to evaluate some documents for relevance before ordering a forensic exam. But when, as in this case, significant costs have already been incurred in producing this material, the allocation of those costs under Rule 37 is the only tool left for the Court to try and ensure proportionality. Thus, in evaluating whether to award sanctions under Rule 37(b) or (c) even if the Court were to determine that the Plaintiffs had acted culpably, by failing to produce social media in a timely fashion, the cumulative nature of the material and its subsequent production has significantly limited, if not eliminated, any prejudice to the Defendants. Moreover, the expense Plaintiffs already incurred must be evaluated in light of the proportionality limits of Rule 26(b)(2)(C) [now, Rule 26(b)(1)], and Rule 37(e)'s caveat precluding sanctions for electronic information lost due to good faith operation of the electronic information system. Having considered all of this, the Court finds that the $29,000 Plaintiffs already incurred to generate the additional material is a sufficient sanction to deter further non-compliance. In combination with the extended discovery deadlines permitting depositions after the material was produced this is a sufficient remedy for any non-compliance with the Court's prior Orders related to production of electronic media.

E. The circumstances of the parties' discovery dispute require an award of costs or attorney's fees associated with the Defendants' Motion to Compel under Rule 37(a).

The Plaintiffs have incurred, and by this Order will bear, the expense of the forensic examination and production of their electronic media totaling over $29,000. The foregoing pages explain the Court's decision not [to] award any further sanction as a result of Plaintiffs' largely complete, but admittedly dilatory discovery response. However, even in cases where the non-complying party does not act in bad faith, Rule 37(a) mandates an award of attorney's fees and costs associated with a motion to compel where discoverable material is produced after the motion, and the non-producing parties conduct was not substantially justified, unless other circumstances make an award of expenses unjust. Fed.R.Civ.P. 37(a)(5)(A). Here, there is no dispute that a large amount of discoverable material was produced after the Defendants filed the motion. Prior to filing, the Defendants certified, and the Court finds, that they attempted to resolve Plaintiffs' non-compliance and were unsuccessful.

Although the Court has found that Defendants failed to establish the level of culpable conduct or prejudice necessary to impose additional sanctions, the Plaintiffs cannot claim that their initial, almost non-existent, production of electronic media was substantially justified. The volume of records produced in their multiple supplements clearly establish both their ability to retrieve responsive documents, and their discoverability. In addition, while the Plaintiffs are individuals and unsophisticated in the burdens of litigation, their counsel are not. Eight lawyers from four different law firms have been engaged on the

Plaintiffs' team. * * * Their inadequate initial response was not substantially justified.

It remains, however, for the Court to determine whether other circumstances would render an award of fees incurred in preparing and litigating the motion unjust. As set forth elsewhere, the Defendants have never requested a specific monetary sanction. At the Court's request, however, counsel submitted an itemized statement of fees associated with their motions to compel electronic production. This statement includes an itemized list of fees incurred between June 20 and August 20, 2014. As modified to reflect the issues addressed by this motion only, those fees total $64,514.00. Given that this statement concluded before the Defendants' voluminous Facebook production, it significantly under-reports the hours spent by counsel evaluating the Plaintiffs' compliance, and certainly understates the costs spent litigating the sanctions motion itself. Nevertheless, after considering the entire scope of the discovery disputes initiated by both sides, the Court finds imposing a fee award of this size would be unjust under the circumstances of this case. Fed.R.Civ.P. 37(a)(5)(A)(iii).

* * *

After considering all the foregoing, the undersigned does not find that an award of all of the fees associated with the motion to compel would be just. But some award of fees is necessary to fulfill the mandate of Rule 37(a) and to discourage the original non-compliance that gave rise to Defendants' original motion to compel. Accordingly, Defendants are DIRECTED to submit by January 14, 2015 affidavits or other support for the reasonableness of the $64,515 fees incurred both as to rate and number of hours. * * *

IV. CONCLUSION

Accordingly, for the foregoing reasons the Defendants' motion for sanctions is GRANTED IN PART and DENIED IN PART. The Plaintiffs shall bear the cost of expert production of electronic media in the amount of $29,220.04. The court shall also award a portion of the fees incurred by the Defendants in bringing the Motion to Compel after evaluating the facts required by Rule 37(a)(5)(A). To the extent Defendants' motion sought other or further relief, it is DENIED.

COMMENTS AND QUESTIONS CONCERNING
FEDERICO V. LINCOLN MILITARY HOUSING, LLC

1.   Magistrate Judge Miller ultimately awarded the defendants $18,000 for the fees they incurred in their motion to compel. The judge recognized that much of the discovery produced was cumulative, the plaintiffs had paid over $29,000 to an expert to organize the document production, and the plaintiffs had limited financial resources. However, the judge concluded that "some award of fees is necessary to discourage the sort of noncompliance which produced the motion [to compel]." *Federico v.*

Lincoln Military Housing, LLC, No. 2:12–CV–80, slip op. at 3 (E.D. Va. May 21, 2015). Do you agree?

2.   Magistrate Judge Miller notes in his opinion that there were 28 contested discovery motions in this action and that, with respect to one sanctions motion: "Combined, the parties' briefing and exhibits on this motion alone totals 2,233 pages." Along with amendments involving discovery, the 2015 amendments to the Federal Rules of Civil Procedure included an amendment to Rule 1 providing that the Rules "should be construed, administered, *and employed by the court and the parties* to secure the just, speedy, and inexpensive determination of every action and proceeding." Have the parties and their counsel met their duties under Rule 1? Who is paying for the 2233 pages of briefs and exhibits on the sanctions motion? *See also* Rule 3.4(e) of the Virginia Rules of Professional Conduct ("A lawyer shall not * * * [m]ake a frivolous discovery request or fail to make reasonably diligent effort to comply with a legally proper discovery request by an opposing party.").

3.   Magistrate Judge Miller lists three bases for possible sanctions in this action:

(1)   payment of expenses on a successful motion to compel (Rule 37(a)(5));

(2)   failure to comply with a court order or disclose or supplement (Rule 37(b) and (c)); and

(3)   common law spoliation.

The judge concludes that, pursuant to Rules 37(a)(5), 37(b), and 37(c), plaintiffs should bear the total cost of their electronic discovery vendor and pay at least a portion of defendants' expenses (attorneys' fees) in bringing their successful discovery motion. However, the judge concludes that plaintiffs' conduct was not such as to support dismissal of the action due to spoliation.

4.   The third basis for sanctions, spoliation, "refers to the destruction or material alteration of evidence or to the failure to preserve property for another's use as evidence in pending or reasonably foreseeable litigation." *Silvestri v. Gen. Motors Corp.*, 271 F.3d 583, 590 (4th Cir. 2001). With respect to spoliation involving electronically stored information, federal law changed with the amendment of Rule 37(e) in 2015. At the time of Judge Miller's ruling, Rule 37(e) simply provided: "Absent exceptional circumstances, a court may not impose sanctions under these rules on a party for failing to provide electronically stored information lost as a result of the routine, good-faith operation of an electronic information system." The Advisory Committee Note to the 2015 amendments to the Federal Rules provides:

> This limited rule has not adequately addressed the serious problems resulting from the continued exponential growth in the volume of such information. Federal circuits have established significantly different standards for imposing sanctions or curative measures on parties who fail to preserve electronically stored information. These developments have caused litigants to

expend excessive effort and money on preservation in order to avoid the risk of severe sanctions if a court finds they did not do enough.

305 F.R.D. 457, 569 (2015). Thus Rule 37(e) was amended to clarify the standard for award of sanctions for failure to preserve electronically stored information.

5.   While the prior version of Rule 37(e) only addressed sanctions "under these rules" (thus permitting sanctions based on the inherent power of the court—with different courts adopting different standards), the 2015 amendment "forecloses reliance on inherent authority or state law to determine when certain measures should be used. The rule does not affect the validity of an independent tort claim for spoliation if state law applies in a case and authorizes the claim." Advisory Committee Note to 2015 Amendment to Rule 37, 305 F.R.D. 457, 569–70 (2015).

6.   The 2015 amendment to Rule 37(e) does not apply to spoliation involving matter other than electronically stored information. Thus standards such as that enunciated in *Silvestri v. General Motors Corp.*, 271 F.3d 583 (4th Cir.2001), still apply to the failure to preserve other types of relevant information. *Silvestri* involved a plaintiff's failure to preserve a wrecked car for inspection in connection with a products liability action. If, though, it is electronically stored information that has not been preserved, the requirements of Rule 37(e) apply to any federal claim for sanctions.

7.   In *Federico*, sanctions would not have been appropriate under either the common law of spoliation applied by Judge Miller or the current version of Rule 37(e) that became effective on December 1, 2015. Judge Miller found that there was little or no prejudice to the defendants, which is required by the current version of Rule 37(e)(1) for the award of any sanctions involving failure to preserve electronically stored information. The judge also found that the plaintiffs had not acted with intent to deprive the defendants of this ESI, as is now required by Rule 37(e)(2) to impose the sanction of dismissal due to the failure to preserve ESI. Did the defendants make a tactical error in seeking dismissal of this action as the sole sanction for failure to preserve the electronically stored information?

8.   How did defense counsel know to send a letter to plaintiffs' counsel asking them to preserve electronic media? At what point in litigation, or anticipated litigation, does a duty to preserve relevant ESI arise? The Advisory Committee Note to the 2015 amendment to Rule 37(e) addresses this question as follows:

> In applying [Rule 37(e)], a court may need to decide whether and when a duty to preserve arose. Courts should consider the extent to which a party was on notice that litigation was likely and that the information would be relevant. A variety of events may alert a party to the prospect of litigation. Often these events provide only limited information about that prospective litigation, however, so that the scope of information that should be preserved may remain uncertain. It is important not to be blinded to this

> reality by hindsight arising from familiarity with an action as it is
> actually filed.

305 F.R.D. 457, 570 (2015). Even before defense counsel sent the letter
asking plaintiffs to preserve relevant ESI, did plaintiffs have reason to
believe that litigation was likely and that their electronic communications
would be relevant to that litigation?

9.   In refusing to infer that plaintiffs deliberately destroyed ESI,
Judge Miller states: "[W]here electronic data is concerned, 'the more logical
inference is that the party was disorganized, or distracted, or technically
challenged, or over-extended,' or all of these. *In re Ethicon, Inc. Pelvic
Repair Systems Prod. Liab. Litis.* 299 F.R.D. 502, 518 (S.D.W.Va. 2014)."
Should such an inference apply regardless of the custodian of the missing
information? *See* Advisory Committee Note to 2015 Amendment to Rule 37,
305 F.R.D. 457, 572 (2015) ("This rule recognizes that 'reasonable steps' to
preserve suffice; it does not call for perfection. The court should be sensitive
to the party's sophistication with regard to litigation in evaluating
preservation efforts; some litigants, particularly individual litigants, may
be less familiar with preservation obligations than others who have
considerable experience in litigation.").

10.   After the plaintiffs produced a minimal amount of responsive ESI,
they engaged an outside vendor to design a protocol to search plaintiffs'
electronic media. Judge Miller does not require that the defendants bear
any of the cost of this vendor, concluding that plaintiffs should have been
able to produce this ESI themselves. Was it fair to impose this entire
expense on the plaintiffs, when the information was sought by the
defendants?

11.   Judge Miller awarded the defendants their attorneys' fees on their
motion to compel, even though the plaintiffs produced the material in
question. What is the basis for such an order?

12.   Rule 37(e)(1) permits the court to, "upon finding prejudice to
another party from loss of the information, * * * order measures no greater
than necessary to cure the prejudice." Did the court employ any such
measures in this action?

13.   Judge Miller notes the difficulty in determining proportionality
(which requires him to decide the significance of particular information
during the pretrial stages of the action): "This potential problem can be
mitigated when a thorough self-directed search allows the Court to
evaluate some documents for relevance before ordering a forensic exam.
But when, as in this case, significant costs have already been incurred in
producing this material, the allocation of those costs under Rule 37 is the
only tool left for the Court to try and ensure proportionality."

The Advisory Committee Note to the 2015 amendment to Rule 37 also
addresses proportionality:

> Another factor in evaluating the reasonableness of
> preservation efforts is proportionality. The court should be
> sensitive to party resources; aggressive preservation efforts can be
> extremely costly, and parties (including governmental parties)

may have limited staff and resources to devote to those efforts. A party may act reasonably by choosing a less costly form of information preservation, if it is substantially as effective as more costly forms. It is important that counsel become familiar with their clients' information systems and digital data—including social media—to address these issues. A party urging that preservation requests are disproportionate may need to provide specifics about these matters in order to enable meaningful discussion of the appropriate preservation regime.

305 F.R.D. 457, 572–73 (2015). The factors now listed in Rule 26(b)(1) for determining proportionality include: "the importance of the issues at stake in the action, the amount in controversy, the parties' relative access to relevant information, the parties' resources, the importance of the discovery in resolving the issues, and whether the burden or expense of the proposed discovery outweighs its likely benefit."

14. How can the defendants establish that the plaintiffs sent relevant, nonprivileged text messages or other electronically stored information if the plaintiffs did not preserve such communications? In many ESI disputes, a party receives in discovery a message not produced by another party— suggesting that relevant data was not preserved or produced by all parties. In a portion of his opinion not included in the text above, Judge Miller notes, "[The defendants] also point to instances of email production by one party of an email copied to, but not produced by another, as evidence that certain Plaintiffs have failed to produce sufficient email." 2014 WL 7447937 at *11.

VIII. THE LAWYER'S ETHICAL DUTIES IN DISCLOSURE AND DISCOVERY

As the *Federico* case illustrates, lawyer and party misconduct—and resulting sanctions—can arise in disputes concerning the alleged failure to preserve electronically stored information. Some of the problems with the discovery of electronically stored information arise due to attorneys' lack of familiarity with ESI. However, ignorance of technology creates a risk for both client and lawyer, because Comment 8 to ABA Model Rule of Professional Conduct 1.1 provides that to "maintain the requisite knowledge and skill [required of all lawyers], a lawyer should keep abreast of changes in the law and its practice, including the benefits and risks associated with relevant technology * * *."

Disputes also frequently arise with respect to other aspects of disclosure and discovery. This is, at least in part, because there are no judges present to supervise disclosure and discovery and there may be litigation and economic incentives for attorney or party misconduct. This section of the chapter considers both the ethical and procedural rules that govern attorneys in such situations and then presents a case study of the difficulties that can arise when those duties are not followed.

A. LAWYERS' ETHICAL DUTIES IN THE DISCOVERY PROCESS

Whether representing a client in litigation or non-litigation matters, lawyers are subject to state ethical rules that govern the attorneys licensed to practice law within that state. In all states but California, these governing rules are based upon the Model Rules of Professional Conduct adopted by the American Bar Association; California is considering adoption of new rules of professional conduct that would be, in part, based on the ABA's Model Rules.

Many of the rules of professional conduct are directed at attorney conduct in litigation, and some directly focus on, or can be implicated by, attorney actions involving disclosure and discovery. The case study that follows, *infra* p. 811, involves an action in the State of Washington, so the following references are to the Washington Rules of Professional Conduct. The Rules cited are identical to the ABA Model Rules of Professional Conduct, while the Rules' headings and comments are virtually identical to those of the Model Rules.

Washington Rule of Professional Conduct 3.4 most directly addresses discovery practice, providing:

A lawyer shall not:

(a) unlawfully obstruct another party's access to evidence or unlawfully alter, destroy or conceal a document or other material having potential evidentiary value. A lawyer shall not counsel or assist another person to do any such act; * * *

(d) in pretrial procedure, make a frivolous discovery request or fail to make reasonably diligent effort to comply with a legally proper discovery request by an opposing party * * *

In addition to these prohibitions, Washington Rule of Professional Conduct 4.4(a) provides: "In representing a client, a lawyer shall not use means that have no substantial purpose other than to embarrass, delay, or burden a third person, or use methods of obtaining evidence that violate the legal rights of such a person."

Finally, Washington Rule of Professional Conduct 3.2 states: "A lawyer shall make reasonable efforts to expedite litigation consistent with the interests of the client." This Rule is explained by the comment after Model Rule 3.2, which contains the following sentences: "The question is whether a competent lawyer acting in good faith would regard the course of action as having some substantial purpose other than delay. Realizing financial or other benefit from otherwise improper delay in litigation is not a legitimate interest of the client."

Consider the application of these Rule provisions to the following situations.

1.   Rule 3.4 is captioned: "Fairness to Opposing Party." Where is the line between an attorney's duty of fairness to opposing parties and

the court and her duty of loyalty to her client? The first comment to Washington Rule of Professional Conduct 1.7 provides: "Loyalty and independent judgment are essential elements in the lawyer's relationship to a client."

2.   Rule 4.4 provides that "a lawyer shall not use means that have no substantial purpose other than to embarrass, delay, or burden a third person." Does this mean that lawyers can use means that, while they may produce relevant discovery for possible use in the action, also delay the action or burden other persons? Isn't the person who must respond to discovery always burdened by preparing a discovery response? Consider the proportionality factors set forth in Rule 26(b)(1), including "whether the burden or expense of the proposed discovery outweighs its likely benefit."

3.   What if arguably-relevant discovery requests will place a heavy financial burden on an impecunious plaintiff? Can the defendant make such requests? In addition to the ethics of such a request, how do "the parties' resources" impact such requests under Federal Rule of Civil Procedure 26(b)(1)?

4.   What might be a "substantial purpose other than delay" that would justify not expediting litigation as required by Rule 3.2? Can defense counsel seek an extension of time to allow her client to gather information relevant to a discovery request? Can defense counsel seek an extension of time to enable her to take a long-planned vacation? What if plaintiff's counsel previously sought extensions of time to respond to defendant's discovery requests?

B. FEDERAL RULE OF CIVIL PROCEDURE 26(g)

The Federal Rules of Civil Procedure also govern attorney conduct during the disclosure and discovery process. In particular, Rule 26(g)(1) provides:

> Every disclosure under Rule 26(a)(1) or (a)(3) and every discovery request, response, or objection must be signed by at least one attorney of record in the attorney's own name—or by the party personally, if unrepresented—and must state the signer's address, e-mail address, and telephone number. By signing, an attorney or party certifies that to the best of the person's knowledge, information, and belief formed after a reasonable inquiry:
>
> (A) with respect to a disclosure it is complete and correct as of the time it is made; and
>
> (B) with respect to a discovery request, response, or objection, it is:
>
> (i)   consistent with these rules and warranted by existing law or by a nonfrivolous argument for

extending, modifying, or reversing existing law, or for establishing new law;

(ii) not interposed for any improper purpose, such as to harass, cause unnecessary delay, or needlessly increase the cost of litigation; and

(iii) neither unreasonable nor unduly burdensome or expensive, considering the needs of the case, prior discovery in the case, the amount in controversy, and the importance of the issues at stake in the action.

Do these certifications sound similar to any other attorney certifications contained elsewhere in the Federal Rules? The Advisory Committee Note to the 1983 Amendment to Rule 26, which added Rule 26(g), states:

Rule 26(g), which parallels the amendments to Rule 11, requires an attorney or unrepresented party to sign each discovery request, response, or objection. Motions relating to discovery are governed by Rule 11. However, since a discovery request, response, or objection usually deals with more specific subject matter than motions or papers, the elements that must be certified in connection with the former are spelled out more completely.

97 F.R.D. 165, 219 (1983).

The Rule 26(g)(1) certification duty is enforced by Rule 26(g)(3):

If a certification violates this rule without substantial justification, the court, on motion or on its own, must impose an appropriate sanction on the signer, the party on whose behalf the signer was acting, or both. The sanction may include an order to pay the reasonable expenses, including attorney's fees, caused by the violation.

Note the manner in which many of the provisions of Rule 26(g) parallel the ethical requirements of the Model Rules of Professional Conduct. Thus Model Rule 3.4(d) prohibits an attorney from making a frivolous discovery request, while Rule 26(g)(1)(B)(i) provides that an attorney's signature represents a certification that the discovery request, response, or objection is "consistent with [the Federal Rules] and warranted by existing law or by a nonfrivolous argument for extending, modifying, or reversing existing law, or for establishing new law." Model Rule 4.4(a) prohibits a lawyer from using means solely to "embarrass, delay, or burden" someone, while Rule 26(g)(1)(B)(ii) interprets an attorney's signature as certifying that the discovery request, response, or objection is "not interposed for any improper purpose, such as to harass, cause unnecessary delay, or needlessly increase the cost of litigation."

The case study in the next section illustrates what can happen when attorneys do not adhere to their Rule 26(g) certifications.

C. WHAT IF ATTORNEYS DON'T FOLLOW THE RULES: *WASHINGTON STATE PHYSICIANS INS. EXCH. & ASS'N V. FISONS CORP.*

The following case study is based on *Washington State Physicians Ins. Exch. & Ass'n v. Fisons Corp.*, 122 Wash. 2d 299 (1993). Although filed in state court, the state procedural rules were modeled on the Federal Rules of Civil Procedure in effect at that time.

In January 1986 two-year old Jennifer Pollock suffered seizures that resulted in severe and permanent brain damage. The seizures were caused by an excess of theophylline in her system. She received the theophylline from the drug Somophyllin Oral Liquid, which consisted primarily of theophylline. An action was brought on behalf of the child against the pediatrician who prescribed the drug and Fisons Corporation, the drug's manufacturer.

The child's claims against the doctor were settled, and the case was set for trial against Fisons. The drug company contended that it did not know that theophylline-based medications were potentially dangerous when given to children with viral infections (such as Jennifer Pollock). The drug company, though, also manufactured the drug Intal, which did not contain theophylline and which the company marketed as an alternative to Somophyllin Oral Liquid. The company's manager of medical communications, in fact, had information about the dangers of theophylline.

Shortly before trial was to begin against Fisons, the Pollocks' counsel received from an anonymous source a June 30, 1981, letter sent by Fisons to a small number of physicians encouraging them to prescribe Intal. This letter discussed an article containing a study confirming reports "of life threatening theophylline toxicity when pediatric asthmatics ... contract viral infections" and referred to theophylline as a "capricious drug."

Fisons was then ordered to produce any documents that it had related to theophylline, which included a July 10, 1985, interoffice memorandum, referring to an "epidemic" of theophylline toxicity and an "alarming increase in adverse reactions such as seizures, permanent brain damage and death."

Neither the 1981 letter nor the 1985 memorandum had been produced in response to the Pollocks' or the doctor's prior discovery requests.

The Pollocks' initial production request had sought various documents concerning "the product" that allegedly contributed to the child's injuries. The Pollocks' request defined this drug as follows:

The term "the product" as used hereinafter in these interrogatories shall mean the product which is claimed to have caused injury or damage to JENNIFER MARIE POLLOCK as alleged in pleadings filed on her behalf, namely, to wit: "Somophyllin" oral liquid.

Interrogatories served on Fisons sought information about both Somophyllin and theophylline, and one of Fisons' marketing brochures stated: "Theophylline. The one name to remember . . . Somophyllin."

However, in a general objection to discovery requests, Fisons stated:

Requests Regarding Fisons Products Other Than Somophyllin Oral Liquid. Fisons objects to all discovery requests regarding Fisons products other than Somophyllin Oral Liquid as overly broad, unduly burdensome, harassing, and not reasonably calculated to lead to the discovery of admissible evidence.

The doctor, too, sought discovery from the drug company, serving the following production request:

Produce genuine copies of any letters sent by your company to physicians concerning theophylline toxicity in children.

The company responded:

Such letters, if any, regarding Somophyllin Oral Liquid will be produced at a reasonable time and place convenient to Fisons and its counsel of record.

In response to requests for correspondence, memoranda, articles and other documents "concerning," "regarding," or "covering" Somophyllin Oral Liquid, the company responded:

Without waiver of these objections and subject to these limitations, Fisons will produce documents responsive to this request at plaintiffs' expense at a mutually agreeable time at Fisons' headquarters.

The Pollocks and the doctor also sought to obtain information from the drug company concerning non-theophylline drugs, requesting:

All documents contained in the files from the regulating department, marketing department, drug surveillance department, pharmaceutical development department, product manager department and the medical departments regarding all cromolyn [Intal] products of Fisons Corporation.

The company responded:

Defendant Fisons objects to this discovery request as not reasonably calculated to lead to the discovery of admissible evidence, as overbroad in time, and as incredibly burdensome and harassing. This discovery request encompasses approximately eighty-five percent of all documents in the subject files and departments—millions of pages of documents. Neither cromolyn * * * nor any cromolyn product, nor the properties or efficacy of cromolyn is at issue in this litigation. Furthermore, Fisons objects to this discovery request as calling for the production of extremely sensitive trade secret and proprietary material.

In seeking a protective order to limit the documents that the company must produce, Fisons' attorneys stated in their memorandum to the court: "In short, Fisons' Regulatory File for Somophyllin Oral Liquid contains all or nearly all documents in Fisons' possession that are reasonably related to plaintiffs' failure-to-warn allegations."

Soon after the two documents implicating theophylline surfaced, Fisons settled with the Pollocks for $6.9 million. The doctor took to trial claims against Fisons for consumer protection, products liability, and fraud, and the jury awarded him approximately $1.1 million for injury to his professional reputation, $2.1 million for pain and suffering, and $450,000 in attorneys' fees. Fisons appealed the judgment and the doctor cross-appealed the trial court's refusal to award Rule 26(g) sanctions.

COMMENTS AND QUESTIONS CONCERNING *WASHINGTON STATE PHYSICIANS INS. EXCH. & ASS'N V. FISONS CORP.*

1.   Should sanctions have been awarded for the failure to produce the June 30, 1981, letter and July 10, 1985, memorandum (both of which were contained in Fisons' files for Intal, rather than Somophyllin)?

2.   If so, against whom should sanctions be awarded; of what type; and in what amount?

3.   Should any additional actions be taken against the drug company's lawyers?

4.   In its opinion the Washington Supreme Court stated:

It appears clear that no conceivable discovery request could have been made by the doctor that would have uncovered the relevant documents, given the * * * [discovery] responses of the drug company. The objections did not specify that certain documents were not being produced. Instead the general objections were followed by a promise to produce requested documents. These responses did not comply with either the spirit or letter of the discovery rules and thus were signed in violation of the certification requirement.

Washington State Physicians Ins. Exch. & Ass'n v. Fisons Corp., 122 Wash. 2d 299, 352 (1993).

Whether or not a person has a potential discovery objection, shouldn't other parties be able to uncover the existence of responsive documents by appropriately worded discovery requests?

5.   Part of the difficulty in *Fisons* was not that defense counsel refused to provide requested documents, but that they did not tell the other parties that they were withholding documents. As amended in 2015, Rule 34(b)(2)(C) provides that an objection "must state whether any responsive materials are being withheld on the basis of that objection. An objection to part of a request must specify the part and permit inspection of the rest."

The Advisory Committee Note to this amendment, 305 F.R.D. 457, 565 (2015) states:

> Rule 34(b)(2)(C) is amended to provide that an objection to a Rule 34 request must state whether anything is being withheld on the basis of the objection. This amendment should end the confusion that frequently arises when a producing party states several objections and still produces information, leaving the requesting party uncertain whether any relevant and responsive information has been withheld on the basis of the objections. The producing party does not need to provide a detailed description or log of all documents withheld, but does need to alert other parties to the fact that documents have been withheld and thereby facilitate an informed discussion of the objection. An objection that states the limits that have controlled the search for responsive and relevant materials qualifies as a statement that the materials have been "withheld."

Would this rule have made a difference in the outcome in *Fisons*? *See also* Washington Rule of Professional Conduct 3.4(c), which is substantively identical to ABA Model Rule 3.4(c) and provides that a lawyer shall not "knowingly disobey an obligation under the rules of a tribunal except for an open refusal based on an assertion that no valid obligation exists."

6.   In 1993, Rule 26(a)(1) of the Federal Rules of Civil Procedure was amended to require that parties automatically disclose the names of individuals "likely to have discoverable information relevant to disputed facts alleged with particularity in the pleadings," as well as documents "that are relevant to disputed facts alleged with particularity in the pleadings." These amendments were adopted over the dissent of several justices, with Justice Scalia writing a dissent that adoption of this amended Rule "would place intolerable strain upon lawyers' ethical duty to represent their clients and not to assist the opposing side." 146 F.R.D. 507, 511 (1993). Rule 26(a)(1) was amended in 2000 to require automatic disclosure of only those witnesses and documents "that the disclosing party may use to support its claims or defenses, unless the use would be solely for impeachment."

7.   Consider the sentiment expressed by Judge Henry Friendly about the lawyer's role in the adversary system: "Under our adversary system the role of counsel is not to make sure the truth is ascertained but to advance his client's cause by any ethical means. Within the limits of professional propriety, causing delay and sowing confusion not only are his right but may be his duty." Friendly, "Some Kind of Hearing," 123 *U.Pa.L.Rev.* 1267, 1288 (1975). *Compare* the second and third sentences of Comment 1 to

Washington Rule of Professional Conduct 1.3 ("A lawyer must * * * act with commitment and dedication to the interests of the client and with diligence in advocacy upon the client's behalf. A lawyer is not bound, however, to press for every advantage that might be realized for a client.") *with* Comment 1 to ABA Model Rule 1.3 (which is identical to the Washington Comment, except that it contains the word "zeal" rather than "diligence"). Why the substitution of "diligence" for "zeal" in the Washington Comment?

8.   How precise must lawyers be in their adherence to governing ethical or professional rules? Is "truthiness" sufficient? *See The Colbert Report*, October 17, 2015 (http://thecolbertreport.cc.com/videos/63ite2/the-word——truthiness).

9.   Finally, consider the following solution to recurrent problems of discovery abuse: "If there is a hell to which disputatious, uncivil, vituperative lawyers go, let it be one in which the damned are eternally locked in discovery disputes with other lawyers of equally repugnant attributes." *Dahl v. City of Huntington Beach*, 84 F.3d 363, 364 (9th Cir. 1996), quoting Judge Wayne E. Alley in *Krueger v. Pelican Prod. Corp.*, No. CIV–87–2385–A (W.D.Okla. Feb. 24, 1989).

IX. CONCLUSION

Disclosure and discovery are essential and distinctive aspects of civil dispute resolution in the United States. Formal disclosure and discovery rules require parties to provide nonprivileged information that is relevant to claims or defenses in the action and proportional to the needs of the case. The parties are required to plan discovery collaboratively through their Rule 26(f) discovery planning conference and to work with each other to resolve discovery disputes before seeking the aid of the court.

Disclosure and discovery are conducted outside the presence of a judge, which requires counsel to police their own behavior and adhere to governing ethical and procedural rules. At the completion of the parties' discovery, the case should be ready for trial or, as the next chapter discusses, the judicial resolution or settlement of the action short of trial.

X. CHAPTER ASSESSMENT

A.   Multiple-Choice Questions. Answer the following questions, reviewing the sections of the chapter noted in connection with each question.

1.   A man and a woman are in a traffic accident, after which the woman files a diversity action against the man in United States District Court. The woman seeks $80,000 in compensatory damages due to the man's alleged negligence. At the time of the accident, the man had automobile collision insurance.

Must the man provide his insurance agreement to the woman?

Review Section II(A) and choose the best answer from the following choices:

(a)   The man need not provide this agreement, because it is not relevant to any claim or defense in the action.

(b)   The man need not provide this agreement, because it is privileged.

(c)   The man must provide this agreement, because it is relevant as to whether he was negligent.

(d)   The man must provide this agreement, because it is a required initial disclosure.

2.   A doctor is working in a hospital emergency room when an ambulance brings in a pedestrian who had been struck by a car. Over a period of several hours, the doctor attends to the pedestrian, who does not appear to have been seriously injured. One week later, though, the pedestrian's condition worsens considerably, and his leg is amputated.

Ten months later, the pedestrian files a diversity action in federal court against the driver who hit him. After interviewing the emergency room doctor, the pedestrian's lawyer decides that the doctor should be called by the pedestrian to testify at trial as to the pedestrian's condition on the day of the accident. Pedestrian's lawyer, though, does not retain the doctor as an expert consultant or trial witness.

At the outset of the discovery period, the driver files a motion seeking an order that (1) the pedestrian identify any physician who might testify at trial on the pedestrian's behalf; (2) the pedestrian or the physician identified provide a written report with any opinions the physician might express at trial, the facts considered by the physician in forming those opinions, and a list of any cases in which the physician provided expert testimony in the last four years; and (3) any physician identified submit to a deposition.

Should the court grant the driver's motion?

Review Sections II(B) and IV and choose the best answer from the following choices:

(a)   The pedestrian must identify the doctor if the pedestrian may use her testimony to support his claims at trial.

(b)   The pedestrian must provide the written report sought by the driver.

(c)   The doctor must provide the written report sought by the driver.

(d)   The doctor must be identified by the pedestrian but need not provide a written report nor submit to a deposition.

3.   The general counsel of a major corporation was asked to investigate a letter that the corporation received from an attorney who alleged that one of the corporation's products is defective; the attorney

also threatened to file suit against the corporation unless he received an immediate settlement on behalf of his injured client. The corporation offered no settlement.

In response to the attorney's letter, the general counsel located an engineer at a second company that builds the allegedly defective sub-assembly for the corporation's products. After interviewing the engineer (who designed the sub-assembly), the general counsel prepared a memorandum for her files, in which she concluded that "this engineer doesn't know what he's doing" and "I really hope that we don't get sued on this, because I can't think of any good defenses."

The attorney who wrote the letter to the corporation brings a diversity action on behalf of his injured client. The general counsel identifies her memorandum in response to a discovery request, but refuses to produce the memorandum. The plaintiff files a motion to compel its production.

Should the court grant the motion to compel production of the memorandum?

Review Sections III(C) and III(D) and choose the best answer from the following choices:

(a) Yes, because the document is not protected by either the attorney-client privilege or the work-product doctrine.

(b) Yes, because the document is within the scope of discovery applicable in the federal courts.

(c) No, because the document is protected by the attorney-client privilege.

(d) No, because the document is protected by the attorney work-product doctrine.

4. A car and a bus are involved in a traffic accident, and the driver of the car brings a diversity action against the bus company in federal district court. Sitting in the front seat of the bus was a passenger, who, quite literally, had a front-row seat to the accident. He is not, though, named as a party in the civil action.

After the parties' Rule 26(f) discovery conference, the driver of the car serves on the bus passenger the following discovery requests: (1) a set of 20 interrogatories and (2) a subpoena and notice setting the deposition of the passenger. The deposition is set at a convenient time for the passenger, who comes to you as an attorney asking whether he must respond to these discovery requests.

Must the passenger respond to the interrogatories and appear for his deposition?

Review Sections VI(A) and (B) and choose the best answer from the following choices:

(a) The passenger must respond to the interrogatories and provide deposition testimony.

(b) The passenger must respond to the interrogatories but need not provide deposition testimony.

(c) The passenger must provide deposition testimony but need not respond to the interrogatories.

(d) The passenger need not respond to the interrogatories and need not provide deposition testimony.

5. A consumer buys a snow blower manufactured by a company that has manufactured such equipment for many years. When starting the snow blower, the consumer reaches near the blade mechanism and his hand is mangled. He brings a diversity action against the company in federal court, asserting products liability claims against the company.

After the parties' Rule 26(f) discovery conference, the consumer serves on the company a document request seeking copies of other consumer complaints about the snow blower that injured the consumer. Thirty days later, without communicating with the company or its attorney, the consumer's attorney files a motion to compel the discovery sought in the document request. Ten days after the motion is filed and served, the company provides the consumer with the complaints requested.

The consumer then seeks an order from the court requiring the company to pay the consumer's reasonable expenses in bringing the motion to compel.

Should the court grant the consumer's motion for attorneys' fees?

Review Section VII(A) and choose the best answer from the following choices:

(a) No, because the consumer's attorney did not attempt to obtain the discovery without court action.

(b) No, because the company provided the discovery sought.

(c) Yes, because the information sought is relevant to consumer's claims in the action.

(d) Yes, because the information was not provided until after the motion was filed.

B. Essay Questions. To test your understanding of this chapter's material, outline or write an answer to the following questions.

1. Discovery Difficulties.

Pamela Prentice is in an automobile accident with a Nickel Plate freight train, which strikes her car as it drives across a railroad track. The only non-party witness to the accident is Willie Witness, who dies after counsel for the Nickel Plate interviews him but before Prentice's counsel can do so. Due to injuries sustained in the accident, Prentice lost all memory concerning the accident.

Prentice brings suit against the Nickel Plate Railroad in federal district court. Prentice's counsel files simultaneously with the complaint the following discovery requests:

(i)   75 interrogatories;

(ii)   a request for "all documents relevant to this case;"

(iii) a request for the statement defense counsel took from Witness; and

(iv) a request that the train engineer immediately be tested for any evidence of illegal drugs or prescription medicines.

In response to the interrogatories and document requests, defendant Nickel Plate sends Prentice's counsel twenty-nine boxes of documents. Unfortunately, several of these boxes break open in transit and the contents mix together. Nickel Plate objects to the request for Witness's statement and does not respond to the request for drug testing.

(a) Discuss any problems with the discovery requests that Prentice served upon the railroad.

(b) Discuss any problems with Nickel Plate's responses to Prentice's discovery.

2.   Gymnastic Gyrations.

Paula Pretzel is a promising college gymnast who apparently injures her back during practice on January 10, 2014, and quits the gymnastics team alleging that "I have no choice because I've been mistreated by our physical therapist, Danielle Defendant." Paula then brings a diversity action in federal district court, asserting a $100,000 tort claim against Danielle for injuries allegedly arising from such mistreatment.

Pursuant to court order, the attorneys for Paula and Danielle hold their Rule 26(f) conference on June 1, 2014. At this conference, Paula's attorney provides Danielle's attorney with a list of individuals with discoverable information which Paula may use to support her claims, several documents upon which Paula may rely, and a calculation of the basis of Paula's $100,000 damage claim. Danielle's attorney does not produce anything for Paula, and Paula's attorney tells her, "That's O.K. I'm sure you'll get me the relevant information when you have time."

On June 2, Paula's attorney files a motion seeking sanctions against Danielle because of her "refusal to comply with federal disclosure requirements." By this motion, Paula seeks an order compelling Danielle to provide the pretrial disclosures required by the Federal Rules of Civil Procedure, an order holding Danielle in contempt of court, and $10,000 in damages.

Before the court can rule on this motion, Danielle provides Paula with the requested disclosures and the judge says that he will "withhold a ruling on this motion for now."

Danielle then files a July 1 request seeking from Paula (1) a psychiatric examination of Paula (to support Danielle's theory that Paula's physical difficulties are "all in Paula's head") and (2) a copy of a statement that Paula's attorney took from Charlene Coach on January 12, 2014, concerning what happened at the January 10, 2014, gymnastics practice. Receiving no response to this request, on August 1, 2004, Danielle files a motion to compel the psychiatric exam and Charlene's statement.

(a)   Should the court provide Paula with any relief in connection with her June 2nd sanctions motion?

(b)   Should the court grant Danielle's August 1st motion to compel?

CHAPTER 11

ADJUDICATION WITHOUT TRIAL: "LET'S END THIS NOW!"

I. INTRODUCTION

Although discovery is provided to enable the parties to prepare their cases for trial, very few civil cases are actually resolved by trial. Recent statistics indicate that only 1.1% of the federal civil actions terminated during the year ending December 31, 2014, reached trial.[1]

Not surprisingly, many civil actions are resolved by settlement. Others, though, are resolved through default judgments, voluntary and involuntary dismissals, and summary judgment, all of which are the subjects of this chapter. Cases not resolved in this manner are considered at pretrial conferences, which are typically followed by pretrial orders. While only a small percentage of civil actions proceed to trial, counsel or the court send many actions to alternative dispute resolution processes such as mediation or arbitration. These alternative dispute resolution (ADR) processes are discussed in the final portion of this chapter.

II. DEFAULT AND DEFAULT JUDGMENTS

Unlike legal thrillers in which the parties vigorously contest a civil action in the courtroom, some cases end because one party or the other does not contest the action at all. If the plaintiff does not pursue the action it filed, or improperly contests that action, it may be dismissed pursuant to Rule 41 of the Federal Rules of Civil Procedure. But if the defendant fails to contest an action filed against it, the court can enter default and default judgment against that defendant pursuant to Rule 55 of the Federal Rules.

Rule 55(a) of the Federal Rules of Civil Procedure provides: "When a party against whom a judgment for affirmative relief is sought has failed to plead or otherwise defend, and that failure is shown by affidavit or otherwise, the clerk must enter the party's default." In some state courts, a party seeking a default judgment simply moves for such a judgment. However, in the federal courts, securing a default judgment is a two step process:

(1) The clerk of courts must enter a Rule 55(a) **default**, a court document attesting that a party "has failed to plead or otherwise defend."

---

[1] Admin. Office of the U. S. Courts, *Federal Judicial Caseload Statistics: December 31, 2014* (2014) (Table C–4) (these statistics do not include land condemnation cases).

(2) The clerk or judge then enters a Rule 55(b) **default judgment**, which can be enforced pursuant to Rule 69 (through a writ of execution, which is used to convert a money judgment into actual money) or Rule 70 (if the judgment is not a money judgment, but an order to a party to take action is needed).

The Rule 55(a) default is simply the clerk's certification that the defendant is not defending the action. The Rule 55(b) default judgment can be more difficult to obtain. Such a final judgment, though, can be turned into monetary or other relief through a Rule 69 or 70 execution on the judgment.

The first question in seeking a Rule 55(b) default judgment is whether that judgment should be sought from the clerk of court or from the judge. Rule 55(b)(1) provides the quickest and simplest way to obtain a default judgment—from the clerk rather than from the judge. Rule 55(b)(1) states:

> If the plaintiff's claim is for a sum certain or a sum that can be made certain by computation, the clerk—on the plaintiff's request, with an affidavit showing the amount due— must enter judgment for that amount and costs against a defendant who has been defaulted for not appearing and who is neither a minor nor an incompetent person.

The prototypical case for entry of default judgment by the clerk is an action seeking to enforce a contract for a set amount. If the defendant agreed to pay the plaintiff $100,000 under a contract and plaintiff's action is based on defendant's failure to pay, the clerk herself can enter judgment against the defendant (assuming the defendant is a competent adult).

But what if the plaintiff filed a tort action and seeks damages for pain and suffering? In that situation, plaintiff's claim would not be "for a sum certain or a sum that can be made certain by computation." So the plaintiff must apply for default judgment to the judge, rather than to the clerk. Rule 55(b)(2) describes how such an application for a default judgment is handled:

> In all other cases [beyond those described in Rule 55(b)(1)], the party must apply to the court for a default judgment. A default judgment may be entered against a minor or incompetent person only if represented by a general guardian, conservator, or other like fiduciary who has appeared.

Rule 55(b)(2) also has specific requirements for the handling of any hearing by the court and requires prehearing notice for those who, at one time or another, appeared in the action:

> If the party against whom a default judgment is sought has appeared personally or by a representative, that party or its

representative must be served with written notice of the application at least 7 days before the hearing. The court may conduct hearings or make referrals—preserving any federal statutory right to a jury trial—when, to enter or effectuate judgment, it needs to:

(A) conduct an accounting;

(B) determine the amount of damages;

(C) establish the truth of any allegation by evidence; or

(D) investigate any other matter.

So, if judgment is properly sought from a competent adult for a "sum certain or a sum that can be made certain by computation," the clerk must enter default judgment. In other cases, only the judge can consider such a motion and in some cases must hold a hearing before entering the default judgment. Figure 11–1 illustrates the situations in which the clerk or the judge can render a final default judgment.

FIGURE 11–1
DEFAULTS AND DEFAULT JUDGMENTS UNDER RULE 55

	Clerk	Judge
(1) Must Enter Default:	If failure to plead or otherwise defend "shown by affidavit or otherwise"	
(2) Can Enter Default Judgment:		
Claim Not for Sum Certain	No	Judge may hold a hearing to determine relief.
Defendant Has Appeared	No	If written notice to defendant 7 days before hearing
Defendant is a Minor	No	If defendant represented by guardian, conservator, or other fiduciary who has appeared
Defendant is Incompetent	No	If defendant represented by guardian, conservator, or other fiduciary who has appeared

Claim for Sum Certain and Defendant is Competent Adult who Hasn't Appeared	Yes	

What if the defendant against whom default judgment was entered has a reasonable excuse for not responding to the civil action and the motions for default and default judgment? For instance, assume that the plaintiff never served the defendant and the defendant did not receive notice of the action or the motions for default and default judgment? Contemplating such situations, Rule 55(c) alerts counsel to the fact that the court "may set aside an entry of default for good cause, and it may set aside a default judgment under Rule 60(b)."

Rule 60(b) provides not only for setting aside default judgments, but extends generally to motions seeking relief from a final judgment, order, or proceeding. It provides:

> On motion and just terms, the court may relieve a party or its legal representative from a final judgment, order or proceeding for the following reasons:
>
> (1) mistake, inadvertence, surprise, or excusable neglect;
>
> (2) newly discovered evidence that, with reasonable diligence, could not have been discovered in time to move for a new trial under Rule 59(b);
>
> (3) fraud (whether previously called intrinsic or extrinsic), misrepresentation, or misconduct by an opposing party;
>
> (4) the judgment is void;
>
> (5) the judgment has been satisfied, released or discharged; it is based on an earlier judgment that has been reversed or vacated; or applying it prospectively is no longer equitable; or
>
> (6) any other reason that justifies relief.

Thus, if the defendant never received notice, its motion to set aside the default and default judgment might be brought under Rule 60(b)(4) (void judgment).

The subsection of Rule 60(b) under which the motion to set aside judgment is made can be relevant to the timeliness of that motion. Rule 60(c)(1) includes strict deadlines for the filing of a Rule 60(b) motion for relief from final judgment: "A motion under Rule 60(b) must be made within a reasonable time—and for reasons (1), (2), and (3) no more than a year after the entry of the judgment or order or the date of the proceeding." Thus if the only reason for the Rule 60(b) motion to set aside judgment is the alleged fraud of the plaintiff, that motion must be filed within one year after the entry of the judgment in question.

However, the best way to avoid worrying about the time limits for Rule 60(b) motions is to promptly respond to the action and provide no basis for a default or default judgment.

Finally, it is important to realize that, even though a default judgment does not address the merits of an action, that judgment is generally considered to be a judgment "on the merits" for the purposes of claim preclusion. Thus the defendant cannot expect to litigate that claim in another action. However, as we will see in Chapter 14, the first court's personal jurisdiction, and possibly subject-matter jurisdiction, can be litigated in the first or second action—but only once.

III. RULE 41 DISMISSALS

Rule 55 defaults and default judgments result when a defendant does not respond to plaintiff's claims. Rule 41 dismissals, though, may occur when the plaintiff does not properly or promptly engage in the action. In some cases, in fact, the plaintiff may consciously decide not to pursue the very action that it filed. Rule 41(a) of the Federal Rules of Civil Procedure provides for plaintiff's voluntary dismissal of its action, while Rule 41(b) allows the defendant to seek involuntary dismissal if the plaintiff fails to prosecute its action or comply with the Rules or a court order.

A. RULE 41(a) VOLUNTARY DISMISSALS

One can imagine why a defendant may not want to actively participate in an action in which she's been sued, but why would a plaintiff not actively prosecute the action that he has filed? Plaintiffs, like the rest of us, sometimes change their minds. The circumstances surrounding a civil action also may have changed. The plaintiff may no longer have the funds, or the patience, to sustain a lawsuit; he and the defendant may have resolved their dispute; or the action may have been assigned to a judge whom plaintiff and his counsel perceive to be hostile to plaintiff or his action.

One federal judge explained why a plaintiff might seek a voluntary dismissal under Rule 41(a) by quoting the poet Oliver Goldsmith:

> For he who fights and runs away
>
> May live to fight another day;
>
> But he who is in battle slain
>
> Can never rise to fight again.[2]

---

[2] *Merit Ins. Co. v. Leatherby Ins. Co.*, 581 F.2d 137, 144 (7th Cir. 1978) (Swygert, J., dissenting). The defendant in this action did not answer the complaint nor file a motion for summary judgment. The *Leatherby* court upheld the plaintiff's right to voluntarily dismiss its action under Rule 41(a)(1), even after the district court granted the defendant's motion to stay the action and compel arbitration and the arbitration had commenced.

In such a situation, the plaintiff can hit the litigation "undo button" and voluntarily dismiss her action. If she moves fast enough, she can do this without the need for agreement of the other parties or the court and, if this is the first voluntary dismissal of this action, her dismissal will be without prejudice to her later refiling of the action. Rule 41(a)(1)(A) provides:

> Subject to Rules 23(e) [class actions], 23.1(c) [derivative actions], 23.2 [class suits involving unincorporated associations], and 66 [receivers] and any applicable federal statute, the plaintiff may dismiss an action without a court order by filing:
>
> > (i)   a notice of dismissal before the opposing party serves either an answer or a motion for summary judgment; * * *

So, if the plaintiff files her notice of dismissal before the defendant serves either an answer or a motion for summary judgment, she can unilaterally dismiss her action simply by filing a notice of dismissal with the court. Why should she only have that right up until the time of an answer or motion for summary judgment? Why can't a plaintiff unilaterally dismiss a certified class action, derivative action, or action involving a receiver? *See* Federal Rule of Civil Procedure 23(e) ("The claims, issues, or defenses of a certified class may be settled, voluntarily dismissed, or compromised only with the court's approval.")

The notice of dismissal is simply a one-sentence pleading in which the plaintiff voluntarily dismisses her action. In the United States District Court for the Southern District of New York, in which *Leonard v. PepsiCo* was decided, the official form for such a voluntary dismissal looks like this:

IN THE UNITED STATES DISTRICT COURT
FOR THE SOUTHERN DISTRICT OF NEW YORK

	) **NOTICE OF VOLUNTARY**
Plaintiff(s)	) **DISMISSAL PURSUANT TO**
v.	) **F.R.C.P. 41(a)(1)(A)(i)**
	)
	) Case No.:
Defendant(s)	)
	)
	)

NOTICE OF VOLUNTARY DISMISSAL PURSUANT TO F.R.C.P. 41(a)(1)(A)(i)

Pursuant to F.R.C.P. 41(a)(1)(A)(i) of the Federal Rules of Civil Procedure, the

plaintiff(s) _____ and or their counsel(s), hereby give notice that the above-captioned action is voluntarily dismissed, without prejudice against the defendant(s) _____.

Date:

_____

Signature of plaintiffs or plaintiff's counsel

_____

Address

_____

City, State & Zip Code

_____

Telephone Number

_____

But, what if the defendant has served its answer or a motion for summary judgment? In that case Rule 41(a)(1)(A)(ii) still permits the plaintiff to voluntarily dismiss her action, but the dismissal requires "a stipulation of dismissal signed by all parties who have appeared." Why, though, would a defendant consent to the voluntary dismissal of plaintiff's action? In the most common situation, the parties have settled their dispute, and the dismissal of the action is one part of that settlement. Even if there has been no settlement, a defendant may believe that it is in its interest to be rid of the action against it. Rule 41(a)(1)(B) provides that unless "the notice or stipulation states otherwise, the dismissal is without prejudice" to the plaintiff refiling that action against defendant.

However, defendant only may agree to stipulate to a dismissal if the stipulation provides that dismissal is with prejudice to the refiling of the action. In addition, Rule 41(a)(1)(B) states that "if the plaintiff previously dismissed any federal-or state-court action based on or including the same claim, a notice of dismissal operates as an adjudication on the merits." Figure 11–2 illustrates the requirements and effects of different Rule 41(a) voluntary dismissals.

FIGURE 11–2
VOLUNTARY DISMISSALS UNDER RULE 41(a)

Plaintiff Initiated/ Granted by Court	Rule 41(a) Provision	Timing	Agreement of Other Parties	Standard	Effect
Plaintiff Can Initiate	41(a)(1)(A)(i)	before opponent's answer or summary judgment motion	not necessary	as of right if filed before answer or summary judgment motion	unless there was a prior dismissal or dismissal states otherwise, without prejudice
Plaintiff Can Initiate	41(a)(1)(A)(ii)	at any time	written stipulation required	as of right with stipulation	unless prior dismissal or dismissal states otherwise, without prejudice
Granted by Court	41(a)(2)	at any time	not necessary	"on terms that the court considers proper"	unless order states otherwise, without prejudice

As discussed in Chapter 9, the defendant can decide to assert its defenses in a preanswer motion (typically a motion to dismiss) or file an answer in which those defenses are included. In most situations, the defendant will choose to file the motion to dismiss, which, if successful, will end the lawsuit (at least in the trial court).

Consider, though, the impact of such a decision on the plaintiff's ability to voluntarily dismiss her action, as illustrated in the 1983–84 effort by the Pennzoil Company to acquire the Getty Oil Company. At the very last moment, it was Texaco Incorporated, not Pennzoil, that acquired Getty (while the Pennzoil-Getty acquisition papers were being drafted).

Pennzoil filed an action in Delaware Chancery Court, unsuccessfully seeking to enjoin Texaco's acquisition of Getty. Pennzoil's attorneys then realized that a Texas jury would be much more sympathetic to Pennzoil than the Delaware Chancery Court. The following excerpt describes how Pennzoil attorney Irv Terrell obtained the Texas jury that rendered a ten billion dollar Pennzoil verdict (ultimately resulting in a three billion dollar settlement for Pennzoil). While reading this excerpt consider both the strategy adopted by Pennzoil's attorneys and the potential impact of such a strategy upon civility within the legal profession. *Compare* Texas Disciplinary Rule of Professional Conduct, § 1.01, Comment 6 ("[A] lawyer should act with competence, commitment and dedication to the interest of the client and with zeal in advocacy upon the client's behalf.") *with* Texas Disciplinary Rule of Professional Conduct, Preamble, ¶ 4 ("A lawyer should demonstrate respect for the legal system and for those who serve it, including judges, other lawyers and public officials.").

T. Petzinger, Jr., *Oil and Honor*
261–62 (1987)

[W]hile studying the unfamiliar (to him) terrain of the Delaware courts, Terrell had come upon a seldom-used rule: If someone fails to file a formal answer to a lawsuit, the lawsuit may be dismissed at any stage of the case—without even asking the judge for permission. Getty Oil had filed a response. So had the trust and the museum. *Texaco hadn't.* As near as Terrell could tell, Pennzoil was now free to drop Texaco from the Delaware lawsuit without even having to ask the judge for permission, then refile the case anywhere in the country where both companies had operations. That, of course, meant [chairman of Pennzoil] Hugh Liedtke's Houston.

While awaiting the decision on the injunction motion, Terrell discussed the move to nonsuit Texaco with the Pennzoil local law firm in Delaware, which agreed that the move just might succeed. However, special security measures were required. The Chancery Court of Delaware is a genteel court, where local custom requires the lawyers on one side of a case to notify their adversaries in advance of any filings. Doing so in this case would obviously permit Texaco to hustle up a piece of paper formally answering Pennzoil's suit.

"Maintain silence," Terrell told his cohorts in Delaware. "We're not gonna follow this gentlemanly rule."

At midnight the day that Judge Brown finally dashed Pennzoil's hope of restoring its deal, Terrell conferred with his partner Jeffers and with Liedtke, who were in Washington appearing before the Federal Trade Commission in yet another effort to thwart the Texaco deal. (It too would fail.) Liedtke gave the go-ahead. Early the following morning, Pennzoil gave the Delaware court clerk a $25,000 check to cover its costs in the case and filed a one-sentence document: "Please take notice that plaintiff, Pennzoil Company, hereby dismisses this action without prejudice as to defendant Texaco Inc. pursuant to Chancery Court Rule 41(a)(1)(I)."

Fifteen minutes later, Terrell filed the case of *Pennzoil Company v. Texaco Incorporated,* Cause #84–05905, in the District Court of Harris County, Texas. In the last paragraph of the twenty-page document, Pennzoil made the greatest damages demand ever seen in Harris County, and probably anywhere in the world: "Pennzoil respectfully prays that upon trial by jury, this Court enter judgment against Texaco in such amount as is proper, but in no event less than $7,000,000,000 actual damages and $7,000,000,000 punitive damages."

The amounts would later be increased to $7.53 billion each, after Pennzoil had more fully refined its case.

————————

B. RULE 41(b) INVOLUNTARY DISMISSALS

In many cases it will not be the plaintiff who wants to voluntarily dismiss its action, but the defendant who seeks dismissal. The first sentence of Rule 41(b) contemplates such a situation: "If the plaintiff fails to prosecute or to comply with these rules or a court order, a defendant may move to dismiss the action or any claim against it."

Other Federal Rules of Civil Procedure provide for the dismissal of an action due to plaintiff's failure to comply with specific rules or governing law. *E.g.,* Rule 12(b) (motion to dismiss); Rule 12(c) (motion for judgment on the pleadings); Rule 37(b) (motion to dismiss for failure to obey a discovery order); Rule 56 (motion for summary judgment). Rule 41 authorizes the court to dismiss an action for not only failure to prosecute the action but for failure to comply with any of the Federal Rules of Civil Procedure or a court order.

Rule 41(b) sets forth no governing standard for when the court should dismiss an action. Plaintiff's failure to prosecute sometimes can be quite clear. *E.g., Peters v. Harrison,* 172 F.3d 53 (7th Cir. 1999) ("On the day of trial * * * Peters failed to return to the courtroom following a recess. Accordingly, the district court dismissed the case for want of prosecution."). In other cases, though, failure to prosecute may be more difficult to determine. *E.g., Lopez v. Cousins,* 435 Fed.Appx. 113 (3rd Cir. 2011) (*per curiam*) (district court abused its discretion in dismissing pro se action because plaintiff did not file opposition to motion for summary judgment after 10 extensions of time to file that opposition). Among the factors that a district court might consider in determining whether to dismiss an action under Rule 41(b) are:

> (1) the extent of the *party's* personal *responsibility;* (2) the *prejudice* to the adversary caused by the failure to meet scheduling orders and respond to discovery; (3) a *history* of dilatoriness; (4) whether the conduct of the party or the attorney was *willful* or in *bad faith;* (5) the effectiveness of sanctions other than dismissal, which entails an analysis of

alternative sanctions; and (6) the *meritoriousness* of the claim or defense.

Poulis v. State Farm Fire & Cas. Co., 747 F.2d 863, 868 (3d Cir. 1984). *See also Link v. Wabash R. Co.*, 370 U.S. 626 (1962).

Rule 41(b) not only provides for involuntary dismissals, but prescribes the effect of specific types of dismissals:

> Unless the dismissal order states otherwise, a dismissal under this subdivision (b) and any dismissal not under this rule— except one for lack of jurisdiction, improper venue, or failure to join a party under Rule 19—operates as an adjudication on the merits.

Thus, if a court never properly could entertain an action, its dismissal will not preclude plaintiff from filing the action in a court that can hear it. Unless the court provides to the contrary in its dismissal order, though, all other Rule 41(b) dismissals preclude refiling of the dismissed action.

A federal district judge has great discretion in determining whether an action should be dismissed under Rule 41(b), because the plaintiff has failed to prosecute, failed to comply with the Rules, or disobeyed a court order. Plaintiffs should not test the patience of the judge, especially by repeatedly failing to respond to court orders, follow the Rules, or otherwise move the action forward. At some point the judge will react like Peter Finch in the movie *Network* and say (or at least think): "I'm mad as Hell, and I'm not going to take this anymore." In that case the Rule 41(b) order of dismissal is likely on its way—and plaintiff's counsel should begin focusing on a Rule 60(b) motion for relief from final judgment and appeal.

IV. SUMMARY JUDGMENT

While Rule 55 default judgments and Rule 41(b) dismissals are due to a party's failure to properly defend or prosecute an action, other case resolutions short of trial are not premised on party inaction or misconduct. An action may be dismissed due to the insufficiency of the allegations of the complaint under Rule 12(b) or under Rule 12(c) after considering the allegations of all the pleadings. Rule 56 provides another opportunity for the judge to decide the case short of trial. After the parties have had an opportunity for discovery, Rule 56 permits a judge to grant summary judgment on the theory that a reasonable jury only could resolve that action in one way. Rule 56(b) provides that, unless a different time is set by local rule or court order, a party may file a motion for summary judgment "at any time until 30 days after the close of all discovery."

Rule 56(a) provides:

> A party may move for summary judgment, identifying each claim or defense—or the part of each claim or defense—on which summary judgment is sought. The court shall grant summary judgment if the movant shows that there is no genuine dispute as to any material fact and the movant is entitled to judgment as a matter of law. * * *

Thus to obtain summary judgment a party must show two things:

- There is no genuine dispute as to any material fact (the factual element of the summary judgment standard); and

- The party bringing the motion (the movant) is entitled to judgment as a matter of law (the legal element of the summary judgment standard).

Rule 56(c)(1)(A) provides that summary judgment motions can be supported or opposed by "depositions, documents, electronically stored information, affidavits or declarations, stipulations (including those made for the purposes of the motion only), admissions, interrogatory answers, or other materials." However, Rule 56(c)(2) states that summary judgment material can be objected to if it "cannot be presented in a form that would be admissible in evidence." Rule 56(c)(4) also contains specific requirements for affidavits or declarations offered in connection with a summary judgment motion: "An affidavit or declaration used to support or oppose a motion must be made on personal knowledge, set out facts that would be admissible in evidence, and show that the affiant or declarant is competent to testify on the matters stated."

When faced with a properly supported summary judgment motion, a party cannot merely assert that it will call witnesses at trial to rebut the moving party's motion. Instead, it's time for the party opposing summary judgment to "put up or shut up."[3] As the United States Court of Appeals for the Fifth Circuit has stated, "Rule 56 * * * say[s] in effect, 'Meet these affidavit facts or judicially die.' "[4]

In the case that follows, the Supreme Court further explains how a party can meet its Rule 56 evidentiary burden.

---

[3]   *Street v. J.C. Bradford & Co.*, 886 F.2d 1472, 1478 (6th Cir. 1989).

[4]   *Southern Rambler Sales, Inc. v. Am. Motors Corp.*, 375 F.2d 932, 937 (5th Cir.), *cert. denied*, 389 U.S. 832 (1967).

A. THE *CELOTEX* STANDARD

Celotex Corporation v. Catrett

United States Supreme Court, 1986
477 U.S. 317

OPINION

■ JUSTICE REHNQUIST delivered the opinion of the Court.

The United States District Court for the District of Columbia granted the motion of petitioner Celotex Corporation for summary judgment against respondent Catrett because the latter was unable to produce evidence in support of her allegation in her wrongful-death complaint that the decedent had been exposed to petitioner's asbestos products. A divided panel of the Court of Appeals for the District of Columbia Circuit reversed, however, holding that petitioner's failure to support its motion with evidence tending to negate such exposure precluded the entry of summary judgment in its favor. This view conflicted with that of the Third Circuit in *In re Japanese Electronic Products*, 723 F.2d 238 (1983), *rev'd on other grounds sub nom. Matsushita Electric Industrial Co. v. Zenith Radio Corp.*, 475 U.S. 574 (1986). We granted certiorari to resolve the conflict, and now reverse the decision of the District of Columbia Circuit.

Respondent commenced this lawsuit in September 1980, alleging that the death in 1979 of her husband, Louis H. Catrett, resulted from his exposure to products containing asbestos manufactured or distributed by 15 named corporations. * * * Petitioner's motion, which was first filed in September 1981, argued that summary judgment was proper because respondent had "failed to produce evidence that any [Celotex] product . . . was the proximate cause of the injuries alleged within the jurisdictional limits of [the District] Court." In particular, petitioner noted that respondent had failed to identify, in answering interrogatories specifically requesting such information, any witnesses who could testify about the decedent's exposure to petitioner's asbestos products. In response to petitioner's summary judgment motion, respondent then produced three documents which she claimed "demonstrate that there is a genuine material factual dispute" as to whether the decedent had ever been exposed to petitioner's asbestos products. The three documents included a transcript of a deposition of the decedent, a letter from an official of one of the decedent's former employers whom petitioner planned to call as a trial witness, and a letter from an insurance company to respondent's attorney, all tending to establish that the decedent had been exposed to petitioner's asbestos products in Chicago during 1970–1971. Petitioner, in turn, argued that the three documents were inadmissible hearsay and thus could not be considered in opposition to the summary judgment motion.

In July 1982, almost two years after the commencement of the lawsuit, the District Court granted all of the motions filed by the various defendants. The court explained that it was granting petitioner's summary judgment motion because "there [was] no showing that the plaintiff was exposed to the defendant Celotex's product in the District of Columbia or elsewhere within the statutory period." Respondent appealed only the grant of summary judgment in favor of petitioner, and a divided panel of the District of Columbia Circuit reversed. The majority of the Court of Appeals held that petitioner's summary judgment motion was rendered "fatally defective" by the fact that petitioner "made no effort to adduce any evidence, in the form of affidavits or otherwise, to support its motion." According to the majority, [Rule 56] of the Federal Rules of Civil Procedure, and this Court's decision in *Adickes v. S.H. Kress & Co.*, 398 U.S. 144, 159 (1970), establish that "the party opposing the motion for summary judgment bears the burden of responding only after the moving party has met its burden of coming forward with proof of the absence of any genuine issues of material fact." The majority therefore declined to consider petitioner's argument that none of the evidence produced by respondent in opposition to the motion for summary judgment would have been admissible at trial. The dissenting judge argued that "[t]he majority errs in supposing that a party seeking summary judgment must always make an affirmative evidentiary showing, even in cases where there is not a triable, factual dispute." According to the dissenting judge, the majority's decision "undermines the traditional authority of trial judges to grant summary judgment in meritless cases."

We think that the position taken by the majority of the Court of Appeals is inconsistent with the standard for summary judgment set forth in Rule 56(c) of the Federal Rules of Civil Procedure [now Rule 56(a), which provides that the court "shall grant summary judgment if the movant shows that there is no genuine dispute as to any material fact and the movant is entitled to judgment as a matter of law"]. Under Rule 56(c), summary judgment is proper "if the pleadings, depositions, answers to interrogatories, and admissions on file, together with the affidavits, if any, show that there is no genuine issue as to any material fact and that the moving party is entitled to a judgment as a matter of law." In our view, the plain language of Rule 56(c) mandates the entry of summary judgment, after adequate time for discovery and upon motion, against a party who fails to make a showing sufficient to establish the existence of an element essential to that party's case, and on which that party will bear the burden of proof at trial. In such a situation, there can be "no genuine issue as to any material fact," since a complete failure of proof concerning an essential element of the nonmoving party's case necessarily renders all other facts immaterial. The moving party is "entitled to a judgment as a matter of law" because the nonmoving party has failed to make a sufficient showing on an essential element of her case with respect to which she has the burden of proof. "[T]h[e] standard [for granting summary judgment] mirrors the standard for a directed verdict under Federal Rule of Civil Procedure 50(a). . . ." *Anderson v. Liberty Lobby, Inc.*, 477 U.S. 242, 250 (1986).

Of course, a party seeking summary judgment always bears the initial responsibility of informing the district court of the basis for its motion, and identifying those portions of "the pleadings, depositions, answers to interrogatories, and admissions on file, together with the affidavits, if any," which it believes demonstrate the absence of a genuine issue of material fact. But unlike the Court of Appeals, we find no express or implied requirement in Rule 56 that the moving party support its motion with affidavits or other similar materials negating the opponent's claim. * * * [R]egardless of whether the moving party accompanies its summary judgment motion with affidavits, the motion may, and should, be granted so long as whatever is before the district court demonstrates that the standard for the entry of summary judgment * * * is satisfied. One of the principal purposes of the summary judgment rule is to isolate and dispose of factually unsupported claims or defenses, and we think it should be interpreted in a way that allows it to accomplish this purpose.

* * *

We do not mean that the nonmoving party must produce evidence in a form that would be admissible at trial in order to avoid summary judgment. Obviously, Rule 56 does not require the nonmoving party to depose her own witnesses. Rule 56(e) permits a proper summary judgment motion to be opposed by any of the kinds of evidentiary materials listed in Rule 56(c), except the mere pleadings themselves, and it is from this list that one would normally expect the nonmoving party to make the showing to which we have referred.

The Court of Appeals in this case felt itself constrained, however, by language in our decision in *Adickes v. S.H. Kress & Co.*, 398 U.S. 144 (1970). There we held that summary judgment had been improperly entered in favor of the defendant restaurant in an action brought under 42 U.S.C. § 1983. In the course of its opinion, the *Adickes* Court said that "both the commentary on and the background of the 1963 amendment conclusively show that it was not intended to modify the burden of the moving party . . . to show initially the absence of a genuine issue concerning any material fact." We think that this statement is accurate in a literal sense, since we fully agree with the *Adickes* Court that the 1963 amendment to Rule 56(e) was not designed to modify the burden of making the showing generally required by Rule 56(c). It also appears to us that, on the basis of the showing before the Court in *Adickes*, the motion for summary judgment in that case should have been denied. But we do not think the *Adickes* language quoted above should be construed to mean that the burden is on the party moving for summary judgment to produce evidence showing the absence of a genuine issue of material fact, even with respect to an issue on which the nonmoving party bears the burden of proof. Instead, as we have explained, the burden on the moving party may be discharged by "showing"—that is, pointing out to the district court— that there is an absence of evidence to support the nonmoving party's case.

* * *

Our conclusion is bolstered by the fact that district courts are widely acknowledged to possess the power to enter summary judgments sua sponte, so long as the losing party was on notice that she had to come forward with all of her evidence. It would surely defy common sense to hold that the District Court could have entered summary judgment sua sponte in favor of petitioner in the instant case, but that petitioner's filing of a motion requesting such a disposition precluded the District Court from ordering it.

Respondent commenced this action in September 1980, and petitioner's motion was filed in September 1981. The parties had conducted discovery, and no serious claim can be made that respondent was in any sense "railroaded" by a premature motion for summary judgment. Any potential problem with such premature motions can be adequately dealt with under Rule 56(f) [now, Rule 56(d)], which allows a summary judgment motion to be denied, or the hearing on the motion to be continued, if the nonmoving party has not had an opportunity to make full discovery.

In this Court, respondent's brief and oral argument have been devoted as much to the proposition that an adequate showing of exposure to petitioner's asbestos products was made as to the proposition that no such showing should have been required. But the Court of Appeals declined to address either the adequacy of the showing made by respondent in opposition to petitioner's motion for summary judgment, or the question whether such a showing, if reduced to admissible evidence, would be sufficient to carry respondent's burden of proof at trial. We think the Court of Appeals with its superior knowledge of local law is better suited than we are to make these determinations in the first instance.

The Federal Rules of Civil Procedure have for almost 50 years authorized motions for summary judgment upon proper showings of the lack of a genuine, triable issue of material fact. Summary judgment procedure is properly regarded not as a disfavored procedural shortcut, but rather as an integral part of the Federal Rules as a whole, which are designed "to secure the just, speedy and inexpensive determination of every action." Fed.Rule Civ.Proc. 1. Before the shift to "notice pleading" accomplished by the Federal Rules, motions to dismiss a complaint or to strike a defense were the principal tools by which factually insufficient claims or defenses could be isolated and prevented from going to trial with the attendant unwarranted consumption of public and private resources. But with the advent of "notice pleading," the motion to dismiss seldom fulfills this function any more, and its place has been taken by the motion for summary judgment. Rule 56 must be construed with due regard not only for the rights of persons asserting claims and defenses that are adequately based in fact to have those claims and defenses tried to a jury, but also for the rights of persons opposing such claims and defenses to demonstrate in the manner provided by the Rule, prior to trial, that the claims and defenses have no factual basis.

The judgment of the Court of Appeals is accordingly reversed, and the case is remanded for further proceedings consistent with this opinion.

It is so ordered.

■ JUSTICE WHITE, concurring.

I agree that the Court of Appeals was wrong in holding that the moving defendant must always support his motion with evidence or affidavits showing the absence of a genuine dispute about a material fact. I also agree that the movant may rely on depositions, answers to interrogatories, and the like, to demonstrate that the plaintiff has no evidence to prove his case and hence that there can be no factual dispute. But the movant must discharge the burden the Rules place upon him: It is not enough to move for summary judgment without supporting the motion in any way or with a conclusory assertion that the plaintiff has no evidence to prove his case.

A plaintiff need not initiate any discovery or reveal his witnesses or evidence unless required to do so under the discovery Rules or by court order. Of course, he must respond if required to do so; but he need not also depose his witnesses or obtain their affidavits to defeat a summary judgment motion asserting only that he has failed to produce any support for his case. It is the defendant's task to negate, if he can, the claimed basis for the suit.

Petitioner Celotex does not dispute that if respondent has named a witness to support her claim, summary judgment should not be granted without Celotex somehow showing that the named witness' possible testimony raises no genuine issue of material fact. It asserts, however, that respondent has failed on request to produce any basis for her case. Respondent, on the other hand, does not contend that she was not obligated to reveal her witnesses and evidence but insists that she has revealed enough to defeat the motion for summary judgment. Because the Court of Appeals found it unnecessary to address this aspect of the case, I agree that the case should be remanded for further proceedings.

■ JUSTICE BRENNAN, with whom THE CHIEF JUSTICE and JUSTICE BLACKMUN join, dissenting.

This case requires the Court to determine whether Celotex satisfied its initial burden of production in moving for summary judgment on the ground that the plaintiff lacked evidence to establish an essential element of her case at trial. I do not disagree with the Court's legal analysis. The Court clearly rejects the ruling of the Court of Appeals that the defendant must provide affirmative evidence disproving the plaintiff's case. Beyond this, however, the Court has not clearly explained what is required of a moving party seeking summary judgment on the ground that the nonmoving party cannot prove its case. This lack of clarity is unfortunate: district courts must routinely decide summary judgment motions, and the Court's opinion will very likely create confusion. For this reason, even if I agreed with the Court's result, I would have written separately to explain more clearly the law in this area. However, because I believe that Celotex did not meet its burden of production under Federal Rule of Civil Procedure 56, I respectfully dissent from the Court's judgment.

I

* * *

If the burden of persuasion at trial would be on the *non-moving* party, the party moving for summary judgment may satisfy Rule 56's burden of production in either of two ways. First, the moving party may submit affirmative evidence that negates an essential element of the nonmoving party's claim. Second, the moving party may demonstrate to the Court that the nonmoving party's evidence is insufficient to establish an essential element of the nonmoving party's claim. If the nonmoving party cannot muster sufficient evidence to make out its claim, a trial would be useless and the moving party is entitled to summary judgment as a matter of law.

Where the moving party adopts this second option and seeks summary judgment on the ground that the nonmoving party—who will bear the burden of persuasion at trial—has no evidence, the mechanics of discharging Rule 56's burden of production are somewhat trickier. Plainly, a conclusory assertion that the nonmoving party has no evidence is insufficient. Such a "burden" of production is no burden at all and would simply permit summary judgment procedure to be converted into a tool for harassment. Rather, as the Court confirms, a party who moves for summary judgment on the ground that the nonmoving party has no evidence must affirmatively show the absence of evidence in the record. This may require the moving party to depose the nonmoving party's witnesses or to establish the inadequacy of documentary evidence. If there is literally no evidence in the record, the moving party may demonstrate this by reviewing for the court the admissions, interrogatories, and other exchanges between the parties that are in the record. Either way, however, the moving party must affirmatively demonstrate that there is no evidence in the record to support a judgment for the nonmoving party.

If the moving party has not fully discharged this initial burden of production, its motion for summary judgment must be denied, and the Court need not consider whether the moving party has met its ultimate burden of persuasion. Accordingly, the nonmoving party may defeat a motion for summary judgment that asserts that the nonmoving party has no evidence by calling the Court's attention to supporting evidence already in the record that was overlooked or ignored by the moving party. * * *

The result in *Adickes v. S.H. Kress & Co.* is fully consistent with these principles. In that case, petitioner was refused service in respondent's lunchroom and then was arrested for vagrancy by a local policeman as she left. Petitioner brought an action under 42 U.S.C. § 1983 claiming that the refusal of service and subsequent arrest were the product of a conspiracy between respondent and the police; as proof of this conspiracy, petitioner's complaint alleged that the arresting officer was in respondent's store at the time service was refused. Respondent subsequently moved for summary judgment on the ground that there was no actual evidence in the record from which a jury could draw an inference of conspiracy. In response, petitioner pointed to a statement from her own deposition and an unsworn statement by a Kress employee, both already in the record and both ignored by respondent, that the policeman who arrested petitioner was in the store at the time she was refused service. We agreed that "[i]f a policeman were present, . . . it would be open to a jury, in light of the sequence that followed, to infer from the circumstances that the policeman and Kress employee had a 'meeting of the minds' and thus reached an understanding that petitioner should be refused service." Consequently, we held that it was error to grant summary judgment "on the basis of this record" because respondent had "failed to fulfill its initial burden" of demonstrating that there was no evidence that there was a policeman in the store.

The opinion in *Adickes* has sometimes been read to hold that summary judgment was inappropriate because the respondent had not submitted affirmative evidence to negate the possibility that there was a policeman in the store. The Court of Appeals apparently read *Adickes* this way and therefore required Celotex to submit evidence establishing that plaintiff's decedent had not been exposed to Celotex asbestos. I agree with the Court that this reading of *Adickes* was erroneous and that Celotex could seek summary judgment on the ground that plaintiff could not prove exposure to Celotex asbestos at trial. However, Celotex was still required to satisfy its initial burden of production.

II

I do not read the Court's opinion to say anything inconsistent with or different than the preceding discussion. My disagreement with the Court concerns the application of these principles to the facts of this case.

Defendant Celotex sought summary judgment on the ground that plaintiff had "failed to produce" any evidence that her decedent had ever been exposed to Celotex asbestos. Celotex supported this motion with a two-page "Statement of Material Facts as to Which There is No Genuine Issue" and a three-page "Memorandum of Points and Authorities" which asserted that the plaintiff had failed to identify any evidence in responding to two sets of interrogatories propounded by Celotex and that therefore the record was "totally devoid" of evidence to support plaintiff's claim.

Approximately three months earlier, Celotex had filed an essentially identical motion. Plaintiff responded to this earlier motion by producing three pieces of evidence which she claimed "[a]t the very least . . . demonstrate that there is a genuine factual dispute for trial:" (1) a letter from an insurance representative of another defendant describing asbestos products to which plaintiff's decedent had been exposed; (2) a letter from T.R. Hoff, a former supervisor of decedent, describing asbestos products to which decedent had been exposed; and (3) a copy of decedent's deposition from earlier workmen's compensation proceedings. Plaintiff also apparently indicated at that time that she intended to call Mr. Hoff as a witness at trial.

Celotex subsequently withdrew its first motion for summary judgment. However, as a result of this motion, when Celotex filed its second summary judgment motion, the record did contain evidence—including at least one witness—supporting plaintiff's claim. Indeed, counsel for Celotex admitted to this Court at oral argument that Celotex was aware of this evidence and of plaintiff's intention to call Mr. Hoff as a witness at trial when the second summary judgment motion was filed. Moreover, plaintiff's response to Celotex' second motion pointed to this evidence—noting that it had already been provided to counsel for Celotex in connection with the first motion—and argued that Celotex had failed to "meet its burden of proving that there is no genuine factual dispute for trial."

On these facts, there is simply no question that Celotex failed to discharge its initial burden of production. Having chosen to base its motion on the argument that there was no evidence in the record to support plaintiff's claim, Celotex was not free to ignore supporting evidence that the record clearly contained. Rather, Celotex was required, as an initial matter, to attack the adequacy of this evidence. Celotex' failure to fulfill this simple requirement constituted a failure to discharge its initial burden of production under Rule 56, and thereby rendered summary judgment improper.

This case is indistinguishable from *Adickes*. Here, as there, the defendant moved for summary judgment on the ground that the record contained no evidence to support an essential element of the plaintiff's claim. Here, as there, the plaintiff responded by drawing the court's attention to evidence that was already in the record and that had been ignored by the moving party. Consequently, here, as there, summary judgment should be denied on the ground that the moving party failed to satisfy its initial burden of production.

■ JUSTICE STEVENS, dissenting.

[Justice Stevens dissented based upon his conclusion that the district court mistakenly had held that Catrett only could defeat summary judgment by offering evidence that her husband had been exposed to asbestos within the District of Columbia.]

COMMENTS AND QUESTIONS CONCERNING
CELOTEX CORP. V. CATRETT

1.   Separate the general principal established or reaffirmed in this case from the resolution of this case itself. Why did the Supreme Court grant certiorari to hear this case, and what did the Court decide?

2.   Justice Rehnquist described Catrett's summary judgment opposition as "a transcript of a deposition of the decedent, a letter from an official of one of the decedent's former employers whom petitioner planned to call as a trial witness, and a letter from an insurance company to respondent's attorney, all tending to establish that the decedent had been exposed to petitioner's asbestos products in Chicago during 1970–1971." Why did these documents not preclude summary judgment in this case?

3.   What could Catrett have done to prevent summary judgment in this case?

4.   In his opinion, Justice Rehnquist quotes the following sentence from *Anderson v. Liberty Lobby*, a second case decided by the Supreme Court as part of the "*Celotex* Trilogy" dealing with summary judgment: "[T]h[e] standard [for granting summary judgment] mirrors the standard for a directed verdict under Federal Rule of Civil Procedure 50(a). . . ." *Anderson v. Liberty Lobby, Inc.*, 477 U.S. 242, 250 (1986).

What is the significance of this fact? Does it make sense to align the standard for summary judgment before trial with the standard for judgment as a matter of law at or after trial?

5.   After the amendment of Rule 56 in 2010, the question in *Celotex* becomes easier to resolve. Rule 56(c)(1) now provides:

A party asserting that a fact cannot be or is genuinely disputed must support the assertion by:

(A) citing to particular parts of materials in the record, including depositions, documents, electronically stored information, affidavits or declarations, stipulations (including those made for purposes of the motion only), admissions, interrogatory answers, or other materials; or

(B) showing that the materials cited do not establish the absence or presence of a genuine dispute, or that an adverse party cannot produce admissible evidence to support the fact.

Justice White said in his concurrence that it "is not enough to move for summary judgment without supporting the motion in any way or with a conclusory assertion that the plaintiff has no evidence to prove his case." Rule 56(c)(1)(A) requires the party to support its summary judgment position by "citing to particular parts of materials in the record * * *." Thus, under both *Celotex* and Rule 56, a party seeking summary judgment need not supply affirmative evidence if it can point to specific parts of the record establishing that a fact cannot be or is not genuinely disputed.

6.   Justice Rehnquist mentions that the motion for summary judgment was not filed until one year after the civil action had been filed. Why is this significant? Rule 56(d) now provides:

If a nonmovant shows by affidavit or declaration that, for specified reasons, it cannot present facts essential to justify its opposition, the court may:

(1)   defer considering the motion or deny it;

(2)   allow time to obtain affidavits or declarations or to take discovery; or

(3)   issue any other appropriate order.

7.   *Celotex* was one of three cases decided by the Supreme Court in its October 1985 term involving summary judgment. In all three cases, the district court granted summary judgment, only to be reversed by the Court of Appeals. Each reversal of summary judgment was, in turn, reversed by the Supreme Court. *Matsushita Elec. Indus. Co. v. Zenith Radio Corp.*, 475 U.S. 574 (1986); *Anderson v. Liberty Lobby, Inc.*, 477 U.S. 242 (1986); *Celotex Corp. v. Catrett*, 477 U.S. 317 (1986). The Supreme Court sent a signal to lower courts with its decisions in the "*Celotex* Trilogy." As Justice Rehnquist observed in *Celotex* itself: "Summary judgment procedure is properly regarded not as a disfavored procedural shortcut, but rather as an integral part of the Federal Rules as a whole, which are designed 'to secure the just, speedy and inexpensive determination of every action.'"

8.   The justices in *Celotex* seem to be in general accord concerning the parameters of summary judgment law and that a party moving for summary judgment need not offer affirmative evidence to be entitled to summary judgment. The disagreements between the justices instead concern whether the Supreme Court itself should decide if there is a factual dispute precluding summary judgment (as Justices Brennan and Blackmun and Chief Justice Burger assert) or whether the Court should remand the action to the lower courts to make that determination (as the rest of the justices conclude).

9.   Why does it matter to Catrett and Celotex whether this action will be decided by the judge on a Rule 56 or Rule 50 motion or by a jury at trial?

B. WHEN ARE FACTUAL DISPUTES "GENUINE"?

1.   YOU WON'T BELIEVE YOUR OWN EYES: *SCOTT V. HARRIS*

Scott v. Harris

United States Supreme Court, 2007
550 U.S. 372

OPINION

■ JUSTICE SCALIA delivered the opinion of the Court.

We consider whether a law enforcement official can, consistent with the Fourth Amendment, attempt to stop a fleeing motorist from continuing his public-endangering flight by ramming the motorist's car from behind. Put another way: Can an officer take actions that place a fleeing motorist at risk of serious injury or death in order to stop the motorist's flight from endangering the lives of innocent bystanders?

I

In March 2001, a Georgia county deputy clocked respondent's vehicle traveling at 73 miles per hour on a road with a 55-mile-per-hour speed limit. The deputy activated his blue flashing lights indicating that respondent should pull over. Instead, respondent sped away, initiating a chase down what is in most portions a two-lane road, at speeds exceeding 85 miles per hour. The deputy radioed his dispatch to report that he was pursuing a fleeing vehicle, and broadcast its license plate number. Petitioner, Deputy Timothy Scott, heard the radio communication and joined the pursuit along with other officers. In the midst of the chase, respondent pulled into the parking lot of a shopping center and was nearly boxed in by the various police vehicles. Respondent evaded the trap by making a sharp turn, colliding with Scott's police car, exiting the parking lot, and speeding off once again down a two-lane highway.

Following respondent's shopping center maneuvering, which resulted in slight damage to Scott's police car, Scott took over as the lead pursuit vehicle. Six minutes and nearly 10 miles after the chase had begun, Scott decided to attempt to terminate the episode by employing a "Precision Intervention Technique ('PIT') maneuver, which causes the fleeing vehicle to spin to a stop." Having radioed his supervisor for permission, Scott was told to " '[g]o ahead and take him out.'" Instead, Scott applied his push bumper to the rear of respondent's vehicle. As a result, respondent lost control of his vehicle, which left the roadway, ran down an embankment, overturned, and crashed. Respondent was badly injured and was rendered a quadriplegic.

Respondent filed suit against Deputy Scott and others under Rev. Stat. § 1979, 42 U.S.C. § 1983, alleging, *inter alia,* a violation of his federal constitutional rights, viz. use of excessive force resulting in an unreasonable seizure under the Fourth Amendment. In response, Scott filed a motion for summary judgment based on an assertion of qualified immunity. The District Court denied the motion, finding that "there are material issues of fact on which the issue of qualified immunity turns which present sufficient disagreement to require submission to a jury." On interlocutory appeal,[2] the United States Court of Appeals for the Eleventh Circuit affirmed the District Court's decision to allow respondent's Fourth Amendment claim against Scott to proceed to trial. Taking respondent's view of the facts as given, the Court of Appeals concluded that Scott's actions could constitute "deadly force" under *Tennessee v. Garner,* 471 U.S. 1 (1985), and that the use of such force in this context "would violate [respondent's] constitutional right to be free from excessive force during a seizure. Accordingly, a reasonable jury could find that Scott violated [respondent's] Fourth Amendment rights." The Court of Appeals further concluded that "the law as it existed [at the time of the incident], was sufficiently clear to give reasonable law enforcement officers 'fair notice' that ramming a vehicle under these circumstances was unlawful." The Court of Appeals thus concluded that Scott was not entitled to qualified immunity. We granted certiorari, and now reverse.

II

In resolving questions of qualified immunity, courts are required to resolve a "threshold question: Taken in the light most favorable to the party asserting the injury, do the facts alleged show the officer's conduct violated a constitutional right? This must be the initial inquiry." *Saucier v. Katz,* 533 U.S. 194, 201 (2001). If, and only if, the court finds a violation of a constitutional right, "the next, sequential step is to ask whether the right was clearly established . . . in light of the specific context of the case." Although this ordering contradicts "[o]ur policy of avoiding unnecessary adjudication of constitutional issues," *United States v. Treasury Employees,* 513 U.S. 454, 478 (1995) (citing *Ashwander v. TVA,* 297 U.S. 288, 346–347 (1936) (Brandeis, J., concurring)), we have said that such a departure from practice is "necessary to set forth principles which will become the basis for a [future] holding that a right is clearly established," *Saucier, supra,* at 201. We therefore turn to the threshold inquiry: whether Deputy Scott's actions violated the Fourth Amendment.

---

[2]   Qualified immunity is "an *immunity from suit* rather than a mere defense to liability; and like an absolute immunity, it is effectively lost if a case is erroneously permitted to go to trial." *Mitchell v. Forsyth,* 472 U.S. 511, 526 (1985). Thus, we have held that an order denying qualified immunity is immediately appealable even though it is interlocutory; otherwise, it would be "effectively unreviewable." *Id.,* at 527. Further, "we repeatedly have stressed the importance of resolving immunity questions at the earliest possible stage in litigation." *Hunter v. Bryant,* 502 U.S. 224, 227 (1991) *(per curiam).*

III

A

The first step in assessing the constitutionality of Scott's actions is to determine the relevant facts. As this case was decided on summary judgment, there have not yet been factual findings by a judge or jury, and respondent's version of events (unsurprisingly) differs substantially from Scott's version. When things are in such a posture, courts are required to view the facts and draw reasonable inferences "in the light most favorable to the party opposing the [summary judgment] motion." *United States v. Diebold, Inc.,* 369 U.S. 654, 655 (1962) *(per curiam); Saucier, supra,* at 201. In qualified immunity cases, this usually means adopting (as the Court of Appeals did here) the plaintiff's version of the facts.

There is, however, an added wrinkle in this case: existence in the record of a videotape capturing the events in question. There are no allegations or indications that this videotape was doctored or altered in any way, nor any contention that what it depicts differs from what actually happened. The videotape quite clearly contradicts the version of the story told by respondent and adopted by the Court of Appeals.[5] For example, the Court of Appeals adopted respondent's assertions that, during the chase, "there was little, if any, actual threat to pedestrians or other motorists, as the roads were mostly empty and [respondent] remained in control of his vehicle." Indeed, reading the lower court's opinion, one gets the impression that respondent, rather than fleeing from police, was attempting to pass his driving test:

> "[T]aking the facts from the non-movant's viewpoint, [respondent] remained in control of his vehicle, slowed for turns and intersections, and typically used his indicators for turns. He did not run any motorists off the road. Nor was he a threat to pedestrians in the shopping center parking lot, which was free from pedestrian and vehicular traffic as the center was closed. Significantly, by the time the parties were back on the highway and Scott rammed [respondent], the motorway had been cleared of motorists and pedestrians allegedly because of police blockades of the nearby intersections."

The videotape tells quite a different story. There we see respondent's vehicle racing down narrow, two-lane roads in the dead of night at speeds that are shockingly fast. We see it swerve around more than a dozen other cars, cross the double-yellow line, and force cars traveling in both directions to their respective shoulders to avoid being hit. We see it run multiple red lights and travel for considerable periods of time in the occasional center left-turn-only lane, chased by numerous

---

[5] Justice STEVENS suggests that our reaction to the videotape is somehow idiosyncratic, and seems to believe we are misrepresenting its contents. We are happy to allow the videotape to speak for itself. See Record 36, Exh. A, available at http://www.supremecourtus.gov/opinions/video/scott_v_harris.html and in Clerk of Court's case file.

police cars forced to engage in the same hazardous maneuvers just to keep up. Far from being the cautious and controlled driver the lower court depicts, what we see on the video more closely resembles a Hollywood-style car chase of the most frightening sort, placing police officers and innocent bystanders alike at great risk of serious injury.

At the summary judgment stage, facts must be viewed in the light most favorable to the nonmoving party only if there is a "genuine" dispute as to those facts. As we have emphasized, "[w]hen the moving party has carried its burden under Rule 56(c) [now, Rule 56(a)], its opponent must do more than simply show that there is some metaphysical doubt as to the material facts. . . . Where the record taken as a whole could not lead a rational trier of fact to find for the nonmoving party, there is no 'genuine issue for trial.' " *Matsushita Elec. Industrial Co. v. Zenith Radio Corp.*, 475 U.S. 574, 586–587 (1986). "[T]he mere existence of *some* alleged factual dispute between the parties will not defeat an otherwise properly supported motion for summary judgment; the requirement is that there be no *genuine* issue of *material* fact." *Anderson v. Liberty Lobby, Inc.*, 477 U.S. 242, 247–248 (1986). When opposing parties tell two different stories, one of which is blatantly contradicted by the record, so that no reasonable jury could believe it, a court should not adopt that version of the facts for purposes of ruling on a motion for summary judgment.

That was the case here with regard to the factual issue whether respondent was driving in such fashion as to endanger human life. Respondent's version of events is so utterly discredited by the record that no reasonable jury could have believed him. The Court of Appeals should not have relied on such visible fiction; it should have viewed the facts in the light depicted by the videotape.

B.

Judging the matter on that basis, we think it is quite clear that Deputy Scott did not violate the Fourth Amendment. * * * The question we need to answer is whether Scott's actions were objectively reasonable.[8]

* * *

The car chase that respondent initiated in this case posed a substantial and immediate risk of serious physical injury to others; no reasonable jury could conclude otherwise. Scott's attempt to terminate the chase by forcing respondent off the road was reasonable, and Scott

---

[8]   Justice STEVENS incorrectly declares this to be "a question of fact best reserved for a jury," and complains we are "usurp[ing] the jury's factfinding function." At the summary judgment stage, however, once we have determined the relevant set of facts and drawn all inferences in favor of the nonmoving party *to the extent supportable by the record,* the reasonableness of Scott's actions—or, in Justice STEVENS' parlance, "[w]hether [respondent's] actions have risen to a level warranting deadly force," is a pure question of law.

is entitled to summary judgment. The Court of Appeals' judgment to the contrary is reversed.

It is so ordered.

■ JUSTICE GINSBURG concurring[, joined the opinion of the Court.]

■ JUSTICE BREYER, concurring.

I join the Court's opinion with one suggestion and two qualifications. Because watching the video footage of the car chase made a difference to my own view of the case, I suggest that the interested reader take advantage of the link in the Court's opinion and watch it. Having done so, I do not believe a reasonable jury could, in this instance, find that Officer Timothy Scott (who joined the chase late in the day and did not know the specific reason why the respondent was being pursued) acted in violation of the Constitution.

Second, the video makes clear the highly fact-dependent nature of this constitutional determination. And that fact dependency supports the argument that we should overrule the requirement, announced in *Saucier v. Katz,* 533 U.S. 194 (2001), that lower courts must first decide the "constitutional question" before they turn to the "qualified immunity question." Instead, lower courts should be free to decide the two questions in whatever order makes sense in the context of a particular case. Although I do not object to our deciding the constitutional question in this particular case, I believe that in order to lift the burden from lower courts we can and should reconsider *Saucier's* requirement as well.

* * *

Third, I disagree with the Court insofar as it articulates a *per se* rule. The majority states: "A police officer's attempt to terminate a dangerous high-speed car chase that threatens the lives of innocent bystanders does not violate the Fourth Amendment, even when it places the fleeing motorist at risk of serious injury or death." This statement is too absolute. As Justice GINSBURG points out, whether a high-speed chase violates the Fourth Amendment may well depend upon more circumstances than the majority's rule reflects. With these qualifications, I join the Court's opinion.

■ JUSTICE STEVENS, dissenting.

Today, the Court asks whether an officer may "take actions that place a fleeing motorist at risk of serious injury or death in order to stop the motorist's flight from endangering the lives of innocent bystanders." Depending on the circumstances, the answer may be an obvious "yes," an obvious "no," or sufficiently doubtful that the question of the reasonableness of the officer's actions should be decided by a jury, after a review of the degree of danger and the alternatives available to the officer. A high-speed chase in a desert in Nevada is, after all, quite different from one that travels through the heart of Las Vegas.

Relying on a *de novo* review of a videotape of a portion of a nighttime chase on a lightly traveled road in Georgia where no pedestrians or other "bystanders" were present, buttressed by uninformed speculation about the possible consequences of discontinuing the chase, eight of the jurors on this Court reach a verdict that differs from the views of the judges on both the District Court and the Court of Appeals who are surely more familiar with the hazards of driving on Georgia roads than we are. The Court's justification for this unprecedented departure from our well-settled standard of review of factual determinations made by a district court and affirmed by a court of appeals is based on its mistaken view that the Court of Appeals' description of the facts was "blatantly contradicted by the record" and that respondent's version of the events was "so utterly discredited by the record that no reasonable jury could have believed him."

* * *

My colleagues on the jury saw respondent "swerve around more than a dozen other cars," and "force cars traveling in both directions to their respective shoulders," but they apparently discounted the possibility that those cars were already out of the pursuit's path as a result of hearing the sirens. * * * At no point during the chase did respondent pull into the opposite lane other than to pass a car in front of him; he did the latter no more than five times and, on most of those occasions, used his turn signal. On none of these occasions was there a car traveling in the opposite direction. In fact, at one point, when respondent found himself behind a car in his own lane and there were cars traveling in the other direction, he slowed and waited for the cars traveling in the other direction to pass before overtaking the car in front of him while using his turn signal to do so. This is hardly the stuff of Hollywood. To the contrary, the video does not reveal any incidents that could even be remotely characterized as "close calls."

In sum, the factual statements by the Court of Appeals quoted by the Court were entirely accurate. That court did not describe respondent as a "cautious" driver as my colleagues imply, but it did correctly conclude that there is no evidence that he ever lost control of his vehicle. That court also correctly pointed out that the incident in the shopping center parking lot did not create any risk to pedestrians or other vehicles because the chase occurred just before 11 p.m. on a weekday night and the center was closed. It is apparent from the record (including the videotape) that local police had blocked off intersections to keep respondent from entering residential neighborhoods and possibly endangering other motorists. I would add that the videos also show that no pedestrians, parked cars, sidewalks, or residences were visible at any time during the chase. The only "innocent bystanders" who were placed "at great risk of serious injury" were the drivers who either pulled off the road in response to the sirens or passed respondent in the opposite direction when he was driving on his side of the road.

* * *

Whether a person's actions have risen to a level warranting deadly force is a question of fact best reserved for a jury. Here, the Court has usurped the jury's factfinding function and, in doing so, implicitly labeled the four other judges to review the case unreasonable. It chastises the Court of Appeals for failing to "vie[w] the facts in the light depicted by the videotape" and implies that no reasonable person could view the videotape and come to the conclusion that deadly force was unjustified. However, the three judges on the Court of Appeals panel apparently did view the videotapes entered into evidence and described a very different version of events:

> "At the time of the ramming, apart from speeding and running two red lights, Harris was driving in a non-aggressive fashion (i.e., without trying to ram or run into the officers). Moreover, . . . Scott's path on the open highway was largely clear. The videos introduced into evidence show little to no vehicular (or pedestrian) traffic, allegedly because of the late hour and the police blockade of the nearby intersections. Finally, Scott issued absolutely no warning (e.g., over the loudspeaker or otherwise) prior to using deadly force."

If two groups of judges can disagree so vehemently about the nature of the pursuit and the circumstances surrounding that pursuit, it seems eminently likely that a reasonable juror could disagree with this Court's characterization of events. Moreover, under the standard set forth in *Garner,* it is certainly possible that "a jury could conclude that Scott unreasonably used deadly force to seize Harris by ramming him off the road under the instant circumstances."

The Court today sets forth a *per se* rule that presumes its own version of the facts: "A police officer's attempt to terminate a dangerous high-speed car chase *that threatens the lives of innocent bystanders* does not violate the Fourth Amendment, even when it places the fleeing motorist at risk of serious injury or death." Not only does that rule fly in the face of the flexible and case-by-case "reasonableness" approach applied in *Garner* and *Graham v. Connor,* 490 U.S. 386 (1989), but it is also arguably inapplicable to the case at hand, given that it is not clear that this chase threatened the life of any "innocent bystande[r]." * * * In my judgment, jurors in Georgia should be allowed to evaluate the reasonableness of the decision to ram respondent's speeding vehicle in a manner that created an obvious risk of death and has in fact made him a quadriplegic at the age of 19.

I respectfully dissent.

COMMENTS AND QUESTIONS CONCERNING *SCOTT V. HARRIS*

1.   Justice Scalia notes that the court of appeals considered this case before entry of final judgment in the district court. Why did the court of appeals hear an interlocutory appeal in this case?

2.   What caused the Supreme Court to post videotape of the car chase on its website? After viewing this police video at http://www. supremecourt.gov/media/media.aspx, do you agree with the eight justices who concluded that there was no "genuine dispute as to any material fact" that would preclude summary judgment under Rule 56(a)? Or is Justice Stevens correct that "the Court has usurped the jury's factfinding function"?

3.   There was clearly a dispute between the parties as to whether Harris "was driving in such fashion as to endanger human life" (so that Deputy Scott did not violate Harris's fourth amendment rights by bumping, and thus "seizing," his car). The question then became whether that factual dispute was "genuine" for the purposes of Rule 56(a). As the majority notes:

> At the summary judgment stage, facts must be viewed in the light most favorable to the nonmoving party only if there is a "genuine" dispute as to those facts. As we have emphasized, "[w]hen the moving party has carried its burden under Rule 56(c) [now, Rule 56(a)], its opponent must do more than simply show that there is some metaphysical doubt as to the material facts. . . . Where the record taken as a whole could not lead a rational trier of fact to find for the nonmoving party, there is no 'genuine issue for trial.'" *Matsushita Elec. Industrial Co. v. Zenith Radio Corp.,* 475 U.S. 574, 586–587 (1986).

Why does Justice Scalia believe that the factual dispute was not genuine so as to preclude summary judgment under Rule 56?

4.   Would this case have been resolved in the same manner without the existence of the police video?

5.   Does the disagreement of the district and court of appeals judges, and Justice Stevens, establish that reasonable people can differ as to just what the videotape shows?

6.   To whom is Justice Stevens referring by his reference to "my colleagues on the jury"? If the Supreme Court were considered a jury, would there be a requirement of juror unanimity? *Compare Wieser v. Chrysler Motors Corp.,* 69 F.R.D. 97, 100 (E.D.N.Y. 1975) ("[I]t is difficult to see how there remains, except through historical custom and usage, any Seventh Amendment requirement of unanimity in a civil case."), *with Masino v. Outboard Marine Corp.,* 88 F.R.D. 251, 252 (E.D.Pa. 1980) *aff'd,* 652 F.2d 330 (3d Cir.), *cert. denied,* 102 U.S. 601 (1981) ("[T]his historical requirement of unanimous jury verdicts in federal courts applies not only to criminal trials, but also to civil cases.").

7.   Several law professors designed an experiment in which 1350 individuals watched the *Scott* videotape. Kahan et al., "Whose Eyes Are

You Going to Believe? *Scott v. Harris* and the Perils of Cognitive Illiberalism," 122 *Harv.L.Rev.* 837 (2009). They found:

> Overall, a majority agreed with the Court's resolution of the key issues, but within the sample there were sharp differences of opinion along cultural, ideological, and other lines. We attribute these divisions to the psychological disposition of individuals to resolve disputed facts in a manner supportive of their group identities. * * * [The Court's] insistence that there was only one "reasonable" view of the facts itself reflected a form of bias— cognitive illiberalism—that consists in the failure to recognize the connection between perceptions of societal risk and contested visions of the ideal society. When courts fail to take steps to counteract that bias, they needlessly invest the law with culturally partisan overtones that detract from the law's legitimacy.

Id. at 838.

The study found that "African Americans, low-income workers, and residents of the Northeast, for example, tended to form more pro-plaintiff views of the facts than did the Court. So did individuals who characterized themselves as liberals and Democrats." *Id.* at 841.

The authors make the following recommendation for judicial resolution of cases such as *Scott*:

> [W]e recommend that a judge engage in a sort of mental double check when ruling on a motion that would result in summary adjudication. * * * Before concluding * * * that no reasonable juror could find such facts, the judge should try to imagine who those potential jurors might be. If, as will usually be true, she cannot identify them, or can conjure only the random faces of imaginary statistical outliers, she should proceed to decide the case summarily. But if instead she can form a concrete picture of the dissenting jurors, and they are people who bear recognizable identity-defining characteristics—demographic, cultural, political, or otherwise—she should stop and think hard. Due humility obliges her to consider whether privileging her own view of the facts risks conveying a denigrating and exclusionary message to members of such subcommunities. If it does, she should choose a different path.

Id. at 898–99.

Do you agree? Can such humility be taught or are judges only likely to display such humility if it was part of their makeup prior to their appointment to the bench? Are these situations in which judges would be well advised to "be very, very careful not to let the facts get mixed up with the truth." Jerry Spinelli, *Maniac Magee* 2 (1990).

8.   A question analogous to that presented in *Scott v. Harris* in the context of summary judgment is presented in the context of jury verdict in *Sioux City & P. R.R. v. Stout*, 84 U.S. 657 (1873), *infra* p. 993. In *Stout* the

Supreme Court addressed the question of why a jury should decide a negligence case in which the facts were undisputed:

> Twelve men of the average of the community, comprising men of education and men of little education, men of learning and men whose learning consists only in what they have themselves seen and heard, the merchant, the mechanic, the farmer, the laborer; these sit together, consult, apply their separate experience of the affairs of life to the facts proven, and draw a unanimous conclusion. This average judgment thus given it is the great effort of the law to obtain. It is assumed that twelve men know more of the common affairs of life than does one man, that they can draw wiser and safer conclusions from admitted facts thus occurring than can a single judge.

84 U.S. at 664. Does the majority in *Scott v. Harris* agree that a jury of six or twelve members know "more of the common affairs of life" than does one person?

2.   SHOULD SUMMARY JUDGMENT HAVE BEEN GRANTED?

Consider whether summary judgment should have been granted in the following case, involving Len Bias, who starred for the University of Maryland basketball team, was drafted second in the 1986 NBA draft, and two days later died of cocaine intoxication. The Court of Appeals described the first claim made by Bias's estate in a federal civil action as follows:

> First, the Estate alleges that, prior to Bias's death, Bias and his parents directed Fentress [Bias's agent] to obtain a one-million dollar life insurance policy on Bias's life, that Fentress represented to Bias and Bias's parents that he had secured such a policy, and that in reliance on Fentress's assurances, Bias's parents did not independently seek to buy an insurance policy on Bias's life. Although the defendants did obtain increased disability coverage for Bias * * * they did not secure any life insurance coverage for Bias prior to his death.

Bias v. Advantage Int'l, Inc., 905 F.2d 1558, 1559–60 (D.C. Cir. 1990).

The defendants argued that the estate suffered no damage, because, even if they had attempted to obtain an insurance policy on Bias, they could not have done so because "Bias was a cocaine user and that no insurer in 1986 would have issued a one-million dollar life insurance policy * * * to a cocaine user unless the applicant made a misrepresentation regarding the applicant's use of drugs, thereby rendering the insurance policy void." 905 F.2d at 1560.

The evidence offered in support of, and in opposition to, defendants' motion for summary judgment included:

- Two of Bias's former teammates "described numerous occasions when they saw Bias ingest cocaine, and [one] testified that he was introduced to cocaine by Bias and that Bias sometimes supplied others with cocaine." 905 F.2d at 1561.

- Each of Bias's parents offered affidavits in which they stated that Bias was not a drug user. *Id.*

- Bias's basketball coach, "Charles 'Lefty' Driesell, * * * testified [at his deposition] that he knew Bias well for four years and never knew Bias to be a user of drugs at any time prior to his death." *Id.*

- "[T]he results of several drug tests administered to Bias during the four years prior to his death * * * may have shown that, on the occasions when the tests were administered, there were no traces in Bias's system of the drugs for which he was tested." *Id.*, at 1561–62.

Based upon this evidence, was there a "genuine dispute as to any material fact" precluding summary judgment? What additional evidence might the estate have offered to support the argument that a genuine dispute as to a material fact existed?

V. PRETRIAL CONFERENCES AND ORDERS

After the parties complete their discovery and the judge rules on any summary judgment motions, the judge will expect the parties to prepare their action for trial. In this process, the judge will invoke Rule 16 of the Federal Rules of Civil Procedure and its authorization of pretrial conferences and pretrial orders. Indeed, the judge will expect the parties to have complied with Rule 16 from the very outset of the action.

A. THE RULE 16(b) SCHEDULING ORDER

Although the judge typically issues many orders over the course of a civil action, there is only one pretrial order required by the Federal Rules. Rule 16(b) requires:

> Except in categories of actions exempted by local rule, the district judge—or a magistrate judge when authorized by local rule—must issue a scheduling order:
>
> (A) after receiving the parties' report under Rule 26(f); or
>
> (B) after consulting with the parties' attorneys and any unrepresented parties at a scheduling conference.

Rule 16(b) thus envisions that the pretrial scheduling order will build upon the planning that the parties have undertaken with each other. Counsel typically will confer, pursuant to Rule 26(f)(1), "as soon as practicable—and in any event at least 21 days before a scheduling conference is to be held or a scheduling order is due under Rule 16(b)." Rule 26(f)(2) provides that, at the Rule 26(f) party conference, "the parties must consider the nature and basis of their claims and defenses and the possibilities for promptly settling or resolving the case; make or arrange for the disclosures required by Rule 26(a)(1); discuss any issues about preserving discoverable information; and develop a proposed discovery plan."

Rule 26(f)(2) requires the parties to submit their written report to the court within 14 days after their conference. The judge then is to issue the Rule 16(b) scheduling order, either after simply considering the report (pursuant to Rule 16(b)(1)(A)) or after "consulting with the parties' attorneys and any unrepresented parties at a scheduling conference" (pursuant to Rule 16(b)(1)(B)). After the scheduling order is entered, counsel and their clients have a road map to further pretrial proceedings in the action. The form order used by United States District Judge Kimba Wood, who decided John Leonard's action against PepsiCo, is typical of the Rule 16(b) scheduling orders entered in the federal courts.

UNITED STATES DISTRICT COURT
SOUTHERN DISTRICT OF NEW YORK

———————————————————— X

)

Plaintiff(s),   )

) ___ Civ. _____ (KMW)

        -against-   )

) **SCHEDULING ORDER**

)

Defendant(s),   )

)

———————————————————— X

APPEARANCES:

Plaintiff(s) by: _____

Defendant(s) by: _____

KIMBA M. WOOD, U.S.D.J.:

It is hereby ordered that:

Pleadings and Parties: Except for good cause shown—

    1.   No additional parties may be jointed after _____

    2.   No additional causes of action or defenses may be asserted after _____.

If the parties do not anticipate the joinder of any additional parties or the assertion of any additional causes of action or defenses, then the parties should insert above the date of the scheduling conference. Otherwise, the Court expects that all parties will be joined and all causes of action and defenses will be asserted **within 90 days of the first scheduling conference.**

Discovery. Except for good cause shown, all discovery shall be commenced in time to be completed by _____. The Court expects discovery to be completed **within 90 days of the first scheduling conference.** In the event that the parties believe that additional time is needed, the parties shall request an extension from the Court, by joint letter, and shall accompany that request with a proposed Amended Scheduling Order, with the extension not to exceed 60 days. Any further extensions will be given only after a showing of good cause that additional time is needed.

Motions. Except for good cause shown, no motions shall be filed or heard after _____. The parties may satisfy this deadline through the submission of a letter to the Court requesting a pre-motion conference. The Court expects that all motions will be filed or heard **within 21 days of the completion of discovery.**

Pretrial Order. A joint pretrial order shall be submitted by _____. The Court expects that a joint pretrial order will be submitted **within 28 days of the completion of discovery.** The pretrial order shall conform to the Court's instructions, a copy of which may be obtained from the Deputy Clerk. It shall be accompanied by **Memorandum of Law**, and, in a case to be tried to a jury, **Proposed <u>Voir Dire</u>** and **Requests to Charge.**

Trial. The parties shall be ready for trial on or after _____. The Court expects that the case will be ready for trial **1 day after the submission of the joint pretrial order.**

Estimated trial time is _____.

Jury: _____. Non-jury: _____. **(Please check.)**

A copy of the Court's Trial Procedures can be downloaded from the Court's website at http://www.nysd.uscourts.gov/judges/USDJ/wood.htm.

Final Pretrial Conference. The Court will schedule a final pretrial conference in jury cases after the parties have filed their joint pretrial order. Non-jury cases will be referred to the designated Magistrate Judge for settlement after the joint pretrial order has been signed.

Mediation. Counsel for the parties have discussed the merits of mediation in regard to this action and wish to employ the free mediation services proved by this Court. **Yes ___ No ____**

Other Directions:

A pending dispositive motion cancels any previously scheduled status conference and adjourns the dates set out in this Scheduling Order as to all parties making or opposing the motion. In the event a dispositive motion is made after the completion of discovery, the dates for submitting the Memoranda of Law, Requests to Charge, Proposed <u>Voir Dire</u>, Pretrial Order and start of trial shall be changed from that shown above to three (3) weeks from the decision on the motion. The final pretrial conference, if any, will be scheduled by the Courtroom Deputy.

At any time after the <u>Ready Trial Date</u>, the Court may call the parties to trial upon <u>forty-eight hours' notice</u>. Therefore, counsel must notify the Court and their adversaries in writing of any potential scheduling conflicts, including, but not limited to, trials and vacations, that would prevent a trial at a particular time. Such notice must come <u>before</u> counsel are notified by the Court of an <u>actual trial date</u>, <u>not after</u>. Counsel should notify the Court and all other counsel in writing, at the earliest possible time of any particular scheduling problems involving out-of-town witnesses or other exigencies.

The parties also have the option of trying this action before the Magistrate Judge assigned to this case. <u>See</u> 28 U.S.C. § 636(c). Such a trial would be identical to a proceeding before this Court in all respects, and the judgment would be directly appealable to the Second Circuit Court of Appeals. Given the nature of this Court's criminal docket, it is more likely that electing to proceed before the Magistrate Judge would result in the parties receiving a firm trial date.

All communications to the Court and all filed papers must identify the name and docket number of the case, followed by the initials of the Judge (KMW), contain the writer's typewritten name, party's name, law firm (if any), business address and telephone number, and be signed by the individual attorney responsible for the matter (unless the party is proceeding <u>pro se</u>). Any letter to the Court must state the manner in which the letter was served on all other counsel.

If either party wishes to change the dates set forth in this Scheduling Order, it must submit a written request to the Court that complies with § 1.E of Judge Wood's Individual Practices.

Signatures:

[Plaintiff's Attorney]	**[Defendant's Attorney]**
Attorney for Plaintiff	**Attorney for Defendant**
[Plaintiff's Name]	**[Defendant's Name]**

SO ORDERED.

Dated: New York, New York

Kimba M. Wood
United States District Judge

B. PRETRIAL CONFERENCES

After the court enters its initial Rule 16(b) scheduling order, there may be several additional conferences with the court before the trial date (which is often set in the scheduling order). To get a sense of why the court might schedule a pretrial conference, consider the purposes for such conferences identified in Rule 16(a). They include:

(1) expediting disposition of the action;

(2) establishing early and continuing control so that the case will not be protracted because of lack of management;

(3) discouraging wasteful pretrial activities;

(4) improving the quality of the trial through more thorough preparation; and

(5) facilitating settlement.

Purposes (1), (2), and (3) all involve judicial efforts to achieve pretrial efficiencies and to move the action to final judgment either at or before trial. Purpose (4) is to involve the parties in pretrial preparation to improve the quality of trial, while purpose (5) is to facilitate resolution of the action through settlement. The assumption behind Rule 16 pretrial conferences and orders is that time spent on pretrial proceedings results in faster and better resolution of civil actions by way of motion, settlement, or trial. As the Advisory Committee Note to the 1983 amendment to Rule 16 states, "Empirical studies reveal that when a trial judge intervenes personally at an early stage to assume judicial control over a case and to schedule dates for completion by the parties of the principal pretrial steps, the case is disposed of by settlement or trial more efficiently and with less cost and delay than when the parties are left to their own devices." 97 F.R.D. 165, 207 (1983).

The many ways in which the court can focus the parties and their counsel on pretrial planning and preparation are set forth in Rule 16(c)(2). This Rule provides that the court "may consider and take appropriate action" on such matters as:

(A) formulating and simplifying the issues, and eliminating frivolous claims or defenses;

(B) amending the pleadings if necessary or desirable;

(C) obtaining admissions and stipulations about facts and documents to avoid unnecessary proof, and ruling in advance on the admissibility of evidence; * * *

(E) determining the appropriateness and timing of summary adjudication under Rule 56;

(F) controlling and scheduling discovery, including orders affecting disclosures and discovery under Rule 26 and Rules 29 through 37; * * *

(I) settling the case and using special procedures to assist in resolving the dispute when authorized by statute or local rule;

(J) determining the form and content of the pretrial order; * * * and

(P) facilitating in other ways the just, speedy, and inexpensive disposition of the action.

Rule 16(c)(1) is to ensure that attorneys have full authority to address the above matters at pretrial conferences. It also authorizes the judge to require that parties or their representatives be available to participate in settlement discussions that may arise at a pretrial conference. Rule 16(c)(1) requires:

> A represented party must authorize at least one of its attorneys to make stipulations and admissions about all matters that can reasonably be anticipated for discussion at a pretrial conference. If appropriate, the court may require that a party or its representative be present or reasonably available by other means to consider possible settlement.

Some pretrial conferences are specifically designated as "settlement conferences." However, most judges raise the question of settlement, at least informally, at virtually all pretrial conferences. Rule 16(c)(1) authorizes the judge to specifically require that each party, or a representative with settlement authority, attend or be available by telephone or otherwise to participate in settlement negotiations.

Not all of the Rule 16(c)(2) matters will be addressed by all judges, nor is it typical for a judge to use a single pretrial conference to address the wide gamut of Rule 16(c) matters. Instead, many judges schedule a series of pretrial conferences with the parties. Some of these conferences may be used by the judge to confirm that the parties are making suitable progress in readying the action for trial. Counsel also may be able to use these conferences to seek the judge's assistance with issues that have arisen in their pretrial preparations. Figure 11–3 shows how pretrial conferences might proceed in a typical action.

FIGURE 11–3
TYPICAL PRETRIAL CONFERENCES AND ORDERS IN A FEDERAL CIVIL ACTION

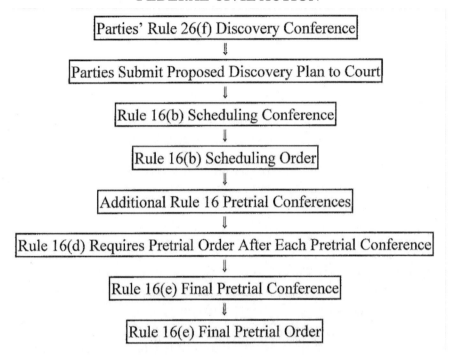

Parties' Rule 26(f) Discovery Conference

⇓

Parties Submit Proposed Discovery Plan to Court

⇓

Rule 16(b) Scheduling Conference

⇓

Rule 16(b) Scheduling Order

⇓

Additional Rule 16 Pretrial Conferences

⇓

Rule 16(d) Requires Pretrial Order After Each Pretrial Conference

⇓

Rule 16(e) Final Pretrial Conference

⇓

Rule 16(e) Final Pretrial Order

C. THE FINAL PRETRIAL ORDER

In most civil actions, there will be many pretrial orders entered over the course of the pretrial proceedings. As the action progresses, there will be mid-course adjustments to the course plotted in the initial scheduling order and later pretrial orders. For instance, the parties may seek more time to conduct discovery, or a party may be granted leave to depose more witnesses than originally contemplated, or the court may permit a party to file a motion not originally planned. Rule 16(d) contemplates such modifications of pretrial proceedings as a case develops. That Rule provides:

> After any conference under this rule, the court should issue an order reciting the action taken. This order controls the course of the action unless the court modifies it.

However, the final pretrial order, issued after the final pretrial conference, is different. Rule 16(e) describes the purpose and timing of the final pretrial conference, as well as the attorneys who must attend:

> The court may hold a final pretrial conference to formulate a trial plan, including a plan to facilitate the admission of evidence. The conference must be held as close to the start of trial as is reasonable, and must be attended by at least one

attorney who will conduct the trial for each party and by any unrepresented party.

Rule 16(f) provides that the court can sanction a party or its attorney who:

(A) fails to appear at a scheduling or other pretrial conference;

(B) is substantially unprepared to participate—or does not participate in good faith—in the conference; or

(C) fails to obey a scheduling or other pretrial order.

In such a situation, Rule 16(f)(1) authorizes the judge to issue any of the sanctions set forth in Rule 37(b)(2)(A)(ii)–(vii), including dismissal of the action and treatment of a failure to obey a scheduling or other pretrial order as contempt of court. In addition to these sanctions, Rule 16(f)(2) provides:

Instead of or in addition to any other sanction, the court must order the party, its attorney, or both to pay the reasonable expenses—including attorney's fees—incurred because of any noncompliance with this rule, unless the noncompliance was substantially justified or other circumstances make an award of expenses unjust.

The purpose of the final pretrial conference, "to formulate a trial plan" in the words of Rule 16(e), is different from that of the pretrial conferences that may have preceded it. The final sentence of Rule 16(e) makes it clear that the final pretrial order issued after the final pretrial conference is to be treated differently by the judge. That Rule provides:

The court may modify the order issued after a final pretrial conference only to prevent manifest injustice.

In the proposed final pretrial order that they submit to the judge, counsel therefore should be sure to address every matter that they believe must be considered at or before trial. The form final pretrial order that follows illustrates the types of matters that counsel must address in such orders.

1. A FORM FINAL PRETRIAL ORDER

The matters to be addressed in final pretrial orders typically are listed in local rules of court or in the standing orders issued by individual judges. Many local rules and standing orders also provide the specific format to be used in preparation of the final pretrial order. Rule 16.1 of the United States District Court for the Western District of Washington provides an example of a form order. Just as the Rule 26(f) Report of the Parties' Planning Meeting, *supra* p. 760, provides a road map for discovery and other pretrial proceedings, orders such as the following govern trial.

Hon. [name of judge]

UNITED STATES DISTRICT COURT
WESTERN DISTRICT OF WASHINGTON AT _____

_____

Plaintiff,   No. _____

vs.

_____   PRETRIAL ORDER

Defendant.

JURISDICTION

Jurisdiction is vested in this court by virtue of: (State the facts and cite the statutes whereby jurisdiction of the case is vested in this court).

CLAIMS AND DEFENSES

The plaintiff will pursue at trial the following claims: (E.g., breach of contract, violation of 28 U.S.C. § 1983). The defendant will pursue the following affirmative defenses and/or claims: (E.g., accord and satisfaction, estoppel, waiver).

ADMITTED FACTS

The following facts are admitted by the parties: (Enumerate every agreed fact, irrespective of admissibility, but with notation of objections as to admissibility. List 1, 2, 3, etc.)

The plaintiff contends as follows: (List 1, 2, 3, etc.)

The defendant contends as follows: (List 1, 2, 3, etc.)

(State contentions in summary fashion, omitting evidentiary detail. Unless otherwise ordered by the court, the factual contentions of a party shall not exceed two pages in length. * * *)

ISSUES OF LAW

The following are the issues of law to be determined by the court: (List 1, 2, 3, etc., and state each issue of law involved. A simple statement of the ultimate issue to be decided by the court, such as "Is the plaintiff entitled to recover?" will not be accepted.) If the parties cannot agree on the issues of law, separate statements may be given in the pretrial order.

EXPERT WITNESSES

(a) Each party shall be limited to _____ expert witness(es) on the issues of _____.

(b) The name(s) and address(es) of the expert witness(es) to be used by each party at the trial and the issue upon which each will testify is:

    (1) On behalf of plaintiff;

    (2) On behalf of defendant.

OTHER WITNESSES

The names and addresses of witnesses, other than experts, to be used by each party at the time of trial and the general nature of the testimony of each are:

(a) On behalf of plaintiff: (E.g., Jane Doe, 10 Elm Street, Seattle, WA; will testify concerning formation of the parties' contract, performance, breach and damage to plaintiff.)

(b) On behalf of defendant: (follow same format).

(As to each witness, expert or others, indicate "will testify," or "possible witness only." Also indicate which witnesses, if any, will testify by deposition. Rebuttal witnesses, the necessity of whose testimony cannot reasonably be anticipated before trial, need not be named.)

EXHIBITS

(a) Admissibility stipulated:

Plaintiff's Exhibits

1.   Photo of port side of ship. (Examples)

2.   Photo of crane motor.

3.   Photo of crane.

Defendant's Exhibits

A–1.   Weather report. (Examples)

A–2.   Log book.

A–3.   X-ray of plaintiff's foot.

A–4.   X-ray of wrist.

(b) Authenticity stipulated, admissibility disputed:

Plaintiff's Exhibits

4.   Inventory Report. (Examples)

Defendant's Exhibits

A–5.   Photograph. (Examples)

(c) Authenticity and admissibility disputed:

Plaintiff's Exhibits

5.   Accountant's report. (Examples)

Defendant's Exhibits

A–6.   Ship's log.

(No party is required to list any exhibit which is listed by another party, or any exhibit to be used for impeachment only. * * *)

ACTION BY THE COURT

(a) This case is scheduled for trial (before a jury) (without a jury) on _____, 20___, at _____.

(b) Trial briefs shall be submitted to the court on or before _____.

(c) (Omit this sub-paragraph in non-jury case.) Jury instructions requested by either party shall be submitted to the court on or before _____. Suggested questions of either party to be asked of the jury by the court on voir dire shall be submitted to the court on or before _____.

(d) (Insert any other ruling made by the court at or before pretrial conference.)

This order has been approved by the parties as evidenced by the signatures of their counsel. This order shall control the subsequent course of the action unless modified by a subsequent order. This order shall not be amended except by order of the court pursuant to agreement of the parties or to prevent manifest injustice.

DATED this _____ day of _____ [insert month], 20___ [insert year].

United States District

Judge/Magistrate Judge

FORM APPROVED

_____

Attorney for Plaintiff

_____

Attorney for Defendant

COMMENTS AND QUESTIONS CONCERNING THE FORM PRETRIAL ORDER

1. What is the advantage of specifying the precise format of the final pretrial order as the federal judges in the Western District of Washington have done? Are there disadvantages to a standard format?

2. Is the completion of form pretrial orders likely to conserve judicial resources? Legal resources? Costs to clients? What must be balanced against any potential savings?

3. The above order requires the parties not only to stipulate to facts and exhibits to be admitted at trial, but to stipulate to "every agreed fact, irrespective of admissibility" and to exhibits as to which there is a dispute as to admissibility but not authenticity. Why does the order require such stipulations concerning matters that may be inadmissible at trial?

4.   In some pretrial orders, counsel are required to estimate the number of days they need to try the case. Based upon such estimates, and, sometimes, subsequent negotiations with the judge, counsel may be restricted to a limited number of trial days in which to present their case. *See General Signal Corp. v. MCI Telecomms. Corp.*, 66 F.3d 1500, 1507–11 (9th Cir. 1995), *cert. denied*, 516 U.S. 1146 (1996); *MCI Commc'ns Corp. v. Am. Tel. & Tel. Co.*, 708 F.2d 1081, 1170–72 (7th Cir.), *cert. denied,* 464 U.S. 891 (1983).

5.   The final section of the form order contemplates the incorporation of judicial rulings into the final pretrial order. Why might judges prefer to make such rulings prior to trial? Why might counsel have a similar preference? Do such pretrial rulings present any potential difficulties?

6.   Judges may require counsel to prepare additional pretrial documents beyond the final pretrial order. The final section of the above order suggests that the parties may be required to prepare trial briefs, proposed jury instructions, and proposed voir dire questions. In cases to be tried to the court rather than to a jury, some judges require counsel to submit proposed findings of fact and conclusions of law either before or after the trial. *See* Fed. R. Civ. P. 52(a).

7.   Final pretrial orders typically are prepared by counsel. After counsel jointly prepare such an order, the proposed order is considered at a pretrial conference and approved for entry by the judge.

2.   WHEN DOES "MANIFEST INJUSTICE" JUSTIFY AMENDMENT OF THE FINAL PRETRIAL ORDER?

What does Rule 16(e) mean by stating that the court "may modify the order issued after a final pretrial conference only to prevent manifest injustice"? Some federal courts have interpreted this standard quite narrowly. As the United States Court of Appeals for the Third Circuit stated in *Ely v. Reading Co.*, 424 F.2d 758, 763–64 (3d Cir. 1970):

> One of the main purposes of the pretrial conference is to formulate the issues to be litigated to aid the parties in preparation for trial. If counsel are permitted to change the positions taken at pretrial obviously the effectiveness of this procedure is destroyed. For this reason the pretrial order is generally binding on the parties. It cannot be modified without the permission of the court and a showing of manifest injustice. The decision of whether or not to permit a change is within the discretion of the trial judge. Appellate interference with this discretion should be kept at a minimum. It should only be exercised where there is a clear abuse of discretion.

In *Youren v. Tintic School Dist.*, 343 F.3d 1296, 1304–05 (10th Cir. 2003), the United States Court of Appeals for the Tenth Circuit also interpreted Rule 16(e) narrowly in rejecting defendants' attempt to assert a statute of limitations defense they had omitted from the final pretrial order:

> The * * * pretrial order "measures the dimensions of the lawsuit, both in the trial court and on appeal." *Tyler v. City of Manhattan,* 118 F.3d 1400, 1403 (10th Cir.1997). "Since the whole purpose of Rule 16 is to clarify the real nature of the dispute at issue, attorneys at a pre-trial conference must make a full and fair disclosure of their views as to what the real issues of the trial will be." *Rios v. Bigler,* 67 F.3d 1543, 1549 (10th Cir.1995). * * *

> Although the defendants included the statute of limitations as an affirmative defense in their answer to the complaint, they did not identify the statute of limitations issue in the pretrial order. Notably, there is a section of the pretrial order with the heading "CONTESTED ISSUES OF LAW," under which the defendants listed three purely legal questions—but the statute of limitations issue was conspicuously not among them. Even more notably, the pretrial order was evidently prepared *exclusively* by the defendants.

* * *

> The statute of limitations issue, therefore, "was not part of the case before the district court." *Gowan,* 148 F.3d at 1192. We thus hold that the defendants waived their statute of limitations affirmative defense by omitting the issue from the pretrial order, and we decline to reach the merits of the defendants' argument on this issue.

Do these cases mean that a party can never be granted leave to amend a final pretrial order? Consider the following case.

Wallin v. Fuller

United States Court of Appeals, Fifth Circuit, 1973
476 F.2d 1204

■ Before RIVES, WISDOM and RONEY, CIRCUIT JUDGES.

OPINION

■ WISDOM, CIRCUIT JUDGE:

This case presents the question whether a trial court should instruct a jury on a theory of liability not mentioned in the pretrial order but supported by evidence introduced at the trial without objection. The district court declined so to instruct the jury. We reverse and remand for a new trial.

Carl Wallin was killed on August 16, 1970, when his Volkswagen, which he was driving, collided with a Pontiac driven by Allen Fuller on a two-lane highway near Lowndesboro, Alabama. Wallin held a policy of insurance with Nationwide Mutual Insurance Company, which contained a standard uninsured motorist clause. Fuller was an uninsured motorist within the meaning of this clause. Marsha Lee Wallin, widow of Carl Wallin, brought suit in federal district court seeking a declaratory judgment against Nationwide under the policy, alleging that Fuller's negligence had caused the collision.

On September 20, 1971, the district court held a pretrial hearing and entered an order specifying the issues agreed upon by the plaintiff, Mrs. Wallin, and defendant, Nationwide. The plaintiff's theory of recovery, as recited in the pretrial order, was that Fuller negligently drove onto his left side of the highway, thus causing the collision with Wallin's car. The defendant denied that Fuller had been negligent. Further, the defendant contended that Wallin had been contributorily negligent in pulling out onto *his* left-hand side of the highway to pass another car when there was insufficient room to pass.

Most of the plaintiff's case at the trial was devoted to showing that the collision had occurred in Wallin's righthand lane, and that Fuller therefore had been on the wrong side of the road. * * *

The defense offered the deposition of George Mayes, who had been riding in Fuller's car at the time of the accident, and called Fuller himself to the stand. Both Mayes and Fuller testified that Wallin had pulled out to pass, and that the cars had collided while Wallin was still in the left lane and Fuller was in his right lane.

The testimony of both Mayes and Fuller revealed a possibility that, even if Wallin had been contributorily negligent, Fuller might have been guilty of subsequent negligence or wanton conduct. Under Alabama law a showing of subsequent negligence or wantonness defeats a defense of contributory negligence. Counsel for the defendant made no objection to the admission of any of this testimony at the trial. Mayes, the passenger, testified at his deposition that Fuller did not slow down when he first became aware that Wallin was trying to pass; that he finally shouted at Fuller to slam on his brakes; and that Fuller then applied his brakes and skidded into Wallin. The defense took the deposition of Mayes on September 8, 1971, before the pretrial hearing. The plaintiff's attorney was present at this deposition, but made no mention of the issues of subsequent negligence and wanton conduct either at the pretrial hearing or when the deposition was introduced into evidence at the trial.

Fuller, called as a witness by the defense, gave testimony on cross-examination by the plaintiff's attorney that tended to corroborate Mayes's version of the events. On recross, asked by the plaintiff's attorney whether the accident would not have happened if he had slowed down the least little bit, Fuller replied: "I guess not." Counsel for the defendant made no objection to any of this examination by the plaintiff's lawyer.

Neither attorney drew the court's attention to the fact that this testimony might show subsequent negligence or wanton conduct, or to the fact that the pretrial order precluded these issues, until after both sides had rested. The defendant then submitted requested written charges to the court. The plaintiff's attorney objected to one of these charges on the ground that it failed to include the issues of subsequent negligence and wanton conduct, and requested leave to amend the pleadings to include these issues. The trial court denied leave to amend, applying the standard of Rule 16 of the Federal Rules of Civil Procedure that, where the issues have been narrowed by a pretrial order, amendment will be permitted only when necessary to prevent "manifest injustice." The court proceeded to submit the case to the jury without instructions as to the legal effect of subsequent negligence or wanton conduct. The jury found for the defendant. The court then denied the plaintiff's motion for a new trial, and the plaintiff brought this appeal.

The pretrial conference serves the purposes of expediting litigation and eliminating surprise at the trial. Rule 16 of the Federal Rules of Civil Procedure establishes that the pre-trial order ordinarily governs the course of the trial. Under the Rule 16 "manifest injustice" standard, the question whether to permit amendment of the pretrial order in the course of the trial is generally a matter within the discretion of the trial judge, and an appellate court will intervene only if the trial judge has acted arbitrarily.

Unbending adherence to the strictures of Rule 16 would, however, frustrate another broad policy of the Federal Rules favoring liberality of amendment. This policy is principally embodied in Rule 15, which deals with amendments to the pleadings. It is unlikely that the pretrial order under Rule 16 was intended to make the pleadings, and therefore Rule 15, obsolete. Even though the parties have the advantage of discovery before the pretrial conference, events not anticipated at the pretrial stage may often occur at the trial. And attorneys would be reluctant to enter agreements at the pretrial conference if later amendments were strictly forbidden.

Courts have therefore widely recognized that Rule 16 must be read in light of Rule 15, and that in some circumstances the policy of Rule 15 should moderate the strictures of Rule 16.

At a minimum the accommodation of Rule 16 to Rule 15 should mean that the more liberal standard of Rule 15 should apply when one of the parties seeks amendment to conform the pleadings to the issues actually raised by the evidence introduced at the trial. Rule 15(b) [now, Rule 15(b)(2)] provides that when issues outside the pleadings are tried by express or implied consent of the parties, "they *shall* be treated in all respects as if they had been raised in the pleadings." Amendment is thus not merely discretionary but mandatory in such a case.

The trial court erred in applying Rule 16 rather than Rule 15(b). Under the standards of Rule 15(b) the defendant impliedly consented to the trial of issues outside the pretrial order, and the pleadings should therefore have been amended. A substantial quantity of evidence tending to establish subsequent negligence or wanton conduct was brought before the jury, through the deposition of Mayes and the testimony of Fuller, without objection by defense counsel. Indeed, both Mayes and Fuller were defense witnesses, and Fuller was himself a defendant. Having deposed Mayes well in advance of the trial, defense counsel cannot complain of having been unaware that the evidence might tend to establish subsequent negligence and wantonness. In these circumstances the failure of the defense to seek to limit the evidence during the trial in accordance with the pretrial order establishes consent to the trial of these issues.

The possibility of prejudice to the opposing party may of course be reason to find a lack of consent to amendment under Rule 15(b). Any danger of prejudice to the defendant in this case could have been averted by the trial court. All witnesses to the accident had testified, as had the investigating officers. It would not have been impractical for the court to have reopened the trial, recalled the witnesses, and granted a short continuance if necessary to enable the defendant to prepare and present a defense.

The defendant, Nationwide Mutual, argues that the testimony of Mayes and Fuller was relevant to the issues of negligence and contributory negligence, and that therefore the admission of this evidence without objection cannot establish consent to the trial of any other issues. It is true that part of this testimony tended to rebut the plaintiff's theory that the collision occurred on Wallin's right side of the road, and tended to show that Wallin might have been contributorily negligent in pulling out to pass. But the testimony as to Fuller's failure to apply his brakes, and the conversation between Mayes and Fuller, was not relevant to the plaintiff's theory of recovery, which was founded solely on the theory that Fuller was on the wrong side of the road. Nor did it establish or rebut the contention that Wallin was contributorily negligent. This evidence was much more strongly relevant to the theories of subsequent negligence and wanton conduct, and this should have been apparent to defense counsel.

* * *

Certainly the plaintiff's attorney should have raised these issues at the pretrial conference. He attended the deposition of Mayes, and was thus well aware before the pretrial conference that there was some evidence of subsequent negligence and wanton conduct. Where a party is aware of an issue before a pretrial conference, his failure to raise it there may in some circumstances be grounds for denying later amendment.

But the failure of the plaintiff's counsel in this case to raise these issues before or during the trial is offset by the failure of the defendant's attorney to attempt to exclude any of the evidence. We find no reason to conclude that the plaintiff's attorney was acting in bad faith by trying to smuggle in issues for the purpose of surprising the defense at the trial. Moreover, we are reluctant to penalize the plaintiff for the errors of her attorney. *See Link v. Wabash R. R. Co.*, 1962, 370 U.S. 626, 646–648, (Black J., dissenting).

We therefore hold that the district court erred in applying the standards of Rule 16 rather than Rule 15(b), and that under Rule 15(b) the plaintiff was entitled to amendment. The judgment of the district court is reversed and the case is remanded for a new trial.

COMMENTS AND QUESTIONS CONCERNING *WALLIN V. FULLER*

1.   Aren't there two Federal Rules at issue in this case: Rule 16(e)'s prohibition of the amendment of final pretrial orders except to prevent "manifest injustice" and Rule 15(b)'s authorization of amendments to include issues raised without objection at trial? How, then, can the Court of Appeals conclude, "At a minimum the accommodation of Rule 16 to Rule 15 should mean that the more liberal standard of Rule 15 should apply when one of the parties seeks amendment to conform the pleadings to the issues actually raised by the evidence introduced at the trial."

2.   What if the complaint had included the theory of liability based upon subsequent negligence or wanton conduct? Would there still be a question as to whether "manifest injustice" had been shown for a Rule 16(e) amendment of the final pretrial order?

3.   Rule 15(b) permits amendments to the pleadings in certain circumstances. In *Youren v. Tintic School Dist.*, 343 F.3d 1296, 1304–05 (10th Cir. 2003), defendants' answers actually included the statute of limitations defense. Thus there was no need to amend the pleadings, but only the final pretrial order. Would it be more unfair to opposing parties to permit an amendment of the final pretrial order in an action in which a matter was never asserted or in an action in which that matter was asserted in the pleadings but not in the final pretrial order?

4.   Judge Wisdom states in his opinion, "Even though the parties have the advantage of discovery before the pretrial conference, events not anticipated at the pretrial stage may often occur at the trial." But, in this case, both counsel knew about the possibility of subsequent negligence or wanton conduct because the deposition of the passenger Mayes had been taken before the final pretrial conference. So does this case present a situation in which "events not anticipated at the pretrial stage" justified an amendment of the pleadings or the final pretrial order?

5.   Judge Wisdom states in his opinion, "Under the Rule 16 'manifest injustice' standard, the question whether to permit amendment of the pretrial order in the course of the trial is generally a matter within the discretion of the trial judge, and an appellate court will intervene only if the trial judge has acted arbitrarily." Has the Court of Appeals therefore concluded that the district judge "acted arbitrarily"?

6.   At the end of his opinion, Judge Wisdom states that "we are reluctant to penalize the plaintiff for the errors of her attorney," citing the dissent of Justice Black in *Link v. Wabash R. R. Co.*, 370 U.S. 626, 646–648 (1962). In *Link* the Supreme Court upheld the sua sponte dismissal of a civil action due to the failure of plaintiff's counsel to attend a pretrial conference after having caused several earlier case delays. Justice Harlan stated for the majority, "[I]f an attorney's conduct falls substantially below what is reasonable under the circumstances, the client's remedy is against the attorney in a suit for malpractice. But keeping this suit alive merely because plaintiff should not be penalized for the omissions of his own attorney would be visiting the sins of plaintiff's lawyer upon the defendant." 370 U.S. at 634 n.10.

In dissent, Justice Black argued:

[T]o say that the sins or faults or delinquencies of a lawyer must always be visited upon his client so as to impose tremendous financial penalties upon him, as here, is to ignore the practicalities and realities of the lawyer-client relationship. * * *

Any general rule that clients must always suffer for the mistakes of their lawyers simply ignores all these problems. If a general rule is to be adopted, I think it would be far better in the interest of the administration of justice, and far more realistic in the light of what the relationship between a lawyer and his client actually is, to adopt the rule that no client is ever to be penalized, as this plaintiff has been, because of the conduct of his lawyer unless notice is given to the client himself that such a threat hangs over his head.

370 U.S. at 646–48.

With which justice do you agree?

VI. SETTLEMENT OF CIVIL ACTIONS

The final pretrial conference and preparation of the final pretrial order focus the parties and their counsel on the strength of both their own case and that of other parties. Rule 16(a)(5) lists as one of the purposes of the pretrial conference the facilitation of settlement, while Rule 16(c)(2)(I) lists as a matter for consideration at a pretrial conference "settling the case and using special procedures to assist in resolving the dispute when authorized by statute or rule."

Studies have found that approximately 60% of civil actions settle.[5] In addition, a study from the 1970s found that attorneys spent about

---

[5]   Flanders, "Blind Umpires—A Response to Professor Resnik," 35 *Hastings L. J.* 505, 517 n.56 (1984). *See also* W. Brazil, *Effective Approaches to Settlement: A Handbook for Lawyers and Judges* 394–97 (1988); Eisenberg et al., "Litigation Outcomes in State and Federal Courts: A Statistical Portrait," 19 *Seattle U. L. Rev.* 433, 444 (1996) (1991–92 settlement rates in contract and non-asbestos tort cases of 62.2% in urban state courts and 64.6% in federal courts).

This does not mean, however, that 40% of civil actions go to trial. To the contrary, only 1.1% of the non-land condemnation federal civil actions terminated during the year ending

15% of their time in settlement discussions—or about as much time as they devoted to any other single litigation task.[6] So settlement is an essential element of both state and federal judicial systems and of the practices of individual lawyers.

By settling an action, the parties themselves set the terms by which their dispute is resolved. By putting the dispute behind them, they also may be able to rebuild their business or personal relationships with each other. Abraham Lincoln described the advantages—for both the parties and their lawyers—of settlement as follows:

> Discourage litigation. Persuade your neighbors to compromise whenever you can. Point out to them how the nominal winner is often the real loser—in fees, expenses, and waste of time. As a peacemaker the lawyer has a superior opportunity of being a good man.

Abraham Lincoln, "Notes for Law Lecture," *in* 2 *Complete Works of Abraham Lincoln* 140, 142 (J. Nicolay & J. Hay ed. 1905).

Settlement of civil actions has become so pervasive, though, that some question whether such high settlement rates are a good thing. Thus Professor Owen Fiss asserts:

> Settlement is for me the civil analogue of plea bargaining: Consent is often coerced; the bargain may be struck by someone without authority; the absence of a trial and judgment renders subsequent judicial involvement troublesome; and although dockets are trimmed, justice may not be done. Like plea bargaining, settlement is a capitulation to the conditions of mass society and should be neither encouraged nor praised.[7]

Professors Andrew McThenia and Thomas Shaffer respond that "Fiss comes close to equating justice with law. * * * We do not believe that law and justice are synonymous. * * * Justice is not usually something people get from the government. And courts * * * are not the only or even the most important places that dispense justice."[8] Taking a middle course, Professor David Luban suggests that "the question cannot be 'for or against settlement?' but 'how much settlement?' " and

---

December 31, 2014, reached trial. Admin. Office of the U. S. Courts, *Federal Judicial Caseload Statistics: December 31, 2014* (2014) (Table C–4). Other actions are resolved by the courts short of trial or are simply dismissed or abandoned by the plaintiffs.

[6]   Trubek et al., "The Costs of Ordinary Litigation," 31 *UCLA L. Rev.* 72, 91 (Table 3) (1983) (15.1% of attorney time devoted to settlement discussions).

[7]   Fiss, "Against Settlement," 93 *Yale L. J.* 1073, 1075 (1984). *See also* Mnookin, "When Not to Negotiate: A Negotiation Imperialist Reflects on Appropriate Limits," 74 *U. Colo. L. Rev.* 1077 (2003) (suggesting that it is appropriate to refuse to negotiate some conflicts, such as between the Taliban and the United States immediately after September 11, 2001).

[8]   McThenia & Shaffer, "For Reconciliation," 94 *Yale L. J.* 1660, 1664–65 (1985). Professor Fiss's reply is set forth in Fiss, "Out of Eden," 94 *Yale L. J.* 1669 (1985). Various arguments favoring settlement are analyzed in Galanter & Cahill, " 'Most Cases Settle': Judicial Promotion and Regulation of Settlements," 46 *Stan. L. Rev.* 1339 (1994).

that settlements open to the public can vindicate some of the same public values promoted by adjudication.[9]

This section of the chapter briefly considers the mechanics of settling a civil action, issues raised by attempts to keep settlement terms confidential, and the role of the judge in settlement facilitation. As you read this material, keep in mind broader questions presented by a system in which a majority of disputes are resolved through settlement and very few cases go to trial.

A. SETTLEMENT MECHANICS

Typically there are at least two separate documents that must be drafted to effectuate the settlement of a civil action: (1) the parties' actual settlement agreement and (2) the notice or court order dismissing the pending litigation. By using two separate documents, the public notice or court order dismissing the action generally need not include the parties' specific settlement terms.[10]

The parties' settlement agreement may be encompassed in a release executed by the plaintiff. The release is just what its title implies: the legal document by which the plaintiff relinquishes all its claims against the defendant.

If a plaintiff has potential tort claims against more than one person and a settlement is reached with fewer than all potential defendants, a covenant not to sue, rather than a release, may be executed with the settling defendants. Such covenants provide that, in return for a valuable consideration, the plaintiff will not sue or continue suit against a particular defendant. They originally were used to avoid inadvertently releasing all tortfeasors from liability through the execution of a release with a single defendant. While tort law in most states now prevents such an inadvertent release of non-settling defendants, many attorneys still use covenants not to sue rather than releases in cases involving multiple tortfeasors.

In some jurisdictions, settling defendants may be concerned that other potential defendants who have not settled will seek contribution from them with respect to a later judgment. In such jurisdictions, the settlement documents may include an agreement by the plaintiff to indemnify the settling defendant if contribution is sought by other potential defendants who are not a party to the present settlement. In addition, a choice of law clause should be used in the covenant or

---

[9] Luban, "Settlements and the Erosion of the Public Realm," 83 *Geo. L. J.* 2619, 2620 (1995).

[10] However, in order to ensure that a federal court will have jurisdiction to enforce the parties' settlement agreement in the future, an order dismissing the action pursuant to Rule 41(a)(2) should be filed with the court and written so that either "the parties' compliance with the terms of the settlement contract (or the court's 'retention of jurisdiction' over the settlement contract) [are] * * * terms set forth in the [dismissal] order." *Kokkonen v. Guardian Life Ins. Co. of Am.*, 511 U.S. 375, 381 (1994).

release to ensure that there is no question as to which state law governs the settlement.

While a release or covenant not to sue may be sufficient to memorialize routine settlements, if the settlement involves significant mutual promises by the parties it is best to draft an actual settlement agreement. This agreement should be signed by the parties and set forth all of the promises underlying the settlement.

Because releases and settlement agreements generally are not filed with the court, a notice, stipulation, or court order dismissing the lawsuit must be prepared and filed with the clerk's office. Rule 41(a)(1)(A)(ii) of the Federal Rules of Civil Procedure provides that, in most cases, a plaintiff "may dismiss an action without a court order by filing * * * a stipulation of dismissal signed by all parties who have appeared."

Rule 41(a)(1)(B) also provides that unless "the notice or stipulation states otherwise, the dismissal is without prejudice."[11] In most cases a precondition to settlement will be the plaintiff's agreement not to refile the same claim against the defendant at a later date. To ensure that there is no later question about this, the notice of dismissal should state that dismissal either is with, or without, prejudice to the refiling of the action.

More complex documentation may be required if the parties have agreed to a structured settlement of the action. Under a structured settlement, the defendant agrees to provide the plaintiff with periodic settlement payments rather than merely give the plaintiff a lump sum payment at the time of settlement. Often structured settlements are designed to ensure long-term care for tort victims, while preventing the plaintiff from squandering a large, initial lump-sum settlement.

Structured settlements can be advantageous to both plaintiffs (who receive periodic payments) and defendants (who can purchase an annuity that will provide a greater sum of money to the plaintiff over time than could be provided in a single lump sum). Another major advantage of a structured settlement is that, under 26 U.S.C. § 104(a)(2), the interest earned on the annuity is not taxable income to the recipient so long as the annuity represents compensation (and not punitive damages) for personal physical injuries or physical sickness. However, if the plaintiff is compensated with a lump sum payment, interest earned from the investment of that payment is generally taxable income.

Thus, in appropriate cases, structured settlements can be advantageous to both plaintiffs and defendants and provide another option in settling a civil action.

---

[11] Rule 41(a)(1)(B) specifies, however, that a notice of dismissal operates as an adjudication upon the merits if the plaintiff had previously filed and dismissed an action based on or including the claim now being dismissed.

B. SETTLEMENT CONFIDENTIALITY

As discussed earlier in Section III(A) of this Chapter, a plaintiff can voluntarily dismiss its action by filing a Rule 41(a)(1)(A)(i) notice of dismissal (if an answer or motion for summary judgment has not been filed) or a Rule 41(a)(1)(A)(ii) stipulation of dismissal (with the written stipulation of all parties to the action). Such a Rule 41(a) notice or stipulation is typically one part of the settlement of a civil action. While there also will be a separate written agreement as to the terms of the settlement, there is no requirement that these settlement terms be filed with the court. Should this be a requirement in a case such as the following?

Schoeps v. Museum of Modern Art

United States District Court, Southern District of New York, 2009
603 F.Supp.2d 673

MEMORANDUM ORDER

■ JED S. RAKOFF, DISTRICT JUDGE.

At the heart of this action are issues of considerable public import. Plaintiffs, heirs of Paul von Mendelssohn-Bartholdy and his wife, claim that two of New York's foremost cultural institutions turned a blind eye to the fact that great works of art in their collections—Pablo Picasso's *Boy Leading a Horse* (1905–1906), now owned by the Museum of Modern Art, and Picasso's *Le Moulin de la Galette* (1900), now owned by the Solomon R. Guggenheim Collection—were sold by von Mendelssohn-Bartholdy against his will because of Nazi duress in the 1930s. The defendant museums, for their part, originated this action (in the form of a declaratory judgment action) to clear their names (or so they said) and to combat what they alleged, in effect, was an effort by plaintiffs and their counsel to use the facade of Nazi iniquities to extort monies from public institutions that were vulnerable to bad publicity.

On February 2, 2009, the morning that trial was to commence, the parties announced in open court that, after over a year of litigation, they had reached a settlement. Counsel for the Museum of Modern Art and the Solomon R. Guggenheim Foundation (the "Museums") indicated that "for a sum certain," which was to remain confidential under the settlement agreement, there would be "complete peace" between the parties and the paintings would remain with the Museums. The Court, after confirming that all affected parties consented to the dismissal of the case with prejudice, accepted the parties' stipulation of dismissal. The Court, however, also asked the parties to submit, under seal, a copy of the signed settlement agreement once executed, so that the Court could determine whether it was appropriate and within the Court's power to make the settlement public. The parties consented.

After receiving the signed agreement, the Court, by Order dated March 6, 2009, directed the parties to submit letters stating whether they objected to making the settlement agreement public and setting forth the grounds for any such objection. By letter that same day, the Museums informed the Court that they no longer had any objection to making the settlement terms public and that they were prepared to waive the confidentiality provision to which the parties had previously agreed. Plaintiffs, however, submitted a letter dated March 13, 2009 stating that they objected to disclosure of the settlement terms. Their letter set forth the general legal principles that weigh against disclosure of settlement agreements, without, however, stating the particular reasons for their objection.

The Court finds the confidentiality provision of the settlement agreement and the plaintiffs' objection to disclosure to be against the public interest and a troubling reversal of the parties' previously stated positions on this issue. From the outset, the parties on both sides portrayed this lawsuit as of considerable public interest because of the importance of establishing the truth concerning the sensitive issues involved. The Museums, when they first brought this action seeking declaratory judgment, stated that they were "prepared to have all factual and legal issues surrounding [plaintiffs'] claims to the Paintings resolved by this Court," Compl. ¶ 8, and they have subsequently reiterated that "they are and remain committed to transparency in their actions," Letter from Evan Davis to the Honorable Jed S. Rakoff dated January 15, 2009. They have portrayed themselves as institutions dedicated to serving the public by enriching its cultural life, see, e.g., Compl. ¶¶ 13–18, and they have characterized the plaintiffs' claims as entirely baseless and, essentially, extortionate, see, e.g., id. ¶¶ 46–55. The plaintiffs, for their part, have claimed loudly throughout that they were vindicating a historical injustice.

Despite these protestations, and despite the fact that the Museums are not-for-profit education corporations who, by their own admission, hold their collections for the public trust, see Compl. ¶ 13, the parties chose to enter into a settlement agreement that—for reasons that remain entirely unexpressed—contained a confidentiality clause. Had the Museums been public agencies of New York State or City, any such provision would have been contrary to New York's Freedom of Information Law ("FOIL"). See N.Y. Pub. Off. L. §§ 84–90. It is hard to see why institutions that proclaim their public status and that seek and receive public support should view themselves as not owing a similar obligation, even if one is not imposed by law. Yet it was only after being pressed by the Court that the Museums retreated from their position of seeking confidentiality and stated that they no longer oppose disclosure.

Plaintiffs, however, for reasons wholly unexplained and seemingly no more compelling than concealing the amount of money going into their pockets, remain opposed. Even after giving allowance for the fact that plaintiffs, who are citizens of foreign countries, may be somewhat unfamiliar with the transparency typical of United States courts, the fact that the plaintiffs, who repeatedly sought to clothe themselves as effectively representatives of victims of one of the most criminal political regimes in history, should believe that there is any public interest in maintaining the secrecy of their settlement baffles the mind and troubles the conscience.

This case is thus very different, in many respects, from the ordinary case that courts of the Second Circuit have had in mind when they have enforced confidentiality provisions in settlement agreements. *See, e.g., Fed. Deposit Ins. Co. v. Ernst & Ernst,* 677 F.2d 230 (2d Cir.1982); *Palmieri v. State of New York,* 779 F.2d 861 (2d Cir.1985). Indeed, one of our sister circuits has noted in dictum that the broad brush of confidentiality should be applied in a more nuanced way than is typically the case. In *Pansy v. Borough of Stroudsburg,* 23 F.3d 772, 785–86 (3d Cir.1994), the Third Circuit wrote,

> Disturbingly, some courts routinely sign orders which contain confidentiality clauses without considering the propriety of such orders, or the countervailing public interests which are sacrificed by the orders. Because defendants request orders of confidentiality as a condition of settlement, courts are willing to grant these requests in an effort to facilitate settlement without sufficiently inquiring into the potential public interest in obtaining information concerning the settlement agreement.

The law of the Second Circuit, however, admits of no such distinctions in this instance. Rather, the Second Circuit strongly endorses the confidentiality of settlement agreements in virtually all cases. *See, e.g., United States v. Glens Falls Newspapers, Inc.,* 160 F.3d 853, 857 (2d Cir.1998) (noting the public interest in settlement of litigation in approving the sealing of settlement documents); *Palmieri,* 779 F.2d at 864 (reversing a district court's modification of a sealing order covering a settlement agreement and citing the "need of our district courts and civil litigants to facilitate efficient resolution of disputes through negotiated settlements").[1]

Given these precedents, the Court has no choice, therefore, but to preserve the confidentiality of the settlement agreement. Nonetheless, the Court will docket a copy of the settlement agreement, under seal, in

---

[1] It is true that a presumption of public access attaches to "judicial documents," which are documents filed with the court that are "relevant to the performance of a judicial function." *United States v. Amodeo,* 44 F.3d 141, 145 (2d Cir.1995). In this case, the settlement agreement, though filed with the Court, is probably not a "judicial document" because it was submitted at the Court's request and was not the basis of any decision or action by the Court. Moreover, even if it were classed as a "judicial document," the Second Circuit has found, in similar cases, that the presumption of access is weak when settlement confidentiality is concerned. *See Glens Falls Newspapers,* 160 F.3d at 858 (the presumption of access to documents pertaining to settlement negotiations is "negligible to nonexistent"); *Gambale v. Deutsche Bank AG,* 377 F.3d 133, 143–44 (2d Cir.2004) (presumption of access to record of counsel's statement of the settlement amount made at a sealed conference is weak).

the hope that the plaintiffs, after they have had a greater opportunity to reflect on their public responsibilities, not just to the courts of the United States that have made judicial processes so freely available to them, but to the public generally, may yet move to unseal it.

SO ORDERED.

COMMENTS AND QUESTIONS CONCERNING
SCHOEPS V. MUSEUM OF MODERN ART

1.   Why was the *Schoeps* case settled "with prejudice"? Would the case have settled whether the dismissal was with or without prejudice?

2.   Why shouldn't private parties be able to settle their private disputes privately?

3.   What is the public interest in this settlement? Why does Judge Rakoff believe that a confidential settlement is "against the public interest"?

4.   Are there people other than the plaintiffs who may move to unseal the settlement agreement that Judge Rakoff included under seal in the court record? Parties desiring confidentiality may file a settlement agreement with the court but request that it be sealed. The use of sealed settlements has been criticized, however, and courts have upheld the right of private parties to have settlements unsealed in certain circumstances. *E.g., Bank of America Nat'l Trust & Sav. Ass'n v. Hotel Rittenhouse Associates,* 800 F.2d 339 (3d Cir. 1986). *See also Janus Films, Inc. v. Miller,* 801 F.2d 578 (2d Cir. 1986).

5.   Why would a judge, as suggested by the United States Court of Appeals for the Third Circuit, "routinely sign orders which contain confidentiality clauses without considering the propriety of such orders, or the countervailing public interests which are sacrificed by the orders"? *Pansy v. Borough of Stroudsburg,* 23 F.3d 772, 785 (3d Cir.1994).

6.   Judge Rakoff notes that "the Second Circuit strongly endorses the confidentiality of settlement agreements in virtually all cases." Why is this so?

7.   What if a private action involves a matter of public safety? Richard Zitran unsuccessfully proposed to the ABA's Ethics 2000 Commission a new provision in the Model Rules of Professional Conduct that would have made it unethical for an attorney to participate in offering or making an agreement restricting the public availability of information the attorney reasonably believed directly concerned a substantial danger to public health or safety. Waldbeser & DeGrave, "Current Development 2002–2003: A Plaintiff's Lawyer's Dilemma: The Ethics of Entering into a Confidential Settlement," 16 *Geo. J. Legal Ethics* 815, 823–24 (2003). The United States District Court for the District of South Carolina has prohibited the sealing of settlement agreements filed with the court, Rule 5.03(E) of the United States District Court for the District of South Carolina, but Rule 5.03 provides that this prohibition does not extend to documents that are not filed with the court.

8. In an effort to deal with the desire of many defendants for settlement confidentiality clauses, a law firm provides in its retainer agreements that clients will not accept settlements with the health care industry that contain "gag clauses." In the event that the client nevertheless agrees to accept such a confidentiality provision, the client must pay the firm's full fees rather than the reduced fees charged those who do not accept settlement confidentiality clauses. Are there ethical difficulties with such fee agreements? Are there practical difficulties? *See* "Engagement Contract May Offer Reduced Fee If Client Rejects Gag Clause in Settlement," 69 *U.S.L.W.* 2215 (Oct. 17, 2000).

9. Despite the controversy they sometimes engender, sealed settlement agreements in federal district courts are rare (occurring in less than one-half of one percent of civil cases) and "generally the only thing kept secret * * * is the amount of settlement." R. Reagan et al., *Sealed Settlement Agreements in Federal District Court* 8 (Federal Judicial Center 2004).

C. THE JUDGE'S ROLE IN SETTLEMENT

While counsel generally negotiate case settlements amongst themselves, there is another individual who is extremely interested in the resolution of cases short of trial: the judge. Judges may be interested in settlements for several reasons. Most importantly, judges realize that private settlements can be tailored to take into account the needs and desires of the parties in a fashion that is not possible within a formal court system. Whether an action is decided at trial by a judge or jury, the possible outcomes typically are (1) a judgment for the defendant (dismissing the action) or (2) a judgment for the plaintiff for a set amount of damages. Creative lawyers, though, may be able to craft a settlement that is much more nuanced and thus more helpful for the parties.

Judges are rightly concerned about the large numbers of cases assigned to them, and each settlement permits the judge to devote more time to cases remaining on the docket. Without the settlement of a large percentage of cases on their dockets, judges would not be able to achieve the goal of Rule 1 of the Federal Rules of Civil Procedure "to secure the just, speedy, and inexpensive determination of every action and proceeding." Indeed, Rule 16(a)(5) lists as a purpose of pretrial conferences "facilitating settlement," while Rule 16(c)(2)(I) includes case settlement within the matters for consideration at pretrial conferences.

Judicial involvement in settlement may take many forms. At one extreme, the judge may set a settlement conference or otherwise require counsel to report concerning the status of any settlement discussions. Pretrial orders commonly summarize the parties' efforts to achieve voluntary settlement. Some judges also assign specific cases to other judicial personnel (such as a federal magistrate judge) to discuss settlement with counsel and attempt to achieve voluntary settlement.

Many judges personally discuss, and encourage, settlement with counsel. Because the authority of the judge is thus brought to bear on counsel, this judicial encouragement is often rewarded with settlement. It also is helpful for counsel to sense how the judge who will try the case evaluates its strengths and weaknesses. This, too, can result in the settlement of cases that otherwise would be tried.

However, direct judicial involvement in settlement has its downside. Counsel may be reluctant to anger the judge who is assigned to try their case and may settle cases they otherwise would take to trial. If, despite judicial intervention, a case is not settled, it may be difficult for the judge to preside evenhandedly at trial (or, even more difficult, to appear to all parties to be presiding evenhandedly). Even if a judge is able to disregard information learned during settlement discussions, counsel still may not believe that he is able to do so.

Professor Leo Levin, a former Director of the Federal Judicial Center, has noted:

> Judicial intervention to promote settlement casts the trial judge in a delicate role. Many lawyers desire more assistance from judges in removing psychological and informational barriers that stand in the way of settlement, but they do not want to lose control over their lawsuits or forgo their rights to proceed to trial. To serve the interests of the parties effectively, the judge must alter the relationship between the disputants so as to encourage—but not coerce—an early settlement. To serve the interests of the court, and indirectly the interests of the public, the judge must not spend more of the court's time than is warranted by the savings in trial time and litigation costs.[12]

Judges therefore must attempt to facilitate settlement of actions short of trial, while maintaining the posture of neutrality that is essential to successfully presiding over trials in the actions that do not settle. The next section of this chapter considers some of the techniques by which judges and others encourage parties to themselves resolve their disputes and civil actions short of trial.

VII. CONSIDER THE ALTERNATIVES

Not only are individual judges interested in the settlement of cases on their dockets, but judicial systems have designed structures to facilitate dispute resolution apart from formal adjudication at trial. These structures are considered forms of "alternative dispute resolution" or ADR. Some also have described ADR as "appropriate

---

[12] Levin, "Foreword" to D. Provine, *Settlement Strategies for Federal District Judges* v (1986). To address such concerns with judicial involvement in settlement, Professor Jeffrey Parness has suggested the adoption of written guidelines governing judicial settlement conferences. Parness, "Improving Judicial Settlement Conferences," 39 *U. C. Davis L. Rev.* 1891 (2006).

dispute resolution," or, as suggested by ADR pioneers Frank Sander and Stephen Goldberg, an effort to make the "forum fit the fuss."[13]

The forms of ADR vary in their formality, expense, and the parties' ability to control the dispute-resolution process.

- The least formal, least expensive ADR technique, and the mechanism over which the parties have the most control, is **negotiation**—in which a lawyer can simply contact the opposing lawyer and try to negotiate a settlement of the parties' dispute.

- A more formal process that involves a third-party is **mediation**, in which a mediator listens to the parties or their lawyers and helps them to settle their dispute.

- A process that involves more formality and expense, and less party control over the outcome, is **arbitration**. An arbitration is convened by a third-party arbitrator, who hears from all parties in sessions not unlike a judicial hearing, although the proceedings are typically a bit less formal and the rules for the admission of evidence may be more relaxed than in a courtroom (permitting, for instance, the admission of hearsay evidence that would be excluded at a judicial trial).

- The most formal ADR proceedings are trials before **private judges**. These private judges are often former judges, who privately contract to hear disputes just as would a sitting "real" judge. The parties may agree that the same rules of evidence and procedure that apply in a courtroom will be applied by the private judge, and the proceedings, although not heard at the courthouse, may appear identical to those in a "real" trial. The parties may prefer to submit their dispute to a private judge because they can maintain confidentiality over the proceedings and those proceedings can be scheduled whenever and wherever the parties decide.

Figure 11–4 shows the spectrum of major ADR procedures, ranging from negotiation (which is the least expensive, least formal, and over which the parties have the most control) to private judges (proceedings before whom are the most expensive, most formal, and over which the parties have the least control).

---

[13] *See* Sander & Goldberg, "Fitting the Forum to the Fuss: A User-Friendly Guide to Selecting an ADR Procedure," 10 *Negotiation J.* 49 (1994).

FIGURE 11–4
FORMALITY, EXPENSE, AND PARTY CONTROL OF
DISPUTE PROCESSING

← ← ←	More Formal, More Expensive & Less Party Control	Less Formal, Less Expensive & More Party Control	→ → →
Private Judges	Arbitration	Mediation	Negotiation

There are two ways in which a party may find itself involved in an alternative dispute resolution process. The parties, themselves, may resort to an ADR process to settle a dispute without resort to state or federal court. If my neighbor's dogs bark all night, or his children repeatedly take a short-cut through my garden, I probably will talk with him to try to resolve such disputes through negotiation. If this doesn't work, I might engage the services of a neighborhood mediation center to see if a third-party mediator could help us to resolve our dispute. Thus ADR processes can be used as an alternative to litigation.

ADR processes, though, also can be an alternative means of resolving civil litigation. Even after the filing of a civil action, the chances are high that this litigation will be resolved by negotiation rather than trial. In addition, many courts have court-annexed dispute resolution programs in which the parties may opt, or be required, to participate. The court may require, for instance, that the parties attempt to settle their action through a court-sponsored mediation or arbitration process before they are entitled to a judicial trial. Consider the difficulties created by such a requirement in the following case.

A. COMPELLED, "MEANINGFUL" PARTICIPATION IN ADR: *GILLING V. EASTERN AIRLINES*

Gilling v. Eastern Airlines, Inc.
United States District Court, District of New Jersey, 1988
680 F.Supp. 169

OPINION

■ SAROKIN, DISTRICT JUDGE.

I.   *Introduction*

In order for the compulsory arbitration program to function properly, it is essential that the parties participate in a meaningful manner. This is particularly so in a case such as this in which one of the parties is a substantial corporation and the other party is one or more individuals. The purposes of the arbitration program are to provide the parties with a quick and inexpensive means of resolving their dispute while, at the same time, reducing the court's caseload.

These purposes are thwarted when a party to the arbitration enters into it with the intention from the outset of rejecting its outcome and demanding a trial de novo. Rather than reducing the cost and promoting efficiency in the system, such an attitude increases the costs and reduces the efficiency. Furthermore, such conduct can serve to discourage the poorer litigant and diminish his or her resolve to proceed to final judgment. Explicit in this court's arbitration program is the need for the parties to participate in good faith. Failure to do so warrants appropriate sanctions by the court.

Here, defendants move for trial de novo after the entry of an adverse arbitration award. The court grants the motion, but imposes sanctions on defendants for failure to participate in the arbitration meaningfully.

II. *Background*

Plaintiffs were passengers aboard a flight of defendant Eastern Air Lines from Miami to Martinique on November 27, 1983. They allege that they were wrongfully ejected from their flight during a stopover in St. Croix after two incidents on board involving knives. Their complaint states claims for breach of contract, negligence, false imprisonment, battery, assault, slander, invasion of privacy, infliction of emotional distress and conversion.

The court referred the matter to compulsory arbitration, as General Rule 47 requires. The arbitrator heard the case on May 20, 1987. The defendants did not attend the arbitration; their appearance was through counsel. Although the parties dispute the extent of defense counsel's presentation at the arbitration, they agree that she presented summaries of the defendants' position and read at least a few passages from deposition testimony and answers to interrogatories. The arbitrator found for each of the plaintiffs.

Within the thirty days allotted by General Rule 47(G)(1), defendants moved for a trial de novo. Plaintiffs opposed the motion, contending that defendants' failure to participate meaningfully in the arbitration as General Rule 47(E)(3) requires deprived them of their right to demand a trial de novo. As the court was unable to evaluate the meaningfulness of the defendants' participation in the arbitration, the court remanded the case to the arbitrator for a factual finding on that question.

On November 12, 1987, the arbitrator made the requested factual findings. He found as a fact that defendants' attorney did not participate in the arbitration proceeding in a meaningful manner:

> I find as a fact that she merely "went through the motions." I find as a fact that the foregoing was a predetermined position taken by her office, even though that position remains obscure to me. I find as a fact that her "participation" in the arbitration proceeding rendered it a sham. . . .

I was . . . flabbergasted when [defendants' counsel] arrived with no witnesses. She stated . . . that all Eastern personnel were on assignment, and that she would render fact summaries and position summaries. While she may have read a few interrogatories and answers [sic] a few lines from one or more deposition transcripts, ninety five percent (95%) of her participation was in fact stating position summaries on behalf of Eastern, and stating fact summaries as to what Eastern's personnel may have said in their own depositions. . . .

I recall another event that occurred at the arbitration proceeding which further buttresses my within findings of fact. At the end of the hearing I asked [defendants' counsel] as to whether she wanted damage awards broken down into compensatory damages and punitive damages, if I should determine to make such damage awards. Her reply to me as best I can paraphrase it now was "Do what you want, or, we don't care what you do, we won't pay it anyway."

After the arbitrator filed his fact findings with the court, the defendants renewed their motion for a trial de novo. Defendants couple their request for a de novo trial with a request that the court vacate the arbitrator's findings.

III. *Discussion*

General Rule 47(E)(3) provides that

the arbitration hearing may proceed in the absence of any party who, after notice, fails to be present. In the event that a party fails to participate in the arbitration process in a meaningful manner, as determined by the arbitrator, the Court may impose appropriate sanctions, including, but not limited to, the striking of any demand for a trial de novo filed by that party.

Defendants ask the court to vacate the arbitrator's finding that they did not participate in the arbitration in a meaningful manner. After examining General Rule 47, the court is unable to discover any standard of review of an arbitrator's findings. The rule simply authorizes the court to devise a sanction "in the event that a party fails to participate in the arbitration process in a meaningful manner, *as determined by the arbitrator.*" General Rule 47(E)(3) (emphasis added). The rule thus appears to place the determination of meaningfulness entirely in the hands and discretion of the arbitrator, without being subject to district court review. *Cf.* F.R.C.P. 72(a) (district court may modify or set aside a magistrate's finding that is "clearly erroneous"); 5 U.S.C. § 706(2)(E) (district court may set aside certain agency actions which are "unsupported by substantial evidence").

However, even if the court does have the authority to disturb an arbitrator's finding of no meaningful participation, it declines to do so in this case. The arbitrator had ample opportunity to observe the conduct of counsel at the arbitration. He had the opportunity to measure the earnestness of the defendants' presentation against the gravity of the plaintiffs' allegations and the defendants' potentially sizeable exposure to liability. Although the defendants are correct that General Rule 47 did not require them to present live testimony, the arbitrator was certainly entitled to factor their decision not to call witnesses into his overall assessment of the meaningfulness of their participation. The arbitrator, examining the totality of the defendants' participation at the arbitration, concluded that the reading of brief position summaries and deposition and interrogatory excerpts did not amount to meaningful participation in the context of this case. The court concludes that this finding was supported by substantial evidence and was not clearly erroneous.

Defendants argue that the enforcement of General Rule 47(E)(3) against them would deprive them of their constitutional right to a jury trial and conflict with the Federal Rules of Civil Procedure. The court notes that compulsory pre-trial arbitration procedures like the one at issue in this case have withstood constitutional attack. *See Kimbrough v. Holiday Inn,* 478 F.Supp. 566 (E.D.Pa.1979); *New England Merchants v. Hughes,* 556 F.Supp. 712 (E.D.Pa.1983); *Rhea v. Massey-Ferguson,* 767 F.2d 266 (6th Cir.1985). In the *New England Merchants* case, the court approved the denial of a demand for trial de novo by a party who refused to participate in arbitration at all.

The court, however, need not reach the defendants' constitutional claim, for the rule does not require the court to deny the application for trial de novo. Rather, it allows the court to choose an "appropriate sanction," only one of which is the rather draconian striking of a demand for trial de novo. While such an extreme sanction may be appropriate where a party absolutely refuses to participate in or even attend arbitration, the court declines to deprive defendants of their day in court because of their limited performance at arbitration, without in any way condoning it.

General Rule 47(E)(3) allows the court to devise an "appropriate sanction." In this case, where the defendants demonstrated such contempt for the arbitration proceeding, it is only fair that they should have to pay for it. The court therefore orders that defendants reimburse plaintiffs for all costs and fees which they incurred in preparing for and participating in the arbitration, as well as costs and fees incurred in opposing defendants' demand for a trial de novo.

The court has determined to impose this more limited sanction, although denial of the trial de novo would have been warranted, because of the lack of clear guidelines as to what participation is "meaningful." However, counsel should be on notice that a trial de novo will not be automatically permitted in those cases in which the party seeking it views the arbitration proceeding merely as a meaningless interlude in the judicial process.

COMMENTS AND QUESTIONS CONCERNING
GILLING V. EASTERN AIRLINES

1.   Judge Sarokin states at the outset of his opinion: "The purposes of the arbitration program are to provide the parties with a quick and inexpensive means of resolving their dispute while, at the same time, reducing the court's caseload." Which is the more significant purpose? If the parties were interested in a "quick and inexpensive means of resolving their dispute," couldn't they participate in a program of their choice outside the court system?

2.   Although the arbitrator's findings made it clear that Eastern Airlines had not participated in the arbitration "in a meaningful manner," won't it be difficult to determine the meaningfulness of participation in other cases?

3.   Assume that defense counsel does not believe that her case will settle short of trial. Can she nevertheless use court-ordered arbitration to her client's advantage?

4.   How should a lawyer resolve the difficulties created if her client says that he will not meaningfully participate in a court-ordered arbitration?

5.   Judge Sarokin states: "Furthermore, [defendants'] conduct can serve to discourage the poorer litigant and diminish his or her resolve to proceed to final judgment." However, aren't poorer litigants discouraged from proceeding to final judgment by the requirement of arbitration, rather than by defendants' behavior in an arbitration proceeding?

B. CONTRACTING OUT OF THE COURTS: PRIVATE AGREEMENTS TO ARBITRATE

Gilling v. Eastern Airlines involved a judicial requirement that the parties engage in an ADR process before the dispute could be heard at trial. The current version of the mandatory arbitration requirement of the United States District Court for the District of New Jersey provides:

> Subject to the exceptions set forth in L.Civ.R. 201.1(d)(2), the Clerk shall designate and process for compulsory arbitration any civil action pending before the Court where the relief sought consists only of money damages not in excess of $150,000 exclusive of interest and costs and any claim for punitive damages.

Rule 201.1(d)(1) of the United States District Court for the District of New Jersey.

In addition to such across-the-board requirements, individual judges may strongly suggest, if not require, that parties engage in an ADR process. Such efforts are, in fact, authorized and encouraged by the Federal Rules. Rule 16(c)(2)(I) provides: "At any pretrial conference, the court may consider and take appropriate action on * * * settling the case and using special procedures to assist in resolving the dispute when authorized by statute or local rule." In addition, Rule 16(c)(2)(L) states: "At any pretrial conference, the court may consider and take appropriate action on * * * adopting special procedures for managing potentially difficult or protracted actions that may involve complex issues, multiple parties, difficult legal questions, or unusual proof problems." Finally, Rule 16(c)(2)(P) more generally states: "At any pretrial conference, the court may consider and take appropriate action on * * * facilitating in other ways the just, speedy, and inexpensive disposition of the action."

But parties often will utilize arbitration or another form of ADR not because the court required this, but because the parties themselves contractually agreed to submit any disputes to arbitration rather than to the courts. Most of us enter into contracts containing arbitration clauses when we finance a car, buy insurance, an airline ticket, or other goods or services, or take a new job. Contract disputes more and more commonly are required to be heard in arbitration rather than in court.

As discussed in Chapter 7 concerning class actions, *supra* pp. 582–594, the Supreme Court has consistently upheld private contracts by which the parties agree to submit contractual disputes to arbitration rather than to the courts. In *AT & T Mobility LLC v. Concepcion*, 563 U.S. 333 (2011), the Court held that the Federal Arbitration Act preempted California law invalidating contracts that precluded class actions in arbitration. More recently, in *American Express Co. v. Italian Colors Restaurant* 133 S.Ct. 2304, 2307 (2013), the Court concluded that "a contractual waiver of class arbitration is enforceable under the Federal Arbitration Act [even] when the plaintiff's cost of individually arbitrating a federal statutory claim exceeds the potential recovery."

There are, however, some limits to the contractual arbitration provisions that the courts will enforce. In a case preceding *Conception*, the United States Court of Appeals for the Ninth Circuit affirmed a district judge's refusal to enforce a contractual arbitration clause he found unconscionable under California law. *Ferguson v. Countrywide Credit Indus., Inc.*, 298 F.3d 778 (9th Cir. 2002). The judge found that the plaintiff employee was in an unequal bargaining position without the ability to negotiate about the clause; the clause required arbitration of claims an employee would be most likely to bring but not those claims the employer would be most likely to bring against the employee; the employee could be required to pay several thousand dollars in arbitration fees; and the contract's one-sided discovery limitations favored the employer.

However, in *Carter v. Countrywide Credit Indus., Inc.*, 362 F.3d 294 (5th Cir. 2004), the United States Court of Appeals for the Fifth Circuit upheld an identical arbitration provision. The Court of Appeals distinguished *Ferguson* as follows:

> [T]he *Ferguson* court explicitly relied on California state law in determining that the arbitration agreement was unconscionable whereas here, both parties acknowledge that Texas law should apply. * * * California law and Texas law differ significantly, with the former being more hostile to the enforcement of arbitration agreements than the latter. * * * Given this dramatic difference between the two states' laws, *Ferguson* is hardly persuasive in applying Texas law.

362 F.3d 294, 301 (5th Cir. 2004).

Is it a good thing that contracts increasingly require that any claim arising from that contract must be resolved in arbitration rather than in a court of law?

VIII. CONCLUSION

Even after the close of discovery, there are many ways that a civil action can be resolved short of trial. If the defendant does not appropriately respond to court orders or its litigation duties, the plaintiff may be able to secure a default judgment against the defendant. The plaintiff may decide to voluntarily dismiss the action pursuant to Rule 41(a), or the defendant may be able to obtain an involuntary dismissal pursuant to Rule 41(b). An action also may be resolved prior to trial through Rule 56 summary judgment, which can be granted to either the plaintiff or defendant (but is most commonly sought by a defendant asserting that "there is no genuine dispute as to any material fact and [it] is entitled to judgment as a matter of law").

The last step before trial in the federal courts is the final pretrial conference, at which a final pretrial order will be discussed and which will provide the roadmap for trial. However, even after the entry of the final pretrial order, the action may be settled—either by negotiation between the parties' counsel or after referral to an ADR procedure. Assuming that settlement does not result from such a procedure, the lawyers will focus on the jury or the judge who will actually resolve the parties' disputed claims. The judge and jury are the subject of the next chapter of this text.

IX. CHAPTER ASSESSMENT

A. Multiple-Choice Questions. Answer the following questions, reviewing the sections of the chapter noted in connection with each question.

1. A patient enters a hospital for a major surgical procedure and signs a form stating that he will "promptly pay all charges for medical treatment provided." After a hospital stay of several weeks, the patient

is discharged, fully recovers, and returns to work full-time. The hospital sends the patient a bill for $80,000 for the medical services, to which the patient does not respond. After unsuccessfully attempting to convince the patient to pay his bill, the hospital files a federal diversity action seeking $80,000 for the unpaid medical bills.

Because the patient neither responds to the complaint nor appears in the action, the clerk enters a default against him. The hospital then files a motion for default judgment, including an affidavit containing the bill and the patient's signed agreement to pay all charges.

Review Section II and choose the best answer from the following choices:

(a) Because the motion is for a sum certain and the patient is a competent adult who has not appeared in the action, the clerk can enter a default judgment against the patient.

(b) Because the patient has not entered an appearance in the action, only the court can enter a default judgment against him.

(c) Because the patient has not entered an appearance in the action, a default judgment only can be entered after a hearing before which the patient is given seven days' notice.

(d) Because the patient has a due process right to contest the hospital bill, neither the clerk nor the court can enter default judgment against him.

2.   An employee files a class action against her employer, alleging that the employer discriminated against a class of 100 employees on the basis of their race. The employer immediately moves to dismiss the class allegations of the complaint. The court permits the parties to engage in two months of discovery and then, after a four-day hearing, certifies the action as a class action. The employee then files a notice with the court that he is dismissing his action without prejudice.

Review Section III(A) and choose the best answer from the following choices:

(a) Because the employer has not filed an answer or a motion for summary judgment, the employee can dismiss her action by filing a notice of dismissal.

(b) Because the employee has not filed her claims in a prior action, she can dismiss her action by filing a notice of dismissal.

(c) Because the action has been certified as a class action, the employee cannot dismiss it without a court order.

(d) Because the court and parties have invested a significant amount of time in this action, the employee cannot dismiss it without a court order.

3.   A car and a bus are in an accident, and the driver of the car files a federal diversity action against the bus company. In its answer,

the bus company pleads a counterclaim seeking recovery for damages to the bus.

The driver files a motion for summary judgment on the bus company's counterclaim. In support of her motion, the driver files an affidavit stating that she was driving within the speed limit, in her lane, and was operating her car safely at the time of the accident. The bus company files no affidavit or other evidence in opposition to the motion for summary judgment, but its attorney asserts in a brief opposing the motion that "the facts at trial will establish that the driver of the car was driving negligently at the time of the accident."

Review Section IV and choose the best answer from the following choices:

(a) Because summary judgment is not available on a counterclaim, the court should deny the motion.

(b) Because there is a genuine dispute as to a material fact, the court should deny the motion.

(c) Because there is no genuine dispute as to a material fact and the car driver is entitled to judgment as a matter of law, the court should grant the motion.

(d) Because the car driver's affidavit is not made on her personal knowledge, the court should grant the motion.

4. An employee brings a wage and hour claim against a company in federal district court. After completion of discovery, the judge sets a date for the final pretrial conference. In his order setting the date, the judge states: "Because I would like to hear from the parties about possible settlement of this action, both the plaintiff and a representative of the defendant with authority to make and accept settlement offers are ordered to be present at the pretrial conference."

The employee, the employee's attorney, and the company's attorney attend the pretrial conference. When the judge asks the company's attorney where the company representative is, the attorney responds, "I'm sorry, Your Honor. I told my client that I would handle this conference by myself, although I don't have authority to discuss settlement today."

Review Section V(B) and (C) and choose the best answer from the following choices:

(a) Because the final pretrial conference is to prepare an action for trial, the judge could not require that a representative of the company be present at the pretrial conference.

(b) Because the company's lawyer was present at the pretrial conference, the judge cannot sanction the company for failing to send a representative to the pretrial conference.

(c) Because a lawyer always has authority to accept or reject settlement offers on behalf of a client, the judge cannot sanction the company.

(d) Because the judge had ordered a representative of the company to attend the pretrial conference, the judge can sanction the company.

5.   A consumer enters into a contract with a company under which the company agrees to provide cable television service to the consumer for a monthly fee. The parties' contract, which was drafted by the company's attorneys, contains a clause providing:

> Any dispute relating to this contract shall be resolved by arbitration, and judgment on the award rendered by the arbitrator(s) may be entered in any court having competent jurisdiction thereof.

One day before the opening of the professional football season, the consumer learns that his television package does not include professional football. The consumer had invited a large group of business associates to his house to watch some games, and he has to cancel this party when he cannot obtain suitable cable service in time for the games. As a result of the cancelled party, the consumer loses several major business clients.

The consumer files a diversity action against the company in federal court. In response to the complaint, the company files a motion asking the judge to compel arbitration pursuant to the arbitration clause of the contract.

Review Section VII(B) and choose the best answer from the following choices:

(a) Because the consumer agreed to submit any contractual disputes to arbitration, the judge should enforce the parties' arbitration clause.

(b) Because arbitration is better suited to the resolution of the parties' claims than are the courts, the judge should enforce the parties' arbitration clause.

(c) Because the consumer has a constitutional right to present his claims to a federal court, the judge should not enforce the parties' arbitration clause.

(d) Because the consumer had no real bargaining power with respect to the company's drafting of this contract, the judge should not enforce the parties' arbitration clause.

B.   Essay Questions.

1.   Can't We Just Start Over?

Two years after an automobile accident involving Peter Plaintiff and Denise Defendant, Plaintiff files a diversity action in federal district court. Plaintiff seeks $150,000 in damages in his complaint. Defendant, who was not hurt in the accident, files an answer in which she includes a counterclaim for $15,000 in damages to her car from the accident.

The action is assigned to Judge Skeptical, who is reputed to favor defendants in personal injury actions and move cases to trial very quickly. Plaintiff's lawyer therefore advises Plaintiff to voluntarily dismiss her action and refile her claims in another federal court.

Please answer the following questions concerning such a possible dismissal.

(a)   What options are available to Plaintiff to voluntarily dismiss her action?

(b)   If Plaintiff does voluntarily dismiss her action, what will be the effect of that dismissal on any future federal action?

(c)   If Plaintiff is able to voluntarily dismiss her action and refile that action in another federal court, what defenses is Defendant likely to assert in that second action?

2.   We Promised You What?

Sally Salesperson worked for many years for Acme, Inc. She became good friends with her former supervisor, Sandra Supervisor, who at the office Holiday Party several years ago told Sally, "Sally, if you reach your sales goals for the next three years, you might get a nice promotion."

Soon thereafter Sandra Supervisor retires and moves to another state. Sally reaches her sales goals for the next three years, and then asks her current supervisor, Stanley Supervisor, about the promotion. Stanley tells Sally that such a promise would be contrary to company policy and denies that Sandra Supervisor or anyone else ever made such a promise.

Sally then files a diversity action in federal court, seeking damages stemming from the alleged contractual breach. During discovery, Sally is deposed and, in answer to the question, "Why did you think that you would be promoted if you met your sales goals for three years?" states: "I think that my former supervisor, Sandra, may have told me that several years ago at the office Holiday Party." Under further questioning, Sally can point to no other evidence that she was promised a promotion. Other than answers to interrogatories and production of a few documents, no additional discovery is conducted.

Sixty days after the close of discovery, Acme, Inc. brings a motion for summary judgment. Acme offers no affidavits or other evidence in support of its motion, but points to Sally's deposition statement as to why she believed she was entitled to a promotion.

In opposition to the motion for summary judgment, Sally points to the allegations of her complaint and argues in his brief that "the jury is much more likely to believe my side of this story than to believe my current supervisor—who has only worked for Acme one year."

    (a)   Should the court grant Acme's motion for summary judgment?

    (b)   What is Sally's best argument in opposition to the motion?

CHAPTER 12

JUDGES AND JURIES: "WHO DECIDES?"

I. INTRODUCTION

Once the final pretrial conference has been held and the final pretrial order entered, the next step in the litigation process is trial. But trial before whom? Will a party's claims or defenses receive a more sympathetic hearing before a judge or a jury? A party may have a right under the Seventh Amendment to demand a trial by jury, but so will other parties. Thus, even if one party prefers a trial to the court (before the judge alone), a jury may hear the case if another party demands such a trial.

Even if a jury hears the case, a judge will preside over the jury trial, making key decisions such as whether specific evidence can be heard by the jury and whether there is a legal basis to take the case from the jury and decide it without the jury's participation. Usually federal civil actions are randomly assigned to individual judges, but the parties may be able to consent to trial by a federal magistrate judge rather than a federal district judge.

Whether the action is assigned to a magistrate or district judge, the parties may ask that judge to step aside, or recuse himself, if his impartiality might reasonably be questioned. If the case was tried to a jury, there also may be a reason to challenge that jury's verdict. However, there are strict limits on the ability of an individual juror to offer evidence to impeach the jury's verdict.

The selection of the trier of fact, and challenges to the judge or jury selected, are governed by statutory and constitutional law—as well as by common law tradition and judicial precedent. "Who decides?" individual cases is not only important to the parties to those cases, but to a judicial system that, in the words of Rule 1, seeks "to secure the just, speedy, and inexpensive determination of every action and proceeding."

II. JUDGE OR JURY?

In certain civil actions, the parties have a choice as to whether their action will be decided by a judge or a jury. They also may have a choice as to the type of federal judge who will decide the facts at trial or preside at a trial that will be decided by a jury.

A. WHICH JUDGE WILL HEAR THE CASE?

In contrast to judges in many state courts, federal district judges are appointed for life, or, as Article III, Section 1 of the Constitution provides, these judges "shall hold their Offices during good Behavior." But Article III district judges are not the only federal trial judges.

The office of United States Magistrate Judge is established by 28 U.S.C. §§ 631–39. In contrast to federal district judges, who are appointed by the President, Sections 631(a) and 631(e) of Title 28 provide for the appointment of magistrate judges by the federal district judges of each United States District Court for a term of eight years (although the term of part-time magistrate judges is four years).

Section 636 of Title 28 defines the jurisdiction and powers of magistrate judges. These judges have the power to try and to impose sentence in certain federal misdemeanor actions, hear pretrial matters in civil and criminal actions when designated to do so by a federal district judge, and, as designated by a district judge, submit to that judge proposed findings and recommendations on specific civil and criminal matters. In addition, with the consent of the parties, Section 636(c) authorizes a magistrate judge to conduct trial proceedings. Several of the opinions included in this text were written by federal magistrate judges, who handle a great amount of discovery and other pretrial matters in many United States District Courts. Parties frequently consent to have their actions tried by a magistrate judge because of the high quality of these judges and because such judges may be able to try an action sooner than the federal district judge to whom the action has been assigned. The major differences between United States district judges and magistrate judges are set forth in Figure 12–1.

FIGURE 12–1
UNITED STATES DISTRICT JUDGES AND
MAGISTRATE JUDGES

	Appointed by:	Term of Office:	Jurisdiction:
District Judge	President	Life ("during good Behavior")	Full civil and criminal jurisdiction (as provided by statute and Article III of the Constitution)
Magistrate Judge	District Court Judges within the District	8 years (full-time Magistrate Judges); 4 years (part-time Magistrate Judges)	Pretrial (as designated by District Judge) and Civil Trials (with party consent). 28 U.S.C. § 636

Not only can the parties consent to have their action tried by an available magistrate judge, 28 U.S.C. § 636(c)(1), but, if they do so, they may appeal from the final judgment entered by that judge "in the same manner as an appeal from any other judgment of a district court." 28 U.S.C. § 636(c)(3). However, the parties still must decide whether to demand that a jury find the contested facts at trial.

B. SHOULD A JURY DECIDE THE FACTS?

There is much popular mythology about whether judges or juries are more sympathetic to certain types of claims and certain types of parties. Stories about "runaway juries" suggest that jurors are easily swayed by emotion, sympathize with plaintiffs, and dislike corporate defendants. Judges, on the other hand, are supposedly less affected by emotional pleas and more understanding of corporate and governmental defendants.

These common preconceptions may or may not be true—depending on the specific judge, jury, parties, and types of claims in question. One comprehensive study of 11 years of national data from the federal courts offered surprising comparisons of actions that were tried to a jury with actions that were tried to a judge. The authors of this study found that, in trials of medical malpractice and products liability actions, the plaintiffs won considerably more often in bench trials than in jury trials. The study also found that, in several types of personal injury actions, the mean recovery in bench trials was higher than in jury trials. Clermont & Eisenberg, "Trial by Jury or Judge: Transcending Empiricism," 77 *Cornell L. Rev.* 1124, 1125–26 (1992).

The experienced trial attorney knows the proclivities of the judge who might try her case and also has a sense of the types of jurors likely to be selected if a jury is demanded. Rather than relying on conventional wisdom or national studies, she will focus on the best decision-makers for her client and choose accordingly. But, first, she must determine whether her client even has the opportunity to demand a jury.

III. THE RIGHT TO JURY TRIAL

In many cases the parties' lawyers will believe it advantageous for one party or another to try its claims before a jury, rather than to a single judge. The question then becomes whether the parties are entitled to demand that a jury try that action or individual claims within the action.

A. THE SEVENTH AMENDMENT RIGHT TO JURY TRIAL

Specific federal statutes provide a right to request a jury to resolve claims under that statute. In many other situations, the right to jury trial is not so clear. In such situations, one or more of the parties may assert the right to a jury under the Seventh Amendment to the United States Constitution.

The Seventh Amendment provides:

> In suits at common law, where the value in controversy shall exceed twenty dollars, the right of trial by jury shall be preserved, and no fact tried by jury, shall be otherwise reexamined in any Court of the United States, than according to the rules of the common law.

The first phrase of the Seventh Amendment ("In suits at common law, where the value in controversy shall exceed twenty dollars, the right of trial by jury shall be preserved") is the Right to Jury Clause that guarantees a right to jury trial in certain cases. The second clause of the Seventh Amendment, the Reexamination Clause, protects facts determined by a jury from later being overturned by a court.

The Right to Jury Clause of the Seventh Amendment is unique in that it does not create a specific right but instead "preserves" rights in existence at the time of the adoption of the Bill of Rights in 1791. At that time, juries were available only in suits filed in courts of law—in which legal relief such as damages could be sought. If a plaintiff needed equitable relief, such as an injunction, that relief had to be sought in a court of equity, in which juries were not available.

So, if a modern plaintiff asserts in a federal diversity action a common law claim for more than $20.00, the parties to that claim will be entitled to a jury. This is because such a claim would have been considered a legal claim in 1791 and such legal claims carried with them a right to a jury. If the plaintiff seeks an injunction, which historically would have been filed in chancery court and not carried with it a right to a jury, there would be no right to jury trial to preserve—and thus no right to jury trial in a modern civil action.

B. MODERN INTERPRETATION OF THE SEVENTH AMENDMENT

What if a civil action includes both legal and equitable claims? In *Beacon Theatres, Inc. v. Westover*, 359 U.S. 500 (1959), Fox West Coast Theaters brought an antitrust action against Beacon Theaters seeking (1) a declaratory judgment that it had not violated antitrust laws and (2) an injunction prohibiting Beacon from instituting suit against it until after the court had determined its declaratory judgment claim. In its answer, Beacon asserted a counterclaim for triple damages under the antitrust laws and demanded a jury trial on the counterclaim. Acting pursuant to Federal Rules of Civil Procedure 42(b) and 57, the district court determined that it would decide Fox's injunction and declaratory judgment claims before convening a jury to try Beacon's counterclaim.

The Supreme Court held that, because the judge would be determining issues common to Fox's equitable claim and Beacon's legal counterclaim (thus binding the jury on these common issues), Judge Westover could not try the equitable, non-jury claim first. The Court concluded, "[A] long-standing principle of equity dictates that only under the most imperative circumstances, circumstances which in view of the flexible procedures of the Federal Rules we cannot now anticipate, can the right to a jury trial of legal issues be lost through prior determination of equitable claims." 359 U.S. at 510–11.

Several years later, in *Dairy Queen, Inc. v. Wood,* 369 U.S. 469 (1962), the Court was faced with a case in which the plaintiff sought temporary and permanent injunctions and an accounting—traditionally an equitable remedy that would be awarded in chancery court. The Court concluded that the defendant was nevertheless entitled to a jury trial:

> The respondents' contention that this money claim is "purely equitable" is based primarily upon the fact that their complaint is cast in terms of an "accounting," rather than in terms of an action for "debt" or "damages." But the constitutional right to trial by jury cannot be made to depend upon the choice of words used in the pleadings. The necessary prerequisite to the right to maintain a suit for an equitable accounting, like all other equitable remedies, is, as we pointed out in *Beacon Theatres*, the absence of an adequate remedy at law. Consequently, in order to maintain such a suit on a cause of action cognizable at law, as this one is, the plaintiff must be able to show that the "accounts between the parties" are of such a "complicated nature" that only a court of equity can satisfactorily unravel them. In view of the powers given to District Courts by Federal Rule of Civil Procedure 53(b) to appoint masters to assist the jury in those exceptional cases where the legal issues are too complicated for the jury adequately to handle alone, the burden of such a showing is considerably increased and it will indeed be a rare case in which it can be met. But be that as it may, this is certainly not such a case. A jury, under proper instructions from the court, could readily determine the recovery, if any, to be had here, whether the theory finally settled upon is that of breach of contract, that of trademark infringement, or any combination of the two. The legal remedy cannot be characterized as inadequate merely because the measure of damages may necessitate a look into petitioner's business records.

369 U.S. at 477–79. Although the district judge could grant a preliminary injunction pending final adjudication of the parties' claims on the merits, 369 U.S. at 479 n.20, because of the common factual issues contained in the parties' legal and equitable claims, the jury had

to first determine the legal claims before the judge considered any equitable claims. 369 U.S. at 479.

In *Dairy Queen* Justice Black noted that the parties' accounts were not too complicated for a jury to understand. But what if they were? In *Ross v. Bernhard*, 396 U.S. 531, 538 (1970), the Supreme Court suggested in a footnote that there might be a "complexity exception" to the Seventh Amendment right to jury trial: "As our cases indicate, the 'legal' nature of an issue is determined by considering, first, the pre-merger custom with reference to such questions; second, the remedy sought; and, third, the practical abilities and limitations of juries."

The possibility of a complexity exception to the Seventh Amendment was considered by the United States Court of Appeals for the Third Circuit in *In re Japanese Elec. Products Antitrust Litig.*, 631 F.2d 1069 (3d Cir. 1980), in which the court was presented with the following question: "In an action for treble damages under the antitrust and antidumping laws, do the parties have a right to trial by jury without regard to the practical ability of a jury to decide the case properly?" 631 F.2d at 1071. The court answered this question as follows:

> In suits at law, a court should deny jury trial on due process grounds only in exceptional cases when the court, after careful inquiry into the factors contributing to complexity, determines that a jury would be unable to understand the case and decide it rationally. Before any such denial, due consideration should be given to the particular strengths of the jury in deciding complex cases, to the possible use of special trial techniques to increase a jury's capabilities, and to methods of reducing the suit's complexity

631 F.2d at 1089.

In a later case the Supreme Court itself quite narrowly limited its suggestion in *Ross* of a complexity exception to the Seventh Amendment:

> This quite distinct inquiry into whether Congress has permissibly entrusted the resolution of certain disputes to an administrative agency or specialized court of equity, and whether jury trials would impair the functioning of the legislative scheme, appears to be what the Court contemplated when, in *Ross v. Bernhard,* 396 U.S. 531, 538, n. 10 (1970), it identified "the practical abilities and limitations of juries" as an additional factor to be consulted in determining whether the Seventh Amendment confers a jury trial right.

Granfinanciera, S.A. v. Nordberg, 492 U.S. 33, 42 (1989).

In creating a new cause of action, Congress can explicitly provide for a jury trial—thus creating a statutory right to jury trial. When Congress is not so clear, or may even appear to have rejected a right to jury trial, the courts must decide whether there is nevertheless a Seventh Amendment constitutional right to jury trial for claims brought under the congressional statute.

If a cause of action existed in 1791, it should be relatively easy to determine whether the claim is legal (with a right to jury trial) or equitable (with no jury). However, what about the many claims created or recognized in the more than 200 years since the adoption of the Seventh Amendment? The Supreme Court has recognized, "The right to a jury trial includes more than the common-law forms of action recognized in 1791; the phrase 'Suits at common law' refers to 'suits in which *legal* rights [are] to be ascertained and determined, in contradistinction to those where equitable rights alone [are] recognized, and equitable remedies [are] administered.' " *Chauffeurs, Teamsters & Helpers, Local No. 391 v. Terry*, 494 U.S. 558, 564 (1990) (quoting *Parsons v. Bedford*, 3 Pet. 433, 447 (1830)).

When faced with an employee's claim for backpay for a union's alleged breach of the duty of fair representation, the Court stated:

> The right [to a jury] extends to causes of action created by Congress. Since the merger of the systems of law and equity, this Court has carefully preserved the right to trial by jury where legal rights are at stake. As the Court noted in *Beacon Theatres, Inc. v. Westover,* 359 U.S. 500, 501 (1959), " 'Maintenance of the jury as a fact-finding body is of such importance and occupies so firm a place in our history and jurisprudence that any seeming curtailment of the right to a jury trial should be scrutinized with the utmost care' " (quoting *Dimick v. Schiedt,* 293 U.S. 474, 486 (1935)).
>
> To determine whether a particular action will resolve legal rights, we examine both the nature of the issues involved and the remedy sought. "First, we compare the statutory action to 18th-century actions brought in the courts of England prior to the merger of the courts of law and equity. Second, we examine the remedy sought and determine whether it is legal or equitable in nature." The second inquiry is the more important in our analysis.

Chauffeurs, Teamsters & Helpers, Local No. 391 v. Terry, 494 U.S. 558, 565 (1990) (quoting *Tull v. United States,* 481 U.S. 412, 417–418 (1987)). In *Terry,* itself, the Court held that the remedy of backpay in a suit alleging breach of the duty of fair representation was legal in nature and that the parties therefore were entitled to a jury on this claim.

C. ASSERTING (OR WAIVING) THE RIGHT TO JURY TRIAL

The fact that a party has a constitutional right to jury trial does not mean that that party cannot waive the right. Rule 38(b) of the Federal Rules of Civil Procedure provides:

> On any issue triable of right by a jury, a party may demand a jury trial by:
>
> > (1) serving the other parties with a written demand—which may be included in a pleading—no later than 14 days after the last pleading directed to the issue is served; and
> >
> > (2) filing the demand in accordance with Rule 5(d).

Rule 38(d) explicitly provides the consequences for not filing a timely demand for jury trial: "A party waives a jury trial unless its demand is properly served and filed."

If a claim is legal, rather than equitable, and a right to jury trial thus attaches, any party can demand a jury on that claim. If a defendant would like a jury determination on a particular claim but the plaintiff already has filed a jury demand on that claim, the defendant need not itself make a jury demand. In order to protect the defendant in such a situation, the final sentence of Rule 38(d) provides: "A proper demand may be withdrawn only if the parties consent."

The right to jury trial is not only claim-specific, but issue-specific as well. Rule 38(c) provides:

> In its demand, a party may specify the issues that it wishes to have tried by a jury; otherwise, it is considered to have demanded a jury trial on all the issues so triable. If the party has demanded a jury trial on only some issues, any other party may—within 14 days after being served with the demand or within a shorter time ordered by the court—serve a demand for a jury trial on any other or all factual issues triable by jury.

It may be difficult to determine in some cases whether a party has a right to a jury. After making such a determination, a party should be careful to assert its demand for a jury on the specific issues in question in a timely and proper manner.

IV. SELECTION AND COMPOSITION OF JURIES

Assuming that the parties have a right to demand a jury, what will that jury look like and how will it be selected? Each United States District Court is required to have a written plan for the random and non-discriminatory selection of jurors from a fair cross section of the community in which the district court sits. 28 U.S.C. § 1863. These plans specify the sources from which the names of prospective jurors are drawn, such as lists of registered voters, drivers, or property owners. *Id.* at § 1863(b)(2). From this pool of prospective jurors the names of individual jurors are randomly drawn and those individuals are sent juror qualification forms to be returned within 10 days. 28 U.S.C. § 1864(a). A judge or the clerk of court then reviews the forms and determines which individuals are qualified to serve as jurors.

Jurors are to be deemed qualified unless they fall within one of the categories for exclusion specified in 28 U.S.C. § 1865(b). They will be considered unqualified, for instance, if they are not physically or mentally capable of satisfactory jury service or are unable to speak English. From those determined to be qualified jurors, names are periodically drawn for specific jury panels. These individuals are summoned to the courthouse and are questioned by the judge, and usually the lawyers, in an effort to select the jury that will try a particular case.

At common law, juries consisted of 12 jurors. This is still the case in many state courts and in federal criminal trials. However, in civil trials in the federal courts there typically are only six jurors. In its 1973 decision in *Colgrove v. Battin*, 413 U.S. 149 (1973), the Supreme Court, by a 5–4 margin, held that six-member federal civil juries were constitutional and did not violate the Rules Enabling Act, 28 U.S.C. §§ 2071–2077, or Federal Rules of Civil Procedure 48 and 83.

In his dissent in *Colgrove*, Justice Marshall cited social science research showing the real-world consequences of reducing juries from 12 to 6 members:

> Although I consider it ultimately irrelevant to the constitutional issue, it is still of some interest that variations in jury size do seem to produce variations in function and result. It is, of course, intuitively obvious that the smaller the size of the jury, the less likely it is to represent a fair cross-section of community viewpoints. What is less obvious but nonetheless statistically demonstrable is that the difference between a 12-man and six-man jury in this respect is quite dramatic and likely to produce different results. Professor Zeisel, perhaps our leading authority on the civil jury, has demonstrated this fact through use of a model in which he assumes that 90% of a hypothetical community shares the same viewpoint, while 10% has a different viewpoint. Of 100 12-man juries picked randomly from such a community, 72 would have at least one member of the minority group, while of the 100 six-man juries so selected, only 47 would have minority representation. Moreover, the differences in minority representation produce significant differences in result. Professor Zeisel posits a case in which the community is divided into six groups of equal size with respect to the monetary value they place on a given personal injury claim,

with one-sixth evaluating the claim at $1,000, another sixth at $2,000, etc. He also assumes that the damages a jury will award lie close to the average assessment of the damages each individual juror would choose. If one accepts these hypotheses, "(i)t is easy to see that the six-member juries show a considerably wider variation of 'verdicts' than the twelve-member juries. For instance, 68.4% of the twelve-member jury evaluations fall between $3,000 and $4,000, while only 51.4% of the six-member jury evaluations fall in this range. Almost 16% of the six-member juries will reach verdicts that will fall into the extreme levels of more than $4,500 or less than $2,500, as against only a little over 4% of the twelve-member juries. * * * This is the result of a more general principle that is by now well known to readers of such statistics as public opinion polls—namely, that the size of any sample is inversely related to its margin of error." Zeisel, . . . And Then There Were None: The Diminution of the Federal Jury, 38 *U.Chi.L.Rev.* 710, 717–718 (1971).

Colgrove v. Battin, 413 U.S. 149, 167 n.1 (1973) (Marshall, J., dissenting). Nevertheless, six-person federal juries were upheld by the majority in *Colgrove*, and they are common in the federal courts.

Rule 48 of the Federal Rules of Civil Procedure provides: "A jury must begin with at least 6 and no more than 12 members, and each juror must participate in the verdict unless excused under Rule 47(c)." Rule 47(c) provides that "[d]uring trial or deliberation, the court may excuse a juror for good cause." Rule 47(c) thus gives the judge authority to excuse a juror if he becomes seriously ill or in the event of a serious family emergency. The fact that the juror is properly excused, however, does not mean that the remaining jurors can render a valid verdict. Typically an alternative juror or two will hear the case and can be substituted for a juror who must be dismissed. If, though, the alternate jurors already have been dismissed because the action has been submitted to the jury for its consideration, there may be fewer than six jurors left to render a verdict. In this situation, the case must be retried unless the parties stipulate to a verdict by fewer than six jurors as is authorized by Rule 48(b) ("Unless the parties stipulate otherwise, the verdict must be unanimous and must be returned by a jury of at least 6 members.").

A. CHALLENGES FOR CAUSE

After their juror qualification forms have been reviewed to determine that individuals are qualified to serve as jurors, a panel of such qualified jurors is called to the courthouse so that individuals can be considered for jury service in a specific civil action. Federal Rule of Civil Procedure 47(a) provides:

The court may permit the parties or their attorneys to examine prospective jurors or may itself do so. If the court examines the jurors, it must permit the parties or their attorneys to make any further inquiry it considers proper, or must itself ask any of their additional questions it considers proper.

This examination by the judge or lawyers (typically, by both) is referred to as "voir dire" (from Law French, "to speak the truth"). This questioning is to determine the suitability of a potential juror serving on the jury in a specific case. Even though it has been determined that an individual meets the statutory qualifications for jury service set forth in 28 U.S.C. § 1865(b), there still may be reasons why that individual should not hear a particular case. For instance, if in a civil rights action against the local police, a potential juror is a police officer, good friend of the plaintiff, or the spouse of one of the lawyers in the case, the judge will dismiss that potential juror from serving on this particular jury "for cause." For cause challenges are appropriate when a juror manifests actual or implied bias or prejudice. *Government of Virgin Islands v. Felix*, 569 F.2d 1274, 1277 n. 5 (3d Cir. 1978).

Because of the seriousness of actual or implied bias, there is no limit to challenges for cause, which are exercised by the judge. In addition to challenges for cause, each party in federal court is given up to three "peremptory challenges," which are exercised by the lawyers for any reason or for no specific reason—so long as they are not exercised for a discriminatory reason based on race or gender (and, perhaps, other protected classes of individuals). The court can limit several plaintiffs or several defendants to three peremptory challenges (in total) or allow additional challenges when there is more than one party on the same side of an action. 28 U.S.C. § 1870.

The differences between for cause and peremptory challenges are shown in Figure 12–2.

FIGURE 12–2
CHALLENGES FOR CAUSE AND PEREMPTORY CHALLENGES

	Challenges for Cause	Peremptory Challenges
Number of Challenges	Unlimited	3 per party (28 U.S.C. § 1870)
Who Exercises Challenges	Judge	Lawyers
Reason for Challenges	Potential juror is prejudiced or biased	No limit, but potential jurors cannot be challenged for unconstitutional, discriminatory reason

B. PEREMPTORY CHALLENGES

Initially, a lawyer may attempt to convince the judge to excuse a potential juror for cause. If the judge does not, the lawyer may need to use one of her limited peremptory challenges to exclude that individual from service on the jury. Just how an attorney can use peremptory challenges is the subject of this subsection of this chapter.

1. PEREMPTORY CHALLENGES: THE TRADITION

Traditionally lawyers prided themselves on their ability to pick (or, actually, unpick) a jury. A major part of this skill was purported to stem from a lawyer's intuition about potential jurors and her ability to "read" people based on their looks, mannerisms, and answers to a few questions from the judge or lawyers during voir dire. In this process, lawyers relied upon stereotypes about different types of people, presuming that individuals had the characteristic views and opinions of the larger groups to which they belonged. In the excerpt from the article that follows, one of America's finest trial lawyers explained the stereotypes and perceptions that guided his own efforts to pick a jury that would be most sympathetic to his clients.

Clarence Darrow, "Attorney for the Defense"
Esquire Magazine, May 1936, at 36, 36–37, 211

Choosing jurors is always a delicate task. The more a lawyer knows of life, human nature, psychology, and the reactions of the human emotions, the better he is equipped for the subtle selection of his so-called "twelve men, good and true." In this undertaking, everything pertaining to the prospective juror needs to be questioned and weighed: his nationality, his business, religion, politics, social standing, family ties, friends, habits of life and thought; the books and newspapers he likes and reads, and many more matters that combine to make a man; all of these qualities and experiences have left their effect on ideas, beliefs and fancies that inhabit his mind. Understanding of all this cannot be obtained too bluntly. It usually requires finesse, subtlety and guesswork. Involved in it all is the juror's method of speech, the kind of clothes he wears, the style of haircut, and, above all, his business associates, residence and origin.

* * *

Let us assume that we represent one of "the underdogs" because of injuries received, or because of an indictment brought by what the prosecutors name themselves, "the state." Then what sort of men will we seek? An Irishman is called into the box for examination. There is no reason for asking about his religion; he is Irish; that is enough. We may not agree with his religion, but it matters not; his feelings go deeper than any religion. You should be aware that he is emotional, kindly and sympathetic. If he is chosen as a juror, his imagination will place him in the dock; really, he is trying himself. You would be guilty of malpractice if you got rid of him, except for the strongest reasons.

An Englishman is not so good as an Irishman, but still, he has come through a long tradition of individual rights, and is not afraid to stand alone; in fact, he is never sure that he is right unless the great majority is against him. The German is not so keen about individual rights except where they concern his own way of life; liberty is not a theory, it is a way of living. Still, he wants to do what is right, and he is not afraid. He has not been among us long, his ways are fixed by his race, his habits are still in the making. We need inquire no further. If he is a Catholic, then he loves music and art; he must be emotional, and will want to help you; give him a chance.

If a Presbyterian enters the jury box and carefully rolls up his umbrella, and calmly and critically sits down, let him go. He is cold as the grave; he knows right from wrong, although he seldom finds anything right. He believes in John Calvin and eternal punishments. Get rid of him with the fewest possible words before he contaminates the others; unless you and your clients are Presbyterians you probably are a bad lot, and even though you may be a Presbyterian, your client most likely is guilty.

If possible, the Baptists are more hopeless than the Presbyterians. They, too, are apt to think that the real home of all outsiders is Sheol, and you do not want them on the jury, and the sooner they leave the better.

The Methodists are worth considering; they are nearer the soil. Their religious emotions can be transmuted into love and charity. They are not half bad; even though they will not take a drink, they really do not need it so much as some of their competitors for the seat next to the throne. If chance sets you down between a Methodist and a Baptist, you will move toward the Methodist to keep warm.

Beware of the Lutherans, especially the Scandinavians; they are almost always sure to convict. Either a Lutheran or Scandinavian is unsafe, but if both in one, plead your client guilty and go down the docket. He learns about sinning and punishing from the preacher, and dares not doubt. A person who disobeys must be sent to hell; he has God's word for that.

* * *

Never take a wealthy man on a jury. He will convict, unless the defendant is accused of violating the anti-trust law, selling worthless stocks or bonds, or something of that kind. Next to the Board of Trade, for him, the penitentiary is the most important of all public buildings. These imposing structures stand for capitalism. Civilization could not possibly exist without them. Don't take a man because he is a "good" man; this means nothing. You should find out what he is good *for*. Neither should a man be accepted because he is a bad sort. There are too many ways of being good or bad. If you are defending, you want imaginative individuals. You are not interested in the morals of the juror. If a man is instinctively kind and sympathetic, take him.

————————

2.   PEREMPTORY CHALLENGES: THE POSSIBILITIES FOR ABUSE

As Clarence Darrow suggests, peremptory challenges traditionally could be exercised for any reason or no reason—and the lawyer exercising those challenges did not have to explain why she struck a particular person from the jury pool. This wide-open approach to peremptory challenges, though, was limited by the Supreme Court in *Batson v. Kentucky*, 476 U.S. 79 (1986). In *Batson* Justice Powell wrote for the Court:

> Although a prosecutor ordinarily is entitled to exercise permitted peremptory challenges "for any reason at all, as long as that reason is related to his view concerning the outcome" of the case to be tried, the Equal Protection Clause forbids the prosecutor to challenge potential jurors solely on account of their race or on the assumption that black jurors as a group will be unable impartially to consider the State's case against a black defendant.

479 U.S. at 89, quoting *United States v. Robinson*, 421 F.Supp. 467, 473 (D. Conn.1976), *mandamus granted sub nom. United States v. Newman*, 549 F.2d 240 (2nd Cir. 1977).

The principle that a prosecutor cannot discriminate against potential jurors on the basis of their race seems quite unsurprising. Practical difficulties, though, are presented as to just how such discrimination can be shown. After its decision in *Purkett v. Elem*, 514 U.S. 765 (1995) (per curiam), the Supreme Court was seen to be backing away from a forceful implementation of *Batson*. The majority stated in *Purkett*:

> The prosecutor's proffered explanation in this case—that he struck juror number 22 because he had long, unkempt hair, a mustache, and a beard—is race neutral and satisfies the prosecution's step two burden of articulating a nondiscriminatory reason for the strike. "The wearing of beards is not a characteristic that is peculiar to any race." *EEOC v. Greyhound Lines, Inc.*, 635 F.2d 188, 190, n.3 (CA3 1980). And neither is the growing of long, unkempt hair. Thus, the inquiry properly proceeded to step three, where the state court found that the prosecutor was not motivated by discriminatory intent.

514 U.S. at 769. The Court thus upheld the overruling by a state judge of a *Batson* challenge to the prosecutor's use of peremptory challenges.

However, in *Miller-El v. Dretke*, 545 U.S. 231 (2005), the Supreme Court held that the defendant had shown racial discrimination in the selection of a state jury. In reading Justice Souter's description of the evidence of racial discrimination, consider the way in which Miller-El's attorneys combined numerous pieces of evidence to build the case of discrimination:

> In the course of drawing a jury to try a black defendant, 10 of the 11 qualified black venire panel members were peremptorily struck. At least two of them, Fields and Warren, were ostensibly acceptable to prosecutors seeking a death verdict, and Fields was ideal. The prosecutors' chosen race-neutral reasons for the strikes do not hold up and are so far at odds with the evidence that pretext is the fair conclusion, indicating the very discrimination the explanations were meant to deny.

> The strikes that drew these incredible explanations occurred in a selection process replete with evidence that the prosecutors were selecting and rejecting potential jurors because of race. At least two of the jury shuffles conducted by the State make no sense except as efforts to delay consideration of black jury panelists to the end of the week, when they might not even be reached. The State has in fact never offered any other explanation. Nor has the State denied that disparate lines of questioning were pursued: 53% of black panelists but only 3% of nonblacks were questioned with a graphic script meant to induce qualms about applying the death penalty (and thus explain a strike), and 100% of blacks but only 27% of nonblacks were subjected to a trick question about the minimum acceptable penalty for murder, meant to induce a disqualifying answer. The State's attempts to explain the prosecutors' questioning of particular witnesses on nonracial grounds fit the evidence less well than the racially discriminatory hypothesis.

> If anything more is needed for an undeniable explanation of what was going on, history supplies it. The prosecutors took their cues from a 20-year-old manual of tips on jury selection, as shown by their notes of the race of each potential juror. By the time a jury was chosen, the State had peremptorily challenged 12% of qualified nonblack panel members, but eliminated 91% of the black ones.

> It blinks reality to deny that the State struck Fields and Warren, included in that 91%, because they were black. The strikes correlate with no fact as well as they correlate with race, and they occurred during a selection infected by shuffling

and disparate questioning that race explains better than any race-neutral reason advanced by the State. The State's pretextual positions confirm Miller-El's claim, and the prosecutors' own notes proclaim that the Sparling Manual's emphasis on race was on their minds when they considered every potential juror.

545 U.S. at 265–66.

Nevertheless, showing that peremptory challenges were based on race or another constitutionally-protected classification can be quite difficult in practice. Consider how the principal of non-discrimination bumps into the realities of courtroom practice in the case that follows.

3.   *BATSON* IN A CIVIL CONTEXT: *J.E.B. V. ALABAMA*

J.E.B. v. Alabama

Supreme Court of the United States, 1994
511 U.S. 127

■ JUSTICE BLACKMUN delivered the opinion of the Court.

In *Batson v. Kentucky,* 476 U.S. 79 (1986), this Court held that the Equal Protection Clause of the Fourteenth Amendment governs the exercise of peremptory challenges by a prosecutor in a criminal trial. The Court explained that although a defendant has "no right to a 'petit jury composed in whole or in part of persons of his own race,'" *id.,* at 85, quoting *Strauder v. West Virginia,* 100 U.S. 303, 305 (1880), the "defendant does have the right to be tried by a jury whose members are selected pursuant to nondiscriminatory criteria." 476 U.S., at 85–86. Since *Batson,* we have reaffirmed repeatedly our commitment to jury selection procedures that are fair and nondiscriminatory. We have recognized that whether the trial is criminal or civil, potential jurors, as well as litigants, have an equal protection right to jury selection procedures that are free from state-sponsored group stereotypes rooted in, and reflective of, historical prejudice.

Although premised on equal protection principles that apply equally to gender discrimination, all our recent cases defining the scope of *Batson* involved alleged racial discrimination in the exercise of peremptory challenges. Today we are faced with the question whether the Equal Protection Clause forbids intentional discrimination on the basis of gender, just as it prohibits discrimination on the basis of race. We hold that gender, like race, is an unconstitutional proxy for juror competence and impartiality.

I

On behalf of relator T.B., the mother of a minor child, respondent State of Alabama filed a complaint for paternity and child support against petitioner J.E.B. in the District Court of Jackson County, Alabama. On October 21, 1991, the matter was called for trial and jury selection began. The trial court assembled a panel of 36 potential jurors, 12 males and 24 females. After the court excused three jurors for cause, only 10 of the remaining 33 jurors were male. The State then used 9 of its 10 peremptory strikes to remove male jurors; petitioner used all but one of his strikes to remove female jurors. As a result, all the selected jurors were female.

Before the jury was empaneled, petitioner objected to the State's peremptory challenges on the ground that they were exercised against male jurors solely on the basis of gender, in violation of the Equal Protection Clause of the Fourteenth Amendment. Petitioner argued that the logic and reasoning of *Batson v. Kentucky,* which prohibits peremptory strikes solely on the basis of race, similarly forbids intentional discrimination on the basis of gender. The court rejected petitioner's claim and empaneled the all-female jury. The jury found petitioner to be the father of the child, and the court entered an order directing him to pay child support. * * * The Alabama Court of Civil Appeals affirmed, relying on Alabama precedent. The Supreme Court of Alabama denied certiorari.

We granted certiorari to resolve a question that has created a conflict of authority—whether the Equal Protection Clause forbids peremptory challenges on the basis of gender as well as on the basis of race. Today we reaffirm what, by now, should be axiomatic: Intentional discrimination on the basis of gender by state actors violates the Equal Protection Clause, particularly where, as here, the discrimination serves to ratify and perpetuate invidious, archaic, and overbroad stereotypes about the relative abilities of men and women.

II

Discrimination on the basis of gender in the exercise of peremptory challenges is a relatively recent phenomenon. Gender-based peremptory strikes were hardly practicable during most of our country's existence, since, until the 20th century, women were completely excluded from jury service. So well entrenched was this exclusion of women that in 1880 this Court, while finding that the exclusion of African-American men from juries violated the Fourteenth Amendment, expressed no doubt that a State "may confine the selection [of jurors] to males." *Strauder v. West Virginia,* 100 U.S., at 310.

* * *

This Court in *Ballard v. United States,* 329 U.S. 187 (1946), first questioned the fundamental fairness of denying women the right to serve on juries. Relying on its supervisory powers over the federal courts, it held that women may not be excluded from the venire in federal trials in States where women were eligible for jury service under local law. In response to the argument that women have no superior or unique perspective, such that defendants are denied a fair trial by virtue of their exclusion from jury panels, the Court explained:

"It is said . . . that an all male panel drawn from the various groups within a community will be as truly representative as if women were included. The thought is that the factors which tend to influence the action of women are the same as those which influence the action of men-personality, background, economic status—and not sex. Yet it is not enough to say that women when sitting as jurors neither act nor tend to act as a class. Men likewise do not act like a class. . . . The truth is that the two sexes are not fungible; a community made up exclusively of one is different from a community composed of both; the subtle interplay of influence one on the other is among the imponderables. To insulate the courtroom from either may not in a given case make an iota of difference. Yet a flavor, a distinct quality is lost if either sex is excluded." *Id.,* at 193–194.

* * *

In 1975, the Court finally repudiated the reasoning of *Hoyt* [*v. Florida,* 368 U.S. 57 (1961),] and struck down, under the Sixth Amendment, an affirmative registration statute nearly identical to the one at issue in *Hoyt.* See *Taylor v. Louisiana,* 419 U.S. 522 (1975). We explained: "Restricting jury service to only special groups or excluding identifiable segments playing major roles in the community cannot be squared with the constitutional concept of jury trial." *Id.* The diverse and representative character of the jury must be maintained " 'partly as assurance of a diffused impartiality and partly because sharing in the administration of justice is a phase of civic responsibility.' " *Id.,* at 530–531, quoting *Thiel v. Southern Pacific Co.,* 328 U.S. 217, 227 (1946) (Frankfurter, J., dissenting).

III

Taylor relied on Sixth Amendment principles, but the opinion's approach is consistent with the heightened equal protection scrutiny afforded gender-based classifications. Since *Reed v. Reed,* 404 U.S. 71 (1971), this Court consistently has subjected gender-based classifications to heightened scrutiny in recognition of the real danger that government policies that professedly are based on reasonable considerations in fact may be reflective of "archaic and overbroad" generalizations about gender, see *Schlesinger v. Ballard,* 419 U.S. 498, 506–507 (1975), or based on "outdated misconceptions concerning the role of females in the home rather than in the 'marketplace and world of ideas.' " *Craig v. Boren,* 429 U.S. 190, 198–199 (1976).

* * *

Certainly, with respect to jury service, African-Americans and women share a history of total exclusion, a history which came to an end for women many years after the embarrassing chapter in our history came to an end for African-Americans.

We need not determine, however, whether women or racial minorities have suffered more at the hands of discriminatory state actors during the decades of our Nation's history. It is necessary only to acknowledge that "our Nation has had a long and unfortunate history of sex discrimination," *id.,* at 684, a history which warrants the heightened scrutiny we afford all gender-based classifications today. * * * [W]e do not weigh the value of peremptory challenges as an institution against our asserted commitment to eradicate invidious discrimination from the courtroom.[7] Instead, we consider whether peremptory challenges based on gender stereotypes provide substantial aid to a litigant's effort to secure a fair and impartial jury.

Far from proffering an exceptionally persuasive justification for its gender-based peremptory challenges, respondent maintains that its decision to strike virtually all the males from the jury in this case "may reasonably have been based upon the perception, supported by history, that men otherwise totally qualified to serve upon a jury in any case might be more sympathetic and receptive to the arguments of a man alleged in a paternity action to be the father of an out-of-wedlock child, while women equally qualified to serve upon a jury might be more sympathetic and receptive to the arguments of the complaining witness who bore the child." Brief for Respondent 10.

We shall not accept as a defense to gender-based peremptory challenges "the very stereotype the law condemns." *Powers v. Ohio,* 499 U.S., at 410. Respondent's rationale, not unlike those regularly expressed for gender-based strikes, is reminiscent of the arguments advanced to justify the total exclusion of women from juries.[10] Respondent offers virtually no support for the conclusion that gender alone is an accurate predictor of juror's attitudes; yet it urges this Court to condone the same stereotypes that justified the wholesale exclusion

---

[7] Although peremptory challenges are valuable tools in jury trials, they "are not constitutionally protected fundamental rights; rather they are but one state-created means to the constitutional end of an impartial jury and a fair trial." *Georgia v. McCollum,* 505 U.S. 42, 57 (1992).

[10] A manual formerly used to instruct prosecutors in Dallas, Texas, provided the following advice: " 'I don't like women jurors because I can't trust them. They do, however, make the best jurors in cases involving crimes against children. It is possible that their "women's intuition" can help you if you can't win your case with the facts.' " Alschuler, The Supreme Court and the Jury: Voir Dire, Peremptory Challenges, and the Review of Jury Verdicts, 56 U.Chi.L.Rev. 153, 210 (1989). Another widely circulated trial manual speculated:

"If counsel is depending upon a clearly applicable rule of law and if he wants to avoid a verdict of 'intuition' or 'sympathy,' if his verdict in amount is to be proved by clearly demonstrated blackboard figures for example, generally he would want a male juror.

"[But] women . . . are desired jurors when plaintiff is a man. A woman juror may see a man impeached from the beginning of the case to the end, but there is at least the chance [with] the woman juror (particularly if the man happens to be handsome or appealing) [that] the plaintiff's derelictions in and out of court will be overlooked. A woman is inclined to forgive sin in the opposite sex; but definitely not her own." 3 M. Belli, *Modern Trials* §§ 51.67 and 51.68, pp. 446–447 (2d ed. 1982).

of women from juries and the ballot box. Respondent seems to assume that gross generalizations that would be deemed impermissible if made on the basis of race are somehow permissible when made on the basis of gender.

Discrimination in jury selection, whether based on race or on gender, causes harm to the litigants, the community, and the individual jurors who are wrongfully excluded from participation in the judicial process. The litigants are harmed by the risk that the prejudice that motivated the discriminatory selection of the jury will infect the entire proceedings. The community is harmed by the State's participation in the perpetuation of invidious group stereotypes and the inevitable loss of confidence in our judicial system that state-sanctioned discrimination in the courtroom engenders.

When state actors exercise peremptory challenges in reliance on gender stereotypes, they ratify and reinforce prejudicial views of the relative abilities of men and women. Because these stereotypes have wreaked injustice in so many other spheres of our country's public life, active discrimination by litigants on the basis of gender during jury selection "invites cynicism respecting the jury's neutrality and its obligation to adhere to the law." *Powers v. Ohio,* 499 U.S., at 412. The potential for cynicism is particularly acute in cases where gender-related issues are prominent, such as cases involving rape, sexual harassment, or paternity. Discriminatory use of peremptory challenges may create the impression that the judicial system has acquiesced in suppressing full participation by one gender or that the "deck has been stacked" in favor of one side. See *id.,* at 413 ("The verdict will not be accepted or understood [as fair] if the jury is chosen by unlawful means at the outset").

In recent cases we have emphasized that individual jurors themselves have a right to nondiscriminatory jury selection. See *Powers, supra, Edmonson, supra,* and *Georgia v. McCollum,* 505 U.S. 42 (1992). Contrary to respondent's suggestion, this right extends to both men and women. See *Mississippi Univ. for Women v. Hogan,* 458 U.S., at 723 (that a state practice "discriminates against males rather than against females does not exempt it from scrutiny or reduce the standard of review"). All persons, when granted the opportunity to serve on a jury, have the right not to be excluded summarily because of discriminatory and stereotypical presumptions that reflect and reinforce patterns of historical discrimination. Striking individual jurors on the assumption that they hold particular views simply because of their gender is "practically a brand upon them, affixed by the law, an assertion of their inferiority." *Strauder v. West Virginia,* 100 U.S. at 308 (1880). It denigrates the dignity of the excluded juror, and, for a woman, reinvokes a history of exclusion from political participation.[14] The message it sends to all those in the courtroom, and all those who may later learn of the discriminatory act, is that certain individuals, for no reason other than gender, are presumed unqualified by state actors to decide important questions upon which reasonable persons could disagree.

IV

Our conclusion that litigants may not strike potential jurors solely on the basis of gender does not imply the elimination of all peremptory challenges. Neither does it conflict with a State's legitimate interest in using such challenges in its effort to secure a fair and impartial jury. Parties still may remove jurors who they feel might be less acceptable than others on the panel; gender simply may not serve as a proxy for bias. Parties may also exercise their peremptory challenges to remove from the venire any group or class of individuals normally subject to "rational basis" review. See *Cleburne v. Cleburne Living Center, Inc.,* 473 U.S., at 439–442; *Clark v. Jeter,* 486 U.S. 456, 461 (1988). Even strikes based on characteristics that are disproportionately associated with one gender could be appropriate, absent a showing of pretext.[16]

If conducted properly, *voir dire* can inform litigants about potential jurors, making reliance upon stereotypical and pejorative notions about a particular gender or race both unnecessary and unwise. *Voir dire* provides a means of discovering actual or implied bias and a firmer basis upon which the parties may exercise their peremptory challenges intelligently.

The experience in the many jurisdictions that have barred gender-based challenges belies the claim that litigants and trial courts are incapable of complying with a rule barring strikes based on gender. As with race-based *Batson* claims, a party alleging gender discrimination must make a prima facie showing of intentional discrimination before the party exercising the challenge is required to explain the basis for the strike. *Batson,* 476 U.S., at 97. When an explanation is required, it need not rise to the level of a "for cause" challenge; rather, it merely must be based on a juror characteristic other than gender, and the proffered explanation may not be pretextual. See *Hernandez v. New York,* 500 U.S. 352 (1991).

---

[14] The popular refrain is that *all* peremptory challenges are based on stereotypes of some kind, expressing various intuitive and frequently erroneous biases. But where peremptory challenges are made on the basis of group characteristics other than race or gender (like occupation, for example), they do not reinforce the same stereotypes about the group's competence or predispositions that have been used to prevent them from voting, participating on juries, pursuing their chosen professions, or otherwise contributing to civic life.

[16] For example, challenging all persons who have had military experience would disproportionately affect men at this time, while challenging all persons employed as nurses would disproportionately affect women. Without a showing of pretext, however, these challenges may well not be unconstitutional, since they are not gender or race based. See *Hernandez v. New York,* 500 U.S. 352 (1991).

Failing to provide jurors the same protection against gender discrimination as race discrimination could frustrate the purpose of *Batson* itself. Because gender and race are overlapping categories, gender can be used as a pretext for racial discrimination. Allowing parties to remove racial minorities from the jury not because of their race, but because of their gender, contravenes well-established equal protection principles and could insulate effectively racial discrimination from judicial scrutiny.

V

Equal opportunity to participate in the fair administration of justice is fundamental to our democratic system. It not only furthers the goals of the jury system. It reaffirms the promise of equality under the law—that all citizens, regardless of race, ethnicity, or gender, have the chance to take part directly in our democracy. When persons are excluded from participation in our democratic processes solely because of race or gender, this promise of equality dims, and the integrity of our judicial system is jeopardized.

In view of these concerns, the Equal Protection Clause prohibits discrimination in jury selection on the basis of gender, or on the assumption that an individual will be biased in a particular case for no reason other than the fact that the person happens to be a woman or happens to be a man. As with race, the "core guarantee of equal protection, ensuring citizens that their State will not discriminate . . . , would be meaningless were we to approve the exclusion of jurors on the basis of such assumptions, which arise solely from the jurors' [gender]." *Batson,* 476 U.S., at 97–98.

The judgment of the Court of Civil Appeals of Alabama is reversed, and the case is remanded to that court for further proceedings not inconsistent with this opinion.

It is so ordered.

■ JUSTICE O'CONNOR, concurring.

I agree with the Court that the Equal Protection Clause prohibits the government from excluding a person from jury service on account of that person's gender. The State's proffered justifications for its gender-based peremptory challenges are far from the " 'exceedingly persuasive' " showing required to sustain a gender-based classification. *Mississippi Univ. for Women v. Hogan,* 458 U.S. 718, 724 (1982). I therefore join the Court's opinion in this case. But today's important blow against gender discrimination is not costless. I write separately to discuss some of these costs, and to express my belief that today's holding should be limited to the *government's* use of gender-based peremptory strikes.

Batson v. Kentucky, 476 U.S. 79 (1986), itself was a significant intrusion into the jury selection process. *Batson* mini hearings are now routine in state and federal trial courts, and *Batson* appeals have proliferated as well. Demographics indicate that today's holding may have an even greater impact than did *Batson* itself. In further constitutionalizing jury selection procedures, the Court increases the number of cases in which jury selection—once a sideshow—will become part of the main event.

For this same reason, today's decision further erodes the role of the peremptory challenge. The peremptory challenge is "a practice of ancient origin" and is "part of our common law heritage." *Edmonson v. Leesville Concrete Co.,* 500 U.S. 614, 639 (1991) (O'CONNOR, J., dissenting). The principal value of the peremptory is that it helps produce fair and impartial juries. *Swain v. Alabama,* 380 U.S. 202, 218–219 (1965). "Peremptory challenges, by enabling each side to exclude those jurors it believes will be most partial toward the other side, are a means of eliminat[ing] extremes of partiality on both sides, thereby assuring the selection of a qualified and unbiased jury." *Holland v. Illinois,* 493 U.S. 474, 484 (1990). The peremptory's importance is confirmed by its persistence: It was well established at the time of Blackstone and continues to endure in all the States.

Moreover, "[t]he essential nature of the peremptory challenge is that it is one exercised without a reason stated, without inquiry and without being subject to the court's control." *Swain,* 380 U.S., at 220. Indeed, often a reason for it cannot be stated, for a trial lawyer's judgments about a juror's sympathies are sometimes based on experienced hunches and educated guesses, derived from a juror's responses at voir dire or a juror's " 'bare looks and gestures.' " *Ibid.* That a trial lawyer's instinctive assessment of a juror's predisposition cannot meet the high standards of a challenge for cause does not mean that the lawyer's instinct is erroneous. Our belief that experienced lawyers will often correctly intuit which jurors are likely to be the least sympathetic, and our understanding that the lawyer will often be unable to explain the intuition, are the very reason we cherish the peremptory challenge. But, as we add, layer by layer, additional constitutional restraints on the use of the peremptory, we force lawyers to articulate what we know is often inarticulable.

In so doing we make the peremptory challenge less discretionary and more like a challenge for cause. We also increase the possibility that biased jurors will be allowed onto the jury, because sometimes a lawyer will be unable to provide an acceptable gender-neutral explanation even though the lawyer is in fact correct that the juror is unsympathetic. Similarly, in jurisdictions where lawyers exercise their strikes in open court, lawyers may be deterred from using their peremptories, out of the fear that if they are unable to justify the strike the court will seat a juror who knows that the striking party thought him unfit. Because I believe the peremptory remains an important litigator's tool and a fundamental part of the process of selecting impartial juries, our increasing limitation of it gives me pause.

Nor is the value of the peremptory challenge to the litigant diminished when the peremptory is exercised in a gender-based manner. We know that like race, gender matters. A plethora of studies make clear that in rape cases, for example, female jurors are somewhat more likely to vote to convict than male jurors. Moreover, though there have been no similarly definitive studies regarding, for example, sexual harassment, child custody, or spousal or child abuse, one need not be a sexist to share the intuition that in certain cases a person's gender and resulting life experience will be relevant to his or her view of the case. " 'Jurors are not expected to come into the jury box and leave behind all that their human experience has taught them.' " *Beck v. Alabama,* 447 U.S. 625, 642 (1980). Individuals are not expected to ignore as jurors what they know as men-or women.

Today's decision severely limits a litigant's ability to act on this intuition, for the import of our holding is that any correlation between a juror's gender and attitudes is irrelevant as a matter of constitutional law. But to say that gender makes no difference as a matter of law is not to say that gender makes no difference as a matter of fact. I previously have said with regard to *Batson:* "That the Court will not tolerate prosecutors' racially discriminatory use of the peremptory challenge, in effect, is a special rule of relevance, a statement about what this Nation stands for, rather than a statement of fact." *Brown v. North Carolina,* 479 U.S. 940, 941–942 (1986) (opinion concurring in denial of certiorari). Today's decision is a statement that, in an effort to eliminate the potential discriminatory use of the peremptory, gender is now governed by the special rule of relevance formerly reserved for race. Though we gain much from this statement, we cannot ignore what we lose. In extending *Batson* to gender we have added an additional burden to the state and federal trial process, taken a step closer to eliminating the peremptory challenge, and diminished the ability of litigants to act on sometimes accurate gender-based assumptions about juror attitudes.

These concerns reinforce my conviction that today's decision should be limited to a prohibition on the government's use of gender-based peremptory challenges. The Equal Protection Clause prohibits only discrimination by state actors. In *Edmonson, supra,* we made the mistake of concluding that private civil litigants were state actors when they exercised peremptory challenges; in *Georgia v. McCollum,* 505 U.S. 42, 50–55 (1992), we compounded the mistake by holding that criminal defendants were also state actors. Our commitment to eliminating discrimination from the legal process should not allow us to forget that not all that occurs in the courtroom is state action. Private civil litigants are just that—*private* litigants. "The government erects the platform; it does not thereby become responsible for all that occurs upon it." *Edmonson,* 500 U.S., at 632 (O'CONNOR, J., dissenting).

Clearly, criminal defendants are not state actors. * * * Limiting the accused's use of the peremptory is "a serious misordering of our priorities," for it means "we have exalted the right of citizens to sit on juries over the rights of the criminal defendant, even though it is the defendant, not the jurors, who faces imprisonment or even death." *McCollum, supra,* 505 U.S., at 61–62 (THOMAS, J., concurring in judgment).

Accordingly, I adhere to my position that the Equal Protection Clause does not limit the exercise of peremptory challenges by private civil litigants and criminal defendants. This case itself presents no state action dilemma, for here the State of Alabama itself filed the paternity suit on behalf of petitioner. But what of the next case? Will we, in the name of fighting gender discrimination, hold that the battered wife—on trial for wounding her abusive husband—is a state actor? Will we preclude her from using her peremptory challenges to ensure that the jury of her peers contains as many women members as possible? I assume we will, but I hope we will not.

■ JUSTICE KENNEDY, concurring in the judgment.

* * *

There is no doubt under our precedents * * * that the Equal Protection Clause prohibits sex discrimination in the selection of jurors. *Duren v. Missouri,* 439 U.S. 357 (1979); *Taylor v. Louisiana,* 419 U.S. 522 (1975). The only question is whether the Clause also prohibits peremptory challenges based on sex. The Court is correct to hold that it does. The Equal Protection Clause and our constitutional tradition are based on the theory that an individual possesses rights that are protected against lawless action by the government. * * * For purposes of the Equal Protection Clause, an individual denied jury service because of a peremptory challenge exercised against her on account of her sex is no less injured than the individual denied jury service because of a law banning members of her sex from serving as jurors. The injury is to personal dignity and to the individual's right to participate in the political process. The neutrality of the Fourteenth Amendment's guarantee is confirmed by the fact that the Court has no difficulty in finding a constitutional wrong in this case, which involves males excluded from jury service because of their gender.

* * *

For these reasons, I concur in the judgment of the Court holding that peremptory strikes based on gender violate the Equal Protection Clause.

■ CHIEF JUSTICE REHNQUIST, dissenting.

[Chief Justice Rehnquist dissented in an opinion in which he stated: "*Batson* is best understood as a recognition that race lies at the core of * * * the Fourteenth Amendment. Not surprisingly, all of our post-*Batson* cases have dealt with the use of peremptory strikes to remove black or racially identified venirepersons, and all have described *Batson* as fashioning a rule aimed at preventing purposeful discrimination against a cognizable racial group."]

■ JUSTICE SCALIA, with whom THE CHIEF JUSTICE and JUSTICE THOMAS join, dissenting.

Today's opinion is an inspiring demonstration of how thoroughly up-to-date and right-thinking we Justices are in matters pertaining to the sexes (or as the Court would have it, the genders), and how sternly we disapprove the male chauvinist attitudes of our predecessors. The price to be paid for this display—a modest price, surely—is that most of the opinion is quite irrelevant to the case at hand. The hasty reader will be surprised to learn, for example, that this lawsuit involves a complaint about the use of peremptory challenges to exclude *men* from a petit jury. To be sure, petitioner, a man, used all but one of *his* peremptory strikes to remove *women* from the jury (he used his last challenge to strike the sole remaining male from the pool), but the validity of *his* strikes is not before us. Nonetheless, the Court treats itself to an extended discussion of the historic exclusion of women not only from jury service, but also from service at the bar (which is rather like jury service, in that it involves going to the courthouse a lot). All this, as I say, is irrelevant, since the case involves state action that allegedly discriminates against men. * * *

The Court also spends time establishing that the use of sex as a proxy for particular views or sympathies is unwise and perhaps irrational. The opinion stresses the lack of statistical evidence to support the widely held belief that, at least in certain types of cases, a juror's sex has some statistically significant predictive value as to how the juror will behave. This assertion seems to place the Court in opposition to its earlier Sixth Amendment "fair cross-section" cases. *See, e.g., Taylor v. Louisiana,* 419 U.S. 522, 532, n. 12 (1975) ("Controlled studies ... have concluded that women bring to juries their own perspectives and values that influence both jury deliberation and result"). But times and trends do change, and unisex is unquestionably in fashion. Personally, I am less inclined to demand statistics, and more inclined to credit the perceptions of experienced litigators who have had money on the line. But it does not matter. The Court's fervent defense of the proposition *il n'y a pas de différence entre les hommes et les femmes* (it stereotypes the opposite view as hateful "stereotyping") turns out to be, like its recounting of the history of sex discrimination against women, utterly irrelevant. Even if sex was a remarkably good predictor in certain cases, the Court would find its use in peremptories unconstitutional.

Of course the relationship of sex to partiality *would have been* relevant if the Court had demanded in this case what it ordinarily demands: that the complaining party have suffered some injury.

Leaving aside for the moment the reality that the defendant himself had the opportunity to strike women from the jury, the defendant would have some cause to complain about the prosecutor's striking male jurors if male jurors tend to be more favorable toward defendants in paternity suits. But if men and women jurors are (as the Court thinks) fungible, then the only arguable injury from the prosecutor's "impermissible" use of male sex as the basis for his peremptories is injury to the stricken juror, not to the defendant. Indeed, far from having suffered harm, petitioner, a state actor under our precedents, has himself actually *inflicted* harm on female jurors. * * *

The core of the Court's reasoning is that peremptory challenges on the basis of any group characteristic subject to heightened scrutiny are inconsistent with the guarantee of the Equal Protection Clause. That conclusion can be reached only by focusing unrealistically upon individual exercises of the peremptory challenge, and ignoring the totality of the practice. Since all groups are subject to the peremptory challenge (and will be made the object of it, depending upon the nature of the particular case) it is hard to see how any group is denied equal protection. That explains why peremptory challenges coexisted with the Equal Protection Clause for 120 years. This case is a perfect example of how the system as a whole is evenhanded. While the only claim before the Court is petitioner's complaint that the prosecutor struck male jurors, for every man struck by the government petitioner's own lawyer struck a woman. To say that men were singled out for discriminatory treatment in this process is preposterous. * * *

[T]he Court says that the only important government interest that could be served by peremptory strikes is "securing a fair and impartial jury."[3] It refuses to accept respondent's argument that these strikes further that interest by eliminating a group (men) which may be partial to male defendants, because it will not accept any argument based on " 'the very stereotype the law condemns.' " This analysis, entirely eliminating the only allowable argument, implies that sex-based strikes do not even rationally further a legitimate government interest, let alone pass heightened scrutiny. That places *all* peremptory strikes based on *any* group characteristic at risk, since they can all be denominated "stereotypes." * * *

Even if the line of our later cases guaranteed by today's decision limits the theoretically boundless *Batson* principle to race, sex, and perhaps other classifications subject to heightened scrutiny (which presumably would include religious belief), much damage has been done. It has been done, first and foremost, to the peremptory challenge system, which loses its whole character when (in order to defend

---

[3] It does not seem to me that even this premise is correct. Wise observers have long understood that the appearance of justice is as important as its reality. If the system of peremptory strikes affects the actual impartiality of the jury not a bit, but gives litigants a greater belief in that impartiality, it serves a most important function. *See, e.g.,* 4 W. Blackstone, Commentaries. In point of fact, that may well be its greater value.

against "impermissible stereotyping" claims) "reasons" for strikes must be given. The right of peremptory challenge " 'is, as Blackstone says, an arbitrary and capricious right; and it must be exercised with full freedom, or it fails of its full purpose.' " *Lewis v. United States*, 146 U.S. 370, 378 (1892), quoting *Lamb v. State*, 36 Wis. 424, 427 (1874). The loss of the real peremptory will be felt most keenly by the criminal defendant, whom we have until recently thought "should not be held to accept a juror, apparently indifferent, whom he distrusted for any reason or for no reason." *Lamb, supra*, at 426. And make no mistake about it: there really is no substitute for the peremptory. *Voir dire* (though it can be expected to expand as a consequence of today's decision) cannot fill the gap. The biases that go along with group characteristics tend to be biases that the juror himself does not perceive, so that it is no use asking about them. It is fruitless to inquire of a male juror whether he harbors any subliminal prejudice in favor of unwed fathers.

And damage has been done, secondarily, to the entire justice system, which will bear the burden of the expanded quest for "reasoned peremptories" that the Court demands. The extension of *Batson* to sex, and almost certainly beyond, will provide the basis for extensive collateral litigation, which especially the criminal defendant (who litigates full time and cost free) can be expected to pursue. While demographic reality places some limit on the number of cases in which race-based challenges will be an issue, every case contains a potential sex-based claim. Another consequence, as I have mentioned, is a lengthening of the *voir dire* process that already burdens trial courts.

* * *

In order, it seems to me, not to eliminate any real denial of equal protection, but simply to pay conspicuous obeisance to the equality of the sexes, the Court imperils a practice that has been considered an essential part of fair jury trial since the dawn of the common law. The Constitution of the United States neither requires nor permits this vandalizing of our people's traditions.

For these reasons, I dissent.

COMMENTS AND QUESTIONS CONCERNING *J.E.B. V. ALABAMA*

1.   When lawyers exercise their peremptory challenges, are they attempting to craft a neutral, unbiased jury? Or are they seeking a jury that will be as sympathetic as possible to their clients?

2.   In its earlier decision in *Edmonson v. Leesville Concrete Co., Inc.*, 500 U.S. 614 (1991), the Supreme Court extended *Batson* to the civil context. The Court held that, because this would violate the equal protection rights of the excluded juror, a private party in a federal civil action could not use peremptory challenges to exclude potential jurors on the basis of their race. Although it was a private party exercising the

peremptory challenges in *Edmonson*, the Court concluded that the exercise of such jury strikes constituted "state action" under the Equal Protection and Due Process Clauses of the Constitution. No state action issue was presented in *J.E.B.*, because the party excising the peremptory challenges in that case was the State of Alabama.

3. Why does Justice Blackmun include so much history in his opinion? Is this history necessary to support his argument that exercising peremptory challenges on the basis of stereotypical views of women or racial minorities is different than exercising peremptory challenges based on stereotypes of other groups? In footnote 14 of his opinion he states:

> The popular refrain is that *all* peremptory challenges are based on stereotypes of some kind, expressing various intuitive and frequently erroneous biases. But where peremptory challenges are made on the basis of group characteristics other than race or gender (like occupation, for example), they do not reinforce the same stereotypes about the group's competence or predispositions that have been used to prevent them from voting, participating on juries, pursuing their chosen professions, or otherwise contributing to civic life.

4. Although they reach different conclusions in the case, Justice O'Connor and Justice Scalia agree that the outcome in *J.E.B.* may fundamentally change the nature of the peremptory challenge. Justice Scalia asserts in his dissent:

> [M]uch damage has been done. It has been done, first and foremost, to the peremptory challenge system, which loses its whole character when (in order to defend against "impermissible stereotyping" claims) "reasons" for strikes must be given. The right of peremptory challenge " 'is, as Blackstone says, an arbitrary and capricious right; and it must be exercised with full freedom, or it fails of its full purpose.' "

Justice O'Connor voices similar reservations:

> Our belief that experienced lawyers will often correctly intuit which jurors are likely to be the least sympathetic, and our understanding that the lawyer will often be unable to explain the intuition, are the very reason we cherish the peremptory challenge. But, as we add, layer by layer, additional constitutional restraints on the use of the peremptory, we force lawyers to articulate what we know is often inarticulable.

Is the limitation of peremptory challenges impossible without destroying the essential nature of such challenges? Would the system be better off with the abolition of all peremptory challenges?

5. Justice Blackmun states: "If conducted properly, *voir dire* can inform litigants about potential jurors, making reliance upon stereotypical and pejorative notions about a particular gender or race both unnecessary and unwise."

If, in a case such as *J.E.B.* a potential juror expressed opinions concerning child support, this could provide a basis for the exercise of challenges by one or more of the lawyers. However, is it likely that potential jurors will express strong feelings suggesting that they are prejudiced against certain types of people?

6.   Is Justice Blackmun correct that the exercise of peremptory challenges on the basis of race and gender can undermine public confidence in the courts? Is the defendant in this case likely to have much confidence in the judicial system after being found to have fathered a child by an all-female jury?

7.   Justice O'Connor wrote a separate opinion to limit the extent of her concurrence in the majority's holding: "I write separately to discuss some of these costs [of the majority decision], and to express my belief that today's holding should be limited to the *government's* use of gender-based peremptory strikes."

Is a distinction between governmental and non-governmental use of peremptory challenges workable? If Justice O'Connor is correct that *Batson* only should apply to the government, does that mean that a private party in a case such as *J.E.B.* can use his peremptory challenges to attempt to create an all-male jury?

8.   Does Justice Blackmun's opinion rest on an assumption that implicit biases and viewpoints do not correspond with race or gender? Compare such a conclusion with the criticism of the Court's near-unanimous decision in *Scott v. Harris*, 550 U.S. 372 (2007), *supra* p. 843, in Kahan et al., "Whose Eyes Are You Going to Believe? *Scott v. Harris* and the Perils of Cognitive Illiberalism," 122 *Harv.L.Rev.* 837 (2009).

In a portion of his dissent not included above, 511 U.S. at 163, Justice Scalia argued:

> [T]he prosecutor presumably violates the Constitution when he selects a male or female police officer to testify because he believes one or the other sex might be more convincing in the context of the particular case, or because he believes one or the other might be more appealing to a predominantly male or female jury. A decision to stress one line of argument or present certain witnesses before a mostly female jury—for example, to stress that the defendant victimized women—becomes, under the Court's reasoning, intentional discrimination by a state actor on the basis of gender.

Do you agree? Are there practical problems with extending the non-discrimination rationale this far?

9.   Look back at Clarence Darrow's description of his use of religious stereotypes in selecting a jury. Could he use peremptory challenges on the basis of religion in a courtroom today? Consider the decision of the United States Court of Appeals for the Seventh Circuit in *United States v. Heron*, 721 F.3d 896 (7th Cir. 2013) *cert. denied*, 134 S. Ct. 1044 (U.S. 2014), in which Judge Diane Wood wrote for the court:

The idea of evaluating the depth of a prospective juror's religious feelings is troubling enough to make us especially reluctant to consider it without a proper exploration in the district court. This is a difficult area, fraught with risks whatever way we turn. Although one might think there would be value in a rule that categorically endorsed all religion-related strikes so long as they were not overtly based on a juror's religious affiliation, upon closer examination we think that such a rule would come with its own problems. The affiliation/practices distinction may often be illusory, since a person's religious affiliation may be hard to distinguish from religious practices and level of devotion. How would we parse, for instance, whether the peremptory strike of a woman wearing a burqa is based on the fact that she is Muslim or on the fact that she is demonstrably devout? We are not confident that we could coherently distinguish between affiliation and "religiosity" in such a case, and the warning against excessive entanglement into religion found in such cases as *Lemon v. Kurtzman,* 403 U.S. 602, 613 (1971), and *Walz v. Tax Comm'n of New York,* 397 U.S. 664, 674–75 (1970), has special force here. Even if the line between affiliation and religiosity were clear, it is unclear why someone's religious affiliation ought to be entitled to greater constitutional protection than that person's religious exercise. These are thorny questions which, given Heron's forfeiture, we are content to save for another day. We also note that Heron in particular faces other serious obstacles: the strike in his case appears to have been based on the religiosity of Juror #9's *mother;* and the religiosity explanation was paired with the "social worker daughter" explanation, which would not have posed a *Batson* problem if raised on its own.

721 F.3d 896 at 902–03.

C. JUROR IMPEACHMENT OF THE JURY'S VERDICT

Significant legal and judicial resources are invested in a jury verdict, which is one reason for protecting such verdicts. Verdict challenges also can lead to uncertainty and lack of public confidence in our judicial system, encourage peripheral efforts to overturn quite legitimate verdicts, and subject individual jurors to public criticism.

Therefore the standard for overturning a verdict because a prospective juror has provided incorrect information during jury selection is quite demanding. The Supreme Court requires the following to overturn a verdict due to a prospective juror's failure to honestly answer a question during jury selection:

> [T]o obtain a new trial in such a situation, a party must first demonstrate that a juror failed to answer honestly a material question on *voir dire,* and then further show that a correct response would have provided a valid basis for a challenge for cause. The motives for concealing information may vary, but

only those reasons that affect a juror's impartiality can truly be said to affect the fairness of a trial.

McDonough Power Equip., Inc. v. Greenwood, 464 U.S. 548, 556 (1984).

Even if there is a basis under *McDonough* to reconsider a jury verdict, there remains the question as to how a party can "demonstrate that a juror failed to answer honestly a material question on *voir dire*." If a juror during voir dire dishonestly denied that she knew any of the parties to an action, the testimony of neighbors or friends might be used to demonstrate that she was, in fact, a good friend of the plaintiff and had lied during voir dire.

But what if the juror had told another juror that she was the plaintiff's best friend? This statement would be highly relevant to any effort to overturn the verdict. But, under a decision by Lord Mansfield that predates the ratification of the United States Constitution, a juror's testimony about alleged juror statements or misconduct within the jury room cannot be used to impeach the jury's verdict. The Mansfield Rule, recognized in most states, is embodied in Federal Rule of Evidence 606(b), which provides:

(1) *Prohibited Testimony of Other Evidence.* During an inquiry into the validity of a verdict or indictment, a juror may not testify about any statement made or incident that occurred during the jury's deliberations; the effect of anything on that juror's or another juror's vote; or any juror's mental processes concerning the verdict or indictment. The court may not receive a juror's affidavit or evidence of a juror's statement on these matters.

(2) *Exceptions.* A juror may testify about whether:

(A) extraneous   prejudicial   information   was improperly brought to the jury's attention;

(B) an outside influence was improperly brought to bear on any juror; or

(C) a mistake was made in entering the verdict on the verdict form.

Consider why Rule 606(b) and the Mansfield Rule protect the judicial system and individual jurors as you read the following case.

1. "WHAT HAPPENS IN THE JURY ROOM STAYS IN THE JURY ROOM":
    WARGER V. SHAUERS

Warger v. Shauers

Supreme Court of the United States, 2014
135 S.Ct. 521

■ JUSTICE SOTOMAYOR delivered the opinion of the Court.

Federal Rule of Evidence 606(b) provides that certain juror testimony regarding what occurred in a jury room is inadmissible "[d]uring an inquiry into the validity of a verdict." The question presented in this case is whether Rule 606(b) precludes a party seeking a new trial from using one juror's affidavit of what another juror said in deliberations to demonstrate the other juror's dishonesty during *voir dire*. We hold that it does.

                                         I

Petitioner Gregory Warger was riding his motorcycle on a highway outside Rapid City, South Dakota, when a truck driven by respondent Randy Shauers struck him from behind. Warger claims he was stopped at the time of the accident, while Shauers claims that Warger suddenly pulled out in front of him. Regardless of the cause of the accident, no one disputes its tragic result: Warger sustained serious injuries that ultimately required the amputation of his left leg.

Warger sued Shauers for negligence in Federal District Court. During jury selection, counsel for both parties conducted lengthy *voir dire* of the prospective jurors. Warger's counsel asked whether any jurors would be unable to award damages for pain and suffering or for future medical expenses, or whether there was any juror who thought, "I don't think I could be a fair and impartial juror on this kind of case." Prospective juror Regina Whipple, who was later selected as the jury foreperson, answered no to each of these questions.

Trial commenced, and the jury ultimately returned a verdict in favor of Shauers. Shortly thereafter, one of the jurors contacted Warger's counsel to express concern over juror Whipple's conduct. The complaining juror subsequently signed an affidavit claiming that Whipple had spoken during deliberations about "a motor vehicle collision in which her daughter was at fault for the collision and a man died," and had "related that if her daughter had been sued, it would have ruined her life."

Relying on this affidavit, Warger moved for a new trial. He contended that Whipple had deliberately lied during *voir dire* about her impartiality and ability to award damages. Thus, he asserted, he had satisfied the requirements of *McDonough Power Equipment, Inc. v. Greenwood,* 464 U.S. 548 (1984), which holds that a party may "obtain a new trial" if he "demonstrate[s] that a juror failed to answer honestly a material question on *voir dire,* and . . . that a correct response would have provided a valid basis for a challenge for cause." *Id.,* at 556.

The District Court refused to grant a new trial, holding that the only evidence that supported Warger's motion, the complaining juror's affidavit, was barred by Federal Rule of Evidence 606(b). As relevant here, that Rule provides that "[d]uring an inquiry into the validity of a verdict," evidence "about any statement made or incident that occurred during the jury's deliberations" is inadmissible. Rule 606(b)(1). The Rule contains three specific exceptions—allowing testimony "about whether (A) extraneous prejudicial information was improperly brought to the jury's attention; (B) an outside influence was improperly brought to bear on any juror; or (C) a mistake was made in entering the verdict on the verdict form," Rule 606(b)(2)—but the District Court found none of these exceptions to be applicable.

The Eighth Circuit affirmed. It first held that Warger's proffered evidence did not fall within the "extraneous prejudicial evidence" exception set forth in Rule 606(b)(2)(A). The court explained that "[j]urors' personal experiences do not constitute extraneous information; it is unavoidable they will bring such innate experiences into the jury room." Next, the court rejected Warger's alternative argument that Rule 606(b) is wholly inapplicable when a litigant offers evidence to show that a juror was dishonest during *voir dire.* Acknowledging that there was a split among the Federal Courts of Appeals on this question, the Eighth Circuit joined those Circuits that had held that Rule 606(b) applies to any proceeding in which the jury's verdict might be invalidated, including efforts to demonstrate that a juror lied during *voir dire.*

We granted certiorari and now affirm.

II

We hold that Rule 606(b) applies to juror testimony during a proceeding in which a party seeks to secure a new trial on the ground that a juror lied during *voir dire.* In doing so, we simply accord Rule 606(b)'s terms their plain meaning. The Rule, after all, applies "[d]uring an inquiry into the validity of a verdict." Rule 606(b)(1). A postverdict motion for a new trial on the ground of *voir dire* dishonesty plainly entails "an inquiry into the validity of [the] verdict": If a juror was dishonest during *voir dire* and an honest response would have provided a valid basis to challenge that juror for cause, the verdict must be invalidated. *See McDonough,* 464 U.S., at 556.

This understanding of the text of Rule 606(b) is consistent with the underlying common-law rule on which it was based. Although some common-law courts would have permitted evidence of jury deliberations to be introduced to demonstrate juror dishonesty during *voir dire,* the majority would not, and the language of Rule 606(b) reflects Congress' enactment of the more restrictive version of the common-law rule.

Rule 606(b) had its genesis in *Vaise v. Delaval,* 1 T.R. 11, 99 Eng. Rep. 944 (K.B. 1785), in which Lord Mansfield held inadmissible an affidavit from two jurors claiming that the jury had decided the case through a game of chance. The rule soon took root in the United States, where it was viewed as both promoting the finality of verdicts and insulating the jury from outside influences, *see McDonald v. Pless,* 238 U.S. 264, 267–268 (1915).

Some versions of the rule were narrower than others. Under what was sometimes known as the "Iowa" approach, juror testimony regarding deliberations was excluded only to the extent that it related to matters that " 'inhere[d] in the verdict,' " which generally consisted of evidence of the jurors' subjective intentions and thought processes in reaching a verdict.[1] A number of courts adhering to the Iowa rule held that testimony regarding jury deliberations is admissible when used to challenge juror conduct during *voir dire.*

But other courts applied a broader version of the anti-impeachment rule. Under this version, sometimes called the "federal" approach, litigants were prohibited from using evidence of jury deliberations unless it was offered to show that an "extraneous matter" had influenced the jury. The "great majority" of appellate courts applying this version of the rule held jury deliberations evidence inadmissible even if used to demonstrate dishonesty during *voir dire.*

* * *

In any event, these decisions predated Congress' enactment of Rule 606(b), and Congress was undoubtedly free to prescribe a broader version of the anti-impeachment rule than we had previously applied. The language of the Rule it adopted clearly reflects the federal approach: As enacted, Rule 606(b) prohibited the use of *any* evidence of juror deliberations, subject only to the express exceptions for extraneous information and outside influences.[2]

For those who consider legislative history relevant, here it confirms that this choice of language was no accident. Congress rejected a prior version of the Rule that, in accordance with the Iowa approach, would have prohibited juror testimony only as to the "effect of anything upon ... [any] juror's mind or emotions ... or concerning his mental processes." [*S*]*ee Tanner v. United States,* 483 U.S. 107, 123–125 (1987) (detailing the legislative history of the Rule). Thus Congress

---

[1] The Iowa rule derived from *Wright v. Illinois & Miss. Tel. Co.,* 20 Iowa 195 (1866), in which the Iowa Supreme Court held that a trial court considering a motion for a new trial should have accepted the affidavits of four jurors who claimed that their damages verdict had been determined by taking the average of the sums each juror thought proper (a "quotient" verdict). The *Wright* court reasoned that, unlike evidence of a juror's subjective intentions in reaching a verdict, whether the verdict had been obtained in this fashion was an "independent fact" and thus could and should be proved by any available evidence.

[2] The additional exception for mistakes made in entering the verdict on the verdict form was adopted in 2006. *See* 547 U.S. 1281, 1286.

"specifically understood, considered, and rejected a version of Rule 606(b)" that would have likely permitted the introduction of evidence of deliberations to show dishonesty during *voir dire. Id.,* at 125.

III

A

Seeking to rebut this straightforward understanding of Rule 606(b), Warger first insists that the proceedings that follow a motion for new trial based on dishonesty during *voir dire* do not involve an "inquiry into the validity of the verdict." His argument is as follows: Under *McDonough,* a party moving for a new trial on the basis of *voir dire* dishonesty need not show that this dishonesty had an effect on the verdict. Although a successful claim will result in vacatur of the judgment, vacatur is simply the *remedy* for the *McDonough* error, just as it may be the remedy for a variety of errors that have nothing to do with the manner in which the jury reached its verdict. Therefore, Warger asserts, the "inquiry begins and ends with what happened during voir dire."

We are not persuaded. Warger, it seems, would restrict Rule 606(b)'s application to those claims of error for which a court must examine the manner in which the jury reached its verdict—claims, one might say, involving an inquiry into the jury's verdict. But the "inquiry" to which the Rule refers is one into the "*validity* of the verdict," not into the verdict itself. The Rule does not focus on the means by which deliberations evidence might be used to invalidate a verdict. It does not say "during an inquiry into jury deliberations," or prohibit the introduction of evidence of deliberations "for use in determining whether an asserted error affected the jury's verdict." It simply applies "[d]uring an inquiry into the validity of the verdict"—that is, during a *proceeding* in which the verdict may be rendered invalid. Whether or not a juror's alleged misconduct during *voir dire* had a direct effect on the jury's verdict, the motion for a new trial requires a court to determine whether the verdict can stand.

B

Next, Warger contends that excluding jury deliberations evidence tending to show that a juror lied during *voir dire* is unnecessary to fulfill Congress' apparent objectives of encouraging full and open debate in the jury room and preventing the harassment of former jurors. He observes that jurors remain free to, and may sometimes be forced to, disclose what happened in the jury room, and that ethical rules limit the ability of parties to harass jurors following trial. But these are arguments against Rule 606(b) generally, not arguments for the particular exception to the Rule that Warger seeks. Congress' enactment of Rule 606(b) was premised on the concerns that the use of deliberations evidence to challenge verdicts would represent a threat to both jurors and finality in those circumstances not covered by the Rule's express exceptions. Warger cannot escape the scope of the Rule Congress adopted simply by asserting that its concerns were misplaced.

C

Nor do we accept Warger's contention that we must adopt his interpretation of Rule 606(b) so as to avoid constitutional concerns. The Constitution guarantees both criminal and civil litigants a right to an impartial jury. And we have made clear that *voir dire* can be an essential means of protecting this right. These principles, Warger asserts, require that parties be allowed to use evidence of deliberations to demonstrate that a juror lied during *voir dire*.

Given the clarity of both the text and history of Rule 606(b), however, the canon of constitutional avoidance has no role to play here. The canon "is a tool for choosing between competing plausible interpretations" of a provision. *Clark v. Suarez Martinez,* 543 U.S. 371, 381 (2005). It "has no application in the absence of . . . ambiguity." *United States v. Oakland Cannabis Buyers' Cooperative,* 532 U.S. 483, 494 (2001). We see none here.

Moreover, any claim that Rule 606(b) is unconstitutional in circumstances such as these is foreclosed by our decision in *Tanner.* In *Tanner,* we concluded that Rule 606(b) precluded a criminal defendant from introducing evidence that multiple jurors had been intoxicated during trial, rejecting the contention that this exclusion violated the defendant's Sixth Amendment right to " 'a tribunal both impartial and mentally competent to afford a hearing.' " 483 U.S., at 126 (quoting *Jordan v. Massachusetts*, 225 U.S. 167, 176 (1912)). We reasoned that the defendant's right to an unimpaired jury was sufficiently protected by *voir dire,* the observations of court and counsel during trial, and the potential use of "nonjuror evidence" of misconduct. 483 U.S., at 127. Similarly here, a party's right to an impartial jury remains protected despite Rule 606(b)'s removal of one means of ensuring that jurors are unbiased. Even if jurors lie in *voir dire* in a way that conceals bias, juror impartiality is adequately assured by the parties' ability to bring to the court's attention any evidence of bias before the verdict is rendered, and to employ nonjuror evidence even after the verdict is rendered.[3]

IV

We further hold, consonant with the Eighth Circuit, that the affidavit Warger sought to introduce was not admissible under Rule 606(b)(2)(A)'s exception for evidence as to whether "extraneous prejudicial information was improperly brought to the jury's attention."

---

[3]   There may be cases of juror bias so extreme that, almost by definition, the jury trial right has been abridged. If and when such a case arises, the Court can consider whether the usual safeguards are or are not sufficient to protect the integrity of the process. We need not consider the question, however, for those facts are not presented here.

Generally speaking, information is deemed "extraneous" if it derives from a source "external" to the jury. *See Tanner,* 483 U.S., at 117. "External" matters include publicity and information related specifically to the case the jurors are meant to decide, while "internal" matters include the general body of experiences that jurors are understood to bring with them to the jury room. *See id.,* at 117–119. Here, the excluded affidavit falls on the "internal" side of the line: Whipple's daughter's accident may well have informed her general views about negligence liability for car crashes, but it did not provide either her or the rest of the jury with any specific knowledge regarding Shauers' collision with Warger.

Indeed, Warger does not argue that Whipple's statements related to "extraneous" information in this sense. Instead, he contends that because Whipple would have been disqualified from the jury had she disclosed her daughter's accident, *any* information she shared with the other jurors was extraneous.

We cannot agree that whenever a juror should have been excluded from the jury, anything that juror says is necessarily "extraneous" within the meaning of Rule 606(b)(2)(A). Were that correct, parties would find it quite easy to avoid Rule 606(b)'s limitations. As discussed above, Congress adopted the restrictive version of the anti-impeachment rule, one that common-law courts had concluded precludes parties from using deliberations evidence to prove juror dishonesty during *voir dire.* But if Warger's understanding of the "extraneous" information exception were accepted, then any time a party could use such evidence to show that a juror's "correct response [during *voir dire*] would have provided a valid basis for a challenge"—a prerequisite for relief under *McDonough*—all evidence of what that juror said during deliberations would be admissible. The "extraneous" information exception would swallow much of the rest of Rule 606(b).

Even if such a result were not precluded by Congress' apparent intent to adopt the restrictive federal approach, it is foreclosed by *Tanner,* which relied upon the doctrine that "treat[s] allegations of the physical or mental incompetence of a juror as 'internal' rather than 'external' matters." 483 U.S., at 118. *Tanner* cited, in particular, cases holding that evidence of jurors' insanity, inability to understand English, and hearing impairments are all "internal" matters subject to exclusion under Rule 606(b). Were we to follow Warger's understanding of the "extraneous information" exception, all these cases, including *Tanner,* would have been wrongly decided: If the jurors were not able to serve on the jury in the first place, or should have been dismissed for their misconduct during the trial, then what they said or did during deliberations would necessarily be "extraneous" and admissible. *Tanner*'s implicit rejection of this view easily extends from the sort of juror incompetence considered in that case to the alleged bias considered here. Whether a juror would have been struck from the jury because of incompetence or bias, the mere fact that a juror would have been struck does not make admissible evidence regarding that juror's conduct and statements during deliberations.

For the foregoing reasons, the judgment of the United States Court of Appeals for the Eighth Circuit is affirmed.

It is so ordered.

2. SHOULD JURORS BE ABLE TO PRESENT EVIDENCE ABOUT DISCRIMINATORY STATEMENTS IN THE JURY ROOM?

The Supreme Court in *Warger v. Shauers* read Federal Rule of Evidence 609(b)(1) broadly and the Rule 606(b)(2) exceptions narrowly, thus precluding juror evidence concerning statements within the jury room. But what if those statements had been discriminatory on the basis of race, gender, or religion?

In footnote 3 of her opinion, Justice Sotomayor states:

> There may be cases of juror bias so extreme that, almost by definition, the jury trial right has been abridged. If and when such a case arises, the Court can consider whether the usual safeguards are or are not sufficient to protect the integrity of the process.

As you read the following case, consider whether, if it were decided under federal law, it would fall within footnote 3 and thus survive the Supreme Court's decision in *Warger v. Shauers*.

Fleshner v. Pepose Vision Institute, P.C.

Supreme Court of Missouri, 2010
304 S.W.3d 81

OPINION

■ MARY R. RUSSELL, JUDGE.

Michelle Fleshner sued her former employer, Pepose Vision Institute, P.C. ("PVI"), for damages resulting from its wrongful termination of her. A jury found PVI liable on Fleshner's claim and awarded her $30,000 in actual damages and $95,000 in punitive damages. This Court granted transfer after disposition by the court of appeals. Jurisdiction is vested in this Court pursuant to article V, section 10 of the Missouri Constitution.

Among its allegations of error, PVI claims that the trial court erred in failing to hold a hearing on its motion for a new trial based on juror misconduct. PVI contends that one juror's anti-Semitic comments about a defense witness deprived it of a jury of 12 fair and impartial jurors. This Court finds that if a juror makes statements evincing ethnic or religious bias or prejudice during jury deliberations, the parties are deprived of their right to a fair and impartial jury and equal protection of the law. Accordingly, the trial court should have held a hearing to determine whether the alleged anti-Semitic comments were made. The overruling of the motion for a new trial was error. The judgment is reversed, and the case is remanded.

* * *

I.   Background

Fleshner worked for PVI, a refractive surgery practice. During the course of her employment, the U.S. Department of Labor investigated PVI to determine whether it failed to pay its employees overtime compensation when they worked more than 40 hours a week. Fleshner received a telephone call at home from a Department of Labor investigator seeking background information about PVI. Fleshner told the investigator about the hours worked by PVI's employees. The next morning she reported her telephone conversation to her supervisor.

Fleshner's employment with PVI was terminated the day after she reported the telephone conversation. Fleshner filed an action against PVI, asserting wrongful termination of employment in violation of public policy and failure to pay overtime compensation in violation of section 290.505, RSMo Supp.2003. As noted, the jury found in favor of Fleshner and awarded her $125,000.

PVI filed motions for a new trial on several bases, including juror misconduct. After the jury was dismissed, a juror approached PVI's attorneys and reported that another juror made anti-Semitic statements during jury deliberations. According to the juror's affidavit, another juror made the following comments directed at a witness for PVI:[2] "She is a Jewish witch." "She is a Jewish bitch." "She is a penny-pinching Jew." "She was such a cheap Jew that she did not want to pay Plaintiff unemployment compensation."

According to an affidavit by one of PVI's attorneys, another juror approached PVI's attorneys and indicated that several anti-Semitic comments were made during deliberations but did not specify what was said. In overruling PVI's motions, the trial court concluded that jury deliberations are sacrosanct and that the juror's alleged comments did not constitute the kind of jury misconduct that would allow the trial court to set aside the verdict and order a new trial.

II.   Analysis

A.   Jury Misconduct in the Form of Anti-Semitic Remarks

PVI alleges that its right to a fair and impartial jury trial was denied when the trial court overruled its motions for a new trial because a juror allegedly made anti-Semitic comments about a witness during jury deliberations. PVI contended in its motions for new trial

---

[2]   The witness is the wife of the president and sole owner of PVI. She serves as PVI's corporate secretary and as a consultant to PVI.

that, as a result of the anti-Semitic comments, it was deprived of its due process rights and did not receive a fair trial.

Standard of Review

This Court will not disturb a trial court's ruling on a motion for a new trial based on juror misconduct unless the trial court abused its discretion. A trial court abuses its discretion if its ruling "is clearly against the logic of the circumstances then before the court and is so arbitrary and unreasonable as to shock the sense of justice and indicate a lack of careful consideration." *Wingate by Carlisle v. Lester E. CoxMed. Ctr.*, 853 S.W.2d 912, 917 (Mo. banc 1993).

Analysis

Both the United States Constitution and Missouri Constitution provide that "no person shall be deprived of life, liberty or property without due process of law." U.S. Const. amend. V; Mo. Const. art. I, sec. 10. "It is axiomatic that 'a fair trial in a fair tribunal is a basic requirement of due process.'" *Caperton v. A.T. Massey Coal Co.*, ___ U.S. ___, ___, (2009) (quoting *In re Murchison*, 349 U.S. 133, 136 (1955)). Moreover, the Missouri Constitution provides for the right to a trial by jury for civil cases. Mo. Const. art. I, sec. 22(a). As this Court has recognized, the right to a trial by jury does not simply provide that 12 jurors will decide the case. If the right to trial by jury is to mean anything, all 12 jurors must be "fair and impartial." *See Catlett v. Ill. Cent. Gulf R.R. Co.*, 793 S.W.2d 351, 353 (Mo. banc 1990). Each juror must "enter the jury box disinterested and with an open mind, free from bias or prejudice."[3] *Catlett*, 793 S.W.2d at 353. While every party is entitled to a fair trial, as a practical matter, our jury system cannot guarantee every party a *perfect* trial.

The general rule in Missouri, referred to as the Mansfield Rule, is that a juror's testimony about jury misconduct allegedly affecting deliberations may not be used to impeach the jury's verdict. "A juror who has reached his conclusions on the basis of evidence presented for his consideration may not have his mental processes and innermost thoughts put on a slide for examination under the judicial microscope." *Baumle v. Smith*, 420 S.W.2d 341, 348 (Mo.1967). In other words, juror testimony is improper if it merely alleges that jurors acted on improper motives, reasoning, beliefs, or mental operations, also known as "matters inherent in the verdict."[4] There are two major policy

---

[3]   Voir dire is the tool for trial courts to weed out those potential jurors who are not fair and impartial. Ideally, the potential jurors' answers to questioning during voir dire would reveal every bias or prejudice. Those potential jurors expressing biases or prejudices would be stricken, while those venirepersons who did not reveal any biases or prejudices would be impaneled to hear and decide the case. In reality, potential jurors are not likely to admit their biases or prejudices, especially those concerning ethnicity and religion, in open court proceedings like voir dire.

[4]   Matters inherent in the verdict include a juror not understanding the law as stated in the instructions, a juror not joining in the verdict, a juror voting a certain way due to misconception of the evidence, a juror misunderstanding the statements of a witness, and a juror being mistaken in his calculations.

considerations for this rule. First, there would be no end to litigation if verdicts could be set aside because one juror reportedly did not correctly understand the law or accurately weigh the evidence. Second, there is no legitimate way to corroborate or refute the mental process of a particular juror.

Over the years, an exception to the rule prohibiting juror testimony has been adopted. Jurors may testify about juror misconduct occurring outside the courtroom. This exception has been used to allow jurors to testify as to whether they gathered evidence independent to that presented at trial. When a juror obtains extrinsic evidence, the trial court conducts a hearing to determine whether the extrinsic evidence prejudiced the verdict.

PVI did not allege juror misconduct occurring outside the courtroom. Instead, PVI asked for a new trial on the basis of juror misconduct occurring *inside* the jury room. PVI alleges that comments made by a juror revealing religious and ethnic bias or prejudice during deliberations prevented it from receiving its constitutional right to a trial by a fair and impartial jury.

Specifically, PVI alleges that, during jury deliberations, a juror made the following statements about the defense witness, who is also the wife of the president of PVI: "She is a Jewish witch." "She is a Jewish bitch." "She is a penny-pinching Jew." "She was such a cheap Jew that she did not want to pay Plaintiff unemployment compensation." Those alleged comments, PVI claims, demonstrate it did not receive a trial by a fair and impartial jury.

While jurors' mental processes and innermost thoughts or beliefs may not be examined, this Court has never considered whether the trial court may hear testimony about juror statements during deliberations evincing ethnic or religious bias or prejudice.

Other jurisdictions that have analyzed similar situations have decided that juror testimony is admissible. The Wisconsin Supreme Court in *After Hour Welding, Inc. v. Laneil Management Co.* determined a trial court may hear juror testimony if it learns that the verdict may have been a result of racial, national origin, religious, or gender bias. 108 Wis.2d 734 (1982). In that case, the defendant moved for a new trial on the basis of jury misconduct. The defendant supported its motion with a juror's affidavit stating that other jurors called a witness who was an officer of the defendant corporation "a cheap Jew." In making its decision, the court recognized that "[w]hile the rule against impeachment of a jury verdict is strong and necessary, it is not written in stone nor is it a door incapable of being opened." *Id.* at 689. The rule "competes with the desire and duty of the judicial system to avoid injustice and to redress the grievances of private litigants." *Id.* The court balanced the interest of privacy for juror discussion against the right to a fair trial and found that when the right to a trial by an impartial jury is impaired by a juror's material prejudice, the interest of juror privacy yields to the right to a fair trial.

Similarly, the Florida Supreme Court considered whether a trial court could hear juror testimony about racial remarks made in jury deliberations. *Powell v. Allstate Ins. Co.*, 652 So.2d 354, 355 (Fla.1995). The trial court held an in-court interview of a juror, who revealed that during deliberations several jurors made derogatory remarks about the plaintiffs, both of whom were black citizens of Jamaican birth. The jury foreperson stated the following, considering it a "joke": "There's a saying in North Carolina, hit a [n* * * * *] and get ten points, hit him when he's moving, get fifteen." *Id.* The court recognized that a juror may not testify as to "any matter which essentially inheres in the verdict or indictment." *Id.* at 356. However, jurors may testify about "overt acts" that might have prejudicially affected the jury's verdict. *Id.* The court concluded that "appeals to racial bias . . . made openly among jurors" constitute "overt acts," and the trial court may hear juror testimony to impeach the verdict. *Id.* at 357.

In *Evans v. Galbraith-Foxworth Lumber Co.*, the Texas Court of Civil Appeals found that when jurors made anti-Semitic comments during jury deliberations, litigants did not receive a fair and impartial trial by jury. 31 S.W.2d 496, 500 (Tex.Civ.App.1929). During deliberations, a juror stated that one of the plaintiffs was "a Jew," that one of the jurors was "a Jew," but that he could not understand why other jurors would be "partial to a Jew." *Id.* at 499. The court explained that, in a situation where jurors make anti-Semitic comments during deliberations, setting aside the verdict is proper:

> It may be clear that eleven (or a lesser number) of the jurors were not, to any degree, influenced by the improper conduct; yet if it remains reasonably doubtful whether one (or a larger number) was, or was not, influenced, the vice remains and the verdict must be set aside because each juror can rightly agree to the verdict only when guided solely by the instructions of the trial judge and the evidence heard in open court.

Id. at 500.

When a juror makes statements evincing ethnic or religious bias or prejudice during deliberations, the juror exposes his mental processes and innermost thoughts. What used to "rest alone in the juror's breast" has now been exposed to the other jurors. *See Baumle*, 420 S.W.2d at 348. The juror has revealed that he is not fair and impartial. Whether the statements may have had a prejudicial effect on other jurors is not necessary to determine. Such statements evincing ethnic or religious bias or prejudice deny the parties their constitutional rights to a trial by 12 fair and impartial jurors and equal protection of the law. *See Powell*, 652 So.2d at 358. The Florida Supreme Court, in criticizing a juror's expression of racial bias, commented, "neither a wronged litigant nor society itself should be without a means to remedy a palpable miscarriage of justice." *Id.* at 356.

Accordingly, if a party files a motion for a new trial alleging there were statements reflecting ethnic or religious bias or prejudice made by a juror during deliberations, the trial court should hold an evidentiary hearing to determine whether any such statements occurred. Juror testimony about matters inherent in the verdict should be excluded. If the trial court finds after conducting a hearing that such biased or prejudicial statements were made during deliberations, then the motion for a new trial should be granted as the parties would have been deprived of their right to a trial by 12 fair and impartial jurors.

Jurors are encouraged to voice their common knowledge and beliefs during deliberations, but common knowledge and beliefs do not include ethnic or religious bias or prejudice. The alleged anti-Semitic comments made during deliberations in this case are "not simply a matter of 'political correctness' to be brushed aside by a thick-skinned judiciary." *Powell,* 652 So.2d at 358. As stated in *United States v. Heller,* "A racially or religiously biased individual harbors certain negative stereotypes which, despite his protestations to the contrary, may well prevent him or her from making decisions based solely on the facts and law that our jury system requires." 785 F.2d 1524, 1527 (11th Cir.1986). Such stereotyping has no place in jury deliberations.

The ethnicity or religion of any party or witness unrelated to the evidence should have no bearing on the outcome of a trial. To allow the verdict to stand without holding a hearing to determine whether the alleged comments were made undermines public confidence in the justice system. The courts must zealously guard the right to a fair and impartial trial and equal protection under the law.

The trial court abused its discretion in failing to hold an evidentiary hearing to determine whether the alleged juror misconduct occurred. The trial court's judgment is reversed, and the case is remanded.

[The second portion of the Court's decision dealt with the standard for causation of termination.]

III. Conclusion

The judgment is reversed, and the case is remanded.

All concur.

COMMENTS AND QUESTIONS CONCERNING *WARGER V. SHAUERS* AND *FLESHNER V. PEPOSE VISION INSTITUTE, P.C.*

1.   Had the Missouri Supreme Court been interpreting Federal Rule of Evidence 606(b), would its decision in *Fleshner* survive the Supreme Court's decision in *Wager v. Shauers?* Is *Fleshner,* in the words of footnote 3

in Justice Sotomayor's opinion in *Wager v. Shauers*, a case of "juror bias so extreme that, almost by definition, the jury trial right has been abridged"?

2.   Why might the Supreme Court have granted certiorari in *Warger v. Shauers*?

3.   In contrast to the unanimity normally required within the federal courts by Federal Rule of Civil Procedure 48(b), nine members of a twelve-person civil jury are sufficient to support a verdict in a Missouri court of record. Mo. Const. art. I § 22(a). Should the party seeking to overturn a Missouri verdict have to show that more than three jurors were affected by discriminatory remarks?

4.   How did the plaintiff Warger attempt to get around the bar on juror testimony created by Federal Rule of Evidence 606(b)?

5.   Did the juror in *Warger* say anything much different to her fellow jurors than what jurors presumably say on a regular basis as they consider the evidence in light of their own life experiences?

6.   Would Federal Rule of Evidence 606(b) bar a judge from considering juror testimony concerning the following matters?

(a)   After its inability to reach a verdict, the jury unanimously decided that it would resolve the case by a coin flip.

(b)   Jurors allege that, "during the course of jury deliberations, there was screaming, hysterical crying, fist banging, name calling, and the use of obscene language. One of the jurors allegedly threw a chair at another, then 'broke down,' crying and claiming that he was a 'sick man.'" *See Jacobson v. Henderson*, 765 F. 3d 12, 14 (2nd Cir. 1985) (*per curiam*).

(c)   One juror tells another at a break in the jury deliberations, "I have a friend who paid me $1000 to look kindly on the plaintiff's testimony in this case. Would you like me to see if he might have $1000 for you?"

(d)   One juror tells the other members of the jury that she has located information relevant to the case on the Internet.

7.   Is the handling of discriminatory juror testimony pursuant to Federal Rule of Evidence 606(b) analogous to the manner in which discriminatory voir dire is treated under *Batson v. Kentucky* and its progeny? Do we presume that jury selection and the jury process have operated properly until presented with direct evidence to the contrary? Peremptory challenges can be made, and jury verdicts supported, for any reason or no reason. However, we will not permit actions based on overtly discriminatory reasons.

8.   You are a juror in a high profile civil action. Are you pleased to learn that you cannot be questioned about what happens in the jury room? Do Federal Rule of Evidence 606(b) and the Mansfield Rule protect only jurors?

9.   What is the standard of review in cases such as these?

V. Judicial Recusal

Not only do the parties to a civil action have a right to an unbiased jury, but they also have a right to an unbiased judge. In bench trials, tried by the judge without a jury, the judge makes all the trial determinations, both factual and legal. Even in a jury trial, though, the judge makes crucial decisions that will impact the case, such as whether to grant dispositive pretrial and post-trial motions, whether to admit certain evidence for the jury to consider, and how to instruct the jury on the law that they should apply in making their factual determinations. So the parties have a right to an unbiased judge in both jury and nonjury cases.

There are two major sources of law that guarantee the parties a right to an unbiased judge. Both state and federal judiciaries are governed by statutes or rules that proscribe inappropriate judicial conduct and the appearance of judicial partiality. Such statutes and rules provide the basis for most challenges to judges, and such claims are raised by a motion asking the judge to step aside, or recuse, himself from the case in question. Indeed, in some situations judicial actions or the appearance of judicial bias can be so clear that the parties can raise a constitutional due process challenge to the judge's continued participation in the action. Both of these challenges will be considered in the next subsections.[1]

A. Federal Statutory Recusal

1. Federal Statutory Recusal Law

Two federal statutes permit parties to seek the recusal of a biased or prejudiced judge. The first of these statutes, 28 U.S.C. § 144, by its terms requires a district judge to recuse himself whenever "a party to any proceeding in a district court makes and files a timely and sufficient affidavit that the judge before whom the matter is pending has a personal bias or prejudice either against him or in favor of any adverse party." However, this statute has been read quite narrowly so as not to require automatic recusal. Instead, Section 144 has been interpreted consistently with 28 U.S.C. § 455(b)(1), which provides for recusal when a judge "has a personal bias or prejudice concerning a party, or personal knowledge of disputed evidentiary facts concerning the proceeding."

Section 455 is the more comprehensive federal recusal statute, applying to all federal judges (not just to judges in federal district

---

[1] In addition to being subject to recusal under rules, statutes, and constitutional provisions, judges' actions both on and off the bench are governed by ethical codes of conduct. Many of these state codes of judicial conduct, which provide a basis for disciplinary action against judges, are based upon the American Bar Association's Model Code of Judicial Conduct. http://www.americanbar.org/groups/professional_responsibility/publications/model_code_of_judicial_conduct.html.

court). It is the federal statute upon which most recusal motions are based. Although Section 455 sets forth a series of circumstances in which a judge is required to recuse, the two major types of situations requiring recusal are contained in Sections 455(a) and (b).

Section 455(a) provides:

> Any justice, judge, or magistrate judge of the United States shall disqualify himself in any proceeding in which his impartiality might reasonably be questioned.

Thus Section 455(a) establishes an objective standard, and a party need not show actual bias or prejudice (as it must under 28 U.S.C. § 144) to successfully obtain a federal judge's recusal.

In addition to the objective appearance of partiality provision of Section 455(a), a series of specific circumstances in which recusal is required are set forth in 28 U.S.C. § 455(b). The party seeking recusal must show specific facts, rather than mere appearances, in order to secure a Section 455(b) recusal. Thus, while a party need not show actual bias to obtain the recusal of a judge under Section 455(a), such a showing is necessary under Section 455(b)(1). The list of situations requiring recusal of a federal judge under Section 455(b) are summarized in Figure 12–3.

FIGURE 12–3
MANDATORY RECUSAL OF FEDERAL JUDGES UNDER 28 U.S.C. SECTION 455

Basis for Recusal	28 U.S.C. § 455 Provision	Can Parties Waive Disqualification?	Can Action by Judge Preclude Recusal?
Impartiality Might Reasonably be Questioned (Objective Standard)	§ 455(a)	Yes, if preceded by full disclosure on record of disqualification basis. 28 U.S.C. § 455(e).	No
Judge Has Personal Bias/ Prejudice about Party or Personal Knowledge of Disputed Facts	§ 455(b)(1)	No	No
Judge, or Lawyer with Whom She Served, was Lawyer in Matter or Judge or such Lawyer was Material Witness	§ 455(b)(2)	No	No

As Government Attorney, Judge was Counsel, Adviser, or Material Witness in Matter or Expressed Opinion on Merits of Controversy	§ 455(b)(3)	No	No
Judge (Himself or as Fiduciary), Spouse, or Minor Child in Household has Financial Interest in Controversy or Party or any Other Interest that could be Substantially Affected by Case Outcome	§ 455(b)(4)	No	Yes, when (1) Substantial Judicial Time devoted to Matter; (2) Financial Interest Discovered After Case Assigned; and (3) Judge, Spouse, or Minor Child in Household has Financial Interest in Party (other than interest that could be Substantially Affected by Outcome), Judge Need Not Recuse if He, Spouse or Child Divests Interest that was Ground for Disqualification. 28 U.S.C. § 455(f).
Judge, Spouse, or Person within 3rd of Relation-ship to Either, or Spouse of Such Person, is (1) Party; or (2) acting as Lawyer in Action; or Judge Knows (3) person has Interest that may be Substantially Affected by Action or (4) is Likely to be Material Witness	28 U.S.C. § 455(b)(5)	No	No

The recusal of a federal district judge under 28 U.S.C. § 455(a) is the subject of the following case.

2. APPLICATION OF FEDERAL STATUTORY RECUSAL LAW: *LIGON V. CITY OF NEW YORK*

Ligon v. City of New York

United States Court of Appeals, Second Circuit, 2013

736 F.3d 118, *vacated in part*, 743 F.3d 362 (2014)

OPINION

■ PER CURIAM.

These cases, motions of which were argued in tandem, deal with an issue of great significance: the constitutional boundaries of practices by the New York City Police Department ("NYPD") that subject citizens to being stopped and frisked. On August 12, 2013, Judge Shira A. Scheindlin, a long-serving and distinguished jurist of the United States District Court for the Southern District of New York, held that the City of New York ("the City") had violated the plaintiffs' Fourth and Fourteenth Amendment rights, and ordered the City to engage in a variety of remedial measures and activities.

On August 27, 2013, the City moved in the district court to stay those remedies, pending an appeal on the merits of the district court's decision. Judge Scheindlin denied the motions. On September 23, 2013, the City moved in this Court to stay the imposition of the district court's remedies. By order dated October 31, 2013, we both granted that stay and, because the appearance of impartiality had been compromised by certain statements made by Judge Scheindlin during proceedings in the district court and in media interviews, we reassigned the cases to a different district judge, to be chosen randomly. We now explain the basis for that order, which is superseded by this opinion.

BACKGROUND

We emphasize that the merits of this litigation are not before us and are not at issue here. Accordingly, we neither express nor intimate any views on the merits of the underlying actions. This opinion deals only with our procedural decision to direct the reassignment of the cases and turns on how the cases came before Judge Scheindlin and the media interviews she gave during the pendency of these lawsuits.

For the sake of clarity, we recite the procedural history that has led us to this point. In January 2008, the plaintiffs in *Floyd* filed a class action alleging that the NYPD violated the Fourth and Fourteenth Amendments through a pattern and practice of stopping and frisking without reasonable suspicion. In March 2012, the plaintiffs in *Ligon* filed a class action alleging that the NYPD violated the Fourth Amendment by engaging in a practice of unlawfully stopping, frisking, and arresting persons for trespass because of their presence in or near buildings enrolled by their landlords in an NYPD crime prevention program known as the Trespass Affidavit Program ("TAP").

When filing, the plaintiffs in *Floyd* marked the case on the appropriate form as related to *Daniels v. City of New York,* an earlier case over which Judge Scheindlin presided. Likewise, the plaintiffs in *Ligon* marked that case as related to *Davis v. City of New York,* over which Judge Scheindlin was also presiding. Because *Daniels,* although terminated a month earlier, and *Davis* had been assigned to Judge Scheindlin, *Floyd* and *Ligon* were forwarded to her, pursuant to Rule 13 of the Local Rules for the Division of Business Among District Judges, and she accepted them both as related cases.

In a decision dated January 8, 2013, and amended on February 14, 2013, Judge Scheindlin granted the *Ligon* plaintiffs' motion for a preliminary injunction, holding that they had "shown a clear likelihood of proving that defendants have displayed deliberate indifference toward a widespread practice of unconstitutional trespass stops by the NYPD outside TAP buildings in the Bronx." In a separate opinion, Judge Scheindlin granted the defendants' motion to stay any remedies until after the "issuance of a final decision regarding the appropriate scope of preliminary injunctive relief, and the appropriate scope of permanent injunctive relief (if any) in *Floyd.*"

On August 12, 2013, following a nine-week trial in *Floyd,* Judge Scheindlin held that the City of New York violated the plaintiffs' rights under the Fourth Amendment and the Equal Protection Clause of the Fourteenth Amendment. The same day, Judge Scheindlin issued an opinion setting forth remedial measures in both *Floyd* and *Ligon* intended to bring the NYPD's use of stop-and-frisk into compliance with the Fourth and Fourteenth Amendments.

On August 16, 2013, the defendants in both cases filed notices of appeal in this court. On August 27, 2013, the City of New York moved in the district court to stay the remedies in *Floyd* and *Ligon,* pending the outcome of the appeals process. On September 17, 2013, Judge Scheindlin denied the City's stay motions. On September 23, 2013, the City moved in this court to stay the district court's August 12, 2013 remedies order.

Following oral argument, this panel, on October 31, 2013, stayed, "the District Court's January 8, 2013 'Opinion and Order,' as well as the August 12, 2013 'Liability Opinion' and 'Remedies Opinion,' each of which may or will have the effect of causing actions to be taken by defendants or designees of the District Court, or causing restraints against actions that otherwise would be taken by defendants." This panel also concluded "that, in the interest, and appearance, of fair and impartial administration of justice, UPON REMAND, these cases shall be assigned to a different District Judge, chosen randomly under the established practices of the District Court for the Southern District of New York. This newly-designated District Judge shall implement this Court's mandate staying all proceedings and otherwise await further action by the Court of Appeals on the merits of the ongoing appeals."

We now explain in greater detail the basis for our decision to reassign the cases.

DISCUSSION

Title 28, United States Code, section 455(a) provides that "[a]ny justice, judge, or magistrate judge of the United States shall disqualify himself in any proceeding in which his impartiality might reasonably be questioned." * * *

The goal of section 455(a) is to avoid not only partiality but also the appearance of partiality. The section does so by establishing an "objective standard 'designed to promote public confidence in the impartiality of the judicial process.' "[13] The rule functions as a critical internal check to ensure the just operation of the judiciary. Our Court, sitting *en banc,* has stated that there exists "unusual circumstances where both for the judge's sake and the appearance of justice, an assignment to a different judge is salutary and in the public interest, especially as it minimizes even a suspicion of partiality."[14] * * *

We emphasize at the outset that we make no findings of misconduct, actual bias, or actual partiality on the part of Judge Scheindlin. Following our review of the record, however, we conclude that her conduct while on the bench, which appears to have resulted in these lawsuits being filed and directed to her, in conjunction with her statements to the media and the resulting stories published while a decision on the merits was pending and while public interest in the outcome of the litigation was high, might cause a reasonable observer to question her impartiality. For this reason, her disqualification is required by section 455(a).

A.

The appearance of partiality stems in the first instance from comments made by Judge Scheindlin that a reasonable observer could interpret as intimating her views on the merits of a case that had yet to be filed, and as seeking to have that case filed and to preside over it after it was filed. These comments were made in the earlier case of *Daniels v. City of New York,* in which the City entered into a settlement agreement requiring it, *inter alia,* to establish policies that prohibited racial profiling. Ten days before Judge Scheindlin's supervisory authority under the settlement agreement was set to expire, she heard argument on a motion brought by the *Daniels* plaintiffs to extend the settlement period. The transcript of the hearing indicates that the City had substantially complied with the relief required by the settlement and that the plaintiffs were seeking information from the City beyond that required to be furnished by the settlement agreement.

---

[13] *SEC v. Drexel Burnham Lambert Inc. (In re Drexel Burnham Lambert Inc.),* 861 F.2d 1307, 1313 (2d Cir.1988) (quoting H.R.Rep. No. 1453, reprinted in 1974 U.S.C.C.A.N. 6351, 6354–55).

[14] *United States v. Robin,* 553 F.2d 8, 9–10 (2d Cir.1977) (en banc).

Observing that the settlement agreement did not entitle the plaintiffs to the relief they sought, Judge Scheindlin counseled:

THE COURT: [. . .] *why don't you file a lawsuit*

Mr. COSTELLO: We did, we are here.

THE COURT: No, you are struggling with the December 31, 2007 deadline in a 1999 case. *And if you got proof of inappropriate racial profiling in a good constitutional case, why don't you bring a lawsuit? You can certainly mark it as related.*

* * *

(TR 10–11) (emphasis added). She returned to the idea of bringing a suit alleging that the City had violated their racial profiling policies and suggested a basis for the suit:

THE COURT: *what I am trying to say—I am sure I am going to get in trouble for saying it, for $65 you can bring that lawsuit.* You can simply—

MR. MOORE: $350

THE COURT: I knew I had it wrong. *The [C]ity violates its own written policy, the City has a policy that violates—they have violated their policy, here is the proof of it, please give us the remedy. Injunction or damages, or whatever lawyers ask for in compliance. So for $350 you can bring that lawsuit and it is timely.*

(TR 14, 15) (emphasis added). And again:

THE COURT: I don't understand why we have to potentially have, you know, months of briefing when it does fit under this stipulation or it doesn't, that Raffo applies or it doesn't that the court has the power to extend the supervision, that we want our immediate appeal to the circuit. *Why do you need that if you have a lawsuit? Bring it. They have a written policy, right?*

MR. GROSSMAN: *Yes, your Honor.*

THE COURT: *If you think they are violating their written policy, sue them.*

(TR 15) (emphasis added).

Judge Scheindlin then advised the plaintiffs that if they filed such a suit, they would successfully obtain relevant documents produced by the government:

THE COURT: . . . There is enough in the public record to craft the suit.

And then *in that suit simply say, we want produced all that was produced in the 1999 lawsuit. I don't know how you could lose getting it.* It may be a question of whether it is still going to be under protective order or not. *But I can hardly imagine not getting it. You know what I am saying? It is so obvious to me that any Judge would require them to reproduce it to you* in the same format that you have it, that you will have it again. Whether or not it remains confidential.

(TR 18) (emphasis added). After the plaintiffs indicated their willingness to bring the new suit, she repeated her earlier suggestion that the cases were related and indicated her willingness to keep the newly filed case:

> MR. MOORE: To the extent that some of the materials have already been made public.
>
> THE COURT: what's public is public,—If you cite to the Rand study, publicly, nobody can criticize you for that. If they do, they weren't acting in good faith. If I can get the Rand study on the internet, it is public—
>
> MR. MOORE: you can go to the NYPD website, your Honor.
>
> THE COURT: *There you go, that's public. You can use that. And as I said before, I would accept it as a related case, which the plaintiff has the power to designate.*
>
> I think this current motion is withdrawn. Thank you.

(TR 42) (emphasis added).

We believe that a reasonable observer viewing this colloquy would conclude that the appearance of impartiality had been compromised. We do not mean to suggest that a district judge can never engage in a colloquy with a party during which the judge advises the party of its legal or procedural options. However, we think, particularly in combination with the public statements described below, that a reasonable observer could question the impartiality of the judge where the judge described a certain claim that differed from the one at issue in the case before her, urged a party to file a new lawsuit to assert the claim, suggested that such a claim could be viable and would likely entitle the plaintiffs to documents they sought, and advised the party to designate it as a related case so that the case would be assigned to her.

B.

This appearance of partiality by Judge Scheindlin at the *Daniels* hearing was exacerbated as a result of interviews she gave to the news media during the course of the *Floyd* litigation. Cases involving public comment by a presiding judge, other than statements in open court, are infrequent. * * * Of course, not every media comment made by a judge is necessarily grounds for recusal. We note that Judge Scheindlin did not specifically mention the *Floyd* or *Ligon* cases in her media interviews. However, a judge's statements to the media may nevertheless undermine the judge's appearance of impartiality with respect to a pending proceeding, even if the judge refrains from specifically identifying that proceeding in his remarks to the media. Because context is always critical, the relevant question at all times remains whether, under the circumstances taken as a whole, a judge's impartiality may reasonably be called into question. Because there is no *scienter* requirement in section 455, the test is not how a judge intended his remarks to be understood, but whether, as a result of the interviews or other extra-judicial statements, the appearance of impartiality might reasonably be questioned.

In late May 2013, at the conclusion of the evidence in *Floyd,* when public interest from reporting on that trial was high, and months before she had produced a decision, Judge Scheindlin made herself available for interviews by the Associated Press, *The New Yorker*, and the *New York Law Journal.* The "lede" of the AP article dated May 18, 2013, read "[t]he federal judge presiding over civil rights challenges to the stop-and-frisk practices of the New York Police Department has no doubt where she stands with the government. 'I know I'm not their favorite judge,' U.S. District Judge Shira A. Scheindlin said during an Associated Press interview Friday." The lengthy profile of Judge Scheindlin in *The New Yorker*, for which she agreed to be interviewed, was titled, "Rights and Wrongs: A Judge Takes on Stop-and-Frisk." The writer, implying that Judge Scheindlin was aligned with the plaintiffs, wrote,

> [t]he primary outlet for Scheindlin's judicial creativity has been an enduring battle she has fought with the N.Y.P.D. A federal judge since 1994, she has been hearing lawsuits against the police for more than a decade. In decision after decision, she has found that cops have lied, discriminated against people of color, and violated the rights of citizens. Now, in the midst of a mayoral race, with the Democratic candidates united in their opposition to the stop-and-frisk policies of the Bloomberg administration, the Floyd case represents Scheindlin's greatest chance yet to rewrite the rules of engagement between the city's police and its people.

While nothing prohibits a judge from giving an interview to the media, and while one who gives an interview cannot predict with certainty what the writer will say, judges who affiliate themselves with news stories by participating in interviews run the risk that the resulting stories may contribute to the appearance of partiality. It is perhaps illustrative of how such situations can get out of the control of the judge that, later in *The New Yorker* piece, the article quotes a former law clerk of Judge Scheindlin: "As one of her former law clerks put it, 'What you have to remember about the judge is that she thinks cops lie.' "

Further, in those two articles, as well as the *New York Law Journal* article, Judge Scheindlin describes herself as a jurist who is skeptical of law enforcement, in contrast to certain of her colleagues, whom she characterizes as inclined to favor the government. Given the heightened and sensitive public scrutiny of these cases, interviews in which the presiding judge draws such distinctions between herself and her colleagues might lead a reasonable observer to question the judge's impartiality. As the First Circuit put it, "the very rarity of such public statements, and the ease with which they may be avoided, make it more likely that a reasonable person will interpret such statements as evidence of bias."[23]

C.

In our previous order, we referenced the Code of Conduct for United States Judges. We now clarify that we did not intend to imply in our previous order that Judge Scheindlin engaged in misconduct cognizable either under the Code of Conduct or under the Judicial Conduct and Disability Act, 28 U.S.C. §§ 372, *et seq.* No such finding is required under section 455, and we do not find that there was any judicial misconduct or violation of any ethical duty.

"To reassign a case on remand, we need only find that the facts might reasonably cause an objective observer to question the judge's impartiality, or absent proof of personal bias requiring recusal [sic], that reassignment is advisable to preserve the appearance of justice."[25] Even where there is reason to believe that a district judge would fairly conduct further proceedings on remand, "in determining whether to reassign a case we consider not only whether a judge could be expected to have difficulty putting aside his previously expressed views, but also whether reassignment is advisable to preserve the appearance of justice."[26] Such a decision "does not imply any personal criticism of the trial judge,"[27] and none is intended here. * * *

Reassigning a case to a different district judge, while not an everyday occurrence, is not unusual in this Circuit. Nor is reassigning a case to a different district judge an unusual occurrence in our sister Circuits. Indeed, as noted in our accompanying opinion, reassignment is simply a mechanism that allows the courts to ensure that cases are decided by judges without even an *appearance* of partiality.

Although the possible recusal of Judge Scheindlin was not raised either by the parties or the judge herself in the district court or this court, there is no barrier to our reassigning the cases *nostra sponte.* Indeed, in numerous cases in recent years, we have found it appropriate

---

[23] *In re Boston's Children First,* 244 F.3d at 170; *see also United States v. Microsoft Corp.,* 253 F.3d 34, 115 (D.C.Cir.2001) ("Judges who covet publicity, or convey the appearance that they do, lead any objective observer to wonder whether their judgments are being influenced by the prospect of favorable coverage in the media.").

[25] *United States v. Londono,* 100 F.3d 236, 242 (2d Cir.1996) (abrogated on other grounds).

[26] *United States v. Campo,* 140 F.3d 415, 420 (2d Cir.1998).

[27] *United States v. Quattrone,* 441 F.3d 153, 192–93 (2d Cir.2006).

to reassign a case without the issue having been raised or briefed by the parties or considered by the district judge. * * * Given the importance of maintaining the judiciary's appearance of impartiality, we think that it is well within our discretion to order reassignment in these cases.

CONCLUSION

This opinion explains the basis for our order of October 31, 2013, directing the reassignment of these cases to a randomly selected district judge and supersedes that order. To reiterate, we have made no findings that Judge Scheindlin has engaged in judicial misconduct. We conclude only that, based on her conduct at the December 21, 2007 hearing and in giving the interviews to the news media in May 2013, Judge Scheindlin's appearance of impartiality may reasonably be questioned within the meaning of 28 U.S.C. § 455 and that "reassignment is advisable to preserve the appearance of justice."[36]

COMMENTS AND QUESTIONS CONCERNING LIGON V. CITY OF NEW YORK

1.   Which party moved for these cases to be reassigned from Judge Scheindlin?

2.   What did Judge Scheindlin do or say that she should not have done or said?

3.   Would the Court of Appeals have reassigned these cases if Judge Scheindlin had not given media interviews concerning her judicial work? The Court of Appeals specifically noted in its opinion that Judge Scheindlin did not mention either of the stop-and-frisk cases in these interviews. The Court did, though, mention that one of the Judge's former clerks allegedly said, "What you have to remember about the judge is that she thinks cops lie."

4.   What if Judge Scheindlin's comments had been made to a pro se plaintiff rather than to the lawyers representing the plaintiffs in this case? The Court of Appeals noted in its opinion: "We do not mean to suggest that a district judge can never engage in a colloquy with a party during which the judge advises the party of its legal or procedural options."

5.   In an opinion issued the same day as the above opinion reassigning the stop-and-frisk cases to another district judge, the Court of Appeals denied a motion by Judge Scheindlin seeking to participate in the matter "as a party, as an intervenor, or as an *amicus curiae* in an appeal of her decisions." *Ligon v. City of New York*, 736 F.3d 166, 168 (2d Cir. 2013). The Court of Appeals concluded:

> We know of no precedent suggesting that a district judge has standing before an appellate court to protest reassignment of a case. While a district judge may believe that he or she has expended a great deal of effort and energy on a case, only to see it reassigned, reassignment is not a legal injury to the district judge.

---

[36]   *Londono*, 100 F.3d at 242.

Rather, reassignment allows the courts to ensure that cases are decided by judges without even an *appearance* of partiality. A district judge has no legal interest in a case or its outcome, and, consequently, suffers no legal injury by reassignment.

736 F.3d at 170–71.

6.   After the election as Mayor of New York City of Bill de Blasio, who had campaigned on a pledge to reform police stop-and-frisk practices, the City withdrew its appeal of Judge Scheindlin's injunction order. In a settlement with the plaintiffs, the City agreed to accept Judge Scheindlin's order, including the appointment of an independent monitor to develop new stop-and-frisk policies, training, supervision, monitoring, and discipline. Weiser & Goldstein, "New York to End Frisking Lawsuit with Settlement," *N. Y. Times*, Jan. 31, 2014, at A1. *See Floyd v. City of New York*, 770 F.3d 1051 (2d Cir. 2014) (granting City's voluntary dismissal with prejudice of its appeal and denying intervention motions by police unions).

B.   WHEN IS RECUSAL CONSTITUTIONALLY REQUIRED?

Most judicial recusal decisions are based on state or federal rules or statutory provisions such as 28 U.S.C. § 455. However, if the challenged judge is not required to recuse under such provisions, there still may be an argument for recusal under the due process protections of the Fifth or Fourteenth Amendments to the Constitution. This is the argument that is made in the following case.

Caperton v. A.T. Massey Coal Co.

Supreme Court of the United States, 2009
556 U.S. 868

■ JUSTICE KENNEDY delivered the opinion of the Court.

In this case the Supreme Court of Appeals of West Virginia reversed a trial court judgment, which had entered a jury verdict of $50 million. Five justices heard the case, and the vote to reverse was 3 to 2. The question presented is whether the Due Process Clause of the Fourteenth Amendment was violated when one of the justices in the majority denied a recusal motion. The basis for the motion was that the justice had received campaign contributions in an extraordinary amount from, and through the efforts of, the board chairman and principal officer of the corporation found liable for the damages.

Under our precedents there are objective standards that require recusal when "the probability of actual bias on the part of the judge or decisionmaker is too high to be constitutionally tolerable." *Withrow v. Larkin,* 421 U.S. 35, 47 (1975). Applying those precedents, we find that, in all the circumstances of this case, due process requires recusal.

I

In August 2002 a West Virginia jury returned a verdict that found respondents A.T. Massey Coal Co. and its affiliates (hereinafter Massey) liable for fraudulent misrepresentation, concealment, and tortious interference with existing contractual relations. The jury awarded petitioners Hugh Caperton, Harman Development Corp., Harman Mining Corp., and Sovereign Coal Sales (hereinafter Caperton) the sum of $50 million in compensatory and punitive damages.

In June 2004 the state trial court denied Massey's post-trial motions challenging the verdict and the damages award, finding that Massey "intentionally acted in utter disregard of [Caperton's] rights and ultimately destroyed [Caperton's] businesses because, after conducting cost-benefit analyses, [Massey] concluded it was in its financial interest to do so." In March 2005 the trial court denied Massey's motion for judgment as a matter of law.

Don Blankenship is Massey's chairman, chief executive officer, and president. After the verdict but before the appeal, West Virginia held its 2004 judicial elections. Knowing the Supreme Court of Appeals of West Virginia would consider the appeal in the case, Blankenship decided to support an attorney who sought to replace Justice McGraw. Justice McGraw was a candidate for reelection to that court. The attorney who sought to replace him was Brent Benjamin.

In addition to contributing the $1,000 statutory maximum to Benjamin's campaign committee, Blankenship donated almost $2.5 million to "And For The Sake Of The Kids," a political organization formed under 26 U.S.C. § 527. The § 527 organization opposed McGraw and supported Benjamin. Blankenship's donations accounted for more than two-thirds of the total funds it raised. This was not all. Blankenship spent, in addition, just over $500,000 on independent expenditures—for direct mailings and letters soliciting donations as well as television and newspaper advertisements—" 'to support . . . Brent Benjamin.' "

To provide some perspective, Blankenship's $3 million in contributions were more than the total amount spent by all other Benjamin supporters and three times the amount spent by Benjamin's own committee. Caperton contends that Blankenship spent $1 million more than the total amount spent by the campaign committees of both candidates combined.

Benjamin won. He received 382,036 votes (53.3%), and McGraw received 334,301 votes (46.7%).

In October 2005, before Massey filed its petition for appeal in West Virginia's highest court, Caperton moved to disqualify now-Justice Benjamin under the Due Process Clause and the West Virginia Code of Judicial Conduct, based on the conflict caused by Blankenship's campaign involvement. Justice Benjamin denied the motion in April

2006. He indicated that he "carefully considered the bases and accompanying exhibits proffered by the movants." But he found "no objective information . . . to show that this Justice has a bias for or against any litigant, that this Justice has prejudged the matters which comprise this litigation, or that this Justice will be anything but fair and impartial." In December 2006 Massey filed its petition for appeal to challenge the adverse jury verdict. The West Virginia Supreme Court of Appeals granted review.

In November 2007 that court reversed the $50 million verdict against Massey. The majority opinion, authored by then-Chief Justice Davis and joined by Justices Benjamin and Maynard, found that "Massey's conduct warranted the type of judgment rendered in this case." It reversed, nevertheless, based on two independent grounds— first, that a forum-selection clause contained in a contract to which Massey was not a party barred the suit in West Virginia, and, second, that res judicata barred the suit due to an out-of-state judgment to which Massey was not a party. Justice Starcher dissented, stating that the "majority's opinion is morally and legally wrong." Justice Albright also dissented, accusing the majority of "misapplying the law and introducing sweeping 'new law' into our jurisprudence that may well come back to haunt us."

Caperton sought rehearing, and the parties moved for disqualification of three of the five justices who decided the appeal. Photos had surfaced of Justice Maynard vacationing with Blankenship in the French Riviera while the case was pending. Justice Maynard granted Caperton's recusal motion. On the other side Justice Starcher granted Massey's recusal motion, apparently based on his public criticism of Blankenship's role in the 2004 elections. In his recusal memorandum Justice Starcher urged Justice Benjamin to recuse himself as well. He noted that "Blankenship's bestowal of his personal wealth, political tactics, and 'friendship' have created a cancer in the affairs of this Court." Justice Benjamin declined Justice Starcher's suggestion and denied Caperton's recusal motion.

The court granted rehearing. Justice Benjamin, now in the capacity of acting chief justice, selected Judges Cookman and Fox to replace the recused justices. Caperton moved a third time for disqualification, arguing that Justice Benjamin had failed to apply the correct standard under West Virginia law—*i.e.,* whether "a reasonable and prudent person, knowing these objective facts, would harbor doubts about Justice Benjamin's ability to be fair and impartial." Caperton also included the results of a public opinion poll, which indicated that over 67% of West Virginians doubted Justice Benjamin would be fair and impartial. Justice Benjamin again refused to withdraw, noting that the "push poll" was "neither credible nor sufficiently reliable to serve as the basis for an elected judge's disqualification."

In April 2008 a divided court again reversed the jury verdict, and again it was a 3-to-2 decision. Justice Davis filed a modified version of his prior opinion, repeating the two earlier holdings. She was joined by Justice Benjamin and Judge Fox. Justice Albright, joined by Judge Cookman, dissented: "Not only is the majority opinion unsupported by the facts and existing case law, but it is also fundamentally unfair. Sadly, justice was neither honored nor served by the majority." The dissent also noted "genuine due process implications arising under federal law" with respect to Justice Benjamin's failure to recuse himself.

Four months later—a month after the petition for writ of certiorari was filed in this Court—Justice Benjamin filed a concurring opinion. He defended the merits of the majority opinion as well as his decision not to recuse. He rejected Caperton's challenge to his participation in the case under both the Due Process Clause and West Virginia law. Justice Benjamin reiterated that he had no " 'direct, personal, substantial, pecuniary interest' in this case.' " Adopting "a standard merely of 'appearances,' " he concluded, "seems little more than an invitation to subject West Virginia's justice system to the vagaries of the day—a framework in which predictability and stability yield to supposition, innuendo, half-truths, and partisan manipulations."

We granted certiorari.

II

It is axiomatic that "[a] fair trial in a fair tribunal is a basic requirement of due process." [*In re*] *Murchison,* [349 U.S. 133, 136 1955.] As the Court has recognized, however, "most matters relating to judicial disqualification [do] not rise to a constitutional level." *FTC v. Cement Institute,* 333 U.S. 683, 702 (1948). The early and leading case on the subject is *Tumey v. Ohio,* 273 U.S. 510 (1927). There, the Court stated that "matters of kinship, personal bias, state policy, remoteness of interest, would seem generally to be matters merely of legislative discretion." *Id.,* at 523.

The *Tumey* Court concluded that the Due Process Clause incorporated the common-law rule that a judge must recuse himself when he has "a direct, personal, substantial, pecuniary interest" in a case. *Ibid.* This rule reflects the maxim that "[n]o man is allowed to be a judge in his own cause; because his interest would certainly bias his judgment, and, not improbably, corrupt his integrity." The Federalist No. 10, p. 59 (J. Cooke ed.1961) (J. Madison). Under this rule, "disqualification for bias or prejudice was not permitted"; those matters were left to statutes and judicial codes. [*Aetna Life Ins. Co. v.*] *Lavoie,* [475 U.S. 813, 820 (1986)]. Personal bias or prejudice "alone would not be sufficient basis for imposing a constitutional requirement under the Due Process Clause." *Lavoie, supra,* at 820.

As new problems have emerged that were not discussed at common law, however, the Court has identified additional instances which, as an objective matter, require recusal. These are circumstances "in which experience teaches that the probability of actual bias on the part of the judge or decisionmaker is too high to be constitutionally tolerable." *Withrow,* 421 U.S., at 47. To place the present case in proper context, two instances where the Court has required recusal merit further discussion.

A

The first involved the emergence of local tribunals where a judge had a financial interest in the outcome of a case, although the interest was less than what would have been considered personal or direct at common law.

This was the problem addressed in *Tumey.* There, the mayor of a village had the authority to sit as a judge (with no jury) to try those accused of violating a state law prohibiting the possession of alcoholic beverages. Inherent in this structure were two potential conflicts. First, the mayor received a salary supplement for performing judicial duties, and the funds for that compensation derived from the fines assessed in a case. No fines were assessed upon acquittal. The mayor-judge thus received a salary supplement only if he convicted the defendant. Second, sums from the criminal fines were deposited to the village's general treasury fund for village improvements and repairs.

The Court held that the Due Process Clause required disqualification "both because of [the mayor-judge's] direct pecuniary interest in the outcome, and because of his official motive to convict and to graduate the fine to help the financial needs of the village." *Id.,* at 535. It so held despite observing that "[t]here are doubtless mayors who would not allow such a consideration as $12 costs in each case to affect their judgment in it." *Id.,* at 532. The Court articulated the controlling principle:

> "Every procedure which would offer a possible temptation to the average man as a judge to forget the burden of proof required to convict the defendant, or which might lead him not to hold the balance nice, clear and true between the State and the accused, denies the latter due process of law." *Ibid.*

The Court was thus concerned with more than the traditional common-law prohibition on direct pecuniary interest. It was also concerned with a more general concept of interests that tempt adjudicators to disregard neutrality.

* * *

B

The second instance requiring recusal that was not discussed at common law emerged in the criminal contempt context, where a judge had no pecuniary interest in the case but was challenged because of a conflict arising from his participation in an earlier proceeding. This Court characterized that first proceeding (perhaps pejoratively) as a " 'one-man grand jury.' " *Murchison,* 349 U.S., at 133.

In that first proceeding, and as provided by state law, a judge examined witnesses to determine whether criminal charges should be brought. The judge called the two petitioners before him. One petitioner answered questions, but the judge found him untruthful and charged him with perjury. The second declined to answer on the ground that he did not have counsel with him, as state law seemed to permit. The judge charged him with contempt. The judge proceeded to try and convict both petitioners.

This Court set aside the convictions on grounds that the judge had a conflict of interest at the trial stage because of his earlier participation followed by his decision to charge them. The Due Process Clause required disqualification. The Court recited the general rule that "no man can be a judge in his own case," adding that "no man is permitted to try cases where he has an interest in the outcome." *Id.,* at 136. It noted that the disqualifying criteria "cannot be defined with precision. Circumstances and relationships must be considered." *Ibid.* These circumstances and the prior relationship required recusal: "Having been a part of [the one-man grand jury] process a judge cannot be, in the very nature of things, wholly disinterested in the conviction or acquittal of those accused." *Id.,* at 137. That is because "[a]s a practical matter it is difficult if not impossible for a judge to free himself from the influence of what took place in his 'grand-jury' secret session." *Id.,* at 138.

* * *

III

Based on the principles described in these cases we turn to the issue before us. This problem arises in the context of judicial elections, a framework not presented in the precedents we have reviewed and discussed.

Caperton contends that Blankenship's pivotal role in getting Justice Benjamin elected created a constitutionally intolerable probability of actual bias. Though not a bribe or criminal influence, Justice Benjamin would nevertheless feel a debt of gratitude to Blankenship for his extraordinary efforts to get him elected. That temptation, Caperton claims, is as strong and inherent in human nature as was the conflict the Court confronted in *Tumey* and [*Ward v.*] *Monroeville*[, 409 U.S. 57 (1972),] when a mayor-judge (or the city) benefited financially from a defendant's conviction, as well as the conflict identified in *Murchison* and *Mayberry*[v. *Pennsylvania,* 400 U.S. 455 (1971),] when a judge was the object of a defendant's contempt.

Justice Benjamin was careful to address the recusal motions and explain his reasons why, on his view of the controlling standard, disqualification was not in order. In four separate opinions issued during the course of the appeal, he explained why no actual bias had been established. He found no basis for recusal because Caperton failed to provide "objective evidence" or "objective information," but merely "subjective belief" of bias. Nor could anyone "point to any actual conduct or activity on [his] part which could be termed 'improper.'" In other words, based on the facts presented by Caperton, Justice Benjamin conducted a probing search into his actual motives and inclinations; and he found none to be improper. We do not question his subjective findings of impartiality and propriety. Nor do we determine whether there was actual bias.

* * *

The difficulties of inquiring into actual bias, and the fact that the inquiry is often a private one, simply underscore the need for objective rules. Otherwise there may be no adequate protection against a judge who simply misreads or misapprehends the real motives at work in deciding the case. The judge's own inquiry into actual bias, then, is not one that the law can easily superintend or review, though actual bias, if disclosed, no doubt would be grounds for appropriate relief. In lieu of exclusive reliance on that personal inquiry, or on appellate review of the judge's determination respecting actual bias, the Due Process Clause has been implemented by objective standards that do not require proof of actual bias. In defining these standards the Court has asked whether, "under a realistic appraisal of psychological tendencies and human weakness," the interest "poses such a risk of actual bias or prejudgment that the practice must be forbidden if the guarantee of due process is to be adequately implemented." *Withrow,* 421 U.S., at 47.

We turn to the influence at issue in this case. Not every campaign contribution by a litigant or attorney creates a probability of bias that requires a judge's recusal, but this is an exceptional case. We conclude that there is a serious risk of actual bias—based on objective and reasonable perceptions—when a person with a personal stake in a particular case had a significant and disproportionate influence in placing the judge on the case by raising funds or directing the judge's election campaign when the case was pending or imminent. The inquiry centers on the contribution's relative size in comparison to the total amount of money contributed to the campaign, the total amount spent in the election, and the apparent effect such contribution had on the outcome of the election.

Applying this principle, we conclude that Blankenship's campaign efforts had a significant and disproportionate influence in placing Justice Benjamin on the case. Blankenship contributed some $3 million to unseat the incumbent and replace him with Benjamin. His contributions eclipsed the total amount spent by all other Benjamin supporters and exceeded by 300% the amount spent by Benjamin's campaign committee. Caperton claims Blankenship spent $1 million more than the total amount spent by the campaign committees of both candidates combined.

Massey responds that Blankenship's support, while significant, did not cause Benjamin's victory. In the end the people of West Virginia elected him, and they did so based on many reasons other than Blankenship's efforts. Massey points out that every major state newspaper, but one, endorsed Benjamin. It also contends that then-Justice McGraw cost himself the election by giving a speech during the campaign, a speech the opposition seized upon for its own advantage.

* * *

Whether Blankenship's campaign contributions were a necessary and sufficient cause of Benjamin's victory is not the proper inquiry. Much like determining whether a judge is actually biased, proving what ultimately drives the electorate to choose a particular candidate is a difficult endeavor, not likely to lend itself to a certain conclusion. This is particularly true where, as here, there is no procedure for judicial factfinding and the sole trier of fact is the one accused of bias. Due process requires an objective inquiry into whether the contributor's influence on the election under all the circumstances "would offer a possible temptation to the average . . . judge to . . . lead him not to hold the balance nice, clear and true." *Tumey, supra,* at 532. In an election decided by fewer than 50,000 votes (382,036 to 334,301), Blankenship's campaign contributions—in comparison to the total amount contributed to the campaign, as well as the total amount spent in the election—had a significant and disproportionate influence on the electoral outcome. And the risk that Blankenship's influence engendered actual bias is sufficiently substantial that it "must be forbidden if the guarantee of due process is to be adequately implemented." *Withrow, supra,* at 47.

The temporal relationship between the campaign contributions, the justice's election, and the pendency of the case is also critical. It was reasonably foreseeable, when the campaign contributions were made, that the pending case would be before the newly elected justice. * * * Just as no man is allowed to be a judge in his own cause, similar fears of bias can arise when—without the consent of the other parties—a man chooses the judge in his own cause. And applying this principle to the judicial election process, there was here a serious, objective risk of actual bias that required Justice Benjamin's recusal.

Justice Benjamin did undertake an extensive search for actual bias. But, as we have indicated, that is just one step in the judicial process; objective standards may also require recusal whether or not actual bias exists or can be proved. Due process "may sometimes bar trial by judges who have no actual bias and who would do their very best to weigh the scales of justice equally between contending parties." *Murchison,* 349 U.S., at 136. The failure to consider objective standards requiring recusal is not consistent with the imperatives of due process. We find that Blankenship's significant and disproportionate influence—coupled with the temporal relationship between the election and the pending case—" ' "offer a possible temptation to the average . . . judge to . . . lead him not to hold the balance nice, clear and true." ' " *Lavoie,* 475 U.S., at 825 (quoting *Monroeville,* 409 U.S., at 60, in turn quoting *Tumey,* 273 U.S., at 532). On these extreme facts the probability of actual bias rises to an unconstitutional level.

IV

Our decision today addresses an extraordinary situation where the Constitution requires recusal. Massey and its *amici* predict that various adverse consequences will follow from recognizing a constitutional violation here—ranging from a flood of recusal motions to unnecessary interference with judicial elections. We disagree. The facts now before us are extreme by any measure. The parties point to no other instance involving judicial campaign contributions that presents a potential for bias comparable to the circumstances in this case.

* * *

This Court's recusal cases are illustrative. In each case the Court dealt with extreme facts that created an unconstitutional probability of bias that " 'cannot be defined with precision.' " *Lavoie,* 475 U.S., at 822 (quoting *Murchison,* 349 U.S., at 136). Yet the Court articulated an objective standard to protect the parties' basic right to a fair trial in a fair tribunal. The Court was careful to distinguish the extreme facts of the cases before it from those interests that would not rise to a constitutional level. In this case we do nothing more than what the Court has done before.

As such, it is worth noting the effects, or lack thereof, of the Court's prior decisions. Even though the standards announced in those cases raised questions similar to those that might be asked after our decision today, the Court was not flooded with *Monroeville* or *Murchison* motions. That is perhaps due in part to the extreme facts those standards sought to address. Courts proved quite capable of applying the standards to less extreme situations.

One must also take into account the judicial reforms the States have implemented to eliminate even the appearance of partiality. Almost every State—West Virginia included—has adopted the American Bar Association's objective standard: "A judge shall avoid impropriety and the appearance of impropriety." ABA Annotated Model Code of Judicial Conduct, Canon 2 (2004); *see* Brief for American Bar Association as *Amicus Curiae* 14, and n. 29. The ABA Model Code's test for appearance of impropriety is "whether the conduct would create in reasonable minds a perception that the judge's ability to carry out judicial responsibilities with integrity, impartiality and competence is impaired." Canon 2A, Commentary; *see also* W. Va.Code of Judicial Conduct, Canon 2A, and Commentary (2009) (same).

The West Virginia Code of Judicial Conduct also requires a judge to "disqualify himself or herself in a proceeding in which the judge's impartiality might reasonably be questioned." Canon 3E(1); *see also* 28 U.S.C. § 455(a) ("Any justice, judge, or magistrate judge of the United States shall disqualify himself in any proceeding in which his impartiality might reasonably be questioned"). Under Canon 3E(1), " '[t]he question of disqualification focuses on whether an objective assessment of the judge's conduct produces a reasonable question about impartiality, not on the judge's subjective perception of the ability to act fairly.' " *State ex rel. Brown v. Dietrick,* 191 W.Va. 169, 174, n. 9 (1994); *see also Liteky v. United States,* 510 U.S. 540, 558 (1994) (KENNEDY, J., concurring in judgment) ("[U]nder [28 U.S.C.] § 455(a), a judge should be disqualified only if it appears that he or she harbors an aversion, hostility or disposition of a kind that a fair-minded person could not set aside when judging the dispute"). Indeed, some States require recusal based on campaign contributions similar to those in this case. *See, e.g.,* Ala.Code §§ 12–24–1, 12–24–2 (2006); Miss.Code of Judicial Conduct, Canon 3E(2) (2008).

These codes of conduct serve to maintain the integrity of the judiciary and the rule of law. The Conference of the Chief Justices has underscored that the codes are "[t]he principal safeguard against judicial campaign abuses" that threaten to imperil "public confidence in the fairness and integrity of the nation's elected judges." Brief for Conference of Chief Justices as *Amicus Curiae* 4, 11. * * *

* * *

"The Due Process Clause demarks only the outer boundaries of judicial disqualifications. Congress and the states, of course, remain free to impose more rigorous standards for judicial disqualification than those we find mandated here today." *Lavoie, supra,* at 828. Because the codes of judicial conduct provide more protection than due process requires, most disputes over disqualification will be resolved without resort to the Constitution. Application of the constitutional standard implicated in this case will thus be confined to rare instances.

* * *

The judgment of the Supreme Court of Appeals of West Virginia is reversed, and the case is remanded for further proceedings not inconsistent with this opinion.

It is so ordered.

■ CHIEF JUSTICE ROBERTS, with whom JUSTICE SCALIA, JUSTICE THOMAS, and JUSTICE ALITO join, dissenting.

I, of course, share the majority's sincere concerns about the need to maintain a fair, independent, and impartial judiciary—and one that appears to be such. But I fear that the Court's decision will undermine rather than promote these values.

Until today, we have recognized exactly two situations in which the Federal Due Process Clause requires disqualification of a judge: when the judge has a financial interest in the outcome of the case, and when the judge is trying a defendant for certain criminal contempts. Vaguer notions of bias or the appearance of bias were never a basis for disqualification, either at common law or under our constitutional precedents. Those issues were instead addressed by legislation or court rules.

Today, however, the Court enlists the Due Process Clause to overturn a judge's failure to recuse because of a "probability of bias." Unlike the established grounds for disqualification, a "probability of bias" cannot be defined in any limited way. The Court's new "rule" provides no guidance to judges and litigants about when recusal will be constitutionally required. This will inevitably lead to an increase in allegations that judges are biased, however groundless those charges may be. The end result will do far more to erode public confidence in judicial impartiality than an isolated failure to recuse in a particular case.

I

There is a "presumption of honesty and integrity in those serving as adjudicators." *Withrow v. Larkin,* 421 U.S. 35, 47 (1975). All judges take an oath to uphold the Constitution and apply the law impartially, and we trust that they will live up to this promise. We have thus identified only *two* situations in which the Due Process Clause requires disqualification of a judge: when the judge has a financial interest in the outcome of the case, and when the judge is presiding over certain types of criminal contempt proceedings.

* * *

Subject to the two well-established exceptions described above, questions of judicial recusal are regulated by "common law, statute, or the professional standards of the bench and bar." *Bracy v. Gramley,* 520 U.S. 899, 904 (1997).

In any given case, there are a number of factors that could give rise to a "probability" or "appearance" of bias: friendship with a party or lawyer, prior employment experience, membership in clubs or associations, prior speeches and writings, religious affiliation, and countless other considerations. We have never held that the Due Process Clause requires recusal for any of these reasons, even though they could be viewed as presenting a "probability of bias." Many state *statutes* require recusal based on a probability or appearance of bias, but "that alone would not be sufficient basis for imposing a *constitutional* requirement under the Due Process Clause." *Lavoie, supra,* at 820. States are, of course, free to adopt broader recusal rules than the Constitution requires—and every State has—but these developments are not continuously incorporated into the Due Process Clause.

II

In departing from this clear line between when recusal is constitutionally required and when it is not, the majority repeatedly emphasizes the need for an "objective" standard. The majority's analysis is "objective" in that it does not inquire into Justice Benjamin's motives or decisionmaking process. But the standard the majority articulates—"probability of bias"—fails to provide clear, workable guidance for future cases. At the most basic level, it is unclear whether the new probability of bias standard is somehow limited to financial support in judicial elections, or applies to judicial recusal questions more generally.

But there are other fundamental questions as well. With little help from the majority, courts will now have to determine:

1. How much money is too much money? What level of contribution or expenditure gives rise to a "probability of bias"?

2. How do we determine whether a given expenditure is "disproportionate"? Disproportionate *to what*?

3. Are independent, non-coordinated expenditures treated the same as direct contributions to a candidate's campaign? What about contributions to independent outside groups supporting a candidate?

4. Does it matter whether the litigant has contributed to other candidates or made large expenditures in connection with other elections?

5. Does the amount at issue in the case matter? What if this case were an employment dispute with only $10,000 at stake? What if the plaintiffs only sought non-monetary relief such as an injunction or declaratory judgment?

6. Does the analysis change depending on whether the judge whose disqualification is sought sits on a trial court, appeals court, or state supreme court?

7. How long does the probability of bias last? Does the probability of bias diminish over time as the election recedes? Does it matter whether the judge plans to run for reelection?

8. What if the "disproportionately" large expenditure is made by an industry association, trade union, physicians' group, or

the plaintiffs' bar? Must the judge recuse in all cases that affect the association's interests? Must the judge recuse in all cases in which a party or lawyer is a member of that group? Does it matter how much the litigant contributed to the association?

9.   What if the case involves a social or ideological issue rather than a financial one? Must a judge recuse from cases involving, say, abortion rights if he has received "disproportionate" support from individuals who feel strongly about either side of that issue? If the supporter wants to help elect judges who are "tough on crime," must the judge recuse in all criminal cases?

10. What if the candidate draws "disproportionate" support from a particular racial, religious, ethnic, or other group, and the case involves an issue of particular importance to that group?

* * *

25. What role does causation play in this analysis? The Court sends conflicting signals on this point. The majority asserts that "[w]hether Blankenship's campaign contributions were a necessary and sufficient cause of Benjamin's victory is not the proper inquiry." But elsewhere in the opinion, the majority considers "the apparent effect such contribution had on the outcome of the election," and whether the litigant has been able to "choos[e] the judge in his own cause." If causation is a pertinent factor, how do we know whether the contribution or expenditure had any effect on the outcome of the election? What if the judge won in a landslide? What if the judge won primarily because of his opponent's missteps?

* * *

39. Does the *judge* get to respond to the allegation that he is probably biased, or is his reputation solely in the hands of the parties to the case?

40. What if the parties settle a *Caperton* claim as part of a broader settlement of the case? Does that leave the judge with no way to salvage his reputation?

These are only a few uncertainties that quickly come to mind. Judges and litigants will surely encounter others when they are forced to, or wish to, apply the majority's decision in different circumstances. Today's opinion requires state and federal judges simultaneously to act as political scientists (why did candidate X win the election?), economists (was the financial support disproportionate?), and psychologists (is there likely to be a debt of gratitude?).

The Court's inability to formulate a "judicially discernible and manageable standard" strongly counsels against the recognition of a novel constitutional right. The need to consider these and countless other questions helps explain why the common law and this Court's constitutional jurisprudence have never required disqualification on such vague grounds as "probability" or "appearance" of bias.

III

A

To its credit, the Court seems to recognize that the inherently boundless nature of its new rule poses a problem. But the majority's only answer is that the present case is an "extreme" one, so there is no need to worry about other cases. The Court repeats this point over and over.

But this is just so much whistling past the graveyard. Claims that have little chance of success are nonetheless frequently filed. The success rate for certiorari petitions before this Court is approximately 1.1%, and yet the previous Term some 8,241 were filed. Every one of the "*Caperton* motions" or appeals or § 1983 actions will claim that the judge is biased, or probably biased, bringing the judge and the judicial system into disrepute. And all future litigants will assert that their case is *really* the most extreme thus far.

Extreme cases often test the bounds of established legal principles. There is a cost to yielding to the desire to correct the extreme case, rather than adhering to the legal principle. That cost has been demonstrated so often that it is captured in a legal aphorism: "Hard cases make bad law."

* * *

* * * Today, the majority * * * departs from a clear, longstanding constitutional rule to accommodate an "extreme" case involving "grossly disproportionate" amounts of money. I believe we will come to regret this decision as well, when courts are forced to deal with a wide variety of *Caperton* motions, each claiming the title of "most extreme" or "most disproportionate."

B

And why is the Court so convinced that this is an extreme case? It is true that Don Blankenship spent a large amount of money in connection with this election. But this point cannot be emphasized strongly enough: Other than a $1,000 direct contribution from Blankenship, *Justice Benjamin and his campaign had no control over how this money was spent.* Campaigns go to great lengths to develop precise messages and strategies. An insensitive or ham-handed ad campaign by an independent third party might distort the campaign's message or cause a backlash against the candidate, even though the candidate was not responsible for the ads. The majority repeatedly characterizes Blankenship's spending as "contributions" or "campaign contributions," but it is more accurate to refer to them as "independent expenditures." Blankenship only "contributed" $1,000 to the Benjamin campaign.

Moreover, Blankenship's independent expenditures do not appear "grossly disproportionate" compared to other such expenditures in this very election. "And for the Sake of the Kids"—an independent group that received approximately two-thirds of its funding from Blankenship—spent $3,623,500 in connection with the election. But large independent expenditures were also made in support of Justice Benjamin's opponent. "Consumers for Justice"—an independent group that received large contributions from the plaintiffs' bar—spent approximately $2 million in this race. And Blankenship has made large expenditures in connection with several previous West Virginia elections, which undercuts any notion that his involvement in this election was "intended to influence the outcome" of particular pending litigation.

It is also far from clear that Blankenship's expenditures affected the outcome of this election. Justice Benjamin won by a comfortable 7-point margin (53.3% to 46.7%). Many observers believed that Justice Benjamin's opponent doomed his candidacy by giving a well-publicized speech that made several curious allegations; this speech was described in the local media as "deeply disturbing" and worse. Justice Benjamin's opponent also refused to give interviews or participate in debates. All but one of the major West Virginia newspapers endorsed Justice Benjamin. Justice Benjamin just might have won because the voters of West Virginia thought he would be a better judge than his opponent. Unlike the majority, I cannot say with any degree of certainty that Blankenship "cho[se] the judge in his own cause." I would give the voters of West Virginia more credit than that.

* * *

It is an old cliché, but sometimes the cure is worse than the disease. I am sure there are cases where a "probability of bias" should lead the prudent judge to step aside, but the judge fails to do so. Maybe this is one of them. But I believe that opening the door to recusal claims under the Due Process Clause, for an amorphous "probability of bias," will itself bring our judicial system into undeserved disrepute, and diminish the confidence of the American people in the fairness and integrity of their courts. I hope I am wrong.

I respectfully dissent.

■ JUSTICE SCALIA, dissenting.

The principal purpose of this Court's exercise of its certiorari jurisdiction is to clarify the law. As THE CHIEF JUSTICE's dissent makes painfully clear, the principal consequence of today's decision is to create vast uncertainty with respect to a point of law that can be raised in all litigated cases in (at least) those 39 States that elect their judges. This course was urged upon us on grounds that it would preserve the public's confidence in the judicial system.

The decision will have the opposite effect. What above all else is eroding public confidence in the Nation's judicial system is the perception that litigation is just a game, that the party with the most resourceful lawyer can play it to win, that our seemingly interminable legal proceedings are wonderfully self-perpetuating but incapable of delivering real-world justice. The Court's opinion will reinforce that perception, adding to the vast arsenal of lawyerly gambits what will come to be known as the *Caperton* claim. The facts relevant to adjudicating it will have to be litigated—and likewise the law governing it, which will be indeterminate for years to come, if not forever. Many billable hours will be spent in poring through volumes of campaign finance reports, and many more in contesting nonrecusal decisions through every available means.

A Talmudic maxim instructs with respect to the Scripture: "Turn it over, and turn it over, for all is therein." Divinely inspired text may contain the answers to all earthly questions, but the Due Process Clause most assuredly does not. The Court today continues its quixotic quest to right all wrongs and repair all imperfections through the Constitution. Alas, the quest cannot succeed—which is why some wrongs and imperfections have been called nonjusticiable. In the best of all possible worlds, should judges sometimes recuse even where the clear commands of our prior due process law do not require it? Undoubtedly. The relevant question, however, is whether we do more good than harm by seeking to correct this imperfection through expansion of our constitutional mandate in a manner ungoverned by any discernable rule. The answer is obvious.

COMMENTS AND QUESTIONS CONCERNING
CAPERTON V. A.T. MASSEY COAL CO.

1.   The American Bar Association, the American Judicature Society, the League of Women Voters, the American Academy of Appellate Lawyers, Public Citizen, and 27 former state chief justices and justices were among the groups that filed or joined in amicus ("friend of the court") briefs supporting Hugh Caperton in his Supreme Court effort to obtain Justice Benjamin's recusal. Justice Sandra Day O'Connor, who after her retirement from the Supreme Court became a leader in merit judicial selection and retention efforts, attended the Supreme Court argument in *Caperton*. L. Leamer, *The Price of Justice* 28 (2013).

The Conference of Chief Justices, which does not take a position on the specifics of a state supreme court decision under review, filed an amicus brief in support of neither party that stated:

The Conference takes the position that, under certain circumstances, the Constitution may require the disqualification of a judge in a particular matter because of extraordinarily out-of-line campaign support from a source that has a substantial stake in the proceedings. As judicial election campaigns become costlier and more politicized, public confidence in the fairness and integrity of the nation's elected judges may be imperiled. Disqualification is an increasingly important tool for assuring litigants that they will receive a fair hearing before an impartial tribunal * * *.

Brief for Conference of Chief Justices as Amicus Curiae Supporting Neither Party, *Caperton v. A.T. Massey Coal Co., Inc.*, 556 U.S. 868 (2009) (No. 08–22).

2. This case was closely followed in the popular media and may have provided the inspiration for John Grisham's novel *The Appeal*. Those favoring state-court non-partisan judicial selection and retention systems such as the "Missouri Plan" have argued that, under such systems, money plays less of a role and excesses such as those highlighted in *Caperton* are less likely to occur. *E.g.*, O'Connor, "The Essentials and Expendables of the Missouri Plan," 74 *Mo. L. Rev.* 479, 488 (2009) ("It is a sad state of affairs when this comes up as a constitutional question when it is so clearly bad policy for a state to allow this to happen. West Virginia cannot possibly benefit from having that much money injected into a judicial campaign; the appearance of bias is high, and it destroys the credibility of that judgment. One cannot help but be skeptical of this judge's impartiality.").

3. Under the Supreme Court's decisions prior to *Caperton*, was it necessary to show that a judge was actually biased in order to obtain recusal? Does the Supreme Court conclude that Justice Benjamin actually was biased in this case?

4. Is it possible to distill a holding from the majority opinion in this case? Is the opinion helpful in guiding judges and courts in future cases?

5. What about the 40 questions raised by Chief Justice Roberts in his dissent? Do such questions mean that the majority was wrong in finding a due process violation? Of the questions excerpted in this text, which do you find the most significant?

6. Rule 2.11 of the ABA Model Code of Judicial Conduct provides that a judge should disqualify himself or herself if:

The judge knows or learns by means of a timely motion that a party, a party's lawyer, or the law firm of a party's lawyer has within the previous [insert number] year[s] made aggregate contributions to the judge's campaign in an amount that is greater than $[insert amount] for an individual or $[insert amount] for an entity [is reasonable and appropriate for an individual or an entity].

However, only five states have adopted a rule requiring judicial recusal due to campaign contributions greater than a specified dollar amount or percentage of the funds raised by the judge in a judicial election.

National Center for State Courts, *Judicial Disqualification Based on Campaign Contributions* (June 5, 2015), http://www.ncsc.org/~/media/f7575d379880490fb7c532c433c6e907.ashx.

7.   On remand from the United States Supreme Court, the Supreme Court of Appeals of West Virginia, in a 4–1 decision, held that the jury verdict was improperly entered by the Circuit Court and remanded the action with instructions that the action be dismissed because it had been filed in the wrong circuit court under the forum selection clause in the parties' contract. *Caperton v. A.T. Massey Coal Co.*, 225 W. Va. 128 (2009). Acting Chief Justice Robin Davis, who wrote the majority opinion, was the only justice who had participated in the judgment that had been reviewed by the United States Supreme Court. The *Caperton* case is chronicled in L. Leamer, *The Price of Justice* (2013).

C. SHOULD THESE JUDGES RECUSE?

Decide whether the judge should, or should not, recuse in the following cases, basing your answers on 28 U.S.C. § 455.

1.   Plaintiff nightclub owners sued challenging the constitutionality of a local ordinance that prohibited nude dancing. The judge granted summary judgment for the government defendants. Thereafter the judge pled guilty to aiding and abetting a felon's possession of a controlled substance, giving that felon (an exotic dancer) his government-issued laptop computer, and the possession of illegal drugs. The judge also was known to have visited nude dance clubs around the time he was considering the action in question, although he did not visit the nightclub that was the subject of the litigation. Plaintiffs sought the retroactive recusal of the judge, who had by this time resigned from the federal bench.

Should the recusal motion be granted? *See Curves, LLC v. Spalding County., Ga.*, 685 F.3d 1284 (11th Cir. 2012) (*per curiam*).

2.   Brazil's Sao Paulo State brought an action alleging that the defendant tobacco companies had conspired to conceal the health risks from smoking, thus preventing it from adopting policies to reduce smoking by its citizens. The defendant tobacco companies filed a motion to recuse the judge. The judge's name mistakenly appeared on a motion of the Louisiana Trial Lawyers Association (LTLA) to file an amicus brief almost nine years before in an action making tobacco claims similar to those in the present case. At the time of the earlier action, the judge was both a member of LTLA and of its executive committee, and he had stepped down as LTLA president six months before the motion was made to file the brief. One of the plaintiffs' lawyers in the present action was on the LTLA committee that approved the filing of the amicus brief in this earlier case. The judge was not involved in the earlier action nor in any other case involving tobacco.

Should the recusal motion be granted? *See Sao Paulo State of Federative Republic of Brazil v. Am. Tobacco Co., Inc.*, 535 U.S. 229 (2002).

3.   An action was filed by two states and several state legislators, seeking rescission of state ratifications of the Equal Rights Amendment ("ERA") and a declaration that the congressional extension of the time period for ratification of the ERA was unconstitutional. Defense counsel, from the United States Department of Justice and for the intervenor National Organization for Women, sought the recusal of the district judge to whom the action was assigned.

The judge was a member of the Church of Jesus Christ of Latter-day Saints and, at the time the action was filed and for six months thereafter, was a Regional Representative of that Church. As Regional Representative, it was the judge's duty to assist in the leadership of the Church within his region, including carrying forth the Church's opposition to the ratification of the Equal Rights Amendment. Members of the Church who advocated in favor of the ERA had been excommunicated from the Church. Other Regional Representatives organized and supported efforts to defeat the ERA. The judge, however, never spoke out on the ERA or the action before him (to which the Church was not a party).

Should the recusal motion be granted? *See State of Idaho v. Freeman*, 507 F. Supp. 706 (D. Idaho 1981).

4.   An action was filed against a federal energy task force, alleging that the task force had not complied with the Federal Advisory Committee Act. The Vice President, as chair of that task force, was sued in his official capacity. After the Supreme Court granted certiorari in the case, one of the parties moved for the recusal of a Justice on the Supreme Court, asserting that the Justice's "impartiality might reasonably be questioned" under 28 U.S.C. § 455(a).

The recusal motion was based on the fact that the Justice had accepted an offer to fly, on a space-available basis on a government plane, with the Vice President for a duck-hunting trip in Louisiana. The Justice's son and son-in-law also joined this trip. Thirteen hunters, plus security personnel, were at the hunting camp, where all meals were eaten in common. Two or three hunters shared each duck blind, although the Justice and Vice President never shared a blind. The Justice and Vice President were never alone, except momentarily, and they never spoke about the case in question (which the Supreme Court decided to hear after the arrangements for the hunting trip were set). Because the Vice President returned to Washington before the Justice, the Justice purchased a commercial ticket home.

Should the recusal motion be granted? *See Cheney v. U.S. Dist. Court for D.C.*, 541 U.S. 913 (2004).

Consider, finally, a practice pointer concerning motions to recuse. If you are planning to file a motion to recuse, you had better plan to win that motion. If not, you may find yourself litigating your case before a judge (no matter how professional and even-handed) whom you have asserted is, by objective standards, partial to another party in the action. As Omar Little said in *The Wire*, "[Y]ou come at the king, you best not miss."

VI. CONCLUSION

One of the most important determinants of litigation success is the person, or group of persons, who will decide the case. In the federal courts, this can be a magistrate judge or a district judge, or the factual disputes can be resolved by a jury. Whoever decides the case, though, counsel must be sure that both the judge and jury are fair and unbiased. In some cases, this may require counsel to seek the recusal of biased judges or challenge partial jurors.

Once an impartial decision-maker is selected, the case proceeds to trial. That is the subject of Chapter 13.

VII. CHAPTER ASSESSMENT

A.   Multiple-Choice Questions. Answer the following questions, reviewing the sections of the chapter noted in connection with each question.

1.   An injured consumer files a products liability action against a manufacturer in federal district court. Because of unfiled judicial vacancies within the district, the district judge to whom the action is assigned will not be able to try the case for at least two years. The consumer, therefore, consents to the assignment of a magistrate judge to try the jury action. The manufacturer, though, refuses to consent to trial before a magistrate judge. When he learns that the manufacturer refused to sign the consent form, the district judge to whom the case is assigned enters an order assigning the action for trial before the magistrate judge.

Can the magistrate judge try this case?

Review Section II(A) and choose the best answer from the following choices:

(a)   Yes, because either party has a right to choose a magistrate judge to hear a civil action.

(b)   Yes, because a district judge has the power to assign a magistrate judge to try a civil action.

(c)   No, because magistrate judges cannot try jury actions.

(d)   No, because all parties must consent before a magistrate judge can try a civil action.

2. A passenger files a diversity action in federal district court against the driver of a bus that crashed. The passenger's complaint asserts several common law and statutory tort claims against the driver, but does not include a demand for a jury trial. Ten days after serving and filing the complaint, the passenger files and serves a jury demand, seeking a jury on the common law tort claims asserted in the passenger's complaint.

The driver answers the complaint, discovery ensues, and the court schedules a final pretrial conference. At that conference, the passenger's counsel informs the judge and the driver's counsel that the passenger is withdrawing her jury demand. Defense counsel object, asserting that such a withdrawal of the jury demand is untimely.

Should Plaintiff's tort claims be tried to a jury?

Review Section III(C) and choose the best answer from the following choices:

(a) Yes, because once a jury demand has been served and filed, that demand only can be withdrawn if all the parties consent.

(b) Yes, because the failure to comply with the requirements of the Federal Rules of Civil Procedure is harmless error that cannot affect a party's constitutional right to a jury trial.

(c) No, because the jury demand was not included in the complaint.

(d) No, because a party cannot restrict its request for a jury to specific claims or issues within a cause of action.

3. The attorneys in a federal diversity action engage in several hours of jury selection. Plaintiff's counsel successfully convinces the judge to dismiss five potential jurors for cause, and she exercises peremptory challenges to dismiss three other jurors.

A potential juror tells the judge that he served as a juror in five other civil cases, and in each case the jury returned a verdict for the defendant. When asked why each verdict was for the defendant, the man replies, "Plaintiffs have the burden of proof, and if they can't meet their burden they lose." The judge then asks the man whether he can be fair in this case and will decide the case on the evidence presented and the instructions given by the judge. The man replies that he will do so.

Should the man be dismissed as a juror?

Review Section IV(A) and (B) and choose the best answer from the following choices:

(a) The judge should dismiss the potential juror for cause.

(b) Although the judge should not dismiss the potential juror for cause, the plaintiff's attorney can dismiss the man with a peremptory challenge.

(c)   The potential juror can be dismissed either by the judge for cause or by the plaintiff's attorney using a peremptory challenge.

(d)   Neither a challenge for cause nor a peremptory challenge are appropriate in this situation.

4.   The lead plaintiff in a nationwide federal class action against several large national banks alleges that these banks have been "rounding down" interest due consumers, costing consumers millions of dollars. The judge certifies the class action and, after discovery and other pretrial proceedings, the action is tried. At the end of the two-week trial, the case is sent to the jury, which returns a verdict for class members in excess of $10,000,000.

After the jury renders its verdict and the jurors leave the courthouse, the bailiff enters the jury room. In one corner of the room he finds a book entitled *How the Banks are Ripping You Off!* He reports his finding to the judge, who informs counsel.

Counsel for the banks move to question the bailiff concerning his discovery and to examine the book.

Should the judge grant this motion?

Review Section IV(C) and choose the best answer from the following choices:

(a)   The bailiff cannot testify because his testimony would bring into question the thought processes of the jurors in reaching their verdict.

(b)   The bailiff cannot testify because he cannot know whether the book had any impact on the jurors' verdict.

(c)   The bailiff can testify, because he is the officer of the court responsible for ensuring the regularity of the jury proceedings.

(d)   The bailiff can testify concerning what he found in the jury room, because his testimony is not barred by Federal Rule of Evidence 606(b) or the Mansfield Rule.

5.   A lawyer was recently appointed as a United States District Judge, after serving for 15 years as an Assistant United States Attorney in the same judicial district. The United States Attorney's Office is quite small, and, although she primarily handled criminal matters, the judge occasionally was assigned to civil cases for short periods of time.

Among the first cases assigned to the judge is a tort action to which she was assigned for one month three years ago while she served as an Assistant United States Attorney. During the time that she was assigned to the action, no court proceedings were scheduled or occurred. The United States now is represented in this action by another Assistant United States Attorney, who has handled the case since it was reassigned to her several years ago.

Although counsel have not sought her recusal, the judge wonders whether she should recuse herself in this action.

Review Section V(A) and choose the best answer from the following choices:

(a) The judge cannot hear the action, because she formerly participated as counsel with respect to the action when she was in the United States Attorney's Office.

(b) The judge cannot hear the action, because a former colleague is handling the action for the United States.

(c) The judge can hear the action, because neither of the parties have asked that she recuse herself.

(d) The judge can hear the action, because she has no personal bias or prejudice concerning either of the parties.

B. Essay Questions. To test your understanding of this chapter's material, outline or write an answer to the following questions.

1. Should There Be a Jury?

On January 10, a borrower filed a federal question action in federal court against a lender pursuant to a federal mortgage privacy act. This recent statute provides that "in the event that a mortgage company or other lender reveals a borrower's personal information to any third party, the borrower can file an action in federal court seeking $1000 for each disclosure of personal information."

On January 30, the lender served and filed an answer, containing both denials of the allegations of the borrower's complaint and a counterclaim denominated as such seeking $100,000 damages for the borrower's failure to make mortgage payments for the past 20 months. Simultaneously with its answer, the lender served and filed a demand for a jury on its counterclaim.

On February 10 of the same year, the borrower served and filed a demand for a jury on its claim under the mortgage privacy act.

(a) Is the borrower entitled to have a jury determine his claim under the mortgage privacy act?

(b) Has the borrower properly demanded a jury?

(c) Is the lender constitutionally entitled to a jury on its counterclaim?

(d) Assuming that the lender is constitutionally entitled to a jury on its counterclaim but the borrower is not entitled to a jury on his claim, is there anything that the judge should do to preserve the lender's right to a jury trial on its counterclaim?

2. Must the Judge Recuse?

One Friday afternoon a federal antitrust action is filed by a start-up business, asserting that a major corporation is monopolizing the start-up's line of business. The start-up seeks a temporary restraining order, and the action is assigned to the only federal judge in the courthouse at that time. After eight hours of hearings that weekend, the judge denies the temporary restraining order. The judge sets a hearing for the start-up's request for a preliminary injunction the next week, and hears eight days of testimony over the next two weeks. During these preliminary injunction hearings, the judge refuses the request of the start-up's attorneys to call five expert witnesses, telling counsel to "concentrate on just one or two experts who actually know what they're talking about and why your client might have a case here."

Three weeks later, on the morning that the judge is planning to rule on the motion for a preliminary injunction, the judge and his wife, a cardiac surgeon, are watching the television during breakfast. A commentator during a local news program states, "Anyone in their right mind should be selling stock in that new start-up company. It's fighting for its life in a local lawsuit, and its chance of prevailing in that action doesn't look good." The judge's wife then tells the judge, "This reminds me, my broker called the first part of last month, and we agreed to buy 20 shares of the start-up company's stock for my investment account."

(a) Must the judge recuse himself pursuant to federal statutory law for any reason?

(b) Regardless of any statutory basis for recusal, would it be unconstitutional for the judge to hear this action?

(c) If the judge is required to recuse himself pursuant to a federal statute, is there any action that the parties or the judge can take so that the judge nevertheless can hear the action?

CHAPTER 13

TRIAL, VERDICTS, AND JUDGMENTS: "THE JURY HAS SPOKEN."

I. INTRODUCTION

Our country rightly prizes the right to jury trial, a right that was considered so important that the Founders included it in the Bill of Rights. Even in jury trials, though, judges play a large role. They decide the evidence that the jury can consider, the witnesses whom the lawyers can call, and the claims that will be presented to the jury. There is, in fact, some tension between the judge and jury, and one of the judge's roles in jury actions is to control the jury so that it acts "reasonably." If it does not, the judge may step in.

Judicial control of jury action can take the form of rulings on pretrial motions to dismiss, motions for summary judgment, or discovery motions. In addition, the final pretrial order governs the trial, limiting the numbers and types of witnesses who will testify, the documents and other exhibits that can be offered, and the length and structure of opening statements, closing arguments, and the evidence presented by all parties. The judge also controls the flow of evidence and rules on motions during trial. The judge even can end the trial by granting a Rule 50(a) motion for judgment as a matter of law, require a new trial by granting a Rule 59 motion for new trial, or overturn a jury verdict by granting a Rule 50(b) renewed motion for judgment as a matter of law.

The Seventh Amendment not only preserves the right to jury trial, but the Reexamination Clause of that amendment provides that "no fact tried by jury * * * shall be otherwise reexamined in any Court of the United States, than according to the rules of the common law." As discussed in this chapter, though, there are many means of judicial control of jury action that do not violate this constitutional provision.

II. THE COURSE OF A CIVIL TRIAL

In order to understand the types, and timing, of judicial control of jury trials, one must understand the typical course of a civil trial. As you know from earlier chapters of this book, a great deal of time and expense is invested in a civil action before it ever reaches the courtroom. In a typical case there is a Rule 26(f) discovery conference involving the attorneys, a Rule 16 scheduling conference and order, party discovery, possible pretrial motions (such as a Rule 12 motion to dismiss or a Rule 56 motion for summary judgment), and a final pretrial conference and final pretrial order.

At the completion of this pretrial activity, the trial—which will be governed by the final pretrial order—awaits. The sequence of events at trial is set forth in Figure 13–1 and includes the following:

- **Jury Selection**, during which the judge and counsel question potential jurors to determine which jurors will be struck from the jury by challenges for cause or peremptory challenges.

- **Opening Statements**, in which counsel give the jurors an overview of the evidence they will hear at trial. Because the plaintiff bears the burden of persuasion (discussed in Section IV(A) of this chapter), plaintiff's counsel typically gives the initial opening statement, followed by the opening statement of the defendant. In some cases defense counsel may not give her opening statement at this time, but may "reserve" her opening statement until right before she presents plaintiff's evidence to the jury.

- **Plaintiff's Evidence** or Case-in-Chief. Because the plaintiff typically must satisfy the burden of persuasion, the plaintiff presents its evidence first. Plaintiff's attorney calls witnesses to testify and offers documents and other exhibits for the consideration of the jury. This portion of the trial is sometimes referred to as plaintiff's case-in-chief, because the plaintiff may be able to present additional (rebuttal) evidence after the defendant has presented its evidence.

- **Defendant's Rule 50(a) Motion for Judgment as a Matter of Law** or, at common law, Motion for a Directed Verdict. The defendant is not required to make such a motion, but Rule 50(a) provides: "If a party has been fully heard on an issue during a jury trial and the court finds that a reasonable jury would not have a legally sufficient evidentiary basis to find for the party on that issue, the court may * * * grant a motion for judgment as a matter of law against the party on a claim or defense that, under the controlling law, can be maintained or defeated only with a favorable finding on that issue." Such motions therefore are appropriate after the plaintiff has presented all its evidence, and, if successful, can lead to the dismissal of portions of plaintiff's case or the entire action.

- **Defendant's Evidence** is presented if a motion for judgment as a matter of law is not granted by the judge. Defense counsel presents defendant's evidence in a manner quite similar to that utilized to present the plaintiff's case-in-chief, calling witnesses and offering exhibits for the consideration of the jury.

- **Plaintiff's Rule 50(a) Motion for Judgment as a Matter of Law** or Motion for a Directed Verdict can be filed by the plaintiff after the defendant has presented all its trial evidence. Because the burden of production must be satisfied by the plaintiff, it is the rare case in which the court will grant such a plaintiff's motion. However, if the court finds under Rule 50(a) "that a reasonable jury would not have a legally sufficient evidentiary basis to find for the [defendant] on [an] issue," the court can enter judgment for the plaintiff and not submit that particular issue or claim to the jury.

- **Plaintiff's Rebuttal Evidence** may be permitted if the defendant's evidence raised matters not addressed in plaintiff's case-in-chief. Rebuttal evidence is not to give the plaintiff "the last word" in presenting trial evidence, but to address new issues raised by the defense evidence.

- **Parties' Closing Arguments** are presented by counsel after the conclusion of the evidence. Typically counsel for plaintiff (on whom rests the burden of persuasion) gives the initial closing argument, followed by defense counsel and, in many cases, followed by a short rebuttal argument in which plaintiff's counsel can address new matters raised by defense counsel in the defendant's closing argument.

- **Judge's Instructions to the Jury** follow the closing arguments in many courts, although in some courts these jury instructions will be given before closing argument. In these instructions the judge provides the jury with the law it is to apply in deciding the case.

- **The Submission of the Case to the Jury and the Jury's Verdict** follow the closing arguments and judge's instructions to the jury.

- **Judge's Entry of Judgment on the Jury Verdict** translates the jury verdict into an enforceable legal judgment entered on the court's docket.

- **Post-Trial Motions** may be filed after the entry of judgment following the jury verdict. These may include a Rule 50(b) renewed motion for judgment as a matter of law (if a Rule 50(a) motion for judgment as a matter of law was filed by that party before the case was submitted to the jury); a Rule 59 motion for new trial; or a later Rule 60(b) motion for relief from judgment.

Most of these same stages of trial apply to nonjury trials as well, although in such cases it is the judge, rather than the jury, who resolves all factual disputes. Instead of a Rule 50(a) motion for judgment as a matter of law, Rule 52(c) provides for a motion for judgment on partial findings. The first sentence of Rule 52(c) provides: "If a party has been fully heard on an issue during a nonjury trial and the court finds against the party on that issue, the court may enter judgment against the party on a claim or defense that, under the controlling law, can be maintained or defeated only with a favorable finding on that issue." Thus there is no reason to hear all the evidence in a case if a party (typically the plaintiff) has offered all its evidence and that evidence is not legally sufficient to establish an essential element of that party's claim.

FIGURE 13–1
THE COURSE OF A CIVIL ACTION

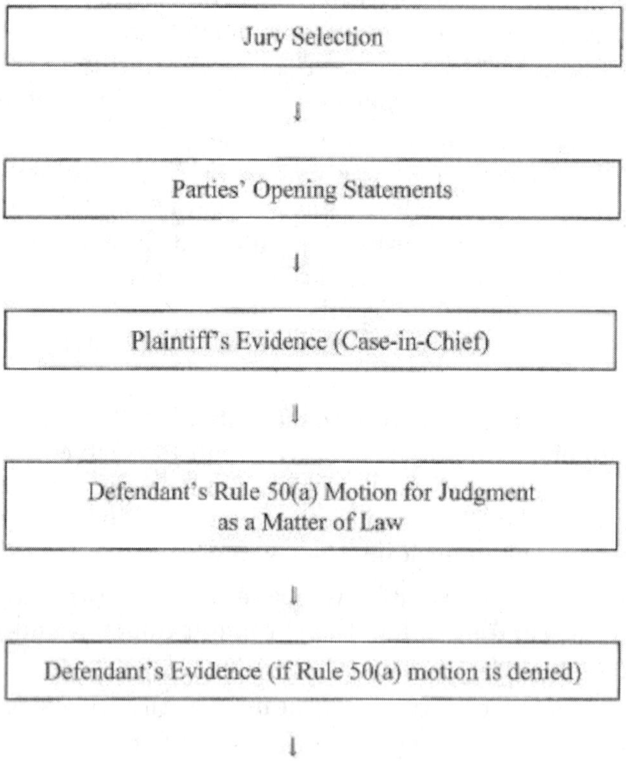

Jury Selection

↓

Parties' Opening Statements

↓

Plaintiff's Evidence (Case-in-Chief)

↓

Defendant's Rule 50(a) Motion for Judgment
as a Matter of Law

↓

Defendant's Evidence (if Rule 50(a) motion is denied)

↓

> **Plaintiff's Rule 50(a) Motion for Judgment as a Matter of Law**
>
> ↓
>
> **Plaintiff's Rebuttal Evidence (if Rule 50(a) motion is denied)**
>
> ↓
>
> **Parties' Closing Arguments**
>
> ⇓
>
> **Judge's Instructions to the Jury**
>
> ⇓
>
> **Submission of Case to Jury and Jury Verdict**
>
> ⇓
>
> **Judge's Entry of Judgment on Jury Verdict**
>
> ⇓
>
> **Post-Trial Motions by Losing Party: (1) Rule 50(b) Renewed Motion for Judgment a Matter of Law; (2) Rule 59 Motion for New Trial**

III. JUDICIAL CONTROL OF JURY TRIALS

Much of the pretrial period is spent on activity narrowing and defining the case that will be presented to the jury. Partial motions to dismiss or for summary judgment may resolve some claims before trial. Discovery should uncover evidence that may cause the parties to either drop or seek to add claims and theories for jury consideration. At the conclusion of pretrial, the final pretrial order will set the ground rules for trial, and the judge may grant motions in limine ("at the threshold") before trial concerning the specific evidence that can, and cannot, be offered at trial.

During trial, it will be the judge who determines what evidence the jury hears, and even after trial, jury discretion is constrained by the judge's jury instructions. While the Seventh Amendment preserves the right to jury trial in certain cases, many of the judge's actions and the procedures surrounding jury trials are to ensure that the jury acts responsibly and stays within its proper scope of decision-making authority.

A. JUDICIAL CONTROL OF THE JURY DURING TRIAL

Rule 16(e) provides for a final pretrial order that, in the words of Rule 16(e), will operate as "a trial plan, including a plan to facilitate the admission of evidence" at trial. This order typically lists all trial witnesses and exhibits, and it may include limits on the length of time the parties will have to present their cases or make opening statements and closing arguments. No matter how detailed the final pretrial order, though, unexpected matters will arise at trial. Witnesses may duplicate the testimony of others, may not be able to testify when they are expected, or may not provide the testamentary foundation for the admission of particular exhibits. In such situations and in many others, the judge must determine whether to cut witnesses, limit the testimony of particular witnesses, or exclude exhibits that the parties assumed would be admitted.

The judge also controls the flow of the case, often in response to the perceived needs of the jury or others. Will the judge recess early or ask the jury to stay late to finish testimony or attempt to reach a verdict? Will the judge require witnesses to be offered in a certain order so out-of-town witnesses can return home or otherwise avoid inconvenience? While the judge does not decide the facts in a jury trial, he will structure and preside over the trial that will provide the basis for the jury's verdict.

The judge also can become quite involved in the presentation of specific trial evidence. The Federal Rules of Evidence govern the admission of evidence in federal trials. Federal Rule of Evidence 614(a) permits the court to "call a witness on its own," while Rule 614(b) provides that the "court may examine a witness regardless of who calls the witness."

There are, though, limits on the extent to which a judge can examine a witness. Judge William Hastie of the United States Court of Appeals for the Third Circuit expressed these limits as follows:

> [P]articularly in a case of this sort where both sides are represented by eminently competent counsel we think it important that the court minimize its own questioning of witnesses, to the end that any such judicial departure from the normal course of trial be merely helpful in clarifying the testimony rather than prejudicial in tending to impose upon the jury what the judge seems to think about the evidence. Not long ago Judge Kalodner, speaking for this court, had occasion to caution that "trial judges should ever keep in mind the

manifest dangers of overparticipation in the examination and cross-examination of witnesses." *See United States v. Neff*, 3 Cir., 1954, 212 F.2d 297, 313. We repeat that admonition.

Groce v. Seder, 267 F.2d 352, 355 (3d Cir. 1959). *See also United States v. Cassiagnol*, 420 F.2d 868, 879 (4th Cir. 1970) ("[T]he judge is entitled to propound questions pertinent to a confused factual issue which requires clarification. He may also intercede because of seeming inadequacy of examination or cross-examination by counsel, or to draw more information from reluctant witnesses or experts who are inarticulate or less than candid. But this privilege or duty is subject to reasonable limitations.").

The judge also may comment upon the evidence offered at trial—within reason. The United States Court of Appeals for the Eighth Circuit in *Hale v. Firestone Tire & Rubber Co.*, 756 F.2d 1322 (8th Cir. 1985), found that a comment by the trial judge was improper, but not sufficiently prejudicial to require a new trial. The court reasoned:

> The one comment made by the district judge before the jury—"Well, I have put air in a lot of tires, but I never had one blow up on me"—was improper. "While remarks made by a district judge within the hearing of the jury are often necessary, the judge should take care not to give the impression that he or she prefers one litigant over another." *Newman v. A.E. Staley Manufacturing Co.*, 648 F.2d 330, 334 (5th Cir.1981). "However, a few improper comments are not necessarily enough to require reversal." *United States v. Singer*, 710 F.2d 431, 436 (8th Cir.1983). Each case must turn on its own facts. The single comment in this case is not sufficient for reversal. The comment was a minor incident in a lengthy trial and is not the type of egregious conduct that alone would require reversal. *United States v. Singer*, 710 F.2d at 436–37 (the judge's excessive questioning because of the inexperience of the prosecutor denied defendant a fair trial); *Newman v. A.E. Staley Manufacturing Co.*, 648 F.2d at 336 (judge's repeated questions and comments before the jury could have influenced the jury); *Pollard v. Fennel*, 400 F.2d 421, 424–26 (4th Cir.1968) (judge's excessive interrogations, leading questions, comments, and vigorous presentation of plaintiff's demonstrative evidence denied defendant a fair trial); *Myers v. George*, 271 F.2d 168 (8th Cir.1959) (judge belittled and ridiculed witnesses).

756 F.2d at 1330.

What if the judge informs the jury that, while he sees the evidence in a certain way, the jury is expected to make its own factual determination. Should the following statement by the judge lead to reversal in a criminal trial:

And now I am going to tell you what I think of the defendant's testimony. You may have noticed, Mr. Foreman and gentlemen, that he wiped his hands during his testimony. It is rather a curious thing, but that is almost always an indication of lying. Why it should be so we don't know, but that is the fact. I think that every single word that man said, except when he agreed with the Government's testimony, was a lie.

Now, that opinion is an opinion of evidence and is not binding on you, and if you don't agree with it, it is your duty to find him not guilty.

Quercia v. United States, 289 U.S. 466, 468–69 (1933).

Judicial questioning or comments can help to organize particular testimony for the jury, especially if an attorney is not asking the key questions or bringing out crucial evidence. But the judge, the authority figure in the courtroom, is not under oath or subject to cross-examination. The judge therefore must be careful in interjecting himself into the trial in a role that could be perceived as adversarial in nature. The Supreme Court has described the delicate balance between the roles of the judge and jury as follows:

In the trial by jury, the right to which is secured by the 7th Amendment, both the court and the jury are essential factors. To the former is committed a power of direction and superintendence, and to the latter the ultimate determination of the issues of fact. Only through the co-operation of the two, each acting within its appropriate sphere, can the constitutional right be satisfied. And so, to dispense with either, or to permit one to disregard the province of the other, is to impinge on that right.

Slocum v. New York Life Ins. Co., 228 U.S. 364, 382 (1913).

B. JUDICIAL CONTROL THROUGH JURY INSTRUCTIONS AND FORMS OF VERDICTS

The purpose of juries is to decide cases by returning a verdict. When judges decide a trial or appellate case, they are required to state reasons for their decisions. This typically is not a requirement for jury verdicts.

In order to restrain the discretion of juries, they are given instructions by the trial judge that set forth the governing law that the jurors are to apply in reaching their verdict. Judges have "standard instructions" with which they charge juries in all cases (for example, admonishing jurors not to talk to others about their deliberations and that nothing that the lawyers or judge says constitutes evidence in the case). Additional standard instructions focus on certain types of claims or issues presented by particular types of cases (for instance, an instruction defining the manner in which a jury should determine proximate cause or apply the law of comparative negligence). *E.g.*, United States Court of Appeals for the Fifth Circuit, *Pattern Jury Instructions: Civil*, http://www.lb5.uscourts.gov/juryinstructions.

Rule 51 of the Federal Rules of Civil Procedure permits an attorney to request that the judge instruct the jury with additional instructions that the attorney believes would be particularly appropriate in the case (and which, not coincidentally, would be particularly helpful in guiding the jury to a verdict favorable to her client). Requested instructions can be drafted by an attorney for a specific case or taken from the pattern jury instructions approved and adopted by several of the United States Courts of Appeal. *See* http://www.lb5.uscourts.gov/juryinstructions/ (containing links to civil jury instructions for several of the United States Courts of Appeals). Because these instructions have been adopted by courts of appeals, district judges within those circuits can give these instructions without concern about appellate reversal for using a particular instruction. If, however, a district judge misstates the law in her jury instructions, the trial court judgment may be reversed unless the misstated instruction constitutes Rule 61 harmless error in light of the instructions in their entirety or other aspects of the case.

Rule 1.17 of the Federal Jury Instructions of the Seventh Circuit provides:

> You may find the testimony of one witness or a few witnesses more persuasive than the testimony of a larger number. You need not accept the testimony of the larger number of witnesses.

https://www.ca7.uscourts.gov/Pattern_Jury_Instr/pattern_jury_instr. html. In an action in which one party called many more witnesses than the other, which attorney might request this instruction?

Rule 51 of the Federal Rules of Civil Procedure sets forth the procedures for requesting specific jury instructions and for objecting to instructions or the failure to give requested instructions. Rule 51(a)(1) provides: "At the close of the evidence or at any earlier reasonable time that the court orders, a party may file and furnish to every other party written requests for the jury instructions it wants the court to give." If the judge asks for requested instructions before the close of the evidence, Rule 51(a)(2) permits counsel to "file requests for instructions on issues that could not reasonably have been anticipated by an earlier time that the court set for requests."

So that counsel can refer to the jury instructions in their closing arguments, Rule 51(b)(1) requires the judge to "inform the parties of its proposed instructions and proposed action on the requests before instructing the jury and before final jury arguments." Rule 51(b)(2) further provides that the judge "must give the parties an opportunity to object on the record and out of the jury's hearing before the instructions and arguments are delivered." If a party does not object to a proposed instruction at this time, an objection will be considered untimely (and thus waived) unless the instruction constitutes plain error because it affects a party's substantial rights. Rule 51(d)(2). *See also* Rule 61. If the asserted error is in the judge's refusal to give a requested instruction, Rule 51(d)(1)(B) provides that the party must have timely objected, "unless the court rejected the request in a definitive ruling on the record."

Jury instructions thus can protect the parties' substantial rights and ensure that different juries decide like cases in a like manner. However, it is difficult for a judge to be certain that the jury actually followed her instructions in reaching a verdict—especially because, under Federal Rule of Evidence 606(b) and the Mansfield Rule, jurors cannot be questioned about statements made during jury deliberations or juror thought processes. *See supra* pp. 923–937.

This problem is exacerbated by the fact that juries typically return general verdicts. These take one of two forms: (1) a verdict for the plaintiff for a certain amount of damages or other relief or (2) a verdict for the defendant. Rule 48(b) further provides: "Unless the parties stipulate otherwise, the verdict must be unanimous and must be returned by a jury of at least 6 members." At least with respect to this unanimity requirement, Rule 48(c) gives the judge and counsel a way to test whether the jury truly was unanimous in its verdict. Rule 48(c) provides:

> After a verdict is returned but before the jury is discharged, the court must on a party's request, or may on its own, poll the jurors individually. If the poll reveals a lack of unanimity or lack of assent by the number of jurors that the parties stipulated to, the court may direct the jury to deliberate further or may order a new trial.

The jury, though, may be unanimous yet not have followed the judge's instructions. Rule 49 provides the judge with two ways to channel the jury's discretion to increase the likelihood that it follows the judge's instructions on the law:

- A Rule 49(a) Special Verdict; or
- A Rule 49(b) General Verdict with Answers to Written Questions.

Rule 49(a) gives the judge discretion to require that the jury return a special verdict, which, in contrast to a general verdict, consists of written findings on each issue of fact. Thus, in a negligence action, the jury could be asked to determine how fast the defendant was driving or whether the plaintiff was within the walkway when struck by defendant's car.

The Rule 49(b) general verdict with answers to written questions is similar, in that the jury is required to answer written questions (sometimes referred to as jury interrogatories) but, in addition, also render a general verdict.

By requiring the jury to answer specific questions, rather than simply return a general verdict for the plaintiff in a certain amount or for the defendant, the hope is that the jury's discretion will be cabined a bit and the jury will be more likely to follow the governing law. In addition, answers to specific factual questions may permit the judge or court of appeals to salvage at least some of the jury's verdict if there is trial error, but that error is confined to certain portions of the jury's special verdict or answers to written questions. Rule 49(b)(3) permits the judge to attempt to harmonize inconsistencies between consistent answers to written jury questions that are inconsistent with a general jury verdict.

Thus, while the Seventh Amendment preserves the right to jury trial, the trial judge is to prevent the jury from acting arbitrarily or unreasonably. Judges do this is by their jury instructions and, in appropriate cases, by utilizing a Rule 49(a) special verdict or a Rule 49(b) general verdict with answers to written questions.

IV. BURDENS OF PRODUCTION AND PERSUASION

Even though the parties may have a right to a jury and the jury has been selected, this does not always mean that the jury will decide the case. The law places on some parties to civil actions both burdens of production and burdens of persuasion. The burden of persuasion requires that a party prove its case before the jury to a specific level of certainty: typically by a preponderance of the evidence in a civil case or beyond a reasonable doubt in a criminal action. The burden of persuasion is what non-lawyers sometimes refer to as a party's "burden of proof."

But any burden of proof encompasses not only the burden of persuasion that must be determined by the jury but also the burden of production, which is sometimes called the "burden of going forward." While a party cannot win its case unless it can convince the jury that it has met its burden of persuasion, the judge will not even submit the case for jury consideration if he is not convinced that a party has met its burden of production. We typically think of such burdens as applying to the claims of plaintiffs, but they also can be placed on defendants seeking to establish affirmative defenses or counterclaims.[1]

The burden of production has been described as a standard requiring that "evidence which would justify a reasonable jury in finding the existence or nonexistence of the fact must be adduced if a judicial ruling for the other party is to be avoided." McNaughton,

---

[1] Specific parties also may be required to assert certain claims or defenses in their pleadings to raise those claims in an action. *E.g. Jones v. Bock*, 549 U.S. 199 (2007), *supra* p. 96.

"Burden of Production of Evidence: A Function of Burden of Persuasion," 68 *Harv.L.Rev.* 1382, 1383 (1955). Thus if a party does not satisfy its burden of production, the judge will take the case from the jury and enter judgment against the party that has not met its burden. One court has characterized procedural burdens as follows: "The burden of proof is to law what inertia is to physics—a built-in bias in favor of the status quo. * * * That is, if you want the court to *do* something, you have to present evidence sufficient to overcome the state of affairs that would exist if the court did nothing." *In re Conservatorship of Hume*, 140 Cal.App.4th 1385, 1388 (4th Dist. 2006).

The burden of production and burden of persuasion are illustrated in Figure 13–2. If the plaintiff does not offer more evidence than "A," it will not have satisfied its burden of production and the trial judge will grant judgment for the defendant. Assuming that the burden of production is met (more evidence than "A" has been offered), the judge should submit the case to the jury. After the jury hears all the evidence, it can only return a verdict for the plaintiff if the plaintiff met its burden of persuasion (offered more than "B" evidence at trial).

FIGURE 13–2[2]
BURDENS OF PRODUCTION AND PERSUASION

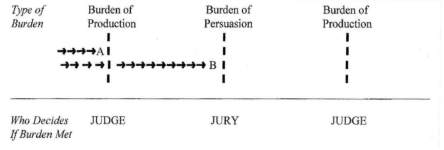

Type of Burden	Burden of Production	Burden of Persuasion	Burden of Production

Who Decides If Burden Met	JUDGE	JURY	JUDGE

These are typically plaintiff's burdens, but how and when can the defendant raise the plaintiff's failure to meet these burdens? The failure of the plaintiff to satisfy the burden of production can be raised by the defendant at two different times by two different motions.

- Federal Rule of Civil Procedure 50(a) allows the defendant to raise plaintiff's failure to meet its burden of production by filing a motion for **judgment as a matter of law**. Rule 50(a)(1) provides that this motion can only be made after "a party has been fully heard on an issue during a jury trial," while Rule 50(a)(2) provides that the motion can be raised "at any time before the case is submitted to the jury." The motion for judgment as a matter of law was called a motion for directed verdict at common law. Older

---

[2] This diagram builds on the diagrams originally offered in 9 J. Wigmore, *Evidence* § 2487 at 298 (McNaughton rev. 1961) and McNaughton, "Burden of Production of Evidence: A Function of Burden of Persuasion," 68 *Harv.L.Rev.* 1382 (1955). *See also* 21B C. Wright & K. Graham, *Federal Practice and Procedure: Evidence* § 5122, at 417 (2nd ed. 2005).

opinions, and some state cases, refer to the motion in that way.

- If a Rule 50(a) motion for judgment as a matter of law is filed before the action is submitted to the jury, the moving party (typically the defendant) can file a Rule 50(b) **renewed motion for judgment as a matter of law** within 28 days after the entry of judgment. These motions were called motions for judgment notwithstanding the verdict at common law (or JNOV motions, based on the Latin phrase "non obstante veredicto"). This language continues to be used in many state procedural systems.

The Rule 50(a) and 50(b) motions are made at different times: The Rule 50(a) motion is made before submission of the case to the jury and the Rule 50(b) motion is made within 28 days after entry of judgment. However, the standard for granting both motions is the same. When faced with either motion, the trial judge should grant the motion if a reasonable jury could only decide the case one way (in favor of the moving party). If a reasonable jury could only decide the action one way, there is no reason for the jury to resolve the case and the judge should enter judgment for the moving party as a matter of law. The timing of the Rule 50(a) and (b) motions is shown in Figure 13–3.

FIGURE 13–3
RULE 50(a) AND 50(b) TRIAL AND POST-TRIAL MOTIONS

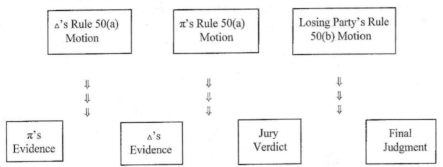

The burden of persuasion typically requires a party (usually the plaintiff) to offer evidence at trial showing that it is more likely than not that all the necessary elements of its claims are true. If this burden of persuasion is met, the jury is to return a verdict for the plaintiff. If the burden of persuasion is not met, the jury's verdict should be for the defendant. Failure to satisfy the burden of persuasion is not raised by party motion, but is the standard that the judge gives to the jury in the jury instructions.[3]

---

[3]   In the event that the jury verdict is against the weight of the evidence, the losing party can file a Rule 59 motion for new trial. *Byrd v. Blue Ridge Rural Elec. Co-op., Inc.*, 356 U.S. 525, 540 (1958) ("The trial judge in the federal system has * * * discretion to grant a new trial if the verdict appears to him to be against the weight of the evidence.").

The application of these burdens is considered in the following sections of this chapter.

A. THE APPLICATION OF THE BURDEN OF PRODUCTION

What does it mean to say that the case should be taken from the jury if there is no "evidence which would justify a reasonable jury in finding the existence or nonexistence of the fact" that must be established for a party to meet its burden of production?[4] Or, in the words of Rule 50(a)(1), that a "party has been fully heard on an issue during a jury trial [but] the court finds that a reasonable jury would not have a legally sufficient evidentiary basis to find for the party on that issue"? Consider the application of this standard in the case that follows.

Lavender v. Kurn

Supreme Court of the United States, 1946
327 U.S. 645

OPINION

■ MR. JUSTICE MURPHY delivered the opinion of the Court.

The Federal Employers' Liability Act permits recovery for personal injuries to an employee of a railroad engaged in interstate commerce if such injuries result "in whole or in part from the negligence of any of the officers, agents, or employees of such carrier, or by reason of any defect or insufficiency, due to its negligence, in its cars, engines, appliances, machinery, track, roadbed, works, boats, wharves, or other equipment." 45 U.S.C. § 51.

Petitioner, the administrator of the estate of L. E. Haney, brought this suit under the Act against the respondent trustees of the St. Louis-San Francisco Railway Company (Frisco) and the respondent Illinois Central Railroad Company. It was charged that Haney, while employed as a switchtender by the respondents in the switchyard of the Grand Central Station in Memphis, Tennessee, was killed as a result of respondents' negligence. Following a trial in the Circuit Court of the City of St. Louis, Missouri, the jury returned a verdict in favor of petitioner and awarded damages in the amount of $30,000. Judgment was entered accordingly. On appeal, however, the Supreme Court of Missouri reversed the judgment, holding that there was no substantial evidence of negligence to support the submission of the case to the jury. We granted certiorari to review the propriety of the Supreme Court's action under the circumstances of this case.

It was admitted that Haney was employed by the Illinois Central, or a subsidiary corporation thereof, as a switchtender in the railroad

---

[4] McNaughton, "Burden of Production of Evidence: A Function of Burden of Persuasion," 68 *Harv.L.Rev.* 1382, 1383 (1955).

yards near the Grand Central Station, which was owned by the Illinois Central. His duties included the throwing of switches for the Illinois Central as well as for the Frisco and other railroads using that station. * * *

The Illinois Central tracks run north and south directly past and into the Grand Central Station. About 2700 feet south of the station the Frisco tracks cross at right angles to the Illinois Central tracks. A westbound Frisco train wishing to use the station must stop some 250 feet or more west of this crossing and back into the station over a switch line curving east and north. The events in issue center about the switch several feet north of the main Frisco tracks at the point where the switch line branches off. This switch controls the tracks at this point.

It was very dark on the evening of December 21, 1939. At about 7:30 p.m. a westbound interstate Frisco passenger train stopped on the Frisco main line, its rear some 20 or 30 feet west of the switch. Haney, in the performance of his duties, threw or opened the switch to permit the train to back into the station. The respondents claimed that Haney was then required to cross to the south side of the track before the train passed the switch; and the conductor of the train testified that he saw Haney so cross. But there was also evidence that Haney's duties required him to wait at the switch north of the track until the train had cleared, close the switch, return to his shanty near the crossing and change the signals from red to green to permit trains on the Illinois Central tracks to use the crossing. The Frisco train cleared the switch, backing at the rate of 8 or 10 miles per hour. But the switch remained open and the signals still were red. Upon investigation Haney was found north of the track near the switch lying face down on the ground, unconscious. An ambulance was called, but he was dead upon arrival at the hospital.

Haney had been struck in the back of the head, causing a fractured skull from which he died. There were no known eye-witnesses to the fatal blow. Although it is not clear there is evidence that his body was extended north and south, the head to the south. Apparently he had fallen forward to the south; his face was bruised on the left side from hitting the ground and there were marks indicating that his toes had dragged a few inches southward as he fell. His head was about 5 ½ feet north of the Frisco tracks. Estimates ranged from 2 feet to 14 feet as to how far west of the switch he lay.

The injury to Haney's head was evidenced by a gash about two inches long from which blood flowed. The back of Haney's white cap had a corresponding black mark about an inch and a half long and an inch wide, running at an angle downward to the right of the center of the back of the head. A spot of blood was later found at a point 3 or 4 feet north of the tracks. The conclusion following an autopsy was that Haney's skull was fractured by "some fast moving small round object." One of the examining doctors testified that such an object might have been attached to a train backing at the rate of 8 or 10 miles per hour. But he also admitted that the fracture might have resulted from a blow from a pipe or club or some similar round object in the hands of an individual.

Petitioner's theory is that Haney was struck by the curled end or tip of a mail hook hanging down loosely on the outside of the mail car of the backing train. This curled end was 73 inches above the top of the rail, which was 7 inches high. The overhang of the mail car in relation to the rails was about 2 to 2 ½ feet. The evidence indicated that when the mail car swayed or moved around a curve the mail hook might pivot, its curled end swinging out as much as 12 to 14 inches. The curled end could thus be swung out to a point 3 to 3 ½ feet from the rail and about 73 inches above the top of the rail. Both east and west of the switch, however, was an uneven mound of cinders and dirt rising at its highest points 18 to 24 inches above the top of the rails. Witnesses differed as to how close the mound approached the rails, the estimates varying from 3 to 15 feet. But taking the figures most favorable to the petitioner, the mound extended to a point 6 to 12 inches north of the overhanging side of the mail car. If the mail hook end swung out 12 to 14 inches it would be 49 to 55 inches above the highest parts of the mound. Haney was 67 ½ inches tall. If he had been standing on the mound about a foot from the side of the mail car he could have been hit by the end of the mail hook, the exact point of contact depending upon the height of the mound at the particular point. His wound was about 4 inches below the top of his head, or 63 ½ inches above the point where he stood on the mound-well within the possible range of the mail hook end.

Respondents' theory is that Haney was murdered. They point to the estimates that the mound was 10 to 15 feet north of the rail, making it impossible for the mail hook end to reach a point of contact with Haney's head. Photographs were placed in the record to support the claim that the ground was level north of the rail for at least 10 feet. Moreover, it appears that the area immediately surrounding the switch was quite dark. Witnesses stated that it was so dark that it was impossible to see a 3-inch pipe 25 feet away. It also appears that many hoboes and tramps frequented the area at night in order to get rides on freight trains. Haney carried a pistol to protect himself. This pistol was found loose under his body by those who came to his rescue. It was testified, however, that the pistol had apparently slipped out of his pocket or scabbard as he fell. Haney's clothes were not disarranged and there was no evidence of a struggle or fight. No rods, pipes or weapons of any kind, except Haney's own pistol, were found near the scene. Moreover, his gold watch and diamond ring were still on him after he was struck. Six days later his unsoiled billfold was found on a high board fence about a block from the place where Haney was struck and near the point where he had been placed in an ambulance. It contained his social security card and other effects, but no money. His wife testified that he "never carried much money, not very much more than $10." Such were the facts in relation to respondents' theory of murder.

Finally, one of the Frisco foremen testified that he arrived at the scene shortly after Haney was found injured. He later examined the fireman's side of the train very carefully and found nothing sticking out or in disorder. In explaining why he examined this side of the train so carefully he stated that while he was at the scene of the accident "someone said they thought that train No. 106 backing in to Grand Central Station is what struck this man" and that Haney "was supposed to have been struck by something protruding on the side of the train." The foreman testified that these statements were made by an unknown Illinois Central switchman standing near the fallen body of Haney. The foreman admitted that the switchman "didn't see the accident." This testimony was admitted by the trial court over the strenuous objections of respondents' counsel that it was mere hearsay falling outside the res gestae rule.

The jury was instructed that Frisco's trustees were liable if it was found that they negligently permitted a rod or other object to extend out from the side of the train as it backed past Haney and that Haney was killed as the direct result of such negligence, if any. The jury was further told that Illinois Central was liable if it was found that the company negligently maintained an unsafe and dangerous place for Haney to work, in that the ground was high and uneven and the light insufficient and inadequate, and that Haney was injured and killed as a direct result of the said place being unsafe and dangerous. This latter instruction as to Illinois Central did not require the jury to find that Haney was killed by something protruding from the train.

The Supreme Court, in upsetting the jury's verdict against both the Frisco trustees and the Illinois Central, admitted that "It could be inferred from the facts that Haney could have been struck by the mail hook knob if he were standing on the south side of the mound and the mail hook extended out as far as 12 or 14 inches." But it held that "all reasonable minds would agree that it would be mere speculation and conjecture to say that Haney was struck by the mail hook" and that "plaintiff failed to make a submissible case on that question." It also ruled that there "was no substantial evidence that the uneven ground and insufficient light were cause or contributing causes of the death of Haney." Finally, the Supreme Court held that the testimony of the foreman as to the statement made to him by the unknown switchmen was inadmissible under the res gestae rule since the switchman spoke from what he had heard rather than from his own knowledge.

We hold, however, that there was sufficient evidence of negligence on the part of both the Frisco trustee and the Illinois Central to justify the submission of the case to the jury and to require appellate courts to abide by the verdict rendered by the jury.

The evidence we have already detailed demonstrates that there was evidence from which it might be inferred that the end of the mail hook struck Haney in the back of the head, an inference that the Supreme Court admitted could be drawn. That inference is not rendered unreasonable by the fact that Haney apparently fell forward toward the main Frisco track so that his head was 5 ½ feet north of the rail. He may well have been struck and then wandered in a daze to the point where he fell forward. The testimony as to blood marks some distance away from his head lends credence to that possibility, indicating that he did not fall immediately upon being hit. When that is added to the evidence most favorable to the petitioner as to the height and swing-out of the hook, the height and location of the mound and the nature of Haney's duties, the inference that Haney was killed by the hook cannot be said to be unsupported by probative facts or to be so unreasonable as to warrant taking the case from the jury.

It is true that there is evidence tending to show that it was physically and mathematically impossible for the hook to strike Haney. And there are facts from which it might reasonably be inferred that Haney was murdered. But such evidence has become irrelevant upon appeal, there being a reasonable basis in the record for inferring that the hook struck Haney. The jury having made that inference, the respondents were not free to relitigate the factual dispute in a reviewing court. Under these circumstances it would be an undue invasion of the jury's historic function for an appellate court to weigh the conflicting evidence, judge the credibility of witnesses and arrive at a conclusion opposite from the one reached by the jury.

It is no answer to say that the jury's verdict involved speculation and conjecture. Whenever facts are in dispute or the evidence is such that fair-minded men may draw different inferences, a measure of speculation and conjecture is required on the part of those whose duty it is to settle the dispute by choosing what seems to them to be the most reasonable inference. Only when there is a complete absence of probative facts to support the conclusion reached does a reversible error appear. But where, as here, there is an evidentiary basis for the jury's verdict, the jury is free to discard or disbelieve whatever facts are inconsistent with its conclusion. And the appellate court's function is exhausted when that evidentiary basis becomes apparent, it being immaterial that the court might draw a contrary inference or feel that another conclusion is more reasonable.

We are unable, therefore, to sanction a reversal of the jury's verdict against Frisco's trustees. Nor can we approve any disturbance in the verdict as to Illinois Central. The evidence was uncontradicted that it was very dark at the place where Haney was working and the surrounding ground was high and uneven. The evidence also showed that this area was entirely within the domination and control of Illinois Central despite the fact that the area was technically located in a public street of the City of Memphis. It was not unreasonable to conclude that these conditions constituted an unsafe and dangerous working place and that such conditions contributed in part to Haney's death, assuming that it resulted primarily from the mail hook striking his head.

* * *

The judgment of the Supreme Court of Missouri is reversed and the case is remanded for whatever further proceedings may be necessary not inconsistent with this opinion.

Reversed.

■ THE CHIEF JUSTICE and MR. JUSTICE FRANKFURTER concur in the result.

■ MR. JUSTICE REED dissents.

■ MR. JUSTICE JACKSON took no part in the consideration or decision of this case.

COMMENTS AND QUESTIONS CONCERNING *LAVENDER V. KURN*

1.   Did the jury in this case have any basis upon which to decide whether Haney was murdered, was hit by something hanging off the train, or met his death in some other manner? Juries decide issues of contested facts, often by determining which of several witnesses to believe. But in this case the dispute arose from the different inferences that could be drawn from facts that were undisputed.

2.   Justice Murphy describes the roles of judge and jury in these Federal Employers' Liability Act cases as follows:

[W]here, as here, there is an evidentiary basis for the jury's verdict, the jury is free to discard or disbelieve whatever facts are inconsistent with its conclusion. And the appellate court's function is exhausted when that evidentiary basis becomes apparent, it being immaterial that the court might draw a contrary inference or feel that another conclusion is more reasonable.

Or, as Justice Murphy wrote for the Court in *Tennant v. Peoria & P.U. Ry.*, 321 U.S. 29, 35 (1944): "Courts are not free to reweigh the evidence and set aside the jury verdict merely because the jury could have drawn different inferences or conclusions or because judges feel that other results are more reasonable."

3.   Justice Murphy's opinion reads a bit like a murder mystery, doesn't it? He cites only three other Supreme Court decisions, while including layers of facts and statements such as "It was very dark on the evening of December 21, 1939." Why would the Supreme Court grant certiorari to decide such a fact-intensive case? How could the Court's decision help lower courts faced with other fact patterns?

4.   In one of the three cases cited in *Lavender*, Justice Roberts, in an opinion joined by Justice Frankfurter, questioned why the Court agreed to hear that case.

> It seems to be thought * * * that any ruling which takes a case from the jury, albeit it will not serve as a precedent, is of such paramount importance as to require review here. I merely state my conviction that the Seventh Amendment envisages trial not by jury, but by court and jury, according to the view of the common law, and that federal and state courts have not usurped power denied them by the fundamental law in directing verdicts where a party failed to adduce proof to support his contention, or in entering judgment notwithstanding a verdict for like reason. But this I do say, that this court does not sit to redress every apparent error committed by competent and responsible courts whose judgments we are empowered to review. And, if we undertake any such task, we shall disenable the court to fulfill its high office in the scheme of our government.

Bailey v. Cent. Vermont Ry., 319 U.S. 350, 358 (1943) (Roberts, J., dissenting).

5.   Along with three prior Supreme Court decisions, the Court in *Lavender*, 327 U.S. at 645, cited Moore, "Recent Trends in Judicial Interpretation in Railroad Cases Under the Federal Employers' Liability Act," 29 *Marquette L.Rev.* 73 (1946). The author of this article asserts:

> This * * * history of the Act portrays the liberalizing tendency of the times leading to the present era of social reform which is the natural product of the age of industrial pioneering. Today, when the facts relative to carrier's negligence are in dispute, or fair-minded men will honestly draw different conclusions from undisputed facts, the case should go to the jury. The jury and not the Court is the fact-finding body, and the jury should be instructed that the duty of the railroad to maintain a high standard of care and to furnish a safe place to work is an absolute and continuing one. In conformity with the 1939 humanitarian amendment to the Federal Employers' Liability Act the enlightened policy of the United States Supreme Court in several recent decisions has been to resolve all inferences in close and doubtful cases in favor of the injured railroad employee. * * *

Id. at 74. Are the railroads, in effect, facing strict liability once these FELA cases are submitted to Depression-era juries? As Justice Frankfurter stated in one of the three Supreme Court decisions cited in *Lavender*: "Perhaps no field of the law comes closer to the lives of so many families in this country than does the law of negligence, imbedded as it is in the Federal Employers' Liability Act." *Tiller v. Atl. Coast Line R. Co.*, 318 U.S. 54, 73 (1943) (Frankfurter, J., concurring).

6.   Once you have read *Pennsylvania RR. v. Chamberlain*, 288 U.S. 333 (1933), *infra* p. 1002, reconsider the outcome in this case. *Chamberlain* is an earlier FELA case in which the Supreme Court reversed a Court of

Appeals decision concluding that the case should go to the jury. The *Chamberlain* Court noted: "We * * * have a case belonging to that class of cases where proven facts give equal support to each of two inconsistent inferences." 288 U.S. at 339. But wasn't that the case in *Lavender* as well?

7.   In the article cited by Justice Murphy in his opinion, the author notes: "New deal Supreme Court justices unquestionabl[y] have bestowed upon railroad workers a new deal to the solution of their claims in line with modem and progressive social thinking." Moore, *supra* note 5, at 94. The only justice who was on the Supreme Court at the time that both *Chamberlain* and *Lavender* were decided was Justice Stone, who separately concurred in *Chamberlain* and died less than one month after *Lavender* was decided.

8.   Justice Frank Murphy, who authored the majority opinion, held a series of local, state, and federal offices before being named by President Roosevelt to the Supreme Court in 1940. As a state trial judge, he presided over the trial of African-Americans charged with murder for repelling a home invasion due to Dr. Ossian Sweet's purchase of a house in an all-white Detroit neighborhood. Clarence Darrow successfully defended the Sweets and their neighbors and friends in two trials before Judge Murphy. *See* K. Boyle, *Arc of Justice* (2004).

Prior to his appointment to the Supreme Court, Murphy served as Mayor of Detroit, Governor-General of, and High Commissioner to, the Philippines, Governor of Michigan, and United States Attorney General. As a member of the Supreme Court, Murphy dissented in *Korematsu v. United States*, 323 U.S. 214 (1944), in which the Court upheld the constitutionality of Japanese internment during World War II. In *Falbo v. United States*, 320 U.S. 549, 561 (1944), he wrote: "The law knows no finer hour than when it cuts through formal concepts and transitory emotions to protect unpopular citizens against discrimination and persecution." Positions such as this led some to refer to "tempering justice with Murphy." *The Oxford Companion to the Supreme Court of the United States* 659 (K. Hall et al. eds. 2d ed. 2005).

B. ARE JURIES ONLY FOR RESOLVING DISPUTED FACTS?

The primary task of civil juries is to resolve disputed issues of fact. But is there still a role for the jury if the facts are not in dispute? Consider the following case.

Sioux City & P. R. Co. v. Stout

United States Supreme Court, 1873
84 U.S. 657

OPINION

Error to the Circuit Court for the District of Nebraska.

Henry Stout, a child six years of age and living with his parents, sued, by his next friend, the Sioux City and Pacific Railroad Company, in the court below, to recover damages for an injury sustained upon a turntable belonging to the said company. The turntable was in an open space, about eighty rods from the company's depot, in a hamlet or settlement of one hundred to one hundred and fifty persons. Near the turntable was a travelled road passing through the depot grounds, and another travelled road near by. On the railroad ground, which was not inclosed or visibly separated from the adjoining property, was situated the company's station-house, and about a quarter of a mile distant from this was the turntable on which the plaintiff was injured. * * * The turntable was not attended or guarded by any servant of the company, was not fastened or locked, and revolved easily on its axis. Two of the boys began to turn it, and in attempting to get upon it, the foot of the child (he being at the time upon the railroad track) was caught between the end of the rail on the turntable as it was revolving, and the end of the iron rail on the main track of the road, and was crushed.

* * *

The jury found a verdict of $7500 for the plaintiff, from the judgment upon which this writ of error was brought.

■ MR. JUSTICE HUNT delivered the opinion of the court.

1st. It is well settled that the conduct of an infant of tender years is not to be judged by the same rule which governs that of an adult. While it is the general rule in regard to an adult, that to entitle him to recover damages for an injury resulting from the fault or negligence of another, he must himself have been free from fault, such is not the rule in regard to an infant of tender years. The care and caution required of a child is according to his maturity and capacity only, and this is to be determined in each case by the circumstances of that case.

But it is not necessary to pursue this subject. The record expressly states that "the counsel for the defendant disclaim resting their defence on the ground that the plaintiff's parents were negligent, or that the plaintiff (considering his tender age) was negligent, but rest their defence on the ground that the company was not negligent, and claim that the injury to the plaintiff was accidental or brought upon himself."

* * *

2d. Was there negligence on the part of the railway company in the management or condition of its turntable?

The charge on this point was an impartial and intelligent one. Unless the defendant was entitled to an order that the plaintiff be nonsuited, or, as it is expressed in the practice of the United States courts, to an order directing a verdict in its favor, the submission was right. If, upon any construction which the jury was authorized to put upon the evidence, or by any inferences they were authorized to draw from it, the conclusion of negligence can be justified, the defendant was not entitled to this order, and the judgment cannot be disturbed. To express it affirmatively, if from the evidence given it might justly be inferred by the jury that the defendant, in the construction, location, management, or condition of its machine had omitted that care and attention to prevent the occurrence of accidents which prudent and careful men ordinarily bestow, the jury was at liberty to find for the plaintiff.

That the turntable was a dangerous machine, which would be likely to cause injury to children who resorted to it, might fairly be inferred from the injury which actually occurred to the plaintiff. There was the same liability to injury to him, and no greater, that existed with reference to all children. When the jury learned from the evidence that he had suffered a serious injury, by his foot being caught between the fixed rail of the road-bed and the turning rail of the table they were justified in believing that there was a probability of the occurrence of such accidents.

So, in looking at the remoteness of the machine from inhabited dwellings, when it was proved to the jury that several boys from the hamlet were at play there on this occasion, and that they had been at play upon the turntable on other occasions, and within the observation and to the knowledge of the employees of the defendant, the jury were justified in believing that children would probably resort to it, and that the defendant should have anticipated that such would be the case.

As it was in fact, on this occasion, so it was to be expected that the amusement of the boys would have been found in turning this table while they were on it or about it. This could certainly have been prevented by locking the turntable when not in use by the company. * * * The evidence is not strong and the negligence is slight, but we are not able to say that there is not evidence sufficient to justify the verdict. We are not called upon to weigh, to measure, to balance the evidence, or to ascertain how we should have decided if acting as jurors. The charge was in all respects sound and judicious, and there being sufficient evidence to justify the finding, we are not authorized to disturb it.

3d. It is true, in many cases, that where the facts are undisputed the effect of them is for the judgment of the court, and not for the decision of the jury. This is true in that class of cases where the existence of such facts come in question rather than where deductions or inferences are to be made from the facts. If a deed be given in evidence, a contract proven, or its breach testified to, the existence of such deed, contract, or breach, there being nothing in derogation of the evidence, is no doubt to be ruled as a question of law. In some cases, too, the necessary inference from the proof is so certain that it may be ruled as a question of law. If a sane man voluntarily throws himself in contact with a passing engine, there being nothing to counteract the effect of this action, it may be ruled as a matter of law that the injury to him resulted from his own fault, and that no action can be sustained by him or his representatives. * * * But these are extreme cases. The range between them is almost infinite in variety and extent. It is in relation to these intermediate cases that the opposite rule prevails. Upon the facts proven in such cases, it is a matter of judgment and discretion, of sound inference, what is the deduction to be drawn from the undisputed facts. Certain facts we may suppose to be clearly established from which one sensible, impartial man would infer that proper care had not been used, and that negligence existed; another man equally sensible and equally impartial would infer that proper care had been used, and that there was no negligence. It is this class of cases and those akin to it that the law commits to the decision of a jury. Twelve men of the average of the community, comprising men of education and men of little education, men of learning and men whose learning consists only in what they have themselves seen and heard, the merchant, the mechanic, the farmer, the laborer; these sit together, consult, apply their separate experience of the affairs of life to the facts proven, and draw a unanimous conclusion. This average judgment thus given it is the great effort of the law to obtain. It is assumed that twelve men know more of the common affairs of life than does one man, that they can draw wiser and safer conclusions from admitted facts thus occurring than can a single judge.

In no class of cases can this practical experience be more wisely applied than in that we are considering. We find, accordingly, although not uniform or harmonious, that the authorities justify us in holding in the case before us, that although the facts are undisputed it is for the jury and not for the judge to determine whether proper care was given, or whether they establish negligence.

> * * *

It has been already shown that the facts proved justified the jury in finding that the defendant was guilty of negligence, and we are of the opinion that it was properly left to the jury to determine that point.

Upon the whole case, the judgment must be

AFFIRMED.

COMMENTS AND QUESTIONS CONCERNING
SIOUX CITY & P. R. CO. V. STOUT

1.   What does it mean that Henry Stout "sued, by his next friend"? *See* Federal Rule of Civil Procedure 17(c).

2.   Justice Hunt describes the circumstances in which a jury may be necessary to infuse the sense of the community into a determination involving undisputed facts:

> Certain facts we may suppose to be clearly established from which one sensible, impartial man would infer that proper care had not been used, and that negligence existed; another man equally sensible and equally impartial would infer that proper care had been used, and that there was no negligence. It is this class of

cases and those akin to it that the law commits to the decision of a jury.

Have you seen such jury determination of community standards in other types of cases?

3.   Justice Hunt describes the special role of the jury in determining community standards:

> Twelve men of the average of the community, comprising men of education and men of little education, men of learning and men whose learning consists only in what they have themselves seen and heard, the merchant, the mechanic, the farmer, the laborer; these sit together, consult, apply their separate experience of the affairs of life to the facts proven, and draw a unanimous conclusion. This average judgment thus given it is the great effort of the law to obtain. It is assumed that twelve men know more of the common affairs of life than does one man, that they can draw wiser and safer conclusions from admitted facts thus occurring than can a single judge.

However, is the jury less likely to have "the butcher, the baker, and the candlestick maker" if there are six, rather than twelve, persons on the jury? *See* Justice Marshall's dissent in *Colgrove v. Battin*, 413 U.S. 149, 167 (1973), *supra* pp. 901–902.

4.   Justice Hunt states in his opinion: "That the turntable was a dangerous machine, which would be likely to cause injury to children who resorted to it, might fairly be inferred from the injury which actually occurred to the plaintiff." Does this mean that, whenever a person is injured by a machine, that machine is dangerous?

5.   Justice Hunt stresses that the duty of judges is not to weigh the evidence or decide the case as if they were a juror, but simply to decide if the jury had stayed within its appropriate role:

> The evidence is not strong and the negligence is slight, but we are not able to say that there is not evidence sufficient to justify the verdict. We are not called upon to weigh, to measure, to balance the evidence, or to ascertain how we should have decided if acting as jurors. The charge was in all respects sound and judicious, and there being sufficient evidence to justify the finding, we are not authorized to disturb it.

Is this merely a matter of common law judicial deference?

V. RULE 50(a) AND (b) MOTIONS FOR JUDGMENT AS A MATTER OF LAW

If a case has not yet been submitted to the jury, the failure of a party to meet its burden of production provides a basis for the judge to keep that case from the jury. If the action has been submitted to the jury, failure to meet the burden of production can provide a basis for the judge to enter judgment contrary to the jury's actual verdict. Rule 50 of the Federal Rules of Civil Procedure authorizes the motions by which such arguments are presented to the court.

Figure 13–4 illustrates how the burden of production is raised at trial by the filing of a Rule 50(a) motion for judgment as a matter of law or a Rule 50(b) renewed motion for judgment as a matter of law. Those motions are considered in the subsections of this chapter that follow.

FIGURE 13–4[5]
RAISING THE BURDEN OF PRODUCTION BY
RULE 50(a) AND (b) MOTIONS

Motion	When Motion Raised	Burden Tested	Standard	Who Decides if Burden is Met
Rule 50(a) Motion for Judgment as a Matter of Law (Motion for a Directed Verdict)	After opposing party "has been fully heard on an issue," Rule 50(a)(1), but "before the case is submitted to the jury." Rule 50(a)(2)	Burden of Production	"If the facts and inferences point so strongly and overwhelmingly in favor of one party that the Court believes that reasonable men could not arrive at a contrary verdict, granting of the motions [for directed verdict or JNOV] is proper." *Boeing Co. v. Shipman*, 411 F.2d 365, 374 (5th Cir. 1969) (en banc).	Judge
Rule 50(b) Renewed Motion for Judgment as a Matter of Law (Motion for Judgment Notwithstanding the verdict or JNOV)	"No later than 28 days after the entry of judgment." Rule 50(b)	Burden of Production	Same as Rule 50(a) standard: "JNOV should not be granted unless the evidence is so clear that reasonable men could reach no other conclusion than the one suggested by the moving party." *Persinger v. Norfolk & W. Ry. Co.*, 920 F.2d 1185, 1189 (4th Cir. 1990).	Judge

---

[5]   There is no specific motion for testing a party's failure to satisfy at trial its burden of persuasion. In most civil actions a party must establish by the preponderance of the evidence at trial all of the elements of that party's claim. A party against whom a jury verdict is returned can file a Rule 59 motion for a new trial because the jury verdict was against the weight of the evidence. *See* note 3, *supra*.

A. RULE 50(a) MOTIONS FOR JUDGMENT AS A MATTER OF LAW

The fact that a trial is held does not necessarily mean that the jury will decide that action. "[T]he party bearing the burden of production ha[s] to put forth enough evidence to make a prima facie case in order to get to the jury." *Dir., Office of Workers' Comp. Programs v. Greenwich Collieries*, 512 U.S. 267, 282 (1994) (Souter, J., dissenting).

Rule 50(a)(1) of the Federal Rules of Civil Procedure provides:

> If a party has been fully heard on an issue during a jury trial and the court finds that a reasonable jury would not have a legally sufficient evidentiary basis to find for the party on that issue, the court may:
>
> (A) resolve the issue against the party; and
>
> (B) grant a motion for judgment as a matter of law against the party on a claim or defense that, under the controlling law, can be maintained or defeated only with a favorable finding on that issue.

Assume, for instance, that a plaintiff must establish defendant's negligence, proximate cause, and damages in order to be successful on his tort claim. If the defendant can establish that, after the submission of all plaintiff's evidence on this issue at trial, the plaintiff has not established "a legally sufficient evidentiary basis" to show proximate cause, the defendant should be able to file a successful Rule 50(a) motion for judgment as a matter of law. Rule 50(a)(2) provides that such a motion "may be made at any time before the case is submitted to the jury." Thus the defendant can make a Rule 50(a) motion either at the conclusion of the plaintiff's case-in-chief or at the conclusion of all evidence (after plaintiff's evidence, defendant's evidence and any rebuttal evidence from plaintiff).

The Rule 50(a)(1) statement of the standard for granting such a motion is not particularly helpful, providing that the motion may be granted if "a reasonable jury would not have a legally sufficient evidentiary basis to find for the party on that issue." The en banc United States Court of Appeals for the Fifth Circuit elaborated on this standard in *Boeing v. Shipman*, 411 F.2d 365, 374–75 (5th Cir. 1969):

> If the facts and inferences point so strongly and overwhelmingly in favor of one party that the Court believes that reasonable men could not arrive at a contrary verdict, granting of the [Rule 50(a) or (b)] motions is proper. On the other hand, if there is substantial evidence opposed to the motions, that is, evidence of such quality and weight that reasonable and fair-minded men in the exercise of impartial judgment might reach different conclusions, the motions should be denied, and the case submitted to the jury. A mere

scintilla of evidence is insufficient to present a question for the jury. The motions for directed verdict and judgment n.o.v. should not be decided by which side has the better of the case, nor should they be granted only when there is a complete absence of probative facts to support a jury verdict. There must be a conflict in substantial evidence to create a jury question. However, it is the function of the jury as the traditional finder of the facts, and not the Court, to weigh conflicting evidence and inferences, and determine the credibility of witnesses.

Juries are typically used to resolve factual disputes. If there are no genuine factual disputes, there may be no need for the jury, and the judge may be able to decide the case as a matter of law.

B. RULE 50(b) RENEWED MOTIONS FOR JUDGMENT AS A MATTER OF LAW

Rule 50(a) permits a party defending against a claim to raise the opposing party's failure to satisfy its burden of production before the case is submitted to the jury. If the party loses that motion, however, Rule 50(b) permits that party to renew the motion after the jury has rendered its verdict. Rule 50(b) provides:

> If the court does not grant a motion for judgment as a matter of law made under Rule 50(a), the court is considered to have submitted the action to the jury subject to the court's later deciding the legal questions raised by the motion. No later than 28 days after the entry of judgment—or if the motion addresses a jury issue not decided by a verdict, no later than 28 days after the jury was discharged—the movant may file a renewed motion for judgment as a matter of law and may include an alternative or joint request for a new trial under rule 59.

While the motions are filed at different times, the standard for granting a Rule 50(b) renewed motion for judgment as a matter of law is the same as for granting a Rule 50(a) motion for judgment as a matter of law. As the United States Court of Appeals for the Fourth Circuit concluded in *Persinger v. Norfolk & W. Ry. Co.*, 920 F.2d 1185, 1189 (4th Cir. 1990):

> JNOV should not be granted unless the evidence is so clear that reasonable men could reach no other conclusion than the one suggested by the moving party. This determination must be made while viewing the evidence in the light most favorable to support the jury verdict, yet more than a "mere scintilla" of evidence is necessary to defeat the motion.

Or, as the Fifth Circuit explained in *Springborn v. Am. Commercial Barge Lines, Inc.*, 767 F.2d 89, 94 (5th Cir. 1985), "[A] motion for j.n.o.v. should be granted only when the facts and inferences point so strongly and overwhelmingly in favor of a moving party that reasonable persons could not arrive at a contrary verdict."

While the standard for the burden of production comes from such case law, Rule 50(b) contains two specific requirements that must be met for the filing of such a motion: (1) a renewed Rule 50(b) motion only can be filed if a Rule 50(a) motion for judgment as a matter of law was made before the case was submitted to the jury and (2) the renewed motion must be filed within 28 days after the entry of judgment.

Why would a judge deny a Rule 50(a) motion for judgment as a matter of law, but then grant a Rule 50(b) renewed motion for judgment as a matter of law? Both motions test whether the plaintiff met its burden of production. If the burden of production was not met, why didn't the judge simply grant the Rule 50(a) motion for judgment as a matter of law before submitting the case to the jury?

Sometimes a judge may not be able to carefully focus on a Rule 50(a) motion in the limited time he has before the trial should resume or the case should be submitted to the jury. If a judge must decide quickly, he may err on the side of caution and deny the motion— presuming that he will have another chance to resolve the burden of production issue in the context of a Rule 50(b) motion after trial. After trial, the judge should have more time to consider this question, and, upon further study and reflection, may conclude that the burden of production was not met and that a Rule 50(b) post-trial motion should be granted.

Another reason why a judge may deny or defer ruling on a Rule 50(a) motion is that the judge may presume that the jury will see the case the same way that he does and therefore return a defense verdict because of the weakness of plaintiff's case. If the plaintiff has not made the minimal showing necessary to satisfy the burden of production, it also has not met the higher burden of persuasion standard of a preponderance of the evidence. This may lead the judge to deny a Rule 50(a) motion or defer ruling on it. If the jury concludes that the plaintiff did not meet the burden of persuasion and returns a defense verdict, the judge need not resolve a Rule 50(b) motion. However, in the event that the jury returns a verdict for the plaintiff, the judge can still decide any Rule 50(b) motion that the defendant may file.

C. BURDEN OF PRODUCTION REDUX: *PENNSYLVANIA RAILROAD V. CHAMBERLAIN*

The standard applied under Rule 50(a) and (b) is difficult to quantify with any precision. We don't want judges to resolve a case if a reasonable jury could decide that case more than one way. On the other hand, if a reasonable jury could reach only one conclusion, why submit the case to the jury and invite it to act unreasonably? *Pennsylvania Railroad v. Chamberlain*, decided before *Lavender v. Kurn, supra* p.

986, is another FELA action in which the railroad argued that the plaintiff had not satisfied its burden of production. Consider how the Supreme Court dealt with this argument, and the two additional possible rationales for keeping this case from the jury.

Pennsylvania R.R. v. Chamberlain

Supreme Court of the United States, 1933
288 U.S. 333

OPINION

■ MR. JUSTICE SUTHERLAND delivered the opinion of the Court.

This is an action brought by respondent against petitioner to recover for the death of a brakeman, alleged to have been caused by petitioner's negligence. The complaint alleges that the deceased, at the time of the accident resulting in his death, was assisting in the yard work of breaking up and making up trains and in the classifying and assorting of cars operating in interstate commerce; that in pursuance of such work, while riding a cut of cars, other cars ridden by fellow employees were negligently caused to be brought into violent contact with those upon which deceased was riding, with the result that he was thrown therefrom to the railroad track and run over by a car or cars, inflicting injuries from which he died.

At the conclusion of the evidence, the trial court directed the jury to find a verdict in favor of petitioner. Judgment upon a verdict so found was reversed by the Court of Appeals, Judge Swan dissenting.

That part of the yard in which the accident occurred contained a lead track and a large number of switching tracks branching therefrom. The lead track crossed a "hump," and the work of car distribution consisted of pushing a train of cars by means of a locomotive to the top of the "hump," and then allowing the cars, in separate strings, to descend by gravity, under the control of hand brakes, to their respective destinations in the various branch tracks. Deceased had charge of a string of two gondola cars, which he was piloting to track 14. Immediately ahead of him was a string of seven cars, and behind him a string of nine cars, both also destined for track 14. Soon after the cars ridden by deceased had passed to track 14, his body was found on that track some distance beyond the switch. He had evidently fallen onto the track and been run over by a car or cars.

The case for respondent rests wholly upon the claim that the fall of deceased was caused by a violent collision of the string of nine cars with the string ridden by deceased. Three employees, riding the nine-car string, testified positively that no such collision occurred. They were corroborated by every other employee in a position to see, all testifying that there was no contact between the nine-car string and that of the deceased. The testimony of these witnesses, if believed, establishes beyond doubt that there was no collision between these two strings of cars, and that the nine-car string contributed in no way to the accident. The only witness who testified for the respondent was one Bainbridge; and it is upon his testimony alone that respondent's right to recover is sought to be upheld. His testimony is concisely stated, in its most favorable light for respondent, in the prevailing opinion below by Judge Learned Hand, as follows:

> The plaintiff's only witness to the event, one Bainbridge, then employed by the road, stood close to the yardmaster's office, near the "hump." He professed to have paid little attention to what went on, but he did see the deceased riding at the rear of his cars, whose speed when they passed him he took to be about eight or ten miles. Shortly thereafter a second string passed which was shunted into another track and this was followed by the nine, which, according to the plaintiff's theory, collided with the deceased's. After the nine cars had passed at a somewhat greater speed than the deceased's, Bainbridge paid no more attention to either string for a while, but looked again when the deceased, who was still standing in his place, had passed the switch and onto the assorting track where he was bound. At that time his speed had been checked to about three miles, but the speed of the following nine cars had increased. They were just passing the switch, about four or five cars behind the deceased. Bainbridge looked away again and soon heard what he described as a "loud crash," not however an unusual event in a switching yard. Apparently this did not cause him at once to turn, but he did so shortly thereafter, and saw the two strings together, still moving, and the deceased no longer in sight. Later still his attention was attracted by shouts and he went to the spot and saw the deceased between the rails. Until he left to go to the accident, he had stood fifty feet to the north of the track where the accident happened, and about nine hundred feet from where the body was found.

The court, although regarding Bainbridge's testimony as not only "somewhat suspicious in itself, but its contradiction * * * so manifest as to leave little doubt," held, nevertheless, that the question was one of fact depending upon the credibility of the witnesses, and that it was for the jury to determine, as between the one witness and the many, where the truth lay. The dissenting opinion of Judge Swan proceeds upon the theory that Bainbridge did not testify that in fact a collision had taken place, but inferred it because he heard a crash, and because thereafter the two strings of cars appeared to him to be moving together. It is correctly pointed out in that opinion, however, that the crash might have come from elsewhere in the busy yard and that Bainbridge was in no position to see whether the two strings of cars were actually together; that Bainbridge repeatedly said he was paying no particular attention; and that his position was such, being 900 feet from the place where the body was found and less than 50 feet from the side of the track in question, that he necessarily saw the strings of cars at such an acute angle that it would be physically impossible even for an attentive observer to tell whether the forward end of the nine-car cut was actually in contact with the rear end of the two-car cut. The dissenting opinion further points out that all the witnesses who were in a position to see testified that there was no collision; that respondent's evidence was wholly circumstantial, and the inferences which might otherwise be drawn from it were shown to be utterly erroneous unless all of petitioner's witnesses were willful perjurers. "This is not a case," the opinion proceeds, "where direct testimony to an essential fact is contradicted by direct testimony of other witnesses, though even there it is conceded a directed verdict might be proper in some circumstances. Here, when all the testimony was in, the circumstantial evidence in support of negligence was thought by the trial judge to be so insubstantial and insufficient that it did not justify submission to the jury."

* * *

We, therefore, have a case belonging to that class of cases where proven facts give equal support to each of two inconsistent inferences; in which event, neither of them being established, judgment, as a matter of law, must go against the party upon whom rests the necessity of sustaining one of these inferences as against the other, before he is entitled to recover.

The rule is succinctly stated in *Smith v. First National Bank in Westfield*, 99 Mass. 605, 611–612, quoted in the *Des Moines National Bank Case*, [145 F. 273, 280 (8th Cir. 1906)]:

> There being several inferences deducible from the facts which appear, and equally consistent with all those facts, the plaintiff has not maintained the proposition upon which alone he would be entitled to recover. There is strictly no evidence to warrant a jury in finding that the loss was occasioned by negligence and not by theft. When the evidence tends equally to sustain either of two inconsistent propositions, neither of them can be said to have been established by legitimate proof. A verdict in favor of the party bound to maintain one of those propositions against the other is necessarily wrong.

That Bainbridge concluded from what he himself observed that the crash was due to a collision between the two strings of cars in question is sufficiently indicated by his statements. But this, of course, proves nothing, since it is not allowable for a witness to resolve the doubt as to which of two equally justifiable inferences shall be adopted by drawing a conclusion, which, if accepted, will result in a purely gratuitous award in favor of the party who has failed to sustain the burden of proof cast upon him by the law.

And the desired inference is precluded for the further reason that respondent's right of recovery depends upon the existence of a particular fact which must be inferred from proven facts, and this is not permissible in the face of the positive and otherwise uncontradicted testimony of unimpeached witnesses consistent with the facts actually proved, from which testimony it affirmatively appears that the fact sought to be inferred did not exist. * * * A rebuttable inference of fact, as said by the court in [*Wabash RR. v. De Tar*, 141 F. 932, 935 (8th Cir. 1905)], "must necessarily yield to credible evidence of the actual occurrence." And, as stated by the court in *George v. Mo. Pac. R.R. Co.*, [213 Mo. App. 668, ___ (Mo. Ct. App. 1923)], supra, "It is well settled that, where plaintiff's case is based upon an inference or inferences, the case must fail upon proof of undisputed facts inconsistent with such inferences." * * *

Not only is Bainbridge's testimony considered as a whole suspicious, insubstantial, and insufficient, but his statement that when he turned shortly after hearing the crash the two strings were moving together is simply incredible, if he meant thereby to be understood as saying that he saw the two in contact; and if he meant by the words "moving together" simply that they were moving at the same time in the same direction but not in contact, the statement becomes immaterial. As we have already seen he was paying slight and only occasional attention to what was going on. The cars were eight or nine hundred feet from where he stood and moving almost directly away from him, his angle of vision being only 3° 33′ from a straight line. At that sharp angle and from that distance, near dusk of a misty evening (as the proof shows), the practical impossibility of the witness being able to see whether the front of the nine-car string was in contact with the back of the two-car string is apparent. And, certainly, in the light of these conditions, no verdict based upon a statement so unbelievable reasonably could be sustained as against the positive testimony to the contrary of unimpeached witnesses, all in a position to see, as this witness was not, the precise relation of the cars to one another. The fact that these witnesses were employees of the petitioner, under the circumstances here disclosed, does not impair this conclusion.

We think, therefore, that the trial court was right in withdrawing the case from the jury. It repeatedly has been held by this court that before evidence may be left to the jury, "there is a preliminary question for the judge, not whether there is literally no evidence, but whether there is any upon which a jury can properly proceed to find a verdict for the party producing it, upon whom the onus of proof is imposed." *Pleasants v. Fant*, 22 Wall. 116, 120, 121. And where the evidence is "so overwhelmingly on one side as to leave no room to doubt what the fact is, the court should give a peremptory instruction to the jury." *Gunning v. Cooley*, 281 U.S. 90, 94. * * * The scintilla rule has been definitely and repeatedly rejected so far as the federal courts are concerned.

Leaving out of consideration, then, the inference relied upon, the case for respondent is left without any substantial support in the evidence, and a verdict in her favor would have rested upon mere speculation and conjecture. This, of course, is inadmissible.

The judgment of the Circuit Court of Appeals is reversed and that of the District Court is affirmed.

■ MR. JUSTICE STONE and MR. JUSTICE CARDOZO concur in the result.

COMMENTS AND QUESTIONS CONCERNING *PENNSYLVANIA R.R. CO. V. CHAMBERLAIN*

1.   The trial court in this case directed a verdict against the plaintiff, so the case was never submitted to the jury. Had this action been filed in the federal courts today, under what rule would the defendant railroad have made its motion?

2.   Justice Sutherland sets forth several possible rationales for the Court's conclusion.

    (a)   The facts gave equal support to conflicting inferences. 288 U.S. at 339 ("We, therefore, have a case belonging to that class of cases where proven facts give equal support to each of two inconsistent inferences; in which event, neither of them being established, judgment, as a matter of law, must go against the party upon whom rests the necessity of sustaining one of these inferences as against the other, before he is entitled to recover.").

    (b)   Bainbridge's testimony could be disregarded because it was physically impossible that he could have seen that the two strings of cars were in contact (and thus had collided). 288 U.S. at 342 ("At that sharp angle and from that distance, near dusk of a misty evening (as the proof shows), the practical impossibility of the witness being able to see whether the front of the nine-car string was in contact with the back of the two-car string is apparent.").

    (c)   Even if Bainbridge's testimony could be considered, it did not create a factual dispute for the jury when compared with the overwhelming, unimpeached testimony to the contrary. 288 U.S. at 342–43 ("And, certainly, in the light of these conditions, no verdict based upon a statement so unbelievable reasonably could be sustained as against the positive testimony to the contrary of unimpeached witnesses, all in a position to see, as this witness was not, the precise relation of the cars to one another.").

Which of these rationales provides the best basis for not permitting the jury to decide this case?

3.   If the proven facts gave truly equal support to conflicting inferences (one of which would not support plaintiff's claims), should the

judge have submitted the case to the jury? Does a jury have any means of resolving such equally plausible inferences? In order to avoid bias to either party, what if the jury simply flipped a coin to determine its verdict?

4.   Will it ever be the case that the likelihood of conflicting inferences is truly equal? While this was one of the bases of the Supreme Court's decision in *Chamberlain*, in *Tennant v. Peoria & P.U. Ry. Co.*, 321 U.S. 29, 35 (1944), the Supreme Court stated: "It is not the function of a court to search the record for conflicting circumstantial evidence in order to take the case away from the jury on a theory that the proof gives equal support to inconsistent and uncertain inferences." *See also* 9B C. Wright & A. Miller, *Federal Practice and Procedure* § 2528, at 460 (3rd ed. 2008) ("Although some courts for a time continued to rely on the *Chamberlain* case and announced that equally probable inferences were not sufficient to reach the jury, that no longer is the rule in federal courts. This undoubtedly reflects the fact that the courts recognize that they lack the ability to say whether two or more reasonable inferences are equal.").

Was it really too much of a stretch for the jury to conclude that Bainbridge saw Chamberlain on a cut of cars; saw that the cars behind Chamberlain were moving fast; heard a loud bang; and then saw the two cuts of cars together with Chamberlain not in sight? If Bainbridge was in a position to see all this, is the inference too strained?

5.   In addition to the question as to what showing a party with the burden of production must make, there is a separate question as to what evidence the district court should consider in determining whether the burden of production standard has been met. The Supreme Court has admonished that, "in entertaining a motion for judgment as a matter of law, the court should review all of the evidence in the record." *Reeves v. Sanderson Plumbing Products, Inc.*, 530 U.S. 133, 150 (2000). But the Court in *Reeves* continued:

> In doing so, however, the court must draw all reasonable inferences in favor of the nonmoving party, and it may not make credibility determinations or weigh the evidence. "Credibility determinations, the weighing of the evidence, and the drawing of legitimate inferences from the facts are jury functions, not those of a judge." *Liberty Lobby*, [477 U.S.] at 255. Thus, although the court should review the record as a whole, it must disregard all evidence favorable to the moving party that the jury is not required to believe. See *Wright & Miller* [§ 2529] 299. That is, the court should give credence to the evidence favoring the nonmovant as well as that "evidence supporting the moving party that is uncontradicted and unimpeached, at least to the extent that that evidence comes from disinterested witnesses." *Id.*, at 300.

Reeves v. Sanderson Plumbing Products, Inc., 530 U.S. 133, 150–51 (2000). So, in effect, a party's own evidence may satisfy the burden of production, but uncontradicted, unimpeached evidence from disinterested witnesses can push that showing below what is necessary to satisfy the burden.

6.   What about the disinterested character of the Railroad's evidence in this case? Justice Sutherland states: "The dissenting opinion [in the court of appeals] further points out that all the witnesses who were in a position to see testified that there was no collision; that respondent's evidence was wholly circumstantial, and the inferences which might otherwise be drawn from it were shown to be utterly erroneous unless all of petitioner's witnesses were willful perjurers." Bainbridge's testimony was countered by that of six or seven Pennsylvania Railroad employees. *Chamberlain v. Pennsylvania R.R.*, 59 F.2d 986, 987 (2d Cir. 1932), *rev'd*, 288 U.S. 333 (1933). Is there any reason to believe that these witnesses were "willful perjurers"?

7.   Justice Sutherland mentions that the dissenting judge in the court of appeals (Judge Swan) noted in his opinion that Chamberlains's "evidence was wholly circumstantial." 288 U.S. at 338. However, such evidence is treated the same as direct evidence. Consider, for instance, the following pattern jury instruction:

> Generally speaking, there are two types of evidence. One is direct evidence, such as testimony of an eyewitness. The other is indirect or circumstantial evidence. Circumstantial evidence is evidence that proves a fact from which you can logically conclude another fact exists. As a general rule, the law makes no distinction between direct and circumstantial evidence, but simply requires that you find the facts from a preponderance of all the evidence, both direct and circumstantial.

United States Court of Appeals for the Fifth Circuit, *Fifth Circuit Pattern Jury Instructions—Civil* No. 3.3 (2014). Or, as more colorfully put by Henry David Thoreau, "Some circumstantial evidence is very strong, as when you find a trout in the milk . . ." 2A C. Wright & P. Henning, *Federal Practice and Procedure Criminal* § 411, at 117 (4th ed. 2009) (quoting Thoreau, *The Journal* (from entry for November 11, 1850) (reprinted in *The Heart of Thoreau's Journals* 40 (O. Shepard ed., Dover Pub. 1961)).

8.   Learned Hand, who wrote the majority opinion for the Court of Appeals, has been described as "the most distinguished lower court judge in the history of America's court system." Frank, "The Great Judge," 108 *Harv.L.Rev.* 931, 931 (1995) (reviewing Gerald Gunter, *Learned Hand: The Man and the Judge* (1994)).

9.   Justice Sutherland notes: "The scintilla rule has been definitely and repeatedly rejected so far as the federal courts are concerned." As the Court previously held in *Gunning v. Cooley*, 281 U.S. 90, 94 (1930), "A mere scintilla of evidence is not enough to require the submission of an issue to the jury." *Black's Law Dictionary* (9th ed. 2009) defines "scintilla" to be "a spark or trace."

10.   Plaintiff is driving through town at 1:00 a.m. Her car is forced off the road by a bus, causing an accident. Rather than offering any direct proof that the bus was owned and operated by the defendant bus company, plaintiff merely offers evidence at trial that the defendant had the only

franchise for operating a public bus on the street in question. Has plaintiff satisfied her burden of production?

VI. MOTIONS FOR A NEW TRIAL AND FOR RELIEF FROM JUDGMENT

The motion for judgment as a matter of law is not the only post-trial motion that a losing party can file after trial. Another common post-trial motion is a Rule 59 motion for a new trial. This motion, like the Rule 50(b) renewed motion for judgment as a matter of law, must be filed within 28 days after entry of judgment. Rule 50(b) authorizes the filing of a motion for new trial along with a renewed motion for judgment as a matter of law, and these motions are frequently filed together by the party that lost at trial.

However, in some situations counsel may not know about a potential challenge to a judgment until more than 28 days after the entry of judgment. Newly discovered evidence may have come to the attention of counsel, or it may only later appear that the judgment was infected with fraud or mistake or that the judgment is void for other reasons. In that event, the losing party may be able to seek relief from the final judgment pursuant to Rule 60(b) of the Federal Rules.

Both Rule 59 and Rule 60 motions are considered in this section of this chapter.

A. THE RULE 59 MOTION FOR A NEW TRIAL

Rule 59(a)(1) of the Federal Rules of Civil Procedure provides:

> The court may, on motion, grant a new trial on all or some of the issues—and to any party—as follows:
>
> > (A) after a jury trial, for any reason for which a new trial has heretofore been granted in an action at law in federal court; or
> >
> > (B) after a nonjury trial, for any reason for which a rehearing has heretofore been granted in a suit in equity in federal court.[6]

---

[6] In a nonjury trial, Rule 52(a)(1) requires that "the court must find the facts specially and state its conclusions of law separately." If a master has been appointed by the judge to handle the trial, Rule 52(a)(4) states that the findings of the master, "to the extent adopted by the court, must be considered the court's findings."

Because it is the judge who determines both the law and facts in a nonjury action, the judge can more easily "fix" any problems that might require an entire new trial if the initial trial had been to a jury. Rule 59(a)(2) provides:

> After a nonjury trial, the court may, on motion for a new trial, open the judgment if one has been entered, take additional testimony, amend findings of fact and conclusions of law or make new ones, and direct the entry of a new judgment.

A party to a nonjury trial can both file a motion for a new trial pursuant to Rule 59(a) (if new testimony is sought) or move to alter or amend judgment pursuant to Rule 59(e) (if a different judgment is sought based upon the existing trial record).

Rule 59(b) further provides that a motion for a new trial must be filed "no later than 28 days after entry of judgment." Moreover, Rule 59(d) authorizes the court, within 28 days after the entry of judgment, to, "on its own, * * * order a new trial for any reason that would justify granting one on a party's motion."[7] Rule 59(d) also states: "After giving the parties notice and an opportunity to be heard, the court may grant a timely motion for a new trial for a reason not stated in the motion."

But what are the reasons "for which a new trial has heretofore been granted in an action at law in federal court" that Rule 59(a)(1)(A) provides as a basis for granting a Rule 59 motion for new trial? The Supreme Court has summarized the grounds for the grant of a new trial as follows:

> The motion for a new trial may invoke the discretion of the court in so far as it is bottomed on the claim that the verdict is against the weight of the evidence, that the damages are excessive, or that, for other reasons, the trial was not fair to the party moving; and may raise questions of law arising out of alleged substantial errors in admission or rejection of evidence or instructions to the jury.

Montgomery Ward & Co. v. Duncan, 311 U.S. 243, 251 (1940).[8]

Thus the two major reasons for granting a new trial after a jury verdict are trial error affecting a party's substantial rights and a jury verdict that is against the weight of the evidence. These two bases for new trial are considered in the next subsections of this chapter.

---

[7]   When might there be a basis for a new trial that causes the judge to act, but which was not the basis of a new trial motion? This might occur if, after a jury verdict, the defendant files only a Rule 50(b) renewed motion for judgment as a matter of law. The judge might determine that, although the plaintiff met its burden of production (so that the Rule 50(b) motion must be denied), there is a basis for a new trial. Even though the defendant did not couple its Rule 50(b) motion with a Rule 59 motion for a new trial, Rule 59(d) authorizes the judge to grant a new trial.

[8]   In addition to situations involving trial error or weight of the evidence, a new trial can be ordered if the jury's verdict is mathematically impossible. The court's ability to upset a verdict for such a reason is limited, though. *Compare Young v. Lukens Steel Co.*, 881 F. Supp. 962, 976 (E.D. Pa. 1994) ("Although jury verdicts can be disturbed when they are subject to mathematical calculations and there is a clear error in the calculation, in a case * * * involving disparate mathematical calculations from which the jury may select, it is beyond the discretion of the court to say that the jury might have miscalculated when its final award was within the amount the jury could have properly awarded and there are no apparent miscalculations.") *with Garfield Aniline Works v. Zendle*, 43 F.2d 537, 538 (3d Cir. 1930) ("Under the evidence, the plaintiff was entitled to $8,448.16 with interest, if he was entitled to anything. The verdict of the jury was excessive, and it was a matter of simple mathematical calculation to determine the amount of interest from December 23, 1924, to April 3, 1929. We do not think that the trial judge erred in reducing the verdict.").

So, in an action involving a single claim for enforcement of a $100,000 liquidated damages clause, the jury could not return a verdict for $50,000.

1. TRIAL ERROR AS THE BASIS FOR A NEW TRIAL: *PINGATORE V. MONTGOMERY WARD & CO.*

Jury verdicts often are challenged on appeal because of alleged error in the jury instructions given by the trial judge, the admission or exclusion of specific evidence, other rulings by the judge, or the actions of counsel. All of these bases for appellate reversal were raised in the case that follows.

Pingatore v. Montgomery Ward & Co.

United States Court of Appeals, Sixth Circuit (1969)
419 F. 2d 1138, *cert. denied*, 398 U.S. 928 (1970)

OPINION

■ ROBERT L. TAYLOR, DISTRICT JUDGE.

This is an appeal by Montgomery Ward and Company, Inc. from a judgment rendered on a verdict of the jury in the amount of $126,000.00 for Mrs. Pingatore and $25,000.00 for Mr. Pingatore. Plaintiffs, by amendment, made F. W. Woolworth a party-defendant and Ward sued Woolworth by cross-claim. A Jury returned a verdict in favor of Woolworth in the original action and the Court dismissed the cross-claim. The trial covered a three weeks' period.

* * *

The parties will be referred to in their status in the Court below.

Statement of the Case

On January 3, 1962, Betty Jean Pingatore and her husband, Daniel F. Pingatore, along with their three children, drove to Ward's store at Seven Mile Road and Gratiot, Detroit. Woolworth operated a store in the same shopping center. Mrs. Pingatore went into Ward's store by way of the breezeway in back of the store, leaving the children and Mr. Pingatore in the car. After exchanging some gifts and making purchases, she walked into the breezeway from the store and as she moved aside to let people pass in the aisle of the breezeway, a rat leaped from the roof of the breezeway, got tangled in her skirts and bit her on the knee. She returned to the car and was taken to the hospital by her husband. The accident was reported to policemen at the hospital. After treatment at Saratoga Hospital, she and her husband returned to Ward's store and told a representative of Ward what had happened. Mr. Pingatore showed the representative where the accident occurred.

Health inspectors of the City of Detroit visited the scene of the accident and found that rats had been living under six-inch skids supporting Ward's merchandise. There was no evidence that rats were harbored on the Woolworth property. The rat problem was discovered by Ward in 1960 or 1961 and had existed in the area for about five or six years. Thirty-six or thirty-seven rats had been killed at one time along the breezeway. There were rat tracks or runways of rats under the pallets.

On January 5, 1962, plaintiff's family physician examined her and found a bite mark on her right knee and a scratch below the knee. * * *

At the trial she was unable to move her right arm or right leg. In a handwriting demonstration she grasped the pen in the index finger and thumb of her right hand and was able to write as her left hand grasped the right and provided movement.

Plaintiff alleged development of conversion hysteria, a traumatic neurosis and a right hemiparesis involving both the arm and leg. Medical examination showed and plaintiff was told that no organic illness was responsible for the paralysis. Some of the doctors described her condition as conversion hysteria, a neurosis which simulated the paralysis of her right arm and leg and the dragging of her foot. One psychiatrist for plaintiff testified that she was not suffering from a neurosis but a psychosis. A doctor for defendant stated she was malingering.

There was testimony by a psychiatrist that he treated her when she was eighteen years of age for anxiety problems When this same psychiatrist examined her shortly after the rat bite of January 3, 1962, he found that she was extremely "anxietous" at that time and had a relatively marked functional loss of the right arm and right leg. She was considerably more "anxietous" at that time than before. This psychiatrist examined and treated her between 70 and 80 times from the date of the rat bite until December, 1967.

Assignments of Error

1.   Defendant contends that the District Judge erred in not granting a continuance because plaintiffs failed to give defendant a list of witnesses, their addresses and the subject matter of their testimony in the list that was furnished on December 14, 1967, as required by the pre-trial order.

Defendant argues that the complaint charged that Mrs. Pingatore was suffering with "conversion hysteria," but that her trouble was psychotic, which is what the layman would call insanity; that her insanity originated when she was less than 2 ½ years old; that the opinion of Dr. Breiner was radically different from her claim of conversion hysteria and failure to comply with the pre-trial order prevented Ward from learning of Dr. Breiner's opinion of long-standing insanity.

Plaintiffs argue that defendant was not prejudiced by their not giving the subject matter of Dr. Breiner's testimony since defendant had obtained all the hospital records pertaining to Mrs. Pingatore long before the trial. Dr. Gass, one of defendant's neurologists, had examined her as late as January 6, 1968, and she had submitted to three medical examinations inaugurated by the defendant since the commencement of the litigation. * * *

On December 27, 1967, plaintiffs' counsel offered to submit plaintiff to another examination by a psychiatrist.

The Question of a continuance addressed itself to the sound discretion of the District Judge. Although the accident occurred on January 3, 1962, the case was not brought to trial until January 10, 1968. Defendant had from December 15, 1967, to January 10, 1968, to discover the testimony of Dr. Breiner. We hold that the District Judge did not abuse his discretion in denying the motion for a continuance.

2. The second assignment of error relates to the exclusion of correspondence by Dr. John Webster, a neurologist who examined Mrs. Pingatore after a referral from Dr. Kasabach, an ear specialist. * * * Dr. Webster was incapacitated, and Dr. Kasabach was dead at the time of the trial. In one letter, Dr. Webster gave a medical history of plaintiff and recommended hospitalization for testing. A second letter summarized the results of the testing. Defendant's counsel read selected parts from the hospital records where the testing was conducted. Since these records were the raw data in Dr. Webster's letters, the claimed error was harmless.

3. Ten errors are assigned to the charge which, as supplemented, contains some forty-six pages. We do not deem it necessary to consider each assignment separately. Although some portions were repetitious, we find no prejudicial error in the charge.

* * *

5. Many errors are assigned to the argument of plaintiffs' counsel, some of which appear to have merit. We recognize that the District Judge has wide discretion in ruling on objections to arguments and that ordinarily his discretion will not be disturbed unless abused.

The affidavit of counsel for Ward relates to the conduct of plaintiffs' counsel in his closing argument to the jury, as follows:

"1. When shouting the words "God" and "damit" and several other times he would bend over and slam the flat of his hand on the counsel table with great force and emphasis, which made a loud noise and aroused and excited the jury.

"2. He placed an empty chair in front of the jury with the chair facing the jury and shouted 'where is the corporation today?

"3. While shouting charges he pointed an accusing finger at the empty chair and at the attorney for Wards.

"4. In a dramatic manner he ripped down from the blackboards, crumpled up and threw on the table behind the blackboards four large sheets of paper, each 36'x 28', taped there with scotch tape by Wards' attorney during the closing argument of Wards' attorney, which four large sheets of paper contained a brief chronological medical history, in large hand printed letters, of plaintiff * * * "

Affiant further stated that Juror No. 3 "was crying during the last part of Mr. Weinstein's closing rebuttal argument."

It is obvious that the foregoing argument was extremely intemperate. Curse words have no place in the courtroom. Reference to Ward as a corporation and a large organization and placing a chair facing the jury and shouting "Where is the corporation today?" was calculated to prejudice the minds of the jury against Ward. Tearing sheets of paper used by opposing counsel in argument and crumpling them while dramatically saying "lies" was deplorable. Counsel's duty is to keep his argument within proper bounds.

The Supreme Court has not tolerated such conduct. In the words of Mr. Justice Stone:

> "Such a bitter and passionate attack on petitioner's conduct of the case, under circumstances tending to stir the resentment and arouse the prejudice of the jury, should have been promptly suppressed. The failure of the trial judge to sustain petitioner's objection or otherwise to make certain that the jury would disregard the appeal, could only have left them with the impression that they might properly be influenced by it in rendering their verdict, and thus its prejudicial effect was enhanced. That the quoted remarks of respondents' counsel so plainly tended to excite prejudice as to be ground for reversal, is, we think not open to argument. The judgments must be reversed, with instructions to grant a new trial." *N.Y. Central R.R. Co. v. Johnson*, 279 U.S. 310, 318 (1929).

In the case of *Brown v. Walter*, 62 F.2d 798 (C.A.2, 1933), Judge Learned Hand, in reversing the trial court for permitting improper argument of counsel for plaintiff, said in part:

> " * * * He argued with much warmth that the whole defence had been fabricated by the insurer—transparently veiled by such provocative phrases as an "unseen hand," and an "unseen force," and the like. This had not the slightest support in the evidence; it was unfair to the last degree. Nobody can read the summation without being satisfied that the real issues were being suppressed, and the picture substituted of an alien and malevolent corporation, lurking in the background and contriving a perjurious defense. A judge, at least in a federal court, is more than a moderator; he is affirmatively charged with securing a fair trial, and he must intervene sua sponte to that end, when necessary. It is not always enough that the other side does not protest; often the protest will only serve to emphasize the evil. Justice does not depend upon legal dialectics so much as upon the atmosphere of the courtroom,

and that in the end depends primarily upon the judge." pp. 799, 800.

* * *

There is substantial evidence to support the verdict of the jury on the question of liability, and this phase of the case is affirmed.

Due to the intemperate argument of counsel for plaintiffs, the case is reversed and remanded for a new trial solely on the issue of the amount of damages. *Gasoline Products Co. v. Champlin Refining Co.*, 283 U.S. 494, 499 (1931). Another trial should not consume as much time since the issue of liability is eliminated.

COMMENTS AND QUESTIONS CONCERNING *PINGATORE V. MONTGOMERY WARD & CO.*

1.   Judge Robert Taylor, who wrote the *Pingatore* opinion for the United States Court of Appeals for the Sixth Circuit, was not a member of the Court of Appeals but a United States District Judge. How was he sitting on the panel of judges that decided this case?

2.   In addition to its challenges to the conduct of plaintiff's counsel, Montgomery Ward raised on appeal 10 objections to jury instructions, an objection to the denial of a continuance and to the failure to admit certain evidence (the substance of which was otherwise in the record), and objections to a statement by Ms. Pingatore that she had been bitten by a rat and an indication of the location of the bite. Might the raising of so many issues on appeal detract from the stronger arguments for appellate reversal?

3.   Note the application of the Harmless Error Rule to some of the trial errors asserted by the defendants. This Rule, set forth in Rule 61 of the Federal Rules of Civil Procedure, provides:

> Unless justice requires otherwise, no error in admitting or excluding evidence—or any other error by the court or a party—is ground for granting a new trial, for setting aside a verdict, or for vacating, modifying, or otherwise disturbing a judgment or order. At every stage of the proceeding, the court must disregard all errors and defects that do not affect any party's substantial rights.

There is no such thing as a perfect trial. The courts are only to intervene in the trial process to ensure a fair trial and the protection of the parties' substantial rights.

4.   Would the court of appeals be better able to review the conduct of plaintiffs' counsel if it had a videotape, as well as a transcript, of his closing argument? The court of appeals relied on an affidavit from counsel for Montgomery Ward as to what transpired in the courtroom, but wouldn't a videotape provide the court with a better sense of tone of voice, gestures, closeness to the jury, and the reaction of jurors? Isn't it especially difficult for a court of appeals applying the abuse of discretion standard of review to reverse a trial judge who was in the courtroom when these events occurred?

5.   What were the worst things said or done by plaintiffs' counsel that resulted in the deprivation of a fair trial for Montgomery Ward:

- the use of "curse words;"
- the use of an empty chair with the shout, "Where is the corporation today?;"
- ripping down papers, crumpling, and throwing them; or
- the combination of all of these words and deeds?

6.   Rule 3.5 of the Michigan Rules of Professional Conduct mirrors the ABA's Model Rules of Professional Conduct and provides that a "lawyer shall not: * * * engage in undignified or discourteous conduct toward the tribunal." A comment to this Rule further states:

> The advocate's function is to present evidence and argument so that the cause may be decided according to law. Refraining from undignified or discourteous conduct is a corollary of the advocate's right to speak on behalf of litigants. * * * An advocate can present the cause, protect the record for subsequent review, and preserve professional integrity by patient firmness no less effectively than by belligerence or theatrics.

Has the overreaching by plaintiff's counsel hurt his clients? Some defense counsel, when liability is clear, will stipulate to liability in an effort to preclude the plaintiff from offering evidence that is directly relevant to liability but that might predispose a jury to a greater damages award.

7.   The court of appeals reversed and remanded the district court judgment "for a new trial solely on the issue of the amount of damages." How will this work? In *Gasoline Products Co. v. Champlin Refining Co.*, 283 U.S. 494 (1931), cited by the Court of Appeals, the Supreme Court stated: "Where the practice permits a partial new trial, it may not properly be resorted to unless it clearly appears that the issue to be retried is so distinct and separable from the others that a trial of it alone may be had without injustice." 283 U.S. at 500. In *Gasoline Products*, itself, the Court held that a new trial limited to damages was improper: "Here the question of damages on the counterclaim is so interwoven with that of liability that the former cannot be submitted to the jury independently of the latter without confusion and uncertainty, which would amount to a denial of a fair trial." *Id.* Are the issues of liability and damages distinct and separable in *Pingatore*?

2.   VERDICTS AGAINST THE WEIGHT OF THE EVIDENCE AS THE BASIS FOR A NEW TRIAL: *VANDER ZEE V. KARABATSOS*

Under Rule 59, district judges can review jury verdicts and grant new trials when a verdict is against the weight of the evidence. In the following case, consider not only the district judge's contingent grant of a motion for a new trial but also the appellate review of that district court determination.

Vander Zee v. Karabatsos

United States Court of Appeals, District of Columbia Circuit, 1978
589 F.2d 723, *cert. denied*, 441 U.S. 962 (1979)

OPINION

■ WILLIAM B. JONES, SENIOR DISTRICT JUDGE:

This case involves an alleged oral contract entered into between the plaintiff-appellant Rein J. Vander Zee and the defendant-appellee Kimon T. Karabatsos. In the trial below, the jury returned a verdict in favor of the plaintiff-appellant. The District Court then overturned the jury's determination by issuing a judgment notwithstanding the verdict (n. o. v.) pursuant to Federal Rule of Civil Procedure 50(b). The Court also contingently granted a new trial under Rule 50(c). Vander Zee has appealed from these rulings. For reasons stated herein, we reverse the entry of judgment n. o. v. and remand for a decision on whether to grant a new trial limited to the issue of damages.

I.   INTRODUCTION

The complaint in this action was brought by Rein J. Vander Zee, an attorney licensed to practice in the District of Columbia and Texas. Appellant Vander Zee is attempting to recover funds that allegedly are owed to him by Kimon Karabatsos, the defendant-appellee.

In early 1975, Vander Zee was approached by William H. Savage, President of Savage/Fogarty, a real estate management firm, in connection with certain leasing difficulties that faced the company. * * * On this occasion, Savage requested Vander Zee to assist the company in renegotiating a lease between the General Services Administration (hereinafter the "GSA") and the Savage/Fogarty Company. The lease involved certain office space located at 1800 North Kent Street, Rosslyn, Virginia. The Savage/Fogarty Company had bought the property at a court ordered bankruptcy sale, and the previous owners' lease with the GSA required renegotiation in view of the bankruptcy and forced sale of the building.

Vander Zee declined Savage's request for direct assistance, explaining that extensive commitments in Texas left him with too little time to "keep on top of" the renegotiation sessions. Vander Zee did, however, offer to help find someone capable of advising Savage/Fogarty on the leasing matter.

Savage accepted Vander Zee's offer to refer a person capable of handling the GSA renegotiations. Indeed, according to Vander Zee, Savage suggested that Vander Zee be compensated for the referral service by splitting the fees eventually earned by the as yet undetermined third party. At trial, Savage denied making such a suggestion.

* * *

Vander Zee * * * contacted Karabatsos, and discussed the matter with him. Having concluded that Karabatsos was an acceptable candidate for the job, Vander Zee arranged a meeting between Karabatsos and William J. Fogarty, who appeared on behalf of the Savage/Fogarty Company. The meeting took place at the "116 Club," a private club in which both Vander Zee and Karabatsos were members.

Subsequent to this introduction, Vander Zee invited Karabatsos to his home for a breakfast meeting. It was on this occasion that the parties allegedly entered an oral agreement that entitled Vander Zee to one third of all compensation earned by Karabatsos for work done in renegotiating the GSA lease.

Vander Zee brought suit in the District Court to enforce the oral agreement. A jury returned a verdict in favor of the plaintiff-appellant Vander Zee, awarding him "(o)ne third (1/3) of total monies received by the defendant and future monies to be received during the term of the lease with G.S.A." The District Judge overturned the jury finding by entering a judgment notwithstanding the verdict. He concluded that there was no substantial evidence of an oral agreement for the splitting of fees between Vander Zee and Karabatsos * * *. The District Court also granted the defendant's motion for a new trial on the grounds that the verdict was against the weight of the evidence. It did not reach the defendant's alternative grounds for a new trial, excessive damages.

II. THE JUDGMENT NOTWITHSTANDING THE VERDICT

A motion for judgment notwithstanding the verdict should not be granted unless the evidence, together with all inferences that can reasonably be drawn therefrom is so one-sided that reasonable men could not disagree on the verdict. * * * [T]he standard for awarding a judgment n. o. v. is the same as that applied when ruling on a motion for a directed verdict. And in *Alden v. Providence Hospital*, 127 U.S.App.D.C. 214, 216 (1967), we carefully delineated that standard:

> * * * Unless the evidence, along with all inferences reasonably to be drawn therefrom, when viewed in the light most favorable to the plaintiff is such that reasonable jurors in fair and impartial exercise of their judgment could not reasonably disagree in finding for the defendant, the motion must be denied.

Application of this standard to the facts of the case before us compels this Court to conclude that the District Court improvidently granted a judgment n. o. v. The record supplies ample evidence to support a jury finding that Vander Zee and Karabatsos entered into an enforceable oral contract. Specifically, the jurors heard Vander Zee testify that Karabatsos agreed to a division of fees at their breakfast meeting in consideration for referral of the Savage/Fogarty business. Rita Crossen backed up Vander Zee's account of the breakfast meeting. Mrs. Crossen, who was married to Vander Zee at the time of the transaction, was present at the meeting and testified that Karabatsos explicitly agreed to a split of the fees.

In addition to this direct testimony, the jury could have drawn inferences from other evidence to conclude that an oral contract existed between the parties. For example, the very occurrence of an early-morning breakfast meeting at the home of Vander Zee, on the day after Karabatsos' introduction to Fogarty, might itself imply that an important discussion between Vander Zee and Karabatsos took place at the time. Additionally, Dompierre's testimony concerning discussions with Karabatsos about a fee splitting arrangement with Vander Zee might support an inference that an oral contract existed between the parties.

Thus, the evidence presented before the Court, along with all reasonable inferences drawn from it, was not so one-sided that no reasonable jurors could find that an oral contract existed between Vander Zee and Karabatsos. The jury properly could have concluded, as it did, that words exchanged at the breakfast meeting manifested the requisite mutual assent of Vander Zee and Karabatsos to enter into a binding contract. A judgment n. o. v. therefore was not appropriate. As Judge Goldberg stated in *Powell v. Lititz Mutual Insurance Co.*, 419 F.2d 62, 64 (5th Cir. 1969):

> A judgment notwithstanding the verdict is permissible only when without weighing the credibility of the witnesses there can be but one reasonable conclusion as to the verdict. In other words, where, as here, there is substantial conflicting evidence a judgment notwithstanding the verdict is improper.

III. THE DECISION TO GRANT A NEW TRIAL

Pursuant to Rule 50(c), the District Judge made a conditional decision on the defendant's motion for a new trial. He granted the motion, on the grounds that the jury's verdict was against the weight of the evidence and was void, being a "miscarriage of justice." He did not reach the alternative grounds of excessive damages that the defendants advanced.

As implied by Rule 50(c)'s language, this Court has the duty to review the appropriateness of the trial court's conditional grant of a new trial * * *, and the Supreme Court has interpreted this language as giving the appellate court the power to grant or deny a new trial in appropriate cases. *Neely v. Eby Construction Co.*, 386 U.S. 317, 323 (1967).

Generally speaking, we review the trial court's Rule 50(c) decision on the motion for a new trial for any abuse of discretion. At one time, this standard of review was applied with little force so that the trial court's decision was nearly unassailable. * * * In recent years, however, this Circuit has followed others in developing a more sophisticated review of new trial determinations. The landmark Third Circuit case of

Lind v. Schenley Industries, Inc., 278 F.2d 79, *cert. denied*, 364 U.S. 835 (1960), started the trend by recognizing that the degree of appellate scrutiny of new trial rulings should depend on the reasons given for the awarding of a new trial. The court distinguished between cases in which a new trial is granted because of some legal error, and cases in which the trial judge simply reweighed evidence already submitted to a jury. While grants of new trial motions based on legal error should be routinely affirmed, the *Lind* court found the second context to be more problematic. As it explained:

> (When the trial court grants a new trial on a "weight of evidence" theory,) the judge takes over, if he does not usurp, the prime function of the jury as the trier of the facts. It then becomes the duty of the appellate (court) tribunal to exercise a closer degree of scrutiny and supervision than is the case where a new trial is granted because of some undesirable or pernicious influence obtruding into the trial. Such a close scrutiny is required in order to protect the litigants' right to jury trial. 278 F.2d at 90.

This Circuit has adopted the *Lind* approach to appellate review of new trial orders in *Taylor v. Washington Terminal Co.*, [133 U.S. App. D.C. 110 (1969)]. As in *Lind*, the *Taylor* court emphasized the concern that a judge's nullification of the jury's verdict may encroach on the jury's important fact-finding function. In view of this danger, we noted that closer appellate scrutiny is required when the trial court Grants a new trial then when the court denied the motion and stands by the jury's conclusion. The *Lind* court, of course, went one step further by pointing out that some reasons for granting new trials deserve more deference than others. When the trial court has ordered a new trial because of legal error, the appellate court should be more inclined to affirm the grant than when the trial court simply weighs the evidence differently than the jury and orders a new trial because the verdict is "against the weight of the evidence."

Applying this standard to the case before the court, we find that we must overturn the trial court's grant for a new trial insofar as it is based on the grounds that the jury's verdict is against the weight of the evidence. As discussed above in the context of the judgment n. o. v., there was testimony to support the jurors' decision that an oral contract existed between Vander Zee and Karabatsos. The trial court's contrary view of the credibility of the witnesses does not justify the granting of a new trial.

The District Court also granted a new trial in order to prevent "a miscarriage of justice." We conclude that this also is an inadequate rationale for a new trial in view of our determination that the alleged contract between Vander Zee and Karabatsos would be valid and enforceable. More troubling, however, is the fact that the District Court specifically did not reach the question whether a new trial should be granted on the issue of damages. Although we have registered our reluctance to perfunctorily affirm grants of new trials based on excessive damages, we recognize that the District Court should have an opportunity to consider this ground for a new trial.

Thus, we must remand this case so that the District Court can make its determination whether a new trial on the damages issue is appropriate.

COMMENTS AND QUESTIONS CONCERNING *VANDER ZEE V. KARABATSOS*

1.   Judge Jones states, "At one time, this standard of review [governing appellate review of district court ruling on new trial motions] was applied with little force so that the trial court's decision was nearly unassailable." Doesn't such appellate deference to the district judge make sense? The judge heard the witnesses testify, while the court of appeals can only review a trial transcript of the district court proceedings. When the district judge grants a new trial, rather than enters judgment against the party that prevailed at trial, why should the court of appeals review that new trial order?

2.   If the district judge grants a Rule 50(b) renewed motion for judgment as a matter of law, why should the judge also rule on a Rule 59 motion for a new trial? Rule 50(c)(1) requires:

> If the court grants a renewed motion for judgment as a matter of law, it must also conditionally rule on any motion for a new trial by determining whether a new trial should be granted if the judgment is later vacated or reversed. The court must state the grounds for conditionally granting or denying the motion for a new trial.

What is the rationale for this requirement?

3.   The effect of a conditional ruling on a motion for new trial is set forth in Rule 50(c)(2):

> Conditionally granting the motion for a new trial does not affect the judgment's finality; if the judgment is reversed, the new trial must proceed unless the appellate court orders otherwise. If the motion for a new trial is conditionally denied, the appellee may assert error in that denial; if the judgment is reversed, the case must proceed as the appellate court orders.

The district judge has heard the trial, and Rule 50(c)(2) provides that, after a grant of a Rule 50(b) motion and conditional grant of a Rule 59 motion for new trial, "the new trial must proceed unless the appellate court orders otherwise" if the court of appeals reverses the Rule 50(b) judgment.

4.   Why should a court of appeals apply a different standard of review depending on the reason given by the district court for granting a new trial?

5.   Judge Jones states that "we have registered our reluctance to perfunctorily affirm grants of new trials based on excessive damages." Why does the court remand the case to the district judge to determine whether a new trial should be granted due to excessive damages?

6.   Rule 50(c) deals with situations in which the district judge grants the renewed motion for judgment as a matter of law. Rule 50(e) deals with the situation in which the district judge denies the Rule 50(b) renewed motion for judgment as a matter of law. In the appeal of such a judgment, why does Rule 50(e) provide that "the prevailing party [in the district court] may, as appellee, assert grounds entitling it to a new trial should the appellate court conclude that the trial court erred in denying the motion"? Note that, if the court of appeals reverses the district court denial of a Rule 50 motion for judgment as a matter of law, Rule 50(e) provides that the court of appeals "may order a new trial, direct the trial court to determine whether a new trial should be granted, or direct the entry of judgment."

B. Remittitur and Additur

In *Gasoline Products Co. v. Champlin Refining Co.*, 283 U.S. 494 (1931), the Supreme Court upheld the ability of the district court to order a partial new trial when "the issue to be retried is so distinct and separable from the others that a trial of it alone may be had without injustice." 283 U.S. at 500. Another way in which a trial judge may attempt to obviate the need for the new trial of an entire action is by conditioning the grant or denial of a new trial upon a party's willingness to accept an amount of damages different from the amount of the jury verdict.

Believing that the size of a jury award cannot be sustained based on the evidence at trial, a judge may agree to grant a new trial unless the plaintiff agrees to accept a lesser amount of damages. This is **remittitur**, under which a new trial is granted unless the plaintiff agrees to remit a specified portion of the jury verdict and accept a lesser amount in damages.

What if the judge believes that the record does not support a verdict as small as the verdict rendered by the jury? In this situation, the judge can order a new trial unless the defendant agrees to an amount of additional damages beyond the amount awarded by the jury. This is **additur**. With respect to both remittur and additur, the question arises as to whether the Seventh Amendment precludes the district judge from, in effect, offering to modify the jury verdict in such fashion.

1. Remittitur

The Reexamination Clause of the Seventh Amendment provides that "no fact tried by a jury, shall be otherwise reexamined in any Court of the United States, than according to the rules of the common law." Despite the potential issues presented by the Reexamination Clause, remittitur has long been recognized in the federal courts. "[F]irst announced by Mr. Justice Story in 1822, the doctrine has been accepted as the law for more than a hundred years and uniformly applied in the federal courts during that time. And, as it finds some support in the practice of the English courts prior to the adoption of the Constitution, we may assume that in a case involving a remittitur * * * the doctrine would not be reconsidered or disturbed at this late day." *Dimick v. Schiedt*, 293 U.S. 474, 484–85 (1935). *See also Blunt v. Little*, 3 F. Cas. 760, 761–62 (C.C.D. Mass. 1822) (Story, J.) ("[I]f it should clearly appear that the jury have committed a gross error, or have acted from improper motives, or have given damages excessive in relation to the person or the injury, it is as much the duty of the court to interfere, to prevent the wrong, as in any other case. * * * After full reflection, I am of opinion, that it is reasonable, that the cause should be submitted to another jury, unless the plaintiff is willing to remit $500 of his damages.").

A partial new trial is only possible if "the issue to be retried is so distinct and separable from the others that a trial of it alone may be had without injustice." *Gasoline Products Co. v. Champlin Refining Co.*, 283 U.S. 494, 500 (1931). Similarly, the Supreme Court has precluded the application of remittitur in situations in which passion and prejudice may have affected both the amount of damages and the jury's determination of liability. The Supreme Court has held:

> [N]o verdict can be permitted to stand which is found to be in any degree the result of appeals to passion and prejudice. Obviously such means may be quite as effective to beget a wholly wrong verdict as to produce an excessive one. A litigant gaining a verdict thereby will not be permitted the benefit of calculation, which can be little better than speculation, as to the extent of the wrong inflicted upon his opponent.

Minneapolis, St. P. & S. S. M. Ry. Co. v. Moquin, 283 U.S. 520, 521–22 (1931).

In cases in which remittitur is appropriate, the court must determine the amount that should be remitted by the plaintiff in order to avoid a new trial. The United States Court of Appeals for the Second Circuit compared the different remittitur standards as follows:

> There are at least three possible rules that district courts have adopted for computing a remittitur. *See generally* 6A *Moore's Federal Practice* ¶ 59.08[7], at 59–192 to–196 (2d ed.1989). The standard that is most intrusive upon jury awards would "reduce the verdict to the lowest amount that could reasonably be found by the jury." 6A *Moore's Federal Practice, supra*, at 59–193. Under this standard, a plaintiff would typically do better by opting for a second trial than he would by accepting the district court's remitted judgment. Thus, this standard not only gives the least weight to the jury's

apparent intent to award a generous verdict, but it also encourages plaintiffs to reject the remittitur and opt for a costly second trial. Perhaps not surprisingly, only one published opinion favoring the adoption of the most intrusive standard could be found. *See Meissner v. Papas*, 35 F.Supp. 676 (E.D.Wis.1940).

Some courts have employed the least intrusive standard, holding that the remitted amount should reduce the verdict only to the maximum that would be upheld by the trial court as not excessive. * * * The benefits of this standard are significant. Compared to the alternatives, it is the most faithful to the jury's verdict. Moreover, the plaintiff is unlikely under this standard to opt for a second trial. * * * For these reasons, the least intrusive standard, which Judge Weinstein employed, seems clearly superior to the most intrusive standard.

Earl v. Bouchard Transp. Co., Inc., 917 F.2d 1320, 1328–29 (2d Cir. 1990).[9]

While the plaintiff has the choice to accept a remitted judgment, if plaintiff does so she cannot later challenge that judgment on appeal. As the Supreme Court held in *Donovan v. Penn Shipping Co., Inc.*, 429 U.S. 648, 649 (1977), "[A] plaintiff cannot 'protest' a remittitur he has accepted in an attempt to open it to challenge on appeal." This rule applies in the federal courts, whether the action is based upon state or federal law. *Id.*, at 649–50.

2. ADDITUR

While remittitur is well established in the federal courts, the Supreme Court has found additur to be unconstitutional. The Court has differentiated additur from remittitur as follows:

The controlling distinction between the power of the court and that of the jury is that the former is the power to determine the law and the latter to determine the facts. * * * Where the verdict is excessive, the practice of substituting a remission of the excess for a new trial is not without plausible support in the view that what remains is included in the verdict along with the unlawful excess—in that sense that it has been found by the jury—and that the remittitur has the

---

[9]   The *Earl* court rejected the third (intermediate) standard for determining the amount to be remitted. "The intermediate standard reduces the excessive jury award to what the trial court believes a 'properly functioning jury, acting free of suggestions by counsel, would have awarded. . . .' *Uris v. Gurney's Inn Corp.*, 405 F.Supp. 744, 747 (E.D.N.Y.1975) (citing 6A *Moore's Federal Practice, supra*, at 59–196)." *Earl v. Bouchard Transp. Co., Inc.*, 917 F.2d 1320, 1329 (2d Cir. 1990). Rejecting this intermediate standard, the Second Circuit concluded that basing remittitur on the maximum amount that would have been upheld by the district court as not excessive was preferable because it was least intrusive on the jury verdict and least likely to lead to appeal. *Id.* at 1330.

effect of merely lopping off an excrescence. But, where the verdict is too small, an increase by the court is a bald addition of something which in no sense can be said to be included in the verdict. When, therefore, the trial court here found that the damages awarded by the jury were so inadequate as to entitle plaintiff to a new trial, how can it be held, with any semblance of reason, that that court, with the consent of the defendant only, may, by assessing an additional amount of damages, bring the constitutional right of the plaintiff to a jury trial to an end in respect of a matter of fact which no jury has ever passed upon either explicitly or by implication? To so hold is obviously to compel the plaintiff to forego his constitutional right to the verdict of a jury and accept "an assessment partly made by a jury which has acted improperly, and partly by a tribunal which has no power to assess."

Dimick v. Schiedt, 293 U.S. 474, 486 (1935).

Despite the unconstitutionality of additur within the federal courts, federal district courts have been held to have the power to increase a jury's award in situations in which damages can be determined as a matter of law. *E.g.*, *Liriano v. Hobart Corp.*, 170 F.3d 264, 272–73 (2d Cir. 1999) ("Under the rule of *Dimick v. Schiedt*, federal courts are denied the same freedom to use additur that is enjoyed by many state court judges. In this case, however, there was no true additur. The district court * * * simply adjusted the jury award to account for a discrete item that manifestly should have been part of the damage calculations and as to whose amount there was no dispute."); *E.E.O.C. v. Massey Yardley Chrysler Plymouth, Inc.*, 117 F.3d 1244, 1252 (11th Cir. 1997) ("Courts recognize an exception to *Dimick* where the jury has found the underlying liability and there is no genuine issue as to the correct amount of damages.").

C. COMBINED POST-TRIAL MOTIONS AND THEIR APPEAL

As you've seen from some of the prior cases in this chapter, both renewed motions for judgment as a matter of law and motions for new trial are often filed by the losing party after trial. Rule 50(b) explicitly provides:

No later than 28 days after the entry of judgment—or, if the motion addresses a jury issue not decided by a verdict, no later than 28 days after the jury was discharged—the movant may file a renewed motion for judgment as a matter of law and may include an alternative or joint request for a new trial under Rule 59.

Rule 50(c) and (e) contain specific directives concerning the manner in which the district court and parties are to consider such Rule 50 and 59 motions. Initially, Rule 50(c)(1) provides:

If the court grants a renewed motion for judgment as a matter of law, it must also conditionally rule on any motion for a new trial by determining whether a new trial should be granted if the judgment is later vacated or reversed. The court must state the grounds for conditionally granting or denying the motion for a new trial.

Why is the district judge required to rule upon a Rule 59 motion for new trial, if she grants a renewed motion for judgment as a matter of law? The judgment as a matter of law ends the litigation in the district court and is a final judgment from which appeal can be taken. However, a conditional ruling on the new trial motion can be helpful in providing the contemporaneous ruling of the district judge in the event that the Rule 50 judgment as a matter of law is reversed on appeal.

But how could a judge grant a renewed motion for judgment as a matter of law, yet not conditionally grant a motion for a new trial? If the only question in the case were the weight of the evidence, it would seem that the grant of a renewed motion for judgment as a matter of law would logically require the conditional grant of a new trial as well. But the weight of the evidence might not be the only issue raised by these post-trial motions.

Assume, for instance, an action in which the jury returns a verdict for the plaintiff and the defendant files both a Rule 50(b) renewed motion for judgment as a matter of law and a Rule 59 motion for a new trial. Assume, further, that the judge grants the renewed motion for judgment as a matter of law because she believes that it was error to permit an expert witness to testify and that, once the expert's testimony is excluded, the plaintiff cannot satisfy his burden of production. In considering the motion for a new trial, though, the judge may reason that, if the grant of the renewed motion for judgment as a matter of law is not affirmed on appeal, this will be because the testimony of the expert should have been admitted. In that case, there would be sufficient evidence to support the plaintiff's verdict, so the judge should conditionally deny the motion for a new trial.

What is the effect of a conditional new trial ruling if the district judge grants a renewed motion for judgment as a matter of law? Rule 50(c)(2) specifically addresses this issue:

> Conditionally granting the motion for a new trial does not affect the judgment's finality; if the judgment is reversed, the new trial must proceed unless the appellate court orders otherwise. If the motion for a new trial is conditionally denied, the appellee may assert error in that denial; if the judgment is reversed, the case must proceed as the appellate court orders.

Thus the conditional ruling on the Rule 59 new trial motion has no impact on the judgment if the Rule 50(b) renewed motion for judgment as a matter of law is granted. Only if the court of appeals reverses the district court's grant of judgment does the conditional grant of a new trial ruling become effective—resulting in a new trial in most cases. If the district judge conditionally denied the new trial motion and the grant of judgment as a matter of law is reversed, the party that lost this motion in the district court can argue that the denial of a new trial was reversible error. In addition, Rule 50(e) provides that a party who successfully brings a Rule 50(b) renewed motion for judgment as a matter of law in the district court may, in the court of appeals, argue that it is entitled to a new trial in the event that the court of appeals determines that judgment was improperly entered in the district court.

Figure 13–5 shows the impact of district court rulings on Rule 50(b) and Rule 59 motions on the appealability of the district court's rulings. As this chart indicates, the grant of a Rule 50(b) motion results in a final, appealable judgment, as does the denial of both the Rule 50(b) and Rule 59 motions. But if the Rule 50(b) motion is denied and the Rule 59 motion is granted, there must be a new trial in the district court. Because such additional proceedings are still required in the district court, there is not yet a final judgment that can be appealed under 28 U.S.C. § 1291.

FIGURE 13–5
FINAL JUDGMENT AFTER RULINGS ON
POST-TRIAL MOTIONS

Rule 50(b) Renewed Motion for Judgment as a Matter of Law	Granted	Granted	Denied	Denied
Rule 59 Motion for New Trial	Granted	Denied	Denied	Granted
Final (Appealable) Judgment?	Yes	Yes	Yes	No

Finally, do not confuse the standard for the grant of a Rule 50(b) renewed motion for judgment as a matter of law with the standard for a Rule 59 motion for new trial. Both motions must be filed within 28 days after judgment. Federal Rules of Civil Procedure 50(b); 50(d); 59(b). But, as the United States Court of Appeals for the Second Circuit concluded in *DLC Mgmt. Corp. v. Town of Hyde Park*, 163 F.3d 124 (2d Cir. 1998), the standards for these two motions are quite different when the argument is made that the evidence at trial does not support the jury's verdict. The Court of Appeals explained, 163 F.3d at 133–34:

> The standards governing a district court's consideration of a Rule 59 motion for a new trial on the grounds that the verdict was against the weight of the evidence differs in two significant ways from the standards governing a Rule 50 motion for judgment as a matter of law. Unlike judgment as a matter of law, a new trial may be granted even if there is substantial evidence supporting the jury's verdict. Moreover, a trial judge is free to weigh the evidence himself, and need not view it in the light most favorable to the verdict winner. A court considering a Rule 59 motion for a new trial must bear in

mind, however, that the court should only grant such a motion when the jury's verdict is "egregious." Accordingly, a court should rarely disturb a jury's evaluation of a witness's credibility.

Parties seeking to overturn a jury verdict therefore should (1) file both a Rule 50(b) renewed motion for judgment as a matter of law and a Rule 59 motion for new trial within 28 days after the entry of judgment on that verdict and (2) be sure to assert the correct, but different, standards as the basis for relief under these two motions.

D. RULE 60(b) MOTION FOR RELIEF FROM JUDGMENT

While Rules 50(b) and 59 provide a basis for challenging a jury verdict within 28 days after judgment has been entered on that verdict, sometimes the basis for challenging a judgment is not that quickly apparent. Rule 60 of the Federal Rules of Civil Procedure provides another basis for seeking relief from judgment in such cases.

Rule 60(b) provides:

On motion and just terms, the court may relieve a party or its legal representative from a final judgment, order, or proceeding for the following reasons:

(1) mistake, inadvertence, surprise, or excusable neglect;

(2) newly discovered evidence that, with reasonable diligence, could not have been discovered in time to move for a new trial under Rule 59(b);

(3) fraud (whether previously called intrinsic or extrinsic), misrepresentation, or misconduct by an opposing party;

(4) the judgment is void;

(5) the judgment has been satisfied, released or discharged; it is based on an earlier judgment that has been reversed or vacated; or applying it prospectively is no longer equitable; or

(6) any other reason that justifies relief.

Some of these grounds for relief from judgment seem more significant than others. Rule 60(b)(1) permits a party to seek relief from judgment due to "mistake, inadvertence, surprise, or excusable neglect." While it seems reasonable to permit relief from judgment for such reasons, are these reasons as significant as the fact that the judgment is void (Rule 60(b)(4)) or that the judgment is based on an earlier judgment that now has been reversed (Rule 60(b)(5))? Rule 60(c)(1) specifies different time periods for seeking relief from judgment based upon the seriousness of the asserted deficiency in the judgment. While Rule 60(c)(1) provides that any Rule 60(b) claim must be filed "within a reasonable time," that section also provides that Rule 60(b) claims based upon the first three bases of claims for relief from judgment must be filed "no more than a year after the entry of the judgment or order or the date of the proceeding." For motions brought under Rule 60(b)(4), (5), and (6), though, the reasonable time for filing the motion can extend beyond one year.

Test yourself concerning the different possible bases for a Rule 60(b) motion by deciding in which of the following cases the judge should relieve a party from final judgment.

(1) Four days before leaving for a family emergency in Nigeria, plaintiff's lawyer had his legal assistant call defense counsel to seek an extension of time to respond to a motion for summary judgment that defense counsel had said he would file. Defense counsel refused to agree to the extension of time, filed the motion for summary judgment the next day, and then asked the court to grant the motion as unopposed. The court granted the motion for summary judgment, and 12 days later, plaintiff's counsel (who had returned from Nigeria) wrote a letter to the court asking that it "rescind" its order. This request was denied, because the plaintiff had not filed a motion for relief from final judgment under Rule 60(b). Plaintiff's counsel then filed a Rule 60(b) motion. Should it be granted pursuant to Rule 60(b)(1)? *See Bateman v. U.S. Postal Serv.*, 231 F.3d 1220 (9th Cir. 2000).

(2) In May defendant filed a motion for summary judgment in a securities fraud action, which motion was opposed by plaintiffs in July. In September and October, defendant belatedly provided plaintiffs with several thousand documents requested in discovery, and plaintiffs rushed to complete a series of depositions before the discovery cutoff. On October 31, defendant filed a second motion for summary judgment on additional claims. The court granted both of defendant's motions for summary judgment on November 14. On November 28, plaintiffs sought relief from judgment under Rule 60(b)(2), attaching to their motion several documents that had been provided to them in September and October. Should the motion be granted pursuant to Rule 60(b)(2)? *See Alpern v. UtiliCorp United, Inc.*, 84 F.3d 1525 (8th Cir. 1996).

(3) At her personal injury trial, plaintiff sought and received damages based on her assertion that she was totally disabled during a specific time period. In another, unrelated criminal case, though, plaintiff testified that she had worked during this time period. Should the court grant the motion for relief from judgment pursuant to Rule 60(b)(3)? *See DiPirro v. United States*, 189 F.R.D. 60 (W.D. N.Y. 1999).

(4) Default judgment was entered against the defendant corporation. A damages award and injunction were entered

based upon that judgment. Several months later, the corporation moved to vacate the judgement as void, asserting that it had no notice of the action and had not been properly served. Should the court grant the motion for relief from judgment pursuant to Rule 60(b)(4)? *See Nature's First Inc. v. Nature's First Law, Inc.*, 436 F. Supp. 2d 368 (D. Conn. 2006).

(5) A man was convicted of third-degree rape, which judgment was affirmed on appeal. Thereafter, the woman who had been found to have been raped filed a civil action for damages. The trial court directed a verdict against the man based upon the rape conviction, and the jury awarded the woman $140,000 in damages. In a later ruling on the criminal conviction, a federal district court overturned the conviction because of the failure of the prosecution to turn over exculpatory evidence. The man then filed a motion for relief from the civil judgment under the state counterpart of Federal Rule of Civil Procedure 60(b)(5). Should the court grant the motion? *See Fahlen v. Mounsey*, 46 Wash. App. 45 (1986).

(6) A naturalized American citizen, who was ill and not able to work, was served in 1942 with a complaint to cancel his certification of naturalization, alleging that he was loyal to Germany rather than the United States. Before the expiration of the time to respond to the complaint, the man was arrested and imprisoned on charges of conspiracy to violate the Selective Service Act. At the time of his arrest, the FBI found a letter written by the man to the ACLU asking for representation in the denaturalization proceeding (which letter was never mailed). Ten days later the federal court entered a default judgment against the man, revoking his American citizenship. The man was convicted of the federal criminal charges and then charged with sedition. Although the initial criminal charges were reversed on appeal and the sedition indictment was dismissed, the man served six and one-half years on these charges. Should the man's Rule 60(b)(6) motion for relief from the denaturalization judgment, filed four and one-half years after its entry, be granted?' *See Klapprott v. United States*, 335 U.S. 601 (1949). What if the motion were based on Rule 60(b)(1) and asserted "excusable neglect"?

VII. CONCLUSION

After an often lengthy pretrial process, civil actions reach trial. These trials may be before a jury, and the Seventh Amendment to the Constitution preserves the right to jury trial in federal court for "suits at common law, where the value in controversy shall exceed twenty dollars."

While the Seventh Amendment preserves juries in many actions in the federal courts, the federal judicial system is designed to limit and channel jury action. Judges determine what evidence the jury will hear, instruct the jury on governing law, comment on trial evidence, and may require the jury to return a Rule 49 special verdict or general verdict with answers to written questions.

If a party does not meet its burden of production, the judge can grant judgment as a matter of law (before the case is even submitted to the jury) or a renewed motion for judgment as a matter of law (after a jury verdict). If a verdict is against the weight of the evidence or there is trial error, the judge can grant a new trial, limited new trial, or remittitur after the jury renders its verdict. Even after final judgment, the court may grant relief from judgment pursuant to Rule 60(b) of the Federal Rules of Civil Procedure.

The jury plays an important part in our system of civil justice. But the jury is only one part of that system, and juries must operate within the framework of that larger judicial system.

VIII. Chapter Assessment

A. Multiple-Choice Questions. Answer the following questions, reviewing the sections of the chapter noted in connection with each question.

1. The passenger in a car sued the car's driver in a federal diversity action, seeking damages stemming from an accident. The driver asserted contributory negligence in her answer. After the conclusion of the evidence at trial, counsel for the passenger submitted to the judge a set of requested jury instructions. The judge rejected these proposed instructions, stating that the judge's "usual instructions packet" would be given. Neither attorney objected to these instructions.

Included in the instructions given by the judge was an instruction providing that the jury should return a verdict for the driver if the passenger was responsible for any contributory negligence. Unbeknown to the judge or the parties, one month before trial the governing law had changed from contributory to comparative negligence (under which negligence by the plaintiff would not necessarily bar plaintiff's recovery).

After the judge instructed the jury, the jury returned a verdict for the driver. Judgment was then entered on the verdict, and the passenger filed a motion for a new trial 25 days later.

Review Section III(B) and VI(A) and choose the best answer from the following choices:

(a) Because the judge must give jury instructions timely requested by the parties, the judge should grant the motion for a new trial.

(b) Because the instruction given by the judge was plain error, the judge should grant the motion for a new trial.

(c) Because the passenger waived any objection to the contributory negligence instruction by not objecting, the judge should deny the motion for a new trial.

(d) Because the motion was untimely, the judge should deny the motion for a new trial.

2.   An attorney files a federal diversity action against a song writer, asserting that he owes her $80,000 for legal services that she provided him. At trial, the attorney is the only person who testifies on her behalf, and her testimony is simply that "sometime last year" the song writer asked her to do legal research concerning the possibility of copyrighting a song. The attorney offers no documents supporting this claim (such as a contract, a legal file, invoices for the legal work, or a letter or memorandum summarizing her alleged legal research). The song writer testifies at trial that he never asked the attorney to do any legal work for him.

At the end of all testimony, the song writer files a Rule 50(a) motion for judgment as a matter of law, which is denied. The jury then returns a verdict for the attorney for $80,000. Fifteen days later, the song writer files both a motion for a new trial pursuant to Rule 59 and a renewed motion for judgment as a matter of law pursuant to Rule 50(b).

Review Sections V(B) and VI(A) and choose the best answer from the following choices:

(a) While the song writer could file either a motion for a new trial or a renewed motion for judgment as a matter of law, he cannot file both motions.

(b) While the song writer can file both a motion for a new trial and a renewed motion for judgment as a matter of law, the motions he filed in this case are untimely.

(c) If the judge grants the renewed motion for judgment as a matter of law she also should rule on the motion for a new trial.

(d) Whether or not the song writer filed a motion for judgment as a matter of law pursuant to Rule 50(a) before the case was submitted to the jury, the song writer can file a Rule 50(b) renewed motion for judgment as a matter of law.

3.   A pedestrian is hit by a car while walking across the street. She files a diversity action in the United States District Court for the District of Maine against the driver of the car. At trial the pedestrian testifies that she was in the crosswalk and was crossing on the "walk" light. The driver and the three other witnesses to the accident testify that the pedestrian was outside the crosswalk and was crossing the street when the crossing light indicated "Don't Walk."

Neither party makes any motions during or immediately after the trial, and the jury returns a verdict for the pedestrian. The driver then files a motion for judgment as a matter of law pursuant to Rule 50 of the Federal Rules of Civil Procedure.

Review Section V and choose the best answer from the following choices:

(a) Even though the driver did not make a motion for judgment as a matter of law before the case was submitted to the jury, he can make a renewed motion for judgment as a matter of law after the jury has rendered its verdict.

(b) If, after all the evidence has been presented, the pedestrian has satisfied his burden of production, the judge can grant a defense motion for judgment as a matter of law or a renewed motion for judgment as a matter of law if the judge believes that the verdict is against the weight of the evidence.

(c) Even though all the witnesses but the pedestrian testified that the driver was not negligent, this factual dispute means that the case was properly submitted to the jury.

(d) All of the above.

4. A consumer was seriously injured while using his power lawn mower and filed a products liability diversity action against the manufacture in federal court. At the final pretrial conference, the judge told counsel they could each call only two expert witnesses to testify concerning the plaintiff's allegation that the lawn mower had malfunctioned. When defense counsel objected, the judge asked her, "Is there anything that a third expert could testify to that could not be covered by the testimony of two other experts?" Defense counsel replied, "No, your honor, but we would like the jury to hear expert testimony from more than just two witnesses." The judge then reaffirmed his decision to only permit two experts per side on the issue of the mower's alleged malfunction.

The plaintiff's evidence at trial included the testimony of the plaintiff, two expert witnesses (who testified that the mower malfunctioned), and two doctors (who testified that the plaintiff's injuries would require continued treatment over the rest of his life). The manufacturer's evidence included testimony from seven employee-engineers who testified as to the manufacturing process, two experts who testified that the mower did not malfunction, and five doctors.

The jury returned a verdict for $500,000 for the consumer, judgment was entered on the verdict, and, twenty days later, the manufacturer filed a motion for a new trial.

Should the judge grant the motion for a new trial?

Review Section VI(A) and choose the best answer from the following choices:

(a) No, because any error in limiting the number of expert witnesses was harmless error.

(b) No, because the motion for a new trial was not timely filed.

(c) Yes, because the trial judge abused his discretion in not admitting the expert testimony.

(d) Yes, because the verdict was against the weight of the evidence.

5. A man files a federal diversity action against a company in the United States District Court for the District of Connecticut. After all the evidence has been presented, the company makes a Rule 50(a) motion for judgment as a matter of law. The court denies this motion. The case is then submitted to the jury, which returns a verdict of $150,000 for the man.

The company files both a Rule 50(b) renewed motion for judgment as a matter of law and a Rule 59 motion for a new trial.

Review Section VI(C) and choose the best answer from the following choices:

(a) If the court grants the renewed motion for judgment as a matter of law and denies the motion for a new trial, the resulting judgment will be a final judgment from which the man can appeal.

(b) If the court grants the renewed motion for judgment as a matter of law and conditionally grants the motion for a new trial, neither party can appeal until after a second trial has been held.

(c) If the court denies both the motion for judgment as a matter of law and the motion for a new trial, the resulting judgment will be a final judgment from which the company can appeal.

(d) Both answers (a) and (c).

B. Essay Questions. To test your understanding of this chapter's material, outline or write an answer to the following questions.

1. Stop, Look and Listen!

After a crossing-grade accident between a car and a train the driver of the car files a diversity action against the railroad that owned and operated the train. At trial, the driver testifies that he never heard the train approaching, that the engineer did not blow a whistle or otherwise warn of the train's approach, and that the crossing gate at the grade crossing did not blink or lower. No other witnesses testified on behalf of the plaintiff.

The railroad's witnesses included the engineer in charge of the train, three other railroad employees on the train, and the driver of another car that stopped for the train. These five individuals uniformly testified that the train's whistle signaled its approach to the crossing, the train slowed, the lights on the crossing gate were blinking, and the gate lowered (although still permitting a car to drive around it onto the track).

At the conclusion of all the evidence, the railroad filed a motion for judgment as a matter of law. The judge summarily denied the motion, and the jury returned a verdict of $200,000 for the plaintiff driver. Twenty-two days after the entry of judgment on the jury's verdict, the railroad filed a renewed motion for judgment as a matter of law and a motion for a new trial. The judge denied the renewed motion for judgment as a matter of law, stating: "The plaintiff's testimony provides at least a scintilla of evidence supporting the verdict, so I am going to deny the railroad's motion." Concerning the motion for a new trial, the judge stated, "Because I am denying the renewed motion for judgment as a matter of law, I will not rule on the motion for a new trial."

(a) Should the judge have granted the railroad's motion for judgment as a matter of law?

(b) Should the judge have granted the railroad's renewed motion for judgment as a matter of law?

(c) Should the judge have ruled on the motion for a new trial?

(d) If the judge had ruled on the motion for a new trial, should the judge have granted or denied that motion?

(e) What, if any, effect would the judge's ruling on the motion for a new trial have had upon the timing of an appeal by the railroad?

2. Trials, New Trials and Damages.

An employee brings a civil action against her employer in federal court, alleging that the employer denied her a promotion because of her religion. At trial the employee testifies that people in her office call center began "treating her differently" once she began wearing a head scarf to work. A former co-worker, who had been fired from her position about the time that the employee was denied the promotion, testifies that she, too, sensed that people began treating the employee differently once she began wearing the head scarf.

In addition to these two witnesses for the employee, the employer called seven trial witnesses. All three members of the committee that considered the promotion testified that the individual who was promoted had significantly greater experience and longevity with the company than the employee and that this individual had taken relevant courses in leadership and supervision that she had not. The committee members also testified that, while meeting the minimum requirements for the promotion, the employee didn't have two of the "preferred" qualifications for the position: fluency in a second language and training in accounting. In addition, the supervisor who accepted the committee's promotion recommendation testified that he did not know the employee nor her religion but found the recommended candidate "highly qualified." Finally, three co-workers of the employee testified that they found her difficult to work with and that she "called in sick pretty frequently."

The jury returned a $2,000,000 verdict for the employee, and the judge entered judgment on that verdict. Twenty days after entry of judgment, the employer filed a motion for a new trial "because the jury's verdict was against the weight of the evidence." One week later, the judge entered an order providing: "Although there has been no motion seeking such relief, I sua sponte order a conditional new trial in this action. Unless the plaintiff agrees to accept $50,000 as her total remedy in this action, I will order a new trial limited to the issue of damages. I find this necessary because I improperly excluded at trial the testimony of an expert offered by the employer as to the monetary loss to the employee from having been denied the promotion."

(a)   Should the judge have granted the employer's motion for a new trial?

(b)   Was the judge's order of a conditional new trial proper?

CHAPTER 14

RESPECT FOR JUDGMENTS: "HAVEN'T WE DONE THIS BEFORE?"

I. INTRODUCTION

As you may remember, there were two lawsuits involving John Leonard and PepsiCo, Inc. stemming from Leonard's claim that PepsiCo owed him a Harrier jet: PepsiCo initially brought a declaratory judgment action in the United States District Court for the Southern District of New York and Leonard then brought suit in state court in Florida. PepsiCo's suit was dismissed for lack of personal jurisdiction and Judge Kimba Wood decided Leonard's action, which had been removed from state to federal court in Florida and then transferred to the Southern District of New York.

Assume that, rather than being transferred to New York, a Florida state court had entered judgment against Leonard. Could Leonard then have filed a new action against PepsiCo in his home state of Washington? What if the Florida judgment had been entered against Leonard in federal court rather than state court? What if the Washington action sought the Harrier jet, but was based on a Washington consumer protection statute that had not been raised in the Florida action?

In all of these scenarios, the second court must determine what, if any, impact the judgment in the first action should have upon the second action. Are the two actions so related that an unfavorable judgment in the first action should bar the second action? Even if the second action is not barred, are there identical issues of fact or law raised in both actions so that there should be no re-litigation of those issues in the second action?

These are the questions that are considered under the common law doctrine of respect for judgments or former adjudication. Initially, the chapter explores the doctrine of claim preclusion or, as it is called in older opinions, res judicata. Claim preclusion generally precludes someone from bringing a second action after judgment has been entered against him in a former action on the same claim. Then the chapter turns to issue preclusion, which often is called collateral estoppel. Issue preclusion, as its name suggests, generally precludes a person from attempting to relitigate an issue that has been determined in a prior action. Finally, the chapter considers the application of claim and issue preclusion when the first and second actions are filed in different court systems.

II. CLAIM PRECLUSION

Rule 1 of the Federal Rules of Civil Procedure provides that those Rules "should be construed, administered, and employed by the court and the parties to secure the just, speedy, and inexpensive determination of every action and proceeding." While claim and issue preclusion are common law doctrines that predate the Federal Rules, these doctrines also strive for the justice, speed, and efficiency that are the ultimate goal of the Federal Rules.

This section of this chapter initially considers the doctrine of claim preclusion, while the next section focuses on issue preclusion. Boiled down to its essentials, the common law doctrine of claim preclusion (or "res judicata," which is the term used in some opinions) provides that you can't sue on the same claim twice. Unfortunately, there are several nuances to the doctrine, which are explored in the following pages.

A. THE DOCTRINE OF CLAIM PRECLUSION

Much of the *Restatement (Second) of Judgments* (1982) is concerned with claim preclusion. Section 17 of that *Restatement* defines the general rules governing claim preclusion as follows:

> A valid and final personal judgment is conclusive between the parties, except on appeal or other direct review, to the following extent:
>
> (1) If the judgment is in favor of the plaintiff, the claim is extinguished and merged in the judgment and a new claim may arise on the judgment;
>
> (2) If the judgment is in favor of the defendant, the claim is extinguished and the judgment bars a subsequent action on that claim; * * *

Merger. Note that the impact of the first judgment is defined differently depending on whether the plaintiff won or lost the first action. If the plaintiff is successful in the first action, "the claim is extinguished and **merged** in the judgment." This is the aspect of claim preclusion that is called "merger," because any second claim is merged in the first action (and therefore cannot be brought). While a second action on the same claim cannot be brought, Section 17(1) provides that, despite merger, "a new claim may arise on the judgment." This means that a second action can be brought to enforce the final judgment obtained in the first action. Assume, for instance, that plaintiff secures a final judgment for $100,000 in Minnesota, but that the defendant has no assets in that state. In that situation, the plaintiff can bring an enforcement action on that $100,000 judgment in a state in which the defendant has assets. But the plaintiff cannot bring a second action on the claim itself.

Bar. What if the plaintiff is unsuccessful in its initial action. In that situation *Restatement* Section 17(2) provides that "the claim is extinguished and the judgment bars a subsequent action on that claim." Thus the aspect of claim preclusion that bars a second action after the plaintiff has lost the initial action is referred to as **bar**. When a final and valid judgment is entered on the merits in the first action, a later action by the plaintiff on that same claim is precluded (unless the second action is simply to enforce an initial judgment in the plaintiff's favor).

The requirements for the application of claim preclusion are:

(1) same claim in first and second action;

(2) same parties in first and second action;

(3) valid judgment in the first action;

(4) final judgment in the first action; and

(5) the judgment in first action was on the merits.

Let's see how these requirements are satisfied in the following case.

B. WHAT'S A "CLAIM" FOR THE PURPOSES OF CLAIM PRECLUSION?

If the basic rule of claim preclusion is that you can't sue on the same claim twice, the question arises as to what's a "claim"? Consider the answer given by the Supreme Court of Maine, and the *Restatement (Second) of Judgments*, in the following case.

Beegan v. Schmidt
Supreme Judicial Court of Maine, 1982
451 A.2d 642

OPINION

■ McKUSICK, CHIEF JUSTICE.

This case comes to the Law Court on appeal from an order of the Superior Court (Kennebec County) dismissing plaintiff Beatrice M. Beegan's suit for breach of express contract against her former dentist, James L. Schmidt. The Superior Court dismissed Beegan's present lawsuit after Dr. Schmidt argued that it was barred by a judgment entered against Beegan in an earlier case she had brought against the same defendant, charging him with negligence and breach of implied contract. We hold that the Superior Court correctly applied the principle of res judicata; and consequently we affirm its dismissal of this second action brought by Beegan against Dr. Schmidt.

In September, 1980, Beegan initiated a civil action in the Superior Court (Kennebec County) against Dr. Schmidt, a dentist practicing in Augusta. Her complaint was in four counts, each of them asking for damages of $70,000 plus interest and costs. Each count alleged the following facts: Beegan "placed herself under the care of the defendant" in the spring of 1975 and employed him "to do any and all things that were required to treat plaintiff's condition and necessary to the maintenance of good dental health in the plaintiff's mouth." Schmidt agreed to do all things necessary for plaintiff's dental health. Schmidt treated Beegan through "the late fall of 1976," but failed to diagnose her various dental diseases, including "severe dental decay [and] gum deterioration." Because of Schmidt's failure to diagnose those problems, Beegan required "extensive dental surgery and treatment" and suffered "permanent impairment and loss of teeth, great pain and suffering of body and mind, dental, periodontal, medical, and drug expenses, loss of time, and other expenses."

* * *

The Superior Court dismissed Beegan's case because she had failed to file her complaint within the two-year limitations period prescribed by the legislature for "malpractice" actions. The Law Court affirmed on November 9, 1981, holding that "[b]oth the claims in negligence and those in implied contract are controlled by the two-year statute of limitations."

Undaunted, Beegan filed a new complaint against dentist Schmidt later in the same month of November, 1981. The 1981 complaint contains the following allegations in two separate counts: On May 7, 1975, Beegan and Schmidt entered into an express contract providing that Schmidt "would repair molars and bicuspids, for the purpose of restoring those specified teeth to a condition whereby root canal work on said teeth would not be required," and that Beegan would pay Schmidt $33 per hour for his services. Schmidt worked on Beegan's teeth through January, 1976. In late 1977 and early 1978, Beegan experienced pain and headaches, consulted other dental practitioners, and discovered that Schmidt had failed to repair the molars and bicuspids which he had undertaken to restore. She then was forced to undergo additional treatment, including root canal surgery, to "restore her mouth to the condition in which it would have been had the defendant performed his contract with the plaintiff." This additional treatment cost Beegan $17,000.

Count I prays for "reasonable" damages. County II further alleges that Beegan engaged Schmidt on January 17, 1976, "for the specific purpose of determining whether or not dental problems were causing her extreme headaches and pain in her neck and head," that Beegan and Schmidt entered into a second express contract whereby Beegan would pay the dentist $30 and he would examine her to determine whether her pain was due to any dental decay, and that Schmidt collected his fee but reported to Beegan that he could find no dental conditions capable of causing the pain she had reported. Count II goes on to allege that Beegan later discovered that decay in the very molars and bicuspids Schmidt had originally agreed to treat was responsible for her pain, and that the pain ultimately forced her not only to have root canal surgery but also to leave her employment, to use prescription painkillers, and to seek psychological and medical treatment. Count II lists Beegan's damages as $17,000 for medical, dental, and psychiatric expenses and $40,000 for loss of wages.

Defendant Schmidt moved to dismiss the 1981 complaint on the ground, *inter alia,* that it was barred as res judicata [claim preclusion] by the final judgment in the 1980 suit between the same two parties. The Superior Court granted Schmidt's motion and dismissed the case without opinion.

The doctrine of res judicata—literally, "thing adjudged"—is a court-made collection of rules designed to ensure that the same matter will not be litigated more than once. Today's case involves the branch of res judicata usually called "bar." Unlike the related rule of collateral estoppel or "issue preclusion," which merely prevents the reopening in a second action of an issue of fact actually litigated and decided in an earlier case, the doctrine of bar, or "claim preclusion," prohibits relitigation of an entire "cause of action" between the same parties or their privies, once a valid final judgment has been rendered in an earlier suit on the same cause of action.

> If a plaintiff brings an action which proceeds to final judgment, his "cause of action" is said to be "merged" in the judgment if he wins and "barred" by it if he loses. This means that what was considered or should have been considered in the first action cannot form the basis of a subsequent action.

Note, Developments in the Law—Res Judicata, 65 *Harv.L.Rev.* 820, 824 (1952). The case now before us presents the question whether the judgment entered against Beegan in her first action against Schmidt bars her from bringing this second case.

In *Kradoska v. Kipp,* Me., 397 A.2d 562, 565 (1979), we summarized the doctrine of bar as it has evolved in this state. The rule, we said,

> has been applied chiefly in the interests of judicial economy to bar relitigation of a cause of action that has already been resolved by a valid prior judgment; the scope of the bar extends to all issues "tried or that might have been tried" in the prior action. *Bray v. Spencer,* 146 Me. 416, 418 (1951). . . . In order for the doctrine to be applied, the court must satisfy itself that 1) the same parties, or their privies, are involved; 2) a valid final judgment was entered in the prior action; and 3) the

matters presented for decision were, or might have been, litigated in the prior action.

The case now before us easily satisfies the three conditions set forth in *Kradoska*. First, the same two parties are involved in this case as in the earlier action. Second, a dismissal for failure to come within an applicable statute of limitations is a "valid final judgment" for res judicata purposes.[2] Third, the issues presented for decision in the instant case could have been presented and decided in the prior action. It is true that the 1981 complaint contains factual allegations not made in 1980, allegations as to the formation and terms of two express contracts allegedly entered into by Dr. Schmidt with Beegan. But by their nature those facts must have been known to Beegan when she filed her 1980 complaint, and therefore her breach of contract claims could have been presented for decision at that time. Similarly, although the legal theory underlying both counts of the 1981 complaint, breach of express contract, differs from the theories relied upon in the 1980 complaint, it was hardly an unknown principle in 1980 and it could equally well have been relied upon in Beegan's original complaint. Nor would the Maine Rules of Civil Procedure have prevented Beegan from incorporating the 1981 allegations and theory of recovery into her 1980 complaint. See M.R.Civ.P. 18(a). Beegan thus could easily have presented for decision in 1980 all of the issues she seeks to litigate by her 1981 complaint.

These conclusions do not end our inquiry, however; in a sense they are mere preliminaries to the issue at the heart of the present case. We have stated that Beegan could have incorporated all of the factual allegations and legal grounds for relief asserted in her 1981 complaint back in 1980. Still to be decided is whether she should have done so; whether her failure to assert those matters in 1980 precludes her from litigating them now. To put it another way, the key question here is whether Beegan's 1981 complaint presents the same "cause of action" that was presented and disposed of in her 1980 action. "The major problem raised by the principle of merger or bar is how much of what could have been considered in the first action, but was not, is also merged or barred—in other words, to what extent a party's present grievances were part of the 'cause of action' already sued on." Note, supra, 65 *Harv.L.Rev.* at 824.

We have acknowledged in an earlier case that "the slippery phrase 'cause of action' all but defies definition." *Kradoska*, supra, 397 A.2d at

---

[2]   In *Kradoska v. Kipp*, Me., 397 A.2d 562, 567 (1979), a dismissal for want of prosecution was held to foreclose relitigation of the same cause of action because such a dismissal "operates as an adjudication on the merits" under M.R.Civ.P. 41(b)(3). By its terms, Rule 41(b)(3) also applies to dismissals for failure to comply with a statute of limitations. *See also Restatement (Second) of Judgments*, supra note 1, § 19 reporter's note, at 168–69 ("The dismissal [on statute of limitations grounds] operates as a bar in the jurisdiction in which it is rendered, even if the plaintiff in the second action seeks to change his theory of recovery and to rely on a longer limitations provision").

568. Recent Maine cases have accepted what is generally known as the transactional test or the "pragmatic concept" of a cause of action, however, and today we reaffirm our commitment to that formula. *Kradoska*, 397 A.2d at 568, approved the definition of "cause of action" used by Professor Field and his collaborators: "The measure of a cause of action is the aggregate of connected operative facts that can be handled together conveniently for purposes of trial." 1 Field, McKusick & Wroth, *Maine Civil Practice* § 18.1, at 360 (2d ed. 1970). * * * *Restatement (Second) of Judgments* § 24 (1982) uses the term "claim" instead of "cause of action," and in its black letter gives a lucid explanation of the dimensions of a claim for res judicata purposes:

> (1) When a valid and final judgment rendered in an action extinguishes the plaintiff's claim pursuant to the rules of merger or bar . . . , the claim extinguished includes all rights of the plaintiff to remedies against the defendant with respect to all or any part of the transaction, or series of connected transactions, out of which the action arose.

> (2) What factual grouping constitutes a "transaction," and what groupings constitute a "series," are to be determined pragmatically, giving weight to such considerations as whether the facts are related in time, space, origin, or motivation, whether they form a convenient trial unit, and whether their treatment as a unit conforms to the parties' expectations or business understanding or usage.

Other courts and commentators state the proposition differently, but all who advocate the transactional test for a cause of action agree on its appropriateness in serving the purposes of the res judicata rule.

Maine cases have always acknowledged that the doctrine of res judicata is justified by concerns for judicial economy and efficiency, the stability of final judgments, and fairness to litigants. The transactional test for a cause of action best advances those goals. Requiring a plaintiff to pursue all rights he may have against a given defendant that grow out of the "transaction or series of transactions" from which his suit arises promotes judicial economy and the public perception of the stability and finality of court decisions. It eases both the financial and psychological burdens on a defendant, who can rest assured that no one will sue him more than once over the same incident or occurrence. And it is fair to the plaintiff, as well: He as well as the defendant will benefit economically—by saving counsel fees and other litigation expenses—if he consolidates as many of his factual allegations and legal theories as possible into one lawsuit. And the rules that have governed civil litigation in Maine since December 1, 1959, provide the plaintiff, as well as the defendant, with "ample procedural means for fully developing the entire transaction in the one action going to the merits to which the plaintiff is ordinarily confined." *Restatement (Second) of Judgments, supra*, § 24 comment a, at 198. * * *

* * *

We have no doubt that Beegan's 1980 and 1981 complaints grow out of only one series of transactions. Both complaints allege essentially the same facts occurring over the same period of time: that Beegan went to Dr. Schmidt for dental work in the spring of 1975, that he was supposed to cure her dental diseases or at least prevent further decay, that he failed to do so, and that his failure resulted in further deterioration in Beegan's condition, ultimately requiring extensive remedial work and leading to related expenses and losses. The basic injury Beegan alleges to have suffered—the unnecessary worsening of her dental problems—is the same in both cases. The damages she requests are the same in both cases—or, to be more precise, the damages she requests in her 1981 complaint are merely a subset of those she demanded in 1980. * * *

* * *

* * * [T]he case we are deciding today is well within the established bounds of Maine res judicata doctrine. * * * Beegan's present lawsuit * * * asks for the same relief she requested earlier and makes no additional factual allegations as to the defendant's wrongful acts. The issues raised in her 1981 complaint both could and should have been presented in her 1980 case. She may not litigate them now.

The entry is:

Judgment affirmed.

All concurring.

COMMENTS AND QUESTIONS CONCERNING *BEEGAN V. SCHMIDT*

1.   Chief Justice McKusick mentions in his opinion that Rule 18(a) of the Maine Rules of Civil Procedure would have permitted the plaintiff to add a claim for breach of an express contract in her first action. Similarly, Rule 18(a) of the Federal Rules of Civil Procedure provides: "A party asserting a claim, counterclaim, crossclaim, or third-party claim may join, as independent or alternative claims, as many claims as it has against an opposing party." Rule 18(a) says that a party "may" join additional claims in a single civil action. Is the Maine Supreme Court saying that additional claims must sometimes be joined? If so, what types of claims?

2.   Chief Justice McKusick relies upon the transactional definition of "claim" from the *Restatement (Second) of Judgments*. What are the advantages of such a definition? Is it clear in this case that the matters asserted in the first and second civil actions were "related in time, space, origin, or motivation," "form[ed] a convenient trial unit," and that "their treatment as a unit conform[ed] to the parties' expectations or business understanding or usage"?

3.   The judgment in the first action appeared to be final and valid, and in footnote 2 of his opinion, the Chief Justice concludes that, under

Maine procedural law, such a dismissal is considered "on the merits." Does it make sense to bar a later action if the merits have not really been considered in the first action? Would the result have been the same under federal law? *See* Federal Rule of Civil Procedure 41(b) ("Unless the dismissal order states otherwise, a dismissal under this subdivision (b) and any dismissal not under this rule—except one for lack of jurisdiction, improper venue, or failure to join a party under Rule 19—operates as an adjudication on the merits.").

4. Chief Justice McKusick summarizes the reasons for recognizing claim preclusion as follows: "Maine cases have always acknowledged that the doctrine of res judicata is justified by concerns for judicial economy and efficiency, the stability of final judgments, and fairness to litigants." In footnote 5 of his opinion, deleted from the preceding text, the Chief Justice also cited *Foss v. Whitehouse,* 94 Me. 491 (1901), quoting from *Foss* the following: "The prohibition is not only against twice recovering, but is against twice vexing. Its purpose is to protect the court as well as the defendant." 94 Me. at 497.

5. Are there any interests that should be balanced against the efficiency, stability of judgments (consistency), and fairness to the defendant dentist that are achieved by applying claim preclusion in this action? Is Beatrice Beegan totally out of luck?

C. WHICH PARTIES ARE "THE SAME" FOR THE PURPOSES OF CLAIM PRECLUSION?

Not only must the claims be the same in the first and second actions for claim preclusion to apply, but the parties also must be the same. Consider the purposes of this requirement as you read the following opinion, in which the defendant Federal Aviation Administration attempted to convince the Supreme Court to recognize a theory of "virtual representation" to expand the definition of "parties."

Taylor v. Sturgell

Supreme Court of the United States, 2008
553 U.S. 880

OPINION

■ JUSTICE GINSBURG delivered the opinion of the Court.

"It is a principle of general application in Anglo-American jurisprudence that one is not bound by a judgment in personam in a litigation in which he is not designated as a party or to which he has not been made a party by service of process." *Hansberry v. Lee,* 311 U.S. 32, 40 (1940). Several exceptions, recognized in this Court's decisions, temper this basic rule. In a class action, for example, a person not named as a party may be bound by a judgment on the merits of the action, if she was adequately represented by a party who actively participated in the litigation. In this case, we consider for the first time whether there is a "virtual representation" exception to the general rule against precluding nonparties. Adopted by a number of courts, including the courts below in the case now before us, the exception so styled is broader than any we have so far approved.

The virtual representation question we examine in this opinion arises in the following context. Petitioner Brent Taylor filed a lawsuit under the Freedom of Information Act seeking certain documents from the Federal Aviation Administration. Greg Herrick, Taylor's friend, had previously brought an unsuccessful suit seeking the same records. The two men have no legal relationship, and there is no evidence that Taylor controlled, financed, participated in, or even had notice of Herrick's earlier suit. Nevertheless, the D.C. Circuit held Taylor's suit precluded by the judgment against Herrick because, in that court's assessment, Herrick qualified as Taylor's "virtual representative."

We disapprove the doctrine of preclusion by "virtual representation," and hold, based on the record as it now stands, that the judgment against Herrick does not bar Taylor from maintaining this suit.

I

The Freedom of Information Act (FOIA) accords "any person" a right to request any records held by a federal agency. 5 U.S.C. § 552(a)(3)(A). No reason need be given for a FOIA request, and unless the requested materials fall within one of the Act's enumerated exemptions, the agency must "make the records promptly available" to the requester, § 552(a)(3)(A). If an agency refuses to furnish the requested records, the requester may file suit in federal court and obtain an injunction "order[ing] the production of any agency records improperly withheld." § 552(a)(4)(B).

The courts below held the instant FOIA suit barred by the judgment in earlier litigation seeking the same records. Because the lower courts' decisions turned on the connection between the two lawsuits, we begin with a full account of each action.

A

The first suit was filed by Greg Herrick, an antique aircraft enthusiast and the owner of an F-45 airplane, a vintage model manufactured by the Fairchild Engine and Airplane Corporation (FEAC) in the 1930's. In 1997, seeking information that would help him restore his plane to its original condition, Herrick filed a FOIA request asking the Federal Aviation Administration (FAA) for copies of any technical documents about the F-45 contained in the agency's records.

To gain a certificate authorizing the manufacture and sale of the F-45, FEAC had submitted to the FAA's predecessor, the Civil Aeronautics Authority, detailed specifications and other technical data about the plane. Hundreds of pages of documents produced by FEAC in the certification process remain in the FAA's records. The FAA denied

Herrick's request, however, upon finding that the documents he sought are subject to FOIA's exemption for "trade secrets and commercial or financial information obtained from a person and privileged or confidential," § 552(b)(4). In an administrative appeal, Herrick urged that FEAC and its successors had waived any trade-secret protection. The FAA thereupon contacted FEAC's corporate successor, respondent Fairchild Corporation (Fairchild). Because Fairchild objected to release of the documents, the agency adhered to its original decision.

Herrick then filed suit in the U.S. District Court for the District of Wyoming. Challenging the FAA's invocation of the trade-secret exemption, Herrick placed heavy weight on a 1955 letter from FEAC to the Civil Aeronautics Authority. The letter authorized the agency to lend any documents in its files to the public "for use in making repairs or replacement parts for aircraft produced by Fairchild." This broad authorization, Herrick maintained, showed that the F-45 certification records held by the FAA could not be regarded as "secre[t]" or "confidential" within the meaning of § 552(b)(4).

Rejecting Herrick's argument, the District Court granted summary judgment to the FAA. The 1955 letter, the court reasoned, did not deprive the F-45 certification documents of trade-secret status, for those documents were never in fact released pursuant to the letter's blanket authorization. The court also stated that even if the 1955 letter had waived trade-secret protection, Fairchild had successfully "reversed" the waiver by objecting to the FAA's release of the records to Herrick.

On appeal, the Tenth Circuit agreed with Herrick that the 1955 letter had stripped the requested documents of trade-secret protection. But the Court of Appeals upheld the District Court's alternative determination—*i.e.,* that Fairchild had restored trade-secret status by objecting to Herrick's FOIA request. On that ground, the appeals court affirmed the entry of summary judgment for the FAA.

In so ruling, the Tenth Circuit noted that Herrick had failed to challenge two suppositions underlying the District Court's decision. First, the District Court assumed trade-secret status could be "restored" to documents that had lost protection. Second, the District Court also assumed that Fairchild had regained trade-secret status for the documents even though the company claimed that status only "*after* Herrick had initiated his request*" for the F-45 records. The Court of Appeals expressed no opinion on the validity of these suppositions.

B

The Tenth Circuit's decision issued on July 24, 2002. Less than a month later, on August 22, petitioner Brent Taylor—a friend of Herrick's and an antique aircraft enthusiast in his own right— submitted a FOIA request seeking the same documents Herrick had unsuccessfully sued to obtain. When the FAA failed to respond, Taylor filed a complaint in the U.S. District Court for the District of Columbia.

Like Herrick, Taylor argued that FEAC's 1955 letter had stripped the records of their trade-secret status. But Taylor also sought to litigate the two issues concerning recapture of protected status that Herrick had failed to raise in his appeal to the Tenth Circuit.

After Fairchild intervened as a defendant, the District Court in D.C. concluded that Taylor's suit was barred by claim preclusion; accordingly, it granted summary judgment to Fairchild and the FAA. The court acknowledged that Taylor was not a party to Herrick's suit. Relying on the Eighth Circuit's decision in *Tyus v. Schoemehl*, 93 F.3d 449 (1996), however, it held that a nonparty may be bound by a judgment if she was "virtually represented" by a party.

The Eighth Circuit's seven-factor test for virtual representation, adopted by the District Court in Taylor's case, requires an "identity of interests" between the person to be bound and a party to the judgment. Six additional factors counsel in favor of virtual representation under the Eighth Circuit's test, but are not prerequisites: (1) a "close relationship" between the present party and a party to the judgment alleged to be preclusive; (2) "participation in the prior litigation" by the present party; (3) the present party's "apparent acquiescence" to the preclusive effect of the judgment; (4) "deliberat[e] maneuver[ing]" to avoid the effect of the judgment; (5) adequate representation of the present party by a party to the prior adjudication; and (6) a suit raising a "public law" rather than a "private law" issue. These factors, the D.C. District Court observed, "constitute a fluid test with imprecise boundaries" and call for "a broad, case-by-case inquiry."

The record before the District Court in Taylor's suit revealed the following facts about the relationship between Taylor and Herrick: Taylor is the president of the Antique Aircraft Association, an organization to which Herrick belongs; the two men are "close associate[s];" Herrick asked Taylor to help restore Herrick's F-45, though they had no contract or agreement for Taylor's participation in the restoration; Taylor was represented by the lawyer who represented Herrick in the earlier litigation; and Herrick apparently gave Taylor documents that Herrick had obtained from the FAA during discovery in his suit.

Fairchild and the FAA conceded that Taylor had not participated in Herrick's suit. The D.C. District Court determined, however, that Herrick ranked as Taylor's virtual representative because the facts fit each of the other six indicators on the Eighth Circuit's list. Accordingly, the District Court held Taylor's suit, seeking the same documents Herrick had requested, barred by the judgment against Herrick.

The D.C. Circuit affirmed. * * *

* * * [T]he D.C. Circuit announced its own five-factor test. The first two factors—"identity of interests" and "adequate representation"—are necessary but not sufficient for virtual representation. In addition, at

least one of three other factors must be established: "a close relationship between the present party and his putative representative," "substantial participation by the present party in the first case," or "tactical maneuvering on the part of the present party to avoid preclusion by the prior judgment."

Applying this test to the record in Taylor's case, the D.C. Circuit found both of the necessary conditions for virtual representation well met. As to identity of interests, the court emphasized that Taylor and Herrick sought the same result—release of the F-45 documents. Moreover, the D.C. Circuit observed, Herrick owned an F-45 airplane, and therefore had "if anything, a stronger incentive to litigate" than Taylor, who had only a "general interest in public disclosure and the preservation of antique aircraft heritage."

Turning to adequacy of representation, the * * * court then concluded that Herrick had adequately represented Taylor even though Taylor had received no notice of Herrick's suit. For this conclusion, the appeals court relied on Herrick's "strong incentive to litigate" and Taylor's later engagement of the same attorney, which indicated to the court Taylor's satisfaction with that attorney's performance in Herrick's case.

The D.C. Circuit also found its "close relationship" criterion met, for Herrick had "asked Taylor to assist him in restoring his F-45" and "provided information to Taylor that Herrick had obtained through discovery"; furthermore, Taylor "did not oppose Fairchild's characterization of Herrick as his 'close associate.' " Because the three above-described factors sufficed to establish virtual representation under the D.C. Circuit's five-factor test, the appeals court left open the question whether Taylor had engaged in "tactical maneuvering."

We granted certiorari to resolve the disagreement among the Circuits over the permissibility and scope of preclusion based on "virtual representation."

II

The preclusive effect of a federal-court judgment is determined by federal common law. *See Semtek Int'l Inc. v. Lockheed Martin Corp.,* 531 U.S. 497, 507–508 (2001). For judgments in federal-question cases—for example, Herrick's FOIA suit—federal courts participate in developing "uniform federal rule[s]" of res judicata, which this Court has ultimate authority to determine and declare. *Id.,* at 508.[4] The federal common law of preclusion is, of course, subject to due process limitations.

* * *

---

[4] For judgments in diversity cases, federal law incorporates the rules of preclusion applied by the State in which the rendering court sits. *See Semtek Int'l Inc. v. Lockheed Martin Corp.,* 531 U.S. 497, 508 (2001).

A

The preclusive effect of a judgment is defined by claim preclusion and issue preclusion, which are collectively referred to as "res judicata."[5] Under the doctrine of claim preclusion, a final judgment forecloses "successive litigation of the very same claim, whether or not relitigation of the claim raises the same issues as the earlier suit." *New Hampshire v. Maine,* 532 U.S. 742, 748 (2001). Issue preclusion, in contrast, bars "successive litigation of an issue of fact or law actually litigated and resolved in a valid court determination essential to the prior judgment," even if the issue recurs in the context of a different claim. *Id.,* at 748–749. By "preclud[ing] parties from contesting matters that they have had a full and fair opportunity to litigate," these two doctrines protect against "the expense and vexation attending multiple lawsuits, conserv[e] judicial resources, and foste[r] reliance on judicial action by minimizing the possibility of inconsistent decisions." *Montana v. United States,* 440 U.S. 147, 153–154 (1979).

A person who was not a party to a suit generally has not had a "full and fair opportunity to litigate" the claims and issues settled in that suit. The application of claim and issue preclusion to nonparties thus runs up against the "deep-rooted historic tradition that everyone should have his own day in court." *Richards,* 517 U.S., at 798. Indicating the strength of that tradition, we have often repeated the general rule that "one is not bound by a judgment *in personam* in a litigation in which he is not designated as a party or to which he has not been made a party by service of process." *Hansberry,* 311 U.S., at 40.

B

Though hardly in doubt, the rule against nonparty preclusion is subject to exceptions. For present purposes, the recognized exceptions can be grouped into six categories.

First, "[a] person who agrees to be bound by the determination of issues in an action between others is bound in accordance with the terms of his agreement." 1 *Restatement (Second) of Judgments* § 40, p. 390 (1980) (hereinafter *Restatement*). For example, "if separate actions involving the same transaction are brought by different plaintiffs against the same defendant, all the parties to all the actions may agree that the question of the defendant's liability will be definitely determined, one way or the other, in a 'test case.'" D. Shapiro, *Civil Procedure: Preclusion in Civil Actions* 77–78 (2001) (hereinafter Shapiro).

Second, nonparty preclusion may be justified based on a variety of pre-existing "substantive legal relationship[s]" between the person to be bound and a party to the judgment. Shapiro 78. Qualifying

---

[5]   These terms have replaced a more confusing lexicon. Claim preclusion describes the rules formerly known as "merger" and "bar," while issue preclusion encompasses the doctrines once known as "collateral estoppel" and "direct estoppel."

relationships include, but are not limited to, preceding and succeeding owners of property, bailee and bailor, and assignee and assignor. These exceptions originated "as much from the needs of property law as from the values of preclusion by judgment." 18A C. Wright, A. Miller, & E. Cooper, *Federal Practice and Procedure* § 4448, p. 329 (2d ed. 2002) (hereinafter Wright & Miller).[8]

Third, we have confirmed that, "in certain limited circumstances," a nonparty may be bound by a judgment because she was "adequately represented by someone with the same interests who [wa]s a party" to the suit. Representative suits with preclusive effect on nonparties include properly conducted class actions and suits brought by trustees, guardians, and other fiduciaries.

Fourth, a nonparty is bound by a judgment if she "assume[d] control" over the litigation in which that judgment was rendered. *Montana,* 440 U.S., at 154. See also 1 *Restatement* § 39. Because such a person has had "the opportunity to present proofs and argument," he has already "had his day in court" even though he was not a formal party to the litigation. *Id.,* Comment *a,* p. 382.

Fifth, a party bound by a judgment may not avoid its preclusive force by relitigating through a proxy. Preclusion is thus in order when a person who did not participate in a litigation later brings suit as the designated representative of a person who was a party to the prior adjudication. And although our decisions have not addressed the issue directly, it also seems clear that preclusion is appropriate when a nonparty later brings suit as an agent for a party who is bound by a judgment.

Sixth, in certain circumstances a special statutory scheme may "expressly foreclos[e] successive litigation by nonlitigants . . . if the scheme is otherwise consistent with due process." *Martin [v. Wilks],* 490 U.S., at 762, n. 2. Examples of such schemes include bankruptcy and probate proceedings, see *ibid.,* and *quo warranto* actions or other suits that, "under [the governing] law, [may] be brought only on behalf of the public at large," *Richards,* 517 U.S., at 804.

III

* * *

The D.C. Circuit, the FAA, and Fairchild have presented three arguments in support of an expansive doctrine of virtual representation. We find none of them persuasive.

---

[8]   The substantive legal relationships justifying preclusion are sometimes collectively referred to as "privity." The term "privity," however, has also come to be used more broadly, as a way to express the conclusion that nonparty preclusion is appropriate on any ground. To ward off confusion, we avoid using the term "privity" in this opinion.

A

The D.C. Circuit purported to ground its virtual representation doctrine in this Court's decisions stating that, in some circumstances, a person may be bound by a judgment if she was adequately represented by a party to the proceeding yielding that judgment. But the D.C. Circuit's definition of "adequate representation" strayed from the meaning our decisions have attributed to that term.

In *Richards,* we reviewed a decision by the Alabama Supreme Court holding that a challenge to a tax was barred by a judgment upholding the same tax in a suit filed by different taxpayers. 517 U.S., at 795–797. The plaintiffs in the first suit "did not sue on behalf of a class," their complaint "did not purport to assert any claim against or on behalf of any nonparties," and the judgment "did not purport to bind" nonparties. There was no indication, we emphasized, that the court in the first suit "took care to protect the interests" of absent parties, or that the parties to that litigation "understood their suit to be on behalf of absent [parties]." In these circumstances, we held, the application of claim preclusion was inconsistent with "the due process of law guaranteed by the Fourteenth Amendment." *Id.,* at 797.

* * *

Our decisions recognizing that a nonparty may be bound by a judgment if she was adequately represented by a party to the earlier suit * * * provide no support for the D.C. Circuit's broad theory of virtual representation.

B

Fairchild and the FAA do not argue that the D.C. Circuit's virtual representation doctrine fits within any of the recognized grounds for nonparty preclusion. Rather, they ask us to abandon the attempt to delineate discrete grounds and clear rules altogether. Preclusion is in order, they contend, whenever "the relationship between a party and a non-party is 'close enough' to bring the second litigant within the judgment." Courts should make the "close enough" determination, they urge, through a "heavily fact-driven" and "equitable" inquiry. Only this sort of diffuse balancing, Fairchild and the FAA argue, can account for all of the situations in which nonparty preclusion is appropriate.

We reject this argument for three reasons. First, our decisions emphasize the fundamental nature of the general rule that a litigant is not bound by a judgment to which she was not a party. Accordingly, we have endeavored to delineate discrete exceptions that apply in "limited circumstances." Respondents' amorphous balancing test is at odds with the constrained approach to nonparty preclusion our decisions advance.

* * *

Our second reason for rejecting a broad doctrine of virtual representation rests on the limitations attending nonparty preclusion based on adequate representation. A party's representation of a nonparty is "adequate" for preclusion purposes only if, at a minimum: (1) the interests of the nonparty and her representative are aligned, and (2) either the party understood herself to be acting in a representative capacity or the original court took care to protect the interests of the nonparty. In addition, adequate representation sometimes requires (3) notice of the original suit to the persons alleged to have been represented. In the class-action context, these limitations are implemented by the procedural safeguards contained in Federal Rule of Civil Procedure 23.

An expansive doctrine of virtual representation, however, would "recogniz[e], in effect, a common-law kind of class action." *Tice,* 162 F.3d, at 972. That is, virtual representation would authorize preclusion based on identity of interests and some kind of relationship between parties and nonparties, shorn of the procedural protections prescribed in *Hansberry, Richards,* and Rule 23. These protections, grounded in due process, could be circumvented were we to approve a virtual representation doctrine that allowed courts to "create *de facto* class actions at will." *Tice,* 162 F.3d, at 973.

Third, a diffuse balancing approach to nonparty preclusion would likely create more headaches than it relieves. Most obviously, it could significantly complicate the task of district courts faced in the first instance with preclusion questions. An all-things-considered balancing approach might spark wide-ranging, time-consuming, and expensive discovery tracking factors potentially relevant under seven- or five-prong tests. And after the relevant facts are established, district judges would be called upon to evaluate them under a standard that provides no firm guidance. Preclusion doctrine, it should be recalled, is intended to reduce the burden of litigation on courts and parties. "In this area of the law," we agree, " 'crisp rules with sharp corners' are preferable to a round-about doctrine of opaque standards." *Bittinger v. Tecumseh Products Co.,* 123 F.3d 877, 881 (C.A.6 1997).

C

Finally, relying on the Eighth Circuit's decision in *Tyus,* 93 F.3d, at 456, the FAA maintains that nonparty preclusion should apply more broadly in "public law" litigation than in "private law" controversies. To support this position, the FAA offers two arguments. First, the FAA urges, our decision in *Richards* acknowledges that, in certain cases, the plaintiff has a reduced interest in controlling the litigation "because of the public nature of the right at issue." When a taxpayer challenges "an alleged misuse of public funds" or "other public action," we observed in *Richards,* the suit "has only an indirect impact on [the plaintiff's] interests." 517 U.S., at 803. In actions of this character, the Court said, "we may assume that the States have wide latitude to establish procedures . . . to limit the number of judicial proceedings that may be entertained." *Ibid.*

Taylor's FOIA action falls within the category described in *Richards,* the FAA contends, because "the duty to disclose under FOIA is owed to the public generally." The opening sentence of FOIA, it is true, states that agencies "shall make [information] available to the public." 5 U.S.C. § 552(a). Equally true, we have several times said that FOIA vindicates a "public" interest. The Act, however, instructs agencies receiving FOIA requests to make the information available not to the public at large, but rather to the "person" making the request. § 552(a)(3)(A). Thus, in contrast to the public-law litigation contemplated in *Richards,* a successful FOIA action results in a grant of relief to the individual plaintiff, not a decree benefiting the public at large.

Furthermore, we said in *Richards* only that, for the type of public-law claims there envisioned, States are free to adopt procedures limiting repetitive litigation. In this regard, we referred to instances in which the first judgment foreclosed successive litigation by other plaintiffs because, "under state law, [the suit] could be brought only on behalf of the public at large." *Id.,* at 804. *Richards* spoke of state legislation, but it appears equally evident that *Congress,* in providing for actions vindicating a public interest, may "limit the number of judicial proceedings that may be entertained." *Id.,* at 803. It hardly follows, however, that *this Court* should proscribe or confine successive FOIA suits by different requesters. Indeed, Congress' provision for FOIA suits with no statutory constraint on successive actions counsels against judicial imposition of constraints through extraordinary application of the common law of preclusion.

The FAA next argues that "the threat of vexatious litigation is heightened" in public-law cases because "the number of plaintiffs with standing is potentially limitless." FOIA does allow "any person" whose request is denied to resort to federal court for review of the agency's determination. 5 U.S.C. § 552(a)(3)(A), (4)(B). Thus it is theoretically possible that several persons could coordinate to mount a series of repetitive lawsuits.

But we are not convinced that this risk justifies departure from the usual rules governing nonparty preclusion. First, *stare decisis* will allow courts swiftly to dispose of repetitive suits brought in the same circuit. Second, even when *stare decisis* is not dispositive, "the human tendency not to waste money will deter the bringing of suits based on claims or issues that have already been adversely determined against others." Shapiro 97. This intuition seems to be borne out by experience: The FAA has not called our attention to any instances of abusive FOIA suits in the Circuits that reject the virtual representation theory respondents advocate here.

IV

For the foregoing reasons, we disapprove the theory of virtual representation on which the decision below rested. The preclusive effects of a judgment in a federal-question case decided by a federal court should instead be determined according to the established grounds for nonparty preclusion described in this opinion.

* * *

* * * We now turn back to Taylor's action to determine whether his suit is such a case, or whether the result reached by the courts below can be justified on one of the recognized grounds for nonparty preclusion.

A

It is uncontested that four of the six grounds for nonparty preclusion have no application here: There is no indication that Taylor agreed to be bound by Herrick's litigation, that Taylor and Herrick have any legal relationship, that Taylor exercised any control over Herrick's suit, or that this suit implicates any special statutory scheme limiting relitigation. Neither the FAA nor Fairchild contends otherwise.

It is equally clear that preclusion cannot be justified on the theory that Taylor was adequately represented in Herrick's suit. Nothing in the record indicates that Herrick understood himself to be suing on Taylor's behalf, that Taylor even knew of Herrick's suit, or that the Wyoming District Court took special care to protect Taylor's interests. Under our pathmarking precedent, therefore, Herrick's representation was not "adequate."

That leaves only the fifth category: preclusion because a nonparty to an earlier litigation has brought suit as a representative or agent of a party who is bound by the prior adjudication. Taylor is not Herrick's legal representative and he has not purported to sue in a representative capacity. He concedes, however, that preclusion would be appropriate if respondents could demonstrate that he is acting as Herrick's "undisclosed agen[t]."

Respondents argue here, as they did below, that Taylor's suit is a collusive attempt to relitigate Herrick's action. The D.C. Circuit considered a similar question in addressing the "tactical maneuvering" prong of its virtual representation test. The Court of Appeals did not, however, treat the issue as one of agency, and it expressly declined to reach any definitive conclusions due to "the ambiguity of the facts." We therefore remand to give the courts below an opportunity to determine whether Taylor, in pursuing the instant FOIA suit, is acting as Herrick's agent. Taylor concedes that such a remand is appropriate.

* * * We note * * * that courts should be cautious about finding preclusion on this basis. A mere whiff of "tactical maneuvering" will not suffice; instead, principles of agency law are suggestive. They indicate that preclusion is appropriate only if the putative agent's conduct of the suit is subject to the control of the party who is bound by the prior adjudication.

B

* * *

[Justice Ginsburg rejected Fairchild's argument that Taylor should bear the burden of proving on remand that he was not acting as Herrick's agent.] Claim preclusion, like issue preclusion, is an affirmative defense. Fed. Rule Civ. Proc. 8(c). Ordinarily, it is incumbent on the defendant to plead and prove such a defense, and we have never recognized claim preclusion as an exception to that general rule. We acknowledge that direct evidence justifying nonparty preclusion is often in the hands of plaintiffs rather than defendants. But "[v]ery often one must plead and prove matters as to which his adversary has superior access to the proof." 2 K. Broun, *McCormick on Evidence* § 337, p. 475 (6th ed. 2006). In these situations, targeted interrogatories or deposition questions can reduce the information disparity. We see no greater cause here than in other matters of affirmative defense to disturb the traditional allocation of the proof burden.

* * *

For the reasons stated, the judgment of the United States Court of Appeals for the District of Columbia Circuit is vacated, and the case is remanded for further proceedings consistent with this opinion.

It is so ordered.

COMMENTS AND QUESTIONS CONCERNING *TAYLOR V. STURGELL*

1.   Justice Ginsburg states: "A person who was not a party to a suit generally has not had a 'full and fair opportunity to litigate' the claims and issues settled in that suit." But what if the person has had a "full and fair opportunity to litigate" the claims? What if the person had notice of the first action? What if that person not only had notice of the first action, but a chance to intervene in that action? *See Martin v. Wilks*, 490 U.S. 755 (1989), *supra* p. 496.

2.   What is Justice Ginsburg's concern with a multi-factor test for determining whether a person who was not a party to a prior judgment is bound by that judgment? Would taking multiple factors into account result in fairer and more accurate determinations of who should be bound by judgments?

3.   Even though a person is not formally bound by a prior judgment due to claim preclusion, will that earlier judgment have any bearing on the adjudication of the second action? Are there other reasons why a person who was not a party to the first action may not bring a second action attempting to establish the position that was rejected in the first action?

4. Justice Ginsburg lists a series of exceptions to the general rule that only parties to a prior action can be bound by the judgment in that action. Among the more common exceptions are those involving persons in privity with a party bound by the first judgment. As Justice Ginsburg notes:

> Qualifying relationships include, but are not limited to, preceding and succeeding owners of property, bailee and bailor, and assignee and assignor. These exceptions originated "as much from the needs of property law as from the values of preclusion by judgment." 18A C. Wright, A. Miller, & E. Cooper, *Federal Practice and Procedure* § 4448, p. 329 (2d ed. 2002).

Assume, for instance, that a neighbor sues me and obtains a judgment establishing an easement across my property. If I leave the property to my daughter in my will, she would be precluded from contesting that easement in new litigation against the neighbor.

5. The Supreme Court remands this case "to give the courts below an opportunity to determine whether Taylor, in pursuing the instant FOIA suit, is acting as Herrick's agent." What sort of evidence might be relevant to this determination? Why should collusion between Taylor and Herrick mean that Taylor should be bound by the Wyoming judgment?

6. On remand, the defendants did not pursue their assertion of claim preclusion. *Taylor v. Babbitt*, 673 F. Supp. 2d 20, 23 n.1 (D.D.C. 2009). The District Court concluded that the requested documents were not protected as trade secrets under the Freedom of Information Act, because they were neither secret nor commercially valuable. *Taylor v. Babbitt*, 760 F. Supp. 2d 90 (D.D.C. 2011). The Court therefore granted summary judgment for the plaintiff Brent Taylor.

D. WHEN IS THE JUDGMENT IN THE FIRST ACTION VALID?

Not only must the first and second actions involve the same claim and same parties, but the first judgment must be valid, final, and "on the merits." In this section, we briefly consider the first of these requirements: that the judgment in the first action must be valid.

1. THE CLAIM PRECLUSION REQUIREMENT OF VALIDITY

Section 1 of the *Restatement (Second) of Judgments* (1982) describes the necessary validity of the first judgment as follows:

> A court has authority to render judgment in an action when the court has jurisdiction of the subject matter of the action, as stated in § 11, and
>
> (1) The party against whom judgment is to be rendered has submitted to the jurisdiction of the court, or
>
> (2) Adequate notice has been afforded the party, as stated in § 2, and the court has territorial jurisdiction of the action, as stated in §§ 4 to 9.

If the first court did not have personal or subject-matter jurisdiction, there is no reason to extend the impact of the first judgment by giving it claim preclusive effect in a later civil action. However, as the next case illustrates, it may not always be easy to determine if the first court had jurisdiction over the first action. Furthermore, the judgment of a court without subject-matter or personal jurisdiction may be used in a later action to establish issue preclusion (concerning the determination that the first court did not have jurisdiction).

2.   *LEMKIN V. HAHN, LOESER & PARKS*

Lemkin v. Hahn, Loeser & Parks

United States District Court, S.D. Ohio, 2011
2011 WL 2555378

OPINION AND ORDER

■ GEORGE C. SMITH, DISTRICT JUDGE.

This matter is before the Court on Defendant Hahn, Loeser & Parks' Motion to Dismiss or, in the alternative, for Summary Judgment. Plaintiff Jack Lemkin filed a response, and this matter is now ripe for review. For the reasons that follow, Defendant's Motion is **GRANTED.**

I.   BACKGROUND

Plaintiff Jack Lemkin brings this action *pro se* against Defendants Hahn, Loeser & Parks ("HLP"), Craig Miller, and Mark Watkins for negligent misrepresentation, fraud, and gross and willful misconduct. According to the Amended Complaint, Defendants Craig Miller and Mark Watkins were once attorneys at Oldham & Oldham, LPA ("O & O"), an Akron law firm which represented clients in matters concerning intellectual property and patent law. Plaintiff claims that on April 8, 1999, Defendant Miller filed a "Provisional Patent" for an adjustable-height pet feeder with the U.S. Patent and Trademark Office. Allegedly submitted along with the "Provisional Patent" were eight drawings which Defendants Miller and Watkins represented were created by Steven Tsengas. However, Plaintiff maintains that he authored seven of those drawings and that he brought this to the attention of Defendant Miller and O & O. Plaintiff claims that although O & O fired Defendant Miller, the "Provisional Patent" was never corrected, even after O & O transferred its clients and files to Defendant HLP in September 2001.

Plaintiff first filed suit against Defendants HLP, Miller, and Watkins in state court alleging negligent misrepresentation and fraud. There, Plaintiff argued that HLP was the successor in interest to O & O, and therefore, HLP was liable for the misconduct of O & O's former employees Miller and Watkins. The state court granted summary judgment in favor of HLP, holding that under Ohio law, HLP had no successor liability.

Later, the state court dismissed the remaining claims against Defendants Miller and Watkins for lack of subject-matter jurisdiction, finding that the remaining claims were claims arising under patent law, the exclusive province of federal court. That dismissal was affirmed by the Ohio Tenth District Court of Appeals * * *.

On July 27, 2010, Plaintiff filed the action now before this Court against Defendants Miller and Watkins—as well as against HLP on a direct liability theory. HLP raises the affirmative defense of res judicata in its Motion. HLP argues that the state court's summary judgment order bars the claims now asserted against HLP because those claims are premised on the same transaction or occurrence which gave rise to the case before the state court. Concerned that the state court decision may not have preclusive effect on the basis that the state court may have lacked subject matter jurisdiction at the time it rendered its summary-judgment decision in favor of HLP, this Court ordered HLP to show cause why its Motion should not be denied for failing to identify a judgment issued by a court of competent jurisdiction. * * *

II. APPLICABLE LAW

A. Patent Law and Exclusive Jurisdiction

Article III of the Constitution gives Congress the exclusive power to define the subject-matter jurisdiction of the lower federal courts. The United States Code provides that "district courts shall have original jurisdiction of any civil action arising under any Act of Congress relating to patents, plant variety protection, copyrights and trademarks. Such jurisdiction shall be exclusive of the courts of the states in patent, plant variety protection and copyright cases." 28 U.S.C. § 1338.

Section 1338 jurisdiction extends over cases in which a well-pleaded complaint[1] establishes either of the following: "federal law creates the cause of action or that the plaintiff's right to relief necessarily depends on resolution of a substantial question of federal patent law, in that patent law is a necessary element of one of the well-pleaded claims." *Christianson v. Colt Indus. Operating Corp.,* 486 U.S. 800, 808 (quoting *Franchise Tax Board of California v. Construction Laborers Vacation Trust,* 463 U.S. 1, 13 (1983)). Notably, though, the Sixth Circuit has noted that "only inventorship, the question of who actually invented the subject matter claimed in a patent, is a question of federal patent law." *E.I. DuPont de Nemours & Co. v. Okuley,* 344 F.3d 578, 528 (6th Cir.2003).

---

[1] Under the well-pleaded complaint rule, "whether a claim arises under patent law must be determined from what necessarily appears in the plaintiff's statement of his own claim in the bill or declaration, unaided by anything alleged in anticipation or avoidance of defenses which it is thought the defendant may interpose." *Christianson v. Colt Indus. Operating Corp.,* 486 U.S. 800, 811 (1988).

B.   Res Judicata and a Court of Competent Jurisdiction

"Federal courts must give the same preclusive effect to a state-court judgment as that judgment receives in the rendering state." *Abbott v. Michigan,* 474 F.3d 324, 330 (6th Cir.2007). As the judgment at issue here—the state court's order granting summary judgment in favor of HLP—was rendered by an Ohio state court, the Ohio law of res judicata applies. "In Ohio, the doctrine of res judicata encompasses the two related concepts of claim preclusion, also known as res judicata or estoppel by judgment, and issue preclusion, also known as collateral estoppel." *State ex rel. Davis v. Pub. Emp. Ret. Bd.,* 120 Ohio St.3d 386 (2008). Under the Ohio doctrine of claim preclusion, "a valid, final judgment rendered upon the merits bars all subsequent actions based upon any claim arising out of the transaction or occurrence that was the subject matter of the previous action." *Grava v. Parkman Twp.,* 73 Ohio St.3d 379 (1995) (expressly adopting *Restatement (Second) of Judgments* (1982) §§ 24–25).

III. DISCUSSION

A.   Did the state court have subject matter jurisdiction?

Res judicata "presupposes a judgment entered by a court of competent jurisdiction." *State ex rel. Rose v. Ohio Dep't of Rehab. & Corr.,* 91 Ohio St.3d 453 (2001). If that judgment upon a cause of action was rendered by a court without subject matter jurisdiction, "a federal court must determine whether to give claim preclusive effect to [that] state court judgment . . . by determining whether the state court would give preclusive effect to such a judgment." *Gargallo v. Merrill Lynch, Pierce, Fenner & Smith, Inc.,* 918 F.2d 658, 660 (6th Cir.1990) (citing *Marrese v. American Acad. of Orthopaedic Surgeons,* 470 U.S. 373, 382 (1985)). In *Gargallo,* the appellee originally filed a collection suit in state court, and the appellant counterclaimed under federal securities laws. The state court dismissed appellant's counterclaims with prejudice for appellant's failure to comply with the court's discovery orders. Later, appellant filed suit against appellee in federal court. The district court dismissed on res judicata grounds because the "issues, facts and evidence" to sustain that action were "identical" to the counterclaims asserted and dismissed with prejudice in state court.

On appeal, the Sixth Circuit faced the issue of whether a district court "may give claim preclusive effect to an Ohio judgment regarding federal securities laws that are within the exclusive jurisdiction of the federal courts" under 15 U.S.C. § 78aa. The Court noted first that a federal court must determine "whether the state court would give preclusive effect to such a judgment" rendered by a court without subject matter jurisdiction, and it determined that Ohio would not give such preclusive effect. *Id.* at 663. The Court then concluded that since the state court lacked subject matter jurisdiction "to resolve the claims brought under federal securities laws, a body of statutes and regulations over which the federal courts have exclusive jurisdiction," it was error to give preclusive effect to that state-court judgment. *Id.* at 664.

In its Show Cause Order, this Court, relying on *Gargallo,* expressed concern that the state court's grant of summary judgment would not have preclusive effect, as that court subsequently dismissed Plaintiff's claims for lack of subject matter jurisdiction over patent law claims. * * *

HLP distinguishes *Gargallo* by pointing out that the state court's grant of summary judgment in favor of HLP was a decision rendered on purely state-law grounds, specifically successor liability under Ohio law, as opposed to the *Gargallo* counterclaim, which was based on federal securities laws. Plaintiff's cause of action against HLP did not arise out of patent law; rather, it was a state-law-based claim of successor liability over which the state court had jurisdiction. Defendant HLP asserts, and the Court agrees with the following:

> In finding that HLP was in fact entitled to summary judgment, the State Court never had to resolve or even consider *any* questions of patent law. . . . The claims were not created by federal patent law, but by HLP's execution of an Asset Purchase Agreement with [O & O], which [Plaintiff] believed made HLP liable for [O & O's] actions as a successor.

In his state complaint, Plaintiff alleged all facts relevant to his claims only against Defendants Miller and Watkins, with HLP characterized in paragraph 3 as the "successor [in] interest" to Miller and Watkins' former law firm. Therefore, Plaintiff's claim against HLP was "merely incidental" to the patent issues raised by Plaintiff.

In *Boggild v. Kenner Products,* the Sixth Circuit noted the distinction between "a patent *claim* which arises under federal statutes relating to patents and which requires the court to interpret the validity and scope of a particular patent within section 1338, and a contract claim in which patent *issues* are merely incidentally implicated." 853 F.2d 465, 468 (6th Cir.1988). There, a defendant's counterclaim challenged the validity of the plaintiff's licensing agreement, alleging "that the terms of the contract, requiring the payment of royalties beyond the existence of the patents, were unenforceable after the patents had expired". *Id.* at 468. The Court determined that the counterclaim "did not implicate the validity or scope of the patents" at issue and, therefore, the counterclaim did not arise out of patent law but, instead, was a matter of contract interpretation. *Id.* "The general rule is that where an action is brought to enforce, set aside, or annul a contract, the action arises out of the contract, and not under the patent laws, even though the contract concerns a patent right." *Combs v. Plough, Inc.,* 681 F.2d 469, 470 (6th Cir.1982) (per curiam).

Here, too, the same logic applies. While Plaintiff's claims against Defendants Miller and Watkins clearly implicate the validity of the patents and Plaintiff's putative role as inventor, his claims against HLP arise out of the contract between O & O and HLP and implicate the issues of whether HLP was O & O's successor in interest. This contract and any attendant liabilities were the only issues examined and ruled upon by the state court. In that decision, the state court held as follows:

> It is clear that the malpractice action against [Defendants Miller and Watkins] arose prior to the September 1, 2001 Closing Date as set forth in the [Asset Purchase] Agreement, and therefore pursuant to Section 3(b) of the Agreement, Hahn Loeser is not responsible for the claim.... Applying the [successor liability] factors set forth in *Welco Indus., Inc. v. Applied Co.* (1993), 67 Ohio St.3d 344, 349, the Court finds that there is no evidence to show that Hahn Loeser entered into a merger with [O & O].

The state court concluded that HLP was not a successor in interest to O & O and, therefore, was not liable for any actions of Defendants Miller and Watkins. On this basis, the state court granted summary judgment in favor of HLP.

This Court is convinced that the state court had subject matter jurisdiction to determine whether, under Ohio law, HLP was O & O's successor in interest. As a result, the state court's grant of summary judgment in favor of HLP is a judgment issued by a court of competent jurisdiction. Now the Court turns its analysis to whether, as a matter of law, HLP's affirmative defense of res judicata is meritorious.

B. Does the state court's judgment have preclusive effect?

The obvious purpose of res judicata is to conserve judicial resources and to protect parties from the cost of litigating and relitigating the same matters in various forums. As noted *supra*, "[f]ederal courts must give the same preclusive effect to a state-court judgment as that judgment receives in the rendering state." *Abbott v. Michigan,* 474 F.3d 324, 330 (6th Cir.2007) (citing 28 U.S.C. § 1738). An Ohio state court granted summary judgment in favor of HLP, so the Ohio law of res judicata applies. Under the Ohio doctrine of claim preclusion, "a valid, final judgment rendered upon the merits bars all subsequent actions based upon any claim arising out of the transaction or occurrence that was the subject matter of the previous action." *Grava v. Parkman Twp.,* 73 Ohio St.3d 379 (1995) (expressly adopting *Restatement (Second) of Judgments* (1982) §§ 24–25). "It has long been the law of Ohio that an existing final judgment or decree between the parties to litigation is conclusive as to all claims which were *or might have been* litigated in a first lawsuit." *Id.* at 229.

In Ohio, a party seeking to invoke the doctrine of res judicata must prove four elements: (1) a prior final, valid decision on the merits by a court of competent jurisdiction; (2) a second action involving the same parties or their privies as the first; (3) a second action raising claims that were or could have been litigated in the first action; and (4) a second action arising out of the transaction or occurrence that was the subject matter of the previous action.

Applying this test, the Court finds that Plaintiff's claims against HLP, under a direct liability theory, could have been raised in the previous state court action. The application of each of the aforementioned factors is as follows:

(1) As examined *supra,* the state court's grant of summary judgment in favor of HLP on the issue of successor liability was a prior, final judgment of a court of competent jurisdiction. In addition, that grant of summary judgment is a decision on the merits.

(2) Plaintiff has added no new defendants to the federal action; therefore, the parties are the same as in the state action. * * *

(3) The state court found that HLP was not liable under a successor liability theory, and that court could have decided whether HLP was liable under a direct liability theory had Plaintiff brought that claim at that time. Therefore, Plaintiff's claim against HLP on a direct liability theory could have been brought against HLP in the earlier state action.

(4) The instant action arose out of the same actions or transactions that were the subject of the earlier action; in fact, the two actions are nearly identical. Both complaints present the same issue of whether Defendants Miller and Watkins improperly credited someone else for Plaintiff's work on two patents. More specifically, both Complaints present the same issue of whether HLP can be held liable for Defendants Miller and Watkins's actions related to the patents and the applications to the U.S. Patent and Trademark Office.

Based on the application of the four res judicata factors to this case, the Court finds that res judicata is applicable and, therefore, Plaintiff's claims in this case asserted against HLP are hereby dismissed.

IV. CONCLUSION

For the foregoing reasons, Defendant Hahn Loeser & Parks' Motion to Dismiss, or In the alternative, for Summary Judgment is hereby **GRANTED.** Plaintiff Jack Lemkin's claims against Hahn Loeser & Parks **only** are dismissed with prejudice. Defendant Hahn, Loeser & Parks shall be terminated as a party to this action, but Plaintiff's claims against Defendants Miller and Watkins remain pending.

* * *

IT IS SO ORDERED.

COMMENTS AND QUESTIONS CONCERNING
LEMKIN V. HAHN, LOESER & PARKS

1.   Isn't there difficulty with applying claim preclusion in this case because the claims in the two actions were not the same? In the first action, Jack Lemkin asserted that Hahn, Loeser & Parks was liable under the theory of successor liability, while in the second action Lemkin asserted that the law firm was directly liable to him. Does this raise a problem for the successful assertion of claim preclusion in the second action?

2.   Why would Congress authorize federal jurisdiction "under any Act of Congress relating to patents," while simultaneously providing that "[n]o State courts shall have jurisdiction over any claim for relief arising under any Act of Congress relating to patents"? *See* 28 U.S.C. § 1338.

3.   Footnote 1 of Judge Smith's opinion states that " 'whether a claim arises under patent law must be determined from what necessarily appears in the plaintiff's statement of his own claim in the bill or declaration, unaided by anything alleged in anticipation or avoidance of defenses which it is thought the defendant may interpose.' *Christianson v. Colt Indus. Operating Corp.*, 486 U.S. 800, 811 (1988)." Does this sound familiar to a case that you read in Chapter 3?

4.   Why did Jack Lemkin's claim against Hahn, Loeser & Parks in his first action not "arise under" federal patent law? Why is this significant?

5.   Why did defendants Craig Miller and Mark Watkins not file a motion for summary judgment based on claim preclusion?

While Judge Smith concludes that the Ohio court had subject-matter jurisdiction over Lemkin's claim against Hahn, Loeser & Parks in the first action, Lemkin's claims against Miller and Watkins were dismissed in that action because they arose under patent law and the state court did not have subject-matter jurisdiction over those claims. Thus the state-court judgment was not a valid judgment that could form the basis for claim preclusion.

6.   Under what authority is claim preclusion considered an affirmative defense? What if this defense had not been included in the answer of Hahn, Loeser & Parks?

7.   Judge Smith cites *Abbott v. Michigan,* 474 F.3d 324, 330 (6th Cir. 2007), for the proposition that "[f]ederal courts must give the same preclusive effect to a state-court judgment as that judgment receives in the rendering state."

The third, and final, sentence of the full faith and credit statute, 28 U.S.C. § 1738, provides: "[The] Acts, records and judicial proceedings * * * shall have the same full faith and credit in every court within the United States and its Territories and Possessions as they have by law or usage in the courts of such State, Territory or Possession from which they are taken." Pursuant to this statute, the Full Faith and Credit Clause of the Constitution (Art. IV, Sec. 1), and the more general concept of full faith and credit, federal and state courts must give full faith and credit to the judgments of both state and federal courts. This does not always mean that the second court must enforce the initial judgment by applying claim preclusion. Instead, the second court must give the same force to that first judgment as would the first court itself. So, if the rendering court would find its own judgment invalid, another court would not be required to apply claim preclusion to enforce that first judgment. The second judge might ask himself "What would the first judge do?" ("WWFJD") if asked to enforce his own judgment.

8.   Although the first court must have had personal and subject-matter jurisdiction for its judgment to have claim preclusive effect in a later action on the same claim, the parties may not be able to collaterally challenge the jurisdiction of the first court. If a party actually litigates the personal or subject-matter jurisdiction of the first court in the first action (and loses on that issue), it cannot later challenge the validity of the first judgment. *Durfee v. Duke*, 375 U.S. 106 (1963), *infra* p. 1106. If you litigate and lose on these jurisdictional issues, you're bound (and can't later challenge the validity of the first judgment).

But what if a party litigates the first action without raising the jurisdictional defense? Under Federal Rule of Civil Procedure 12(h)(1), the defense of lack of personal jurisdiction is waived if it is omitted from a Rule 12(b) motion to dismiss or the answer. Similar waiver usually occurs with respect to subject-matter jurisdiction. As the Supreme Court noted in *Travelers Indem. Co. v. Bailey*, 557 U.S. 137, 152–53 (2009): "Those orders are not any the less preclusive because the attack is on the Bankruptcy Court's conformity with its subject-matter jurisdiction, for '[e]ven subject-matter jurisdiction . . . may not be attacked collaterally.' *Kontrick v. Ryan*, 540 U.S. 443, 455, n.9 (2004)." The Supreme Court thus has referred to the "well-settled principle that res judicata may be pleaded as a bar, not only as respects matters actually presented to sustain or defeat the right asserted in the earlier proceeding, 'but also as respects any other available matter which might have been presented to that end'." *Chicot County Drainage Dist. v. Baxter State Bank,* 308 U.S. 371, 378 (1940) (quoting *Grubb v. Public Utilities Commission*, 281 U.S. 470, 478 (1930)).

Nevertheless, Section 12 of the *Restatement (Second) of Judgments* (1982) still leaves open the possibility of collateral challenge to the subject-matter jurisdiction of the first court if the question of subject-matter jurisdiction was not litigated in the first action and if (1) the first court's subject-matter jurisdiction "was so plainly beyond the court's jurisdiction that its entertaining the action was a manifest abuse of authority;" or (2) "allowing the judgment to stand would substantially infringe the authority of another tribunal or agency of government;" or (3) the first court did not have the "capability to make an adequately informed determination of a question concerning its own jurisdiction and as a matter of procedural fairness the party seeking to avoid the judgment should have opportunity belatedly to attack the court's subject matter jurisdiction." *See also Restatement (Second) of Conflict of Laws* § 97 (rev. 1988), *infra* pp. 1114–1115.

If the defendant did not enter an appearance in the first action, there are additional ways in which to collaterally challenge that action. Such challenge may be possible under *Pennoyer v. Neff*, 95 U.S. 714, 733 (1988); if the defendant received no notice of the first action (as required by *Mullane v. Central Hanover Bank & Trust Co.*, 339 U.S. 306 (1950)); or if the first judgment was procured by fraud. *See* Section IV(B), *infra*.

3. SHOULD CLAIM PRECLUSION APPLY?

After an investor became indebted to an investment firm, the firm filed a contract action in state court seeking the money the investor allegedly owed. The investor included in his state court answer a counterclaim brought under the federal securities laws, even though the federal courts have exclusive subject-matter jurisdiction over such claims. Because the investor refused to comply with discovery orders and the firm's discovery requests, the state court ultimately dismissed the investor's counterclaim "with prejudice" under a state rule modeled on Rule 37 of the Federal Rules of Civil Procedure.

After unsuccessfully appealing the dismissal of his state-court counterclaim, the investor filed a federal action asserting the same federal securities claim that he had asserted in his state counterclaim against the investment firm.

(a) What is the investment firm's best argument that claim preclusion should be applied by the federal court?

(b) What is the investor's best argument as to why claim preclusion should not be applied?

(c) Should the judge apply claim preclusion on these facts? *See Gargallo v. Merrill Lynch, Pierce, Fenner & Smith, Inc.*, 918 F.2d 658 (6th Cir. 1990).

E. WHEN IS THE JUDGMENT IN THE FIRST ACTION FINAL?

Not only must the initial judgment be valid for claim preclusion to apply, but that judgment also must be final. An order granting a preliminary injunction, denying a motion to dismiss, or involving other pretrial matters would not provide a sufficient basis upon which to base claim preclusion in a later civil action. As we will see in Chapter 15, a final judgment for appellate review purposes "generally is one which ends the litigation on the merits and leaves nothing for the court to do but execute the judgment." *Catlin v. United States*, 324 U.S. 229, 233 (1945). A similar common sense approach is taken with respect to finality for claim preclusion purposes. It would make little sense to extend the impact of an order to another civil action if the impact of that order is still tentative in the action in which it was rendered.

In most cases it's easy to determine whether a final judgment was entered in the first action. However, what if the judgment in the first action was appealed? Should there be no claim preclusive impact from that judgment until the appellate process runs its course? The *Restatement (Second) of Judgments* concludes that the "better view" (and the view adopted in the federal courts) is that an appeal does not suspend the possibility of claim preclusion based on that appealed judgment. *Restatement (Second) of Judgments* § 13 cmt. f (1982). *See also* 18A C. Wright, A. Miller & E. Cooper, *Federal Practice and Procedure* § 4433, at 78 (2nd ed. 2002) ("The Supreme Court long ago seemed to establish the rule that a final judgment retains all of its res judicata consequences pending decision of the appeal, apart from the virtually nonexistent situation in which the 'appeal' actually involves a full trial de novo.").

While this is the more efficient way to apply claim preclusion, what if the first judgment is reversed on appeal? Federal Rule of Civil Procedure 60(b)(5) specifically contemplates such a situation, providing that a federal district court "may relieve a party or its legal representative from a final judgment * * * [if] * * * the judgment * * * is based on an earlier judgment that has been reversed or vacated." A Rule 60(b)(5) motion "must be made within a reasonable time," Rule 60(c)(1), but there is no one-year limitation on the filing of such a motion as there is on motions for relief from final judgment under Rule 60(b)(1), (2), or (3).

F. WHEN IS THE JUDGMENT IN THE FIRST ACTION "ON THE MERITS?"

The final requirement for claim preclusion, that the judgment be "on the merits," is more of a conclusion than a test that logically can be applied to different types of judgments. Not surprisingly, a judgment is "on the merits" if the judgment is entered after a full trial and the return of a jury verdict. But what claim preclusive effect is given other district court dispositions short of trial?

The final sentence of Rule 41(b) of the Federal Rules of Civil Procedure would seem to provide a clear answer for federal court dismissals, providing:

> Unless the dismissal order states otherwise, a dismissal under this subdivision (b) and any dismissal not under this rule— except one for lack of jurisdiction, improper venue, or failure to join a party under Rule 19—operates as an adjudication on the merits.[1]

---

[1]   *See also Restatement (Second) of Judgments* § 20 (1982):

   (1) A personal judgment for the defendant, although valid and final, does not bar another action by the plaintiff on the same claim:

   (a) When the judgment is one of dismissal for lack of jurisdiction, for improper venue, or for nonjoinder or misjoinder of parties; or

   (b) When the plaintiff agrees to or elects a nonsuit (or voluntary dismissal) without prejudice or the court directs that the plaintiff be nonsuited (or that the action be otherwise dismissed) without prejudice; or

So even a default judgment, in a case that has never reached trial, is considered a "judgment on the merits" for the purposes of claim preclusion. But does this mean that every dismissal, except for lack of personal or subject-matter jurisdiction, improper venue, or failure to join a party under Rule 19, has claim preclusive effect on a later filing of the same claim? Unfortunately, no, as the Supreme Court explained in *Semtek Int'l Inc. v. Lockheed Martin Corp.*, 531 U.S. 497, 501–03 (2001):

> The original connotation of an "on the merits" adjudication is one that actually "pass[es] directly on the substance of [a particular] claim" before the court. *Restatement [(Second) of Judgments]* § 19, Comment *a*, at 161. That connotation remains common to every jurisdiction of which we are aware. *See ibid.* ("The prototyp[ical] [judgment on the merits is] one in which the merits of [a party's] claim are in fact adjudicated [for or] against the [party] after trial of the substantive issues"). And it is, we think, the meaning intended in those many statements to the effect that a judgment "on the merits" triggers the doctrine of res judicata or claim preclusion. *See, e.g., Parklane Hosiery Co. v. Shore,* 439 U.S. 322, 326, n. 5 (1979) ("Under the doctrine of res judicata, a judgment on the merits in a prior suit bars a second suit involving the same parties or their privies based on the same cause of action").

> But over the years the meaning of the term "judgment on the merits" "has gradually undergone change," R. Marcus, M. Redish, & E. Sherman, *Civil Procedure: A Modern Approach* 1140–1141 (3d ed. 2000), and it has come to be applied to some judgments (such as the one involved here) that do *not* pass upon the substantive merits of a claim and hence do *not* (in many jurisdictions) entail claim-preclusive effect.

In considering the federal diversity action before it in *Semtek*, the Supreme Court concluded:

> [T]he effect of the "adjudication upon the merits" default provision of Rule 41(b)—and, presumably, of the explicit order in the present case that used the language of that default provision—is simply that, unlike a dismissal "without prejudice," the dismissal in the present case barred refiling of the same claim in the United States District Court for the Central District of California."

531 U.S. at 506.

With respect to the effect of the federal dismissal on a later action filed in Maryland, the Supreme Court held that, because California law

---

(c) When by statute or rule of court the judgment does not operate as a bar to another action on the same claim, or does not so operate unless the court specifies, and no such specification is made.

did not give claim preclusive effect to a dismissal for failure to meet the statute of limitations, the district court dismissal would not bar the Maryland action. The Court did note, though, "This federal reference to state law will not obtain, of course, in situations in which the state law is incompatible with federal interests. If, for example, state law did not accord claim-preclusive effect to dismissals for willful violation of discovery orders, federal courts' interest in the integrity of their own processes might justify a contrary federal rule." 531 U.S. at 509.

While federal courts in diversity actions thus must look to the claim preclusive effect given by state courts, Rule 41(b) remains the default option in federal question actions. Looking at Rule 41, consider the claim preclusive effects of judgments entered after the following dismissals of federal question actions:

(1) The court enters a default judgment dismissing an action;

(2) The court dismisses an action for lack of personal jurisdiction;

(3) The court dismisses an action pursuant to Rule 37(b) for failure to comply with a discovery order;

(4) The court dismisses an action under Rule 12(b)(6) for failure to state a claim;

(5) The court grants a motion for summary judgment dismissing an action;

(6) The court grants a Rule 50(a) motion for judgment as a matter of law dismissing an action; or

(7) The court enters judgment for the defendant after the jury has returned a defense verdict at the conclusion of trial.

G. WHAT CLAIMS AND DEFENSES ARE AVAILABLE IN A LATER ACTION ON THE FIRST JUDGMENT?

The basic rule of claim preclusion is that you can't sue twice on the same claim. But does this mean that there can be no later civil action involving that first judgment? No, it does not.

1. EXECUTION ON THE INITIAL JUDGMENT

Assume that a plaintiff obtains a final, valid judgment on the merits against a defendant. Plaintiff's counsel will enjoy passing on this good news to the plaintiff, but the plaintiff will have a question: "When do I get my money?" A judgment is merely a court document, and if the defendant does not voluntarily pay the judgment, plaintiff's counsel will have to execute on that judgment to convert it into the money damages that are the object of most civil actions. Rule 69 of the Federal Rules of Civil Procedure provides that federal courts follow state procedure in executing on a judgment, unless there is specific federal law governing a particular type of execution.

If the defendant has assets in the state in which the initial judgment was obtained, it should not be difficult to execute on that judgment. But what if the defendant has no assets in that state? For instance, the plaintiff may have obtained judgment against a defendant who was merely "passing through" a state but, because he was served with process while in the state, is subject to transient personal jurisdiction as recognized in *Burnham v. Superior Court*, 495 U.S. 186 (1990), *supra* p. 262. If the defendant has no property within the state in which judgment was rendered, the plaintiff may seek to enforce the judgment against the defendant in a state where the defendant has property that can be the basis for execution on the judgment.

But will execution on the first court's judgment be considered the filing of the same claim that was filed in the first action, so that the second action is barred by res judicata? No, and, in fact, the *Restatement of Judgments* specifically acknowledges that an action to **enforce** an initial judgment is not barred by claim preclusion. Section 18(1) of the *Restatement (Second) of Judgments* provides:

> When a valid and final personal judgment is rendered in favor of the plaintiff * * * [t]he plaintiff cannot thereafter maintain an action on the original claim or any part thereof, although he may be able to maintain an action upon the judgment * * *.

2.   DEFENSES MUST BE ASSERTED IN THE INITIAL ACTION

In the event that the plaintiff needs to bring a second action to enforce the initial judgment, are there any limitations on the defenses that the defendant can raise in the enforcement action? Here, too, the *Restatement (Second) of Judgments* provides an answer. Section 18(2) of the *Restatement* provides:

> When a valid and final personal judgment is rendered in favor of the plaintiff, * * * [i]n an action upon the judgment, the defendant cannot avail himself of defenses he might have interposed, or did interpose, in the first action.

Note that Section 18 presumes that the first judgment was "valid," which means that, under Section 1 of the *Restatement (Second)*, the defendant submitted to the jurisdiction of the court or received notice of the first action and is subject to the personal jurisdiction of the court. In that event, the defendant in an action to enforce the first judgment cannot raise any defense (1) that it actually raised in the first action or (2) that it "might have" raised in that action. As the Supreme Court stated in *Cromwell v. Sac Cnty.*, 94 U.S. 351, 352 (1876):

> In the [case of a second action on the same claim], the judgment, if rendered upon the merits, constitutes an absolute bar to a subsequent action. It is a finality as to the claim or demand in controversy, concluding parties and those in privity

with them, not only as to every matter which was offered and received to sustain or defeat the claim or demand, but as to any other admissible matter which might have been offered for that purpose. * * * If * * * defenses were not presented in the action, and established by competent evidence, the subsequent allegation of their existence is of no legal consequence. The judgment is as conclusive, so far as future proceedings at law are concerned, as though the defenses never existed.

Thus, just as plaintiffs cannot hold back matters in the initial action, defendants also must assert their defenses in that action or be precluded from asserting them in a second action to enforce the initial (valid and final) judgment.

3. DEFENDANT'S FAILURE TO INTERPOSE A COUNTERCLAIM IN THE FIRST ACTION

A defendant may not only lose a defense in a later action by failing to assert that defense in a prior action. Even more significantly, a defendant may lose a potential counterclaim by failing to assert it in the first action.

Section 22 of the *Restatement (Second) of Judgments* provides that, in most cases, there is no requirement to assert a counterclaim in an action unless a compulsory counterclaim statute or rule requires the assertion of the counterclaim.[2] In the federal courts, Rule 13(a)(1) is just such a compulsory counterclaim rule, requiring that:

A pleading must state as a counterclaim any claim that— at the time of its service—the pleader has against an opposing party if the claim:

(A) arises out of the transaction or occurrence that is the subject matter of the opposing party's claim; and

(B) does not require adding another party over whom the court cannot acquire jurisdiction.

Thus, while there generally is no common law requirement that counterclaims arising from the same transaction or occurrence that is the subject of the plaintiff's claims be asserted, Rule 13(a) or its state-court equivalent requires the filing of such counterclaims in most cases.

---

[2]   The one other situation in which a mandatory counterclaim may be required absent a mandatory counterclaim rule or statute is if the "relationship between the counterclaim and the plaintiff's claim is such that successful prosecution of the second action would nullify the initial judgment or would impair rights established in the initial action." *Restatement (Second) of Judgments* § 22(2)(b) (1982). These situations rarely occur. "The [mandatory] counterclaim must be such that its successful prosecution in a subsequent action would nullify the judgment, for example, by allowing the defendant to enjoin enforcement of the judgment, or to recover on a restitution theory the amount paid pursuant to the judgment * * *, or by depriving the plaintiff in the first action of property rights vested in him under the first judgment * * *." *Restatement (Second) of Judgments* § 22 cmt. f (1982).

4.   HYPOTHETICALS CONCERNING THE PRECLUSION OF DEFENSES AND COUNTERCLAIMS

Answer the following hypotheticals concerning the possible preclusion of defenses and counterclaims. All hypotheticals stem from an accident involving a car and a truck and the negligence action brought by the driver of the car against the driver of the truck. Assume that the truck driver received notice of the first action and was subject to personal jurisdiction in that action.

a.   Presume that the truck driver did not appear in the first suit and a default judgment was entered against him. The car driver then files suit to enforce this judgment in another state. In this second action, can the truck driver raise the defense that the car driver was contributorily negligent?

b.   Presume again that the truck driver did not appear in the first action and a default judgment was entered against him. Can the truck driver file a separate lawsuit against the car driver based upon the car driver's alleged negligence?

c.   Presume that the truck driver defended the first suit on the grounds that the car driver was negligent. If judgment is entered for the truck driver in this action, can the truck driver then file a separate action against the car driver seeking recovery due to the car driver's negligence?

d.   Presume again that the truck driver defended the first action on the grounds that the car driver was negligent. If the jury finds for the car driver and a judgment is entered against the truck driver, could the truck driver bring a second suit against the car driver based upon the car driver's alleged negligence—assuming that contributory negligence is a complete defense to a negligence action in this state?

e.   Presume that, after the car driver files his initial suit against the truck driver, the parties settle the lawsuit and the truck driver pays $10,000 to the car driver. Can the truck driver then sue the car driver based upon the car driver's alleged negligence?

III. ISSUE PRECLUSION

Whether or not claim preclusion applies, an issue may have been decided in an initial action that is the same as an issue in a later action. Issue preclusion (or "collateral estoppel") is the doctrine under which a party may be precluded from relitigating that issue in the later action.

Section 17(3) of the *Restatement (Second) of Judgments* provides:

A valid and final personal judgment is conclusive between the parties, except on appeal or other direct review, to the following extent:

* * *

> (3) A judgment in favor of either the plaintiff or the defendant is conclusive, in a subsequent action between them on the same or a different claim, with respect to any issue actually litigated and determined if its determination was essential to that judgment.

So, in order for issue preclusion to apply, the classic definition of issue preclusion requires:

(1)   same issue in first and second action;

(2)   same parties in first and second action;

(3)   valid judgment in the first action;

(4)   final judgment in the first action;

(5)   the issue subject to preclusion was litigated and determined in the first action; and

(6)   the issue subject to preclusion was essential to the first judgment.

As we will see, the traditional requirement that the parties be the same in both actions (the requirement of "mutuality") has been discarded in some situations in many courts. This, and the other requirements for issue preclusion, will be considered in turn.[3]

A.   WHAT'S THE "SAME ISSUE" FOR THE PURPOSES OF ISSUE PRECLUSION?

Under what circumstances might a party attempt to use issue preclusion (collateral estoppel) to avoid relitigation of an issue that was decided between the same parties in an earlier action? Consider the following example. A seller sues to recover an installment payment due under the parties' contract. The buyer's sole defense is that the contract is unenforceable because it has not been reduced to writing as required by the statute of frauds. After a bench trial, the judge determines that the statute of frauds does not apply and enters judgment for the seller. In a second action to enforce later installment payments under the contract, the buyer again raises the statute of frauds defense. Because this is the same issue that was decided in the first action and the other requirements for issue preclusion are met, the seller should be able to assert issue preclusion successfully on this issue in the second action. *See Restatement (Second) of Judgments* § 27, ill. 6 (1982).

---

[3]   The issue preclusion requirements that the first judgement is valid and final are the same as the validity and finality requirements for the application of claim preclusion, *supra* pp. 1057, 1066. These requirements therefore will not be discussed again at this point in the text.

While validity and finality are required for the application of both claim and issue preclusion, the claim preclusion requirement that the first judgment is "on the merits" is not a requirement for issue preclusion. Can you think of an issue decided in an action not dismissed on the merits that might be of use in a latter collateral estoppel motion?

Are there situations, though, in which it is more difficult to determine if the same issue is presented in the first and later actions? Consider the following sets of cases.

1. DEFENSIVE ISSUE PRECLUSION (IN WHICH ISSUE PRECLUSION IS ASSERTED DEFENSIVELY BY THE DEFENDANT)

> Case No. 1: A businessman borrows money from the federal government but does not repay those funds. The United States brings a civil fraud action against the businessman. After a bench trial, the judge finds that the United States has not proven fraud and dismisses the action on that basis.

> Case No. 2: The United States then brings a criminal fraud action against the businessman, based upon his failure to repay the loan.

Assuming that the definition of fraud is the same for both civil and criminal purposes, can the businessman collaterally estop the United States on the factual issues concerning fraud in the second (criminal) action?

What if the criminal action goes to judgment first?

> Case No. 1: The United States brings a criminal fraud action against the businessman. After a bench trial, the judge dismisses the action based on her finding that the United States did not prove fraud.

> Case No. 2: The United States then brings a civil fraud action against the businessman, based upon his failure to repay the loan.

Can the businessman collaterally estop the United States on the factual issues concerning fraud in the second (civil) action?

2. OFFENSIVE ISSUE PRECLUSION (IN WHICH ISSUE PRECLUSION IS ASSERTED OFFENSIVELY BY THE PLAINTIFF)

> Case No. 1: A businessman borrows money from the federal government but does not repay those funds. The United States brings a criminal fraud action against the businessman, and the businessman is convicted of this crime.

> Case No. 2: The United States then brings a civil fraud action against the businessman, seeking damages resulting from his failure to repay the loan.

Assuming that the definition of fraud is the same for both criminal and civil purposes, can the United States collaterally estop the businessman on the factual issues concerning fraud in the second (civil) action?

What if the order of the actions is reversed?

Case No. 1: The United States brings a civil fraud action against the businessman, seeking damages resulting from his failure to repay the loan. The jury returns a damages verdict for the United States.

Case No. 2: The United States follows its civil action with a criminal prosecution for fraud involving the failure to repay the loan.

Can the United States collaterally estop the businessman on the factual issues concerning fraud in the second (criminal) action?

In most cases it will not be difficult to determine whether an issue in the second action is the same as an issue decided in the first action. In making that determination, though, it may be necessary to consider the procedural posture in which that issue was determined. Deciding a certain fact under a preponderance of the evidence standard in a civil action is not the same as deciding that issue under a beyond a reasonable doubt standard in a criminal action. Preclusion cannot be applied in a criminal action based on the successful assertion of a matter in an earlier civil action. However, the establishment of an issue in an initial criminal action could serve as the basis for issue preclusion in a later civil action. If the issue is initially determined in a criminal action, that determination should provide the basis for issue preclusion in either a later civil or criminal action—so long as the other requirements for issue preclusion are met.

B. WHEN IS AN ISSUE "LITIGATED AND DETERMINED" IN A PRIOR ACTION?

Sometimes the question may not be whether the same issue is presented in the current and a prior action, but whether that issue was decided in the first action. This can be a problem when the first action was resolved by a general jury verdict, as illustrated in the next case. Underlying the reasoning of the court is the fact that, at the time of this action, Indiana law provided that contributory negligence was a complete bar to recovery in negligence actions such as this.

Illinois Central Gulf Railroad Company v. Parks

Court of Appeals of Indiana, First District, 1979
181 Ind. App. 141

OPINION

■ LYBROOK, JUDGE.

[Following an accident in which an Illinois Central train crashed into the car that Jessie Parks was driving and in which Bertha Parks was a passenger, the Parks filed two lawsuits in state court:

(1) The present action, in which Jessie Parks sought damages for his own personal injuries; and

(2) A separate, companion action, in which Bertha Parks sought damages for her personal injuries and Jessie sought damages for the loss of Bertha's services and consortium due to the injuries to Bertha.

The jury in the companion action returned a verdict of $30,000 for Bertha and a verdict for the Illinois Central on Jessie's claim. Based upon these verdicts, the Illinois Central filed a motion for summary judgment in the present case. It argued that, because the jury in the first action ruled against Jessie while returning a $30,000 verdict for Bertha, that jury had determined that Jessie was contributorily negligent and judgment should be entered against him in the present action. Jessie Parks also filed a motion for summary judgment, asserting that, because Bertha had been awarded $30,000 in the first action, that jury had determined that the Illinois Central was negligent and that its negligence was the proximate cause of Jessie's and Bertha's injuries.

The trial judge granted Jessie's motion and denied the motion of the Illinois Central, concluding that "the issues to be determined at the trial of this cause will be whether the plaintiff [Jessie] was guilty of contributory negligence, whether the contributory negligence of the plaintiff proximately contributed to the accident, injuries and damages complained of and whether plaintiff sustained injuries and damages." The Illinois Central then filed its interlocutory appeal.]

We begin, as did the railroad in its brief to this court, with the definitive and often-quoted statement on the law of Res judicata in this state from the opinion of Judge Shake in *Town of Flora v. Indiana Service Corporation*, (1944) 222 Ind. 253, 256–57:

> There are two well defined branches of the rule of Res judicata. The subject has often been confused by the loose use of descriptive terms. One branch of the subject [claim preclusion] deals with prior adjudication as a bar. Under it a cause of action finally determined between the parties on the merits by a court of competent jurisdiction, cannot again be litigated by new proceedings before the same or any other tribunal, except by way of review according to law. Such a judgment or decree so rendered is a complete bar to any subsequent action on the same claim or cause of action, between the same parties, or those in privity with them. Every question which was within the issues, and which, under the issues, might have been proved, will be presumed to have been proved and adjudicated. This rule is perhaps best described as "estoppel by judgment."
>
> The other branch of the subject [issue preclusion] applies where the causes of action are not the same, but where some fact or question has been determined and adjudicated in the former suit, and the same fact or question is again put in issue in a subsequent suit between the same parties. In such cases

the former adjudication of the fact or question, if properly presented and relied on, will be held conclusive on the parties in the latter suit, regardless of the identity of the causes of action, or the lack of it, in the two suits. When the second action between the same parties is on a different cause of action, claim, or demand, it is well settled that the judgment in the first suit operates as an estoppel only as to the point or question actually litigated and determined, and not as to other matters which might have been litigated and determined. In such cases the inquiry must always be as to the point or question actually litigated and determined in the original action. This branch of the subject may appropriately be described as "estoppel by verdict or finding."

Illinois Central Gulf's first allegation of error is an attempt to apply estoppel by judgment [claim preclusion] in the case at bar, but the railroad concedes its own argument by admitting that Jessie's cause of action for loss of services and consortium as a derivative of Bertha's personal injuries is a distinct cause of action from Jessie's claim for damages for his own personal injuries.

Estoppel by judgment precludes the relitigation of a Cause of action finally determined between the parties, and decrees that a judgment rendered is a complete bar to any subsequent action on the same claim or cause of action. Jessie's cause of action in the case at bar is a different cause of action from the one he litigated in the companion case; therefore, estoppel by judgment does not apply.

Estoppel by verdict [issue preclusion], however, does apply. Using Judge Shake's terminology, the causes of action are not the same but, if the case at bar were to go to trial on all the issues raised in the pleadings and answer, some facts or questions determined and adjudicated in the companion case would again be put in issue in this subsequent action between the same parties.

To protect the integrity of the prior judgment by precluding the possibility of opposite results by two different juries on the same set of facts, *Nichols* [*v. Yater*, 147 Ind. App. 141 (1970)], the doctrine of estoppel by verdict allows the judgment in the prior action to operate as an estoppel as to those facts or questions actually litigated and determined in the prior action. The problem at hand, then, is to determine what facts or questions were actually litigated and determined in the companion case.

We agree with three concessions made by Illinois Central Gulf as to the effect of the verdict in the prior case: 1) that the verdict in favor of Bertha established, among other things, that the railroad was negligent and that its negligence was a proximate cause of the accident and Bertha's injuries; 2) that, inasmuch as Jessie's action for loss of services and consortium was derivative, if Jessie sustained any such loss it was proximately caused by the railroad's negligence; and 3) that, in order for the jury to have returned a verdict against Jessie, it had to have decided that he either sustained no damages or that his own negligence was a proximate cause of his damages.

This third proposition places upon the railroad the heavy burden outlined by Judge Shake in *Flora, supra,* 222 Ind. at 257–58:

> (W)here a judgment may have been based upon either or any of two or more distinct facts, a party desiring to plead the judgment as an estoppel by verdict or finding upon the particular fact involved in a subsequent suit must show that it went upon that fact, or else the question will be open to a new contention. The estoppel of a judgment is only presumptively conclusive, when it appears that the judgment could not have been rendered without deciding the particular matter brought in question. It is necessary to look to the complete record to ascertain what was the question in issue.

The railroad argues that, because Jessie's evidence as to his loss of services and consortium was uncontroverted, the jury's verdict had to be based upon a finding of contributory negligence. Illinois Central Gulf made this same argument in the companion case in relation to a related issue and Jessie countered, as he does here, with his contention that, although the evidence was uncontroverted, it was minimal and, thus, could have caused the jury to find no compensable damages. We reviewed the complete record in the companion case and held that the jury verdict against Jessie in that cause could mean that he had failed his burden of proving compensable damages. * * *

We hold that Illinois Central Gulf has failed its burden of showing that the judgment against Jessie in the prior action could not have been rendered without deciding that Jessie was contributorily negligent in the accident which precipitated the two lawsuits. Consequently, the trial court was correct in granting partial summary judgment estopping the railroad from denying its negligence and in limiting the issues at trial to whether Jessie was contributorily negligent, whether any such contributory negligence was a proximate cause of the accident, and whether Jessie sustained personal injuries and compensable damages.

* * *

Finding no error in the trial court's interlocutory order, we affirm. Affirmed.

■ LOWDERMILK, P. J., and ROBERTSON, J., concur.

COMMENTS AND QUESTIONS CONCERNING ILLINOIS CENTRAL GULF RAILROAD CO. V. PARKS

1. Why isn't Jessie's claim for personal injuries barred by claim preclusion? Would it be under Section 24 of the *Restatement (Second) of*

Judgments, because the two actions arise from the same "transaction, or series of connected transactions?" *See Beegan v. Schmidt, supra* p. 1039.

2.   Does the apparent problem with applying issue preclusion stem from the general verdicts that the jury returned in the first case? Is there a way to lessen these problems by determining just what the first jury actually determined?

3.   What are we concerned about in cases such as this—efficiency or consistency in the determinations in the separate actions? Which goal is more important?

4.   If the jury in the first action concluded that Jessie suffered no damages (and therefore returned a verdict for the Illinois Central), how could a jury in the second action return a damages award for him?

5.   While rejecting the Illinois Central's attempt to preclude Jessie on the issue of contributory negligence, the Indiana Court of Appeals upheld the trial court's imposition of issue preclusion against the Illinois Central. On what issue? How are the requirements for issue preclusion on these issues satisfied?

6.   What will the trial look like now that the trial judge's order on issue preclusion has been affirmed?

C. WHEN IS AN ISSUE "ESSENTIAL" TO THE FIRST JUDGMENT?

In some cases it's clear that the issue presented in the second action was litigated and decided in the first action. But what if there was more than one basis for the first judgment? Issue preclusion only can apply if the issue on which preclusion is sought was essential to the first judgment.

Assume that a judge dismisses a state court action in a written opinion concluding both that (1) the state court has no subject-matter jurisdiction over the action and (2) the defendant is not subject to personal jurisdiction in that state. The plaintiff then files the same action in federal court in that same state.

First, be sure to understand why the plaintiff can file the same action in a federal court without running afoul of claim preclusion. Then assume that the defendant seeks to dismiss the action based on the determination in the first action that the defendant is not subject to personal jurisdiction in that state. Should the federal judge grant this motion?

The issue and parties are the same in both actions, there was a final and valid judgment in the first action, and the lack of personal jurisdiction over the defendant in that state was litigated and determined in the first action. Why must that issue also have been essential to the first judgment—especially when the first judge actually wrote an opinion discussing why the defendant was not subject to personal jurisdiction?

The federal judge, following the *Restatement (Second) of Judgments*, would not grant this motion to dismiss. Section 27 of the *Second Restatement* provides:

> When an issue of fact or law is actually litigated and determined by a valid and final judgment, and the determination is essential to the judgment, the determination is conclusive in a subsequent action between the parties, whether on the same or a different claim.

In some cases, issue preclusion can raise issues similar to those presented by dicta in a judicial opinion. We assume that a judge may not focus as carefully on dicta, or anything not essential to the outcome of his opinion, as he would if there were a single, essential reason for reaching the conclusion that he does.

The *Restatement (Second) of Judgments* § 27, cmt. I (1982) lists several reasons why, if a judgment is based on the determination of two or more issues, either of which could independently support the judgment, neither of those issues is considered essential for issue preclusion:

> First, a determination in the alternative may not have been as carefully or rigorously considered as it would have if it had been necessary to the result, and in that sense it has some of the characteristics of dicta. Second, and of critical importance, the losing party, although entitled to appeal from both determinations, might be dissuaded from doing so because of the likelihood that at least one of them would be upheld and the other not even reached. If he were to appeal solely for the purpose of avoiding the application of the rule of issue preclusion, then the rule might be responsible for increasing the burdens of litigation on the parties and the courts rather than lightening those burdens. * * * There may be causes where, despite these considerations, the balance tips in favor of preclusion because of the fullness with which the issue was litigated and decided in the first action. But since the question of preclusion will almost always be a close one if each case is to rest on its own particular facts, it is in the interest of predictability and simplicity for the result of nonpreclusion to be uniform.

When a judgment rests on two or more bases, the adversarial process simply breaks down. The judge may not focus as much on alternative bases for a conclusion as he otherwise might, the losing party may not have any incentive to appeal, and the winning party may not vigorously argue on appeal in support of multiple, alternative grounds of decision.

These situations are treated differently in the *Restatement (Second) of Judgments* and the earlier *Restatement (First) of Judgments*. The

Restatement (First) concluded: "It seems obvious that it should not be held that neither [alternative ground] is material, and hence both should be held to be material." *Restatement (First) of Judgments* § 68 cmt. n (1942).

While disagreeing with the "obvious" conclusion of the first *Restatement* that all alternative grounds are essential to an initial judgment, the *Restatement (Second)* does follow the *Restatement (First)* when one or more of those alternative grounds are affirmed on appeal. Comment o to Section 27 of the *Second Restatement* provides:

> If the judgment of the court of first instance was based on a determination of two issues, either of which standing independently would be sufficient to support the result, and the appellate court upholds both of these determinations as sufficient, and accordingly affirms the judgment, the judgment is conclusive as to both determinations. * * * [T]he losing party has here obtained an appellate decision on the issue, and thus the balance weighs in favor of preclusion.

> If the appellate court upholds one of these determinations as sufficient but not the other, and accordingly affirms the judgment, the judgment is conclusive as to the first determination

> If the appellate court upholds one of these determinations as sufficient and refuses to consider whether or not the other is sufficient and accordingly affirms the judgment, the judgment is conclusive as to the first determination.

Test your understanding of the *Restatement (Second)* by answering the following questions.

(1) A borrower brought a declaratory judgment action against a bank, alleging that the terms of the borrower's loan were illegal under federal law. After trial, the jury returned a general verdict for the bank plus answers to written questions. In these written questions, the jury accepted both of the bank's defenses, finding that (1) the borrower fraudulently procured the loan and (2) the loan complied with federal law.

The borrower then brought a second action against the bank, alleging that another loan, obtained with the first loan, did not comply with federal law. The bank moved for summary judgment, seeking to estop the borrower with the jury's finding from the first action that the borrower obtained the loan fraudulently. Should issue preclusion be applied?

(2) Assume the same loan as described in the first problem. Also assume that the borrower appealed the first judgment and the court of appeals affirmed that judgment on both grounds relied upon by the jury. Should issue preclusion be applied in the second action?

(3) Assume the same loan as described in the first problem. Also assume that the borrower appealed the first judgment and the court of appeals affirmed that judgment on only the issue of the borrower's fraud. Should issue preclusion be applied in the second action?

D. MUST THE PARTIES ALWAYS BE THE SAME FOR ISSUE PRECLUSION TO APPLY?

For claim preclusion to apply, the parties must be the same in the first and the second actions (or be in privity with a party to the first action). However, because the claim also must be the same in the first and second actions, the parties' identity typically is not an issue with respect to claim preclusion.

At common law the parties in the first and second actions also had to be identical for issue preclusion to apply, just as is required for the application of claim preclusion. The Supreme Court stated more than 100 years ago in *Bigelow v. Old Dominion Copper Mining and Smelting Co.*, 225 U.S. 111, 127 (1912): "It is a principle of general elementary law that the estoppel of a judgment must be mutual."

However, the underlying rationale for the requirement of mutuality was not so clear, and exceptions to the requirement began to appear in both federal and state courts.

> By far the most common [exceptions] in the 20th Century involved a judgment in favor of an employee in an action for negligence, followed by an action against the employer to recover for the same negligence. If the employee won the first action, the employer can assert claim preclusion; if the employee lost, the employer is free to relitigate all issues but the maximum recovery by the plaintiff is limited to the amount of the judgment in the first action. Other relationships commonly involved in narrow exception cases have included the driver of an automobile and an owner sued under an owner's liability statute, a subcontractor and a contractor liable for proper performance of the entire contract, a contractor and a property owner subject to a nondelegable duty to protect others against injury, a primary obligor and a surety or guarantor, and businesses that have extended comparable warranties or similar protections in successive sales transactions.

18A C. Wright, A. Miller & E. Cooper, *Federal Practice and Procedure* § 4463, at 681 (2nd ed. 2002).

To prohibit non-mutual issue preclusion in such indemnification situations would create unfairness—leading the courts to create exceptions to the issue preclusion requirement of mutuality.

An apparent exception to this rule of mutuality had been held to exist where the liability of the defendant is altogether dependent upon the culpability of one exonerated in a prior suit, upon the same facts when sued by the same plaintiff. The unilateral character of the estoppel of an adjudication in such cases is justified by the injustice which would result in allowing a recovery against a defendant for conduct of another, when that other has been exonerated in a direct suit. The cases in which it has been enforced are cases where the relation between the defendants in the two suits has been that of principal and agent, master and servant, or indemnitor and indemnitee.

Bigelow v. Old Dominion Copper Mining & Smelting Co., 225 U.S. 111, 127 (1912).

Efforts to circumvent the requirement of mutuality outside indemnification situations continued throughout the middle and later parts of the 20th Century. These cases sought to expand the number of persons who could assert issue preclusion—not the number of persons against whom issue preclusion could be asserted. With or without mutuality, only a person who was a party to the first action can be bound—through claim or issue preclusion—by a judgment in that action.

Consider the following case concerning the possibility of non-mutual offensive collateral estoppel in the federal courts.

1.   *PARKLANE HOSIERY CO. INC. V. SHORE*

Parklane Hosiery Company, Inc. v. Shore

United States Supreme Court, 1979
439 U.S. 322

OPINION

■ MR. JUSTICE STEWART delivered the opinion of the Court.

This case presents the question whether a party who has had issues of fact adjudicated adversely to it in an equitable action may be collaterally estopped from relitigating the same issues before a jury in a subsequent legal action brought against it by a new party.

The respondent brought this stockholder's class action against the petitioners in a Federal District Court. The complaint alleged that the petitioners, Parklane Hosiery Co., Inc. (Parklane), and 13 of its officers, directors, and stockholders, had issued a materially false and misleading proxy statement in connection with a merger. The proxy statement, according to the complaint, had violated §§ 14(a), 10(b), and 20(a) of the Securities Exchange Act of 1934, as amended, 15 U.S.C. §§ 78n(a), 78j(b), and 78t(a), as well as various rules and regulations promulgated by the Securities and Exchange Commission (SEC). The complaint sought damages, rescission of the merger, and recovery of costs.

Before this action came to trial, the SEC filed suit against the same defendants in the Federal District Court, alleging that the proxy statement that had been issued by Parklane was materially false and misleading in essentially the same respects as those that had been alleged in the respondent's complaint. Injunctive relief was requested. After a 4-day trial, the District Court found that the proxy statement was materially false and misleading in the respects alleged, and entered a declaratory judgment to that effect. The Court of Appeals for the Second Circuit affirmed this judgment.

The respondent in the present case then moved for partial summary judgment against the petitioners, asserting that the petitioners were collaterally estopped from relitigating the issues that had been resolved against them in the action brought by the SEC.[2] The District Court denied the motion on the ground that such an application of collateral estoppel would deny the petitioners their Seventh Amendment right to a jury trial. The Court of Appeals for the Second Circuit reversed, holding that a party who has had issues of fact determined against him after a full and fair opportunity to litigate in a nonjury trial is collaterally estopped from obtaining a subsequent jury trial of these same issues of fact. The appellate court concluded that "the Seventh Amendment preserves the right to jury trial only with respect to issues of fact, [and] once those issues have been fully and fairly adjudicated in a prior proceeding, nothing remains for trial, either with or without a jury." Because of an inter-circuit conflict, we granted certiorari.

The threshold question to be considered is whether, quite apart from the right to a jury trial under the Seventh Amendment, the petitioners can be precluded from relitigating facts resolved adversely to them in a prior equitable proceeding with another party under the general law of collateral estoppel. Specifically, we must determine whether a litigant who was not a party to a prior judgment may nevertheless use that judgment "offensively" to prevent a defendant from relitigating issues resolved in the earlier proceeding.[4]

---

[2] A private plaintiff in an action under the proxy rules is not entitled to relief simply by demonstrating that the proxy solicitation was materially false and misleading. The plaintiff must also show that he was injured and prove damages. *Mills v. Electric Auto-Lite Co.*, 396 U.S. 375, 386–390. Since the SEC action was limited to a determination of whether the proxy statement contained materially false and misleading information, the respondent conceded that he would still have to prove these other elements of his prima facie case in the private action. The petitioners' right to a jury trial on those remaining issues is not contested.

[4] In this context, offensive use of collateral estoppel occurs when the plaintiff seeks to foreclose the defendant from litigating an issue the defendant has previously litigated unsuccessfully in an action with another party. Defensive use occurs when a defendant seeks to prevent a plaintiff from asserting a claim the plaintiff has previously litigated and lost against another defendant.

A.

Collateral estoppel, like the related doctrine of res judicata,[5] has the dual purpose of protecting litigants from the burden of relitigating an identical issue with the same party or his privy and of promoting judicial economy by preventing needless litigation. *Blonder-Tongue Laboratories, Inc. v. University of Illinois Foundation*, 402 U.S. 313, 328–329. Until relatively recently, however, the scope of collateral estoppel was limited by the doctrine of mutuality of parties. Under this mutuality doctrine, neither party could use a prior judgment as an estoppel against the other unless both parties were bound by the judgment. Based on the premise that it is somehow unfair to allow a party to use a prior judgment when he himself would not be so bound,[7] the mutuality requirement provided a party who had litigated and lost in a previous action an opportunity to relitigate identical issues with new parties.

By failing to recognize the obvious difference in position between a party who has never litigated an issue and one who has fully litigated and lost, the mutuality requirement was criticized almost from its inception. Recognizing the validity of this criticism, the Court in *Blonder-Tongue Laboratories, Inc. v. University of Illinois Foundation, supra*, abandoned the mutuality requirement, at least in cases where a patentee seeks to relitigate the validity of a patent after a federal court in a previous lawsuit has already declared it invalid. The "broader question" before the Court, however, was "whether it is any longer tenable to afford a litigant more than one full and fair opportunity for judicial resolution of the same issue." 402 U.S., at 328. The Court strongly suggested a negative answer to that question:

> "In any lawsuit where a defendant, because of the mutuality principle, is forced to present a complete defense on the merits to a claim which the plaintiff has fully litigated and lost in a prior action, there is an arguable misallocation of resources. To the extent the defendant in the second suit may not win by asserting, without contradiction, that the plaintiff had fully and fairly, but unsuccessfully, litigated the same claim in the prior suit, the defendant's time and money are diverted from alternative uses—productive or otherwise—to relitigation of a decided issue. And, still assuming that the issue was resolved correctly in the first suit, there is reason to be concerned about the plaintiff's allocation of resources. Permitting repeated

---

[5] Under the doctrine of res judicata, a judgment on the merits in a prior suit bars a second suit involving the same parties or their privies based on the same cause of action. Under the doctrine of collateral estoppel, on the other hand, the second action is upon a different cause of action and the judgment in the prior suit precludes relitigation of issues actually litigated and necessary to the outcome of the first action.

[7] It is a violation of due process for a judgment to be binding on a litigant who was not a party or a privy and therefore has never had an opportunity to be heard. *Blonder-Tongue Laboratories, Inc. v. University of Illinois Foundation*, 402 U.S. 313, 329; *Hansberry v. Lee*, 311 U. S. 32, 40.

litigation of the same issue as long as the supply of unrelated defendants holds out reflects either the aura of the gaming table or 'a lack of discipline and of disinterestedness on the part of the lower courts, hardly a worthy or wise basis for fashioning rules of procedure.' *Kerotest Mfg. Co. v. C-O-Two Co.*, 342 U.S. 180, 185 (1952). Although neither judges, the parties, nor the adversary system performs perfectly in all cases, the requirement of determining whether the party against whom an estoppel is asserted had a full and fair opportunity to litigate is a most significant safeguard." *Id.*, at 329.[10]

B

The *Blonder-Tongue* case involved defensive use of collateral estoppel—a plaintiff was estopped from asserting a claim that the plaintiff had previously litigated and lost against another defendant. The present case, by contrast, involves offensive use of collateral estoppel—a plaintiff is seeking to estop a defendant from relitigating the issues which the defendant previously litigated and lost against another plaintiff. In both the offensive and defensive use situations, the party against whom estoppel is asserted has litigated and lost in an earlier action. Nevertheless, several reasons have been advanced why the two situations should be treated differently.

First, offensive use of collateral estoppel does not promote judicial economy in the same manner as defensive use does. Defensive use of collateral estoppel precludes a plaintiff from relitigating identical issues by merely "switching adversaries." *Bernhard v. Bank of America Nat. Trust & Savings Assn.*, 19 Cal.2d, at 813.[12] Thus defensive collateral estoppel gives a plaintiff a strong incentive to join all potential defendants in the first action if possible. Offensive use of collateral estoppel, on the other hand, creates precisely the opposite incentive. Since a plaintiff will be able to rely on a previous judgment against a defendant but will not be bound by that judgment if the defendant wins, the plaintiff has every incentive to adopt a "wait and see" attitude, in the hope that the first action by another plaintiff will result in a favorable judgment. Thus offensive use of collateral estoppel will likely increase rather than decrease the total amount of litigation, since potential plaintiffs will have everything to gain and nothing to lose by not intervening in the first action.

---

[10] The Court also emphasized that relitigation of issues previously adjudicated is particularly wasteful in patent cases because of their staggering expense and typical length. 402 U.S., at 334, 348. Under the doctrine of mutuality of parties an alleged infringer might find it cheaper to pay royalties than to challenge a patent that had been declared invalid in a prior suit, since the holder of the patent is entitled to a statutory presumption of validity. *Id.*, at 338.

[12] Under the mutuality requirement, a plaintiff could accomplish this result since he would not have been bound by the judgment had the original defendant won.

A second argument against offensive use of collateral estoppel is that it may be unfair to a defendant. If a defendant in the first action is sued for small or nominal damages, he may have little incentive to defend vigorously, particularly if future suits are not foreseeable. *The Evergreens v. Nunan*, 141 F.2d 927, 929 (CA2); cf. *Berner v. British Commonwealth Pac. Airlines*, 346 F.2d 532 (CA2) (application of offensive collateral estoppel denied where defendant did not appeal an adverse judgment awarding damages of $35,000 and defendant was later sued for over $7 million). Allowing offensive collateral estoppel may also be unfair to a defendant if the judgment relied upon as a basis for the estoppel is itself inconsistent with one or more previous judgments in favor of the defendant.[14] Still another situation where it might be unfair to apply offensive estoppel is where the second action affords the defendant procedural opportunities unavailable in the first action that could readily cause a different result.[15]

C

We have concluded that the preferable approach for dealing with these problems in the federal courts is not to preclude the use of offensive collateral estoppel, but to grant trial courts broad discretion to determine when it should be applied. The general rule should be that in cases where a plaintiff could easily have joined in the earlier action or where, either for the reasons discussed above or for other reasons, the application of offensive estoppel would be unfair to a defendant, a trial judge should not allow the use of offensive collateral estoppel.

In the present case, however, none of the circumstances that might justify reluctance to allow the offensive use of collateral estoppel is present. The application of offensive collateral estoppel will not here reward a private plaintiff who could have joined in the previous action, since the respondent probably could not have joined in the injunctive action brought by the SEC even had he so desired. Similarly, there is no unfairness to the petitioners in applying offensive collateral estoppel in this case. First, in light of the serious allegations made in the SEC's complaint against the petitioners, as well as the foreseeability of subsequent private suits that typically follow a successful Government judgment, the petitioners had every incentive to litigate the SEC

---

[14] In Professor Currie's familiar example, a railroad collision injures 50 passengers all of whom bring separate actions against the railroad. After the railroad wins the first 25 suits, a plaintiff wins in suit 26. Professor Currie argues that offensive use of collateral estoppel should not be applied so as to allow plaintiffs 27 through 50 automatically to recover. Currie, *supra*, 9 Stan.L.Rev., at 304. *See Restatement (Second) of Judgments* § 88(4), *supra*.

[15] If, for example, the defendant in the first action was forced to defend in an inconvenient forum and therefore was unable to engage in full scale discovery or call witnesses, application of offensive collateral estoppel may be unwarranted. Indeed, differences in available procedures may sometimes justify not allowing a prior judgment to have estoppel effect in a subsequent action even between the same parties, or where defensive estoppel is asserted against a plaintiff who has litigated and lost. The problem of unfairness is particularly acute in cases of offensive estoppel, however, because the defendant against whom estoppel is asserted typically will not have chosen the forum in the first action. *See id.*, § 88(2) and Comment d.

lawsuit fully and vigorously.[18] Second, the judgment in the SEC action was not inconsistent with any previous decision. Finally, there will in the respondent's action be no procedural opportunities available to the petitioners that were unavailable in the first action of a kind that might be likely to cause a different result.[19]

We conclude, therefore, that none of the considerations that would justify a refusal to allow the use of offensive collateral estoppel is present in this case. Since the petitioners received a "full and fair" opportunity to litigate their claims in the SEC action, the contemporary law of collateral estoppel leads inescapably to the conclusion that the petitioners are collaterally estopped from relitigating the question of whether the proxy statement was materially false and misleading.

II

The question that remains is whether, notwithstanding the law of collateral estoppel, the use of offensive collateral estoppel in this case would violate the petitioners' Seventh Amendment right to a jury trial.

A

"[T]he thrust of the [Seventh] Amendment was to preserve the right to jury trial as it existed in 1791." *Curtis v. Loether*, 415 U.S. 189, 193. At common law, a litigant was not entitled to have a jury determine issues that had been previously adjudicated by a chancellor in equity.

Recognition that an equitable determination could have collateral-estoppel effect in a subsequent legal action was the major premise of this Court's decision in *Beacon Theatres, Inc. v. Westover*, 359 U.S. 500. In that case the plaintiff sought a declaratory judgment that certain arrangements between it and the defendant were not in violation of the antitrust laws, and asked for an injunction to prevent the defendant from instituting an antitrust action to challenge the arrangements. The defendant denied the allegations and counterclaimed for treble damages under the antitrust laws, requesting a trial by jury of the issues common to both the legal and equitable claims. The Court of Appeals upheld denial of the request, but this Court reversed, stating: "[T]he effect of the action of the District Court could be, as the Court of Appeals believed, 'to limit the petitioner's opportunity fully to try to a jury every issue which has a bearing upon its treble damage suit,' for determination of the issue of clearances by the judge might 'operate

---

[18] After a 4-day trial in which the petitioners had every opportunity to present evidence and call witnesses, the District Court held for the SEC. The petitioners then appealed to the Court of Appeals for the Second Circuit, which affirmed the judgment against them. Moreover, the petitioners were already aware of the action brought by the respondent, since it had commenced before the filing of the SEC action.

[19] It is true, of course, that the petitioners in the present action would be entitled to a jury trial of the issues bearing on whether the proxy statement was materially false and misleading had the SEC action never been brought—a matter to be discussed in Part II of this opinion. But the presence or absence of a jury as factfinder is basically neutral, quite unlike, for example, the necessity of defending the first lawsuit in an inconvenient forum.

either by way of res judicata or collateral estoppel so as to conclude both parties with respect thereto at the subsequent trial of the treble damage claim.' " *Id.*, at 504.

It is thus clear that the Court in the *Beacon Theatres* case thought that if an issue common to both legal and equitable claims was first determined by a judge, relitigation of the issue before a jury might be foreclosed by res judicata or collateral estoppel. To avoid this result, the Court held that when legal and equitable claims are joined in the same action, the trial judge has only limited discretion in determining the sequence of trial and "that discretion . . . must, wherever possible, be exercised to preserve jury trial." *Id.*, at 510.

Both the premise of *Beacon Theatres*, and the fact that it enunciated no more than a general prudential rule were confirmed by this Court's decision in *Katchen v. Landy*, 382 U.S. 323. In that case the Court held that a bankruptcy court, sitting as a statutory court of equity, is empowered to adjudicate equitable claims prior to legal claims, even though the factual issues decided in the equity action would have been triable by a jury under the Seventh Amendment if the legal claims had been adjudicated first. The Court stated:

> "Both *Beacon Theatres* and *Dairy Queen* recognize that there might be situations in which the Court could proceed to resolve the equitable claim first even though the results might be dispositive of the issues involved in the legal claim." *Id.*, at 339.

Thus the Court in *Katchen v. Landy* recognized that an equitable determination can have collateral-estoppel effect in a subsequent legal action and that this estoppel does not violate the Seventh Amendment.

B

Despite the strong support to be found both in history and in the recent decisional law of this Court for the proposition that an equitable determination can have collateral-estoppel effect in a subsequent legal action, the petitioners argue that application of collateral estoppel in this case would nevertheless violate their Seventh Amendment right to a jury trial. The petitioners contend that since the scope of the Amendment must be determined by reference to the common law as it existed in 1791, and since the common law permitted collateral estoppel only where there was mutuality of parties, collateral estoppel cannot constitutionally be applied when such mutuality is absent.

The petitioners have advanced no persuasive reason, however, why the meaning of the Seventh Amendment should depend on whether or not mutuality of parties is present. A litigant who has lost because of adverse factual findings in an equity action is equally deprived of a jury trial whether he is estopped from relitigating the factual issues against the same party or a new party. In either case, the party against whom estoppel is asserted has litigated questions of fact, and has had the facts determined against him in an earlier proceeding. In either case there is no further factfinding function for the jury to perform, since the common factual issues have been resolved in the previous action.

The Seventh Amendment has never been interpreted in the rigid manner advocated by the petitioners. On the contrary, many procedural devices developed since 1791 that have diminished the civil jury's historic domain have been found not to be inconsistent with the Seventh Amendment. *See Galloway v. United States*, 319 U.S. 372, 388–393 (directed verdict does not violate the Seventh Amendment); *Gasoline Products Co. v. Champlin Refining Co.*, 283 U.S. 494, 497–498 (retrial limited to question of damages does not violate the Seventh Amendment even though there was no practice at common law for setting aside a verdict in part); *Fidelity & Deposit Co. v. United States*, 187 U.S. 315, 319–321 (summary judgment does not violate the Seventh Amendment).[23]

The *Galloway* case is particularly instructive. There the party against whom a directed verdict had been entered argued that the procedure was unconstitutional under the Seventh Amendment. In rejecting this claim, the Court said:

> "The Amendment did not bind the federal courts to the exact procedural incidents or details of jury trial according to the common law in 1791, any more than it tied them to the common-law system of pleading or the specific rules of evidence then prevailing. Nor were 'the rules of the common law' then prevalent, including those relating to the procedure by which the judge regulated the jury's role on questions of fact, crystalized in a fixed and immutable system. . . .

> "The more logical conclusion, we think, and the one which both history and the previous decisions here support, is that the Amendment was designed to preserve the basic institution of jury trial in only its most fundamental elements, not the great mass of procedural forms and details, varying even then so widely among common-law jurisdictions." 319 U.S., at 390, 392.

The law of collateral estoppel, like the law in other procedural areas defining the scope of the jury's function, has evolved since 1791. Under the rationale of the *Galloway* case, these developments are not repugnant to the Seventh Amendment simply for the reason that they did not exist in 1791. Thus if, as we have held, the law of collateral

---

[23] The petitioners' reliance on *Dimick v. Schiedt*, 293 U.S. 474, is misplaced. In the *Dimick* case the Court held that an increase by the trial judge of the amount of money damages awarded by the jury violated the *second* clause of the Seventh Amendment, which provides that "no fact tried by a jury, shall be otherwise reexamined in any Court of the United States, than according to the rules of the common law." Collateral estoppel does not involve the "re-examination" of any fact decided by a jury. On the contrary, the whole premise of collateral estoppel is that once an issue has been resolved in a prior proceeding, there is no further factfinding function to be performed.

estoppel forecloses the petitioners from relitigating the factual issues determined against them in the SEC action, nothing in the Seventh Amendment dictates a different result, even though because of lack of mutuality there would have been no collateral estoppel in 1791.

The judgment of the Court of Appeals is

Affirmed.

[Justice Rehnquist, without reaching the question as to whether nonmutual offensive collateral estoppel would be appropriate in a case not implicating the Seventh Amendment, dissented. He stated:

> The right of trial by jury in civil cases at common law is fundamental to our history and jurisprudence. Today, however, the Court reduces this valued right, which Blackstone praised as "the glory of the English law," to a mere "neutral" factor and in the name of procedural reform denies the right of jury trial to defendants in a vast number of cases in which defendants, heretofore, have enjoyed jury trials. Over 35 years ago, Mr. Justice Black lamented the "gradual process of judicial erosion which in one hundred fifty years has slowly worn away a major portion of the essential guarantee of the Seventh Amendment." *Galloway v. United States*, 319 U.S. 372, 397 (1943) (dissenting opinion). Regrettably, the erosive process continues apace with today's decision.

439 U.S. at 338.]

COMMENTS AND QUESTIONS CONCERNING *PARKLANE HOSIERY CO. INC. V. SHORE*

1.   What if the Parklane defendants had prevailed in the SEC's action against them? If this issue had been essential to the first court's judgment, could the defendants collaterally estop Shore on the issue of the allegedly misleading nature of the proxy statement in the second action?

2.   The Supreme Court abandoned the requirement of mutuality of the parties in its earlier decision in *Blonder-Tongue Laboratories, Inc. v. University of Illinois Foundation*, 402 U.S. 313 (1971). Are there reasons that mutuality might not be required for the defensive assertion of collateral estoppel, but still required if a plaintiff attempted to use non-mutual collateral estoppel offensively? If the major concern of a judicial system is efficiency, why might that system endorse defensive non-mutual collateral estoppel but not offensive non-mutual collateral estoppel? Were there reasons why *Blonder-Tongue* was a particularly good case in which to abandon mutuality?

3.   Is it unfair to bind a party to a determination in a prior action that cannot bind the party asserting issue preclusion? Does non-mutual collateral estoppel raise due process questions? Does it raise questions under the famous legal maxim, "What's sauce for the goose is sauce for the gander"?

4.   In footnote 14 of his opinion, Justice Stewart refers to Professor Brainerd Currie's hypothetical in which 50 passengers bring 50 separate actions against a railroad and the actions are tried separately and result in defense verdicts—until a plaintiff finally prevails in the 26th action. The remaining 24 plaintiffs then attempt to use the 26th judgment as the basis for collateral estoppel against the railroad in actions 27–50. Are there real-world realities that would discourage a group of plaintiffs from bringing their actions one-by-one in the hope of creating a judgment that could be used for estoppel purposes? Are there ways in which a court, court system, or the railroad could counter such a strategy?

5.   Justice Stewart writes in *Parklane*:

> We have concluded that the preferable approach for dealing with these problems [of offensive non-mutual collateral estoppel] in the federal courts is not to preclude the use of offensive collateral estoppel, but to grant trial courts broad discretion to determine when it should be applied. The general rule should be that in cases where a plaintiff could easily have joined in the earlier action or where, either for the reasons discussed above or for other reasons, the application of offensive estoppel would be unfair to a defendant, a trial judge should not allow the use of offensive collateral estoppel.

What are the boundaries on district court discretion in such cases?

6.   The Court's first limitation on offensive non-mutual collateral estoppel is that it should not be available "where a plaintiff could easily have joined in the earlier action." Will this limit many of the opportunities for the use of offensive non-mutual collateral estoppel? Consider, though, situations such as *Parklane* in which the first judgment is obtained by the government (perhaps in a criminal antitrust, fraud, or securities action) and plaintiffs attempt to use that judgment as a basis for collateral estoppel in their own private actions.

7.   The second restriction on a district court's discretion to permit offensive non-mutual collateral estoppel is when "the application of offensive estoppel would be unfair to a defendant." In *Parklane*, Justice Stewart concludes that "there will in the respondent's action be no procedural opportunities available to the petitioners that were unavailable in the first action of a kind that might be likely to cause a different result." In footnote 19 of his opinion he simply states that "the presence or absence of a jury as factfinder is basically neutral." What is Justice Stewart's authority for this conclusion? Is this consistent with the Court's decisions in *Beacon Theatres, Inc. v. Westover*, 359 U.S. 500 (1959), and *Dairy Queen v. Wood*, 369 U.S. 469 (1962)? Do you agree?

2.   MUTUALITY OF ESTOPPEL HYPOTHETICALS

Presume that, after a bus crash, Passenger sues Driver for Driver's alleged negligence, with final judgment being entered for Driver in a court of general jurisdiction.

(1) Can Driver collaterally estop a second passenger in a later suit brought against the Driver alleging the same negligence on which there was a special jury finding for Driver in the first action?

(2) Presume that the jury rendered a special verdict in the first action, finding that Passenger was contributorily negligent (contributory negligence being a complete defense in that jurisdiction). If Passenger brings a new action against the bus company, can that new defendant estop Passenger in that action on the issue of Passenger's negligence?

(3) Presume that Passenger obtains a jury verdict and final judgment against Driver in the first action and that no other plaintiffs could have joined in this first action. Can another passenger bring her own action and collaterally estop Driver on the issue of Driver's negligence in that second action?

E. WHEN IS NON-MUTUAL OFFENSIVE COLLATERAL ESTOPPEL UNFAIR TO THE DEFENDANT?

The Supreme Court in *Parklane* limited non-mutual offensive collateral estoppel to situations in which such issue preclusion is fair to the defendant against whom preclusion is invoked. Justice Stewart identified as one specific unfairness: "Allowing offensive collateral estoppel may * * * be unfair to a defendant if the judgment relied upon as a basis for the estoppel is itself inconsistent with one or more previous judgments in favor of the defendant." 439 U.S. at 330. While reading the following opinion, consider the difficulties posed by multiple, inconsistent prior judgments and the potential unfairness of applying any of those judgments against the defendant.

State Farm Fire & Cas. Co. v. Century Home Components, Inc.

Oregon Supreme Court, 1976
275 Or. 97

OPINION

■ HOLMAN, JUSTICE.

Defendant appeals from judgments entered in 13 actions for damages resulting from a fire. These actions were among 48 cases consolidated for a single hearing in the court below on the issue of collateral estoppel. The ruling of the trial court that defendant was collaterally estopped from contesting liability in each of the 48 actions forms the basis for defendant's appeal.

The fire giving rise to this litigation started early one Sunday morning in the summer of 1968. Defendant constructed prefabricated housing in a large shed. Plaintiffs' property was stored in a warehouse which was located approximately 60 feet from defendant's shed and which was connected thereto by a wooden loading dock. On the side of defendant's shed was a wooden box, called a skip box, into which sawdust from a neighboring saw was customarily deposited. On the Saturday evening preceding the fire, defendant's janitor had dumped a mix of linseed oil and dry sawdust into the box. No employees were present at the time the fire started. Whatever its cause and point of origin, and these are in dispute, the fire spread via the loading dock and caused substantial damage to defendant's shed, the warehouse and its contents.

Shortly thereafter various actions, eventually totaling over 50, were filed against defendant to recover for losses from the fire. Three of these actions proceeded separately through trial to final judgment. In each case the plaintiffs alleged essentially that defendant was negligent with respect to both the start and spread of the fire. The first case to come to trial resulted in a jury verdict for defendant. On appeal this court reversed the judgment for error in failing to compel defendant to produce a statement needed by the plaintiff for purposes of impeaching a defense witness, and remanded for a new trial. *Pacific N. W. Bell v. Century Home*, 261 Or. 333 (1972). During the pendency of the foregoing appeal the second case was tried and produced another jury verdict for defendant. *Sylwester v. Century Home Components, Inc.*, No. 92582 (Circuit Court of Oregon for Lane County). No appeal was taken from that judgment and it became final. Shortly thereafter the third case was tried and a jury verdict was returned for the plaintiff. This judgment was affirmed on appeal. *Hesse v. Century Home*, 267 Or. 53 (1973). The *Pacific N. W. Bell* case was subsequently retried, this time to the court sitting without a jury, and the court found for the plaintiff. We affirmed on appeal.

Following entry of final judgment in both *Hesse* and *Pacific N. W. Bell*, the present plaintiffs filed amended and supplemental complaints, conforming their allegations to those in the foregoing cases, and asserted that the judgments therein should operate to preclude defendant from again litigating the question of liability. Defendant alleged in defense that it would be unfair to bar relitigation in view of the similarity of issues between those cases and *Sylwester* and of the existence of the jury verdict and judgment in defendant's favor in *Slywester*. In the consolidated hearing on the question of collateral estoppel the parties submitted the records and transcripts of all three cases. The trial court rendered its ruling in favor of plaintiffs, finding inter alia:

> * * * That the allegations of the second amended and supplemental complaint raising the issue of collateral estoppel have been established by the greater weight of the evidence,

and that the affirmative allegations of the answer thereto have not been established by the evidence. * * *.

To summarize the posture of these cases, the question of defendant's negligence has been tried four times and three final judgments have been rendered. Defendant has procured one favorable judgment (and two jury verdicts) and the claimants have received two judgments. The present plaintiffs, who were not parties to any of the previous actions, seek to utilize the prior claimants' judgments to establish conclusively defendant's negligence and its responsibility for any loss caused by the fire.

* * *

Defendant does not challenge the trial court's conclusion that the issues in *Hesse* and *Pacific N. W. Bell* were identical with the issues in the present cases and that the question of defendant's negligence with respect to the cause and spreading of the fire was decided adversely to defendant in both actions. Nor does it deny, at least with respect to the second *Pacific N. W. Bell* trial, that it had a full and fair opportunity to litigate the issue of negligence. Defendant's only contention is that the trial court erroneously concluded that no unfairness would result from collaterally estopping defendant in the present circumstances.

* * *

The "multiple-claimant anomaly" was first hypothesized by Brainerd Currie as one instance where, absent mutuality, the unrestrained application of collateral estoppel might produce unfair results. Currie, "Mutuality of Collateral Estoppel: Limits of the Bernhard Doctrine," 9 *Stan.L.Rev.* 281 (1957). Currie posed the situation of a train wreck resulting in 50 separate claims being filed against the railroad for negligence. If the defendant railroad won the first 25 cases and subsequently lost the 26th, Currie characterized as an "absurdity" the notion that the remaining 24 claimants could ride in on the strength of the 26th plaintiff's judgment and estop the defendant on the issue of negligence. The reason was that the 26th judgment would clearly seem to be an aberration. Currie then reasoned that, if we should be unwilling to give preclusive effect to the 26th judgment, we should not afford such effect to an adverse judgment rendered in the first action brought because "we have no warrant for assuming that the aberrational judgment will not come as the first in the series." Currie, *Supra* at 289. Currie thus concluded that, absent mutuality, collateral estoppel should not be applied where a defendant potentially faces more than two successive actions. Currie, *Supra* at 308.

Those courts which have discarded the rule of mutuality and permit the offensive assertion of collateral estoppel have generally rejected Currie's solution to the multiple-claimant anomaly in situations where the first judgment is adverse to the defendant, and have precluded a defendant from relitigating multiple claims where it has been concluded that the defendant had in actuality the incentive and complete opportunity to contest the issue fully in the first action. Currie's reservations were based on the apprehension that the first judgment might well be an aberration, but this view failed to recognize that the very notion of collateral estoppel demands and assumes a certain confidence in the integrity of the end result of our adjudicative process. There is no foundation in either experience or policy for accepting the suggestion that a decision rendered after a full and fair presentation of the evidence and issues should be considered either substantially suspect or infected with variables indicating the question might be decided differently in another go-around. Currie subsequently conceded the untenability of his initial position and retreated from it, stating that

> * * * so long as we retain sufficient faith in the institution of trial by jury to retain it for civil cases at all, what warrant is there for mistrusting the verdict for purposes of collateral estoppel when there is no suggestion that there has been compromise or other impropriety? Currie, "Civil Procedure: The Tempest Brews," 53 *Calif.L.Rev.* 25, 36 (1965).

Thus, once it is accepted that the propriety of collateral estoppel is dependent upon the existence of a prior full and fair opportunity to present a case, there seems little reason to limit its application simply because there are multiple claimants in the picture. Although in our adversary system "there is always a lingering question whether the party might have succeeded in proving his point if he had only been given a second chance at producing evidence," *James Talcott, Inc. v. Allahabad Bank, Ltd.*, 444 F.2d 451, 463 (5th Cir.), *cert. denied*, 404 U.S. 940 (1971), the unsubstantiated and conjectural possibility that a party might receive a favorable judgment somewhere down the road is an insufficient reason for refusing to apply collateral estoppel. As we stated in *In re Gygi*, 541 P.2d 1392, 1395 (1975),

> * * * the prior judgment is treated as conclusive, not because it is actually conclusive evidence of the ultimate truth as to those issues necessarily determined, but because of the public interest in the finality of judgments and in the efficient administration of justice. * * *.

The deference we lend prior adjudications is based on our reasonable confidence as to their correctness, rather than on a conviction of their unassailable truth. One of the purposes of the doctrine is to protect the authority of judicial decisions, and this purpose would obviously be ill-served by refusing to give effect to a prior determination on the hypothetical possibility of a contrary decision if the case were continuously retried. *See* Hazard, "Res Nova in Res Judicata," 44 *S.Cal.L.Rev.* 1036, 1041–044 (1971).

As the foregoing discussion would indicate, however, we are not free to disregard incongruous results when they are looking us in the eye. If the circumstances are such that our confidence in the integrity of the determination is severely undermined, or that the result would likely be different in a second trial, it would work an injustice to deny the litigant another chance. Thus, where it is apparent that the verdict was the result of a jury compromise, the losing party should not be precluded by the judgment. *Berner v. British Commonwealth Pacific Airlines, Ltd.*, 346 F.2d 532, 540–41 (2d Cir. 1965), *cert. denied*, 382 U.S. 983 (1966); *Taylor v. Hawkinson*, 47 Cal.2d 893, 896 (1957); *Restatement (Second) of Judgments* § 88(5) (Tent.Draft No. 2, 1975). In *Berner* the additional circumstance that the award of damages of $35,000 was so small in comparison to the $500,000 prayer of the complaint might well have caused the airlines to consider the judgment an actual "victory" and to accept that determination rather than incur the additional expense of appealing for a new trial to rectify whatever errors may have been committed during the course of the trial. It has also been held that if the prior determination was manifestly erroneous the judgment should not be given preclusive effect. *Henderson v. Bardahl Int'l Corp.*, 72 Wash.2d 109 (1967); *Restatement (Second) of Judgments* § 88(7) and comment I. (Tent.Draft No. 2, 1975). And the existence of newly discovered or crucial evidence that was not available to the litigant at the first trial would provide a basis for denying preclusion where it appears the evidence would have a significant effect on the outcome. *See Costello v. Pan American World Airways, Inc.*, 295 F.Supp. 1384, 1389 (SDNY 1969); *Restatement (Second) of Judgments* § 88(7) and comment I. (Tent.Draft No. 2, 1975).

Those courts and commentators which have considered the question are in virtually unanimous agreement that where outstanding determinations are actually inconsistent on the matter sought to be precluded, it would be patently unfair to estop a party by the judgment it lost. Although Currie's initial perceptions provoked much discussion, the problem has remained largely academic because inconsistent verdicts are rarely encountered. Our research has disclosed only one case where inconsistent determinations by separate trial courts were asserted as a reason for denying collateral estoppel. In *Blumcraft of Pittsburgh v. Kawneer Co.*, 482 F.2d 542 (5th Cir. 1973), a patent infringement suit, the court held the plaintiff collaterally estopped, even though inconsistent determinations as to the patent's validity had been reached by separate courts. The court in that case read the U.S. Supreme Court's opinion in *Blonder-Tongue Laboratories, Inc. v. University of Illinois Foundation*, 402 U.S. 313 (1972), to require only one condition for the application of collateral estoppel, which was the existence of one full and fair opportunity to contest the patent's validity. Having concluded that the plaintiff had received such an opportunity in the case it lost, the court held that collateral estoppel was mandated notwithstanding the existence of inconsistent determinations. Although the result may be justified in view of the peculiar nature of patent cases, the complexity of the determination, and the need for finality due to the prohibitive costs of such litigations as were discussed in *Blonder-Tongue*, we are unable to accept the court's reasoning in *Blumcraft*. As we discuss below, the existence of a full and fair opportunity to contest the issue in the adverse case is not the only criterion in this state for the application of estoppel. The court must also consider the fairness under all the circumstances of precluding a party.

We agree with the commentators to the extent at least that, where there are extant determinations that are inconsistent on the matter in issue, it is a strong indication that the application of collateral estoppel would work an injustice. There seems to be something fundamentally offensive about depriving a party of the opportunity to litigate the issue again when he has shown beyond a doubt that on another day he prevailed. As stated by the Tentative Draft of *Restatement (Second) of Judgments*:

> * * * Giving a prior determination of an issue conclusive effect in subsequent litigation is justified not merely as avoiding further costs of litigation but also by underlying confidence that the result reached is substantially correct. Where a determination relied on as preclusive is itself inconsistent with some other adjudication of the same issue, that confidence is generally unwarranted. * * * *Restatement (Second) of Judgments* § 88(4), comment F. (Tent. Draft No. 2, 1975).

Plaintiffs in the present case contend that the determinations are not "inconsistent" because the issues in *Hesse* and *Pacific N. W. Bell* were not identical with the issues in *Sylwester*. It is true, as plaintiffs point out, that the phrasing of the allegations of negligence differed and that certain specifications of negligence were not submitted to the jury in *Slywester*. We do not give much weight to variations in the wording of the pleadings, however, where essentially the same acts and omissions are alleged. To concentrate on slight discrepancies in the allegations of negligence would put defendant at a distinct disadvantage, for claimants could modify the wording after each judgment for defendant until one claimant prevailed, after which all remaining claimants could conform their complaints to that of the prevailing claimant and could then successfully claim that the prior judgments for defendant were based upon different issues.

The thrust of plaintiffs' argument must be that the jury in *Hesse* and the court in *Pacific N. W. Bell* adjudicated defendant negligent in respects which were not considered by the jury in *Sylwester*. The records of the cases, however, do not permit such a conclusion. Since the jury in *Hesse* returned a general verdict, we do not know in which respects it found defendant negligent and, given the substantial similarity of some of the allegations and the basic thrust of the negligence alleged, we are unable to conclude that it found defendant

negligent on the basis of conduct not submitted to the jury in *Sylwester*.
* * *

Plaintiffs argue that the jury instructions create a misleading impression of the *Sylwester* case because the emphasis at trial concerned whether the fire started by spontaneous combustion, whereas the focus in *Pacific N. W. Bell* was not how the fire started but whether it originated in defendant's skip box, regardless of its cause. The court in *Sylwester* did, however, instruct the jury as to defendant's duty regardless of the cause of the fire. Where the matter was submitted, we cannot hazard the guess that the jury disregarded its duty and failed to consider the issue.

Plaintiffs also argue that if the prior results are inconsistent, such inconsistency should not be afforded much weight because the only relevant consideration is whether defendant had a full and fair opportunity to litigate the case which it lost, and contend that this condition has been amply satisfied. We first point out that both *Bahler* and our subsequent decisions have made clear that the question whether preclusion would be fair under all the circumstances is independent of, and in addition to, whether a party had a full and fair opportunity to present its case in the action resulting in an adverse judgment. The latter consideration relates to the circumstances affecting the preparation and conduct of the trial of the prior case and those that might bear upon the strategy and conduct of a second trial, whereas the former relates to variables (not necessarily connected to the actual trials) concerning the equity and justice of applying collateral estoppel in a given case.

In addition, plaintiffs' argument, if taken too literally, would prove too much, since defendant presumably also had a full and fair opportunity to litigate the case it won. Plaintiffs maintain, however, that the circumstances of the second *Pacific N. W. Bell* trial clearly indicate that it was the better tried of all the cases. They assert that the issues were more clearly defined, there was substantially more money at stake than in *Sylwester* ($146,935 compared to $21,355), defendant brought in additional experts to testify at considerable expense, the evidence regarding the fire, and particularly its origin, was more fully developed, and defendant was aware that the outcome might have a significant effect on the cases waiting in the wings.

The only relevant implication of plaintiffs' position is that, since the second *Pacific N. W. Bell* trial was more fully tried, the result must be substantially better than the jury verdict in *Sylwester*. We decline the invitation to decide which case was the better tried, in which case the evidence more truly presented the facts, and which "full and fair opportunity" by defendant resulted in the "correct" decision. The existence of conflicting determinations of similar issues demonstrates that different bodies can legitimately draw different conclusions. As noted previously, the application of collateral estoppel is a matter of policy, not a quest for certainty.

We conclude that the prior determinations are basically inconsistent and that the circumstances are such that it would be unfair to preclude defendants from relitigating the issue of liability.

Reversed and remanded.

COMMENTS AND QUESTIONS CONCERNING *STATE FARM FIRE & CAS. CO. V. CENTURY HOME COMPONENTS, INC.*

1.   After prevailing in the first action (*Pacific N. W. Bell v. Century Home*), why didn't the defendant use non-mutual collateral estoppel based on the finding in the first action that it was not negligent?

2.   After a small-scale disaster of this nature, are there alternatives to the filing of more than 50 separate actions? Justice Holman notes in his opinion: "Although Currie's initial perceptions provoked much discussion, the problem has remained largely academic because inconsistent verdicts are rarely encountered." Would claims such as this be appropriate for class action treatment? Even if the claims were filed individually, is it likely that many of them would reach final judgment?

3.   The Oregon Supreme Court concluded that non-mutual offensive collateral estoppel was not appropriate in this action because it would be unfair to the defendant in light of the prior inconsistent judgments. Justice Holman stated: "There seems to be something fundamentally offensive about depriving a party of the opportunity to litigate the issue again when he has shown beyond a doubt that on another day he prevailed." Do you agree?

4.   Might the attempt at non-mutual offensive collateral estoppel against Century Home Components fail for another reason (other than unfairness to the defendant) under the Supreme Court's test in *Parklane*?

5.   Both Justice Stewart in *Parklane* and Justice Holman in *Century Home Components* cite Professor Currie's example involving the 27th passenger attempting to use non-mutual offensive collateral estoppel against the defendant railroad after the first 25 passengers lost their actions. Professor Currie, though, took this hypothetical one step further to argue that, because the aberrational judgment may be the first judgment, collateral estoppel should not be employed whenever a defendant faces more than two potential actions against it.

Justice Holman answered this hypothetical as follows:

> There is no foundation in either experience or policy for accepting the suggestion that a decision rendered after a full and fair presentation of the evidence and issues should be considered either substantially suspect or infected with variables indicating the question might be decided differently in another go-around. Currie subsequently conceded the untenability of his initial position and retreated from it, stating that

* * * so long as we retain sufficient faith in the institution of trial by jury to retain it for civil cases at all, what warrant is there for mistrusting the verdict for purposes of collateral estoppel when there is no suggestion that there has been compromise or other impropriety? Currie, "Civil Procedure: The Tempest Brews," 53 *Calif.L.Rev.* 25, 36 (1965).

Why doesn't the Oregon Supreme Court have confidence in using the *Pacific N. W. Bell* and *Hesse* judgments as a basis for collateral estoppel in the present cases?

6.   Why didn't the Court consider it significant that the pleadings in the present actions were most similar to those in *Hesse* and *Pacific N. W. Bell*? What about identifying one of the prior actions as having been "better tried" and using the judgment in that case as the basis for issue preclusion in other actions?

7.   Justice Holman differentiated between ultimate truth and judicial finality as follows:

As we stated in *In re Gygi*, 541 P.2d 1392, 1395 (1975),

> * * * the prior judgment is treated as conclusive, not because it is actually conclusive evidence of the ultimate truth as to those issues necessarily determined, but because of the public interest in the finality of judgments and in the efficient administration of justice. * * *.

In a somewhat similar vein, Justice Jackson described the United States Supreme Court: "We are not final because we are infallible, but we are infallible because we are final." *Brown v. Allen*, 344 U.S. 443, 540 (U.S. 1953).

8.   Do you agree with Justice Holman's statement that "the application of collateral estoppel is a matter of policy, not a quest for certainty"? What are the implications of this statement for issue and claim preclusion? For our systems of civil justice?

F. EXCEPTIONS TO CLAIM AND ISSUE PRECLUSION

As with any rules, there are exceptions to the doctrines of claim and issue preclusion. While these doctrines are to promote finality, consistency, and efficiency, those goals should not be achieved at the expense of justice for individual litigants. Thus several, limited exceptions to both claim and issue preclusion have been recognized.

Section 26 of the *Restatement (Second) of Judgments* recognizes several specific exceptions to the general requirement that parties cannot split their claims into separate civil actions. Section 26 provides:

(1) When any of the following circumstances exists, the general rule of § 24 [precluding claim splitting] does not apply to extinguish the claim, and part or all of the claim subsists as a possible basis for a second action by the plaintiff against the defendant:

(a) The parties have agreed in terms or in effect that the plaintiff may split his claim, or the defendant has acquiesced therein; or

(b) The court in the first action has expressly reserved the plaintiff's right to maintain the second action; or

(c) The plaintiff was unable to rely on a certain theory of the case or to seek a certain remedy or form of relief in the first action because of the limitations on the subject matter jurisdiction of the courts or restrictions on their authority to entertain multiple theories or demands for multiple remedies or forms of relief in a single action, and the plaintiff desires in the second action to rely on that theory or to seek that remedy or form of relief; or

(d) The judgment in the first action was plainly inconsistent with the fair and equitable implementation of a statutory or constitutional scheme, or it is the sense of the scheme that the plaintiff should be permitted to split his claim; or

(e) For reasons of substantive policy in a case involving a continuing or recurrent wrong, the plaintiff is given an option to sue once for the total harm, both past and prospective, or to sue from time to time for the damages incurred to the date of suit, and chooses the latter course; or

(f) It is clearly and convincingly shown that the policies favoring preclusion of a second action are overcome for an extraordinary reason, such as the apparent invalidity of a continuing restraint or condition having a vital relation to personal liberty or the failure of the prior litigation to yield a coherent disposition of the controversy.

The first two exceptions allowing claim splitting occur if (a) the parties have agreed or acquiesced in splitting or (b) the court expressly reserved this right for the plaintiff in the first action. Subsection (c) does not preclude a second action if the plaintiff could not rely on a theory or seek certain relief in the first action; for instance, if the first action is a state-court antitrust action the plaintiff still can bring a second federal antitrust action in the federal courts (which have exclusive jurisdiction over such claims). Illustration 6 for Section 26(d) of the *Restatement (Second)* illustrates subsection (c) and involves a student who loses a civil rights claim against a school system but does not appeal that judgment. If another student is later successful in challenging that same policy in the Supreme Court, the original student will not be precluded from bringing his initial claim again. Subsection (e) may be triggered by a series of contract breaches that can be redressed by separate actions as the breaches occur. Finally, Subsection

(f) is a general catch-all exception permitting claim splitting if there is an "extraordinary reason" supporting separate actions. Such a reason might exist, for instance, if the defendant concealed crucial facts or otherwise engaged in fraud that caused the plaintiff to bring a more confined claim in the first action than he would have had he known the facts concealed by the defendant.

In addition to these possible exceptions to claim preclusion, Section 28 of the *Restatement (Second) of Judgments* contains specific exceptions to the application of issue preclusion.[4] Section 28 provides:

> Although an issue is actually litigated and determined by a valid and final judgment, and the determination is essential to the judgment, relitigation of the issue in a subsequent action between the parties is not precluded in the following circumstances:
>
> (1) The party against whom preclusion is sought could not, as a matter of law, have obtained review of the judgment in the initial action; or
>
> (2) The issue is one of law and (a) the two actions involve claims that are substantially unrelated, or (b) a new determination is warranted in order to take account of an intervening change in the applicable legal context or otherwise to avoid inequitable administration of the laws; or
>
> (3) A new determination of the issue is warranted by differences in the quality or extensiveness of the procedures followed in the two courts or by factors relating to the allocation of jurisdiction between them; or
>
> (4) The party against whom preclusion is sought had a significantly heavier burden of persuasion with respect to the issue in the initial action than in the subsequent action; the burden has shifted to his adversary; or the adversary has a significantly heavier burden than he had in the first action; or
>
> (5) There is a clear and convincing need for a new determination of the issue (a) because of the potential adverse impact of the determination on the public interest or the interests of persons not themselves parties in the initial action, (b) because it was not sufficiently foreseeable at the time of the initial action that the issue would arise in the context of a subsequent action, or (c)

---

[4]   Section 28 contains specific exceptions to the assertion of issue preclusion by a party to the former action. In addition, Section 29 of the *Restatement (Second) of Judgments* contains further restrictions on the assertion of non-mutual issue preclusion in circumstances in which the party to the first action "lacked full and fair opportunity to litigate the issue in the first action or other circumstances justify affording him an opportunity to relitigate the issue."

because the party sought to be precluded, as a result of the conduct of his adversary or other special circumstances, did not have an adequate opportunity or incentive to obtain a full and fair adjudication in the initial action.

The classic example of exception (1) arises if a defendant unsuccessfully asserts in a criminal prosecution that his constitutional rights were violated but then is acquitted of the criminal charges. Because the defendant could not appeal after he was acquitted, he cannot be estopped based on the finding that there was no constitutional violation of his rights in a later civil rights action brought against the police.

Exception (2), to "avoid inequitable administration of the laws," might be applied if a taxpayer unsuccessfully sued the city seeking a refund, but then another taxpayer convinced an appellate court that the tax is invalid. In that situation, a court could invoke Section 28(2) rather than bind the first taxpayer in a second challenge to the city tax.

Exception (3) would apply to preclude the estoppel of a party in a state or federal trial court based upon an earlier adjudication in a municipal court with limited procedures. Pairs of cases falling within Exception (4) are discussed in Section III(A) of this text, *supra*. While it is generally possible to collaterally estop a party based on an issue from an earlier criminal adjudication, estoppel is not possible if the burden of persuasion is higher in the second action (as is the case when the first case is a civil action followed by a criminal prosecution).

Finally, Exception (5) is a more general exception to issue preclusion if there is "a clear and convincing need for a new determination of the issue" for certain reasons, including "the potential adverse impact of the determination on the public interest or the interests of persons not themselves parties in the initial action." It might, for instance, be possible to argue that a city government should not be estopped based on an old judgment if the factual context has changed and the public will be adversely affected by foreclosing litigation of the issue formerly decided.

It is important to know that there are specific possible exceptions to the application of both claim and issue preclusion. However, these are limited exceptions that only apply in specific situations. Counsel should not count on such exceptions, but should assume that claims and issues lost in one action may be used to preclude their clients in future actions as well.

IV. RESPECT FOR JUDGMENTS ACROSS COURT SYSTEMS

Until now, our discussion of respect for judgments has presumed that both the initial judgment and the second action are within the same court system. But what if the first judgment was from a different court system than the one that is asked to respect that judgment? What if, for example, the initial judgment was rendered by a court in Illinois and it is a Texas court that is asked to give effect to that judgment?

Article IV, Section 1, of the United States Constitution, the Constitution's Full Faith and Credit Clause, directly addresses this situation:

> Full Faith and Credit shall be given in each State to the public Acts, Records, and judicial Proceedings of every other State. And the Congress may by general Laws prescribe the manner in which such Acts, Records and Proceedings shall be proved, and the Effect thereof.

The Supreme Court has explained the manner in which the Full Faith and Credit Clause extends the common law doctrine of respect for judgments from one state to another:

> Regarding judgments * * * the full faith and credit obligation is exacting. A final judgment in one State, if rendered by a court with adjudicatory authority over the subject matter and persons governed by the judgment, qualifies for recognition throughout the land. For claim and issue preclusion (res judicata) purposes, in other words, the judgment of the rendering State gains nationwide force.

Baker by Thomas v. Gen. Motors Corp., 522 U.S. 222, 233 (1998).

The Full Faith and Credit Clause makes the states "integral parts of a single nation throughout which a remedy upon a just obligation might be demanded as of right, irrespective of the state of its origin." *Milwaukee County v. M.E. White Co.*, 296 U.S. 268, 277 (1935). Thus the second court, located in another state, generally must give the same effect to a judgment as would the rendering state court.

Pursuant to the Full Faith and Credit Clause, Congress enacted the full faith and credit statute, 28 U.S.C. § 1738, the final sentence of which states:

> Such Acts, records and judicial proceedings [of any State, Territory, or Possession] or copies thereof, so authenticated, shall have the same full faith and credit in every court within the United States and its Territories and Possessions as they have by law or usage in the courts of such State, Territory or Possession from which they are taken.

The federal courts thus must give the same effect to a state court judgment as would the state court itself. In addition, although different theories have been advanced to support this conclusion, "State courts generally recognize the obligation to honor federal judgments without cavil." 18B C. Wright, A. Miller & E. Cooper, *Federal Practice and Procedure* § 4468, at 69 (2nd ed. 2002). Not surprisingly, federal courts apply principles of respect for judgments in recognizing the judgments of other federal courts. As stated in the *Restatement (Second) of Conflict of Laws* § 93 (rev. 1988) ("Recognition of Sister State and Federal Court Judgments"), with certain exceptions (such as lack of notice or finality), "A valid judgment rendered in one State of the United States must be recognized in a sister State."

But what if a state or federal court is asked to preclude a party based upon a judgment from a court outside the United States? There is no equivalent to the Full Faith and Credit Clause binding courts around the world to respect foreign judgments, but U.S. courts will enforce some of these judgments under the doctrine of comity.

> Comity is a recognition which one nation extends within its own territory to the legislative, executive, or judicial acts of another. It is not a rule of law, but one of practice, convenience, and expediency. Although more than mere courtesy and accommodation, comity does not achieve the force of an imperative or obligation. Rather, it is a nation's expression of understanding which demonstrates due regard both to international duty and convenience and to the rights of persons protected by its own laws. Comity should be withheld only when its acceptance would be contrary or prejudicial to the interest of the nation called upon to give it effect.

Somportex Ltd. v. Philadelphia Chewing Gum Corp., 453 F.2d 435, 440 (3d Cir. 1971).

United States courts do not extend comity to the judgments of all foreign nations, such as those "rendered under a judicial system that does not provide impartial tribunals or procedures compatible with due process of law." *Restatement (Third) of Foreign Relations Law* § 482 (1987).

The following case illustrates how a state court must respect a final, valid judgment issued by another state.

A. *DURFEE V. DUKE*

Durfee v. Duke

Supreme Court of the United States, 1963
375 U.S. 106

OPINION

■ MR. JUSTICE STEWART delivered the opinion of the Court.

The United States Constitution requires that "Full Faith and Credit shall be given in each State to the * * * judicial Proceedings of every other State." The case before us presents questions arising under this constitutional provision and under the federal statute enacted to implement it.

In 1956 the petitioners brought an action against the respondent in a Nebraska court to quiet title to certain bottom land situated on the

Missouri River. The main channel of that river forms the boundary between the States of Nebraska and Missouri. The Nebraska court had jurisdiction over the subject matter of the controversy only if the land in question was in Nebraska. Whether the land was Nebraska land depended entirely upon a factual question—whether a shift in the river's course had been caused by avulsion or accretion. The respondent appeared in the Nebraska court and through counsel fully litigated the issues, explicitly contesting the court's jurisdiction over the subject matter of the controversy.[5] After a hearing the court found the issues in favor of the petitioners and ordered that title to the land be quieted in them. The respondent appealed, and the Supreme Court of Nebraska affirmed the judgment after a trial de novo on the record made in the lower court. The State Supreme Court specifically found that the rule of avulsion was applicable, that the land in question was in Nebraska, that the Nebraska courts therefore had jurisdiction of the subject matter of the litigation, and that title to the land was in the petitioners. The respondent did not petition this Court for a writ of certiorari to review that judgment.

Two months later the respondent filed a suit against the petitioners in a Missouri court to quiet title to the same land. Her complaint alleged that the land was in Missouri. The suit was removed to a Federal District Court by reason of diversity of citizenship. The District Court after hearing evidence expressed the view that the land was in Missouri, but held that all the issues had been adjudicated and determined in the Nebraska litigation, and that the judgment of the Nebraska Supreme Court was res judicata and "is now binding upon this court." The Court of Appeals reversed, holding that the District Court was not required to give full faith and credit to the Nebraska judgment, and that normal res judicata principles were not applicable because the controversy involved land and a court in Missouri was therefore free to retry the question of the Nebraska court's jurisdiction over the subject matter. We granted certiorari to consider a question important to the administration of justice in our federal system. For the reasons that follow, we reverse the judgment before us.

The constitutional command of full faith and credit, as implemented by Congress, requires that "judicial proceedings * * * shall have the same full faith and credit in every court within the United States * * * as they have by law or usage in the courts of such State * * * from which they are taken." Full faith and credit thus generally requires every State to give to a judgment at least the res judicata effect which the judgment would be accorded in the State which rendered it. "By the Constitutional provision for full faith and credit, the local doctrines of res judicata, speaking generally, become a part of national

---

[5] This is, therefore, not a case in which a party, although afforded an opportunity to contest subject-matter jurisdiction, did not litigate the issue. *Cf. Chicot County Drainage Dist. v. Baxter State Bank*, 308 U.S. 371.

jurisprudence, and therefore federal questions cognizable here." *Riley v. New York Trust Co.*, 315 U.S. 343, 349.

It is not questioned that the Nebraska courts would give full res judicata effect to the Nebraska judgment quieting title in the petitioners. It is the respondent's position, however, that whatever effect the Nebraska courts might give to the Nebraska judgment, the federal court in Missouri was free independently to determine whether the Nebraska court in fact had jurisdiction over the subject matter, i.e., whether the land in question was actually in Nebraska.

In support of this position the respondent relies upon the many decisions of this Court which have held that a judgment of a court in one State is conclusive upon the merits in a court in another State only if the court in the first State had power to pass on the merits—had jurisdiction, that is, to render the judgment. As Mr. Justice Bradley stated the doctrine in the leading case of *Thompson v. Whitman*, 18 Wall. 457, "we think it clear that the jurisdiction of the court by which a judgment is rendered in any State may be questioned in a collateral proceeding in another State, notwithstanding the provision of the fourth article of the Constitution and the law of 1790, and notwithstanding the averments contained in the record of the judgment itself." 18 Wall., at 469. * * *

However, while it is established that a court in one State, when asked to give effect to the judgment of a court in another State, may constitutionally inquire into the foreign court's jurisdiction to render that judgment, the modern decisions of this Court have carefully delineated the permissible scope of such an inquiry. From these decisions there emerges the general rule that a judgment is entitled to full faith and credit—even as to questions of jurisdiction—when the second court's inquiry discloses that those questions have been fully and fairly litigated and finally decided in the court which rendered the original judgment.

With respect to questions of jurisdiction over the person, this principle was unambiguously established in *Baldwin v. Iowa State Traveling Men's Ass'n*, 283 U.S. 522. There it was held that a federal court in Iowa must give binding effect to the judgment of a federal court in Missouri despite the claim that the original court did not have jurisdiction over the defendant's person, once it was shown to the court in Iowa that that question had been fully litigated in the Missouri forum. "Public policy," said the Court, "dictates that there be an end of litigation; that those who have contested an issue shall be bound by the result of the contest; and that matters once tried shall be considered forever settled as between the parties. We see no reason why this doctrine should not apply in every case where one voluntarily appears, presents his case and is fully heard, and why he should not, in the absence of fraud, be thereafter concluded by the judgment of the tribunal to which he has submitted his cause." 283 U.S., at 525–526.

Following the *Baldwin* case, this Court soon made clear in a series of decisions that the general rule is no different when the claim is made that the original forum did not have jurisdiction over the subject matter. *Davis v. Davis*, 305 U.S. 32; *Stoll v. Gottlieb*, 305 U.S. 165; *Treinies v. Sunshine Mining Co.*, 308 U.S. 66; *Sherrer v. Sherrer*, 334 U.S. 343. In each of these cases the claim was made that a court, when asked to enforce the judgment of another forum, was free to retry the question of that forum's jurisdiction over the subject matter. In each case this Court held that since the question of subject-matter jurisdiction had been fully litigated in the original forum, the issue could not be retried in a subsequent action between the parties.

* * *

* * * In *Treinies*, the rule was succinctly stated: "One trial of an issue is enough. 'The principles of res judicata apply to questions of jurisdiction as well as to other issues,' as well to jurisdiction of the subject matter as of the parties." 308 U.S., at 78.

The reasons for such a rule are apparent. In the words of the Court's opinion in *Stoll v. Gottlieb, supra*, "We see no reason why a court in the absence of an allegation of fraud in obtaining the judgment, should examine again the question whether the court making the earlier determination on an actual contest over jurisdiction between the parties, did have jurisdiction of the subject matter of the litigation. * * * Courts to determine the rights of parties are an integral part of our system of government. It is just as important that there should be a place to end as that there should be a place to begin litigation. After a party has his day in court, with opportunity to present his evidence and his view of the law, a collateral attack upon the decision as to jurisdiction there rendered merely retries the issue previously determined. There is no reason to expect that the second decision will be more satisfactory than the first." 305 U.S., at 172.

To be sure, the general rule of finality of jurisdictional determinations is not without exceptions. Doctrines of federal pre-emption or sovereign immunity may in some contexts be controlling. *Kalb v. Feuerstein*, 308 U.S. 433; *United States v. United States Fidelity & Guaranty Co.*, 309 U.S. 506.[12] But no such overriding considerations

---

[12] It is to be noted, however, that in neither of these cases had the jurisdictional issues actually been litigated in the first forum.

THE RESTATEMENT OF CONFLICT OF LAWS recognizes the possibility of such exceptions:

"Where a court has jurisdiction over the parties and determines that it has jurisdiction over the subject matter, the parties cannot collaterally attack the judgment on the ground that the court did not have jurisdiction over the subject matter, unless the policy underlying the doctrine of res judicata is outweighed by the policy against permitting the court to act beyond its jurisdiction. Among the factors appropriate to be considered in determining that collateral attack should be permitted are that

"(a) the lack of jurisdiction over the subject matter was clear;

are present here. While this Court has not before had occasion to consider the applicability of the rule of *Davis, Stoll, Treinies,* and *Sherrer* to a case involving real property, we can discern no reason why the rule should not be fully applicable.

It is argued that an exception to this rule of jurisdictional finality should be made with respect to cases involving real property because of this Court's emphatic expressions of the doctrine that courts of one State are completely without jurisdiction directly to affect title to land in other States. This argument is wide of the mark. Courts of one State are equally without jurisdiction to dissolve the marriages of those domiciled in other States. But the location of land, like the domicile of a party to a divorce action, is a matter "to be resolved by judicial determination." *Sherrer v. Sherrer*, 334 U.S., at 349. The question remains whether, once the matter has been fully litigated and judicially determined, it can be retried in another State in litigation between the same parties. Upon the reason and authority of the cases we have discussed, it is clear that the answer must be in the negative.

It is to be emphasized that all that was ultimately determined in the Nebraska litigation was title to the land in question as between the parties to the litigation there. Nothing there decided, and nothing that could be decided in litigation between the same parties or their privies in Missouri, could bind either Missouri or Nebraska with respect to any controversy they might have, now or in the future, as to the location of the boundary between them, or as to their respective sovereignty over the land in question. Either State may at any time protect its interest by initiating independent judicial proceedings here. *Cf. Missouri v. Nebraska*, 196 U.S. 23.

For the reasons stated, we hold in this case that the federal court in Missouri had the power and, upon proper averments, the duty to inquire into the jurisdiction of the Nebraska courts to render the decree quieting title to the land in the petitioners. We further hold that when that inquiry disclosed, as it did, that the jurisdictional issues had been fully and fairly litigated by the parties and finally determined in the Nebraska courts, the federal court in Missouri was correct in ruling that further inquiry was precluded. Accordingly the judgment of the Court of Appeals is reversed, and that of the District Court is affirmed. It is so ordered.

Judgment of Court of Appeals reversed and judgment of District Court affirmed.

"(b) the determination as to jurisdiction depended upon a question of law rather than of fact;

"(c) the court was one of limited and not of general jurisdiction;

"(d) the question of jurisdiction was not actually litigated;

"(e) the policy against the court's acting beyond its jurisdiction is strong."

RESTATEMENT, CONFLICT OF LAWS, § 451(2) (Supp.1948) [now, *Restatement (Second) of Conflict of Laws* § 97 (rev. 1988)].

■ MR. JUSTICE BLACK, concurring.

Petitioners and respondents dispute the ownership of a tract of land adjacent to the Missouri River, which is the boundary between Nebraska and Missouri. Resolution of this question turns on Whether the land is in Nebraska or Missouri. Neither State, of course, has power to make a determination binding on the other as to which State the land is in. U.S.Const. Art. III, § 2; 28 U.S.C. § 1251(a). However, in a private action brought by these Nebraska petitioners, the Nebraska Supreme Court has held that the disputed tract is in Nebraska. In the present suit, brought by this Missouri respondent in Missouri, the United States Court of Appeals has refused to be bound by the Nebraska court's judgment. I concur in today's reversal of the Court of Appeals' judgment, but with the understanding that we are not deciding the question whether the respondent would continue to be bound by the Nebraska judgment should it later be authoritatively decided, either in an original proceeding between the States in this Court or by a compact between the two States under Art. I, § 10, that the disputed tract is in Missouri

COMMENTS AND QUESTIONS CONCERNING *DURFEE V. DUKE*

1.   What might Julia Duke have done to prevent a Nebraska state court from entering a judgment against her that she could not later collaterally attack?

2.   In reaching its decision, the Supreme Court reversed a judgment of the United States Court of Appeals for the Eighth Circuit. In the opinion for the Court of Appeals, then Judge Harry Blackmun wrote:

> After careful consideration we conclude that, for a land case such as this, a policy of careful recognition of jurisdictional limitations and of permitting inquiry into the basis of subject-matter jurisdiction outweighs any conflicting res judicata principle. We feel that as a matter of basic legal philosophy the question of excessive judicial action by way of claimed jurisdiction over land presents a fundamental and classic situation where validity may be a proper subject of inquiry despite opposing considerations in favor of the termination of litigation.

Duke v. Durfee, 308 F.2d 209, 220 (8th Cir. 1962) *rev'd*, 375 U.S. 106 (1963). Why did the Supreme Court disagree?

3.   In his opinion Justice Stewart states: "Full faith and credit thus generally requires every State to give to a judgment at least the res judicata effect which the judgment would be accorded in the State which rendered it." Thus, if the judgment or decree could have been modified by the rendering court, the second court could modify the judgment as well. As Section 73 of the *Restatement (Second) of Judgments* (1982) states:

[Generally], a judgment may be set aside or modified if:

> (1) The judgment was subject to modification by its own terms or by applicable law, and events have occurred subsequent to the judgment that warrant modification of the contemplated kind; or

> (2) There has been such a substantial change in the circumstances that giving continued effect to the judgment is unjust.

Can you think of judgments or decrees that are not infrequently modified?

4.   There was an issue concerning the course of the Missouri River on Nebraska's border with Iowa in *Owen Equipment & Erection Co. v. Kroger*, 437 U.S. 365 (1978), *supra* p. 707 (Question 3). In both *Owen Equipment* and *Durfee*, the question was whether the Missouri River had moved by accretion or avulsion.

In an original suit in the Supreme Court between Iowa and Nebraska concerning their boundary, these two terms and their impact were described as follows:

> It is settled law that when grants of land border on running water, and the banks are changed by that gradual process known as "accretion," the riparian owner's boundary line still remains the stream, although, during the years, by this accretion, the actual area of his possessions may vary. * * *

> It is equally well settled that where a stream, which is a boundary, from any cause suddenly abandons its old and seeks a new bed, such change of channel works no change of boundary; and that the boundary remains as it was, in the center of the old channel, although no water may be flowing therein. This sudden and rapid change of channel is termed, in the law, "avulsion." * * *

Nebraska v. Iowa, 143 U.S. 359, 360–61 (1892).

5.   Why does Justice Black separately concur?

B. WHEN CAN A PARTY COLLATERALLY CHALLENGE PERSONAL OR SUBJECT-MATTER JURISDICTION?

In footnote 12 to his opinion in *Durfee v. Duke*, Justice Stewart cites to the *Restatement of Conflict of Laws* as to when a party can collaterally attack a prior judgment because the rendering court did not have subject-matter jurisdiction. This section discusses the limited situations in which a party can challenge a prior judgment because the first court did not have subject-matter or personal jurisdiction over the party challenging the first judgment.

1. DEFENDANT LITIGATES AND LOSES ISSUE OF JURISDICTION IN FIRST ACTION

If a party unsuccessfully challenges subject-matter or personal jurisdiction in an action, a later jurisdictional challenge is typically precluded. *Durfee v. Duke* (with respect to subject-matter jurisdiction) and *Baldwin v. Iowa State Traveling Men's Ass'n* (with respect to personal jurisdiction) hold that if you litigate the issue in the first proceeding and lose, you are precluded from raising that issue in a later action.

2. DEFENDANT APPEARS IN FIRST ACTION, BUT DOESN'T CHALLENGE JURISDICTION

What if the party appeared in the first action, but did not raise the issue of lack of personal or subject-matter jurisdiction in that action? Here, too, the party (typically the defendant in the first action) will be precluded from later challenging the first court's jurisdiction. Pursuant to Federal Rule of Civil Procedure 12(h)(1), the defense of personal jurisdiction is waived if not included in a pre-answer motion or in the answer.

While Rule 12(h)(3) provides that a court can dismiss an action if it determines "at any time that it lacks subject-matter jurisdiction," the defendant who appears in an action but fails to raise the question of subject-matter jurisdiction will have a difficult time later raising lack of subject-matter jurisdiction in the first action. Although rules in this area varied in earlier times, the Supreme Court has referred to the "well-settled principle that res judicata may be pleaded as a bar, not only as respects matters actually presented to sustain or defeat the right asserted in the earlier proceeding, 'but also as respects any other available matter which might have been presented to that end'." *Chicot County Drainage Dist. v. Baxter State Bank,* 308 U.S. 371, 378 (1940) (quoting *Grubb v. Public Utilities Commission*, 281 U.S. 470, 478 (1930)). *See also Travelers Indem. Co. v. Bailey,* 557 U.S. 137, 152 (2009) ("[O]nce the 1986 Orders became final on direct review (whether or not proper exercises of bankruptcy court jurisdiction and power), they became res judicata to the ' "parties and those in privity with them, not only as to every matter which was offered and received to sustain or defeat the claim or demand, but as to any other admissible matter which might have been offered for that purpose." ' *Nevada v. United States,* 463 U.S. 110, 130 (1983) (quoting *Cromwell v. County of Sac,* 94 U.S. 351, 352 (1877)).."). In addition, Section 18(2) of the *Restatement (Second) of Judgments* provides: "When a valid and final personal judgment is rendered in favor of the plaintiff, * * * [i]n an action upon the judgment, the defendant cannot avail himself of defenses he might have interposed, or did interpose, in the first action."

3. DEFENDANT DEFAULTS IN FIRST ACTION

Assume that the defendant does not even enter an appearance in the first action. Can he later challenge the personal or subject-matter jurisdiction of the first court? There may be several bases upon which to collaterally attack such a judgment on due process grounds. As you'll remember from *Mullane v. Central Hanover Bank & Trust Co.*, 339 U.S. 306, 314 (1950), *supra* p. 210, "An elementary and fundamental requirement of due process in any proceeding which is to be accorded finality is notice reasonably calculated, under all the circumstances, to apprise interested parties of the pendency of the action and afford them an opportunity to present their objections." Thus a defendant who does not receive notice of an action may challenge the judgment in that action in a later proceeding.

Having not done so in the first action, a defendant also can later challenge a default judgment because the first court could not constitutionally exercise personal jurisdiction. *Pennoyer v. Neff*, 95 U.S. 714, 733 (1988), *supra* p. 243 ("Since the adoption of the Fourteenth Amendment to the Federal Constitution, the validity of such judgments may be directly questioned, and their enforcement in the State resisted, on the ground that proceedings in a court of justice to determine the personal rights and obligations of parties over whom that court has no jurisdiction do not constitute due process of law.").

Finally, the defendant generally can challenge the first judgment if it was procured by fraud. *See Baldwin v. Iowa State Traveling Men's Ass'n*, 283 U.S. 522, 525–26 (1931) ("[T]hose who have contested an issue shall be bound by the result * * *. We see no reason why this doctrine should not apply * * * where one *voluntarily* appears, presents his case and is fully heard, and why he should not, *in the absence of fraud*, be thereafter concluded by the judgment of the tribunal to which he has submitted his cause.") (emphasis added). Thus the plaintiff cannot forcibly or fraudulently bring a defendant into a jurisdiction, obtain a judgment against that person, and later attempt to enforce that judgment in another jurisdiction. *Cf. Burnham v. Superior Court of California*, 495 U.S. 604, 613 (1990).

In contrast to these challenges to personal jurisdiction, collateral attacks on the subject-matter jurisdiction of the first court are not constitutionally based. They therefore are more difficult to sustain— even when the defendant did not appear in the first action. In footnote 12 of his opinion in *Durfee v. Duke* Justice Stewart cites Section 451(2) of the *Restatement of Conflict of Laws*, which lists several factors relevant to permitting a collateral attack due to lack of subject-matter jurisdiction. These factors are now contained in Comment d to Section 97 of the *Restatement (Second) of Conflict of Laws* (rev. 1988), which provides:

Whether a party should be permitted to attack a judgment collaterally involves weighing the policy underlying the rules of res judicata against the policy prohibiting a court from exceeding the powers conferred upon it. Important factors to be considered in determining whether there are sufficient grounds of public policy for denying the judgment the effect of res judicata are whether (1) the lack of jurisdiction or competence was so clear that the court's entertaining the action was a manifest abuse of authority, (2) allowing the judgment to stand would substantially infringe the authority of another tribunal or agency of government, or (3) the judgment was rendered by a court lacking capability to make an adequately informed determination of a question concerning its own jurisdiction, and as a matter of procedural fairness the party seeking to avoid the judgment should have the opportunity belatedly to attack the court's jurisdiction or competence.

See also Restatement (Second) of Judgments § 12 (1982) (containing the same three-factor test).

A party's opportunity to challenge the personal or subject-matter jurisdiction of a court in a later action is set forth in Figure 14–1.

FIGURE 14–1
OPPORTUNITY TO CONTEST JURISDICTION IN 2ND
SUIT (COLLATERAL ATTACK)

	Personal Jurisdiction	Subject-Matter Jurisdiction
Defendant Litigates (and Loses) Issue in First Action	Preclusion: *Baldwin v. Iowa State Traveling Men's Ass'n*, 283 U.S. 522 (1931)	Preclusion: *Durfee v. Duke*, 375 U.S. 106 (1963)
Defendant Appears in First Action, But Doesn't Litigate Jurisdictional Issue	Preclusion: FRCP 12(h)(1); *Restatement (Second) of Judgments* § 18(2)	Preclusion: *Chicot County Drainage Dist. v. Baxter State Bank*, 308 U.S. 371 (1940); *Restatement (Second) of Judgments* § 18(2)
Defendant Defaults in First Action	Challenge may be possible if (1) no notice (*Mullane*); (2) no personal jurisdiction (*Pennoyer v. Neff*); or (3) fraud.	Challenge may be possible under factors in *Restatement (Second) of Conflict of Laws* § 97 and *Restatement (Second) of Judgments* § 12.

V. CONCLUSION

Not only does a judgment typically end trial court proceedings in a civil action, but its impact may be magnified by extending the effect of that judgment to other civil actions. Through the application of claim preclusion, that judgment may preclude a future action on the same claim. If specific issues were determined in that initial action, parties to that action may be precluded from relitigating those issues in other actions. Through the Full Faith and Credit Clause and full faith and credit statute, these principals of respect for judgment apply not only within a single judicial system but across judicial systems.

There are limited situations in which a party can successfully collaterally challenge a prior judgment that is asserted against it in a later civil action. The best way to challenge a trial court judgment is on direct appeal of that judgment to the appropriate court of appeals. Appeals are the subject of the next, and final, chapter of this text.

VI. CHAPTER ASSESSMENT

A.   Multiple-Choice Questions. Answer the following questions, reviewing the sections of the chapter noted in connection with each question.

1.   While traveling on their honeymoon, a woman and a man, citizens of California, are injured in a 2015 automobile accident with a car driven by a citizen of Oregon. The woman files a negligence action against the driver in Oregon state court, seeking damages for injuries that she sustained in the accident. There is a trial, the jury returns a verdict against the woman, and the judge enters a judgment against the woman based on that verdict.

The woman and man then file a diversity action against the driver in Oregon federal court seeking damages for the driver's alleged negligence in the 2015 accident. The driver asserts claim preclusion and seeks the dismissal of the diversity action.

Assuming that Oregon has adopted the *Restatement (Second)* definition of "claim," review Sections II(B) and IV and choose the best answer from the following choices.

(a) Claim preclusion should be applied to bar the federal action brought by the man.

(b) Claim preclusion should be applied to bar the federal action brought by the woman.

(c) Claim preclusion should be applied to bar the federal action brought by both the man and the woman.

(d) Because the first judgment was rendered in a state, not federal, court, the doctrine of claim preclusion cannot be applied even if the requirements for claim preclusion were otherwise met.

2.   A woman brings a civil action against a man in the United States District Court for the District of Arizona, seeking damages for her medical bills stemming from a September 1, 2014, automobile accident involving the two parties. The man, a citizen of Arizona, is served in Arizona but does not respond to the complaint or otherwise appear in the action. The court therefore enters a default and a default judgment against him on March 15, 2015.

On April 15, 2015, the woman brings another civil action against the man in the same federal district court, seeking damages for destruction of her car in the same September 1, 2014, automobile accident.

The man includes the defense of res judicata (claim preclusion) in his answer to this second action. He then files a motion for summary judgment based upon the first (default) judgment, attaching a copy of the first judgment to his motion.

Review Section II(F) and choose the best answer from the following choices:

(a)   The court should grant the motion for summary judgment.

(b)   The court should deny the motion for summary judgment, because the first judgment is a default judgment.

(c)   The court should deny the motion for summary judgment, because the first judgment is not considered to be on the merits.

(d)   The court should deny the motion for summary judgment, because the woman never raised a claim for property damage in her first lawsuit.

3.   Daniel Defendant is convicted in federal district court of criminal tax fraud, an essential element of which is "to intentionally understate on a tax return the amount that was legally owed to the United States of America."

Defendant files an appeal of the criminal judgment entered against him, which remains pending.

The United States then brings a civil action against Defendant, seeking repayment of the taxes that it claims Defendant should have paid. The United States seeks to collaterally estop Defendant on the issue that he did "intentionally understate on a tax return the amount that was legally owed to the United States of America."

Review Section III(A) and choose the best answer from the following choices:

(a)   Because the first judgment is on appeal, it cannot be used as a basis for issue preclusion in the federal courts.

(b)   Because the burden of persuasion is different in the two actions, there cannot be issue preclusion in the second action.

(c)   While there could be issue preclusion if the first judgment had been in a civil action and the second action had been a criminal prosecution, issue preclusion cannot be based on a criminal judgment to determine an issue in a later civil action.

(d)   Issue preclusion can be applied in the second action.

4.   A man sues a woman in the United States District Court for the District of Kansas concerning a May 1, 2014, automobile accident between them. After the pleadings are closed, there is a bench trial (to the judge, with no jury), and the judge enters judgment for the woman. In his written opinion, the judge states: "After listening to all the testimony in this case, I conclude both that (1) the plaintiff suffered no damages in the parties' accident and (2) the plaintiff was himself (contributorily) negligent concerning this accident." The man appeals, and the U. S. Court of Appeals for the 10th Circuit affirms the judgment for the woman, stating in its brief opinion: "While the District Court concluded that this case should be dismissed both due to plaintiff's lack of damages and contributory negligence, we need not reach the question of negligence and affirm solely on the basis that the plaintiff suffered no damages in this accident."

The woman then files an action in the United States District Court for the District of Colorado against the man for her damages from the accident.

Review Section III(C) and choose the best answer from the following choices:

(a)   Because the woman did not assert her claim for damages stemming from the accident in the first lawsuit, she cannot assert that claim in the second action.

(b)   Because the issues in the two actions were different, involving negligence and contributory negligence, issue preclusion is not possible between the two actions.

(c)   Because the Kansas district judge dismissed the first action both because the man did not suffer damages and because he was negligent, the woman can successfully collaterally estop the man on the issue of his negligence in the second (Colorado) lawsuit.

(d)   Had the first (Kansas) action not been appealed, the woman could have successfully collaterally estopped the man in the second (Colorado) action.

5.   A protester was arrested at a public rally after refusing to move from an intersection where he and others were blocking traffic. The protester was charged with disorderly conduct and a criminal action was filed against him in state court. The protester filed a motion to dismiss the charges, alleging that the city had violated his civil rights. The judge denied the protester's motion, the case was tried, and the jury returned a verdict of acquittal.

The protester then filed a civil rights action against the city in federal court. The city filed a motion for summary judgment, attaching the record of the criminal proceedings and invoking issue preclusion against the protester on the issue of whether his civil rights had been violated.

Review Section III(F) and choose the best answer from the following choices:

(a) Because the protester could not appeal the first action, the city should not be able to successfully assert issue preclusion against him in his civil rights action.

(b) Because the first action was a criminal and the second action a civil action, the city should not be able to successfully assert issue preclusion against the protester in his civil rights action.

(c) Because the burden of persuasion is higher in a criminal than in a civil action, the city should be able to successfully assert issue preclusion against the protester in his civil rights action.

(d) Because the protester had every incentive to litigate the criminal action, the city should be able to successfully assert issue preclusion against him in his civil rights action.

B.   Essay Questions. To test your understanding of this chapter's material, outline or write an answer to the following questions.

1.   Pile-up on the Interstate—and in the Courts.

Randy Reckless (a citizen of Missouri) drives trucks for a trucking company incorporated and with its principal place of business in Missouri. He and his truck are involved in a major accident on an interstate highway in Missouri. The accident involves seven cars, including cars driven by Peter Driver (in which Polly Passenger was a passenger), Tommy Texan, and Kathy Kansas.

As a result of this crash, the trucking company is sued in the following actions:

1)   Peter Driver, a citizen of Colorado, sues the company for the personal injuries he suffered in the crash in California state court, which action is dismissed for lack of personal jurisdiction.

2)   Tommy Texan, a citizen of Texas, sues the company in the United States District Court for the Eastern District of Missouri, and a jury returns a verdict for the company. However, 20 days after the verdict is returned, Tommy moves for judgment as a matter of law and for a new trial. The trial judge denies the motion for judgment as a matter of law and grants the motion for a new trial.

3)   Kathy Kansas, a Kansas citizen, sues the company in the United States District Court for the District of Kansas. The jury returns a verdict for $250,000 in Kathy's favor. After judgment is entered on

that $250,000 verdict, the company appeals the judgment, which appeal is still pending.

4)   The United States brings a criminal prosecution against the company in United States District Court for the Eastern District of Missouri. Relying on company records that indicate that the truck that crashed had never had a safety inspection and that Randy had numerous other driving accidents, the jury convicts the trucking company under a federal highway safety act that requires a finding that the company acted in a "criminally negligent manner on the nation's highways."

5)   Polly Passenger, a citizen of Colorado and the wife of Peter Driver (who brought lawsuit #1), sues the company in state court in Missouri seeking damages for the injuries she suffered in the crash.

Please answer the following questions:

(a)   Can the company make use of judgment #1 in Passenger's current action (#5)?

(b)   Can the company make use of use of judgment #2 in Passenger's current action (#5)?

(c)   Can Passenger make use of judgment #3 in her current lawsuit (#5)?

(d)   Can Passenger make use of judgment #4 in her current lawsuit (#5)?

2.   "Ethanol for America!"

Dandy Defendant urges Midwesterners to "invest in ethanol—the fuel of the future!" After hundreds of Iowa and Nebraska citizens do just that, the profitability of ethanol drops precipitously because of overbuilding of ethanol plants and a steep rise in corn prices. Eileen, an Iowa citizen, sues Dandy, a Nebraska citizen, in Iowa state court seeking recovery for the $100,000 she lost due to her investment in his company "Ethanol For America." Dandy files a motion to dismiss, and the Iowa state court dismisses this action on the grounds that (1) it does not have personal jurisdiction over Dandy and (2) the Iowa state court in which Eileen filed her lawsuit does not have subject-matter jurisdiction for claims for more than $50,000 and therefore cannot hear this action.

After the dismissal of her Iowa state action, Eileen files the same claim against Dandy in Nebraska state court. Because she refuses to provide deposition testimony, the court dismisses the action. Eileen appeals to the Nebraska Supreme Court, which appeal remains pending.

Eileen's father then files a claim against Dandy in Nebraska state court. Dandy does not respond to the complaint, and the court enters a default judgment against Dandy.

While her appeal to the Nebraska Supreme Court is still pending, Eileen files the same claim she previously asserted against Dandy in the United States District Court for the Southern District of Iowa. Both Dandy and Eileen move for summary judgment, based upon the previous three civil actions.

Answer the following questions, presuming that the state procedural rules and statutes in Iowa and Nebraska are identical to those of the federal courts.

(a) Can Dandy use the Iowa state court judgment against Eileen to assert either claim or issue preclusion in the Iowa federal action?

(b) Can Dandy use the Nebraska state court judgment against Eileen to assert claim or issue preclusion in the Iowa federal action?

(c) Can Eileen use the Nebraska state court judgment that her father obtained against Dandy to assert claim or issue preclusion in the Iowa federal action?

CHAPTER 15

APPEALS: "IF AT FIRST YOU DON'T SUCCEED . . . ."

I. INTRODUCTION

At some point trial-court proceedings must end, but this does not mean that the litigation will not continue in the appellate courts. This chapter considers appeals in the United States Courts of Appeal. As illustrated by Figure 1–2 in Chapter 1, *supra* p. 7, the 94 federal district courts are grouped within 12 United States Courts of Appeal that are geographically spread across the country. These are the First through Eleventh United States Courts of Appeal and the United States Court of Appeals for the District of Columbia Circuit (in which there is only a single district court: the United States District Court for the District of Columbia).[1]

Before considering just what a federal appeal is, it is important to realize what such an appeal is not. Appeals are *not*:

- to immediately challenge every ruling of the trial judge as that ruling is made;

- to retry the case presented in the trial court in the court of appeals; or

- to introduce new evidence or argument that wasn't presented to the trial court.

The following sections of this chapter consider just what a civil appeal is. In particular, it considers:

- *Why* should a losing party appeal? (Appeals consume both time and money.)

- *What* can be appealed? (Some errors are harmless.)

- *Who* can appeal? (A party may lose particular claims or arguments but still obtain the full relief it sought in the district court.)

- *When* can you appeal? (Federal appeals are possible only from final judgments.)

- *Where* and *How* can you appeal? (Federal appeals are governed by the Federal Rules of Appellate Procedure,

---

[1] In addition to these 12 courts of appeals with jurisdiction over appeals from specific geographic areas, the United States Court of Appeals for the Federal Circuit has nationwide jurisdiction to consider appeals in specific types of cases involving such matters as international trade, government contracts, claims against the United States, federal personnel, patents, and trademarks.

while Title 28, the Federal Rules of Civil Procedure, and judicial precedent provide appellate standards of review.)[2]

II. WHY SHOULD A LOSING PARTY APPEAL?

You think that your client has a very good case, but the district judge or jury disagrees and rules for another party. You have properly preserved strong issues for appeal in the district court record. The court of appeals has the power to reverse the final judgment of the district court, allowing your client to snatch victory from the jaws of defeat. Why would a party *not* appeal in such circumstances?

Appeals, like all litigation, consume great amounts of time and money. Even more importantly, only a small fraction of district court judgments are reversed on appeal. In the 12-month period ending December 31, 2014, there were reversals in only 12.3% of the appeals terminated on the merits from private party civil actions that were not prisoner petitions.[3]

Thus the fact that the losing party can appeal does not mean that an appeal should be taken. Good issues in the district court may not be particularly strong issues on appeal, especially because of the deference granted trial court rulings under many of the appellate court standards of review. Even if an appellate reversal can be achieved, this vindication may take years and require great investments of time and money. An appeal also might lead an opposing party to file a cross-appeal, seeking appellate review of issues on which your client—the appellant—prevailed.[4]

Thus, as with many litigation decisions, the decision to appeal must be thoughtfully considered with one's client. Counsel and client must consider the possible benefits from a successful appeal, such as an appellate reversal of unfavorable trial court determinations. However, the likely costs and possible negative outcomes (such as an appellate affirmance or successful cross-appeal by an opposing party) also must be considered. Only after a careful cost-benefit analysis should the decision be made to appeal, or not to appeal, a final judgment of the district court.

---

[2] The "Five Ws and One H" ("What," "Who," "Why," "When," "Where," and "How") provide a helpful guide not only for reporters but for attorneys planning pretrial investigations, civil litigation, and appeals. As Rudyard Kipling wrote in *The Elephant's Child*,

I keep six honest serving-men:

(They taught me all I knew)

Their names are What and Where and When

And How and Why and Who.

[3] Admin. Office of the U.S. Courts, *Federal Judicial Caseload Statistics: Dec. 31, 2014* (2014) (Table B–5). The corresponding percentage of reversals in appeals from private prisoner petitions was only 3.0%. *Id.*

[4] The party (plaintiff or defendant) that originally appeals is the "appellant," while the other party (opposing the appeal) is the "appellee."

III. WHAT CAN BE APPEALED?

Courts of appeal can review errors in the federal district courts, but only if the asserted error was properly preserved in the district court record. The courts of appeal are to review rulings of the district court—not to provide a forum in which to raise new arguments for the first time. As the United States Court of Appeals for the Fifth Circuit has explained: "[I]f a litigant desires to preserve an argument for appeal, the litigant must press and not merely intimate the argument during the proceedings before the district court. If an argument is not raised to such a degree that the district court has an opportunity to rule on it, we will not address it on appeal." *F.D.I.C. v. Mijalis*, 15 F.3d 1314, 1327 (5th Cir. 1994).

The trial lawyer therefore must "make a record" by raising in the district court any issues that may be raised on appeal. If, for instance, an objection will be raised to the decision of a trial court to give, or not to give, a specific jury instruction, Rule 51(d) of the Federal Rules of Civil Procedure requires that a proper objection must be made in the trial court.[5]

But even if a party properly made a record in the trial court, thus preserving that matter for appeal, that objection may not provide a basis for appellate reversal of the trial court ruling. Section 2111 of Title 28 states: "On the hearing of any appeal * * *, the court shall give judgment after an examination of the record without regard to errors or defects which do not affect the substantial rights of the parties." In addition, Rule 61 of the Federal Rules of Civil Procedure, the "harmless error rule," provides:

> Unless justice requires otherwise, no error in admitting or excluding evidence—or any other error by the court or a party—is ground for granting a new trial, for setting aside a verdict, or for vacating, modifying, or otherwise disturbing a judgment or order. At every stage of the proceeding, the court must disregard all errors and defects that do not affect any party's substantial rights.

Thus a party may be able to successfully appeal a district court order that incorrectly precludes an expert from testifying or from offering her expert conclusions at trial. However, it is likely that the exclusion at trial of minor parts of that proposed testimony would be

---

[5] The significance of the record is illustrated by this colloquy in the United States Supreme Court:

Mr. Dabney: Your Honor, in the real world, a business competitor-

Justice Breyer: No, I'm not interested in the real world. I am interested in the record.

Transcript of Oral Argument at 7, *Already, LLC v. Nike, Inc.*, 133 S.Ct. 721 (2012) (No. 11–982).

considered harmless error under Rule 61 and Section 2111 and therefore not provide a basis for successful appeal.[6]

The Supreme Court has explained the rationale for the harmless error rule as follows:

> This Court has long held that " '[a litigant] is entitled to a fair trial but not a perfect one,' for there are no perfect trials." *Brown v. United States*, 411 U.S. 223, 231–232 (1973), quoting *Bruton v. United States*, 391 U.S. 123, 135 (1968), and *Lutwak v. United States*, 344 U.S. 604, 619 (1953). Trials are costly, not only for the parties, but also for the jurors performing their civic duty and for society which pays the judges and support personnel who manage the trials. It seems doubtful that our judicial system would have the resources to provide litigants with perfect trials, were they possible, and still keep abreast of its constantly increasing case load. Even this straightforward products liability suit extended over a three-week period.

McDonough Power Equip., Inc. v. Greenwood, 464 U.S. 548, 553 (1984).

On rare occasions, though, trial court error may so affect a party's substantial rights, and be so clear, that an appellate court will consider the asserted error on appeal, even though objection was not properly made in the trial court. With respect to jury instructions, Rule 51(d)(2) provides: "A court may consider a plain error in the instructions that has not been preserved as required by Rule 51(d)(1) if the error affects substantial rights."[7]

So if you're going to forget an objection in the trial court, you and your client may be rescued on appeal if the court's error was so clearly wrong that it's considered plain error. But, in a more typical situation, counsel must be sure to make her objection in the trial court to preserve the issue in the record for later appeal.

---

[6]   *See also* Federal Rule of Evidence 103(a), which provides that a party "may claim error in a ruling to admit or exclude evidence only if the error affects a substantial right of the party [and there has been a timely and specific trial court objection]."

[7]   *Cf. United States v. Marcus*, 560 U.S. 258 (2010), involving plain error in the criminal context:

> [A]n appellate court may, in its discretion, correct an error not raised at trial only where the appellant demonstrates that (1) there is an "error"; (2) the error is "clear or obvious, rather than subject to reasonable dispute"; (3) the error "affected the appellant's substantial rights, which in the ordinary case means" it "affected the outcome of the district court proceedings"; and (4) "the error seriously affect[s] the fairness, integrity or public reputation of judicial proceedings."

560 U.S. at 262 (quoting *Puckett v. United States,* 556 U.S. 129, 135 (2009)).

In addition, lack of subject-matter jurisdiction can be raised at any time by either the parties or the court. *See* Federal Rule of Civil Procedure 12(h)(3) ("If the court determines at any time that it lacks subject-matter jurisdiction, the court must dismiss the action.").

IV. WHO CAN APPEAL?

Not only are there limited matters that can be considered by the United States Courts of Appeal, but only a limited number of parties can raise those issues on appeal. Only losing parties in a United States District Court can appeal a final judgment to the appropriate United States Court of Appeals. And those losing parties only can appeal final judgments—not opinions, orders, or rulings entered by the trial judge before final judgment.

Consider, for instance, an action in which a plaintiff asserts federal statutory claims, a state common law claim, and a state statutory claim in federal district court. The district court awards damages, a permanent injunction, costs and attorneys' fees on the federal claims and additional damages on the state common law claim. While the court also finds that the defendant violated the state statute, it awards no damages or other relief against the defendant on that claim. The court of appeals ultimately held in this case that the defendant lacked standing to appeal the finding that defendant had violated the state statute:

> "[T]he law is well-settled that a party lacks standing to appeal from a judgment by which it is not aggrieved." *See Penda Corp. v. United States*, 44 F.3d 967, 971 (Fed.Cir.1994). The district court's judgment in this case did not award damages, an injunction, or attorney's fees based on the Florida statutory claim, nor did PODS seek a declaratory judgment on this claim. Porta Stor has identified no other basis to conclude that it was aggrieved by the district court's judgment, and therefore it lacks standing to appeal the jury's verdict on the Florida Deceptive and Unfair Trade Practices Act. *See id.* at 972 ("Courts . . . have not recognized standing to appeal where a party does not seek reversal of the judgment but asks only for review of unfavorable findings.").

PODS, Inc. v. Porta Stor, Inc., 484 F.3d 1359, 1366 (Fed. Cir. 2007).

For similar reasons, the United States Court of Appeals for the Fifth Circuit found that a plaintiff had no standing to appeal a judgment based on a finding that her constitutional rights had been violated and awarding her "nominal damages, a temporary restraining order, a preliminary injunction, a rescission of the speaker policy [she had challenged], attorney's fees and a judgment in [her] favor." *Ward v. Santa Fe Indep. Sch. Dist.*, 393 F.3d 599, 605 (5th Cir. 2004). The Court of Appeals stated:

> It is a central tenet of appellate jurisdiction that a party who is not aggrieved by a judgment of the district court has no standing to appeal it. Thus, a prevailing party generally may not appeal a judgment in its favor. *Lindheimer v. Illinois Bell Tel. Co.*, 292 U.S. 151, 176 (1934) ("The Company was

successful in the District Court and has no right of appeal from the decree in its favor"); *See also In re DES Litig.*, 7 F.3d 20, 23 (2d Cir.1993) ("Ordinarily, a prevailing party cannot appeal from a district court judgment in its favor"). Rather, a prevailing party has standing to appeal only if it can demonstrate an adverse effect resulting from the judgment in its favor. *See e.g. Aetna Cas. & Sur. Co. v. Cunningham*, 224 F.2d 478, 480–81 (5th Cir.1955) (prevailing party had standing to appeal where grounds for district court judgment rendered it dischargeable in bankruptcy); *In re DES Litig.*, *supra*, 7 F.3d at 23 (a prevailing party may appeal if aggrieved by the collateral estoppel effects of the district court's opinion.)

393 F.3d at 603. As Judge Posner noted in an opinion for the Seventh Circuit Court of Appeals, "A winning party cannot appeal merely because the court that gave him his victory did not say things that he would have liked to hear, such as that his opponent is a lawbreaker. * * * Judgments are appealable; opinions are not." *Chathas v. Local 134 Int'l Bhd. of Elec. Workers*, 233 F.3d 508, 512 (7th Cir. 2000).

There are, though, rare situations in which a party may receive all the relief it sought in the trial court but nevertheless have standing to appeal. In *Aetna Cas. & Sur. Co. v. Cunningham*, 224 F.2d 478 (5th Cir. 1955), the plaintiff Aetna received all the damages it sought, prevailing on a contract claim against Cunningham but not on a fraud claim seeking the same amount of damages as Aetna recovered on the contract claim. Although it received judgment for all the damages it sought, Aetna nevertheless appealed because a judgment based solely on its contract claim would be dischargeable in bankruptcy. As the United States Court of Appeals for the Fifth Circuit concluded: "[A]mount is not the sole measure of the relief to which a party may be entitled. The judgment may have different qualities and legal consequences dependent on the claim on which it is based." 224 F.2d at 480. Accordingly, "Aetna was denied judgment of the quality to which it laid claim, [making] it * * * a party aggrieved on appeal." 224 F.2d at 480.

Many trial court determinations are within the discretion of the trial judge and, even if the judge abuses his discretion, many rulings will never be presented to an appellate court. Assume, for example, that a trial judge denied defendant's motion to dismiss, but the jury later returned a verdict for the defendant. The defendant will not be able to appeal the denial of the motion to dismiss, because it later obtained a trial court judgment based on the jury verdict. However, what if the plaintiff appeals the judgment entered for the defendant? In that situation, the defendant can argue to the court of appeals that the district court judgment must be affirmed because of both the jury verdict and the denial of the motion to dismiss.

Federal courts of appeal review federal trial court judgments, not trial court opinions. Moreover, appeals can be taken only by a party who lost in the district court—although others may be interested in the action, some of whom even may suffer injury resulting from the activity challenged in the civil action. Thus being a losing party in the trial court may not be all bad news. Even though you lost your claim or action in that court, as a losing party you should be able to pursue an appeal to a United States Court of Appeals.

V. WHEN CAN YOU APPEAL?

You've decided what you'd like to appeal, confirmed that you are a losing party with the ability to appeal, and determined that it is worth your client's time and money to invest in an appeal. The next question is when you can take your appeal to the appropriate United States Court of Appeals. The "when" question is governed by the final judgment rule, which is considered in this section.

A. THE FINAL JUDGMENT RULE

Prior to and during trial, the trial judge makes many decisions, some of which can provide the basis for later appellate review. But just when those decisions should be subject to review is a separate question. Should the losing party be able to appeal individual decisions or orders as they are entered? Although this is more possible in some state courts,[8] the federal system employs a unitary appeal—under which all trial court decisions are appealed together only after final judgment has been entered in the district court.

Section 1291 of 28 U.S.C. provides:

> The courts of appeal (other than the United States Court of Appeals for the Federal Circuit) shall have jurisdiction of appeals from all final decisions of the district courts of the United States * * *, except where a direct review may be had in the Supreme Court.[9]

---

[8] *E.g.*, N.Y. C.P.L.R. 5701 (McKinney 1999) ("An appeal may be taken to the appellate division as of right in an action, originating in the supreme court or a county court: * * * 2. from an order not specified in subdivision (b), where the motion it decided was made upon notice and it: * * * (iv) involves some part of the merits; or (v) affects a substantial right * * *."); Del. S. Ct. Rule 42(b)(ii) and (iii) (Although interlocutory appeals "should be exceptional, not routine, * * * in deciding whether to certify an interlocutory appeal, the trial court should consider whether * * * (G) Review of the interlocutory order may terminate the litigation; or (H) Review of the interlocutory order may serve considerations of justice.").

[9] While Section 1291 refers to appeals from all "final decisions of the district courts of the United States," the Judiciary Act of 1789 referred to appeals from "final judgments and decrees." The change in statutory language from "judgments" to "decisions" has been held not to have changed the substance of the earlier appeals provision. 15A C. Wright, A. Miller & E. Cooper, *Federal Practice & Procedure* § 3906, at 256–66 (2nd ed. 1992). Thus the doctrine continues to be known as the "final judgment rule" even though 28 U.S.C. § 1291 refers to appeals from "final decisions of the district courts."

This jurisdictional statute creates what is known as the "final judgment rule," which, with certain narrow exceptions discussed in the next subsection, restricts federal appellate jurisdiction to appeals from final judgments rendered in the United States District Courts.

As interpreted by the Supreme Court in *Catlin v. United States*, 324 U.S. 229, 233 (1945), "A 'final decision' generally is one which ends the litigation on the merits and leaves nothing for the court to do but execute the judgment." As the Court later explained in *Richardson-Merrell, Inc. v. Koller*, 472 U.S. 424, 429–30 (1985):

> Title 28 U.S.C. § 1291 grants the courts of appeals jurisdiction of appeals from all "final decisions of the district courts," except where a direct appeal lies to this Court. The statutory requirement of a "final decision" means that "a party must ordinarily raise all claims of error in a single appeal following final judgment on the merits." *Firestone Tire & Rubber Co. v. Risjord*, 449 U.S. 368, 374 (1981). As the Court noted in *Firestone*, the final judgment rule promotes efficient judicial administration while at the same time emphasizing the deference appellate courts owe to the district judge's decisions on the many questions of law and fact that arise before judgment. Immediate review of every trial court ruling, while permitting more prompt correction of erroneous decisions, would impose unreasonable disruption, delay, and expense. It would also undermine the ability of district judges to supervise litigation. In § 1291 Congress has expressed a preference that some erroneous trial court rulings go uncorrected until the appeal of a final judgment, rather than having litigation punctuated by "piecemeal appellate review of trial court decisions which do not terminate the litigation." *United States v. Hollywood Motor Car Co.*, 458 U.S. 263, 265, (1982).

So, before jurisdiction will exist for an appeal, counsel must await a final judgment in the district court that "ends the litigation on the merits and leaves nothing for the court to do but execute the judgment." *Catlin v. United States*, 324 U.S. at 233.

B. EXCEPTIONS TO THE FINAL JUDGMENT RULE

The final judgment rule is not difficult to apply in most cases, and it is usually easy to determine when an appeal can be taken. There are, though, a small number of exceptions to the rule that have been recognized to avoid party unfairness. Provisions of Title 28 of the United States Code, the Federal Rules of Civil Procedure, and federal case law all contain well-recognized exceptions to the final judgment rule.

1. Statutory Exceptions to the Final Judgment Rule. Congress, itself, has recognized several exceptions to the final judgment rule. These exceptions, within Title 28 of the United States Code, provide that specific interlocutory decisions may be appealed before a final judgment has been entered in the district court.

Interlocutory Orders Involving Injunctions. Initially, Section 1292(a)(1) extends federal appellate jurisdiction to "[i]nterlocutory orders of the district courts of the United States * * *, or of the judges thereof, granting, continuing, modifying, refusing or dissolving injunctions, or refusing to dissolve or modify injunctions, except where a direct review may be had in the Supreme Court." This grant of appellate jurisdiction is not as broad as it might seem. "Temporary restraining orders ordinarily cannot be appealed, and appeal is permitted from interlocutory orders that grant—and in some cases orders that refuse to grant—permanent injunctive relief. In addition, there is substantial uncertainty over the nature of the mandatory orders that qualify as 'injunctions' [for the purposes of Section 1292(a)]." 16 C. Wright, A. Miller & E. Cooper, *Federal Practice & Procedure* § 3921, at 13–14 (3rd ed. 2012). As Justice Brennan noted in an opinion upholding appellate jurisdiction:

> Because § 1292(a)(1) was intended to carve out only a limited exception to the final-judgment rule, we have construed the statute narrowly to ensure that appeal as of right under § 1292(a)(1) will be available only in circumstances where an appeal will further the statutory purpose of "permit[ting] litigants to effectually challenge interlocutory orders of serious, perhaps irreparable, consequence."

Carson v. Am. Brands, Inc., 450 U.S. 79, 84 (1981) (quoting *Baltimore Contractors, Inc. v. Bodinger*, 348 U.S. 176, 181 (1955)).

Discretionary Review of Certified Questions. While an aggrieved party has a right to appeal interlocutory orders falling within Section 1291(a)(1), 28 U.S.C. § 1292(b) provides the possibility of discretionary appeals if both the district court and court of appeals conclude that an interlocutory appeal is appropriate. Section 1292(b) provides:

> When a district judge, in making in a civil action an order not otherwise appealable under this section, shall be of the opinion that such order involves a controlling question of law as to which there is substantial ground for difference of opinion and that an immediate appeal from the order may materially advance the ultimate termination of the litigation, he shall so state in writing in such order. The Court of Appeals which would have jurisdiction of an appeal of such action may thereupon, in its discretion, permit an appeal to be taken from such order, if application is made to it within ten days after the entry of the order * * *.

A discretionary appeal under Section 1292(b) might be granted if a close, controlling question has been decided, but significant proceedings in the district court are still necessary before entry of a final judgment. Assume, for example, that, after considering several possible statutes of limitation that might apply to a complex fraud action, a federal district judge concludes that the applicable statute of limitations does not bar that action and that extensive discovery and trial proceedings on the merits are in order. In such a case the defendant might be able to immediately appeal the judge's order under Section 1292(b) if:

(1) The district judge in his order finding that the plaintiff has satisfied the statute of limitations states that:

(a) his order involves a "controlling question of law as to which there is substantial ground for difference of opinion;" and

(b) "an immediate appeal from the order may materially advance the ultimate termination of the litigation;"

(2) The defendant applies within 10 days after entry of the district court order to the court of appeals to permit an appeal; and

(3) The court of appeals exercises its discretion to permit the interlocutory appeal.

Discretionary appeals pursuant to Section 1292(b) are possible only if the losing party, district court, and court of appeals all agree that an appeal prior to final judgment is appropriate. Such appeals can save the district court and the parties the necessity of extended district court proceedings in an action in which the court of appeals ultimately concludes that the district court order should be reversed.

Mandamus. Congress also has recognized the power of the federal courts to entertain interlocutory appeals in aid of their appellate jurisdiction. The All Writs Act, 28 U.S.C. § 1651(a), provides: "The Supreme Court and all courts established by Act of Congress may issue all writs necessary or appropriate in aid of their respective jurisdictions and agreeable to the usages and principles of law." The most significant of these writs are writs of mandamus.

Chief Justice Warren described the limited situations in which a writ of mandamus might permit an appeal from an interlocutory district court order:

The peremptory writ of mandamus has traditionally been used in the federal courts only "to confine an inferior court to a lawful exercise of its prescribed jurisdiction or to compel it to exercise its authority when it is its duty to do so." *Roche v. Evaporated Milk Assn.*, 319 U.S. 21, 26 (1943). While the courts have never confined themselves to an arbitrary and technical definition of "jurisdiction," it is clear that only exceptional circumstances amounting to a judicial "usurpation of power" will justify the invocation of this extraordinary remedy. *De Beers Consol. Mines, Ltd. v. United States*, 325 U.S. 212, 217 (1945). Thus the writ has been invoked where unwarranted judicial action threatened "to embarrass the executive arm of the government in conducting foreign relations," *Ex parte Republic of Peru*, 318 U.S. 578, 588 (1943), where it was the only means of forestalling intrusion by the federal judiciary on a delicate area of federal-state relations, *State of Maryland v. Soper*, 270 U.S. 9 (1926), where it was necessary to confine a lower court to the terms of an appellate tribunal's mandate, *United States v. United States Dist. Court*, 334 U.S. 258 (1948), and where a district judge displayed a persistent disregard of the Rules of Civil Procedure promulgated by this Court, *La Buy v. Howes Leather Co.*, 352 U.S. 249 (1957).

Will v. United States, 389 U.S. 90, 95–96 (1967).[10]

2.   Exceptions to the Final Judgment Rule in the Federal Rules of Civil Procedure. In addition to the congressionally-enacted exceptions to the final judgment rule in 28 U.S.C. §§ 1292 and 1651, the Federal Rules of Civil Procedure expressly address final judgments in two significant respects.[11]

Rule 54(b): Judgment on Multiple Claims or Involving Multiple Parties. What if a civil action involves multiple claims or parties? Can a party appeal one portion of an action before all claims have been decided by the trial judge? Rule 54(b) of the Federal Rules of Civil Procedure permits the district judge to enter final judgment on fewer than all claims and to determine that there is no just reason for delay, thus allowing a losing party to appeal that portion of the action before entry of a final judgment. The first sentence of Rule 54(b) provides:

> When an action presents more than one claim for relief—whether as a claim, counterclaim, or third-party claim—or when multiple parties are involved, the court may direct entry of a final judgment as to one or more, but fewer than all, claims or parties only if the court expressly determines that there is no just reason for delay.

The second sentence of Rule 54(b) provides that, absent such an express determination by the district judge to enter final judgment on

---

[10] As in *Will v. United States*, the appellee in mandamus actions in the United States Court of Appeals is typically the federal judge who allegedly exceeded or failed to exercise his or her jurisdiction and whose action is being challenged by the petition for a writ of mandamus.

[11] 28 U.S.C. § 1292(e) provides: "The Supreme Court may prescribe rules, in accordance with section 2072 of this title [the Rules Enabling Act], to provide for an appeal of an interlocutory decision to the courts of appeals that is not otherwise provided for under subsection (a), (b), (c), or (d)."

fewer than all claims or parties, final judgment is not to be entered before all claims have been determined:

> Otherwise [if there is no Rule 54(b) determination that there is no just reason for delay], any order or other decision, however designated, that adjudicates fewer than all the claims or the rights and liabilities of fewer than all the parties does not end the action as to any of the claims or parties and may be revised at any time before the entry of a judgment adjudicating all the claims and all the parties' rights and liabilities.

Rule 54(b) does not provide a right to appeal the dismissal or other resolution of individual claims. However, it recognizes the possibility of appeal if the district judge determines there is no just reason to delay appellate consideration of the final resolution of a claim until the entry of final judgment on all claims and involving all parties.

Rule 23(f): Orders Granting or Denying Class Certification. The Federal Rules also recognize the possibility of an immediate appeal of orders granting or denying class action certification. The Advisory Committee described the rationale for this exception to the final judgment rule as follows:

> An order denying certification may confront the plaintiff with a situation in which the only sure path to appellate review is by proceeding to final judgment on the merits of an individual claim that, standing alone, is far smaller than the costs of litigation. An order granting certification, on the other hand, may force a defendant to settle rather than incur the cost of defending a class action and run the risk of potentially ruinous liability. These concerns can be met at low cost by establishing in the court of appeals a discretionary power to grant interlocutory review in cases that show appeal-worthy certification issues.

Advisory Committee Note to 1998 Amendment to Rule 23, 167 F.R.D. 523, 565 (1998).

Rule 23(f) therefore provides:

> A court of appeals may permit an appeal from an order granting or denying class-action certification under this rule if a petition for permission to appeal is filed with the circuit clerk within 14 days after the order is entered. An appeal does not stay proceedings in the district court unless the district judge or the court of appeals so orders.

As with Rule 54(b), Rule 23(f) does not create a right to an interlocutory appeal. It does, though, give the courts of appeal discretion to permit an appeal from orders granting or denying class certification.

3. The Collateral Order Doctrine. When faced with situations in which a party will suffer harm absent the opportunity to immediately appeal, the Supreme Court has recognized the possibility of interlocutory appeals in a narrow set of circumstances.

The most significant judicially-crafted exception to the final judgment rule is the "collateral order doctrine" recognized by the Supreme Court in *Cohen v. Beneficial Industrial Loan Corp.*, 337 U.S. 541 (1949). In *Cohen* the Court held that a district court order refusing to apply state security bond and fee-shifting requirements in a stockholder derivative action was appealable as "fall[ing] in that small class which finally determine claims of right separable from, and collateral to, rights asserted in the action, too important to be denied review and too independent of the cause itself to require that appellate consideration be deferred until the whole case is adjudicated." 337 U.S. at 546.

The Supreme Court later described the collateral order exception to the final judgment rule as follows:

> The collateral order doctrine is a "narrow exception," *Firestone* [*Tire & Rubber Co. v. Risjord*], 449 U.S., at 374, whose reach is limited to trial court orders affecting rights that will be irretrievably lost in the absence of an immediate appeal. To fall within the exception, an order must at a minimum satisfy three conditions: It must "conclusively determine the disputed question," "resolve an important issue completely separate from the merits of the action," and "be effectively unreviewable on appeal from a final judgment." *Coopers & Lybrand v. Livesay*, 437 U.S. 463, 468 (1978).

> *Richardson-Merrell, Inc. v. Koller*, 472 U.S. 424, 430–31 (1985).

Relying upon the doctrine developed in *Cohen v. Beneficial Industrial Loan Corp.*, the Supreme Court has permitted appeals from interlocutory orders denying the President absolute immunity from a civil damage action challenging presidential actions, *Nixon v. Fitzgerald*, 457 U.S. 731, 741–43 (1982), denying a claim of qualified immunity turning on an issue of law and asserted by the Attorney General, *Mitchell v. Forsyth*, 472 U.S. 511, 524–30 (1985), and denying a motion to dismiss an indictment on double jeopardy grounds. *Abney v. United States*, 431 U.S. 651, 656–62 (1977). Why does interlocutory appeal make sense in such cases?

The overwhelming majority of orders issued by federal district courts are non-appealable interlocutory orders. However, if an order satisfies the *Cohen* test for the collateral order exception to the final judgment rule, it may be possible to obtain appellate review of such order before the entry of a final judgment in the district court.

The most significant exceptions to the final judgment rule are summarized in Figure 15–1.

FIGURE 15–1
EXCEPTIONS TO 28 U.S.C. § 1291 FINAL JUDGMENT RULE

Exception	Exception Type	Exception Authority	Application
Interlocutory Orders involving Injunctions	Statutory	28 U.S.C. § 1292(a)	order "granting, continuing, modifying, refusing or dissolving injunctions or refusing to dissolve or modify injunctions"
Discretionary Review of Certified Questions	Statutory	28 U.S.C. § 1292(b)	district judge certifies order that "involves a controlling question of law as to which there is substantial ground for difference of opinion and that an immediate appeal * * * may materially advance the ultimate termination of the litigation" and court of appeals permits appeal
Mandamus	Statutory	28 U.S.C. § 1651(a) (All Writs Act)	"to confine an inferior court to a lawful exercise of its prescribed jurisdiction or to compel it to exercise its authority when it is its duty to do so" *Roche v. Evaporated Milk Assn.*, 319 U.S. 21, 26 (1943).
Class Certification Orders	Federal Rules of Civil Procedure	FRCP 23(f)	order "granting or denying class-action certification"
Judgment on Multiple Claims or involving Multiple Parties	Federal Rules of Civil Procedure	FRCP 54(b)	district court may "direct entry of a final judgment as to one or more, but fewer than all, claims or parties * * * expressly determin[ing] that there is no just reason for delay"

Collateral Order Doctrine	Judicial	*Cohen v. Beneficial Industrial Loan Corp.*, 337 U.S. 541 (1949)	"order must conclusively determine the disputed question, resolve an important issue completely separate from the merits of the action, and be effectively unreviewable on appeal from a final judgment" *Coopers & Lybrand v. Livesay*, 437 U.S. 463, 468 (1978).

VI. WHERE AND HOW DO YOU APPEAL?

Once the district judge issues the final judgment or an exception to the final judgment rule has been identified, the action can be appealed. The Federal Rules of Appellate Procedure address how and where an appeal is perfected. Federal case law and the Federal Rules of Civil Procedure provide the standard of review to be applied by the appellate courts. Both the governing provisions of the Federal Rules of Appellate Procedure and the standard of review are addressed in this section.

A. APPEALS UNDER THE FEDERAL RULES OF APPELLATE PROCEDURE

Just as the Federal Rules of Civil Procedure provide the governing procedural rules for federal district courts, the Federal Rules of Appellate Procedure "govern procedure in the United States courts of appeals." Federal Rule of Appellate Procedure 1(a)(1).

The first sentence of Federal Rule of Appellate Procedure 3(a)(1) provides: "An appeal permitted by law as of right from a district court to a court of appeals may be taken only by filing a notice of appeal with the district clerk within the time allowed by Rule 4." Rule 4(a)(1)(A) provides that, in most cases, "In a civil case * * * the notice of appeal required by Rule 3 must be filed with the district clerk within 30 days after entry of the judgment or order appealed from."[12]

Thus counsel must wait for the entry of the final judgment pursuant to Rule 58 of the Federal Rules of Civil Procedure. A judge's statement, orally or in an opinion, that he is granting a dispositive

---

[12] The exceptions to the 30-day period of Rule 4(a)(1) are appeals taken by the United States, a U.S. agency, or certain current or former U.S. officers or employees (all of which are given 60 days to file the notice) or by an inmate confined in an institution (for whom filing is considered accomplished when the notice of appeal is deposited in the institution's internal mail system). In addition, Federal Rule of Appellate Procedure 4(a)(4) lists certain trial-court motions that extend the period for filing the notice of appeal (such as a Rule 50(b) renewed motion for judgment as a matter of law, Rule 59 motion for a new trial, and Rule 54 motion for attorney's fees if the court extends the time to appeal in connection with that motion).

motion is not a substitute for the entry of final judgment required by Rule 58. Federal Rule of Appellate Procedure 4(a)(2) addresses the situation in which a party prematurely files a notice of appeal based on a judge's ruling but before final judgment is entered: "A notice of appeal filed after the court announces a decision or order—but before the entry of the judgment or order—is treated as filed on the date of and after the entry."

In addition to the initial appeal filed by a losing party, Rule 4(a)(3) of the Federal Rules of Appellate Procedure provides for the possibility of cross-appeals:

> If one party timely files a notice of appeal, any other party may file a notice of appeal within 14 days after the date when the first notice was filed, or within the time otherwise prescribed by this Rule 4(a), whichever period ends later.

Assume, for instance, that the trial judge has both (1) dismissed the plaintiff's action and (2) dismissed defendant's counterclaim. In this situation, the defendant might not consider it worthwhile to maintain an appeal seeking review of the dismissal of the counterclaim. However, once the plaintiff files her appeal, the defendant will be put to the expense of an appeal seeking reversal of the dismissal of plaintiff's claim. In this event, it may cost little more for the defendant to appeal the dismissal of his counterclaim at the same time. The defendant therefore may decide to file a cross-appeal once the plaintiff has filed her original appeal.

Form 1 of the Appendix of Forms of the Federal Rules of Appellate Procedure is a one-sentence document that illustrates how simple the notice of appeal is:

> Notice is hereby given that [(here name all parties taking the appeal), (plaintiffs) (defendants) in the above named case] hereby appeal to the United States Court of Appeals for the _____ Circuit (from the final judgment) (from an order (describing it)) entered in this action on the _____ day of _____, 20___.

The record on appeal is defined by Federal Rule of Appellate Procedure 10(a) as follows:

> The following items constitute the record on appeal:
>
> (1) the original papers and exhibits filed in the district court;
>
> (2) the transcript of proceedings, if any; and
>
> (3) a certified copy of the docket entries prepared by the district clerk.

In the United States Courts of Appeal, the appeal typically is heard by a panel of three judges from that circuit, although Rule 35(a) of the Federal Rules of Appellate Procedure provides for the possibility of hearings or rehearings *en banc* by all the judges of that circuit in situations in which:

(1) en banc consideration is necessary to secure or maintain uniformity of the court's decisions; or

(2) the proceeding involves a question of exceptional importance.

The court of appeals panel may decide the appeal by a written, reported decision, by a written decision that is provided to the parties but not published, or by a per curiam opinion. The United States Courts web page defines "per curiam" as follows: "Latin, meaning 'for the court.' In appellate courts, often refers to an unsigned opinion." http://www.uscourts.gov/Common/Glossary.aspx. Such opinions are written to resolve the specific appeal before the court, typically without providing a comprehensive analysis to serve as precedent in other actions. Just such a short-and-to-the-point per curiam opinion was issued by a three-judge panel of the United States Court of Appeals for the Second Circuit in *Leonard v. PepsiCo, Inc.*:

Leonard v. Pepsico, Inc.
United States Court of Appeals, Second Circuit, 2000
210 F.3d 88

■ Before: FEINBERG, JACOBS and HALL,* CIRCUIT JUDGES.

OPINION

■ PER CURIAM.

In 1995, defendant-appellee Pepsico, Inc. conducted a promotion in which it offered merchandise in exchange for "points" earned by purchasing Pepsi Cola. A television commercial aired by Pepsico depicted a teenager gloating over various items of merchandise earned by Pepsi points, and culminated in the teenager arriving at high school in a Harrier Jet, a fighter aircraft of the United States Marine Corps. For each item of merchandise sported by the teenager (a T shirt, a jacket, sunglasses), the ad noted the number of Pepsi points needed to get it. When the teenager is shown in the jet, the ad prices it as 7 million points.

Plaintiff-appellant John D. R. Leonard alleges that the ad was an offer, that he accepted the offer by tendering the equivalent of 7 million points, and that Pepsico has breached its contract to deliver the Harrier jet. Pepsico characterizes the use of the Harrier jet in the ad as a hyperbolic joke ("zany humor"), cites the ad's reference to offering

---

* The Honorable Cynthia Holcomb Hall, of the United States Court of Appeals for the Ninth Circuit, sitting by designation.

details contained in the promotional catalog (which contains no Harrier fighter plane), and argues that no objective person would construe the ad as an offer for the Harrier jet.

The United States District Court for the Southern District of New York (Wood, J.) agreed with Pepsico and granted its motion for summary judgment on the grounds (1) that the commercial did not amount to an offer of goods; (2) that no objective person could reasonably have concluded that the commercial actually offered consumers a Harrier Jet; and (3) that the alleged contract could not satisfy the New York statute of frauds.

We affirm for substantially the reasons stated in Judge Wood's opinion. *See* 88 F.Supp.2d 116 (S.D.N.Y.1999).

B. THE STANDARD OF REVIEW IN THE UNITED STATES COURTS OF APPEAL[13]

Once the appeal has been properly noticed, counsel must turn her attention to the briefing and argument of the appeal. Much of counsel's focus will be on many of the same arguments made (unsuccessfully) in the federal district court. However, these arguments must be viewed through a different lens on appeal. Specifically, the court of appeals will only consider relevant arguments pursuant to the appropriate standard or scope of review. In fact, Federal Rules of Appellate Procedure 28(a)(9)(B) and 29(b)(5) require that appellate briefs in the United States Courts of Appeal include a statement of the applicable standard of review.

Counsel may argue to a district judge that a defendant's action was negligent or that the judge should not admit particular evidence during trial. In the court of appeals, however, the argument usually is not that the defendant was negligent nor that the judge was wrong—but that the decisions of the trial judge were clearly erroneous or an abuse of discretion. The appropriate standard of review in the federal court of appeals depends on the determination that is challenged on appeal. The court of appeals will apply a different standard of review depending upon whether it is reviewing a district judge's findings of fact in a bench trial, a district judge's conclusions of law in a bench trial, a district judge's entry of judgment based upon a jury verdict, or a district judge's entry of pretrial orders. Each of these situations, and corresponding standard of review on appeal, will be considered in turn.

1. De Novo Review of Trial Court Conclusions of Law. When the district court, sitting without a jury, enters conclusions of law, there is usually no reason for a court of appeals to defer to those

---

[13] *See generally* Childress, "A Primer on Standards of Review in Federal Civil Actions," 293 F.R.D. 156 (2013).

legal conclusions. This is not a situation where it would make sense to "give due regard to the trial court's opportunity to judge the witnesses' credibility" as Rule 52(a)(6) requires with respect to factual findings. The standard of review concerning trial court conclusions of law, therefore, is one of "de novo," independent, or plenary appellate review. Justice Blackmun explained why de novo review is appropriate in such cases:

> Independent appellate review of legal issues best serves the dual goals of doctrinal coherence and economy of judicial administration. District judges preside alone over fast-paced trials: Of necessity they devote much of their energy and resources to hearing witnesses and reviewing evidence. Similarly, the logistical burdens of trial advocacy limit the extent to which trial counsel is able to supplement the district judge's legal research with memoranda and briefs. Thus, trial judges often must resolve complicated legal questions without benefit of "extended reflection [or] extensive information." Coenen, "To Defer or Not to Defer: A Study of Federal Circuit Court Deference to District Court Rulings on State Law," 73 *Minn.L.Rev.* 899, 923 (1989).

> Courts of appeals, on the other hand, are structurally suited to the collaborative juridical process that promotes decisional accuracy. With the record having been constructed below and settled for purposes of the appeal, appellate judges are able to devote their primary attention to legal issues. As questions of law become the focus of appellate review, it can be expected that the parties' briefs will be refined to bring to bear on the legal issues more information and more comprehensive analysis than was provided for the district judge. Perhaps most important, courts of appeals employ multijudge panels, *see* 28 U.S.C. §§ 46(b) and (c), that permit reflective dialogue and collective judgment.

Salve Regina Coll. v. Russell, 499 U.S. 225, 231–32 (1991).

Thus, when reviewing a conclusion of law reached by a district court, the court of appeals considers that legal determination without any deference to the district court—considering it de novo or "anew."

2. Clearly Erroneous Review of Trial Court Findings of Fact. When a district judge finds facts in a bench (nonjury) trial, those fact findings will be reviewed by a court of appeals under a clearly erroneous standard. Federal Rule of Civil Procedure 52(a)(1) requires that in "an action tried on the facts without a jury or with an advisory jury, the court must find the facts specially and state its conclusions of law separately." Rule 52(a)(6) specifies the appellate standard of review for these factual findings: "Findings of fact, whether based on oral or other evidence, must not be set aside unless clearly erroneous, and the reviewing court must give due regard to the trial court's opportunity to judge the witnesses' credibility." The Supreme Court has stated that a "finding is 'clearly erroneous' when although there is evidence to support it, the reviewing court on the entire evidence is left with the definite and firm conviction that a mistake has been committed." *United States v. U.S. Gypsum Co.*, 333 U.S. 364, 395 (1948). This deference to district court findings of fact contrasts with appellate review of district court conclusions of law (to which there is no deference).

3. Abuse of Discretion Review of Trial Court Rulings. In addition to the entry of findings of fact or conclusions of law at the conclusion of bench trials, district judges enter many additional orders. The Supreme Court differentiates the standard of review in these three situations as follows: "For purposes of standard of review, decisions by judges are traditionally divided into three categories, denominated questions of law (reviewable de novo), questions of fact (reviewable for clear error), and matters of discretion (reviewable for " 'abuse of discretion')." *Pierce v. Underwood*, 487 U.S. 552, 558 (1988). The Court in *Pierce* further described the situations in which the courts of appeal apply abuse of discretion review:

> It is especially common for issues involving what can broadly be labeled "supervision of litigation," which is the sort of issue presented here, to be given abuse-of-discretion review. *See, e.g., Hensley v. Eckerhart*, 461 U.S. 424, 437 (1983) (attorney's fees); *National Hockey League v. Metropolitan Hockey Club, Inc.*, 427 U.S. 639, 642 (1976) (discovery sanctions); *see generally* 1 S. Childress & M. Davis, *Standards of Review* §§ 4.1–4.20, pp. 228–286 (1986).

Pierce v. Underwood, 487 U.S. at 588.

Whether to limit discovery, grant a motion to amend the pleadings, give parties additional time to complete discovery, or limit the number of trial witnesses are all discretionary decisions subject to appellate review under the abuse of discretion standard. The court of appeals does not decide whether it would have made the same decision as did the district court, but, instead, whether the district court's decision is within a broad range of appropriate decisions. Thus if a district judge cannot be convinced to rule favorably on such an issue in the district court, there is only a limited chance that the court of appeals will reverse such a district court order.

4. Reasonableness Review of Jury Determinations. What if the trial in the district court is heard by a jury? Rule 50(a)(1) permits a trial judge to take a case from a jury, or overturn a jury determination, in the following situation: "If a party has been fully heard on an issue during a jury trial and the court finds that a reasonable jury would not have a legally sufficient evidentiary basis to find for the party on that issue." The same standard applies to the review of jury determinations in the federal courts of appeal. 9B C. Wright & A. Miller, *Federal*

Practice & Procedure § 2524, at 234–36 (3rd ed. 2008) ("[T]he analysis that is employed is the same in the trial court and on appeal * * *.").

The Supreme Court has described the showing that must be made to determine, as a matter of law, that a reasonable jury could not return a verdict for a party:

> If the defendant in a run-of-the-mill civil case moves for summary judgment or for a directed verdict based on the lack of proof of a material fact, the judge must ask himself not whether he thinks the evidence unmistakably favors one side or the other but whether a fair-minded jury could return a verdict for the plaintiff on the evidence presented. The mere existence of a scintilla of evidence in support of the plaintiff's position will be insufficient; there must be evidence on which the jury could reasonably find for the plaintiff.

Anderson v. Liberty Lobby, Inc., 477 U.S. 242, 252 (1986). Thus the courts of appeal are most deferential to district court findings by a jury, only reversing such determinations upon a determination that no reasonable jury could have reached that determination on the evidence presented.

These different appellate standards of review thus span the spectrum from de novo review (providing no deference to the trial court) to the reasonableness review of jury determinations (providing the greatest deference to the trial court determination and upholding the jury verdict so long as a reasonable jury could have reached the jury's result). These standards are illustrated in Figure 15–2.

FIGURE 15–2
APPELLATE STANDARDS OF REVIEW

Decision of Judge or Jury	Trial Court Determination	Appellate Standard of Review	Amount of Deference to Trial Court
Judge (Bench Trial)	Conclusion of Law	De Novo	No Deference to Trial Court
Judge (Bench Trial)	Finding of Fact	Clearly Erroneous (Rule 52(a)(6))	"[T]he reviewing court on the entire evidence is left with the definite and firm conviction that a mistake has been committed." *United States v. U.S. Gypsum Co.*, 333 U.S. 364, 395 (1948).

Judge (in Bench or Jury Trial)	Pretrial order in "supervision of litigation." *Pierce v. Underwood*, 487 U.S. 552, 559 (1988)	Abuse of Discretion	Question is not whether judge was "right or wrong," but whether judge appropriately acted within a broad range of discretion.
Jury	Jury Finding or Verdict	Reasonableness Review	Most Deference to Trial Court: Could fair-minded jury "return a verdict for the plaintiff on the evidence presented?" *Anderson v. Liberty Lobby, Inc.*, 477 U.S. 242, 252 (1986).

Assume that in an action ultimately tried by the judge (a bench trial), the defendant appeals a final judgment challenging (1) the trial judge's conclusion of law on a particular issue; (2) the trial judge's findings of certain facts; and (3) the trial judge's exclusion of expert evidence at trial. In such an appeal, separate standards of review will apply to the appellate review of the different types of trial court determinations. Through what appellate lens will the court of appeals consider issues 1, 2, and 3?

VII. CONCLUSION

As you have seen in this chapter, there are a separate set of rules and procedures governing appeals in the United States Courts of Appeals. Just as importantly, specific actions must be taken in the United States District Court to make an appropriate record and preserve issues for appeal. Many of the decisions of district judges are discretionary and only can be reversed on appeal in situations in which the district judge abused his discretion. While an appeal may be possible, counsel therefore must do everything possible to ensure success in the district court in the first instance. At the end of the day, it's much better to be an appellee than an appellant or, better yet, to obtain a successful judgment in the district court that is not appealed.

VIII. CHAPTER ASSESSMENT

A. Multiple-Choice Questions. Answer the following questions and check your answers by reviewing the sections of the chapter noted in connection with each question.

1. A plaintiff motorist files a federal diversity action against a truck company, seeking damages resulting from a traffic accident. In its

answer the company includes a counterclaim, seeking damages allegedly caused by the motorist's negligence in the same accident. After trial, the jury returns a verdict for the company on plaintiff's claim and a verdict for the plaintiff motorist on the defendant's counterclaim.

That same day, the court enters judgment on both claims. Thirty days later, the plaintiff motorist files a notice of appeal to appeal the judgment against her on her claim. Ten days after the filing of plaintiff's notice, the defendant company files a notice of appeal to appeal the judgment against it on its counterclaim.

Review Section IV and VI(a) and choose the best answer from the following choices:

(a) Although the filing of the plaintiff's notice of appeal was timely, the filing of defendant's notice of appeal was not and the defendant cannot challenge the dismissal of its counterclaim in the court of appeals.

(b) Although the filing of the plaintiff's notice of appeal was timely, the filing of defendant's notice of appeal was not but defendant can nevertheless challenge the dismissal of its counterclaim in the court of appeals.

(c) Both notices of appeal were timely filed.

(d) Neither notice of appeal was timely filed.

2.   A plaintiff filed a diversity action in federal district court, alleging that the defendant negligently injured plaintiff in a traffic accident. After the completion of discovery and pretrial, a three-day jury trial was held. The jury returned a verdict for the defendant and the judge entered judgment on that verdict.

Ten days after the judge entered judgment for the defendant based upon the jury verdict, the plaintiff filed a motion for a new trial pursuant to Rule 59 of the Federal Rules of Civil Procedure. The judge granted that motion, entering an order for a new trial.

Review Section V(A) and choose the best answer from the following choices:

(a) Because the plaintiff did not agree to an immediate appeal, the defendant cannot appeal at this time.

(b) Because the order granting the motion for a new trial is not a final judgment, the defendant cannot appeal at this time.

(c) Because the action was fully tried in the district court, the defendant can appeal at this time.

(d) Because the order granting the motion for a new trial falls within an exception to the final order doctrine, the defendant can appeal at this time.

3. A retailer filed a federal diversity action against a manufacturer, alleging that the manufacturer failed to provide the retailer with the goods specified in the parties' contract. After completing discovery, counsel for the parties met with the judge at a Rule 16 final pretrial conference. At this conference the judge (1) denied a motion by the defendant manufacturer to grant summary judgment and dismiss the action; (2) denied the plaintiff retailer's motion to dismiss a defense counterclaim; (3) told the parties that they would only have two days per side to present their cases at trial; and (4) limited the parties to two expert witnesses per side.

All of these rulings were incorporated into a single order filed the day after the pretrial conference.

Review Section V(A) and choose the best answer from the following choices:

(a) Because these rulings were incorporated into a single written order, all four of the judge's rulings can be appealed at this time.

(b) Because it involved the denial of a motion seeking the dismissal of the action, the ruling on the motion for summary judgment can be appealed at this time although the other rulings cannot.

(c) Because there has been no final judgment, none of the judge's four rulings can be appealed at this time.

(d) Because they involve pretrial rulings, none of the judge's four rulings can be appealed either at this time or after trial.

4. After the completion of discovery, a defendant filed a motion for summary judgment. After the summary judgment motion was briefed by the parties, the federal district judge held oral argument on the motion. At the conclusion of the oral argument, the judge stated from the bench: "After considering your briefs and argument, I have concluded that there is no genuine dispute of any material fact and the defendant is entitled to judgment as a matter of law. I therefore will grant the motion for summary judgment."

That same afternoon, counsel for the plaintiff filed a notice of appeal in the district court. One week later a written judgment for the defendant was filed by the judge with the clerk of court.

Review Section VI(A) and choose the best answer from the following choices:

(a) Because the judge announced her decision immediately after the summary judgment argument, this was the final judgment in this action and the notice of appeal was timely filed.

(b) Because the plaintiff filed his notice of appeal after the judge announced her decision but before the final judgment was entered, the notice of appeal will be treated as if it was timely filed.

(c)   Because the plaintiff did not file his notice of appeal after entry of the final judgment, the notice of appeal was not timely filed.

(d)   Because the plaintiff filed his notice of appeal in the district court rather than in the court of appeals, the court of appeals cannot hear this action.

5.   After a two-day bench trial, the district judge filed factual findings and conclusions of law. On the basis of these findings of fact and conclusions of law, the district judge entered judgment for the plaintiff. Twenty-five days after the entry of judgment, the defendant filed a notice of appeal, then challenged in his appellate brief both the district court judge's specific findings of fact and conclusions of law.

Review Section VI(B) and choose the best answer from the following choices:

(a)   The court of appeals should review the district court conclusions of law under a de novo standard of review and the district court's findings of fact under a clearly erroneous standard.

(b)   The court of appeals should review the district court conclusions of law under a clearly erroneous standard of review and the district court's findings of fact under a de novo standard.

(c)   The court of appeals should review both the district court conclusions of law and findings of fact under a de novo standard of review.

(d)   The court of appeals should review both the district court conclusions of law and findings of fact under a clearly erroneous standard of review.

B.   Essay Questions. To test your understanding of this chapter's material, outline or write an answer to the following questions.

1.   Who Can Appeal and When?

Paula Pupil and eight other students and their parents filed an action in United States District Court challenging the alleged failure of their city school district to accommodate children with learning disabilities. Over the plaintiffs' objections, the judge bifurcated the liability and damages phases of the action. The judge then tried the liability phase of the action, involving the nine students in six different city schools.

After a two-month trial, the judge issued oral findings of fact and conclusions of law determining that, although the school district did not violate the federal constitutional or statutory rights of any student, it did violate the rights asserted by visually-impaired elementary and junior-high school students on their pendent state-law claim.

The district judge then scheduled two additional months of proceedings on the appropriate remedy, with these hearings to begin in three weeks. Under the pendent state-law claim, the prevailing plaintiffs could recover remedies identical to those available under their federal constitutional and statutory claims.

(a) Can the school district appeal the district judge's ruling against it before the district judge holds two months of proceedings on the appropriate remedy for the visually-impaired elementary and junior-high school students?

(b) Can the non-visually impaired students appeal at this time the judge's conclusion that their rights were not violated under federal constitutional, federal statutory, or state common law?

(c) Can the visually-impaired students appeal at this time the judge's ruling against them with respect to their federal constitutional and statutory claims?

(d) Assuming that the school district can appeal at this time the judge's determination that the district violated the rights of the visually-impaired elementary and junior-high students, what standard of review will the court of appeals apply to its review of that ruling?

2. When Does an Interlocutory Order Become an Appealable Collateral Order?

A woman filed a products liability action against a corporation, alleging that she suffered birth defects because her mother took a drug manufactured by the company. The plaintiff was represented by eight lawyers from four separate law firms. Right before trial, the company filed a motion to disqualify plaintiff's lead counsel. The motion was based on the alleged actions of plaintiff's counsel in (1) release to the media of information and allegations about defendant's drug in an effort to prejudice the jury pool and expose potential jurors to inadmissible evidence and (2) improper efforts to obtain from a secretary at the lead counsel's law firm a written statement that, contrary to her prior oral statements, she did not hear plaintiff's mother say that she never took any drugs manufactured by the company. The district judge held four days of evidentiary hearings on the company's motion, ultimately disqualifying plaintiff's lead counsel because of these two actions.

Plaintiff's counsel file an interlocutory appeal, asserting that the court of appeals can hear this appeal under the collateral order exception to the final judgment rule. Does the court of appeals have jurisdiction to hear this appeal? *See Richardson-Merrell, Inc. v. Koller,* 472 U.S. 424 (1985).

INDEX

References are to Pages